MILLENNIUM

From The Undisputed Leader In Accounting Instruction

Introducing The Most Complete High School Accounting Instructional Package.

Century 21 Accounting
First-Year Course

- *Right For The Way You Teach Now*
- *Ready To Adapt For Your Needs In The Future*
- *Not Just Pieces, But A Fully-Integrated Teaching/Learning System*

Century 21 Accounting
First-Year Course
General Journal Approach

Automated
Accounting 6.0

Century 21 Accounting
Advanced Course

Now, The Future Of Accounting Is In Your Hands.

Open The Door To The Future.

Think about how the world has changed since you started teaching. Now you have less time than ever before. There's a bewildering array of new technology available. Students raised on MTV don't relate well to the old instructional methods.

Imagine…

Now imagine a future where you spend more time teaching and less time with preparation and paperwork. Imagine a new approach to technology which allows you to harness its power easily. Imagine your students interacting easily with the material as participants rather than spectators.

Suddenly, The Future Is Here.

The new editions of *Century 21 Accounting* will help give you all you imagined and more. Starting right now, the tools you need for the next century are in your hands.

Use The Only First-Year Text With 3 Complete Accounting Cycles.

Our unique approach allows the accounting cycle to be applied 3 times during the course so your students learn the material in a real-world way.

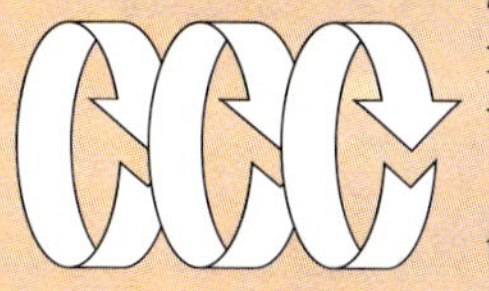

Students begin to get the concepts they need early in the course, rather than saving them for the end where they may never be covered.

Choose The First-Year Version That Fits The Way You Teach.

We are the only publisher who offers you two choices:

- *Century 21 Accounting* (traditional multi-column journal approach)

OR

- *Century 21 Accounting—General Journal* (general journal/special journals approach)

Either way, we have everything you need to cover more material better with these two new *Century 21 Accounting* instructional packages.

Computer Applications Flow Directly From Manual Concepts.

We will help you guide your students smoothly from understanding concepts to manual applications to computer applications. The new edition of *Century 21 Accounting* continues to be the only instructional package that integrates automated accounting right into the text.

The Way Accounting Will Be Taught From Now On.

An Easier Way To A More Successful Tomorrow

The new edition of *Century 21 Accounting* is easy for you to use. It's based on the proven principles and concepts which you are used to teaching. But, while it is as comfortable as your favorite slippers, it will change the way high school accounting is taught from this day forward.

Because the learning is interactive and intuitive, your students will be able to jump right in and begin to build skills and confidence. But don't take our word for it, check out these features for yourself.

More Transactions Than Any Other Text.

Other texts provide many problems but relatively few actual transactions. *Century 21 Accounting* has a better method. We give your students a carefully selected group of problems with an appropriate number of transactions. The language and construction of problems are always the same. This focus on complete problems and consistent presentation reflects the real world of accounting.

The Computer Advantage.

The new edition of *Century 21 Accounting* is the only instructional package which continues to integrate automated accounting right into the text. This feature is valuable to your students because it allows them to work specially iconed regular chapter problems with automated accounting software.

The mini-chapters integrate manual and automated accounting and provide students the opportunity to complete 31 problems, 3 reinforcement activities, and 3 simulations with our *Automated Accounting 6.0* software.

Additionally, the Application Program disk provides 23 problems; the Spreadsheet Template enables the student to work 17 problems; and the Tutorial is used with 20 different chapters.

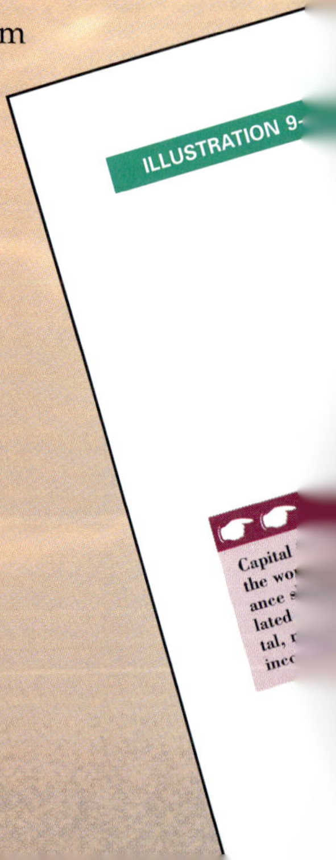

Now Your Students Can Check Their Own Progress.

With our new Audit Your Understanding feature at the end of each part of the chapter, it's easy for students to see how well they understand the work that they have covered. Students can uncover the gaps in knowledge and take the necessary corrective action by themselves. It's a confidence-builder for them; it's a time-saver for you.

AUDIT YOUR UNDERSTANDING

Challenge Your Students To Think For Themselves.

Every chapter ends with a critical-thinking feature that you may use to stretch your students and help them assimilate the material covered.

CASES FOR CRITICAL THINKING

The cases also encourage the use of language and writing skills, which provides an important cross-discipline opportunity.

Put Your Students On The Job.

Give your students "on the job" training and hands-on experience with our three "real-life" simulations. Available in both manual and automated versions, *Video Transfer, Viking Marine*, and *Western Rider* are fictitious but realistic companies which let your students do real accounting and learn by putting theory into practice.

We Place Math In The Spotlight.

All math formulas are featured in boxes and noted with icons to emphasize their importance.

MATHEMATICS

Prepare Your Students For A Changing World.

Take Your Classroom Into The Boardroom.

Interviews with top business people give your students the "facts of life" about the importance of accounting in a future career. These vivid profiles also highlight various multicultural groups.

Give Your Class An Ethical Overview Of Business.

Our Professional Business Ethics feature raises important, relevant questions for discussion. Topics include truthfulness on resumes, software pirating, and what is and isn't a legitimate business expense. Students are given a 3-step checklist to help evaluate each situation.

PROFESSIONAL BUSINESS ETHICS

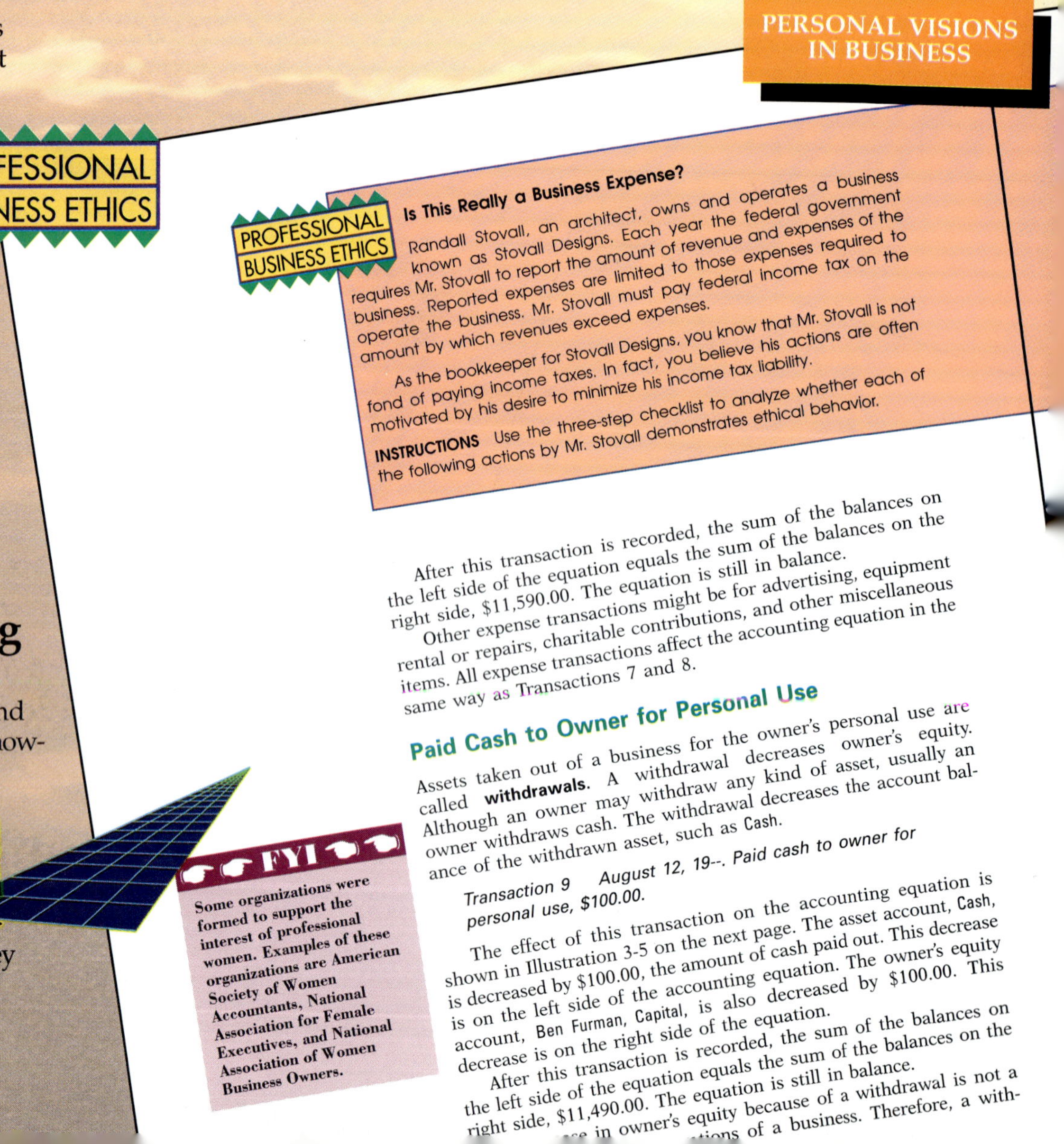

PERSONAL VISIONS IN BUSINESS

PROFESSIONAL BUSINESS ETHICS

Is This Really a Business Expense?

Randall Stovall, an architect, owns and operates a business known as Stovall Designs. Each year the federal government requires Mr. Stovall to report the amount of revenue and expenses of the business. Reported expenses are limited to those expenses required to operate the business. Mr. Stovall must pay federal income tax on the amount by which revenues exceed expenses.

As the bookkeeper for Stovall Designs, you know that Mr. Stovall is not fond of paying income taxes. In fact, you believe his actions are often motivated by his desire to minimize his income tax liability.

INSTRUCTIONS Use the three-step checklist to analyze whether each of the following actions by Mr. Stovall demonstrates ethical behavior.

After this transaction is recorded, the sum of the balances on the left side of the equation equals the sum of the balances on the right side, $11,590.00. The equation is still in balance.

Other expense transactions might be for advertising, equipment rental or repairs, charitable contributions, and other miscellaneous items. All expense transactions affect the accounting equation in the same way as Transactions 7 and 8.

Paid Cash to Owner for Personal Use

Assets taken out of a business for the owner's personal use are called **withdrawals**. A withdrawal decreases owner's equity. Although an owner may withdraw any kind of asset, usually an owner withdraws cash. The withdrawal decreases the account balance of the withdrawn asset, such as Cash.

Transaction 9 August 12, 19--. Paid cash to owner for personal use, $100.00.

The effect of this transaction on the accounting equation is shown in Illustration 3-5 on the next page. The asset account, Cash, is decreased by $100.00, the amount of cash paid out. This decrease is on the left side of the accounting equation. The owner's equity account, Ben Furman, Capital, is also decreased by $100.00. This decrease is on the right side of the equation.

After this transaction is recorded, the sum of the balances on the left side of the equation equals the sum of the balances on the right side, $11,490.00. The equation is still in balance.

... in owner's equity because of a withdrawal is not a ... of a business. Therefore, a with-

FYI

Some organizations were formed to support the interest of professional women. Examples of these organizations are American Society of Women Accountants, National Association for Female Executives, and National Association of Women Business Owners.

Show How Accounting Can Lead To An Exciting Career.

Many different accounting and accounting-related careers are showcased throughout the text. This helps students set career goals and demonstrates the ultimate value of the skills and information which they will learn in your class.

The BCCI Scandal and the Savings & Loan Crisis are merely two examples of how important it will be for your students to have a sense of their ethical responsibilities as they leave the classroom for the real world of business.

Increasing international competition makes understanding of various cultures a top priority. Your students need to acquire an appreciation for the many opportunities accounting will provide them in the future. *Century 21 Accounting* helps you cover all these important topics and more in the exciting, new student editions.

Give Your Class A Global Perspective.

In selected chapters, we provide practical information relating to accounting and business practices in the global community. In today's ever-smaller world, this is a must for your students.

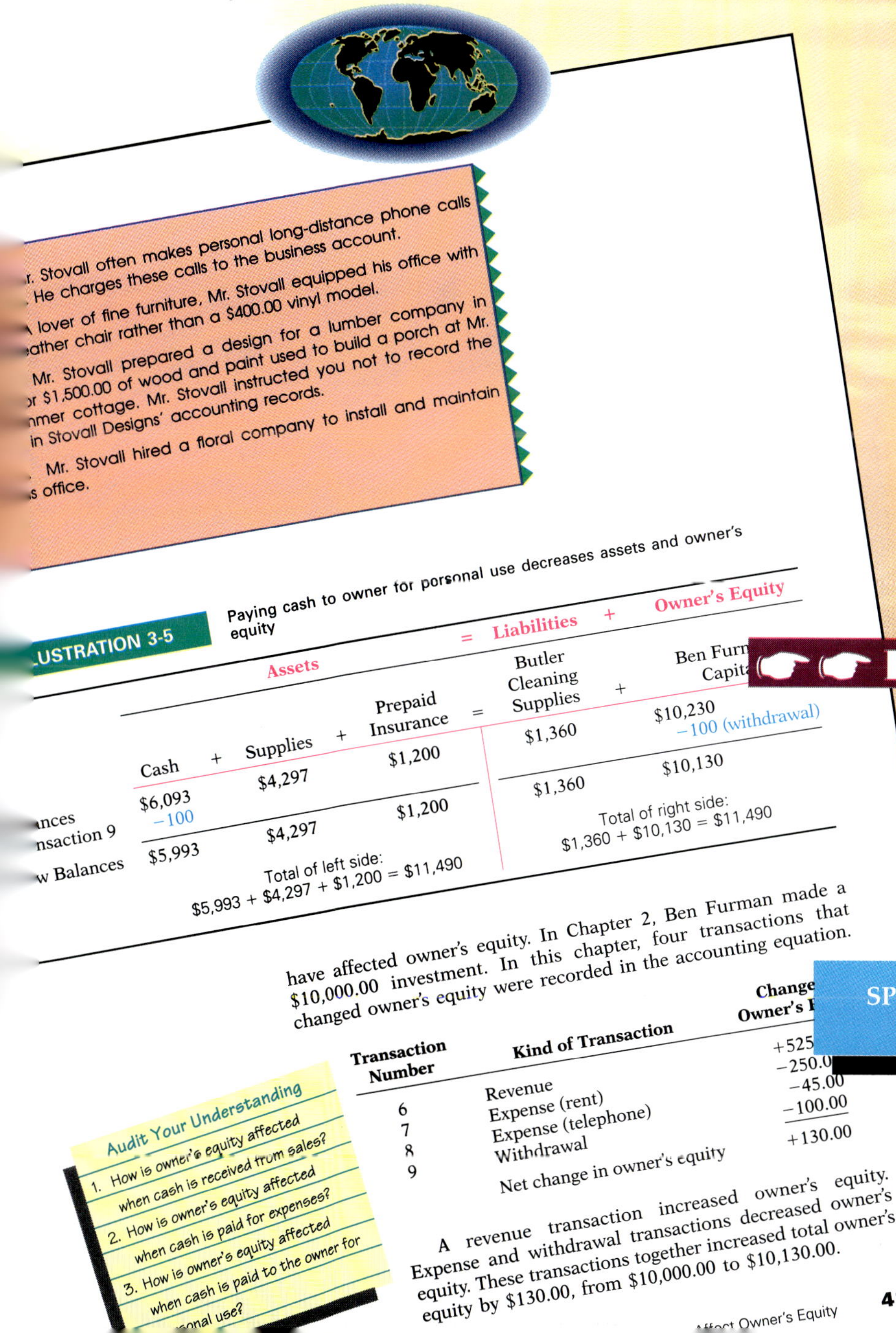

r. Stovall often makes personal long-distance phone calls . He charges these calls to the business account.

lover of fine furniture, Mr. Stovall equipped his office with eather chair rather than a $400.00 vinyl model.

Mr. Stovall prepared a design for a lumber company in or $1,500.00 of wood and paint used to build a porch at Mr. nmer cottage. Mr. Stovall instructed you not to record the in Stovall Designs' accounting records.

Mr. Stovall hired a floral company to install and maintain s office.

USTRATION 3-5 — Paying cash to owner for personal use decreases assets and owner's equity

	Assets					=	Liabilities	+	Owner's Equity
	Cash	+	Supplies	+	Prepaid Insurance	=	Butler Cleaning Supplies	+	Ben Furn Capita
nces	$6,093		$4,297		$1,200		$1,360		$10,230
nsaction 9	−100								−100 (withdrawal)
w Balances	$5,993		$4,297		$1,200		$1,360		$10,130
	Total of left side: $5,993 + $4,297 + $1,200 = $11,490						Total of right side: $1,360 + $10,130 = $11,490		

have affected owner's equity. In Chapter 2, Ben Furman made a $10,000.00 investment. In this chapter, four transactions that changed owner's equity were recorded in the accounting equation.

Transaction Number	Kind of Transaction	Change Owner's E
6	Revenue	+525
7	Expense (rent)	−250.0
8	Expense (telephone)	−45.00
9	Withdrawal	−100.00
	Net change in owner's equity	+130.00

A revenue transaction increased owner's equity. Expense and withdrawal transactions decreased owner's equity. These transactions together increased total owner's equity by $130.00, from $10,000.00 to $10,130.00.

Audit Your Understanding
1. How is owner's equity affected when cash is received from sales?
2. How is owner's equity affected when cash is paid for expenses?
3. How is owner's equity affected when cash is paid to the owner for onal use?

41 ...ffect Owner's Equity

Broaden Your Students' Awareness Of Multicultural Issues.

This feature exposes your class to the many different cultures in our country and world. It shows the contributions of each as well as the advantages of having different cultures within one harmonious society.

We Highlight The Important Information.

These short, impactful FYI features are sprinkled throughout each chapter to emphasize important points and provide interesting information about accounting and business.

Spreadsheet Options Illustrate Flexibility.

This feature shows your class a variety of ways to use spreadsheets. They may use their spreadsheet software to duplicate the examples given and may create new sets of data so they can do "What If" scenarios.

Gain The Freedom and Flexibility To Teach Your Best.

Our New Wraparound Format Puts Everything You Need For Daily Teaching Right At Your Fingertips.

MULTICULTURAL AWARENESS

The MULTICULTURAL AWARENESS feature is intended to expose students to the concept that our society is composed of people from many different cultural backgrounds. These features show both past contributions of many cultures and benefits of a culturally diverse society. Teachers should (1) have students read the brief feature; (2) discuss the concepts explored in the feature; (3) clarify any terms or questions that students may have; and (4) do the additional multicultural activity.

provides. Write the accounting equation on the board and explain the analyzing procedure. Present the accounting equation as a review of a basic algebraic concept, the equation. Remind students that an equation must always have equal amounts on each side.

APPLY

- Review the importance of keeping a business' financial information separate from the owner's personal financial information.
- Draw the accounting equation on the board and show how changes on one side can affect the other side.

Guided Practice

Invite a student to the board. Have the class list assets they own while the student lists them. Continue this for equities and liabilities. It is important to encourage students to participate in class. Participation gives students a sense of importance and enhances the learning process.

Independent Practice

Assign Terms 1–7 and Questions 1–3.

ASSESS

- Assess student understanding by checking solutions to the Independent Practice activities.
- Ask students why personal and business items should be kept separate.
- Write the accounting equation on the board. Then write a mathematical equation and omit one number. Ask students to furnish the missing number and explain how they arrived at that answer.

A = L + OE
10 = 5 + ___

20

MULTICULTURAL AWARENESS

Professional Organizations

Professional organizations provide important social and economic benefits to their members. For example, the National Association of Black Accountants is a professional organization. Members of this association are CPAs, accountants, and accounting students. The organizational purpose is to unite accountants and accounting students who have similar interests and ideals, who are committed to professional and academic excellence, who possess a sense of professional and civic responsibility, and who are concerned with enhancing opportunities for minorities in the accounting profession. Activities include free income tax preparation, student scholarships, high school and university career seminars, regional student conferences, technical seminars and lecturers, a speakers' bureau, a placement service, and publication of a journal and newsletter.

A person who chooses to start a business m sions. To make these decisions, a businessp information about the business. To provide t records and reports relating to the business n to create useful records and reports, financial kept in an organized way. Planning, recording, preting financial information is known as acc process for providing financial information th management is known as an accounting system

THE BUSINESS

A business that performs an activity for a fee is cal **ness.** Ben Furman worked for a service business th for a fee. Mr. Furman wants to be in control of hi earnings. Therefore, he decided to start his own business. A business owned by one person is calle **ship.** A proprietorship is also referred to as a sole Mr. Furman has named his new proprietorship Ru will rent office space and the equipment used to business.

Since a new business is being started, Mr. Furman the accounting system that will be used to keep Rugca ing records. In the accounting system, Mr. Furman m ful to keep Rugcare's accounting records separate fro personal financial records. For example, Mr. Furman ov and a personal car. Rugcare's financial records must information about Mr. Furman's house, car, or othe belongings. For example, Mr. Furman must use one account for his personal expenses and another checking a Rugcare. The financial records for Rugcare and Mr. Furn sonal belongings must be kept separate. The accounting *Business Entity*, is applied when a business' financial info is recorded and reported separately from the owner's financial information. *(CONCEPT: Business Entity)*

Accounting concepts are described throughout this textb when an application of a concept first occurs. When additio applications occur, a concept reference, such as *(CONCEPT: B ness Entity)*, indicates an application of a specific accounting co cept. A brief description of each accounting concept used in th text is also provided in Appendix A.

FYI A complete list of accounting concepts is in Appendix A.

THE ACCOUNTING EQUATION

A business has many items that have value. Rugcare will own ite such as cash and supplies that will be used to conduct daily op ations. Anything of value that is owned is called an **asset.** Asse have value because they can be used to acquire other assets or b used to operate a business. For example, Rugcare will use cash t

20

PART 2 Accounting for a Service Business Organized as a Proprietorship

MULTICULTURAL AWARENESS ACTIVITY

For additional exposure to diversity in professional organizations, explain to students that most professions have their own professional organizations. Furthermore, in many professions, such as accounting, people of similar minority or ethnic backgrounds often form additional professional organizations. Ask students to research professional organizations for different professions and to identify professional organizations organized for particular minority or ethnic groups. Students may wish to do this research as a group activity.

New "Wraparound" Teacher's Editions

Our new Teacher's Editions give you the same basic concepts in the same proven way that you've probably relied on since you started teaching high school accounting. But now, we've given you more help than ever before. And we've wrapped it right around every page so it's in front of you, every minute of every teaching day. This makes it easier to keep your class on schedule and makes your preparation time more productive.

TEACHING TIPS

APPLIED SKILLS

You told us how helpful our Teaching Tips are. So we gave you more of them than ever before—in the margins, just where you need them the most.

Lesson Plans Keep You On Course Every Day.

Now, your lesson plans are in the margins, so you'll never need to hunt for them or spend time preparing for class the old-fashioned way.

FOCUS

TEACH

APPLY

ASSESS

CLOSURE

Special Interleaf Pages Organize Each Unit and Chapter.

Now, planning your presentation of material is simpler and more rewarding because the material is laid out for you. Each unit and chapter has a Teacher Overview so you know where you want to go right from the start.

UNIT & CHAPTER OVERVIEWS

The points you want to emphasize, and appropriate teaching techniques for them, come immediately to mind.

You'll also like the chapter grids that correlate Enabling Performance tasks with lesson plans, chapter activities, and tests. The grids ensure appropriate teaching, application, and assessment of tasks to be mastered.

GRIDS

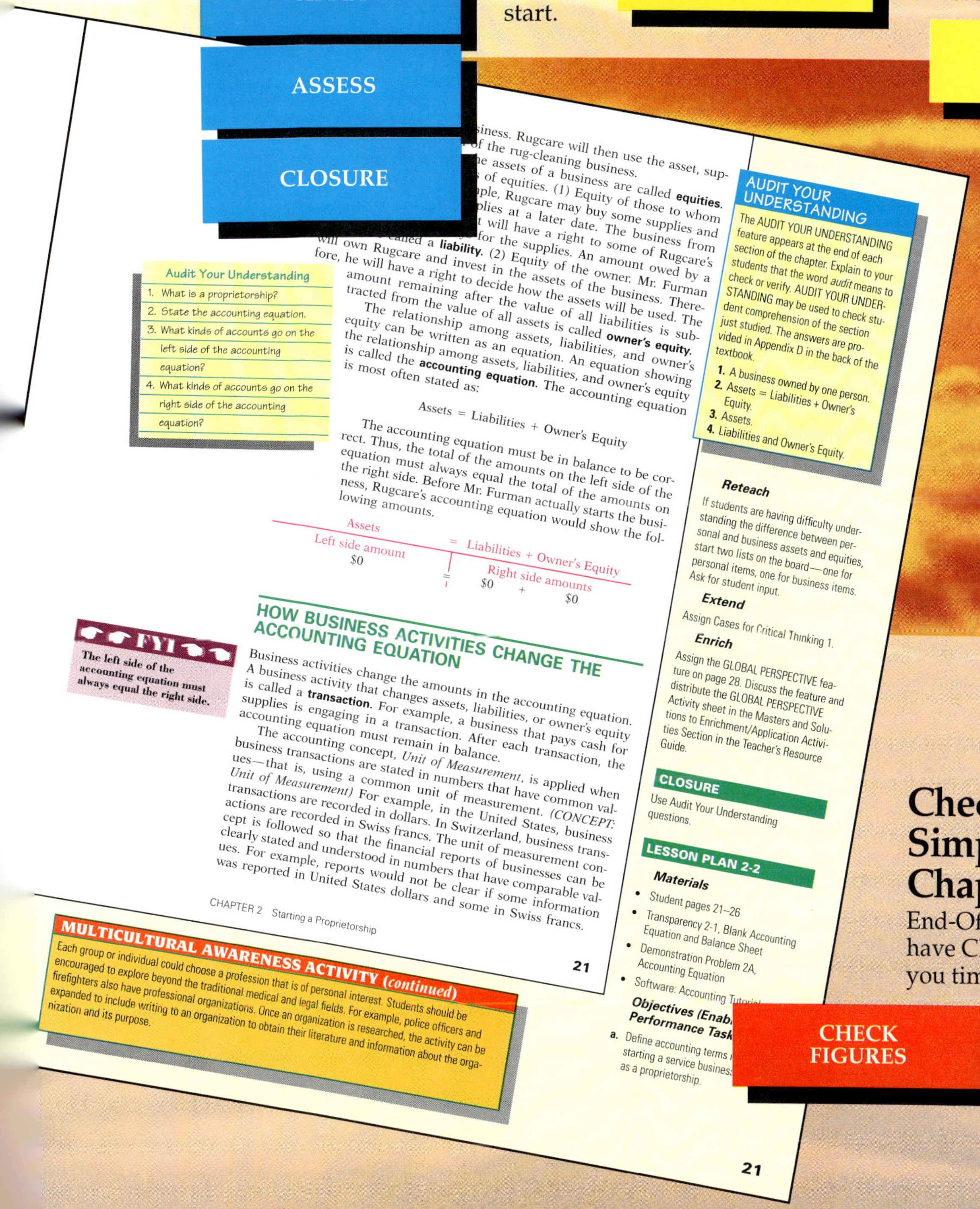

Check Figures Simplify Use Of Chapter Problems.

End-Of-Chapter Problems have Check Figures to save you time. This will mean you have more time to concentrate on helping your students master the concepts.

CHECK FIGURES

A Complete Package Of Teacher Support To Save You Time.

Teacher's Resource Guide
Now you can make more effective presentations with less preparation time. Includes Enrichment materials, Test Masters, blank ruling masters and solutions to tests.

TEACHER'S RESOURCE GUIDE

Bring complex concepts to life with skillfully designed **Transparency Masters**. Includes 90 all-new masters, with at least one per chapter.

TRANSPARENCIES

Test-giving is easier with the right **Printed Tests**. Both Problem Tests and Objective Tests are available.

TESTS

Working Papers with Demonstration and Recycling Problems provide additional problems you can use to demonstrate concepts within each chapter, and we've included rulings for the Recycling Problems.

WORKING PAPERS

New Teaching Support Options Help You Use Your Time More Effectively.

Now, *Century 21 Accounting* makes more help available. You can select the individual products you need to help you implement your instructional plan and give you more planning choices.

MICROEXAM

MicroExam. Now tests are easier to prepare and give with this test bank. It supplies 50 questions for each chapter and makes it simple to modify the tests or add your own.

ELECTRONIC AUDITOR

Electronic Auditor means you won't have to check your students' automated problems the time-consuming manual way ever again. This software does it for you, effortlessly and accurately.

VIDEO

Enhance your classroom instruction with the power of sight, sound, and motion. **Video Cassettes** involve your class in a way that no oral or written presentation can and make the material easier to understand. We make it easy for you to match this exciting new product with your own teaching style. The technology of tomorrow is available to you now from *Century 21 Accounting's* unsurpassed package of teacher support options.

The Most Advanced Package For Advanced Accounting Instruction.

- Builds Upon The First-Year Course With The Same Approach And Features
- Continuity Helps Your Second-Year Students Learn Faster
- All New Package Helps You Teach More Efficiently

A Complete Package To Help You Achieve Your Teaching Goals

Realistic Software For The Real World Beyond The Classroom.

- Provides Hands-On Experience With Computer Business Applications
- State-Of-The-Art Appearance And Function
- Works Like Popular Commercial Packages
- Uses Mouse Or Keyboard

BUILT-IN FEATURES

Automated Accounting 6.0 has the "look and feel" of the software which is employed in business accounting today, but its simple format and many built-in features make it easier to learn and faster to use.

FOR FIRST & SECOND YEAR STUDENTS

Automated Accounting 6.0 is the one single program that works with problem templates from both First-Year and Advanced Accounting. So you only have to buy one software program for both courses.

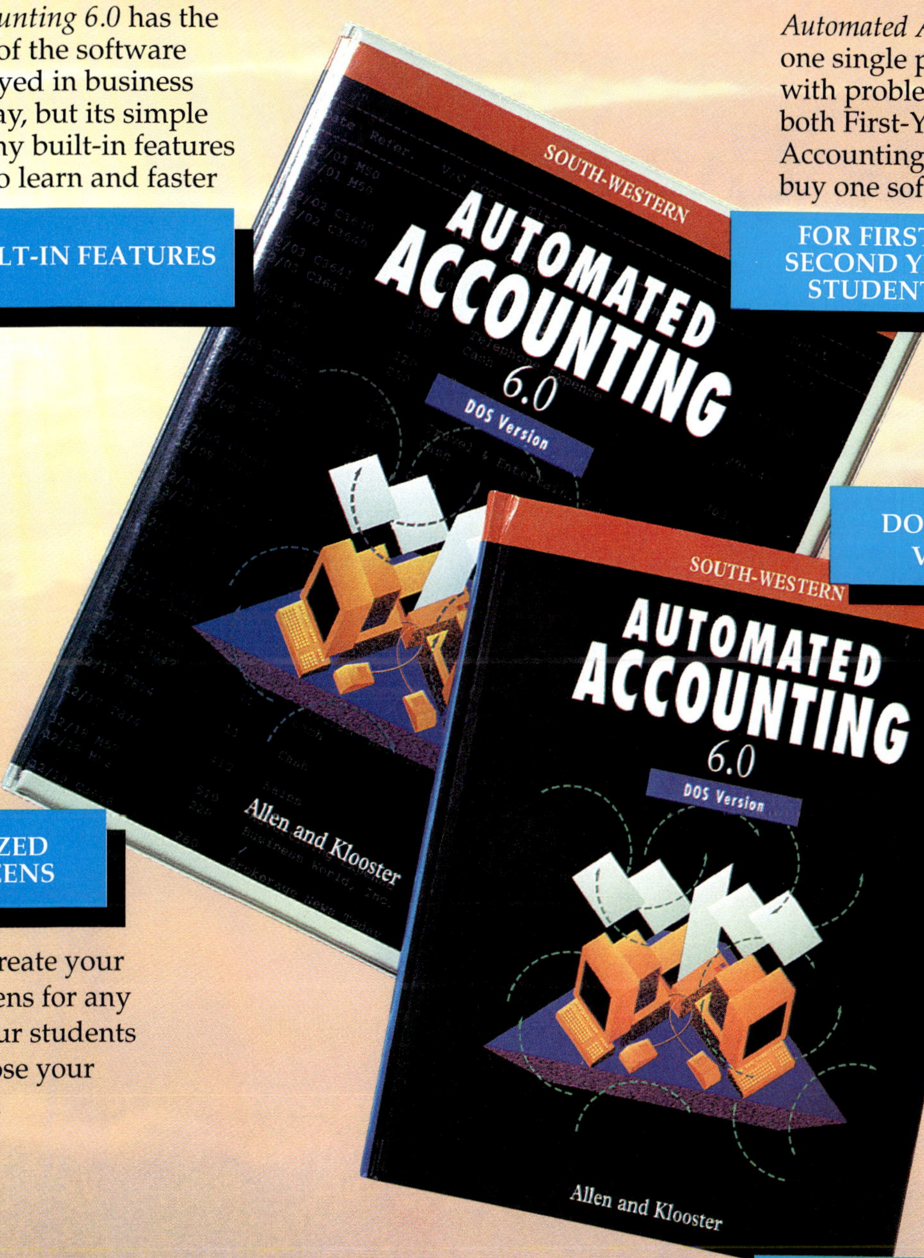

DOS AND MAC VERSIONS

Whichever kind of computers your class uses, we have the software to match it.

CUSTOMIZED HELP SCREENS

Now you can create your own Help Screens for any problem, so your students don't have to lose your personal touch.

SEPARATE TEXT AVAILABLE

If you wish to teach a separate course in Automated Accounting, a specially designed text is available with additional problems.

Your Success Is The Bottom Line.

We know that no matter how good your teaching materials and support may be, you are the one who makes it happen for your students in the classroom.

For that reason, these new editions of *Century 21 Accounting* are dedicated to you.

We invite you to examine this text, and we welcome your comments or questions.

For help, or just to tell us how you feel about the enhancements we've made, please give us a call at 1-800-543-7972.

We are looking forward to hearing from you.

SOUTH WESTERN PUBLISHING CO.

ISBN 0-538-62998-3

Stock No. BA20FAEG95

CENTURY 21 Accounting

ADVANCED COURSE

WRAPAROUND TEACHER'S EDITION

SIXTH EDITION

Kenton E. Ross, CPA
Professor of Accounting
East Texas State University
Commerce, Texas

Robert D. Hanson
Associate Dean
College of Business Administration
Central Michigan University
Mount Pleasant, Michigan

Claudia Bienias Gilbertson, CPA
Teaching Professor
Anoka-Ramsey Community College
Coon Rapids, Minnesota

Mark W. Lehman, CPA
Instructor
School of Accountancy
Mississippi State University
Starkville, Mississippi

South-Western Publishing Co.
BE27FW

Teacher's Edition Photo Credits:

Photography by Alan Brown/Photonics: pages T3, T4 (middle, bottom), 23A, 163A, 221A, 321A, 401A, 565A

Haworth, Inc.: page T4 (top)

Photography by Erik VonFischer/Photonics: page T5

Courtesy of Hewlett-Packard Company: page 491A

Cover Design: The Optimum Group

Internal Design: Lesiak/Crampton Design

ISBN: 0-538-63182-1

1 2 3 4 5 6 7 8 9 0 KI 99 98 97 96 95 94

Printed in the United States of America

I(T)P

International Thomson Publishing

South-Western Publishing Co. is an ITP Company. The ITP trademark is used under license.

TEACHER'S EDITION CONTENTS

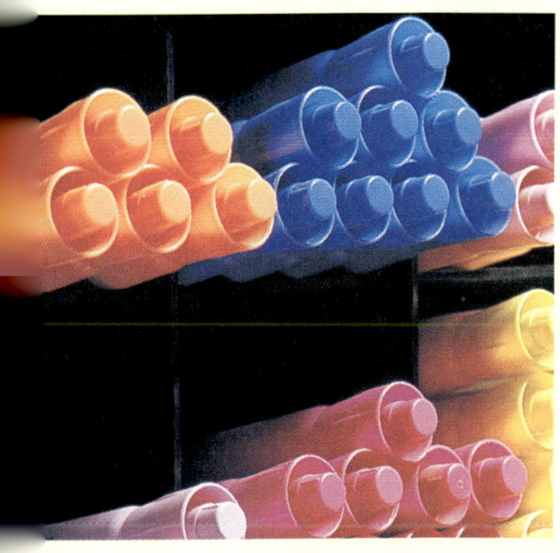

PART 4

PART 5

PART 6

PART 7

PART 8

INSTRUCTIONAL STRATEGIES

BREAKTHROUGH EDITION

How do you teach advanced accounting, covering advanced, college preparatory topics, increased use of spreadsheet and accounting software, and focus on multicultural issues, ethical dilemmas, global (international) topics, communications activities, careers, and math applications? The answer is to use this new 6th Edition of *CENTURY 21 ACCOUNTING, Advanced Course*. The text has been completely redesigned to provide you and your students with a textbook and supplemental items to facilitate teaching and learning. Many new features support various approaches to teaching accounting.

1. Traditional: *CENTURY 21 ACCOUNTING, Advanced Course,* continues to support the traditional course in which accounting procedures are done manually within the framework of the accounting cycle.
2. Automated: Frequent integrated accounting topics show how manual concepts are practiced in an automated environment. *Automated Accounting 6.0* and higher software is used for illustrations and for solving textbook problems.
3. Contemporary curriculum: All of the features of the traditional course can be taught and automated accounting concepts can be integrated. However, with the new *CENTURY 21 ACCOUNTING, Advanced Course* you can also devote time to issues that concern educators today and concepts that are increasingly being integrated in college accounting courses. The textbook provides opportunities to focus on multicultural issues, ethical dilemmas, global (international) topics, communications activities, careers, math applications, and spreadsheet topics, without neglecting any of the traditional and automated accounting topics.

The textbook has new, relevant topics and features. This wraparound teacher's edition provides lesson plans, answers, and teaching tips and suggestions. All these enhancements make accounting easy to teach so that you can put your energies into the classroom where they benefit your students most. As you examine the new edition of *CENTURY 21 ACCOUNTING, Advanced Course* you will find the familiar basic skills and procedures of accounting still there, but greatly enhanced with new features.

INNOVATIVE ENHANCEMENTS FOR STUDENTS

Many new enhancements have been made to the student text and student support materials.

New Graphic Design

A new, larger trim size provides spacious margins and more readable pages.

Emphasis on Critical Thinking

Critical thinking activities are emphasized in the content of the text and through Professional Business Ethics and Global Perspective activities which require thoughtful analysis of the situations described. Also critical thinking analysis has been added to end-of-chapter activities.

End-of-Chapter Activities

Two new activities have been added—Cases for Critical Thinking and Applied Communications. Cases for Critical Thinking require application and synthesis of accounting knowledge acquired in the chapter to new situations encountered by accounting professionals. Applied Communication activities require students to accurately communicate solutions to accounting activities.

Also, each end-of-chapter activity is correlated with the enabling performance tasks so students can see that they have met the learning objectives.

Special Features

New special interest features have been added to this edition. These features may be used as part of the accounting instruction to add interest to the course. However, if the instructor prefers, these features can be omitted without affecting the integrity of the course.

Multicultural Awareness

Student awareness of many cultural groups and their contributions to accounting is heightened in these articles. Teacher annotations suggest additional activities for further appreciation of multicultural contributions.

Professional Business Ethics

Business courses are often criticized for teaching business concepts but ignoring the ethical application of these concepts. Professional Business Ethics exposes students to ethical issues in the workplace. A three-step checklist, first presented in Chapter 1, is used for solving the ethical dilemmas presented in each case.

Global Perspective

Students learn practical aspects of doing business in the international environment. Additional student worksheets are presented in the Teacher's Resource Guide (TRG) as blackline masters for additional exploration of these topics.

Personal Visions in Business

Interviews with successful businesspeople take students out of the classroom and into the community and beyond. Personal Visions in Business emphasize the importance of business/accounting study for success and highlight contributions of individuals with diverse cultural backgrounds.

Careers in Accounting

Information about accounting positions and the job world in general appear frequently. Job titles and descriptions of duties are correlated with the *Dictionary of Occupational Titles.*

Spreadsheet Options

Students discover various uses of spreadsheets that are relevant in current accounting practice.

FYI (For Your Information)

FYI notes in the margins of the student edition emphasize points to remember and provide enrichment information about accounting and business. Students will eagerly turn the pages to discover each new FYI.

Audit Your Understanding

Questions at the end of each section of each chapter provide an informal review of comprehension. Answers are printed in the wraparound teacher's edition. Answers are also printed in Appendix D of the student edition for self-checking.

Applied Math

All formulas are highlighted and icons in the end-of-chapter activities indicate the first occurrence of each math skill. A full grid of math competencies and their first occurrence in the end-of-chapter activities is presented in the Applied Math Grid section in this teacher edition.

Applied Communications

Selected chapters have new Applied Communications activities that require responding to a situation in a written or verbal mode.

Glossary

The glossary presents every term defined in the text and its definition, including a reference to the page on which the term is defined.

Technology Enhancements

Technology has been integrated into this text through the use of software. As with other special features, instructors may choose to omit these activities without sacrificing the integrity of the accounting course.

Integrating Automated Accounting Topics is a new technology feature. These topics are mini-chapters that explain the application of *Automated Accounting 6.0* program software. Described in each are the procedures for completing input forms and instructions for automating selected problems from the chapters in the text.

Along with the new mini-chapters on automated accounting, students are given the opportunity to use the following software in conjunction with end-of-chapter activities.

- *Automated Accounting 6.0*
- *Spreadsheet Templates*

A comprehensive grid for using all software is in the Teacher's Resource Guide in the Lesson Plans section.

STUDENT SUPPORT MATERIALS

Two major supplements exist outside the textbook to aid student understanding and reinforcement of skills.

Working Papers and Study Guides

Using the working papers is the most efficient method of assuring that students complete problems accurately and in the least time possible. Beginning balances for ledger accounts and work sheet trial balances are provided where required. This eliminates tedious copying work before a problem can be started. Each workbook provides the following:

- An objective, short-answer study guide for each chapter.
- Sufficient ruled paper for completing the Application Problems, Enrichment Problems, and Reinforcement Activities 1, 2, and 3.
- Input forms for completing the Integrating Automated Accounting Problems.

Simulations

A variety of business simulations may be used with *CENTURY 21 ACCOUNTING, Advanced Course.* Business simulations should be used at intervals to integrate all the principles studied up to a certain point. Use of at least one simulation a semester is recommended. Simulations provide a capstone experience for each accounting cycle as well as provide realistic exposure to the business world.

The first two simulations are available in both manual and automated versions; the cost accounting simulation is a manual version only. Separate teacher's keys are needed for the manual and automated versions.

Students gain realistic exposure to the business world by working with original source documents in both the manual and automated versions of the Galleria, Inc., and Four Seasons, Inc. simulations.

Automated simulations require *Automated Accounting 6.0* plus the appropriate template disk. The template disk is recommended since the beginning balances and the charts of accounts for general ledger and subsidiary ledgers are already entered for the students.

The simulations available are:

Galleria, Inc., a departmentalized merchandising business organized as a corporation, is recommended for use after Chapter 5. One month's transactions are recorded in the books of account using realistic source documents.

Four Seasons, Inc., a merchandising business organized as a corporation, is recommended for use after Chapter 14. One month's transactions are recorded in the books of account using realistic source documents.

Bombay Leather, Inc., a manufacturing business organized as a corporation, is recommended for use after Chapter 20. One month's cost accounting transactions are recorded in the books of account. This set is available in manual version only.

INNOVATIVE ENHANCEMENTS FOR TEACHERS

With this edition, we have also enhanced the teacher support materials with many new features. The major enhancement is the Wraparound Teacher's Edition.

Wraparound Annotated Teacher's Edition

The wraparound annotated teacher's edition contains the complete student text and an examination guide, teacher information, lesson plans and margin notes on reduced student pages, and chapter and part interleaf pages.

Using the Wraparound Teacher's Edition

The wraparound teacher's edition has margin notes on reduced student pages that contain lesson plans for each section of each chapter, teaching suggestion boxes that address relevant topics, answers to end-of-chapter activities, and check figures.

Lesson Plans

Lesson plans are printed in the margins of the wraparound teacher's edition. Most chapters have two or more lesson plans and they are positioned to show how each chapter can be broken down into several smaller parts. Abbreviated lesson plans are also printed in the TRG as blackline masters.

The lesson plans have been designed to satisfy the needs of teachers following various formats. The following parts are included in each lesson plan:

- ***Materials.*** Each lesson plan begins with a list of the items needed to complete the lesson, such as student pages covered and applicable software.
- ***Goals.*** Specific enabling performance tasks covered by each lesson plan are listed.
- ***Focus.*** Focus provides motivation for student learning and a setting or background for the work to be done as well as a transition from past lessons to the current one.
- ***Teach.*** Suggestions describes how the teacher presents material to the students and emphasizes important concepts.
- ***Apply.*** The use of specific transparencies and how to prepare students for Guided and Independent Practice.

  Guided Practice. The instructor and students do the suggested guided practice activities together. The teacher's role is to demonstrate, monitor, observe, and answer questions. Students follow the demonstration step-by-step until readiness for independent practice activities is achieved.

  Independent Practice. Students perform suggested independent practice activities by themselves. The teacher does not normally intervene with instructional assistance.
- ***Assess.*** Each lesson plan ends with suggestions for informally assessing student comprehension as the lesson progresses.

  Reteach. Reteaching suggestions are used if students are having difficulty understanding the material to present the material in a different way.

  Extend/Enrich. Suggestions for extension and enrichment activities take students beyond the traditional assignments to stretch their ability and knowledge.
- ***Closure.*** Closure suggestions describe ways to review and reinforce the material.
- ***Assess.*** The last lesson plan for each chapter lists tests that can be used for formal assessment.

Teaching Suggestions

In addition to the lesson plans, marginal boxes describe various teaching strategies or tips. These can be categorized in three general areas:

1. *Suggestions Related to Building Student Skills.* Blue boxes describe actions the teacher can take to build applied skills in the following areas:
   - Communications
   - Building Study Skills
   - Language Arts
   - Word Processing
   - Writing Across the Curriculum
2. *Suggestions Related to Other Teaching Methodology.* Black boxes describe actions the teacher can take to reinforce concepts developed in the chapter. They can be categorized in the following areas:
   - Accounting Pedagogy
   - Assessment by Portfolio
   - Different Learning Abilities (covering Gifted Students, Limited English Proficiency (LEP)

Students, Specific Learning Disability (SLD) Students, At-Risk Students, and Visually-Impaired Students)
- Different Learning Styles (covering print learners, visual learners, auditory learners, tactile learners, and kinesthetic learners)
- Cooperative Learning
- Expanding Beyond the Classroom
- Applying Visuals
- Teaching Tip

3. *Suggestions Related to Student Features.* Color coordinated boxes highlight special student features and their benefits. Additional optional activities, such as the Multicultural Awareness, are suggested.
- Multicultural Awareness
- Professional Business Ethics
- Global Perspective
- Careers in Accounting
- Personal Visions in Business
- Spreadsheet Options
- Audit Your Understanding
- Software Focus

Check Figures

Check figures are given for end-of-chapter activities and reinforcement activities. When student solutions match these check figures, it can be assumed that the student's solutions are significantly correct. A blackline master of check figures is provided in the TRG to use as a student handout if desired.

OTHER TEACHER SUPPORT MATERIALS

We have also greatly enhanced our other teacher support material with new ideas to make organizing your lessons easier.

Teacher's Resource Guide

Some of the teacher aids available in this resource guide:

1. Lesson plans
2. Schedules for planning the year's work
3. Blackline masters for
   - Accounting forms
   - 3-step checklist for ethical decisions
   - Check figures handout
   - Assessment by portfolio
   - Resume checklist
4. Competency-based education outline and competency statements
   - Personal attributes for success in business
   - Branch accounting
5. Test section
   - Blackline masters for Chapter Problem Tests
   - Answers for Chapter Problem Tests
   - Blackline masters for Unit Objective Tests
   - Answers for Unit Objective Tests
6. Integrating Automated Accounting section with solutions to all automated problems

Teacher's Editions of the Working Papers and Study Guides

The teacher's editions provide full solutions for all problems in the end-of-chapter sections of each student chapter, including reinforcement activities and integrating automated accounting problems.

Chapter Problem Tests

Solutions and blackline masters of the problem tests are provided in the TRG. Multiple copies of both sets of problem tests may be purchased from the publisher.

Unit Objective Tests

Answer keys and blackline masters of the objective tests are provided in the TRG. Multiple copies of the objective tests may be purchased from the publisher.

Simulation Keys

Each simulation has a separate key. Manual and automated versions of the simulation have separate keys. The automated keys show solutions to the input forms and required output.

MicroExam

This test preparation software can be used to produce objective tests or daily quizzes for one or more chapters. Problems may be selected by question or randomly generated. Answer key strips are also generated by the software.

Electronic Auditor

This piece of software will check student solutions to automated problems.

ORGANIZATION OF THE TEXT

The student text is organized in a logical manner. Learning progresses from the simple to the complex using a spiral approach as shown in the eight parts of the textbook.

Scope and Sequence

The textbook begins with a merchandising business organized as a corporation, which is where the first-year course ends.

Part 1: The accounting framework, accounting concepts, ethics, and communications

Part 2: Departmentalized business, including payroll

Part 3: Accounting control systems (inventory and voucher systems)

Part 4: General accounting adjustments

Part 5: Corporation accounting

Part 6: Management accounting

Part 7: Cost accounting

Part 8: Accounting for partnerships and not-for-profit organizations

Part Opener Page

Each part in the student edition begins with a page that lists the goals for the part so students understand the purpose of that part.

In the wraparound teacher's edition, the part opener also gives an overview of all the chapters in that part. An additional interleave page lists all special features for both student edition and teacher edition to assist the instructor in planning the lessons.

Chart of Accounts

Each part begins with a chart of accounts to provide a point of reference to account titles and account numbers.

Chapter Opener Page

Each chapter in the student edition begins with a page that shows a photograph related to the chapter, a list of the enabling performance tasks (goals/learning objectives) for the chapter, and a preview of the accounting terms to be defined within the chapter.

In the wraparound teacher's edition, an additional interleave page features planning grids to assist the instructor in teaching the content of that chapter.

Smaller Parts

Each chapter can be divided into smaller parts based on the lesson plans in the margins of the wraparound teacher's edition.

Enabling Performance Tasks (EPTs)

The Enabling Performance Tasks describe what the student will be able to achieve and demonstrate proficiency in after completing the chapter. End-of-chapter activities are labeled to show which EPTs are demonstrated by each activity.

Emphasis on Vocabulary

Accounting terms are carefully defined in complete sentences ending with the term printed in bold type.

Illustrations

The chapters are copiously illustrated to demonstrate the concepts presented in the chapter.

End-of-Chapter Activities

These activities include Accounting Terms, Questions for Individual Study, Cases for Critical Thinking, and Application, Mastery, and Challenge Problems. Applied Communications activities are interspersed throughout the text. Recycling Problems for students who need additional reinforcement are included in Appendix C.

Reinforcement Activities

Reinforcement Activities in the middle and end of each accounting cycle provide an opportunity to synthesize all learnings from the part and complete an entire accounting cycle project.

Simulations

Three accounting simulations, Galleria, Inc., Four Seasons, Inc., and Bombay Leather, Inc. provide realistic simulations of daily business activities for students to apply the principles learned in an accounting cycle.

Special Features

This edition includes many new features that are specifically described in the section titled "Innovative Enhancements for Students." These include Multicultural Awareness, Professional Business Ethics, Global Perspective, Personal Visions in Business, Careers in Accounting, Spreadsheet Options, FYI (For Your Information), Audit Your Understanding, Applied Math, Applied Communications, and Integrating Automated Accounting Topics.

USING SOFTWARE AND TECHNOLOGY

After manual accounting procedures are mastered, computer software may be used as an enrichment activity to facilitate the processing of accounting data and experience the use of computers in accounting.

Two software packages are available to use with *CENTURY 21 ACCOUNTING, Advanced Course* to augment teacher instruction: *Spreadsheet Template for CENTURY 21 ACCOUNTING* and *Automated Accounting 6.0* or higher, and the accompanying templates.

All activities for which software may be used are designated by an icon next to the activity in the text. This makes identification easy for both the teacher and student. Also, software applicable to individual chapters is noted in lesson plans and interleave pages.

Each software package and its documentation is available from South-Western Publishing Company.

A complete correlation grid for using software is in the Teacher's Resource Guide.

Spreadsheet Template

Spreadsheet Template for CENTURY 21 ACCOUNTING, First-Year and Advanced Courses may be used with selected Application Problems and Enrichment Problems. In order to use the templates, Lotus® 1-2-3® or Microsoft® Works™ are needed for DOS computers. For Macintosh computers, Microsoft Works for the Macintosh™ or Microsoft Excel® are needed.

Thirty-seven problems from *CENTURY 21 ACCOUNTING, Advanced Course* may be used with spreadsheet software.

Automated Accounting

Automated Accounting, 6.0 or higher may be used to complete selected Application Problems, Enrichment Problems, Reinforcement Activities, and Simulations. The *CENTURY 21 ACCOUNTING, Advanced Course Template Disk* is also needed to complete the *Automated Accounting* problems and reinforcement activities in the text. Separate templates are needed for each simulation that is completed.

A total of 21 problems, 2 reinforcement activities, and 2 simulations from *CENTURY 21 ACCOUNTING* that may be automated using *Automated Accounting 6.0.*

It is suggested that the text that accompanies *Automated Accounting 6.0.* be used as reference. The correlation for that text is listed in the last column of the grid.

Startup

To boot the *Automated Accounting 6.0* software, key A1 at the prompt. Students will be prompted to enter the path to which a template file can be retrieved. After the file is retrieved, a help screen will appear. This student help screen contains step-by-step instructions for completing the problem. Direct your students to print a copy to use throughout the completion of the problem. You may want to file a copy of the help screen for reference.

The student text for *Automated Accounting 6.0* gives complete operational instructions for the software.

Documentation

Teachers who plan to use the *Automated Accounting 6.0* software in conjunction with *CENTURY 21 ACCOUNTING,* should also obtain at least one copy of the Automated Accounting student text and teacher's manual as complete documentation for the software. The student text gives instructions for using the software, including all software operations. The teacher's manual gives additional instructions including how to use the *Electronic Auditor 6.0.*

Saving Work in Progress on Template Disk

The keying of accounting data often must be halted before all data have been entered. For example, students may only be partially finished keying data for a computer application when a class period ends. *Automated Accounting 6.0* allows students to save a problem at any stage of completion. The software also allows the student to save a problem under more than one name. See the student text for complete instructions.

Building and Solving Additional Problems

Additional problems can be added to the template disk. Complete documentation of the procedures for doing so are in the teacher's manual.

Electronic Auditor 6.0. The *Electronic Auditor* helps you check your students' work. The software will compare student data files (stored on data disks or a hard disk) with solution data files stored on the *Electronic Auditor 6.0.* In addition, a summary report of the results will be provided.

You may also add solutions to the *Electronic Auditor 6.0* for problems you create. Once added, these solutions will appear in the solutions directory and can be used to check your student's solutions.

A full explanation of how to use the *Electronic Auditor 6.0* is provided in the teacher's manual.

STRATEGIES FOR OPTIMIZING INDIVIDUAL LEARNING

The student population not only reflects the cultural diversity in American society as a whole, but it also consists of students with different abilities and different styles of learning. Many of these individual student differences require an adjustment in teaching style or presentation. This section describes teaching strategies for students with different learning abilities and different learning styles, and suggests cooperative learning strategies.

Teaching Strategies for Students with Different Learning Abilities

Classrooms typically contain students with a wide variation of ability, intelligence, and motivation. Although the instructor must direct a majority of the instruction to the "average" student, optimal learning will occur only when the curriculum is modified to meet the needs of each individual student.

The first and greatest challenge facing the instructor is identifying the special abilities of each student. Whereas physical disabilities are usually relatively easy to identify, learning disabilities can be very difficult to detect and classify. Classifying students solely on examination scores and prior classroom performance may be misleading and should be avoided. For example, poor subject examination scores and short attention spans may be the symptoms of either a student with a specific learning disability or a gifted student who is bored.

The correct assessment of students should be a combined effort of the instructor, the school counselor or special education instructor, and the student. Together, this team can design an individualized program that will challenge the student while providing adequate opportunity to achieve attainable goals.

Gifted Students

Advanced accounting courses will typically consist of the better first-year accounting students. One objective of programs for gifted students should be the development of leadership skills. Current literature suggests that four skill areas are involved in the development of effective leadership.

1. Cognition—The ability to identify, research, and learn factual knowledge.
2. Problem Solving—The ability to identify problems and develop creative solutions.
3. Interpersonal Communication—The ability to work with other people.
4. Decision Making—The ability to develop and implement realistic goals, and evaluate performance of the goals.

Different hemispheres of the brain control these functions. Cognition and Problem Solving are typically associated with left-brain functions; Interpersonal Communication and Decision Making are associated with right-brain functions. Therefore, effective leadership training must target development of both hemispheres. Most students will enter the classroom with stronger development in some skill areas more than others. Thus, a student lacking interpersonal communication skills should undertake projects to develop those skills.

The Professional Business Ethics and Applied Communications activities in the student textbook provide opportunities for gifted students to develop these leadership skills. Encourage gifted students to extend these activities by developing related activities.

Gifted students may need to move through the accounting program at an accelerated pace. It may not be appropriate for gifted students to work every problem provided. For example, after a chapter has been reviewed, gifted students may demonstrate mastery by working only the mastery or recycling problem. Others may need to work one or more of the application problems. The challenge problem should always be assigned to gifted students to provide the "stretch" for exploring alternatives to the chapter content.

Limited-English-Proficiency Students

Limited-English-Proficiency (LEP) students are individuals whose native or dominant language is a language other than English. Although these students may be involved in special English-as-a-Second-Language (ESL) classes, the instructor can significantly improve learning by adopting several strategies.

1. Provide students with translations of key terms prior to presenting each chapter. Encourage students to use dictionaries.
2. Create visual instructional methods, such as posters and bulletin boards, that reinforce accounting concepts in both English and the other dominant language(s).
3. Use simple words in oral presentations and testing materials. Avoid polysyllabic words. Simplify the non-technical vocabulary.
4. At early levels, LEP students have limited comprehension of English and can respond with one or two word answers. Assess understanding by having students match, choose, move, draw, or point. Students at this level can respond to directions that require them to name, list, categorize, label, or reply with one or two words.
5. LEP students, like visual learners, require a variety of visual clues to support the lesson and help them understand abstract ideas. Use transparencies, textbook illustrations, and software demonstrations to provide these clues.
6. Allow for longer pauses when you ask questions. Non-native speakers need more time to formulate their answers.
7. Stress accounting terms so that LEP students learn the language of accounting.
8. Speak directly. Avoid negative constructions and passive verbs, such as "Don't forget that Cash is not debited in this transaction." Instead, say "Remember to credit Cash in this transaction."
9. Rather than asking students whether they understand what you have said, ask them to restate what you have said in their own words.
10. Adjust the length of time allotted to complete assignments and tests. Remember that the primary objective is to assess knowledge of accounting rather than the ability to translate and comprehend the question or problem.
11. Coordinate classroom activities with the school's ESL support staff.
12. Don't misinterpret a nod as understanding. The nod may instead mean that the listener did not understand.
13. Be cautious if there are no interruptions or questions. It may mean that very little has been understood.
14. In some cultures, "Yes" is the response to every question. It may mean "I heard your question" rather than "I understand."
15. In some cultures, giggling or inappropriate laughter may indicate embarrassment at poor comprehension rather than disrespect for the teacher.

Specific Learning Disability (SLD) Students

Instructors need not be reminded that adolescence is a period of turmoil and adjustment. What many instructors often view as adolescent behavior may, however, be caused by a student's specific learning disability (SLD). The correct assessment of SLD students is difficult because adolescent behavior is similar to the typical characteristics of SLD students.

Passive Learners

When faced with making a decision, SLD students avoid making a decision in favor of waiting for a teacher to provide specific direction.

Poor Self-Concept

Years of failure cause SLD students to have low self-esteem, thus reducing their confidence that they can achieve academic success.

Inept Social Skills

SLD students often have difficulty making and keeping friends.

Attention Deficits

SLD students often lack the ability to concentrate on one topic for an extended period.

Lack of Motivation

Years of failure have conditioned SLD students to doubt their abilities and, therefore, view their efforts as being futile.

Once an SLD student is correctly assessed, the instructor should work with the student to develop an individualized program. The basic objective of the program should be the development of functional (life) skills. The student should be counseled to established challenging yet attainable goals and provide frequent feedback as to the attainment of these goals. The student's academic success should be measured on the demonstrated ability to learn as much as the mastery of a defined body of knowledge.

Several general instructional strategies are effective in teaching SLD students:

1. When asking questions during class, ask SLD students questions that they can likely answer successfully. Save more difficult or unstructured questions for better students.
2. Rotate instructional materials rather than trying to complete a single text. Supplemental instructional materials may include additional texts, business magazines, government publications, etc.
3. Incorporate current literature (magazines and newspapers) to identify current topics of interest to students.
4. Encourage students to maintain a daily log or journal that describes their academic progress. Students can share this log, if they desire, with the teacher when updating their individual program.
5. When feasible, SLD students should become involved in work-study programs that are consistent with course content. When work-study opportunities are unavailable, simulations can be used to provide a simulated work environment. Field trips are an excellent method to expose students to the business world.

At-Risk Students

Many environmental factors may negatively impact a student's ability and motivation to succeed academically. Any student who is a potential dropout may be classified as an at-risk student. At-risk students typically are deficient in mathematics, reading, and language skills. These students provide a unique challenge to the accounting instructor since the instructor has little, if any, power to correct problems in the home environment.

Effective instructional strategies for at-risk students should be based on the premise that all individuals have a need for achievement and social acceptance. Within the accounting classroom, these needs can be fulfilled by developing a curriculum that promotes academic success and acceptance by the instructor. Techniques for working with at-risk students include:

1. Develop a personal profile of the student. Avoid placing too much significance on past academic performance as this may represent a symptom rather than the underlying problem.
2. Together with the student, develop an individualized program that allows the student to attain both short-term and long-term goals. When identifying goals, consider the student's anticipated career goals.
3. Utilize the lesson plans provided in the teacher's edition to divide each chapter into smaller parts to create short units that provide frequent opportunities for assessment and goal attainment.
4. Modify presentation strategies to include more visual displays and supplement explanations with current, realistic examples.
5. Organize field trips and mentor programs to expose students to the business environment.

Visually Impaired Students

Students with mild visual impairments are typically mainstreamed and may elect to enroll in accounting. The nature and degree of students' visual impairments will vary. A student's visual impairment may include a difficulty in reading print, an inability to distinguish colors, a sensitivity to light, and a limited field of vision. The instructor must identify each student's exact impairment and adapt teaching strategies appropriately.

Many sources exist for providing alternative teaching materials. Most states have schools for the blind and rehabilitation service agencies that can enlarge the textbook and working papers. Consult these organizations to identify the latest technologies available for assisting the students.

The instructor and student should develop an individualized program that establishes a time frame for achieving specific learning objectives. The learning objectives should be consistent with the student's anticipated career goals. The time frame should consider the student's impairment and the availability of technical assistance, such as enlarged materials and closed circuit television. The use of software should not be overlooked for visually impaired students, particularly if oversized monitors with larger displays are available.

Teaching Strategies for Students with Different Learning Styles

There are many different learning styles. Some people learn best from reading material. Others need to see a demonstration or learn by feeling. Still others may learn best from auditory cues. It is important to remember, however, that no matter what learning style works best for any individual, learning style is not an indicator of intelligence. Two people of similar levels of intelligence may learn best in two different styles of learning. Learning style is also not necessarily a rigid behavior. Many individuals may have a dominant learning style; however, most also have the flexibility to adapt learning style to the demands of the material to be learned. Different learning styles include print, visual, auditory, tactile, and kinesthetic learning.

Print Learners

The print learner prefers to see the data in print—preferably printed in words. For example, for learning transaction analysis, a print learner would prefer to study the illustration in the textbook which shows a T account.

Visual Learners

The visual learner needs to "see" the concept. One way for the learner to "see" the concept is mental visualization. Illustrations and visual aids are important to the visual learner.

Auditory Learners

The auditory learner will best learn by hearing. Auditory learners who read a textbook chapter benefit from hearing reinforcement of key concepts spoken out loud. Auditory learners also benefit from verbalizing concepts, such as listing steps involved in a journal entry or verbally explaining a formula and/or calculations to other students in a small group.

Tactile Learners

The tactile learner learns best by touching or handling objects. Tactile learners may benefit from using the computer to key journal entries and then print reports. Tactile learners should also be given the opportunity to journalize transactions from at least one simulation that contains source documents which must be handled to analyze, journalize, and file.

Kinesthetic Learners

The kinesthetic learner learns best by taking an active part in the instruction. Motion is an important part of kinesthetic learning. A student might draw a T account in the air or use a finger to draw a T account on the back of the hand or arm. Provide the opportunity to perform calculations to solve formulas using drills or prepared worksheets.

COOPERATIVE LEARNING

Cooperative learning activities should be an integral part of accounting pedagogical strategies. Cooperative learning involves small heterogeneous groups of students who work together to share the responsibility for learning. Cooperative learning activities should be designed with the following goals in mind.

1. All students should be able to participate.
2. Groups should be heterogeneous.
3. Each student needs to be held accountable for his or her contribution to the group.

Cooperative learning is more successful with heterogeneous rather than homogeneous groups. Research further supports cooperative learning as a teaching strategy to increase students' motivation, achievement, and behavior. The teacher should select team members for a cooperative learning activity. Group composition should include a mixture of gender, ability level, cultural or ethnic background, and learning style. For example, placing a visual learner with an auditory learner enhances and strengthens the group's performance. Group members should be rotated frequently.

The time needed to complete an activity will vary among groups. Therefore, the teacher needs to provide additional activities to be completed by groups as they finish. These activities might include, for example, specific questions about the activity. These additional activities are often referred to as debriefing.

Cooperative learning promotes the development of higher-order thinking skills where brighter students explain concepts or principles to slower students. Using higher-order thinking skills to articulate ideas in accounting will normally result in material's being learned more effectively with improved retention rates.

To be successful, each student must be held accountable for his/her contribution to the cooperative learning activity. A variety of evaluation methods may be employed. These methods may include (1) a short quiz taken individually, (2) teacher observation of individual contributions to a group activity, or (3) bonus points assigned to individuals only if all group members do well individually. Performance on cooperative learning activities in accounting should range from no more than 5 to 10 percent of the final grade.

One of the goals of cooperative learning is to have students work out the roles of the group members themselves. Some groups will assign a role to an individual, such as when a representative of the group will need to record results and present them to the class, and sometimes individuals within a group will assume roles within the group without being asked to do so.

Some cooperative learning activities are as follows:

1. *Research project.* Assign students to groups of two. Each group researches the financial statements (through the annual report) of a company in which they are interested, perhaps because they are familiar with the product. Students look for a list of specific items such as what kinds of stock is the corporation authorized to issue, what categories of assets are listed on the balance sheet, what is the total of current liabilities, did net income increase/decrease from the previous period, etc. The group must then plan and deliver a presentation of the data to the entire class. Additional time outside of class is needed to complete research and prepare presentation.
2. *Divide the class into groups of two students each.* Have one student describe a transaction while the other student analyzes it. Have students alternate roles.
3. *Divide the class into two groups.* Each group stands and faces each other. The teacher or a student moderator states an accounting term. The first student to raise a hand has the opportunity to give the correct definition. The group with the most correctly defined terms is declared the winner. As an alternative to this game, the teacher or moderator may read the definition of a term, such as "Anything of value that is owned," while the groups must identify the term. The answer should be given in a question format, such as "What is an asset?" if you wish to imitate a popular television game show.
4. *Reinforcement Activities.* Assign reinforcement activities as homework. Divide the class into groups of two students each. Each pair of students exchange and evaluate each other's work in class. Students are permitted to correct their work based on their partner's evaluation.
5. *Divide the class into groups of four or five students each.* Using Cases for Critical Thinking, each group analyzes the cases and arrives at agreed-upon solutions. One member of each group is appointed the recorder and presents the group's analysis to the class.
6. *Divide the class into auditing groups of three or four students per group.* Each auditing group is responsible for assisting other class members as well as correcting homework assignments. A lead auditor is appointed by the group and is responsible for turning in completed homework assignments for each group member to the teacher.

SUGGESTIONS FOR TEACHING PROFESSIONAL BUSINESS ETHICS

Businesses have recently become aware of the severe implications of the unethical behavior of employees. In response, many businesses have begun training their employees to make ethical decisions and establishing company codes of conduct. The message from businesses today is clear—employees must be capable of making ethical decisions to protect the business from legal liability and to maximize long-term profits.

Most students' principles of right and wrong are well established prior to their enrolling in high school accounting. Thus, the presentation of business ethics does not involve the teaching of right and wrong. Instead, students need to learn how to apply their principles of right and wrong to business situations.

Professional Business Ethics

There are seven Professional Business Ethics features in this text to give instructors an opportunity to teach ethics in the accounting class.

Causes of Unethical Behavior

Chapter 1 provides an introduction to business ethics. The major causes of unethical behavior are presented to assist students in recognizing the forces that can cause unethical behavior. Recognizing the causes of unethical behavior is the first step in making business decisions that prevent employees from being placed in compromising situations.

Steps for Analyzing Ethical Situations

A three-step checklist is presented to help students analyze the ethics of an action. This approach encourages students to collect pertinent information that will provide a basis for their decision. Ultimately, students' decisions are based on their personal ethics applied to the facts of the situation.

Assessment

Correct solutions are generally obvious if the action is either illegal or violates a business or professional standard. For example, most students will agree that it is unethical to dispose of hazardous waste into the water supply. However, students may challenge compliance with other laws and standards. A class discussion of whether the truck drivers of a business should be required to drive the speed limit and wear safety belts may demonstrate many students' willingness to disregard selected laws.

Many of the situations in the Professional Business Ethics activities provide situations where the line between right and wrong is unclear. As a result, students will likely differ on their decision as to whether the action is ethical. Answers to Professional Business Ethics activities should be graded based on the students' analysis of the facts and the objective support for their decisions. The students' decisions about whether a case demonstrates ethical behavior should not be graded. Therefore, no conclusions are provided with the solutions.

Teachers can adopt several strategies to cover a Professional Business Ethics activity. The activity can be presented initially as a classroom discussion. Alternately, the activity can be assigned as an individual or group project. Whichever method is used, students should be given the opportunity to discuss the case in class. This exchange of ideas enables students to observe how other individuals make and support their decisions. When asking questions and making observations, the instructor should be careful not to reveal his or her personal bias.

Communication Skills

The Professional Business Ethics activities provide an opportunity for students to practice communication skills. For example, the Professional Business Ethics activity in Chapter 1 requires students to evaluate the ethical behavior of an accountant who, while serving as a member of a zoning board, votes against a zoning request of a client's competitor. Students could assume the position of zoning board chairperson and prepare the appropriate message to the CPA. In this case, the students would also be required to identify the correct method of communication.

Solutions for Professional Business Ethics

Chapter 1: Mixing Politics and Business

Students are required to evaluate the ethical behavior of an accountant who, while serving as a member of a zoning board, votes against a zoning request of a clients' competitor. Students may contend that the accountant's actions violate the conflicts of interest clause of Rule 102 of the AICPA's Rules of the Code of Professional Conduct. Some students may contend, however, that the accountant was not involved "in the performance of professional services" as a member of the zoning board.

This first Professional Business Ethics activity has been completed in the chapter for the students to walk them through the three-step checklist for analyzing ethical behavior. The Professional Business Ethics activities in future chapters will not provide answers in the textbook.

Since personal ethics are unique, students' solutions will vary. Although there is no one correct solution, the solution given illustrates the use of the three-step checklist.

Guide students through this checklist and encourage different solutions from them.

Chapter 7: At What Price Safety?

Students will evaluate a company's use of a less reliable part to reduce its costs and increase profits. The new part still exceeds government quality standards. Students must weigh the benefit of less costly cars against a slightly higher risk of serious injury. Although students will generally agree that using a less reliable part is unethical, the company's compliance with the government standard may complicate their decision.

Because personal ethics are unique, students' solutions will vary. Although no one correct solution exists, the following solution illustrates the use of the three-step checklist.

1. Is the action illegal? No. The new part still exceeds government quality standards.
2. Does the action violate company or professional standards? No. No company or professional standards apply.
3. Who is affected, and how, by the action? *(See Table 1.)*

TABLE 1

PEOPLE AFFECTED	NEGATIVE	POSITIVE
Webster Industries	Increases the risk of potential litigation.	Reduces production costs and increases profits by $40.00 per unit.
Stockholders		Increases return on investment.
Car Manufacturer		Lower costs promote higher sales and profits.
Car Owners	Increases slightly the chance of incurring a serious injury if involved in an accident.	Reduces the cost of a car by $60.00.

Chapter 10: Is Salary Expense a Picnic?

This activity requires students to evaluate the ethical behavior of an accountant who, at the direction of management, records an expense in violation of a government contract. Students should determine that the accountant's action is illegal since it violates a government contract. In addition, the accountant has violated Rule 102 of the AICPA's Code of Professional Conduct.

Some students may contend that the expense is justified because it will result in a net savings for the government. Without permission from the government, however, the company is violating the contract. This action could result in the company's disqualification for future contracts.

1. Is the action illegal? Yes. The expenditure does not qualify as a cost according to the government contract.
2. Does the action violate company or professional standards? Yes. The accountant has violated Rule 102 of the AICPA's Code of Professional Ethics. The recording of the expenditure against the government contract involves the accountant in a misstatement of the facts.
3. Who is affected, and how, by the action? Because the action is illegal and also violates professional standards, no evaluation of this question is necessary.

Chapter 13: Ups and Downs of CEO Compensation

This activity focuses on the ethics involved in excessive management compensation in the form of stock options. The issue of excessive management compensation was being debated by the government as this textbook was being written. In most cases, "excessive" compensation results when corporate officers exercise stock options.

The instructor may need to introduce this activity by analyzing the journal entries involved in the issuance of stock options. No transaction was recorded when the CEO's options were issued. The following transaction was recorded when the options were exercised (assuming a $10.00 par value): Cash was debited for $2,500,000 (200,000 × $25); Common Stock was credited for $1,000,000 (20,000 × $10); Paid-in Capital in Excess of Par was credited for $1,500,000.

No transaction was recorded for the subsequent sale of the stock on the stock exchange. As the entry illustrates, using stock options for officer compensation results in no "expense" to the corporation. The additional supply of shares outstanding may, however, have a slight downward influence on the stock's market price.

Because personal ethics are unique, students' solutions will vary. Although no one correct solution exists, the following solution illustrates the use of the three-step checklist.

1. Is the action illegal? No. No laws limit the salary that any individual can earn in private business.
2. Does the action violate company or professional standards? No. No company or professional standards apply.
3. Who is affected, and how, by the action? *(See Table 2.)*

TABLE 2

PEOPLE AFFECTED	NEGATIVE	POSITIVE
CEO		Provides a substantial increase in salary if CEO can improve company's profitability.
Employees	May resent the high salary provided to the CEO.	
Teletron Industries		Provides CEO with incentive to improve profitability. Stock options are not recorded as an expense.
Stockholders	May slightly reduce the market price of stock when options are exercised.	Increases the wealth of stockholders only if CEO is successful in increasing profitability.

Chapter 16: Smooth Sailing with Client Referrals

This activity requires students to evaluate the ethical behavior of a CPA who accepts a referral fee in the form of a gift. Students should determine that the CPA's action violates the AICPA's Code of Professional Conduct and, therefore, is unethical. The following solution illustrates the use of the three-step checklist.

1. Is the action illegal? No. Accepting a gift is not illegal.
2. Does the action violate company or professional standards? Yes, the gift is a referral fee. Because the client was not informed of the referral fee, the action violates Rule 503(C) of the AICPA's Code of Professional Conduct.
3. Who is affected, and how, by the action? Because the action violates professional standards, no evaluation of this question is necessary.

Chapter 18: Legislate Competition Away

Students are required to evaluate the ethical behavior of an industrial association that influences Congress to enact trade restrictions that prevent foreign companies from marketing their product domestically. This type of trade restriction was being used with increasing regularity when this textbook was being written. Students' reaction to this activity may depend upon the employment situation of family members. For example, the son of an unemployed auto worker is likely to approve of the action.

Because personal ethics are unique, students' solutions will vary. Although no one correct solution exists, the following solution illustrates the use of the three-step checklist.

1. Is the action illegal? No. The law was enacted by Congress.
2. Does the action violate company or professional standards? No. No company or professional standards apply.
3. Who is affected, and how, by the action? *(See Table 3.)*

TABLE 3

PEOPLE AFFECTED	NEGATIVE	POSITIVE
American manufacturers	Foreign governments may establish similar laws against American manufacturers in other industries.	Increases market for product and improves profitability. American employees are employed and stockholders earn a higher return on investment.
Foreign manufacturers	Decreases market for their product and reduces profitability. Foreign employees are terminated and stockholders earn a lower return on investment.	
Government		Increases tax revenues.
Customers	Increases the cost of the electronic equipment.	

Chapter 23: Keeping a Trade Secret

Students are required to evaluate the behavior of a professional accountant and his relationship with his client.

Because personal ethics are unique, students' solutions will vary. Although no one correct solution exists, the following solution illustrates the use of the three-step checklist.

1. Is the action illegal? No.
2. Does the action violate company or professional standards? Yes. The client/accountant relationship is confidential.
3. Who is affected, and how, by the action? *(See Table 4.)*

TABLE 4

PEOPLE AFFECTED	NEGATIVE	POSITIVE
Accountant	Lose standing in professional associations for revealing confidential information.	Friend may get contract for a job.
Client	Confidentiality of relationship was broken.	Client may get cheaper bids.
Bidders	Did not have access to other bids so that they could adjust their prices.	
Accountant's friend	May lose reputation if others in the building industry find out he had inside information.	May get contract that pays a lot of money.

SUGGESTIONS FOR TEACHING APPLIED COMMUNICATIONS

Chapter 1 contains a brief introduction to the importance of communication and language arts skills for career success. Several accounting organizations have emphasized that successful accounting professionals must possess good oral and written communication skills. Since effective communication is a skill developed with practice, this textbook has incorporated several opportunities for students to develop their skills. There are eight Applied Communications activities that are interspersed throughout the chapters in the end-of-chapter section after the Cases for Critical Thinking. Suggested solutions are printed in the margin of this Annotated Teacher's Edition.

Students' knowledge of communication and language arts skills will vary. You may consider asking an English or communications instructor to assist you in reviewing communication skills that students have learned previously in other classes.

Whether preparing an outline for an oral presentation or a letter for a written assignment, students should be encouraged to use word processing software to prepare their messages. Word processing software is now used extensively by both public and private accountants and proficiency in its use is essential. By using word processing to complete Applied Communications activities, you will be able to emphasize the importance of computer skills from the first week of the semester.

Assessment

Since the activities allow students to prepare unique messages, there are no "correct" answers. Your students may create excellent solutions that differ significantly from the sample solution. Thus, evaluate each student's solution on its ability to transmit the message in an efficient, effective, and professional manner. The activities should be evaluated for both content and format. Each instructor must determine the importance of errors.

Revising Written Documents

A significant amount of learning occurs when students are provided the opportunity to correct mistakes in their original written documents. Require students to revise documents and incorporate your suggestions. The revised document should be graded and, if necessary, revised again. Teachers should consider adjusting the student's grade for successful revisions. For example, the grade on the first and revised documents may be averaged.

Cases for Critical Thinking

Most of the Cases for Critical Thinking in this textbook require students to prepare a written answer. You can adapt these cases to further reinforce students' communication skills. Rather than simply answering the questions, require students to prepare an oral or written message to an individual or business mentioned in the case. For example, Case 2 of Chapter 1 requires a decision as to whether Roger, the accountant in the case, should take the CPA's advice regarding the handling of business papers after transactions have been recorded. Vary the requirements of each activity by requiring different types of oral and written messages.

ASSESSMENT BY PORTFOLIO

Assessment by portfolio is a growing education trend in assessing student performance. A portfolio enables the teacher to assess student goals and accomplishments while providing the student with the opportunity to collect information that will help set and accomplish current and future goals.

A portfolio should be organized across the curriculum with each discipline making a contribution. A complete portfolio should include the following:

1. A resume.
2. Copies of personal information such as social security card and driver's license.
3. A completed job application to use as a guide.
4. Copies of awards and achievements.
5. Samples of letters of applications, cover memos to attach with a resume, and thank you letters for interviews.
6. Reference letters.
7. Copies of performance in skills, communications, and any other evaluation that would contribute to success in a job.

The accounting class can contribute as many of these items to the portfolio as the instructor desires. Most instructors will want to have accounting students complete a resume (number 1) and documentation of performance (number 7).

A resume is an important component of a student portfolio. Students should revise the resume they wrote in the first-year accounting course for inclusion in the portfolio. Writing a resume is an Applied Communications activity in Chapter 2 which provides the opportunity for Writing Across the Curriculum. This can be a positive writing experience for students and is a good way to start off the school year.

Documenting performance in accounting should include a variety of accounting material that is produced by the student. A portfolio might include items such as problems the student has completed, a personal journal describing references and procedures the student used to complete the problem, and a summary report on what was learned from the project. The portfolio should be based on the accounting cycle to produce the most desirable results. Each documentation of performance should have an evaluation sheet that the student completes to explain what activity has been accomplished. The instructor should review and sign this evaluation. A sample PORTFOLIO ASSESSMENT sheet is in the Teacher's Resource Guide.

The portfolio should be an example of the student's best work that will reflect the skills and knowledge the student has learned. Each student should have a binder or folder so that the work may be organized and presented in an attractive manner. Suggested organization of the portfolio is as follows:

1. Table of contents.
2. Personal information (resume, job applications, etc.).
3. Documentation of performance (work samples, personal journals).

The following is a guideline for content coverage in the portfolio.

Objective

The student will demonstrate the skills necessary to record business transactions and analyze the financial condition of a departmentalized merchandising business. (The wording of the objective will change depending on the part of the textbook that is being evaluated.)

Documentation of Performance

1. The major component of the portfolio is a complete accounting problem that encompasses the entire accounting cycle. The problem should include journals, ledgers, a work sheet, and financial statements. There should be examples for each major component of the advanced course: departmentalized business, corporation ownership

structure, manufacturing business, and partnership and not-for-profit organization, with an emphasis on financial statement analysis.

2. A daily personal journal should be kept in which the student records activities such as the number of problem instructions completed each day, references necessary to perform various tasks, how difficult tasks were solved, what equipment was used, and any other activity that contributed to the successful completion of the assignment.
3. A written report is another important part of the portfolio. The report should include experiences encountered by the student while completing the activity, such as instructions that took more or less time to complete than anticipated, accessibility to equipment, student time management and organization skills that enabled the project to flow smoothly, and how things could have been done differently. A second part of the report should include an analysis of the business in the problem such as are the component percentages acceptable for that type of business, is the chart of accounts appropriate for the business, and suggestions on how to make the business operate more efficiently from an accounting point of view.

Assessment

1. The accounting problem should be complete and in correct format, all words should be spelled correctly, the information should be neat and accurate, and the problem should be submitted in an orderly fashion.
2. The personal journal should be set up on a daily basis and entries should be recorded for each day. Personal experiences should be documented neatly and accurately. Language arts skills should be evaluated (grammar, spelling, punctuation, and sentence structure).
3. The written report should be in complete sentences and word processed or typewritten. It should be an accurate assessment of the student's experience. Language arts skills should be evaluated (grammar, spelling, punctuation, and sentence structure).
4. The student will complete a PORTFOLIO ASSESSMENT and describe the project. The teacher should then complete the evaluation portion of the assessment sheet.

CENTURY 21 ACCOUNTING—A COMPLETE COMPETENCY-BASED ACCOUNTING PROGRAM

CENTURY 21 ACCOUNTING is organized into a complete competency-based instructional program. A competency-based instructional program is an organization of subject matter consisting of one or more courses designed to lead students to predetermined goals and objectives. A competency-based instructional program identifies what the student must "do" to successfully complete the program. A minimum acceptable level of performance is clearly specified before instruction and learning begin. In a competency-based instructional program, attention is focused on learner outcomes rather than on teaching activities. The teaching activities or delivery of instruction is directed toward the predetermined goals and objectives. A competency-based instructional program may be used effectively in a traditional classroom setting. The competency-based *CENTURY 21 ACCOUNTING* program model is given in Figure 1.

USING THE COMPETENCY-BASED ACCOUNTING PROGRAM

Program Goals

Program goals are general, student-oriented competency statements which take two or more general behavioral goals to demonstrate. The complete *CENTURY 21 ACCOUNTING* program has the following program goals.

1. Know accounting as it relates to careers.
2. Know accounting terminology.
3. Understand accounting concepts, principles, and practices.
4. Apply accounting procedures.

Learning outcomes that demonstrate knowledge involve recall of previously learned subject matter. Being able to identify the correct definition of an accounting term would be an example of a learning outcome that demonstrates knowledge. Knowledge represents the lowest level of learning outcomes.

Learning outcomes that demonstrate understanding involve the ability to interpret subject matter. Being able to distinguish between correct and incorrect accounting principles and practices would be an example of a learning outcome that demonstrates understanding. Understanding goes one step beyond the simple remembering of material. Understanding assumes the knowledge level of learning.

Learning outcomes that demonstrate application involve the ability to use learned material in realistic situations. Being able to record transactions in a journal would be an example of a learning outcome that demonstrates application. Application represents a higher level of learning than either knowledge or understanding levels of learning.

General Behavioral Goals

General behavioral goals are student-oriented behavioral statements which take one or more terminal performance objectives to demonstrate. General

FIGURE 1

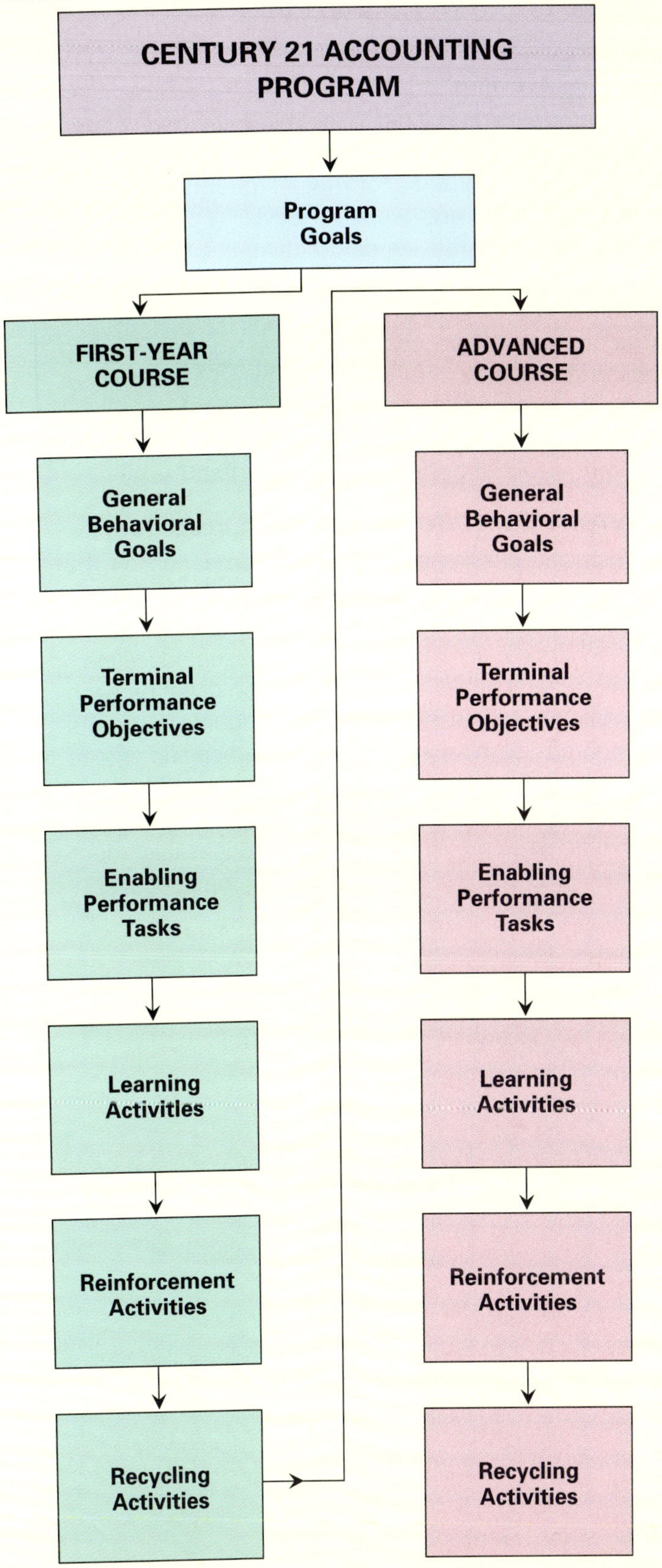

behavioral goals specify the content required to satisfy the learning outcomes described in the program goals.

Terminal Performance Objectives

Terminal performance objectives are statements that indicate the behavior a student will demonstrate upon successful completion of a learning experience. Terminal performance objectives consists of three basic elements.

1. The condition under which the performance is to take place.
2. The behavior (things to be done) expected of a student.
3. The criteria (standards) used to determine how well the behavior is to be done.

Determining Criteria (Standards) of Performance

A terminal performance objective specifies the minimum level of performance needed to demonstrate successful completion of a block of subject matter. The minimum level of performance may be related to grading standards or to employment standards. For example, a minimum of 75 percent of the behavior specified in the terminal performance objective may meet school requirements for a grade of C. However, a higher minimum (perhaps 95 percent) may be required to meet the minimum acceptable employment standards.

Many schools now require that the criteria specified in a terminal performance objective be based on minimum employment standards. Using employment standards allows schools to better communicate with prospective employers concerning the specific behaviors students have obtained and those that may require on-the-job training to meet the minimum requirements of the position.

To establish the minimum level of performance required for employment, teachers must follow local employment standards. The establishment of an advisory committee made up of prospective employers of accounting graduates is an approach often used to determine the minimum levels of performance required for employment. An advisory committee may also be used to review the behaviors specified in the terminal performance objectives. Local condition may require that additional behaviors be specified or may allow the deletion of some of the behaviors.

The evaluation of performance for grading purposes under a competency-based instructional program is the same as for noncompetency-based programs. Local school grading standards are followed. A student may perform at a level satisfactory to pass the course but may not perform at a level necessary for employment. Typically, a student achieving minimum employment standards earns a C for the course. A grade of D means a student gets credit for the course but does not meet minimum employment standards.

Availability of Terminal Performance Objectives

Teachers should distribute copies of terminal performance objectives to all students before they begin their study of each part of the accounting program. Each terminal performance objective should be reviewed with students so that they understand the specific behaviors required.

Level of Specificity of Terminal Performance Objectives

The writing of terminal performance objectives related to specific evaluation instruments is fully explained in the TRG.

Enabling Performance Tasks

Enabling performance tasks are the steps a student must go through to prepare for the successful demonstration of the behavior specified in terminal performance objectives. Enabling performance tasks are performance statements designed to guide the student through the learning experiences required.

Learning Activities

Learning activities are teacher-directed activities planned for one or more students so that they may be able to demonstrate predetermined terminal performance objectives. The learning activities should be directed to the knowledge, understanding, and application specified in the terminal performance objectives.

Reinforcement Activities

Reinforcement activities should be provided in a competency-based instructional program to strengthen student learnings. In a competency-based accounting program, each reinforcement activity should cover a complete accounting cycle.

Recycling Activities

Some students do not reach the minimum level of performance specified in a terminal performance objective as easily as others. For these students, additional learning activities are needed. Recycling activities are the student-oriented learning activities used by students who need more practice than most students. Not all students need to complete recycling activities. After students have completed the teacher-directed recycling activities, they should be given a second opportunity to demonstrate performance on the terminal performance objective for which they did not reach the minimum level of performance on the first try.

CENTURY 21 ACCOUNTING, Advanced Course

The specific elements within each component in the competency-based program model are provided in outline form in the TRG. This material is provided as a guide for teachers conducting competency-based education.

The general behavioral goals are also given on each part opener within the textbook to guide students through the learning experiences. The specific criteria (standards) of performance have been purposely omitted from the terminal performance objectives to allow each teacher to provide for local differences in student abilities, job requirements, and school conditions.

APPLIED MATHEMATICS GRID

Basic applied mathematic skills are not specifically identified in *CENTURY 21 ACCOUNTING* since all problems apply the basic skills that are listed in the following table. Adding columns of numbers is demonstrated in all chapters that contain journalizing, posting, work sheets, and financial statements. Subtracting numbers is demonstrated in chapters that involve posting, calculating net income/net loss on work sheets, and preparing financial statements. Multiplying numbers is demonstrated in chapters that cover payroll, depreciation, sales tax, discounts, and interest. Dividing numbers is demonstrated in chapters that include component percentages, depreciation, and interest. Finding unknown numbers is covered in chapters in which transactions are analyzed using the accounting equation.

The Mathematics icon appears in the end-of-chapter activities the first time a specific math skill that demonstrates a specific accounting skill is introduced. The following grid depicts the math skill and the first application in the end-of-chapter activities of that skill. Repeated applications are not noted.

APPLIED MATHEMATICS GRID

Applied Mathematics/Accounting Skill	Application
Chapter 2	
A: Calculating purchases discount and amount due	Prob. 2-3
Chapter 3	
A: Calculating sales discount	Prob. 3-2
B: Calculating sales tax	Prob. 3-2
C: Calculating sales invoice amount due	Prob. 3-2
D: Proving cash	Prob. 3-3
Chapter 4	
A: Calculating accumulated vacation time and other benefit hours	Prob. 4-1
B: Calculating regular time, overtime, and total earnings	Prob. 4-2
C: Calculating sales commission	Prob. 4-4
D: Calculating employee deductions	Prob. 4-5
E: Calculating net pay	Prob. 4-5
F: Calculating payroll tax liabilities	Prob. 4-8
Chapter 5	
A: Calculating estimated ending inventory	Prob. 5-1
B: Calculating component percentage of total cost of merchandise sold	Prob. 5-2
C: Calculating component percentage of total gross profit on operations	Prob. 5-2
D: Calculating estimated uncollectible accounts expense	Prob. 5-7
E: Calculating component percentage of total operating expenses	Prob. 5-5
F: Calculating component percentage for net income before federal income tax	Prob. 5-6
G: Calculating component percentages for a departmental statement of gross profit and an income statement	Prob. 5-7
Chapter 7	
A: Estimating merchandise inventory using the gross profit method	Prob. 7-4
B: Estimating merchandise inventory using the retail method	Prob. 7-4
C: Calculating merchandise inventory turnover ratio	Prob. 7-5
D: Calculating average number of days' sales in merchandise inventory	Prob. 7-5
Chapter 8	
A: Estimating uncollectible accounts expense using a percentage of net sales	Prob. 8-2
B: Estimating uncollectible accounts expense using a percentage of total sales on account	Prob. 8-3
C: Estimating the balance of Allowance for Uncollectible Accounts by aging accounts receivable	Prob. 8-4
D: Estimating the balance of Allowance for Uncollectible Accounts by using a percentage of the accounts receivable account balance	Prob. 8-5
E: Calculating the accounts receivable turnover ratio	Prob. 8-8

(continued on page T-24)

(continued from page T-23)

APPLIED MATHEMATICS GRID

Applied Mathematics/Accounting Skill	Application
Chapter 9	
A: Calculating depreciation using the straight-line method	Prob. 9-2
B: Calculating loss or gain on disposal of plant assets	Prob. 9-4
C: Calculating depreciation using the declining-balance method	Prob. 9-6
D: Calculating depreciation using the sum-of-the-years-digits method	Prob. 9-6
E: Calculating depreciation using the production-unit method	Prob. 9-7
F: Calculating depreciation using MACRS	Prob. 9-8
G: Calculating depletion expense	Prob. 9-9
H: Calculating property tax	Prob. 9-10
Chapter 10	
A: Calculating interest	Prob. 10-1
B: Calculating maturity dates	Prob. 10-1
C: Calculating bank discount and proceeds	Prob. 10-1
Chapter 11	
A: Calculating interest	Prob. 11-3
B: Calculating maturity dates	Prob. 11-C
C: Calculating unearned rent	Prob. 11-C
Chapter 12	
A: Calculating the value of common and preferred stock	Prob. 12-3
B: Calculating dividends for common and preferred stock	Prob. 12-3
Chapter 13	
A: Calculating paid-in capital in excess of par/stated value	Prob. 13-1
B: Calculating discount on capital stock	Prob. 13-1
C: Calculating paid-in capital from sale of treasury stock	Prob. 13-2
D: Calculating interest on bonds	Prob. 13-C
E: Calculating bond sinking fund deposits	Prob. 13-C
Chapter 14	
A: Calculating federal income tax	Prob. 14-1
B: Calculating component percentages	Prob. 14-3
C: Calculating earnings per share	Prob. 14-3
D: Calculating equity per share	Prob. 14-4
E: Calculating price-earnings ratio	Prob. 14-4
F: Calculating accounts receivable turnover ratio	Prob. 14-5
G: Calculating rate earned on average stockholders' equity	Prob. 14-5
H: Calculating rate earned on average total assets	Prob. 14-5
Chapter 15	
A: Calculating projected quarterly sales	Prob. 15-1
B: Calculating projected quarterly ending inventory	Prob. 15-1
C: Calculating projected quarterly purchases	Prob. 15-1
D: Calculating projected quarterly expenses	Prob. 15-2
E: Calculating projected federal income tax expense	Prob. 15-2
F: Calculating projected quarterly cash receipts	Prob. 15-3
G: Calculating projected quarterly cash payments	Prob. 15-3
Chapter 16	
A: Calculating contribution margin	Prob. 16-1
B: Calculating contribution margin rate	Prob. 16-2
C: Calculating breakeven point	Prob. 16-2
D: Calculating contribution margin per unit	Prob. 16-3
E: Calculating sales required to maintain planned net income	Prob. 16-4
F: Calculating sales mix	Prob. 16-6

(continued on page T-25)

(continued from page T-24)

APPLIED MATHEMATICS GRID

Applied Mathematics/Accounting Skill	Application
Chapter 17	
A: Calculating trend analysis	Prob. 17-1
B: Calculating component percentages	Prob. 17-2
C: Calculating rate earned on average total assets	Prob. 17-3
D: Calculating rate earned on average stockholders's equity	Prob. 17-3
E: Calculating rate earned on net sales	Prob. 17-3
F: Calculating earnings per share	Prob. 17-3
G: Calculating price-earnings ratio	Prob. 17-3
H: Calculating accounts receivable turnover ratio	Prob. 17-4
I: Calculating average number of days for payment	Prob. 17-4
J: Calculating merchandise inventory turnover ratio	Prob. 17-4
K: Calculating average number of days' sales in merchandise inventory	Prob. 17-4
L: Calculating working capital	Prob. 17-5
M: Calculating current ratio	Prob. 17-5
N: Calculating acid-test ratio	Prob. 17-5
O: Calculating debt ratio	Prob. 17-6
P: Calculating equity ratio	Prob. 17-6
Q: Calculating equity per share	Prob. 17-6
Chapter 18	
A: Calculating component percentages	Prob. 18-3
Chapter 19	
A: Estimating direct labor cost	Prob. 19-C
B: Calculating the factory overhead applied rate	Prob. 19-2
C: Calculating applied factory overhead	Prob. 19-3
D: Calculating manufacturing cost per unit	Prob. 19-3
Chapter 21	
A: Calculating share of partnership equity	Prob. 21-2
B: Calculating equity greater than partner's investment	Prob. 21-4
C: Calculating goodwill	Prob. 21-5
Chapter 22	
A: Calculating distribution of partnership net income using:	
Fixed percentage	Prob. 22-1
Percentage of total equity	Prob. 22-1
Interest on equity	Prob. 22-1
Salaries	Prob. 22-1
Combination of methods	Prob. 22-1
B: Calculating distribution of partnership deficit	Prob. 22-1
C: Calculating distribution of loss and gain on realization	Prob. 22-4
Chapter 24	
A: Calculating excess of revenues over expenditures	Prob. 24-1

SPECIAL FEATURES GRID

CENTURY 21 ACCOUNTING has been expanded to cover many contemporary special features. The following grid illustrates the features and their location.

SPECIAL FEATURES GRID

Chapter	Professional Business Ethics	Spreadsheet Options	Multicultural Awareness	Global Perspective	Personal Visions in Business	Careers in Accounting	Applied Communications
1	Mixing Politics and Business		Asian American Business				Writing a Report About a Job in the Classifieds
2				International Terms of Sale			Writing a Resume
3					Al Parker, Polyfab Display Co.	Auditor	
4		Using the Titles Command					
5			Hispanic American Businesses		Debra Miller, M.D.		
6				International Banking		Accounting Clerk	Writing a Report About Computer Viruses
7	At What Price Safety?		Korean American Businesses		James Martinez, Martinez Personnel Systems, Inc.		
8		Copying a Relative Cell Reference	Native American Businesses				
9				International Introductions			
10	Is Salary Expense a Picnic?					Financial Securities Clerk	
11					Cynthia Reed, Branches Medical, Inc.		Writing a Memo Concerning an Audit
12			Diverse Work Force	International Packages and Customs Inspections			Preparing a Personal Introduction for a Speaker

(continued on page T-27)

(continued from page T-26)

SPECIAL FEATURES GRID

Chapter	Professional Business Ethics	Spreadsheet Options	Multicultural Awareness	Global Perspective	Personal Visions in Business	Careers in Accounting	Applied Communications
13	Ups and Downs of CEO Compensation						
14		Printing Spreadsheets and Graphs			Dr. Yoshi Tsuchiya, Hamagami Laboratory	Audit Clerk	
15			Calculators		Bonnie Combs, Bonnie's Hallmark		Creating a Presentation About Why Everyone Needs to Take Accounting
16	Smooth Sailing with Client Referrals					Budget Accountant	
17				International Organizations			
18	Legislate Competition Away		Women Business Owners				
19				International Travel		Accountant, Cost	
20		Using the Numerical Format Option			Glenn D. Southard, Southard Insurance Agency		Writing a Report Comparing Competition
21			Minority Recruiting				Identifying Expenses and Writing a Report Including a Pie Chart
22				International Mail		Revenue Officer	
23	Keeping a Trade Secret						
24					Ruth Smith, American Indian Heritage Center of Texas	Auditor, County or City	

SOFTWARE CORRELATION

After manual accounting procedures are mastered, computer software may be used as an enrichment activity to facilitate the processing of accounting data and experience the use of computers in accounting.

Two software packages are available to use with *CENTURY 21 ACCOUNTING, Advanced Course* to augment teacher instruction: *SPREADSHEET TEMPLATE FOR CENTURY 21 ACCOUNTING* and *AUTOMATED ACCOUNTING 6.0* or higher and the accompanying templates.

All activities for which software may be used are designated by an icon next to the activity in the text. This makes identification easy for both the teacher and student.

Each software package and its documentation is available from South-Western Publishing Company.

Spreadsheet Template: *SPREADSHEET TEMPLATE FOR CENTURY 21 ACCOUNTING, First-Year and Advanced Courses* may be used with selected Application Problems and Enrichment Problems. In order to use the templates, Lotus® 1-2-3® or Microsoft® Works™ are needed for DOS computers. For Macintosh computers, Microsoft Works for the Macintosh™ or Microsoft Excel® are needed.

Thirty-seven problems from *CENTURY 21 ACCOUNTING* may be used with spreadsheet software.

Automated Accounting: *AUTOMATED ACCOUNTING 6.0* or higher may be used to complete selected Application Problems, Enrichment Problems, Integrating Automated Accounting Problems, Reinforcement Activities, and Simulations. The *CENTURY 21 ACCOUNTING, First-Year Course Template Disk* is also needed to complete the *AUTOMATED ACCOUNTING* problems and reinforcement activities in the text. Separate templates are needed for each simulation that is completed.

A total of 22 problems, 2 reinforcement activities, and 2 simulations from *CENTURY 21 ACCOUNTING* may be automated using *AUTOMATED ACCOUNTING 6.0.*

It is suggested that the text that accompanies *AUTOMATED ACCOUNTING 6.0, Advanced Course* be used as reference. The correlation for that text is listed in the last column of the grid.

CENTURY 21 ACCOUNTING Text Advanced Course Chapter	CENTURY 21 ACCOUNTING Text Advanced Course Template Problems	CENTURY 21 ACCOUNTING Spreadsheet Template	AUTOMATED ACCOUNTING 6.0 Text Advanced Course Chapter
1			1
2	2-1, 2-2, 2-4, 2-5, 2-M		
Integrating Automated Accounting Topic 1			
3	3-1, 3-3, 3-M, 3-C		2
Integrating Automated Accounting Topic 2			
4		4-1, 4-4, 4-5	4
5	5-7, 5-M	5-1, 5-3, 5-M	3
Integrating Automated Accounting Topic 3			
Reinforcement Activity 1 Galleria, Inc. Simulation (A separate template disk is needed)			
6			
7		7-1, 7-2, 7-3, 7-4	7
Integrating Automated Accounting Topic 4 Problem DB-4			
8		8-4	
9	9-1, 9-6, 9-8, 9-C	9-6, 9-7, 9-8	5
Integrating Automated Accounting Topic 5			
10		10-1	
11			

(continued on page T-29)

(continued from page T-28)

CENTURY 21 ACCOUNTING Text Advanced Course Chapter	CENTURY 21 ACCOUNTING Text Advanced Course Template Problems	CENTURY 21 ACCOUNTING Spreadsheet Template	AUTOMATED ACCOUNTING 6.0 Text Advanced Course Chapter
12		12-M	6
13			
14	14-2, 14-M	14-1, 14-M	
Integrating Automated Accounting Topic 6			
Reinforcement Activity 2 Four Seasons, Inc. Simulation (A separate template disk is needed)			
15	15-C	15-1, 15-2, 15-3	9
Integrating Automated Accounting Topic 7			
16		16-1, 16-3, 16-4, 16-5, 16-6	
17		17-1, 17-2, 17-M	10
18	18-2, 18-M	18-M	
19		19-1	
20		20-3	
21		21-4, 21-5	8
22		22-1, 22-M	
23			
24	24-1	24-M	12

LOCATION OF ANSWERS AND SOLUTIONS

Due to the abundance of teacher support material available with this course, the table below is provided to guide you in locating solutions to student activities.

KEY TO LOCATION OF ANSWERS AND SOLUTIONS	
Item	**Found In**
Audit Your Understanding Questions	Margins of Wraparound Teacher's Edition Appendix D of Student Text
Accounting Terms	Margins of Wraparound Teacher's Edition
Questions for Understanding	Margins of Wraparound Teacher's Edition
Cases for Critical Thinking	Margins of Wraparound Teacher's Edition
Applied Communications	Margins of Wraparound Teacher's Edition
Application Problems	Check figures in Margins of Wraparound Teacher's Edition Balance of Solution in Teacher's Edition of Working Papers
Mastery Problems	Check figures in Margins of Wraparound Teacher's Edition Balance of Solution in Teacher's Edition of Working Papers
Challenge Problems	Check figures in Margins of Wraparound Teacher's Edition Balance of Solution in Teacher's Edition of Working Papers
Recycling Problems	Check figures in Margins of Wraparound Teacher's Edition Balance of Solution in Teacher's Edition of Demonstration and Recycling Problems
Reinforcement Activities	Check figures in Margins of Wraparound Teacher's Edition Balance of Solution in Teacher's Edition of Working Papers
Integrating Automated Accounting Problems	Check figures in Margins of Wraparound Teacher's Edition Input Form Solutions in Teacher's Edition of Working Papers and repeated in TRG Reports in TRG
Study Guides	Teacher's Edition of Working Papers
Tests	TRG
Manual Simulations	Key for manual simulations
Automated Simulations	Key for automated simulations

PROFESSIONAL REFERENCES AND RESOURCES

Periodicals

Accounting Horizons, American Accounting Association, Sarasota, FL.

Accounting News, Warren, Gorham & Lamont, New York, NY.

Accounting, Organizations and Society, Pergamon Press, Inc., Tarrytown, NY.

Accounting Review, American Accounting Association, Sarasota, FL.

Accounting Technology (formerly *Computers in Accounting*), Faulkner & Gray, Eleven Penn Plaza, 17th Floor, New York, NY 10001.

Accounting Today, Lebhar-Friedman, Inc., New York, NY.

American Accounting Association Newsletter, Sarasota, FL.

Black Enterprise, New York, NY. (Multicultural awareness)

CPA Digest, CPA Services, Inc., Brookfield, WI.

CPA Journal, New York State Society of CPAs, New York, NY.

Forbes, New York, NY (Business news).

Fortune, New York, NY (Business news).

Hispanic, Washington, D.C. (Multicultural awareness)

Inc. (Business)

Journal of Accountancy, AICPA, Jersey City, NJ.

Journal of Accounting Education, Pergamon Press, Inc., Tarrytown, NY.

Journal of Business Ethics, Kluwer Academic Publishers, Norwell, CA.

Nattive, A. "Cooperative Learning: An Overview." *Journal of Humanistic Education*. 1988.

Management Accounting, National Association of Accountants, 10 Paragon Drive, Montvale, NJ.

Multicultural Review, Greenwood Press Inc., Westport, CT. (Multicultural awareness)

Multinational Business, Economist Newspaper, New York NY. (Global business)

Native Peoples, Phoenix, AZ. (Multicultural awareness)

Practical Accountant, Faulkner & Gray, Inc., New York, NY.

Transpacific, Malibu, CA. (Multicultural awareness)

Wall Street Journal, New York, NY. (Business newspaper)

Working Woman, New York, NY. (Multicultural awareness)

Books

AICPA. *A Survey of Perceptions, Knowledge and Attitudes Towards CPAs and the Accounting Profession*, 1986.

AICPA. *Accounting Trends and Techniques*, 1991.

AICPA. *FASB Accounting Standards*.

AICPA. *Upward Mobility of Women Special Committee: Report to the AICPA Board of Directors*.

African America: Portrait of a People. Detroit: Visible Ink Press, 1994.

Albrecht, W. Steve. *Ethical Issues in the Practice of Accounting*. Cincinnati: South-Western Publishing Co., 1992.

AT&T, *International Telephone Guide*.

Bieg, Bernard J., and B. Lewis Keeling. *Payroll Accounting*. (Revised Annually). Cincinnati: South-Western Publishing Co.

Bloom, Benjamin S., ed., et. al. *Taxonomy of Educational Objectives: Handbook I, Cognitive Domain*. White Plains: Longman, Inc., 1977.

Cantlon, T. *Structuring the Classroom Successfully for Cooperative Team Learning*. Portland, OR: Prestige Publishers, 1991.

Champagne, Duane. *Native America: Portrait of a People*. Detroit: Visible Ink Press, 1994.

Chatfield, Michael. *A History of Accounting Thought*. Second Edition. Huntington, NY: Robert E. Krieger Publishing, 1977.

Cohen, E. *Designing Group Work*. New York: Teachers College Press, 1986.

Diamond, Michael A. *Financial Accounting*. Third Edition. Cincinnati: South-Western Publishing Co., 1993.

Duranti, Luciana. "The Odyssey of Records Managers." *ARMA Quarterly*, July, 1989.

Ehrlich, Virginia Z. *Gifted Children: A Guide for Parents and Teachers*. Unionville, NY: Trillium Press, 1985.

Elashmawi, Farid, and Philip R. Harris. *Multicultural Management: New Skills for Global Success*. Houston: Gulf Publishing Company, 1993.

Estes, Ralph. *Dictionary of Accounting*. Second Edition. Cambridge: The MIT Press, 1986.

Evans, Thomas G., Martin E. Taylor, and Oscar Holzmann. *International Accounting and Reporting*. Cincinnati: South-Western Publishing Co., 1985.

Fess, Philip E., and Carl S. Warren. *Accounting Principles*. Seventeenth Edition. Cincinnati: South-Western Publishing Co., 1993.

Gelinas, Ulric J., Jr., Allan E. Oram, and William P. Wiggins. *Accounting Information Systems*. Second Edition. Cincinnati: South-Western Publishing Co., 1993.

Gibson, Charles H. *Financial Statement Analysis: Using Financial Accounting Information*. Fifth Edition. Cincinnati: South-Western Publishing Co., 1992.

Gilbertson, Claudia. *Accounting: Learning and Instruction*. Second Edition. Cincinnati: South-Western Publishing Co., 1992.

Gordon, Gus. *Understanding Financial Statements*. Cincinnati: South-Western Publishing Co., 1992.

Gronlund, Norman E. *Stating Objectives for Classroom Instruction*. 3d. ed. New York: Macmillan Publishing Co., Inc., 1985.

Hamilton, D. *Cooperative Learning in the Classroom*. Bloomington, IN: Phi Delta Kappa Educational Foundation, 1990.

Harrell, Earl, and Cassandra Harrell. *Surviving in the Workplace: A Resource for Individuals, Educational Institutions, and Businesses for Promoting Safety and Awareness in the Workplace*. Milwaukee: E.T. Publishing Company, 1994.

Harris, Philip R., and Robert T. Moran. *Managing Cultural Differences*. Houston: Gulf Publishing Company, 1992.

Heintz, James, and Robert Parry. *College Accounting*. Fourteenth Edition. Cincinnati: South-Western Publishing Co., 1993.

Hendrickson, Aletha. *Writing for Accountants*. Cincinnati: South-Western Publishing Co., 1993.

Henke, Emerson O. *Introduction to Nonprofit Organization Accounting*. Fourth Edition. Cincinnati: South-Western Publishing Co., 1992.

Johnson, D., and R. Johnson. *Cooperation and Competition*. Hillsdale, NJ: Lawrence Eribaum, 1987.

Johnson, D., and R. Johnson. *Social Skills for Successful Group Work*. Educational Leadership, 1990.

Kagan, S. *Cooperative Learning Resources for Teachers*. San Juan Capistrano: Resources for Teachers, 1989.

Langenderfer, Harold Q., Willis C. Stevenson, Herbert C. Sieg, and James B. Bower. *Federal Income Taxation*. (Revised Annually). Cincinnati: South-Western Publishing Co.

Langenderfer, Harold Q., Willis C. Stevenson, Herbert C. Sieg, and James B. Bower. *Personal Income Taxation.* (Revised Annually). Cincinnati: South-Western Publishing Co.

Lerner, Janet. *Learning Disabilities: Theories, Diagnosis, and Teaching Strategies*, Fifth Edition. Boston: Houghton Mifflin, 1988.

Mager, Robert F. *Preparing Instructional Objectives.* 2d. ed., rev. Belmont: Pitman Learning, Inc., 1984.

Magill, Harry T., and Gary J. Previts. *CPA Professional Responsibilities: A Guide.* Cincinnati: South-Western Publishing Co., 1991.

Marzano, Robert J. *A Different Kind of Classroom: Teaching with Dimensions of Learning.* Association for Supervision and Curriculum Development, Alexandria, VA, 1992.

McCabe and McCabe. *Writing Effective Resumes, A Complete Guide.* Cincinnati: South-Western Publishing Co., 1993.

Miller, Sidney R., and Patrick J. Schloss. *Career-Vocational Education for Handicapped Youth.* Rockville, MD: Aspen Systems Corporation, 1982.

Moran, Robert T., and William G. Stripp. *Dynamics of Successful International Business Negotiations.* Houston: Gulf Publishing Company, 1991.

Moran, Robert T., Philip R. Harris, and William G. Stripp. *Developing the Global Organization.* Houston: Gulf Publishing Company, 1993.

Nash, John F., and Cynthia D. Heagy. *Accounting Information Systems.* Third Edition. Cincinnati: South-Western Publishing Co., 1993.

National Society of Public Accountants. *Portfolio of Accounting Systems for Small and Medium-Sized Businesses.* Revised. Englewood Cliffs, NJ: Prentice Hall, 1977.

Parker, Jeanette P. *Instructional Strategies for Teaching the Gifted.* Boston: Allyn and Bacon, 1989.

Sarkees, Michelle Donnelly, and John L. Scott. *Vocation Special Needs*, Second Edition. American Technical Publishers, 1986.

Secretary's Commission on Achieving Necessary Skills. *What Work Requires of Schools: A SCANS Report for America 2000.* Washington, DC: U.S. Department of Labor, 1991.

Sheth, Jagdish N., and Abdolreza Eshghi, eds. *Global Accounting Perspectives.* Cincinnati: South-Western Publishing Co., 1989.

Shim, Jay K., and Joel G. Siefel. *Encyclopedic Dictionary of Accounting & Finance.* Englewood Cliffs, NJ: Prentice Hall, 1989.

Simons, George F., Carmen Vazquez, and Philip R. Harris. *Transcultural Leadership: Empowering the Diverse WorkForce.* Houston: Gulf Publishing Company, 1993.

Skousen, K. Fred, Harold Q. Langenderfer, and W. Steve Albrecht. *Accounting Principles and Applications.* Cincinnati: South-Western Publishing Co., 1993.

Slavin, R. *Using Student Team Learning.* Baltimore: John Hopkins University Press, 1986.

Swartz, R. *The Effects of Attitudes and Aptitudes in Predicting Final Course Grades: Implications for Multi-Group Organization in Business Communication Classes.* Unpublished paper presented in Teacher Education 883, Michigan State University, East Lansing, 1987.

U.S. Department of Commerce. *Basic Guide to Exporting.* 1986.

U.S. Department of Labor. *Dictionary of Occupational Titles.*

U.S. Department of Labor. *Occupational Outlook Handbook.*

Weirich, Thomas R., and Alan Reinstein. *Accounting and Auditing Research: A Practical Guide.* Third Edition. Cincinnati: South-Western Publishing Co., 1992.

Zedlitz. *Getting a Job, Process Kit.* Third Edition. Cincinnati: South-Western Publishing Co., 1993.

Technology

AICPA. *The Bottom Line: Inside Accounting Today*, 1987. (Video)

AICPA. *It All Adds Up*, 1989. (Video)

AICPA. *A License to Succeed*, 1990. (Video)

AICPA. *Luca Pacioli: Unsung Hero of the Renaissance.* (Video)

AICPA. *Serving America: A Tradition of Excellence*, 1986. (Video)

AICPA. *TOTAL (Total On-line Tax and Accounting Library)* (Tax and accounting on-line database)

Dun & Bradstreet Information Services. *Dun's Direct Access* (On-line database of U.S. companies)

Excel (spreadsheet software)

Lotus (spreadsheet software)

Mead Data Central, Inc. LEXIS/NEXIS (On-line database)

Pagemaker (desktop publishing software)

Research Institute of America. OnPoint CD-ROM Tax Library (Tax research CD-ROM database)

Ventura Publisher (desktop publishing software)

Windows (operating system software)

WordPerfect (word processing software)

Works (integrated software)

CENTURY 21 Accounting

CENTURY 21 Accounting

ADVANCED COURSE

SIXTH EDITION

Kenton E. Ross, CPA
Professor of Accounting
East Texas State University
Commerce, Texas

Robert D. Hanson
Associate Dean
College of Business Administration
Central Michigan University
Mount Pleasant, Michigan

Claudia Bienias Gilbertson, CPA
Teaching Professor
Anoka-Ramsey Community College
Coon Rapids, Minnesota

Mark W. Lehman, CPA
Instructor
School of Accountancy
Mississippi State University
Starkville, Mississippi

South-Western Publishing Co.
BE27FA

Vice-President/Editor-in-Chief: Dennis M. Kokoruda
Senior Developmental Editor: Carol Volz
Art Director: John Robb
Design Coordinator: Darren Wright
Marketing Manager: Larry Qualls
Coordinating Editor: Mark Beck
Production Manager: Carol Sturzenberger
Senior Production Editor: Mark Cheatham
Production Editor: Kimberlee Kusnerak
Production Editor I: Denise Wheeler
Associate Director/Photo Editing: Devore Nixon
Photo Editor: Kimberly A. Larson

Cover Design: The Optimum Group

Internal Design: Lesiak/Crampton Design

ISBN: 0-538-63174-0

Library of Congress Catalog Card Number: 93-084971

1 2 3 4 5 6 7 8 9 0 D 99 98 97 96 95 94

Printed in the United States of America

I(T)P
International Thomson Publishing

South-Western Publishing Co. is an ITP Company. The ITP trademark is used under license.

Preface

This advanced-course accounting text expands on topics learned in the first-year course while adding new topics about management accounting, cost accounting, not-for-profit accounting, and financial analysis. The study of a second year of accounting helps qualify students for jobs and careers at higher levels than one year of study would allow. It is also excellent background and preparation for college business and accounting courses and business majors. Research has proven that students who have successfully completed two years of high school accounting are more successful in their first year of college accounting than students without that background. In addition, the cost, budgeting, and financial analysis topics are useful tools for the new entrepreneur.

How to Use This Text

This textbook is carefully designed to function as a learning tool. The overall organization is in eight parts, with one or more chapters in each part. Part 1 is a special part that has only one chapter. The remaining seven parts consist of two to four chapters on related topics. For each part, a business is identified and described and that business is used to illustrate all the concepts for the rest of that part. In addition, each of these parts begins with a chart of accounts that is used throughout the part; it is an excellent preview for the part and serves as a convenient reference as you study each chapter.

Each chapter begins with a set of enabling performance tasks, or learning objectives, that describe what you will be able to do after studying the chapter. The task statements preview the chapter. A list of new terms that are defined and used within the chapter is also printed at the start of the chapter. Begin your study of each chapter by reading the enabling performance tasks and new accounting terms.

Each chapter has a number of headings that should be previewed to help you understand the chapter. These headings can also function as a topical outline for a chapter if your studying method includes taking notes in outline format. Abundant illustrations highlight concepts in the chapter narrative. Note that each illustration has both an illustration number that is referenced within the narrative of the chapter and a descriptive caption that describes what is being illustrated. All new accounting vocabulary terms are printed in bold type within the sentences that define the terms so these definitions can be easily found.

Several features within the chapter enhance the learning experience. Audit Your Understanding questions at the end of each short section of a chapter provide questions for assessing your grasp of the concepts covered. Self-check answers are provided in Appendix D. FYI (For Your Information) boxes in the margins emphasize important points from the chapter and sometimes present additional interesting information about accounting and business.

Special Features

The following special features appear throughout the textbook:

Multicultural Awareness: This feature describes the contributions of a variety of cultures to accounting and business. Some of these features focus on historical contributions while others describe a situation in the United States today. This feature will help strengthen your awareness of the value of diversity in the work force and society.

Professional Business Ethics: The news medias are full of stories about unethical behavior in business and the effect of this unethical behavior on businesses and individuals. Boxed features throughout the text present ethical dilemmas that employees and business owners encounter in real life. Chapter 1 discusses ethical behavior in general and presents a three-step checklist as a model for analyzing ethical decisions.

Global Perspective: Global business topics provide information and activities to enhance preparation for working in the global economy. These topics provide practical real-life information about trading across national boundaries and furnish activities to demonstrate how this information is applied.

Personal Visions in Business: These personality profiles describe individuals in the business world today from a variety of occupations and cultural backgrounds. The individuals portrayed describe how an accounting background can be useful when starting and maintaining your own business and what they have learned about business from their own experiences.

Careers in Accounting: This feature presents a list of job duties for different job titles. This feature can help you select the kinds of jobs you might want to pursue based on the responsibilities of each job.

Spreadsheet Options: Features of spreadsheet software can help streamline business practices. The Spreadsheet Options feature describes some of the techniques used by businesses to make their financial reporting and analysis more efficient.

Applied Mathematics: If accounting is the language of business, then numbers are probably the words of the language. Many different mathematical calculations are involved in accounting for a business. Within a chapter, each time a new mathematical calculation is presented the formula is highlighted by a color box and the Applied Math icon appears beside it. The Applied Math icon is repeated next to end-of-chapter activities that first apply each calculation.

AUDIT YOUR UNDERSTANDING

Audit Your Understanding questions: At the end of each short section of a chapter, a list of questions is provided for assessing your grasp of the concepts covered. Self-check answers are provided in Appendix D.

FYI

FYI (For Your Information): Boxes in the margins emphasize important points from the chapter and sometimes present additional interesting information about accounting and business.

End-of-Chapter Activities

The end of each chapter provides questions, cases, and problems for practicing the new skills learned in the chapter and demonstrating your grasp of the concepts. Each section identifies the enabling performance tasks to be performed. The identifying task letters are placed in parentheses next to the heading of each activity.

The first section at the end of each chapter presents a list of all the new accounting terms defined in the chapter. You should be sure you know the meaning of each of these terms. This activity is followed by questions that help you review the concepts in the chapter. The next section, called Cases for Critical Thinking, describes case scenarios, based on chapter concepts, for which you are required to stretch your knowledge to provide the best answer or select the best alternative from those presented. Frequent Applied Communications sections furnish opportunities for honing your communication skills in the context of topics that are related to accounting.

The remaining end-of-chapter activities are application, mastery, and challenge problems. Application Problems apply your new accounting skills as you complete a problem for each section of the chapter. The Mastery Problem is a further application of all the new skills from the chapter in one single problem. The Challenge Problem concludes the chapter by stretching your knowledge to cover new applications. A Recycling Problem is available at the end of the textbook, in Appendix C, to use for additional practice or review. Reinforcement Activities and simulations for each of the three accounting cycles are milestone activities that synthesize all the activities from the chapters in the part.

Software

There are two pieces of software that may be used to complete end-of-chapter activities. Each piece of software is represented by an icon. These icons are placed on the appropriate problems that may be completed using the computer.

AUTOMATED

Automated Accounting: This icon identifies a problem that is appropriate for solving using the *Automated Accounting 6.0* or higher software. A template for this problem is available that contains the chart of accounts and opening balances for selected problems.

Spreadsheet Template: This icon identifies a problem for which a template file is available that can be used with commercial spreadsheet software to solve the problem.

All problems that are identified as being appropriate for solving with the use of software can also be completed manually with pencil and paper.

Reference Material

Reference material at the end of the book includes four appendices, a glossary of terms, and an index. Appendix A briefly describes the preparation and use of a statement of cash flows. Appendix B includes information about using a ten-key calculator and computer keypad. Appendix C presents a recycling problem for each chapter in the textbook for additional practice or review. Appendix D provides the answers to the Audit Your Understanding questions in each chapter so that the questions can be used for self-review. The glossary of terms lists all the terms defined in the text and their definitions for easy reference. The index shows the page location for each topic in the text. This can be useful if you need to look up a topic but do not know where to find it.

ACKNOWLEDGMENTS

We thank the following individuals who contributed to the review process for this edition:

Mrs. Linda Songer
Orange Park High School
Orange Park, Florida

Mr. Joe McFarland
Shasta High School
Redding, California

Mrs. Judith Depew
Turpin High School
Turpin, Oklahoma

Mr. Robert J. Metz
Springville-Griffith Institute
Springville, New York

Ms. Carolyn Alexander
Langham Creek High School
Houston, Texas

Ms. Linda L. White
Waynesboro Area High School
Waynesboro, Pennsylvania

Mr. Dan Miller
Jersey Shore High School
Jersey Shore, Pennsylvania

Ms. Judy Sams
Buckingham County High School
Buckingham, Virginia

Mr. Bill King
Douglas Byrd High School
Fayetteville, North Carolina

Mr. Robert Greer
John Jay High School
San Antonio, Texas

We also appreciate the ongoing feedback provided by the classroom professionals who use CENTURY 21 ACCOUNTING every day.

ACKNOWLEDGMENTS

Contents

PART 1

Professional Accounting

PART 2

Departmentalized Accounting

PART 3

Accounting Control Systems

PART 4

General Accounting Adjustments

PART 5

Corporation Accounting

PART 6

Management Accounting

PART 7

Cost Accounting

PART 8

Other Accounting Systems

PHOTO CREDITS

SWP: pages 4, 6, 31, 610, 641

Photography by Alan Brown/Photonics: pages 27, 53, 64, 88, 91, 116, 136, 151, 167, 170, 192, 206, 215, 225, 226, 277, 280, 281, 306, 325, 327, 344, 364, 370, 393, 405, 407, 436, 438, 441, 462, 515, 569, 586, 587, 634, A-1, B-1

Lori Adamski Peek/Tony Stone Worldwide: page 66

Photo by Ron Samardge: page 74

Laurence Monneret/Tony Stone Worldwide: page 83

Photos © Todd Joyce: pages 140, 207, 383, 422, 542

Michele Burgess/The Stock Market: page 246

Haworth, Inc.: page 249

Photography by Erik VonFischer/Photonics: pages 312, 463

©1993 Paul Morris: page 315

Comstock, Inc.: page 355

Alastair Black/Tony Stone Images: page 495

Alan Levenson/Tony Stone Worldwide: page 496

Photo courtesy Bergen Brunswig Corporation: page 521

Courtesy of Hewlett-Packard Company: page 534

David Woods/The Stock Market: page 547

Arthur Meyerson Photography: page 570

David C. Frazier/The Stock Solution: page 609

Dan DeWilde for SWP: page 645

Courtesy of International Business Machines Corporation: page C-1

PART 1 OVERVIEW

STUDENT EDITION

STUDENT FEATURES

Professional Business Ethics

Mixing Politics and Business, page 18

Multicultural Awareness

Asian-American Businesses, page 7

Audit Your Understanding

This student activity can be found on pages 8, 11, and 21

APPLIED SKILLS

Applied Communications

Page 23

TEACHER'S EDITION

APPLIED SKILLS

Communications, page 17
Language Arts, page 13
Writing Across the Curriculum, page 16
Building Study Skills, page 14
Word Processing, page 12

TEACHING STRATEGIES

Accounting Pedagogy, page 4
Different Learning Abilities, page 11
Cooperative Learning, page 10
Expanding Beyond the Classroom, pages 4, 19
Applying Visuals, page 5
Teaching Tip, pages 7, 15, 18, 20

ASSESSMENT

MicroExam software

SOFTWARE

Study Guide Software
MicroExam
WordPerfect (word processing)
Windows (operating system)

BIBLIOGRAPHY

AICPA. *A Survey of Perceptions, Knowledge and Attitudes Towards CPAs and the Accounting Profession,* 1986.

Albrecht, W. Steve. *Ethical Issues in the Practice of Accounting.* Cincinnati: South-Western Publishing Co., 1992.

Bloom, Benjamin S., ed., et. al. *Taxonomy of Educational Objectives: Handbook I, Cognitive Domain.* White Plains: Longman, Inc., 1977.

Estes, Ralph, *Dictionary of Accounting.* Second Edition. Cambridge: The MIT Press, 1986.

Gilbertson, Claudia. *Accounting: Learning and Instruction.* Second Edition. Cincinnati: South-Western Publishing Co., 1992.

Hendrickson, Aletha. *Writing for Accountants.* Cincinnati: South-Western Publishing Co., 1993.

McCabe and McCabe. *Writing Effective Resumes,* A Complete Guide. Cincinnati: South-Western Publishing Co., 1993.

Periodicals

Accounting Review, American Accounting Association, Sarasota, FL

Fortune, New York, NY (Business news)

Hispanic, Washington, D.C. (Multicultural awareness)

Practical Accountant, Faulkner & Gray, Inc., New York, NY

Wall Street Journal, New York, NY (Business newspaper)

Technology

AICPA. *A License to Succeed,* 1990. (video)

PART 1 OPENER

CHAPTER 1
Accounting Framework and Concepts

PART 1

Professional Accounting

GENERAL GOALS

1. Know terminology related to the framework of accounting and the forms of business organization.
2. Understand the framework of accounting, the forms of business organization, and how accounting standards are developed.
3. Understand applications of accounting concepts.
4. Understand that success in the accounting profession depends on the ability to communicate and make ethical decisions.

OVERVIEW

Part 1 lays the foundation for the accounting program. In Chapter 1, an overview is presented that introduces students to the accounting framework and the various fields of accounting and careers in the accounting profession. The forms of business organization are discussed as well as the accounting concepts as outlined by the Financial Accounting Standards Board (FASB). Two important and timely topics are also presented—communication skills and ethics.

Good communication skills play an important role for today's worker. Employers seek individuals with good written and oral communication skills. Chapter 1 introduces students to the importance of effective communication. As the chapters progress, students are given the opportunity to apply their skills in the end-of-chapter Applied Communications activities. Students are also given opportunities to apply their writing skills in portfolio assessment, writing across the curriculum, and practicing language arts skills as suggested in the margin of the teacher's edition. All communication activities are accounting-related to be more meaningful and applicable to the subject area.

Ethical decision making skills also play an important role for today's worker. Chapter 1 discusses business ethics and some of the causes of unethical behavior. A three-step checklist is outlined for making ethical decisions which gives students a framework to stretch their critical thinking skills. Throughout the text, the student feature Professional Business Ethics gives students the opportunity to apply this three-step checklist and analyze situations that they may encounter in the real world.

CHAPTER 1 OVERVIEW

Chapter 1 describes the accounting framework; the accounting fields—financial, managerial, cost, tax, systems, auditing, and personal financial services; accounting professions—private, public, and not-for-profit; communication skills and ethics; the forms of business organization —proprietorship, partnership, and corporation; and accounting standards.

The eleven commonly accepted accounting concepts that guide the work of professional accountants as established by the Financial Accounting Standards Board (FASB) are discussed. Examples of the

GUIDE TO ACHIEVING LEARNING OBJECTIVES

	TEACH	APPLY	EXTEND/ENRICH					
Enabling Performance Tasks	**Lesson Plans**	**Application Problems**	**Mastery Problems**	**Challenge Problems**	**Cases for Critical Thinking**	**Recycling Problems**	**Reinforcement Activity**	
a. Define accounting terms related to the framework of accounting and the forms of business organization.	1-1, 1-2 1-3							
b. Identify the framework of accounting.	1-1							
c. Describe how communication skills are important in reporting accounting information.	1-2							
d. Describe how individuals make ethical business decisions.	1-2							
e. Identify the forms of business organizations, how accounting standards are developed, and the applications of accounting concepts.	1-3				Cases 1, 2			

ENRICHMENT

SPECIAL FEATURES
Professional Business Ethics, page 18
Multicultural Awareness, page 7
Applied Communications, page 23

application of these concepts are provided. These examples are designed to help students understand the underlying accounting assumptions and principles that form the basis for the step-by-step procedures followed in an accounting system.

Chapter 1 is an informational chapter. Therefore, end-of-chapter problems are not included. However, Cases for Critical Thinking and an Applied Communications activity are provided.

	INFORMAL ASSESSMENT		FORMAL ASSESSMENT			
	Study Guide	**Audit Your Understanding**	**Chapter MicroExam**	**Chapter Problem Test**	**Unit Objective Test**	**Portfolio**
	Unit A				✓	
	Units B, C					

NEW, REVIEW, AND EXTENSION

ACTIVITIES/CONCEPTS/TRANSACTIONS	NEW	REVIEW/ EXTENSION
Accounting fields		✓
Accounting profession		✓
Communication skills in accounting		✓
Ethical decision-making		✓
3-step checklist for making ethical decisions		✓
Forms of business organization		✓
Accounting concepts		✓

TEACHING MATERIALS

TEACHING MATERIALS
Teacher's Wraparound Edition of Text
Teacher's Resource Guide
Teacher's Edition of Working Papers
MicroExam

TEACHING STRATEGIES: ACCOUNTING PEDAGOGY

This textbook introduces enabling performance tasks at the beginning of each chapter. These tasks are the steps that the student must undertake in order to demonstrate mastery of the content of the chapter.

1

Accounting Framework and Concepts

ENABLING PERFORMANCE TASKS

After studying Chapter 1, you will be able to:

a Define accounting terms related to the framework of accounting and the forms of business organization.

b Identify the framework of accounting.

c Describe how communication skills are important in reporting accounting information.

d Describe how individuals make ethical business decisions.

e Identify the forms of business organizations, how accounting standards are developed, and the applications of accounting concepts.

TERMS PREVIEW

accounting • accounting system • accounting records • financial accounting • managerial accounting • cost accounting • tax accounting • auditing • auditor • personal financial planning • management advisory services • ethics • proprietorship • partnership • corporation • share of stock • capital stock • stockholder

TEACHING STRATEGIES: EXPANDING BEYOND THE CLASSROOM

This chapter is informational and motivational for students. Arrange to have a guest speaker from a local employment agency or accounting firm speak to the class about the accounting profession in general and specifically about employment in private, public, and governmental/not-for-profit accounting.

All types of organizations need reliable financial information to operate successfully. To be successful, businesses must be able to achieve two objectives: (1) provide the kind and quality of merchandise or services their customers want and (2) earn a reasonable profit. To achieve these two objectives, business owners and managers must have reliable financial information to evaluate their current operations and to plan future operations. Business owners and managers use financial information to help them answer many important questions. Are profits adequate? Are costs reasonable or too high? If costs are too high, which ones can be reduced and how? Should selling prices be increased or decreased? Should new or different products be sold? Should new equipment be bought?

Objectives of governmental and other not-for-profit organizations, such as schools, churches, and social clubs, differ from those of business organizations. The major objective is to provide the best services possible for the least cost. Although the objectives differ from profit-oriented businesses, managers of governmental and other not-for-profit organizations also need reliable financial information to manage their organizations successfully. These managers use financial information to help them answer questions important to their organizations. Are costs reasonable for the services provided? If costs are too high, which ones can be reduced and how? Are adequate funds available from taxes, dues, or donations to provide the level of services desired by members of the organization? Should the level of services be increased or decreased? Should taxes or assessments be increased to pay for additional services? Providing financial information that will help managers answer these questions is an important function.

FYI

The term data typically refers to an unorganized collection of facts. In contrast, the term information refers to facts that have been organized in a manner that brings meaning to the reader. Accounting converts data into information.

THE ACCOUNTING FRAMEWORK

Planning, recording, analyzing, and interpreting financial information is called **accounting.** The accounting framework in Illustration 1-1 presents the many sources and users of accounting information.

ILLUSTRATION 1-1 The accounting framework

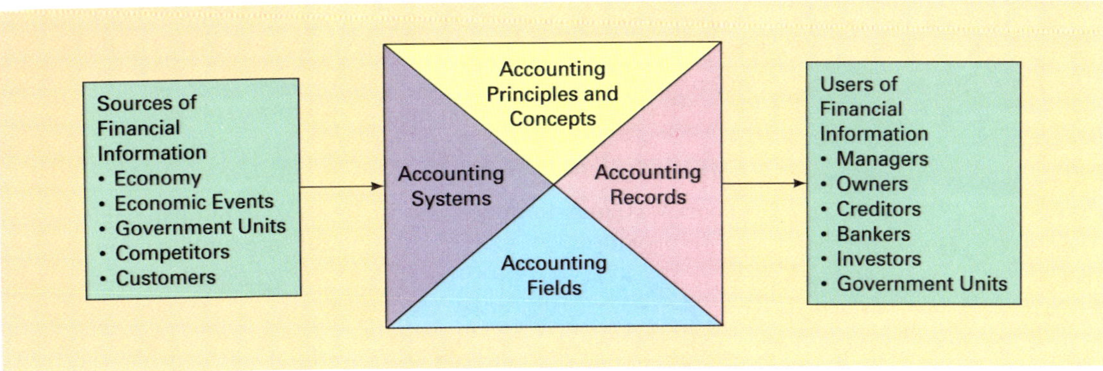

TEACHING STRATEGIES: APPLYING VISUALS

Direct students to Illustration 1-1. Review the accounting framework.

LESSON PLAN 1-1

Materials

- Student pages 5–8

Objectives (Enabling Performance Tasks)

a. Define accounting terms related to the framework of accounting and the forms of business organization.

b. Identify the framework of accounting.

FOCUS

- The advanced accounting course should develop the students' knowledge and appreciation for the accounting profession while reinforcing and extending accounting procedures learned in the first-year accounting course. In this lesson, the accounting framework and fields are presented. Explain that this material provides an overview of topics that will be expanded in later chapters of the text.
- Introduce vocabulary: accounting, accounting system, accounting records, financial accounting, managerial accounting, cost accounting, tax accounting, auditing, auditor, personal financial planning.

TEACH

Cover student pages 5–8 "The Accounting Framework" and "Accounting Fields." Explain that accounting transforms data into information. Data may be obtained from a variety of sources. Information created by the accounting system is reported to many different types of people. Discuss the accounting framework. Explain the various accounting fields.

APPLY

Refer students to Illustration 1-1. Ask students to expand the components of the framework using their personal experiences. For example, a student may know of an accountant who specializes in a field of accounting not presented in the framework.

Guided Practice

Guide students to learning more about one field of accounting. Assist them in writing to accounting organizations requesting literature that more fully describes the field.

Independent Practice

Assign Terms 1–10 and Questions 1–4.

ASSESS

Assess student understanding by checking the solutions to the Independent Practice activities.

Reteach

Lead students in a discussion of one group of users of information shown on the accounting framework, Illustration 1-1. The following are examples of questions you might ask to get the discussion started. What accounting report would be useful to a sales manager? What would be the source of the data? What accounting fields would be required to process the data?

Enrich

Assign students to read the MULTICULTURAL AWARENESS feature on page 7. Discuss with them how an understanding and appreciation of history and other cultures contributes to understanding civilization today.

CLOSURE

Use Audit Your Understanding questions.

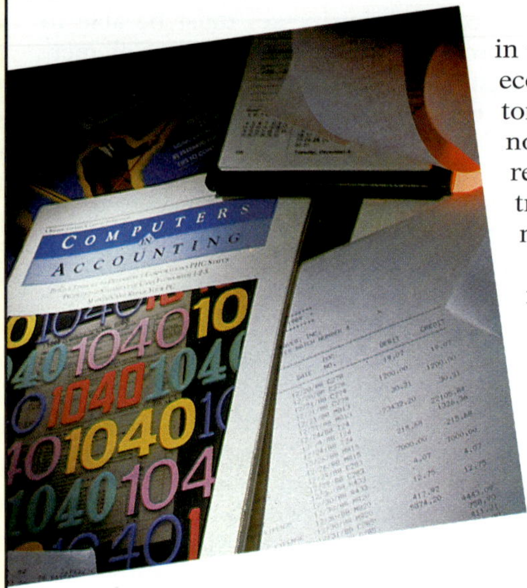

A successful business must understand the environment in which it operates. Information concerning the economy, economic events, government units, competitors, and customers is critical to effective business planning. The economic events, such as sales, collections of accounts receivable, or cash payments for operating and administrative expenses, are the most common financial information collected.

Accountants assist businesses to collect, organize, and interpret accounting financial information. A planned process for providing financial information that will be useful to management is called an **accounting system.** The accounting system will vary based on the type and form of business organization.

Organized summaries of a business' financial activities are called **accounting records.** Many individuals and organizations need information about the financial activities of a business. An accounting system will, therefore, produce a variety of accounting records. Users of accounting records include managers, owners, creditors, bankers, investors, and government units.

ACCOUNTING FIELDS

FYI

The government's first regulation of accounting information began in 1917 with the Federal Reserve Board's publication of "Uniform Accounts."

Several accounting fields have emerged as a result of the varied uses of accounting information. Prominent accounting fields are financial accounting, managerial accounting, cost accounting, tax accounting, accounting systems, auditing, and personal financial planning.

Financial Accounting

The recording of a business' financial activities and the periodic preparation of financial reports is called **financial accounting.** Financial accounting provides financial reports primarily for use by persons *external* to the organization. External users of financial accounting information include creditors, investors, bankers, governmental units, auditors, and personal financial planners. Chapters 2 through 5, 8 through 14, and 21 through 24 of this textbook present financial accounting concepts and procedures.

Managerial Accounting

The analysis, measurement, and interpretation of financial accounting information is called **managerial accounting.** Managerial accounting provides information for *internal* decision making concerning daily operations as well as planning and control of future operations. Chapters 15 through 17 of this textbook describe managerial accounting concepts and procedures.

MULTICULTURAL AWARENESS

Asian American Businesses

The Census Bureau's Survey of minority-owned business enterprises shows a pronounced increase in the number of minority business enterprises. From 1982 to 1987, minority-owned businesses increased from 742,000 to 1,214,000.

Census information also shows that among all minorities, Asian Americans had the largest growth rate in the number of businesses owned. Asian Americans increased the number of businesses owned by 89%. Korean Americans owned more businesses than any other Asian Americans. For every 1,000 Korean Americans in the general population, 102 businesses were owned.

Cost Accounting

The determination and control of costs of a business enterprise is called **cost accounting.** Cost accounting provides information for *internal* decision making concerning the costs of operating merchandising and manufacturing businesses. Owners and managers use cost information for controlling current operations and planning for the future. Chapters 18 through 20 of this textbook describe the cost accounting concepts and procedures.

Tax Accounting

The preparation of tax returns as well as tax planning is called **tax accounting.** Tax accountants use financial statement information to prepare tax returns. Even not-for-profit organizations are required to submit informational tax returns. Tax accountants must keep up to date on changes in tax regulations as well as court decisions on tax cases. This knowledge enables tax accountants to minimize a business' tax liability and assure that the business or organization complies with tax laws.

Accounting Systems

Accounting systems create accounting reports containing financial, managerial, cost, and tax information. The systems accountant works in the design and implementation of accounting systems. A systems accountant must be familiar with the uses and various types of computers which might make the accounting system more efficient. Integrating Automated Accounting Topics 1 through 7 of this textbook describe the use of computers in accounting systems. Chapters 6 and 7 of this textbook describe accounting systems used to control assets.

Auditing

The independent reviewing and issuing of an opinion on the reliability of accounting records is called **auditing.** A person who examines the records which support the financial records of a business to assure that generally accepted accounting principles (GAAP) are being followed is called an **auditor**. Also, an auditor is responsible for determining whether policies and procedures prescribed by management are being followed.

The auditor's opinion is necessary for our economic system to operate efficiently. The auditor's opinion enables external users to be confident of the information reported in financial statements. With this confidence, individuals and businesses are more likely to enter into economic transactions.

Personal Financial Planning

Assisting individuals in managing their personal investments is called **personal financial planning**. Most individuals attempt to invest

MULTICULTURAL AWARENESS

The MULTICULTURAL AWARENESS feature is intended to expose students to the concept that our society is composed of people from many different cultural backgrounds. These features show both past contributions of many cultures and benefits of a culturally diverse society. (1) Read the feature. (2) Discuss the specific information in the feature. (3) Clarify any terms or questions.

TEACHING STRATEGIES: TEACHING TIP

This chapter provides an opportunity to evaluate how much students remember from the first-year accounting course. A review of the complete accounting cycle may be appropriate. An optional REVIEW PROJECT is provided in the Teacher's Resource Guide.

AUDIT YOUR UNDERSTANDING

The AUDIT YOUR UNDERSTANDING feature appears at the end of each section of the chapter. Explain to your students that the word *audit* means to check or verify. AUDIT YOUR UNDERSTANDING may be used to check student comprehension of the section just studied. The answers are provided in Appendix D in the back of the textbook.

1. The economy, economic events, government units, competitors, and customers.
2. Managers, owners, creditors, bankers, investors, and government units.
3. Financial accounting, managerial accounting, cost accounting, tax accounting, accounting systems, auditing, and personal financial planning.
4. To assist individuals to interpret financial information and determine which investments will maximize their investment income.

LESSON PLAN 1-2

Materials

- Student pages 8–12
- 3-Step Checklist for Making Ethical Decisions (TRG)

Objectives (Enabling Performance Tasks)

a. Define accounting terms related to the framework of accounting and the forms of business organization.

c. Describe how communication skills are important in reporting accounting information.

d. Describe how individuals make ethical business decisions.

FOCUS

- The accounting framework and the fields of accounting were introduced earlier in this chapter. This lesson presents the career opportunities in the accounting profession and the professional certification required for success in certain accounting fields. Explain that other qualities necessary for success, such as communication skills and ethics, will also be discussed.
- Introduce vocabulary: management advisory services, ethics.

Audit Your Understanding

1. What are the sources of information that are critical to business planning?
2. What individuals might use the financial records of a business?
3. What are the prominent accounting fields?
4. What is the role of the accountant in personal financial planning?

a portion of their income to pay for future expenditures, such as their children's education and retirement. The increasing variety and complexity of investment opportunities requires many individuals to seek professional assistance. Accountants can assist individuals to interpret financial information and determine which investments will maximize their investment income.

FYI

Knowledge of accounting is necessary for individuals to effectively manage their personal investments.

ACCOUNTING PROFESSION

Accounting is a growing profession. The demand for accountants remains strong because of the number, size, and complexity of businesses, governmental units, and other not-for-profit organizations. Continual change in government regulations and federal tax reporting requirements keep the demand for accountants high. Accounting employment is usually in private accounting, public accounting, or governmental/not-for-profit accounting.

Private Accounting

Persons employed in private accounting work for only one business. These persons may perform a variety of duties. In small organizations they may do all of the summarizing, analyzing, and interpreting of financial information for management. In large organizations, accountants typically specialize in one field of accounting, such as financial, managerial, cost, or tax.

Public Accounting

FYI

Most public accounting firms are organized as partnerships.

Persons employed in public accounting may work independently or as a member of a public accounting firm. Public accountants sell services to individuals, businesses, governmental units, and not-for-profit organizations. Auditing and tax accounting have historically been the primary services provided by public accountants. As the business environment becomes more complex, organizations have increasingly hired public accountants to solve a variety of business problems. Management advice provided to an organization by a public accountant is called **management advisory services**. Management advisory services is the fastest growing service provided by public accountants.

Governmental/Not-for-Profit Accounting

Some persons employed in governmental/not-for-profit accounting work for a governmental agency (federal, state, county, or city). The Internal Revenue Service is an example of a governmental agency that employs large numbers of accountants. Some accountants may also work for other not-for-profit organizations such as hospitals, churches, or foundations.

Colleges and universities also employ accountants to teach future accounting professionals. In addition to teaching accounting classes, accounting instructors provide management advisory services and conduct research to improve accounting principles and procedures.

PROFESSIONAL CERTIFICATION

FYI

The educational and experience requirements for the CPA exam for your state may be obtained from your state's board of public accountancy.

There are many professional accounting certifications available, the most widely recognized being the Certified Public Accountant (CPA). A public accountant who has the required education and experience and passes a required examination is designated as a CPA.

The American Institute of Certified Public Accountants (AICPA) prepares the examination for all states in the United States. However, each state establishes its own education and experience requirements. Thus, candidates are granted the CPA designation upon successfully completing the examination and meeting the requirements specified by the state in which they wish to practice. The CPA certificate signifies professional status in public accounting and is required to issue an audit opinion.

Many private accountants specialize in managerial and cost accounting. These accountants are often referred to as management accountants. A private accountant who has the required education and experience and passes a required examination is designated as a Certified Management Accountant (CMA). The CMA certificate is granted by the Institute of Management Accountants (IMA).

Large businesses are required to hire public accountants to perform an audit and issue an audit opinion. However, most large businesses also hire private accountants to assist the public accountants and audit the operational efficiency of the business. These accountants are referred to as internal auditors. A private accountant who has the required education and experience and passes a required examination is designated as a Certified Internal Auditor (CIA). The certificate is granted by the Institute of Internal Auditors (IIA).

The professional certification for accounting instructors is a doctoral degree in accounting. Some colleges and universities also require accounting instructors to have a minimum amount of previous accounting experience and CPA professional certification.

THE IMPORTANCE OF COMMUNICATION AND ETHICS IN ACCOUNTING

The knowledge of accounting will provide a person with an important skill necessary for success in any profession or business. Yet, accounting knowledge alone will not assure success. The ability to communicate and make ethical decisions will increase a person's chances of achieving professional success.

TEACH

Cover student pages 8–12 "Accounting Profession," "Professional Certification," "The Importance of Communication and Ethics in Accounting," and "Community Service." Emphasize that many career opportunities exist within the accounting profession. Discuss the various career options for accountants. Emphasize that an accountant can specialize in one field of accounting (e.g. managerial accounting) and be in private, public, or governmental accounting. Describe the professional certification required for success in certain accounting fields. Explain why communication skills and ethics are important to accountants. Review the six causes of unethical behavior and the three-step checklist for making ethical decisions. Discuss the importance of community service to accountants.

APPLY

Bring in a variety of classified advertisements for accounting positions. Discuss the qualifications required for each position. You may wish to involve the students by asking them to help gather sample advertisements.

Guided Practice

Guide students through using the three-step checklist to analyze ethical situations they face in their personal lives. Use situations familiar to the students, such as those related to school, youth organizations, family, and work. Give a brief description of a situation. Then, as a group, apply each step and decide if the action is ethical.

Independent Practice

Assign Terms 11–12 and Questions 5–10.

TEACHING STRATEGIES: EXPANDING BEYOND THE CLASSROOM

Assign a student to contact a professional accounting association. Instruct the student to request information such as membership enrollment, activities performed by the association, etc.

ASSESS

Assess student understanding by checking the solutions to the Independent Practice activities.

Reteach

List the accounting fields on the board. Discuss how a public accountant would provide professional services within each of the accounting fields.

Extend

Discuss the PROFESSIONAL BUSINESS ETHICS feature on page 18. You may wish to distribute copies of the 3-Step Checklist for Making Ethical Decisions. A blackline master is furnished in the Blackline Masters section of the Teacher's Resource Guide.

Enrich

Have students identify newspaper or magazine articles that describe how an individual made an ethical or unethical decision. You may wish to distribute copies of the 3-Step Checklist for Making Ethical Decisions. A blackline master is furnished in the Blackline Masters section of the Teacher's Resource Guide. Assist students in applying the three-step checklist to the individual's decision. Ask the students if they agree with the individual's decision.

CLOSURE

Use Audit Your Understanding questions.

FYI

Accountants consistently judge listening as one of the most important communication skills required by today's accountant.

Communication Skills

Accountants need technical skills to process financial information and prepare accounting records. In addition, accountants need effective communication skills to interpret the accounting information for individuals who have little or no accounting knowledge. To an accountant, communication skills are as important as technical skills in achieving career success.

Regular practice is needed to develop effective communication skills. Therefore, this textbook presents a variety of business situations that require preparation of an oral or written message.

Business Ethics

All persons are faced daily with making decisions between right and wrong. The principles of right and wrong that guide an individual in making decisions are called **ethics**. A person's ethics are developed from relationships with family, friends, teachers, and other individuals that influence the person's life.

All employees will be challenged to apply ethics in making business decisions. Many of these decisions will be difficult to make.

Causes of Unethical Behavior. Unethical behavior occurs when an individual disregards his or her principles of right and wrong by choosing the wrong action. An understanding of the causes of unethical behavior is critical to preventing unethical behavior. Six causes of unethical behavior are listed below.

1. *Excessive emphasis on profits.* The salaries of managers are often based on their ability to increase profits. Managers may feel pressured to make decisions that will earn them a higher salary.
2. *Misplaced business loyalty.* Some individuals develop a misplaced dedication to their employer. They make decisions that benefit the business without considering the negative impact on others.
3. *Personal advancement.* Individuals sometimes develop a "whatever it takes" attitude toward their personal careers. They make decisions that will advance their personal careers, regardless of the impact on the business or other individuals.
4. *Expectation of not getting caught.* Individuals can make unethical decisions because they know the chance of getting caught is small.
5. *Unethical business environment.* Managers establish the ethical environment within a business. Managers who make ethical decisions are more likely to have employees who also make ethical decisions.
6. *Unwillingness to take a stand.* Individuals are often unwilling to take a stand against unethical behavior because they fear losing their jobs, missing a deserved promotion, or alienating other employees.

TEACHING STRATEGIES: COOPERATIVE LEARNING

Newspapers and magazines regularly report on illegal or unethical actions by individuals and businesses. Select a group of five students to collect examples from the local media of illegal or unethical actions. Each member of the group should find an example and write a summary of these actions and analyze the ethics involved. Allow five days for the collection of material. Appoint a group leader to present the findings to the class.

Making Ethical Decisions. Analyzing a situation is the first step in deciding whether an action is ethical. The following three-step checklist for making ethical decisions will serve as a guide in collecting all relevant information regarding an action.

1. *Is the action illegal?* An action should not be considered if it violates international, federal, state, or local laws.
2. *Does the action violate company or professional standards?* An action may be legal yet violate the standards of the business or profession. Violating these standards may affect the employee's job security and professional certification and have a negative effect on the business.

   Several professional accounting organizations have adopted codes of professional conduct to assist their members in making ethical decisions. These codes have been written by the organizations' members to encourage its members to act and uphold the professional image of the accounting profession. The AICPA's Rules of the Code of Professional Conduct are summarized in Illustration 1-2 on page 12.
3. *Who is affected, and how, by the action?* If an action is legal and complies with business and professional standards, the next step is to determine how the action will affect a variety of people. The people to be considered include employees and owners, customers, the local community, and society.

Opportunities to analyze common business situations are provided throughout this textbook. Use the three-step checklist and the AICPA's Rules of the Code of Professional Conduct to help determine whether each action demonstrates ethical behavior.

FYI

Prior to 1978, the Code of Professional Conduct prohibited advertising of any kind. The U.S. Department of Justice, contending that the ban on advertising restricted free competition, successfully pressured the AICPA to modify the Code.

TEACHING STRATEGIES: DIFFERENT LEARNING ABILITIES

Limited English Proficiency (LEP) Students. Provide students with translations of key terms prior to presenting each chapter. Encourage students to use dictionaries.

COMMUNITY SERVICE

Accountants, lawyers, bankers, and other business professionals are leaders within the economic community. These business professionals also have a responsibility to accept other leadership roles in the community. Accountants can provide a variety of civic and charitable organizations with leadership, especially in the management of the organizations' assets and the preparation of necessary financial statements.

Activities in civic and charitable organizations provide many benefits to both accountants and the community. The community benefits because organizations are better able to provide services to the community. Accountants benefit through their development of professional skills and the satisfaction of helping others. Taking leadership roles in civic and charitable organizations allows accountants to develop the leadership and communication skills necessary to attain professional success. Leadership skills, like communication skills, can be developed through practice. By making ethical decisions in their leadership roles, accountants have the opportunity to influence the decisions of other individuals.

Audit Your Understanding

1. How are private and public accounting similar? How are they different?
2. What are three professional certifications available to accountants?
3. When does unethical behavior occur?
4. What groups of people should be considered when evaluating an ethical situation?

AUDIT YOUR UNDERSTANDING

1. Similar: both typically specialize in one field of accounting. Different: private accountants work for only one business; public accountants sell professional services to many businesses.
2. Certified Public Accountant (CPA), Certified Management Accountant (CMA), and Certified Internal Auditor (CIA).
3. When an individual disregards his or her principles of right and wrong by choosing the wrong action.
4. Employees, owners, customers, the local community, and society.

APPLIED SKILLS: WORD PROCESSING

If you wish to integrate word processing into your accounting course, you may direct students to answer the end-of-chapter Accounting Terms, Questions for Individual Study, and Cases for Critical Thinking using their word processing software.

LESSON PLAN 1-3

Materials

- Student pages 12–21
- Assess: MicroExam Chapter 1, Objective Test No. 1

Objectives (Enabling Performance Tasks)

a. Define accounting terms related to the framework of accounting and the forms of business organization.

e. Identify the forms of business organizations, how accounting standards are developed, and the applications of accounting concepts.

FOCUS

- Explain that this lesson reviews some of the foundation of accounting that was presented in the first-year course. The specific topics that will be reviewed are forms of business organizations, accounting standards, and accounting concepts. Explain that information presented in this lesson will be applied throughout the remainder of the textbook.
- Introduce vocabulary: proprietorship, partnership, corporation, share of stock, capital stock, stockholder.

ILLUSTRATION 1-2 AICPA's Rules of the Code of Professional Conduct

AMERICAN INSTITUTE OF CERTIFIED PUBLIC ACCOUNTANTS (AICPA) RULES

Rule 101 — Independence
A member in public practice shall be independent in the performance of professional services.

Rule 102 — Integrity and Objectivity
In the performance of any professional service, a member shall maintain objectivity and integrity, shall be free of conflicts of interest, and shall not knowingly misrepresent facts or subordinate his or her judgment to others.

Rule 201 — General Standards
A. *Professional Competence.* Undertake only those professional services that the member or the member's firm can reasonably expect to be completed with professional competence.
B. *Due Professional Care.* Exercise due professional care in the performance of professional service.
C. *Planning and Supervision.* Adequately plan and supervise the performance of professional services.
D. *Sufficient Relevant Data.* Obtain sufficient relevant data to afford a reasonable basis for conclusions or recommendations in relation to any professional services performed.

Rule 202 — Compliance with Standards
A member who performs auditing, management advisory, tax, or other professional services shall comply with standards issued by organizations approved by the Institute.

Rule 203 — Accounting Principles
A member shall not express an opinion on financial statements that contain a departure from accounting principles issued by organizations approved by the Institute.

Rule 301 — Confidential Client Information
A member in public practice shall not disclose any confidential client information without the specific consent of the client.

Rule 302 — Contingent Fees
A member in public practice shall not perform an audit or prepare a tax return for a contingent fee. A contingent fee is an arrangement in which the fee to be charged is dependent upon a specific result being attained.

Rule 501 — Acts Discreditable
A member shall not commit an act discreditable to the profession.

Rule 502 — Advertising and Other Forms of Solicitation
A member in public practice shall not seek to obtain clients by advertising or other forms of solicitation in a manner that is false, misleading, or deceptive. Solicitation by the use of coercion, over-reaching, or harassing conduct is prohibited.

Rule 503 — Commissions and Referral Fees
A. *Prohibited Commissions.* A member in public practice shall not for a commission recommend any product or service to an audit client.
B. *Disclosure of Permitted Commissions.* A member in public practice who is not prohibited by this rule from receiving a commission shall disclose that fact to his or her client.
C. *Referral Fees.* Any member who accepts a referral fee for recommending the services of another CPA to any person or entity shall disclose the referral fee to the client.

Rule 505 — Form of Practice and Name
A member may practice public accounting only in the form of a proprietorship, a partnership, or a professional corporation. A member shall not practice public accounting under a firm name that is misleading. A firm may not designate itself as "Members of the American Institute of Certified Public Accountants" unless all of its partners are members of the Institute.

Adapted from the Code of Professional Conduct as amended May 20, 1991 (used and adapted with permission).

FORMS OF BUSINESS ORGANIZATION

The accounting information recorded, reported, analyzed, and interpreted may vary according to the type and form of business organization. A business is organized as either a (1) proprietorship, (2) partnership, or (3) corporation.

Proprietorship

A business owned by one person is called a **proprietorship.** A proprietorship is also referred to as a sole proprietorship. A proprietorship has a number of advantages and disadvantages.

Advantages of a Proprietorship

1. A proprietorship is easy to establish.
2. The money needed to start a proprietorship need not be large.
3. A proprietorship provides complete independence for the owner. The owner has the satisfaction of making all decisions and assumes all profits or losses.

Disadvantages of a Proprietorship

1. A proprietorship has limited potential for growth. Proprietorships are limited to the investment of the owner. Frequently, this investment is too small for future growth.
2. A proprietorship depends on the managerial skills of only one person. If the owner has limited managerial skills, the business may fail.
3. A proprietorship has unlimited liability. The owner is personally liable for all business debts.

FYI

Approximately 50% of all new accountants today are women.

Partnership

A business in which two or more persons combine their assets and skills is called a **partnership.** A partnership has a number of advantages and disadvantages.

Advantages of a Partnership

1. A partnership is easy to establish.
2. The number of partners is unlimited. A partnership agreement is generally established which specifies each partner's investment, duties, and share of the business' profit or loss.
3. A partnership has growth potential. Combining the assets and skills of more than one person increases investment and adds to the business' growth potential.

Disadvantages of a Partnership

1. Partners have unlimited liability. As with a proprietorship, each of the owners (partners) is liable for all business debts.
2. Conflicts may develop among partners in managing a partnership. The partners may not agree on the solution to partnership problems. This potential for conflict often makes partnership management decisions difficult and ineffective.

Corporation

An organization with the legal rights of a person and which may be owned by many persons is called a **corporation.** The ownership of a profit-making corporation is divided into units. Each unit of ownership in a corporation is called a **share of stock.** Total shares

TEACH

Cover student pages 12–21 "Forms of Business Organization," "Accounting Standards," and "Accounting Concepts." Discuss the advantages and disadvantages of each form of business organization. Emphasize the differences among the forms of business organizations. Identify the organizations involved in developing accounting principles. Discuss the role of each of the professional accounting organizations. Review the eleven accounting concepts.

APPLY

List the three forms of business organizations on the board. Write the headings Advantages and Disadvantages under each business. As each is discussed, write a brief statement of the advantage or disadvantage under the appropriate heading until the chart is complete.

Guided Practice

Guide students through Cases for Critical Thinking 1 and 2. Ask a volunteer to read Case 1 to the class. Direct students to the list of concepts in the textbook. As a group, review each concept to determine which applies to Case 1. Then, decide if the person is following an accepted accounting concept and explain why or why not. All students should agree with the decision before proceeding to the next case. Repeat the process for Case 2.

Independent Practice

- Assign Terms 13–18 and Questions 11–18.
- Assign Study Guide 1.

APPLIED SKILLS: LANGUAGE ARTS

Paraphrasing, writing complete sentences, and identifying subjects. For additional practice in language arts skills, direct students to answer the Questions for Individual Study at the end of the chapter. Students should write the answers in their own words and in complete sentences. To further practice language arts skills ask students to underline the subject(s) in each sentence of their answers.

ASSESS

Assess student understanding by checking the solutions to the Independent Practice activities.

Reteach

- Display transparencies of the owners' equity sections of each form of business organization. Discuss the accounts used by each organization to reteach the differences in ownership.
- Write the eleven accounting concepts on the board. Ask for student volunteers to interpret each of the concepts. Give them five minutes to prepare an oral response.
- Depending on the length of time since students completed the first-year course, a review of the complete accounting cycle may be appropriate. An optional REVIEW PROJECT is provided in the Teacher's Resource Guide.

Extend

Break the class into small groups. Have the students discuss why various businesses that they are familiar with are best suited for the proprietorship, partnership, or corporation form of business organization. Each group should elect one member to act as group spokesperson and one person to act as the group's recorder.

Enrich

Assign the Applied Communications special feature on page 23.

FYI

Corporations can range from small local businesses owned by a few stockholders to large international businesses with thousands of stockholders.

of ownership in a corporation are called **capital stock.** An owner of one or more shares of a corporation is called a **stockholder.** A corporation has a number of advantages and disadvantages.

Advantages of a Corporation

1. A corporation, with the legal right to act as a person, may buy, own, and sell property in its corporate name.
2. A corporation's life is independent of its owners. A corporation's life may be for a specified time, which is renewable, or it may be unlimited.
3. Unlike a proprietorship or partnership, a stockholder is not liable for a corporation's debts. Thus, a stockholder can never lose more than the amount paid for stock.
4. A corporation has growth potential. Additional stock may be issued to provide funds for future growth.

Disadvantages of a Corporation

1. The net income of a corporation is subject to double taxation—first as corporate income and later as stockholders' personal income. A corporation's net income, after payment of income tax, may be distributed to stockholders. This net income distribution is considered personal income to the stockholders and thus is subject to personal income tax.
2. A corporation has greater government regulation than either proprietorships or partnerships. Corporations come into existence under state and federal laws. Corporations are generally required to prepare more reports for both federal and state governments.

ACCOUNTING STANDARDS

FYI

The Financial Accounting Standards Board (FASB), consisting of seven individuals, is located in Stamford, Connecticut.

The accounting profession is guided by principles and concepts to provide standardization and consistency in the work performed. A number of organizations provide assistance and influence in the development of these principles and concepts.

The Financial Accounting Standards Board (FASB) is responsible for the development of standards for financial accounting and reporting. When problems occur, the FASB studies the issues and develops recommended solutions which are distributed for review by the various accounting organizations and individual accountants. Once accepted by the accounting profession, the FASB publishes statements of financial accounting standards and financial accounting concepts. These statements are recognized by the professional accountant as generally accepted accounting principles (GAAP) which must be followed.

The Governmental Accounting Standards Board (GASB) is responsible for the development of standards to be followed by state and municipal governments. Some of the GASB standards also apply to not-for-profit organizations. The GASB operates similar to

APPLIED SKILLS: BUILDING STUDY SKILLS

Outlining. Good study skills play an important role in learning accounting. Stress the importance of using an outline when studying. Assign students to outline the chapter using the headings as their guide.

the FASB in studying issues, developing recommended solutions, seeking industry review, and issuing governmental accounting standards.

The American Institute of Certified Public Accountants (AICPA) is an organization of practicing certified public accountants (CPAs). The AICPA is the oldest and most influential of all organizations which guide the development of accounting principles and concepts. Administering and grading the uniform CPA examination is one of the primary roles of the AICPA.

The Institute of Management Accountants (IMA) is an organization of accountants concerned with how accounting information is used within an enterprise to direct business operations. The Institute of Internal Auditors (IIA) assists internal auditors to develop techniques useful in improving the accounting system of their business.

The American Accounting Association (AAA) is an organization comprised primarily of accounting instructors. The AAA promotes the improvement of accounting education and publishes numerous journals that enable accounting instructors to share the results of their accounting research.

The Securities and Exchange Commission (SEC) is a government agency established by an act of Congress. This agency issues regulations that must be followed in the preparation of financial statements and other reports filed with the Commission. The primary role of the SEC is to regulate the issuance of stock by corporations and the trading of stock by the general public.

The Internal Revenue Service (IRS) is a government agency which issues regulations defining income for federal income taxation. Accounting for income tax has an influence on the development of accounting practices and concepts.

FYI

The forerunner of the AICPA, the American Association of Public Accountants, was formed in 1887. The AICPA's Journal of Accountancy was first published in 1905. Each month the Journal informs AICPA members of techniques useful in improving the quality of professional services.

FYI

Corporations whose stock is publicly traded must submit an annual report to the Securities and Exchange Commission (SEC). The report includes audited financial statements and management's analysis of the corporation's operations.

ACCOUNTING CONCEPTS

Accounting employees follow concepts commonly accepted by the profession as guides for reporting and interpreting accounting information. The accounting procedures described in this textbook are based on the application of accepted concepts. Eleven commonly accepted concepts are described in this chapter.

CONCEPT: Accounting Period Cycle

Changes in financial information are reported for a specific period of time in the form of financial statements.

Periodically, accounting records are summarized and reported to business owners and managers. The time period for which financial statements are prepared depends on the needs of the business. An accounting period may be one month, three months, six months, or one year. For tax purposes every business prepares financial statements at the end of each year.

CLOSURE

Use Audit Your Understanding questions.

ASSESS

- Administer a MicroExam test for Chapter 1.
- Administer Objective Test No. 1.

TEACHING STRATEGIES: TEACHING TIP

The first few days in class will set the tone for the entire term. Therefore, involve students in identifying the importance of accounting information in various organizations. Have students identify how accounting information is used in familiar organizations, such as the business where they work, a family member's employer, and the local school system. Stress the importance of good accounting records and the decisions that are made based on these records.

CONCEPT: Adequate Disclosure

Financial statements contain all information necessary to understand a business' financial condition.

Accurate and up-to-date financial information about a business is needed by many persons. These persons include owners, managers, lenders, and investors. All important financial information must be adequately and completely disclosed on financial statements.

A business reports only the total liabilities of $200,000.00 on its balance sheet. However, the total liabilities include $50,000.00 in current liabilities and $150,000.00 in long-term liabilities. Therefore, the balance sheet does not adequately disclose the nature of the liabilities. The critical information not disclosed is that $50,000.00 is current and due within a few months.

APPLIED SKILLS: WRITING ACROSS THE CURRICULUM

Writing paragraphs and short essays. The Cases for Critical Thinking are short, practical applications of the accounting principles developed in the chapter. Some cases are planned to present problems related to the chapter but not specifically discussed and answered in the chapter. These cases present an opportunity for critical thinking and decision making. These cases also require more than a short objective-type response. Therefore they provide ideal practice in writing paragraphs and short essays.

FYI

Corporations normally use the report form of a balance sheet.

CONCEPT: Business Entity

Financial information is recorded and reported separately from the owner's personal financial information.

A business owner usually owns personal items as well as business items. A business' financial records and reports must not be mixed with an owner's personal records and reports. For example, a business owner may buy insurance to protect the business and insurance to protect the owner's home. Only the insurance obtained for the business is recorded in the business' financial records. The insurance purchased for the owner's personal home is recorded in the owner's personal financial records. One bank account is used for the business and another for the owner. A business exists separately from its owner.

CONCEPT: Consistent Reporting

The same accounting procedures are followed in the same way in each accounting period.

Business decisions are based on the financial information reported on financial statements. Business decisions are often made by comparing current financial statements with previous financial statements. Accounting information recorded and reported differently each accounting period makes comparisons from one accounting period to another impossible. Unless a change is necessary to make information more easily understood, accounting information is reported in a consistent way for each accounting period.

A business reported the following on its income statement for August:

Sales	$200,000.00
Operating Expenses	−$170,000.00
Net Income from Operations	$ 30,000.00

The same business reported the following on its income statement for September:

Sales	$200,000.00
Cost of Merchandise Sold	−$120,000.00
Gross Profit on Sales	$ 80,000.00
Operating Expenses	−$ 50,000.00
Net Income from Operations	$ 30,000.00

The two income statements are reported differently. Thus, the reader cannot compare all items on the two reports.

APPLIED SKILLS: COMMUNICATIONS

Surveys of business managers show that communication skills are one of the most desired traits in new employees. The APPLIED COMMUNICATIONS activity provides an opportunity for students to practice their communication and language arts skills on topics that directly relate to accounting. This activity requires students to identify a want ad for an accounting or business job they would like to pursue. Students should write why they believe they would like the job and how their anticipated qualifications would prepare them to succeed in that position.

CONCEPT: Going Concern

Financial statements are prepared with the expectation that a business will remain in operation indefinitely.

New businesses are started with the expectation that they will be successful. Accounting records and financial statements are designed as though businesses will continue indefinitely.

A business bought store equipment for $30,000.00. The store equipment is expected to last 10 years. Yearly depreciation, therefore, is recorded and reported based on the expected life of the equipment. After six years of the expected 10 year life of the equipment, the book value (cost less accumulated depreciation) of the equipment is $13,200.00. If the business ended operations and the equipment had to be sold, the amount received may be less than $13,200.00. However, accounting records are maintained with the expectation that the business will remain in operation indefinitely, and the cost will be allocated over the useful life of the equipment. The equipment value, therefore, remains $13,200.00 on the records regardless of what the equipment may be worth when sold.

A business is expected to continue indefinitely even if the owner retires or sells the business. If a business is sold, the new owner is expected to continue the business' operations.

FYI

The six largest accounting firms in the United States are referred to as the Big Six. They are:

- **Arthur Andersen & Co.**
- **Coopers & Lybrand**
- **Deloitte & Touche**
- **Ernst & Young**
- **KMPG Peat Marwick**
- **Price Waterhouse**

CONCEPT: Historical Cost

The actual amount paid for merchandise or other items bought is recorded.

The actual amount paid for an item in a business transaction may be different from the value.

Office equipment is valued at $20,000.00 and advertised at a sale price of $18,000.00. A business arranges to buy the equipment for $17,000.00. The amount recorded in the accounting records for the office equipment is the historical cost, $17,000.00—the actual amount paid.

Business A bought a computer for $12,000.00. The historical cost of the computer according to the accounting records of Busi-

Professional Business Ethics

This first Professional Business Ethics activity has been completed for the students to walk them through the three-step checklist of analyzing ethical behavior. The Professional Business Ethics activities in future chapters will not provide answers in the student textbook. Since personal ethics are unique, students' solutions will vary. Although there is no one correct solution, the solution given illustrates the use of the three-step checklist. Guide students through this checklist and encourage different solutions from them.

PROFESSIONAL BUSINESS ETHICS

Mixing Politics and Business

A CPA serves on the zoning board of Centerville. The board is reviewing a rezoning request for a large section of property to permit Dave's Department Store, a national discount retailer, to build a store. The CPA, knowing the possible negative impact the new store would have on many of the firm's small retail clients, votes against the rezoning request. Without the support of the zoning board, the land cannot be developed to build a store. Centerville is a small town and this is the only piece of undeveloped land. Therefore, Dave's Department Store is unable to build a store and plans are canceled.

INSTRUCTIONS Use the three-step checklist to analyze whether the CPA's vote against the retailer demonstrated ethical behavior. This first activity has been completed for you as follows.

1. *Is the action illegal?* No. The action is not illegal, although it does demonstrate a possible inappropriate use of political power.
2. *Does the action violate company or professional standards?* Maybe. The CPA has conflict between the interests of the community as a member of the zoning board and the interests of the clients as a CPA. However, the CPA is not involved in providing professional services to a client in the role on the zoning board.

ness A is $12,000.00. Business A decides two months later to sell the computer. Business A sells the computer to Business B for $9,000.00. For Business B, the historical cost of the computer is $9,000.00.

CONCEPT: Matching Expenses with Revenue

Revenue from business activities and expenses associated with earning that revenue are recorded in the same accounting period.

FYI

The fastest growth in new jobs in the U.S. is in service businesses. Between 1970 and 1988, the service sector grew 67%.

Business activities for an accounting period are summarized in financial statements. To adequately report how a business performed during an accounting period, all revenue earned as a result of business operations must be reported. Likewise, all expenses incurred during the same accounting period in producing the revenue must be reported. Matching expenses with revenue gives a true picture of business operations for an accounting period.

A business had sales of $100,000.00 in December. Expenses recorded for December were $80,000.00. Depreciation of $5,000.00 for December was not recorded with the expenses. To report accurate financial information, all expenses associated with earning revenue must be recorded in the same accounting period. Therefore, $85,000.00 should have been reported as expenses associated with earning the revenue of $100,000.00. The matching of expenses with revenue results in an accurate report of net income, $15,000.00, for

TEACHING STRATEGIES: TEACHING TIP

Instruct students to clip accounting employment advertisements from local and national newspapers. Use these advertisements for class discussion. The advertisements will demonstrate the variety and quantity of accounting positions available within your community as well as across the nation.

3. *Who is affected, and how, by the action?* (Because the answer to question 2 is uncertain, analysis of this question is necessary.)

People Affected	*Negative*	*Positive*
CPA	Conflict of interest may damage reputation.	Protects the fees earned by providing professional fees to current clients.
CPA's clients		Protected from competition.
Centerville	Prevents residents from having access to lower cost merchandise.	Protects the interests of current businesses and their employees.
Dave's Department Store	Unfairly prohibited from entering market and increasing sales/profits.	
Landowner	Owner does not profit from sale of land.	

TEACHING STRATEGIES: EXPANDING BEYOND THE CLASSROOM

Stress the importance of accounting in everyday jobs. Students need to realize that accounting is important for everyone, not just people who are going to be accountants. Set up a day where several people from the community are invited to be members of a professional panel. Try to get a person such as a hair stylist who can tell students how important it is to understand accounting to keep track of the books. A builder might explain to students how costs are tracked for building a house and the role accounting plays. This could be a good recruiting tool to emphasize the importance of accounting in everyday living.

December ($100,000.00 sales *minus* total expenses of $85,000.00 *equals* $15,000.00 net income).

CONCEPT: Materiality

Business activities creating dollar amounts large enough to affect business decisions should be recorded and reported as separate items in accounting records and financial statements.

Business transactions are recorded in accounting records and reported in financial statements in dollar amounts. How the amounts are recorded and reported depends on the amount involved and the relative importance of the time needed to make business decisions. Dollar amounts which are large will generally be considered in making decisions about future operations. A separate accounting record, therefore, is kept for these items. Dollar amounts which are small and not considered important in decision making may be combined with other amounts in the accounting records and financial statements.

Buying an office desk lamp for $20.00 should be accounted for as an asset and depreciated over its useful life. However, if the lamp has an estimated useful life of five years, recording $4.00 depreciation ($20.00 ÷ 5 years) each year represents an amount small enough to have little importance in decision making. Therefore, the entire cost of the lamp may be recorded as an expense in the accounting period the lamp is purchased.

TEACHING STRATEGIES: TEACHING TIP

Share information with the guidance counselors on the importance of accounting for all students. Educate them to the fact that students who are going on to college will benefit from taking a high school accounting course even though they are not planning to be accountants. Anyone majoring in Business Administration will take an accounting course in college. Those entering legal studies will also take an accounting course. Students going directly into the work force will have a better chance of employment with an accounting background.

Buying a computer system for $20,000.00 represents an amount large enough to significantly affect the amount of net income reported if recorded as an expense. Therefore, the computer should be recorded as an asset and depreciated each year of its useful life.

CONCEPT: Objective Evidence

A source document is prepared for each transaction.

Only business transactions that actually did occur should be recorded in accounting records. The amounts recorded in accounting records must be accurate and true. One way to check the accuracy of accounting records is to check the original business papers containing details of transactions. For example, a check is the original business paper for cash payments. A sales invoice is the original business paper for goods sold. A receipt is the original business paper for cash received. Every entry in accounting records is supported by a business paper. When accounting information reported on financial statements needs to be checked or verified, an accountant can first check the accounting record. If the details of an entry need further checking, an accountant may then check the business papers as the objective evidence that the transaction did occur.

CONCEPT: Realization of Revenue

Revenue is recorded at the time goods or services are sold.

A business may sell either goods or services. Cash may be received at the time of sale or an agreement may be made to receive payment at a later date. Regardless of when cash is actually received, the sale amount is recorded in the accounting records at the time of sale.

A business sells office furniture for $2,000.00. The business agrees to an initial payment of $400.00 with the remaining balance to be divided into four monthly payments of $400.00 each. The full $2,000.00 of revenue is recorded at the time of sale even though $1,600.00 will be paid later.

FYI

After the year 2000, the AICPA will require all new members to have 150 hours of college education, including a bachelor's degree.

CONCEPT: Unit of Measurement

Business transactions are stated in numbers that have common values—that is, using a common unit of measurement.

All transactions are recorded in accounting records in terms of money. Useful nonfinancial information may also be recorded to describe the nature of a business transaction.

If part of the accounting information is financial and part is nonfinancial, financial statements will not be clear. A shoe store owner reporting only the number of shoes sold (nonfinancial) and the dollar amounts (financial) paid for expenses cannot determine net income. If the number of shoes sold and the expenses are both reported in dollar amounts (financial), the profit can be calculated.

Total expenses (financial) subtracted from money taken in from shoe sales (financial) equals profit. All values recorded in accounting records and reported on financial statements are reported in a common unit of measurement—the dollar.

Throughout this textbook, materials and procedures are described which apply to one or more of the concepts. In the chapters that follow, each time a concept application occurs, a concept reference is given.

Audit Your Understanding

1. Which form(s) of business organization exposes its owners to unlimited liability?
2. Which form(s) of business organization is subjected to double taxation?
3. What is the primary function of the FASB?
4. What are the names of three professional accounting organizations?
5. What accounting concept is applied if a new computer keyboard bought for $60 is recorded as a miscellaneous expense?

AUDIT YOUR UNDERSTANDING

1. Proprietorship and partnership.
2. Corporation.
3. Development of standards for financial accounting and reporting.
4. American Institute of Certified Public Accountants (AICPA); Institute of Management Accountants (IMA); American Accounting Association (AAA).
5. Materiality concept.

ACCOUNTING TERMS

1. **accounting:** Planning, recording, analyzing, and interpreting financial information. (p. 5)
2. **accounting system:** A planned process for providing financial information that will be useful to management. (p. 6)
3. **accounting records:** Organized summaries of a business' financial activities. (p. 6)
4. **financial accounting:** The recording of a business' financial activities and the periodic preparation of financial reports. (p. 6)
5. **managerial accounting:** The analysis, measurement, and interpretation of financial accounting information. (p. 6)
6. **cost accounting:** The determination and control of costs of a business enterprise. (p. 7)
7. **tax accounting:** The preparation of tax returns as well as tax planning. (p. 7)
8. **auditing:** The independent reviewing and issuing of an opinion on the reliability of accounting records. (p. 7)
9. **auditor:** A person who examines the records which support the financial records of a business to assure that generally accepted accounting principles (GAAP) are being followed. (p. 7)
10. **personal financial planning:** Assisting individuals in managing their personal investments. (p. 7)
11. **management advisory services:** Management advice provided to an organization by a public accountant. (p. 8)

TERMS *(cont'd)*

12. ethics: The principles of right and wrong that guide an individual in making decisions. (p. 10)

13. proprietorship: A business owned by one person. (p. 13)

14. partnership: A business in which two or more persons combine their assets and skills. (p. 13)

15. corporation: An organization with the legal rights of a person and which may be owned by many persons. (p. 13)

16. share of stock: Each unit of ownership in a corporation. (p. 13)

17. capital stock: Total shares of ownership in a corporation. (p. 14)

18. stockholder: An owner of one or more shares of a corporation. (p. 14)

QUESTIONS FOR INDIVIDUAL STUDY

1. Financial accounting, managerial accounting, cost accounting, tax accounting, accounting systems, auditing, and personal financial planning. (p. 6)

2. Creditors, investors, bankers, governmental units, auditors, and personal financial planners. (p. 6)

3. To provide information for internal decision making concerning daily operations as well as planning and control of future operations. (p. 6)

4. To provide information for internal decision making concerning the costs of operating merchandising and manufacturing businesses. (p. 7)

5. The state in which the accountant wishes to practice. (p. 9)

6. An accountant must have the required education and experience and pass a required examination. (p. 9)

7. To interpret the accounting information for individuals who have little or no accounting knowledge. (p. 10)

8. From relationships with family, friends, teachers, and other individuals that influence the person's life. (p. 10)

9. (a) Is the action illegal? (b) Does the action violate company or professional standards? (c) Who is affected, and how, by the action? (p. 11)

ACCOUNTING TERMS EPT(a)

What is the meaning of each of the following?

1. **accounting**
2. **accounting system**
3. **accounting records**
4. **financial accounting**
5. **managerial accounting**
6. **cost accounting**
7. **tax accounting**
8. **auditing**
9. **auditor**
10. **personal financial planning**
11. **management advisory services**
12. **ethics**
13. **proprietorship**
14. **partnership**
15. **corporation**
16. **share of stock**
17. **capital stock**
18. **stockholder**

QUESTIONS FOR INDIVIDUAL STUDY EPT(b,c,d,e)

1. What are the prominent accounting fields?
2. What external units use a business' financial accounting information?
3. How is managerial accounting information used?
4. How is cost accounting information used?
5. Who grants candidates the Certified Public Accountant (CPA) designation?
6. What is required for an accountant to obtain the Certified Management Accountant (CMA) designation?
7. Why must accountants have effective communication skills?
8. How are a person's ethics developed?
9. What is the three-step checklist for collecting information for making an ethical decision?
10. How does taking leadership in civic and charitable organizations help accountants?
11. What are three advantages of the proprietorship form of business organization?
12. What are two disadvantages of a partnership form of business organization?
13. What are four advantages of a corporate form of business organization?
14. What accounting organization is responsible for the development of standards for financial accounting and reporting?
15. What accounting organization is responsible for the administering and grading of the CPA examination?
16. What accounting organization is primarily concerned with how accounting information is used within an enterprise for directing business operations?
17. What is the primary role of the Securities and Exchange Commission (SEC)?
18. What governmental agency issues regulations for determining income for federal income taxation?

CASES FOR CRITICAL THINKING EPT(e)

CASE 1 Susan Bosley operates a video tape rental service. She records and reports accounting information on the basis of one-month accounting periods. The money earned from rentals is recorded in the accounting records at the time the tapes are rented to customers. Expenses for operating the business are recorded in the accounting records when actually paid. Is Ms. Bosley following accepted accounting concepts? Explain.

CASE 2 Roger Desantis does the accounting for Excell Office Supply. After transactions are recorded, Mr. Desantis destroys the business papers containing the information for the entries. David Engels, a CPA, suggests that the business papers be kept for future reference. Mr. Desantis argues that once a transaction has been recorded, the business paper is of no value. With whom do you agree? Explain.

10. Accountants benefit through their development of professional skills and the satisfaction of helping others. Taking leadership roles in civic and charitable organizations allows accountants to develop leadership and communication skills. (p. 11)

11. (a) A proprietorship is easy to establish. (b) The money needed to start a proprietorship need not be large. (c) A proprietorship provides complete independence for the owner. (p. 13)

12. (a) Partners have unlimited liability. (b) Conflicts may develop among partners in managing a partnership. (p. 13)

APPLIED COMMUNICATIONS

Accounting is the language of business. Completing this advanced accounting course will enable you to pursue a wide variety of business-related careers. Several accounting career opportunities are presented in this chapter. Although you are several years away from earning a college degree, you should begin to identify the career fields in accounting and business of special interest to you.

INSTRUCTIONS:

Select a classified advertisement from the newspaper for an accounting or business position in which you would be interested. Write why you would like that job and how your anticipated qualifications upon graduation would match that position.

QUESTIONS *(cont'd)*

13. (a) A corporation, with the legal right to act as a person, may buy, own, and sell property in its corporate name. (b) A corporation's life is independent of its owners. (c) Unlike a proprietorship or partnership, a stockholder is not liable for a corporation's debts. (d) A corporation has good growth potential. (p. 14)

14. The Financial Accounting Standards Board (FASB). (p. 14)

15. The American Institute of Certified Public Accountants (AICPA). (p. 15)

16. The Institute of Management Accountants (IMA). (p. 15)

17. Regulate the issuance of stock by corporations and the trading of stock by the general public. (p. 15)

18. The Internal Revenue Service. (p. 15)

CASES FOR CRITICAL THINKING

Case 1 No. The matching expenses with revenue concept states that revenue from business activities and expenses associated with earnings be recorded in the same accounting period. Ms. Bosley may have expenses that would not be paid until the next accounting period.

Case 2 Mr. Engels. The objective evidence accounting concept states that each transaction is supported by a business document that proves the transaction did occur. When accounting information reported on financial statements needs to be checked or verified, an accountant first checks the accounting record. If the details of an entry need further checking, it is possible to go to the business paper as the objective evidence that the transaction did occur.

APPLIED COMMUNICATIONS

Students' solutions will vary. The instructor should consider the following items when grading the activity: (1) insight into the accounting profession and business, (2) support for their decision, (3) matching their anticipated qualifications with the job requirements, (4) writing style, and (5) mechanics (grammar, spelling, punctuation, sentence structure).

STUDENT EDITION

STUDENT FEATURES

Careers In Accounting

Auditor, page 65

Spreadsheet Options

Using The Titles Command, page 94

Multicultural Awareness

Hispanic American Businesses, page 123

Global Perspective

International Terms of Sale, page 43

Personal Visions In Business

Al Parker, page 74
Debra Miller, M.D., page 140

Audit Your Understanding

This student activity can be found on pages 32, 38, 45, 70, 76, 97, 104, 109, 121, 130, 141

APPLIED SKILLS

Applied Communications

Page 47

Applied Math

Pages 40, 41, 48, 73, 79, 93, 97, 101, 102, 119, 121, 123, 134, 135

SOFTWARE APPLICATIONS

Automated Accounting 6.0 Problems 2-1, 2-2, 2-4, 2-5, 2-M, 3-1, 3-3, 3-M, 3-C, 5-7, 5-M, Reinforcement Activity 1
Spreadsheet Template Problems 4-1, 4-4, 4-5, 5-1, 5-3, 5-M

TEACHER'S EDITION

APPLIED SKILLS

Communications, page 31
Language Arts, pages 27, 68, 102, 136
Writing Across the Curriculum, pages 29, 74, 95, 139
Building Study Skills, pages 36, 76, 123
Word Processing, pages 36, 77, 108, 127

TEACHING STRATEGIES

Accounting Pedagogy, pages 26, 27, 64, 83, 88, 116
Assessment by Portfolio, pages 31, 142
Different Learning Abilities, pages 38, 54, 55, 56, 68, 84, 96, 138
Different Learning Styles, pages 34, 40, 41, 42, 45, 66, 69, 75
Cooperative Learning, pages 35, 60, 64, 85, 103, 135
Expanding Beyond the Classroom, pages 44, 104, 124
Applying Visuals, pages 35, 71, 98, 143
Teaching Tip, pages 26, 28, 30, 33, 34, 37, 59, 65, 71, 72, 73, 75, 86, 90, 98, 105, 106, 117, 118, 126, 128, 132
Software Focus, pages 44, 53, 76, 83, 93, 129
Safety and Health, page 58
Simulation, page 149
Milestone, page 150
Reinforcement Activity, page 150

ASSESSMENT

Assessment by Portfolio
MicroExam software for each chapter
Problem Test for each chapter
Unit Objective Test No. 2 (2–5)

SOFTWARE

Automated Accounting 6.0
Electronic Auditor
MicroExam
Lotus (spreadsheet)
WordPerfect (word processing)
Windows (operating system)

BIBLIOGRAPHY

AICPA. *FASB Accounting Standards.*
Bieg, Bernard J., and B. Lewis Keeling. *Payroll Accounting.* (Revised Annually). Cincinnati: South-Western Publishing Co.
Gibson, Charles H. *Financial Statement Analysis: Using Financial Accounting Information.* Fifth Edition. Cincinnati: South-Western Publishing Co., 1992.
Marzano, Robert J. *A Different Kind of Classroom: Teaching with Dimensions of Learning.* Association for Supervision and Curriculum Development, Alexandria, VA, 1992.
Miller, Sidney R., and Patrick J. Schloss. *Career-Vocational Education for Handicapped Youth.* Aspen Systems Corporation, 1982.
Nash, John F., and Cynthia D. Heagy. *Accounting Information Systems.* Third Edition. Cincinnati: South-Western Publishing Co., 1993.
U.S. Department of Labor. *Occupational Outlook Handbook.*

Periodicals

Accounting Technology (formerly *Computers in Accounting*), Faulkner & Gray, Eleven Penn Plaza, 17th Floor, New York, NY 10001
Black Enterprise, New York, NY (Multicultural awareness)
Forbes, New York, NY (Business news)
Practical Accountant, Faulkner & Gray, Inc., New York, NY
Wall Street Journal, New York, NY (Business newspaper)

Technology

AICPA. *Serving America: A Tradition of Excellence,* 1986. (Video)

PART 2 OPENER

PART 2

Departmentalized Accounting

GENERAL GOALS

1. Know accounting terminology related to a departmentalized merchandising business organized as a corporation.
2. Understand accounting concepts and practices related to a departmentalized merchandising business organized as a corporation.
3. Demonstrate accounting procedures for a departmentalized merchandising business organized as a corporation.

OVERVIEW

This part is a review of an accounting cycle for a merchandising business organized as a corporation. To prepare students for this part, an optional REVIEW PROJECT is provided in the Teacher's Resource Guide. This REVIEW PROJECT covers a complete accounting cycle for a merchandising business organized as a corporation.

The organization and content provide students with both a review of what was learned in a first year of accounting study and expanded learnings through applications applied to a departmental accounting system.

Chapter 2 describes purchases and cash payments. After Chapter 2, Integrating Automated Accounting Topic 1 is presented to integrate computer application of the manual procedures that have been introduced in Chapter 2. For those teachers who wish to fully integrate the program, *Automated Accounting 6.0* may be used to actually automate selected problems in the text.

Chapter 3 describes sales and cash receipts followed by Integrating Automated Accounting Topic 2.

Chapter 4 describes departmental payroll. Chapter 5 describes financial reporting for a departmentalized business followed by Integrating Automated Accounting Topic 3.

Chapters 2–5 review the entire accounting cycle for a corporation. It is important that the student see the entire accounting cycle as it applies to a particular form of business. It is also important that the student apply these concepts through the completion of the simulation, Galleria, Inc., and/or the reinforcement activity.

CHAPTER 2 OVERVIEW

In preparation for this chapter, an optional REVIEW PROJECT is provided in the Teacher's Resource Guide. This REVIEW PROJECT covers a complete accounting cycle for a merchandising business organized as a corporation. This project will serve as a review in preparation for this course. If you choose to use this project, duplicate the REVIEW PROJECT narrative and accompanying blank forms for each student. A blank 10-column work sheet is included in the Teacher's Resource Guide if the 10-column work sheet is preferred.

GUIDE TO ACHIEVING LEARNING OBJECTIVES

	TEACH	APPLY	EXTEND/ENRICH					
Enabling Performance Tasks	**Lesson Plans**	**Application Problems**	**Mastery Problems**	**Challenge Problems**	**Cases for Critical Thinking**	**Recycling Problems**	**Reinforcement Activity**	
a. Define accounting terms related to departmental purchases and cash payments.	2-1, 2-2, 2-3							
b. Identify accounting concepts and practices related to departmental purchases and cash payments.	2-1, 2-2, 2-3				Case 1			
c. Perform file maintenance.	2-1	2-1	2-M			2-R1		
d. Journalize and post departmental purchases and cash payments.	2-2, 2-3	2-2, 2-3, 2-4	2-M	2-C		2-R1	1	
e. Reconcile a bank statement.	2-3	2-5	2-M		Case 2	2-R2	1	

ENRICHMENT

SPECIAL FEATURES
Global Perspective, page 43
Applied Communications, page 47
TECHNOLOGY CONNECTION
Automated Accounting 6.0 Problems 2-1, 2-2, 2-4, 2-5, 2-M

NEW, REVIEW, AND EXTENSION

ACTIVITIES/CONCEPTS/TRANSACTIONS	NEW	REVIEW/ EXTENSION
Corporation accounting		✓
Journalizing and posting using special journals		✓
Recording departmentalized transactions	✓	
Recording purchases of merchandise on account		✓
Recording cash payments for expenses		✓
Recording purchase of merchandise for cash		✓
Recording cash payments for purchases on account		✓
Recording purchases discounts		✓
Recording replenishing a petty cash fund		✓
Reconciling a bank statement		✓
Recording purchases returns and allowances		✓

Chapter 2 provides a review of accounting practices and procedures learned in the first year of accounting study. Departmentalized accounting is then introduced to expand student understanding of accounting systems. Purchases, purchases returns and allowances, and cash payment journals are used to record transactions. Each transaction is fully explained and illustrated using T accounts and the appropriate journal.

	INFORMAL ASSESSMENT		**FORMAL ASSESSMENT**			
	Study Guide	**Audit Your Understanding**	**Chapter MicroExam**	**Chapter Problem Test**	**Unit Objective Test**	**Portfolio**
	Unit A	✓	✓		✓	
	Unit B	✓	✓		✓	
				✓		
				✓		✓
				✓		✓

TEACHING MATERIALS

Teacher's Wraparound Edition of Text
Teacher's Resource Guide
Teacher's Edition of Working Papers
MicroExam

APPLIED MATHEMATICS

APPLIED MATH/ACCOUNTING SKILL	APPLICATION
Calculating purchases discount	Prob. 2-3

MasterSport

CHART OF ACCOUNTS

Balance Sheet Accounts

(1000) ASSETS

1100	Current Assets
1105	Cash
1110	Petty Cash
1115	Accounts Receivable
1120	Allowance for Uncollectible Accounts
1125-1	Merchandise Inventory—Golf
1125-2	Merchandise Inventory—Tennis
1130	Supplies—Office
1135	Supplies—Store
1140	Prepaid Insurance
1200	Plant Assets
1205	Office Equipment
1210	Accumulated Depreciation—Office Equipment
1215	Store Equipment
1220	Accumulated Depreciation—Store Equipment

(2000) LIABILITIES

2105	Accounts Payable
2110	Employee Income Tax Payable—Federal
2115	Employee Income Tax Payable—State
2120	Federal Income Tax Payable
2125	FICA Tax Payable
2130	Sales Tax Payable
2135	Unemployment Tax Payable—Federal
2140	Unemployment Tax Payable—State
2145	Health Insurance Premiums Payable
2150	Life Insurance Premiums Payable
2155	Dividends Payable

(3000) STOCKHOLDERS' EQUITY

3105	Capital Stock
3110	Retained Earnings
3115	Dividends
3120-1	Income Summary—Golf
3120-2	Income Summary—Tennis
3125	Income Summary—General

Income Statement Accounts

(4000) OPERATING REVENUE

4105-1	Sales—Golf
4105-2	Sales—Tennis
4110-1	Sales Discount—Golf
4110-2	Sales Discount—Tennis
4115-1	Sales Returns and Allowances—Golf
4115-2	Sales Returns and Allowances—Tennis

(5000) COST OF MERCHANDISE

5105-1	Purchases—Golf
5105-2	Purchases—Tennis
5110-1	Purchases Discount—Golf
5110-2	Purchases Discount—Tennis
5115-1	Purchases Returns and Allowances—Golf
5115-2	Purchases Returns and Allowances—Tennis

(6000) OPERATING EXPENSES

6100	Selling Expenses
6105	Advertising Expense
6110	Credit Card Fee Expense
6115	Depreciation Expense—Store Equipment
6120-1	Salary Expense—Golf
6120-2	Salary Expense—Tennis
6125	Supplies Expense—Store
6200	Administrative Expenses
6205	Depreciation Expense—Office Equipment
6210	Insurance Expense
6215	Miscellaneous Expense
6220	Payroll Taxes Expense
6225	Rent Expense
6230	Salary Expense—Administrative
6235	Supplies Expense—Office
6240	Uncollectible Accounts Expense

(7000) INCOME TAX

7105	Federal Income Tax Expense

The chart of accounts for MasterSport is illustrated above for ready reference as you study Part 2 of this textbook.

TEACHING STRATEGIES: ACCOUNTING PEDAGOGY

A chart of accounts for the business that is used to illustrate each part of this textbook is provided at the beginning of each part. Charts of accounts are extremely important to companies because they drive the accounting system. Employees usually cannot even receive reimbursement for expenses without knowing which account the expense should be charged to. Pedagogically, the chart of accounts provides the following information: (1) Classification for each account—needed to determine how a transaction is analyzed. (2) Permanent accounts (balance sheet accounts) and temporary accounts (income statement accounts)—assist in analyzing transactions and recording closing entries. (3) Account number for every general ledger account—critical information in automated accounting, since transactions are entered by account number rather than account title.

TEACHING STRATEGIES: CHART OF ACCOUNTS

This first chart of accounts is for a merchandising business organized as a corporation. Because the business is also departmentalized, many accounts are divided into departments. In the Assets section, there is a merchandise inventory account for each department. In the stockholders' equity section, there is an income summary account for each department and also a general income summary account. The Operating Revenue and Cost of Merchandise accounts are all departmentalized.

The Operating Expenses section is divided into selling and administrative expenses. Within the selling expenses Salary Expense is divided to indicate the salaries for the two different departments. The other selling expenses are not clearly distributed to one department or another. Administrative expenses are expenses of the business that do not clearly relate to the sales effort, such as salaries and supplies of the office staff.

TEACHING STRATEGIES: TEACHING TIP

Emphasize that students should refer to this chart of accounts throughout their study of Part 2. It will help them determine classification of accounts, which accounts are temporary and permanent accounts, and what account numbers to use for automated accounting. It will also be a useful reference for performing file maintenance activities.

2

Recording Departmental Purchases and Cash Payments

TEACHING STRATEGIES: ACCOUNTING PEDAGOGY

This textbook presents review material to prepare students for the advanced accounting course. The review material is broken into small parts so that students are not overloaded. All important corporate terms are reviewed where appropriate.

ENABLING PERFORMANCE TASKS

After studying Chapter 2, you will be able to:

a Define accounting terms related to departmental purchases and cash payments.

b Identify accounting concepts and practices related to departmental purchases and cash payments.

c Perform file maintenance.

d Journalize and post departmental purchases and cash payments.

e Reconcile a bank statement.

TERMS PREVIEW

asset • liability • equities • owner's equity • accounting equation • source document • journal • special journal • double-entry accounting • account • ledger • general ledger • subsidiary ledger • controlling account • file maintenance • departmental accounting system • merchandising business • posting • debit memorandum • contra account • contra balance • cash discount • purchases discount • petty cash • bank statement

APPLIED SKILLS: LANGUAGE ARTS

Paraphrasing, writing complete sentences, and identifying direct objects. For additional practice in language arts skills, direct students to answer the Accounting Terms and Questions For Individual Study at the end of the chapter. Students should write the answers in their own words and in complete sentences. To further practice language arts skills ask students to underline the direct object(s) in each sentence of their answers.

LESSON PLAN 2-1

Materials

- Student pages 28–32
- Software: *Automated Accounting 6.0* or higher; CENTURY 21 ACCOUNTING Template, Advanced Course

Objectives (Enabling Performance Tasks)

a. Define accounting terms related to departmental purchases and cash payments.

b. Identify accounting concepts and practices related to departmental purchases and cash payments.

c. Perform file maintenance.

FOCUS

- In the first-year accounting course, the accounting concepts and practices related to recording, summarizing, and reporting the financial information for a merchandising business organized as a corporation were presented. Explain that this lesson will review the accounting equation, the use of special journals and the general journal, the use of general and subsidiary ledgers, and the chart of accounts numbering system and file maintenance.
- Introduce vocabulary: asset, liability, equities, owner's equity, accounting equation, source document, journal, special journal, double-entry accounting, account, ledger, general ledger, subsidiary ledger, controlling account, file maintenance.

Financial information for a business can be recorded, summarized, and reported in a variety of ways. The way in which information is kept and reported is determined by the size, type, and complexity of the business. When designing financial records, the business should also consider the types of decisions that will be made based on the financial statements. If managers want to use financial statements to assist in making decisions for individual departments, information for each department must be recorded separately. However, the same accounting concepts and practices must be followed regardless of the procedures used.

ACCOUNTING PRINCIPLES

Anything of value that is owned is called an **asset.** An amount owed by a business is called a **liability.** Financial rights to the assets of a business are called **equities.** The amount remaining after the value of all liabilities is subtracted from the value of all assets is called **owner's equity.** In a corporation the value of the owner's equity is referred to as stockholders' equity.

FYI

Total assets must always equal total liabilities plus owner's equity.

An equation showing the relationship among assets, liabilities, and owner's equity is called an **accounting equation.** The accounting equation may be stated as assets = equities. More commonly the equation is stated as assets = liabilities + owner's equity. The accounting equation is shown in the T account.

Accounting Equation		
(LEFT side) Assets	=	(RIGHT side) Liabilities + Owner's Equity

The equation is often viewed as forming a "T." Assets are listed on the left side of the T account and equities (liabilities and owner's equity) on the right side of the T account. Total assets must always equal total liabilities plus owner's equity.

ACCOUNTING RECORDS

Accounting records show changes and the current account balance of each asset, liability, and owner's equity (or stockholders' equity) account. In the United States, the amounts are stated in dollars and cents. *(CONCEPT: Unit of Measurement)*

The concept reference above indicates the application of a specific accounting concept. For a complete statement and explanation of the concepts, refer to Chapter 1.

Information about business transactions is first obtained from original business papers. A business paper from which information is obtained for a journal entry is called a **source document.** A source document describes in detail the information about a transaction. Each journal entry must be supported by a source document proving that a transaction did occur. *(CONCEPT: Objective Evidence)* Common source documents include receipts, checks, cash register tapes, invoices, and memorandums.

TEACHING STRATEGIES: TEACHING TIP

Review classifying accounts, recognizing the balance side of each account, and recognizing the increase and decrease side of each account.

Journals

A form for recording transactions in chronological order is called a **journal.** A journal used to record only one kind of transaction is called a **special journal.** A business with many daily transactions may use special journals. MasterSport uses four special journals along with a general journal to record its transactions.

1. Purchases journal—for all purchases on account
2. Cash payments journal—for all cash payments
3. Sales journal—for all sales on account
4. Cash receipts journal—for all cash receipts

A general journal is used for all other transactions.

All journals include amount columns for recording the dollars and cents of a transaction. *(CONCEPT: Unit of Measurement)* The general journal, for example, has two amount columns. The *left* amount column is labeled Debit. The *right* amount column is labeled Credit. An entry recorded in the debit column is known as a debit. Likewise, an entry recorded in the credit column is known as a credit. The "T" previously described in the accounting equation is also present in a general journal's debit and credit amount columns as shown in Illustration 2-1.

ILLUSTRATION 2-1 Relationship of "T" in the accounting equation and general journal

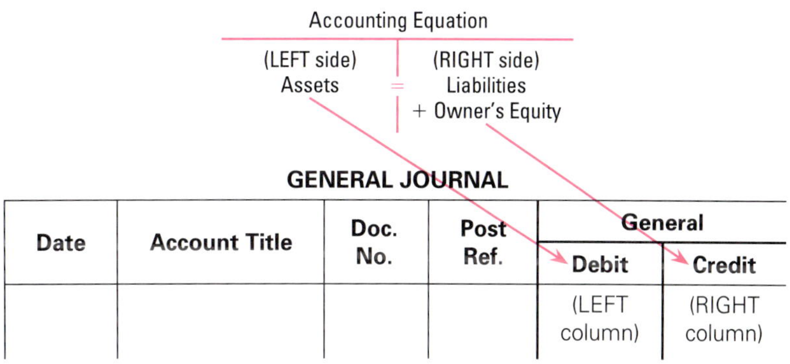

The recording of debit and credit parts of a transaction is called **double-entry accounting.** The accounting equation is the basis for all double-entry accounting. Two accounting principles are common to double-entry accounting. (1) The total value of things owned by a business (assets) *equals* the total value of claims of outsiders (liabilities) and claims of owners (owner's equity). (2) Debits equal credits for each business transaction recorded.

Accounts

Transactions are journalized in chronological order. Periodically, information is sorted to summarize like kinds of information. A

TEACH

Cover student pages 28–32 "Accounting Principles," "Accounting Records," and "General and Subsidiary Ledger File Maintenance." Review the accounting equation and explain how it is the basis for double-entry accounting. Review the use of the four special journals and the general journal. Explain the relationship of the accounting equation to the amount columns in a general journal. Review the general ledger account form and the normal balances of the different classifications of accounts. Explain how the general ledger controlling account summarizes all accounts in a subsidiary ledger. Emphasize that the total of the subsidiary accounts must equal the balance in the appropriate controlling account. Review the chart of accounts numbering system and explain how to assign the unused middle number to a new general ledger account.

APPLY

Write the accounting equation on the board and discuss how the "T" of the equation relates to the debit and credit columns of the general journal and general ledger accounts. Refer students to Illustrations 2-1 and 2-2. Review the procedure for assigning the unused middle number to a new ledger account.

Guided Practice

Guide students through the assigning of an account number if a new account is added between the first and second accounts in the Selling Expenses section of the chart of accounts on page 26. Ask students to determine the unused middle number between account numbers 6110 and 6115. All students should know why 6112.5 cannot be used for the new account. Ask students to assign an account number to a new account added after the last Selling Expense account, 6125. All students should know why 6130 is the number assigned.

Independent Practice

Assign Terms 1–15, Questions 1–7, and Problem 2-1.

APPLIED SKILLS: WRITING ACROSS THE CURRICULUM

Writing paragraphs and short essays. The Cases for Critical Thinking are short, practical applications of the accounting principles developed in the chapter. Some cases are planned to present problems related to the chapter but not specifically discussed and answered in the chapter. These cases present an opportunity for critical thinking and decision making. These cases also require more than a short objective-type response. Therefore they provide ideal practice in writing paragraphs and short essays.

ASSESS

Assess student understanding by checking the solutions to the Independent Practice activities.

Reteach

Place the accounting equation and a list of accounts on the board. Select accounts from the chart of accounts on page 26. Ask students to classify each account and place it under the appropriate element of the equation. Using T accounts, ask students to indicate the increase and decrease sides of each account.

Extend

Use *Automated Accounting 6.0* or higher with CENTURY 21 ACCOUNTING Template, Advanced Course, with Problem 2-1.

Enrich

Assign the Applied Communications special feature on page 47. This activity provides the opportunity to prepare a resume. Guide students through the steps of completing a resume.

CLOSURE

Use Audit Your Understanding questions.

TEACHING STRATEGIES: TEACHING TIP

Review the four questions used to analyze a transaction.

1. What accounts are affected?
2. How is each account classified?
3. How is each account balance changed?
4. How is each amount entered in the accounts?

record summarizing all the information pertaining to a single item in the accounting equation is called an **account.** The basic elements of an account form are the two amount columns used to record debit and credit amounts from a journal. The two amount columns form a "T" as shown in Illustration 2-2.

ILLUSTRATION 2-2 Two amount columns of an account

Debit	Credit
(LEFT column)	(RIGHT column)

FYI

The normal balance side is the increase side.

The amount in an account is known as an account balance. Each business transaction causes a change in two or more account balances. Increases in an account balance are recorded in the same column as its normal balance. Decreases in an account balance are recorded in the column opposite its normal balance. The normal balances of different classifications of accounts are shown in Illustration 2-3.

ILLUSTRATION 2-3 Normal balances of accounts

Assets = Liabilities + Owner's Equity

Account	DEBIT column	CREDIT column
Any Asset Account	Normal balance Increase +	Decrease −
Any Liability Account	Decrease −	Normal balance Increase +
Any Capital Account	Decrease −	Normal balance Increase +
Any Revenue Account	Decrease −	Normal balance Increase +
Any Expense Account	Normal balance Increase +	Decrease −

Asset account balances are increased by debits and decreased by credits. Liability and capital account balances as well as revenue account balances are increased by credits and decreased by debits. Expense account balances are increased by debits and decreased by credits.

Ledgers

A group of accounts is called a **ledger.** A ledger that contains all accounts needed to prepare financial statements is called a **general ledger.** A ledger that is summarized in a single general ledger account is called a **subsidiary ledger.** An account in a general ledger that summarizes all accounts in a subsidiary ledger is called a **controlling account.** Two subsidiary ledgers and two general ledger controlling accounts are commonly used.

Subsidiary Ledgers	Controlling Accounts
Accounts Receivable Ledger	Accounts Receivable
Accounts Payable Ledger	Accounts Payable

Accounts for customers who buy merchandise on account are kept in an accounts receivable ledger. Separate accounts are kept in an accounts payable ledger for vendors to whom money is owed.

GENERAL AND SUBSIDIARY LEDGER FILE MAINTENANCE

MasterSport, the business described in Part 2, uses a general ledger account numbering system that meets three needs. (1) A separate numeric listing is provided for each ledger division. (2) A predesigned arrangement of numbers is provided within each ledger division. (3) Enough account number digits are provided to allow the addition of new accounts. The procedure for arranging accounts in a general ledger, assigning account numbers, and keeping records current is called **file maintenance.**

The general ledger chart of accounts on page 26 has seven divisions. The first digit of each four-digit account number shows the general ledger division in which the account is located. The accounts in some divisions, such as Assets, are divided into categories. The second digit of the account number shows the category in which the account is located. The last two digits show the location of a specific account with respect to other accounts in that division and category.

MasterSport uses a four-digit numbering system for general ledger accounts with each account number initially assigned sequentially by 5s. Assigning account numbers by 5s allows adding new accounts easily. New accounts can be added between existing account numbers without renumbering all accounts.

Adding a New General Ledger Account

A numbering system must contain enough digits to allow addition of new accounts without changing the numbers of existing accounts. A new account is assigned the unused middle number between two existing accounts.

APPLIED SKILLS: COMMUNICATIONS

Surveys of business managers show that communication skills are one of the most desired traits in new employees. The APPLIED COMMUNICATIONS activity provides an opportunity for students to practice their communication and language arts skills on topics that directly relate to accounting. This activity is repeated from the first year course. This activity requires the student to research the preparation of a resume and then prepare a personal resume. You may want to bring reference books into the classroom rather than go to the library. Another alternative is to duplicate the Resume Checklist in the Teacher's Resource Guide and distribute copies as a guide to what is contained in a successful resume.

If students have already completed a resume, use this opportunity to update and revise to reflect current information. The resume should be keyed, one page in length, and in the most current style.

TEACHING STRATEGIES: ASSESSMENT BY PORTFOLIO

The student resume and resume checklist prepared in the Applied Communications activity are the first items that should be included in a student's portfolio if you are using portfolios in your assessment program.

When no exact middle number is available, the nearest even whole number is used.

MasterSport decided to add a new account Equipment Repair Expense between the two existing accounts Depreciation Expense—Office Equipment, 6205, and Insurance Expense, 6210. The unused middle number between 6205 and 6210 is 6207.5. The number 6107.5 contains five digits and cannot be assigned in a four-digit numbering system. Therefore, account number 6108, the nearest *even whole number,* is used. The new account is placed in the general ledger as shown below.

6205 Depreciation Expense—Office Equipment (existing account)
6208 EQUIPMENT REPAIR EXPENSE (NEW ACCOUNT)
6210 Insurance Expense (existing account)

New accounts that are added after the last account in a division are assigned the next number in sequence. Dividends Payable, *2155,* is the last existing account in the liabilities division. If MasterSport decides to add a new liability account after Dividends Payable, the new account would be assigned number 2160.

2155 Dividends Payable (existing account)
2160 NEW ACCOUNT

Deleting a General Ledger Account

When an account is no longer needed, it is removed from the general ledger chart of accounts. The account number is then available for a new general ledger account.

Subsidiary Ledger File Maintenance

The numbering system used for subsidiary ledger accounts must meet the same three needs as the system for general ledger accounts. MasterSport uses a three-digit numbering system for its subsidiary ledger accounts. MasterSport's subsidiary ledgers generally require more file maintenance than a general ledger. Therefore, subsidiary ledger account numbers are assigned by 10s to provide more numbers for adding new accounts between existing accounts. MasterSport uses the same file maintenance procedures for the subsidiary ledgers as for the general ledger.

Audit Your Understanding

1. How is the accounting equation most commonly stated?
2. What are the three needs met by MasterSport's account numbering system?

DEPARTMENTAL ACCOUNTING

Management decisions depend on accounting information about each phase of a business. Accounting information about the kinds of merchandise that produce the greatest or the least profit is

AUDIT YOUR UNDERSTANDING

The AUDIT YOUR UNDERSTANDING feature appears at the end of each section of the chapter. Explain to your students that the word audit means to check or verify. AUDIT YOUR UNDERSTANDING may be used to check student comprehension of the section just studied. The answers are provided in Appendix D in the back of the textbook.

1. Assets = Liabilities + Owner's Equity
2. (1) A separate numeric listing is provided for each ledger division. (2) A predesigned arrangement of numbers is provided within each ledger division. (3) Enough account number digits are provided to allow the addition of new accounts.

LESSON PLAN 2-2

Materials

- Student pages 32–38
- Blackline Master for Departmental Purchases Journal (TRG)
- Blackline Master for Departmental Purchases Returns and Allowances Journal (TRG)
- Software: *Automated Accounting 6.0* or higher; CENTURY 21 ACCOUNTING Template, Advanced Course

Objectives (Enabling Performance Tasks)

a. Define accounting terms related to departmental purchases and cash payments.
b. Identify accounting concepts and practices related to departmental purchases and cash payments.
d. Journalize and post departmental purchases and cash payments.

FYI

CPAs are the key to helping small businesses avoid many pitfalls of doing business.

needed. When a business has two or more departments, accounting information is needed about how well each department is doing.

An accounting system showing accounting information for two or more departments is called a **departmental accounting system.** In a departmental accounting system, gross profit is calculated for each department. The general ledger, therefore, must include a number of separate departmental accounts. Shoe stores, furniture stores, computer stores, department stores, and sporting goods stores are examples of firms that commonly organize on a departmental basis.

A business that purchases and sells goods is called a **merchandising business.** MasterSport, the merchandising business described in Part 2, is a corporation organized on a departmental basis. The business sells golf equipment and tennis equipment.

> A business may have two types of equipment: (1) equipment purchased for sale to customers and (2) equipment used in the operation of the business. MasterSport purchases and sells golf and tennis equipment. MasterSport also has office equipment and store equipment that is used in the operation of the business.

MasterSport uses a departmental accounting system. Accounting information is recorded and reported for two departments: (1) Golf and (2) Tennis. Sales are made to individuals as well as to clubs and school systems. The separate departmental accounts for MasterSport are in the chart of accounts, page 26. The accounts for the golf department are indicated by a -1 after the account number. Accounts for the tennis department are indicated by a -2 after the account number. For example, Merchandise Inventory—Golf is assigned number 1125-1 and Merchandise Inventory—Tennis is assigned number 1125-2. The basic four digit account number for Merchandise Inventory is 1125. A fifth digit, -1 or -2, is used only to identify departmental accounts.

DEPARTMENTAL PURCHASES ON ACCOUNT

A business with more than one department records a purchase on account in the same way as a business with a single department except for two differences. (1) Each purchase invoice has a notation placed on it showing to which department the purchase applies. (2) Each department has a separate Purchases Debit column in the purchases journal.

FYI

Only purchases of merchandise on account are recorded in the purchases journal.

Journalizing Purchases on Account

All departmental purchases on account are recorded in a purchases journal. MasterSport's purchases journal has special Purchases Debit columns for each department—Golf and Tennis. MasterSport's purchases journal is shown in Illustration 2-4.

FOCUS

- In the first-year accounting course, purchases transactions were recorded for a merchandising business organized as a corporation. In this lesson, purchases transactions will be recorded for a departmentalized merchandising business organized as a corporation. Explain that when a business has two or more departments, accounting information is needed about how well each department is doing.
- Introduce vocabulary: departmental accounting system, merchandising business, posting, debit memorandum, contra account, contra balance.

TEACH

Cover student pages 32–38 "Departmental Accounting," "Departmental Purchases on Account," and "Departmental Purchases Returns and Allowances." Present the departmental purchases journal and explain that the journal has a separate Purchases Debit column for each department. Review the procedures for analyzing and recording a departmental purchases on account transaction and the steps in posting from a purchases journal. Present the departmental purchases returns and allowances journal and explain that the journal has a separate Purchases Returns and Allowances Credit column for each department. Review the procedures for analyzing and recording a departmental purchases returns and allowances transaction and the steps in posting from a purchases returns and allowances journal. Explain how a contra balance is shown in a vendor's account.

TEACHING STRATEGIES: TEACHING TIP

Use the overhead projector or chalkboard to provide a comparison between the chart of accounts used in Part 2, a departmental merchandising business, and the chart of accounts used for a nondepartmental merchandising business. Students should determine which accounts are different and why these accounts are needed in a business that maintains departmental records.

APPLY

Use T accounts on the overhead projector or chalkboard to show how each transaction in this lesson is analyzed. Refer students to Illustrations 2-4, 2-5, 2-6, and 2-7 as journalizing and posting using a departmental purchases journal are presented. Refer students to Illustration 2-8 as journalizing and posting using a departmental purchases returns and allowances journal are presented.

Guided Practice

Guide students through the T account analysis of the March 1–15 transactions in Problem 2-2. Have students draw T accounts on a sheet of paper and analyze the first transaction. All students should agree with the analysis before proceeding to the next transaction. Repeat the process until all transactions have been analyzed. The balance of Problem 2-2 can be assigned as Independent Practice.

Independent Practice

Assign Terms 16–21, Questions 8–10, and Problem 2-2.

TEACHING STRATEGIES: TEACHING TIP

Review the five steps in posting.

1. The date is written in the Date column of the account.
2. The journal page number is written in the Post. Ref. column of the account.
3. The amount is written in the Debit or Credit amount column of the account.
4. The new account balance is calculated and recorded in the Balance Debit or Credit column of the account.
5. The account number is placed in the Post. Ref. column (or in parentheses below the column total) of the journal to show to which account an amount has been posted.

ILLUSTRATION 2-4 Departmental purchases journal

PURCHASES JOURNAL PAGE 6

	DATE		ACCOUNT CREDITED	PURCH. NO.	POST. REF.	1 ACCOUNTS PAYABLE CREDIT	2 PURCHASES DEBIT GOLF	3 PURCHASES DEBIT TENNIS	
1	19-- June	1	Tennis Warehouse	336		845 00		845 00	1
2									2

June 1, 19--. Purchased tennis equipment on account from Tennis Warehouse, $845.00. Purchase Invoice No. 336.

GENERAL LEDGER

Purchases—Tennis	
845.00	

Accounts Payable	
	845.00

ACCOUNTS PAYABLE LEDGER

Tennis Warehouse	
	845.00

The source document for this transaction is a purchase invoice. *(CONCEPT: Objective Evidence)*

In the general ledger, Purchases—Tennis is increased by an $845.00 debit. Accounts Payable is increased by an $845.00 credit. In the accounts payable ledger, Tennis Warehouse, is increased by an $845.00 credit.

The details of Purchase Invoice No. 336 are recorded on line 1 of the purchases journal, Illustration 2-4. The date, *19--, June 1,* is written in the Date column. The vendor name, *Tennis Warehouse,* is written in the Account Credited column. The purchase invoice number, *336,* is recorded in the Purch. No. column. Since only purchase invoice numbers are recorded in the column, no identifying letter is necessary. The credit amount, *$845.00,* is recorded in the Accounts Payable Credit column. The debit amount, *$845.00,* is recorded in the Purchases Debit Tennis column.

Posting from a Purchases Journal

Transferring information from a journal entry to a ledger account is called **posting.** MasterSport keeps vendor accounts in an accounts payable ledger. Individual amounts in the Accounts Payable Credit column of the purchases journal are posted often to the appropriate vendor accounts. The purchases journal is abbreviated as *P* in the Post. Ref. column of the ledger accounts. Posting line 1 from the purchases journal to an accounts payable ledger is shown in Illustration 2-5.

The date, *19--, June 1,* is written in the account's Date column. The journal page number, *P6,* is recorded in the Post. Ref. column. The amount, *$845.00,* is recorded in the Credit column. Since there is no previous balance in this account, the amount in the Credit column is also the balance of the account. Therefore, this amount, *$845.00,* is also recorded in the Credit Balance column. The vendor number, *270,* is entered in the Post. Ref. column of the purchases journal to show that posting has been completed for this line.

TEACHING STRATEGIES: DIFFERENT LEARNING STYLES

Auditory Learner. The auditory learner will best learn by hearing. When introducing the T account to an auditory learner, have the student say out loud that the "left side is the debit side of the account." Repeating this statement a few times will increase the chances of its being reinforced. Repeat the process with the statement the "right side is the credit side of the account."

ILLUSTRATION 2-5 Posting from a purchases journal to an accounts payable ledger account

PURCHASES JOURNAL — PAGE 6

	DATE		ACCOUNT CREDITED	PURCH. NO.	POST. REF.	1 ACCOUNTS PAYABLE CREDIT	2 PURCHASES DEBIT GOLF	3 PURCHASES DEBIT TENNIS	
1	19-- June	1	Tennis Warehouse	336	270	845 00		845 00	1
2									2
3									3

VENDOR Tennis Warehouse — VENDOR NO. 270

DATE		ITEM	POST. REF.	DEBIT	CREDIT	CREDIT BALANCE
19-- June	1		P6		845 00	845 00

The purchases journal is proved and ruled at the end of each month. A journal is proved by adding each column and then proving that the sum of the debit column totals equals the sum of the credit column totals. Double lines are then ruled across the amount columns to show that the totals have been verified as correct. Each amount column total is posted to the general ledger account named in the column heading. Posting an amount column total from the purchases journal to a general ledger is shown in Illustration 2-6.

ILLUSTRATION 2-6 Posting a total from a purchases journal to a general ledger account

PURCHASES JOURNAL — PAGE 6

	DATE		ACCOUNT CREDITED	PURCH. NO.	POST. REF.	1 ACCOUNTS PAYABLE CREDIT	2 PURCHASES DEBIT GOLF	3 PURCHASES DEBIT TENNIS	
24		30	Golf-Tee, Inc.	359	230	1 390 00	1 390 00		24
25		30	Totals			27 830 00	9 360 00	18 470 00	25
26						(2105)			26
27									27
28									28

ACCOUNT Accounts Payable — ACCOUNT NO. 2105

DATE		ITEM	POST. REF.	DEBIT	CREDIT	BALANCE DEBIT	BALANCE CREDIT
19-- June	1	Balance	✓				8 680 00
	30		P6		27 830 00		36 510 00

TEACHING STRATEGIES: APPLYING VISUALS

Direct the students to Illustrations 2-5 and 2-6 to review posting.

ASSESS

Assess student understanding by checking the solutions to the Independent Practice activities.

Reteach

Make transparencies of the departmental purchases and purchases returns and allowances journals from the accounting forms masters provided in the Blackline Masters section of the Teacher's Resource Guide. Refer students to Recycling Problem 2-R1. Ask students to use T accounts to analyze the November 5, 8, 10, 14, and 15 purchases and purchases returns and allowances transactions. Use the transparencies to demonstrate how the transactions are journalized.

Extend

- Assign Cases for Critical Thinking 1.
- Use *Automated Accounting 6.0* or higher with CENTURY 21 ACCOUNTING Template, Advanced Course, with Problem 2-2.

CLOSURE

Use Audit Your Understanding questions.

TEACHING STRATEGIES: COOPERATIVE LEARNING

Select a group of three students to prepare a bulletin board that includes the five steps for posting. Allow five days for this project. Appoint a spokesperson to make a presentation to the class of these five steps and how they are necessary to posting correctly.

FYI

An account number under a column total shows that the total was posted.

To indicate that the posting came from the purchases journal, page 6, *P6* is recorded in the ledger account's Post. Ref. column. The account number, *2105,* is recorded in parentheses immediately below the purchases journal's column total to show that the amount has been posted.

MasterSport's departmental purchases journal, Illustration 2-7, is shown after all posting has been completed.

APPLIED SKILLS: WORD PROCESSING

If you wish to integrate word processing in your accounting course, you may direct students to answer the end-of-chapter Accounting Terms, Questions for Individual Study, and Cases for Critical Thinking using their word processing software.

ILLUSTRATION 2-7 Departmental purchases journal after posting has been completed

PURCHASES JOURNAL PAGE 6

	DATE		ACCOUNT CREDITED	PURCH. NO.	POST. REF.	1 ACCOUNTS PAYABLE CREDIT	2 PURCHASES DEBIT GOLF	3 PURCHASES DEBIT TENNIS	
1	19-- June	1	Tennis Warehouse	336	270	845 00		845 00	1
23		30	EZ Golf	358	220	2 920 00	2 920 00		23
24		30	Golf-Tee, Inc.	359	230	1 390 00	1 390 00		24
25		30	Totals			27 830 00	9 360 00	18 470 00	25
26						(2105)	(5105-1)	(5105-2)	26
27									27
28									28

DEPARTMENTAL PURCHASES RETURNS AND ALLOWANCES

Merchandise may be returned to a vendor for several reasons. The merchandise may be unsatisfactory. The merchandise may not be what was ordered. Also, merchandise may be received in damaged condition. When merchandise is returned, the vendor usually gives the buyer credit.

Journalizing Purchases Returns and Allowances

MasterSport records all purchases returns and allowances in a purchases returns and allowances journal. MasterSport's purchases returns and allowances journal is shown in Illustration 2-8.

Details of a purchases return or allowance may be stated in a letter or on a preprinted form. A form prepared by the customer showing the price deduction taken by the customer for returns and allowances is called a **debit memorandum.** When returning merchandise or requesting an adjustment, MasterSport issues a debit memorandum. The debit memorandum is used as the source document for a purchases returns and allowances transaction. *(CONCEPT: Objective Evidence)*

APPLIED SKILLS: BUILDING STUDY SKILLS

Before students journalize transactions, they should first analyze each transaction into debit and credit parts using T accounts. The additional practice helps students master the debit/credit concepts.

ILLUSTRATION 2-8 Departmental purchases returns and allowances journal

PURCHASES RETURNS AND ALLOWANCES JOURNAL — PAGE 6

	DATE		ACCOUNT DEBITED	DEBIT MEMO. NO.	POST. REF.	1 ACCOUNTS PAYABLE DEBIT	2 PURCHASES RETURNS AND ALLOWANCES CREDIT GOLF	3 PURCHASES RETURNS AND ALLOWANCES CREDIT TENNIS	
1	19-- June	3	*Key Tennis Company*	22	240	54 50		54 50	1
2		4	*EZ Golf*	23	220	126 30	126 30		2
3		7	*Champion Tennis Supply*	24	210	96 00		96 00	3
4		8	*Tennis Warehouse*	25	270	49 50		49 50	4
5		13	*Golf-Tee, Inc.*	26	230	176 00	176 00		5
6		20	*Nelson Racquets, Inc.*	27	250	65 00		65 00	6
7		23	*University Tennis*	28	280	560 00		560 00	7
8		27	*Super Pro Tennis*	29	260	240 00		240 00	8
9		30	*Totals*			1 367 30	302 30	1 065 00	9
10						(2105)	(5115-1)	(5115-2)	10
11									11
12									12
13									13

TEACHING STRATEGIES: TEACHING TIP

It is important that transactions are always analyzed using T accounts. Students who establish the habit of analyzing transactions will have fewer problems understanding journalizing in future chapters. If working with the entire class, put the T accounts on the board and fill them in as students analyze a transaction. If working with an individual student, have that student put T accounts on a piece of paper. Avoid placing T accounts side be side on the board. Place T accounts one below another. With this stacked arrangement students can more easily check the analysis to determine if debits equal credits for the transaction.

FYI

The normal balance of a contra account is opposite that of the related account.

An account that reduces a related account on a financial statement is called a **contra account.** Purchases—Tennis is a cost account. An account showing deductions from a purchases account is a contra cost account. Purchases Returns and Allowances—Tennis is one of MasterSport's contra cost accounts. Purchases returns and allowances are kept in a separate account and not deducted directly from the purchases account. This procedure helps the business see what proportion of the merchandise was returned to vendors.

June 3, 19--. Returned tennis equipment to Key Tennis Company, $54.50, from Purchase Invoice No. 333. Debit Memorandum No. 22.

The source document for this transaction is a debit memorandum. *(CONCEPT: Objective Evidence)*

In the general ledger, Accounts Payable is decreased by a $54.50 debit. Purchases Returns and Allowances—Tennis is increased by a $54.50 credit. In the accounts payable ledger, the vendor account, Key Tennis Company, is decreased by a $54.50 debit.

GENERAL LEDGER

Accounts Payable

Debit	Credit
54.50	

Purchases Returns and Allowances—Tennis

Debit	Credit
	54.50

ACCOUNTS PAYABLE LEDGER

Key Tennis Company

Debit	Credit
54.50	

The details of Debit Memorandum No. 22 are recorded on line 1 of the purchases returns and allowances journal, Illustration 2-8. The date, *19--, June 3,* is written in the Date column. The vendor name, *Key Tennis Company,* is written in the Account Debited column. The debit memorandum number, *22,* is recorded in the Debit Memo. No. column. The debit memorandum amount, *$54.50,* is recorded in the Accounts Payable Debit column. The credit amount, *$54.50,* is recorded in the Purchases Returns and Allowances Credit Tennis column.

Posting from a Purchases Returns and Allowances Journal

Purchases returns and allowances are posted in the same manner as purchases on account. Each amount written in the Accounts Payable Debit column is posted often to the vendor account written in the Account Debited column. The purchases returns and allowances journal is abbreviated as *PR* in the Post. Ref. column of the ledger accounts. To indicate that posting came from the purchases returns and allowances journal, page 6, *PR6* is recorded in the Post. Ref. column of the account. The vendor number for Key Tennis Company, *240,* is recorded in the Post. Ref. column on line 1 of the journal to indicate completion of posting.

Sometimes a purchases return or allowance is made after a vendor has been paid in full. This situation might occur if an invoice is paid very soon after it is received. When this happens, the vendor account after posting has a debit balance instead of a normal credit balance. This debit balance reduces the amount to be paid for future purchases. An account balance that is opposite the normal balance is called a **contra balance.** A contra balance is shown by enclosing the amount in parentheses in the account's Balance column.

A purchases returns and allowances journal is proved, ruled, and posted at the end of each month. Each amount column total is posted to the general ledger account named in the column heading. The account number is written below the journal's column total to show that the amount has been posted. MasterSport's departmental purchases returns and allowances journal, Illustration 2-8, is shown after all posting has been completed.

FYI

A purchase allowance is given for a part of the purchase price of merchandise that is not returned.

Audit Your Understanding

1. What general ledger accounts are affected, and how, by a purchase of merchandise on account by MasterSport's tennis department?
2. What general ledger accounts are affected, and how, by a purchases return of tennis equipment?

DEPARTMENTAL CASH PAYMENTS

Most of MasterSport's cash payments are made by check. Therefore, checks are the source documents for most cash payments. *(CONCEPT: Objective Evidence)* All cash payments are recorded in a cash payments journal. MasterSport's cash payments journal, shown in Illustration 2-9, has two debit columns—General Debit and Accounts Payable Debit. The journal also has four credit columns—General Credit, a Purchases Discount Credit column for each of the two departments, and Cash Credit.

Cash Payment on Account

Purchases on account are expected to be paid within the credit period agreed upon. A seller may encourage early payment by allowing a deduction from the invoice amount. A deduction that a vendor allows on the invoice amount to encourage prompt payment is called a **cash discount.** A cash discount on purchases taken by a customer is called a **purchases discount.**

AUDIT YOUR UNDERSTANDING

1. Purchases—Tennis is debited; Accounts Payable is credited.
2. Accounts Payable is debited; Purchases Returns and Allowances—Tennis is credited.

LESSON PLAN 2-3

Materials

- Student pages 38–45
- Blackline Master for Departmental Cash Payments Journal (TRG)
- Software: *Automated Accounting 6.0* or higher; CENTURY 21 ACCOUNTING Template, Advanced Course
- Assess: Problem Test Chapter 2, MicroExam Chapter 2

Objectives (Enabling Performance Tasks)

a. Define accounting terms related to departmental purchases and cash payments.
b. Identify accounting concepts and practices related to departmental purchases and cash payments.
d. Journalize and post departmental purchases and cash payments.
e. Reconcile a bank statement.

TEACHING STRATEGIES: DIFFERENT LEARNING ABILITIES

Specific Learning Disability (SLD) Students. When asking questions during class, ask SLD students questions that they can likely answer successfully. Save more difficult or unstructured questions for better students.

ILLUSTRATION 2-9 Departmental cash payments journal

CASH PAYMENTS JOURNAL — PAGE 11

	DATE		ACCOUNT TITLE	CK. NO.	POST. REF.	1 GENERAL DEBIT	2 GENERAL CREDIT	3 ACCOUNTS PAYABLE DEBIT	4 PURCH. DISCOUNT CR. GOLF	5 PURCH. DISCOUNT CR. TENNIS	6 CASH CREDIT	
1	19-- June	1	Champion Tennis Supply	315	210			525 00		10 50	514 50	1
2		1	Golf-Tee, Inc.	316	230			225 00	4 50		220 50	2
3		1	Supplies—Office	317	1130	136 00					136 00	3
4		1	Rent Expense	318	6225	1 500 00					1 500 00	4
5		3	EZ Golf	319	220			440 00	8 80		431 20	5
6		4	Supplies—Store	320	1135	89 50					89 50	6
7		4	Miscellaneous Expense	321	6215	39 00					39 00	7
8		4	University Tennis	322	280			860 00		17 20	842 80	8

CASH PAYMENTS JOURNAL — PAGE 12

	DATE		ACCOUNT TITLE	CK. NO.	POST. REF.	1 GENERAL DEBIT	2 GENERAL CREDIT	3 ACCOUNTS PAYABLE DEBIT	4 PURCH. DISCOUNT CR. GOLF	5 PURCH. DISCOUNT CR. TENNIS	6 CASH CREDIT	
2		30	Supplies—Office	350	1130	164 00					402 00	2
3			Supplies—Store		1135	136 00						3
4			Advertising Expense		6105	56 00						4
5			Miscellaneous Expense		6215	46 00						5
6		30	Miscellaneous Expense	351	6215	73 00					73 00	6
7		30	Miscellaneous Expense	M18	6215	12 80					12 80	7
8		30	Credit Card Fee Expense	M19	6110	340 00					340 00	8
9		30	Totals			19 520 00	1 730 00	43 930 00	141 30	331 50	61 247 20	9
10						(✓)	(✓)	(2105)	(5110-1)	(5110-2)	(1105)	10
11												11
12												12
13												13

FYI

The "n" in 2/10, n/30 represents the word "net."

A purchases discount is usually stated as a percentage. For example, the terms of an invoice may be written as *2/10, n/30.* The expression 2/10 means that 2% of the invoice amount may be deducted from the amount due if payment is made within 10 days of the invoice date. The expression n/30 means that payment of the total invoice amount must be made within 30 days of the invoice date. No discount can be deducted, however, if payment is made after 10 days from the invoice date. MasterSport takes advantage of all discounts allowed by vendors.

A purchases discount reduces the net amount of cash paid for a purchase. The account Purchases Discount—Tennis is in the cost of merchandise division of MasterSport's general ledger. Purchases discounts are kept in separate accounts and not deducted directly from the purchases accounts. This procedure helps the business see what proportion of purchases on account were allowed purchases discounts. An account that reduces a related account on a financial statement is known as a contra account. The purchases discount accounts are contra cost accounts.

FOCUS

- Journalizing departmental purchases transactions was presented earlier in this chapter. In this lesson, cash payments transactions will be journalized in a departmental cash payments journal. Explain that the procedures for reconciling a bank statement will be reviewed.
- Introduce vocabulary: cash discount, purchases discount, petty cash, bank statement.

TEACH

Cover student pages 38–45 "Departmental Cash Payments" and "Bank Statements." Present the departmental cash payments journal and explain that the journal contains a separate Purchases Discount Credit column for each department. Demonstrate how to calculate a discount and the steps to follow in calculating the amount due on a cash payment on account. Review the procedures for analyzing and recording the departmental cash payment transactions and the steps in posting from a cash payments journal. Review the procedures for reconciling a bank statement and journalizing bank charges.

APPLY

Use T accounts on the overhead projector or chalkboard to show how each transaction in this lesson is analyzed. Refer students to Illustration 2-9 as journalizing and posting using a departmental cash payments journal are presented. Refer students to Illustration 2-10 as reconciling a bank statement is reviewed. Ask students who have checking accounts to explain how they reconcile their bank statements.

Guided Practice

- Guide students through the procedures for calculating the purchases discounts and amounts due on Purchase Invoices Nos. 226 and 227 in Problem 2-3. Write the formulas on the board for reference. Working as a group, have the students calculate the amounts for Invoice No. 226. Have them verify the amounts by comparing them with the answers given as the example. Next, have students calculate the amounts for Invoice No. 227. When all students agree on the correct amounts, direct students to record the amounts on the form in the working papers. The balance of Problem 2-3 can be completed as Independent Practice.
- Guide students through the T account analysis of the November 1–15 transactions in Problem 2-4. Have students draw T accounts on a sheet of paper and analyze the first transaction. All students should agree with the analysis before proceeding to the next transaction. Repeat the process until all transactions have been analyzed. The balance of Problem 2-4 can be completed as Independent Practice.

Independent Practice

- Assign Terms 22–25; Questions 11–16; Problems 2-3, 2-4, and 2-5.
- Assign Study Guide 2 and Mastery Problem 2-M.

June 1, 19--. Paid cash on account to Champion Tennis Supply, $514.50, covering Purchase Invoice No. 331 for tennis equipment for $525.00, less 2% discount, $10.50. Check No. 315.

The source document for this transaction is a check. *(CONCEPT: Objective Evidence)*

GENERAL LEDGER

Accounts Payable	
525.00	

Cash	
	514.50

Purchases Discount—Tennis	
	10.50

ACCOUNTS PAYABLE LEDGER

Champion Tennis Supply	
525.00	

In the general ledger, Accounts Payable is decreased by a $525.00 debit. Cash is decreased by a $514.50 credit. Purchases Discount—Tennis is increased by a $10.50 credit. In the accounts payable ledger, Champion Tennis Supply is decreased by a $525.00 debit.

The entry on line 1, Illustration 2-9, shows the cash payment to Champion Tennis Supply in which there is a purchases discount. The date, *19--, June 1,* is written in the Date column. The vendor name, *Champion Tennis Supply,* is written in the Account Title column. The check number, *315,* is entered in the Ck. No. column. The debit amount, *$525.00,* is recorded in the Accounts Payable Debit column. The credit amount, *$10.50,* is recorded in the Purchases Discount Credit Tennis column. The credit amount, *$514.50,* is recorded in the Cash Credit column.

An additional calculation is necessary when a discount is taken after a purchase return or allowance has been granted. The discount is calculated on the amount owed at the time the invoice is paid. Therefore, the amount of the return or allowance must be deducted from the amount of the original purchase *before* the discount can be calculated.

June 1, 19--. Paid cash on account to Golf-Tee, Inc., $220.50, covering Purchase Invoice No. 332 for golf equipment for $275.00, less Debit Memorandum No. 20 for $50.00, and less 2% discount, $4.50. Check No. 316.

The source document for this transaction is a check. *(CONCEPT: Objective Evidence)*

FYI

The proper use of a calculator is explained in Appendix B.

GENERAL LEDGER

Accounts Payable	
225.00	

Cash	
	220.50

Purchases Discount—Golf	
	4.50

ACCOUNTS PAYABLE LEDGER

Golf-Tee, Inc.	
225.00	

The amount owed at the time the invoice is paid is calculated as shown below.

Original Purchase Invoice Amount (P332)	–	Purchases Return (DM20)	=	Purchase Invoice Amount After Return
$275.00	–	50.00	=	$225.00

TEACHING STRATEGIES: Different Learning Styles

Kinesthetic Learner. Kinesthetic learners learn best by taking an active part in the instruction. When introducing the T account to a kinesthetic learner, have the student draw a T account in the air or have the student use a finger to draw a T account on the back of the hand or arm. Next, have the student label the left side with the word "DEBIT" and the right side with the word "CREDIT."

At the time of payment, the total amount owed is $225.00. Therefore, the purchases discount is calculated on $225.00 as shown below.

Purchase Invoice Amount After Return	×	Purchases Discount Rate	=	Purchases Discount
$225.00	×	2%	=	$4.50

The amount due after the purchases discount is calculated as shown below.

Purchase Invoice Amount After Return	−	Purchases Discount	=	Total Amount Due
$225.00	−	$4.50	=	$220.50

This transaction is journalized the same way as a payment of cash when there is no purchases return or allowance. The only difference is the way in which the amounts are calculated. This transaction is shown on line 2 of page 11 of the cash payments journal in Illustration 2-9.

Buying Supplies for Cash

Supplies—Office	
136.00	

Cash	
	136.00

June 1, 19--. Paid cash for office supplies, $136.00. Check No. 317.

Supplies—Office is increased by a $136.00 debit. Cash is decreased by a $136.00 credit.

The entry on line 3 of page 11 of the cash payments journal, Illustration 2-9, shows the cash payment for supplies. The date, *1*, is written in the Date column. The account title, Supplies—Office, is written in the Account Title column. The check number, *317*, is entered in the Ck. No. column. The debit amount, *$136.00*, is recorded in the General Debit column. The credit amount, *$136.00*, is recorded in the Cash Credit column.

Cash Payment of an Expense

Rent Expense	
1,500.00	

Cash	
	1,500.00

June 1, 19--. Paid cash for rent, $1,500.00. Check No. 318.

Rent Expense is increased by a $1,500.00 debit. Cash is decreased by a $1,500.00 credit.

The entry on line 4 of page 11 of the cash payments journal, Illustration 2-9, shows the cash payment for an expense. The date, *1*, is written in the Date column. The account title, Rent Expense, is entered in the Account Title column. The check number, *318*, is recorded in the Ck. No. column. The debit amount, *$1,500.00*, is recorded in the General Debit column. The credit amount, *$1,500.00*, is recorded in the Cash Credit column.

ASSESS

Assess student understanding by checking the solutions to the Independent Practice activities.

Reteach

- Make a transparency of the departmental cash payments journal from the accounting forms masters provided in the Blackline Masters section of the Teacher's Resource Guide. Refer students to Recycling Problem 2-R1. Ask students to use T accounts to analyze the November 1, 2, 4, and 12 cash payments transactions. Use the transparency to demonstrate how the transactions are journalized.
- Assign Recycling Problems 2-R1 and 2-R2.

Extend

- Assign Cases for Critical Thinking 2.
- Assign Challenge Problem 2-C. (The challenge is to record purchases at net amount and use the Discounts Lost account.)
- Use *Automated Accounting 6.0* or higher with CENTURY 21 ACCOUNTING Template, Advanced Course, with Problems 2-4, 2-5, and 2-M.

Enrich

Assign and discuss the GLOBAL PERSPECTIVE feature on page 43.

CLOSURE

Use Audit Your Understanding questions.

ASSESS

- Administer Problem Test Chapter 2.
- Administer a MicroExam test for Chapter 2.

TEACHING STRATEGIES: DIFFERENT LEARNING STYLES

Print Learner. The print learner prefers to see the data in print—preferably words. When introducing the T account, a print learner would prefer to study the illustration in the textbook which shows a T account, labelled with the words "DEBIT" and "CREDIT."

Cash Payment to Replenish Petty Cash

MasterSport deposits all cash receipts in a bank. Some money, however, is kept on hand for making small cash payments and for making change at the cash register.

An amount of cash kept on hand and used for making small payments is called **petty cash.** MasterSport has a petty cash fund of $500.00. A petty cash fund is replenished whenever the amount on hand becomes low. MasterSport replenishes petty cash whenever the fund drops below $100.00. Regardless of the amount remaining, the petty cash fund is always replenished on the last business day of each fiscal period. This procedure assures that all expenses are recorded during the fiscal period in which they occurred. *(CONCEPT: Matching Expenses with Revenue)*

To replenish petty cash, a check is written for the amount spent from the fund. The check is cashed and the money placed back in the petty cash fund.

FYI

Petty Cash is debited to establish but not to replenish the fund.

TEACHING STRATEGIES: DIFFERENT LEARNING STYLES

Visual Learner. The visual learner needs to "see" the concept. One way for the learner to "see" the concept is mental visualization. When introducing the T account, have the student (with eyes closed) picture a T account. The student should be able to see both sides of the account. Next, the student should visualize the word "DEBIT" on the left side of the account. Finally, the student should visualize the word "CREDIT" on the right side of the account. Once this concept takes on a visual form, the student will be able to access it when needed.

Supplies—Office	
164.00	

Supplies—Store	
136.00	

Advertising Expense	
56.00	

Miscellaneous Expense	
46.00	

Cash	
	402.00

June 30, 19--. Paid cash to replenish the petty cash fund, $402.00: office supplies, $164.00; store supplies, $136.00; advertising, $56.00; miscellaneous expense, $46.00. Check No. 350.

The accounts increased by debits are: Supplies—Office, $164.00; Supplies—Store, $136.00; Advertising Expense, $56.00; and Miscellaneous Expense, $46.00. Cash is decreased by a $402.00 credit, the total amount needed to replenish petty cash. When Check No. 350 is cashed and the $402.00 is placed back in the petty cash fund, the fund again totals $500.00.

The entry on lines 2 through 5 of page 12 of the cash payments journal, Illustration 2-9, shows the cash payment to replenish petty cash. The date, *30,* is written once in the Date column, line 2. The account titles are written in the Account Title column. The check number, *350,* is recorded once in the Ck. No. column, line 2. The debit amounts are recorded in the General Debit column. The credit amount is entered in the Cash Credit column on the first line of the entry.

Posting from a Cash Payments Journal

Cash payments are posted in a similar manner as purchases on account and purchases returns and allowances. MasterSport posts often to the general ledger each amount written in the General Debit and General Credit columns of the cash payments journal. Also, each amount written in the Accounts Payable Debit column is posted often to the accounts payable ledger. The cash payments journal is abbreviated as *CP* in the Post. Ref. column of the ledger accounts.

At the end of each month, the cash payments journal is proved and ruled. Totals of the special amount columns are then posted to their respective accounts in the general ledger. The general ledger account number for each respective account is written in paren-

Global Perspective

INTERNATIONAL TERMS OF SALE

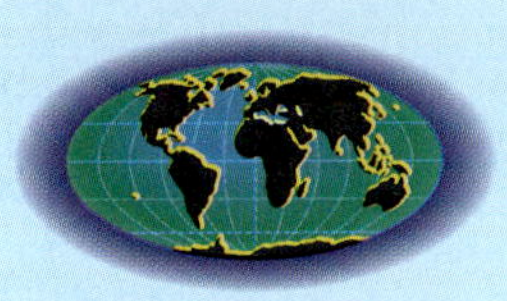

Terms of sale for international business are very similar to those used in the United States. However, it is important to make sure that all parties understand the terms before business is complete.

Selected international terms of sale are described below.

- C.I.F. (Cost, Insurance, Freight) to the named port of import. Under this method, the seller quotes a price for the goods. The price includes insurance, all transportation, and all miscellaneous charges to the point of unloading the goods from the vessel.
- F.A.S. (Free AlongSide a ship at the named U.S. port of export). Under this term, the seller quotes a price for goods that includes charges for delivery of the goods alongside a vessel at the port. The seller handles the cost of the unloading and wharf charges. All charges once goods are delivered to the vessel, including loading, ocean transportation, and insurance, are the responsibility of the buyer.
- F.O.B. VESSEL (named port of export). The seller quotes a price that includes all expenses up to, and including, delivery of goods upon an overseas vessel that is provided by or for the buyer. Once the goods are loaded "on board," all subsequent charges are the sole responsibility of the buyer.
- EX ("EX" means "from" the named point of origin) such as EX FACTORY. Under this term, the price quoted applies only at the point of origin, and the seller agrees to place the goods at the disposal of the buyer at the specified place on the date or within the period fixed. All other charges are the responsibility of the buyer.

GLOBAL PERSPECTIVE ACTIVITY:

Research the following terms of sale. Tell what the initials represent and what the actual terms involve.

1. F.O.B. (named port of exportation)
2. F.O.B. (named inland point of origin)
3. C. and F.

FYI

A check mark means don't post.

theses immediately below the total. A check mark is recorded in parentheses below the totals of the General Debit and General Credit columns to show that these totals are not posted. MasterSport's departmental cash payments journal, Illustration 2-9, is shown after all posting has been completed.

BANK STATEMENTS

Banks keep detailed records of their depositors' checking accounts. Records are kept of all deposits, all checks paid, and bank charges for maintaining an account. Bank charges include service charges and credit card fees.

A report of deposits, withdrawals, and bank balance sent to a depositor by a bank is called a **bank statement.** Bank statements are commonly sent to depositors monthly. A bank usually includes all canceled checks listed on the statement.

Reconciling a Bank Statement

A depositor should check the bank statement for accuracy as soon as it is received. Any errors found should be reported immediately to the bank. The bank balance is compared with the checkbook bal-

Global Perspective

The GLOBAL PERSPECTIVE feature is intended to expose students to some of the ways in which accounting and business in general differ in other countries. This GLOBAL PERSPECTIVE feature allows students to explore international terms of sale. The GLOBAL PERSPECTIVE ACTIVITY requires students to expand their thinking beyond the terms of sale that are described in the feature.

Answers to Global Perspective Activity

1. F.O.B. (named port of exportation) Free on Board. The quoted price includes the costs of transporting the goods to the named point.
2. F.O.B. (named inland point of origin) Free on Board. The quoted price applies only at a designated inland shipping point. The seller is responsible for loading goods onto the transport vessel, the buyer for all subsequent expenses.
3. C. and F. (Cost and Freight) to the named port of import. Under this method, the seller quotes a price for the goods that includes the cost of transportation to the named point of unloading the goods from the vessel.

ance. Bringing information on a bank statement and a checkbook into agreement is reconciling a bank statement.

MasterSport uses the steps and the form shown in Illustration 2-10 when reconciling the bank statement each month.

An adjusted checkbook balance and an adjusted bank balance must be the same. The reconciliation, Illustration 2-10, shows that both balances are the same, $32,878.75.

TEACHING STRATEGIES: EXPANDING BEYOND THE CLASSROOM

Bank personnel may be invited to speak to the class about banking services. Or invite someone from a local business to describe to the class how a petty cash fund is used and controlled.

ILLUSTRATION 2-10 Printed form for reconciling a bank statement

RECONCILIATION OF BANK STATEMENT Date *June 30, 19--*

1. Enter CHECKBOOK BALANCE as shown on check stub.
2. Enter and add bank charges to obtain TOTAL BANK CHARGES.
3. Deduct TOTAL BANK CHARGES from CHECKBOOK BALANCE to obtain ADJUSTED CHECKBOOK BALANCE.
4. Enter BANK BALANCE as shown on bank statement.
5. Enter and add the amounts of any outstanding deposits recorded on the check stubs but not listed on the bank statement to obtain TOTAL OUTSTANDING DEPOSITS.
6. Add TOTAL OUTSTANDING DEPOSITS to BANK BALANCE to obtain TOTAL.
7. Sort all checks included in the statement numerically or by date issued.
   a. Check off on the check stubs of the checkbook each of the checks paid by the bank.
   b. Enter the check numbers and amounts of checks still outstanding.
   c. Add the outstanding checks to obtain TOTAL OUTSTANDING CHECKS.
8. Deduct TOTAL OUTSTANDING CHECKS from TOTAL to obtain ADJUSTED BANK BALANCE.
9. The ADJUSTED CHECKBOOK BALANCE and the ADJUSTED BANK BALANCE should agree, proving that both the checkbook balance and the bank balance are correct.

(1) CHECKBOOK BALANCE .... $ *33,231.55*

BANK CHARGES

Description	Amount	
Service Charge	*12*	*80*
Credit Card Fee	*340*	*00*

(2) DEDUCT TOTAL BANK CHARGES .... $ *352.80*

(3) ADJUSTED CHECKBOOK BALANCE .. $ *32,878.75*

(4) BANK BALANCE .... $ *20,525.23*

OUTSTANDING DEPOSITS

Date	Amount	
6/30	*12,828*	*52*

(5) ADD TOTAL OUTSTANDING DEPOSITS .... $ *12,828.52*

(6) TOTAL .... $ *33,353.75*

OUTSTANDING CHECKS

CK. NO.	Amount	
350	*402*	*00*
351	*73*	*00*

(7) DEDUCT TOTAL OUTSTANDING CHECKS .... $ *475.00*

(8) ADJUSTED BANK BALANCE .... $ *32,878.75*

Journalizing Bank Charges

All bank charges listed on a bank statement are considered cash payments. Even though no checks are issued, each bank charge is recorded in a cash payments journal.

MasterSport has two bank charges. One charge is a bank service charge for maintaining a checking account. The other charge is a credit card fee based on a percentage of the total of credit card sales deposited with the bank. No checks are available to serve as source documents for journalizing these two bank charges. Therefore, memorandums are prepared showing the details of each service charge. *(CONCEPT: Objective Evidence)*

SOFTWARE FOCUS

Software may be used for independent practice or enrichment/extension as the instructor deems appropriate. For this chapter, *Automated Accounting 6.0* or higher may be used with Problems 2-1, 2-2, 2-4, 2-5, and 2-M.

Miscellaneous Expense	
12.80	

Cash	
	12.80

June 30, 19--. Received bank statement showing June bank service charge, $12.80. Memorandum No. 18.

The source document for this transaction is a memorandum. *(CONCEPT: Objective Evidence)*

Miscellaneous Expense is increased by a $12.80 debit. Cash is decreased by a $12.80 credit.

Credit Card Fee Expense	
340.00	

Cash	
	340.00

June 30, 19--. Recorded credit card fee expense for June, $340.00. Memorandum No. 19.

The source document for this transaction is a memorandum. *(CONCEPT: Objective Evidence)*

Credit Card Fee Expense is increased by a $340.00 debit. Cash is decreased by a $340.00 credit.

The bank service charge and credit card fee expense are recorded on lines 7 and 8 of page 12 of the cash payments journal, Illustration 2-9. The date is written in the Date column. The account titles are written in the Account Title column. The memorandum numbers are recorded in the Ck. No. column and identified by the letter *M*. The debit amounts are entered in the General Debit column. The credit amounts are entered in the Cash Credit column.

Audit Your Understanding

1. What general ledger accounts are affected, and how, by a cash payment on account transaction for tennis equipment which includes a purchases discount?
2. Why is a petty cash fund always replenished on the last day of each fiscal period?
3. What source document does MasterSport use for the two bank charge transactions shown on the bank statement?

AUDIT YOUR UNDERSTANDING

1. Accounts Payable is debited; Cash and Purchases Discount—Tennis are credited.
2. To assure that all expenses are recorded during the fiscal period in which they occurred.
3. Memorandum

TEACHING STRATEGIES: DIFFERENT LEARNING STYLES

Tactile Learner. Tactile learners need to handle or touch materials to learn concepts. Using play money, have the student touch the right side of the desk and place an amount of money on it to reinforce an amount in the right side or credit side of an account. Repeat the process for the left/debit side.

ACCOUNTING TERMS

1. **asset:** Anything of value that is owned. (p. 28)
2. **liability:** An amount owed by a business. (p. 28)
3. **equities:** Financial rights to the assets of a business. (p. 28)
4. **owner's equity:** The amount remaining after the value of all liabilities is subtracted from the value of all assets. (p. 28)
5. **accounting equation:** An equation showing the relationship among assets, liabilities, and owner's equity. (p. 28)
6. **source document:** A business paper from which information is obtained for a journal entry. (p. 28)
7. **journal:** A form for recording transactions in chronological order. (p. 29)
8. **special journal:** A journal used to record only one kind of transaction. (p. 29)
9. **double-entry accounting:** The recording of debit and credit parts of a transaction. (p. 29)
10. **account:** A record summarizing all the information pertaining to a single item in the accounting equation. (p. 30)
11. **ledger:** A group of accounts. (p. 31)
12. **general ledger:** A ledger that contains all accounts needed to prepare financial statements. (p. 31)
13. **subsidiary ledger:** A ledger that is summarized in a single general ledger account. (p. 31)
14. **controlling account:** An account in a general ledger that summarizes all accounts in a subsidiary ledger. (p. 31)
15. **file maintenance:** The procedure for arranging accounts in a general ledger, assigning account numbers, and keeping records current. (p. 31)
16. **departmental accounting system:** An accounting system showing accounting information for two or more departments. (p. 33)
17. **merchandising business:** A business that purchases and sells goods. (p. 33)
18. **posting:** Transferring information from a journal entry to a ledger account. (p. 34)
19. **debit memorandum:** A form prepared by the customer showing the price deduction taken by a customer for returns and allowances. (p. 36)
20. **contra account:** An account that reduces a related account on a financial statement. (p. 37)
21. **contra balance:** An account balance that is opposite the normal balance. (p. 38)

ACCOUNTING TERMS EPT(a)

What is the meaning of each of the following?

1. **asset**
2. **liability**
3. **equities**
4. **owner's equity**
5. **accounting equation**
6. **source document**
7. **journal**
8. **special journal**
9. **double-entry accounting**
10. **account**
11. **ledger**
12. **general ledger**
13. **subsidiary ledger**
14. **controlling account**
15. **file maintenance**
16. **departmental accounting system**
17. **merchandising business**
18. **posting**
19. **debit memorandum**
20. **contra account**
21. **contra balance**
22. **cash discount**
23. **purchases discount**
24. **petty cash**
25. **bank statement**

QUESTIONS FOR INDIVIDUAL STUDY EPT(b)

1. What determines how financial information and records are kept and reported?
2. Which accounting concept is being applied when each journal entry is supported with a source document to prove that a transaction did occur?
3. What two accounting principles are common to double-entry accounting?
4. What is the normal balance side of asset accounts? of liability accounts? of the capital account? of revenue accounts? of cost accounts? of expense accounts?
5. What is the title of the general ledger controlling account that summarizes all accounts in an accounts receivable subsidiary ledger?
6. What is the title of the general ledger controlling account that summarizes all accounts in an accounts payable subsidiary ledger?
7. Why does MasterSport assign subsidiary ledger account numbers by 10s while assigning general ledger account numbers by 5s?
8. For what reasons might merchandise be returned to a vendor?
9. Why does MasterSport record purchases returns and allowances amounts in a separate account?
10. What source document does MasterSport use for a purchases returns and allowances transaction?
11. Why would a seller allow a deduction from an invoice amount?
12. When the terms of a purchase invoice are 2/10, n/30, what payment options are available?
13. How often does MasterSport replenish its petty cash fund?
14. What three items do banks keep records of for their depositors' checking accounts?
15. What is meant by reconciling a bank statement?
16. What two bank charges are paid by MasterSport?

CASES FOR CRITICAL THINKING EPT(b,e)

CASE 1 Maria Hector manages a card and gift shop. The shop's general ledger includes a single sales account and a single purchases account. Periodically, Ms. Hector has an accountant review her accounting records and procedures. The accountant recommends that Ms. Hector change to a departmental accounting system. The accountant recommends that separate revenue and cost accounts be kept for the two types of merchandise sold—cards and gifts. Ms. Hector objects to the accountant's recommendation. She sees no advantage to complicating the accounting system by having separate departmental revenue and cost accounts. With whom do you agree? Why?

CASE 2 Scott Peper manages a hardware store. He has found that his bank statement and checkbook reconcile without error month after month. In order to save the time spent reconciling his bank statement each month, Mr. Peper decides to make the reconciliation once every six months. His daughter, who helps with the business' accounting, disagrees with this practice. With whom do you agree? Why?

22. **cash discount:** A deduction that a vendor allows on an invoice amount to encourage prompt payment. (p. 38)
23. **purchases discount:** A cash discount on purchases taken by a customer. (p. 38)
24. **petty cash:** An amount of cash kept on hand and used for making small payments. (p. 42)
25. **bank statement:** A report of deposits, withdrawals, and bank balance sent to a depositor by a bank. (p. 43)

APPLIED COMMUNICATIONS

A resume provides a statement of your education, experience, and qualifications for a prospective employer. Your resume should be accurate, honest, and perfect in every respect.

Your resume should include all work experience along with the companies and dates of employment. Education, activities, and interests are all important items that should be included. It is preferable to limit the resume to one typed page.

INSTRUCTIONS:

1. Go to the library and research how to prepare an appropriate resume.
2. Prepare a personal resume that you could send to a prospective employer.

APPLICATION PROBLEMS

EPT(c,d,e)

PROBLEM 2-1 Performing file maintenance activities; adding general ledger accounts

AUTOMATED

The following is Jason Supply Company's partial general ledger chart of accounts.

Administrative Expenses		Accounts Added
6205	Depreciation Expense—Office Equipment	Payroll Taxes Expense
6210	Rent Expense	Salary Expense—Administrative
6215	Supplies Expense—Office	Utilities Expense

INSTRUCTIONS:

Add the three new administrative expense accounts to the general ledger chart of accounts using the unused middle number method.

PROBLEM 2-2 Journalizing and posting departmental purchases on account and purchases returns and allowances

AUTOMATED

Sound Stop, Inc., has two departments: Compact Discs and Tapes. The general ledger and accounts payable ledger are given in the working papers accompanying this textbook. The balances are recorded as of March 1 of the current year.

INSTRUCTIONS:

1. Journalize the following transactions completed during March of the current year. Use page 3 of a purchases journal and a purchases returns and allowances journal. Source documents are abbreviated as follows: debit memorandum, DM; purchase invoice, P.

Mar. 1. Purchased tapes on account from Raymond Wholesalers, $1,350.00. P283.
2. Purchased compact discs on account from Artex Music, $965.00. P284.
4. Purchased tapes on account from Castle Records and Tapes, $2,130.00. P285.
6. Returned compact discs to Dade, Inc., $165.00, from P280. DM36.
9. Purchased compact discs on account from Delta Distributors, $845.00. P286.
13. Purchased compact discs on account from Music Unlimited, $1,135.00. P287.
15. Returned tapes to Raymond Wholesalers, $100.00, from P283. DM37.
Posting. Post the items that are to be posted individually. Post from the journals in this order: purchases journal and purchases returns and allowances journal.
18. Purchased tapes on account from Quality Tapes, $268.00. P288.
20. Returned compact discs to Artex Music, $120.00, from P284. DM38.
23. Purchased tapes on account from Castle Records and Tapes, $993.00. P289.
24. Returned tapes to Park Recording Company, $55.00, from P281. DM39.
27. Purchased compact discs on account from Dade, Inc., $1,045.00. P290.
30. Purchased tapes on account from Raymond Wholesalers, $1,360.00. P291.
31. Returned tapes to Castle Records and Tapes, $150.00, from P289. DM40.
Posting. Post the items that are to be posted individually.

CHECK FIGURES

Complete solutions to the problems may be found in the Teacher's Edition of the Working Papers.

Problem 2-1 Account Numbers: Payroll Taxes Expense, 6208; Salary Expense—Administrative, 6213; Utilities Expense, 6220

Problem 2-2 Purchases Journal totals: 10,091; 3,990; 6,101. Purchases Returns and Allowances Journal totals: 590; 285; 305

QUESTIONS FOR INDIVIDUAL STUDY

1. Size, type, and complexity of the business. (p. 28)
2. Objective Evidence concept. (p. 28)
3. (a) The total value of things owned by a business (assets) equals the total value of claims of outsiders (liabilities) and claims of owners (owner's equity). (b) Debits equal credits for each business transaction recorded. (p. 29)
4. The normal balance side of (a) asset accounts is the debit side, (b) liability accounts is the credit side, (c) the capital account is the credit side, (d) revenue accounts is the credit side, (e) cost accounts is the debit side, and (f) expense accounts is the debit side. (p. 30)
5. Accounts Receivable. (p. 31)
6. Accounts Payable. (p. 31)
7. Because MasterSport's subsidiary ledgers require more file maintenance than the general ledger, more numbers are provided for adding new accounts between existing accounts. (p. 32)
8. The merchandise may be unsatisfactory. The merchandise may not be what was ordered. The merchandise may be received in damaged condition. (p. 36)
9. This procedure helps the business see what proportion of the merchandise was returned to vendors. (p. 37)
10. Debit memorandum. (p. 37)
11. To encourage prompt payment. (p. 38)
12. A 2% discount may be deducted if payment is made within 10 days of the invoice date. Payment of the total invoice amount must be made within 30 days of the invoice date. (p. 39)
13. Whenever the amount on hand in the fund drops below $100.00 and on the last business day of each fiscal period. (p. 42)
14. Deposits, checks paid, and miscellaneous charges for maintaining an account. (p. 43)
15. Bringing information on a bank statement and a checkbook into agreement. (p. 44)
16. Service charge and credit card fee expense. (p. 44)

CASES FOR CRITICAL THINKING

Case 1 The accountant. Department records would make it possible to determine gross profit for the two departments. This information would help make decisions about the efficiency of each phase of the business and would call attention to where changes might result in greater profits.

Case 2 Mr. Peper's daughter is correct. Cash should be checked often and regularly. The bank statement should be reconciled immediately when received. Banks generally require that errors or inquiries be reported within 60 days of the statement date. Most businesses have considerably more cash transactions than any other single kind of transaction. Therefore, if errors are made, there is more chance of making them with cash transactions. Also, a bank may make errors in its records of deposits and withdrawals.

APPLIED COMMUNICATIONS

The resume should be keyed, one page in length, and in the most current style. Individual student resumes will vary; however, they should include the following elements: (1) Name, address, telephone number, social security number. (2) Education, including grade average, courses, any special skills. (3) Work experience and any special training. (4) Relevant school activities. (5) Honors or awards. The instructor should also consider writing style and mechanics (grammar, spelling, punctuation) when grading this activity.

2. Prove and rule the purchases journal. Post the totals.
3. Prove and rule the purchases returns and allowances journal. Post the totals.

PROBLEM 2-3 Calculating purchases discounts and amounts due

MATHEMATICS

Hopkins Lumber Company, a departmental merchandising business, takes advantage of all purchases discounts allowed by vendors. The following purchases on account are to be paid within the discount period.

Purchase Invoice No.	Purchase Invoice Amount	Purchases Discount Rate
226	$1,240.00	2%
227	945.00	1%
228	936.00	2%
229	1,560.00	2%
230	1,475.00	1%
231	780.00	1%
232	650.00	2%
233	295.00	2%

INSTRUCTIONS:

Use a form similar to the following. Calculate and record the purchases discount in Column 4 and the total amount paid in Column 5 for each purchase invoice number. The amounts calculated for Purchase Invoice No. 226 are given as an example.

1	2	3	4	5
Purchase Invoice No.	Invoice Amount	Discount Rate	Purchases Discount	Amount Due
226	$1,240.00	2%	*$24.80*	*$1,215.20*

PROBLEM 2-4 Journalizing and posting departmental cash payments

AUTOMATED

Tyler Nursery and Craft has two departments: Crafts and Plants. The general ledger and accounts payable ledger are given in the working papers accompanying this textbook. The balances are recorded as of November 1 of the current year.

INSTRUCTIONS:

1. Journalize the following transactions completed during November of the current year. Use page 21 of a cash payments journal. All of the vendors from which merchandise is purchased on account offer terms of 2/10, n/30. Source documents are abbreviated as follows: check, C; memorandum, M.

Nov. 1. Paid cash for miscellaneous expense, $150.00. C303.
2. Paid cash for rent, $1,300.00. C304.
4. Paid cash on account to Wholesale Crafts, Inc., $867.30, covering P287 for crafts for $885.00, less discount, $17.70. C305.
5. Paid cash for advertising, $83.50. C306.
8. Paid cash for supplies, $95.50. C307.
10. Paid cash on account to Northtown Plants, $1,225.00, covering P288 for plants for $1,250.00, less discount, $25.00. C308.
13. Paid cash on account to Century Crafts, Inc., $943.74, covering P289 for crafts for $963.00, less discount, $19.26. C309.
15. Paid cash for miscellaneous, $33.50. C310.
Posting. Post the items that are to be posted individually.
21. Paid cash for supplies, $52.00. C311.

Nov. 23. Paid cash on account to Evergreen Trees & Shrubs, $1,803.20, covering P290 for plants for $1,840.00, less discount, $36.80. C312.
27. Paid cash on account to Evergreen Trees & Shrubs, $1,430.80, covering P292 for plants for $1,460.00, less discount, $29.20. C313.
30. Paid cash to replenish the petty cash fund, $212.00: supplies, $89.00; advertising, $83.40; miscellaneous, $39.60. C314.
30. Received bank statement showing November bank service charge, $14.30. M26.
30. Recorded credit card fee expense for November, $488.20. M27.

Posting. Post the items that are to be posted individually.

2. Prove and rule the cash payments journal. Post the totals.

PROBLEM 2-5 Reconciling a bank statement

AUTOMATED

On October 31 of the current year, Perry's Auto, Inc., received a bank statement dated October 29. The following information is obtained from the bank statement and from the records of the business.

Bank statement balance	$31,820.00
Bank service charge	8.80
Bank credit card charge	325.20
Outstanding deposit:	
October 27	7,152.75
Outstanding checks:	
No. 361	89.50
No. 362	1,460.25
Checkbook balance on Check Stub No. 363	37,757.00

INSTRUCTIONS:

Prepare a bank statement reconciliation on a form similar to the one in this chapter. Use October 31 of the current year as the date.

ENRICHMENT PROBLEMS EPT(c,d,e)

MASTERY PROBLEM 2-M Performing file maintenance activities; journalizing departmental purchases and cash payments; reconciling a bank statement

AUTOMATED

Blaine Camera, Inc. has two departments: Cameras and Accessories.

The following is Blaine Camera's partial general ledger chart of accounts.

6205	Depreciation Expense—Office Equipment
6210	Miscellaneous Expense
6215	Salary Expense—Administrative
6220	Supplies Expense—Office
6225	Supplies Expense—Store

INSTRUCTIONS:

1. Add Insurance Expense and Uncollectible Accounts Expense to the general ledger chart of accounts using the unused middle number method described in this chapter.

2. Journalize the following transactions completed during November of the current year. Use page 11 of a purchases journal and a purchases returns and allowances journal and page 21 of a cash payments journal. All of the vendors from which merchandise is purchased on account offer terms of 2/10, n/30. Source documents are abbreviated as follows: check, C; debit memorandum, DM; purchase invoice, P.

Nov. 1. Paid cash for advertising, $95.00. C273.
1. Paid cash for rent, $1,250.00. C274.
2. Purchased accessories on account from Standish Photo Supplies, $800.00. P262.

CHECK FIGURES *(cont'd)*

Problem 2-3 Amounts Due: $1,215.20; 935.55; 917.28; 1,528.80; 1,460.25; 772.20; 637.00; 289.10

Problem 2-4 Cash Payments Journal totals: 2,429.00; 6,398.00; 36.96; 91.00; 8,699.04

Problem 2-5 Adjusted balance, $37,423.00

Mastery Problem 2-M Purchases Journal totals: 4,660.40; 2,974.40; 1,686.00. Purchases Returns and Allowances Journal totals: 295.50; 88.00; 207.50. Cash Payments Journal totals: 2,166.80; 4,680.00; 40.16; 22.40; 6,784.24. Adjusted balances, $18,277.00

Nov. 3. Paid cash on account to National Camera Outlet, $490.00, covering P259 for cameras for $500.00, less discount, $10.00. C275.
3. Purchased cameras on account from Jens Wholesale Cameras, $840.00. P263.
5. Paid cash on account to Standish Photo Supplies, $632.10, covering P261 for accessories for $645.00, less discount, $12.90. C276.
7. Returned cameras to Jens Wholesale Cameras, $88.00, from P263. DM28.
10. Purchased cameras on account from Focal Camera Distributors, $388.00. P264.
11. Paid cash for store supplies, $82.50. C277.
14. Paid cash on account to Standish Photo Supplies, $800.00, covering P262 for accessories; no discount. C278.
16. Returned accessories to Quality Film Company, $132.50, from P260. DM29.
17. Purchased accessories on account from Farmer Camera Supply, Inc., $550.00. P265.
17. Paid cash on account to Focal Camera Distributors, $380.24, covering P264 for cameras for $388.00, less discount, $7.76. C279.
18. Paid cash on account to Jens Wholesale Cameras, $752.00, covering P263 for cameras for $840.00, less DM28 for $88.00; no discount. C280.
18. Returned accessories to Farmer Camera Supply, Inc., $75.00, from P265. DM30.
19. Purchased cameras on account from Jens Wholesale Cameras, $1,120.00. P266.
21. Paid cash for office supplies, $62.30. C281.
23. Purchased accessories on account from Quality Film Company, $336.00. P267.
24. Paid cash on account to Farmer Camera Supply, Inc., $465.50, covering P265 for accessories for $550.00, less DM30 for $75.00, and less discount, $9.50. C282.
24. Purchased cameras on account from National Camera Outlet, $626.40. P268.
26. Paid cash on account to Jens Wholesale Cameras, $1,097.60, covering P266 for cameras for $1,120.00, less discount, $22.40. C283.
28. Paid cash for store supplies, $53.00. C284
30. Paid cash to replenish the petty cash fund, $221.00: office supplies, $57.10; advertising, $62.50; miscellaneous, $101.40. C285.

3. Prepare a bank statement reconciliation. Use November 30 of the current year as the date. The bank statement is dated November 29. The following information is obtained from the bank statement and from the records of the business.

Bank statement balance	$16,578.00
Bank service charge	20.20
Bank credit card charge	382.80
Outstanding deposit:	
November 29	3,070.60
Outstanding checks:	
No. 283	1,097.60
No. 284	53.00
No. 285	221.00
Checkbook balance on Check Stub No. 286	18,680.00

4. Continue journalizing the following transactions.

Nov. 30. Received bank statement showing November bank service charge, $20.20. M31.
30. Recorded credit card fee expense for November, $382.80. M32.

5. Prove and rule the journals.

CHALLENGE PROBLEM 2-C Journalizing purchases at net amount and using the account Discounts Lost

Introductory remarks: Some businesses record purchases at the net amount to be paid when the cash discount is taken. For example, merchandise is purchased for $1,000.00 with a 2% discount allowed if the account is paid within 10 days. The discount will reduce the price from $1,000.00 to $980.00. To record this purchase on account transaction, Purchases is deb-

CHECK FIGURES *(cont'd)*

Challenge Problem 2-C Purchases Journal totals: 4,567.19; 2,914.91; 1,652.28. Purchases Returns and Allowances Journal totals: 289.59; 86.24; 203.35. Cash Payments Journal totals: 2,197.84; 4,586.40; 6,784.24

ited for $980.00 and Accounts Payable is credited for $980.00. When the account is paid, Accounts Payable is debited for $980.00 and Cash is credited for $980.00. Purchases returns and allowances are also recorded at the discounted amount.

If the discount period expires before payment is made, then the entry in the cash payments journal for the example above would be as follows: Accouts Payable is debited for $980.00, Discounts Lost is debited for $20.00, and Cash is credited for $1,000.00. Because almost all cash discounts are taken, there are few entries involving the discounts lost account. For this reason, no special amount column is provided for the account in the cash payments journal. Instead, the amounts debited to this account are recorded in the General Debit column.

INSTRUCTIONS:

1. Journalize the transactions for Mastery Problem 2-M following the method described above. Use page 11 of a purchases journal and a purchases returns and allowances journal and page 21 of a cash payments journal. All of the vendors from which merchandise is purchased on account offer terms of 2/10, n/30.
2. Prove and rule the journals.

Safety and Health Considerations

ELECTRICAL EQUIPMENT

The following rules protect the operator of the equipment, other persons in the environment, and the equipment itself.

1. Do not unplug equipment by pulling on the electrical cord. Instead, grasp the plug at the outlet and remove it.
2. Do not stretch electrical cords across an aisle where someone might trip over them.
3. Avoid food and beverages near equipment where a spill might result in an electrical short.
4. Do not attempt to remove the cover of equipment for any reason while the power is turned on.
5. Do not attempt to repair equipment while it is plugged in. To avoid damage most repairs should be done by an authorized service technician.
6. Always turn the power off when finished using equipment.
7. Do not overload extension cords.
8. Follow manufacturer recommendations for safe use.
9. Replace frayed electrical cords immediately.

MICROCOMPUTERS

1. To avoid damage to the drives, do not insert pencils or other implements in floppy disk drives.
2. To prevent overheating, avoid blocking air vents.
3. Position keyboards to prevent bumping or dropping them off the work surface.

MONITORS

1. Most manufacturers advise repair by authorized service technicians only.
2. Adjust brightness and focus for comfortable viewing.
3. Avoid glare on the monitor screen.
4. Do not leave fingerprints on the screen. Keep the screen clear of dust. Only use a soft cloth for cleaning the screen.

PRINTERS

1. Do not let jewelry, ties, scarves, loose sleeves, or other clothing get caught in the machinery. This could result in damage to the machinery and could cause personal injury.
2. Exercise caution when using toxic chemicals such as toner in order to avoid spills.

DISKETTES

1. Write/protect all program software to avoid accidental erasure.
2. Do not bend or fold diskettes.
3. Do not write on a diskette with a hard or sharp-pointed pen or pencil; use a felt-tip marker.
4. Do not touch exposed surfaces of diskettes.
5. Be sure the disk drive is not running when you insert or remove a diskette.
6. Keep diskettes away from extreme hot or cold temperatures. Do not leave diskettes in a car during very hot or cold weather.
7. Keep diskettes away from magnetic fields such as transformers and magnets.
8. Store diskettes in the storage envelopes.
9. Keep diskettes away from smoke, ashes, and dust, including chalk dust.
10. Do not leave diskettes in the disk drive for prolonged periods, such as overnight.

52

Recording Departmental Purchases and Cash Payments

Decisions about present and future operations of a business depend on current, accurate, and complete financial information. Producing financial information requires an accounting system with an organized set of recording and reporting procedures.

An accounting system may be either manual or automated. An accounting system in which data are recorded and reported mostly by hand is **manual accounting**. An accounting system in which data are recorded and reported mostly by using automated machines is referred to as **automated accounting**. Regardless of the accounting system used, accounting concepts are the same and are applied in the same way in each accounting period.

MasterSport, the departmentalized merchandising business described in Part 2, uses a manual accounting system. MasterSport's manual recording procedures for purchases and cash payments are described in Chapter 2. Integrating Automated Accounting Topic 1 describes procedures for using automated software to record MasterSport's purchases and cash payments. The Automated Accounting Problems contain instructions for using automated accounting software to solve Problem 2-1, Problem 2-2, Problem 2-4, Problem 2-5, and Mastery Problem 2-M in Chapter 2.

TEACHING STRATEGIES: ACCOUNTING PEDAGOGY

This textbook introduces manual accounting concepts before automated accounting concepts. It is important that students master accounting theory before relying on the computer to do the repetitive functions.

SOFTWARE FOCUS

The Automated Accounting Problems in this Integrating Automated Accounting topic use Application Problems 2-1, 2-2, 2-4, 2-5, and Mastery Problem 2-M, Chapter 2, which students have already completed manually. Refer students back to these problems so they may complete the input forms. The problem instructions in *Automating Accounting 6.0* will lead students through automating the problems.

LESSON PLAN A1

Materials

- Student pages 53–60
- Input forms for Automating Application Problems 2-1, 2-2, 2-4, 2-5, and Mastery Problem 2-M are provided in the working papers that accompany this textbook. If additional input forms are needed, blackline masters are provided in the Blackline Masters Section of the Teacher's Resource Guide.
- Complete solutions for automated problems are provided in the Teacher's Resource Guide.
- Software: *Automated Accounting 6.0* or higher; CENTURY 21 ACCOUNTING Template, Advanced Course

Objectives

- Perform file maintenance activities using an automated accounting system.
- Journalize purchases and cash payments transactions using an automated accounting system.
- Reconcile a bank statement using an automated accounting system.

FOCUS

- In Chapter 2, manual journalizing and posting procedures for departmental purchases and cash payments were described. Emphasize that automated accounting software may be used to speed the journalizing and posting procedures. Explain that using automated accounting software, however, does not change accounting concepts. Only the methods change.
- Introduce vocabulary: manual accounting, automated accounting, data base, template, file maintenance, menu, journal entry transmittal, batch.

FYI

The accounting cycle is the same in both automated accounting and manual accounting. Only procedures change.

AUTOMATED ACCOUNTING

Automated accounting is based on the same accounting concepts as manual accounting. Likewise, an accounting cycle is the same in both automated accounting and manual accounting. Only the procedures differ.

General Ledger Data Base

A prearranged file in which data can be entered and retrieved is a **data base.** In automated accounting the general ledger is a data base. A model of a computer application stored on a computer disk for repeated use is a **template**. MasterSport stores its general ledger data base as a template.

To perform automated accounting procedures, a data base is retrieved from the template disk. The file is then renamed which allows the template to remain in its original format. Changes to the original template should be made only when necessary to update the file for future use.

File Maintenance

MasterSport's general ledger chart of accounts is on page 26. Automated accounting uses the same general ledger account titles and account numbers as manual accounting with one exception. Departmental accounts in an automated system are designated with a decimal (.) rather than a dash (—) followed by a department number. For example, the accounts for the golf department are indicated by a .1 after the account number. Accounts for the tennis department are indicated by a .2 after the account number.

MasterSport's four-digit numbering system is described in Chapter 2. The procedure for arranging accounts in a general ledger, assigning account numbers, and keeping records current is known as **file maintenance**.

Adding a New General Ledger Account. A new account is assigned the unused middle number between two existing accounts. When no exact middle number is available, the nearest even whole number is used.

On June 1, MasterSport added a new account, Equipment Repair Expense, between the two existing accounts Depreciation Expense—Office Equipment, 6205, and Insurance Expense, 6210. The unused middle number between 6205 and 6210 is 6207.5. The number 6207.5 contains five digits and cannot be assigned in a four-digit numbering system. Therefore, account number 6208, the nearest *even whole number,* was used. The new account, Equipment Repair Expense, is placed in the general ledger as shown below.

6205 Depreciation Expense—Office Equipment (existing account)
6208 EQUIPMENT REPAIR EXPENSE (new account)
6210 Insurance Expense (existing account)

TEACHING STRATEGIES: DIFFERENT LEARNING ABILITIES

At-Risk Students. Teachers report that at-risk students are particularly successful when completing activities at the computer. Completing automated problems adds reality to the task at hand. Students can work at their own pace and experience immediate satisfaction. Encourage at-risk students to work at the computer as often as possible.

General ledger file maintenance activities are recorded on a chart of accounts input form. The data needed to add the new account, Equipment Repair Expense, is entered on line 1 of the chart of accounts input form shown in Illustration T1-1.

ILLUSTRATION T1-1 Entry for file maintenance

RUN DATE 06/01/-- (MM DD YY)

CHART OF ACCOUNTS
Input Form

	1 ACCOUNT NUMBER	2 ACCOUNT TITLE	
1	6208	Equipment Repair Expense	1
2			2
3			3
4			4
5			5
6			6

New accounts that are added after the last account in a division are assigned the next number in sequence. Dividends Payable, *2155,* is the last existing account in the liabilities division. If MasterSport decides to add a new liability account after Dividends Payable, the new account would be assigned number 2160.

MasterSport uses the same file maintenance procedures for the subsidiary ledgers as for the general ledger. A three-digit numbering system is used for its subsidiary ledger accounts. MasterSport's subsidiary ledgers generally require more file maintenance than a general ledger. Therefore, subsidiary ledger account numbers are assigned by 10s to provide more numbers for adding new accounts between existing accounts.

Processing File Maintenance Data. In automated accounting the activities are arranged so that each activity may be selected using a keyboard or some other input device such as a mouse. A list of options from which an activity may be selected is a **menu.** MasterSport's software has a menu bar and a series of pull-down windows. The menu bar shown in Illustration T1-2 on page 56 contains six different menus.

To process file maintenance data, the data are keyed from the chart of accounts input form as shown for Equipment Repair Expense in Illustration T1-3 on page 56. An input form is also known as a **journal entry transmittal.**

After all file maintenance data have been keyed, a revised chart of accounts is displayed and checked for accuracy. The revised chart of accounts is then printed and filed for future reference.

TEACH

Cover student pages 53–60 "Automated Accounting," "Recording Departmental Purchases and Cash Payments," "Processing Journal Entries," and "Reconciling a Bank Statement." Review the chart of accounts numbering system and explain how to assign the unused middle number to a new general ledger account. Point out that similar procedures are used for assigning new subsidiary ledger account numbers. It is important to emphasize that *Automated Accounting 6.0* software limits account titles to 25 characters. When students are completing input forms, account titles may need to be abbreviated.

While explaining the procedures for journalizing and posting purchases on account transactions, make the students aware that the automated accounting software automatically records the credit to Accounts Payable. Likewise, when journalizing and posting cash payments transactions the software automatically records the credit to Cash. Point out that purchases returns and allowances transactions are recorded on a general journal input form. Review the procedures for reconciling a bank statement.

APPLY

Make a transparency of the chart of accounts input form from the accounting forms masters provided in the Blackline Masters Section of the Teacher's Resource Guide to point out and explain the three steps that are followed when completing a chart of accounts input form.

Guided Practice

Students should be at the computers. Guide students through booting the software and loading Automating Problem A2-1 from the template. Instruct students to complete the file maintenance activities as you go step-by-step through the procedures.

Independent Practice

Assign Automating Application Problems 2-2, 2-4, 2-5, and Mastery Problem 2-M.

TEACHING STRATEGIES: DIFFERENT LEARNING ABILITIES

Gifted Students. Students who are gifted often enjoy the challenge of working on the computer. Give gifted students an opportunity to automate other chapter problems after the assignment has been completed. It will challenge them to start a problem from scratch. Additional information for using *Automated Accounting 6.0* software is available with the software.

ILLUSTRATION T1-2 Menu bar

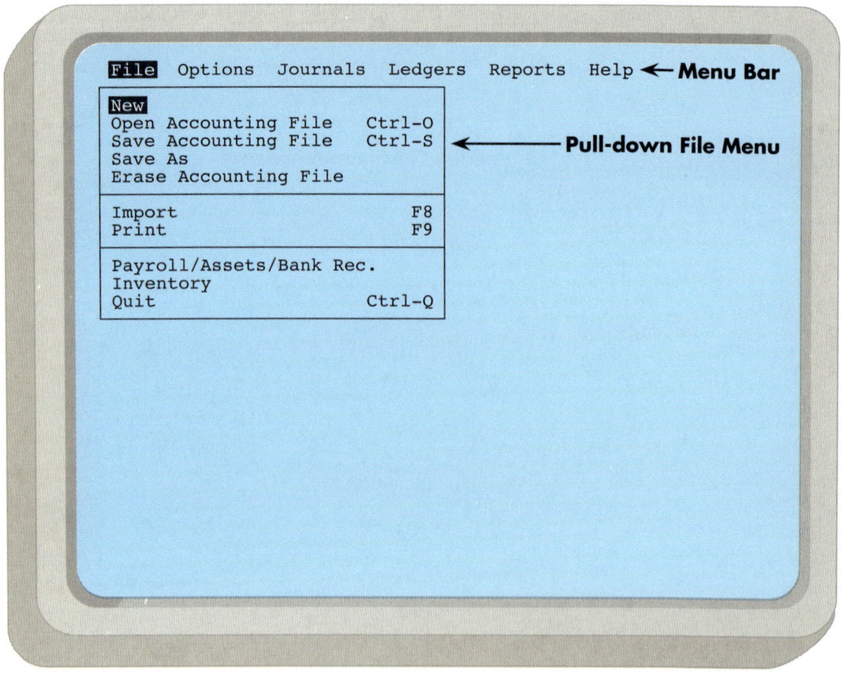

ILLUSTRATION T1-3 Data entry window for file maintenance

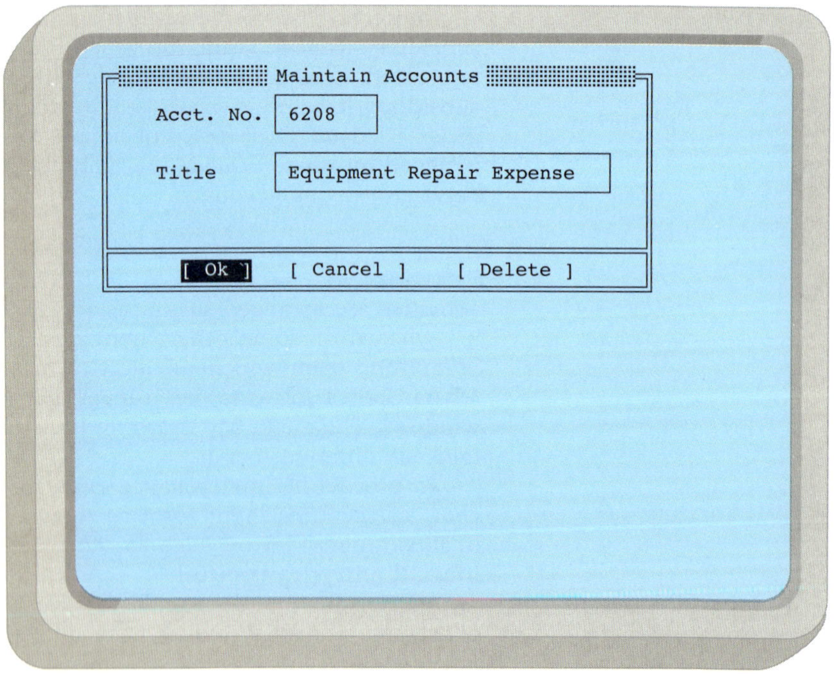

TEACHING STRATEGIES: DIFFERENT LEARNING ABILITIES

Limited English Proficiency (LEP) Students. LEP Teachers report that LEP students are particularly successful using software to complete accounting problems. LEP students are independent, work at their own pace, and do not feel the need to compete with other students in the classroom. LEP students can successfully complete automated problems because the problems do not require strong verbal skills.

RECORDING DEPARTMENTAL PURCHASES AND CASH PAYMENTS

MasterSport's accounting system has two departments: (1) Golf and (2) Tennis. MasterSport's departmental purchases and cash payments transactions are analyzed in Chapter 2.

FYI

Batching organizes daily transactions into categories which makes keying the information more manageable.

Purchases on Account

A group of journal entries is a **batch**. MasterSport batches all purchases on account transactions and records them on a purchases journal input form.

June 1, 19--. Purchased tennis equipment on account from Tennis Warehouse, $845.00. Purchase Invoice No. 336.

The journal entry to record this transaction is on line 1 of the purchases journal input form shown in Illustration T1-4. The software automatically records the credit to Accounts Payable for a purchases on account transaction.

ILLUSTRATION T1-4

Purchases journal input form with transaction entered

RUN DATE 06/30/-- (MM DD YY)

PURCHASES JOURNAL
Input Form

	DATE MM/DD	VENDOR NO.	INVOICE NO.	INVOICE AMOUNT	ACCOUNT NO.	DEBIT	CREDIT	
1	06/01	270	P336	845 00	5105.2	845 00		1
2	/							2
25	/							25

NOTE: A credit to Accounts Payable is made automatically by the software.

Purchases Returns and Allowances

MasterSport batches purchases returns and allowances on a general journal input form.

June 3, 19--. Returned tennis equipment to Key Tennis Company, $54.50, from Purchase Invoice No. 333. Debit Memorandum No. 22.

The journal entry to record this transaction is recorded on lines 1 and 2 of the general journal input form shown in Illustration T1-5.

ASSESS

Assess student understanding by checking the solutions to the Independent Practice activities.

Reteach

Review Illustrations T1-1 through T1-7. These illustrations can be used to reinforce the procedures for performing file maintenance, recording purchases and cash payments transactions, and reconciling bank statements using automated accounting software.

Extend

Assign the students to write a few paragraphs about the importance of saving your data often and of creating backup files when using an automated accounting system. Students should discuss some of the reasons that may cause data to be lost and the consequences of lost data.

CLOSURE

Review the steps for performing file maintenance, recording purchases and cash payments transactions, and reconciling bank statements using automated accounting software.

ILLUSTRATION T1-5

General journal input form with transaction entered

RUN DATE 06/30/-- (MM DD YY)

GENERAL JOURNAL
Input Form

	DATE MM/DD	REFERENCE	ACCOUNT NO.	CUSTOMER/ VENDOR NO.	DEBIT	CREDIT	
1	06/03	DM22	2115	240	54 50		1
2	/		5115.2			54 50	2
25	/						25
				PAGE TOTALS			
				FINAL TOTALS			

SAFETY AND HEALTH

Put write/protect tabs on all templates and software to avoid accidental erasure. A Safety and Health page is given in the Teacher's Resource Guide and on page 52 of this text.

Cash Payment on Account

MasterSport batches cash payments transactions and records them on a cash payments input form.

June 1, 19--. Paid cash on account to Champion Tennis Supply, $514.50, covering Purchase Invoice No. 331 for tennis equipment for $525.00, less 2% discount, $10.50. Check No. 315.

The journal entry to record this transaction is on line 1 of the cash payments journal input form shown in Illustration T1-6. The software automatically records the credit to Cash for a cash payments transaction.

ILLUSTRATION T1-6

Cash payments input form with transactions recorded

FYI

For illustration purposes, check numbers have been omitted from this input form.

RUN DATE 06/30/-- (MM DD YY)

CASH PAYMENTS JOURNAL
Input Form

	DATE MM/DD	VENDOR NO.	CHECK NO.	ACCOUNTS PAY. DEBIT	ACCOUNT NO.	DEBIT	CREDIT	
1	06/01	210	C315	525 00	5110.2		10 50	1
2	/01	230	C316	225 00	5110.1		4 50	2
3	/01		C317		1130	136 00		3
4	/01		C318		6225	1500 00		4
5	/30		C350		1130	164 00		5
6	/				1135	136 00		6
7	/				6105	56 00		7
8	/				6215	46 00		8
9	/30		C351		6215	73 00		9
25	/							25

NOTE: A credit to Cash is made automatically by the software.

June 1, 19--. Paid cash on account to Golf-Tee, Inc., $220.50, covering Purchase Invoice No. 332 for golf equipment for $275.00, less Debit Memorandum No. 20 for $50.00, and less 2% discount, $4.50. Check No. 316.

An additional calculation is necessary when a discount is taken after a purchase return or allowance has been granted. The amount of the return or allowance must be deducted from the amount of the original purchase *before* the discount can be calculated.

The journal entry to record this transaction is on line 2 of the cash payments journal input form shown in Illustration T1-6.

TEACHING STRATEGIES: TEACHING TIP

It is important for students to save a template file under another name before they begin work. This will keep the template file intact for future use.

Buying Supplies for Cash

June 1, 19--. Paid cash for office supplies, $136.00. Check No. 317.

The journal entry to record this transaction is on line 3 of the cash payments journal input form shown in Illustration T1-6.

FYI

The run date is usually the date of the last transaction or the last day of a fiscal period.

Cash Payment for an Expense

June 1, 19--. Paid cash for rent, $1,500.00. Check No. 318.

The journal entry to record this transaction is on line 4 of the cash payments journal input form shown in Illustration T1-6.

Cash Payment to Replenish Petty Cash

June 30, 19--. Paid cash to replenish the petty cash fund, $402.00: office supplies, $164.00; store supplies, $136.00; advertising, $56.00; miscellaneous expense, $46.00. Check No. 350.

The journal entry to record this transaction is on lines 5–8 of the cash payments journal input form shown in Illustration T1-6.

PROCESSING JOURNAL ENTRIES

After all transactions have been journalized, data from each input form are keyed and posted.

A general journal report, cash payments journal report, and purchases journal report are then displayed, verified for accuracy, printed, and filed for future reference.

RECONCILING A BANK STATEMENT

To reconcile a bank statement using automated accounting software, a data entry window is displayed on the monitor for entering bank reconciliation data. The following information is obtained from the June 30 bank statement and from the records of MasterSport.

Bank statement balance	$20,525.23
Checkbook balance	33,231.55
Bank charges:	
Service charge	12.80
Credit Card Fee	340.00
Outstanding deposit	12,828.52
Outstanding checks:	
No. 350	402.00
No. 351	73.00

The bank statement reconciliation data are keyed and the bank statement reconciliation report is printed, as shown in Illustration T1-7, and is filed for future reference.

FYI

Automated Accounting 6.0 **software is broken into three modules. Module 1—general ledger, accounts payable, accounts receivable, financial statement analysis, and budgeting. Module 2—payroll, plant asset accounting, and bank reconciliation. Module 3—inventory accounting.**

TEACHING STRATEGIES: COOPERATIVE LEARNING

Using automated accounting software to complete accounting problems is an ideal cooperative learning experience. Students working in groups can collaborate on completing input forms and keying data.

ILLUSTRATION T1-7 Bank statement reconciliation

```
                          MasterSport
                      Bank Reconciliation
                           06/30/--

Checkbook Balance                                       33231.55
                                              352.80
                                           -----------
Less Bank Charges                                         352.80
                                                      -----------
Adjusted Checkbook Balance                              32878.75
                                                      ===========

Bank Balance                                            20525.23
                                            12828.52
                                           -----------
Plus Outstanding Deposits                               12828.52
                                350          402.00
                                351           73.00
                                           -----------
Less Outstanding Checks                                   475.00
                                                      -----------
Adjusted Bank Balance                                   32878.75
                                                      ===========
```

AUTOMATED ACCOUNTING PROBLEMS

AUTOMATING APPLICATION PROBLEM 2-1 Performing file maintenance activities; adding general ledger application accounts

INSTRUCTIONS:

1. Prepare a chart of accounts input form for Problem 2-1, Chapter 2. Use June 1 of the current year as the run date.
2. Load the *Automated Accounting 6.0* or higher software. Select data base A2-1 (Advanced Course Problem 2-1) from the CENTURY 21 ACCOUNTING Advanced Course Template. Read the Problem Instructions screen.
3. Select File from the menu bar and choose the Save As menu command. Key the path to the drive and directory that contains your data files. Save the data base with a file name of XXX2-1 (where XXX are your initials).
4. Key the data from the chart of accounts input form.
5. Display/print the revised chart of accounts report.

AUTOMATING APPLICATION PROBLEM 2-2 Recording departmental purchases on account and purchases returns and allowances

INSTRUCTIONS:

1. Journalize transactions from Problem 2-2, Chapter 2 on a general journal input form and a purchases journal input form. Use March 31 of the current year as the run date.
2. Load the *Automated Accounting 6.0* or higher software. Select data base A2-2 from the CENTURY 21 ACCOUNTING Advanced Course Template. Read the Problem Instructions screen.
3. Select File from the menu bar and choose the Save As menu command. Key the path to the drive and directory that contains your data files. Save the data base with a file name of XXX2-2 (where XXX are your initials).
4. Key the data from the general journal input form and purchases journal input form.
5. Display/print the general journal report and the purchases journal report.

CHECK FIGURES

- Automating Application Problem 2-2: General Journal totals 590.00; Purchases Journal totals 10,091
- Automating Application Problem 2-4: Cash Payments Journal totals 8,827

AUTOMATING APPLICATION PROBLEM 2-4 Journalizing and posting departmental cash payments

INSTRUCTIONS:

1. Journalize transactions from Problem 2-4, Chapter 2, on a cash payments journal input form. Use November 30 of the current year as the run date.
2. Load the *Automated Accounting 6.0* or higher software. Select data base A2-4 from the CENTURY 21 ACCOUNTING Advanced Course Template. Read the Problem Instructions screen.
3. Use the Save As command and rename your data base file.
4. Key the data from the cash payments journal input form.
5. Display/print the cash payments journal report.

AUTOMATING APPLICATION PROBLEM 2-5 Reconciling a bank statement

INSTRUCTIONS:

1. Load the *Automated Accounting 6.0* or higher software. Select the Payroll/Assets/Bank Reconciliation command.
2. Select data base A2-5. Read the Problem Instructions screen.

Bank statement balance	$31,820.00
Bank service charge	8.80
Bank credit card charge	325.20
Outstanding deposit:	
October 27	7,152.75
Outstanding checks:	
No. 361	89.50
No. 362	1,460.25
Checkbook balance on Check Stub No. 363	37,757.00

3. Use the Save As command and rename your data base file.
4. Key the bank statement reconciliation data.
5. Display/print the bank statement reconciliation.

CHECK FIGURES *(cont'd)*

- Automating Application Problem 2-5: Adjusted balances 37,423
- Automating Mastery Problem 2-M: General Journal totals 295.50; Purchases Journal totals 4,660.40; Cash Payments Journal totals 6,846.80; Adjusted balances: 18,277.00

AUTOMATING MASTERY PROBLEM 2-M Performing file maintenance activities; journalizing departmental purchases and cash payments; reconciling a bank statement

INSTRUCTIONS:

1. Journalize transactions from Mastery Problem 2-M, Chapter 2 on the appropriate input forms. Use November 30 of the current year as the run date.
2. Load the *Automated Accounting 6.0* or higher software. Select data base A2-M from the CENTURY 21 ACCOUNTING Advanced Course Template. Read the Problem Instructions screen.
3. Use the Save As command and rename your data base file.
4. Key the data from the chart of accounts input form.
5. Display/print the revised chart of accounts report.
6. Key the data from the general journal input form, purchases input form, and cash payments journal input form.
7. Display/print each journal report.
8. Save your file.
9. The following information is obtained from the bank statement and from the records of the business.

Bank statement balance	$16,578.00
Bank service charge	20.20
Bank credit card charge	382.80
Outstanding deposit:	
November 29	3,070.60
Outstanding checks:	
No. 283	1,097.60
No. 284	53.00
No. 285	221.00
Checkbook balance on Check Stub No. 286	18,680.00

10. To complete the bank reconciliation, select File from the menu bar and then select the Payroll/Assets/Bank Rec. command. Select File and then the Open Data File command to retrieve data base A2-M from the template disk.
11. Use the Save As command and rename your data base file.
12. Key the bank statement reconciliation data.
13. Display/print the bank statement reconciliation.

63

CHAPTER 3 OVERVIEW

Chapter 3 continues the study of departmentalized accounting to expand student understanding of accounting systems. Sales, sales returns and allowances, and cash receipts journals are used to record transactions. Each transaction is fully explained and illustrated using T accounts and the appropriate journal. Proving cash is reviewed and the importance of the order of posting from special journals is emphasized.

GUIDE TO ACHIEVING LEARNING OBJECTIVES

	TEACH	APPLY	EXTEND/ENRICH					
Enabling Performance Tasks	**Lesson Plans**	**Application Problems**	**Mastery Problems**	**Challenge Problems**	**Cases for Critical Thinking**	**Recycling Problems**	**Reinforcement Activity**	
a. Define accounting terms related to departmental sales and cash receipts.	3-1, 3-2							
b. Identify accounting concepts and practices related to departmental sales and cash receipts.	3-1, 3-2				Cases 1, 2			
c. Journalize and post departmental sales and cash receipts.	3-1, 3-2	3-1, 3-3	3-M	3-C		3-R	1	
d. Prove cash.	3-2	3-3	3-M			3-R	1	

ENRICHMENT

SPECIAL FEATURES
Personal Visions in Business, page 74
Careers in Accounting, page 65
TECHNOLOGY CONNECTION
Automated Accounting 6.0 Problems 3-1, 3-3, 3-M, 3-C

NEW, REVIEW, AND EXTENSION

ACTIVITIES/CONCEPTS/TRANSACTIONS	NEW	REVIEW/ EXTENSION
Journalizing and posting using special journals		✓
Recording departmentalized transactions	✓	
Recording sales of merchandise on account		✓
Recording cash and credit card sales		✓
Recording cash receipts for sales on account		✓
Sales discounts		✓
Recording sales returns and allowances		✓
Proving cash		✓

	INFORMAL ASSESSMENT		FORMAL ASSESSMENT			
	Study Guide	Audit Your Understanding	Chapter MicroExam	Chapter Problem Test	Unit Objective Test	Portfolio
	Unit A	✓	✓		✓	
	Unit B	✓	✓		✓	
				✓		✓
				✓		✓

TEACHING MATERIALS

Teacher's Wraparound Edition of Text
Teacher's Resource Guide
Teacher's Edition of Working Papers
MicroExam

APPLIED MATHEMATICS

APPLIED MATH/ACCOUNTING SKILL	APPLICATION
Calculating sales discount	Prob. 3-2
Calculating sales tax	Prob. 3-2
Calculating sales invoice amount due	Prob. 3-2
Proving cash	Prob. 3-3

TEACHING STRATEGIES: ACCOUNTING PEDAGOGY

This textbook continues to present review material in manageable blocks so that students do not become frustrated with an overload of learning.

3

Recording Departmental Sales and Cash Receipts

ENABLING PERFORMANCE TASKS

After studying Chapter 3, you will be able to:

a Define accounting terms related to departmental sales and cash receipts.

b Identify accounting concepts and practices related to departmental sales and cash receipts.

c Journalize and post departmental sales and cash receipts.

d Prove cash.

TERMS PREVIEW

credit memorandum • sales discount • proving cash

TEACHING STRATEGIES: COOPERATIVE LEARNING

Select a group of three students to create a bulletin board using source documents described in the first accounting cycle. Allow five days for completion of the activity. Appoint a spokesperson to report to the class as to where the documents came from, what each document represents, and how each document is used. These documents can be collected from local businesses or documents from obsolete business simulations may be used. Documents such as receipts, checks, and cash register tapes can be collected through personal daily activities.

CAREERS IN ACCOUNTING

AUDITOR

- *Reviews data regarding assets, equity, liabilities, income, and expenditures*
- *Counts cash on hand, inspects notes receivable and payable, and inspects cancelled checks*
- *Inspects items in books of original entry to determine if acceptable accounting procedure was followed in recording transactions*
- *Verifies journal and ledger entries*
- *Prepares reports for management concerning financial status of the company*

Managers use departmental data to make decisions relating to business operations. A departmental accounting system used to record purchases and cash payments data provides valuable information. In order to have comprehensive departmental data, however, sales and cash receipts data should also be recorded separately for each department. For example, gross profit from operations for each department is one type of valuable information for management decision making. Departmental gross profit from operations helps business managers decide if each department is earning an appropriate profit. If not, departmental information can help managers determine which items are causing the problem. To determine departmental gross profit from operations, the business must keep records of departmental sales and cost of merchandise sold.

DEPARTMENTAL SALES ON ACCOUNT

MasterSport makes sales on account to individuals, clubs, leagues, and schools. MasterSport sells merchandise in two departments. The golf department sells golf equipment such as clubs, bags, balls, and carts. The tennis department sells tennis equipment including racquets, balls, bags, and nets.

Journalizing Sales on Account

MasterSport records all departmental sales on account in a sales journal. The journal has one debit column—Accounts Receivable Debit. The journal also has three credit columns—Sales Tax Payable Credit and special Sales Credit columns for Golf and Tennis. MasterSport's departmental sales journal is shown in Illustration 3-1.

ILLUSTRATION 3-1 Departmental sales journal

SALES JOURNAL — PAGE 6

	DATE		ACCOUNT DEBITED	SALE NO.	POST. REF.	1 ACCOUNTS RECEIVABLE DEBIT	2 SALES TAX PAYABLE CREDIT	3 SALES CREDIT GOLF	4 SALES CREDIT TENNIS	
1	19-- June	1	Golden Golf League	101		294 00	14 00	280 00		1
26		30	Swanville Schools	126		200 00		200 00		26
27										27
28										28

MasterSport's sales invoice is prepared in duplicate for each sale on account. *(CONCEPT: Objective Evidence)* Each sales invoice shows the amount of merchandise sold by the department.

The customer is given the original copy of the sales invoice. The duplicate copy is the source document for journalizing the trans-

TEACHING STRATEGIES: TEACHING TIP

Use an overhead projector to compare sales and cash receipts journals used in a nondepartmental merchandising business and a departmental merchandising business. Students should determine why additional amount columns are needed for journals used by a departmental business.

CAREERS IN ACCOUNTING

The CAREERS IN ACCOUNTING feature box, AUDITOR, comes from the Dictionary of Occupational Titles (DOT). The entry number for this job title is D.O.T. 160.167-054. Bring this dictionary to class and explain its purpose and how to use it. The career feature is designed to expose students to the exploration of different careers in accounting. The feature gives a realistic description of actual job duties. This feature can be used to demonstrate that the skills learned in this course are relevant.

LESSON PLAN 3-1

Materials

- Student pages 65–70
- Blackline Master for Departmental Sales Journal (TRG)
- Blackline Master for Departmental Sales Returns and Allowances Journal (TRG)
- Software: *Automated Accounting 6.0* or higher; CENTURY 21 ACCOUNTING Template, Advanced Course

Objectives (Enabling Performance Tasks)

a. Define accounting terms related to departmental sales and cash receipts.

b. Identify accounting concepts and practices related to departmental sales and cash receipts.

c. Journalize and post departmental sales and cash receipts.

FOCUS

- In Chapter 2, purchases and cash payments transactions were recorded for a departmentalized merchandising business organized as a corporation. Explain that in order to have comprehensive departmental data, sales and cash receipts data should also be recorded separately for each department. In this lesson, departmental sales will be journalized and posted. Explain that the procedures are similar to those learned in the first-year accounting course.
- Introduce vocabulary: credit memorandum.

TEACH

Cover student pages 65–70 "Departmental Sales on Account" and "Departmental Sales Returns and Allowances." Present the departmental sales journal and explain that the journal has a separate Sales Credit column for each department. Explain how sales tax is calculated on a sale. Discuss what types of organizations may be exempt from paying sales tax. Review the procedures for analyzing and recording a departmental sales on account transaction and the steps in posting from a sales journal. Present the departmental sales returns and allowances journal and explain that there is a separate Sales Returns and Allowances Debit column for each department. Explain that sales tax must be calculated on the amount of the return. Review the procedures for analyzing and recording a departmental sales return transaction and the steps in posting from a sales returns and allowances journal.

APPLY

Use T accounts on the overhead projector or chalkboard to show how each transaction in this lesson is analyzed. Refer students to Illustrations 3-1, 3-2, 3-3, and 3-4 as journalizing and posting using a departmental sales journal are presented. Refer students to Illustration 3-5 as journalizing and posting using a departmental sales returns and allowances journal are presented. Have students survey return policies of local merchandising businesses and report back to class.

Guided Practice

Guide students through the T account analysis of the September 1–15 transactions in Problem 3-1. Have students draw T accounts on a sheet of paper and analyze the first transaction. All students should agree with the analysis before proceeding to the next transaction. Repeat the process until all transactions have been analyzed. The balance of Problem 3-1 can be completed as Independent Practice.

Independent Practice

Assign Term 1, Questions 1–9, and Problem 3-1.

---

action. MasterSport records all departmental sales at the time of sale regardless of when payment is made. *(CONCEPT: Realization of Revenue)*

GENERAL LEDGER

Accounts Receivable	
294.00	

Sales Tax Payable	
	14.00

Sales—Golf	
	280.00

ACCOUNTS RECEIVABLE LEDGER

Golden Golf League	
294.00	

FYI

A liability account is increased by a credit.

June 1, 19--. Sold golf equipment on account to Golden Golf League, $280.00, plus sales tax, $14.00; total, $294.00. Sales Invoice No. 101.

The source document for this transaction is a sales invoice. *(CONCEPT: Objective Evidence)*

Accounts Receivable is increased by a $294.00 debit. Sales Tax Payable is increased by a $14.00 credit. Sales—Golf is increased by a $280.00 credit. In the accounts receivable ledger, Golden Golf League is increased by a $294.00 debit.

The details of Sales Invoice No. 101 are recorded on line 1 of the sales journal, Illustration 3-1. The date, *19--, June 1,* is written in the Date column. The customer name, *Golden Golf League,* is written in the Account Debited column. The sales invoice number, *101,* is recorded in the Sale No. column. Since only sales invoice numbers are recorded in this column, no identifying letter is necessary. The debit amount, *$294.00,* is entered in the Accounts Receivable Debit column. The credit amount, *$14.00,* is entered in the Sales Tax Payable Credit column. The credit amount, *$280.00,* is entered in the Sales Credit Golf column.

The state in which MasterSport is located has a sales tax of 5.0%. However, not all customers are required to pay a sales tax. Many agencies supported by local and state government and non-profit educational institutions are exempt from paying a sales tax. These exemptions vary from state to state. Line 26 of the sales journal, Illustration 3-1, shows a sale on account to a school that is not required to pay sales tax.

Posting from a Sales Journal

MasterSport keeps customer accounts in an accounts receivable ledger. Individual amounts in the Accounts Receivable Debit column of the sales journal are posted often to the appropriate customer accounts. Posting line 1 from the sales journal to an accounts receivable ledger account is shown in Illustration 3-2.

The date, *19--, June 1,* is written in the account's Date column. To indicate that the posting came from page 6 of the sales journal, *S6,* is recorded in the Post. Ref. column of the subsidiary ledger account. The amount, *$294.00,* is entered in the Debit column. The account balance, *$294.00,* is entered in the Debit Balance column. The customer number, *140,* is recorded in the Post. Ref. column of the sales journal to show that posting is completed for this line.

The sales journal is proved and ruled at the end of each month. Each amount column total is posted to the general ledger account named in the column heading. Posting a column total from the

TEACHING STRATEGIES: DIFFERENT LEARNING STYLES

Auditory Learner. When learning how to post, the auditory learner would prefer to hear the steps involved in posting. This can be done via a live lecture or a taped tutorial. To reinforce learning, the student could recite the posting steps to another student or group of students.

ILLUSTRATION 3-2

Posting from a sales journal to an accounts receivable ledger

SALES JOURNAL — PAGE 6

	DATE		ACCOUNT DEBITED	SALE NO.	POST. REF.	1 ACCOUNTS RECEIVABLE DEBIT	2 SALES TAX PAYABLE CREDIT	3 SALES CREDIT GOLF	4 SALES CREDIT TENNIS	
1	19-- June	1	Golden Golf League	101	140	294 00	14 00	280 00		1
2										2
3										3

CUSTOMER *Golden Golf League* — CUSTOMER NO. *140*

DATE		ITEM	POST. REF.	DEBIT	CREDIT	DEBIT BALANCE
19-- June	1		S6	294 00		294 00

sales journal to a general ledger account is shown in Illustration 3-3.

To indicate that the posting came from the sales journal, page 6, *S6* is written in the Post. Ref. column of the ledger account. The general ledger account number, *1115,* is written in parentheses immediately below the column total in the sales journal to show that the amount has been posted. All amount column totals are posted in the same way.

ILLUSTRATION 3-3

Posting a total from a sales journal to a general ledger

SALES JOURNAL — PAGE 6

	DATE		ACCOUNT DEBITED	SALE NO.	POST. REF.	1 ACCOUNTS RECEIVABLE DEBIT	2 SALES TAX PAYABLE CREDIT	3 SALES CREDIT GOLF	4 SALES CREDIT TENNIS	
26		30	Swanville Schools	126	170	200 00		200 00		26
27		30	Totals			19 336 50	905 55	8 990 65	9 440 30	27
28						(1115)				28
29										29

ACCOUNT *Accounts Receivable* — ACCOUNT NO. *1115*

DATE		ITEM	POST. REF.	DEBIT	CREDIT	BALANCE DEBIT	BALANCE CREDIT
19-- June	1	Balance	✓			18 182 20	
	30		S6	19 336 50		37 518 70	

ASSESS

Assess student understanding by checking the solutions to the Independent Practice activities.

Reteach

Make transparencies of the departmental sales and sales returns and allowances journals from the accounting forms masters provided in the Blackline Masters section of the Teacher's Resource Guide. Refer students to Recycling Problem 3-R. Ask students to use T accounts to analyze the April 1, 5, 8, and 22 sales on account and sales returns and allowances transactions. Use the transparencies to demonstrate how the transactions are journalized.

Extend

- Assign Cases for Critical Thinking 1.
- Use *Automated Accounting 6.0* or higher with CENTURY 21 ACCOUNTING Template, Advanced Course, with Problem 3-1.

Enrich

Assign the PERSONAL VISIONS IN BUSINESS feature on page 74.

CLOSURE

Use Audit Your Understanding questions.

MasterSport's sales journal, after all posting has been completed, is shown in Illustration 3-4.

ILLUSTRATION 3-4 Departmental sales journal after posting has been completed

SALES JOURNAL PAGE 6

	DATE		ACCOUNT DEBITED	SALE NO.	POST. REF.	1 ACCOUNTS RECEIVABLE DEBIT	2 SALES TAX PAYABLE CREDIT	3 SALES CREDIT GOLF	4 SALES CREDIT TENNIS	
1	19-- June	1	Golden Golf League	101	140	294 00	14 00	280 00		1
2		1	Lawrence Bissell	102	110	2352 00	112 00		2240 00	2
3		1	Eastside Sports Center	103	120	903 00	43 00		860 00	3
25		30	Eastside Sports Center	125	120	262 50	12 50	250 00		25
26		30	Swanville Schools	126	170	200 00		200 00		26
27		30	Totals			19336 50	905 55	8990 65	9440 30	27
28						(1115)	(2130)	(4105-1)	(4105-2)	28
29										29
30										30

APPLIED SKILLS: LANGUAGE ARTS

Paraphrasing, writing complete sentences, identifying singular and plural nouns. For additional practice in language arts skills, direct students to define the terms at the end of the chapter. Students should write the definitions in their own words and in complete sentences. To further practice language arts skills ask students to underline the singular nouns and circle the plural nouns in their definitions.

DEPARTMENTAL SALES RETURNS AND ALLOWANCES

Merchandising businesses normally have some merchandise returned. A customer may have received the wrong size, the wrong style, or damaged or unsatisfactory goods. Merchandise may be returned by a customer for a credit on account or a cash refund. Credit may also be granted without having the damaged or unsatisfactory merchandise returned. An allowance may be given because of a shortage in the shipment.

Journalizing Sales Returns and Allowances

MasterSport records all sales returns and allowances in a sales returns and allowances journal. MasterSport's departmental sales returns and allowances journal is shown in Illustration 3-5.

A vendor usually informs a customer in writing when a sales return or a sales allowance is granted. Details of a sales return or allowance may be stated in a letter or on a preprinted form. A form prepared by the vendor showing the amount deducted for returns and allowances is called a **credit memorandum.** When a customer returns merchandise or requests an allowance, MasterSport issues a credit memorandum. A credit memorandum is the source document for a sales returns and allowances transaction. *(CONCEPT: Objective Evidence)*

FYI

A contra revenue account has a normal debit balance.

An account that reduces a related account on a financial statement is known as a contra account. Sales—Tennis is a revenue account. Therefore, an account showing deductions from a sales account is a contra revenue account. Sales Returns and Allowances—

TEACHING STRATEGIES: DIFFERENT LEARNING ABILITIES

Limited English Proficiency (LEP) Students. Adjust the length of time allotted to complete assignments and tests. Remember that the primary objective is to assess knowledge of accounting rather than the ability to translate and comprehend the question or problem.

ILLUSTRATION 3-5 Departmental sales returns and allowances journal

SALES RETURNS AND ALLOWANCES JOURNAL — PAGE 6

	DATE		ACCOUNT CREDITED	CREDIT MEMO. NO.	POST. REF.	1 ACCOUNTS RECEIVABLE CREDIT	2 SALES TAX PAYABLE DEBIT	3 SALES RETURNS AND ALLOWANCES DEBIT GOLF	4 SALES RETURNS AND ALLOWANCES DEBIT TENNIS	
1	19-- June	2	Galaxy Tennis Club	43	130	136 50	6 50		130 00	1
2		7	Swanville Schools	44	170	88 00		88 00		2
3		15	Golden Golf League	45	140	34 13	1 63	32 50		3
4		21	Lawrence Bissell	46	110	89 25	4 25		85 00	4
5		22	Eastside Sports Center	47	120	71 40	3 40	68 00		5
6		24	Par Golf Club	48	160	136 50	6 50	130 00		6
12		30	Helen Vega	54	180	52 50	2 50		50 00	12
13		30	Totals			1 168 35	53 35	480 00	635 00	13
14						(1115)	(2130)	(4115-1)	(4115-2)	14

Tennis is one of MasterSport's contra revenue accounts. Sales returns and allowances are kept in a separate account and not deducted directly from the sales account. This procedure helps the business see what proportion of the merchandise sold was returned by customers. *(CONCEPT: Adequate Disclosure)*

June 2, 19--. Granted credit to Galaxy Tennis Club for tennis equipment returned, $130.00, plus sales tax, $6.50, from Sales Invoice No. 100; total, $136.50. Credit Memorandum No. 43.

GENERAL LEDGER

Sales Tax Payable

Debit	Credit
6.50	

Sales Returns and Allowances—Tennis

Debit	Credit
130.00	

Accounts Receivable

Debit	Credit
	136.50

ACCOUNTS RECEIVABLE LEDGER

Galaxy Tennis Club

Debit	Credit
	136.50

Sales Tax Payable is decreased by a $6.50 debit. The contra revenue account, Sales Returns and Allowances—Tennis, is increased by a $130.00 debit. Accounts Receivable is decreased by a $136.50 credit. In the accounts receivable ledger, Galaxy Tennis Club is decreased by a $136.50 credit.

Details of Credit Memorandum No. 43 are recorded on line 1 of the sales returns and allowances journal, Illustration 3-5. The date, *19--, June 2,* is written in the Date column. The customer name, *Galaxy Tennis Club,* is recorded in the Account Credited column. The credit memorandum number, *43,* is entered in the Credit Memo. No. column. The credit amount, *$136.50,* is written in the Accounts Receivable Credit column. The debit amount, *$6.50,* is recorded in the Sales Tax Payable Debit column. The debit amount, *$130.00,* is entered in the Sales Returns and Allowances Debit Tennis column.

Posting from a Sales Returns and Allowances Journal

FYI

The abbreviation SR is used to indicate the sales returns and allowances journal in the Post. Ref. column of ledger accounts.

Sales returns and allowances are posted in the same manner as sales on account. Each amount written in the Accounts Receivable Credit column is posted to the customer account written in the Account Credited column. The amount in the Accounts Receivable Credit column, line 1, is posted as a credit to Galaxy Tennis Club's

TEACHING STRATEGIES: DIFFERENT LEARNING STYLES

Kinesthetic Learner. When learning how to post, the kinesthetic learner would prefer to participate in the posting process. This can be done by using a transparency of the ledger account and having each student complete one or more steps of the posting process at the overhead projector. Other students can be completing the posting process individually on printed ledger accounts.

TEACHING STRATEGIES: DIFFERENT LEARNING STYLES

Print Learner. When learning how to post, the print learner would prefer to see the process in print. This can be done by distributing a handout which explains the steps in the posting process. Allow the student to study the handout.

AUDIT YOUR UNDERSTANDING

The AUDIT YOUR UNDERSTANDING feature appears at the end of each section of the chapter. Explain to your students that the word *audit* means to check or verify. AUDIT YOUR UNDERSTANDING may be used to check student comprehension of the section just studied. The answers are provided in Appendix D in the back of the textbook.

1. Accounts Receivable is debited; Sales Tax Payable and Sales—Golf are credited.
2. Sales Tax Payable and Sales Returns and Allowances—Tennis are debited; Accounts Receivable is credited.

LESSON PLAN 3-2

Materials

- Student pages 70–76
- Blackline Master for Departmental Cash Receipts Journal (TRG)
- Software: *Automated Accounting 6.0* or higher; CENTURY 21 ACCOUNTING Template, Advanced Course
- Assess: Problem Test Chapter 3, MicroExam Chapter 3

Objectives (Enabling Performance Tasks)

a. Define accounting terms related to departmental sales and cash receipts.
b. Identify accounting concepts and practices related to departmental sales and cash receipts.
c. Journalize and post departmental sales and cash receipts.
d. Prove cash.

FOCUS

- Journalizing and posting departmental sales transactions were presented earlier in this chapter. In this lesson, cash receipts transactions will be journalized and posted. Explain that the procedure for proving cash will be reviewed.
- Introduce vocabulary: sales discount, proving cash.

account in the accounts receivable ledger. To indicate that the posting came from page 6 of the sales returns and allowances journal, *SR6* is recorded in the Post. Ref. column of the subsidiary ledger account. The customer number, *130,* is written in the Post. Ref. column of the sales returns and allowances journal to show that posting is completed for this line.

Sometimes a sales return or allowance is granted after a sale on account has been paid in full by a customer. This situation might occur if a sales invoice is paid very soon after the sale is made. When this happens, the customer account after posting has a credit balance instead of a normal debit balance. The credit balance, a contra balance, reduces the amount to be received from a customer for future sales on account. When a three-column account form is used, a contra balance in a customer account is shown by enclosing the amount in parentheses.

Audit Your Understanding

1. What general ledger accounts are affected, and how, when golf equipment is sold on account?
2. What general ledger accounts are affected, and how, when tennis equipment that was sold on account is returned?

A sales returns and allowances journal is proved, ruled, and posted at the end of each month in the same manner as a sales journal. Each amount column total is posted to the general ledger account named in the column heading. The account number is written in parentheses below the column total in the journal to show that the amount has been posted. MasterSport's departmental sales returns and allowances journal, after all posting has been completed, is shown in Illustration 3-5.

DEPARTMENTAL CASH RECEIPTS

MasterSport keeps a record of all cash receipts. The sources of most cash receipts are (1) cash received on account from customers and (2) cash and credit card sales.

MasterSport records all cash receipts in a cash receipts journal. The journal has five credit columns—General Credit, Accounts Receivable Credit, Sales Tax Payable Credit, Sales Credit Golf, and Sales Credit Tennis. The journal also has five debit columns—General Debit, Sales Tax Payable Debit, Sales Discount Debit Golf, Sales Discount Debit Tennis, and Cash Debit. MasterSport's departmental cash receipts journal is shown in Illustration 3-6.

FYI

The cash receipts journal has both a Sales Tax Payable Credit and a Sales Tax Payable Debit column.

Cash Receipts on Account

Each customer is expected to pay the amount due within the credit terms agreed upon. To encourage early payment, a deduction on the invoice amount may be granted. A deduction that a vendor allows on the invoice amount to encourage prompt payment is known as a cash discount. A cash discount on sales is called a **sales discount.** MasterSport sells on account using terms 2/10, n/30. These terms mean that a 2% sales discount may be deducted if sales on account are paid within 10 days of the invoice date. All sales on account must be paid within 30 days of the invoice date.

ILLUSTRATION 3-6 Departmental cash receipts journal

CASH RECEIPTS JOURNAL — PAGE 11

	DATE		ACCOUNT TITLE	DOC. NO.	POST. REF.	GENERAL DEBIT (1)	GENERAL CREDIT (2)	ACCOUNTS RECEIVABLE CREDIT (3)	SALES TAX PAYABLE DEBIT (4)	SALES TAX PAYABLE CREDIT (5)	SALES CREDIT GOLF (6)	SALES CREDIT TENNIS (7)	SALES DISCOUNT DEBIT GOLF (8)	SALES DISCOUNT DEBIT TENNIS (9)	CASH DEBIT (10)	
1	19-- June	1	Par Golf Club	R89	160			1785 00	1 70				34 00		1749 30	1
2		4	✓	T4	✓					690 00	5860 00	7940 00			14490 00	2
3		6	Golden Golf League	R90	140			290 00	30				6 00		283 70	3
4		7	Lawrence Bissell	R91	110			2352 00	2 24					44 80	2304 96	4
5		8	Eastside Sports Center	R92	120			446 25	43					8 50	437 32	5
6		9	Eastside Sports Center	R93	120			903 00	86					17 20	884 94	6
7		11	✓	T11	✓					532 50	4370 00	6280 00			11182 50	7

CASH RECEIPTS JOURNAL — PAGE 12

	DATE		ACCOUNT TITLE	DOC. NO.	POST. REF.	GENERAL DEBIT (1)	GENERAL CREDIT (2)	ACCOUNTS RECEIVABLE CREDIT (3)	SALES TAX PAYABLE DEBIT (4)	SALES TAX PAYABLE CREDIT (5)	SALES CREDIT GOLF (6)	SALES CREDIT TENNIS (7)	SALES DISCOUNT DEBIT GOLF (8)	SALES DISCOUNT DEBIT TENNIS (9)	CASH DEBIT (10)	
2		30	Swanville Schools	R108	170			399 00					7 98		391 02	2
3		30	✓	T30	✓					587 50	5620 00	6130 00			12337 50	3
4		30	Totals					19706 10	15 30	2621 50	24520 00	27910 00	147 00	169 00	74426 30	4
5								(1115)	(2130)	(2130)	(4105-1)	(4105-2)	(4110-1)	(4110-2)	(1105)	5

FYI

When multiplying a percentage, move the decimal two places to the left.

At the time a sale is made, Sales Tax Payable is credited for the sales tax liability on the total sales invoice amount. When payment is received within a discount period, the sales tax liability is reduced by the amount of sales tax on the sales discount. Three amounts must be calculated when cash is received on account within a discount period: (1) sales discount, (2) reduction in sales tax payable, and (3) cash received. When MasterSport receives cash on account, a receipt is prepared as the source document. *(CONCEPT: Objective Evidence)*

The amount of cash received when payment is made within a discount period is calculated as shown below.

Sales Discount:

Sales Invoice Amount	×	Sales Discount Rate	=	Sales Discount
$1,700.00	×	2%	=	$34.00

Sales Tax Liability Reduction:

Sales Discount	×	Sales Tax Rate	=	Reduction in Sales Tax Payable
$34.00	×	5%	=	$1.70

Cash Received:

Total Invoiced Amount	–	Sales Discount	–	Sales Tax Reduction	=	Cash Received
$1,785.00	–	$34.00	–	$1.70	=	$1,749.30

TEACHING STRATEGIES: APPLYING VISUALS

Direct students to Illustration 3-6 to review journalizing and posting using a departmental cash receipts journal.

TEACH

Cover student pages 70–76 "Departmental Cash Receipts," "Proving Cash," and "Order of Posting from Journals." Present the departmental cash receipts journal and explain that the journal contains a separate Sales Credit column and Sales Discount Debit column for each department. Demonstrate how to calculate the cash received when payment is made within a discount period. Demonstrate the additional calculation necessary when a customer takes a discount after being granted a return or an allowance. Review the procedures for analyzing and recording the departmental cash receipts on account transactions. Explain the procedures for analyzing and recording the cash and credit card sales transactions. Review the steps in posting from a cash receipts journal. Review the steps to prove cash. Explain the recommended order in which to post special journals and the general journal.

TEACHING STRATEGIES: TEACHING TIP

Use the chalkboard or overhead transparency to demonstrate the calculations to determine the amount of cash received when payment is made within a discount period. Reinforce the procedure by using several examples with different sales discount rates.

APPLY

Use T accounts on the overhead projector or chalkboard to show how each transaction in this lesson is analyzed. Refer students to Illustration 3-6 as journalizing and posting using a departmental cash receipts journal are presented.

Guided Practice

- Guide students through the procedures for calculating the sales tax, sales discounts, and amounts due on Sales Invoices Nos. 183 and 184 in Problem 3-2. Write the formulas on the board for reference. Working as a group, have the students calculate the amounts for Invoice 183. Have them verify the amounts by comparing them with the answers given as the example. Next, have students calculate the amounts for Invoice 184. When all students agree on the correct amounts, direct students to record the amounts on the form in the working papers. The balance of Problem 3-2 can be completed as Independent Practice.
- Guide students through the T account analysis of the November 1–15 transactions in Problem 3-3. Have students draw T accounts on a sheet of paper and analyze the first transaction. All students should agree with the analysis before proceeding to the next transaction. Repeat the process until all transactions have been analyzed. The balance of Problem 3-3 can be completed as Independent practice.

Independent Practice

- Assign Terms 2–3; Questions 10–16; Problems 3-2 and 3-3.
- Assign Study Guide 3 and Mastery Problem 3-M.

GENERAL LEDGER

Cash	
1,749.30	

Sales Tax Payable	
1.70	

Sales Discount—Golf	
34.00	

Accounts Receivable	
	1,785.00

ACCOUNTS RECEIVABLE LEDGER

Par Golf Club	
	1,785.00

June 1, 19--. Received cash on account from Par Golf Club, $1,749.30, covering Sales Invoice No. 96 for golf equipment for $1,785.00 ($1,700.00 plus sales tax, $85.00), less 2% discount, $34.00, and less sales tax, $1.70. Receipt No. 89.

Cash is increased by a $1,749.30 debit. Sales Tax Payable is decreased by a $1.70 debit, the sales tax on the sales discount amount. Sales Discount—Golf is increased by a $34.00 debit. Accounts Receivable is decreased by a $1,785.00 credit. In the accounts receivable ledger, Par Golf Club is decreased by a $1,785.00 credit.

The details of Receipt No. 89 are recorded on line 1 on page 11 of the cash receipts journal, Illustration 3-6. The date, *19--, June 1,* is written in the Date column. The customer name, *Par Golf Club,* is written in the Account Title column. The document number, *R89,* is recorded in the Doc. No. column. The credit amount, *$1,785.00,* is entered in the Accounts Receivable Credit column. The debit amount, *$1.70,* is entered in the Sales Tax Payable Debit column. The debit amount, *$34.00,* is entered in the Sales Discount Debit Golf column. The debit amount, *$1,749.30,* is entered in the Cash Debit column.

An additional calculation is necessary when a customer takes a discount after being granted a return or an allowance. The discount is calculated on the amount owed at the time the invoice is paid. Therefore, the amount of the return or allowance must be deducted from the amount of the original sale *before* the discount can be calculated.

June 8, 19--. Received cash on account from Eastside Sports Center, $437.32, covering Sales Invoice No. 97 for $525.00 ($500.00 plus sales tax, $25.00), less Credit Memorandum No. 42 for $78.75 ($75.00 plus sales tax, $3.75), less 2% discount, $8.50, and less sales tax, $0.43. Receipt No. 92.

GENERAL LEDGER

Cash	
437.32	

Sales Tax Payable	
.43	

Sales Discount—Golf	
8.50	

Accounts Receivable	
	446.25

ACCOUNTS RECEIVABLE LEDGER

Eastside Sports Center	
	446.25

The amount owed at the time the invoice is paid is calculated as follows.

TEACHING STRATEGIES: TEACHING TIP

Using the chalkboard or overhead projector to show T accounts is an excellent way to demonstrate analyzing transactions as this is a very visual activity. The procedure can be reinforced by having students draw T accounts at their desks while you are drawing them on the chalkboard or overhead.

	Amount of Sale	Sales Tax	Total Receivable
Original Sales Invoice Amount (S97)	$500.00	$25.00	$525.00
less Sales Return (CM42)	− 75.00	− 3.75	− 78.75
equals Sales Invoice Amount After Return	$425.00	+ $21.25 =	$446.25

The actual amount received at the time of payment is calculated as shown below.

Sales Discount:

Sales Invoice Amount	×	Sales Discount Rate	=	Sales Discount
$425.00	×	2%	=	$8.50

Sales Tax Liability Reduction:

Sales Discount	×	Sales Tax Rate	=	Reduction in Sales Tax Payable
$8.50	×	5%	=	$0.43

Cash Received:

Total Sales Amount After Return	−	Sales Discount	−	Sales Tax Reduction	=	Cash Received
$446.25	−	$8.50	−	$0.43	=	$437.32

This transaction is journalized the same way as a receipt of cash when there is no sales return or allowance. The only difference is the way in which the amounts are calculated. This transaction is shown on line 5 of page 11 of the cash receipts journal in Illustration 3-6.

Cash and Credit Card Sales

MasterSport sells merchandise to customers for cash. Also, merchandise is sold to customers who have a credit card that shows they have an account with a bank credit card system. MasterSport's bank accepts credit card slips in much the same way it accepts checks for deposit. The bank increases MasterSport's bank account balance by the total amount of the credit card sales slips deposited. Because the bank account balance is increased at the time of deposit, MasterSport records credit card sales and cash sales as one transaction. Sales transactions involving cash and credit cards, therefore, are all recorded as cash sales.

MasterSport uses a cash register to record all cash and credit card sales. Each transaction is printed on a paper tape that is given to a customer as a receipt. The cash register also internally accumulates data about total sales.

FYI

Most credit card sales are completed using a computer.

ASSESS

Assess student understanding by checking the solutions to the Independent Practice activities.

Reteach

- Make a transparency of the departmental cash receipts journal from the accounting forms masters provided in the Blackline Masters section of the Teacher's Resource Guide. Refer students to Recycling Problem 3-R. Ask students to calculate the sales tax and discount amounts and to use T accounts to analyze the April 2, 5, and 9 cash receipts transactions. Use the transparency to demonstrate how the transactions are journalized.
- Assign Recycling Problem 3-R.

Extend

- Assign Cases for Critical Thinking 2.
- Assign Challenge Problem 3-C. (The challenge is to journalize transactions without sales tax.)
- Use *Automated Accounting 6.0* or higher with CENTURY 21 ACCOUNTING Template, Advanced Course, with Problem 3-3, Mastery Problem 3-M, and Challenge Problem 3-C.

Enrich

Assign the CAREERS IN ACCOUNTING feature on page 65. Have students discuss what a career as an auditor might be like.

CLOSURE

Use Audit Your Understanding questions.

ASSESS

- Administer Problem Test Chapter 3.
- Administer a MicroExam test for Chapter 3.

TEACHING STRATEGIES: TEACHING TIP

Encourage students to develop good study habits. At the end of each class, review what has been covered. Urge students to write summary notes that can later be used to study for a test.

A credit card slip is prepared for credit card sales. However, the sale is still recorded on the cash register.

At the end of each week, the cash register prints a total of all cash and credit card sales for the week. The tape is removed from the cash register and identified with a *T* and the date. MasterSport uses a cash register tape as the source document for cash and credit card sales. *(CONCEPT: Objective Evidence)*

Cash	
14,490.00	

Sales Tax Payable	
	690.00

Sales—Golf	
	5,860.00

Sales—Tennis	
	7,940.00

June 4, 19--. Recorded cash and credit card sales, golf equipment, $5,860.00; tennis equipment, $7,940.00; plus sales tax, $690.00; total, $14,490.00. Cash Register Tape No. 4.

Cash is increased by a $14,490.00 debit. Sales Tax Payable is increased by a $690.00 credit. Sales—Golf is increased by a $5,860.00 credit. Sales—Tennis is increased by a $7,940.00 credit.

The details of Cash Register Tape No. 4 are recorded on line 2 of page 11 of the cash receipts journal, Illustration 3-6. The date, *4*, is written in the Date column. A check mark is placed in the Account Title column to show that no account title needs to be written for this transaction. The cash register

Personal Visions in Business

This special student feature introduces students to successful entrepreneurs or business professionals. Each profile gives a flavor of what the actual business world is like and some of the opportunities available to students who study accounting. These features can be used to motivate students to pursue professional business careers in a wide variety of fields. The subjects of these profiles have been carefully chosen to represent the full spectrum of diverse ethnic and racial backgrounds of professional business people. As an optional activity, students can be encouraged to seek out and interview successful business people in their own communities.

■ Al Parker ■

POLYFAB DISPLAY CO.

Al Parker and partner Steve Lawwill founded Polyfab Display Company. Polyfab takes raw plastic and forms it into useful shapes. Polyfab specializes in plastic signs, displays, and graphics, especially items in retail locations.

Parker started the company with $2,000 of his own savings. He and Lawwill got their first contract before they even had any machinery which could form plastic into any shape at all.

Parker is fond of saying that persistence is the key to business success; he often quotes President Calvin Coolidge on persistence: "Nothing in the world can take the place of persistence. Talent will not; nothing is more common than unsuccessful men with talent. Genius will not; the world is full of educated derelicts. Persistence and determination alone are omnipotent." Parker believes so strongly in the value of persistence that his plant is located on Persistence Drive!

Like many new entrepreneurs, Parker and Lawwill kept their full-time day jobs and worked in their own new company at night. In the first year of operation, once they had quit their old jobs, both partners concentrated on selling during the day and then took turns sleeping while they produced the products during the evening and early morning hours.

Parker took accounting courses in college; however, even with a good business education background, he was still surprised in the early days of the business. One surprise was the number of permits the government required of the business. Also, once Polyfab began hiring other employees, it was surprising how much extra cash was required for employee taxes, such as FICA tax, unemployment tax, workers' compensation, and other benefits paid for workers.

Polyfab has worked with many large businesses, including Circuit City Stores, USA Today, J.C. Penney, May Co. Stores, and Hallmark Cards. The company has a national presence in the Point of Purchase Display Industry and is ranked among the fastest growing minority-owned companies in the country.

Personal Visions in Business

APPLIED SKILLS: WRITING ACROSS THE CURRICULUM

Writing paragraphs and short essays. The Cases for Critical Thinking are short, practical applications of the accounting principles developed in the chapter. Some cases are planned to present problems related to the chapter but not specifically discussed and answered in the chapter. These cases present an opportunity for critical thinking and decision making. These cases also require more than a short objective-type response. Therefore they provide ideal practice in writing paragraphs and short essays.

FYI

Sales transactions involving credit cards are recorded as cash sales.

tape number, *T4,* is recorded in the Doc. No. column. A check mark is also placed in the Post. Ref. column to show that amounts on this line do not need to be posted individually. The amount credited to Sales Tax Payable, *$690.00,* is entered in the Sales Tax Payable Credit column. The amount credited to Sales—Golf, *$5,860.00,* is entered in the Sales Credit Golf column. The amount credited to Sales—Tennis, *$7,940.00,* is entered in the Sales Credit Tennis column. The amount debited to Cash, *$14,490.00,* is entered in the Cash Debit column.

TEACHING STRATEGIES: DIFFERENT LEARNING STYLES

Tactile Learner. The tactile learner can use a group of index cards to represent the general ledger. Each card should represent an account and should have 3 vertical lines to distinguish between the debit and credit columns, and balance columns. Have the tactile learner post each example of a journal entry to the appropriate cards (accounts).

Posting from a Cash Receipts Journal

Individual amounts are posted often from the cash receipts journal. MasterSport posts each amount written in the General Debit and Credit columns of the cash receipts journal to the general ledger. Also, each amount in the Accounts Receivable Credit column is posted to the accounts receivable ledger. To indicate that the posting came from page 11 of the cash receipts journal, *CR11* is recorded in the Post. Ref. column of the ledger account. The respective ledger account number is recorded in the Post. Ref. column of the journal to indicate completion of posting.

Transactions involving entries in the General Debit and Credit columns of a cash receipts journal are described in Chapter 10.

At the end of the month, the cash receipts journal is proved and ruled. Totals of the special amount columns are then posted to their respective accounts in the general ledger. The general ledger account number is written in parentheses immediately below the total. A check mark is placed in parentheses below the totals of the General Debit and Credit columns to show that the totals are not posted. MasterSport's departmental cash receipts journal, page 12, after all posting has been completed, is shown in Illustration 3-6.

TEACHING STRATEGIES: TEACHING TIP

As you review the calculations for proving cash, have the students look back at the illustrations identified as the source of information.

FYI

The cash balance on hand must equal the checkbook balance.

PROVING CASH

Determining that the amount of cash agrees with the accounting records is called **proving cash.** MasterSport's cash proof at the end of June is calculated as shown below.

Cash on hand at the beginning of the month....... (June 1 balance of cash account in general ledger)	$23,580.00
Plus total cash received during the month......... (Cash Debit column total, cash receipts journal, Illustration 3-6)	74,426.30
Equals Total	$98,006.30
Less total cash paid during the month .... (Cash Credit column total, cash payments journal, Illustration 2-9, Chapter 2)	61,247.20
Equals cash on hand at end of the month	$36,759.10

TEACHING STRATEGIES: DIFFERENT LEARNING STYLES

Visual Learner. When learning how to post, the visual learner would prefer to see how the posting process works. To encourage visual learners, therefore, the instructor could use a transparency to assist in the lecture. The transparency could be a blank transparency that the instructor completes.

AUDIT YOUR UNDERSTANDING

1. Cash, Sales Tax Payable, and Sales Discount—Golf are debited; Accounts Receivable is credited.
2. Cash is debited; Sales Tax Payable, Sales—Golf, and Sales—Tennis are credited.
3. Cash on hand at the beginning of the month plus total cash received during the month less total cash paid during the month equals cash on hand at the end of the month.

Audit Your Understanding

1. What general ledger accounts are affected, and how, when cash is received within a discount period for a sale of golf equipment on account?
2. What general ledger accounts are affected, and how, when a cash and credit card sales transaction for both golf and tennis equipment is recorded?
3. How is the cash proof at the end of a month calculated?

The last check written in June was Check No. 351. The checkbook balance on the next unused check stub is $36,759.10. Since the checkbook balance is the same as the cash balance on hand, cash is proved.

ORDER OF POSTING FROM JOURNALS

Businesses post transactions affecting vendor and customer accounts often during the month so that balances of subsidiary ledger accounts are kept up to date. General ledger account balances are needed only when financial statements are prepared. Therefore, posting to general ledger accounts may be done less frequently than posting to subsidiary ledgers. However, all transactions, including special amount column totals, must be posted at the end of a fiscal period. The recommended order in which to post journals is listed below.

1. Sales journal.
2. Sales returns and allowances journal.
3. Purchases journal.
4. Purchases returns and allowances journal.
5. General journal.
6. Cash receipts journal.
7. Cash payments journal.

This posting order generally places the debits and credits in the accounts in the order the transactions occurred.

APPLIED SKILLS: BUILDING STUDY SKILLS

A Quick Reference Guide (QRG) can be a useful study tool for several reasons. A QRG is simply a sheet of paper or notecard on which important information is written. When students create a QRG for an accounting topic, learning is reinforced because (1) the concept is reinforced through the act of writing it down; (2) students gain confidence in their knowledge of the subject; (3) repeated use of a QRG reinforces the concept so students find that after a while they do not need to rely on the QRG. Creating a QRG also provides additional writing practice and often calls on students to order steps within a sequence. Direct students to prepare a QRG for the recommended order of posting. Students should use a QRG when they complete end-of-chapter problems, reinforcement activities, and simulations.

SOFTWARE FOCUS

Software may be used for independent practice or enrichment/extension as the instructor deems appropriate. For this chapter, *Automated Accounting 6.0* or higher may be used with Problems 3-1 and 3-3, Mastery Problem 3-M, and Challenge Problem 3-C.

ACCOUNTING TERMS EPT(a)

What is the meaning of each of the following?

1. **credit memorandum**
2. **sales discount**
3. **proving cash**

QUESTIONS FOR INDIVIDUAL STUDY EPT(b)

1. Besides departmental purchases and cash payments, what other data must be recorded separately for each department in order for a business to have comprehensive departmental data?
2. What is one type of management information available through a departmental accounting system?
3. What two types of information are needed to determine departmental gross profit from operations?
4. Which accounting concept is being applied when all departmental sales are recorded at the time of sale?
5. Why might a customer return merchandise?
6. What is the source document for sales returns and allowances?
7. Why are sales returns and allowances kept in a separate account and not deducted directly from the sales account?
8. When might a customer account in the subsidiary ledger have a credit balance instead of its normal debit balance?
9. When a three-column subsidiary account form is used, how is a contra balance indicated in a customer account?
10. What two types of cash receipts are recorded by MasterSport?
11. Why does MasterSport offer a sales discount on sales on account?
12. What three amounts must be calculated when cash is received on account within a discount period?
13. Why does MasterSport record credit card sales and cash sales as one transaction?
14. Why is a check mark placed in the Post. Ref. column of the cash receipts journal for a cash and credit card sale transaction?
15. Why do businesses post transactions affecting vendor and customer accounts frequently during the month?
16. What is the recommended order in which to post journals?

CASES FOR CRITICAL THINKING EPT(b)

CASE 1 Outdoor Adventures specializes in hiking, camping, and fishing gear. All accounting records are kept on a departmental basis. When merchandise is returned by a customer or an allowance is granted, a journal entry is made debiting the appropriate sales account and crediting Accounts Receivable and the customer account. Do you agree or disagree with this accounting procedure? Why?

CASE 2 Ogden's, Inc. sells a complete line of hardware products. To encourage early payment for sales on account, a sales discount is granted. When cash is received on account within a discount period, a sales discount amount and a sales tax on the discount amount are deducted from the invoice amount. The manager suggests that the business not record any sales tax for sales on account at the time of sale. Sales tax would only be recorded at the end of the fiscal period or when sales tax is due. The manager feels that this procedure would be easier and take less time because a sales tax would not need to be figured each time a sales discount is calculated. The accountant disagrees with the manager's suggestion. With whom do you agree? Why?

APPLIED SKILLS: Word Processing

If you wish to integrate word processing in your accounting course, you may direct students to answer the end-of-chapter Accounting Terms, Questions for Individual Study, and Cases for Critical Thinking using their word processing software.

ACCOUNTING TERMS

1. **credit memorandum:** A form prepared by the vendor showing the amount deducted for returns and allowances. (p. 68)
2. **sales discount:** A cash discount on sales. (p. 70)
3. **proving cash:** Determining that the amount of cash on hand agrees with the accounting records. (p. 75)

QUESTIONS FOR INDIVIDUAL STUDY

1. Sales and cash receipts data for each department. (p. 65)
2. Gross profit from operations for each department. (p. 65)
3. Records of departmental sales and cost of merchandise sold. (p. 65)
4. Realization of Revenue concept. (p. 66)
5. The customer may have received the wrong size, the wrong style, or damaged or unsatisfactory goods. (p. 68)
6. A credit memorandum. (p. 68)
7. This procedure helps the business see what proportion of the merchandise sold was returned by customers. (p. 69)
8. When a sales return or allowance is granted after a sale on account has been paid in full by a customer. (p. 70)
9. The contra balance amount is enclosed in parentheses. (p. 70)
10. (a) Cash received on account from customers and (b) cash and credit card sales. (p. 70)
11. To encourage early payment. (p. 70)
12. (a) Sales discount. (b) Reduction in sales tax payable. (c) Cash received. (p. 71)
13. Because the bank account balance is increased for the total amount of the credit card sales slips deposited and the total cash deposited. (p. 73)
14. To show that amounts on the line do not need to be posted individually. (p. 75)
15. So that balances of subsidiary ledger accounts are kept up to date. (p. 78)
16. (a) Sales journal. (b) Sales returns and allowances journal. (c) Purchases journal. (d) Purchases returns and allowances journal. (e) General journal. (f) Cash receipts journal. (g) Cash payments journal. (p. 76)

CASES FOR CRITICAL THINKING

Case 1 Disagree. When the sales account is debited for a return or allowance, the balance of the sales account at the end of the fiscal period will represent net sales only. The income statement will not disclose the volume of sales returns and allowances. This omission would be considered a violation of the adequate disclosure accounting concept. Management should be informed of the volume of sales returns and allowances. A special account entitled Sales Returns and Allowances should be established for each department. The balance of the account should be shown on the income statement as a reduction in sales for each respective department.

Case 2 The accountant. The procedure currently being used by the business maintains a current status of sales and sales tax owed in all accounts at all times. However, the procedure recommended by the manager is not incorrect and is used by some businesses for the reasons stated by the manager.

CHECK FIGURES

Complete solutions to the problems can be found in the Teacher's Edition of the Working Papers.

Problem 3-1 Sales Journal totals: 2,286.80; 95.80; 926.00; 1,265.00. Sales Returns and Allowances Journal totals: 164.85; 7.85; 82.00; 75.00

Problem 3-2 Total Cash Received: $2,109.45; 1,286.25; 956.97; 740.88; 391.02; 967.26; 288.12; 1,193.64

Problem 3-3 Cash Receipts Journal totals: 3,519.60; 3.35; 2,282.00; 21,430.00; 24,210.00; 34.64; 32.40; 51,371.21

APPLICATION PROBLEMS EPT(c,d)

PROBLEM 3-1 Journalizing and posting departmental sales on account and sales returns and allowances

AUTOMATED

Little Alps Ski Shop has two departments: Ski Clothing and Ski Equipment. The general ledger and accounts receivable ledger are given in the working papers accompanying this textbook. The balances are recorded as of September 1 of the current year.

INSTRUCTIONS:

1. Journalize the following transactions completed during September of the current year. Use page 9 of a sales journal and a sales returns and allowances journal. The sales tax rate is 5%. Source documents are abbreviated as follows: credit memorandum, CM; sales invoice, S.

Sept. 1. Sold ski clothing on account to Sarah Webster, $145.00, plus sales tax, $7.25; total, $152.25. S142.

3. Sold ski equipment on account to Nancy Varez, $320.00, plus sales tax, $16.00; total, $336.00. S143.

3. Sold ski equipment on account to Robert Godeen, $435.00, plus sales tax, $21.75; total, $456.75. S144.

5. Granted credit to Sarah Webster for ski clothing returned, $30.00, plus sales tax, $1.50, from S142; total, $31.50. CM24.

8. Sold ski clothing on account to Sarah Webster, $88.00, plus sales tax, $4.40; total, $92.40. S145.

12. Granted credit to Robert Godeen for ski equipment returned, $75.00, plus sales tax, $3.75, from S144; total, $78.75. CM25.

15. Granted credit to Sarah Webster for ski clothing returned, $28.00, plus sales tax, $1.40, from S145; total, $29.40. CM26.

Posting. Post the items that are to be posted individually. Post from the journals in this order: sales journal and sales returns and allowances journal.

17. Sold ski equipment on account to Jane Pilley, $235.00, plus sales tax, $11.75; total, $246.75. S146.

20. Sold ski clothing on account to Lyle Sanders, $65.00, plus sales tax, $3.25; total, $68.25. S147.

23. Sold ski clothing on account to Barry Zmolek, $98.00, plus sales tax, $4.90; total, $102.90. S148.

26. Granted credit to Lyle Sanders for ski clothing returned, $24.00, plus sales tax, $1.20, from S147; total, $25.20. CM27.

27. Sold ski clothing on account to Robert Godeen, $145.00, plus sales tax, $7.25; total, $152.25. S149.

29. Sold ski equipment on account to Coleraine School District, $275.00. No sales tax. S150.

30. Sold ski clothing on account to Nancy Varez, $385.00, plus sales tax, $19.25; total, $404.25. S151.

Posting. Post the items that are to be posted individually.

2. Prove and rule the sales journal. Post the totals.

3. Prove and rule the sales returns and allowances journal. Post the totals.

PROBLEM 3-2 Calculating sales tax, sales discounts, and amounts due

Bischoff's Limited, a departmental merchandising business, charges a 5% sales tax on all sales. A 2% sales discount is granted to customers for early payment of their accounts. The following selected sales on account are paid within the discount period.

MATHEMATICS

Sales Invoice No.	Sales Invoice Amount
183	$2,050.00
184	1,250.00
185	930.00
186	720.00
187	380.00
188	940.00
189	280.00
190	1,160.00

INSTRUCTIONS:

Use a form similar to the following. Calculate and record the following amounts: sales tax, Column 3; amount due before discount, Column 4; sales discount, Column 5; reduction in sales tax payable, Column 6; total cash received, Column 7. The amounts calculated for Sales Invoice No. 183 are given as an example.

1	2	3	4	5	6	7
Sales Invoice No.	**Sales Invoice Amount**	**Sales Tax**	**Amount Due Before Discount**	**Sales Discount**	**Sales Tax Reduction**	**Total Cash Received**
183	*$2,050.00*	*$102.50*	*$2,152.50*	*$41.00*	*$2.05*	*$2,109.45*

PROBLEM 3-3 Journalizing and posting departmental cash receipts

Russell, Inc. has two departments: Furniture and Carpeting. The general ledger and accounts receivable ledger are given in the working papers accompanying this textbook. The balances are recorded as of November 1 of the current year.

AUTOMATED

INSTRUCTIONS:

MATHEMATICS

1. Journalize the following transactions completed during November of the current year. Use page 21 of a cash receipts journal. Russell, Inc. offers terms of 2/10, n/30. The sales tax rate is 5%. Source documents are abbreviated as follows: receipt, R; cash register tape, T.

Nov. 1. Received cash on account from Katherine Heinze, $782.04, covering S102 for carpeting for $798.00 ($760.00 plus sales tax, $38.00), less discount, $15.20, and less sales tax, $0.76. R87.

2. Received cash on account from Dale Richter, $267.54, covering S103 for furniture for $273.00 ($260.00 plus sales tax, $13.00), less discount, $5.20, and less sales tax, $0.26. R88.

5. Recorded cash and credit card sales: furniture, $4,620.00; carpeting, $4,130.00; plus sales tax, $437.50; total, $9,187.50. T5.

8. Received cash on account from Anne Minton, $288.12, covering S104 for carpeting for $399.00 ($380.00 plus sales tax, $19.00), less CM21 for $105.00 ($100.00 plus sales tax, $5.00), less discount, $5.60, and less sales tax, $0.28. R89.

10. Received cash on account from Mark Kipper, $436.30, covering S105 for furniture for $445.20 ($424.00 plus sales tax, $21.20), less discount, $8.48, and less sales tax, $0.42. R90.

Nov. 12. Recorded cash and credit card sales: furniture, $4,680.00; carpeting, $5,120.00; plus sales tax, $490.00; total, $10,290.00. T12.

15. Received cash on account from Edward Pacetti, $185.22, covering S106 for furniture for $189.00 ($180.00 plus sales tax, $9.00), less discount, $3.60, and less sales tax, $0.18. R91.

Posting. Post the items that are to be posted individually.

19. Recorded cash and credit card sales: furniture, $4,510.00; carpeting, $6,230.00; plus sales tax, $537.00; total, $11,277.00. T19.

22. Received cash on account from Yoko Saga, $275.77, covering S107 for furniture for $281.40 ($268.00 plus sales tax, $13.40), less discount, $5.36, and less sales tax, $0.27. R92.

25. Received cash on account from Anne Minton, $596.82, covering S108 for carpeting for $609.00 ($580.00 plus sales tax, $29.00), less discount, $11.60, and less sales tax, $0.58. R93.

26. Recorded cash and credit card sales: furniture, $4,750.00; carpeting, $5,490.00; plus sales tax, $512.00; total $10,752.00. T26.

29. Received cash on account from Edward Pacetti, $257.25, covering S109 for furniture for $262.50 ($250.00 plus sales tax, $12.50), less discount, $5.00, and less sales tax, $0.25. R94.

30. Received cash on account from Yoko Saga, $360.15, covering S110 for furniture for $420.00 ($400.00 plus sales tax, $20.00), less CM22 for $52.50 ($50.00 plus sales tax, $2.50), less discount, $7.00, and less sales tax, $0.35. R95.

30. Recorded cash and credit card sales: furniture, $2,870.00; carpeting, $3,240.00; plus sales tax, $305.50; total $6,415.50. T30.

Posting. Post the items that are to be posted individually.

2. Prove the cash receipts journal.

3. Prove cash. The cash balance on hand on November 1 was $43,340.00. The total of the cash credit column of the cash payments journal is $38,310.00. The balance on the next unused check stub is $56,401.21.

4. Rule the cash receipts journal. Post the totals.

ENRICHMENT PROBLEMS — EPT (c,d)

MASTERY PROBLEM 3-M Journalizing departmental sales, sales returns and allowances, and cash receipts

McKinney's Clothing Store has two departments: Men's Clothing and Women's Clothing.

AUTOMATED

INSTRUCTIONS:

1. Journalize the following transactions completed during June of the current year. Calculate and record sales tax on all sales and sales returns and allowances as described in this chapter. Use page 6 of a sales journal and a sales returns and allowances journal and page 11 of a cash receipts journal. McKinney's offers its customers terms of 2/10, n/30. The sales tax rate is 5%. Source documents are abbreviated as follows: credit memorandum, CM; receipt, R; sales invoice, S; cash register tape, T.

June 1. Sold men's clothing on account to Jason Gunn, $660.00, plus sales tax. S134.

3. Sold men's clothing on account to Kara Wilder, $430.00, plus sales tax. S135.

CHECK FIGURES *(cont'd)*

Mastery Problem 3-M Sales Journal totals: 3,487.90; 129.00; 2,170.00; 1,188.00. Sales Returns and Allowances Journal totals: 170.10; 8.10; 95.00; 67.00. Cash Receipts Journal totals: 4,026.75; 3.84; 2,020.50; 19,860.00; 20, 550.00; 54.30; 22.40; 46,376.71

Challenge Problem 3-C Sales Journal totals: 3,358.00; 2,170.00; 1,188.00. Sales Returns and Allowances Journal totals: 162.00; 95.00; 67.00. Cash Receipts Journal totals: 3,835.00; 19,860.00; 20,550.00; 27.15; 11.20; 44,206.65

80

June 4. Received cash on account from William Hodges, covering S132 for women's clothing ($360.00 plus sales tax), less discount and less sales tax. R83.

4. Recorded cash and credit card sales: men's clothing, $2,280.00; women's clothing, $2,520.00; plus sales tax. T4.

6. Received cash on account from Robin Vaughn, covering S131 for men's clothing ($640.00 plus sales tax), less discount and less sales tax. R84.

8. Granted credit to Kara Wilder for men's clothing returned, $95.00, plus sales tax, from S135. CM28.

9. Received cash on account from Kara Wilder, covering S133 for women's clothing ($399.00 plus sales tax), less discount and less sales tax. R85.

11. Received cash on account from Jason Gunn, covering S134 for men's clothing ($660.00 plus sales tax), less discount and less sales tax. R86.

11. Sold men's clothing on account to Paul Reed, $840.00, plus sales tax. S136.

11. Recorded cash and credit card sales: men's clothing, $4,720.00; women's clothing, $5,030.00; plus sales tax. T11.

13. Received cash on account from Kara Wilder, covering S135 for men's clothing ($430.00 plus sales tax), less CM28 ($95.00 plus sales tax), less discount and less sales tax. R87.

15. Sold women's clothing on account to Linda Baron, $428.00, plus sales tax. S137.

17. Sold men's clothing on account to Robin Vaughn, $240.00, plus sales tax. S138.

18. Recorded cash and credit card sales: men's clothing, $5,130.00; women's clothing, $4,980.00; plus sales tax. T18.

21. Received cash on account from Paul Reed, covering S136 for men's clothing ($840.00 plus sales tax), less discount and less sales tax. R88.

21. Granted credit to Linda Baron for women's clothing returned, $67.00, plus sales tax, from S137. CM29.

25. Received cash on account from Linda Baron, covering S137 for women's clothing ($428.00 plus sales tax), less CM29 ($67.00 plus sales tax), less discount and less sales tax. R89.

25. Recorded cash and credit card sales: men's clothing, $4,750.00; women's clothing, $4,910.00; plus sales tax. T25.

27. Received cash on account from Robin Vaughn, covering S138 for men's clothing ($240.00 plus sales tax), less discount and less sales tax. R90.

28. Sold women's clothing on account to Royalton Schools, $760.00; no sales tax. S139.

30. Recorded cash and credit card sales: men's clothing, $2,980.00; women's clothing, $3,110.00; plus sales tax. T30.

2. Prove and rule the sales journal and the sales returns and allowances journal.

3. Prove the cash receipts journal.

4. Prove cash. The cash balance on hand on June 1 was $37,940.00. The total of the cash credit column of the cash payments journal is $31,120.86. The balance on the next unused check stub is $53,195.85.

5. Rule the cash receipts journal.

CHALLENGE PROBLEM 3-C Journalizing departmental sales, sales returns and allowances, and cash receipts

Assume that McKinney's Clothing Store, the business described in Mastery Problem 3-M, is located in a state that does not charge a retail sales tax. Also, assume that McKinney's offers customers terms of 1/10, n/30. The journals with the proper headings are given in the working papers.

AUTOMATED

INSTRUCTIONS:

1. Journalize the transactions given in Mastery Problem 3-M without sales tax. Use page 6 of a sales journal and a sales returns and allowances journal and page 11 of a cash receipts journal.
2. Prove and rule the journals.

Recording Departmental Sales and Cash Receipts

TEACHING STRATEGIES: ACCOUNTING PEDAGOGY

This textbook introduces the manual accounting concept of journalizing purchases, cash payments, sales, and cash receipts before using the computer to journalize and post. It is important that students master accounting theory before using the computer.

MasterSport's manual recording procedures for sales and cash receipts are described in Chapter 3. Integrating Automated Accounting Topic 2 describes procedures for using automated accounting software to record MasterSport's transactions. The Automated Accounting Problems contain instructions for using automated accounting software to solve Problem 3-1, Problem 3-3, Mastery Problem 3-M, and Challenge Problem 3-C from Chapter 3.

RECORDING DEPARTMENTAL SALES AND CASH RECEIPTS

Departmental sales are recorded at the time of sale regardless of when payment is received. MasterSport's departmental sales and cash receipts transactions are analyzed in Chapter 3.

SOFTWARE FOCUS

The Automated Accounting Problems in this Integrating Automated Accounting topic use Application Problems 3-1, 3-3, Mastery Problem 3-M, and Challenge Problem 3-C, Chapter 3, which students have already completed manually. Refer students back to these problems to complete the input forms. The problem instructions in *Automated Accounting 6.0* will lead students through automating the problems.

LESSON PLAN A2

Materials

- Student pages 83–86
- Input forms for Automating Application Problems 3-1, 3-3, Mastery Problem 3-M, and Challenge Problem 3-C are provided in the working papers that accompany this textbook. If additional input forms are needed, blackline masters are provided in the Blackline Masters Section of the Teacher's Resource Guide.
- Complete solutions for automated problems are provided in the Teacher's Resource Guide.
- Software: *Automated Accounting 6.0* or higher; CENTURY 21 ACCOUNTING Template, Advanced Course

Objective

Journalize sales and cash receipts transactions using an automated accounting system.

FOCUS

In Chapter 3, manual journalizing and posting procedures for departmental sales and cash receipts were described. Emphasize that automated accounting software may be used to speed the journalizing and posting procedures. Explain that using automated accounting software, however, does not change accounting concepts. Only the methods change.

TEACH

Cover student pages 83–86 "Recording Departmental Sales and Cash Receipts" and "Processing Journal Entries." While explaining the procedures for journalizing and posting sales on account transactions, make the students aware that the automated accounting software automatically records the debit to Accounts Receivable. Likewise, when journalizing and posting cash receipts transactions, the software automatically records the debit to Cash. Point out that sales returns and allowances transactions are recorded on a general journal input form.

Sales on Account

MasterSport uses a separate sales account for each of its two departments—golf and tennis. Sales on account transactions are batched and recorded on a sales journal input form.

June 1, 19--. Sold golf equipment on account to Golden Golf League, $280.00, plus sales tax, $14.00; total, $294.00. Sales Invoice No. 101.

The journal entry to record this transaction is recorded on lines 1 and 2 of the sales journal input form shown in Illustration T2-1.

ILLUSTRATION T2-1

Sales journal input form

RUN DATE 06/30/-- (MM DD YY)

SALES JOURNAL
Input Form

	DATE MM/DD	CUSTOMER NO.	INVOICE NO.	INVOICE AMOUNT	ACCOUNT NO.	DEBIT	CREDIT	
1	06/01	140	S101	294 00	4105.1		280 00	1
2	/				2130		14 00	2
3	/01	110	S102	2352 00	4105.2		2240 00	3
4	/				2130		112 00	4
5	/01	120	S103	903 00	4105.2		860 00	5
6	/				2130		43 00	6
25	/							25

NOTE: A debit to Accounts Receivable is made automatically by the software.

Sales Returns and Allowances

MasterSport batches sales returns and allowances transactions and records them on a general journal input form.

June 2, 19--. Granted credit to Galaxy Tennis Club for tennis equipment returned, $130.00, plus sales tax, $6.50, from Sales Invoice No. 100; total, $136.50. Credit Memorandum No. 43.

The journal entry to record this transaction is recorded on lines 1–3 of the general journal input form shown in Illustration T2-2.

Cash Receipts on Account

MasterSport batches cash receipts transactions and records them on a cash receipts journal input form.

June 1, 19--. Received cash on account from Par Golf Club, $1,749.30, covering Sales Invoice No. 96 for golf equipment for $1,785.00 ($1,700.00 plus sales tax, $85.00), less 2% discount, $34.00, and less sales tax, $1.70. Receipt No. 89.

FYI

A journal entry should not be split on two different input forms.

TEACHING STRATEGIES: DIFFERENT LEARNING ABILITIES

Visually-Impaired Students. The use of software should not be overlooked for visually impaired students, particularly if oversized monitors with larger displays are available.

ILLUSTRATION T2-2 General journal input form

RUN DATE 06/30/-- (MM DD YY)

GENERAL JOURNAL
Input Form

	DATE MM/DD	REFERENCE	ACCOUNT NO.	CUSTOMER/ VENDOR NO.	DEBIT	CREDIT	
1	06/02	CM43	4115.2		130.00		1
2	/		2130		6.50		2
3	/		1115	130		136.50	3
4	/07	CM44	4115.1		88.00		4
5	/		1115	170		88.00	5
6	/15	CM45	4115.1		32.50		6
7	/		2130	140	1.63		7
8	/		1115			34.13	8
9	/21	CM46	4115.2		85.00		9
10	/		2130		4.25		10
11	/		1115	110		89.25	11
12	/22	CM47	4115.1		68.00		12
13	/		2130		3.40		13
14	/		1115	120		71.40	14
15	/24	CM48	4115.1		130.00		15
16	/		2130		6.50		16
17	/		1115	160		136.50	17
25	/						25
				PAGE TOTALS			
				FINAL TOTALS			

The journal entry to record this transaction is recorded on lines 1 and 2 of the cash receipts journal input form shown in Illustration T2-3.

June 8, 19--. Received cash on account from Eastside Sports Center, $437.32, covering Sales Invoice No. 97 for $525.00 ($500.00 plus sales tax, $25.00), less Credit Memorandum No. 42 for $78.75 plus sales tax, $3.75), less 2.0% discount, $8.50, and less sales tax, $0.43. Receipt No. 92.

The journal entry to record this transaction is on lines 10 and 11 of the cash receipts input form shown in Illustration T2-3.

Cash and Credit Card Sales

June 4, 19--. Recorded cash and credit card sales: golf equipment, $5,860.00; tennis equipment, $7,940.00; plus sales tax, $690.00; total, $14,490.00. Cash Register Tape No. 4.

The journal entry to journalize this transaction is on lines 3 through 5 of the cash receipts journal input form shown in Illustration T2-3.

TEACHING STRATEGIES: COOPERATIVE LEARNING

Using automated accounting software to complete accounting problems is an ideal cooperative learning experience. Students working in groups can collaborate on completing input forms and keying data.

APPLY

Use T accounts on the overhead projector or chalkboard to show how each transaction in this lesson is analyzed. Refer students to Illustration T2-1 as journalizing sales on account transactions is presented. Refer students to Illustration T2-2 as journalizing sales returns and allowances transactions is presented. Refer students to Illustration T2-3 as journalizing cash receipts transactions is presented.

Guided Practice

Guide students through the journalizing of the first 5 transactions in Automating Application Problems 3-1 and 3-3. Have students analyze the first transaction using T accounts. Have them journalize the transaction on their input form. All students should agree with the analysis before proceeding to the next transaction. Repeat the process until all transactions have been analyzed and journalized. The balance of Automating Application Problems 3-1 and 3-3 can be completed as Independent Practice.

Independent Practice

Assign Automating Application Problems 3-1, 3-3, and Mastery Problem 3-M.

ASSESS

Assess student understanding by checking the solutions to the Independent Practice activities.

Reteach

Make transparencies of the sales journal, general journal, and cash receipts journal input forms from the accounting forms masters provided in the Blackline Masters Section of the Teacher's Resource Guide. Refer students to Challenge Problem 3-C. Ask students to use T accounts to analyze the transactions. Use the transparencies to demonstrate how the transactions are journalized on the input forms.

Extend

Assign Automating Challenge Problem 3-C.

CLOSURE

Review the steps for recording sales on account, sales returns and allowances, and cash receipts transactions using automated accounting software.

ILLUSTRATION T2-3 Cash receipts journal input form

RUN DATE 06/30/-- (MM DD YY)

CASH RECEIPTS JOURNAL
Input Form

	DATE MM/DD	CUSTOMER NO.	REFERENCE	ACCOUNTS REC. CREDIT	ACCOUNT NO.	DEBIT	CREDIT	
1	06/01	160	R89	1785 00	2130	1 70		1
2	/				4110.1	34 00		2
3	/04		T4		4105.1		5860 00	3
4	/				4105.2		7940 00	4
5	/				2130		690 00	5
6	/06	140	R90	290 00	2130	30		6
7	/				4110.1	6 00		7
8	/07	110	R91	2352 00	2130	2 24		8
9	/				4110.2	44 80		9
10	/08	120	R92	446 25	2130	43		10
11	/				4110.2	8 50		11
12	/09	120	R93	903 00	2130	86		12
13	/				4110.2	17 20		13
14	/11		T11		4105.1		4370 00	14
15	/				4105.2		6280 00	15
16	/				2130		532 50	16
25	/							25

NOTE: A debit to Cash is made automatically by the software.

FYI

To avoid damage to disk drives on the computer, do not insert any implements such as pencils in the disk drive.

PROCESSING JOURNAL ENTRIES

After all transactions have been journalized, data from each input form are keyed and posted. A general journal report, sales journal report, and cash receipts journal report are then displayed, verified for accuracy, printed, and filed for future reference.

AUTOMATED ACCOUNTING PROBLEMS

AUTOMATED

AUTOMATING APPLICATION PROBLEM 3-1 Journalizing and posting departmental sales on account and sales returns and allowances

INSTRUCTIONS:

1. Journalize transactions from Problem 3-1, Chapter 3, on appropriate input forms. Use September 30 of the current year as the run date.
2. Load the *Automated Accounting 6.0* or higher software. Select data base A3-1 (Advanced Course Problem 3-1) from the CENTURY 21 ACCOUNTING Advanced Course Template. Read the Problem Instructions screen.
3. Use the Save As command and rename your data base file.
4. Key the data from the general journal input form and the sales journal input form.
5. Display/print the general journal report and the sales journal report.

CHECK FIGURES

- Automating Application Problem 3-1: General Journal totals 164.85; Sales Journal totals 2,286.80
- Automating Application Problem 3-3: Cash Receipts Journal totals 51,441.60
- Automating Mastery Problem 3-M: General Journal totals 170.10; Sales Journal totals 3,487.90; Cash Receipts Journal totals 46,457.25
- Automating Challenge Problem 3-C: General Journal totals 162.00; Sales Journal totals 3,358.00; Cash Receipts Journal totals 44,245.00

TEACHING STRATEGIES: Teaching Tip

It is important for students to save a template file under another name before they begin work. This will keep the template file intact for future use.

AUTOMATING APPLICATION PROBLEM 3-3 Journalizing and posting departmental cash receipts

AUTOMATED

INSTRUCTIONS:

1. Journalize transactions from Problem 3-3, Chapter 3, on appropriate input forms. Use November 30 of the current year as the run date.
2. Load the *Automated Accounting 6.0* or higher software. Select data base A3-3 from the CENTURY 21 ACCOUNTING Advanced Course Template. Read the Problem Instructions screen.
3. Use the Save As command and rename your data base file.
4. Key the data from the cash receipts journal input form.
5. Display/print the cash receipts journal report.

AUTOMATING MASTERY PROBLEM 3-M Journalizing departmental sales, sales returns and allowances, and cash receipts

AUTOMATED

INSTRUCTIONS:

1. Journalize transactions from Problem 3-M, Chapter 3, on appropriate input forms. Use June 30 of the current year as the run date.
2. Load the *Automated Accounting 6.0* or higher software. Select data base A3-M from the CENTURY 21 ACCOUNTING Advanced Course Template. Read the Problem Instructions screen.
3. Use the Save As command and rename your data base file.
4. Key the data from the input forms.
5. Display/print the general journal report, sales journal report, and cash receipts journal report.

AUTOMATING CHALLENGE PROBLEM 3-C Recording departmental sales, sales returns and allowances, and cash receipts

AUTOMATED

INSTRUCTIONS:

1. Journalize transactions from Problem 3-C, Chapter 3, on appropriate input forms.
2. Load the *Automated Accounting 6.0* or higher software. Select data base A3-C from the CENTURY 21 ACCOUNTING Advanced Course Template. Read the Problem Instructions screen.
3. Use the Save As command and rename your data base file.
4. Key the data from the input forms.
5. Display/print the general journal report, sales journal report, and cash receipts journal report.

87

CHAPTER 4 OVERVIEW

Chapter 4 presents calculating and recording payroll data. Partial income tax withholding tables for a bi-weekly payroll period are shown in this chapter. An 8% FICA rate has been assumed for all payroll calculations. The employer's unemployment tax rates are calculated on the first $7,000.00 earned by each employee. The federal unemployment tax rate is 0.8%; the state unemployment tax rate is 5.4%. Since Congress may change any of these rates at any point in time, it is recommended that amounts and rates

GUIDE TO ACHIEVING LEARNING OBJECTIVES

	TEACH	APPLY	EXTEND/ENRICH					
Enabling Performance Tasks	**Lesson Plans**	**Application Problems**	**Mastery Problems**	**Challenge Problems**	**Cases for Critical Thinking**	**Recycling Problems**	**Reinforcement Activity**	
a. Define accounting terms related to a departmental payroll system.	4-1, 4-2, 4-3							
b. Identify accounting concepts and practices related to a departmental payroll system.	4-1, 4-2, 4-3				Cases 1, 2			
c. Complete payroll records.	4-2	4-1, 4-2, 4-3, 4-4, 4-5, 4-6	4-M	4-C		4-R		
d. Journalize payroll transactions.	4-3	4-7, 4-8	4-M			4-R	1	

ENRICHMENT

SPECIAL FEATURES
Spreadsheet Options, page 94
TECHNOLOGY CONNECTION
Spreadsheet Template Problems 4-1, 4-4, 4-5

NEW, REVIEW, AND EXTENSION

ACTIVITIES/CONCEPTS/TRANSACTIONS	NEW	REVIEW/ EXTENSION
Recording payroll transactions		✓
Recording employee benefits	✓	
Calculating commissions	✓	
Calculating hours worked and total earnings from time cards		✓
Preparing a payroll register		✓
Preparing employee earnings records		✓
Recording employer payroll taxes		✓
Paying withholding and payroll taxes		✓

given in the textbook be used. Regardless of rates, the accounting procedures remain the same.

The time cards prepared in Problem 4-3 and the commissions records prepared in Problem 4-4 are needed to complete Problem 4-5. The payroll register prepared in Problem 4-5 is needed to complete Problems 4-6 and 4-7.

	INFORMAL ASSESSMENT		FORMAL ASSESSMENT			
	Study Guide	**Audit Your Understanding**	**Chapter MicroExam**	**Chapter Problem Test**	**Unit Objective Test**	**Portfolio**
	Unit B	✓	✓		✓	
	Units A, C	✓	✓		✓	
				✓		
				✓		✓

TEACHING MATERIALS

Teacher's Wraparound Edition of Text
Teacher's Resource Guide
Teacher's Edition of Working Papers
MicroExam

APPLIED MATHEMATICS

APPLIED MATH/ACCOUNTING SKILL	APPLICATION
Calculating accumulated vacation time and other benefit hours	Prob. 4-1
Calculating regular, overtime, and total earnings	Prob. 4-2
Calculating sales commission	Prob. 4-4
Calculating employee deductions	Prob. 4-5
Calculating net pay	Prob. 4-5

4

Calculating and Recording Departmental Payroll Data

TEACHING STRATEGIES: ACCOUNTING PEDAGOGY

This textbook introduces the complete payroll system for a departmentalized business. Covering payroll at this early stage of the text allows for students to actually apply payroll procedures in a business simulation at the end of the part.

ENABLING PERFORMANCE TASKS

After studying Chapter 4, you will be able to:

a Define accounting terms related to a departmental payroll system.

b Identify accounting concepts and practices related to a departmental payroll system.

c Complete payroll records.

d Journalize payroll transactions.

TERMS PREVIEW

salary • pay period • payroll • payroll taxes • employee benefits • payroll register • withholding allowance • tax base • employee earnings record • automatic check deposit

FYI

Salaries are usually stated as a fixed amount as either weekly, biweekly, semimonthly, or monthly. Salaried workers do not normally receive overtime pay.

Employees are an essential element of the business world. Most businesses cannot operate successfully without competent employees. Employees provide services to a business in exchange for money. The money paid for employee services is called a **salary.** Employers are required by federal, state, and local laws to keep accurate records of the money paid to employees and of other payments related to employee services. Financial records must be maintained for the business and for each employee. The period covered by a salary payment is called a **pay period.** The total amount earned by all employees for a pay period is called a **payroll.**

In addition to salaries, a business must pay taxes based on the payroll. Taxes based on the payroll of a business are called **payroll taxes.** Payroll taxes are reported as separate items because the taxes represent a business transaction with dollar amounts large enough to affect business decisions. Therefore, all payroll taxes are reported as separate items in accounting records and financial statements. *(CONCEPT: Materiality)*

FYI

Compensation for employee services is known as wages. Wages are normally stated as hourly, weekly, or piecework. Employees who receive wages are usually paid for overtime.

Employers are required by law to withhold certain payroll taxes from employee salaries each pay period. Periodically, employers must pay government agencies all payroll taxes withheld from employee salaries as well as the employer payroll taxes. A business must also provide a yearly report to each employee showing the total salary earned and the total taxes withheld. Therefore, a business must keep records of each employee's earnings, amounts withheld, and net amount paid. Payroll records also must show the total amount of payroll taxes that a business must pay.

Payroll information a business must keep and report is specified by federal, state, and local governments. However, the payroll system used by individual businesses may differ. A business protects itself by keeping complete and accurate payroll records showing all required information.

EMPLOYEE BENEFITS

Payments to employees for nonworking hours and to insurance and retirement programs are called **employee benefits.** Employee benefits are provided by most businesses as a reward for continuous service. These benefits generally include vacation time, sick leave time, and personal leave time with pay after a period of continuous employment. Employee benefits may also include payments by the employer for health insurance and retirement. The number and type of employee benefits vary among businesses. Regardless of the type and number of employee benefits, records must be maintained of each employee's benefits earned, used, and available. MasterSport has three employee benefits. (1) Vacation time. (2) Sick leave time. (3) Personal leave time. The time available to MasterSport's employees is outlined in the schedule shown in Illustration 4-1.

LESSON PLAN 4-1

Materials

- Student pages 89–97
- Blackline Master for Benefits Record (TRG)
- Blackline Master for Commissions Record (TRG)
- Software: Spreadsheet Template

Objectives (Enabling Performance Tasks)

a. Define accounting terms related to a departmental payroll system.

b. Identify accounting concepts and practices related to a departmental payroll system.

FOCUS

- In the first-year accounting course, the accounting concepts and practices related to a payroll system were presented. Explain that this lesson will review the basic payroll procedures. In addition, the payroll for a departmentalized business will be prepared.
- Introduce vocabulary: salary, pay period, payroll, payroll taxes, employee benefits.

TEACH

Cover student pages 89–97 "Employee Benefits," "Employee Earnings," and "Preparing a Departmental Payroll." Explain the basic types of employee benefits provided by most businesses. Emphasize that employee benefits are determined by individual businesses and not required by law. Provide examples of jobs that are hourly, salary, and commission. Explain the benefits authorization form and benefits record used by MasterSport. Demonstrate how accumulated hours available are calculated. Explain the use of a time card and the procedures used by the accounting department to complete the payroll time card. Explain commissions and describe how MasterSport's commissions record is completed. Demonstrate how commissions are calculated. List the various deductions made by businesses from employee earnings.

ILLUSTRATION 4-1 Employee benefits schedule

MasterSport
Employee Benefits Schedule

	1	2	3	4
Benefits	**Earned After 12 Months**	**Biweekly After 12 Months**	**Minimum Time Blocks**	**Maximum Carry Over**
Vacation time hours.........	40	4	4	120
Sick leave time hours........	0	2	1	80
Personal leave time hours....	0	1	1	24

FYI

A biweekly pay period means once every two weeks; a semimonthly pay period means twice a month.

Vacation Time

MasterSport pays its employees every two weeks. A two-week pay period is referred to as a biweekly pay period. MasterSport's employees are entitled to one week (40 hours) of paid vacation time after completing one full year of employment. Beginning with the second year of employment, employees earn four paid vacation hours for each biweekly pay period of at least 80 hours. Beginning in the second year of employment, employees may take vacation time in blocks of hours. Vacation time may be taken in blocks of at least four hours each or up to the maximum number of hours accumulated. Employees who do not use their full number of paid vacation hours in one year may carry over the unused hours to the following year. Each employee may accumulate up to three weeks (120 hours) of paid vacation time.

Sick Leave Time

Beginning with the second year of employment, MasterSport's employees are allowed two paid sick leave hours for each biweekly pay period of at least 80 hours. Sick leave time must be taken in blocks of at least one hour each or up to the maximum number of hours accumulated. Sick leave time may accumulate up to a maximum of 80 hours.

Personal Leave Time

MasterSport's employees are allowed one paid personal leave hour for each biweekly pay period of at least 80 hours beginning with the second year of employment. Personal leave time is to be used for required time away from business for personal reasons. Personal leave time must be taken in blocks of at least one hour at a

TEACHING STRATEGIES: TEACHING TIP

Conduct a survey of selected local businesses to determine types of employee benefits available and the records kept. This survey can either be conducted by the teacher or by a selected group of students. The findings from this survey should be reported to the class.

time and cannot exceed eight hours at a time. Personal leave time may accumulate up to a maximum of 24 hours.

FYI

The terms wages and salaries are often used interchangeably. Regardless of whether a payroll consists of wages, salaries, or a combination of both, payroll accounting procedures are the same.

EMPLOYEE EARNINGS

An employee's pay rate is usually stated as a rate per hour, day, week, month, or year. The pay rate is sometimes based on pieces produced per unit of time, such as number of pieces produced per hour.

MasterSport has a biweekly pay period of 80 hours. The basic salary may be supplemented by other types of earnings. For example, in addition to a basic biweekly salary, an employee may receive commissions, cost-of-living adjustments, a share of profits, or a bonus.

MasterSport has three types of employee earnings. First, an hourly salary is paid biweekly to sales clerks and accounting department employees. Second, a biweekly salary is paid to each of the two department supervisors and the store manager. Third, a monthly commission is also paid to each of the department supervisors.

PREPARING A DEPARTMENTAL PAYROLL

MasterSport's payroll system shows the amount of employee benefits, salaries, and withholdings for each employee and each department.

Benefits Authorization

A benefits authorization form is used to record and authorize employee benefits. MasterSport pays employee benefits biweekly on 80 hours of continuous work. Employee benefits are not paid for hours in excess of 80 hours per pay period.

At the beginning of the pay period, the accounting department records employee benefits in the Hours Avail. column of a benefits authorization form. Each employee authorization form is then forwarded to the appropriate department supervisor or store manager. The department supervisor or store manager records employee benefits hours used on the benefits authorization form as they are used during each pay period. Sales clerks and accounting department employees must have their employee benefits authorized by their department supervisor. Department supervisors must have their employee benefits authorized by the store manager.

At the end of the pay period, the completed benefits authorization forms are returned to the accounting department. Virginia Ames' benefits authorization form, completed by department supervisor Marilyn Caulder for the pay period ended July 2, is shown in Illustration 4-2.

APPLY

Ask working students to share with the class the benefits that they receive from their employer. Refer students to Illustration 4-3 as the benefits record is presented. Select a student who works for a business using a time card to review the procedures for completing the time card. Refer students to Illustration 4-4.

Guided Practice

- Guide students through calculating total earnings for Employees Nos. 1 and 2 in Problem 4-2. Working as a group, have the students calculate the amounts for Employee No. 1. Have students verify the amounts by comparing them with the answers given as the example. Next, have students calculate the amounts for Employee No. 2. When all students agree on the correct amounts, direct students to record the amounts on the form in the working papers. The balance of Problem 4-2 can be completed as Independent Practice.
- Guide students through Instructions 1-4 for Employee 3, Janet Aguilar, in Problem 4-3. Refer students to Illustration 4-1 for the employee benefits and the working papers for Aguilar's benefits authorization form. Working as a group, have students complete Aguilar's benefits record. When all students agree, direct them to record the amounts on Aguilar's benefits record and time card in the working papers. Next, as a group, have students calculate Aguilar's hours worked. When all agree, direct students to record the amounts on Aguilar's time card. Finally, have students calculate Aguilar's earnings. When all agree, direct students to record the amounts on the time card. The balance of Problem 4-3 can be completed as Independent Practice.

Independent Practice

Assign Terms 1–5; Questions 1–7; Problems 4-1, 4-2, 4-3, and 4-4.

ASSESS

Assess student understanding by checking the solutions to the Independent Practice activities.

Reteach

Make transparencies of the benefits record and commissions record from the accounting forms masters provided in the Blackline Masters section of the Teacher's Resource Guide. Use data from Recycling Problem 4-R, Instructions 1–2, and the transparencies to demonstrate how to complete these forms.

Extend

- Assign Cases for Critical Thinking 1.
- Assign the Spreadsheet Template for Problems 4-1 and 4-4.

CLOSURE

Use Audit Your Understanding questions.

ILLUSTRATION 4-2 Benefits authorization

BENEFITS AUTHORIZATION

EMPLOYEE NO. *7* EMPLOYEE *Virginia C. Ames*

PAY PERIOD ENDED *7/2/--* DEPARTMENT *Golf*

	HOURS AVAIL.	M	T	W	T	F	S	M	T	W	T	F	S	HOURS USED
VACATION	*32*			*8*										*8*
SICK LEAVE	*40*							*4*						*4*
PERSONAL LEAVE	*24*										*1*			*1*

MANAGER (only if needed) ______ *Marilyn A. Caulder* DEPARTMENT SUPERVISOR ______ *7/2/--* DATE

Ms. Ames' benefits authorization shows the hours available at the beginning of the pay period. The form also shows the authorized vacation, sick leave, and personal leave time used during the pay period. Eight hours of vacation time were used on Wednesday of the first week. Four hours of sick leave time were used on Monday, and one hour of personal leave time was used on Thursday of the second week. The department supervisor signs and forwards the benefits authorization to the accounting department.

FYI

Beginning hours available plus hours earned minus hours used equals accumulated hours available on the benefits record.

Benefits Record

Detailed information about each employee's benefits is summarized in a benefits record. A benefits record is used to summarize total benefits earned, used, and available at the end of each pay period.

MasterSport keeps its benefits records on printed sheets. One sheet is used for each employee. Each sheet covers a calendar year. Since a biweekly payroll system has 26 pay periods in a calendar year, MasterSport's benefits record has 26 lines. One line is used to summarize employee benefits for each pay period. Accumulated employee benefits available at the end of one calendar year are brought forward and recorded on the next year's benefits record. Virginia Ames' benefits record for the current year is shown in Illustration 4-3.

For the first pay period ended January 2, Virginia Ames' accumulated hours available from the last pay period of the previous year are entered in the Begin. Hours Avail. columns, columns 1, 5, and 9. Accumulated vacation time hours available, *74,* are taken from column 4 of the previous year's benefits record. These hours are entered on line 1 in the Vacation Time Begin. Hours Avail. column, column 1, of the current benefits record. The accumulated sick leave time hours, *28,* are taken from column 8 of the previous year's benefits record. These hours are entered on line 1 in the Sick Leave Time Begin. Hours Avail. column, column 5, of the current benefits record. The accumulated personal leave time hours, *23,* are taken from column 12 of the previous year's benefits record. These hours are entered on line 1 in the Personal Leave Time Begin. Hours

ILLUSTRATION 4-3 Benefits record

BENEFITS RECORD

EMPLOYEE NO. *7* EMPLOYEE NAME *Virginia C. Ames* DEPARTMENT *Golf*

DATE OF INITIAL EMPLOYMENT *April 6, 1981* YEAR *19--*

		1	2	3	4	5	6	7	8	9	10	11	12
	PAY PERIOD ENDED	VACATION TIME				SICK LEAVE TIME				PERSONAL LEAVE TIME			
		BEGIN. HOURS AVAIL.	HOURS EARNED	HOURS USED	ACC. HOURS AVAIL.	BEGIN. HOURS AVAIL.	HOURS EARNED	HOURS USED	ACC. HOURS AVAIL.	BEGIN. HOURS AVAIL.	HOURS EARNED	HOURS USED	ACC. HOURS AVAIL.
1	*1/2*	*74*	*4*	*8*	*70*	*28*	*2*	*0*	*30*	*23*	*1*	*0*	*24*
2	*1/16*	*70*	*4*	*0*	*74*	*30*	*2*	*4*	*28*	*24*	*1*	*4*	*21*
11	*5/21*	*26*	*4*	*4*	*26*	*34*	*2*	*0*	*36*	*25*	*1*	*0*	*26*
12	*6/4*	*26*	*4*	*0*	*30*	*36*	*2*	*0*	*38*	*26*	*1*	*4*	*23*
13	*6/18*	*30*	*4*	*2*	*32*	*38*	*2*	*0*	*40*	*23*	*1*	*0*	*24*
14	*7/2*	*32*	*4*	*8*	*28*	*40*	*2*	*4*	*38*	*24*	*1*	*1*	*24*
15													

SOFTWARE FOCUS

Software may be used for independent practice or enrichment/extension as the instructor deems appropriate. For this chapter, the Spreadsheet Template may be used with Problems 4-1, 4-4, and 4-5.

Avail. column, column 9, of the current benefits record. Beginning hours available *plus* hours earned *minus* hours used *equals* the accumulated hours available at the end of a pay period. For example, the vacation time accumulated hours available for the pay period ended January 2 are calculated as shown below.

Vacation Time Beginning Hours Available	+	Vacation Time Hours Earned	−	Vacation Time Hours Used	=	Vacation Time Accumulated Hours Available
74	+	4	−	8	=	70

The hours available at the end of one pay period are carried forward as the beginning hours available for the next pay period. For example, 70 vacation hours are available after the pay period ended January 2. The number of hours, *70,* is carried forward on the benefits record, line 2, column 1, as the next period's beginning vacation hours available. Sick leave time and personal leave time are recorded in the same way.

After each employee benefits record is completed, the employee benefits hours available are recorded on each employee benefits authorization form. The accounting department sends the benefits authorization forms to the appropriate department supervisor or store manager for use during the next pay period. The accounting department also records employee benefits on employee time cards.

Payroll Time Card

MasterSport is open for business six days a week from 9:00 a.m. until 6:00 p.m. However, employees usually work only a five-day week of 40 hours. Days worked during a week vary so that enough

93

Spreadsheet Options

The SPREADSHEET OPTIONS feature is intended to expose students to a variety of ways to use spreadsheets. As an optional activity, students may use their spreadsheet software to duplicate the example shown in the spreadsheet options feature. They may also create new sets of data to do what-if analyses.

Spreadsheet Options

USING THE TITLES COMMAND

The preparation of a payroll requires many mathematical calculations. However, the calculations are usually the same for every payroll period. The formulas for the spreadsheet can be set up and used for each pay period for the new payroll data. As a result, a payroll register is an excellent application for an electronic spreadsheet.

A payroll register requires more space than displayed by most spreadsheets. By using the spreadsheet titles command, part of the spreadsheet can be locked or frozen on the screen. Other parts of the spreadsheet can then be scrolled while the frozen part stays in view. Therefore, the spreadsheet titles command is an effective tool to view specific columns of a large spreadsheet.

The spreadsheet in the first illustration shows the deductions portion of a payroll register. To key $20.00 as a deduction in the Other Deductions column for Jereme Wagner, the amount would be keyed in cell T30. However, when the cursor is moved to cell T30, the horizontal and vertical titles of the payroll register scroll off the screen. This screen shows that it is impossible to verify that the $20.00 deduction is being keyed in the correct cell.

The second screen illustration shows the same spreadsheet after a titles command is executed. Notice that Rows 1-9 and Columns A-C are locked on the screen. The horizontal and vertical titles of the payroll register are now visible when the cell pointer is on cell T30. It is now easy to see that the $20.00 deduction was correctly input for Jereme Wagner in the Other Deductions column.

```
T30: (,2) [W10] 20                                                        READY

     M     N          O     P    Q          R          S          T          U     V
25         0.00     680.00       86.00      34.00      54.40                 174.40
26         0.00     596.75       48.00      29.84      47.74      10.00      135.58
27       820.00       0.00       84.00      41.00      65.60                 190.60
28         0.00     688.00       63.00      34.40      55.04                 152.44
29         0.00     560.00       68.00      28.00      44.80                 140.80
30         0.00     560.00       68.00      28.00      44.80      20.00      160.80
31         0.00     600.00       51.00      30.00      48.00                 129.00
32       756.50       0.00       95.00      37.83      60.52                 193.35
33    ------------------ ----------------------------------------------
34    7,172.25 7,957.88  1,442.00     756.52 1,210.41     130.00 3,538.93
35    ================== ==============================================
```

```
T30: (,2) [W10] 20                                                        READY

     A     B          C          Q          R          S          T          U     V
1
2       Pay Period Ended:
3       Date of Payment:
4                                                Deductions
5                             ---------------------------------------------
6                               Federal    State
7    Empl.                      Income     Income     FICA
8    No.  Employee's Name       Tax        Tax        Tax        Other      Total
9    -----------------------  ---------------------------------------------
25    21 Peters, John            86.00      34.00      54.40                 174.40
26    22 Rackley, William        48.00      29.84      47.74      10.00      135.58
27    17 Read, Elliot            84.00      41.00      65.60                 190.60
28     9 Rudis, Alan             63.00      34.40      55.04                 152.44
29    16 Thomas, Prentiss        68.00      28.00      44.80                 140.80
30    18 Wagner, Jereme          68.00      28.00      44.80      20.00      160.80
31    20 Welch, Randy            51.00      30.00      48.00                 129.00
32    23 Williams, Grady         95.00      37.83      60.52                 193.35
33                            ---------------------------------------------
34                            1,442.00     756.52 1,210.41     130.00 3,538.93
35                            =============================================
```

employees are available for each of the six days the business is open. For example, one employee may work Monday through Friday while another employee may work Tuesday through Saturday.

MasterSport's sales clerks and accounting employees are paid an hourly salary for the two regular 40-hour work weeks in each pay period. All time worked in excess of 8 hours in any one day is considered overtime. Employees are paid 1½ times the regular rate for overtime hours. MasterSport uses a time clock to record regular and overtime hours worked by each employee paid an hourly salary.

In MasterSport's time-clock system, a payroll time card is inserted in the time clock each time an employee arrives for work and leaves work. A time clock records the time on a payroll time card when a card is inserted.

Virginia Ames' time card for the pay period ended July 2 is shown in Illustration 4-4.

FYI

Each employee must complete a Form W-4, Employees Withholding Allowance Certificate.

ILLUSTRATION 4-4

Payroll time card

NAME Virginia C. Ames
DEPARTMENT Golf
EMPLOYEE NO. 7
PAY PERIOD ENDED 7/2/--

MORNING		AFTERNOON		OVERTIME		HOURS	
IN	OUT	IN	OUT	IN	OUT	REG	OT
M 9:00	M 1:01	M 2:00	M 6:03	M 7:00	M 9:02	8	2
T 8:58	T 1:00	T 1:59	T 6:00			8	
						V8	
T 8:59	T 1:02	T 2:01	T 6:00			8	
F 9:00	F 1:00	F 2:00	F 6:01			8	
M 8:57	M 1:00					4S4	
T 8:59	T 12:58	T 2:00	T 6:00			8	
W 9:01	W 1:02	W 2:00	W 6:02			8	
T 9:03	T 12:59	T 3:01	T 6:00			7P1	
F 9:00	F 1:01	F 2:00	F 6:01	F 6:29	F 9:31	8	3

	HOURS	RATE	AMOUNT
REGULAR	80	6.00	480.00
OVERTIME	5	9.00	45.00
TOTAL HOURS	85	TOTAL EARNINGS	525.00

The time card shows that Ms. Ames had a total of 80 *regular* hours for the biweekly pay period. Her lunch period is from 1:00 to 2:00 p.m. daily. Her time card also shows that she worked 5 *overtime* hours—2 hours on Monday of the first week and 3 hours on Friday of the second week.

At the end of the biweekly pay period, the accounting department enters the authorized employee benefit hours on the payroll time cards. The employee benefits hours are shown by the first letter of the benefit written next to the hours. Ms. Ames' time card, Illustration 4-4, shows *V8* written in the Hours Reg column for

APPLIED SKILLS: WRITING ACROSS THE CURRICULUM

Writing paragraphs and short essays. The Cases for Critical Thinking are short, practical applications of the accounting principles developed in the chapter. Some cases are planned to present problems related to the chapter but not specifically discussed and answered in the chapter. These cases present an opportunity for critical thinking and decision making. These cases also require more than a short objective-type response. Therefore they provide ideal practice in writing paragraphs and short essays.

Wednesday of the first week. Ms. Ames gets credit for 8 regular hours for the day even though the hours represented vacation time. *S4* is written next to the 4 hours of regular hours worked on Monday of the second week to show that 4 hours were used for sick leave time. *P1* is written next to the 7 hours of regular time worked on Thursday of the second week to show that 1 hour was used for personal leave time.

The number of hours for Ms. Ames is determined to be 85. Using the 85 hours, Ms. Ames' biweekly earnings are calculated. Ms. Ames' regular salary is $480.00 (80 hours × $6.00 per hour). Ms. Ames' overtime pay is $45.00 (5 hours × $6.00 × 1.5). The regular salary, $480.00, *plus* the overtime salary, $45.00, *equals* the total earnings, $525.00.

TEACHING STRATEGIES: DIFFERENT LEARNING ABILITIES

At-Risk Students. Together with the student, develop an individualized program that allows the student to attain both short-term and long-term goals. When identifying goals, consider the student's anticipated career goals.

Commissions Record

Supervisors for each of the two departments—golf and tennis—are paid a regular biweekly salary. They are not paid for overtime hours. However, to encourage increased sales, the supervisors are paid a 1% commission on the department's monthly net sales.

The store manager is paid a regular biweekly salary and receives no salary for overtime hours. The store manager, however, normally receives an annual bonus based on the sales record for both departments.

Commissions for the previous month's net sales are included with the first biweekly pay period of a month. A commissions record is used to record the data necessary to calculate each department supervisor's commission. MasterSport's commissions record for Marilyn Caulder, golf department supervisor, is shown in Illustration 4-5.

ILLUSTRATION 4-5 Commissions record

COMMISSIONS RECORD

EMPLOYEE NO. *3* EMPLOYEE NAME *Marilyn A. Caulder*

COMMISSION *1%* MONTH *June* YEAR *19--*

DEPT. *Golf* REGULAR BIWEEKLY SALARY *$450.00*

Sales			
Sales on Account		$ *8,990.65*	
Cash and Credit Card Sales		*24,520.00*	
Total Sales		$ *33,510.65*	
Less: Sales Discounts	$ *147.00*		
Sales Returns and Allowances	*480.00*	*627.00*	
Net Sales			$ *32,883.65*
Commission on Net Sales			$ *328.84*

General information is recorded at the top of the form. The sales on account for June, *$8,990.65,* are obtained from the sales journal, Illustration 3-4, Chapter 3. The cash and credit card sales for June, *$24,520.00,* are obtained from the cash receipts journal, Illustration 3-6, Chapter 3. The sales discount amount for June, *$147.00,* is also obtained from the cash receipts journal, Illustration 3-6. The sales returns and allowances for June, *$480.00,* are obtained from the sales returns and allowances journal, Illustration 3-5, Chapter 3. Commission on net sales for Marilyn Caulder is calculated as shown below.

Net Sales	×	Commission Rate	=	Commission on Net Sales
$32,883.65	×	1%	=	$328.84

Payroll Deductions

MasterSport is required by law to withhold two federal taxes from each employee's pay: federal income tax and FICA tax. FICA tax is also known as social security tax. FICA is the abbreviation for the Federal Insurance Contributions Act.

Some cities and states also require that employers deduct amounts for income and other taxes from employee earnings. Laws for handling state, city, and county taxes vary.

Some businesses also have deductions from employee earnings for health insurance, life insurance, pension plans, and savings deposits. MasterSport makes deductions from its employee salaries for federal income tax, state income tax, FICA tax, health insurance, and life insurance.

Audit Your Understanding

1. Why are payroll taxes reported as separate items in accounting records and financial statements?
2. Why are employee benefits provided by most businesses?
3. If an employee of MasterSport has a regular salary rate of $8.00 and works 5 hours of overtime during the biweekly period, what is the employee's overtime pay for the period?
4. What two federal taxes are withheld from an employee's pay?

COMPLETING PAYROLL RECORDS

A business must complete a number of payroll records in order to provide the payroll information required by governmental agencies.

Preparing a Payroll Register

A business form used to record payroll information is called a **payroll register.** A payroll register summarizes the payroll for one pay period and shows total earnings, amounts withheld, and net pay for all employees.

MasterSport prepares a separate payroll register for each biweekly payroll. MasterSport's payroll register for the biweekly pay period ended July 2 is shown in Illustration 4-6.

AUDIT YOUR UNDERSTANDING

The AUDIT YOUR UNDERSTANDING feature appears at the end of each section of the chapter. Explain to your students that the word *audit* means to check or verify. AUDIT YOUR UNDERSTANDING may be used to check student comprehension of the section just studied. The answers are provided in Appendix D in the back of the textbook.

1. Because the taxes represent a business transaction with dollar amounts large enough to affect business decisions.
2. As a reward for continuous service.
3. $60.00 (5 hours times $8.00 times 1.5)
4. Federal income tax and FICA tax.

LESSON PLAN 4-2

Materials

- Student pages 97–104
- Blackline Master for Payroll Register (TRG)
- Blackline Master for Employee Earnings Record (TRG)
- Software: Spreadsheet Template

Objectives (Enabling Performance Tasks)

a. Define accounting terms related to a departmental payroll system.
b. Identify accounting concepts and practices related to a departmental payroll system.
c. Complete payroll records.

FOCUS

- In the first-year course, a payroll register and employee earnings records were completed. In this lesson, a payroll register and employee earnings records for a departmental payroll system will be prepared. Explain that some of the information used to complete these payroll records comes from the commissions records and time cards presented earlier in this chapter.
- Introduce vocabulary: payroll register, withholding allowance, tax base, employee earnings record.

TEACHING STRATEGIES: APPLYING VISUALS

Direct students to Illustration 4-6 to review preparing a payroll register.

TEACH

Cover student pages 97–104 "Completing Payroll Records." Present the payroll register and explain how it is completed. Emphasize the columns that are special for a departmental payroll system. Explain how information from the commissions records and time cards is used to complete the payroll register. When presenting the Deductions columns, review the use of tax tables and show students how to find tax amounts. Also, review calculating payroll taxes using percentages. Demonstrate how to calculate net pay. Explain how the payroll register is proved and ruled. Point out that check numbers are not recorded in the check number column until the checks are actually written. Present the employee earnings record and explain how it is completed. Explain that information needed to complete the employee earnings record is obtained from the payroll register. Explain how to calculate accumulated earnings. Emphasize that accumulated earnings are the earnings the employee has made up to the current pay period. Total earnings are added to the accumulated earnings—not the net pay column.

ILLUSTRATION 4-6 Payroll register (left side)

PAY PERIOD ENDED *July 2, 19--* PAYROLL REGISTER

	1	2	3	4	5	6	7	8	9	
						EARNINGS				
	EMPL. NO.	EMPLOYEE NAME	MARITAL STATUS	NO. OF ALLOWANCES	TOTAL HOURS	REGULAR	OVERTIME	COMMISSION	TOTAL	
1	*7*	*Ames, Virginia C.*	*M*	*3*	*85*	*480 00*	*45 00*		*525 00*	1
2	*10*	*Caulder, Marilyn A.*	*S*	*1*	*—*	*450 00*		*328 84*	*778 84*	2
3	*16*	*Cole, David M.*	*M*	*2*	*82*	*440 00*	*16 50*		*456 50*	3
4	*9*	*Fabel, Sean L.*	*S*	*1*	*80*	*464 00*			*464 00*	4
5	*15*	*Felice, Jeffrey R.*	*M*	*2*	*—*	*600 00*			*600 00*	5
6	*11*	*Fye, Amy L.*	*M*	*3*	*83*	*448 00*	*25 20*		*473 20*	6
15	*8*	*Roberts, Claud P.*	*S*	*1*	*82*	*464 00*	*17 40*		*481 40*	15
16						*7 090 00*	*194 10*	*674 30*	*7 958 40*	16
17										17
18										18

Entering Basic Employee Data in a Payroll Register. The last day of the biweekly payroll period, *July 2,* is entered at the top of the payroll register. The date of payment, *July 9,* is also entered at the top of the payroll register. The time between the end of a pay period and the date of payment is needed to prepare the payroll records and payroll checks. Employee No., Name, Marital Status, and No. of Allowances are taken from personnel records kept for each employee. The payroll register, Illustration 4-6, line 1, columns 1-4, shows the basic employee data for Virginia Ames.

For each person supported, including the employee, an employee is entitled to a reduction in the amount on which income tax is calculated. A deduction from total earnings for each person legally supported by a taxpayer is called a **withholding allowance**.

Entering Data from Time Cards in a Payroll Register. The time card, Illustration 4-4, shows the hours worked and the earnings for Virginia Ames. This payroll information is entered in the payroll register on the line with the employee's name. The payroll register, line 1, columns 5-9, shows the information from Virginia Ames' time card.

Entering Data from Commissions Records in a Payroll Register. The commissions record, Illustration 4-5, shows information about Marilyn Caulder's commission for June. Department supervisors do not account for their hourly time on a time card. A line is therefore drawn through the Total Hours column, column 5, as shown on line 2 of the payroll register. Each department supervisor's salary remains the same for each biweekly pay period. Therefore, the salary amount is recorded in the Regular Earnings column, column 6. Commissions from the commissions records are entered in the

TEACHING STRATEGIES: TEACHING TIP

Provide extensive practice in calculating payroll earnings, deductions, and net pay. Placing payroll data on an overhead projector or chalkboard and having students make calculations and use withholding tables at their desks provides a valuable learning experience.

ILLUSTRATION 4-6 Payroll register (right side)

DATE OF PAYMENT *July 9, 19--* PAYROLL REGISTER

	10	11	12	13	14	15	16	17	18	19	
	DEPARTMENT		ADMIN. SALARIES	DEDUCTIONS					PAID		
	GOLF	TENNIS		FEDERAL INCOME TAX	STATE INCOME TAX	FICA TAX	OTHER	TOTAL	NET PAY	CHECK NO.	
1	525 00			28 00	26 25	42 00	H 28 00 L 12 80	137 05	387 95	246	1
2	778 84			98 00	38 94	62 31	H 16 00	215 25	563 59	247	2
3			456 50	28 00	22 83	36 52	H 28 00	115 35	341 15	248	3
4		464 00		52 00	23 20	37 12	H 16 00 L 12 80	141 12	322 88	249	4
5			600 00	51 00	30 00	48 00	H 28 00 L 12 80	169 80	430 20	250	5
6		473 20		20 00	23 66	37 86	H 28 00	109 52	363 68	251	6
15	481 40			55 00	24 07	38 51	H 16 00	133 58	347 82	260	15
16	3695 04	2742 86	1520 50	667 00	397 92	636 67	H 360 00 L 64 00	2125 59	5832 81		16
17											17
18											18

Commission Earnings column, column 8. Regular Earnings, column 6, and Commission Earnings, column 8, are added together to determine Total Earnings for the biweekly pay period.

Entering Departmental and Administrative Salaries in a Payroll Register. Time cards and commissions records show the department to be charged for each employee's total earnings. Total earnings are entered in columns 10 or 11 of the payroll register according to the department in which the employee works. Salaries of non-sales employees, such as accounting department employees, are entered in the Admin. Salaries column, column 12. The store manager's salary is also entered in column 12 on line 5.

The payroll register, line 1, column 10, shows that Virginia Ames' salary is charged to the golf department. The entry on line 4, column 11, shows that Sean Fabel's salary is charged to the tennis department.

Entering Deductions for Employee Federal Income Tax. The federal income tax amount to be withheld from each employee's total earnings is determined from withholding tables furnished by the federal government. Partial federal income tax tables for biweekly payroll periods are shown in Illustration 4-7.

Tax rates change from time to time. Rates used in this textbook are those in effect at the time this book was written.

An employee's total earnings, marital status, and number of withholding allowances claimed determine the federal income tax amount to be withheld. For example, Virginia Ames' total earnings for the biweekly pay period ended July 2 are $525.00. Virginia is married and claims 3 allowances. The two columns at the left of

APPLY

Refer students to Illustration 4-6 as the procedures for preparing the payroll register are presented. Ask students to use the federal income tax tables in Illustration 4-7 to locate the amount of tax withheld for each employee. Ask students to verify the calculation of net pay for each employee in the payroll register shown in Illustration 4-6.

Guided Practice

- Guide students through the completion of line 1 of the payroll register in Problem 4-5 for Employee No. 3, Janet Aguilar. Students will need Aguilar's time card completed in Problem 4-3. Working as a group, have students record Aguilar's earnings in the payroll register provided in the working papers. Then, refer students to the tax tables in Illustration 4-7 to determine Aguilar's withholding tax. When students agree, have them record the amount in the payroll register. Next, have students calculate the state income tax and FICA tax on Aguilar's earnings. When the students agree, direct them to record the amounts in the payroll register. Finally, have students record the amounts for dental and health insurance and determine net pay. Be sure that all students have recorded the correct amounts in their payroll registers. The balance of Problem 4-5 can be completed as Independent Practice.
- Guide students through the completion of the employee earnings record for Janet Aguilar in Problem 4-6. Students will need the payroll register completed in Problem 4-5. Working as a group, have students use the information from the payroll register to complete Aguilar's employee earnings record. Students should agree on each amount before they record it on the record. The balance of Problem 4-6 can be completed as Independent Practice.

Independent Practice

Assign Terms 6–9; Questions 8–11; Problems 4-5 and 4-6.

ASSESS

Assess student understanding by checking the solutions to the Independent Practice activities.

Reteach

Make transparencies of the payroll register and employee earnings record from the accounting forms masters provided in the Blackline Masters section of the Teacher's Resource Guide. Using the information from Recycling Problem 4-R, Instructions 3 and 4, demonstrate how to complete lines 1 and 2 of the payroll register for Employees Nos. 1 and 2. Demonstrate how to complete the employee earnings record for Employee No. 2. Accumulated earnings for the first three pay periods is $1,575.00.

Extend

Assign the Spreadsheet Template for Problem 4-5.

Enrich

Assign the SPREADSHEET OPTIONS feature on page 94.

CLOSURE

Use Audit Your Understanding questions.

ILLUSTRATION 4-7 Sections of income tax withholding tables for biweekly pay period

BIWEEKLY PAYROLL PERIOD — SINGLE PERSONS

And the wages are–		And the number of withholding allowances claimed is–										
At least	But less than	0	1	2	3	4	5	6	7	8	9	10
		The amount of income tax to be withheld shall be–										
430	440	59	48	37	25	14	3					
440	450	61	49	38	27	16	4					
450	460	62	51	40	28	17	6					
460	470	64	52	41	30	19	7					
470	480	65	54	43	31	20	9					
480	490	67	55	44	33	22	10					
490	500	68	57	46	34	23	12	1				
500	520	70	59	48	37	25	14	3				
520	540	73	62	51	40	28	17	6				
540	560	76	65	54	43	31	20	9				
560	580	79	68	57	46	34	23	12	1			
580	600	82	71	60	49	37	26	15	4			
600	620	85	74	63	52	40	29	18	7			
620	640	88	77	66	55	43	32	21	10			
640	660	91	80	69	58	46	35	24	13	1		
660	680	94	83	72	61	49	38	27	16	4		
680	700	97	86	75	64	52	41	30	19	7		
700	720	100	89	78	67	55	44	33	22	10		
720	740	104	92	81	70	58	47	36	25	13	2	
740	760	109	95	84	73	61	50	39	28	16	5	
760	780	115	98	87	76	64	53	42	31	19	8	
780	800	121	101	90	79	67	56	45	34	22	11	
800	820	126	105	93	82	70	59	48	37	25	14	3
820	840	132	111	96	85	73	62	51	40	28	17	6
840	860	137	116	99	88	76	65	54	43	31	20	9

BIWEEKLY
SINGLE PERSONS

BIWEEKLY PAYROLL PERIOD — MARRIED PERSONS

And the wages are–		And the number of withholding allowances claimed is–										
At least	But less than	0	1	2	3	4	5	6	7	8	9	10
		The amount of income tax to be withheld shall be–										
380	390	40	29	18	6							
390	400	42	30	19	8							
400	410	43	32	21	9							
410	420	45	33	22	11							
420	430	46	35	24	12	1						
430	440	48	36	25	14	3						
440	450	49	38	27	15	4						
450	460	51	39	28	17	6						
460	470	52	41	30	18	7						
470	480	54	42	31	20	9						
480	490	55	44	33	21	10						
490	500	57	45	34	23	12						
500	520	59	48	36	25	14	3					
520	540	62	51	39	28	17	6					
540	560	65	54	42	31	20	9					
560	580	68	57	45	34	23	12					
580	600	71	60	48	37	26	15	3				
600	620	74	63	51	40	29	18	6				
620	640	77	66	54	43	32	21	9				
640	660	80	69	57	46	35	24	12	1			
660	680	83	72	60	49	38	27	15	4			
680	700	86	75	63	52	41	30	18	7			
700	720	89	78	66	55	44	33	21	10			
720	740	92	81	69	58	47	36	24	13	2		
740	760	95	84	72	61	50	39	27	16	5		
760	780	98	87	75	64	53	42	30	19	8		
780	800	101	90	78	67	56	45	33	22	11		
800	820	104	93	81	70	59	48	36	25	14	3	
820	840	107	96	84	73	62	51	39	28	17	6	
840	860	110	99	87	76	65	54	42	31	20	9	

BIWEEKLY
MARRIED PERSONS

the tax table for married persons show ranges of earnings amounts. The total earnings amount, *$525.00,* is in the range of "at least 520 but less than 540." The withholding amount, *$28.00,* is found on the same line in the column at the right with a *3* at the top. The federal income tax deduction, *$28.00,* is recorded in the payroll register, line 1, column 13.

Entering Deductions for Employee State Income Tax. The state in which MasterSport operates has an income tax on the total earn-

FYI

When an employee's earnings exceed the tax base, no more FICA tax is deducted.

ings of its residents. The state provides withholding tables to employers to determine the state income tax amount to be withheld from employee earnings. The state income tax deduction can also be calculated by using a percentage of total earnings. Ms. Ames' state income tax deduction, *$26.25,* is entered in the payroll register, line 1, column 14.

Entering Deductions for Employee FICA Tax. The FICA tax is calculated on employee earnings paid in a calendar year. The maximum amount of earnings on which a tax is calculated is referred to as a tax base. Congress sets the tax base and the tax rates for FICA tax. An act of Congress can change the tax base and tax rate at any time.

Congress has limited the amount of FICA tax that each individual must pay. The FICA tax is not calculated on total earnings over a specific maximum amount. The maximum amount of earnings on which a tax is calculated is called a **tax base**.

The FICA tax rate is a combination of two different tax rates: (1) a tax for old-age, survivors, and disability and (2) a tax for Medicare. The two taxes also have different tax bases. The FICA tax rates and bases used in this text are shown below.

	Tax Rate	Tax Base
Old-age, survivors, and disability	6.5%	Earnings up to $55,500
Medicare	1.5%	Earnings up to $130,200
Total	8.0%	

Therefore, the effective FICA tax rate for earnings up to the tax base of $55,500 is 8.0% (6.5% + 1.5%). The additional FICA tax rate for earnings from $55,500 to $130,200 is 1.5%.

Accounting procedures are the same regardless of changes in tax bases and tax rates. Therefore, the FICA tax rates and the tax bases shown above are assumed for all payroll calculations in this textbook.

Virginia Ames' FICA tax deduction for the biweekly pay period ended July 2 is calculated as shown below.

Total Earnings	×	FICA Tax Rate	=	FICA Tax Deduction
$525.00	×	8%	=	$42.00

Ms. Ames' FICA tax deduction, *$42.00,* is recorded in the payroll register on line 1, column 15.

Entering Employee Other Deductions. Besides income taxes and FICA tax, some employees have two other deductions.

1. *Health insurance.* This deduction is $16.00 per biweekly pay period for each insured single employee claiming one allowance. The deduction is $28.00 for each married employee and each single employee claiming more than one dependent. This deduction is written in the payroll register, column 16. The health insurance deduction is identified by writing the letter *H* in front of the amount.
2. *Life insurance.* This deduction is $12.80 per biweekly pay period for employees desiring life insurance. Not all employees have life insurance premiums deducted from their earnings. This amount is written in the payroll register, column 16. The deduction is identified by writing the letter *L* in front of the amount.

Ms. Ames' deductions for health insurance, *H28.00,* and life insurance, *L12.80,* are entered in the payroll register, line 1, column 16.

APPLIED SKILLS: LANGUAGE ARTS

Paraphrasing, writing complete sentences, and identifying adjectives and the words they modify. For additional practice in language arts skills, direct students to answer the Accounting Terms and Questions for Individual Study at the end of the chapter. Students should write the answers in their own words and in complete sentences. To further practice language arts skills ask students to underline the adjectives and circle the words they modify in their definitions.

Calculating Net Pay in a Payroll Register

After all deductions are entered in the payroll register, the amounts for deductions are added and the total is written in column 17. The net pay is then figured by subtracting the total deductions, column 17, from total earnings, column 9. The net pay for Virginia Ames is calculated as shown below.

Total Earnings (column 9)	–	Total Deductions (column 17)	=	Net Pay (column 18)
$525.00	–	$137.05	=	$387.95

Ms. Ames' net pay, *$387.95,* is entered in the payroll register, line 1, column 18.

Proving a Payroll Register's Accuracy

FYI

The check number column of the payroll register is not completed until the check has been written.

When the net pay has been entered for all employees, each payroll register amount column is totaled. The Total Deductions column is subtracted from the Total Earnings column. The result should equal the total of the Net Pay column. If the totals do not agree, the errors must be found and corrected. Proving the accuracy of MasterSport's payroll register for pay period ended July 2 is shown below.

Total Earnings (column 9)	–	Total Deductions (column 17)	=	Net Pay (column 18)
$7,958.40	–	$2,125.59	=	$5,832.81

The net pay, *$5,832.81,* is the same as the total of the Net Pay column. The payroll register is proved. After the payroll register is proved, double lines are ruled below all amount column totals to show the totals have been verified as correct.

Preparing an Employee Earnings Record

A business must send a quarterly report to federal and state governments showing employee taxable earnings and taxes withheld from employee earnings. Detailed information about each employee's earnings is summarized in a single record for each employee. A business form used to record details affecting payments made to an employee is called an **employee earnings record.** An employee's total earnings and deductions for each pay period are summarized on one line of the employee earnings record.

MasterSport keeps its employee earnings records on printed cards. A new earnings record is prepared for each employee each quarter. Virginia Ames' earnings record for the third quarter is shown in Illustration 4-8.

TEACHING STRATEGIES: COOPERATIVE LEARNING

Divide the class into groups of four or five students each. Using Cases for Critical Thinking, each group analyzes the cases and arrives at agreed-upon solutions. One member of each group is appointed the recorder and presents the group's analysis to the class. This cooperative learning activity should not take more than 20 to 25 minutes of class time.

ILLUSTRATION 4-8 Employee earnings record

EARNINGS RECORD FOR QUARTER ENDED *Sept. 30, 19--*

EMPLOYEE NO. *7* NAME *Ames, Virginia C.* SOCIAL SECURITY NO. *512-36-7216*

MARITAL STATUS *M* WITHHOLDING ALLOWANCES *3* HOURLY RATE *$6.00* SALARY

DEPARTMENT *Golf* POSITION *Salesclerk*

1	2	3	4	5	6	7	8	9	10
PAY PERIOD		TOTAL EARNINGS	DEDUCTIONS					NET PAY	ACCUMULATED EARNINGS
NO.	ENDED		FEDERAL INCOME TAX	STATE INCOME TAX	FICA TAX	OTHER	TOTAL		6,340 00
1	7/2	525 00	28 00	26 25	42 00	H 28 00 L 12 80	137 05	387 95	6,865 00
2									
3									

The biweekly pay period ended July 2 is the first pay period of the third quarter ended September 30. Virginia Ames' salary and deductions are shown in the first entry on her earnings record.

Information needed to complete the amount columns of an employee earnings record is obtained from amount columns of a payroll register. Ms. Ames' payroll information is obtained from the payroll register, Illustration 4-6, line 1.

The Accumulated Earnings column of the employee earnings record shows the accumulated earnings since the beginning of the fiscal year. Accumulated earnings are often referred to as year-to-date earnings. Accumulated earnings are needed for each employee because certain payroll taxes do not apply after an employee's earnings reach a specified amount. For example, employers pay federal and state unemployment taxes only on the first $7,000.00 of each

FYI

Total earnings are added to the accumulated earnings column, not the net pay column, on the earnings record.

AUDIT YOUR UNDERSTANDING

1. The Other Deductions column.
2. Total Earnings minus Total Deductions equals Net Pay
3. Total earnings for the pay period.

LESSON PLAN 4-3

Materials

- Student pages 104–109
- Assess: Problem Test Chapter 4, MicroExam Chapter 4

Objectives (Enabling Performance Tasks)

a. Define accounting terms related to a departmental payroll system.

b. Identify accounting concepts and practices related to a departmental payroll system.

d. Journalize payroll transactions.

FOCUS

- Recording a payroll was presented earlier in this chapter. In this lesson, information from those payroll records will be used to journalize payroll transactions. Explain that the procedures for journalizing a departmental payroll are similar to the procedures presented in the first-year accounting course.
- Introduce vocabulary: automatic check deposit.

Audit Your Understanding

1. In which column(s) of the payroll register are the deductions for health and life insurance recorded?
2. What is the formula for calculating net pay on the payroll register?
3. What amount is added to the accumulated earnings to get the new accumulated earnings to date?

employee's earnings during a calendar year. FICA taxes also are paid only on a maximum amount determined by law.

The first entry in the Accumulated Earnings column, *$6,340.00,* is Ms. Ames' accumulated earnings for the first two quarters ended June 30. The total earnings for the pay period ended July 2, *$525.00,* are added to the accumulated earnings to get the new accumulated earnings to date. The new accumulated earnings amount, *$6,865.00,* is entered on the same line as the other payroll information for the pay period ended July 2.

PAYING A PAYROLL

MasterSport pays its employees biweekly by check. A special payroll checking account and special payroll checks are used.

Payroll Bank Account

After a biweekly payroll register has been completed, a check is written on MasterSport's general checking account payable to *Payroll* for the total net pay. This check is deposited in a special payroll checking account against which payroll checks are written for each employee's net pay.

FYI

A special payroll check account for writing checks for individual employee net pay provides an internal control. Only payroll checks are written from this account.

The amount of the biweekly deposit to the payroll account equals the sum of the biweekly salary payments. The special payroll account balance, therefore, is reduced to zero as soon as all employees have cashed their payroll checks. Because the special payroll bank account has a balance only until all payroll checks are cashed, no special account is needed in the general ledger.

Automatic Check Deposit

Employees may authorize an employer to deposit payroll checks directly in their checking account at a specified bank. Depositing payroll checks directly to an employee's checking or savings account in a specific bank is called **automatic check deposit.** When automatic check deposit is used, the employer sends the check to the employee's bank for deposit.

In addition to automatic check deposit, electronic funds transfer (EFT) can also be used. The net pay amount is transferred electronically from the employer's account directly to the employee's bank account. Electronic funds transfer eliminates the need for preparing payroll checks. Under this system, each employee receives a statement of earnings and deductions similar to the detachable stub on a payroll check.

The use of automatic check deposit or electronic funds transfer for payroll does not change the accounting procedures for recording payroll. *(CONCEPT: Consistent Reporting)*

TEACHING STRATEGIES: EXPANDING BEYOND THE CLASSROOM

Research Activity. Assign students to make a written report on EFT. A local bank will be a good source of information. The student should explain how the EFT is set up with a local bank, how it works, charges, and so on.

JOURNALIZING A PAYROLL

A business' payroll register contains the information needed to journalize a payroll.

Journalizing Payment of a Payroll

The source document for journalizing a payroll payment is the check written for the net payroll amount. *(CONCEPT: Objective Evidence)*

> *July 9, 19--. Paid cash for biweekly payroll, $5,832.81 (total payroll: golf, $3,695.04; tennis, $2,742.86; administrative, $1,520.50; less deductions: employee income tax—federal, $667.00; employee income tax—state, $397.92; FICA tax, $636.67; health insurance, $360.00; life insurance, $64.00). Check No. 370.*

The total net amount paid to all employees for the pay period is the total of column 18 of the payroll register, Illustration 4-6. The department and administrative salaries for the pay period are the totals of columns 10-12 of the payroll register. The deductions are the totals of columns 13-16 of the payroll register.

Salary Expense—Golf	
3,695.04	

Salary Expense—Tennis	
2,742.86	

Salary Expense—Administrative	
1,520.50	

Employee Income Tax Payable—Federal	
	667.00

Employee Income Tax Payable—State	
	397.92

FICA Tax Payable	
	636.67

Health Insurance Premiums Payable	
	360.00

Life Insurance Premiums Payable	
	64.00

Cash	
	5,832.81

Salary Expense—Golf is increased by a $3,695.04 debit. Salary Expense—Tennis is increased by a $2,742.86 debit. Salary Expense—Administrative is increased by a $1,520.50 debit. Employee Income Tax Payable—Federal is increased by a $667.00 credit. Employee Income Tax Payable—State is increased by a $397.92 credit. FICA Tax Payable is increased by a $636.67 credit. Health Insurance Premiums Payable is increased by a $360.00 credit. Life Insurance Premiums Payable is increased by a $64.00 credit. Cash is decreased by a $5,832.81 credit.

TEACH

Cover student pages 104–109 "Paying a Payroll," "Journalizing a Payroll," and "Paying Withholding and Payroll Taxes." Explain the use of a payroll bank account. Explain the advantages of using automatic check deposit or electronic funds transfer. Review the cash payments journal presented in Chapter 2 and explain how to journalize payment of the payroll. Explain how the information for this entry is taken from the payroll register. Describe the three payroll taxes paid by the business and show how they are calculated. Explain that the total of these three taxes is the amount debited to payroll taxes expense. Present the general journal and review how to record the payroll taxes transaction in the journal. Explain when a business must pay payroll taxes and how the payments are recorded in the cash payments journal. Emphasize that employee income tax and FICA tax are paid in one payment.

TEACHING STRATEGIES: TEACHING TIP

Make liberal use of T accounts on the overhead projector or chalkboard to help students review transaction analysis procedures applied to payroll entries.

APPLY

Use T accounts on the overhead projector or chalkboard to show how each transaction in this lesson is analyzed. Refer students to Illustration 4-9 as journalizing payment of the payroll is presented. Refer students to Illustration 4-10 as journalizing employer payroll taxes is discussed. Refer students back to Illustration 4-9 as journalizing payment of withholding and payroll taxes is presented.

Guided Practice

- Guide students through the T account analysis of the payment of the payroll transaction in Problem 4-7, Instruction 1. Students will need the payroll register completed in Problem 4-5. Have students draw T accounts on a sheet of paper. Working as a group, analyze the payment of the payroll transaction. Be sure all students agree with the analysis.
- Guide students through the calculation of the employer payroll taxes in Problem 4-7, Instruction 2. Students will need the payroll register completed in Problem 4-5. Working as a group, have students calculate the employer payroll taxes. Be sure all students have calculated the correct amounts. The balance of Problem 4-7 can be completed as Independent Practice.

Independent Practice

- Assign Term 10; Questions 12–15; Problems 4-7 and 4-8.
- Assign Study Guide 4 and Mastery Problem 4-M.

The journal entry for MasterSport's payroll payment on July 9 is shown on lines 11-18 of the cash payments journal, Illustration 4-9.

ILLUSTRATION 4-9 Journal entry to record payment of a payroll

CASH PAYMENTS JOURNAL — PAGE *13*

	DATE	ACCOUNT TITLE	CK. NO.	POST. REF.	1 GENERAL DEBIT	2 GENERAL CREDIT	3 ACCOUNTS PAYABLE DEBIT	4 PURCH. DISCOUNT CR. GOLF	5 PURCH. DISCOUNT CR. TENNIS	6 CASH CREDIT	
11	9	*Salary Expense—Golf*	*370*		*3,695.04*					*5,832.81*	11
12		*Salary Expense—Tennis*			*2,742.86*						12
13		*Salary Expense—Admin.*			*1,520.50*						13
14		*Emp. Inc. Tax Pay.—Fed.*				*667.00*					14
15		*Emp. Inc. Tax Pay.—State*				*397.92*					15
16		*FICA Tax Payable*				*636.67*					16
17		*Health Ins. Premiums Pay.*				*360.00*					17
18		*Life Ins. Premiums Pay.*				*64.00*					18

CASH PAYMENTS JOURNAL — PAGE *14*

	DATE	ACCOUNT TITLE	CK. NO.	POST. REF.	1 GENERAL DEBIT	2 GENERAL CREDIT	3 ACCOUNTS PAYABLE DEBIT	4 PURCH. DISCOUNT CR. GOLF	5 PURCH. DISCOUNT CR. TENNIS	6 CASH CREDIT	
22	28	*Emp. Inc. Tax Pay.—Fed.*	*390*		*1,299.00*					*3,509.50*	22
23		*FICA Tax Payable*			*2,210.50*						23
24	29	*Unemploy. Tax Pay.—Fed.*	*391*		*290.48*					*290.48*	24
25	29	*Unemploy. Tax Pay.—State*	*392*		*1,960.71*					*1,960.71*	25
26											26
27											27

Journalizing Employer Payroll Taxes

Most employers have three separate payroll taxes. (1) Employer FICA tax. (2) Federal unemployment tax. (3) State unemployment tax. Unemployment taxes are used to pay qualified workers cash benefits for limited periods of unemployment.

Employees in a few states also have deductions from their earnings for state unemployment tax. Employees do not pay federal unemployment tax.

FYI

Payroll deductions are recorded as liabilities for the employer.

Employer payroll taxes expense is based on a percentage of employee earnings. The employer FICA tax is calculated at the same rate (8%) and on the same tax base ($50,000.00) used in calculating the FICA tax for employees. The federal unemployment tax is

TEACHING STRATEGIES: TEACHING TIP

Review how information from the payroll register is used to journalize payment of a payroll. Emphasize the following: Total earnings are debit amounts to salary expense accounts. Net pay is a credit amount for cash. All other columns provide the credit parts of the entry. These credits become liabilities; therefore, add payable to the end of each column heading.

6.2% of the first $7,000.00 earned by each employee. An employer generally can deduct from federal unemployment payments the amounts paid to state unemployment funds. This deduction cannot be more than 5.4% of taxable earnings. The effective federal unemployment tax rate in most states is, therefore, 0.8% on the first $7,000.00 earned by each employee. (Federal 6.2% − deductible for state 5.4% = 0.8%.) All of the unemployment tax on the first $7,000.00 of salary is paid by the employer.

None of MasterSport's employees has earned $7,000.00 by the pay period ended July 2. Therefore, MasterSport's federal unemployment tax is 0.8% of $7,958.40 total earnings, or $63.67. MasterSport's state unemployment tax is 5.4% of $7,958.40 total earnings, or $429.75.

Jeffrey Felice, manager, would have earned over $7,000.00 by July 2 had he worked since the beginning of the year. However, he started work at MasterSport on March 1 of the current year.

Payroll Taxes Expense
Debit: 1,130.09

FICA Tax Payable
Credit: 636.67

Unemployment Tax Payable—Federal
Credit: 63.67

Unemployment Tax Payable—State
Credit: 429.75

July 9, 19--. Recorded employer payroll taxes, $1,130.09, for the biweekly pay period ended July 2. Taxes owed are: FICA tax, $636.67; federal unemployment tax, $63.67; state unemployment tax, $429.75. Memorandum No. 42.

The source document for journalizing this transaction is a memorandum. *(CONCEPT: Objective Evidence)*

Payroll Taxes Expense is increased by a $1,130.09 debit. FICA Tax Payable is increased by a $636.67 credit. Unemployment Tax Payable—Federal is increased by a $63.67 credit. Unemployment Tax Payable—State is increased by a $429.75 credit.

The journal entry to record the employer payroll taxes for the pay period ended July 2 and paid on July 9 is shown on lines 1–4 of the general journal, Illustration 4-10.

ILLUSTRATION 4-10

Journal entry to record employer payroll taxes

GENERAL JOURNAL — PAGE 7

	DATE		ACCOUNT TITLE	DOC. NO.	POST. REF.	DEBIT	CREDIT	
1	19-- July	9	Payroll Taxes Expense	M42		1 130 09		1
2			FICA Tax Payable				636 67	2
3			Unemploy. Tax Payable—Fed.				63 67	3
4			Unemploy. Tax Payable—State				429 75	4
5								5
6								6
7								7
8								8
9								9
10								10

ASSESS

Assess student understanding by checking the solutions to the Independent Practice activities.

Reteach

- Using amounts from the completed payroll register for Recycling Problem 4-R (solution in Teacher's Resource Guide) and T accounts on the chalkboard, analyze the transaction to pay the payroll. Using the same payroll register and the tax rates given in Recycling Problem 4-R, Instruction 6, demonstrate how the employer's payroll taxes are calculated.
- Assign Recycling Problem 4-R.

Extend

- Assign Cases for Critical Thinking 2.
- Assign Challenge Problem 4-C. (The challenge is to calculate employee benefits available for a semimonthly payroll system.)

Enrich

Assign the students to write a brief report on some of the advantages and disadvantages of using automatic check deposit and electronic funds transfer.

CLOSURE

Use Audit Your Understanding questions.

ASSESS

- Administer Problem Test Chapter 4.
- Administer a MicroExam test for Chapter 4.

APPLIED SKILLS: WORD PROCESSING

If you wish to integrate word processing in your accounting course, you may direct students to answer the end-of-chapter Accounting Terms, Questions for Individual Study, and Cases for Critical Thinking using their word processing software.

PAYING WITHHOLDING AND PAYROLL TAXES

Employers must pay to federal, state, and local governments all payroll taxes withheld from employee earnings as well as the employer payroll taxes. The frequency of payments is determined by the amount owed.

Journalizing Payment of Federal Income Tax and FICA Tax Liability

FYI

A deposit coupon, Form 8109, must accompany payment of employee income tax and FICA tax to the federal government.

If the amount owed for federal income tax and FICA tax is less than $500.00 a quarter, payment is due at the end of the quarter. If the amount owed is between $500.00 and $3,000.00 by the end of any month, payment is due by the 15th of the following month. If the amount owed is $3,000.00 or more within a month, payment is due three banking days following specified payment periods. The federal government identifies eight specified payment periods in which unpaid taxes of $3,000.00 or more are due. The eight specified payment periods are the 3d, 7th, 11th, 15th, 19th, 22d, 25th, and the last day of each month.

FYI

Employees do not pay federal unemployment tax.

At the end of MasterSport's second biweekly pay period ended July 16 and paid on July 23, federal income tax and FICA tax liabilities for the month exceed $3,000.00. Therefore, payment must be made three banking days following the July 25 specified payment period or July 28.

July 28, 19--. Paid cash for liability for employee federal income tax, $1,299.00, and for FICA tax, $2,210.50; total, $3,509.50. Check No. 390.

Employee Income Tax Payable—Federal	
1,299.00	

FICA Tax Payable	
2,210.50	

Cash	
	3,509.50

The source document for journalizing payment of the federal income tax and FICA tax liability is a check.

Employee Income Tax Payable—Federal is decreased by a $1,299.00 debit. FICA Tax Payable is decreased by a $2,210.50 debit. This FICA tax amount includes both the amounts withheld from employees and the employer's share. Cash is decreased by a $3,509.50 credit.

The entry for payment of these liabilities is shown on lines 22 and 23 of the cash payments journal, Illustration 4-9.

MasterSport's liability for state income tax withholding is paid at the end of each quarter.

Journalizing Payment of Federal Unemployment Tax Liability

If the annual federal unemployment tax is $100.00 or less, payment is due annually by January 31 of the following year. If the annual tax is over $100.00, quarterly payments are required in the month following the end of the quarter.

MasterSport's federal unemployment tax for the second quarter is $290.48. Payment is required during the first month of the following quarter, July.

Unemployment Tax Payable—Federal	
290.48	

Cash	
	290.48

July 29, 19--. Paid cash for federal unemployment tax liability for quarter ended June 30, $290.48. Check No. 391.

The source document for this transaction is a check. *(CONCEPT: Objective Evidence)*

Unemployment Tax Payable—Federal is decreased by a $290.48 debit. Cash is decreased by a $290.48 credit.

The journal entry for payment of the federal unemployment tax is shown on line 24 of the cash payments journal, Illustration 4-9.

Audit Your Understanding

1. When a payroll is journalized, which general ledger account is credited for the total net amount paid to all employees?
2. What three separate payroll taxes do most employers have?
3. What determines the frequency of payments of withholding and payroll taxes?

Journalizing Payment of State Unemployment Tax Liability

Requirements for paying state unemployment taxes vary. Usually, employers are required to pay the state unemployment tax during the month following each calendar quarter.

MasterSport's state unemployment tax for the second quarter is $1,960.71.

July 29, 19--. Paid cash for state unemployment tax liability for quarter ended June 30, $1,960.71. Check No. 392.

Unemployment Tax Payable—State	
1,960.71	

Cash	
	1,960.71

The source document for this transaction is a check. *(CONCEPT: Objective Evidence)*

Unemployment Tax Payable—State is decreased by a $1,960.71 debit. Cash is decreased by a $1,960.71 credit.

The journal entry for payment of this liability is shown on line 25 of the cash payments journal, Illustration 4-9.

AUDIT YOUR UNDERSTANDING

1. Cash
2. (1) Employer FICA tax; (2) federal unemployment tax; (3) state unemployment tax.
3. The amount owed.

ACCOUNTING TERMS EPT(a)

What is the meaning of each of the following?

1. **salary**
2. **pay period**
3. **payroll**
4. **payroll taxes**
5. **employee benefits**
6. **payroll register**
7. **withholding allowance**
8. **tax base**
9. **employee earnings record**
10. **automatic check deposit**

QUESTIONS FOR INDIVIDUAL STUDY EPT(b)

1. Which accounting concept is being applied when payroll expenses are reported as separate items in accounting records and financial statements?
2. Who specifies the payroll information a business must keep and report?
3. What are MasterSport's three employee benefits?
4. On what basis might employee earnings be stated?
5. An employee's salary may be supplemented by what other types of earnings?
6. What are the three types of employee earnings paid by MasterSport?
7. When are commissions paid to MasterSport's department supervisors?
8. Why do the payroll date and the date of payment differ on MasterSport's payroll register?
9. How does MasterSport determine the federal income tax to be withheld from each employee's pay?
10. How many employee earnings records does MasterSport use for each employee?
11. Where is the information obtained for completing an employee earnings record?
12. Which accounting concept is being applied when a check is used as the source document for a payroll payment?
13. How is employer FICA tax figured?
14. What is the source document for journalizing employer payroll taxes?
15. What accounts are affected, and how, by payment of the federal unemployment tax liability?

CASES FOR CRITICAL THINKING EPT(b)

CASE 1 Barbara's Boutique keeps its accounting records on a departmental basis. All general ledger accounts that affect gross profit on sales are identified by department. However, the operating expenses connected with sales are not kept on a departmental basis. As the salary expense is the largest single selling expense, the accounting department recommends that the business consider setting up special salary expense accounts for each of the sales departments. The store manager disagrees with the recommendation because salesclerks do not work solely in individual departments. The store manager feels that it would not be feasible to identify salary expenses by department. Therefore, the decision was made to continue using one salary expense account for all departments. Do you agree or disagree with the decision? Why?

CASE 2 MasterSport uses one account, Payroll Taxes Expense, in which to record all of the expenses for FICA tax, federal unemployment tax, and state unemployment tax. Sports Den uses three expense accounts—FICA Tax Expense, Federal Unemployment Tax Expense, and State Unemployment Tax Expense—when recording the business' three payroll tax expenses. Which system of recording taxes is more desirable? Explain your answer.

ACCOUNTING TERMS

1. **salary:** The money paid for employee services. (p. 89)
2. **pay period:** The period covered by a salary payment. (p. 89)
3. **payroll:** The total amount earned by all employees for a pay period. (p. 89)
4. **payroll taxes:** Taxes based on the payroll of a business. (p. 89)
5. **employee benefits:** Payments to employees for nonworking hours and to insurance and retirement programs. (p. 89)
6. **payroll register:** A business form used to record payroll information. (p. 97)
7. **withholding allowance:** A deduction from total earnings for each person legally supported by a taxpayer. (p. 98)
8. **tax base:** The maximum amount of earnings on which a tax is calculated. (p. 101)
9. **employee earnings record:** A business form used to record details affecting payments made to an employee. (p. 103)
10. **automatic check deposit:** Depositing payroll checks directly to an employee's checking or savings account in a specific bank. (p. 104)

QUESTIONS FOR INDIVIDUAL STUDY

1. Materiality concept. (p. 89)
2. Federal, state, and local governments. (p. 89)
3. Vacation time, sick leave time, and personal leave time. (p. 89)
4. As a rate per hour, day, week, month, or year or on pieces produced per unit of time. (p. 91)
5. Commissions, cost-of-living adjustments, a share of profits, or a bonus. (p. 91)
6. (a) An hourly salary is paid biweekly to salesclerks and accounting department employees. (b) A biweekly salary is paid to each of the two department supervisors and the store manager. (c) A monthly commission is paid to each of the department supervisors. (p. 91)
7. Commissions for the previous month's net sales are included with the first biweekly pay period of a month. (p. 96)
8. Time is needed between the end of a pay period and the date of payment to prepare the payroll records and payroll checks. (p. 98)
9. From withholding tables furnished by the federal government. (p. 99)
10. One card is used per quarter. (p. 103)
11. From amount columns of a payroll register. (p. 103)
12. Objective Evidence concept. (p. 105)
13. The tax is figured at the same rate and on the same tax base used in calculating the FICA tax for employees. (p. 106)
14. Memorandum. (p. 107)
15. Unemployment Tax Payable—Federal is debited; Cash is credited. (p. 109)

APPLICATION PROBLEMS EPT(c,d)

PROBLEM 4-1 Preparing a benefits record

SPREADSHEET

McGarvie's provides the same employee benefits as those described for MasterSport in Illustration 4-1 in this chapter.

INSTRUCTIONS:

Prepare Meredith Byer's benefits record for the first four biweekly pay periods of the current year. Use the following information.

Employee No.: 14 Employee Name: Meredith K. Byer
Department: Auto Parts Date of Initial Employment: November 1, 1987

Pay Period	Regular Hours	Employee Benefits Available			Employee Benefits Used		
1/2	80	V64	S73	P15	V8	S0	P4
1/16	80	______	______	______	V0	S4	P2
1/30	80	______	______	______	V16	S0	P0
2/13	80	______	______	______	V0	S2	P3

V = Vacation time; S = Sick leave time; P = Personal leave time

PROBLEM 4-2 Calculating employee earnings

MATHEMATICS

The following information for each employee is taken from the time cards.

Employee Number	Hours Worked		Regular Rate
	Regular	Overtime	
1	*80*	*4*	*$7.75*
2	80	2	6.00
3	80	0	8.25
4	80	5	7.00
5	80	1	8.50

INSTRUCTIONS:

Use a form similar to the following. For each employee, calculate the amount of regular, overtime, and total earnings. Overtime hours are paid at 1½ times the regular rate. The amounts calculated for Employee No. 1 are given as an example.

Employee Number	Hours Worked		Regular Rate	Earnings		Total Earnings
	Regular	Overtime		Regular	Overtime	
1	*80*	*4*	*$7.75*	*$620.00*	*$46.50*	*$666.50*

PROBLEM 4-3 Recording employee benefits and calculating earnings on time cards

Lind's has two departments: Paint and Wallpaper. A biweekly payroll system of 26 pay periods per year is used. Salesclerks and employees in the accounting department are paid on an hourly basis and receive 1½ times the regular hourly pay rate for all hours worked in excess of 8 hours in any one day. A time card is used for hourly employees to record hours worked.

CASES FOR CRITICAL THINKING

Case 1 Disagree. Salary expenses for a departmentalized business should be kept on a departmental basis. This procedure allows management to review salaries by department to assure that salaries are kept consistent with salary policies. Even though salesclerks do not work solely in one department, salary expenses can still be identified by department. One method is to record a salesclerk's employee number on the sales slips for each department. The sales slips can then be sorted by salesclerks. At the end of the pay period, the percentage of each salesclerk's salary devoted to the sales in each department can be determined. For example, if 30 percent of the sales of one salesclerk were in department A, then 30 percent of that salesclerk's salary is charged to department A.

Case 2 MasterSport's use of a single account provides a means of summarizing the total of all payroll tax expenses. Sports Den's procedure provides a means of summarizing the total of each kind of tax. Since this same information can be found in MasterSport's separate payroll tax liability accounts, no real advantage is provided by keeping separate payroll tax expense accounts.

CHECK FIGURES

Complete solutions to the problems can be found in the Teacher's Edition of the Working Papers.

Problem 4-1 Pay Period Ended 2/13—Acc. Hours. Avail.: Vacation, 56; sick leave, 75; personal leave, 10.

Problem 4-2 Total Earnings Column: 666.50; 498.00; 660.00; 612,50; 692.75

Problem 4-3 Overtime amount: Aguilar, $47.25; Parker, $39.00; Sabo, $43.88

Lind's provides the same employee benefits as those described for MasterSport in this chapter. The employee benefits provided are shown in Illustration 4-1 in this chapter. A benefits authorization form similar to the one shown in Illustration 4-2 is also used.

Time cards and benefits authorization forms for selected employees of Lind's are provided in the working papers. The time cards and employee benefits authorizations are for the biweekly pay period ended March 12 of the current year.

INSTRUCTIONS:

1. Prepare an employee benefits record for each employee.
2. Record employee benefits hours on time cards for each employee.
3. Calculate regular, overtime, and total hours worked by each employee on the time cards.
4. Complete each time card by calculating regular, overtime, and total earnings.

The time cards prepared in this problem are needed to complete Problem 4-5.

CHECK FIGURES (cont'd)

Problem 4-4 Commissions: Blake, $197.11; Byrum, $202.20

Problem 4-5 Total Earnings: Regular, $2,660.00; Overtime, $130.13; Commission, $399.31; Total, $3,189.44

PROBLEM 4-4 Preparing departmental commissions records

SPREADSHEET

MATHEMATICS

Lind's employs a departmental supervisor for each of its two departments. Departmental supervisors are paid a biweekly salary and receive monthly commissions of 1% of net sales. Commissions are paid for the previous month in the first pay period of the current month. The following data are from the accounting records for the month ended February 28 of the current year.

a. Paint department: sales on account, $8,623.40; cash and credit card sales, $12,936.20; sales discount, $148.90; sales returns and allowances, $1,699.30.

b. Wallpaper department: sales on account, $7,223.89; cash and credit card sales, $13,987.11; sales discount, $337.17; sales returns and allowances, $654.33.

INSTRUCTIONS:

Prepare a commissions record similar to the one in this chapter for each of the following departmental supervisors. Use February of the current year as the month.

a. Paint department
Employee name: Jacqueline A. Blake
Employee number: 9
Regular salary: $540.00

b. Wallpaper department
Employee name: Lawrence M. Byrum
Employee number: 14
Regular salary: $520.00

The commissions records prepared in this problem are needed to complete Problem 4-5.

PROBLEM 4-5 Completing a payroll register

SPREADSHEET

MATHEMATICS

The time cards prepared in Problem 4-3 and the commissions records prepared in Problem 4-4 are needed to complete this problem.

Lind's partially completed payroll register for the pay period ended March 12 is provided in the working papers. Use the following additional data.

a. A deduction for federal income tax is to be made from each employee's total earnings. Use the appropriate income tax withholding tables shown in Chapter 4, Illustration 4-7.

b. A deduction of 5% for state income tax is to be made from each employee's total earnings.

c. A deduction of 8% for FICA tax is to be made from each employee's total earnings.

d. All employees have dental insurance, $9.40, and health insurance, $13.20, deducted from their pay each biweekly pay period. These deductions are to be recorded in the Other Deductions column of the payroll register. The letter *D* is to be written in front of the dental insurance deduction. The letter *H* is to be written in front of the health insurance deduction. Both the dental and health insurance deductions are written on one line of the payroll register for each employee.

INSTRUCTIONS:

Complete the payroll register for the pay period ended March 12 and paid on March 19 of the current year.

The payroll register prepared in Problem 4-5 is needed to complete Problems 4-6 and 4-7.

PROBLEM 4-6 Completing an employee earnings record

The payroll register prepared in Problem 4-5 is needed to complete this problem.

A partially completed employee earnings record for each of Lind's employees is provided in the working papers.

INSTRUCTIONS:

Complete the employee earnings record for each employee. This pay period is the sixth of the first quarter of the current year.

PROBLEM 4-7 Journalizing payment of a departmental payroll

The payroll register prepared in Problem 4-5 is needed to complete this problem.

INSTRUCTIONS:

1. Record the March 19 payroll payment on page 6 of a cash payments journal. The source document is Check No. 463.
2. Record the employer payroll taxes on page 6 of a general journal. Use March 19 of the current year as the date. The source document is Memorandum No. 41. Employer tax rates are: FICA, 8%; federal unemployment, 0.8%; and state unemployment, 5.4%.

PROBLEM 4-8 Calculating and journalizing payment of payroll tax liabilities

Use the following payroll data for Walker's for the first quarter of the current year. Employer tax rates are: FICA, 8%; federal unemployment, 0.8%; and state unemployment, 5.4%.

Period	Total Earnings	FICA Tax Withheld	Federal Income Tax Withheld
March	$ 7,742.00	$619.36	$911.02
First Quarter	25,346.10	—	—

INSTRUCTIONS:

1. Calculate the liability for federal income tax and FICA tax for the month of March. Include both the FICA tax withheld and the employer liability for FICA tax. Record the payment of federal income tax withholding and FICA tax on page 7 of a cash payments journal. The payment is made on April 15 using Check No. 492 as the source document.
2. Calculate the federal unemployment tax liability for the first quarter. Record the payment on page 8 of a cash payments journal. The payment is made on April 30 using Check No. 515 as the source document.
3. Calculate the state unemployment tax liability for the first quarter. Record the payment on page 8 of a cash payments journal. The payment is made on April 30 using Check No. 516 as the source document.

CHECK FIGURES *(cont'd)*

Problem 4-6 Accumulated Earnings: Blake, $3,902.31; Byrum, $3,816.50; Parker, $3,343.10; Sabo, $3,240.78

Problem 4-7 FICA, $255.16; Unempl.—Fed., $25.52; Unempl.—State, $172.23

Problem 4-8 Empl. Inc. Tax, $911.02; FICA Tax Pay., $1,238.72; Unempl.—Fed., $2202.77; Unempl.—State, $1,368.69

ENRICHMENT PROBLEMS

EPT (c,d)

MASTERY PROBLEM 4-M Completing payroll records, journalizing payment of a payroll, and journalizing payroll taxes

McCarron's Sewing Store has two departments: Fabric and Supplies. A biweekly payroll system of 26 pay periods per year is used. Salesclerks and employees in the accounting department are paid on an hourly basis and receive 1½ times the regular hourly pay rate for all hours worked in excess of 8 hours in any one day. A time card is used for hourly employees to record hours worked.

Department supervisors are paid a biweekly salary and receive monthly commissions of 1% of net sales. Commissions are paid for the previous month in the first pay period of the next month.

McCarron's Sewing Store provides the same employee benefits as those described for MasterSport in this chapter. The employee benefits provided are in the employee benefits schedule shown in Illustration 4-1 in this chapter. A benefits authorization form similar to the one shown in Illustration 4-2 is also used.

McCarron's Sewing Store's partially completed payroll records for selected employees are provided in the working papers. The payroll records are for the pay period ended February 13 and paid on February 20 of the current year.

INSTRUCTIONS:

1. Complete the benefits record for each employee and record employee benefits hours used on the time cards.
2. Calculate regular, overtime, and total hours worked by each employee.
3. Complete each time card by calculating regular, overtime, and total earnings.
4. Complete the commissions record for each departmental supervisor. The following data are from the accounting records for the month ended January 31 of the current year.
   a. Fabric department: sales on account, $5,443.89; cash and credit card sales, $8,017.02; sales discount, $85.86; sales returns and allowances, $296.66.
   b. Supplies department: sales on account, $5,209.33; cash and credit card sales, $9,903.55; sales discount, $156.67; sales returns and allowances, $1,302.31.
5. Complete the payroll register for the pay period ended February 13 and paid February 20 of the current year. Use the following additional data to complete the payroll register.
   a. A deduction for federal income tax is to be made from each employee's total earnings. Use the appropriate income tax withholding tables shown in Illustration 4-7 in this chapter.
   b. A deduction of 5% for state income tax is to be made from each employee's total earnings.
   c. A deduction of 8% for FICA tax is to be made from each employee's total earnings.
   d. All employees have health insurance, $14.80, and life insurance, $8.20, deducted from their pay each biweekly pay period. The letter *H* is to be written in front of the health insurance deduction. The letter *L* is to be written in front of the life insurance deduction.
6. Complete the employee earnings record for each employee. This pay period is the fourth of the first quarter of the current year.
7. Journalize the February 20 payroll payment on page 4 of a cash payments journal. The source document is Check No. 143.
8. Journalize the employer payroll taxes on page 4 of a general journal. Use February 20 of the current year as the date. The source document is Memorandum No. 14. Employer tax rates are: FICA, 8%; federal unemployment, 0.8%; and state unemployment, 5.4%. The employee FICA tax withheld and the employer share of FICA tax will not be equal due to rounding differences.

CHALLENGE PROBLEM 4-C Preparing a benefits record

Rancourt's uses a semimonthly payroll system. Three employee benefits are provided. (1) Vacation time. (2) Sick leave time. (3) Personal leave time. The time available is outlined in the following employee benefits schedule.

CHECK FIGURES *(cont'd)*

Mastery Problem 4-M
Commissions: Brown, $130.78; Ostenbauer, $136.54. Total Earnings: $3,861.83. Total Deductions: $1,020.05. Net Pay: $2,841.78. FICA tax, $308.95. Unempl.—Fed., $30.89. Unempl.—State, $208.54

Challenge Problem 4-C Acc. Hours Avail: Vacation, 33⅔; sick leave, 20⅓; personal leave, 12.

RANCOURT'S EMPLOYEE BENEFITS				
Benefits	**Earned After 12 Months**	**Semimonthly After 12 Months**	**Minimum Time Blocks**	**Maximum Carry Over**
Vacation time hours.........	40	$3\frac{1}{3}$	4	120
Sick leave time hours........	0	$1\frac{2}{3}$	1	80
Personal leave time hours....	0	1	1	24

INSTRUCTIONS:

Prepare Arthur Delgado's benefits record for the first four semimonthly pay periods of the current year. Use the following information.

Employee No.: 7 Employee Name: Arthur J. Delgado

Department: Men's Shoes Date of Initial Employment: June 5, 1986

Pay Period	Regular Hours	Employee Benefits Available			Employee Benefits Used		
1/15	80	V32 1/3	S25 2/3	P15	V0	S4	P2
1/31	80	______	______	______	V4	S0	P3
2/15	80	______	______	______	V8	S8	P0
2/29	80	______	______	______	V0	S0	P2

V = Vacation time; S = Sick leave time; P = Personal leave time

CHAPTER 5 OVERVIEW

Chapter 5 completes the accounting cycle for a merchandising business organized as a corporation. Financial reporting for a departmentalized business is described and illustrated.

Several enhancements have been made to this chapter. Critical thinking skills have been incorporated through the presentation of financial statement analysis. The term percentage ratio has been changed to component percentage to reflect more common usage. Students will calculate component percentages for cost of merchandise sold, gross profit on operations, total operating expenses, and net income before federal income tax.

The account title Bad Debts Expense has been changed to Uncollectible Accounts Expense to reflect more common usage and parallel more closely the title of the contra asset account, Allowance for Uncollectible Accounts. The definition of dividends has been included in this chapter.

GUIDE TO ACHIEVING LEARNING OBJECTIVES

	TEACH	APPLY	EXTEND/ENRICH					
Enabling Performance Tasks	**Lesson Plans**	**Application Problems**	**Mastery Problems**	**Challenge Problems**	**Cases for Critical Thinking**	**Recycling Problems**	**Reinforcement Activity**	
a. Define accounting terms related to financial reporting for a departmentalized business.	5-1, 5-2, 5-3							
b. Identify accounting concepts and practices related to financial reporting for a departmentalized business.	5-1, 5-2, 5-3				Cases 1, 2			
c. Prepare selected interim and end-of-fiscal-period work for a departmentalized business.	5-1, 5-2, 5-3	5-1, 5-3, 5-4, 5-7	5-M	5-C		5-R1, 5-R2	1	
d. Analyze financial statements using selected component percentages.	5-1, 5-3	5-2, 5-3, 5-5, 5-6, 5-7	5-M			5-R1, 5-R2	1	

ENRICHMENT

SPECIAL FEATURES
Multicultural Awareness, page 123
Personal Visions in Business, page 140
TECHNOLOGY CONNECTION
Automated Accounting 6.0 Problems 5-7, 5-M
Spreadsheet Template Problems 5-1, 5-3, 5-M

NEW, REVIEW, AND EXTENSION

ACTIVITIES/CONCEPTS/TRANSACTIONS	NEW	REVIEW/ EXTENSION
Calculating estimated merchandise inventory		✓
Preparing an interim departmental statement of gross profit	✓	
Preparing schedules of accounts payable and accounts receivable		✓
Completing a work sheet		✓
Preparing an income statement for a corporation		✓
Preparing a statement of stockholders' equity		✓
Preparing a balance sheet for a corporation		✓
Calculating component percentages		✓
Recording adjusting entries for a corporation		✓
Recording closing entries for a corporation		✓
Preparing a post-closing trial balance		✓

Challenge Problem 5-C uses a 10-column work sheet. A 10-column work sheet may be used for any of the problems in this text. A master ruling of a 10-column work sheet is available in the Teacher's Resource Guide.

In this edition, account titles are included on the working papers for financial statements and also on the problem tests. This change recognizes that in actual practice the format for financial statements varies from company to company.

Chapters 2–5 present the entire cycle for a merchandising business organized as a corporation. It is important that the student see the entire accounting cycle. It is also important that the student apply these concepts through the completion of the simulation, Galleria, and/or the reinforcement activity.

	INFORMAL ASSESSMENT		**FORMAL ASSESSMENT**			
	Study Guide	**Audit Your Understanding**	**Chapter MicroExam**	**Chapter Problem Test**	**Unit Objective Test**	**Portfolio**
	Unit A	✓	✓		✓	
	Units B, C	✓	✓		✓	
				✓		✓
				✓		✓

TEACHING MATERIALS

- Teacher's Wraparound Edition of Text
- Teacher's Resource Guide
- Teacher's Edition of the Working Papers
- MicroExam
- Key for Galleria, Inc.

APPLIED MATHEMATICS

APPLIED MATH/ACCOUNTING SKILL	APPLICATION
Calculating estimated ending merchandise inventory	Prob. 5-1
Calculating component percentages	Prob. 5-2
Estimating uncollectible accounts expense	Prob. 5-7

TEACHING STRATEGIES: ACCOUNTING PEDAGOGY

This textbook covers complete financial statement preparation including Statement of Stockholder's Equity. Students are given the opportunity to perform financial statement analysis which will help improve their critical thinking skills.

5

Financial Reporting for a Departmentalized Business

ENABLING PERFORMANCE TASKS

After studying Chapter 5, you will be able to:

a Define accounting terms related to financial reporting for a departmentalized business.

b Identify accounting concepts and practices related to financial reporting for a departmentalized business.

c Prepare selected interim and end-of-fiscal-period work for a departmentalized business.

d Analyze financial statements using selected component percentages.

TERMS PREVIEW

fiscal period • departmental statement of gross profit • interim departmental statement of gross profit • periodic inventory • perpetual inventory • gross profit method of estimating an inventory • component percentage • schedule of accounts receivable • schedule of accounts payable • trial balance • work sheet • plant assets • depreciation expense • income statement • statement of stockholders' equity • capital stock • retained earnings • dividends • balance sheet • adjusting entries • closing entries • post-closing trial balance • accounting cycle

The financial information recorded by a business is summarized and reported on financial statements. The financial statements of a business are then analyzed to evaluate the financial position and progress of the business. The managers of the business use the financial statements to make financial decisions for future operations. The financial statements are also used in the preparation of tax reports, which must be completed at least once a year. Therefore, financial statements are prepared at least once a year. A business may, however, prepare financial statements more often. The length of time for which a business summarizes and reports financial information is called a **fiscal period.** *(CONCEPT: Accounting Period Cycle)* A fiscal period can be one month, three months, six months, or twelve months. The length of the fiscal period a business uses is determined by the business. MasterSport uses a calendar-year fiscal period.

FYI

Accountants spend up to 90 percent of their time writing while on the job.

A departmentalized business prepares the same financial statements in the same form as a nondepartmentalized business. In addition, a departmentalized business usually prepares reports about how well each department is doing. A statement prepared at the end of a fiscal period showing the gross profit for each department is called a **departmental statement of gross profit.**

A departmental statement of gross profit provides a manager with information about revenue and costs for each department. A review of this information may show a need to (1) change merchandise selling prices, (2) change suppliers of merchandise, (3) change or add products, or (4) discontinue a department.

INTERIM DEPARTMENTAL STATEMENT OF GROSS PROFIT

Gross profit information reflects changes between costs and selling prices. A departmental statement of gross profit also provides information that can be used to quickly determine potential profits. Therefore, a departmental statement of gross profit is often prepared at the end of each month even though the fiscal period is for more than one month. A statement showing gross profit for each department for a portion of a fiscal period is called an **interim departmental statement of gross profit.** MasterSport prepares monthly interim departmental statements of gross profit.

Determining an Ending Merchandise Inventory

To prepare an interim departmental statement of gross profit, both beginning and ending inventory amounts are needed. The ending inventory for one month is also the beginning inventory for the next month.

Two principal methods are used to determine actual quantities of merchandise on hand. A merchandise inventory determined by counting, weighing, or measuring items of merchandise on hand is called a **periodic inventory.** A periodic inventory is sometimes

LESSON PLAN 5-1

Materials

- Student pages 117–121
- Blackline Master for Estimated Merchandise Inventory Sheet—Gross Profit Method (TRG)
- Blackline Master for Interim Departmental Statement of Gross Profit (TRG)
- Software: Spreadsheet Template

Objectives (Enabling Performance Tasks)

a. Define accounting terms related to financial reporting for a departmentalized business.

b. Identify accounting concepts and practices related to financial reporting for a departmentalized business.

c. Prepare selected interim and end-of-fiscal-period work for a departmentalized business.

d. Analyze financial statements using selected component percentages.

TEACHING STRATEGIES: TEACHING TIP

Determine if any of the students have helped with taking a periodic inventory in a store or factory in which they may have worked. Bring realism to the class by having these students give a brief report of their experiences.

FOCUS

- In the first-year accounting course, the concepts and procedures related to end-of-fiscal-period work for a merchandising business organized as a corporation were presented. Explain that a departmentalized merchandising business prepares the same financial statements as a nondepartmentalized business. In addition, a departmentalized business prepares reports about how well each department is doing. In this lesson, the concepts and procedures related to preparing interim financial reports will be presented to show how well each department is doing for a portion of a fiscal period. The end-of-fiscal-period work for a departmentalized business will be presented later in this chapter.
- Introduce vocabulary: fiscal period, departmental statement of gross profit, interim departmental statement of gross profit, periodic inventory, perpetual inventory, gross profit method of estimating an inventory, component percentage.

TEACH

Cover student pages 117–121 "Interim Departmental Statement of Gross Profit." Explain the purpose of an interim departmental statement of gross profit. Review the difference between periodic and perpetual inventory. Explain the gross profit method of estimating merchandise inventory and show how an estimated merchandise inventory sheet is prepared. Explain the sections of an interim departmental statement of gross profit and show how the component percentages of cost of merchandise sold and gross profit on operations are calculated. Describe how acceptable levels of performance are determined.

FYI

Many large merchandising businesses use a computer to keep a perpetual inventory.

referred to as a physical inventory. A merchandise inventory determined by keeping a continuous record of increases, decreases, and balance on hand is called a **perpetual inventory.** A perpetual inventory is sometimes referred to as a book inventory.

The cost of merchandise inventory is relatively easy to determine at any time when a perpetual inventory is kept. However, keeping a perpetual inventory may not be practical for a merchandising business with numerous items of merchandise. For a periodic inventory, a physical count of merchandise is made. However, a monthly periodic inventory may not be practical. When a perpetual inventory is not kept and a monthly periodic inventory is not practical, merchandise inventory may be estimated. Estimating inventory by using the previous year's percentage of gross profit on operations is called the **gross profit method of estimating an inventory.**

Estimating an Ending Merchandise Inventory

Because of the numerous items of merchandise, MasterSport determines its monthly ending inventory by using the gross profit method of estimating an inventory. An estimated merchandise inventory sheet is used to record the necessary data.

The golf department's estimated inventory sheet prepared on June 30 is shown in Illustration 5-1.

ILLUSTRATION 5-1 Estimated merchandise inventory sheet

ESTIMATED MERCHANDISE INVENTORY SHEET
Gross Profit Method

DEPARTMENT *Golf* DATE *6/30/--*

1	Beginning inventory, January 1		$ 186,434.61
2	Net purchases to date		56,550.10
3	Merchandise available for sale		$ 242,984.71
4	Net sales to date	$ 186,848.80	
5	Less estimated gross profit (Net sales × Estimated gross profit 45.0 %)	84,081.96	
6	Estimated cost of merchandise sold		102,766.84
7	Estimated ending inventory		$ 140,217.87

MasterSport's estimated merchandise inventory sheet is prepared using the following procedures.

Line 1: The beginning inventory, January 1, is obtained from the general ledger. The balance of Merchandise Inventory—Golf, $186,434.61, is the actual merchandise inventory on hand at the

TEACHING STRATEGIES: TEACHING TIP

Provide extensive practice on estimating merchandise inventory. Illustrate the procedures on an overhead projector or chalkboard. Have students practice the procedures with a variety of net sales and net purchases amounts. Also vary the estimated gross profit percentage to emphasize the significance of the percentage in arriving at an estimated ending inventory.

beginning of the fiscal period. The amount is the result of the periodic inventory count from December 31 of the previous year.

Even when estimated inventory methods are used, a periodic inventory is usually taken at least once a year.

Line 2: The net purchases to date, $56,550.10, is obtained from general ledger accounts. The amount is calculated as shown below.

Purchases—Golf	$59,430.60
Less Purchases Discount—Golf	− 1,090.20
	$58,340.40
Less Purchases Returns and Allowances—Golf	− 1,790.30
Equals net purchases to date (January 1–June 30)	$56,550.10

Line 3: The merchandise available for sale, $242,984.71, is calculated by adding lines 1 and 2.

Line 4: The net sales to date, $186,848.80, is obtained from general ledger accounts. The amount is calculated as shown below.

Sales—Golf	$190,540.20
Less Sales Discounts—Golf	− 680.60
	$189,859.60
Less Sales Returns and Allowances—Golf	− 3,010.80
Equals net sales to date (January 1–June 30)	$186,848.80

Line 5: The estimated gross profit, $84,081.96, is calculated by multiplying the amount on line 4 by 45.0%. The percentage used is a gross profit estimate based on records of previous years' operations.

Line 6: The estimated cost of merchandise sold, $102,766.84, is calculated by subtracting the amount on line 5 from the amount on line 4.

Line 7: The estimated ending inventory, $140,217.87, is calculated by subtracting the amount on line 6 from the amount on line 3. The June 30 estimated merchandise inventory for the golf department, $140,217.87, is used on the interim departmental statement of gross profit. The same procedure is used to calculate the estimated ending merchandise inventory for the tennis department.

Preparing an Interim Departmental Statement of Gross Profit

MasterSport's interim departmental statement of gross profit for the month ended June 30 is shown in Illustration 5-2.

Data are organized into three sections. (1) Operating Revenue. (2) Cost of Merchandise Sold. (3) Gross Profit on Operations. The beginning inventory for each department is the estimated ending inventory from the interim departmental statement of gross profit for the month ended May 31 of the current year.

APPLY

Refer students to Illustration 5-1 as the preparation of the estimated merchandise inventory sheet is presented. Refer students to Illustration 5-2 as analyzing an interim departmental statement of gross profit is discussed.

Guided Practice

- Guide students through the preparation of an estimated merchandise inventory sheet for the Equipment Department in Problem 5-1. Working as a group, have the students determine the amounts to be recorded on each line. When all students agree on the correct amounts, direct students to record the amounts on the inventory sheet provided in the working papers. The balance of Problem 5-1 can be completed as Independent Practice.
- Guide students through the calculation of component percentages for Businesses 1 and 2 in Problem 5-2. Working as a group, have students calculate the component percentages for Business 1. Have students verify the percentages by comparing them with the percentages given as the example. Next, have students calculate the component percentages for Business 2. When all students agree on the correct amounts, direct students to record the percentages on the form provided in the working papers. The balance of Problem 5-2 can be completed as Independent Practice.

Independent Practice

Assign Terms 1–7; Questions 1–10; Problems 5-1, 5-2, and 5-3.

ASSESS

Assess student understanding by checking the solutions to the Independent Practice activities.

Reteach

- Make transparencies of the estimated merchandise inventory sheet—gross profit method and the interim departmental statement of gross profit ruling from the accounting forms masters provided in the Blackline Masters section of the Teacher's Resource Guide. Use information from Problem 5-R1 and the first transparency to demonstrate how to prepare the estimated merchandise inventory sheet for the Men's Shoes Department. Then, use the second transparency to demonstrate how to prepare the Men's Shoes Department portion of the interim departmental statement of gross profit and calculate the component percentages for that department.
- Assign Recycling Problem 5-R1.

Extend

- Assign Cases for Critical Thinking 1.
- Assign the Spreadsheet Template for Problems 5-1 and 5-3.

Enrich

Assign the PERSONAL VISIONS IN BUSINESS feature on page 140.

CLOSURE

Use Audit Your Understanding questions.

ILLUSTRATION 5-2 Interim departmental statement of gross profit

MasterSport
Interim Departmental Statement of Gross Profit
For Month Ended June 30, 19--

	Golf		*% of Net Sales	Tennis		*% of Net Sales	Total		*% of Net Sales
Operating Revenue:									
Net Sales		$32,883.65	100.0		$36,546.30	100.0		$69,429.95	100.0
Cost of Merchandise Sold:									
Est. Mdse. Inv., June 1.	$149,387.48			$141,799.62			$291,187.10		
Net Purchases	8,916.40			17,073.50			25,989.90		
Mdse. Available for Sale.	$158,303.88			$158,873.12			$317,177.00		
Less Est. End. Inv., June 30. .	140,217.87			138,772.66			278,990.53		
Cost of Merchandise Sold . . .		18,086.01	55.0		20,100.46	55.0		38,186.47	55.0
Gross Profit on Operations		$14,797.64	45.0		$16,445.84	45.0		$31,243.48	45.0

*Rounded to nearest 0.1%

Analyzing an Interim Departmental Statement of Gross Profit

FYI

Interim financial statements provide information for periods of time less than a year such as monthly, quarterly, or semiannually.

To help a manager analyze financial information, relationships between items in a financial statement are calculated. The percentage relationship between one financial statement item and the total that includes that item is called a **component percentage.** Component percentages may be shown in a separate column on a financial statement. Four basic components are included in every sales dollar. (1) Cost of merchandise sold. (2) Gross profit on operations. (3) Total operating expenses. (4) Net income before federal income tax.

MasterSport analyzes its interim departmental statement of gross profit monthly by calculating a component percentage for cost of merchandise sold and gross profit on operations. The component percentages for operating expenses and net income are calculated and analyzed at the end of each fiscal period.

Cost of Merchandise Sold. Because the cost of merchandise sold is a significant cost, management attempts to keep this cost as low as possible. MasterSport's interim departmental statement of gross profit, Illustration 5-2, shows that the component percentage for total cost of merchandise sold is 55.0%. This component percentage is calculated as shown below.

Total Cost of Merchandise Sold	÷	Total Net Sales	=	Total Cost of Merchandise Sold Component Percentage
$38,186.47	÷	$69,429.95	=	55.0%

A component percentage for cost of merchandise sold is also calculated for each department.

Gross Profit on Operations. The excess of net sales over cost of merchandise sold is gross profit on operations. Gross profit on operations must be large enough to cover total operating expenses and produce a net income. Analysis of the interim departmental statement of gross profit, Illustration 5-2, shows that the component percentage for total gross profit on operations is 45.0%. This component percentage is calculated as shown below.

Total Gross Profit on Operations	÷	Total Net Sales	=	Total Gross Profit on Operations Component Percentage
$31,243.48	÷	$69,429.95	=	45.0%

FYI

Interim statements allow managers to make decisions and implement changes as soon as a problem is detected.

The component percentage for gross profit on operations is also calculated for each department.

Determining Acceptable Levels of Performance. For component percentages to be useful, a business must know acceptable levels of performance. To determine acceptable levels of performance, businesses generally make comparisons with previous performance and with industry performance standards that are published by industry organizations. Based on these sources, MasterSport determines that an acceptable component percentage for departmental and total cost of merchandise sold should not be more than 55.0%. MasterSport further determines that an acceptable component percentage for departmental and total gross profit on operations should not be less than 45.0%.

An analysis of the interim departmental statement of gross profit for the month ended June 30 indicates acceptable levels of performance. The component percentage for total cost of merchandise sold, 55.0%, is not more than 55.0%. The component percentage for total gross profit on operations, 45.0%, is not less than 45.0%. The component percentage for cost of merchandise sold and gross profit on operations for each department also indicate acceptable levels of performance.

Audit Your Understanding

1. What additional information beyond regular financial statements does a departmentalized business provide management?
2. What are the two principal methods for determining quantities of merchandise on hand?
3. What are the three sections of an interim departmental statement of gross profit?

PROVING THE ACCURACY OF POSTING TO SUBSIDIARY LEDGERS

MasterSport prepares a report showing the total of all accounts receivable ledger accounts. A listing of customer accounts, account balances, and total amount due from all customers is called a

AUDIT YOUR UNDERSTANDING

The AUDIT YOUR UNDERSTANDING feature appears at the end of each section of the chapter. Explain to your students that the word *audit* means to check or verify. AUDIT YOUR UNDERSTANDING may be used to check student comprehension of the section just studied. The answers are provided in Appendix D in the back of the textbook.

1. Reports about how well each department is doing.
2. Periodic inventory and perpetual inventory
3. Operating Revenue; Cost of Merchandise Sold; Gross Profit on Operations.

LESSON PLAN 5-2

Materials

- Student pages 121–130
- Blackline Master for 8-Column Work Sheet (TRG)

Objectives (Enabling Performance Tasks)

a. Define accounting terms related to financial reporting for a departmentalized business.

b. Identify accounting concepts and practices related to financial reporting for a departmentalized business.

c. Prepare selected interim and end-of-fiscal-period work for a departmentalized business.

FOCUS

- In the first-year accounting course, the concepts and procedures related to end-of-fiscal-period work for a merchandising business organized as a corporation were presented. Explain that the end-of-fiscal-period work for a departmentalized business is very similar to that of a nondepartmentalized business. In this lesson, the procedures for proving the accuracy of posting to subsidiary ledgers will be reviewed. Also, the procedures for preparing a work sheet for a departmentalized merchandising business will be presented.
- Introduce vocabulary: schedule of accounts receivable, schedule of accounts payable, trial balance, work sheet, plant assets, depreciation expense.

TEACH

Cover student pages 121–130 "Proving the Accuracy of Posting to Subsidiary Ledgers" and "Work Sheet for a Departmentalized Business." Review the preparation of the schedules of accounts receivable and accounts payable. Emphasize that the total of each schedule must equal the balance of the corresponding controlling account in the general ledger. Begin the presentation of the work sheet for a departmentalized business by reviewing the procedures for preparing the trial balance. Next, review how adjustments are planned on the work sheet. Show how the uncollectible accounts expense is calculated. Present the use of the departmental income summary accounts to adjust the two merchandise inventory accounts. Remind students that the inventory amount in the trial balance is the balance at the beginning of the period. Review the supplies, prepaid insurance, depreciation expense, and federal income tax expense adjustments. Emphasize that these adjustments are the same for either a departmentalized or nondepartmentalized business organized as a corporation. Review the steps to complete the work sheet—extend amounts to the balance sheet and income statement columns and calculate net income or net loss.

schedule of accounts receivable. The total on a schedule of accounts receivable must equal the balance of the general ledger controlling account, Accounts Receivable. MasterSport's schedule of accounts receivable is shown in Illustration 5-3.

ILLUSTRATION 5-3 Schedule of accounts receivable

MasterSport
Schedule of Accounts Receivable
June 30, 19--

Lawrence Bissell	$ 950.60
Eastside Sports Center	644.70
Galaxy Tennis Club	1,785.00
Golden Golf League	1,592.50
Mary Lynch	245.70
Par Golf Club	1,391.25
Swanville Schools	775.25
Helen Vega	3,675.00
William Wenz	2,695.00
Total Accounts Receivable	$13,755.00

FYI

A controlling account is an account in a general ledger that summarizes all accounts in a subsidiary ledger.

MasterSport also prepares a report showing the total of all accounts payable ledger accounts. A listing of vendor accounts, account balances, and total amount due all vendors is called a **schedule of accounts payable.** The total on a schedule of accounts payable must equal the balance of the controlling account, Accounts Payable. MasterSport's schedule of accounts payable is shown in Illustration 5-4.

The balances of both controlling accounts, Accounts Receivable and Accounts Payable, agree with the totals shown on the two schedules. Therefore, posting to subsidiary ledgers is assumed to be correct.

ILLUSTRATION 5-4 Schedule of accounts payable

MasterSport
Schedule of Accounts Payable
June 30, 19--

Champion Tennis Supply	$ 3,660.60
E-Z Golf	9,420.00
Golf Tee, Inc.	1,590.00
Key Tennis Company	1,514.30
Nelson Racquets, Inc.	10,840.00
Tennis Warehouse	3,610.40
University Tennis	725.00
Total Accounts Payable	$31,360.30

WORK SHEET FOR A DEPARTMENTALIZED BUSINESS

If debits equal credits in journals and if posting is done correctly, debits will equal credits in a general ledger. A proof of the equality of debits and credits in a general ledger is called a **trial balance.**

A trial balance is most often prepared as part of the end-of-fiscal-period activities. Another of these activities is the completion of a work sheet. A columnar accounting form used to summarize the general ledger information needed to prepare financial statements is called a **work sheet.**

MasterSport completes the end-of-fiscal-period work as of December 31 each year. *(CONCEPT: Accounting Period Cycle)*

MULTICULTURAL AWARENESS

Hispanic American Businesses

The Census Bureau's Survey of minority-owned business enterprises shows a pronounced increase in the number of minority business enterprises. From 1982 to 1987, minority-owned businesses increased from 742,000 to 1,214,000.

Census information also shows that among all minorities, Hispanic Americans had a large growth rate in the number of businesses owned. Hispanic Americans increased the number of businesses owned by 81% during the 1980s. Cuban Americans owned more businesses than any other Hispanic Americans. Cuban Americans owned 63 businesses for every 1,000 Cuban Americans in the general population. An 81% growth rate is a remarkable indication of the prevalence of Hispanic American businesses compared to a 14% growth rate in new businesses in the general population.

Trial Balance on a Departmental Work Sheet

A trial balance is prepared in the Trial Balance columns of the work sheet. General ledger accounts are listed in the Account Title column in the same order in which they appear in the general ledger. All accounts are listed regardless of whether there is a balance or not. MasterSport's trial balance for the current year ended December 31 is on the work sheet shown in Illustration 5-5, pages 124 and 125.

After all general ledger accounts and balances have been entered, the Trial Balance columns are totaled and checked for equality. The two column totals, $1,302,612.99, are the same. The Trial Balance columns are ruled as shown on line 58 of the work sheet.

Adjustments on a Departmental Work Sheet

Some general ledger accounts are not up to date. For example, uncollectible accounts expense has not been recorded. The entries needed to bring accounts up to date are planned in the Adjustments columns of the work sheet.

Uncollectible Accounts Expense Adjustment. Merchandise is sometimes sold on account to customers who later are unable to pay the amounts owed. Amounts that cannot be collected from customers are business expenses. Accurate financial reporting requires that expenses be recorded in the fiscal period in which the expenses contribute to earning revenue. *(CONCEPT: Matching Expenses with Revenue)*

MasterSport has found from past experience that approximately 1% of the total sales on account will be uncollectible. Total sales on account for the current year are $210,940.00. Therefore, MasterSport's uncollectible accounts expense is calculated as shown below.

Total Sales on Account	×	Percentage	=	Estimated Uncollectible Accounts Expense
$210,940.00	×	1%	=	$2,109.40

MULTICULTURAL AWARENESS

The MULTICULTURAL AWARENESS feature is intended to expose students to the concept that our society is composed of people from many different cultural backgrounds. These features show both past contributions of many cultures and benefits of a culturally diverse society. (1) Read the feature. (2) Discuss the specific information in the feature. (3) Clarify any terms or questions.

APPLIED SKILLS: BUILDING STUDY SKILLS

Direct students to create a Quick Reference Guide (QRG) on a small card or sheet of paper to use as an aid in analyzing adjustments. Students should write the four questions to analyze an adjustment on an index card to use as a QRG. Have them use this QRG whenever they analyze adjustments.

APPLY

Refer students to Illustrations 5-3 and 5-4 when the schedules of accounts receivable and accounts payable are reviewed. Refer students to Illustration 5-5 as preparation of the work sheet is discussed. Use T accounts on the overhead projector or chalkboard to analyze each adjustment in this lesson.

Guided Practice

Guide students through the T account analysis of the adjustments in Problem 5-7, Instruction 1. Refer students to the work sheet provided in the working papers for general ledger account balances. Have students draw T accounts on a sheet of paper and analyze the first adjustment. All students should agree with the analysis before proceeding to the next adjustment. Repeat the process until all adjustments have been analyzed. The balance of Problem 5-7, Instruction 1, can be completed as Independent Practice.

Independent Practice

Assign Terms 8–13; Questions 11–12; Problems 5-4 and 5-7, Instruction 1.

ILLUSTRATION 5-5 Departmental work sheet

MasterSport
Work Sheet
For Year Ended December 31, 19--

	ACCOUNT TITLE	1 TRIAL BALANCE DEBIT	2 TRIAL BALANCE CREDIT	3 ADJUSTMENTS DEBIT	4 ADJUSTMENTS CREDIT	5 INCOME STATEMENT DEBIT	6 INCOME STATEMENT CREDIT	7 BALANCE SHEET DEBIT	8 BALANCE SHEET CREDIT	
1	*Cash*	434400						434400		1
2	*Petty Cash*	50000						50000		2
3	*Accounts Receivable*	1285500						1285500		3
4	*Allowance for Uncoll. Accts.*		24060		(a) 210940				235000	4
5	*Merchandise Inventory—Golf*	18643461		(b) 1842039				20485500		5
6	*Merchandise Inventory—Tennis*	19984460			(c) 936000			19048460		6
7	*Supplies—Office*	1270000			(d) 995000			275000		7
8	*Supplies—Store*	1433000			(e) 779000			654000		8
9	*Prepaid Insurance*	985000			(f) 565000			420000		9
10	*Office Equipment*	1690000						1690000		10
11	*Accum. Depr.—Office Equipment*		596000		(g) 149000				745000	11
12	*Store Equipment*	3890000						3890000		12
13	*Accum. Depr.—Store Equipment*		1800000		(h) 300000				2100000	13
14	*Accounts Payable*		3816030						3816030	14
15	*Employee Income Tax Payable—Federal*		268075						268075	15
16	*Employee Income Tax Payable—State*		111819						111819	16
17	*Federal Income Tax Payable*				(i) 119007				119007	17
18	*FICA Tax Payable*		336070						336070	18
19	*Sales Tax Payable*		313964						313964	19
20	*Unemployment Tax Payable—Federal*		2360						2360	20
21	*Unemployment Tax Payable—State*		15930						15930	21
22	*Health Insurance Premiums Payable*		226116						226116	22
23	*Life Insurance Premiums Payable*		35019						35019	23
24	*Dividends Payable*		3000000						3000000	24
25	*Capital Stock*		34000000						34000000	25
26	*Retained Earnings*		4221050						4221050	26
27	*Dividends*	3000000						3000000		27
28	*Income Summary—Golf*				(b) 1842039		1842039			28

TEACHING STRATEGIES: EXPANDING BEYOND THE CLASSROOM

Invite an auditor to talk about the importance of the accuracy of the data on the work sheet.

29	Income Summary—Tennis			(c) 9360 00		9360 00				29
30	Income Summary—General									30
31	Sales—Golf		351032 81				351032 81			31
32	Sales—Tennis		438341 75				438341 75			32
33	Sales Discount—Golf	1605 85				1605 85				33
34	Sales Discount—Tennis	2005 25				2005 25				34
35	Sales Ret. and Allow.—Golf	4950 50				4950 50				35
36	Sales Ret. and Allow.—Tennis	6181 80				6181 80				36
37	Purchases—Golf	215745 68				215745 68				37
38	Purchases—Tennis	231766 62				231766 62				38
39	Purchases Discount—Golf		4058 95				4058 95			39
40	Purchases Discount—Tennis		4334 55				4334 55			40
41	Purchases Ret. and Allow.—Golf		8282 48				8282 48			41
42	Purchases Ret. and Allow.—Tennis		8897 52				8897 52			42
43	Advertising Expense	5192 88				5192 88				43
44	Credit Card Fee Expense	5950 00				5950 00				44
45	Depr. Expense—Store Equipment			(h) 3000 00		3000 00				45
46	Salary Expense—Golf	90924 19				90924 19				46
47	Salary Expense—Tennis	72627 02				72627 02				47
48	Supplies Expense—Store			(e) 7790 00		7790 00				48
49	Depr. Expense—Office Equipment			(g) 1490 00		1490 00				49
50	Insurance Expense			(f) 5650 00		5650 00				50
51	Miscellaneous Expense	5958 48				5958 48				51
52	Payroll Taxes Expense	21426 92				21426 92				52
53	Rent Expense	18056 40				18056 40				53
54	Salary Expense—Admin.	43667 19				43667 19				54
55	Supplies Expense—Office			(d) 9950 00		9950 00				55
56	Uncollectible Accounts Expense			(a) 2109 40		2109 40				56
57	Federal Income Tax Expense	10800 00		(i) 1190 07		11990 07				57
58		1302612 99	1302612 99	58959 86	58959 86	777398 25	833368 45	551424 60	495454 40	58
59	Net Income after Fed. Inc. Tax					55970 20			55970 20	59
60						833368 45	833368 45	551424 60	551424 60	60
61										61
62										62
63										63
64										64

ASSESS

Assess student understanding by checking the solutions to the Independent Practice activities.

Reteach

Make a transparency of the 8-column work sheet from the accounting forms masters provided in the Blackline Masters section of the Teacher's Resource Guide. Use data from Problem 5-R2, Instruction 1, and the transparency to demonstrate how to prepare a work sheet for a departmentalized business.

Extend

Assign Cases for Critical Thinking 2.

Enrich

Assign students to read the MULTICULTURAL AWARENESS feature on page 123. Discuss with them how an understanding and appreciation of history and other cultures contributes to understanding civilization today.

CLOSURE

Use Audit Your Understanding questions.

TEACHING STRATEGIES: TEACHING TIP

Review the four questions to analyze an adjustment.

1. What is the balance of the account?
2. What should the balance be for the account?
3. What must be done to correct the account balance?
4. What adjustment is made?

Uncollectible Accounts Expense

Debit		Credit	
Adj. (a)	2,109.40		

Allowance for Uncollectible Accounts

Debit		Credit	
		Dec. 31 Bal.	240.60
		Adj. (a)	2,109.40
		(New Bal.	*2,350.00)*

MasterSport estimates that of the $210,940.00 sales on account during the year, $2,109.40 will eventually be uncollectible.

An adjustment is made to record the estimated uncollectible accounts expense for the fiscal year. The effect of MasterSport's uncollectible accounts expense adjustment is shown in the T accounts.

Uncollectible Accounts Expense is increased by a $2,109.40 debit. Allowance for Uncollectible Accounts, a contra asset account, is increased by a $2,109.40 credit. The Allowance for Uncollectible Accounts balance represents the total estimated amount that MasterSport believes will not be collected from accounts receivable. This estimated amount is not deducted from the Accounts Receivable balance until MasterSport knows for sure which customers will not pay. The estimated uncollectible accounts amount, therefore, is recorded in a separate account titled Allowance for Uncollectible Accounts.

FYI

When multiplying by a percentage, use the decimal 0.45 for 45.0%.

Entries related to uncollectible accounts expense are described in Chapter 8.

The uncollectible accounts expense adjustment is recorded on the work sheet, lines 4 and 56, Illustration 5-5. The adjustment is labeled *(a)* because it is the first adjustment recorded.

Merchandise Inventory Adjustments. The merchandise inventory account balance in a trial balance is the beginning inventory for a fiscal period. The amount of the ending inventory is determined by taking a periodic inventory at the end of a fiscal period.

FYI

Each department has a merchandise inventory account and an income summary account.

The beginning golf merchandise inventory, $186,434.61, for MasterSport is shown on line 5 in the Trial Balance Debit column of the work sheet in Illustration 5-5. The beginning tennis merchandise inventory, $199,844.60, is shown on line 6 in the Trial Balance Debit column of the work sheet.

Merchandise Inventory—Golf

Debit		Credit	
Dec. 31 Bal.	186,434.61		
Adj. (b)	18,420.39		
(New Bal.	*204,855.00)*		

Income Summary—Golf

Debit		Credit	
		Adj. (b)	18,420.39

The actual periodic inventory on December 31 shows that the cost of golf merchandise inventory is $204,855.00. To bring MasterSport's golf merchandise inventory up to date, the balance of Merchandise Inventory—Golf needs to be increased by $18,420.39 ($204,855.00 ending inventory *less* $186,434.61 beginning inventory).

The account Merchandise Inventory—Golf is debited for $18,420.39. Income Summary—Golf is credited for $18,420.39. The balance of Merchandise Inventory—Golf after this adjustment, $204,855.00, is equal to the actual ending inventory. The account is up to date.

Income Summary—Tennis

Debit		Credit	
Adj. (c)	9,360.00		

Merchandise Inventory—Tennis

Debit		Credit	
Dec. 31 Bal.	199,844.60	Adj. (c)	9,360.00
(New Bal.	*190,484.60)*		

A similar adjustment is made for Merchandise Inventory—Tennis. The actual periodic inventory on December 31 shows that the cost of tennis merchandise inventory is $190,484.60. To bring MasterSport's tennis merchandise inventory up to date, the balance of

Merchandise Inventory—Tennis needs to be decreased by $9,360.00 ($199,844.60 beginning inventory *less* $190,484.60 ending inventory).

Income Summary—Tennis is debited for $9,360.00. Merchandise Inventory—Tennis is credited for $9,360.00. The balance of Merchandise Inventory—Tennis after this adjustment, $190,484.60, is equal to the actual ending inventory. The account is up to date.

The two inventory adjustments are entered on the work sheet, lines 5, 6, 28, and 29, Illustration 5-5. The Merchandise Inventory—Golf adjustment is labeled *(b)*. The Merchandise Inventory—Tennis adjustment is labeled *(c)*.

APPLIED SKILLS: WORD PROCESSING

If you wish to integrate word processing into your accounting course, you may direct students to answer the end-of-chapter Accounting Terms, Questions for Individual Study, and Cases for Critical Thinking using their word processing software.

Supplies Adjustments. The supplies inventory account balance in a trial balance includes two items. (1) The account balances on January 1. (2) The cost of supplies bought during the year. The account balances do not reflect the cost of any supplies used during the year which is an operating expense. The amount of the ending inventory is determined by taking a periodic inventory at the end of a fiscal period.

FYI

The adjustment for supplies is the actual amount of supplies used.

MasterSport's office supplies account balance, $12,700.00, is shown on line 7 in the Trial Balance Debit column of the work sheet, Illustration 5-5. The store supplies account balance, $14,330.00, is shown on line 8 in the Trial Balance Debit column of the work sheet.

The actual periodic inventory on December 31 shows that the cost of office supplies inventory is $2,750.00. To bring MasterSport's office supplies inventory up to date, the balance of Supplies—Office needs to be decreased by $9,950.00 (December 31 balance, $12,700.00, *less* ending inventory, $2,750.00).

Supplies Expense—Office

Adj. (d)	9,950.00		

Supplies—Office

Dec. 31 Bal.	12,700.00	Adj. (d)	9,950.00
(New Bal.	*2,750.00)*		

Supplies Expense—Office is increased by a $9,950.00 debit. Supplies—Office is decreased by a $9,950.00 credit. The balance of Supplies—Office after this adjustment, $2,750.00, is equal to the actual ending inventory. The account is up to date.

A similar adjustment is made for store supplies inventory.

The two supplies adjustments are entered on the work sheet, lines 7, 8, 48, and 55, Illustration 5-5. The Supplies—Office adjustment is labeled *(d)*. The Supplies—Store adjustment is labeled *(e)*.

Prepaid Insurance Adjustment. The prepaid insurance account balance includes two items. (1) The account balance on January 1. (2) The amount of insurance premiums paid during the year. The account balance does not reflect the amount of any insurance used during the year, an operating expense. The amount of unexpired insurance is determined at the end of a fiscal period.

Insurance Expense

Adj. (f)	5,650.00		

Prepaid Insurance

Dec. 31 Bal.	9,850.00	Adj. (f)	5,650.00
(New Bal.	*4,200.00)*		

MasterSport's prepaid insurance account balance, $9,850.00, is shown on line 9 in the Trial Balance Debit column of the work sheet, Illustration 5-5. The actual unexpired prepaid insurance on December 31 is $4,200.00. To bring MasterSport's prepaid insurance account up to date, the balance of Prepaid Insurance must be decreased by $5,650.00 (December 31 balance, $9,850.00, *less* unexpired insurance, $4,200.00).

Insurance Expense is increased by a $5,650.00 debit. Prepaid Insurance is decreased by a $5,650.00 credit. The balance of Prepaid Insurance after this adjustment, $4,200.00, is equal to the actual unexpired prepaid insurance. The account is up to date.

The Prepaid Insurance adjustment is entered on the work sheet, lines 9 and 50, Illustration 5-5. The adjustment is labeled *(f)*.

FYI

Contra asset accounts are needed to record depreciation. Depreciation is not recorded in the asset account itself.

TEACHING STRATEGIES: TEACHING TIP

Explain that the amount of federal income tax expense in the trial balance column of the work sheet represents the total amount of estimated quarterly installments made throughout the period. The adjustment represents any additional tax owed. The amount extended to the income statement column is the total amount owed for the period.

Depreciation Expense Adjustments. Assets which will be used for a number of years in the operation of a business are called **plant assets.** Plant assets are not bought for resale to customers in the normal course of business. Plant assets decrease in value because of use and because of the passage of time as they become older and new models become available. The portion of a plant asset's cost that is transferred to an expense account in each fiscal period during a plant asset's useful life is called **depreciation expense.** The decrease in the value of equipment because of use and passage of time is an operating expense. *(CONCEPT: Matching Expenses with Revenue)* The amount of depreciation is an estimate. The actual decrease in equipment value is not known until equipment is disposed of or sold. For this reason, the *estimated* depreciation is recorded in a separate contra asset account for each type of equipment.

Calculating the amount of depreciation is described more fully in Chapter 9.

Depreciation Expense—Office Equipment

Adj. (g)	1,490.00		

Accumulated Depreciation—Office Equipment

		Dec. 31 Bal.	5,960.00
		Adj. (g)	1,490.00
		(New Bal.	*7,450.00)*

MasterSport estimates that the yearly depreciation on office equipment is $1,490.00. To bring MasterSport's office equipment depreciation expense account up to date, the balance of Depreciation Expense—Office Equipment must be increased by $1,490.00.

Depreciation Expense—Office Equipment is increased by a $1,490.00 debit. Accumulated Depreciation—Office Equipment is increased by a $1,490.00 credit.

A similar adjustment is made for Depreciation Expense—Store Equipment.

The two depreciation expense adjustments are entered on the work sheet, lines 11, 13, 45, and 49, Illustration 5-5. The Depreciation Expense—Office Equipment adjustment is labeled *(g)*. The Depreciation Expense—Store Equipment adjustment is labeled *(h)*.

FYI

The adjustment for federal income tax is for corporations only.

Federal Income Tax Expense Adjustment. Corporations anticipating federal income taxes of $500.00 or more are required to pay estimated taxes each quarter. The estimated tax is paid in quarterly installments in April, June, September, and December. Even though a corporation pays a quarterly estimated tax, the actual income tax must be calculated at the end of each fiscal year.

MasterSport estimated $10,800.00 federal income tax for the current year. Each quarterly income tax payment is recorded in a cash payments journal as a debit to Federal Income Tax Expense and a credit to Cash. At the end of the fiscal year, MasterSport determines

Federal Income Tax Expense			
Dec. 31 Bal.	10,800.00		
Adj. (i)	1,190.07		
(New Bal.	*11,990.07)*		

Federal Income Tax Payable			
		Adj. (i)	1,190.07

that the federal income tax is $11,990.07. To bring MasterSport's federal income tax expense account up to date, the balance of Federal Income Tax Expense must be increased by $1,190.07 (federal income tax amount, $11,990.07, *less* December 31 balance in Federal Income Tax Expense, $10,800.00).

Federal Income Tax Expense is increased by a $1,190.07 debit. Federal Income Tax Payable is increased by a $1,190.07 credit. The balance of Federal Income Tax Expense after this adjustment, $11,990.07, is equal to the total federal income tax for the fiscal year. The account is up to date.

The Federal Income Tax Expense adjustment is entered on the work sheet, lines 17 and 57. The adjustment is labeled *(i)*.

FYI

The amount of federal income tax expense in the trial balance column of the work sheet represents the total amount of estimated quarterly installments made throughout the period.

Calculating federal income tax at the end of a fiscal period is described in more detail in Chapter 14.

Debits must equal credits in a work sheet's Adjustments columns. After all adjustments have been entered on a work sheet, the Adjustments columns are totaled and checked for equality. The two column totals, $58,959.86, are the same. The work sheet's Adjustments columns are ruled as shown on line 58 of the work sheet, Illustration 5-5.

SOFTWARE FOCUS

Software may be used for independent practice or enrichment/extension as the instructor deems appropriate. For this chapter, the following software may be used: *Automated Accounting 6.0* or higher with Problem 5-7, Mastery Problem 5-M, and Reinforcement Activity 1; Spreadsheet Template with Problems 5-1 and 5-3 and Mastery Problem 5-M.

Balance Sheet Columns on a Work Sheet

The asset, liability, and stockholders' equity account balances are extended to the Balance Sheet columns of a work sheet. For those accounts affected by adjustments, new balances are calculated and extended. For example, Allowance for Uncollectible Accounts, line 4 of the work sheet, Illustration 5-5, has a Trial Balance Credit balance of $240.60. The Adjustments Credit column amount of $2,109.40 makes the new account balance $2,350.00 ($240.60 *plus* $2,109.40). The new credit balance, $2,350.00, is extended to the Balance Sheet Credit column.

The two Balance Sheet columns are totaled. These two totals are out of balance by the amount of change in stockholders' equity resulting from a net income or a net loss. MasterSport's two balance sheet column totals are shown on line 58 of the work sheet.

Income Statement Columns on a Work Sheet

The balances of all revenue, cost, and expense accounts are extended to the Income Statement columns on a work sheet. The amounts in the Adjustments columns for Income Summary—Golf and Income Summary—Tennis are also extended to the Income Statement columns. This procedure is shown on MasterSport's work sheet, lines 28 and 29, Illustration 5-5.

The two Income Statement columns are totaled. These two totals are out of balance by the amount of change in stockholders' equity resulting from a net income or net loss. MasterSport's two Income Statement column totals are shown on line 58 of the work sheet.

Net Income on a Work Sheet

The difference between the two Income Statement column totals on the work sheet is the net income or net loss for a fiscal period. If the credit column total is larger than the debit column total, the difference is the increase in stockholders' equity resulting from a net income. If the debit column total is larger than the credit column total, the difference is the decrease in stockholders' equity resulting from a net loss.

MasterSport's two Income Statement column totals result in a net income calculated as shown below.

Income Statement Credit column total (line 58)	$833,368.45
Less Income Statement Debit column total (line 58)	−777,398.25
Equals net income for the fiscal period	$ 55,970.20

The net income, $55,970.20, is written under the work sheet's Income Statement Debit column total, line 59, to make the two Income Statement columns balance. The words *Net Income after Fed. Inc. Tax* are written in the Account Title column on the same line.

The difference between the two Balance Sheet column totals on the work sheet is the net income or net loss for a fiscal period. If the debit column total is larger than the credit column total, the difference is an increase in stockholders' equity resulting from a net income. If the credit column total exceeds the debit column total, the difference is a decrease in stockholders' equity resulting from a net loss.

MasterSport's net income, $55,970.20, is written under the Balance Sheet Credit column total, line 59, to make the two Balance Sheet columns balance.

When a net loss occurs, the net loss amount is written on a work sheet in the Income Statement Credit and Balance Sheet Debit columns.

After the net income amount is written in the two work sheet columns, the last four columns are totaled again. These new totals are shown on line 60, Illustration 5-5. The totals for each pair of columns must be the same. The two Income Statement totals are the same, $833,368.45. The two Balance Sheet totals are the same, $551,424.60. If the totals of each pair of columns are equal, the work sheet is assumed to be correct.

When the same net income or net loss amount makes the Income Statement columns and Balance Sheet columns balance, the work sheet is ruled as shown on line 60. If columns do not balance, errors must be found and corrected before final ruling is done.

Audit Your Understanding

1. What two reports are prepared to prove the accuracy of posting to subsidiary ledgers?
2. What general ledger accounts are affected, and how, by the uncollectible accounts expense adjustment?
3. What account balances are extended to the Balance Sheet columns of a work sheet?

AUDIT YOUR UNDERSTANDING

1. Schedule of accounts receivable and schedule of accounts payable.
2. Uncollectible Accounts Expense is debited; Allowance for Uncollectible Accounts is credited.
3. Asset, liability, and stockholders' equity.

FINANCIAL STATEMENTS FOR A DEPARTMENTALIZED BUSINESS

Financial statements are prepared to report the financial progress and condition of a business. *(CONCEPT: Adequate Disclosure)* MasterSport prepares four financial statements at the end of the annual fiscal period. *(CONCEPT: Accounting Period Cycle)* (1) Departmental statement of gross profit. (2) Income statement. (3) Statement of stockholders' equity. (4) Balance sheet. In preparing financial statements, MasterSport applies accounting principles the same way from one accounting period to the next. *(CONCEPT: Consistent Reporting)*

Departmental Statement of Gross Profit

MasterSport's departmental statement of gross profit for the fiscal year ended December 31 is shown in Illustration 5-6.

ILLUSTRATION 5-6 Departmental statement of gross profit

MasterSport
Departmental Statement of Gross Profit
For Year Ended December 31, 19--

	Golf		*% of Net Sales	Tennis		*% of Net Sales	Total		*% of Net Sales
Operating Revenue:									
Net Sales		$344,476.46	100.0		$430,154.70	100.0		$774,631.16	100.0
Cost of Merchandise Sold:									
Mdse. Inventory, Jan. 1	$186,434.61			$199,844.60			$386,279.21		
Net Purchases	203,404.25			218,534.55			421,938.80		
Mdse. Available for Sale	$389,838.86			$418,379.15			$808,218.01		
Less Ending Inv., Dec. 31	204,855.00			190,484.60			395,339.60		
Cost of Merchandise Sold		184,983.86	53.7		227,894.55	53.0		412,878.41	53.3
Gross Profit on Operations		$159,492.60	46.3		$202,260.15	47.0		$361,752.75	46.7

*Rounded to nearest 0.1%

The departmental statement of gross profit prepared at the end of a fiscal period is similar to the monthly interim departmental statement of gross profit. However, monthly interim departmental statements of gross profit use estimated ending inventories. The annual departmental statement of gross profit uses the actual ending periodic inventories.

Data needed to complete the departmental statement of gross profit are taken from the Trial Balance, Income Statement, and Balance Sheet columns of the work sheet.

MasterSport analyzes the annual departmental statement of gross profit in the same way as the interim departmental statement

LESSON PLAN 5-3

Materials

- Student pages 131–143
- Blackline Master for Departmental Statement of Gross Profit (TRG)
- Blackline Master for General Journal (TRG)
- Software: Spreadsheet Template
- *Automated Accounting 6.0* or higher; CENTURY 21 ACCOUNTING Template, Advanced Course
- Assess: Problem Test Chapter 5, MicroExam Chapter 5, Objective Test 2

Objectives (Enabling Performance Tasks)

a. Define accounting terms related to financial reporting for a departmentalized business.
b. Identify accounting concepts and practices related to financial reporting for a departmentalized business.
c. Prepare selected interim and end-of-fiscal-period work for a departmentalized business.
d. Analyze financial statements using selected component percentages.

FOCUS

- The end-of-fiscal-period work for a departmentalized business was begun earlier in this chapter with the preparation of the schedules of accounts receivable and accounts payable and the work sheet. In this lesson, the financial statements for a departmentalized business will be prepared and analyzed. Explain that these statements are similar to those prepared by a nondepartmentalized business. Also, the adjusting and closing entries will be journalized and a post-closing trial balance will be prepared.
- Introduce vocabulary: income statement, statement of stockholders' equity, capital stock, retained earnings, dividends, balance sheet, adjusting entries, closing entries, post-closing trial balance, accounting cycle.

TEACH

Cover student pages 131–143 "Financial Statements for a Departmentalized Business," "Adjusting and Closing Entries for a Departmentalized Business," "Post-Closing Trial Balance for a Departmentalized Business," and "Summary of Accounting Cycle." Present the departmental statement of gross profit and explain how it is similar to the interim statement introduced earlier in this chapter. Review the steps for preparing an income statement, a statement of stockholders' equity, and a balance sheet. Review the definition of component percentage, explain how component percentages are used to analyze the income statement, and show how the component percentages are calculated. Describe how component percentages are used to determine levels of performance. Review the steps for journalizing adjusting and closing entries. Explain that the departmental income summary accounts are closed into the general income summary account. Explain where to obtain the information for each closing entry. Review the purpose and preparation of a post-closing trial balance.

FYI

A component percentage is usually carried out one decimal place.

of gross profit. Component percentages for the total cost of merchandise sold and gross profit on operations are calculated. The same component percentages are also calculated for each department.

MasterSport uses the same performance standards for the annual departmental statement of gross profit as for the interim departmental statement of gross profit. For comparative purposes, MasterSport's acceptable and actual component percentages are shown in Illustration 5-7.

ILLUSTRATION 5-7

Income statement acceptable component percentages

Income Statement Items	Acceptable Component Percentages	Actual Component Percentages
Net sales	100.0%	100.0%
Cost of merchandise sold	not more than 55.0%	53.3%
Gross profit on operations	not less than 45.0%	46.7%
Total operating expenses	not more than 38.0%	37.9%
Net income before federal income tax	not less than 7.0%	8.8%

The component percentage for total cost of merchandise sold should not be more than 55.0%. The component percentage for total gross profit on operations should not be less than 45.0%. The same performance standards are used for each department.

An analysis of the annual departmental statement of gross profit indicates acceptable levels of performance. The component percentage for total cost of merchandise sold, 53.3%, is not more than 55.0%. The component percentage for total gross profit on operations, 46.7%, is not less than 45.0%. The component percentages for total cost of merchandise sold and total gross profit on operations for each department also indicate acceptable levels of performance.

Income Statement

A financial statement showing the revenue and expenses for a fiscal period is called an **income statement.** An income statement reports financial progress of a business for a fiscal period. MasterSport's income statement for the fiscal year ended December 31 is shown in Illustration 5-8.

The data used to prepare MasterSport's income statement are obtained from the work sheet's Trial Balance, Income Statement, and Balance Sheet columns.

Besides analyzing the component percentages for cost of merchandise sold and gross profit on operations for a fiscal year, MasterSport also analyzes the component percentages for total

TEACHING STRATEGIES: TEACHING TIP

Provide extensive practice in calculating the various component percentages presented in this chapter. Emphasize the importance of component percentages in comparing performance levels with historical data as well as industry standards.

ILLUSTRATION 5-8 Income statement

MasterSport
Income Statement
For Year Ended December 31, 19--

					% of Net Sales
Operating Revenue:					
Sales			$789,374.56		
Less: Sales Discount		$ 3,611.10			
Sales Returns and Allow.		11,132.30	14,743.40		
Net Sales				$774,631.16	100.0
Cost of Merchandise Sold:					
Merchandise Inventory, Jan. 1, 19--			$386,279.21		
Purchases		$447,512.30			
Less: Purchases Discount	$ 8,393.50				
Purchases Returns and Allow.	17,180.00	25,573.50			
Net Purchases			421,938.80		
Total Cost of Mdse. Avail. for Sale			$808,218.01		
Less Mdse. Inventory, Dec. 31, 19--			395,339.60		
Cost of Merchandise Sold				412,878.41	53.3
Gross Profit on Operations				$361,752.75	46.7
Operating Expenses:					
Selling Expenses:					
Advertising Expense		$ 5,192.88			
Credit Card Fee Expense		5,950.00			
Depreciation Exp.—Store Equip.		3,000.00			
Salary Expense—Golf		90,924.19			
Salary Expense—Tennis		72,627.02			
Supplies Expense—Store		7,790.00			
Total Selling Expenses			$185,484.09		
Administrative Expenses:					
Depreciation Exp.—Office Equip.		$ 1,490.00			
Insurance Expense		5,650.00			
Miscellaneous Expense		5,958.48			
Payroll Taxes Expense		21,426.92			
Rent Expense		18,056.40			
Salary Expense—Admin.		43,667.19			
Supplies Expense—Office		9,950.00			
Uncollectible Accounts Expense		2,109.40			
Total Administrative Expense			108,308.39		
Total Operating Expenses				293,792.48	37.9
Net Income before Federal Inc. Tax				$ 67,960.27	8.8
Less Federal Income Tax Exp.				11,990.07	1.6
Net Income after Federal Inc. Tax				$ 55,970.20	7.2

operating expenses, net income before and after income tax, and federal income tax. Comparisons with previous performance and with industry performance standards that are published by indus-

APPLY

Refer students to the financial statements shown in Illustrations 5-6, 5-8, 5-9, and 5-10, respectively, as the departmental statement of gross profit, income statement, statement of stockholders' equity, and balance sheet are presented. Refer students to Illustrations 5-11 and 5-12 as journalizing adjusting and closing entries is discussed.

Guided Practice

Guide students through the calculation of component percentages and the determination of performance levels for Businesses 1 and 2 in Problem 5-5 and 5-6. Working as a group, have students calculate the component percentage and determine the performance level for Business 1 in Problem 5-5. Have students verify their calculations by comparing their answers with those given as the example. Next, have students calculate the component percentage and determine the performance level for Business 2. When all students agree on the correct amounts, direct students to record their answers on the form provided in the working papers. Repeat the process for Businesses 1 and 2 in Problem 5-6. The balance of Problems 5-5 and 5-6 can be completed as Independent Practice.

Independent Practice

- Assign Terms 14–23; Questions 13–18; Problems 5-5, 5-6, and 5-7, Instructions 2–7.
- Assign Study Guide 5 and Mastery Problem 5-M.

ASSESS

Assess student understanding by checking the solutions to the Independent Practice activities.

Reteach

- Make transparencies of the departmental statement of gross profit ruling and the general journal from the accounting forms masters provided in the Blackline Masters section of the Teacher's Resource Guide. Use data from the work sheet completed in Recycling Problem 5-R2 (solution in the TRG) and the transparencies to demonstrate how to prepare the departmental statement of gross profit and calculate the component percentages and to record the closing entries for a departmental business.
- Assign Recycling Problem 5-R2.

Extend

- Assign Challenge Problem 5-C. (The challenge is to use a 10-column work sheet.)
- Assign Reinforcement Activity 1.
- Assign the Spreadsheet Template for Mastery Problem 5-M.
- Use *Automated Accounting 6.0* or higher with CENTURY 21 ACCOUNTING Template, Advanced Course, with Problem 5-7, Mastery Problem 5-M, and Reinforcement Activity 1.

Enrich

Assign GALLERIA, Inc. A Business Simulation.

try organizations are used to determine acceptable levels of performance. From these sources, MasterSport determines acceptable component percentages for the end of the fiscal period. For comparative purposes, MasterSport's acceptable and actual component percentages are shown in Illustration 5-7. The component percentages for these items are shown in a separate column on the income statement. The component percentages for total gross profit on operations and total cost of merchandise sold are obtained from the departmental statement of gross profit. The component percentage for total operating expenses is calculated as shown below.

Total Operating Expenses	÷	Net Sales	=	Total Operating Expenses Component Percentage
$293,792.48	÷	$774,631.16	=	37.9%

The component percentage for net income before federal income tax is calculated as shown below.

Net Income Before Federal Income Tax	÷	Net Sales	=	Net Income Before Federal Income Tax Component Percentage
$67,960.27	÷	$774,631.16	=	8.8%

The last two items on the income statement, federal income tax expense and net income after federal income tax, are important. Since the tax rate is set by the Internal Revenue Service, MasterSport does not have much control over these two items. However, MasterSport is interested in what portion of each sales dollar is paid to the federal government for income taxes. Therefore, the component percentages for federal income tax and net income after federal income tax are calculated. The component percentages for federal income tax and for net income after federal income tax are shown in the component percentage column of the income statement.

The component percentage for federal income tax is calculated as shown below.

Federal Income Tax	÷	Net Sales	=	Federal Income Tax Component Percentage
$11,990.07	÷	$774,631.16	=	1.6%

The component percentage for net income after federal income tax is calculated as shown below.

Net Income After Federal Income Tax	÷	Net Sales	=	Net Income After Federal Income Tax Component Percentage
$55,970.20	÷	$774,631.16	=	7.2%

FYI

Account titles should be abbreviated only when there is not enough room to write them in full.

An analysis of MasterSport's income statement for the year ended December 31 indicates acceptable levels of performance. The component percentage for cost of merchandise sold, 53.3%, is acceptable based on the performance standard of not more than 55.0%. The component percentage for gross profit on operations, 46.7%, is acceptable based on the performance standard of not less than 45.0%. The component percentage for total operating expenses, 37.9%, is acceptable based on the performance standard of not more than 38.0%. The component percentage for net income before federal income tax, 8.8%, is acceptable based on the performance standard of not less than 7.0%.

Statement of Stockholders' Equity

A financial statement that shows changes in a corporation's ownership for a fiscal period is called a **statement of stockholders' equity.** MasterSport's statement of stockholders' equity for the fiscal year ended December 31 is shown in Illustration 5-9.

ILLUSTRATION 5-9 Statement of stockholders' equity

MasterSport
Statement of Stockholders' Equity
For Year Ended December 31, 19--

Capital Stock:			
$170.00 Per Share			
January 1, 19–, 2,000 Shares Issued		$340,000.00	
Issued during Current Year, None		-0-	
Balance, December 31, 19–, 2,000 Shares Issued			$340,000.00
Retained Earnings:			
Balance, January 1, 19–		$ 42,210.50	
Net Income after Federal Income Tax for 19–	$55,970.20		
Less Dividends Declared during 19–	30,000.00		
Net Increase during 19–		25,970.20	
Balance, December 31, 19–			68,180.70
Total Stockholders' Equity, December 31, 19–			$408,180.70

CLOSURE

- Use Audit Your Understanding Questions.
- Review Summary Illustration 5-14, Summary of Accounting Cycle.

ASSESS

- Administer Problem Test Chapter 5.
- Administer a MicroExam test for Chapter 5.
- Administer Objective Test 2.

TEACHING STRATEGIES: COOPERATIVE LEARNING

Explain what component percentages measure. Assign students to groups of three. Each group is to plan, prepare, and deliver a presentation to NON ACCOUNTANTS. The presentation should explain what component percentages are and how they are used to analyze financial statements. Time frame: Class time = 30 minutes over a few class periods; additional time outside of class will be required to prepare the presentation.

A statement of stockholders' equity contains two major sections. (1) Capital Stock. Total shares of ownership in a corporation are called **capital stock.** (2) Retained Earnings. An amount earned by a corporation and not yet distributed to stockholders is called **retained earnings.**

The first section shows that MasterSport started the fiscal year with $340,000.00 capital stock. This capital stock consisted of 2,000 shares of stock issued prior to January 1. During the year, MasterSport did not issue any additional stock. Thus, at the end of the fiscal year, MasterSport still had $340,000.00 capital stock. This information is obtained from the previous year's statement of stockholders' equity and the capital stock account.

The second section of MasterSport's statement of stockholders' equity shows that the business started the fiscal year with $42,210.50 retained earnings. This amount represents previous years' earnings that have been kept in the business. For the current fiscal year ended December 31, MasterSport earned net income after federal income tax of $55,970.20. This amount is obtained from line 59 of the work sheet, Illustration 5-5.

APPLIED SKILLS: LANGUAGE ARTS

Paraphrasing, writing complete sentences. For additional practice in language arts skills, direct students to answer the Questions for Individual Study at the end of the chapter. Students should write the answers in their own words and in complete sentences.

Net income increases the retained earnings of a corporation. Some income may be retained by a corporation for business expansion. Some income may be distributed to stockholders as a return on their investment. Earnings distributed to stockholders are called **dividends.**

MasterSport's board of directors declared dividends of $30,000.00 during the year. The amount of dividends declared is obtained from line 27 of the Balance Sheet Debit column of the work sheet. The amount of dividends declared, $30,000.00, is subtracted from the amount of net income for the year, $55,970.20, to obtain the net increase in Retained Earnings for the year, $25,970.20. The net increase in Retained Earnings, $25,970.20, is added to the January 1 balance of Retained Earnings, $42,210.50, to obtain the December 31 balance, $68,180.70. MasterSport's capital stock, $340,000.00, plus retained earnings, $68,180.70, equals total stockholders' equity on December 31, $408,180.70.

Declaration and payment of dividends is described in Chapter 12.

Balance Sheet

A financial statement that reports assets, liabilities, and owner's equity on a specific date is called a **balance sheet.** A balance sheet reports the financial condition of a business on a specific date. MasterSport's balance sheet for December 31 is shown in Illustration 5-10.

Data used in preparing a balance sheet are obtained from two sources. (1) Balance Sheet columns of the work sheet. (2) Statement of Stockholders' Equity. On a balance sheet, the total assets must equal the total liabilities plus stockholders' equity. MasterSport's balance sheet, Illustration 5-10, has total assets of $490,624.60

ILLUSTRATION 5-10 Balance sheet

MasterSport
Balance Sheet
December 31, 19--

ASSETS			
Current Assets:			
Cash		$ 43,440.00	
Petty Cash		500.00	
Accounts Receivable	$12,855.00		
Less Allowance for Uncollectible Accounts	2,350.00	10,505.00	
Merchandise Inventory—Golf		204,855.00	
Merchandise Inventory—Tennis		190,484.60	
Supplies—Office		2,750.00	
Supplies—Store		6,540.00	
Prepaid Insurance		4,200.00	
Total Current Assets			$463,274.60
Plant Assets:			
Office Equipment	$16,900.00		
Less Accumulated Depreciation—Office Equipment	7,450.00	$ 9,450.00	
Store Equipment	$38,900.00		
Less Accumulated Depreciation—Store Equipment	21,000.00	17,900.00	
Total Plant Assets			27,350.00
Total Assets			$490,624.60
LIABILITIES			
Current Liabilities:			
Accounts Payable		$ 38,160.30	
Employee Income Tax Payable—Federal		2,680.75	
Employee Income Tax Payable—State		1,118.19	
Federal Income Tax Payable		1,190.07	
FICA Tax Payable		3,360.70	
Sales Tax Payable		3,139.64	
Unemployment Tax Payable—Federal		23.60	
Unemployment Tax Payable—State		159.30	
Health Insurance Premiums Payable		2,261.16	
Life Insurance Premiums Payable		350.19	
Dividends Payable		30,000.00	
Total Liabilities			$ 82,443.90
STOCKHOLDERS' EQUITY			
Capital Stock		$340,000.00	
Retained Earnings		68,180.70	
Total Stockholders' Equity			408,180.70
Total Liabilities and Stockholders' Equity			$490,624.60

and total liabilities and stockholders' equity of the same amount. Because the two amounts are the same, MasterSport's balance sheet is in balance and assumed to be correct.

Financial analysis of balance sheet items is described in Chapter 17.

ADJUSTING AND CLOSING ENTRIES FOR A DEPARTMENTALIZED BUSINESS

Account balances are changed only by posting journal entries. Journal entries recorded to update general ledger accounts at the end of a fiscal period are called **adjusting entries.** At the end of a fiscal period, the temporary account balances are transferred to an income summary account. This procedure summarizes, in one account, the effect of operating the business. Journal entries used to prepare temporary accounts for a new fiscal period are called **closing entries.**

TEACHING STRATEGIES: DIFFERENT LEARNING ABILITIES

Specific Learning Disability (SLD) Students. Encourage students to maintain a daily log or journal that describes their academic progress. Students can share this log, if they desire, with the teacher when updating their individual program.

Journalizing Adjusting Entries

MasterSport's adjusting entries made on December 31 are shown in Illustration 5-11.

MasterSport uses information in the Adjustments columns of the work sheet, Illustration 5-5, to journalize adjusting entries.

The words *Adjusting Entries* are written on line 1 in the Account Title column. This statement identifies a group of adjusting entries. Therefore, a source document or explanation is not written for each individual adjusting entry.

FYI

Do not skip lines between adjusting entries.

ILLUSTRATION 5-11 Adjusting entries

GENERAL JOURNAL PAGE 8

	DATE		ACCOUNT TITLE	DOC. NO.	POST. REF.	DEBIT	CREDIT	
1			*Adjusting Entries*					1
2	19-- Dec.	31	Uncollectible Accounts Expense			2 109 40		2
3			Allowance for Uncoll. Accounts				2 109 40	3
4		31	Merchandise Inventory—Golf			18 420 39		4
5			Income Summary—Golf				18 420 39	5
6		31	Income Summary—Tennis			9 360 00		6
7			Merchandise Inventory—Tennis				9 360 00	7
8		31	Supplies Expense—Office			9 950 00		8
9			Supplies—Office				9 950 00	9
10		31	Supplies Expense—Store			7 790 00		10
11			Supplies—Store				7 790 00	11
12		31	Insurance Expense			5 650 00		12
13			Prepaid Insurance				5 650 00	13
14		31	Depreciation Exp.—Office Equip.			1 490 00		14
15			Accum. Depr.—Office Equip.				1 490 00	15
16		31	Depreciation Exp.—Store Equip.			3 000 00		16
17			Accum. Depr.—Store Equip.				3 000 00	17
18		31	Federal Income Tax Expense			1 190 07		18
19			Federal Income Tax Payable				1 190 07	19
20								20

After the adjusting entries are posted, general ledger accounts will have up-to-date balances as of December 31.

Journalizing Closing Entries

MasterSport's closing entries made on December 31 are shown in Illustration 5-12.

ILLUSTRATION 5-12 Closing entries

GENERAL JOURNAL PAGE 9

	DATE		ACCOUNT TITLE	DOC. NO.	POST. REF.	DEBIT	CREDIT	
1			*Closing Entries*					1
2	19-- Dec.	31	*Income Summary—Golf*			18 420 39		2
3			*Sales—Golf*			351 032 81		3
4			*Sales—Tennis*			438 341 75		4
5			*Purchases Discount—Golf*			4 058 95		5
6			*Purchases Discount—Tennis*			4 334 55		6
7			*Purchases Ret. and Allow.—Golf*			8 282 48		7
8			*Purchases Ret. and Allow.—Tennis*			8 897 52		8
9			*Income Summary—General*				833 368 45	9
10		31	*Income Summary—General*			777 398 25		10
11			*Income Summary—Tennis*				9 360 00	11
12			*Sales Discount—Golf*				1 605 85	12
13			*Sales Discount—Tennis*				2 005 25	13
14			*Sales Returns and Allow.—Golf*				4 950 50	14
15			*Sales Returns and Allow.—Tennis*				6 181 80	15
16			*Purchases—Golf*				215 745 68	16
17			*Purchases—Tennis*				231 766 62	17
18			*Advertising Expense*				5 192 88	18
19			*Credit Card Fee Expense*				5 950 00	19
20			*Depreciation Exp.—Store Equip.*				3 000 00	20
21			*Salary Expense—Golf*				90 924 19	21
22			*Salary Expense—Tennis*				72 627 02	22
23			*Supplies Expense—Store*				7 790 00	23
24			*Depreciation Exp.—Office Equip.*				1 490 00	24
25			*Insurance Expense*				5 650 00	25
26			*Miscellaneous Expense*				5 958 48	26
27			*Payroll Taxes Expense*				21 426 92	27
28			*Rent Expense*				18 056 40	28
29			*Salary Expense—Administrative*				43 667 19	29
30			*Supplies Expense—Office*				9 950 00	30
31			*Uncollectible Accounts Expense*				2 109 40	31
32			*Federal Income Tax Expense*				11 990 07	32
33		31	*Income Summary—General*			55 970 20		33
34			*Retained Earnings*				55 970 20	34
35		31	*Retained Earnings*			30 000 00		35
36			*Dividends*				30 000 00	36

APPLIED SKILLS: WRITING ACROSS THE CURRICULUM

Writing paragraphs and short essays. The Cases for Critical Thinking are short, practical applications of the accounting principles developed in the chapter. Some cases are planned to present problems related to the chapter but not specifically discussed and answered in the chapter. These cases present an opportunity for critical thinking and decision making. These cases also require more than a short objective-type response. Therefore they provide ideal practice in writing paragraphs and short essays.

139

Information to journalize closing entries is obtained from the Income Statement columns of the work sheet. MasterSport records four closing entries to prepare the general ledger for the next fiscal period.

1. The closing entry for MasterSport's income statement credit balance accounts on December 31 is shown on lines 1–9, Illustration 5-12. Income statement credit balance accounts are the departmental income summary accounts with a credit balance (Income Summary—Golf), the revenue accounts (Sales—Golf and Sales—Tennis), and the contra cost accounts (Purchases Discount—Golf, Purchases Discount—Tennis, Purchases Returns and Allowances—Golf, and Purchases Returns and Allowances—Tennis). Information needed for closing income statement credit balance accounts is obtained from the Income Statement Credit column of the work sheet, as shown in Illustration 5-5.
2. The closing entry for MasterSport's income statement debit balance accounts on December 31 is shown on lines 10–32, Illustration 5-12. Income statement debit balance accounts are the departmental income summary accounts with a debit balance (Income Summary—Tennis), the contra revenue accounts (Sales Discount—Golf, Sales Discount—Tennis, Sales Returns and Allowances—Golf, and Sales Returns and Allowances—Tennis), the cost accounts (Purchases—Golf and Purchases—Tennis), and expense accounts. Information needed for closing income statement debit balance accounts is obtained from the Income Statement Debit column of the work sheet, as shown in Illustration 5-5.

Personal Visions in Business

This special student feature introduces students to successful entrepreneurs or business professionals. Each profile gives a flavor of what the actual business world is like and some of the opportunities available to students who study accounting. These features can be used to motivate students to pursue professional business careers in a wide variety of fields. The subjects of these profiles have been carefully chosen to represent the full spectrum of diverse ethnic and racial backgrounds of professional business people. As an optional activity, students can be encouraged to seek out and interview successful business people in their own communities.

■ Debra Miller ■

DEBRA MILLER, M.D.

Dr. Debra Miller has always been in the medical field. Miller worked as a nurse before entering medical school to train to be a doctor. She now has her own medical practice.

Miller had no real concept of what it would take to run a business when she started her medical practice. She did not know about accounts receivable, the wages and taxes for employees, the federal taxes she would have to pay, and what it would cost to run a medical practice.

"It costs a lot of money to run a medical practice!" says Miller. She was surprised when she started out that her top three expenses—rent, employee wages and benefits, and malpractice insurance—consumed half of all her revenue.

Miller found that it is not realistic for a doctor to hope "to just practice medicine." It is surprising how complicated worker's compensation and unemployment tax requirements can be to follow. "The complications involved in receiving payments from health insurance plans are staggering," Miller declared. "I also learned," she said, "that there are a lot of legal requirements to meet. And ignorance of the law is not a valid defense in a court of law."

Miller advises anyone who plans to work in the business world to study accounting, business law, and finance courses. "Running a business," she says, "involves more than just balancing a checkbook. I have to rely on my accountant whose advice I accept without question."

Personal Visions in Business

FYI

Only temporary accounts are closed.

3. The closing entry to record MasterSport's net income in the retained earnings account and close the income summary account on December 31 is shown on lines 33–34, Illustration 5-12. The Income Summary—General account balance is equal to the net income (or net loss) for the fiscal period. A corporation's net income is recorded in the retained earnings account. Information needed for this entry is obtained from line 59 of MasterSport's work sheet, as shown in Illustration 5-5.
4. The closing entry for MasterSport's dividends account on December 31 is shown on lines 35-36, Illustration 5-12. The debit balance of a dividends account is the total amount of dividends declared during a fiscal period. Since dividends decrease the earnings retained by a corporation, the dividends account is closed to Retained Earnings. Information needed for closing MasterSport's dividends account is obtained from line 27 of the Balance Sheet Debit column of the work sheet, as shown in Illustration 5-5.

After closing entries are posted, all temporary accounts have zero balances and are prepared for a new fiscal period.

POST-CLOSING TRIAL BALANCE FOR A DEPARTMENTALIZED BUSINESS

Debits must always equal credits in general ledger accounts. The trial balance recorded on the work sheet, Illustration 5-5, proves that debits do equal credits before adjusting and closing entries are posted. After adjusting and closing entries are posted, equality of general ledger debits and credits is proved again. This procedure assures that the equality of debits and credits has been maintained in preparation for a new fiscal period.

A trial balance prepared after the closing entries are posted is called a **post-closing trial balance.** MasterSport's post-closing trial balance prepared on December 31 is shown in Illustration 5-13, page 142.

The total of debit balances, $521,424.60, is the same as the total of credit balances. The equality of general ledger debits and credits is proved. MasterSport's general ledger is ready for the next fiscal period.

Audit Your Understanding

1. What four financial statements does MasterSport prepare at the end of its fiscal period?
2. What is the formula for calculating the component percentage for total operating expenses?
3. What are the two major sections of a statement of stockholders' equity?

AUDIT YOUR UNDERSTANDING

1. Departmental statement of gross profit; income statement; statement of stockholders' equity; balance sheet.
2. Total Operating Expenses divided by Net Sales equals Total Operating Expenses Component Percentage.
3. Capital Stock and Retained Earnings.

SUMMARY OF ACCOUNTING CYCLE

Accounting procedures used by MasterSport, a departmentalized merchandising business, are described in Chapters 2 through 5. The procedures used for the fiscal year ended December 31 are followed each year. The series of accounting activities included in recording financial information for a fiscal period is called an **accounting cycle.** Accounting cycle procedures provide information for prepar-

ILLUSTRATION 5-13 Post-closing trial balance

MasterSport Post-Closing Trial Balance December 31, 19--		
Account Title	**Debit**	**Credit**
Cash	$ 43,440.00	
Petty Cash	500.00	
Accounts Receivable	12,855.00	
Allowance for Uncollectible Accounts		$ 2,350.00
Merchandise Inventory—Golf	204,855.00	
Merchandise Inventory—Tennis	190,484.60	
Supplies—Office	2,750.00	
Supplies—Store	6,540.00	
Prepaid Insurance	4,200.00	
Office Equipment	16,900.00	
Accumulated Depreciation—Office Equipment		7,450.00
Store Equipment	38,900.00	
Accumulated Depreciation—Store Equipment		21,000.00
Accounts Payable		38,160.30
Employee Income Tax Payable—Federal		2,680.75
Employee Income Tax Payable—State		1,118.19
Federal Income Tax Payable		1,190.07
FICA Tax Payable		3,360.70
Sales Tax Payable		3,139.64
Unemployment Tax Payable—Federal		23.60
Unemployment Tax Payable—State		159.30
Health Insurance Premiums Payable		2,261.16
Life Insurance Premiums Payable		350.19
Dividends Payable		30,000.00
Capital Stock		340,000.00
Retained Earnings		68,180.70
Totals	$521,424.60	$521,424.60

TEACHING STRATEGIES: ASSESSMENT BY PORTFOLIO

An ideal specimen for inclusion in a portfolio to demonstrate mastery of the procedures and concepts involved in the complete accounting cycle is an extended activity that simulates the accounting cycle. For this part, the accounting cycle for a departmentalized business, you may wish to have students complete and include in their portfolios either Reinforcement Activity 1 or *Galleria: A Business Simulation.* You may also wish to include both a manual version and an automated version for either or both of these activities.

ing interim and end-of-fiscal-period financial statements. *(CONCEPT: Accounting Period Cycle.)*

MasterSport's complete accounting cycle is shown in Illustration 5-14.

An accounting cycle begins with source documents proving that transactions did occur. *(CONCEPT: Objective Evidence)* MasterSport's fiscal year cycle includes preparation of a monthly interim departmental statement of gross profit. An interim departmental statement of gross profit provides management with information about the operating efficiency of each department. A cycle also includes preparation of financial statements at the end of a fiscal period to give a complete and accurate picture of the financial operations of a business. *(CONCEPT: Adequate Disclosure)* An accounting cycle is completed when the general ledger is proved by a post-closing trial balance.

SUMMARY ILLUSTRATION 5-14

Accounting cycle

1 Source documents describe transactions. The documents are verified for accuracy.

2 Entries are recorded in journals from information on the source documents.

3 Entries in journals are posted to ledgers.

4 From accounting records, an interim departmental statement of gross profit is prepared.

5 Schedules of accounts receivable and accounts payable are prepared from the subsidiary ledgers.

6 A trial balance is prepared and a work sheet is completed to summarize a business' financial condition.

7 From data on the work sheet, financial statements are prepared.

8 From data on the work sheet, adjusting and closing entries are journalized and posted.

9 A post-closing trial balance is prepared to check the equality of debits and credits in a general ledger.

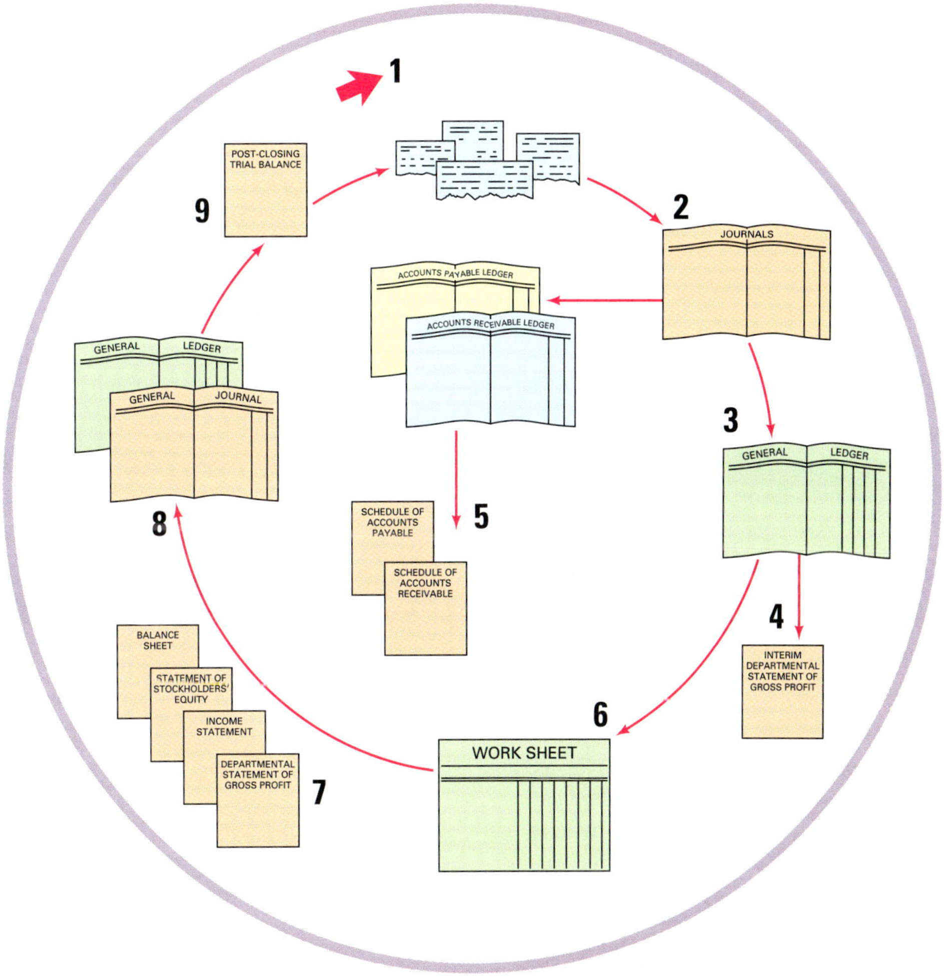

TEACHING STRATEGIES: APPLYING VISUALS

Direct students to Summary Illustration 5-14. Review the summary of the accounting cycle.

ACCOUNTING TERMS

1. **fiscal period:** The length of time for which a business summarizes and reports financial information. (p. 117)
2. **departmental statement of gross profit:** A statement prepared at the end of a fiscal period showing the gross profit for each department. (p. 117)
3. **interim departmental statement of gross profit:** A statement showing gross profit for each department for a portion of a fiscal period. (p. 117)
4. **periodic inventory:** A merchandise inventory determined by counting, weighing, or measuring items of merchandise on hand. (p. 117)
5. **perpetual inventory:** A merchandise inventory determined by keeping a continuous record of increases, decreases, and balance on hand. (p. 118)
6. **gross profit method of estimating an inventory:** Estimating inventory by using the previous year's percentage of gross profit on operations. (p. 118)
7. **component percentage:** The percentage relationship between one financial statement item and the total that includes that item. (p. 120)
8. **schedule of accounts receivable:** A listing of customer accounts, account balances, and total amount due from all customers. (pp. 121-122)
9. **schedule of accounts payable:** A listing of vendor accounts, account balances, and total amount due all vendors. (p. 122)
10. **trial balance:** A proof of the equality of debits and credits in a general ledger. (p. 123)
11. **work sheet:** A columnar accounting form used to summarize the general ledger information needed to prepare financial statements. (p. 123)
12. **plant assets:** Assets which will be used for a number of years in the operation of a business. (p. 128)
13. **depreciation expense:** The portion of a plant asset's cost that is transferred to an expense account in each fiscal period during a plant asset's useful life. (p. 128)
14. **income statement:** A financial statement showing the revenue and expenses for a fiscal period. (p. 132)
15. **statement of stockholders' equity:** A financial statement that shows changes in a corporation's ownership for a fiscal period. (p. 135)
16. **capital stock:** Total shares of ownership in a corporation. (p. 136)
17. **retained earnings:** An amount earned by a corporation and not yet distributed to stockholders. (p. 136)
18. **dividends:** Earnings distributed to stockholders. (p. 136)
19. **balance sheet:** A financial statement that reports assets, liabilities, and owner's equity on a specific date. (p. 136)
20. **adjusting entries:** Journal entries recorded to update general ledger accounts at the end of a fiscal period. (p. 138)
21. **closing entries:** Journal entries used to prepare temporary accounts for a new fiscal period. (p. 138)
22. **post-closing trial balance:** A trial balance prepared after the closing entries are posted. (p. 141)
23. **accounting cycle:** The series of accounting activities included in recording financial information for a fiscal period. (p. 141)

ACCOUNTING TERMS EPT(a)

What is the meaning of each of the following?

1. **fiscal period**
2. **departmental statement of gross profit**
3. **interim departmental statement of gross profit**
4. **periodic inventory**
5. **perpetual inventory**
6. **gross profit method of estimating an inventory**
7. **component percentage**
8. **schedule of accounts receivable**
9. **schedule of accounts payable**
10. **trial balance**
11. **work sheet**
12. **plant assets**
13. **depreciation expense**
14. **income statement**
15. **statement of stockholders' equity**
16. **capital stock**
17. **retained earnings**
18. **dividends**
19. **balance sheet**
20. **adjusting entries**
21. **closing entries**
22. **post-closing trial balance**
23. **accounting cycle**

QUESTIONS FOR INDIVIDUAL STUDY EPT(b)

1. Why is one year a common length of time for summarizing and reporting accounting information?
2. Which accounting concept is being applied when a business summarizes and reports financial information for a fiscal period?
3. What possible changes might a manager make after reviewing the gross profit for each department?
4. How often is an interim departmental statement of gross profit generally prepared?
5. How does a business determine an ending inventory when neither a periodic inventory is taken nor a perpetual inventory is kept?
6. How does MasterSport determine its ending inventory at the end of each month?
7. What information is used to determine an estimated gross profit percentage?
8. How does MasterSport determine the beginning inventory when preparing an interim departmental statement of gross profit?
9. What four basic components are included in every sales dollar?
10. How large must gross profit on operations be?
11. Which accounting concept is being applied when expenses are recorded in the fiscal period in which the expenses contribute to earning revenue?
12. When recording the inventory adjustment on a work sheet, how is the amount of the ending inventory determined?
13. Which accounting concept is being applied when financial statements are prepared to report the financial progress and condition of a business?
14. Which accounting concept is being applied when a business applies accounting principles the same way from one accounting period to the next?
15. What is the major difference between the two departmental statements of gross profit prepared by MasterSport?
16. Where does MasterSport obtain the data needed to prepare a departmental statement of gross profit?
17. Where is information obtained to journalize adjusting entries?
18. Where is information obtained to journalize closing entries?

CASES FOR CRITICAL THINKING

EPT(b)

CASE 1 The following data are obtained from financial information for Cardoza's for the month ended August 31 of the current year.

Beginning inv., Jan. 1	$98,000.00
Net purchases for the period, Jan. 1 to Aug. 31	42,500.00
Net sales for the period, Jan. 1 to Aug. 31	66,800.00

You are asked to report the estimated ending inventory on August 31 using the gross profit method for estimating inventory. What will you report?

CASE 2 Rose Hill Decorating is a departmentalized business. An interim departmental statement of gross profit is prepared monthly. A departmental statement of gross profit is prepared at the end of each fiscal year. The manager suggests that the accountant extend the statements of gross profit by including a division of all expenses by department. The accountant indicates that the time required to divide the expenses by department would not add significantly to the information available for decision making. Do you agree or disagree with the accountant? Why?

APPLICATION PROBLEMS

EPT(c,d)

PROBLEM 5-1 Estimating ending merchandise inventory

SPREADSHEET

MATHEMATICS

Strom's Dive Shop has two departments: Equipment and Accessories. The following data are obtained from the accounting records on January 31 of the current year.

	Equipment	Accessories
Beginning inventory, January 1	$145,000.00	$153,000.00
Net purchases for January	14,300.00	14,100.00
Net sales for January	49,200.00	53,400.00
Gross profit on operations as a percent of sales .	43.0%	43.0%

INSTRUCTIONS:

Prepare an estimated merchandise inventory sheet, similar to the one in this chapter, for each department for the month ended January 31.

PROBLEM 5-2 Calculating component percentages for cost of merchandise sold and gross profit on operations

MATHEMATICS

The data on page 146 are obtained from the interim departmental statements of gross profit for six businesses.

QUESTIONS FOR INDIVIDUAL STUDY

1. Because businesses must prepare tax reports at least once a year. (p. 117)
2. Accounting Period Cycle concept. (p. 117)
3. A review of this information may show a need to (a) change merchandise selling prices, (b) change suppliers of merchandise, (c) change or add products, or (d) discontinue a department. (p. 117)
4. Monthly. (p. 117)
5. The ending merchandise inventory may be estimated. (p. 118)
6. By using the gross profit method of estimating an inventory. (p. 118)
7. Records from previous years' operations. (p. 119)
8. The beginning inventory is the estimated ending inventory from the interim departmental statement of gross profit for the previous month. (p. 119)
9. (a) Cost of merchandise sold. (b) Gross profit on operations. (c) Total operating expenses. (d) Net income before federal income tax. (p. 120)
10. Large enough to cover total operating expenses and produce a net income. (p. 121)
11. Matching Expenses with Revenue concept. (p. 123)
12. By taking a periodic inventory at the end of a fiscal period. (p. 126)
13. Adequate Disclosure concept. (p. 131)
14. Consistent Reporting concept. (p. 131)
15. Monthly interim departmental statements of gross profit use estimated ending inventories. The annual departmental statement of gross profit uses the actual ending periodic inventories. (p. 131)
16. From the Trial Balance, Income Statement, and Balance Sheet columns of the work sheet. (p. 131)
17. From the Adjustments columns of the work sheet. (p. 138)
18. From the Income Statement columns of the work sheet. (p. 140)

CHECK FIGURES

Complete solutions to the problems can be found in the Teacher's Edition of the Working Papers.

Problem 5-1 Equipment, $131,256.00; Accessories, $136,662.00

Problem 5-2 Component Percentages: (1) 100.0%, 60.0%, 40.0%; (2) 100.0%, 66.7%, 33.3%; (3) 100.0%, 46.2%, 53.8%; (4) 100.0%, 53.1%, 46.9%; (5) 100.0%, 55.6%, 44.4%; (6) 100.0%, 51.4%, 48.6%

CASES FOR CRITICAL THINKING

Case 1 Nothing can be reported because the previous year's percentage of gross profit on operations is missing.

Case 2 Agree. The major information needed by a manager to review how well each department is doing is the gross profit on operations. (Additional time would be required both for dividing the expenses and for preparing the statements.)

Business	Component	Amount
1	Total Net Sales Total Cost of Merchandise Sold Total Gross Profit on Operations	$200,000.00 120,000.00 80,000.00
2	Total Net Sales Total Cost of Merchandise Sold Total Gross Profit on Operations	$120,000.00 80,000.00 40,000.00
3	Total Net Sales Total Cost of Merchandise Sold Total Gross Profit on Operations	$130,000.00 60,000.00 70,000.00
4	Total Net Sales Total Cost of Merchandise Sold Total Gross Profit on Operations	$160,000.00 85,000.00 75,000.00
5	Total Net Sales Total Cost of Merchandise Sold Total Gross Profit on Operations	$180,000.00 100,000.00 80,000.00
6	Total Net Sales Total Cost of Merchandise Sold Total Gross Profit on Operations	$210,000.00 108,000.00 102,000.00

Use a form similar to the following.

1	2	3	4
Business	**Component**	**Amount**	**Component Percentage**
1	Total Net Sales Total Cost of Merchandise Sold Total Gross Profit on Operations	$200,000.00 120,000.00 80,000.00	*100.0%* *60.0%* *40.0%*

INSTRUCTIONS:

Calculate component percentages for total cost of merchandise sold and total gross profit on operations for each business. Round percentage calculations to the nearest 0.1%. Enter the component percentages in Column 4. The component percentages for Business 1 are given as examples.

PROBLEM 5-3 Preparing an interim departmental statement of gross profit; calculating component percentages

SPREADSHEET

Parts Plus has two departments: Truck Parts and Auto Parts. The following data are obtained from the accounting records on March 31 of the current year.

	Truck Parts	Auto Parts
Beginning inventory, January 1	$154,640.00	$166,500.00
Estimated beginning inventory, March 1	131,344.00	135,660.00
Net purchases, January 1 to February 28	23,360.00	24,840.00
Net sales, January 1 to February 28	77,760.00	92,800.00
Net purchases for March	13,497.20	9,978.40
Net sales for March	29,200.00	33,600.00
Gross profit on operations as a percent of sales	40.0%	40.0%

CHECK FIGURES *(cont'd)*

Problem 5-3 Est. End. Inv.: Truck, $127,321.20; Auto, $125,478.40. Gross Profit on Oper.: Truck, $11,680; Auto, $13,440; Total, $25,120.

Problem 5-4 Total Accounts Payable, $9,066.70; Total Accounts Receivable, $6,907.20

Problem 5-5 Component % and Performance: (1) 29.4-A (2) 29.5-A (3) 28.0-U (4) 24.7-A (5) 31.4-U 6) 27.4-A

INSTRUCTIONS:

1. Prepare an estimated merchandise inventory sheet, similar to the one in this chapter, for each department for the month ended March 31 of the current year.
2. Prepare an interim departmental statement of gross profit. Calculate and record component percentages for departmental and total cost of merchandise sold and gross profit on operations. Round percentage calculations to the nearest 0.1%.

PROBLEM 5-4 Preparing subsidiary schedules

On December 31 of the current year, Gabriel's Gourmet Shop has the following vendor and customer accounts and balances.

Vendor	Account Balance	Customer	Account Balance
Barnett Co.	$2,250.40	Mary Anacker	$1,310.20
Gould Associates	1,520.30	Alice Conroy	820.70
Hills Supply	936.80	Raymond Gaetz	826.10
Kroy Enterprises	1,262.50	John Klem	1,304.20
Swedberg, Inc.	826.10	Irma Musgrove	619.60
Williamson Products	2,270.60	Richard Wimer	2,026.40

INSTRUCTIONS:

1. Prepare a schedule of accounts payable. Compare the schedule total with the balance, $9,066.70, of the general ledger controlling account Accounts Payable. If the totals are not the same, find and correct the errors.
2. Prepare a schedule of accounts receivable. Compare the schedule total with the balance, $6,907.20, of the general ledger controlling account Accounts Receivable. If the totals are not the same, find and correct the errors.

PROBLEM 5-5 Calculating and analyzing component percentage for total operating expenses

The following data are obtained from the income statements of six businesses.

Business	Net Sales	Total Operating Expenses	Performance Standard—Not more than:
1	*$148,000.00*	*$43,500.00*	*32.0%*
2	*175,500.00*	*51,750.00*	*30.0%*
3	*130,300.00*	*36,500.00*	*26.0%*
4	*145,600.00*	*35,930.00*	*25.0%*
5	*185,300.00*	*58,250.00*	*30.0%*
6	*163,900.00*	*44,980.00*	*28.0%*

Use a form similar to the following.

1	2	3	4	5	6
Business	Net Sales	Total Operating Expenses	Performance Standard—Not more than:	Component Percentage	Performance Level
1	$148,000.00	$43,500.00	32.0%	*29.4%*	*A*

INSTRUCTIONS:

1. Calculate the component percentage for total operating expenses for each business. Round percentage calculations to the nearest 0.1%. Record the component percentage in Column 5.
2. Determine the performance level for each business by comparing the component percentage with the performance standard. If the performance level is acceptable, write an *A* in Column 6. If the performance level is unacceptable, write a *U* in Column 6. The component percentage and performance level for Business 1 are given as examples.

PROBLEM 5-6 Calculating and analyzing component percentages for net income before federal income tax

The income statements of six businesses show the following information.

Business	Net Sales	Net Income Before Federal Income Tax	Performance Standard—Not less than:
1	*$155,200.00*	*$16,130.00*	*10.0%*
2	*193,100.00*	*24,150.00*	*12.0%*
3	*138,920.00*	*13,940.00*	*9.0%*
4	*161,750.00*	*10,820.00*	*8.0%*
5	*174,600.00*	*8,200.00*	*6.0%*
6	*143,838.00*	*16,447.50*	*11.0%*

Use a form similar to the following.

1	2	3	4	5	6
Business	Net Sales	Net Income Before Federal Income Tax	Performance Standard—Not less than:	Component Percentage	Performance Level
1	$155,200.00	$16,130.00	10.0%	*10.4%*	*A*

INSTRUCTIONS:

1. Calculate the component percentage for net income before federal income tax for each business. Round percentage calculations to the nearest 0.1%. Record the component percentage in Column 5.
2. Determine the performance level by comparing the component percentage with the performance standard. If the performance level is acceptable, write an *A* in Column 6. If the performance level is unacceptable, write a *U* in Column 6. The component percentage and performance level for Business 1 are given as examples.

CHECK FIGURES *(cont'd)*

Problem 5-6 Component % and Performance: (1) 10.4-A (2) 12.5-A (3) 10.0-A (4) 6.7-U (5) 4.7-U (6) 11.4-A

Problem 5-7 Net Income after Fed. Inc. Tax, $61,003.62. Total Stockholders' Equity, $386,678.62. Total Assets, $432,261.28.

Mastery Problem 5-M Net Income after Fed. Inc. Tax, $59,607.35. Total Stockholders' Equity, $484,607.35. Total Assets, $534,235.20

PROBLEM 5-7 Preparing end-of-fiscal-period work for a departmentalized business

AUTOMATED

The Music Box has two departments: Books and Instruments. The general ledger accounts and balances for December 31 of the current year are recorded on a work sheet in the working papers accompanying this textbook.

INSTRUCTIONS:

1. Complete the departmental work sheet for the year ended December 31 of the current year. Record the adjustments on the work sheet using the information on the next page.

MATHEMATICS

Adjustment Information, December 31

Uncollectible accounts expense estimated as 1.0% of sales on account. Sales on account for year, $125,910.00.

Merchandise inventory—books	$168,820.10
Merchandise inventory—instruments	173,450.80
Office supplies inventory	4,930.60
Store supplies inventory	5,720.40
Value of prepaid insurance	4,600.00
Annual depreciation expense—office equipment	1,280.00
Annual depreciation expense—store equipment	2,800.00
Federal income tax expense for the year	13,667.88

2. Prepare a departmental statement of gross profit. Calculate and record component percentages for cost of merchandise sold and gross profit on operations. Round percentage calculations to the nearest 0.1%.
3. Prepare an income statement. Record the component percentages for cost of merchandise sold and gross profit on operations from the departmental statement of gross profit. Calculate and record the component percentages for total operating expenses and net income before and after federal income tax. Round percentage calculations to the nearest 0.1%.
4. Prepare a statement of stockholders' equity. Use the following additional information.

January 1 balance of capital stock account (2,000 shares issued for $100.00 per share)	$200,000.00
No additional capital stock issued.	
January 1 balance of retained earnings account	155,675.00
Dividends declared during the current year	30,000.00

5. Prepare a balance sheet.
6. Journalize the adjusting entries. Use page 15 of a general journal.
7. Journalize the closing entries. Continue using page 15 of a general journal. Do not skip a line between the adjusting and closing entries.

SIMULATION

To give students an opportunity to apply accounting concepts from the departmentalized accounting cycle, assign students to complete *Galleria: A Business Simulation. Galleria* may also be automated using *Automated Accounting 6.0* or higher.

ENRICHMENT PROBLEMS

EPT(c,d)

MASTERY PROBLEM 5-M Preparing end-of-fiscal-period work for a departmentalized business

AUTOMATED

SPREADSHEET

Zabel's Gift Shop has two departments: Gifts and Plants. The general ledger accounts and balances on December 31 of the current year are recorded on a work sheet in the working papers accompanying this textbook.

INSTRUCTIONS:

1. Complete the departmental work sheet for the year ended December 31 of the current year. Record the adjustments on the work sheet using the following information.

Adjustment Information, December 31

Uncollectible accounts expense estimated as 1.0% of sales on account. Sales on account for year, $197,040.00.

Merchandise inventory—gifts	$205,380.20
Merchandise inventory—plants	236,520.80
Office supplies inventory	6,010.30
Store supplies inventory	4,220.50
Value of prepaid insurance	2,800.00
Annual depreciation expense—office equipment	1,200.00
Annual depreciation expense—store equipment	2,600.00
Federal income tax expense for the year	13,202.45

2. Prepare a departmental statement of gross profit. Calculate and record component percentages for cost of merchandise sold and gross profit on operations. Round percentage calculations to the nearest 0.1%.
3. Prepare an income statement. Record the component percentages for cost of merchandise sold and gross profit on operations from the departmental statement of gross profit. Calculate and record the component percentages for total operating expenses and net income before and after federal income tax. Round percentage calculations to the nearest 0.1%.
4. Prepare a statement of stockholders' equity. Use the following additional information.

January 1 balance of capital stock account . . . . (1,500 shares issued for $200.00 per share)	$300,000.00
No additional capital stock issued.	
January 1 balance of retained earnings account	155,000.00
Dividends declared during the current year	30,000.00

5. Prepare a balance sheet.
6. Journalize the adjusting entries. Use page 18 of a general journal.
7. Journalize the closing entries. Continue using page 18 of a general journal. Do not skip a line between the adjusting and closing entries.

TEACHING STRATEGIES: REINFORCEMENT ACTIVITY

Reinforcement Activity 1 is the complete accounting cycle for a departmentalized business. A blackline master for an audit test for Reinforcement Activity 1 is available in the Teacher's Resource Guide. In addition, *Automated Accounting 6.0* or higher can be used to automate Reinforcement Activity 1.

CHALLENGE PROBLEM 5-C Preparing a 10-column work sheet for a departmentalized business

Introductory remarks: Some businesses choose to use a work sheet that has 10 columns instead of the 8-column work sheet used by MasterSport. A 10-column work sheet has Adjusted Trial Balance Debit and Credit columns. These columns are used to recalculate account balances after the adjustments have been entered on the work sheet. If an account balance was not changed by the adjustments, the balance is transferred to the Adjusted Trial Balance column unchanged. If an account balance was adjusted, the new balance is transferred to the Adjusted Trial Balance columns. The Adjusted Trial Balance Debit and Credit columns are totaled. The total of the debit column must equal the total of the credit column. Once the columns are equal, the amounts in the Adjusted Trial Balance columns are transferred to either the Balance Sheet or Income Statement columns. The work sheet is completed as usual.

Discount Hardware has two departments: Hardware and Housewares. The general ledger accounts and balances for December 31 of the current year are recorded on a work sheet in the working papers accompanying this textbook.

INSTRUCTIONS:

Complete the departmental work sheet for the year ended December 31 of the current year. Record the adjustments on the work sheet using the following information.

Adjustment Information, December 31

Uncollectible accounts expense estimated as 1.0% of sales on account. Sales on account for year, $35,000.00.	
Merchandise inventory—hardware	$115,430.00
Merchandise inventory—housewares	97,680.00
Supplies inventory	2,377.00
Value of prepaid insurance	500.00
Federal income tax expense for the year	4,795.18

CHECK FIGURES *(cont'd)*

Challenge Problem 5-C Net Income after Fed. Inc. Tax, $27,172.71

MILESTONE

These first five chapters of the textbook are the foundation for subsequent learning. It is assumed that these chapters have been mastered as the chapters to follow will expand upon this foundation with concepts of increasing complexity.

Completing End-of-Fiscal-Period Work for a Departmental Business

MasterSport's manual accounting procedures for completing end-of-fiscal-period work are described in Chapter 5. Integrating Automated Accounting Topic 3 describes procedures for using automated accounting software to complete MasterSport's end-of-fiscal-period work. The Automated Accounting Problems contain instructions for using automated accounting software to solve Problem 5-7 and Mastery Problem 5-M, Chapter 5.

PROCESSING A TRIAL BALANCE

A trial balance is prepared to prove the equality of debits and credits in the general ledger and to use for planning adjustments. MasterSport's general ledger is in balance and is assumed to be correct as shown in Illustration T3-1.

TEACHING STRATEGIES: ACCOUNTING PEDAGOGY

This textbook introduces the manual accounting concept of closing entries before using automated accounting to perform closing entries. It is important that students master accounting theory before relying on the computer to do the repetitive functions.

LESSON PLAN A3

Materials

- Student pages 151–154
- Input forms for Automating Application Problem 5-7 and Mastery Problem 5-M are provided in the working papers that accompany this textbook. If additional input forms are needed, blackline masters are provided in the Blackline Masters Section of the Teacher's Resource Guide.
- Complete solutions for automated problems are provided in the Teacher's Resource Guide.
- Software: *Automated Accounting 6.0* or higher; CENTURY 21 ACCOUNTING Template, Advanced Course

Objective

Complete end-of-fiscal-period work using an automated accounting system.

FOCUS

In Chapter 5, the manual procedures for completing end-of-fiscal-period work for a departmentalized business were described. Emphasize that using an automated accounting system speeds the processing of end-of-fiscal-period work by (1) eliminating the need to prepare a work sheet, (2) having all financial reports prepared by a computer, and (3) having the software generate closing entries.

ILLUSTRATION T3-1 Trial balance

MasterSport
Trial Balance
12/31/--

Acct. Number	Account Title	Debit	Credit
1105	Cash	43440.00	
1110	Petty Cash	500.00	
1115	Accounts Receivable	12855.00	
1120	Allow. for Uncoll. Accts.		240.60
1125.1	Mdse. Inventory--Golf	186434.61	
1125.2	Mdse. Inventory--Tennis	199844.60	
1130	Supplies--Office	12700.00	
1135	Supplies--Store	14330.00	
1140	Prepaid Insurance	9850.00	
1205	Office Equipment	16900.00	
1210	Acc. Depr.--Office Equip.		5960.00
1215	Store Equipment	38900.00	
1220	Acc. Depr.--Store Equip.		18000.00
2105	Accounts Payable		38160.30
2110	Empl. Inc. Tax Pay.--Fed.		2680.75
2115	Empl. Inc. Tax Pay.--St.		1118.19
2125	FICA Tax Payable		3360.70
2130	Sales Tax Payable		3139.64
2135	Unemployment Tax Pay.--Fed.		23.60
2140	Unemployment Tax Pay.--St.		159.30
2145	Health Ins. Premiums Pay.		2261.16
2150	Life Ins. Premiums Pay.		350.19
2155	Dividends Payable		30000.00
3105	Capital Stock		340000.00
3110	Retained Earnings		42210.50
3115	Dividends	30000.00	
4105.1	Sales--Golf		351032.81
4105.2	Sales--Tennis		438341.75
4110.1	Sales Discount--Golf	1605.85	
4110.2	Sales Discount--Tennis	2005.25	
4115.1	Sales Ret. & All.--Golf	4950.50	
4115.2	Sales Ret. & All.--Tennis	6181.80	
5105.1	Purchases--Golf	215745.68	
5105.2	Purchases--Tennis	231766.62	
5110.1	Pur. Disc.--Golf		4058.95
5110.2	Pur. Disc.--Tennis		4334.55
5115.1	Pur. Ret. & All.--Golf		8282.48
5115.2	Pur. Ret. & All.--Tennis		8897.52
6105	Advertising Expense	5192.88	
6110	Credit Card Fee Expense	5950.00	
6120.1	Salary Expense--Golf	90924.19	
6120.2	Salary Expense--Tennis	72627.02	
6215	Miscellaneous Expense	5958.48	
6220	Payroll Taxes Expense	21426.92	
6225	Rent Expense	18056.40	
6230	Salary Expense--Admin.	43667.19	
7105	Federal Income Tax Exp.	10800.00	
	Totals	1302612.99	1302612.99

UPDATING GENERAL LEDGER ACCOUNTS

At the end of a fiscal period, some general ledger accounts do not contain up-to-date balances.

SOFTWARE FOCUS

The Automated Accounting Problems in this Integrating Automated Accounting topic use Application Problem 5-7 and Mastery Problem 5-M, Chapter 5, which students have already completed manually. Refer students back to these problems to complete the input forms. The problem instructions in *Automated Accounting 6.0* will lead students through automating the problems.

FYI

Dollar signs and cent signs are not keyed when using *Automated Accounting 6.0* software. When the cents are zero (.00), key only the dollar amount. The software automatically assigns the .00.

Journalizing Adjusting Entries

MasterSport plans adjustments using the trial balance. MasterSport's adjusting entries are analyzed in Chapter 5. The adjusting entries are journalized on the general journal input form shown in Illustration T3-2. The two totals are compared to assure that debits equal credits. As the two totals are the same, $58,959.86, the adjusting entries are assumed to be correct.

ILLUSTRATION T3-2

General journal input form with adjusting entries recorded

RUN DATE 12/31/-- (MM DD YY)

GENERAL JOURNAL
Input Form

	DATE MM/DD	REFERENCE	ACCOUNT NO.	CUSTOMER/ VENDOR NO.	DEBIT	CREDIT	
1	12/31	Adj.Ent.	6240		2109.40		1
2	/		1120			2109.40	2
3	/31	Adj.Ent.	1125.1		18420.39		3
4	/		3120.1			18420.39	4
5	/31	Adj.Ent.	3120.2		9360.00		5
6	/		1125.2			9360.00	6
7	/31	Adj.Ent.	6235		9950.00		7
8	/		1130			9950.00	8
9	/31	Adj.Ent.	6125		7790.00		9
10	/		1135			7790.00	10
11	/31	Adj.Ent.	6210		5650.00		11
12	/		1140			5650.00	12
13	/31	Adj.Ent.	6205		1490.00		13
14	/		1210			1490.00	14
15	/31	Adj.Ent.	6115		3000.00		15
16	/		1220			3000.00	16
17	/31	Adj.Ent.	7105		1190.07		17
18	/		2120			1190.07	18
25	/						25
				PAGE TOTALS	58959.86	58959.86	
				FINAL TOTALS	58959.86	58959.86	

Processing Adjusting Entries

After all adjusting entries have been journalized and posted, the general journal report for adjusting entries is displayed. The report is checked for accuracy by comparing the totals on the report, *$58,959.86*, with the totals on the general journal input form, *$58,959.86*. As the totals are the same, the general journal report is assumed to be correct. The general journal report is printed, as shown in Illustration T3-3, and filed for future reference.

TEACH

Cover student pages 151–154 "Processing a Trial Balance," "Updating General Ledger Accounts," "Processing Financial Statements," and "Closing the Ledger." This lesson introduces students to end-of-fiscal-period procedures using automated accounting software. As the lesson progresses, review the definitions of fiscal period, trial balance, adjusting entries, income statement, component percentage, and post-closing trial balance.

End-of-fiscal-period work is completed using the same basic procedures for both manual and automated methods. However, the component percentages are automatically produced by the software. Analyzing acceptable component percentages is an important student critical thinking skill. Because using an automated accounting system speeds the processing of end-of-fiscal-period work, students can spend more time analyzing component percentages.

Adjusting entries are recorded on an input form in the same manner as they are recorded in a journal. Closing entries are easy when using automated accounting software. No additional input of data is necessary to perform closing entries. The *Automated Accounting 6.0* software contains instructions for closing temporary accounts.

TEACHING STRATEGIES: COOPERATIVE LEARNING

Using automated accounting software to complete accounting problems is an ideal cooperative learning experience. Students working in groups can collaborate on completing input forms and keying data.

APPLY

Guided Practice

Students should be at the computers. Guide students through booting the software and loading Automating Application Problem 5-7 from the template. Instruct students to complete the end-of-fiscal-period work as you go step-by-step through the procedures.

Independent Practice

Assign Automating Mastery Problem 5-M.

ASSESS

Assess student understanding by checking solutions to Automating Mastery Problem 5-M. Have students list the steps for completing end-of-fiscal-period work.

Reteach

For students who have difficulty completing end-of-fiscal-period work, make a list of the steps and photocopy. Students should use this guide to review and study the procedures.

Extend

Assign the students to complete Reinforcement Activity 1 using the automated accounting software.

Enrich

Have the students complete GALLERIA, INC.: An Automated Business Simulation.

CLOSURE

As a whole-class activity, close the lesson by having students take turns describing the various steps for the end-of-fiscal-period procedures.

ILLUSTRATION T3-3 General journal report for adjusting entries

MasterSport
General Journal
12/31/--

Date	Refer.	V/C	Acct.	Title	Debit	Credit
12/31	Adj.Ent.		6240	Uncoll. Accounts Expense	2109.40	
12/31	Adj.Ent.		1120	Allow. for Uncoll. Accts.		2109.40
12/31	Adj.Ent.		1125.1	Mdse. Inventory--Golf	18420.39	
12/31	Adj.Ent.		3120.1	Income Summary--Golf		18420.39
12/31	Adj.Ent.		3120.2	Income Summary--Tennis	9360.00	
12/31	Adj.Ent.		1125.2	Mdse. Inventory--Tennis		9360.00
12/31	Adj.Ent.		6235	Supplies Expense--Office	9950.00	
12/31	Adj.Ent.		1130	Supplies--Office		9950.00
12/31	Adj.Ent.		6125	Supplies Expense--Store	7790.00	
12/31	Adj.Ent.		1135	Supplies--Store		7790.00
12/31	Adj.Ent.		6210	Insurance Expense	5650.00	
12/31	Adj.Ent.		1140	Prepaid Insurance		5650.00
12/31	Adj.Ent.		6205	Depr. Exp.--Office Equip.	1490.00	
12/31	Adj.Ent.		1210	Acc. Depr.--Office Equip.		1490.00
12/31	Adj.Ent.		6115	Depr. Exp.--Store Equip.	3000.00	
12/31	Adj.Ent.		1220	Acc. Depr.--Store Equip.		3000.00
12/31	Adj.Ent.		7105	Federal Income Tax Exp.	1190.07	
12/31	Adj.Ent.		2120	Federal Income Tax Pay.		1190.07
				Totals	58959.86	58959.86

PROCESSING FINANCIAL STATEMENTS

After the adjusting entries have been verified, MasterSport prepares the following financial statements. (1) Departmental statements of gross profit. (2) Income statement. (3) Retained earnings statement. (The retained earnings statement prepared by MasterSport's automated accounting software is similar to the statement of stockholder's equity prepared in MasterSport's manual system described in Chapter 5.) (4) Balance sheet.

FYI

When using automated accounting software, closing the ledger does not require journal entries. The software performs the closing activities after the command to close is chosen.

CLOSING THE LEDGER

MasterSport closes all temporary accounts at the end of each fiscal period. In manual accounting systems, closing entries are manually recorded in a journal and posted to the general ledger accounts. In automated accounting systems, the automated accounting software contains instructions for closing temporary accounts. After the period-end closing option has been selected to close temporary accounts, the post-closing trial balance is printed as shown in Illustration T3-4, and filed for future reference.

SAFETY AND HEALTH

To avoid damage to the computer and monitor, do not attempt to make any repairs but call a manufacturer's service representative. A Safety and Health page is given in the Teacher's Resource Guide. This page may be duplicated and given to students.

ILLUSTRATION T3-4 Post-closing trial balance

MasterSport
Trial Balance
12/31/--

Acct. Number	Account Title	Debit	Credit
1105	Cash	43440.00	
1110	Petty Cash	500.00	
1115	Accounts Receivable	12855.00	
1120	Allow. for Uncoll. Accts.		2350.00
1125.1	Mdse. Inventory--Golf	204855.00	
1125.2	Mdse. Inventory--Tennis	190484.60	
1130	Supplies--Office	2750.00	
1135	Supplies--Store	6540.00	
1140	Prepaid Insurance	4200.00	
1205	Office Equipment	16900.00	
1210	Acc. Depr.--Office Equip.		7450.00
1215	Store Equipment	38900.00	
1220	Acc. Depr.--Store Equip.		21000.00
2105	Accounts Payable		38160.30
2110	Empl. Inc. Tax Pay.--Fed.		2680.75
2115	Empl. Inc. Tax Pay.--St.		1118.19
2120	Fed. Income Tax Payable		1190.07
2125	FICA Tax Payable		3360.70
2130	Sales Tax Payable		3139.64
2135	Unempl. Tax Pay.--Federal		23.60
2140	Unempl. Tax Pay.--State		159.30
2145	Health Ins. Premiums Pay.		2261.16
2150	Life Ins. Premiums Pay.		350.19
2155	Dividends Payable		30000.00
3105	Capital Stock		340000.00
3110	Retained Earnings		68180.70
	Totals	521424.60	521424.60

TEACHING STRATEGIES: TEACHING TIP

It is important for students to save a template file under another name before they begin work. This will keep the template file intact for future use.

AUTOMATED ACCOUNTING PROBLEMS

AUTOMATING APPLICATION PROBLEM 5-7 Preparing end-of-fiscal-period work for a departmentalized business

AUTOMATED

INSTRUCTIONS:

1. Load the *Automated Accounting 6.0* or higher software. Select data base A5-7 (Advanced Course Problem 5-7) from the CENTURY 21 ACCOUNTING Advanced Course Template. Read the Problem Instructions Screen.
2. Use the Save As command and rename your data base file.
3. Display/print a chart of accounts.
4. Display/print a trial balance.
5. Record adjusting entries on a general journal input form using the following information. Use December 31 of the current year as the run date.

Adjustment Information, December 31

Uncollectible accounts expense estimated as 1.0% of sales on account. Sales on account for year, $125,910.00.

Merchandise inventory—books	$168,820.10
Merchandise inventory—instruments	173,450.80
Office supplies inventory	4,930.60

CHECK FIGURES

- Automating Application Problem 5-7: Trial Balance totals 1,162,547.08; General Journal totals 44,007.18; Gross Profit Department 1 177,987.20; Gross Profit Department 2 156,303.80; Gross Profit Consolidated 334,291.00; Net Income after Income Tax 61,003.62; Total Liabilities & Equity 432,261.28; Retained Earnings (End of Period) 186,678.62; Post-Closing Trial Balance totals 457,071.18

Adjustment Information, December 31

Store supplies inventory	5,720.40
Value of prepaid insurance	4,600.00
Annual depreciation expense—office equipment	1,280.00
Annual depreciation expense—store equipment	2,800.00
Federal income tax expense for the year	13,667.88

6. Key the adjusting entries from the general journal input form.
7. Display/print the general journal report.
8. Display/print the statement of gross profit for Department 1 and Department 2.
9. Display/print the consolidated gross profit statement.
10. Display/print the income statement, balance sheet, and retained earnings statement.
11. Perform period-end closing.
12. Display/print the post-closing trial balance.

CHECK FIGURES *(cont'd)*

- Automating Mastery Problem 5-M: Trial Balance totals 1,293,498.20; General Journal totals 52,034.65; Gross Profit Department 1 173,144.20; Gross Profit Department 2 169,932.80; Gross Profit Consolidated 343,077.00; Net Income after Income Tax 59,607.35; Total Liabilities & Equity 534,235.20; Retained Earnings (End of Period) 184,607.35; Post-Closing Trial Balance totals 561,256.40

AUTOMATING MASTERY PROBLEM 5-M Preparing end-of-fiscal-period work for a departmentalized business

AUTOMATED

INSTRUCTIONS:

1. Load the *Automated Accounting 6.0* or higher software. Select data base A5-M from the CENTURY 21 ACCOUNTING Advanced Course Template. Read the Problem Instructions Screen.
2. Use the Save As command and rename your data base file.
3. Display/print a chart of accounts.
4. Display/print a trial balance.
5. Record adjusting entries on a general journal input form using the information below. Use December 31 of the current year as the run date.

Adjustment Information, December 31

Uncollectible accounts expense estimated as 1.0% of sales on account.
Sales on account for year, $197,040.00.

Merchandise inventory—gifts	$205,380.20
Merchandise inventory—plants	236,520.80
Office supplies inventory	6,010.30
Store supplies inventory	4,220.50
Value of prepaid insurance	2,800.00
Annual depreciation expense—office equipment	1,200.00
Annual depreciation expense—store equipment	2,600.00
Federal income tax expense for the year	13,202.45

6. Key the adjusting entries from the general journal input form.
7. Display/print the general journal report.
8. Display/print the statement of gross profit for Department 1 and Department 2.
9. Display/print the consolidated gross profit statement.
10. Display/print the income statement, balance sheet, and retained earnings statement.
11. Perform period-end closing.
12. Display/print the post-closing trial balance.

REINFORCEMENT ACTIVITY 1

Processing and Reporting Departmentalized Accounting Data

This activity reinforces selected learnings from Part 2, Chapters 2 through 5. The complete accounting cycle is for a departmentalized merchandising business organized as a corporation.

CAMPUS BOOKS, INC.

Campus Books, Inc., has two departments: Books and Supplies. Campus Books is open for business Monday through Saturday. A monthly rent is paid on the building. The business owns the office and store equipment.

Campus Books sells books and supplies to individuals and schools. Cash sales and sales on account are made. The business uses a national credit card service in addition to its own company credit card.

Campus Books' fiscal year is January 1 through December 31. During the fiscal year, a monthly interim departmental statement of gross profit is prepared.

Campus Books uses the chart of accounts shown on the following page. The journals and ledgers used by Campus Books are similar to those illustrated in Part 2. The journal and ledger forms are provided in the working papers accompanying this textbook. Beginning balances have been recorded in the ledgers.

PREPARING AN INTERIM DEPARTMENTAL STATEMENT OF GROSS PROFIT

Campus Books prepares an interim departmental statement of gross profit each month. The following data are obtained from the accounting records at the end of November of the current year.

	Books	Supplies
Beginning inventory, January 1	$164,164.20	$147,840.30
Estimated beginning inventory, November 1	180,205.05	157,195.78
Net purchases, January 1 to October 31	133,839.60	130,449.20
Net sales, January 1 to October 31	214,179.55	220,170.40
Net purchases for November	13,007.20	14,162.58
Net sales for November	19,480.60	20,240.30
Gross profit on operation as a percent of sales	45.0%	45.0%

INSTRUCTIONS:

1. Use the gross profit method of estimating an inventory to prepare an estimated merchandise inventory sheet for each department for the month ended November of the current year.
2. Prepare an interim departmental statement of gross profit for the month ended November 30 of the current year. Calculate and record component percentages for departmental and total cost of merchandise sold and gross profit on operations. Round percentage calculations to the nearest 0.1%.

TEACHING STRATEGIES: REINFORCEMENT ACTIVITY

Reinforcement Activity 1 covers the complete accounting cycle for a departmentalized merchandising business organized as a corporation. Blackline masters for audit tests for Reinforcement Activity 1 are available in the Teacher's Resource Guide. In addition, *Automated Accounting 6.0* or higher can be used to automate Reinforcement Activity 1.

TEACHING STRATEGIES: ASSESSMENT BY PORTFOLIO

If you intend to use Reinforcement Activity 1 as part of an assessment by portfolio evaluation, advise students that their work on this activity will be included in their portfolio.

CAMPUS BOOKS, INC.
GENERAL LEDGER CHART OF ACCOUNTS

Balance Sheet Accounts

(1000) ASSETS

1100 Current Assets

1105 Cash
1110 Petty Cash
1115 Accounts Receivable
1120 Allowance for Uncollectible Accounts
1125-1 Merchandise Inventory—Books
1125-2 Merchandise Inventory—Supplies
1130 Supplies—Office
1135 Supplies—Store
1140 Prepaid Insurance

1200 Plant Assets

1205 Office Equipment
1210 Accumulated Depreciation—Office Equipment
1215 Store Equipment
1220 Accumulated Depreciation—Store Equipment

(2000) LIABILITIES

2105 Accounts Payable
2110 Employee Income Tax Payable—Federal
2115 Employee Income Tax Payable—State
2120 Federal Income Tax Payable
2125 FICA Tax Payable
2130 Sales Tax Payable
2135 Unemployment Tax Payable—Federal
2140 Unemployment Tax Payable—State
2145 Health Insurance Premiums Payable
2150 Dividends Payable

(3000) STOCKHOLDERS' EQUITY

3105 Capital Stock
3110 Retained Earnings
3115 Dividends
3120-1 Income Summary—Books
3120-2 Income Summary—Supplies
3125 Income Summary—General

Income Statement Accounts

(4000) OPERATING REVENUE

4105-1 Sales—Books
4105-2 Sales—Supplies
4110-1 Sales Discount—Books
4110-2 Sales Discount—Supplies
4115-1 Sales Returns and Allowances—Books
4115-2 Sales Returns and Allowances—Supplies

(5000) COST OF MERCHANDISE

5105-1 Purchases—Books
5105-2 Purchases—Supplies
5110-1 Purchases Discount—Books
5110-2 Purchases Discount—Supplies
5115-1 Purchases Returns and Allowances—Books
5115-2 Purchases Returns and Allowances—Supplies

(6000) OPERATING EXPENSES

6100 Selling Expenses

6105 Advertising Expense
6110 Credit Card Fee Expense
6115 Depreciation Expense—Store Equipment
6120-1 Salary Expense—Books
6120-2 Salary Expense—Supplies
6125 Supplies Expense—Store

6200 Administrative Expenses

6205 Depreciation Expense—Office Equipment
6210 Insurance Expense
6215 Miscellaneous Expense
6220 Payroll Taxes Expense
6225 Rent Expense
6230 Salary Expense—Administrative
6235 Supplies Expense—Office
6240 Uncollectible Accounts Expense

(7000) INCOME TAX

7105 Federal Income Tax Expense

SUBSIDIARY LEDGERS CHARTS OF ACCOUNTS

Accounts Receivable Ledger

110 Marcella Amco
120 Matthew Barasso
130 Tanya Dockman
140 Brian Fadstad
150 Gilmore Public Schools
160 Belinda Judd
170 Janelle Kamschorr
180 Donald Lindgren
190 Renville Public Schools

Accounts Payable Ledger

210 A-1 Supplies
220 CBG Distributors
230 Grandway Products
240 H & B Books
250 Maryland Books & Supplies
260 Oliver Books, Inc.
270 Strup Supplies

RECORDING TRANSACTIONS

INSTRUCTIONS:

3. Journalize the following transactions completed during December of the current year. Calculate and record sales tax on all sales and sales returns and allowances as described in Chapter 3. The sales tax rate is 5.0%. No sales tax is charged on sales to schools. Campus Books offers its customers terms of 2/10, n/30. All of the vendors from which merchandise is purchased on account offer terms of 2/10, n/30. Source documents are abbreviated as follows: check, C; credit memorandum, CM; debit memorandum, DM; memorandum, M; purchase invoice, P; receipt, R; sales invoice, S; cash register tape, T.

Dec. 1. Paid cash for monthly payroll, $7,859.71 (total payroll: books, $4,522.20; supplies, $4,310.40; administrative, $2,630.25, less deductions: employee income tax—federal, $1,204.51; employee income tax—state, $537.60; FICA tax, $917.03; health insurance, $944.00). C340.

1. Recorded employer payroll taxes, $964.38, for the monthly pay period ended November 30. Taxes owed are: FICA tax, $917.03; federal unemployment tax, $6.11; state unemployment tax, $41.24, M40.

1. Paid cash for rent, $1,200.00. C341.

2. Paid cash for office supplies, $135.00. C342.

2. Granted credit to Gilmore Public Schools for supplies returned, $250.00, from S94. CM31.

2. Purchased books on account from Oliver Books, Inc., $1,933.00. P115.

3. Granted credit to Belinda Judd for books returned, $75.00, plus sales tax, from S95. CM32.

3. Recorded cash and credit card sales: books, $2,478.00; supplies, $2,588.50; plus sales tax. T3.

   Posting. Post the items that are to be posted individually. Post from the journals in this order: sales journal, sales returns and allowances journal, purchases journal, purchases returns and allowances journal, general journal, cash receipts journal, cash payments journal.

5. Returned books to H & B Books, $1,435.00, from P112. DM58.

5. Sold books on account to Matthew Barasso, $880.00, plus sales tax. S97.

5. Received cash on account from Tanya Dockman, $493.92, covering S92 for supplies for $504.00 ($480.00 plus sales tax), less discount, and less sales tax. R139.

6. Paid cash on account to CBG Distributors, $2,185.50, covering P111 for books for $2,230.10, less discount. C343.

7. Paid cash on account to H & B Books, $3,915.25, covering P112 for books for $5,430.15, less DM58, and less discount. C344.

7. Returned books to Oliver Books, Inc., $300.00, from P115. DM59.

8. Received cash on account from Gilmore Public Schools, $5,870.40, covering S94 for supplies for $6,240.20, less CM31, and less discount. R140.

8. Received cash on account from Belinda Judd, $180.07, covering S95 for books for $262.50 ($250.00 plus sales tax), less CM32, less discount, and less sales tax. R141.

8. Received cash on account from Renville Public Schools, $9,389.87, covering S96 for books for $9,581.50, less discount. R142.

8. Paid cash on account to Maryland Books & Supplies, $554.09, covering P113 for supplies for $565.40, less discount. C345.

TEACHING STRATEGIES: COOPERATIVE LEARNING

Divide the class into groups of two students each. After completing the recording of transactions as a homework assignment, students evaluate each other's work in class. Students are permitted to correct their work based on their partner's evaluation. This cooperative learning activity should not take more than 15 to 20 minutes of class time. The same kind of group activity can be used after students have completed the end-of-fiscal-period work.

Dec. 9. Paid cash on account to Oliver Books, Inc., $4,821.80, covering P114 for books for $4,920.20, less discount. C346.

9. Granted credit to Matthew Barasso for books returned, $100.00, plus sales tax, from S97. CM33.

10. Recorded cash and credit card sales: books, $4,946.50; supplies, $3,650.00; plus sales tax. T10.

Posting. Post the items that are to be posted individually.

12. Paid cash on account to Oliver Books, Inc., $1,600.34, covering P115 for books for $1,933.00, less DM59, and less discount. C347.

13. Sold supplies on account to Marcello Amco, $450.00, plus sales tax. S98.

15. Paid cash for liability for federal employee income tax, $1,240.80, and for FICA tax, $1,582.90; total, $2,823.70. C348.

15. Paid cash for quarterly federal income tax estimate, $1,200.00. C349. (Debit Federal Income Tax Expense; credit Cash.)

15. Received cash on account from Matthew Barasso, $802.62, covering S97 for books for $924.00 ($880.00 plus sales tax), less CM33, less discount, and less sales tax. R143.

17. Recorded cash and credit card sales: books, $3,820.60; supplies, $3,240.50; plus sales tax. T17.

Posting. Post the items that are to be posted individually.

22. Sold supplies on account to Renville Public Schools, $4,750.00; no sales tax. S99.

22. Purchased supplies on account from Strup Supplies, $1,647.00. P116.

22. Purchased supplies on account from A-1 Supplies, $1,278.50. P117.

23. Sold books on account to Brian Fadstad, $1,720.00, plus sales tax. S100.

23. Sold supplies on account to Janelle Kamschorr, $920.00, plus sales tax. S101.

23. Received cash on account from Marcello Amco, $463.05, covering S98 for supplies for $472.50 ($450.00 plus sales tax), less discount, and less sales tax. R144.

24. Purchased books on account from CBG Distributors, $1,500.00. P118.

24. Recorded cash and credit card sales: books, $4,160.10; supplies, $3,420.50; plus sales tax. T24.

Posting. Post the items that are to be posted individually.

26. Sold supplies on account to Donald Lindgren, $540.00, plus sales tax. S102.

26. Returned supplies to A-1 Supplies, $265.00, from P117. DM60.

27. Purchased books on account from Maryland Books & Supplies, $2,440.50. P119.

27. Purchased supplies on account from Grandway Products, $3,157.99. P120.

28. Sold books on account to Donald Lindgren, $650.00, plus sales tax. S103.

4. Prepare a bank statement reconciliation. Use December 29 of the current year as the date. The following information is obtained from the bank statement and from the records of the business.

Bank statement balance	$48,363.56
Bank service charge	11.40
Bank credit card charge	354.20
Outstanding deposit: December 29	7,959.63
Outstanding checks:	
No. 348	2,823.70
349	1,200.00
Checkbook balance on Check Stub No. 349	52,665.09

SOFTWARE FOCUS

Automated Accounting 6.0 can be used to complete Reinforcement Activity 1 using the computer.

160

5. Continue journalizing the following transactions.

Dec. 30. Received bank statement showing December bank service charge, $11.40. M41.
30. Recorded credit card fee expense for December, $354.20. M42.
31. Granted credit to Renville Public Schools for supplies returned, $1,500.00, from S99. CM34.
31. Sold books on account to Gilmore Public Schools, $6,200.00; no sales tax. S104.
31. Paid cash to replenish petty cash fund, $415.00: store supplies, $145.00; advertising, $160.00; miscellaneous, $110.00. C350.
31. Recorded cash and credit card sales: books, $3,580.40; supplies, $2,480.00; plus sales tax. T31.

Posting. Post the items that are to be posted individually.

COMPLETING JOURNALS

INSTRUCTIONS:

6. Prove and rule the sales journal and the sales returns and allowances journal. Post the totals of the special columns.
7. Prove and rule the purchases journal and the purchases returns and allowances journal. Post the totals of the special columns.
8. Prove the cash receipts journal and the cash payments journal.
9. Prove cash. The balance on the next unused check stub is $61,397.91.
10. Rule the cash receipts journal. Post the totals of the special columns.
11. Rule the cash payments journal. Post the totals of the special columns.

END-OF-FISCAL-PERIOD WORK

INSTRUCTIONS:

12. Prepare a schedule of accounts receivable and a schedule of accounts payable. Compare each schedule total with the balance of the controlling account in the general ledger. The total and the balance should be the same.
13. Prepare a trial balance on a work sheet.
14. Complete the work sheet. Record the adjustments on the work sheet using the following information.

Adjustment Information, December 31

Uncollectible accounts expense estimated as 1.0% of sales on account. Sales on account for year, $241,257.00.	
Merchandise inventory—books	$174,469.25
Merchandise inventory—supplies	151,439.85
Office supplies inventory	4,635.00
Store supplies inventory	3,960.00
Value of prepaid insurance	4,400.00
Annual depreciation expense—office equipment	870.00
Annual depreciation expense—store equipment	940.00
Federal income tax expense for the year	5,013.75

161

15. Prepare a departmental statement of gross profit. Calculate and record component percentages for cost of merchandise sold and gross profit on operations. Round percentage calculations to the nearest 0.1%.
16. Prepare an income statement. Record the component percentages for cost of merchandise sold and gross profit on operations from the departmental statement of gross profit. Calculate and record the component percentages for total operating expenses and net income before and after federal income tax. Round component percentage calculations to the nearest 0.1%.
17. Prepare a statement of stockholders' equity. Use the following additional information.

January 1 balance of capital stock account . . . . (3,000 shares issued for $100.00 per share)	$300,000.00
No additional capital stock issued.	
January 1 balance of retained earnings account	97,525.70

18. Prepare a balance sheet.
19. Use page 13 of a general journal. Journalize and post the adjusting entries.
20. Continue using page 13 of a general journal. Journalize and post the closing entries. Do not skip a line between the adjusting and closing entries.
21. Prepare a post-closing trial balance.

162

Galleria, Inc., is a departmentalized merchandising business organized as a corporation. This business simulation covers the realistic transactions completed by Galleria, Inc. which has two departments: Furniture and Interiors. The activities included in the accounting cycle for Galleria, Inc. are listed below.

This simulation is available from the publisher in either manual or automated versions.

Activities in Galleria, Inc.:

1. Recording transactions in special journals and a general journal.
2. Calculating and recording departmental payroll data.
3. Preparing a bank reconciliation.
4. Posting items to be posted individually to a general journal and subsidiary ledgers.
5. Proving and ruling journals.
6. Posting column totals to a general ledger.
7. Preparing schedules of accounts receivable and accounts payable.
8. Preparing a trial balance on a work sheet.
9. Planning adjustments and completing a work sheet.
10. Preparing financial statements.
11. Journalizing and posting adjusting entries.
12. Journalizing and posting closing entries.
13. Preparing a post-closing trial balance.

PART 3 OVERVIEW

STUDENT EDITION

STUDENT FEATURES

Professional Business Ethics

At What Price Safety? page 204

Careers In Accounting

Accounting Clerk, page 168

Multicultural Awareness

Korean American Business Enterprises, page 195

Global Perspective

International Banking, page 180

Personal Visions In Business

James Martinez, page 207

Audit Your Understanding

This student activity can be found on pages 174, 179, 184, 198, 203, 208

APPLIED SKILLS

Applied Communications

Page 187

Applied Math

Pages 206, 207, 208, 212

SOFTWARE APPLICATIONS

Automated Accounting 6.0 Problems Integrating Automated Accounting Topic 4 Problem DB-4
Spreadsheet Template Problems 7-1, 7-2, 7-3, 7-4

TEACHER'S EDITION

APPLIED SKILLS

Communications, page 184
Language Arts, pages 176, 205
Writing Across the Curriculum, pages 173, 194
Building Study Skills, page 208
Word Processing, pages 185, 193

TEACHING STRATEGIES

Accounting Pedagogy, pages 166, 167, 192, 215
Different Learning Abilities, pages 192, 216
Different Learning Styles, pages 199, 206, 207, 208
Cooperative Learning, pages 182, 199, 218
Expanding Beyond the Classroom, pages 172, 196
Applying Visuals, pages 185, 202
Teaching Tip, pages 166, 169, 171, 173, 175, 178, 195, 197, 201, 220
Software Focus, pages 198, 219
Safety and Health, page 217

ASSESSMENT

MicroExam software for each chapter
Problem Test for each chapter
Unit Objective Test No. 3 (6-7)

SOFTWARE

Automated Accounting 6.0
MicroExam
Lotus (spreadsheet)
WordPerfect (word processing)
Works (integrated software)

BIBLIOGRAPHY

AICPA. *Upward Mobility of Women Special Committee: Report to the AICPA Board of Directors.*
Cantlon, T. *Structuring the Classroom Successfully for Cooperative Team Learning.* Portland, OR: Prestige Publishers, 1991.
Chatfield, Michael. *A History of Accounting Thought.* Second Edition. Huntington, NY: Robert E. Krieger Publishing, 1977.
Gelinas, Ulric J., Jr., Allan E. Oram, and William P. Wiggins. *Accounting Information Systems.* Second Edition. Cincinnati: South-Western Publishing Co., 1993.
Kagan, S. *Cooperative Learning Resources for Teachers.* San Juan Capistrano: Resources for Teachers, 1989.
Swartz, R. *The Effects of Attitudes and Aptitudes in Predicting Final Course Grades: Implications for Multi-Group Organization in Business Communication Classes.* Unpublished paper presented in Teacher Education 883, Michigan State University, East Lansing, 1987.
U.S. Department of Labor. *Dictionary of Occupational Titles.*

Periodicals

American Accounting Association Newsletter, Sarasota, FL.
Journal of Accountancy, AICPA, Jersey City, NJ.
Native Peoples, Phoenix, AZ. (Multicultural awareness)

Technology

AICPA. *Luca Pacioli: Unsung Hero of the Renaissance.* (Video)
AICPA. *TOTAL (Total On-line Tax and Accounting Library).* (Tax and accounting on-line database)

PART 3 OPENER

CHAPTER 6
A Voucher System

CHAPTER 7
Inventory Planning and Valuation

INTEGRATING AUTOMATED ACCOUNTING—TOPIC 4
Inventory Planning and Valuation

PART 3

Accounting Control Systems

GENERAL GOALS

1. Know accounting terminology related to selected accounting control systems.
2. Understand accounting concepts and practices related to selected accounting control systems.
3. Demonstrate accounting procedures for selected accounting control systems.

OVERVIEW

Part 3 introduces accounting control systems and their importance to management. Of particular concern to management are procedures to control and protect assets. Many businesses, therefore, use two specific control systems to protect assets—vouchers and inventory planning and valuation.

Chapter 6 introduces vouchers as a system of controlling cash payments. Vouchers are described and the procedures for using a voucher system are thoroughly discussed.

Chapter 7 establishes the importance of managing inventory. Procedures for maintaining inventory must be established in order for a business to be successful. This chapter covers all the important elements of maintaining inventory. After Chapter 7, Integrating Automated Accounting Topic 4 is presented to integrate computer application of the manual procedures that have been introduced in Chapter 7. For those teachers who wish to fully integrate the program, *Automated Accounting 6.0* may be used to actually automate selected problems in the text.

CHAPTER 6 OVERVIEW

Chapter 6 introduces vouchers as one method of accounting control systems. Steps for preparing the voucher are illustrated including recording the voucher in the voucher register. Activities such as canceling vouchers, preparing voucher checks, and recording checks in the check register are described.

GUIDE TO ACHIEVING LEARNING OBJECTIVES

	TEACH	APPLY	EXTEND/ENRICH				
Enabling Performance Tasks	**Lesson Plans**	**Application Problems**	**Mastery Problems**	**Challenge Problems**	**Cases for Critical Thinking**	**Recycling Problems**	**Reinforcement Activity**
a. Define accounting terms related to a voucher system.	6-1, 6-2						
b. Identify accounting concepts and practices related to a voucher system.	6-1, 6-2, 6-3				Cases 1, 2		
c. Prepare a voucher.	6-1	6-4					
d. Journalize data from vouchers in a voucher register.	6-1	6-1	6-M	6-C		6-R	
e. Journalize voucher payment transactions in a check register.	6-2	6-2	6-M	6-C		6-R	
f. Journalize purchases returns and allowances and payroll transactions in a voucher system.	6-3	6-3, 6-4	6-M	6-C		6-R	

ENRICHMENT

SPECIAL FEATURES
Global Perspective, page 180
Careers in Accounting, page 168
Applied Communications, page 187

Students will need the voucher register prepared in Problem 6-1 to complete Problem 6-2. Challenge Problem 6-C includes an explanation of the net method of recording purchases. This problem requires the student to use the net method of recording purchases within a voucher system.

	INFORMAL ASSESSMENT		FORMAL ASSESSMENT			
	Study Guide	**Audit Your Understanding**	**Chapter MicroExam**	**Chapter Problem Test**	**Unit Objective Test**	**Portfolio**
	Unit A	✓	✓		✓	
	Units B, D	✓	✓		✓	
				✓		
	Unit C			✓		
	Unit C			✓		
	Unit C			✓		

NEW, REVIEW, AND EXTENSION

ACTIVITIES/CONCEPTS/TRANSACTIONS	NEW	REVIEW/ EXTENSION
Using a voucher system	✓	
Preparing a voucher	✓	
Journalizing vouchers in a voucher register		✓
Journalizing a voucher for a purchase on account		✓
Journalizing a voucher for cash payment of an expense		✓
Proving, ruling, and posting a voucher register		✓
Voucher checks		✓
Journalizing cash payments in a check register		✓
Proving, ruling, and posting a check register		✓
Journalizing a voucher for purchases returns and allowances on account		✓
Journalizing a voucher for a payroll transaction		✓

TEACHING MATERIALS

Teacher's Wraparound Edition of the Text
Teacher's Resource Guide
Teacher's Edition of Working Papers
MicroExam

TEACHING STRATEGIES: ACCOUNTING PEDAGOGY

A chart of accounts for the business that is used to illustrate each part of this textbook is provided at the beginning of each part. Charts of accounts are extremely important to companies because they drive the accounting system. Employees usually cannot even receive reimbursement for expenses without knowing which account the expense should be charged to. Pedagogically, the chart of accounts provides the following information: (1) Classification for each account—needed to determine how a transaction is analyzed. (2) Permanent accounts (balance sheet accounts) and temporary accounts (income statement accounts)—assists in analyzing transactions and recording closing entries. (3) Account number for every general ledger account—critical information in automated accounting, since transactions are entered by account number rather than account title.

CHART OF ACCOUNTS

This chart of accounts is for a merchandising business organized as a corporation. Because the business is not departmentalized, accounts are not divided into departments as they were for Mastersport in Part 2. The liabilities section reflects the fact that OfficeMart uses a voucher system for controlling cash payments. In the stockholders' equity section, there is only one income summary account since the company is not departmentalized.

The Operating Expenses section is divided into selling and administrative expenses. Administrative expenses are expenses of the business that do not clearly relate to the sales effort, such as salaries and supplies of the office staff.

OFFICEMART, INC.

CHART OF ACCOUNTS

Balance Sheet Accounts

(1000) ASSETS

1100 Current Assets

1105 Cash
1110 Petty Cash
1115 Accounts Receivable
1120 Allowance for Uncollectible Accounts
1125 Merchandise Inventory
1130 Supplies—Sales
1135 Supplies—Administrative
1140 Prepaid Insurance

1200 Plant Assets

1205 Delivery Equipment
1210 Accumulated Depreciation—Delivery Equipment
1215 Office Equipment
1220 Accumulated Depreciation—Office Equipment
1225 Store Equipment
1230 Accumulated Depreciation—Store Equipment

(2000) LIABILITIES

2100 Current Liabilities

2105 Vouchers Payable
2110 Employee Income Tax Pay.—Federal
2115 Employee Income Tax Pay.—State
2120 Federal Income Tax Payable
2125 FICA Tax Payable
2130 Sales Tax Payable
2135 Unemployment Tax Pay.—Federal
2140 Unemployment Tax Pay.—State
2145 Dividends Payable

(3000) STOCKHOLDERS' EQUITY

3105 Capital Stock
3110 Retained Earnings
3115 Dividends
3120 Income Summary

Income Statement Accounts

(4000) OPERATING REVENUE

4105 Sales
4110 Sales Discount
4115 Sales Returns and Allowances

(5000) COST OF MERCHANDISE

5105 Purchases
5110 Purchases Discount
5115 Purchases Returns and Allowances

(6000) OPERATING EXPENSES

6100 Selling Expenses

6105 Advertising Expense
6110 Delivery Expense
6115 Depreciation Expense—Delivery Equipment
6120 Depreciation Expense—Store Equipment
6125 Miscellaneous Expense—Sales
6130 Salary Expense—Sales
6135 Supplies Expense—Sales

6200 Administrative Expenses

6205 Depreciation Expense—Office Equipment
6210 Insurance Expense
6215 Miscellaneous Expense—Administrative
6220 Payroll Taxes Expense
6225 Rent Expense
6230 Salary Expense—Administrative
6235 Supplies Expense—Administative
6240 Uncollectible Accounts Expense
6245 Utilities Expense

(7000) INCOME TAX EXPENSE

7105 Federal Income Tax Expense

The chart of accounts for OfficeMart, Inc. is illustrated above for ready reference as you study Part 3 of this textbook.

TEACHING STRATEGIES: TEACHING TIP

Emphasize that students should refer to this chart of accounts throughout their study of Part 3. It will help them determine classification of accounts, which accounts are temporary and permanent accounts, and what account numbers to use for automated accounting. It will also be a useful reference for performing file maintenance activities.

6

A Voucher System

ENABLING PERFORMANCE TASKS

After studying Chapter 6, you will be able to:

a Define accounting terms related to a voucher system.

b Identify accounting concepts and practices related to a voucher system.

c Prepare a voucher.

d Journalize data from vouchers in a voucher register.

e Journalize voucher payment transactions in a check register.

f Journalize purchases returns and allowances and payroll transactions in a voucher system.

TERMS PREVIEW

voucher • voucher system • voucher register • voucher check • check register

TEACHING STRATEGIES: ACCOUNTING PEDAGOGY

This textbook introduces cash control systems. Internal control procedures are necessary to operate a successful business. Because the voucher system is one of the most effective means of internal control, it is important that students are exposed early in the course to this form of internal control.

CAREERS IN ACCOUNTING

The CAREERS feature box, ACCOUNTING CLERK, comes from the Dictionary of Occupational Titles (DOT). The entry number for this job title is D.O.T. 216.482-010. Bring this dictionary to class and explain its purpose and how to use it. The career feature is designed to expose students to the exploration of different careers in accounting. The feature gives a realistic description of actual job duties. This feature can be used to demonstrate that the skills learned in this course are relevant.

LESSON PLAN 6-1

Materials

- Student pages 168–174
- Blackline Master for Voucher Register (TRG)

Objectives (Enabling Performance Tasks)

a. Define accounting terms related to a voucher system.
b. Identify accounting concepts and practices related to a voucher system.
c. Prepare a voucher.
d. Journalize data from vouchers in a voucher register.

FOCUS

- Explain that many businesses use specific procedures to control and protect the asset cash. In this lesson, a set of procedures for approving all cash payments will be presented. A special business form used to show this approval and the special journal in which the form is recorded will be introduced.
- Introduce vocabulary: voucher, voucher system, voucher register.

CAREERS IN ACCOUNTING

ACCOUNTING CLERK

- ***Compiles and sorts documents supporting business transactions***
- ***Calculates and records charges***
- ***Prepares vouchers, invoices, and checks***
- ***Verifies and posts details of business transactions***

An accounting system includes procedures for the recording and reporting of accurate and up-to-date financial information useful to management. In addition, an accounting system should include procedures to assist management in controlling daily operations. Of particular concern to management are procedures and records to control and protect assets. One asset that should be controlled and protected is cash. Cash is the asset most likely to be misused because ownership is easily transferred. Also, transactions generally affect the cash account more often than other general ledger accounts. Many businesses, therefore, use specific cash control procedures.

Cash control procedures include storing cash in a safe place, making bank deposits regularly, and approving all cash payments. Cash payments are approved before being paid to ensure that the goods or services were ordered, have been received, and the amounts due are correct. In small businesses the owner or manager usually approves cash payments. In large businesses several persons may have authority to approve cash payments. A business form used to show an authorized person's approval for a cash payment is called a **voucher.** A set of procedures for controlling cash payments by preparing and approving vouchers before payments are made is called a **voucher system.** In a voucher system *NO* check can be issued without a properly authorized voucher.

Any business paper used to authorize an accounting entry may be referred to as a voucher. However, when a voucher system is used, *voucher* refers only to the cash payments approval form.

A VOUCHER

A voucher is prepared for each invoice received from a vendor. An invoice is checked for accuracy before a voucher is prepared.

August 1, 19--. Purchased merchandise on account from O'Riley Company, $3,500.00. Voucher No. 647.

Purchases	
3,500.00	

Vouchers Payable	
	3,500.00

When a voucher system is used, the source document for an approved cash payment is the voucher. The source document for this transaction is Voucher No. 647. *(CONCEPT: Objective Evidence)*

In a voucher system, the general ledger liability account, Vouchers Payable, is used instead of Accounts Payable. Accounts Payable has been used to record only amounts of items bought on account. In a voucher system, Vouchers Payable is used to record *ALL* amounts to be paid by check. Since Vouchers Payable is a liability account, the normal balance of Vouchers Payable is on the credit side of the account. Also, an accounts payable ledger is not kept. Instead, vouchers needing to be paid are kept in an unpaid vouchers file. The unpaid vouchers file shows all amounts owed and to whom amounts are owed.

FYI

In a voucher system, the vouchers payable account replaces the accounts payable account.

Verifying an Invoice

OfficeMart, a merchandising business, sells office furniture and supplies. When OfficeMart receives an invoice, a verification form is stamped on the invoice, as shown in Illustration 6-1.

OfficeMart's receiving clerk verifies that the items were received in the correct quantities. A clerk in OfficeMart's purchasing department verifies that the terms and prices are correct. The calculations on the invoice are also verified. Each person doing a part of the work places a check mark next to the items verified and initials the verification form to show responsibility for that part.

ILLUSTRATION 6-1

Verification of an invoice

INVOICE

O'RILEY COMPANY
1257 N. Rosemount Dr.
Chicago, IL 60640-5234

NO. 6384
DATE: July 31 19--
TERMS: 2/10, n/30 ✓

TO: OfficeMart
9424 Lincoln Street
Duluth, MN 55804-5478

QUANTITY	DESCRIPTION	UNIT PRICE	AMOUNT
✓ 10	Executive Desks, ED3060	300.00 ✓	3,000.00 ✓
✓ 50	Chair Mats, 6M3648	10.00 ✓	500.00 ✓

Date rec'd. 8/1/--
MATERIAL RECEIVED C.M.G.
TERMS APPROVED BAH
PRICES APPROVED BAH
FIGURES CHECKED BAH
Voucher No. 647

THANK YOU FOR YOUR ORDER!

INVOICE TOTAL 3,500.00 ✓

Preparing a Voucher from an Invoice

A form is printed on the outside of a voucher to summarize the contents and provide space for approving payments. The outside of OfficeMart's voucher for the invoice from O'Riley Company is shown in Illustration 6-2. After the invoice is summarized on the voucher, the voucher is folded so that related documents can be placed inside the fold. For this reason a voucher is sometimes known as a voucher jacket.

When a business uses a voucher system, consecutive voucher numbers are often preprinted on each blank voucher. OfficeMart uses prenumbered voucher forms and must account for all voucher numbers. Therefore, the prenumbered vouchers serve as an additional control within OfficeMart's voucher system.

FYI

The unpaid voucher file shows all amounts owed and to whom they are owed.

TEACH

Cover student pages 168–174 "A Voucher" and "A Voucher Register." Stress the purpose of a voucher system as a means of controlling cash payments. Introduce the vouchers payable account. Discuss the verification form stamped on an invoice. Explain how a voucher is prepared from an invoice. Emphasize the importance of each part of a voucher. When discussing Section 1, review terms of sale and calculating due dates and emphasize that checks are written two days before they are due. Introduce the voucher register and explain that the register replaces the purchases journal. Describe how approved vouchers are recorded in the voucher register. Emphasize that an account title is written in the account title column if there is not a special column in the voucher register. Describe the unpaid vouchers file. Review the procedures for proving, ruling, and posting a voucher register.

APPLY

Draw a T account on the board for Vouchers Payable and label the sides. Refer students to Illustration 6-2 as preparation of a voucher is discussed. Refer students to Illustration 6-5 as journalizing in a voucher register is described.

Guided Practice

Guide students through the T account analysis of the transactions in Problem 6-1, Instruction 1. Have students draw T accounts on a sheet of paper and analyze the first transaction. All students should agree with the analysis before proceeding to the next transaction. Repeat the process until all transactions have been analyzed. The balance of Problem 6-1 can be completed as Independent Practice.

Independent Practice

Assign Terms 1–3, Questions 1–8, and Problem 6-1.

TEACHING STRATEGIES: TEACHING TIP

Stress the purpose of a voucher system as a means of controlling cash payments. In addition, point out the system of approvals and verification that enables a voucher system to serve as a control mechanism.

ASSESS

Assess student understanding by checking the solutions to the Independent Practice activities.

Reteach

Make transparencies of the voucher register from the accounting forms masters provided in the Blackline Masters Section of the Teacher's Resource Guide. Refer students to Recycling Problem 6-R. Ask students to use T accounts to analyze the May 1, 2, 4, and 14 purchases and expense transactions. Use the transparencies to demonstrate how the transactions are journalized.

Extend

Assign Cases for Critical Thinking 1.

Enrich

Assign the CAREERS IN ACCOUNTING feature on page 168. Have students discuss what a career as an accounting clerk might be like.

CLOSURE

Use Audit Your Understanding questions.

ILLUSTRATION 6-2 Outside of a voucher for an invoice

Section 1

Vchr. No. 647

Date 8/1/-- Due Date 8/10/-- Payment Date 8/8/--

To O'Riley Company

Address 1257 N. Rosemount Dr. (Street)
Chicago, (City) IL (State) 60640-3234 (ZIP)

Section 2

ACCOUNTS DEBITED	AMOUNT
PURCHASES	3,500 00
SUPPLIES—SALES	
SUPPLIES—ADMIN.	
MISCELLANEOUS EXPENSE—SALES	
MISCELLANEOUS EXPENSE—ADMIN.	
RENT EXPENSE	
SALARY EXPENSE—SALES	
SALARY EXPENSE—ADMIN.	
TOTAL DEBITS	3,500 00

ACCOUNTS CREDITED	AMOUNT
VOUCHERS PAYABLE	3,500 00
EMPLOYEE INC. TAX PAY.—FEDERAL	
EMPLOYEE INC. TAX PAY.—STATE	
FICA TAX PAYABLE	
TOTAL CREDITS	3,500 00

Section 3

Voucher Approved by *Laura Post*

Section 4

Recorded in Voucher Register Page ______ by ______

Section 5

Paid { Date ______ Check No. ______ Amount $ ______ Approved by ______

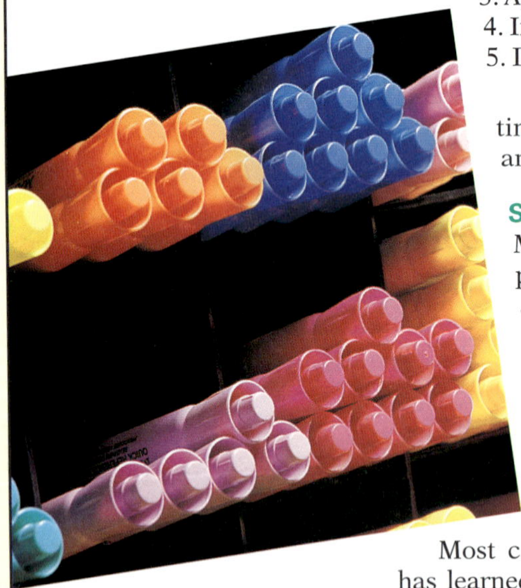

The outside of OfficeMart's voucher has five sections for recording information.

1. Information about the payee.
2. Information about the accounts affected.
3. Approval of the voucher.
4. Information about where the voucher is recorded.
5. Information about payment of the voucher.

Sections 1, 2, and 3 of the voucher are completed at the time a voucher is prepared. The completion of Sections 4 and 5 is described later in this chapter.

Section 1 of a Voucher—Payee Information. OfficeMart's accounting clerk obtains information about the payee from the verified invoice, Illustration 6-1. The accounting clerk enters the information in Section 1 of the voucher, as shown in Illustration 6-2.

The due date of Voucher No. 647 is calculated using information on the invoice. The invoice is dated July 31. The invoice terms, 2/10, n/30, indicate that a 2% discount can be taken by paying the invoice within ten days. Therefore, to take the discount, the invoice must be paid no later than August 10.

Most cash payments are mailed. From experience, OfficeMart has learned that most checks are received within two days. Therefore, OfficeMart writes and mails checks two days before the due date. Thus, the payment date for Voucher No. 647 is August 8.

After Section 1 of the voucher is completed, the voucher number, *647,* is recorded on the verification stamp on the invoice, as shown in Illustration 6-1.

FYI

A schedule of vouchers payable is prepared in the same manner as a schedule of accounts payable. All unpaid vouchers are listed on a schedule and totaled. The total of all unpaid vouchers should equal the total of the vouchers payable account.

Section 2 of a Voucher—Accounts Affected. As previously described, two accounts are affected by this transaction: the cost account, Purchases, is debited; the liability account, Vouchers Payable, is credited. Section 2 of the voucher lists several preprinted account titles. Purchases is preprinted under the heading Accounts Debited. Vouchers Payable is preprinted under the heading Accounts Credited. Therefore, only the amount of the invoice, *$3,500.00,* must be entered in Section 2, as shown in Illustration 6-2. Total Debits and Total Credits are also calculated and entered.

Titles of the accounts that are most often affected by cash payments are printed on the voucher form. If additional account titles are needed, they are entered on the blank lines in Section 2.

Section 3 of a Voucher—Voucher Approval. As a double check, someone is usually authorized to approve vouchers before they are journalized. Laura Post, accountant, is authorized to approve vouchers for OfficeMart. When Miss Post verifies that the voucher is correct, she approves it by signing her name in Section 3, as shown in Illustration 6-2.

TEACHING STRATEGIES: TEACHING TIP

Use an overhead projector to display transparencies of a purchases journal and a cash payments journal. Record the following transactions in the journals: (a) purchase on account, (b) miscellaneous expense, (c) cash payment on account, (d) purchases returns and allowances, and (e) payroll. Show how these entries will be recorded in these journals. Then use transparencies for a voucher register and a check register. Demonstrate how the same transactions will be recorded in these registers. Help students recognize the similarities and differences between recording these transactions in previously studied journals and in the registers described in this chapter.

A VOUCHER REGISTER

A voucher is recorded after it has been approved. A journal used to record vouchers is called a **voucher register.** A voucher register is similar to and replaces a purchases journal. Vouchers are recorded in the voucher register as they are approved. Since OfficeMart's vouchers are prenumbered, all vouchers can be accounted for. A missing voucher number shows that a voucher has not been recorded.

FYI

For internal control, the person who approves vouchers is not the same person who prepares vouchers.

OfficeMart's voucher register is shown in Illustration 6-3 on pages 172 and 173. Special columns are provided for Vouchers Payable Credit, Purchases Debit, Supplies—Sales Debit, and Supplies—Administrative Debit. For accounts with no special amount columns, information is recorded in the General columns.

Journalizing a Voucher in a Voucher Register's Special Columns

The entry for Voucher No. 647 is shown in Illustration 6-3. The date of the voucher, *19--, Aug. 1,* is written in the Date column. The name of the payee, *O'Riley Company,* is written in the Payee column. The voucher number, *647,* is recorded in the Vchr. No. column. This information is obtained from Section 1 of the voucher.

ILLUSTRATION 6-3 Voucher recorded in a voucher register (left page)

VOUCHER

	DATE		PAYEE	VCHR. NO.	PAID DATE	PAID CK. NO.	1 VOUCHERS PAYABLE CREDIT	
1	19-- Aug.	1	O'Riley Company	647			3 500 00	1
2								2
3								3
4								4
5								5

The credit amount, *$3,500.00,* is written in the Vouchers Payable Credit column. The debit amount, *$3,500.00,* is written in the Purchases Debit column. This information is obtained from Section 2 of the voucher.

Section 4 of a Voucher—Where Voucher is Recorded

The person who records the voucher in the voucher register also completes Section 4 of the voucher. A notation is made indicating the page on which the information is recorded in the voucher register. The person's initials are also recorded in the space provided on the voucher. Placing the voucher register page number on the voucher provides easy reference to where the entry is located in the voucher register. Section 4 of Voucher No. 647 is shown in Illustration 6-4.

FYI

In a voucher register, special amount columns are used for frequently occurring transactions.

ILLUSTRATION 6-4 Notation on voucher showing where voucher is recorded

Recorded in Voucher Register Page 21 by G. R. S.

After Voucher No. 647 is journalized and the notation is made in Section 4, the voucher is filed in an unpaid vouchers file. The vouchers are placed in this file according to the payment date. Filing the vouchers by payment date makes it easier to determine which vouchers need to be paid each day. This method helps assure payment of invoices within the discount period. Thus, Voucher No. 647 is filed under the date on which it is to be paid, August 8.

Payment of a voucher is described later in this chapter.

TEACHING STRATEGIES: EXPANDING BEYOND THE CLASSROOM

Stress the importance of accounting in everyday jobs. Students need to realize that accounting is important for everyone, not just people who are going to be accountants. Set up a day where several people from the community are invited to be members of a professional panel. Try to get a person such as a hair stylist who can tell students how important it is to understand accounting to keep track of the books. A builder might explain to students how costs are tracked for building a house and the role accounting plays.

ILLUSTRATION 6-3 Voucher recorded in a voucher register (right page)

REGISTER PAGE 21

	2	3	4			5	6	
	PURCHASES DEBIT	SUPPLIES—SALES DEBIT	SUPPLIES—ADMINISTRATIVE DEBIT	GENERAL ACCOUNT TITLE	POST. REF.	GENERAL DEBIT	GENERAL CREDIT	
1	3 500 00							1
2								2
3								3
4								4
5								5

TEACHING STRATEGIES: TEACHING TIP

Draw T accounts on the chalkboard to show the analysis of each transaction as it is presented.

Journalizing a Voucher in a Voucher Register's General Columns

OfficeMart's voucher register has special debit amount columns for Purchases Debit, Supplies—Sales Debit, and Supplies—Administrative Debit. When an account other than these four is affected, the information is recorded in the General columns.

August 2, 19--. Received invoice for sales miscellaneous expense from Glenhill Company, $40.00. Voucher No. 648.

Miscellaneous Expense—Sales	
40.00	

Vouchers Payable	
	40.00

This voucher is prepared in the same way as described for Voucher No. 647, Illustration 6-2.

The entry for Voucher No. 648 is shown on line 2 of the voucher register, Illustration 6-5, pages 174–175.

The date, *2,* is written in the Date column. The name of the payee, *Glenhill Company,* is written in the Payee column. The voucher number, *648,* is recorded in the Vchr. No. column. The credit amount, *$40.00,* is recorded in the Vouchers Payable Credit column. Since OfficeMart's voucher register does not have a special debit amount column for Miscellaneous Expense—Sales, the debit amount, *$40.00,* is recorded in the General Debit column. When an amount is recorded in a general amount column, an account title must also be written in the Account Title column. The account to be debited, *Miscellaneous Expense—Sales,* is written in the Account Title column.

A notation is made on Voucher No. 648 in Section 4 to show where the voucher was recorded and by whom.

APPLIED SKILLS: WRITING ACROSS THE CURRICULUM

Writing paragraphs and short essays. The Cases for Critical Thinking are short, practical applications of the accounting principles developed in the chapter. Some cases are planned to present problems related to the chapter but not specifically discussed and answered in the chapter. These cases present an opportunity for critical thinking and decision making. These cases also require more than a short objective-type response. Therefore they provide ideal practice in writing paragraphs and short essays.

Proving, Ruling, and Posting a Voucher Register

Separate amounts recorded in a voucher register's General Debit and General Credit columns are posted individually during the month. As each amount is posted, the account number is written in the voucher register's Post. Ref. column. OfficeMart's voucher register after posting is completed is shown in Illustration 6-5, pages 174 and 175.

FYI

There are about 400,000 CPAs in the United States. About 35,000 new CPAs enter the work force each year.

ILLUSTRATION 6-5 Voucher register (left page)

VOUCHER

	DATE		PAYEE	VCHR. NO.	PAID DATE	PAID CK. NO.	1 VOUCHERS PAYABLE CREDIT	
1	19-- Aug.	1	O'Riley Company	647	Aug. 8	783	3,500.00	1
2		2	Glenhill Company	648			40.00	2
3		4	Jacobs Equipment	649	Aug. 11	784	973.91	3
4		5	Salem Wholesale Instruments	650			451.00	4
5		7	Bob's Delivery Service	651	Aug. 17	786	63.00	5
6		7	Ramsey, Inc.	652	See Vchr. 655		180.00	6
7		10	Superior Office Supplies	653			87.00	7
8		12	Kuker Company	654	Aug. 19	788	276.00	8
9		12	Ramsey, Inc.	655			95.00	9
10								10
11		14	Petty Cash Custodian, OfficeMart	656	Aug. 14	785	212.50	11
12								12
26		31	Payroll	694	Aug. 31	800	4,331.96	26
27								27
28								28
29								29
30								30
31		31	Totals				105,077.41	31
32							(2105)	32
33								33
34								34
35								35
36								36

AUDIT YOUR UNDERSTANDING

The AUDIT YOUR UNDERSTANDING feature appears at the end of each section of the chapter. Explain to your students that the word *audit* means to check or verify. AUDIT YOUR UNDERSTANDING may be used to check student comprehension of the section just studied. The answers are provided in Appendix D in the back of the textbook.

1. Vouchers Payable.
2. To serve as an additional control; all vouchers can be accounted for.
3. Purchases journal.
4. When the vouchers are approved.

Audit Your Understanding

1. In a voucher system, what general ledger account is used to record all amounts to be paid by check?
2. What is the purpose of using prenumbered voucher forms?
3. A voucher register is similar to and replaces what journal?
4. When are vouchers recorded in the voucher register?

At the end of each month, OfficeMart's voucher register is proved and ruled. The procedures for proving and ruling a voucher register are the same as those previously described for special journals.

Totals of special amount columns are posted to the general ledger accounts listed in the column headings. Totals of General Debit and General Credit amount columns are not posted. Posting procedures for a voucher register's column totals are the same as previously described for special journals.

LESSON PLAN 6-2

Materials

- Student pages 174–179
- Blackline Master for Check Register (TRG)

Objectives (Enabling Performance Tasks)

a. Define accounting terms related to a voucher system.

b. Identify accounting concepts and practices related to a voucher system.

e. Journalize voucher payment transactions in a check register.

A CHECK REGISTER

OfficeMart pays each voucher by check. A check is prepared for the amount of each voucher less any purchases discount. The check and voucher are presented to a person authorized to approve payment. A check with space for writing details about a

ILLUSTRATION 6-5 Voucher register (right page)

REGISTER PAGE 21

	2	3	4			5	6	
	PURCHASES DEBIT	SUPPLIES—SALES DEBIT	SUPPLIES—ADMINISTRATIVE DEBIT	GENERAL				
				ACCOUNT TITLE	POST. REF.	DEBIT	CREDIT	
1	3 500 00							1
2				*Miscellaneous Expense—Sales*	6125	40 00		2
3	973 91							3
4	451 00							4
5		63 00						5
6	180 00							6
7			87 00					7
8	276 00							8
9				*Vouchers Payable*	2105	180 00		9
10				*Purchases Returns and Allowances*	5115		85 00	10
11		40 00	55 25	*Advertising Expense*	6105	47 00		11
12				*Miscellaneous Expense—Administrative*	6215	70 25		12
26				*Salary Expense—Sales*	6130	3 000 00		26
27				*Salary Expense—Administrative*	6230	2 854 00		27
28				*Employee Income Tax Payable—Federal*	2110		878 10	28
29				*Employee Income Tax Payable—State*	2115		175 62	29
30				*FICA Tax Payable*	2125		468 32	30
31	53 806 91	1 224 00	1 452 25			56 175 25	75 810 00	31
32	(5105)	(1130)	(1135)			(√)	(√)	32
33								33
34								34
35								35
36								36

cash payment is called a **voucher check.** OfficeMart prepares voucher checks in duplicate. The original copy is given to the payee and OfficeMart keeps the duplicate copy.

OfficeMart does not prepare check stubs when checks are written. Instead, the duplicate check is used as the source document for a cash payment transaction. *(CONCEPT: Objective Evidence)*

OfficeMart's procedures for keeping a record of the checking account balance are explained later in this chapter.

Preparing a Voucher Check

On August 8, vouchers to be paid on that day are removed from the unpaid vouchers file. Included in this group is Voucher No. 647. To pay Voucher No. 647, OfficeMart's cash payments clerk prepares Check No. 783, as shown in Illustration 6-6 on page 176.

Each voucher check provides space in which details about the cash payment are shown. OfficeMart's voucher checks have space

FYI

The stub of a voucher check must be removed by the payee before cashing the check.

FOCUS

- Preparing vouchers for all cash payments and journalizing the vouchers in a voucher register were presented earlier in this chapter. In this lesson, the journal used in a voucher system to record cash payments will be described.
- Introduce vocabulary: voucher check, check register.

TEACH

Cover student pages 174–179 "A Check Register." Describe preparing a voucher check with a detachable stub. Introduce the check register and explain the use of the bank columns. Emphasize that the register replaces the cash payments journal. Describe how checks are recorded in the check register and how the new bank balance is calculated. Emphasize that the date of payment and check number must also be recorded in the voucher register as shown in the Paid columns of Illustration 6-5. Review proving, ruling, and posting a check register.

TEACHING STRATEGIES: TEACHING TIP

Prepare a bulletin board display. Obtain or prepare an invoice for a purchase of merchandise on account transaction. Prepare two journals: (a) a purchases journal and (b) a voucher register. Show how the transaction would be recorded in each of these two journals. In addition, prepare the outside of a voucher to be displayed near the voucher register. Also, a check can be prepared for payment of the invoice. The entry for the cash payment can be shown in two journals: (a) a cash payments journal and (b) a check register.

APPLY

Refer students to Illustration 6-9 as the check register is discussed.

Guided Practice

Guide students through the T account analysis of the transactions in Problem 6-2, Instruction 2. Have students draw T accounts on a sheet of paper and analyze the first transaction. All students should agree with the analysis before proceeding to the next transaction. Repeat the process until all transactions have been analyzed. The balance of Problem 6-2 can be completed as Independent Practice.

Independent Practice

Assign Terms 4–5, Questions 9–13, and Problem 6-2.

ILLUSTRATION 6-6 Voucher check

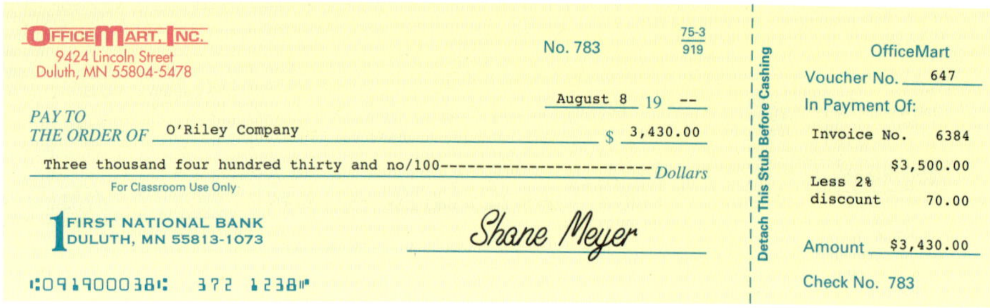
OFFICEMART, INC.
9424 Lincoln Street
Duluth, MN 55804-5478
No. 783 75-3/919
August 8 19 --
PAY TO THE ORDER OF O'Riley Company $ 3,430.00
Three thousand four hundred thirty and no/100---------------------- Dollars
For Classroom Use Only
FIRST NATIONAL BANK
DULUTH, MN 55813-1073
Shane Meyer
⑆0919000381⑆ 372 1238⑈
Detach This Stub Before Cashing
OfficeMart
Voucher No. 647
In Payment Of:
Invoice No. 6384
$3,500.00
Less 2% discount 70.00
Amount $3,430.00
Check No. 783

at the right in which the details are recorded. On Check No. 783, the information includes the items listed below.

1. OfficeMart's voucher number, *647*.
2. Payee's invoice number, *6384*.
3. Amount of invoice, *$3,500.00*.
4. Amount of discount, *$70.00*.
5. Net amount for which check is written, *$3,430.00*.

Before a payee deposits or cashes a voucher check, the stub showing details of the transaction is removed. The stub is kept by the payee as a record of the check.

Section 5 of a Voucher—Payment of a Voucher

The person who prepares the check also completes part of Section 5 of the voucher. A notation is made indicating the date paid, the check number, and the amount. The payment notation for Voucher No. 647 is shown in Illustration 6-7.

ILLUSTRATION 6-7 Notation on voucher showing approval of payment

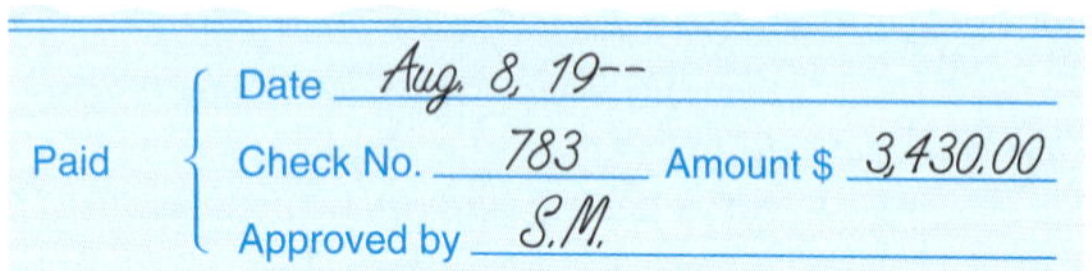
Paid
Date Aug. 8, 19--
Check No. 783 Amount $ 3,430.00
Approved by S.M.

FYI

When a payment is approved, a notation must be made in the Paid columns of the voucher register.

The manager, Shane Meyer, verifies that the information on the check and voucher agrees and is accurate. When he is satisfied that the payment is in order, he signs the check and initials Section 5 of the voucher, as shown in Illustration 6-7.

Information about this payment must also be recorded in the voucher register. The person who prepares the check usually makes this notation. The date on which this voucher is paid, *Aug. 8,* and the check number, *783,* are written in the Paid columns of the voucher register. This information is written on the same line as the

APPLIED SKILLS: LANGUAGE ARTS

Paraphrasing, writing complete sentences, and identifying verbs. For additional practice in language arts skills, direct students to answer the Accounting Terms and Questions for Individual Study at the end of the chapter. Students should write the answers in their own words and in complete sentences. To further practice language arts skills, ask students to underline all verbs in their answers.

original entry for Voucher No. 647 as shown on line 1 of Illustration 6-5.

The check is given or sent to the payee, and the voucher is filed in the paid vouchers file according to the name of the vendor.

Journalizing Cash Payments in a Check Register

A journal used in a voucher system to record cash payments is called a **check register.** OfficeMart's check register is shown in Illustration 6-8. This check register is similar to and replaces a cash payments journal.

ILLUSTRATION 6-8 Check recorded in a check register

CHECK REGISTER — PAGE 19

	DATE		PAYEE	CK. NO.	VCHR. NO.	1 VOUCHERS PAYABLE DEBIT	2 PURCHASES DISCOUNT CREDIT	3 CASH CREDIT	4 BANK DEPOSITS	5 BANK BALANCE	
1	19-- Aug.	8	Brought Forward		√	23 109 90	268 30	22 841 60		97 768 13	1
2		8	O'Riley Company	783	647	3 500 00	70 00	3 430 00		94 338 13	2
3											3

Maintaining Bank Columns in a Check Register. OfficeMart does not use a checkbook with check stubs. OfficeMart needs some way to know the checking account balance. Therefore, OfficeMart uses a check register to maintain the checking account balance.

OfficeMart's check register, Illustration 6-8, has two Bank columns, *Deposits* and *Balance.* These two Bank columns are used to keep an up-to-date record of cash in OfficeMart's checking account. The Bank Deposits column is used to record the amounts deposited in the checking account. The Bank Balance column shows the checking account balance after each check and deposit is recorded in the check register.

FYI

Vouchers provide internal control. No checks can be issued without an authorized voucher.

Journalizing Checks in a Check Register. OfficeMart prepares a voucher for each approved cash payment. Therefore, each check is issued in payment of a voucher. Checks are recorded in the check register in the order they are written.

In OfficeMart's voucher system, only three general ledger accounts are affected by a cash payment: Vouchers Payable, Purchases Discount, and Cash. Therefore, OfficeMart's check register has only three special amount columns: Vouchers Payable Debit, Purchases Discount Credit, and Cash Credit. Each check is recorded in a check register as a debit to the liability account, Vouchers Payable, and a credit to the asset account, Cash. If a discount is taken for prompt payment, the discount amount is recorded as a credit to the contra cost account, Purchases Discount.

August 8, 19--. Paid cash to O'Riley Company, $3,430.00, covering Voucher No. 647 for $3,500.00, less 2% discount, $70.00. Check No. 783.

ASSESS

Assess student understanding by checking the solutions to the Independent Practice activities.

Reteach

Make a transparency of the check register from the accounting forms masters provided in the Blackline Masters Section of the Teacher's Resource Guide. Refer students to Recycling Problem 6-R. Ask students to use T accounts to analyze the May 8, 14, and 22 cash payments transactions. Use the transparency to demonstrate how the transactions are journalized in the check register. Also, show how the payment notation is recorded in the voucher register.

Extend

Assign Cases for Critical Thinking 2.

Enrich

Assign and discuss the GLOBAL PERSPECTIVE feature on page 180.

CLOSURE

Use Audit Your Understanding questions.

Vouchers Payable	
3,500.00	Vchr. 647 3,500.00

Purchases Discount	
	70.00

Cash	
	3,430.00

The liability account, Vouchers Payable, is debited for $3,500.00. The contra cost account, Purchases Discount, is credited for $70.00. Cash is credited for the net amount paid, $3,430.00.

The check register entry to record Check No. 783 is shown on line 2 of Illustration 6-8.

The date, *8*, is recorded in the Date column. The name of the payee, *O'Riley Company*, is written in the Payee column. The check number, *783*, is entered in the Ck. No. column. The number of the voucher being paid, *647*, is entered in the Vchr. No. column. The debit to Vouchers Payable, *$3,500.00*, is recorded in the Vouchers Payable Debit column. The credit to Purchases Discount, *$70.00*, is recorded in the Purchases Discount Credit column. The credit to Cash, *$3,430.00*, is recorded in the Cash Credit column. A new checking account balance is calculated. The previous balance, $97,768.13, *minus* this payment, $3,430.00, *equals* the new balance, $94,338.13. The new balance, *$94,338.13*, is recorded in the Bank Balance column.

FYI

The Bank Balance column of a check register shows the up-to-date record of cash in the checking account.

TEACHING STRATEGIES: TEACHING TIP

Gather examples of vouchers, voucher registers, and check registers from your school and/or local businesses. Create a bulletin board collage of these forms to illustrate that a voucher system is designed according to the needs of each business.

Proving, Ruling, and Posting a Check Register

At the end of each month, the check register's special amount columns are proved, ruled, and posted. OfficeMart's check register after it has been posted is shown in Illustration 6-9.

ILLUSTRATION 6-9 Ruling and posting a check register

CHECK REGISTER PAGE *19*

	DATE		PAYEE	CK. NO.	VCHR. NO.	1 VOUCHERS PAYABLE DEBIT	2 PURCHASES DISCOUNT CREDIT	3 CASH CREDIT	4 BANK DEPOSITS	5 BANK BALANCE	
1	19-- Aug.	8	Brought Forward		✓	23109 90	268 30	22841 60		97768 13	1
2		8	O'Riley Company	783	647	3500 00	70 00	3430 00		94338 13	2
3		11	Jacobs Equipment	784	649	973 91	19 48	954 43		93383 70	3
4		14	Petty Cash Cust., OfficeMart	785	656	212 50		212 50		93171 20	4
5		14	Deposit		✓				18767 15	111938 35	5
22		31	Payroll	800	694	4331 96		4331 96		95373 21	22
23		31	Deposit		✓				19294 78	114667 99	23
24		31	Totals			103452 22	566 88	102885 34			24
25						(2105)	(5110)	(1105)			25
26											26

Procedures for posting from OfficeMart's check register are the same as those previously described for special journals. However, no separate amounts are posted individually because the check register does not have a General Debit or General Credit column. The three special amount column totals are posted to the general ledger accounts listed in the column headings. After each total is posted, the account number is written in parentheses below the column total.

FYI

The Bank Deposit and Balance columns of a check register are neither ruled nor posted.

The two Bank columns are used to summarize the status of the checking account balance. These two columns are neither ruled nor posted.

A deposit in the checking account is shown on line 5 of Illustration 6-9. The Deposits column does not need to be totaled and posted because each cash receipt is recorded in the cash receipts journal and posted from that journal. At the end of each month, cash is proved by comparing the last amount in the check register's Balance column with the balance in the general ledger cash account. Cash is proved if the two amounts are the same.

Starting a New Page of a Check Register

Audit Your Understanding

1. A check register is similar to and replaces what journal?
2. In what order are paid vouchers filed in the paid vouchers file?
3. In a voucher system, where is the checking account balance maintained?
4. What account is debited for each check recorded in a check register?

A new page of a check register may be needed either during a month or at the start of a new month. When a new page is started during a month, the totals of the Vouchers Payable Debit, Purchases Discount Credit, and Cash Credit columns are brought forward from the previous page. The balance of the Bank Balance column is also brought forward. No amount is brought forward for the Bank Deposits column. This procedure is shown on line 1 of the check register in Illustration 6-8, page 177.

OfficeMart begins a new page of the check register at the beginning of each month. Only the balance of the Bank Balance column is brought forward. The totals of the special amount columns are not brought forward because they were posted at the end of the previous month. A new page of a check register started at the beginning of a month is shown in Illustration 6-10.

ILLUSTRATION 6-10 Starting a new page of a check register at the beginning of a month

CHECK REGISTER — PAGE 20

	DATE		PAYEE	CK. NO.	VCHR. NO.	1 VOUCHERS PAYABLE DEBIT	2 PURCHASES DISCOUNT CREDIT	3 CASH CREDIT	4 BANK DEPOSITS	5 BANK BALANCE	
1	19-- Sept.	1	Brought Forward		✓					114 667 99	1
2											2

USING A VOUCHER SYSTEM FOR SELECTED TRANSACTIONS

A voucher was prepared for each transaction described previously in this chapter. Each voucher was paid in full when due. Some transactions, however, require different procedures. Two examples are purchases returns and allowances and payroll transactions.

AUDIT YOUR UNDERSTANDING

1. Cash payments journal.
2. According to the name of the vendor.
3. In a check register.
4. Vouchers Payable.

LESSON PLAN 6-3

Materials

- Student pages 179–185
- Blackline Master for Voucher Register (TRG)
- Blackline Master for Check Register (TRG)
- Assess: Problem Test Chapter 6, MicroExam Chapter 6

Objectives (Enabling Performance Tasks)

b. Identify accounting concepts and practices related to a voucher system.

f. Journalize purchases returns and allowances and payroll transactions in a voucher system.

Global Perspective

The GLOBAL PERSPECTIVE feature is intended to expose students to some of the ways in which accounting and business in general differ in other countries. This GLOBAL PERSPECTIVE feature allows students to explore international banking services. The GLOBAL PERSPECTIVE activity requires students to research international banking services provided by local banks.

Answers to Global Perspective Activity

Locating a bank that provides international banking services should be a relatively easy task. There should be at least one large bank in a nearby city that provides all services listed in the Activity questions. Student answers will vary depending on the bank that is used.

Global Perspective

INTERNATIONAL BANKING

International business transactions usually require the use of international services from a commercial bank. More than 300 U.S. banks have international banking departments to assist customers with international business. Most of these banks that deal with international commerce are located in large cities.

Most international banking specialists maintain relationships with foreign banks to cover the banking portion of the transaction from its inception to its conclusion. These banking specialists give assistance to companies to guide them through the procedures of conducting business and receiving or giving payment. If individual companies had to deal directly with foreign banks, it would not be very efficient due to barriers such as language, cultural differences, and currency exchange values.

Some specific services that are offered by commercial banks are:

- Exchange of currency
- Assistance in financing exports
- Collection of invoices, drafts, letters of credit, and other foreign receivables

GLOBAL PERSPECTIVE ACTIVITY:

Contact a local bank that has an international department. Find out the following information.

1. With what countries does the bank have specialized relationships?
2. Does the bank handle letters of credit? If so, what is the procedure to negotiate a letter of credit?
3. Is financial assistance available to exporters? If so, what are the guidelines?
4. Will the bank transfer money to other countries?
5. Does the bank provide export counseling?

Purchases Returns and Allowances

A purchases returns and allowances transaction reduces the total amount owed for an invoice. Therefore, the voucher record for that invoice must be changed to show the reduction in the amount owed.

August 12, 19--. Issued Debit Memorandum No. 98 to Ramsey, Inc. for return of merchandise purchased, $85.00. Cancel Voucher No. 652. Voucher No. 655.

Vouchers Payable

Debit		Credit	
Vchr. 655	180.00	Vchr. 652	180.00
		Vchr. 655	95.00

Purchases Returns and Allowances

Debit		Credit	
		Vchr. 655	85.00

Voucher No. 655 is prepared for this transaction and is the source document for the entry. *(CONCEPT: Objective Evidence)*

The liability account, Vouchers Payable, is debited for $180.00 to cancel Voucher No. 652. Vouchers Payable is credited for $95.00, the difference between Voucher No. 652 ($180.00) and Debit Memorandum No. 98 ($85.00). The contra cost account, Purchases Returns and Allowances, is credited for $85.00, the amount of merchandise returned.

OfficeMart follows five steps in changing the original amount owed for Voucher No. 652 because of the purchases return.

1 Remove Voucher No. 652 from the unpaid vouchers file. Write *Canceled* across Section 5 to show cancellation of the voucher.

FYI

A canceled voucher is placed inside the new voucher.

2 Prepare Voucher No. 655 as shown in Illustration 6-11. Place the canceled Voucher No. 652 and Debit Memorandum No. 98 inside of Voucher No. 655.

ILLUSTRATION 6-11

Outside of a voucher for the return of merchandise purchased

Vchr. No. 655

Date 8/12/-- Due Date 8/16/-- Payment Date 8/14/--

To Ramsey, Inc.

Address 1237 Cardinal Road (Street)
Springbrook, (City) WI (State) 54824-3291 (ZIP)

ACCOUNTS DEBITED	AMOUNT	
PURCHASES		
SUPPLIES—SALES		
SUPPLIES—ADMIN.		
MISCELLANEOUS EXPENSE—SALES		
MISCELLANEOUS EXPENSE—ADMIN.		
RENT EXPENSE		
SALARY EXPENSE—SALES		
SALARY EXPENSE—ADMIN.		
Vouchers Payable	180	00
TOTAL DEBITS	180	00

ACCOUNTS CREDITED	AMOUNT	
VOUCHERS PAYABLE	95	00
EMPLOYEE INC. TAX PAY.—FEDERAL		
EMPLOYEE INC. TAX PAY.—STATE		
FICA TAX PAYABLE		
Purchases Returns and Allowances	85	00
TOTAL CREDITS	180	00

Voucher Approved by *Laura Post*

Recorded in Voucher Register Page ________ by ________

Paid { Date ________ Check No. ________ Amount $ ________ Approved by ________ }

3 Write the words, *See Vchr. 655,* in the voucher register's Paid columns on the same line as Voucher No. 652. This notation is shown on line 6 of Illustration 6-5.

4 Record Voucher No. 655 in the voucher register as shown on lines 9 and 10 of Illustration 6-5. The date, *12,* is recorded in the Date column. The name of the payee, *Ramsey, Inc.,* is written in the Payee column. The voucher number, *655,* is entered in the Vchr. No. column. The new credit amount, *$95.00,* is entered in the Vouchers Payable Credit column. The title of the account debited, *Vouchers Payable,* is written in the General Account Title column. The amount of the canceled Voucher No. 652, *$180.00,* is recorded in the General Debit column.

FOCUS

The procedures for preparing, recording, and paying vouchers were presented earlier in this chapter. Explain that some transactions, such as purchases returns and allowances and payroll, require different procedures. In this lesson, the steps used to record these two transactions using a voucher system will be described.

TEACH

Cover student pages 179–185 "Using a Voucher System for Selected Transactions" and "Advantages of a Voucher System." Discuss the purchases returns and allowances transaction. Go through each step in canceling a voucher. Explain that canceled vouchers are placed inside the new voucher. Describe recording the new voucher in a voucher register and canceling the original voucher for purchases returns and allowances transactions. Emphasize that the due date for canceled vouchers remains the same for the new voucher. Explain how a voucher is prepared for a payroll transaction and journalized in a voucher register. Describe how payment of the payroll is journalized in the check register and a notation is made in the voucher register. Engage students in a conversation about the advantages of a voucher system.

APPLY

Refer students to Illustrations 6-5 and 6-11 as canceling and recording a new voucher for a purchases returns and allowances transaction are explained. Refer students to the voucher in Illustration 6-12 and the voucher register in Illustration 6-5 as the payroll transaction is discussed.

Guided Practice

Guide students through the T account analysis of the transactions in Problem 6-3. Have students draw T accounts on a sheet of paper and analyze the first transaction. All students should agree with the analysis before proceeding to the next transaction. Repeat the process until all transactions have been analyzed. The balance of Problem 6-3 can be completed as Independent Practice.

Independent Practice

- Assign Questions 14–16 and Problems 6-3 and 6-4.
- Assign Study Guide 6 and Mastery Problem 6-M.

On the next line, the title of the account credited, *Purchases Returns and Allowances,* is written in the General Account Title column. The amount of the return, *$85.00,* is recorded in the General Credit column. A notation is made in Section 4 on Voucher No. 655 showing the voucher register page number on which this voucher is recorded.

5 File Voucher No. 655 by its payment date in the unpaid vouchers file. The payment date is based on the terms of the original invoice. Therefore, Voucher No. 655 has the same payment date as canceled Voucher No. 652.

FYI

Information from a payroll register is summarized on the inside of a voucher.

Payroll

OfficeMart pays its employees semimonthly. A payroll register is prepared showing details for each payroll. The payroll register is prepared in a similar way as described in Part 2. Information from a payroll register is used in preparing a voucher for payroll.

August 31, 19--. Recorded voucher for semimonthly payroll for period ended August 31, $4,331.96 (total payroll: sales, $3,000.00; administrative, $2,854.00; less deductions: employee income tax payable—federal, $878.10; employee income tax payable—state, $175.62; FICA tax payable, $468.32). Voucher No. 694.

Salary Expense—Sales	
3,000.00	

Salary Expense—Administrative	
2,854.00	

Vouchers Payable	
	4,331.96

Employee Income Tax Payable—Federal	
	878.10

Employee Income Tax Payable—State	
	175.62

FICA Tax Payable	
	468.32

The analysis of this payroll transaction is shown in the T accounts.

A payroll register is needed for several purposes, as described in Part 2. Therefore, the payroll register cannot be placed inside a voucher for payroll. For this reason information from the payroll register is summarized on the inside of Voucher No. 694, as shown in Illustration 6-12.

The outside of Voucher No. 694 is shown in Illustration 6-13.

The voucher register entry to record Voucher No. 694 is shown on lines 26 to 30 in Illustration 6-5, pages 174 and 175.

August 31, 19--. Paid cash for semimonthly payroll, $4,331.96, covering Voucher No. 694. Check No. 800.

Vouchers Payable	
4,331.96	Vchr. 694 4,331.96

Cash	
	4,331.96

Section 5 of Voucher No. 694 is completed to show that the voucher has been paid. Voucher No. 694 is then placed in the paid vouchers file.

The check register entry to record Check No. 800 is shown on line 22 in Illustration 6-9, page 178.

A notation of the payment of Voucher No. 694 is made in the voucher register, as shown on line 26 in Illustration 6-5, pages 174 and 175.

TEACHING STRATEGIES: COOPERATIVE LEARNING

Divide the class into groups of four or five students each. Using Cases for Critical Thinking, each group analyzes the cases and arrives at agreed-upon solutions. One member of each group is appointed the recorder and presents the group's analysis to the class. This cooperative learning activity should not take more than 20 to 25 minutes of class time.

ILLUSTRATION 6-12 Inside of a voucher for payroll

VOUCHER Vchr. No. 694

Payment Date August 31 19 --

Date August 31 19 -- Terms ______ Due August 31 19 --

To Payroll

Address ______

City ______ State ______ ZIP ______

For the following: Enclose all invoices or other papers.

DATE	VOUCHER DETAILS		AMOUNT
Aug. 31	Payroll for period ended 8/31/--		
	Salary Expense--Sales		$3,000.00
	Salary Expense--Administrative		2,854.00
	Deductions:		
	Employee Inc. Tax Pay.--Federal	$878.10	
	Employee Inc. Tax Pay.--State	175.62	
	FICA Tax Payable	468.32	1,522.04
	Net cash payment		$4,331.96

OFFICEMART, INC.

ILLUSTRATION 6-13 Outside of a voucher for payroll

Vchr. No. 694

Date 8/31/-- Due Date 8/31/-- Payment Date 8/31/--

To Payroll

Address ______ Street

City State ZIP

ACCOUNTS DEBITED	AMOUNT	
PURCHASES		
SUPPLIES—SALES		
SUPPLIES—ADMIN.		
MISCELLANEOUS EXPENSE—SALES		
MISCELLANEOUS EXPENSE—ADMIN.		
RENT EXPENSE		
SALARY EXPENSE—SALES	3,000	00
SALARY EXPENSE—ADMIN.	2,854	00
TOTAL DEBITS	5,854	00

ACCOUNTS CREDITED	AMOUNT	
VOUCHERS PAYABLE	4,331	96
EMPLOYEE INC. TAX PAY.—FEDERAL	878	10
EMPLOYEE INC. TAX PAY.—STATE	175	62
FICA TAX PAYABLE	468	32
TOTAL CREDITS	5,854	00

Voucher Approved by *Laura Post*

Recorded in Voucher Register Page *21* by *G.R.S.*

Paid { Date *Aug. 31, 19--* Check No. *800* Amount $ *4,331.96* Approved by *S.M.*

ASSESS

Assess student understanding by checking the solutions to the Independent Practice activities.

Reteach

- Make transparencies of the voucher register and check register from the accounting forms masters provided in the Blackline Masters Section of the Teacher's Resource Guide. Refer students to Recycling Problem 6-R. Ask students to use T accounts to analyze the May 8, 14, 15, and 16 transactions related to purchases returns and allowances and payroll. Use the transparencies to demonstrate how the transactions are journalized in the registers. Also, show how the notations for canceling and paying vouchers are made in the voucher register.
- Assign Recycling Problem 6-R.

Extend

Assign Challenge Problem 6-C. (The challenges are to bring totals forward, use Discounts Lost, calculate discounts and record net amount, and number vouchers and checks.)

Enrich

Assign the APPLIED COMMUNICATIONS special feature on page 187.

CLOSURE

- Use Audit Your Understanding questions.
- Review Summary Illustration 6-14, "Summary of a Voucher System."

ASSESS

- Administer Problem Test Chapter 6.
- Administer a MicroExam test for Chapter 6.

FYI

More than 70 percent of all corporations in the United States gross less than $500,000 a year.

An entry is made in OfficeMart's general journal for the employer's payroll taxes. This entry is the same as described in Part 2. Later, when payroll taxes are due, vouchers are prepared, approved, and paid. One voucher is prepared for total payroll taxes owed to the federal government. Another voucher is prepared for total payroll taxes owed to the state government.

ADVANTAGES OF A VOUCHER SYSTEM

A voucher system has the following advantages for businesses that make many cash payments.

FYI

The unpaid and paid voucher files replace the accounts payable ledger.

1. Authorizing and approving all cash payments is limited to a few persons. This procedure helps protect and control cash.
2. Providing a voucher jacket is a convenient method of filing invoices and related business papers for future reference. This is especially true when invoices received from vendors are of different sizes.
3. Filing unpaid vouchers according to their payment dates helps assure payment of invoices within the discount periods.
4. Using an unpaid vouchers file and a paid vouchers file eliminates posting to an accounts payable ledger.
5. Using a paid vouchers file provides three different and easy ways to find information about a paid voucher.
   a. *If only the voucher number is known,* look in the voucher register for that number and find the payee's name on the same line. The voucher will be in the paid vouchers file under the name of the payee.
   b. *If only the check number used to pay the voucher is known,* look in the check register for the check number. The payee's name is on the same line. The voucher will be in the paid vouchers file under the name of the payee.
   c. *If only the name of the payee is known,* look in the paid vouchers file where vouchers are filed under the name of the payee.

The chart shown in Illustration 6-14 summarizes the steps followed when using a voucher system.

Audit Your Understanding

1. What accounts are affected, and how, when a debit memorandum is issued for the return of merchandise purchased and the original voucher is canceled?
2. What is the first step in canceling a voucher?
3. Where is the information obtained for preparing a voucher for payroll?
4. What is the advantage of filing unpaid vouchers according to their payment dates?

AUDIT YOUR UNDERSTANDING

1. Vouchers Payable is debited; Purchases Returns and Allowances is credited.
2. Remove the voucher from the unpaid voucher file and write Canceled across Section 5.
3. A payroll register.
4. The procedure helps assure payment of invoices within the discount periods.

APPLIED SKILLS: COMMUNICATIONS

Surveys of business managers show that communication skills are one of the most desired traits in new employees. The APPLIED COMMUNICATIONS activity provides an opportunity for students to practice their communication and language arts skills on topics that directly relate to accounting. This activity requires students to prepare a report about computer viruses. In addition to learning about computer viruses, students learn how to do research in current periodicals. The instructor may need to assist students in the research process.

SUMMARY ILLUSTRATION 6-14

Summary of a voucher system

1 A voucher is prepared from a verified invoice or other source document. The voucher is then approved for payment.

2 Data from the approved voucher are recorded in a voucher register.

3 A check is prepared to pay a voucher. The check is approved and signed.

4 Data from the signed check are recorded in the check register. The cash balance is calculated and recorded in the check register after each check or deposit.

5 A payment notation is entered on the voucher and in the voucher register.

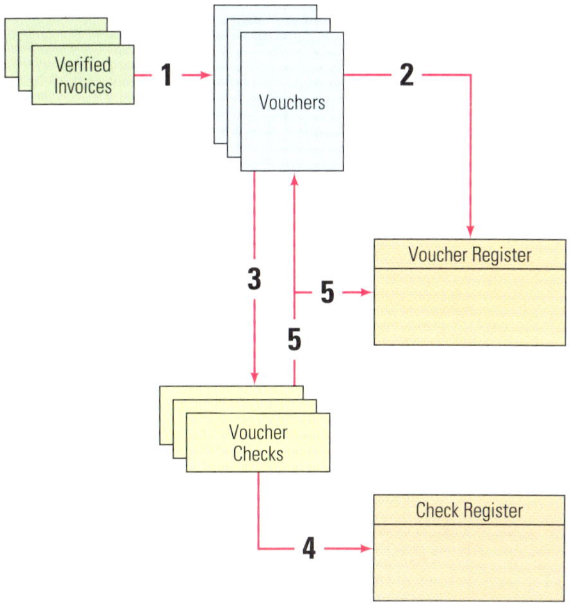

TEACHING STRATEGIES: Applying Visuals

Direct students to Summary Illustration 6-14 to review the steps followed when using a voucher system.

APPLIED SKILLS: Word Processing

If you wish to integrate word processing into your accounting course, you may direct students to answer the end-of-chapter Accounting Terms, Questions for Individual Study, and Cases for Critical Thinking using their word processing software.

ACCOUNTING TERMS

1. **voucher:** A business form used to show an authorized person's approval for a cash payment. (p. 168)
2. **voucher system:** A set of procedures for controlling cash payments by preparing and approving vouchers before payments are made. (p. 168)
3. **voucher register:** A journal used to record vouchers. (p. 171)
4. **voucher check:** A check with space for writing details about a cash payment. (p. 175)
5. **check register:** A journal used in a voucher system to record cash payments. (p. 177)

QUESTIONS FOR INDIVIDUAL STUDY

1. Procedures used to control and protect cash include storing cash in a safe place, making bank deposits regularly, and approving all cash payments. (p. 168)
2. Vouchers Payable is used in place of Accounts Payable. (p. 168)
3. The invoice is verified for such details as quantities received, terms, prices, and calculations. (p. 169)
4. To summarize the contents and provide space for approving payments. (p. 169)
5. Section 1 shows information about the payee. Section 2 shows information about the accounts affected. Section 3 shows information about the approval of the voucher. (pp. 170–171)
6. Unpaid vouchers are filed in the unpaid vouchers file according to the payment date. (p. 172)
7. In the General columns. (p. 173)
8. The totals of special amount columns are posted as totals at the end of the period. (p. 174)
9. A copy of the voucher check is the source document for an entry in a check register. (p. 175)
10. The date paid and the check number are recorded in the voucher register when the voucher is paid. (p. 176)
11. These two columns are used to keep an up-to-date record of cash in OfficeMart's checking account. (p. 177)
12. Vouchers Payable Debit, Purchases Discount Credit, and Cash Credit. (p. 177)

ACCOUNTING TERMS EPT(a)

What is the meaning of each of the following?

1. **voucher**
2. **voucher system**
3. **voucher register**
4. **voucher check**
5. **check register**

QUESTIONS FOR INDIVIDUAL STUDY EPT(b)

1. What three procedures are used to control and protect cash?
2. What account title is used in place of Accounts Payable when a voucher system is used?
3. What items are verified on an invoice before a voucher is prepared?
4. When preparing a voucher from an invoice, why is a form printed on the outside of the voucher?
5. What information is shown in Sections 1, 2, and 3 of a voucher?
6. In what order are unpaid vouchers filed in the unpaid vouchers file?
7. Where are account titles and amounts recorded that cannot be recorded in one of the special amount columns of a voucher register?
8. Which amounts in a voucher register are posted as totals?
9. What is the source document for an entry in a check register?
10. When a voucher is paid, what information is recorded in the voucher register?
11. Why does OfficeMart use the Bank Deposits and Bank Balance columns in its check register?
12. Which three special amount columns are used in OfficeMart's check register?
13. What amounts are posted from OfficeMart's check register?
14. When a purchases return is made, how is the new voucher amount calculated?
15. What is the source of information used in preparing a voucher for payroll?
16. What are five advantages of using a voucher system?

CASES FOR CRITICAL THINKING EPT(b)

CASE 1 Kelly White, the bookkeeper for Greenfield, Inc. is setting up a voucher system for Greenfield. In her planning, she is trying to decide how many columns to use in the voucher register. She is also trying to decide what headings to use for the special columns in the voucher register. What should Ms. White consider in making her decision about these special columns?

CASE 2 The Harper Company uses a voucher system for cash payments. Jonathan Bartell, the bookkeeper, receives and verifies the invoices. He then prepares the voucher and enters the voucher in the voucher register. When the voucher is due, Mr. Bartell prepares and signs the check and enters the payment in the check register. What is your opinion of the procedure Harper Company follows for its voucher system? Explain.

APPLIED COMMUNICATIONS

Information is the key to a successful business. The loss of information can inhibit the ability of accountants to prepare reports and managers to make business decisions. Computer viruses can cause the information in computer files to be destroyed and, therefore, are a serious problem for businesses of all sizes.

INSTRUCTIONS:

1. Go to the library and research computer viruses.
2. Write a short report about computer viruses. Include the following items:
   a. Describe one particular computer virus.
   b. Where did the virus originate?
   c. How do you prevent your computer from getting a virus?
   d. What should you do if a virus is detected?

APPLICATION PROBLEMS EPT(c,d,e,f)

PROBLEM 6-1 Journalizing vouchers in a voucher register

TeleTronics uses a voucher register similar to the one described in this chapter.

INSTRUCTIONS:

1. Journalize the following transactions completed during September of the current year. Use page 9 of a voucher register. The abbreviation for voucher is V.

Sept. 1. Purchased merchandise on account from Eastern Company, $3,100.00. V87.
2. Received invoice for September rent from Post Real Estate Developers, $1,150.00. V88.
5. Bought sales supplies on account from Supra Supply Company, $258.00. V89.
8. Received invoice for advertising from Newport News, $87.50. V90.
11. Purchased merchandise on account from Hoyer Company, $3,347.75. V91.
18. Received invoice for delivery service from Rapid Rabbit, $235.15. V92.
19. Purchased merchandise on account from Beggen Company, $1,973.00. V93.
23. Bought office equipment on account from Syracuse Company, $1,315.00. V94.
25. Received invoice for utilities from Northside Electric Cooperative, $185.00. V95.
29. Bought administrative supplies on account from Northern Supply, $317.00. V96.
30. Received invoice for miscellaneous sales expense from Manley Maintenance Company, $25.00. V97.

2. Prove and rule the voucher register.

The voucher register prepared in Problem 6-1 is needed to complete Problem 6-2.

PROBLEM 6-2 Journalizing cash payments and deposits in a check register

The voucher register prepared in Problem 6-1 is needed to complete Problem 6-2.

TeleTronics uses a check register similar to the one described in this chapter.

QUESTIONS (cont'd)

13. The three special amount column totals are posted to the general ledger accounts listed in the column headings. (p. 178)

14. The new voucher amount equals the old voucher amount minus the debit memorandum amount. (p. 180)

15. The payroll register. (p. 182)

16. (a) Authorizing and approving all cash payments is limited to a few persons. (b) The voucher jacket is a convenient method of filing invoices and related business papers. (c) Filing unpaid invoices according to their payment dates helps assure payment of invoices within the discount periods. (d) The unpaid vouchers file and the paid vouchers file eliminate posting to an accounts payable ledger. (e) The paid vouchers file provides information about a paid voucher. (p. 184)

CASES FOR CRITICAL THINKING

Case 1 Ms. White should consider what accounts are debited and how often each account is used. To do this, Ms. White could examine transactions from previous months. The accounts that are used most often are those that should be considered for special columns in the voucher register.

Case 2 One person, Mr. Bartell, is totally responsible for ALL aspects of the system. Because of this, it would be possible for Mr. Bartell to enter an unauthorized invoice into the system. He could then issue a check for this unauthorized invoice and cash the check himself. The invoice and voucher should be approved by persons who do not authorize, prepare, approve, or sign the checks. By dividing the responsibility, more employees are involved in each transaction. With more employees involved, illegal acts are more difficult to hide.

APPLIED COMMUNICATIONS

Students' solutions will vary. In addition to the required information, the instructor should consider the following items when grading the activity: (1) understanding of computer viruses, (2) conciseness and completeness, (3) writing style, and (4) mechanics (grammar, spelling, punctuation).

CHECK FIGURES

See Teacher's Edition of the Working Papers for complete solutions.

Problem 6-1 Total Vouchers Payable Credit column: $11,993.40

Problem 6-2 Check Register totals: Vouchers Payable Debit, $8,388.40; Purchases Discount Credit, $128.96; Cash Credit, $8,259.44. September 30 Bank Balance, $16,868.23

INSTRUCTIONS:

1. Use page 9 of a check register. Record the bank balance brought forward on September 1 of the current year, $19,443.13.
2. Continue using page 9 of the check register. Journalize the following cash payments and deposits completed during September of the current year. As each cash payment is journalized, make the appropriate notation in the voucher register. Source documents are abbreviated as follows: check, C; voucher, V.

Sept. 2. Paid cash to Post Real Estate Developers, $1,150.00, covering V88. C83.
8. Paid cash to Newport News, $87.50, covering V90. C84.
9. Paid cash to Eastern Company, $3,038.00, covering V87 for $3,100.00, less 2% discount, $62.00. C85.
13. Paid cash to Supra Supply Company, $258.00, covering V89. C86.
18. Paid cash to Rapid Rabbit, $235.15, covering V92. C87.
19. Paid cash to Hoyer Company, $3,280.79, covering V91 for $3,347.75, less 2% discount, $66.96. C88.
24. Made a deposit in the checking account, $5,684.54.
25. Paid cash to Northside Electric Cooperative, $185.00, covering V95. C89.
30. Paid cash to Manley Maintenance Company, $25.00, covering V97. C90.

3. Prove and rule the check register.

PROBLEM 6-3 Journalizing purchases returns and allowances in a voucher register

Nygren Supply Company uses a voucher register similar to the one described in this chapter.

CHECK FIGURES *(cont'd)*

Problem 6-3 Amounts in Vouchers Payable Credit column: $2,700.00, $2,500.00, $1,778.00, $1,428.00

Problem 6-4 Accounts credited in the voucher: Vouchers Payable, $3,120.97; Employee Inc. Tax Pay.—Federal, $632.63; Employee Inc. Tax. Pay.—State, $126.53, FICA Tax Payable, $337.40

INSTRUCTIONS:

Journalize the following transactions completed during February of the current year. Use page 2 of a voucher register. When a voucher is canceled, make appropriate notations in the voucher register. Source documents are abbreviated as follows: debit memorandum, DM; voucher, V.

Feb. 1. Purchased merchandise on account from Hamline Corporation, $2,700.00. V10.
4. Issued DM2 to Hamline Corporation for return of merchandise purchased, $200.00. Cancel V10. V11.
15. Purchased merchandise on account from Moorhead, Inc., $1,778.00. V12.
17. Issued DM3 to Moorhead, Inc., for return of merchandise purchased, $350.00. Cancel V12. V13.

PROBLEM 6-4 Preparing and journalizing a voucher for payroll

Bowman Service Center uses a voucher form and a voucher register similar to the ones described in this chapter. Bowman Service Center's payroll register for May 15 of the current year shows the following information. The abbreviation for voucher is V.

May 15. Recorded voucher for semimonthly payroll for period ended May 15, $3,120.97 (total payroll: sales, $2,530.53; administrative, $1,687.00, less deductions: employee income tax payable—federal, $632.63; employee income tax payable—state, $126.53; FICA tax payable, $337.40). V51.

INSTRUCTIONS:

1. Prepare a voucher for the payroll on May 15 of the current year.
2. Use page 5 of a voucher register. Journalize the voucher for the payroll. Assume the voucher has been approved. After the voucher is journalized, complete Section 4 of the voucher.

ENRICHMENT PROBLEMS EPT(d,e,f)

MASTERY PROBLEM 6-M Journalizing transactions in a voucher system

Jameson Company uses a voucher register and a check register similar to the ones described in this chapter.

INSTRUCTIONS:

1. Use page 20 of a check register. Record the bank balance brought forward on November 1 of the current year, $11,676.77.
2. Journalize the following transactions completed during November of the current year. Use page 22 of a voucher register and page 20 of a check register. When a voucher is paid or canceled, make appropriate notations in the voucher register. Source documents are abbreviated as follows: check, C; debit memorandum, DM; voucher, V.

Nov. 1. Purchased merchandise on account from Georgia Company, $975.00. V68.
2. Bought administrative supplies on account from Supply World, $216.80. V69.
4. Bought store equipment on account from Equipment Plus, $1,998.00. V70.
8. Purchased merchandise on account from North Heights Corporation, $1,695.15. V71.
8. Paid cash to Georgia Company, $955.50, covering V68 for $975.00, less 2% discount, $19.50. C57.
10. Made a deposit in the checking account, $3,579.00.
14. Received invoice for delivery service from Quick Delivery, $24.10. V72.
14. Paid cash to Quick Delivery, $24.10, covering V72. C58.
14. Issued DM10 to North Heights Corporation for return of merchandise purchased, $225.00. Cancel V71. V73.
15. Paid cash to North Heights Corporation, $1,440.75, covering V73 for $1,470.15, less 2% discount, $29.40. C59.
16. Recorded voucher for semimonthly payroll for period ended November 15, $1,459.64 (total payroll: sales, $1,183.50; administrative, $789.00; less deductions: employee income tax payable—federal, $295.88; employee income tax payable—state, $59.18; FICA tax payable, $157.80). V74.
16. Paid cash for semimonthly payroll, $1,459.64, covering V74. C60.
22. Paid cash to Supply World, $216.80, covering V69. C61.
25. Bought office equipment on account from Fischer Equipment, $2,350.00. V75.
29. Made a deposit in the checking account, $1,170.15.
30. Purchased merchandise on account from Georgia Company, $2,258.50. V76.

3. Prove and rule both the voucher register and the check register.

CHECK FIGURES *(cont'd)*

Mastery Problem 6-M Voucher Register Vouchers Payable total, $12,447.34; Check Register Vouchers Payable total, $4,145.69; November 30 Bank Balance, $12,329.13

CHALLENGE PROBLEM 6-C Journalizing purchase invoices at the net amount in a voucher system

CHECK FIGURES *(cont'd)*

Challenge Problem 6-C
Voucher Register Vouchers Payable total, $5,011.00; Check Register Vouchers Payable total, $4,985.00; December 31 Bank Balance, $8,910.00

Cayman Company uses a voucher system. All of the vendors with whom Cayman Company does business offer terms of 2/10, n/30. Cayman has a policy of paying all invoices within the discount period. The business records invoice vouchers at the net amount (invoice total less a 2% discount). Thus, a $1,000.00 invoice, allowing a 2% discount of $20.00, is recorded at the net amount, $980.00. **Purchases** is debited and **Vouchers Payable** is credited for $980.00. A purchases discount account is not used.

If an invoice *is not* paid within the discount period, the discount is lost by Cayman Company. This loss is recorded in an account titled **Discounts Lost.** Thus, if the $1,000.00 invoice described above *is not* paid within the discount period, the business must pay the full $1,000.00. However, one of the controls in a voucher system is that *no* check can be written for more than the voucher amount. Therefore, in order for a check to be written for the full $1,000.00, the original voucher must be canceled. A new voucher for $1,000.00 must be prepared, approved, and recorded.

This new voucher would include a debit to **Discounts Lost** of $20.00, a debit to **Vouchers Payable** of $980.00 (the amount of the original voucher), and a credit to **Vouchers Payable** of $1,000.00. Once this voucher is approved, a check can be written for $1,000.00 to pay the full amount due.

If an invoice is recorded at its net amount, then all purchases returns and allowances are recorded at net amounts. A $1,000.00 invoice recorded at net with a 2% discount, has a $100.00 purchase return and allowance. Thus, the $100.00 return is discounted by 2% and recorded as $98.00. For the return, **Vouchers Payable** is debited $980.00 (the amount of original voucher), **Purchases Returns and Allowances** is credited for $98.00, and **Vouchers Payable** is credited for $882.00 (the amount of the new voucher).

Cayman's voucher register is similar to the one described for OfficeMart in this chapter. However, the third amount column is titled *Discounts Lost* and there is only one Supplies Debit column because there is only one supplies account. Cayman's check register has two special amount columns: Vouchers Payable Debit and Cash Credit.

INSTRUCTIONS:

1. Use page 20 of a check register. Record the amounts brought forward on December 11 of the current year.

Vouchers Payable Debit.	$1,395.00
Cash Credit	1,395.00
Bank Balance	8,500.00

2. Journalize the following transactions completed during December of the current year. Use page 25 of a voucher register. Assume that for all purchases of merchandise, equipment, or supplies the invoice terms are 2/10, n/30. When a voucher is paid or canceled, make appropriate notations in the voucher register. Number vouchers consecutively starting with Voucher No. 109. Source documents are abbreviated as follows: check, C; debit memorandum, DM; voucher, V.

Dec. 11. Purchased merchandise on account from Knotts Company, $2,000.00.
15. Made a deposit in the checking account, $1,000.00.
15. Bought supplies on account from Fairgate Supply Company, $200.00.
18. Bought store equipment on account from Hightop Company, $1,000.00.
18. Paid cash to Knotts Company covering V109. C80.
19. Purchased merchandise on account from Neal Company, $500.00.
22. Made a deposit in the checking account, $2,000.00.
25. Paid cash to Hightop Company covering V111. C81.
26. Paid cash to Fairgate Supply Company covering V110. C82.

Dec. 28. Bought supplies on account from Peerless Supply Company, $300.00.
28. Issued DM30 to Neal Company for return of merchandise purchased, $50.00. Cancel V112.
29. Made a deposit in the checking account, $1,000.00.
31. Paid cash to Neal Company covering V115. C83.

3. Prove and rule both the voucher register and the check register.

CHAPTER 7 OVERVIEW

Chapter 7 lays the groundwork for describing the importance of inventory systems. Periodic and perpetual inventory are covered as well as calculating the cost of inventory using fifo, lifo, weighted-average, and lower of cost or market inventory costing methods. Merchandise inventory cost is estimated using the gross profit and retail methods and the merchandise inventory turnover ratio is calculated.

GUIDE TO ACHIEVING LEARNING OBJECTIVES

	TEACH	APPLY	EXTEND/ENRICH					
Enabling Performance Tasks	**Lesson Plans**	**Application Problems**	**Mastery Problems**	**Challenge Problems**	**Cases for Critical Thinking**	**Recycling Problems**	**Reinforcement Activity**	
a. Define accounting terms related to planning and costing inventory.	7-1, 7-2, 7-3							
b. Identify accounting concepts and practices related to planning, counting, and costing inventory.	7-1, 7-2, 7-3				Cases 1, 2			
c. Determine the cost of merchandise inventory using selected costing methods.	7-2	7-1, 7-2, 7-3	7-M	7-C		7-R		
d. Estimate the cost of merchandise inventory using selected estimating methods.	7-3	7-4	7-M			7-R		
e. Calculate merchandise inventory turnover ratio and average number of days' sales in merchandise inventory.	7-3	7-5	7-M			7-R		

ENRICHMENT

SPECIAL FEATURES
Professional Business Ethics, page 204
Multicultural Awareness, page 195
Personal Visions in Business, page 207
TECHNOLOGY CONNECTION
Automated Accounting 6.0 Integrating Automated Accounting Topic 4, Problem DB-4
Spreadsheet Template Problems 7-1, 7-2, 7-3, 7-4

NEW, REVIEW, AND EXTENSION

ACTIVITIES/CONCEPTS/TRANSACTIONS	NEW	REVIEW/ EXTENSION
Goods in transit	✓	
Goods on consignment	✓	
Inventory stock record		✓
Periodic inventory		✓
Calculating cost of inventory		✓
Fifo inventory costing method		✓
Lifo inventory costing method		✓
Weighted-average inventory costing method		✓
Lower of cost or market inventory costing method	✓	
Gross profit method of estimating inventory		✓
Retail method of estimating inventory	✓	
Calculating merchandise inventory turnover ratio	✓	
Calculating average number of days' sales in mechandise inventory	✓	

	INFORMAL ASSESSMENT		FORMAL ASSESSMENT			
	Study Guide	Audit Your Understanding	Chapter MicroExam	Chapter Problem Test	Unit Objective Test	Portfolio
	Unit A	✓	✓		✓	
	Unit B	✓	✓		✓	
				✓		
				✓		
				✓		

TEACHING MATERIALS

Teacher's Wraparound Edition of the Text
Teacher's Resource Guide
Teacher's Edition of Working Papers
MicroExam

APPLIED MATHEMATICS

APPLIED MATH/ACCOUNTING SKILL	APPLICATION
Estimating merchandise inventory using the gross profit method	Prob. 7-4
Estimating merchandise inventory using the retail method	Prob. 7-4
Calculating merchandise inventory turnover ratio	Prob. 7-5
Calculating average number of days' sales in merchandise inventory	Prob. 7-5

TEACHING STRATEGIES: ACCOUNTING PEDAGOGY

This textbook continues to emphasize the importance of internal control systems by dedicating a chapter to inventory planning and valuation. Analysis of inventory including turnover ratio and average number of days' sales in merchandise inventory is covered in this chapter. This information is covered in this chapter where it is appropriate and not in isolation. This is a critical thinking skill that is important for advanced accounting students.

7

Inventory Planning and Valuation

ENABLING PERFORMANCE TASKS

After studying Chapter 7, you will be able to:

a Define accounting terms related to planning and costing inventory.

b Identify accounting concepts and practices related to planning, counting, and costing inventory.

c Determine the cost of merchandise inventory using selected costing methods.

d Estimate the cost of merchandise inventory using selected estimating methods.

e Calculate merchandise inventory turnover ratio and average number of days' sales in merchandise inventory.

TERMS PREVIEW

consignment • consignee • consignor • stock record • stock ledger • purchase order • inventory record • first-in, first-out inventory costing method • last-in, first-out inventory costing method • weighted-average inventory costing method • lower of cost or market inventory costing method • retail method of estimating inventory • merchandise inventory turnover ratio • average number of days' sales in merchandise inventory

TEACHING STRATEGIES: DIFFERENT LEARNING ABILITIES

Specific Learning Disability (SLD) Students. Many students will ultimately work in inventory-related jobs. Simulating the inventory of a business will enable students to actively participate in the accounting for inventory. For example, students could establish a classroom store carrying school supplies, snacks, or other low cost items. The students would record the purchase and sales transactions and update the perpetual inventory. Students would periodically take inventory and reconcile the periodic and perpetual inventory quantities.

A successful business must maintain an adequate amount of merchandise inventory that customers are willing to buy. A business may fail if too much or too little merchandise inventory is kept on hand. Business managers frequently analyze sales and inventory transactions to assist them in planning future inventory purchases. The cost of merchandise inventory on hand provides business managers with important information used to make effective business decisions.

NATURE OF MERCHANDISE INVENTORY

Merchandise is continually being purchased and sold. The actual merchandise inventory changes from day to day. The flow of inventory costs through a business' records is shown in Illustration 7-1.

ILLUSTRATION 7-1

Flow of inventory costs through a business' records

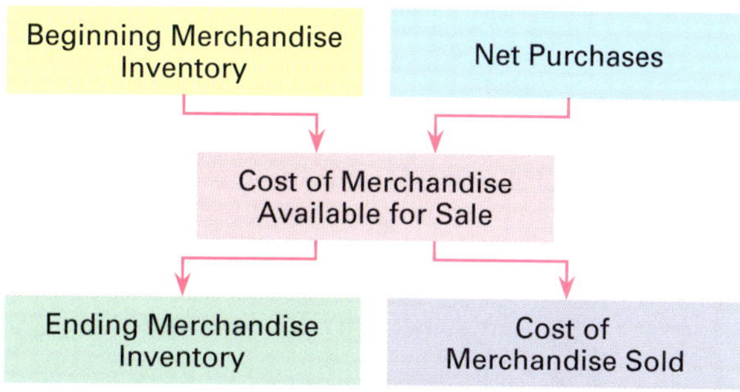

The cost of the merchandise available for sale consists of two elements.

1. The cost of the beginning merchandise inventory.
2. The cost of the net purchases added to the inventory during the fiscal period.

At the end of each fiscal period, the cost of the merchandise available for sale is divided into two parts.

1. The cost of the ending merchandise inventory. The ending merchandise inventory represents a *current* asset that will be charged as costs in *future* fiscal periods.
2. The cost of the merchandise sold during the *current* fiscal period. This cost materially affects the amount of net income reported for the fiscal period. *(CONCEPT: Adequate Disclosure)*

FYI

Cost of Merchandise Available for Sale less Ending Merchandise Inventory equals Cost of Merchandise Sold.

Effect of Errors in Costing an Inventory

The cost of both beginning and ending merchandise inventory affects items on an income statement, a statement of stockholders' equity, and a balance sheet. The effect is shown in Illustration 7-2.

LESSON PLAN 7-1

Materials

- Student pages 193–198
- Blackline Master for Stock Record (TRG)
- 3-Step Checklist for Making Ethical Decisions (TRG)
- Software: Spreadsheet Template

Objectives (Enabling Performance Tasks)

a. Define accounting terms related to planning and costing inventory.

b. Identify accounting concepts and practices related to planning, counting, and costing inventory.

FOCUS

- The two principal methods used to determine actual quantities of merchandise inventory—periodic inventory and perpetual inventory—were introduced in Chapter 5. In this lesson, the procedures for determining the inventory count using these two methods will be presented.
- Introduce vocabulary: consignment, consignee, consignor, stock record, stock ledger, purchase order, inventory record.

APPLIED SKILLS: WORD PROCESSING

If you wish to integrate word processing into your accounting course, you may direct students to answer the end-of-chapter Accounting Terms, Questions for Individual Study, and Cases for Critical Thinking using their word processing software.

TEACH

Cover student pages 193–198 "Nature of Merchandise Inventory" and "Inventory Count." Review the flow of inventory costs through a business' records. Discuss the effect of errors in costing merchandising inventory. Explain the importance of accurately reporting inventory. Discuss what goods are included in a count of inventory. Emphasize the difference between FOB shipping point and FOB destination. Explain perpetual inventory. Describe the use of a stock record. Explain periodic inventory. Discuss the five steps in completing the inventory record. Ask students if they have ever participated in taking inventory for a business. If any have, ask them to explain the process they followed.

APPLY

Refer students to Illustrations 7-3 and 7-4, respectively, as the stock record and inventory record are discussed.

Guided Practice

Guide students through the preparation of the stock record for exterior doors, Stock No. EX472 in Problem 7-1. Working as a group, have the students complete the heading of the record and record the July 1 balance. Direct students to record the correct information on the stock record provided in the working papers. Continue working as a group to record the July 5 transaction in Instruction 2. When all students agree on how the information should be recorded, direct them to record the sale on the stock record in the working papers. Continue the procedure for the July 9, 14, and 17 transactions. The balance of Problem 7-1 can be completed as Independent Practice.

Independent Practice

Assign Terms 1–7, Questions 1–13, and Problem 7-1.

ILLUSTRATION 7-2 Effect of errors in costing merchandise inventory

Reports and Items Affected	If Ending Inventory is	
	Understated	**Overstated**
Income Statement:		
Cost of Merchandise Sold	Overstated	Understated
Gross Profit	Understated	Overstated
Net Income	Understated	Overstated
Statement of Stockholders' Equity:		
Net Income	Understated	Overstated
Retained Earnings	Understated	Overstated
Stockholders' Equity	Understated	Overstated
Balance Sheet:		
Merchandise Inventory	Understated	Overstated
Total Assets	Understated	Overstated
Stockholders' Equity	Understated	Overstated

FYI

If merchandise inventory cost is not accurate, information reported on financial statements will not be accurate.

An accurate merchandise inventory cost must be determined to adequately report the financial progress and condition of a merchandising business. *(CONCEPT: Adequate Disclosure)* If the inventory is understated, the net income will be understated. As a result, total assets and total stockholders' equity will be understated. If the inventory is overstated, the reverse will be true, and additional income tax must be paid on the overstated income. In neither situation will accurate information be reported on financial statements. *(CONCEPT: Adequate Disclosure)*

Amounts Included in the Cost of Inventory

The amounts used to determine the cost of merchandise inventory should include two costs.

1. The price paid to vendors for the merchandise. The price paid includes the purchase invoice amount less discounts, returns, and allowances granted by the vendors.
2. The costs involved in getting the merchandise to the place of business and ready for sale. This cost includes transportation charges paid by the buyer.

Goods Included in a Count of Inventory

Items in the merchandise inventory of a merchandising business are frequently referred to as *goods*. Typically, a business counts as part of its inventory all goods legally owned by the business. When title to goods passes to the buyer, the goods become part of the inventory of the buyer regardless of where the goods are physically located.

FYI

FOB shipping point means that even though the goods are in transit, they are part of the inventory of the buyer.

Goods in Transit. A vendor's terms of sale may include the provision *FOB shipping point*. FOB is an abbreviation for the phrase *Free*

APPLIED SKILLS: WRITING ACROSS THE CURRICULUM

Writing paragraphs and short essays. The Cases for Critical Thinking are short, practical applications of the accounting principles developed in the chapter. Some cases are planned to present problems related to the chapter but not specifically discussed and answered in the chapter. These cases present an opportunity for critical thinking and decision making. These cases also require more than a short objective-type response. Therefore they provide ideal practice in writing paragraphs and short essays.

On Board. FOB shipping point means that the buyer pays the transportation charges. Under FOB shipping point terms, the title to the goods passes to the buyer as soon as the vendor delivers the goods to a transportation business. These goods in transit, but not yet received by the buyer, are part of the inventory of the *buyer.*

If the terms of sale are *FOB destination,* the vendor pays the transportation charges. Title to these goods passes to the buyer when the goods are received by the buyer. These goods in transit, but not yet received by the buyer, are part of the inventory of the *vendor.*

FYI

FOB destination means that even though the goods are in transit, they are part of the inventory of the vendor.

MULTICULTURAL AWARENESS

Korean American Businesses

Korean immigrants to America sometimes form savings groups called "kyes" to facilitate starting a business. These groups are prevalent in South Korea and are used in America to finance small Korean-owned businesses.

Members of the group contribute to a pool of money on a regular basis. Periodically, a member of the group receives the whole pool. Each member of the group is pledged to continue to contribute until the last member of the group has had a chance to receive the pool. These funds are then usually used to start a business.

Surveys show that nearly half of all Koreans in the United States are self-employed and have started their first business within four years of arriving.

Goods on Consignment.

Goods which are given to a business to sell, but for which title to the goods remains with the vendor, are called a **consignment.** The person or business who receives goods on consignment is called the **consignee.** The person or business who gives goods on consignment is called the **consignor.**

The consignee agrees to receive, care for, and attempt to sell the consigned goods. If the goods are sold, the consignee deducts a commission from the sale amount, and the remainder is sent to the consignor. In a consignment, title to the goods does not pass to the consignee. The goods on consignment are part of the inventory of the consignor.

A consignee agrees to give goods on consignment due care and to make adequate attempts to sell the goods. Therefore, a consignee has implied liabilities if anything should happen to the goods before they are sold. A consignee often reports the cost of consigned goods as an attachment or footnote to the balance sheet.

MULTICULTURAL AWARENESS

The MULTICULTURAL AWARENESS feature is intended to expose students to the concept that our society is composed of people from many different cultural backgrounds. These features show both past contributions of many cultures and benefits of a culturally diverse society. (1) Read the feature. (2) Discuss the specific information in the feature. (3) Clarify any terms or questions.

INVENTORY COUNT

Costing an inventory starts with determining the number of each item on hand. Sometimes the number on hand is obtained by physically counting the individual items. Sometimes the number on hand is obtained by keeping a continuous record showing the number purchased and sold for each merchandise item.

TEACHING STRATEGIES: TEACHING TIP

Review the definition of perpetual inventory: A merchandise inventory determined by keeping a continuous record of increases, decreases, and balance on hand.

Perpetual Inventory

Merchandise inventory determined by keeping a continuous record of increases, decreases, and balance on hand is known as a perpetual inventory. OfficeMart, Inc. is a supplier of office furniture, equipment, and supplies. OfficeMart keeps a perpetual inventory.

A perpetual inventory provides day-to-day records about the quantity of merchandise on hand. Based on the records, management knows when the inventory is low and additional merchandise should be ordered. A record is kept of the number on hand, purchases, and sales of each kind of merchandise. A form used to show the kind of merchandise, quantity received, quantity sold, and bal-

FYI

A periodic inventory should be taken once each year to check the accuracy of a perpetual inventory.

TEACHING STRATEGIES: TEACHING TIP

End-of-chapter problems for Chapter 7 include a large amount of computational work. Students should be encouraged to use calculators to allow them to focus their attention on the procedures rather than on the arithmetic.

ASSESS

Assess student understanding by checking the solutions to the Independent Practice activities.

Reteach

Make a transparency of a stock record from the accounting forms masters provided in the Blackline Masters Section of the Teacher's Resource Guide. Using information and transactions similar to those given in Problem 7-1, Instructions 1 and 2, demonstrate how to keep perpetual inventory stock records.

Extend

- Assign Cases for Critical Thinking 1 and 2.
- Assign the Spreadsheet Template for Problem 7-1.

Enrich

Discuss the PROFESSIONAL BUSINESS ETHICS feature on page 204. You may wish to distribute copies of the 3-Step Checklist for Making Ethical Decisions. A Blackline Master is furnished in the Blackline Masters Section of the Teacher's Resource Guide.

CLOSURE

Use Audit Your Understanding questions.

ance on hand is called a **stock record.** A file of stock records for all merchandise on hand is called a **stock ledger.**

In addition to other information on a stock record, a notation is made of the minimum balance at which a reorder is to be placed. For example, OfficeMart determines that two weeks are required to order and to receive shipment of boxes of $3^1/_2''$ diskettes from a vendor. OfficeMart also determines that in a two-week period, an average of 300 boxes of diskettes will be sold. Therefore, OfficeMart has established 300 boxes, or units, as the minimum balance before a reorder is sent to a vendor. Each reorder is to be for 1,000 units.

OfficeMart's stock record for the diskettes is shown in Illustration 7-3.

ILLUSTRATION 7-3 Stock record

STOCK RECORD

Description *3½" Computer Diskettes (boxes)* Stock No. *F106*
Reorder *1,000* Minimum *300* Location *Bin 26*

1	2	3	4	5	6	7
INCREASES			DECREASES			BALANCE
DATE	PURCHASE INVOICE NO.	QUANTITY	DATE	SALES INVOICE NO.	QUANTITY	QUANTITY
19-- Jan. 1						*700*
			Jan. 16	*1761*	*120*	*580*
			Feb. 21	*1923*	*310*	*270*
			Mar. 6	*2071*	*230*	*40*
Mar. 9	*669*	*1,000*				*1,040*
			Dec. 15	*2967*	*160*	*670*

FYI

Goods and services made in one country and sent to another are known as exports.

On January 1, the corporation had 700 boxes of diskettes on hand as shown in column 7 of the stock record card. On January 16, 120 boxes were sold. This decrease is recorded on the stock record as shown in columns 4–6. On February 21, another 310 boxes were sold. After the decrease on February 21, OfficeMart had 270 boxes remaining as shown in column 7. That quantity on hand, *270,* is below the minimum count of 300. Therefore, on February 21 a purchase order for 1,000 boxes was prepared and sent to a vendor. On March 6, another 230 boxes were sold, and the balance was reduced to 40.

A completed form authorizing a seller to deliver goods with payment to be made later is called a **purchase order.** OfficeMart prepares purchase orders for all purchases.

On March 9, 1,000 boxes of diskettes were received from the vendor and recorded on the stock record as shown in columns 1-3. The new balance of boxes on hand, *1,040,* was recorded in column 7.

TEACHING STRATEGIES: EXPANDING BEYOND THE CLASSROOM

Invite to class a local business person whose business maintains a perpetual inventory. Ask the speaker to explain how the perpetual inventory is used, and to show students the inventory forms used. Have students compare and contrast the forms with those in the textbook to recognize similarities and differences.

Merchandise purchases are recorded on the stock record only when the goods are received. Thus, the 1,000 units ordered on February 21 were not recorded on the stock record until March 9, the day the units were received.

On December 31, when a merchandise inventory count is needed, OfficeMart uses the last amount shown in column 7 of each stock record. For example, in Illustration 7-3, inventory count for boxes of 3½" diskettes is 670.

Unit prices change from time to time. Therefore, OfficeMart does not record unit prices on stock records. When needed, unit prices are obtained from copies of purchase invoices.

Periodic Inventory

A merchandise inventory determined by counting, weighing, or measuring items of merchandise on hand is known as a periodic inventory. Counting, weighing, or measuring merchandise on hand for a periodic inventory is commonly referred to as "taking an inventory." For businesses with a large quantity of merchandise on hand, taking a merchandise inventory count is expensive. For this reason, businesses usually take a periodic merchandise inventory only once each fiscal period.

TEACHING STRATEGIES: TEACHING TIP

Review the definition of periodic inventory: A merchandise inventory determined by counting, weighing, or measuring items of merchandise on hand.

FYI

Deciding the quantity of merchandise on hand and procedures for ordering, receiving, and maintaining inventory is inventory management.

When only a periodic inventory is used, a business must check carefully each day to determine if the quantity of any inventory item is low. However, the low quantity of a merchandise item can be overlooked. When this happens, the business may not have the merchandise when customers want it. For this reason, OfficeMart uses the perpetual inventory method. Errors can occur, however, even when the perpetual inventory method is used. Therefore, OfficeMart takes a periodic inventory once each year to check the accuracy of the perpetual inventory.

A form used during a periodic inventory to record information about each item of merchandise on hand is called an **inventory record.** OfficeMart uses an inventory record for a periodic inventory as shown in Illustration 7-4.

ILLUSTRATION 7-4 Inventory record

INVENTORY RECORD

DATE *October 31, 19--* ITEM *Computer Diskettes (boxes)*

1 STOCK NUMBER	2 DESCRIPTION	3 NO. OF UNITS ON HAND	4 UNIT PRICE	5 TOTAL COST
F106	*3½" Diskettes*	*670*	*4.70*	*3,149.00*
F107	*5¼" Diskettes*	*360*	*5.10*	*1,836.00*
	Total			*172,796.00*

TEACHING STRATEGIES: TEACHING TIP

Ask students if they have ever participated in taking inventory for a business. If any have, ask them to explain the process they followed.

AUDIT YOUR UNDERSTANDING

The AUDIT YOUR UNDERSTANDING feature appears at the end of each section of the chapter. Explain to your students that the word *audit* means to check or verify. AUDIT YOUR UNDERSTANDING may be used to check student comprehension of the section just studied. The answers are provided in Appendix D in the back of the textbook.

1. (1) Cost of beginning merchandise inventory. (2) Cost of the net purchases added to the inventory during the fiscal period.
2. Understated.
3. (1) By physically counting the items. (2) By keeping a continuous record showing the number purchased and sold for each item.
4. Once each fiscal period.

LESSON PLAN 7-2

Materials

- Student pages 198–203
- Software: Spreadsheet Template

Objectives (Enabling Performance Tasks)

a. Define accounting terms related to planning and costing inventory.

b. Identify accounting concepts and practices related to planning, counting, and costing inventory.

c. Determine the cost of merchandise inventory using selected costing methods.

FOCUS

- The two methods for determining inventory count were discussed earlier in this chapter. Explain that after the inventory count has been determined, the next step is to calculate the cost of merchandise inventory. In this lesson, various inventory costing methods will be presented.
- Introduce vocabulary: first-in, first-out inventory costing method; last-in, first-out inventory costing method; weighted-average inventory costing method; lower of cost or market inventory costing method.

Audit Your Understanding

1. The cost of merchandise available for sale consists of what two elements?
2. If ending merchandise inventory is understated, will the net income be overstated or understated?
3. What two procedures may be used to determine the number of inventory items on hand?
4. How often do businesses usually take a periodic merchandise inventory?

The inventory record is completed in five steps.

1 The stock numbers and descriptions are recorded on the form in columns 1 and 2.

2 The actual number of units on hand is written in column 3.

3 The unit price is recorded in column 4. The data are obtained from purchase invoices.

4 The total cost for each item is calculated and recorded in column 5. Total cost for each item is calculated by multiplying the unit price, column 4, by the number of items on hand, column 3.

5 Column 5 is totaled. The total of column 5, *$172,796.00*, is the total cost of the ending merchandise inventory.

The periodic inventory count is compared to the perpetual inventory, and any differences are adjusted on the stock records.

INVENTORY COST

Once OfficeMart takes a periodic inventory, a dollar cost is determined for each item. *(CONCEPT: Unit of Measurement)* The unit prices are obtained from purchase invoices. For example, in Illustration 7-4 the 670 F106 boxes of diskettes have a unit price of $4.70 and a total cost of $3,149.00. The 360 F107 boxes of diskettes have a unit price of $5.10 and a total cost of $1,836.00.

Various methods may be used to determine the cost of merchandise inventory. A business usually uses a specific method that best matches the revenue and costs for that business during the fiscal period. *(CONCEPT: Matching Expenses with Revenue)*

FYI

Fifo uses the most recent purchase prices to determine the cost of merchandise inventory.

First-In, First-Out Inventory Costing Method

Using the price of merchandise purchased first to calculate the cost of merchandise sold first is called the **first-in, first-out inventory costing method.** *Fifo* is an abbreviation for first in, first out. The fifo method of determining the cost of merchandise on hand assumes that the merchandise purchased *first* (first in) is the merchandise sold *first* (first out). Thus, the fifo method uses the most recent purchase prices to determine the cost of merchandise inventory. For example, OfficeMart has an inventory of 700 3-ring binders on November 30. If OfficeMart used the fifo method, the binders would be costed as shown in Illustration 7-5.

Of the 700 units on hand, 500 binders are assumed to be from the most recent purchase, November, at $1.25 each. The remaining 200 units are assumed to have been purchased on the next most recent date, June, at $1.20 each. None is considered to be part of the 500 units in beginning inventory at $1.00 each. The total cost, using the fifo method, is $865.00. The binders in the beginning

SOFTWARE FOCUS

Software may be used for independent practice or enrichment/extension as the instructor deems appropriate. For this chapter, the following software may be used: *Automated Accounting 6.0* or higher with Application Problem 4; Spreadsheet Template with Problems 7-1, 7-2, 7-3, and 7-4.

TEACH

Cover student pages 198–203 "Inventory Cost" and "Lower of Cost or Market Inventory Costing Method." Explain the fifo, lifo, and weighted-average inventory costing methods and give some examples of each. Explain how the costing methods affect the cost on ending inventory during a period of increasing and decreasing prices. Emphasize how the cost of ending inventory affects the cost of merchandise sold and net income on the income statement. Explain the lower of cost or market inventory costing method and give some examples.

ILLUSTRATION 7-5 Inventory costs calculated using the fifo method

Fifo Inventory Costing Method				
Purchase			Ending Inventory	
Date	Units	Unit Price	Units	Total Cost
January, beginning inventory....	500	$1.00	0	0.00
June	500	1.20	200	$240.00
November	500	1.25	500	625.00
Totals......................			700	$865.00

inventory are the *first in.* Therefore, the business assumes that the binders in beginning inventory are also the *first out,* or first sold.

Last-In, First-Out Inventory Costing Method

Using the price of merchandise purchased last to calculate the cost of merchandise sold first is called the **last-in, first-out inventory costing method.** *Lifo* is an abbreviation for last in, first out. The lifo method of determining the cost of merchandise on hand assumes that the merchandise purchased *last* (last in) is the merchandise sold *first* (first out). Thus, the lifo method uses the earliest purchase prices to determine the cost of merchandise inventory. If OfficeMart used the lifo method, the 700 binders would be costed as shown in Illustration 7-6.

FYI

If a business sells two items—posters and frames—the weighted average price per unit for posters and frames would be calculated separately.

ILLUSTRATION 7-6 Inventory costs calculated using the lifo method

Lifo Inventory Costing Method				
Purchase			Ending Inventory	
Date	Units	Unit Price	Units	Total Cost
January, beginning inventory....	500	$1.00	500	$500.00
June	500	1.20	200	240.00
November	500	1.25	0	0.00
Totals......................			700	$740.00

Of the 700 units currently on hand, 500 units are assumed to be the units in the beginning inventory at $1.00 per unit. The remaining 200 units are assumed to have been purchased on the next earliest date, June, at $1.20 each. None is considered to be part of the 500 units purchased on the most recent date, November, at $1.25 each. The total cost, using the lifo method, is $740.00. The binders purchased in November are the *last in.* Therefore, the busi-

TEACHING STRATEGIES: DIFFERENT LEARNING STYLES

Print Learner. When learning formulas, the print learner would prefer to be able to study the formula as given in the textbook or as printed on a separate handout. The print material should show the formula as well as an example of performing the calculations.

TEACHING STRATEGIES: COOPERATIVE LEARNING

Divide the class into two groups. Each group stands and faces the other. The teacher chooses selected Accounting Terms from Chapters 6 and 7. The teacher gives the term. The first student who raises his or her hand has the opportunity to give the correct definition. The group with the most correctly defined terms is declared the winner. This cooperative learning activity should not take more than 20 to 25 minutes of class time.

APPLY

Use an overhead projector or chalkboard to demonstrate the calculation of merchandise inventory using the fifo, lifo, and weighted-average inventory costing methods. Have students compare the inventory amounts for the three different methods and explain why the amounts differ. Demonstrate the calculation of merchandise inventory using the lower of cost or market inventory costing method.

Guided Practice

Guide students through the calculations to determine inventory costs for Stock Nos. A10 and B21 in Problem 7-2. Working as a group, have the students calculate the inventory costs for Stock No. A10 using the fifo method. Have them verify the costs by comparing the amounts with the answers given as the example. Repeat the procedure for Stock No. A10 using the lifo and weighted-average methods. Next, have students calculate the inventory costs for Stock No. B21 using the fifo method. When all students agree on the correct amounts, direct students to record the costs on the form in the working papers. Repeat the procedure for Stock No. B21 using the lifo and weighted-average methods. The balance of Problem 7-2 can be completed as Independent Practice.

Independent Practice

Assign Terms 8–11, Questions 14–18, and Problems 7-2 and 7-3.

ness assumes that the binders purchased in November are also the *first out,* or first sold.

Weighted-Average Inventory Costing Method

Using the average cost of beginning inventory plus merchandise purchased during a fiscal period to calculate the cost of merchandise sold is called the **weighted-average inventory costing method.** This method is based on the assumption that the cost is an average of the price paid for similar items purchased during the accounting period. If OfficeMart used the weighted-average method, the 700 binders would be costed as shown in Illustration 7-7.

ILLUSTRATION 7-7 Inventory costs calculated using the weighted-average method

Weighted-Average Inventory Costing Method
Quantity on Hand, 700 units

Purchase			Total Cost
Date	**Units**	**Unit Price**	
January, beginning inventory. . . .	500	$1.00	$ 500.00
June	500	1.20	600.00
November	500	1.25	625.00
Totals.	1,500		$1,725.00

Total of Beginning Inventory and Purchases	÷	Total Units	=	Weighted-Average Price per Unit
$1,725.00	÷	1,500	=	$1.15

Units in Ending Inventory	×	Weighted-Average Price per Unit	=	Cost of Ending Inventory
700	×	$1.15	=	$805.00

FYI

Goods and services produced in one country and brought into another country are imports.

The total cost, *$1,725.00,* is divided by the total units purchased, *1,500,* to calculate the weighted-average cost per unit, *$1.15.* The 700 units currently on hand are assumed to have been purchased at an average cost of $1.15 each. Therefore, the total cost of ending merchandise inventory using the weighted-average method is $805.00.

Costing Inventory During Periods of Changing Prices

In the situations for costing inventory previously described in this chapter, prices increased from $1.00 to $1.25 each. Sometimes prices decrease and the results change when using the previously described inventory costing methods.

Costing Inventory During a Period of Increasing Prices. Three ways of costing an inventory of 700 ring binders during a period of increasing prices are summarized in Illustration 7-8.

ILLUSTRATION 7-8 Summary of three methods of costing inventory during periods of increasing prices

Summary of Three Methods of Costing Inventory of 700 units of Ring Binders during a Period of Increasing Prices

Purchase		Fifo Method		Lifo Method		Weighted-Average Method
Date	Unit Price	Units	Cost	Units	Cost	
Jan., begin. inv. June Nov.	$1.00 1.20 1.25	0 200 500	0.00 $240.00 625.00	500 200 0	$500.00 240.00 0.00	Average Cost $1.15
Totals		700	$865.00	700	$740.00	$805.00

FYI

The goal of the Japanese concept, the just-in-time (JIT) system, is to minimize inventory. Materials should be received only when they are needed for production; they should not be kept in inventory.

The cost of the ending inventory affects the cost of merchandise sold amount on an income statement. The higher the ending inventory, the lower the cost of merchandise sold amount, and vice versa. Therefore, during a period of *increasing prices,* the fifo method usually will result in the lowest cost of merchandise sold. The lifo method usually will result in the highest cost of merchandise sold.

The higher the cost of merchandise sold, the lower the net income reported on financial statements, and vice versa. Therefore, during a period of *increasing prices,* the fifo method usually will result in the highest reported net income. The lifo method usually will result in the lowest reported net income.

Costing Inventory During a Period of Decreasing Prices. If OfficeMart determined the cost of inventory during a period of decreasing prices, the three inventory costing methods would be summarized as shown in Illustration 7-9.

ILLUSTRATION 7-9 Summary of three methods of costing inventory during periods of decreasing prices

Summary of Three Methods of Costing Inventory of 700 units of Ring Binders during a Period of Decreasing Prices

Purchase		Fifo Method		Lifo Method		Weighted-Average Method
Date	Unit Price	Units	Cost	Units	Cost	
Jan., begin. inv. June Nov.	$1.25 1.20 1.00	0 200 500	0.00 $240.00 500.00	500 200 0	$625.00 240.00 0.00	Average Cost $1.15
Totals		700	$740.00	700	$865.00	$805.00

During a period of *decreasing prices,* as shown in Illustration 7-9, the fifo method usually results in the lowest merchandise inventory cost. This lower inventory cost results in a higher cost of merchandise sold and a lower net income. During a period of *decreasing prices,* the lifo method usually results in the highest merchandise

ASSESS

Assess student understanding by checking the solutions to the Independent Practice activities.

Reteach

- Use data from Recycling Problem 7-R to calculate the inventory costs for Stock Nos. A12, B70, and D62 using the fifo, lifo, and weighted-average inventory costing methods.
- Assign Recycling Problem 7-R, Instructions 1–3.

Extend

Assign the Spreadsheet Template for Problems 7-2 and 7-3.

Enrich

Assign students to read the MULTICULTURAL AWARENESS feature on page 195. Discuss with them how an understanding and appreciation of history and other cultures contributes to understanding civilization today.

CLOSURE

Use Audit Your Understanding questions.

TEACHING STRATEGIES: TEACHING TIP

Use the overhead projector or chalkboard to demonstrate the calculation of merchandise inventory using the fifo, lifo, and weighted-average inventory costing methods. Have students compare the inventory amounts for the three different methods and explain why the amounts differ.

inventory cost. This higher inventory cost results in a lower cost of merchandise sold and a higher net income.

A comparison of three methods of costing inventory during periods of increasing or decreasing prices is shown in Illustration 7-10.

TEACHING STRATEGIES: APPLYING VISUALS

Direct students to Illustration 7-10 to review the comparison of the three methods of costing inventory.

ILLUSTRATION 7-10

Comparison of three methods of costing inventory

Comparison of Three Methods of Costing Inventory during Periods of Increasing or Decreasing Prices

Prices are	Total Inventory Cost Using		
	Fifo Method	Lifo Method	Weighted-Average Method
Increasing	$865.00	$740.00	$805.00
Decreasing	$740.00	$865.00	$805.00

The weighted-average method usually results in a total cost between the fifo and lifo methods in both periods of increasing and decreasing prices. For businesses that purchase items with frequent fluctuations in price, the weighted-average method results in more consistent reporting of merchandise inventory costs.

FYI

The higher the cost of merchandise sold, the lower the net income reported on financial statements. The lower the cost of merchandise sold, the higher the net income.

Each business selects the method of costing merchandise inventory that best fits the policies and goals of that business. Businesses select one method of costing merchandise inventory and use it for a number of years. In this way, the information on a series of financial statements can be compared easily. *(CONCEPT: Consistent Reporting)*

LOWER OF COST OR MARKET INVENTORY COSTING METHOD

Using the lower of cost or market price to calculate the cost of ending merchandise inventory is called the **lower of cost or market inventory costing method.** When merchandise is purchased, the unit price is used to record inventory costs. *(CONCEPT: Historical Cost)* If the unit price is higher than the market price at the end of a fiscal period, the inventory cost is reduced to the current market price. However, if the unit price is lower than the market price, the inventory cost is maintained at the unit price.

Two amounts are needed to apply the lower of cost or market method. (1) The cost of the inventory using the fifo, lifo, or weighted-average method. (2) The current market price of the inventory. These two amounts are then compared, and the lower of the two is used to cost the inventory. For example, OfficeMart uses the weighted-average method of costing inventory. The weighted-

TEACHING STRATEGIES: DIFFERENT LEARNING STYLES

Tactile Learner. Suggest using a calculator with a printed tape to perform mathematical calculations. Better calculators also print the operational signs of calculations (+, −, etc.) for students to trace the steps in a calculation.

average cost and the current market price for 700 ring binders are shown in Illustration 7-11. The weighted-average cost is $805.00 and the current market price is $770.00. Using the lower of cost or market method, the market price of the binders is lower than the weighted-average cost. Therefore, the market value of $770.00 is used as the cost of the binders.

ILLUSTRATION 7-11

Inventory costs using lower of cost or market method

Lower of Cost or Market Inventory Costing Method			
Costing Method	**Cost**	**Market Price (700 units × 1.10 current market price)**	**Lower of Cost or Market**
Weighted-Average	$805.00	$770.00	$770.00
Fifo	865.00	770.00	770.00
Lifo	740.00	770.00	740.00

Audit Your Understanding

1. What inventory costing method does a business usually use?
2. Which inventory costing method uses the earliest purchase prices to determine the cost of merchandise inventory?
3. During a period of increasing prices, what inventory costing method will result in the highest reported net income?
4. What two amounts are needed to apply the lower of cost or market inventory costing method?

If OfficeMart used the fifo method, the fifo cost would be $865.00. The $770.00 market price is lower than the fifo cost, so the market price would be used instead of the fifo cost. If OfficeMart used the lifo method, the lifo cost would be $740.00. The lifo cost is lower than the market price, so the lifo cost would be used to cost the inventory.

ESTIMATING THE COST OF MERCHANDISE INVENTORY

A business that prepares monthly interim financial statements needs a cost for monthly ending merchandise inventory. Taking a monthly periodic inventory is usually too expensive to be worthwhile. Therefore, monthly ending inventories may be estimated.

Two methods that may be used to estimate an ending merchandise inventory are the (1) gross profit method and (2) retail method.

Gross Profit Method of Estimating Inventory

Estimating inventory by using the previous years' percentage of gross profit on operations is known as the gross profit method of estimating inventory. The gross profit method of estimating inventory is based on the assumption that a continuing relationship exists between gross profit and net sales. Based on experience in previous fiscal periods, a gross profit to net sales percentage is calculated.

FYI

Monthly ending inventories are estimated because taking a monthly periodic inventory is too time consuming and expensive.

AUDIT YOUR UNDERSTANDING

1. A method that best matches the revenue and costs for that business during the fiscal period.
2. The last-in, first-out (lifo) method.
3. The first-in, first-out (fifo) method.
4. (1) The cost of the inventory using the fifo, lifo, or weighted-average method. (2) The current market price of the inventory.

LESSON PLAN 7-3

Materials

- Student pages 203–208
- Software: Spreadsheet Template
- Assess: Problem Test Chapter 7, MicroExam Chapter 7

Objectives (Enabling Performance Tasks)

a. Define accounting terms related to planning and costing inventory.
b. Identify accounting concepts and practices related to planning, counting, and costing inventory.
d. Estimate the cost of merchandise inventory using selected estimating methods.
e. Calculate merchandise inventory turnover ratio and average number of days' sales in merchandise inventory.

Professional Business Ethics

The PROFESSIONAL BUSINESS ETHICS feature stimulates critical thinking and decision making. It may be used in many ways such as an individual assignment, a class discussion, or a small group cooperative learning project. When these ethics cases are discussed in class, students can also gain a sense of individual diversity as students demonstrate individual opinions. If you wish to integrate word processing in your accounting course, you may direct students to word process their answers. If you wish to include the creation of tables, you might direct students to format their responses to resemble the ethical decision-making grid in a 3-column table. A Blackline Master of the 3-Step Checklist for Making Ethical Decisions is furnished in the Teacher's Resource Guide. Suggested solutions for the PROFESSIONAL BUSINESS ETHICS feature are provided in the front of this teacher's edition.

FOCUS

- The gross profit method of estimating inventory was introduced in Chapter 5. In this lesson, the gross profit method will be reviewed and another method, the retail method, will be presented. Also, two measures of the speed with which merchandise inventory is sold will be discussed.
- Introduce vocabulary: retail method of estimating inventory, merchandise inventory turnover ratio, average number of days' sales in merchandise inventory.

TEACH

Cover student pages 203–208 "Estimating the Cost of Merchandise Inventory" and "Merchandise Inventory Turnover." Review the gross profit method of estimating inventory. Explain the retail method of estimating inventory and give some examples. Demonstrate how to calculate the merchandise inventory turnover ratio and explain what the ratio means. Demonstrate how to calculate average number of days' sales in merchandise inventory and discuss how managers use this information.

PROFESSIONAL BUSINESS ETHICS

At What Price Safety?

Webster Industries assembles safety systems for cars. The safety system substantially reduces severe injuries to drivers involved in accidents.

Webster has begun purchasing an important component for this system at a $100 savings. The new component, however, increases the system's estimated failure rate from 12 to 15 failures per 10,000 accidents. Despite this increase, the company still continues to meet the government's safety standard of 20 failures per 10,000 accidents.

Webster has reduced the unit sales price of its safety system by $60. However, the savings for the new component is $100. Therefore, Webster still earns an additional $40 profit per unit. The car manufacturer is passing the $60 savings on to its customers to promote an increase in sales volume.

INSTRUCTIONS Use the three-step checklist to analyze whether Webster Industries' use of the new component demonstrates ethical behavior.

OfficeMart's estimated ending merchandise inventory on October 31 using the gross profit method is calculated as shown in Illustration 7-12.

ILLUSTRATION 7-12 Estimating ending merchandise inventory using the gross profit method

ESTIMATED MERCHANDISE INVENTORY SHEET
Gross Profit Method

COMPANY *OfficeMart, Inc.* DATE *10/31/--*

1	Beginning inventory, January 1		$ *158,930.00*
2	Net purchases to date		*762,440.00*
3	Merchandise available for sale		$ *921,370.00*
4	Net sales to date	$ *1,296,000.00*	
5	Less estimated gross profit. (Net sales × Estimated gross profit *42.5* %)	*550,800.00*	
6	Estimated cost of merchandise sold		*745,200.00*
7	Estimated ending inventory		$ *176,170.00*

1 January 1 beginning inventory, *$158,930.00*, line 1, is obtained from the merchandise inventory account in the general ledger.

2 Net purchases to date, *$762,440.00*, line 2, is obtained from the purchases, purchases discount, and purchases returns and allowances accounts in the general ledger.

3 Merchandise available for sale, *$921,370.00*, line 3, is calculated by adding the amounts on lines 1 and 2.

4 Net sales to date, *$1,296,000.00,* line 4, is obtained from the sales, sales discount, and sales returns and allowances accounts in the general ledger.

5 Estimated gross profit, *$550,800.00,* line 5, is calculated by multiplying the amount on line 4 by 42.5%. The percentage, *42.5%,* is an average of the gross profit percentages from OfficeMart's income statements for the past three years.

6 Estimated cost of merchandise sold, *$745,200.00,* line 6, is calculated by subtracting the amount on line 5 from the amount on line 4.

7 Estimated ending inventory, *$176,170.00,* line 7, is calculated by subtracting the amount on line 6 from the amount on line 3.

FYI

Estimated gross profit is calculated by multiplying the net sales to date by the average of gross profit percentage.

An ending merchandise inventory amount calculated using the gross profit method is an estimate and is not absolutely accurate. However, when preparing monthly interim financial statements the estimated amount is sufficiently accurate without taking a periodic inventory.

Retail Method of Estimating Inventory

Estimating inventory by using a percentage based on both cost and retail prices is called the **retail method of estimating inventory.** To use the retail method, separate records must be kept of both cost and retail prices for net purchases, net sales, and beginning merchandise inventory.

An estimated ending merchandise inventory, using the retail method, is calculated for Shaver, Inc. as shown in Illustration 7-13.

ILLUSTRATION 7-13 Estimating ending merchandise inventory using the retail method

ESTIMATED MERCHANDISE INVENTORY SHEET
Retail Method

COMPANY *Shaver, Inc.* DATE *12/31/--*

		Cost	Retail
1	Beginning inventory, January 1	$ *315,800.00*	$ *542,200.00*
2	Net purchases to date	*192,540.00*	*331,200.00*
3	Merchandise available for sale	$ *508,340.00*	$ *873,400.00*
4	Net sales to date		*347,600.00*
5	Estimated ending inventory at retail		$ *525,800.00*
6	Estimated ending inventory at cost (Inventory at Retail × percentage *58.2* %)	$ *306,015.60*	

1 January 1 beginning inventory at cost, *$315,800.00,* line 1, is obtained from the merchandise inventory account in the general ledger. Beginning inventory at retail, *$542,200.00,* is obtained from the separate record of retail prices.

APPLY

Write each formula on the chalkboard or overhead projector and demonstrate all calculations.

Guided Practice

- Guide students through the calculation of the estimated ending inventory for Foley, Inc., in Problem 7-4. Working as a group, calculate the estimated ending inventory using the gross profit method. When all students agree, have them record the amount on the form provided in the working papers. Use the same procedure to calculate the estimated ending inventory using the retail method. The balance of Problem 7-4 can be completed as Independent Practice.
- Guide students through the calculation of the merchandise inventory turnover ratio and average number of days' sales in merchandise inventory for Corporation A in Problem 7-5. Working as a group, calculate the merchandise inventory turnover ratio for Corporation A. When all students agree with the ratio, direct them to write the correct answer on the form in the working papers. Use the same procedure to calculate the average number of days' sales in merchandise inventory for Corporation A. The balance of Problem 7-5 can be completed as Independent Practice.

Independent Practice

- Assign Terms 12–14, Questions 19–20, and Problems 7-4 and 7-5.
- Assign Study Guide 7 and Mastery Problem 7-M.

APPLIED SKILLS: LANGUAGE ARTS

Paraphrasing, writing complete sentences, and identifying active and passive verbs. For additional practice in language arts skills, direct students to answer the Accounting Terms and Questions for Individual Study at the end of the chapter. Students should write the answers in their own words and in complete sentences. To further practice language arts skills, ask students to underline all active verbs and circle all passive verbs in their answers.

ASSESS

Assess student understanding by checking the solutions to the Independent Practice activities.

Reteach

- Use data from Recycling Problem 7-R to calculate the corporation's estimated ending inventory using the gross profit and retail methods of estimating inventory.
- Assign Recycling Problem 7-R, Instructions 4–7.

Extend

- Assign Challenge Problem 7-C. (The challenge is to calculate adjusted unit and total prices including freight and cash discounts.)
- Assign the Spreadsheet Template for Problem 7-4.

Enrich

- Assign the PERSONAL VISIONS IN BUSINESS feature on page 207.
- Have students obtain the annual reports of several familiar public corporations. Use the information in the financial statements to calculate the merchandise inventory turnover ratio and the average number of days' sales in merchandise inventory. On the chalkboard, have students compare the amounts for corporations in different industries. Discuss how businesses in different industries will have significantly different ratios.

CLOSURE

Use Audit Your Understanding questions.

ASSESS

- Administer Problem Test Chapter 7.
- Administer a MicroExam test for Chapter 7.

2 Net purchases to date at cost, *$192,540.00,* line 2, is obtained from the purchases, purchases discount, and purchases returns and allowances accounts in the general ledger. Net purchases to date at retail, *$331,200.00,* is obtained from the separate record of retail prices.

3 Merchandise available for sale at cost, *$508,340.00,* and at retail, *$873,400.00,* line 3, is calculated by adding lines 1 and 2.

4 Net sales to date at retail, *$347,600.00,* line 4, is obtained from the sales, sales discount, and sales returns and allowances accounts in the general ledger.

5 Estimated ending inventory at retail, *$525,800.00,* line 5, is calculated by subtracting line 4 from line 3.

6 Estimated ending inventory at cost, *$306,015.60,* line 6, is calculated by multiplying the amount on line 5 by 58.2%. The percentage of merchandise available for sale at cost to merchandise available for sale at retail, *58.2%,* is calculated from the amounts on line 3.

Merchandise Available for Sale at Cost	÷	Merchandise Available for Sale at Retail	=	Percentage
$508,340.00	÷	$873,400.00	=	58.2%

FYI

The gross profit method is easier to use because separate retail records are not needed.

Many businesses that need to estimate ending merchandise inventory use the gross profit method rather than the retail method. The gross profit method does not require that separate records be kept at cost and retail prices as is true of the retail method. OfficeMart uses a perpetual inventory. Therefore, monthly ending inventories are available from the stock record cards without estimating or taking a monthly inventory.

MERCHANDISE INVENTORY TURNOVER

The more rapidly a business sells merchandise, the more chance a business has of making a satisfactory net income. For example, more revenue results from selling 100 ring binders per day than from selling 60 binders per day. Two measures of the speed with which merchandise inventory is sold are (1) merchandise inventory turnover ratio and (2) average number of days' sales in merchandise inventory.

Merchandise Inventory Turnover Ratio

The number of times the average amount of merchandise inventory is sold during a specific period of time is called the **merchandise**

TEACHING STRATEGIES: DIFFERENT LEARNING STYLES

Auditory Learner. The auditory learner can reinforce the learning of formulas by verbally explaining the formula and/or calculations to other students in a small group. In a group of three, for example, each student should get the opportunity to "teach" the formula to the other two students. Through this process, each student in the group will "teach" the formula once and "learn" the formula two times.

inventory turnover ratio. A merchandise inventory turnover ratio expresses a relationship between an average inventory and the cost of merchandise sold. Merchandise inventory represents a large investment for most merchandising businesses. Therefore, a low merchandise inventory turnover ratio usually indicates a low return on investment.

OfficeMart's merchandise inventory turnover ratio for the current fiscal year is calculated as follows.

January 1 Merchandise Inventory	+	December 31 Merchandise Inventory	÷	2	=	Average Merchandise Inventory
($168,365.00	+	$173,325.00)	÷	2	=	$170,845.00

Cost of Merchandise Sold	÷	Average Merchandise Inventory	=	Merchandise Inventory Turnover Ratio
$925,368.00	÷	$170,845.00	=	5.4 times

■ James Martinez ■

MARTINEZ PERSONNEL SYSTEMS, INC.

James Martinez owns Martinez Personnel Systems, Inc., the personnel company he started from scratch. Martinez, a Hispanic-American, has a degree in business from Wright State University where his course of studies included a year of accounting courses. Even though Martinez has studied accounting, his company uses the services of a CPA. However, monthly, quarterly, and yearly reports are prepared internally. Martinez says that his accounting courses helped him to know how to prepare the regular reports and also to relate to his CPA and banks.

Like many new businesses, Martinez Personnel Systems was started from family savings. Although Martinez thought he had enough money to start a business, a little luck and a lot of persistence landed a large contract just as more cash was needed to develop his business.

When he started his business Martinez was surprised by the initial loneliness after being used to working in a larger company with many coworkers to talk to and be with. Martinez says, "As a sole owner of a business just starting out, you are alone a lot and have to learn how to deal with it."

When Martinez was ready to open his personnel business he invited a number of prospective clients to a grand opening reception. However, the week before the reception the furniture company told him that the office furniture he had ordered months before would not be delivered in time. "They told me not to worry," Martinez said. "They said that they would send some loaner furniture for the reception. Thinking it would be similar to what I had ordered, I relaxed. Imagine my surprise when the folding chairs and tables arrived from the furniture company as a substitute for office furniture! But we survived that day to become very successful. In fact, I am opening my third branch office soon."

In his personnel company, Martinez has the opportunity to interview many young people who are looking for jobs. He finds that many lack confidence in what they believe they can do. To build confidence Martinez recommends participating in as many extracurricular activities in school as possible and volunteering for community and church projects. Taking an active role in these activities helps build the confidence that will make you a more valuable employee.

Personal Visions in Business

Personal Visions in Business

This special student feature introduces students to successful entrepreneurs or business professionals. Each profile gives a flavor of what the actual business world is like and some of the opportunities available to students who study accounting. These features can be used to motivate students to pursue professional business careers in a wide variety of fields. The subjects of these profiles have been carefully chosen to represent the full spectrum of diverse ethnic and racial backgrounds of professional business people. As an optional activity, students can be encouraged to seek out and interview successful business people in their own communities.

TEACHING STRATEGIES: DIFFERENT LEARNING STYLES

Kinesthetic Learner. The kinesthetic learner should have the opportunity to perform the calculations to solve the formula. One way to accomplish this is to develop several examples using different amounts for beginning and ending inventory. The student should calculate the merchandise inventory turnover ratio for each example.

APPLIED SKILLS: BUILDING STUDY SKILLS

Direct students to prepare a Quick Reference Guide (QRG) by writing the formulas for calculating merchandise inventory turnover ratio and average number of days' sales in merchandise inventory on an index card. Students should use this QRG as a reference.

FYI

A low merchandise inventory turnover ratio usually indicates a low return on investment.

A 5.4 merchandise inventory turnover ratio means that the business sold the average merchandise inventory 5.4 times during the current year. OfficeMart compares its merchandise inventory turnover ratio with those published by national trade associations. Businesses similar to OfficeMart have an average merchandise inventory turnover ratio of 7.0 times. OfficeMart's turnover ratio of 5.4 is below the industry standard of 7.0. To correct this situation, OfficeMart's managers should consider taking action to better control the quantity of merchandise inventory on hand.

Average Number of Days' Sales in Merchandise Inventory

The period of time needed to sell an average amount of merchandise inventory is called **average number of days' sales in merchandise inventory.** The average number of days' sales in merchandise inventory based on a 5.4 merchandise inventory turnover ratio is calculated as shown below.

Days in Year	÷	Merchandise Inventory Turnover Ratio	=	Average Number of Days' Sales in Merchandise Inventory
365	÷	5.4	=	68 days

FYI

The higher the number of days in merchandise inventory, the longer merchandise tends to remain unsold.

The average number of days' sales in merchandise inventory is rounded to the nearest day. This level of accuracy provides managers with adequate information to make sound business decisions. An average of 68 days means that, on average, each item in merchandise inventory is sold 68 days after it is purchased. Published averages from trade associations show that businesses similar to OfficeMart have an average number of days' sales in merchandise inventory of 53 days. OfficeMart's average of 68 is above the industry standard of 53 days. OfficeMart's management should seek ways to increase its turnover of merchandise inventory.

The higher the number of days in merchandise inventory, the longer merchandise tends to remain unsold. A business can reduce the merchandise inventory turnover ratio and the number of days' sales in merchandise inventory by reducing the size of the inventory kept on hand. However, a lower inventory level may not meet the demands of customers. A business also can improve its turnover ratio and the number of days' sales in merchandise inventory by increasing the amount of merchandise sold during a month or a year.

Audit Your Understanding

1. The gross profit method of estimating inventory is based on what assumption?
2. To use the retail method of estimating inventory, what records must be kept?
3. What does a merchandise inventory turnover ratio of 5.0 mean?
4. How is the average number of days' sales in merchandise inventory calculated?

AUDIT YOUR UNDERSTANDING

1. That a continuing relationship exists between gross profit and net sales.
2. Separate records of both cost and retail prices for net purchases, net sales, and beginning merchandise inventory.
3. That the business sold the average merchandise inventory five times during the current year.
4. Days in year (365) divided by merchandise inventory turnover ratio equals average number of days' sales in merchandise inventory.

TEACHING STRATEGIES: DIFFERENT LEARNING STYLES

Visual Learner. Formulas, such as those used to calculate merchandise inventory turnover ratio, should be illustrated on the chalkboard to assist visual learners. The instructor should also complete the calculations for a few examples using different amounts for beginning and ending inventory to show the process to visual learners.

ACCOUNTING TERMS EPT(a)

What is the meaning of each of the following?

1. **consignment**
2. **consignee**
3. **consignor**
4. **stock record**
5. **stock ledger**
6. **purchase order**
7. **inventory record**
8. **first-in, first-out inventory costing method**
9. **last-in, first-out inventory costing method**
10. **weighted-average inventory costing method**
11. **lower of cost or market inventory costing method**
12. **retail method of estimating inventory**
13. **merchandise inventory turnover ratio**
14. **average number of days' sales in merchandise inventory**

QUESTIONS FOR INDIVIDUAL STUDY EPT(b)

1. What two elements make up the cost of the merchandise available for sale?
2. At the end of a fiscal period, the cost of merchandise available for sale is divided into what two parts?
3. Which accounting concept is being applied when an accurate merchandise inventory cost must be determined to adequately report the financial progress and condition of a merchandising business?
4. What items on financial statements are affected, and how, when an ending merchandise inventory is understated?
5. What two amounts are used to determine the cost of merchandise inventory?
6. Who has title to goods that are in transit with terms of FOB shipping point?
7. Who has title to goods that are in transit with terms of FOB destination?
8. Who has title to goods that are on consignment?
9. When does OfficeMart reorder an inventory item?
10. How can the number of items on hand be determined when a perpetual inventory is kept?
11. Why do businesses with large merchandise inventories usually take a periodic inventory only once each fiscal period?
12. How will errors in a perpetual inventory be discovered?
13. Where does OfficeMart obtain the unit prices for items listed on an inventory record?
14. Which accounting concept is being applied when a business chooses a method of costing inventories?
15. Which merchandise is assumed to be sold first when a business uses the fifo method?
16. Which merchandise is assumed to be sold first when a business uses the lifo method?
17. What is the formula for calculating the average cost per unit of merchandise when the weighted-average method is used?
18. During a period of increasing prices, which method of costing inventories usually gives the highest inventory cost?
19. Why might a business use the gross profit method instead of the retail method to estimate monthly ending inventory?
20. What can be interpreted from a merchandise inventory turnover ratio of 6 times?

ACCOUNTING TERMS

1. **consignment:** Goods which are given to a business to sell, but for which title to the goods remains with the vendor. (p. 195)
2. **consignee:** The person or business who receives goods on consignment. (p. 195)
3. **consignor:** The person or business who gives goods on consignment. (p. 195)
4. **stock record:** A form used to show the kind of merchandise, quantity received, quantity sold, and balance on hand. (p. 196)
5. **stock ledger:** A file of stock records for all merchandise on hand. (p. 196)
6. **purchase order:** A completed form authorizing a seller to deliver goods with payment to be made later. (p. 196)
7. **inventory record:** A form used during a periodic inventory to record information about each item of merchandise on hand. (p. 197)
8. **first-in, first-out inventory costing method:** Using the price of merchandise purchased first to calculate the cost of merchandise sold first. (p. 198)
9. **last-in, first-out inventory costing method:** Using the price of merchandise purchased last to calculate the cost of merchandise sold first. (p. 199)
10. **weighted-average inventory costing method:** Using the average cost of beginning inventory plus merchandise purchased during a fiscal period to calculate the cost of merchandise sold. (p. 200)
11. **lower of cost or market inventory costing method:** Using the lower of cost or market price to calculate the cost of ending merchandise inventory. (p. 202)
12. **retail method of estimating inventory:** Estimating inventory by using a percentage based on both cost and retail prices. (p. 205)
13. **merchandise inventory turnover ratio:** The number of times the average amount of merchandise inventory is sold during a specific period of time. (p. 206)
14. **average number of days' sales in merchandise inventory:** The period of time needed to sell an average amount of merchandise inventory. (p. 208)

QUESTIONS FOR INDIVIDUAL STUDY

1. (a) Cost of the beginning merchandise inventory. (b) Cost of the net purchases added to the inventory during the fiscal period. (p. 193)
2. (a) Cost of the ending merchandise inventory. (b) Cost of merchandise sold during the current fiscal period. (p. 193)
3. Adequate Disclosure concept. (p. 194)
4. Net income, total assets, and stockholders' equity will be understated. (p. 194)
5. (a) Price paid to vendors for the merchandise. The price paid includes purchase invoice amount less discounts, returns, and allowances. (b) Costs involved in getting the merchandise to the place of business and ready for sale. The cost includes transportation charges paid by the buyer. (p. 194)
6. The buyer. (p. 195)
7. The vendor. (p. 195)
8. The consignor. (p. 195)
9. When the number on hand reaches the minimum amount noted on the stock record card. (p. 196)
10. By using the last line on each of the stock record cards. (p. 197)
11. Taking a periodic inventory is expensive. (p. 197)
12. By taking a periodic inventory once a year and comparing the results to the perpetual inventory. (p. 197)
13. From purchase invoices. (p. 198)
14. Matching Expenses with Revenue concept. (p. 198)
15. The merchandise purchased first (first-in). (p. 198)
16. The merchandise purchased last (last-in). (p. 199)
17. Total cost ÷ total units purchased = weighted-average price per unit. (p. 200)
18. Fifo method. (p. 201)
19. Because the gross profit method does not require that separate records be kept at cost and retail prices. (p. 206)
20. The business sold the average merchandise inventory 6 times during the fiscal period. Also, an average item remains in merchandise inventory approximately 61 days before it is sold. (p. 208)

CASES FOR CRITICAL THINKING — EPT(b)

CASE 1 Quitman, Inc. keeps a perpetual merchandise inventory. A new member of the board of directors notices that two employees work full time keeping the inventory records. The director suggests that the corporation stop using the perpetual inventory system and take a periodic inventory once a year when information is needed for financial statements. The director also suggests that the salaries saved by eliminating the positions of the two inventory employees will be more than the cost of an annual periodic inventory. What is your opinion of this suggestion? Explain your answer.

CASE 2 Hastings, Inc. sells many different items of sports equipment. The corporation takes a periodic inventory once every three months for use in preparing quarterly financial statements. A newly employed accountant suggests that the corporation change over to a perpetual inventory. What would you recommend? Explain your recommendation.

APPLICATION PROBLEMS — EPT(c,d,e)

PROBLEM 7-1 Keeping perpetual inventory records

SPREADSHEET

Western Hardware, Inc. keeps a perpetual merchandise inventory.

INSTRUCTIONS:

1. Complete the heading of a stock record for each of the following two inventory items. Also, record the balance on July 1 of the current year for each item.

   Exterior door; Stock No. EX472; reorder, 30; minimum, 5; location, Bin 20; number on hand July 1, 21.
   Storm shutter; Stock No. S398; reorder, 40; minimum, 10; location, Bin 92; number on hand July 1, 26.

2. Record on the stock records the merchandise items received and sold during July of the current year. Source documents are abbreviated as follows: sales invoice, S; purchase invoice, P.

July 3. Sold 15 storm shutters, S321.
5. Sold 12 exterior doors, S322.
9. Sold 5 doors, S323.
10. Sold 6 shutters, S324.
14. Received 30 doors, P1216.
15. Received 40 shutters, P1217.
17. Sold 10 doors, S325.
20. Sold 20 shutters, S326.
21. Sold 10 doors, S327.
21. Sold 8 shutters, S328.
25. Sold 12 doors, S329.
26. Sold 13 shutters, S330.
28. Received 40 shutters, P1218.
30. Received 30 doors, P1219.

PROBLEM 7-2 Determining cost of inventory using fifo, lifo, and weighted-average methods

Accounting records at Glenden, Inc. show the following purchases and periodic inventory counts.

Stock No.	January 1 Inventory		First Purchase		Second Purchase		Third Purchase		Fourth Purchase		December 31 Inventory
	No.	Unit Price	No.	Unit Price	No.	Unit Price	No.	Unit Price	No.	Unit Price	
A10	8	$5.00	8	$6.00	8	$7.00	10	$8.00	10	$6.00	20
B21	10	6.00	10	6.00	12	6.00	12	5.00	12	5.00	30
C45	15	3.00	20	4.00	20	4.00	20	5.00	20	6.00	52
D70	6	9.00	10	9.00	10	8.00	10	7.00	10	6.00	35
E39	12	4.00	5	4.00	5	6.00	10	5.00	5	4.00	20

INSTRUCTIONS:

1. Calculate the inventory costs using the fifo, lifo, and weighted-average inventory costing methods. Use a form similar to the following. The inventory cost for Stock No. A10 is given as an example.

Stock No.	Dec. 31 Inventory	Inventory Costing Method					
		Fifo		Lifo		Weighted-Average	
		Unit Price	Total Cost	Unit Price	Total Cost	Unit Price	Total Cost
A10	20	*10 @ $6.00* *10 @ 8.00*	*$140.00*	*8 @ $5.00* *8 @ 6.00* *4 @ 7.00*	*$116.00*	*20 @ $6.45*	*$129.00*
B21							
Total Cost							

2. Total the three Total Cost columns.
3. Which of the three methods of costing inventory results in the highest inventory cost for Glenden, Inc.? Which results in the lowest inventory cost?

PROBLEM 7-3 Determining cost of inventory using lower of cost or market method

Tempson, Inc. obtained the following information from its records on December 31 of the current year.

Stock No.	Inventory	Cost	Market Price
S40	10	$ 4.70	$ 5.10
R23	25	2.15	2.00
Q10	10	22.00	19.00
T55	11	8.00	9.50
A40	8	17.00	15.00
W16	20	2.50	3.25
X58	15	10.00	12.00

CASES FOR CRITICAL THINKING

Case 1 This suggestion is not necessarily a good one. Benefits of keeping a perpetual inventory are: (a) The business can easily establish reordering minimums for various merchandise items. The perpetual inventory method helps alert the business to the need to reorder individual items. (b) Actual inventory information is available for use on monthly interim financial statements without taking a periodic inventory or estimating ending inventories. If a business has relatively few different items of merchandise which can be counted easily and quickly, a perpetual inventory is not needed and a periodic inventory will be sufficient. However, most merchandising businesses carry many items of merchandise and can benefit from a perpetual inventory.

Case 2 Recommend changing to a perpetual inventory which is checked once a year with a periodic inventory. With the large number of different items, taking a periodic inventory is expensive. Quarterly inventories are easily obtained from a perpetual inventory system. The cost of taking three periodic inventories per year can be saved with a perpetual system. The money saved can be used to employ personnel to keep the perpetual inventory. In addition, a perpetual inventory system makes it easier to keep track of which individual items need to be reordered before all are sold.

CHECK FIGURES

See Teacher's Edition of the Working Papers for complete solutions.

Problem 7-1 Ending balance: Item EX472—32; Item S398—44

Problem 7-2 Total cost of ending inventory: fifo, $919.00; lifo, $862.00; weighted-average, $888.84

Problem 7-3 Total cost of inventory using lower of cost or market: $695.00

INSTRUCTIONS:

1. Calculate the inventory cost for each item of merchandise using the lower of cost or market inventory costing method. Use a form similar to the following. The inventory cost for Stock No. S40 is given as an example.

Stock No.	Inventory	Price to Use		Lower of Cost or Market
		Cost	Market	
S40	10	$4.70		*$47.00*
Total				

2. Total the Lower of Cost or Market column.

PROBLEM 7-4 Estimating ending merchandise inventory

SPREADSHEET

MATHEMATICS

The following information is obtained from the records of two corporations.

Item	Foley, Inc.		Songer, Inc.	
	Cost	Retail	Cost	Retail
Beginning merchandise inventory...	$19,800.00	$ 32,980.00	$ 35,200.00	$ 50,400.00
Net purchases to date..........	65,100.00	107,800.00	110,600.00	157,700.00
Net sales to date...............	—	87,900.00	—	128,000.00
Gross profit percentage..........	40%		30%	

INSTRUCTIONS:

1. Calculate the estimated ending inventory for the two corporations using the gross profit method of estimating inventory. Use July 31 of the current year as the date.
2. Calculate the estimated ending inventory for the two corporations using the retail method of estimating inventory. Round the percentage to the nearest 0.1%.

PROBLEM 7-5 Calculating merchandise inventory turnover ratio and average number of days' sales in merchandise inventory

MATHEMATICS

Selected information for three corporations is given below.

Item	Corporation		
	A	B	C
Beginning merchandise inventory...	$ 30,700.00	$ 40,000.00	$ 54,400.00
Ending merchandise inventory	34,900.00	39,300.00	45,200.00
Cost of merchandise sold	308,300.00	422,100.00	428,300.00

INSTRUCTIONS:

1. For each corporation, calculate the merchandise inventory turnover ratio. Round the ratio to the nearest 0.1.
2. For each corporation, calculate the average number of days' sales in merchandise inventory. Round the amount to the nearest day.
3. Which corporation has the best merchandise inventory turnover ratio?

CHECK FIGURES *(cont'd)*

Problem 7-4 Estimated ending inventory: Gross profit method, $32,160.00, $56,200.00; Retail method, $31,886.64, $56,150.10

Problem 7-5 Merchandise inventory turnover ratio: 9.4 times, 10.6 times, 8.6 times. Average number of days' sales in merchandise inventory: 39 days, 34 days, 42 days. Best merchandise inventory turnover ratio: Corporation B.

ENRICHMENT PROBLEMS

EPT(c,d,e)

MASTERY PROBLEM 7-M Determining cost of merchandise inventory; estimating cost of merchandise inventory using estimating methods; calculating merchandise inventory turnover ratio and average number of days' sales in merchandise inventory

On December 31 of the current year, Sowell, Inc. took a periodic inventory. The following information is obtained from Sowell's records.

Stock No.	January 1 Inventory		First Purchase		Second Purchase		December 31 Inventory	Market Price
	No.	Unit Price	No.	Unit Price	No.	Unit Price		
R46	14	$ 7.00	15	$ 8.00	15	$ 9.00	18	$ 9.50
S10	16	5.00	10	5.00	10	8.00	26	4.75
T76	8	12.00	15	11.00	15	11.00	25	10.00
U92	7	8.00	7	8.00	7	8.00	10	8.00
V17	5	4.00	10	6.00	10	7.00	5	6.00

INSTRUCTIONS:

1. Calculate the inventory costs using the fifo, lifo, and weighted-average inventory costing methods. Use a form similar to the following.

Stock No.	Dec. 31 Inventory	Inventory Costing Method					
		Fifo		Lifo		Weighted-Average	
		Unit Price	Total Cost	Unit Price	Total Cost	Unit Price	Total Cost
Total Costs							

2. Total the three Total Cost columns.
3. Sowell uses the lifo inventory costing method to determine the cost of inventory. Use the market price given in the form at the beginning of the problem to determine the cost of inventory using the lower of cost or market. Total the Lower of Cost or Market column. Use a form similar to the following.

Stock No.	Lifo Cost	Market Price			Lower of Cost or Market
		Inventory	Unit Price	Total Cost	
Total					

4. Calculate the corporation's estimated ending inventory using the gross profit method of estimating inventory. The following information is obtained from the corporation's records on December 31 of the current year.

CHECK FIGURES *(cont'd)*

Mastery Problem 7-M Total cost of ending inventory: fifo, $709.00; lifo, $643.00; weighted-average, $686.19. Total cost of ending inventory using lower of cost or market: $603.50. Estimated ending inventory: Gross profit, $26,980.00; Retail, $27,000.00. Merchandise inventory turnover ratio: 2.6 times. Average number of days' sales in merchandise inventory: 140 days.

Item	Cost	Retail
Beginning merchandise inventory..........	$21,200.00	$ 35,000.00
Net purchases to date..................	68,000.00	113,700.00
Net sales to date......................	—	103,700.00
Gross profit percentage................	40%	

5. Calculate the corporation's estimated ending inventory using the retail method of estimating inventory. Round the percentage to the nearest 0.1%.
6. Use the information and the estimated inventory calculated in Instruction 4. Calculate the corporation's merchandise inventory turnover ratio. Round the ratio to the nearest 0.1.
7. Calculate the corporation's average number of days' sales in merchandise inventory. Round the amount to the nearest day.

CHECK FIGURES *(cont'd)*

Challenge Problem 7-C

Adjusted unit price percentage: 1.03.
Adjusted total costs: A69, $103.00; V56, $92.70; X28, $123.60; W12, $61.80; S92, $41.20.

CHALLENGE PROBLEM 7-C Determining the unit price of merchandise inventory purchases

Minder, Inc. recently received a shipment of merchandise inventory. Minder maintains a perpetual inventory using unit prices including freight and cash discounts. The following information is from the purchase invoice for the shipment.

Stock No.	Quantity	Unit Price	Total Cost
A69	50	$2.00	$100.00
V56	15	6.00	90.00
X28	30	4.00	120.00
W12	20	3.00	60.00
S92	5	8.00	40.00
Subtotal			$410.00
Freight			20.50
Cash Discount			(8.20)
Total Cost			$422.30

INSTRUCTIONS:

1. Divide the total cost by the subtotal. Round the percentage to the nearest 0.1%.
2. Calculate the adjusted unit price of each item by multiplying the percentage calculated in Instruction 1 by the unit price of the item.
3. Calculate the adjusted total cost for each item by multiplying the quantity by the adjusted unit price.

Inventory Planning and Valuation

Merchandise inventory is usually the largest current asset of a merchandising business. Therefore, selecting an inventory system that provides for accurate and up-to-date inventory valuations is an important element in the operation of a merchandising business. Inventory planning and valuation may be accomplished by using either a manual or an automated inventory system. OfficeMart, Inc., the business described in Chapter 7, uses manual procedures for inventory planning and valuation. Bixler, Inc., the business described in Integrating Automated Accounting Topic 4, uses automated accounting software. This automated accounting software has an automated inventory system for inventory planning and valuation.

The Automated Accounting Problem contains instructions for using automated accounting software to complete an inventory problem.

INVENTORY TRANSACTIONS

Bixler uses a one-month fiscal period. All inventory transactions are entered daily on an inventory transactions input form. Inventory

TEACHING STRATEGIES: ACCOUNTING PEDAGOGY

This textbook presents input forms for students to complete before going to the computer to key data. This procedure encourages student organization and time management skills.

LESSON PLAN A4

Materials

- Student pages 215–221
- Input forms for Automating Application Problem 4 are provided in the working papers that accompany this textbook. If additional input forms are needed, blackline masters are provided in the Blackline Masters Section of the Teacher's Resource Guide.
- Complete solutions for automated problems are provided in the Teacher's Resource Guide.
- Software: *Automated Accounting 6.0* or higher; CENTURY 21 ACCOUNTING Template, Advanced Course.

Objective

Accomplish inventory planning and valuation using an automated accounting system.

FOCUS

In Chapter 7, manual procedures for inventory planning and valuation were described. Emphasize that automated accounting software may be used to speed the inventory transactions processing and reports preparation procedures. Explain that using automated accounting software, however, does not change accounting concepts. Only the methods change.

TEACH

Cover student pages 215–220 "Inventory Transactions," "Inventory Exceptions," "Inventory Valuation," and "Yearly Sales." Point out that inventory transactions are entered daily on an inventory transactions input form but data are keyed and processed weekly. Inventory transactions include items sold, ordered, and received. Explain the importance of keeping accurate inventory records and preparing timely inventory exceptions reports. Review the three inventory costing methods—average cost, LIFO, FIFO—described in Chapter 7.

transactions include items sold, ordered, and received. Inventory transaction data are keyed and processed weekly. Bixler's completed inventory transactions input form for the week ended January 31 is shown in Illustration T4-1.

ILLUSTRATION T4-1

Inventory transactions input form

RUN DATE *01/31/--* (MM DD YY)

INVENTORY TRANSACTIONS
Input Form

	DATE MM/DD	STOCK NUMBER	QUANTITY SOLD	SELLING PRICE	QUANTITY ORDERED	QUANTITY RECEIVED	COST PRICE	
1	01/25	142	2	119.50				1
2	/25	148			4			2
3	/25	315				2	163.00	3
4	/25	426			2			4
5	/26	146				2	402.00	5
6	/26	316	2	239.00				6
7	/26	316			4			7
8	/27	148				4	550.00	8
9	/27	422	1	299.50				9
10	/28	148	3	825.00				10
11	/28	316				4	205.00	11
12	/29	315	2	239.00				12
13	/29	426				2	163.00	13
14	/30	144	3	299.00				14
15	/30	146	3	599.50				15
25	/							25
		TOTALS	16		10	14		

The run date, *01/31/--*, is entered in the space provided at the top of the form. Lines 1–4 show quantity sold, ordered, and received on January 25. Lines 5–15 show the inventory transactions completed during the remainder of the week ended January 31.

At the end of the week, the inventory transactions data are processed using automated accounting software. File is selected from the menu bar. Inventory is then selected from the File menu to load the inventory module. File is again selected from the menu bar, and the Open Data File command is chosen to retrieve the inventory data base from the template disk.

The Transactions option is selected from the menu bar. The Inventory Transactions command is then selected to display the data entry window for entering inventory transaction data. Line 1 of Illustration T4-1 is shown entered in the Inventory Transactions data entry window shown in Illustration T4-2.

After all lines on the input form have been keyed, the Reports option is selected from the menu bar, and Inventory Transactions

FYI

Keep diskettes away from extreme hot or cold temperatures. Do not leave diskettes in a car during very hot or cold weather.

TEACHING STRATEGIES: DIFFERENT LEARNING ABILITIES

Visually Impaired Students. You should orient visually impaired students with the computer atw their individual work stations. This will make them more comfortable and confident in their surroundings.

ILLUSTRATION T4-2 Inventory transactions data entry window

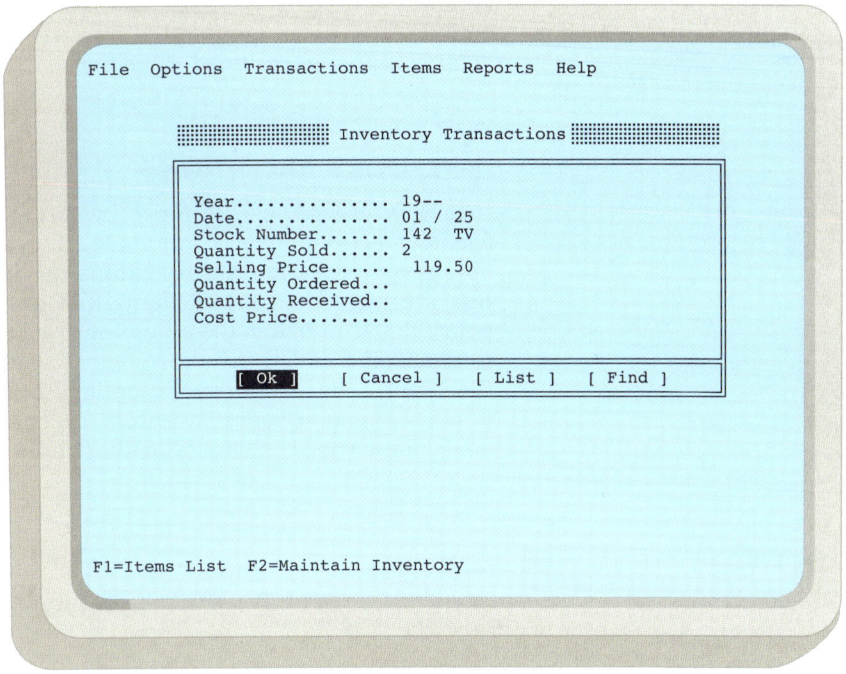

is then selected from the Reports menu. Bixler's inventory transactions report for the week ended January 31 is shown in Illustration T4-3.

ILLUSTRATION T4-3 Inventory transactions report

Bixler, Inc.
Inventory Transactions
01/31/--

Date	Stock No.	Description	Quantity Sold	Selling Price	Quan. Ord.	Quan. Recd.	Cost Price
01/25	142	TV	2	119.50			
01/25	148	TV			4		
01/25	315	VCR				2	163.00
01/25	426	Stereo			2		
01/26	146	TV				2	402.00
01/26	316	VCR	2	239.00			
01/26	316	VCR			4		
01/27	148	TV				4	550.00
01/27	422	Stereo	1	299.50			
01/28	148	TV	3	825.00			
01/28	316	VCR				4	205.00
01/29	315	VCR	2	239.00			
01/29	426	Stereo				2	163.00
01/30	144	TV	3	299.00			
01/30	146	TV	3	599.50			
		Totals	16		10	14	

APPLY

Guided Practice

Guide students through the preparation of an inventory transactions input form. Write a variety of inventory transactions on the chalkboard or overhead projector. Working as a group, have the students determine the amounts to be recorded in each column. When all students agree on the correct entry, direct the students to record the amounts on their inventory transactions input forms. When all transactions are correctly recorded, the input forms may be totaled and checked for accuracy.

Independent Practice

Assign Automating Application Problem 4.

HEALTH AND SAFETY

To prevent the computer from overheating, avoid blocking air vents. A Safety and Health page is given in the Teacher's Resource Guide. This page may be duplicated and given to students.

ASSESS

Assess student understanding by checking solutions to Automating Application Problem 4.

Reteach

Make a transparency of an inventory transactions input form from the accounting forms masters provided in the Blackline Masters Section of the Teacher's Resource Guide. Refer students back to Automating Application Problem 4. Use the transparency to demonstrate how the transactions are recorded.

Extend

In small groups, have the students discuss some of the problems that may occur if too little or too much inventory is kept on hand.

CLOSURE

As a whole-class activity, close the lesson by having students take turns describing the purpose of the various inventory reports.

The inventory transactions report is checked for accuracy by comparing the report totals with the totals on the inventory transactions input form. As the totals are the same, the inventory transactions report is assumed to be correct.

INVENTORY EXCEPTIONS

Inventory exceptions are those inventory items that require management action. Bixler's automated inventory system provides an option for preparing an exceptions report. This report lists items that are out of stock and items that are at or below the reorder point. Bixler prepares the exceptions report at the end of each week to determine which inventory items are to be ordered. To process the report, the Inventory Exceptions option is selected from the Reports menu. Bixler's inventory exceptions report for the week ended January 31 is shown in Illustration T4-4.

ILLUSTRATION T4-4 Inventory exceptions report

Bixler, Inc.
Inventory Exceptions
01/31/--

Stock No.	Description	Unit Meas.	On Hand	On Order	Reorder Point	Exceptional Condition
142	TV	Ea	2		3	At/below reorder point
144	TV	Ea	0		3	Out of stock
148	TV	Ea	1		2	At/below reorder point
422	Stereo	Ea	3		4	At/below reorder point

INVENTORY VALUATION

FYI

Dollar signs and cent signs are not keyed when using *Automated Accounting 6.0* software. When the cents are zero (.00), key only the dollar amount. The software automatically assigns the .00.

Various methods are used to determine the cost of merchandise inventory. Bixler's automated inventory system provides options for determining inventory cost using the average cost, LIFO, or FIFO costing methods. These reports are processed by selecting Inventory Valuation from the Report menu.

Bixler prepares three inventory valuation reports by making selections from the Reports menu as follows. (1) Average cost shown in Illustration T4-5. (2) Last-In-First-Out (LIFO) shown in Illustration T4-6. (3) First-In-First-Out (FIFO) shown in Illustration T4-7 on page 220.

YEARLY SALES

Bixler's automated inventory system provides an option for preparing a yearly sales report. This report accumulates total sales

TEACHING STRATEGIES: COOPERATIVE LEARNING

Using automated accounting software to complete accounting problems is an ideal cooperative learning experience. Students working in groups can collaborate on completing input forms and keying data.

ILLUSTRATION T4-5 Inventory valuation (average cost)

Bixler, Inc.
Inventory Valuation (Average Cost)
01/31/--

Stock No.	Description	On Hand	Cost	Value At Cost	Retail Price	Value At Retail
142	TV	2	82.00	164.00	119.50	239.00
146	TV	3	400.67	1202.01	599.50	1798.50
148	TV	1	550.00	550.00	825.00	825.00
315	VCR	4	160.00	640.00	239.00	956.00
316	VCR	6	204.33	1225.98	239.00	1434.00
422	Stereo	3	250.00	750.00	299.50	898.50
424	Stereo	4	300.00	1200.00	449.50	1798.00
426	Stereo	5	305.20	1526.00	599.50	2997.50
	Total Inventory Value			7257.99		10946.50

ILLUSTRATION T4-6 Inventory valuation (LIFO)

Bixler, Inc.
Inventory Valuation (Last-in-First-Out)
01/31/--

Stock No.	Description	On Hand	Cost	Value At Cost	Retail Price	Value At Retail
142	TV	2	82.00	164.00	119.50	239.00
146	TV	3	400.00	1200.00	599.50	1798.50
148	TV	1	550.00	550.00	825.00	825.00
315	VCR	4	160.00	640.00	239.00	956.00
316	VCR	2	203.00	406.00	239.00	478.00
316	VCR	4	205.00	820.00	239.00	956.00
422	Stereo	3	250.00	750.00	299.50	898.50
424	Stereo	4	300.00	1200.00	449.50	1798.00
426	Stereo	3	400.00	1200.00	599.50	1798.50
426	Stereo	2	163.00	326.00	599.50	1199.00
	Total Inventory Value			7256.00		10946.50

SOFTWARE FOCUS

The Automated Accounting Problem in this Integrating Automated Accounting topic has not been completed manually. Students should complete the input forms before going to the computer. The problem instructions in *Automated Accounting 6.0* will lead students through automating the problem.

throughout the year. Therefore, Bixler's yearly sales report prepared at the end of January would contain total sales for the month of January. A yearly sales report prepared at the end of February would contain total sales for the months of January and February.

The Yearly Sales option is selected from the Reports menu to prepare a yearly sales report. The report may be prepared in stock number sequence or yearly sales sequence. Bixler's yearly sales

ILLUSTRATION T4-7 Inventory valuation (FIFO)

Bixler, Inc.
Inventory Valuation (First-in-First-Out)
01/31/--

Stock No.	Description	On Hand	Cost	Value At Cost	Retail Price	Value At Retail
142	TV	2	82.00	164.00	119.50	239.00
146	TV	1	400.00	400.00	599.50	599.50
146	TV	2	402.00	804.00	599.50	1199.00
148	TV	1	550.00	550.00	825.00	825.00
315	VCR	2	160.00	320.00	239.00	478.00
315	VCR	2	163.00	326.00	239.00	478.00
316	VCR	2	203.00	406.00	239.00	478.00
316	VCR	4	205.00	820.00	239.00	956.00
422	Stereo	3	250.00	750.00	299.50	898.50
424	Stereo	4	300.00	1200.00	449.50	1798.00
426	Stereo	3	400.00	1200.00	599.50	1798.50
426	Stereo	2	163.00	326.00	599.50	1199.00
	Total Inventory Value			7266.00		10946.50

TEACHING STRATEGIES: TEACHING TIP

It is important for students to save a template file under another name before they begin work. This will keep the template file intact for future use.

report prepared in stock number sequence is shown in Illustration T4-8.

ILLUSTRATION T4-8 Yearly sales report

Bixler, Inc.
Yearly Sales
01/31/--

Stock No.	Description	Unit Meas.	Yearly Quantity	Yearly Amount
142	TV	Ea	6	717.00
144	TV	Ea	6	1794.00
146	TV	Ea	5	2997.50
148	TV	Ea	3	2475.00
315	VCR	Ea	4	956.00
316	VCR	Ea	5	1195.00
422	Stereo	Ea	3	898.50
424	Stereo	Ea	2	899.00
426	Stereo	Ea	3	1798.50
			37	13730.50

AUTOMATED ACCOUNTING PROBLEM

AUTOMATING APPLICATION PROBLEM 4 Inventory planning and valuation

Cycle Mart, Inc. uses an automated inventory system similar to the one described for Bixler, Inc.

INSTRUCTIONS:

1. Enter the inventory transactions for the week ended June 30 on an inventory transactions input form. Use June 30 of the current year as the run date.

CHECK FIGURES

Automating Application Problem 4: Inventory Transactions totals 16; 18; 13; Inventory Exceptions Stock No. 110; Inventory Valuation (Average Cost) Total Value At Cost 2,602.29; Inventory Valuation (LIFO) Total Value At Cost 2,600.00; Inventory Valuation (FIFO) Total Value At Cost 2,604.50; Total Yearly Sales 28,555.50

June 28. Ordered 3 bicycles, Stock Number 110.
28. Sold 4 bicycles, Stock Number 115; selling price $225.00.
28. Sold 2 bicycles, Stock Number 110; selling price $159.50.
28. Ordered 6 bicycles, Stock Number 115.
29. Sold 5 bicycles, Stock Number 120; selling price $299.50.
29. Received 3 bicycles, Stock Number 110; cost, $123.00.
29. Sold 3 bicycles, Stock Number 110; selling price $159.50.
29. Ordered 4 bicycles, Stock Number 120.
30. Received 6 bicycles, Stock Number 115; cost, $152.00.
30. Sold 2 bicycles, Stock Number 120; selling price $299.50.
30. Received 4 bicycles, Stock Number 120; cost, $205.00.
30. Ordered 5 bicycles, Stock Number 110.

2. Load the *Automated Accounting 6.0* software. Select File from the menu bar, and then select the Inventory command. Select data base DB-4 from the *CENTURY 21 ACCOUNTING Advanced Course* template. Read the Problem Instructions screen.
3. Key the data from the inventory transactions input form.
4. Display/print an inventory transactions report.
5. Display/print an inventory exceptions report.
6. Display/print inventory valuation reports for average cost, LIFO, and FIFO.
7. Display/print a yearly sales report in stock number sequence.

PART 4 OVERVIEW

STUDENT EDITION

STUDENT FEATURES

Professional Business Ethics

Is Salary Expense A Picnic? page 286

Careers In Accounting

Financial Securities Clerk, page 295

Spreadsheet Options

Copying A Relative Cell Reference, page 239

Multicultural Awareness

Native American Businesses, page 229

Global Perspective

International Introductions, page 255

Personal Visions In Business

Cynthia Reed, page 315

Audit Your Understanding

This student activity can be found on pages 228, 236, 240, 252, 261, 270, 284, 292, 300, 311, 314, 317

APPLIED SKILLS

Applied Communications, page 319
Applied Mathematics, pages 230, 231, 233, 234, 237, 238, 242, 243, 250, 251, 256–258, 260, 262–266, 268–270, 272–275, 282–284, 290, 292, 293, 297, 303, 309, 310, 312, 315, 320, 321

SOFTWARE APPLICATIONS

Automated Accounting 6.0 Problems 9-1, 9-6, 9-8, 9-C
Spreadsheet Template Problems 8-4, 9-6, 9-7, 9-8, 10-1

TEACHER'S EDITION

APPLIED SKILLS

Communications, page 319
Language Arts, pages 237, 269, 299, 311
Writing Across the Curriculum, pages 238, 260, 298, 309
Building Study Skills, pages 231, 287, 310
Word Processing, pages 239, 258, 297, 317

TEACHING STRATEGIES

Accounting Pedagogy, pages 224, 225, 246, 277, 280, 306
Different Learning Abilities, pages 234, 249, 298, 307
Different Learning Styles, pages 228, 234–236, 253, 259, 264, 266, 268
Cooperative Learning, pages 232, 268, 289, 314
Expanding Beyond the Classroom, pages 230, 290
Applying Visuals, pages 232, 266, 296, 317
Teaching Tip, pages 224, 226, 227, 229, 230, 233, 247, 250, 255, 258, 262, 267, 278, 281–283, 285, 291, 294, 299, 306, 308, 312, 313
Software Focus, pages 225, 246, 277, 293

ASSESSMENT

Assessment by Portfolio
MicroExam software for each chapter
Problem Test for each chapter
Unit Objective Test No. 4 (8–11)

SOFTWARE

Automated Accounting 6.0
MicroExam
Lotus (spreadsheet)
WordPerfect (word processing)
Ventura Publisher (desktop publishing software)

BIBLIOGRAPHY

AICPA. *Accounting Trends and Techniques,* 1991.
Cohen, E. *Designing Group Work.* New York: Teachers College Press, 1986.
Diamond, Michael A. *Financial Accounting.* Third Edition. Cincinnati: South-Western Publishing Co., 1993.
Fess, Philip E., and Carl S. Warren. *Accounting Principles.* Seventeenth Edition. Cincinnati: South-Western Publishing Co., 1993.
Gronlund, Norman E. *Stating Objectives for Classroom Instruction.* 3d ed. New York: Macmillan Publishing Co., Inc., 1985.
Lerner, Janet. *Learning Disabilities: Theories, Diagnosis, and Teaching Strategies.* Fifth Edition. Boston: Houghton Mifflin, 1988.
Sheth, Jagdish N., and Abdolreza Eshghi, eds. *Global Accounting Perspectives.* Cincinnati: South-Western Publishing Co., 1989.

Periodicals

CPA Digest, CPA Services, Inc., Brookfield, WI.
Journal of Accounting Education, Pergamon Press, Inc., Tarrytown, NY.
Transpacific, Malibu, CA. (Multicultural awareness)

Technology

AICPA. *It All Adds Up,* 1989. (Video)
Dun & Bradstreet Information Services. *Dun's Direct Access.* (On-line database of U.S. companies)

PART 4 OPENER

PART 4

General Accounting Adjustments

GENERAL GOALS

1. Know accounting terminology related to general accounting adjustments.
2. Understand accounting concepts and practices related to general accounting adjustments.
3. Demonstrate accounting procedures for general accounting adjustments.

OVERVIEW

Part 4 explores various general accounting adjustments. Adjustments sometimes involve more than just calculating amounts. Procedures for calculating some adjustments involve various aspects of accounting that must be explored before the actual adjustment figure is calculated.

Chapter 8 describes accounting for uncollectible accounts and the various methods of writing off accounts. These methods of writing off accounts lead directly to the adjusting entries for uncollectible accounts.

Chapter 9 explains plant assets and the methods for depreciating them. Depletion and property taxes are also covered in this chapter. A general description of the procedures for calculating depreciation using the MACRS method is also presented. The Internal Revenue Service requires that for most plant assets placed in service after 1986, the IRS' Modified Accelerated Cost Recovery System (MACRS) depreciation method be used for income tax computation purposes. This is a depreciation method with prescribed periods of useful life for various classes of assets. Most businesses use one of the generally accepted accounting methods for recording depreciation. The MACRS method is generally used only for the preparation of federal income tax returns. Therefore, generally accepted accounting practices for the preparation of financial statements are emphasized in this text. More detailed information describing MACRS depreciation method can be obtained from the Internal Revenue Service.

After Chapter 9, Integrating Automated Accounting Topic 5 is presented to integrate computer application of the manual procedures that have been introduced in Chapter 9. For those teachers who wish to fully integrate the program, *Automated Accounting 6.0* may be used to actually automate selected problems in the text.

Chapter 10 introduces accounting for notes payable, prepaid expenses, and accrued expenses. The procedures for calculating adjusting entries and recording reversing entries are covered for these topics. Chapter 11 then looks at the same aspects of notes receivable, unearned revenue, and accrued revenue.

CHAPTER 8 OVERVIEW

Chapter 8 covers the important topic of accounting for uncollectible accounts. All businesses must understand the procedures for writing off uncollectible accounts.

The direct write-off method of determining uncollectible accounts expense is explained. The entry to write off the account and the entry to collect a written-off account are illustrated.

GUIDE TO ACHIEVING LEARNING OBJECTIVES

	TEACH	APPLY	EXTEND/ENRICH					
Enabling Performance Tasks	**Lesson Plans**	**Application Problems**	**Mastery Problems**	**Challenge Problems**	**Cases for Critical Thinking**	**Recycling Problems**	**Reinforcement Activity**	
a. Define accounting terms related to uncollectible accounts.	8-1, 8-2, 8-3							
b. Identify accounting concepts and practices related to uncollectible accounts.	8-1, 8-2, 8-3				Cases 1, 2			
c. Calculate estimated uncollectible accounts expense.	8-2	8-2, 8-3, 8-4, 8-5	8-M	8-C		8-R	RA2	
d. Analyze and journalize entries related to uncollectible accounts.	8-1, 8-2	8-1, 8-2, 8-3, 8-4, 8-5, 8-6, 8-7	8-M	8-C		8-R	RA2	
e. Calculate and analyze accounts receivable turnover ratios.	8-3	8-8					RA2	

ENRICHMENT

SPECIAL FEATURES
Spreadsheet Options, page 239
Multicultural Awareness, page 229

TECHNOLOGY CONNECTION
Spreadsheet Template Problem 8-4

NEW, REVIEW, AND EXTENSION

ACTIVITIES/CONCEPTS/TRANSACTIONS	NEW	REVIEW/ EXTENSION
Uncollectible accounts		✓
Writing off an uncollectible account		✓
Direct write-off method	✓	
Collecting a written-off account		✓
Allowance method of recording uncollectible accounts expense		✓
Estimating uncollectible accounts expense using a percentage of net sales		✓
Estimating uncollectible accounts expense using a percentage of total sales on account		✓
Estimating uncollectible accounts expense using a percentage of net sales		✓
Estimating the balance of Allowance for Uncollectible Accounts using a percentage of accounts receivable		✓
Estimating the balance of Allowance for Uncollectible Accounts by aging accounts receivable		✓
Accounts receivable turnover ratio	✓	
Average number of days for payment	✓	

The allowance method of determining uncollectible accounts expense is also covered in detail. Percentage of sales method and percentage of accounts receivable method, including aging accounts receivable, are the focus of the discussions.

The accounts receivable turnover ratio is described, calculated, and analyzed.

	INFORMAL ASSESSMENT		FORMAL ASSESSMENT			
	Study Guide	**Audit Your Understanding**	**Chapter MicroExam**	**Chapter Problem Test**	**Unit Objective Test**	**Portfolio**
	Unit A	✓	✓		✓	
	Unit C	✓	✓		✓	
				✓		✓
	Unit B			✓		✓
				✓		✓

TEACHING MATERIALS

Teacher's Wraparound Edition of Text
Teacher's Resource Guide
Teacher's Edition of Working Papers
MicroExam

APPLIED MATHEMATICS

APPLIED MATH/ACCOUNTING SKILL	APPLICATION
Estimating uncollectible accounts expense using a percentage of net sales	Prob. 8-2
Estimating uncollectible accounts expense using a percentage of total sales on account	Prob. 8-3
Estimating the balance of Allowance for Uncollectible Accounts by aging accounts receivable	Prob. 8-4
Estimating the balance of Allowance for Uncollectible Accounts by using a percentage of the accounts receivable account balance	Prob. 8-5
Calculating the accounts receivable turnover ratio	Prob. 8-8

TEACHING STRATEGIES: Accounting Pedagogy

A chart of accounts for the business that is used to illustrate each part of this textbook is provided at the beginning of each part. Charts of accounts are extremely important to companies because they drive the accounting system. Employees usually cannot even receive reimbursement for expenses without knowing which account the expense should be charged to.

Pedagogically, the chart of accounts provides the following information: (1) Classification for each account—needed to determine how a transaction is analyzed. (2) Permanent accounts (balance sheet accounts) and temporary accounts (income statement accounts)—assist in analyzing transactions and recording closing entries. (3) Account number for every general ledger account—critical information in automated accounting, since transactions are entered by account number rather than account title.

CHART OF ACCOUNTS

This chart of accounts is for a merchandising business organized as a corporation. Appliance Center's chart of accounts is similar to that of OfficeMart's described in Part 3. The Liabilities section is divided into current and long-term liabilities. Appliance Center does not use the voucher system for controlling cash payments.

The Operating Expenses section is divided into administrative, selling, and warehouse expenses. Administrative expenses are expenses of the business that do not clearly relate to the sales effort, such as salaries and supplies of the office staff. Warehouse expenses are expenses of the business that can be directly attributed to the warehousing of merchandise inventory.

Appliance Center's chart of accounts distinguishes between revenues and expenses that occur that are not the result of everyday business transactions. The classifications Other Revenue and Other Expenses are used to account for those transactions that are not directly related to the selling of merchandise inventory.

Appliance Center, Inc.

CHART OF ACCOUNTS

Balance Sheet Accounts

(1000) ASSETS

1100 Current Assets

1105 Cash
1110 Petty Cash
1115 Notes Receivable
1120 Interest Receivable
1125 Accounts Receivable
1130 Allowance for Uncollectible Accounts
1135 Merchandise Inventory
1140 Supplies—Administrative
1145 Supplies—Sales
1150 Supplies—Warehouse
1155 Prepaid Insurance
1160 Prepaid Interest

1200 Plant Assets

1205 Land
1215 Building
1220 Accumulated Depreciation—Building
1225 Office Equipment
1230 Accumulated Depreciation—Office Equipment
1235 Store Equipment
1240 Accumulated Depreciation—Store Equipment
1245 Warehouse Equipment
1250 Accumulated Depreciation—Warehouse Equipment

(2000) LIABILITIES

2100 Current Liabilities

2105 Notes Payable
2110 Interest Payable
2115 Accounts Payable
2120 Employee Income Tax Payable
2125 Federal Income Tax Payable
2130 FICA Tax Payable
2135 Salaries Payable
2140 Sales Tax Payable
2145 Unearned Rent
2150 Unemployment Tax Payable—Federal
2155 Unemployment Tax Payable—State

2200 Long-Term Liability

2205 Mortgage Payable

(3000) STOCKHOLDERS' EQUITY

3105 Capital Stock
3110 Retained Earnings
3115 Income Summary

Income Statement Accounts

(4000) OPERATING REVENUE

4105 Sales
4110 Sales Discount
4115 Sales Returns and Allowances

(5000) COST OF MERCHANDISE

5105 Purchases
5110 Purchases Discount
5115 Purchases Returns and Allowances

(6000) OPERATING EXPENSES

6100 Administrative Expenses

6105 Depreciation Expense—Building
6110 Depreciation Expense—Office Equipment
6115 Insurance Expense
6120 Miscellaneous Expense—Administrative
6125 Payroll Taxes Expense
6130 Property Tax Expense
6135 Salary Expense—Administrative
6140 Supplies Expense—Administrative
6145 Uncollectible Accounts Expense

6200 Selling Expenses

6205 Advertising Expense
6210 Credit Card Fee Expense
6215 Depreciation Expense—Store Equipment
6220 Miscellaneous Expense—Sales
6225 Salary Expense—Sales
6230 Supplies Expense—Sales

6300 Warehouse Expenses

6305 Depreciation Expense—Warehouse Equipment
6310 Miscellaneous Expense—Warehouse
6315 Salary Expense—Warehouse
6320 Supplies Expense—Warehouse

(7000) OTHER REVENUE

7105 Gain on Plant Assets
7110 Interest Income
7115 Rent Income

(8000) OTHER EXPENSES

8105 Interest Expense
8110 Loss on Plant Assets

(9000) INCOME TAX

9105 Federal Income Tax Expense

The chart of accounts for Appliance Center, Inc. is illustrated above for ready reference as you study Part 4 of this textbook.

TEACHING STRATEGIES: Teaching Tip

Emphasize that students should refer to this chart of accounts throughout their study of Part 4. It will help them determine classification of accounts, which accounts are temporary and permanent accounts, and what account numbers to use for automated accounting. It will also be a useful reference for performing file maintenance activities.

8

Accounting for Uncollectible Accounts

TEACHING STRATEGIES: ACCOUNTING PEDAGOGY

This textbook covers analysis of accounting for uncollectible accounts including book value of accounts receivable and turnover ratio. This information is covered in this chapter where it is appropriate and not in isolation. This is a critical thinking skill that is important for advanced accounting students.

ENABLING PERFORMANCE TASKS

After studying Chapter 8, you will be able to:

a Define accounting terms related to uncollectible accounts.

b Identify accounting concepts and practices related to uncollectible accounts.

c Calculate estimated uncollectible accounts expense.

d Analyze and journalize entries related to uncollectible accounts.

e Calculate and analyze accounts receivable turnover ratios.

TERMS PREVIEW

uncollectible accounts • writing off an account • direct write-off method of recording losses from uncollectible accounts • allowance method of recording losses from uncollectible accounts • aging accounts receivable • accounts receivable turnover ratio • book value of accounts receivable

SOFTWARE FOCUS

Software may be used for independent practice or enrichment/extension as the instructor deems appropriate. For this chapter, the Spreadsheet Template may be used with Problem 8-4.

In today's economy, many business transactions are completed on account rather than for cash. Businesses offer credit terms to attract new customers, increase sales to current customers, and encourage customer loyalty. Before a business sells merchandise on account, the business should investigate the customer's credit rating to ensure the customer will pay promptly.

Regardless of the care taken in granting credit, some customers will not pay when payment is due. Accounts receivable that cannot be collected are called **uncollectible accounts.** Uncollectible accounts are sometimes referred to as bad debts.

FYI

A credit rating is an evaluation of an individual's willingness and ability to pay debts. Credit ratings are usually kept by the local credit bureau.

When a sale on account is made to a customer, the amount is recorded in a general ledger account titled Accounts Receivable. The amount remains recorded in this asset account until paid or until specifically known to be uncollectible.

When a customer account is known to be uncollectible, the account is no longer an asset. An uncollectible account should be canceled and removed from the assets of the business. Canceling the balance of a customer account because the customer does not pay is called **writing off an account**.

DIRECT WRITE-OFF METHOD OF RECORDING UNCOLLECTIBLE ACCOUNTS EXPENSE

An amount owed by a specific customer is part of the accounts receivable account balance until paid or until written off as uncollectible. An uncollectible account is closed by transferring the balance to a general ledger account titled Uncollectible Accounts Expense.

Northwest Cleaners dry cleans clothing for its customers. The business has few sales on account. The business has a small number of accounts receivable and very few of these accounts become uncollectible. Therefore, Northwest Cleaners records uncollectible accounts expense only when a specific account is actually known to be uncollectible. Recording uncollectible accounts expense only when an amount is actually known to be uncollectible is called the **direct write-off method of recording losses from uncollectible accounts.**

Writing Off an Uncollectible Account—Direct Write-Off Method

On November 15, Northwest Cleaners learned that James Nordquist is unable to pay his account. Northwest Cleaners decides that Mr. Nordquist's account is uncollectible.

November 15, 19--. Wrote off James Nordquist's past-due account as uncollectible, $50.00. Memorandum No. 21.

LESSON PLAN 8-1

Materials

- Student pages 226–229
- Blackline Master for General Journal (TRG)
- Blackline Master for Cash Receipts Journal (TRG)

Objectives (Enabling Performance Tasks)

a. Define accounting terms related to uncollectible accounts.

b. Identify accounting concepts and practices related to uncollectible accounts.

d. Analyze and journalize entries related to uncollectible accounts.

FOCUS

- Explain that no matter how carefully a business checks the credit of customers, some accounts receivable will not be collected. Two methods of recording uncollectible accounts expense are presented in Chapter 8. In this lesson, the direct write-off method will be explained.
- Introduce vocabulary: uncollectible accounts, writing off an account, direct write-off method of recording losses from uncollectible accounts.

TEACHING STRATEGIES: TEACHING TIP

Explain that uncollectible accounts are the same as bad debts. If a business cannot collect from customers, that amount becomes an expense to the business.

GENERAL LEDGER
Uncollectible Accounts Expense

Write off	50.00		

Accounts Receivable

Bal.	54,789.05	Write off	50.00
(New Bal.	*54,739.05)*		

ACCOUNTS RECEIVABLE LEDGER
James Nordquist

Bal.	50.00	Write off	50.00
(New Bal. zero)			

Uncollectible Accounts Expense is increased by a $50.00 debit. Accounts Receivable is decreased by a $50.00 credit. In the accounts receivable ledger, James Nordquist's account is decreased by a $50.00 credit.

The journal entry to record this transaction is shown in Illustration 8-1.

After this entry is journalized and posted, the balance of Accounts Receivable no longer includes the $50.00 as part of the business' assets. Also, James Nordquist's account has a zero balance and is written off.

ILLUSTRATION 8-1 Journal entry to write off an uncollectible account—direct write-off method

GENERAL JOURNAL — PAGE 11

	DATE		ACCOUNT TITLE	DOC. NO.	POST. REF.	DEBIT	CREDIT	
1	19-- Nov.	15	Uncollectible Accounts Expense	M21		50 00		1
2			Accounts Rec./James Nordquist		/		50 00	2

FYI

Uncollectible accounts are sometimes referred to as bad debts.

Collecting a Written-Off Account—Direct Write-Off Method

Sometimes a customer's written-off account is later collected. When the account is written off, the balance is recorded as an expense. When the account is later collected, the amount is recorded as other revenue.

January 21, 19--. Received cash in full payment of James Nordquist's account, previously written off as uncollectible, $50.00. Memorandum No. 54 and Receipt No. 49.

Northwest Cleaners needs a complete record of accounts receivable. Therefore, two journal entries are recorded for the collection of a written-off account receivable. (1) A general journal entry to reopen the customer account. (2) A cash receipts journal entry to record the cash received on account.

The analysis of the entry to reopen a customer account is shown in the T accounts.

GENERAL LEDGER
Accounts Receivable

Bal.	54,789.05	Write off	50.00
Reopen	50.00		

Collection of Uncollectible Accounts

		Reopen	50.00

ACCOUNTS RECEIVABLE LEDGER
James Nordquist

Bal.	50.00	Write off	50.00
Reopen	50.00		
(New Bal.	*50.00)*		

Accounts Receivable is increased by a $50.00 debit. Collection of Uncollectible Accounts is increased by a $50.00 credit. In the accounts receivable ledger, James Nordquist's account is increased by a $50.00 debit and is reopened.

The account Collection of Uncollectible Accounts is used for recording collection of previously written-off accounts. The account is closed to Income Summary at the end of a fiscal period and is reported on an income statement as part of Other Revenue.

TEACH

Cover student pages 226–229 "Direct Write-Off Method of Recording Uncollectible Accounts Expense." Explain that uncollectible accounts are the same as bad debts. If a business cannot collect from customers, that amount becomes an expense to the business. Describe how to analyze and journalize writing off an uncollectible account using the direct write-off method. Emphasize that when this method is used an uncollectible account expense is recorded only when a specific account is actually known to be uncollectible. Discuss how to analyze and journalize collecting a written-off account when the direct write-off method has been used. Explain the need for the two journal entries.

APPLY

Draw T accounts on the chalkboard to analyze writing off an uncollectible account using the direct write-off method. Label the balance and transaction as shown in the textbook. Leave the accounts on the board as collecting a written-off account using the direct write-off method is presented. Add additional T accounts as needed. Label each entry as it is analyzed. When all of the transactions are analyzed, students should be able to see a complete picture of the activity that occurred in the accounts.

Guided Practice

Guide students through the T account analysis of the transactions in Problem 8-1. Have students draw T accounts on a sheet of paper and analyze the first transaction. All students should agree with the analysis before proceeding to the next transaction. Repeat the process until all transactions have been analyzed. The balance of Problem 8-1 can be assigned as Independent Practice.

Independent Practice

Assign Terms 1–3, Questions 1–5, and Problem 8-1.

TEACHING STRATEGIES: TEACHING TIP

Explain the need for two journal entries to record the collection of a written-off account receivable. (1) A general journal entry to reopen the customer account. (2) A cash receipts journal entry to record the cash received on account.

The journal entry to reopen Mr. Nordquist's account is shown in Illustration 8-2.

ILLUSTRATION 8-2

Journal entry to reopen customer account previously written off as uncollectible

GENERAL JOURNAL PAGE 1

	DATE		ACCOUNT TITLE	DOC. NO.	POST. REF.	DEBIT	CREDIT	
18		21	Accounts Receivable/James Nordquist	M54	/	50 00		18
19			Collection of Uncoll. Accounts				50 00	19
20								20
21								21
22								22

The analysis of the entry for cash received on account from Mr. Nordquist is shown in the T accounts.

GENERAL LEDGER

Cash

Debit		Credit	
Received	50.00		

Accounts Receivable

Debit		Credit	
Bal.	54,789.05	Write off	50.00
Reopen	50.00	Received	50.00

ACCOUNTS RECEIVABLE LEDGER

James Nordquist

Debit		Credit	
Bal.	50.00	Write off	50.00
Reopen	50.00	Received	50.00
(New Bal. zero)			

Cash is increased by a $50.00 debit. Accounts Receivable is decreased by a $50.00 credit. In the accounts receivable ledger, the customer account is decreased by a $50.00 credit.

The journal entry to record cash received on account is shown in Illustration 8-3.

After both these entries are journalized and posted, James Nordquist's account shows a complete history.

1. A $50.00 debit balance resulting from a sale on account.
2. A $50.00 credit when the account was written off as uncollectible.
3. A $50.00 debit when the account was reopened
4. A $50.00 credit when cash was received on account.

Audit Your Understanding

1. What is meant by writing off an account?
2. What account is debited when an uncollectible account is written off using the direct write-off method?
3. What two general journal entries are recorded for the collection of a written-off account receivable?
4. What general ledger account is credited when an uncollectible account is reopened using the direct write-off method when payment is received?

ASSESS

Assess student understanding by checking the solutions to the Independent Practice activities.

Reteach

Make transparencies of the general journal and cash receipts journal from the accounting forms masters provided in the Blackline Masters Section of the Teacher's Resource Guide. Refer students to Recycling Problem 8-R. (Note: The instructions state to use the allowance method. However, the transactions can be analyzed using the direct write-off method.) Ask students to use T accounts to analyze the transactions using the direct write-off method. Use the transparencies to demonstrate how the transactions are journalized.

Enrich

Assign students to read the MULTICULTURAL AWARENESS feature on page 229. Discuss with them how an understanding and appreciation of history and other cultures contributes to understanding civilization today.

CLOSURE

Use Audit Your Understanding questions.

AUDIT YOUR UNDERSTANDING

The AUDIT YOUR UNDERSTANDING feature appears at the end of each section of the chapter. Explain to your students that the word *audit* means to check or verify. AUDIT YOUR UNDERSTANDING may be used to check student comprehension of the section just studied. The answers are provided in Appendix D in the back of the textbook.

1. Canceling the balance of a customer account because the customer does not pay.
2. Uncollectible Accounts Expense.
3. (1) A general journal entry to reopen the customer account. (2) A cash receipts journal entry to record the cash received on account.
4. Collection of Uncollectible Accounts.

TEACHING STRATEGIES: DIFFERENT LEARNING STYLES

Auditory Learner. To reinforce the learning of journal entries, the auditory learner should verbally repeat the analysis of the transaction. The student should also verbally list the steps involved in making the entry.

ILLUSTRATION 8-3 Journal entry to record cash received for an account previously written off as uncollectible

CASH RECEIPTS JOURNAL — PAGE 2

	DATE	ACCOUNT TITLE	DOC. NO.	POST. REF.	1 GENERAL DEBIT	2 GENERAL CREDIT	3 ACCOUNTS RECEIVABLE CREDIT	4 SALES CREDIT	5 SALES TAX PAYABLE DEBIT	6 SALES TAX PAYABLE CREDIT	7 SALES DISCOUNT DEBIT	8 CASH DEBIT	
12	21	James Nordquist	R49				50 00					50 00	12
13													13
14													14
15													15

ALLOWANCE METHOD OF RECORDING UNCOLLECTIBLE ACCOUNTS EXPENSE

Some businesses use the direct write-off method and record uncollectible accounts expense only when a specific customer account is determined to be uncollectible. However, when the direct write-off method is used, the expense may be recorded in a fiscal period different from the fiscal period of the sale. Uncollectible accounts expense should be recorded in the same fiscal period in which the sales revenue is received. *(CONCEPT: Matching Expenses with Revenue)*

At the time sales on account are made, a business has no way of knowing for sure which customer will not pay an amount due. Therefore, an estimate is made based on past history of uncollectible accounts expense for a business. Crediting the estimated value of uncollectible accounts to a contra account is called the **allowance method of recording losses from uncollectible accounts.** Two methods are commonly used to estimate uncollectible accounts expense. (1) Percentage of sales method. (2) Percentage of accounts receivable method.

Percentage of Sales Method

The *percentage of sales method* assumes that a percentage of each sales dollar will become an uncollectible account. Therefore, emphasis is placed on estimating a percentage of sales that will not be collected. This estimated amount is charged to Uncollectible Accounts Expense. Two variations of this method are used. (1) Estimating uncollectible accounts expense by using a percentage of net sales. (2) Estimating uncollectible accounts expense by using a percentage of total sales on account.

Estimating Uncollectible Accounts Expense by Using a Percentage of Net Sales. Past experience of Morgan, Inc. indicates that approximately 0.5% of net sales will prove to be uncollectible. On

MULTICULTURAL AWARENESS

Native American Businesses

The Census Bureau's survey of minority-owned business enterprises shows a pronounced increase in the number of minority business enterprises. From 1982 to 1987, minority-owned businesses increased from 742,000 to 1,214,000.

Census information also shows that among all minorities, Native Americans had a large growth rate in the number of businesses owned. The number of businesses owned by Native Americans increased by 58%.

LESSON PLAN 8-2

Materials

- Student pages 229–236
- Blackline Master for General Journal (TRG)
- Blackline Master for Cash Receipts Journal (TRG)
- Software: Spreadsheet Template

Objectives (Enabling Performance Tasks)

a. Define accounting terms related to uncollectible accounts.
b. Identify accounting concepts and practices related to uncollectible accounts.
c. Calculate estimated uncollectible accounts expense.
d. Analyze and journalize entries related to uncollectible accounts.

MULTICULTURAL AWARENESS

The MULTICULTURAL AWARENESS feature is intended to expose students to the concept that our society is composed of people from many different cultural backgrounds. These features show both past contributions of many cultures and benefits of a culturally diverse society. (1) Read the feature. (2) Discuss the specific information in the feature. (3) Clarify any terms or questions.

TEACHING STRATEGIES: TEACHING TIP

Review the definition of contra account: An account that reduces a related account on a financial statement.

FOCUS

- The direct write-off method of recording uncollectible accounts expense was presented earlier in this chapter. In this lesson, the allowance method will be described. The allowance method estimates the uncollectible accounts expense based on past history. Two common methods of estimating uncollectible accounts expense will be presented.
- Introduce vocabulary: allowance method of recording losses from uncollectible accounts, aging accounts receivable.

December 31, Morgan calculated its estimated uncollectible accounts expense as shown below.

Total Sales	−	Sales Discount	−	Sales Returns and Allowances	=	Net Sales
$114,897.55	−	$755.51	−	$856.29	=	$113,285.75

Net Sales	×	Percentage	=	Estimated Uncollectible Accounts Expense
$113,285.75	×	0.5%	=	$566.43

Morgan estimated that of the $113,285.75 net sales, $566.43 eventually will prove to be uncollectible. The adjusting entry made at the end of the fiscal period affects two accounts: Uncollectible Accounts Expense and Allowance for Uncollectible Accounts. Morgan does not yet know which customer accounts in the accounts receivable ledger will become uncollectible. Therefore, the amount cannot be recorded directly in accounts receivable.

Uncollectible Accounts Expense

Debit		Credit	
Adj.	566.43		

Allowance for Uncollectible Accounts

Debit		Credit	
		Bal.	25.87
		Adj.	566.43
		(New Bal.	*592.30)*

Uncollectible Accounts Expense is increased by a $566.43 debit. The contra asset account, Allowance for Uncollectible Accounts, is increased by a $566.43 credit.

Before the adjustment is made, Morgan's general ledger shows Allowance for Uncollectible Accounts with a $25.87 credit balance. This balance is what remains of estimates made in previous fiscal periods but not yet specifically identified by customer. The new balance of the allowance account is $592.30 (previous balance, $25.87, *plus* adjustment, $566.43).

At the end of a fiscal period, an adjustment for uncollectible accounts expense is planned on a work sheet. This adjustment for Morgan, Inc., is shown in the Adjustments columns of the partial work sheet in Illustration 8-4.

TEACHING STRATEGIES: TEACHING TIP

Adjustments often prove to be a challenge to accounting students. Therefore, additional drill and practice may be needed to produce mastery of this topic. The use of T accounts may help students understand the effect of the adjusting entry on the financial statement. A short drill at the beginning of each class period reviewing the topic of the previous day may also be helpful. For example, provide students with amounts similar to those found in Problem 8-2. Changing the amounts is an easy way to provide new practice materials each day. Have students analyze the amounts according to different methods of calculating uncollectible accounts expense.

ILLUSTRATION 8-4 Uncollectible accounts expense adjustment on a work sheet

Morgan, Inc.
Work Sheet
For Year Ended December 31, 19--

	ACCOUNT TITLE	1 TRIAL BALANCE DEBIT	2 TRIAL BALANCE CREDIT	3 ADJUSTMENTS DEBIT	4 ADJUSTMENTS CREDIT	5 INCOME STATEMENT DEBIT	6 INCOME STATEMENT CREDIT	7 BALANCE SHEET DEBIT	8 BALANCE SHEET CREDIT	
4	*Allowance for Uncoll. Accts.*		25 87		(a) 566 43					4
49	*Uncollectible Accounts Exp.*			(a) 566 43						49

On line 49 of the work sheet, Uncollectible Accounts Expense is debited for $566.43 in the Adjustments Debit column. On line 4,

TEACHING STRATEGIES: EXPANDING BEYOND THE CLASSROOM

Invite a representative from a local business that sells on credit to address the class. The presentation can focus on the way the business handles uncollectible accounts.

Allowance for Uncollectible Accounts is credited for $566.43 in the Adjustments Credit column.

Estimating Uncollectible Accounts Expense by Using a Percentage of Total Sales on Account. Peper, Inc. bases its estimate of uncollectible accounts expense on a percentage of total sales on account. Peper's past records show that approximately 1% of total sales on account during a fiscal period will become uncollectible. During the current year, the business had total sales on account of $126,603.91. Peper estimates that 1% of the total sales on account, *$1,266.04,* will eventually prove uncollectible. Uncollectible accounts expense for Peper is calculated as shown below.

Total Sales on Account	×	Percentage	=	Estimated Uncollectible Accounts Expense
$126,603.91	×	1%	=	$1,266.04

Uncollectible Accounts Expense

Debit		Credit	
Adj.	1,266.04		

Allowance for Uncollectible Accounts

Debit		Credit	
		Bal.	393.66
		Adj.	1,266.04
		(New Bal.	*1,659.70)*

Uncollectible Accounts Expense is increased by a $1,266.04 debit. Allowance for Uncollectible Accounts is increased by a $1,266.04 credit.

The allowance account's previous balance, *$393.66,* is the estimated uncollectible amount recorded in previous fiscal periods but not yet actually written off. The new balance of the allowance account is $1,659.70 (previous balance, $393.66, *plus* adjustment, $1,266.04).

The balance of Allowance for Uncollectible Accounts may increase from year to year. If the increase is large, this may indicate that an incorrect percentage is being used to calculate the uncollectible amount. When this occurs, a new percentage should be calculated based on actual experience for the past two or three years.

Regardless of the method used to calculate the amount, the adjustment is entered on a work sheet in the same way as previously described. The same two general ledger accounts are affected, Allowance for Uncollectible Accounts and Uncollectible Accounts Expense.

Percentage of Accounts Receivable Method

FYI

2/10, n/30 means that a 2% discount is given if paid in 10 days. The entire amount must be paid in 30 days.

The *percentage of accounts receivable method* assumes that a percentage of the accounts receivable account balance is uncollectible. Therefore, emphasis is placed on estimating a percentage of accounts receivable that will not be collected. An amount that will bring the balance of Allowance for Uncollectible Accounts up to the estimated amount is recorded in that account. Two variations of this method are used. (1) Estimating the amount of uncollectible accounts by aging accounts receivable. (2) Estimating the amount of uncollectible accounts by using a percentage of the accounts receivable account balance.

TEACH

Cover student pages 229–236 "Allowance Method of Recording Uncollectible Accounts Expense." Present the allowance method of recording uncollectible accounts expense. Emphasize that uncollectible accounts expense is estimated. Discuss the percentage of sales method and explain how to estimate uncollectible accounts expense using either a percentage of net sales or a percentage of total sales on account. Discuss the percentage of accounts receivable method and explain how to estimate the balance of Allowance for Uncollectible Accounts either by aging accounts receivable or by using a percentage of the accounts receivable account balance. Emphasize that the older the account receivable, the greater the likelihood that it will become uncollectible in the future. Explain how to write off an uncollectible account using the allowance method. Discuss the two entries recorded for the collection of a written-off account.

APPLIED SKILLS: BUILDING STUDY SKILLS

Before students journalize transactions, they should first analyze each transaction into debit and credit parts using T accounts. The additional practice helps students master the debit/credit concepts.

APPLY

Write each formula on the chalkboard or overhead projector and demonstrate all calculations. Draw T accounts to analyze each transaction as it is presented. Refer students to Illustration 8-4 to show how an uncollectible accounts expense adjustment is recorded on a work sheet.

Guided Practice

- Guide students through the calculation of the estimated amount for the uncollectible accounts adjusting entry in Problem 8-2, Instruction 1. Working as a group, write the formula on the board and have students complete the calculations. All students should agree on the estimated amount. The balance of Problem 8-2 can be completed as Independent Practice.
- Guide students through the T account analysis of the transactions in Problems 8-6 and 8-7. Have students draw T accounts on a sheet of paper and analyze the first transaction. All students should agree with the analysis before proceeding to the next transaction. Repeat the process until all transactions have been analyzed. The balance of Problems 8-6 and 8-7 can be completed as Independent Practice.

Independent Practice

Assign Terms 4–5; Questions 6–11; and Problems 8-2, 8-3, 8-4, 8-5, 8-6, and 8-7.

TEACHING STRATEGIES: APPLYING VISUALS

Direct students to Illustrations 8-5 and 8-6 to review aging accounts receivable.

FYI

The older the account receivable, the greater the likelihood that it will become uncollectible in the future.

Estimating the Balance of Allowance for Uncollectible Accounts by Aging Accounts Receivable. Analyzing accounts receivable according to when they are due is called **aging accounts receivable.** Rosedale, Inc. ages accounts receivable at the end of each fiscal period to provide information for the uncollectible accounts expense adjustment. Rosedale sells on terms of 2/10, n/30. Rosedale expects customers to pay in full within 30 days. If cash has not been received within 30 days, reminders are mailed to the customers. If cash has not been received after 60 days, special attempts are made to collect the amount due. If an amount has not been collected from a customer after 90 days, the business stops selling on account to that customer until collection has been made. Also, after an account is 90 days or more overdue, the business notifies the local credit bureau which adds the information to its files.

Rosedale's schedule of accounts receivable by age is shown in Illustration 8-5.

ILLUSTRATION 8-5 Schedule of accounts receivable by age

Customer	Account Balance	Not Yet Due	Days Account Balance Past Due			
			1–30	31–60	61–90	Over 90
Louise Asmus	$ 735.51	$ 735.51				
Mark Darby	132.58		132.58			
Ann Gabriel	99.55					99.55
Kathy Quay	238.00	200.00	38.00			
Thomas Yost	133.67				133.67	
Totals	$12,891.97	$8,734.08	$2,952.90	$749.54	$238.45	$217.00
Percentages	—	0.1%	0.2%	0.4%	10.0%	80.0%

Based on past records, Rosedale determines that a percentage of each accounts receivable age group will become uncollectible in the future. For example, as shown in Illustration 8-5, 0.4% of the accounts receivable overdue 31-60 days will probably become uncollectible. Also, 80.0% of the accounts overdue more than 90 days probably will become uncollectible.

Using these percentages, Rosedale calculated the total amount of estimated uncollectible accounts receivable as shown in Illustration 8-6.

Of the total accounts receivable on December 31, *$12,891.97*, the business estimated that $215.09 will prove to be uncollectible in the future.

Rosedale's general ledger shows that Allowance for Uncollectible Accounts has a $40.78 credit balance. This balance is what remains of estimates made in previous fiscal periods but not yet specifically identified by customer. However, the current balance for the

TEACHING STRATEGIES: COOPERATIVE LEARNING

Assign a group of students to gather information on charge sales. A local department store can provide information on their credit cards. The group should present information such as how to apply for a card, payment terms, and so on. Encourage each team member to participate in the presentation.

ILLUSTRATION 8-6 Estimating the balance of Allowance for Uncollectible Accounts by aging accounts receivable

Age Group	Amount	Percentage	Uncollectible
Not yet due	$ 8,734.08	0.1%	$ 8.73
1–30 days	2,952.90	0.2%	5.91
31–60 days	749.54	0.4%	3.00
61–90 days	238.45	10.0%	23.85
Over 90 days	217.00	80.0%	173.60
Totals	$12,891.97	—	$215.09

allowance account should be $215.09. The additional amount to be recorded is calculated as shown below.

Estimated Balance of Allowance for Uncollectible Accounts	−	Current Balance of Allowance for Uncollectible Accounts	=	Estimated Addition to Allowance for Uncollectible Accounts
$215.09	−	$40.78	=	$174.31

Uncollectible Accounts Expense	
Adj. 174.31	

Allowance for Uncollectible Accounts	
	Bal. 40.78
	Adj. 174.31
	(New Bal. 215.09)

Uncollectible Accounts Expense is increased by a $174.31 debit. Allowance for Uncollectible Accounts is increased by a $174.31 credit. The new balance of the allowance account is $215.09 (previous balance, $40.78, *plus* adjustment, $174.31).

The aging accounts receivable method is based on amounts still owed by customers at the time the uncollectible accounts expense is estimated. Until recent years, some businesses did not use the aging method because of the additional work required in analyzing accounts receivable for the aging schedule. However, with the increased availability of computers to make the calculations, more businesses use the aging method.

FYI

The journal entry to write off an uncollectible account is the same regardless of the allowance method used to calculate the estimated amount.

Estimating the Balance of Allowance for Uncollectible Accounts by Using a Percentage of the Accounts Receivable Account Balance. Appliance Center, Inc. is a merchandising business that sells appliances. Appliance Center expects to make money and continue in business indefinitely. *(CONCEPT: Going Concern)* Appliance Center estimates its amount of uncollectible accounts expense by using a percentage of the accounts receivable account balance at the end of a fiscal period. This method assumes that a percentage of the current amount still to be collected from customers will prove to be uncollectible.

On December 31, Appliance Center's accounts receivable account balance is $45,462.79. Appliance Center's past experience

ASSESS

Assess student understanding by checking the solutions to the Independent Practice activities.

Reteach

- Make transparencies of the general journal and cash receipts journal from the accounting forms masters provided in the Blackline Masters Section of the Teacher's Resource Guide. Refer students to Recycling Problem 8-R. Ask students to use T accounts to analyze the transactions using the allowance method. Use the transparencies to demonstrate how the transactions are journalized.
- Assign Recycling Problem 8-R.

Extend

- Assign Cases for Critical Thinking 1 and 2
- Assign the Spreadsheet Template for Problem 8-4.

Enrich

Assign the SPREADSHEET OPTIONS feature on page 239.

CLOSURE

Use Audit Your Understanding questions.

TEACHING STRATEGIES: TEACHING TIP

Emphasize that regardless of the allowance method used to calculate the estimated uncollectible accounts expense, the accounts affected by the adjustment are the same.

TEACHING STRATEGIES: DIFFERENT LEARNING ABILITIES

Gifted Students. This part presents a variety of accounting concepts, such as accounts receivable, plant assets, notes payable and receivable, prepaid and accrued expenses, and unearned and accrued revenue. Using gifted students as tutors for other students can be an effective way of teaching the topics students find most difficult. Allow the gifted students to complete one of these chapters while the class completes the first two chapters of the part. The gifted students can then assist you in presenting the concepts and procedures in their chapter to the class. Encourage the students to use visual aids and develop methods to assess student learning.

indicates that approximately 3% of the accounts receivable account balance will be uncollectible. The estimated addition to the balance of Allowance for Uncollectible Accounts is calculated as shown below.

Balance of Accounts Receivable Account	×	Percentage	=	Estimated Balance of Allowance for Uncollectible Accounts
$45,462.79	×	3%	=	$1,363.88
Estimated Balance of Allowance for Uncollectible Accounts	−	**Current Balance of Allowance for Uncollectible Accounts**	=	**Estimated Addition to Allowance for Uncollectible Accounts**
$1,363.88	−	$74.34	=	$1,289.54

Uncollectible Accounts Expense

Debit		Credit	
Adj.	1,289.54		

Allowance for Uncollectible Accounts

Debit		Credit	
		Bal.	74.34
		Adj.	1,289.54
		(New Bal.	*1,363.88)*

Uncollectible Accounts Expense is increased by a $1,289.54 debit. Allowance for Uncollectible Accounts is increased by a $1,289.54 credit. The new balance of the allowance account is $1,363.88 (previous balance, $74.34, *plus* adjustment, $1,289.54).

Writing Off an Uncollectible Account—Allowance Method

The procedures for writing off an account are the same regardless of the allowance method used to calculate the estimated uncollectible accounts expense. When a specific customer account is known to be uncollectible, the account balance is written off. Appliance Center determined that Candace Rhode will not pay the amount she owes, *$42.80*. The balance is no longer *estimated* to be uncollectible, it is *actually determined* to be uncollectible.

January 5, 19--. Wrote off Candace Rhode's past-due account as uncollectible, $42.80. Memorandum No. 71.

GENERAL LEDGER

Allowance for Uncollectible Accounts

Debit		Credit	
Write off	42.80	Bal.	1,363.88

Accounts Receivable

Debit		Credit	
Bal.	45,462.79	Write off	42.80

ACCOUNTS RECEIVABLE LEDGER

Candace Rhode

Debit		Credit	
Bal.	42.80	Write off	42.80
(New Bal. zero)			

Allowance for Uncollectible Accounts is decreased by a $42.80 debit. Accounts Receivable is decreased by a $42.80 credit. In the accounts receivable ledger, the customer account is also decreased by a $42.80 credit. After this entry is journalized and posted, Candace Rhode's account has a zero balance, and the account is written off.

In a previous fiscal period, an adjusting entry was recorded for estimated uncollectible accounts expense resulting in an Allowance for Uncollectible Accounts balance of $1,363.88. This balance is the estimated amount of uncollectible accounts. The $42.80 debit entry in this account removes an amount that is no longer estimated but is actual.

TEACHING STRATEGIES: TEACHING TIP

Emphasize that the procedures for writing off an account are the same regardless of the allowance method used to calculate the estimated uncollectible accounts expense.

TEACHING STRATEGIES: DIFFERENT LEARNING STYLES

Kinesthetic Learner. When covering journal entries with a kinesthetic learner, the instructor should give the student journal paper and have the student complete the entries as the instructor demonstrates on a transparency or chalkboard.

FYI

Embezzlement is the taking of an asset fraudulently by the person who has responsibility for the asset.

Uncollectible Accounts Expense is not affected when a business writes off an account using the allowance method. The expense is recorded in an adjusting entry at the end of a previous fiscal period.

The journal entry to write off an uncollectible account is the same regardless of the allowance method used to calculate the estimated amount. The journal entry to record this transaction is shown in Illustration 8-7.

ILLUSTRATION 8-7 Journal entry to write off an uncollectible account—allowance method

GENERAL JOURNAL PAGE 1

	DATE		ACCOUNT TITLE	DOC. NO.	POST. REF.	DEBIT	CREDIT	
4		5	*Allowance for Uncollectible Accts.*	*M71*		42 80		4
5			*Accounts Rec./Candace Rhode*				42 80	5
6								6

The aging accounts receivable method and the percentage of the accounts receivable account balance method are similar. Both methods are based on *actual* amounts owed by customers at the end of a fiscal period.

Collecting a Written-Off Account—Allowance Method

Later in the year, Appliance Center received a check in full payment of the amount owed by Candace Rhode.

April 5, 19--. Received cash in full payment of Candace Rhode's account, previously written off as uncollectible, $42.80. Memorandum No. 92 and Receipt No. 280.

Appliance Center's records must show a complete history of Ms. Rhode's credit dealings. Therefore, two journal entries are recorded for the collection of a written-off account receivable. (1) A general journal entry to reopen the customer account. (2) A cash receipts journal entry to record the cash received on account.

GENERAL LEDGER

Accounts Receivable

Bal.	45,462.79	Write off	42.00
Reopen	42.80		

Allowance for Uncollectible Accounts

Write off	42.80	Bal.	1,363.88
		Reopen	42.80

ACCOUNTS RECEIVABLE LEDGER

Candace Rhode

Bal.	42.80	Write off	42.80
Reopen	42.80		
(New Bal.	*42.80)*		

The analysis of the entry to reopen Ms. Rhode's account is shown in the T accounts.

Accounts Receivable is increased by a $42.80 debit. Allowance for Uncollectible Accounts is increased by a $42.80 credit. In the accounts receivable ledger, Candace Rhode's account is increased by a $42.80 debit and is reopened. The account balances now appear as they were before Ms. Rhode's account was written off as uncollectible.

The journal entry to reopen Ms. Rhode's account is shown in Illustration 8-8.

TEACHING STRATEGIES: DIFFERENT LEARNING STYLES

Print Learner. When covering journal entries with a print learner, the instructor should discuss the entries, using the textbook examples and referring to the textbook. The print learner can later go back and study the entries.

TEACHING STRATEGIES: DIFFERENT LEARNING STYLES

Tactile Learner. Tactile learners may benefit from using the computer to key journal entries and then print reports. A ruler can be positioned on the input forms as a guide when keying the entries. The student should also be encouraged to place a finger on each account title in the journal entries report and trace it over to the amount in the amount column of the report to check it for accuracy. Tactile learners should also be given the opportunity to journalize transactions from at least one simulation that contains source documents which must be handled to analyze, journalize, and file.

AUDIT YOUR UNDERSTANDING

1. Matching Expenses with Revenue concept.
2. Total sales minus sales discount minus sales returns and allowances equals net sales.
3. (1) Estimating the amount of uncollectible accounts by aging accounts receivable. (2) Estimating the amount of uncollectible accounts by using a percentage of the accounts receivable account balance.
4. Allowance for Uncollectible Accounts.

LESSON PLAN 8-3

Materials

- Student pages 236–240
- Assess: Problem Test Chapter 8, MicroExam Chapter 8

Objectives (Enabling Performance Tasks)

a. Define accounting terms related to uncollectible accounts.

b. Identify accounting concepts and practices related to uncollectible accounts.

e. Calculate and analyze accounts receivable turnover ratios.

ILLUSTRATION 8-8 Journal entry to reopen customer account previously written off as uncollectible

GENERAL JOURNAL PAGE 4

	DATE		ACCOUNT TITLE	DOC. NO.	POST. REF.	DEBIT	CREDIT	
1	19-- Apr.	5	Accounts Receivable/Candace Rhode	M92	/	42 80		1
2			Allow. for Uncollectible Accounts				42 80	2
3								3

Audit Your Understanding

1. Which accounting concept is being applied when the allowance method of recording uncollectible accounts expense is used?
2. What is the formula for calculating net sales?
3. What are two variations of the percentage of accounts receivable method of estimating uncollectible accounts expense?
4. What general ledger account is credited when an uncollectible account is reopened using the allowance method when payment is received?

The analysis of the entry for cash received on account from Ms. Rhode is shown in the T accounts.

GENERAL LEDGER

Cash

Received	42.80		

Accounts Receivable

Bal.	45,462.79	Write off	42.80
Reopen	42.80	**Received**	**42.80**

ACCOUNTS RECEIVABLE LEDGER

Candace Rhode

Bal.	42.80	Write off	42.80
Reopen	42.80	**Received**	**42.80**
(New Bal. zero)			

Cash is increased by a $42.80 debit. Accounts Receivable is decreased by a $42.80 credit. In the accounts receivable ledger, the customer account is decreased by a $42.80 credit.

The journal entry to record cash received on account is similar to the entry shown in Illustration 8-3.

ACCOUNTS RECEIVABLE TURNOVER RATIO

Appliance Center needs cash to purchase additional merchandise to sell to customers and to pay for operating expenses. If amounts due from customers are not collected promptly, too large a share of the assets of the business are in accounts receivable and not immediately usable. Any business selling on account needs prompt collection from credit customers.

Appliance Center needs to know how promptly customers are making payments on account. If the customers are not paying promptly, the business will adopt new procedures to speed collections. One means of analyzing the collection efficiency of a business is to calculate the accounts receivable turnover ratio. The

TEACHING STRATEGIES: DIFFERENT LEARNING STYLES

Visual Learner. When covering journal entries with a visual learner, the instructor should discuss the entries, using a transparency or the chalkboard to record the entry. In addition, the student should be asked to mentally picture each part of the entry before the instructor actually writes it on the transparency or chalkboard.

number of times the average amount of accounts receivable is collected during a specified period is called the **accounts receivable turnover ratio**.

FYI

An accounts receivable turnover ratio can be calculated monthly or annually.

Some businesses calculate an accounts receivable turnover ratio monthly. With monthly rates, a business can take steps at the end of each month to improve collection practices. However, some businesses find that an annual ratio is sufficient. The annual ratio is used to revise collection policies for the next fiscal year.

Calculating the Accounts Receivable Turnover Ratio

The difference between the balance of Accounts Receivable and its contra account, Allowance for Uncollectible Accounts, is called the **book value of accounts receivable**. Appliance Center calculated its book value of accounts receivable as shown below.

Total Accounts Receivable	−	Allowance for Uncollectible Accounts	=	Book Value of Accounts Receivable
$45,462.79	−	$1,363.88	=	$44,098.91

The accounts receivable turnover ratio is calculated by dividing net sales on account by the average book value of accounts receivable. Appliance Center calculated its accounts receivable turnover ratio for the current year as shown below.

(Beginning Book Value of Accounts Receivable	+	Ending Book Value of Accounts Receivable)	÷	2	=	Average Book Value of Accounts Receivable
($48,912.31	+	$44,098.91)	÷	2	=	$46,505.61

Net Sales on Account	÷	Average Book Value of Accounts Receivable	=	Accounts Receivable Turnover Ratio
$330,312.85	÷	$46,505.61	=	7.1 times

An accounts receivable turnover ratio of 7.1 times means that Appliance Center turns over (or collects) its average accounts receivable about seven times a year.

Appliance Center sells on account to customers on terms of n/30. These terms mean that Appliance Center expects customers

FOCUS

- Two methods of writing off uncollectible accounts were presented earlier in this chapter. Explain that in addition to determining which accounts are uncollectible, a business needs to know how promptly customers are making payments on account. In this lesson, one means of analyzing the collection efficiency of a business will be presented.
- Introduce vocabulary: accounts receivable turnover ratio, book value of accounts receivable.

TEACH

Cover student pages 236–240 "Accounts Receivable Turnover Ratio." Explain the procedure for calculating accounts receivable turnover ratio. Discuss what the turnover ratio means. Explain the procedure for calculating average number of days for payment. Discuss how a business analyzes accounts receivable turnover ratios and uses the analysis to make business decisions.

APPLIED SKILLS: LANGUAGE ARTS

Practicing punctuation skills. Special handouts for practicing punctuation skills can be created easily using word processing software. Key in some text, either something that you have written yourself or that has appeared in a newspaper or magazine. After checking to be sure you have keyed it correctly, use the change feature of the word processor to change all punctuation to an underline. This will create an answer space for students to supply the correct punctuation. Student solutions can then be compared with the original copy for correctness. For additional challenge, the answer blanks can be omitted.

APPLY

Write each formula on the chalkboard or overhead projector and demonstrate all calculations.

Guided Practice

Guide students through the procedures for calculating the accounts receivable turnover ratios for Businesses A and B in Problem 8-8, Instruction 1. Write the formulas on the board for reference. Working as a group, calculate the ratio for Business A. All students should agree on the ratio before repeating the process for Business B. The balance of Problem 8-8 can be completed as Independent Practice.

Independent Practice

- Assign Terms 6–7, Questions 12–15, and Problem 8-8.
- Assign Study Guide 8 and Mastery Problem 8-M.

ASSESS

Assess student understanding by checking the solutions to the Independent Practice activities.

Reteach

Set up a table of information similar to the one in Problem 8-8 but use different amounts. Write the formulas on the board and demonstrate how to calculate the accounts receivable turnover ratio for the first business. Then ask for volunteers to come to the board and calculate the ratios for the remaining businesses as the rest of the students do the calculations at their desks.

Extend

Assign Challenge Problem 8-C. (The challenge is to estimate uncollectible accounts expense by aging Accounts Receivable.)

FYI

The terms of sale offered by a business determines the expected accounts receivable turnover ratio.

to pay amounts owed within 30 days. The expected accounts receivable turnover ratio is 12.0 times, or one-twelfth of a year (30 days). This expected number of days for payment is calculated as shown below.

Days in Year	÷	Expected Accounts Receivable Turnover Ratio	=	Expected Average Number of Days for Payment
365	÷	12.0	=	30

Appliance Center calculated its actual number of days for payment as shown below.

Days in Year	÷	Accounts Receivable Turnover Ratio	=	Actual Average Number of Days for Payment
365	÷	7.1	=	51

Appliance Center's customers are taking an average of about 51 days to pay their accounts in full.

Analyzing Accounts Receivable Turnover Ratios

Most of Appliance Center's customers do pay their accounts, but they take much longer than the expected 30 days. Appliance Center's accounts receivable turnover ratios and collection periods for the past several years are shown below.

Appliance Center, Inc.—Accounts Receivable Turnover Ratios

Year	19X1	19X2	19X3	19X4	19X5	19X6	19X7
Ratio	6.2	6.4	6.0	6.4	6.8	6.8	7.1
Days for Payment	59	57	61	57	54	54	51

From 19X1 to 19X7, the accounts receivable turnover ratio has risen from 6.2 to 7.1 times. In 19X1, customers took an average of 59 days to pay their accounts in full. In 19X7, customers are taking an average of 51 days to pay their accounts in full, eight fewer days than in 19X1. However, the 19X7 turnover ratio, 7.1 times, is still much lower than the expected rate of 12.0.

APPLIED SKILLS: WRITING ACROSS THE CURRICULUM

Writing paragraphs and short essays. The Cases for Critical Thinking are short, practical applications of the accounting principles developed in the chapter. Some cases are planned to present problems related to the chapter but not specifically discussed and answered in the chapter. These cases present an opportunity for critical thinking and decision making. These cases also require more than a short objective-type response. Therefore they provide ideal practice in writing paragraphs and short essays.

SPREADSHEET OPTIONS

COPYING A RELATIVE CELL REFERENCE

Mathematical calculations on a spreadsheet are made using formulas. The spreadsheet copy command increases the efficiency of creating formulas. On most spreadsheet templates, many of the formulas contain the same logic. For example, the amounts in cells F7–F11 calculate the estimated uncollectible amount for each of the five age groups. Each formula multiplies an age group's amount by that age group's percentage. Therefore, the basic formula, multiply one cell's value times another, is the same. Only the cell reference changes.

The copy command eliminates the need to manually create each of the five formulas. Rather, a single formula is created and copied to create the remaining four formulas. When the spreadsheet was created, the formula +B7*D7 was keyed at cell F7, as shown on the prompt line in the upper left corner of the screen. The formula was then copied to cells F8–F11, creating the following formulas:

F7: +B7*D7
F8: +B8*D8
F9: +B9*D9
F10: +B10*D10
F11: +B11*D11

When copied to cell F8, the spreadsheet automatically modified the cell addresses in the formula by one row. Thus, the formula +B7*D7 at F7 was changed to +B8*D8 when copied to F8. This is known as a relative cell reference because the formula changed to reflect where it was moved.

```
F7: (C2) [W12] +B7*D7                                                    READY

            A                  B          C     D          E          F        G
1   McMillan Corporation
2   Aging of Accounts Receivable
3   June 30, 19--
4
5        Age Group           Amount          Percentage          Uncollectible
6   -----------------------------------------------------------------------------
7   Net yet due            $53,241.00            1.0%               $532.41
8   1-30 days              $42,112.00            2.0%               $842.24
9   31-60 days              $5,324.00            4.0%               $212.96
10  61-90 days              $1,236.00           10.0%               $123.60
11  Over 90 days            $7,453.00           25.0%             $1,863.25
12                       ------------                          ------------
13  Totals                $109,366.00                             $3,574.46
14                       ============
15
16  Current balance of Allowance for
17    Uncollectible Accounts..........................           $1,342.00
18                                                            ------------
19  Required change in account balance.................           $2,232.46
20                                                            ============
```

With the exception of 19X3, the turnover ratio has been steadily increasing. On the average, customers have been paying their accounts in full in a fewer number of days each year. Appliance Center wants this favorable trend to continue.

Appliance Center needs to plan additional ways to encourage customers to pay their accounts in less time. The goal is to have a turnover ratio of 12.0 times as compared to the present rate of 7.1.

SPREADSHEET OPTIONS

The SPREADSHEET OPTIONS feature is intended to expose students to a variety of ways to use spreadsheets. As an optional activity, students may use their spreadsheet software to duplicate the example shown in the spreadsheet options feature. They may also create new sets of data to do what-if analysis.

CLOSURE

Use Audit Your Understanding questions.

ASSESS

- Administer Problem Test Chapter 8.
- Administer a MicroExam test for Chapter 8.

APPLIED SKILLS: WORD PROCESSING

If you wish to integrate word processing into your accounting course, you may direct students to answer the end-of-chapter Accounting Terms, Questions for Individual Study, and Cases for Critical Thinking using their word processing software.

AUDIT YOUR UNDERSTANDING

1. A business needs cash to purchase additional merchandise to sell and to pay for operating expenses.
2. Total accounts receivable minus allowance for uncollectible accounts equals book value of accounts receivable.
3. Net sales on account divided by average book value of accounts receivable equals accounts receivable turnover ratio.
4. Days in year (365) divided by accounts receivable turnover ratio equals actual average number of days for payment.

Audit Your Understanding

1. Why do most businesses need prompt payment from customers?
2. How is the book value of accounts receivable calculated?
3. How is the accounts receivable turnover ratio calculated?
4. How is the actual average number of days for payment calculated?

The business might take several steps to create a more favorable accounts receivable turnover ratio.

1. Send statements of account to customers more often, including a request for prompt payment.
2. Do not sell on account to any customer who has an account for which payment is overdue more than 30 days.
3. Encourage more cash sales and fewer sales on account.
4. Conduct a more rigorous credit check on new customers before extending credit to them.

Sometimes a demand for quicker payment can result in loss of business. Some customers might start buying from competitors. A business must weigh a change in credit policies against the effect the change will have on total sales.

ACCOUNTING TERMS

1. **uncollectible accounts:** Accounts receivable that cannot be collected. (p. 226)
2. **writing off an account:** Canceling the balance of a customer account because the customer does not pay. (p. 226)
3. **direct write-off method of recording losses from uncollectible accounts:** Recording uncollectible accounts expense only when an amount is actually known to be uncollectible. (p. 226)
4. **allowance method of recording losses from uncollectible accounts:** Crediting the estimated value of uncollectible accounts to a contra account. (p. 229)
5. **aging accounts receivable:** Analyzing accounts receivable according to when they are due. (p. 232)
6. **accounts receivable turnover ratio:** The number of times the average amount of accounts receivable is collected during a specified period. (p. 237)
7. **book value of accounts receivable:** The difference between the balance of Accounts Receivable and its contra account, Allowance for Uncollectible Accounts. (p. 237)

ACCOUNTING TERMS EPT(a)

What is the meaning of each of the following?

1. **uncollectible accounts**
2. **writing off an account**
3. **direct write-off method of recording losses from uncollectible accounts**
4. **allowance method of recording losses from uncollectible accounts**
5. **aging accounts receivable**
6. **accounts receivable turnover ratio**
7. **book value of accounts receivable**

QUESTIONS FOR INDIVIDUAL STUDY EPT(b)

1. Why should the amount of an uncollectible account be removed from the assets of a business?
2. In the direct write-off method, how is an uncollectible account closed?
3. What general ledger accounts are affected, and how, when an uncollectible account is written off using the direct write-off method?
4. What general ledger accounts are affected, and how, when an uncollectible account is reopened using the direct write-off method when payment is received?
5. Why is the customer account reopened when cash is received for an account previously written off as uncollectible?
6. What are the two methods commonly used to estimate uncollectible accounts expense for a fiscal period?
7. What is the formula for estimating uncollectible accounts expense based on net sales?
8. What general ledger accounts are affected, and how, when an adjustment is made using the allowance method of calculating uncollectible accounts expense?

QUESTIONS FOR INDIVIDUAL STUDY

1. The value of the uncollectible account is no longer an asset and should not be recorded in an asset account. (p. 226)
2. The uncollectible account is closed by transferring the balance to Uncollectible Accounts Expense. (p. 226)
3. Uncollectible Accounts Expense is debited; Accounts Receivable is credited. (p. 227)
4. Accounts Receivable is debited; Collection of Uncollectible Accounts is credited. (p. 227)
5. To provide information in the customer account that will give a complete history of the customer's credit activities. (p. 227)
6. (a) Percentage of sales method. (b) Percentage of accounts receivable method. (p. 229)

QUESTIONS FOR INDIVIDUAL STUDY

EPT(b)

9. If the allowance for uncollectible accounts account balance increase is large from year to year, what is the probable cause?
10. What general ledger accounts are affected, and how, when an uncollectible account is written off using the allowance method?
11. When using the allowance method, what general ledger accounts are affected, and how, if an account is reopened because payment is received?
12. What is the formula for calculating average book value of accounts receivable?
13. What is the formula for calculating the accounts receivable turnover ratio?
14. If a business desires an accounts receivable turnover ratio of 12.0 times and actually has a turnover ratio of 6.0 times, how can this be interpreted?
15. How can a business decide if an accounts receivable turnover ratio of 6.0 times is acceptable or not?

CASES FOR CRITICAL THINKING

EPT(b)

CASE 1 Westermen, Inc. sells merchandise for cash and on account. The business uses the direct write-off method of recording uncollectible accounts expense. For the past two years, the amount of uncollectible accounts written off each year has been about 1.0% of the net sales on account. Net sales on account last year were $416,228.00. An accountant recommends that the business change to the allowance method of recording uncollectible accounts expense. However, management is reluctant to accept the recommendation because the business has used the direct write-off method for a long time and personnel fully understand it. What do you recommend and why?

CASE 2 The following entries were made in each of the years shown. What effect will the entries in each of these years have on the financial statements of the business?

19X1 Adjusting entry; debit **Uncollectible Accounts Expense,** credit **Allowance for Uncollectible Accounts,** $2,000.00.

19X2 Wrote off Gerald Garland's account as uncollectible, $550.00.

19X3 Reopened Gerald Garland's account; received payment in full for the account, $550.00.

APPLICATION PROBLEMS

EPT(c,d,e)

PROBLEM 8-1 Journalizing entries to write off uncollectible accounts—direct write-off method

Kelley, Inc. uses the direct write-off method of recording uncollectible accounts expense.

INSTRUCTIONS:

Journalize the following transactions completed during the current year. Use page 2 of a general journal and page 3 of a cash receipts journal. Source documents are abbreviated as follows: memorandum, M; receipt, R.

Jan. 20. Wrote off Belinda Rafferty's past-due account as uncollectible, $265.48. M15.
Feb. 15. Wrote off Ervin Bond's past-due account as uncollectible, $52.00. M21.
Apr. 10. Received cash in full payment of Stephanie Byrd's account, previously written off as uncollectible, $178.43. M34 and R89.
June 14. Wrote off Duane Comb's past-due account as uncollectible, $89.97. M68.

7. Total sales − sales discount − sales returns and allowances = Net sales × percentage = Estimated uncollectible accounts expense. (p. 230)

8. Uncollectible Accounts Expense is debited; Allowance for Uncollectible Accounts is credited. (p. 230)

9. The percentage used to calculate the annual amount of uncollectible accounts expense is probably incorrect. (p. 231)

10. Allowance for Uncollectible Accounts is debited; Accounts Receivable is credited. (p. 234)

11. Accounts Receivable is debited; Allowance for Uncollectible Accounts is credited. (p. 235)

12. (Beginning book value of accounts receivable + ending book value of accounts receivable) ÷ 2 = Average book value of accounts receivable. (p. 237)

13. Net sales on account ÷ average book value of accounts receivable = Accounts receivable turnover ratio. (p. 237)

14. A turnover ratio of 6.0 times means that the customers are taking an average of 1/6 of a year to pay their accounts in full. One-sixth of a year is about 60 days (365 ÷ 6). A desired turnover ratio of 12.0 means that the customers should be taking an average of 1/12 of a year to pay their accounts in full. One-twelfth of a year is about 30 days. The customers are taking longer than desired to pay their accounts. The actual turnover ratio, 6.0 times, is not a desirable one for this business. (pp. 237–238)

15. The acceptability is measured against how quickly the business expects customers to pay their accounts. For example, if a business has terms of n/60, the customers are expected to pay their accounts in not more than 60 days. Thus, a turnover ratio of 6.0 would be acceptable. However, if terms are n/30, then customers are expected to pay in 30 days, and a turnover ratio of 6.0 is not acceptable. (p. 238)

CHECK FIGURES

See Teacher's Edition of the Working Papers for complete solutions.

Problem 8-1 Accounts debited in general journal: Jan. 20, Feb. 15, and June 14, Uncollectible Accounts Expense; Apr. 10, Oct. 5, and Nov. 1, Accounts Receivable.

CASES FOR CRITICAL THINKING

Case 1 Generally accepted accounting practice is to record significant amounts of expenses in the same fiscal period as the revenue earned from paying the expenses. If it is determined the amount is sizable and significant, the business would be wise to consider changing to the allowance method. *(CONCEPT: Materiality)*

Case 2 19X1 Income statement: The adjusting entry will increase expenses and reduce net income. Balance sheet: The entry also will decrease the book value of accounts receivable and thus reduce the total assets. 19X2 Income statement: The income statement will not be affected by this entry. Balance sheet: Both Allowance for Uncollectible Accounts and Accounts Receivable will be reduced the same amount. The book value of Accounts Receivable will remain the same. No change caused on the balance sheet by this entry.

19X3 Income statement: No changes in income statement accounts caused by entries in 19X3. Balance sheet: The entries in 19X3 will affect the book value of Accounts Receivable. The entry to reopen the customer's account will increase Accounts Receivable and Allowance for Uncollectible Accounts. The entry to record cash received on account will decrease Accounts Receivable. The balance of Allowance for Uncollectible Accounts remains unchanged, and Accounts Receivable is decreased. The book value of accounts receivable shown on the balance sheet will be decreased.

Oct. 5. Received cash in full payment of Belinda Rafferty's account, previously written off as uncollectible, $265.48. M104 and R135.

Nov. 1. Received cash in full payment of Bischoff, Inc.'s account, previously written off as uncollectible, $217.53. M127 and R139.

PROBLEM 8-2 Estimating amount of uncollectible accounts expense by using a percentage of net sales—allowance method; journalizing the adjusting entry

MATHEMATICS

Lynum, Inc. has the following general ledger account balances on December 31 of the current year before adjusting entries are recorded.

Accounts Receivable	$ 23,731.39
Allowance for Uncollectible Accounts	427.16
Sales	248,900.13
Sales Discount	1,496.90
Sales Returns and Allowances	2,082.14

INSTRUCTIONS:

1. Calculate the estimated amount for the uncollectible accounts expense adjusting entry on December 31. The corporation estimates that the amount of uncollectible accounts expense is equal to 0.5% of net sales.
2. Journalize the adjusting entry for uncollectible accounts expense on December 31 of the current year. Use page 12 of a general journal.

PROBLEM 8-3 Estimating amount of uncollectible accounts expense by using a percentage of total sales on account—allowance method; journalizing the adjusting entry

MATHEMATICS

Brook, Inc. has a total of $188,717.32 in sales on account for the current year.

INSTRUCTIONS:

1. Calculate the estimated amount for the uncollectible accounts expense adjusting entry on December 31. The corporation estimates that the amount of uncollectible accounts expense is equal to 1% of sales on account.
2. Journalize the adjusting entry for uncollectible accounts expense on December 31 of the current year. Use page 12 of a general journal.

PROBLEM 8-4 Estimating the balance of Allowance for Uncollectible Accounts by aging accounts receivable—allowance method; journalizing the adjusting entry

SPREADSHEET

MATHEMATICS

The following information has been obtained from the records of Kersten, Inc.

Customer	Account Balance	Not Yet Due	Days Account Balance Past Due			
			1–30	31–60	61–90	Over 90
Eric Bales	$ 518.28	$ 518.28				
Catherine Kosta	421.75		$ 421.75			
Holden Ostling	430.99	400.00	30.99			
Marie Phillips	120.84					120.84
Totals	$14,662.05	$8,619.18	$2,254.83	$862.57	$2,574.57	$350.90
Percentages	—	0.1%	0.2%	0.3%	0.8%	50.0%

INSTRUCTIONS:

1. Calculate the estimated balance of **Allowance for Uncollectible Accounts.** Prepare a list of estimated uncollectible amounts in each age group similar to the list in Illustration 8-6.
2. Journalize the adjusting entry for uncollectible accounts expense on December 31 of the current year. Use page 12 of a general journal. The balance of **Allowance for Uncollectible Accounts** on December 31 before adjusting entries are recorded is $63.24.

PROBLEM 8-5 Estimating the balance of Allowance for Uncollectible Accounts by using a percentage of the accounts receivable account balance—allowance method; journalizing the adjusting entry

Use the information given in Problem 8-4.

INSTRUCTIONS:

1. Calculate the estimated balance of **Allowance for Uncollectible Accounts**. Kersten, Inc. estimates that 2% of the accounts receivable account balance will become uncollectible in the future.
2. Journalize the adjusting entry for uncollectible accounts expense on December 31 of the current year. Use page 12 of a general journal.

PROBLEM 8-6 Journalizing entries to write off uncollectible accounts—allowance method

Microware, Inc. uses the allowance method of recording uncollectible accounts expense.

INSTRUCTIONS:

Journalize the following transactions completed during the current year. Use page 2 of a general journal. The abbreviation for memorandum is M.

Feb. 11. Wrote off William Mahler's past-due account as uncollectible, $77.00. M12.
Apr. 15. Wrote off Marilyn Burgquist's past-due account as uncollectible, $119.58. M21.
July 20. Wrote off David Martin's past-due account as uncollectible, $27.50. M39.
Oct. 10. Wrote off Linda Hilton's past-due account as uncollectible, $48.13. M61.

PROBLEM 8-7 Journalizing entries for collection of written off accounts—allowance method

Microware, Inc. uses the allowance method of recording uncollectible accounts expense.

INSTRUCTIONS:

Journalize the following transactions completed during the current year. Use page 4 of a general journal and page 7 of a cash receipts journal. Source documents are abbreviated as follows: memorandum, M; receipt, R.

Apr. 2. Received cash in full payment of William Mahler's account, previously written off as uncollectible, $77.00. M17 and R43.
May 14. Received cash in full payment of Marilyn Burgquist's account, previously written off as uncollectible, $119.58. M25 and R47.
Dec. 5. Received cash in full payment of Linda Hilton's account, previously written off as uncollectible, $48.13. M81 and R103.

PROBLEM 8-8 Calculating accounts receivable turnover ratios

The following information has been obtained from the records of four businesses.

Business	For Current Year			Last Year's Turnover Ratio
	Beginning Book Value of Accounts Receivable	Ending Book Value of Accounts Receivable	Net Sales on Account	
A	$ 18,201.18	$ 15,820.93	$ 119,320.36	8.0
B	27,160.52	27,320.42	130,754.25	6.0
C	34,058.33	29,725.77	158,648.50	5.0
D	106,432.28	127,718.74	1,301,322.50	9.0

INSTRUCTIONS:

1. For each business, calculate the accounts receivable turnover ratio for the current year.

CHECK FIGURES *(cont'd)*

Problem 8-2 Uncollectible Accounts Expense: $1,226.61

Problem 8-3 Uncollectible Accounts Expense: $1,887.17

Problem 8-4 Estimated uncollectible accounts: $211.77. Uncollectible Accounts Expense: $148.53.

Problem 8-5 Uncollectible Accounts Expense: $230.00

Problem 8-6 Account debited: Allowance for Uncollectible Accounts. Account credited: Accounts Receivable.

Problem 8-7 Account debited in general journal: Accounts Receivable. Account credited in general journal: Allowance for Uncollectible Accounts.

Problem 8-8 Accounts receivable turnover ratios: Co. A, 7.0; Co. B, 4.8; Co. C, 5.0; Co. D, 11.1. Best turnover ratio: Last year, Co. D, Current year, Co. D. Worst turnover ratio: Last year, Co. C, Current year, Co. B. Greatest improvement: Co. D. Least amount of improvement: Co. B.

2. Answer the following questions.
   a. Which business had the best turnover ratio last year? This current year?
   b. Which business had the worst turnover ratio last year? This current year?
   c. Which business had the greatest amount of improvement in the turnover ratio from last year to this year?
   d. Which business had the least amount of improvement in its turnover ratio from last year to this year?

CHECK FIGURES *(cont'd)*

Mastery Problem 8-M Uncollectible Accounts Expense: $3,775.40. Ending balance of Allowance for Uncollectible Accounts: $3,813.98.

Challenge Problem 8-C Estimated uncollectible accounts: $891.94. Uncollectible Accounts Expense: $753.36.

ENRICHMENT PROBLEMS

EPT(c,d)

MASTERY PROBLEM 8-M Journalizing entries for uncollectible accounts—allowance method; calculating and journalizing the adjusting entry for uncollectible accounts expense

Northern, Inc. uses the allowance method of recording uncollectible accounts expense.

INSTRUCTIONS:

1. Journalize the following transactions completed during the current year. Use page 1 of a general journal and page 1 of a cash receipts journal. Source documents are abbreviated as follows: memorandum, M; receipt, R.

Jan. 9. Wrote off Jane Martinez' past-due account as uncollectible, $634.65. M20.
Mar. 4. Wrote off Jason Young's past-due account as uncollectible, $782.50. M29.
Mar. 28. Received cash in full payment of Jane Martinez' account, previously written off as uncollectible, $634.65. M40 and R24.
June 20. Wrote off Allison Aanerud's past-due account as uncollectible, $617.16. M58.
Oct. 7. Wrote off Meredith Darst's past-due account as uncollectible, $808.15. M74.
Dec. 11. Received cash in full payment of Jason Young's account, previously written off as uncollectible, $782.50. M82 and R92.

2. Journalize the adjusting entry for uncollectible accounts expense on December 31 of the current year. Northern, Inc. has the following account balances on December 31 before adjusting entries are recorded.

Accounts Receivable	$ 20,171.68
Sales	380,065.10
Sales Discount	1,605.70
Sales Returns and Allowances	919.82

   Northern estimates that the amount of uncollectible accounts expense is equal to 1% of net sales.

3. If all the entries recorded in the general journal and cash receipts journal were posted, including the adjusting entry, what would be the new balance of Allowance for Uncollectible Accounts? The January 1 balance of Allowance for Uncollectible Accounts, before the transactions for the year were recorded, was $1,463.89.

CHALLENGE PROBLEM 8-C Estimating and journalizing uncollectible accounts expense by aging accounts receivable—allowance method; calculating and journalizing the adjusting entry for uncollectible accounts expense

Use the information given in Mastery Problem 8-M. A partial schedule of accounts receivable by age is given as follows.

Customer	Account Balance	Not Yet Due	Days Account Balance Past Due			
			1–30	31–60	61–90	Over 90
Totals	$22,171.68	$15,234.64	$2,307.65	$898.90	$2,640.87	$1,089.62
Percentages	—	0.2%	0.6%	1.0%	7.0%	60.0%

INSTRUCTIONS:

1. Journalize the transactions given in Problem 8-M. Use page 1 of a general journal and page 1 of a cash receipts journal.
2. Journalize the adjusting entry for uncollectible accounts expense on December 31 of the current year. Estimate the balance of **Allowance for Uncollectible Accounts** by using the provided partial schedule of accounts receivable by age. The January 1 balance of **Allowance for Uncollectible Accounts,** before the transactions for the year were recorded, was $1,563.89.

245

CHAPTER 9 OVERVIEW

Chapter 9 discusses buying and recording plant assets. Calculating the adjusting entries for plant assets using the straight-line method of calculating and recording depreciation is included as well as the declining-balance, sum-of-the-years-digits, and production-unit methods of calculating depreciation. These methods are compared and contrasted. Selling and disposing of plant assets are also covered. A general description of the procedures for calculating depreciation using the MACRS method is also presented.

GUIDE TO ACHIEVING LEARNING OBJECTIVES

	TEACH	APPLY	EXTEND/ENRICH					
Enabling Performance Tasks	**Lesson Plans**	**Application Problems**	**Mastery Problems**	**Challenge Problems**	**Cases for Critical Thinking**	**Recycling Problems**	**Reinforcement Activity**	
a. Define accounting terms related to plant assets and depreciation.	9-1, 9-3							
b. Identify accounting concepts and practices related to accounting for plant assets and depreciation.	9-1, 9-2, 9-3				Cases 1, 2			
c. Record plant asset information on plant asset records.	9-1	9-1, 9-2, 9-3	9-M					
d. Calculate depreciation expense for a plant asset.	9-1, 9-3	9-2, 9-6, 9-7, 9-8, 9-9	9-M	9-C		9-R1, 9-R2	RA2	
e. Journalize entries for buying and disposing of plant assets.	9-1, 9-2	9-1, 9-4, 9-5	9-M	9-C		9-R1	RA2	
f. Journalize entries for depreciation.	9-1, 9-2, 9-3	9-3, 9-4	9-M	9-C		9-R1	RA2	
g. Calculate and record property tax expense.	9-3	9-10				9-R3		

ENRICHMENT

SPECIAL FEATURES
Global Perspective, page 255
TECHNOLOGY CONNECTION
Automated Accounting 6.0 Problems 9-1, 9-6, 9-8, 9-C
Spreadsheet Template Problem 9-6, 9-7, 9-8

NEW, REVIEW, AND EXTENSION

ACTIVITIES/CONCEPTS/TRANSACTIONS	NEW	REVIEW/ EXTENSION
Completing a plant asset record	✓	
Buying a plant asset for cash or on account		✓
Calculating depreciation expense		✓
Straight-line depreciation method		✓
Adjusting entry for depreciation expense		✓
Disposing of plant assets		✓
Gain/loss on plant assets		✓
Trading a plant asset	✓	
Selling land and buildings		✓
Declining-balance depreciation method		✓
Sum-of-the-years-digits depreciation method		✓
Production-unit depreciation method		✓
Modified Accelerated Cost Recovery System	✓	
Depletion		✓
Property Tax		✓

To provide more versatile dates used in illustrative problems, the years are reported as 19X1, 19X2, etc., rather than an actual year. This change still permits students to work with problems involving multiple years, such as depreciation problems, yet retains the effect of working with current years beyond the textbook's first year of publication.

The plant asset records used in Problem 9-1 are needed to complete Problems 9-2, 9-3, and 9-4. The depreciation tables completed in Problem 9-2 are needed to complete Problem 9-3.

	INFORMAL ASSESSMENT		FORMAL ASSESSMENT			
	Study Guide	**Audit Your Understanding**	**Chapter MicroExam**	**Chapter Problem Test**	**Unit Objective Test**	**Portfolio**
	Unit B	✓	✓		✓	
	Units A, C	✓	✓		✓	
				✓		
				✓		✓
				✓		✓
				✓		✓
				✓		

TEACHING MATERIALS

Teacher's Wraparound Edition of Text
Teacher's Resource Guide
Teacher's Edition of Working Papers
MicroExam

APPLIED MATHEMATICS

APPLIED MATH/ACCOUNTING SKILL	APPLICATION
Calculating depreciation using the straight-line method	Prob. 9-2
Calculating loss or gain on disposal of plant assets	Prob. 9-4
Calculating depreciation using the declining-balance method	Prob. 9-6
Calculating depreciation using the sum-of-the-years-digits method	Prob. 9-6
Calculating depreciation using the production-unit method	Prob. 9-7
Calculating depreciation using MACRS	Prob. 9-8
Calculating depletion expense	Prob. 9-9
Calculating property tax	Prob. 9-10

TEACHING STRATEGIES: ACCOUNTING PEDAGOGY

This textbook presents depreciation of plant assets as an important accounting procedure that eventually affects tax reporting at the end of the fiscal period. It is important for students to understand the traditional methods of depreciation as well as alternative methods such as MACRS. It is equally important for students to understand how to make the appropriate adjusting entries.

9

Accounting for Plant Assets

ENABLING PERFORMANCE TASKS

After studying Chapter 9, you will be able to:

a Define accounting terms related to plant assets and depreciation.

b Identify accounting concepts and practices related to accounting for plant assets and depreciation.

c Record plant asset information on plant asset records.

d Calculate depreciation expense for a plant asset.

e Journalize entries for buying and disposing of plant assets.

f Journalize entries for depreciation.

g Calculate and record property tax expense.

TERMS PREVIEW

plant asset record • straight-line method of depreciation • book value of a plant asset • declining-balance method of depreciation • sum-of-the-years-digits method of depreciation • production-unit method of depreciation • Modified Accelerated Cost Recovery System • depletion • real property • personal property • assessed value

SOFTWARE FOCUS

Software may be used for independent practice or enrichment/extension as the instructor deems appropriate. For this chapter, the following software may be used: *Automated Accounting 6.0* or higher with Problems 9-1, 9-6, 9-8, and Challenge Problem 9-C; Spreadsheet Template with Problems 9-6, 9-7, and 9-8.

FYI

Current assets are assets expected to be exchanged for cash or consumed within a year. Plant assets are assets that will be used for a number of years in the operation of a business.

A business owns a variety of assets, all of which are used to help the business earn a profit. Some assets such as cash, accounts receivable, and supplies are exchanged for cash or consumed within a year. Cash and other assets expected to be exchanged for cash or consumed within a year are known as current assets. Other assets such as land, buildings, and equipment are expected to help the business earn a profit for more than one year. Assets which will be used for a number of years in the operation of a business are known as plant assets. Plant assets are sometimes referred to as fixed assets or long-term assets.

An office equipment business may sell such things as desks, chairs, file cabinets, and typewriters. These items are for sale to customers and are not used in the operation of the business. Therefore, equipment purchased for sale to customers is classified as merchandise rather than as plant assets.

PLANT ASSET RECORD

A business keeps a separate record of each plant asset owned. An accounting form on which a business records information about each plant asset is called a **plant asset record.** Appliance Center uses a printed card as its plant asset record. The plant asset record is shown in Illustration 9-1.

ILLUSTRATION 9-1

Plant asset record

1

PLANT ASSET RECORD — General Ledger Account No. *1225*

Description *Copying Machine* — General Ledger Account *Office Equipment*

Date Bought *January 2, 19--* — Serial Number *X3492D194* — Original Cost *$1,680.00*

Estimated Useful Life *5 years* — Estimated Salvage Value *$230.00* — Annual Depreciation *$290.00*

2

Disposed of: Discarded ______ Sold ______ Traded ______

Date ______ Disposal Amount ______

3

YEAR	ANNUAL DEPRECIATION EXPENSE	ACCUMULATED DEPRECIATION	ENDING BOOK VALUE

Appliance Center's plant asset record has three sections. Section 1 is prepared when a plant asset is bought. Information in this section shows the description, general ledger account title and number, date bought, serial number, and information needed to calculate annual depreciation expense for the plant asset. Section 2 provides space for recording disposition of the plant asset. Section 3 provides space for recording annual depreciation expense.

Calculating depreciation and disposing of plant assets are described later in this chapter.

LESSON PLAN 9-1

Materials

- Student pages 247–253
- Blackline Master for Cash Payments Journal (TRG)
- Blackline Master for Plant Asset Record (TRG)
- Software: *Automated Accounting 6.0* or higher; Accounting Textbook Template, Advanced Course

Objectives (Enabling Performance Tasks)

a. Define accounting terms related to plant assets and depreciation.
b. Identify accounting concepts and practices related to accounting for plant assets and depreciation.
c. Record plant asset information on plant asset records.
d. Calculate depreciation expense for a plant asset.
e. Journalize entries for buying and disposing of plant assets.
f. Journalize entries for depreciation.

TEACHING STRATEGIES: TEACHING TIP

Begin this chapter by reviewing adjustments described in Chapter 5, including adjustments for depreciation. This will help students understand that Chapter 9 is an expansion of something they already know.

FOCUS

- Adjustments for depreciation of plant assets were planned on the work sheet in Chapter 5. Explain that Chapter 9 is an expansion of what students already know. In this lesson, journalizing buying plant assets, preparing a plant asset record, calculating depreciation using the straight-line method, and recording depreciation will be presented.
- Introduce vocabulary: plant asset record, straight-line method of depreciation, book value of a plant asset.

BUYING PLANT ASSETS

When a plant asset is bought, a journal entry is recorded and information is placed on a plant asset record.

Buying a Plant Asset for Cash

FYI

Plant assets are sometimes referred to as fixed assets or long-term assets.

Appliance Center needs a new copying machine. Because the copying machine is to be used in the office, the plant asset is classified as office equipment.

Appliance Center has three kinds of plant assets—office equipment, store equipment, and warehouse equipment. Separate general ledger accounts are used for each of these plant assets.

Office Equipment	
1,680.00	

Cash	
	1,680.00

January 2, 19--. Paid cash for new copying machine, $1,680.00. Check No. 62.

Office Equipment is increased by a $1,680.00 debit. Cash is decreased by a $1,680.00 credit.

The journal entry to record this transaction is shown in Illustration 9-2.

ILLUSTRATION 9-2 Journal entry to record buying a plant asset for cash

CASH PAYMENTS JOURNAL — PAGE 1

	DATE		ACCOUNT TITLE	CK. NO.	POST. REF.	1 GENERAL DEBIT	2 GENERAL CREDIT	3 ACCOUNTS PAYABLE DEBIT	4 PURCHASES DISCOUNT CREDIT	5 CASH CREDIT	
1	19-- Jan.	2	Office Equipment	62		1 680 00				1 680 00	1

A plant asset record is also prepared for this new plant asset as shown in Illustration 9-1.

The plant asset record is filed in alphabetic order along with all the other plant asset records for office equipment.

Buying a Plant Asset on Account

Not all plant assets are bought for cash. Appliance Center sometimes buys a plant asset on one date and pays for it on a later date.

GENERAL LEDGER

Office Equipment	
3,300.00	

Accounts Payable	
	3,300.00

ACCOUNTS PAYABLE LEDGER

Discount Computers	
	3,300.00

January 2, 19--. Bought an office computer on account from Discount Computers, $3,300.00. Memorandum No. 70.

Office Equipment is increased by a $3,300.00 debit. Accounts Payable is increased by a $3,300.00 credit. In the accounts payable ledger, Discount Computers is also increased by a $3,300.00 credit.

The journal entry to record this transaction is shown in Illustration 9-3.

This transaction does not involve the purchase of merchandise. Therefore, the entry is *not* recorded in a purchases journal.

ILLUSTRATION 9-3

Journal entry to record buying a plant asset on account

GENERAL JOURNAL PAGE 1

	DATE		ACCOUNT TITLE	DOC. NO.	POST. REF.	DEBIT	CREDIT	
1	19-- Jan.	2	Office Equipment	M70		3 300 00		1
2			Accts. Pay./Discount Computers		/		3 300 00	2

The procedure for preparing the computer's plant asset record is similar to the procedure previously described for preparing the plant asset record for the copying machine.

CALCULATING DEPRECIATION USING THE STRAIGHT-LINE METHOD

FYI

Land is not subject to depreciation.

Plant assets may wear out, no longer be needed in the operation of a business, or become outdated by new models. In order to match revenue with the expenses incurred to earn the revenue, the cost of a plant asset should be allocated to an expense account over the useful life of the plant asset. *(CONCEPT: Matching Expenses with Revenue)* The portion of a plant asset's cost that is transferred to an expense account in each fiscal period during a plant asset's useful life is known as depreciation expense.

Land, because of its permanent nature, is not subject to depreciation. Increases or decreases in land value are usually recorded only when land is sold or otherwise disposed of.

Three factors are used to calculate a plant asset's annual depreciation expense. (1) Original cost. (2) Estimated salvage value. (3) Estimated useful life.

Original Cost

The original cost of a plant asset includes all costs paid to make the asset usable to a business. These costs include the purchase price, delivery costs, and any necessary installation costs. *(CONCEPT: Historical Cost)*

Estimated Salvage Value

When plant assets are disposed of, often some part of the original value still remains. When a plant asset is bought, only an estimate of the final value can be made. The estimated salvage value is the amount an owner expects to receive when a plant asset is removed from use. Salvage value is also referred to as residual value, scrap value, or trade-in value.

Until a plant asset is disposed of, most businesses have difficulty determining a plant asset's *exact* salvage value. Thus, until actually disposed of, a plant asset's salvage value can only be *estimated.*

TEACH

Cover student pages 247–253 "Plant Asset Record," "Buying Plant Assets," "Calculating Depreciation Using the Straight-Line Method," and "Recording Depreciation." Explain the purpose of a plant asset record. Describe the procedure for journalizing buying a plant asset for cash and on account. Discuss the procedure for calculating depreciation using the straight-line method for a year and for part of a year. Emphasize that salvage value and useful life used in calculating depreciation expense are only estimates. Explain the procedure for recording annual depreciation expense on a plant asset record. Discuss the adjusting entry to journalize annual depreciation expense.

TEACHING STRATEGIES: DIFFERENT LEARNING ABILITIES

Limited English Proficiency (LEP) Students. Throughout the course, stress the accounting terms so that LEP students learn the language of accounting.

APPLY

Draw T accounts on the chalkboard to analyze the transactions for buying a plant asset. Use the overhead projector or chalkboard to demonstrate the calculation of depreciation using the straight-line method. Refer students to Illustration 9-4 as recording annual depreciation expense on a plant asset record is discussed.

Guided Practice

- Guide students through the T account analysis of the transactions in Problem 9-1. Have students draw T accounts on a sheet of paper and analyze the first transaction. All students should agree with the analysis before proceeding to the next transaction. Repeat the process until all transactions have been analyzed. The balance of Problem 9-1 can be assigned as Independent Practice.
- Guide students through the calculation of a depreciation table using the straight-line method for the plant asset bought on January 2 in Problem 9-1. Working as a group, calculate the amounts for the first year. All students should agree with the amounts before proceeding to the second year. Repeat the process until the table is complete.

Independent Practice

Assign Terms 1–3; Questions 1–8; and Problems 9-1, 9-2, and 9-3.

Because salvage value is used to calculate a plant asset's annual depreciation, the most accurate estimate possible is made when a plant asset is bought.

Estimated Useful Life

FYI

Estimated salvage value and estimated useful life of an asset are just what the titles imply—they are estimates only.

The estimated useful life is the number of years a plant asset is expected to be useful to a business. A plant asset's useful life differs from one situation to another. Most businesses use past experience as the basis for estimating a plant asset's useful life. If a calculator usually lasts five years for a specific business, then five years is the estimated useful life of a new calculator for that business. Sometimes, however, a business has difficulty estimating a plant asset's useful life. The Internal Revenue Service issues guidelines which give estimated useful life for many plant assets.

Calculating Depreciation Expense

Charging an *equal* amount of depreciation expense for a plant asset in each year of useful life is called the **straight-line method of depreciation.** Appliance Center uses the straight-line method.

Other methods of calculating depreciation are described later in this chapter. Regardless of the method used, the accounts debited and credited for depreciation are the same.

Appliance Center bought a computer on January 2 for $3,300.00. Estimated salvage value is $300.00. Estimated useful life is 5 years. Annual depreciation expense is calculated.

Original Cost	–	Estimated Salvage Value	=	Estimated Total Depreciation Expense
$3,300.00	–	$300.00	=	$3,000.00
Estimated Total Depreciation Expense	÷	**Years of Estimated Useful Life**	=	**Annual Depreciation Expense**
$3,000.00	÷	5	=	$600.00

Annual depreciation expense may also be calculated using an annual percentage rate. In the above example, the plant asset has an estimated useful life of 5 years. Therefore, the annual depreciation rate is 20% (100% *divided by* 5 *equals* .20 or 20%). Estimated total depreciation expense, $3,000.00, *times* depreciation rate, 20%, *equals* annual depreciation expense, $600.00.

Calculating Depreciation Expense for Part of a Year

FYI

19X1 is used to indicate year one instead of using an actual year.

A calendar month is the smallest unit of time used to calculate depreciation. A plant asset may be placed in service at a date other than the first day of a fiscal period. In such cases, depreciation

TEACHING STRATEGIES: TEACHING TIP

The mathematics of calculating depreciation and preparing depreciation tables is involved and often complicated. For these reasons, much of the work on end-of-chapter problems should be done in class so that you can help students immediately.

FYI

Depreciation expense is calculated to the nearest first of a month.

expense is calculated to the nearest first of a month. To calculate depreciation expense for part of a year, the annual depreciation expense is divided by 12 to determine depreciation expense for a month. The monthly depreciation is then multiplied by the number of months the plant asset is used that year.

Appliance Center bought a cabinet on August 8, 19X1. The original cost is $700.00, estimated salvage value is $100.00, and estimated useful life is 5 years. The estimated depreciation expense for 19X1 is calculated as shown below.

STEP 1:

Original Cost	–	Estimated Salvage Value	=	Estimated Total Depreciation Expense
$700.00	–	$100.00	=	$600.00

STEP 2:

Estimated Total Depreciation Expense	÷	Years of Estimated Useful Life	=	Annual Depreciation Expense
$600.00	÷	5	=	$120.00

STEP 3:

Annual Depreciation Expense	÷	Months in a Year	=	Monthly Depreciation Expense
$120.00	÷	12	=	$10.00

STEP 4:

Monthly Depreciation Expense	×	Number of Months Asset Is Used	=	Partial Year's Depreciation Expense
$10.00	×	5	=	$50.00

The depreciation expense for the part of the year Appliance Center used the cabinet is $50.00.

RECORDING DEPRECIATION

Appliance Center records annual depreciation expense in two places for each plant asset. (1) On the plant asset record. (2) As part of the adjusting entries which are posted to general ledger accounts.

Recording Annual Depreciation Expense on a Plant Asset Record

On December 31, Appliance Center recorded the annual depreciation expense on each plant asset record. This information is placed on a plant asset record as shown in Illustration 9-4.

In section 3 of the plant asset record, the year is recorded in the Year column. The depreciation expense for the plant asset is recorded in the Annual Depreciation Expense column. The annual depreciation expense for the cabinet bought August 8, 19X1, is

FYI

An asset cannot be depreciated once its book value equals the estimated salvage value.

ASSESS

Assess student understanding by checking the solutions to the Independent Practice activities.

Reteach

Make transparencies of the cash payments journal and plant asset record from the accounting forms masters provided in the Blackline Masters Section of the Teacher's Resource Guide. Refer students to Recycling Problem 9-R1. Ask students to use T accounts to analyze the January 5 and March 3, 19X1, transactions. Use the transparencies to demonstrate how the transactions are journalized and the information is recorded on the plant asset records. Next, demonstrate the calculation of depreciation tables using the straight-line method for both plant assets.

Extend

Assign Cases for Critical Thinking 1.

Enrich

Use *Automated Accounting 6.0* or higher with Accounting Textbook Template, Advanced Course with Problem 9-1.

CLOSURE

Use Audit Your Understanding questions.

ILLUSTRATION 9-4 Depreciation expense recorded on a plant asset record

PLANT ASSET RECORD

Description	*Cabinet*			General Ledger Account No.	*1225*
				General Ledger Account	*Office Equipment*
Date Bought	*August 8, 19X1*	Serial Number	*Z769D2*	Original Cost	*$700.00*
Estimated Useful Life	*5 years*	Estimated Salvage Value	*$100.00*	Annual Depreciation	*$120.00*

Disposed of: Discarded ______ Sold ______ Traded ______

Date ______ Disposal Amount ______

YEAR	ANNUAL DEPRECIATION EXPENSE	ACCUMULATED DEPRECIATION	ENDING BOOK VALUE
19X1	*50.00*	*50.00*	*650.00*
19X2	*120.00*	*170.00*	*530.00*
19X3	*120.00*	*290.00*	*410.00*
19X4	*120.00*	*410.00*	*290.00*
19X5	*120.00*	*530.00*	*170.00*
19X6	*70.00*	*600.00*	*100.00*

$120.00. However, the amount recorded in the Annual Depreciation Expense column is $50.00, the depreciation expense for the months that the cabinet was used in 19X1. The amount of accumulated depreciation is recorded in the Accumulated Depreciation column. The Accumulated Depreciation is the sum of the previous year's Accumulated Depreciation and the Annual Depreciation Expense for the current year. For example, Accumulated Depreciation for 19X2, $170.00, *plus* Annual Depreciation Expense for 19X3, $120.00, *equals* Accumulated Depreciation for 19X3, $290.00. The original cost of a plant asset minus accumulated depreciation is called the **book value of a plant asset.** A new book value is calculated and recorded in the Ending Book Value column.

At the end of the estimated useful life, the cabinet should be depreciated down to its estimated salvage value. Illustration 9-4 verifies that at the end of the fifth year, the ending book value is equal to the estimated salvage value, *$100.00.* The calculation for depreciation uses an *estimated* useful life. The *actual* useful life of the cabinet may exceed the estimate made when the asset was put into use. If a plant asset is used longer than the estimated useful life, depreciation is *not* recorded once the book value equals the estimated salvage value.

Appliance Center follows the same procedures in recording depreciation information on all plant asset records.

Audit Your Understanding

1. What journal is used for recording buying a plant asset on account when special journals are used?
2. Over what period should the cost of a plant asset be allocated to an expense account?
3. What two formulas are used to calculate annual depreciation for a plant asset using the straight-line method?
4. How is the book value of a plant asset calculated?
5. What accounts are affected, and how, when an adjusting entry is made to record the total estimated depreciation expense for store equipment?

Journalizing Annual Depreciation Expense

After depreciation expense is recorded on the plant asset records, depreciation amounts for the year are

AUDIT YOUR UNDERSTANDING

The AUDIT YOUR UNDERSTANDING feature appears at the end of each section of the chapter. Explain to your students that the word *audit* means to check or verify. AUDIT YOUR UNDERSTANDING may be used to check student comprehension of the section just studied. The answers are provided in Appendix D in the back of the textbook.

1. General journal.
2. Over the useful life of the plant asset.
3. (1) Original cost minus estimated salvage value equals estimated total depreciation expense. (2) Estimated total depreciation expense divided by years of estimated useful life equals annual depreciation expense.
4. Original cost of a plant asset minus accumulated depreciation equals book value of a plant asset.
5. Depreciation Expense—Store Equipment is debited; Accumulated Depreciation—Office Equipment is credited.

totaled. For example, the total for all of Appliance Center's office equipment depreciation expense from plant assets records is $11,571.00.

Depreciation Expense—Office Equipment	
Dec. 31 Adj. 11,571.00	

Accumulated Depreciation—Office Equipment	
	Jan. 1 Bal. 37,434.00
	Dec. 31 Adj. 11,571.00
	Dec. 31 Bal. 49,005.00

An adjusting entry is made to record the total estimated depreciation expense for a fiscal year.

Depreciation Expense—Office Equipment is increased by a $11,571.00 debit. Accumulated Depreciation—Office Equipment is increased by a $11,571.00 credit.

The adjusting entry is shown in Illustration 9-5.

A similar adjusting entry for depreciation expense is recorded for store equipment, warehouse equipment, and building.

ILLUSTRATION 9-5 Adjusting entry to journalize office equipment depreciation expense

GENERAL JOURNAL PAGE *13*

	DATE		ACCOUNT TITLE	DOC. NO.	POST. REF.	DEBIT	CREDIT	
1			*Adjusting Entries*					1
22		*31*	*Depr. Exp.—Office Equipment*			*11 571 00*		22
23			*Accum. Depr.—Office Equipment*				*11 571 00*	23
24								24

DISPOSING OF PLANT ASSETS

Appliance Center usually disposes of plant assets in one of three ways.

FYI

Discard means to throw away.

1. The plant asset is discarded because no useful life remains.
2. The plant asset is sold because it is no longer needed even though it might still be usable.
3. The plant asset is traded for another plant asset of the same kind.

Discarding a Plant Asset with No Book Value

If a plant asset has a salvage value of zero and the total accumulated depreciation is equal to the original cost value, the plant asset has no book value.

When a plant asset with no book value is discarded, a journal entry is recorded that removes the original cost of the plant asset and its related accumulated depreciation.

Appliance Center discarded a storage cabinet that had no book value.

January 5, 19X6. Discarded storage cabinet: original cost, $275.00; total accumulated depreciation through December 31, 19X5, $275.00. Memorandum No. 72.

LESSON PLAN 9-2

Materials

- Student pages 253–262
- Blackline Master for General Journal (TRG)
- Blackline Master for Cash Receipts Journal (TRG)
- Blackline Master for Cash Payments Journal (TRG)

Objectives (Enabling Performance Tasks)

b. Identify accounting concepts and practices related to accounting for plant assets and depreciation.

e. Journalize entries for buying and disposing of plant assets.

f. Journalize entries for depreciation.

TEACHING STRATEGIES: DIFFERENT LEARNING STYLES

Auditory Learner. The auditory learner can reinforce the learning of formulas by verbally explaining the formula and/or calculations to other students in a small group. In a group of three, for example, each student should get the opportunity to "teach" the formula to the other two students. Through this process, each student in the group will "teach" the formula once and "learn" the formula two times.

FOCUS

Journalizing buying plant assets was presented earlier in this chapter. In this lesson, the procedures for disposing of plant assets will be described.

TEACH

Cover student pages 253–262 "Disposing of Plant Assets." Discuss the reasons for disposing of a plant asset. Emphasize that a fully depreciated asset may continue to be used by a business. However, no additional depreciation expense is recorded. Explain the procedure for journalizing each of the ways of disposing of a plant asset. Emphasize that when an asset is disposed of during the year, two journal entries are required. Show how to calculate the loss or gain on the disposal of a plant asset. The journal entry for trade-in of a plant asset is more complicated than other entries. Explain trade-in step-by-step so students can follow. Explain that land is considered to be a permanent plant asset. Therefore, annual depreciation is not recorded.

Accumulated Depreciation—Office Equipment

Debit	Credit
275.00	Bal. 275.00

Office Equipment

Debit	Credit
Bal. 275.00	275.00

Accumulated Depreciation—Office Equipment is decreased by a $275.00 debit. This debit cancels the total depreciation recorded for the cabinet. Office Equipment is decreased by a $275.00 credit. This credit cancels the original cost, *$275.00,* recorded when the cabinet was bought. When this entry is journalized and posted, all amounts for the discarded cabinet are removed from the two accounts.

The journal entry to record this transaction is shown in Illustration 9-6. A notation is made in section 2 of the plant asset record for discarding this plant asset with no book value as shown in Illustration 9-7.

ILLUSTRATION 9-6 Journal entry to record discarding a plant asset with no book value

GENERAL JOURNAL — PAGE 1

	DATE		ACCOUNT TITLE	DOC. NO.	POST. REF.	DEBIT	CREDIT	
7		5	Accum. Depr.—Office Equipment	M72		275 00		7
8			Office Equipment				275 00	8
9								9
10								10

The date on which the cabinet was discarded, January 5, 19X6, is written in the space for the disposition date. The book value at the time the cabinet was discarded, *zero,* is written in the space for disposal amount.

ILLUSTRATION 9-7 Plant asset record showing discarding of a plant asset

PLANT ASSET RECORD

General Ledger Account No. *1225*
Description *Storage Cabinet* — General Ledger Account *Office Equipment*
Date Bought *January 3, 19X1* — Serial Number *AX5034* — Original Cost *$275.00*
Estimated Useful Life *5 years* — Estimated Salvage Value *zero* — Annual Depreciation *$55.00*

Disposed of: Discarded ✓ — Sold ______ — Traded ______
Date *January 5, 19X6* — Disposal Amount *zero*

YEAR	ANNUAL DEPRECIATION EXPENSE	ACCUMULATED DEPRECIATION	ENDING BOOK VALUE
19X1	55.00	55.00	220.00
19X2	55.00	110.00	165.00
19X3	55.00	165.00	110.00
19X4	55.00	220.00	55.00
19X5	55.00	275.00	—

Global Perspective

INTERNATIONAL INTRODUCTIONS

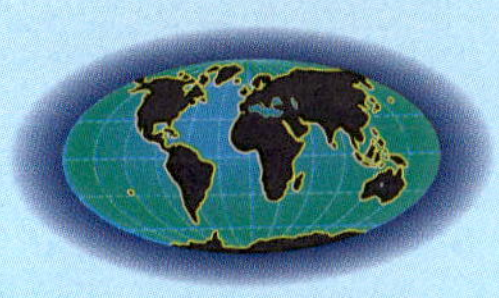

International business dictates that introductions be made in a culturally acceptable manner. People from other countries may decide from your first meeting whether they want to do business with you or not. Therefore, it is very important that introductions be handled correctly.

Introductions between Westerners and people in other countries often require different approaches, some of which follow.

- Do not use first names with foreign business associates until invited to do so.
- In some countries, bowing is part of the culture. Do not bow unless you know it is acceptable. They may think you are making fun of their customs.
- In Japan, address a person by adding Mr. or Mrs. to their last name.
- Chinese names appear in the reverse order of names in the United States. The family name or "last" name precedes the first name. For example, Mr. Wu Ho is called Mr. Wu because Ho is his first name.
- People from India prefer to be addressed by their last names and their titles (such as Dr. or Mr.).
- For people from the Middle East, address them as their name appears on their business card. Usually Mr. or Sheik will be used. If they are members of a royal family, use Your Excellency.
- In Latin America, address a person as Señor, Señora, or Señorita, followed by the last name. If they have a title such as doctor, be sure to use it.

GLOBAL PERSPECTIVE ACTIVITY:

Research introductions and cultures with regard to meeting foreign businesspeople. Find the appropriate introduction for meeting someone from Germany, South Africa, and England.

Discarding a Plant Asset with a Book Value

Appliance Center discarded a table that is damaged beyond repair. The table still has a book value.

> *June 30, 19X6. Discarded office table: original cost, $200.00; total accumulated depreciation through December 31, 19X5, $140.00; additional depreciation to be recorded through June 30, 19X6, $20.00. Memorandum No. 92.*

Two entries are recorded for discarding a plant asset with a book value. (1) A journal entry to record depreciation expense for part of a year. (2) A journal entry to discard a plant asset with a book value.

Journal Entry to Record Depreciation Expense for Part of a Year. A plant asset may be disposed of at any time during its useful life. When a plant asset is disposed of, its depreciation expense from the beginning of the current fiscal year to the date of disposal is recorded. For example, adjusting entries for depreciation expense were last recorded on December 31, 19X5. The table was discarded on June 30, 19X6. Before entries are made for the disposal of the table, six months' depreciation expense must be recorded. The six months' depreciation expense is for the period from January 1 to June 30, 19X6. The annual depreciation expense for the table is $40.00.

Global Perspective

The GLOBAL PERSPECTIVE feature is intended to expose students to some of the ways in which accounting and business in general differ in other countries. This GLOBAL PERSPECTIVE feature allows students to explore international customs for handling introductions.

The GLOBAL PERSPECTIVE activity requires students to research introductions and cultures for meeting foreign business people from a variety of countries. Student responses will vary depending on the countries that are chosen. Have students report their findings to the class.

TEACHING STRATEGIES: TEACHING TIP

Emphasize that when an asset is disposed of during the year, two journal entries are required. (1) A journal entry to record depreciation for part of the year. (2) A journal entry to record disposal of the plant asset.

APPLY

Draw T accounts on the chalkboard to analyze each transaction for disposing of a plant asset. Write each formula on the board and demonstrate all calculations.

Guided Practice

Guide students through the T account analysis of the transactions in Problem 9-4. Students will need the plant assets records used in Problem 9-3. Have students draw T accounts on a sheet of paper and analyze the first transaction. All students should agree with the analysis before proceeding to the next transaction. Repeat the process until all transactions have been analyzed. The balance of Problem 9-4 can be assigned as Independent Practice.

Independent Practice

Assign Questions 9–16 and Problems 9-4 and 9-5.

Depreciation Expense—Office Equipment

Debit	Credit
Add. Depr. 20.00	

Accumulated Depreciation—Office Equipment

Debit	Credit
	Bal. 140.00
	Add. Depr. 20.00
	(New Bal. 160.00)

Depreciation Expense—Office Equipment is increased by a $20.00 debit. Accumulated Depreciation—Office Equipment is increased by a $20.00 credit.

The journal entry to record the six months' depreciation expense is shown on lines 4-5 of the general journal in Illustration 9-8. A notation is made in section 3 of the plant asset record to record depreciation expense for part of a year for this office table.

ILLUSTRATION 9-8

Journal entries to record depreciation expense for part of a year and to discard a plant asset with book value

GENERAL JOURNAL — PAGE 6

	DATE		ACCOUNT TITLE	DOC. NO.	POST. REF.	DEBIT	CREDIT	
4		30	*Depr. Exp.—Office Equipment*	*M92*		20 00		4
5			*Accum. Depr.—Office Equipment*				20 00	5
6		30	*Accum. Depr.—Office Equipment*	*M92*		160 00		6
7			*Loss on Plant Assets*			40 00		7
8			*Office Equipment*				200 00	8
9								9

Journal Entry to Discard a Plant Asset with a Book Value.

When an asset with a book value is discarded, a journal entry is recorded that achieves the following effects in the accounts.

1. Removes the original cost of the plant asset and its related accumulated depreciation.
2. Recognizes the loss on disposal of the asset.

FYI

A loss from discarding a plant asset is not an operating expense. Loss on Plant Assets is classified as an Other Expense.

After the partial year's depreciation expense is recorded, an entry is made for discarding the table. Discarding a plant asset with a book value is a loss to the business. The amount of the loss on the table is calculated as shown below.

Original Cost	–	Accumulated Depreciation	=	Book Value of Plant Asset
$200.00	–	$160.00	=	$40.00

Accumulated Depreciation—Office Equipment

Debit	Credit
160.00	Bal. 160.00

Loss on Plant Assets

Debit	Credit
40.00	

Office Equipment

Debit	Credit
Bal. 200.00	200.00

Accumulated Depreciation—Office Equipment is decreased by a $160.00 debit. Loss on Plant Assets is increased by a $40.00 debit. Office Equipment is decreased by a $200.00 credit.

A loss from discarding a plant asset is not an operating expense. Therefore, Loss on Plant Assets is classified as an Other Expense as shown in Appliance Center's chart of accounts.

The journal entry to record this transaction is shown on lines 6-8 of the general journal, Illustration 9-8. A notation is made in section 2 of the plant asset record for discarding this office table.

Selling a Plant Asset for Less than Book Value

When a plant asset is sold for less than book value, a journal entry is recorded that achieves the following effects in the accounts.

1. Removes the original cost of the plant asset and its related accumulated depreciation.
2. Recognizes the cash received.
3. Recognizes the loss on disposal of the asset.

Cash	
185.00	

Accumulated Depreciation—Office Equipment	
400.00	Bal. 400.00

Loss on Plant Assets	
15.00	

Office Equipment	
Bal. 600.00	600.00

Appliance Center sold a typewriter bought in 19X2.

January 4, 19X6. Received cash from sale of typewriter, $185.00: original cost, $600.00; total accumulated depreciation through December 31, 19X5, $400.00. Receipt No. 60.

Cash is increased by a $185.00 debit. Accumulated Depreciation—Office Equipment is decreased by a $400.00 debit. Loss on Plant Assets is increased by a $15.00 debit. Office Equipment is decreased by a $600.00 credit.

The amount of the loss is calculated as shown below.

Book Value of Asset Sold			–	Value of Asset Received	=	Loss on Disposal
Cost		$600.00				
Accum. Depr.	–	400.00				
Book Value		$200.00	–	Cash $185.00	=	$15.00 Loss

FYI

It is important to keep plant asset records up to date. Always record the sale of an asset in the plant asset record as soon as possible after the asset has been removed from use.

The typewriter sold by Appliance Center had a book value of $200.00 on January 4, 19X6. However, the amount of cash received for the typewriter was $185.00, $15.00 less than the book value.

The journal entry to record this transaction in a cash receipts journal is shown in Illustration 9-9. A notation is made in section 2 of the plant asset record to record the sale of the typewriter for less than book value.

ILLUSTRATION 9-9 Journal entry to record the sale of a plant asset for less than book value

CASH RECEIPTS JOURNAL — PAGE 1

	Date		Account Title	Doc. No.	Post. Ref.	1 General Debit	2 General Credit	3 Accounts Receivable Credit	4 Sales Credit	5 Sales Tax Payable Debit	6 Sales Tax Payable Credit	7 Sales Discount Debit	8 Cash Debit	
1	19X6 Jan.	4	Accum. Depr.—Office Equip.	R60		400 00							185 00	1
2			Loss on Plant Assets			15 00								2
3			Office Equipment				600 00							3
4														4

ASSESS

Assess student understanding by checking the solutions to the Independent Practice activities.

Reteach

- Make transparencies of the general, cash receipts, and cash payments journals from the accounting forms masters provided in the Blackline Masters Section of the Teacher's Resource Guide. Refer students to Recycling Problem 9-R1. Ask students to use T accounts to analyze the January 3, March 5, and June 29, 19X3, transactions. Use the transparencies to demonstrate how the transactions are journalized.
- Assign Recycling Problem 9-R1.

Enrich

Assign and discuss the GLOBAL PERSPECTIVE feature on page 255.

CLOSURE

Use Audit Your Understanding questions.

Selling a Plant Asset for More than Book Value

Appliance Center sold a warehouse cart for more than its book value.

> *March 31, 19X6. Received cash from sale of warehouse cart, $700.00: original cost, $1,500.00; total accumulated depreciation through December 31, 19X5, $840.00; additional depreciation to be recorded through March 31, 19X6, $35.00. Memorandum No. 99 and Receipt No. 75.*

Two entries are recorded for selling a plant asset for more than book value. (1) A journal entry to record depreciation expense for part of a year. (2) A journal entry to record the sale of a plant asset for more than book value.

TEACHING STRATEGIES: TEACHING TIP

Emphasize the steps to follow in analyzing a journal entry for disposing of a plant asset. (1) Record depreciation expense for part of year to date of disposal. (2) Remove the original cost of the plant asset and its related accumulated depreciation. (3) Recognize any cash received, if applicable. (4) Recognize any gain or loss, if applicable.

Depreciation Expense—Warehouse Equipment	
Add. Depr. 35.00	

Accumulated Depreciation—Warehouse Equipment	
	Bal. 840.00
	Add. Depr. 35.00
	(New Bal. 875.00)

Journal Entry to Record Depreciation Expense for Part of a Year. Annual depreciation expense for the warehouse cart is $140.00. Depreciation for three months, one-fourth of a year, is $35.00.

Depreciation Expense—Warehouse Equipment is increased by a $35.00 debit. Accumulated Depreciation—Warehouse Equipment is increased by a $35.00 credit.

This journal entry is similar to the entry on lines 4-5 of the general journal, Illustration 9-8. A notation is made in section 3 of the plant asset record to record depreciation expense for part of a year for this warehouse cart.

Journal Entry to Record the Sale of a Plant Asset for More than Book Value. When a plant asset is sold for more than book value, a journal entry is recorded that achieves the following effects in the accounts.

FYI

A gain from the sale of plant assets is not operating revenue. Gain on Plant Assets is classified as Other Revenue.

1. Removes the original cost of the plant asset and its related accumulated depreciation.
2. Recognizes the cash received.
3. Recognizes the gain on disposal of the asset.

After depreciation expense is recorded for part of a year, a journal entry is made for the sale of the plant asset. The warehouse equipment is sold for $700.00. The ending book value is $625.00. The gain of $75.00 is calculated as shown below.

Value of Asset Received	–	Book Value of Asset Sold			=	Gain on Disposal
		Cost		$1,500.00		
		Accum. Depr.	–	875.00		
Cash $700.00	–	Book Value		$ 625.00	=	$75.00 Gain

APPLIED SKILLS: WORD PROCESSING

If you wish to integrate word processing in your accounting course, you may direct students to answer the end-of-chapter Accounting Terms, Questions for Individual Study, and Cases for Critical Thinking using their word processing software.

Cash	
700.00	

Accumulated Depreciation—Warehouse Equipment	
875.00	Bal. 875.00

Warehouse Equipment	
Bal. 1,500.00	1,500.00

Gain on Plant Assets	
	75.00

Cash is increased by a $700.00 debit. Accumulated Depreciation—Warehouse Equipment is decreased by an $875.00 debit. Warehouse Equipment is decreased by a $1,500.00 credit. Gain on Plant Assets is increased by a $75.00 credit.

A gain from the sale of plant assets is not operating revenue. Therefore, Gain on Plant Assets is classified as Other Revenue as shown in Appliance Center's chart of accounts.

The journal entry to record this transaction is shown in Illustration 9-10. A notation is made in section 2 of the plant asset record to record the sale of the warehouse cart for more than book value.

ILLUSTRATION 9-10 Journal entry to record the sale of a plant asset for more than book value

CASH RECEIPTS JOURNAL PAGE 6

	DATE	ACCOUNT TITLE	DOC. NO.	POST. REF.	1 GENERAL DEBIT	2 GENERAL CREDIT	3 ACCOUNTS RECEIVABLE CREDIT	4 SALES CREDIT	5 SALES TAX PAYABLE DEBIT	6 SALES TAX PAYABLE CREDIT	7 SALES DISCOUNT DEBIT	8 CASH DEBIT	
21	31	Accum. Depr.—Warehouse Equip.	R75		875 00							700 00	21
22		Warehouse Equipment				1 500 00							22
23		Gain on Plant Assets				75 00							23
24													24

TEACHING STRATEGIES: DIFFERENT LEARNING STYLES

Kinesthetic Learner. The kinesthetic learner should have the opportunity to perform the calculations to solve the formula. One way to accomplish this is to develop data about several depreciable assets. The student should calculate the depreciation table for each asset using the three different methods of calculating depreciation expense.

Trading a Plant Asset

Businesses often buy a new plant asset by paying cash and trading in a similar plant asset. For example, Appliance Center needed a new store counter. The vendor agreed to take cash and an old store counter in trade.

June 27, 19X6. Paid cash, $850.00, plus old store counter for new store counter: original cost of old counter, $1,000.00; total accumulated depreciation through December 31, 19X5, $720.00; additional depreciation to be recorded through June 27, 19X6, $45.00 Memorandum No. 130 and Check No. 154.

Two entries are recorded for the trading of a plant asset. (1) A journal entry to record depreciation expense for part of a year. (2) A journal entry to record the trade-in of an old plant asset for a new plant asset.

Depreciation Expense—Store Equipment	
Add. Depr. 45.00	

Accumulated Depreciation—Store Equipment	
	Bal. 720.00 Add. Depr. 45.00 *(New Bal. 765.00)*

Journal Entry to Record Depreciation Expense for Part of a Year. Additional depreciation expense for the first six months of 19X6 is recorded first.

Depreciation Expense—Store Equipment is increased by a $45.00 debit. Accumulated Depreciation—Store Equipment is increased by a $45.00 credit.

FYI

The entry for a trade-in is somewhat more complicated than the entry for a sale or discard of an asset. Follow the step-by-step procedures as outlined, and the entry will be easy to complete.

The journal entry to record the additional depreciation expense is similar to the one shown on lines 4-5 of the general journal, Illustration 9-8. A notation is made in section 3 of the plant asset record to record depreciation expense for part of a year for the old counter.

Journal Entry to Record Trade-In of an Old Plant Asset for a New Plant Asset. When an old plant asset is traded for a new plant asset, a journal entry is recorded that achieves the following effects in the accounts.

1. Removes the original cost of the old plant asset and its related accumulated depreciation.
2. Recognizes the cash paid.
3. Records the new plant asset at its original cost.

The new plant asset's original cost equals the cash *actually* paid plus the book value of the asset traded. *(CONCEPT: Historical Cost)* The original cost of the new counter is calculated as follows.

APPLIED SKILLS: WRITING ACROSS THE CURRICULUM

Writing paragraphs and short essays. The Cases for Critical Thinking are short, practical applications of the accounting principles developed in the chapter. Some cases are planned to present problems related to the chapter but not specifically discussed and answered in the chapter. These cases present an opportunity for critical thinking and decision making. These cases also require more than a short objective-type response. Therefore they provide ideal practice in writing paragraphs and short essays.

	Book Value of Asset Traded		+	Cash Paid	=	Original Cost of New Asset
Cost		$1,000.00				
Accum. Depr.	–	765.00				
Book Value		$ 235.00	+	Cash $850.00	=	$1,085.00 New Counter

Store Equipment

Debit		Credit	
Bal.	1,000.00	Trade-in	1,000.00
New Equip.	1,085.00		

Accumulated Depreciation—Store Equipment

Debit		Credit	
	765.00	Bal.	765.00

Cash

Debit		Credit	
			850.00

Store Equipment is decreased by a $1,000.00 credit, the original cost of the old counter. Store Equipment is also increased by a $1,085.00 debit, the original cost of the new counter. Accumulated Depreciation—Store Equipment is decreased by a $765.00 debit, total depreciation recorded to date on the traded item. Cash is decreased by a $850.00 credit.

The journal entry to record the trade-in of the old counter for the new counter is shown in Illustration 9-11 on page 261. A notation is made in section 2 of the old counter's plant asset record to show the trade-in. A new plant asset record is prepared for the new counter.

Selling Land and Buildings

FYI

Any gain or loss on the disposal of land is recorded at the time it is disposed of.

Land is considered to be a permanent plant asset. Therefore, the useful life is not estimated, and annual depreciation is not recorded for land. The book value of land is the original cost. *(CONCEPT: Historical Cost)*

Land is seldom discarded (abandoned). Usually land is sold at the same time as the buildings on the land are sold. Any gain or loss on the disposal of land is recorded at the time the land is disposed of.

ILLUSTRATION 9-11 Journal entry to record the trade-in of a plant asset

CASH PAYMENTS JOURNAL — PAGE 12

	DATE	ACCOUNT TITLE	CK. NO.	POST. REF.	1 GENERAL DEBIT	2 GENERAL CREDIT	3 ACCOUNTS PAYABLE DEBIT	4 PURCHASES DISCOUNT CREDIT	5 CASH CREDIT	
18	27	Store Equipment	154		1 085 00				850 00	18
19		Accum. Depr.—Store Equipment			765 00					19
20		Store Equipment				1 000 00				20

Cash	
97,000.00	

Accumulated Depreciation—Building	
85,000.00	Bal. 85,000.00

Land	
Bal. 25,000.00	25,000.00

Building	
Bal. 150,000.00	150,000.00

Gain on Plant Assets	
	7,000.00

Entries to record discarding (tearing down) or selling buildings are handled the same as for any other plant asset. Buildings are seldom traded for new buildings. But if a building is traded for another building, the entry is the same as for other plant assets.

Fidelity Company sold land with a building for $97,000.00.

January 2, 19X6. Received cash from sale of land and building, $97,000.00 ($30,000.00 for land and $67,000.00 for building): original cost of land, $25,000.00; original cost of building, $150,000.00; total accumulated depreciation on building through December 31, 19X5, $85,000.00. Receipt No. 105.

If the sales contract does not specify separate amounts received for land and buildings, a professional appraisal may be used to determine the separate amounts.

An adjusting entry on December 31, 19X5, brought the depreciation expense and accumulated depreciation on the building up to date. Therefore, no additional entries are needed for depreciation expense. A journal entry is needed that achieves the following effects in the accounts.

1. Removes the original cost of the land and building and the building's related accumulated depreciation.
2. Recognizes the cash received.
3. Recognizes the gain on disposal of the plant assets.

Cash is increased by a $97,000.00 debit. Accumulated Depreciation—Building is decreased by a $85,000.00 debit. Land is decreased by a $25,000.00 credit. Building is decreased by a $150,000.00 credit. Gain on Plant Assets is increased by a $7,000.00 credit.

The amount of the gain is calculated as shown on the next page.

The journal entry to record this transaction is shown in Illustration 9-12. A notation is made in section 2 of the plant asset records to record the sales of the land and building for more than book value.

Audit Your Understanding

1. What three ways might a plant asset be disposed of?
2. When a plant asset is sold for less than book value, a journal entry is recorded that achieves what three effects in the accounts?
3. What is the formula used to calculate the loss recognized on the sale of a plant asset for less than the book value?
4. What is the book value of land?

AUDIT YOUR UNDERSTANDING

1. (1) Discarded because no useful life remains. (2) Sold because the plant asset is no longer needed even though it might still be usable. (3) Traded for another plant asset of the same kind.
2. (1) Removes the original cost of the plant asset and its related accumulated depreciation. (2) Recognizes the cash received. (3) Recognizes the loss on disposal of the asset.
3. Book value of asset sold minus value of asset received equals loss on disposal.
4. The original cost of the land.

Asset Sold	Value of Asset Received	–	Book Value of Asset Sold		=	Gain on Disposal
Land	Cash $30,000.00	–	Book Value	$ 25,000.00	=	$5,000.00 Gain
Building			Cost	$ 150,000.00		
			Accum. Depr. –	85,000.00		
	Cash $67,000.00	–	Book Value	$ 65,000.00	=	$2,000.00 Gain
Total Gain on Plant Assets						$7,000.00

ILLUSTRATION 9-12 Journal entry to record the sale of land and building for more than book value

CASH RECEIPTS JOURNAL PAGE 23

	DATE		ACCOUNT TITLE	DOC. NO.	POST. REF.	1 GENERAL DEBIT	2 GENERAL CREDIT	3 ACCOUNTS RECEIVABLE CREDIT	4 SALES CREDIT	5 SALES TAX PAYABLE DEBIT	6 SALES TAX PAYABLE CREDIT	7 SALES DISCOUNT DEBIT	8 CASH DEBIT	
1	19X6 Jan.	2	Accum. Depr.—Building	R105		85 000 00							97 000 00	1
2			Land				25 000 00							2
3			Building				150 000 00							3
4			Gain on Plant Assets				7 000 00							4
5														5

OTHER METHODS OF CALCULATING DEPRECIATION

Appliance Center uses the straight-line method of depreciation. An equal amount of depreciation expense is recorded each year during the useful life of a plant asset.

Many plant assets depreciate more in the early years of useful life than in later years. For example, an automobile's market price will decrease more the first year of service than in later years. Therefore, charging more depreciation expense in the early years of a plant asset may be more accurate than charging the same amount each year. Three methods other than the straight-line method of depreciation may be used.

1. Declining-balance method of calculating depreciation.
2. Sum-of-the-years-digits method of calculating depreciation.
3. Production-unit method of calculating depreciation.

Regardless of the method used to calculate the amount of depreciation expense, the general ledger accounts affected are the same.

Declining-Balance Method of Depreciation

Multiplying the book value at the end of each fiscal period by a constant depreciation rate is called the **declining-balance method of depreciation.** Although the rate is the same each year, the book

LESSON PLAN 9-3

Materials

- Student pages 262–271
- Software: Spreadsheet Template; *Automated Accounting 6.0* or higher; Accounting Textbook Template, Advanced Course
- Assess: Problem Test Chapter 9, MicroExam Chapter 9

Objectives (Enabling Performance Tasks)

a. Define accounting terms related to plant assets and depreciation.
b. Identify accounting concepts and practices related to accounting for plant assets and depreciation.
d. Calculate depreciation expense for a plant asset.
f. Journalize entries for depreciation.
g. Calculate and record property tax expense.

TEACHING STRATEGIES: TEACHING TIP

Emphasize that each business selects the method of calculating depreciation that is most accurate for that specific business. Also, businesses do not switch arbitrarily from one method to another.

FYI

The greatest depreciation expense is recorded in the first year when the declining-balance method is used.

value declines from one year to the next because of the increasing accumulated depreciation. The greatest book value exists during the first year. Therefore, the greatest depreciation expense is recorded in the first year. Because the smallest book value exists during the last year, the least depreciation expense is recorded in the last year.

The declining-balance depreciation rate is greater than the straight-line rate. Because of the ease in calculating, many businesses use a declining-balance rate that is twice the straight-line rate. For example, if a plant asset has an estimated useful life of 5 years, then the declining-balance rate is calculated as shown below.

Estimated Total Depreciation Expense	÷	Years of Estimated Useful Life	=	Straight-Line Rate
100%	÷	5	=	20%

Straight-Line Rate	×	2	=	Declining-Balance Rate
20%	×	2	=	40%

Depreciation expense calculated using both the declining-balance and the straight-line methods is shown in Illustration 9-13.

ILLUSTRATION 9-13

Comparison of two methods of calculating annual depreciation expense for the same plant asset

Plant asset: Cash Register
Original cost: $2,000.00
Estimated salvage value: $175.00
Estimated useful life: 5 years

Year	Straight-Line Method			Declining-Balance Method		
	Beg. Book Value	Annual Depr.	End. Book Value	Beg. Book Value	Annual Depr.	End. Book Value
1	$2,000.00	$ 365.00	$1,635.00	$2,000.00	$ 800.00	$1,200.00
2	1,635.00	365.00	1,270.00	1,200.00	480.00	720.00
3	1,270.00	365.00	905.00	720.00	288.00	432.00
4	905.00	365.00	540.00	432.00	172.80	259.20
5	540.00	365.00	175.00	259.20	84.20	175.00
Total Depr.	—	$1,825.00	—	—	$1,825.00	—

FYI

Many businesses use a declining-balance rate that is twice the straight-line rate.

When using the declining-balance method, the annual depreciation expense is calculated using the beginning book value for each year. The beginning book value is the same as the ending book value from the previous year. More depreciation expense is recorded in the earlier years of a plant asset. The annual depreciation expense for the first year using the declining-balance method is calculated as shown on page 264.

FOCUS

- The straight-line method of calculating depreciation was presented earlier in this chapter. In this lesson, other methods of calculating depreciation will be described. In addition, the procedure for calculating and paying property tax will be explained.
- Introduce vocabulary: declining-balance method of depreciation, sum-of-the-years-digits method of depreciation, production-unit method of depreciation, Modified Cost Recovery System, depletion, real property, personal property, assessed value.

TEACH

Cover student pages 262–271 "Other Methods of Calculating Depreciation," "Calculating Depreciation Expense for Income Tax Purposes," "Depletion," and "Calculating and Paying Property Tax." Explain the procedure for calculating depreciation expense using each of the three other methods. Explain that the rate used in the declining-balance method of depreciation stays the same each year. Since the book value of the plant asset decreases each year, the amount of annual depreciation also decreases each year. Remind students that a plant asset is not to be depreciated below its estimated salvage value. Emphasize that for sum-of-the-years-digits method the fraction for the first year uses the last year's digit for the numerator. Explain the procedure for calculating depreciation expense for income tax purposes. Remind students that salvage value is not used in the calculation. Explain the procedure for calculating depletion expense for a natural resource plant asset. Describe how governmental units assess property value and calculate property taxes.

Beginning Book Value	×	Rate	=	Annual Depreciation Expense
$2,000.00	×	40%	=	$800.00

The ending book value for the first year is calculated as shown below.

Beginning Book Value	–	Annual Depreciation Expense	=	Ending Book Value
$2,000.00	–	$800.00	=	$1,200.00

FYI

A plant asset is never depreciated below its estimated salvage value.

When using the declining-balance method, a different amount of depreciation expense is recorded each year. Special care must be taken in calculating depreciation expense for the last year of useful life. A plant asset is never depreciated below its estimated salvage value. Therefore, in the last year, only enough depreciation expense is recorded to reduce the book value of the plant asset to its salvage value. For example, in Illustration 9-13, depreciation expense in the fifth year is $84.20 and the ending book value is $175.00.

When using the straight-line method, the same amount, *$365.00,* is recorded as the depreciation expense for each year of the plant asset's useful life. The straight-line method results in a book value equal to salvage value at the end of the last year of useful life.

Sum-of-the-Years-Digits Method of Depreciation

FYI

When using the sum-of-the-years-digits method, the fraction for the first year uses the last year's digit for the numerator.

Another method of calculating depreciation is based on a fraction derived from the years' digits for the useful life of a plant asset. Using fractions based on years of a plant asset's useful life is called the **sum-of-the-years-digits method of depreciation.** The fractions are determined as shown below for the plant asset in Illustration 9-14.

	Years' Digits	Fraction
	1	5/15
	2	4/15
	3	3/15
	4	2/15
	5	1/15
Total	15	

The years' digits are added (1 + 2 + 3 + 4 + 5 = 15). Then, using the sum of the years' digits, a fraction is created for each year with the years' digits in reverse order. Year 1 has a fraction of 5/15. Year 5 has a fraction of 1/15.

TEACHING STRATEGIES: DIFFERENT LEARNING STYLES

Print Learner. When learning formulas, the print learner would prefer to be able to study the formula as given in the textbook or as printed on a separate handout. The print material should show the formula as well as an example of performing the calculations.

ILLUSTRATION 9-14 Calculating depreciation expense using the sum-of-the-years-digits method

Plant asset: Cash Register Original cost: $2,000.00 Estimated salvage value: $175.00 Estimated total depreciation: $1,825.00 Estimated useful life: 5 years			
Year	**Fraction ×**	**Total Depreciation =**	**Year's Annual Depreciation**
1	5/15	$1,825.00	$ 608.33
2	4/15	1,825.00	486.67
3	3/15	1,825.00	365.00
4	2/15	1,825.00	243.33
5	1/15	1,825.00	121.67
Total	—	—	$1,825.00

The first year's depreciation is calculated as shown below.

Original Cost	–	Estimated Salvage Value	=	Estimated Total Depreciation Expense
$2,000.00	–	$175.00	=	$1,825.00
Estimated Total Depreciation Expense	×	**Year's Fraction**	=	**Annual Depreciation Expense**
$1,825.00	×	5/15	=	$608.33

The depreciation expense for each year is calculated by multiplying the total depreciation expense times the fraction for that year. The sum-of-the-years-digits method results in a last year ending book value equal to the plant asset's salvage value. The depreciation expense is calculated using the year's fractions as shown in Illustration 9-14.

Comparison of Three Methods of Depreciation

A comparison of three methods of calculating depreciation expense is shown in Illustration 9-15. The total depreciation expense for the 5 years is $1,825.00.

The straight-line method is relatively easy to calculate. The same amount of depreciation expense is recorded for each of the 5 years of estimated life.

The declining-balance method is relatively easy to calculate. This method records a greater depreciation expense in the early years than is true of the straight-line method.

The sum-of-the-years-digits method is not as easy to use as the straight-line or declining-balance methods. This method also records a greater depreciation expense in the early years than is true of the straight-line method.

APPLY

Write each formula on the board and demonstrate all calculations. Refer students to Illustration 9-15 for a comparison of three methods of calculating depreciation expense.

Guided Practice

Guide students through the calculation of the depreciation expense using the three methods in Problem 9-6. Working as a group, calculate the expense and prepare the depreciation table for the first year for each method. When students agree with the amounts, direct the students to complete the first year of the table provided in the working papers. Repeat the process for the second year. The balance of Problem 9-6 can be completed as Independent Practice.

Independent Practice

- Assign Terms 4–11; Questions 17–20; and Problems 9-6, 9-7, 9-8, 9-9, and 9-10.
- Assign Study Guide 9 and Mastery Problem 9-M.

TEACHING STRATEGIES: APPLYING VISUALS

Direct students to Illustration 9-15 to review the comparison of three methods of calculating depreciation expense.

ASSESS

Assess student understanding by checking the solutions to the Independent Practice activities.

Reteach

- Using information from Recycling Problem 9-R2, demonstrate how to calculate depreciation expense using the straight-line, declining-balance, and sum-of-the-years-digits methods.
- Assign Recycling Problems 9-R2 and 9-R3.

Extend

- Assign Cases for Critical Thinking 2.
- Assign Challenge Problem 9-C.
- Assign the Spreadsheet Template for Problems 9-6, 9-7, and 9-8.

Enrich

- Ask a volunteer to call the local courthouse and find out information about the way in which property is assessed, tax rates determined, and property taxes calculated.
- Use *Automated Accounting 6.0* or higher with Accounting Textbook Template, Advanced Course with Problems 9-6, 9-8, and Challenge Problem 9-C.

ILLUSTRATION 9-15 Comparison of three methods of calculating annual depreciation expense for the same plant asset

Plant asset: Cash Register
Original cost: $2,000.00
Estimated salvage value: $175.00
Estimated useful life: 5 years

Year	Straight-Line Method	Declining-Balance Method	Sum-of-the-Years-Digits Method
1	$ 365.00	$ 800.00	$ 608.33
2	365.00	480.00	486.67
3	365.00	288.00	365.00
4	365.00	172.80	243.33
5	365.00	84.20	121.67
Totals	$1,825.00	$1,825.00	$1,825.00
Ending Book Value	$ 175.00	$ 175.00	$ 175.00

FYI

The formulas for most depreciation methods are calculated in a similar fashion. After the total depreciation expense is calculated, that amount is divided by estimated life, whether it be in units or years.

Production-Unit Method of Depreciation

Sometimes the useful life of a plant asset depends on how much the asset is used. For example, an automobile will wear out faster if driven 80,000 miles a year rather than 60,000. Calculating estimated annual depreciation expense based on the amount of production expected from a plant asset is called the **production-unit method of depreciation.**

Mariah Delivery Service owns a small truck. The original cost of the truck is $18,200.00, estimated salvage value is $2,000.00, and estimated useful life is 90,000 miles. The depreciation rate for the truck is calculated as shown below.

Original Cost	−	Estimated Salvage Value	=	Estimated Total Depreciation Expense
$18,200.00	−	$2,000.00	=	$16,200.00
Estimated Total Depreciation Expense	÷	**Estimated Useful Life**	=	**Depreciation Expense Per Mile Driven**
$16,200.00	÷	90,000 miles	=	$0.18

The annual depreciation expense for the truck during its useful life is shown in Illustration 9-16.

Annual depreciation expense for the first year is calculated as shown below.

Total Miles Driven	×	Depreciation Rate	=	Annual Depreciation Expense
9,000	×	$0.18	=	$1,620.00

TEACHING STRATEGIES: DIFFERENT LEARNING STYLES

Tactile Learner. Suggest using a calculator with a printed tape to perform mathematical calculations. Better calculators also print the operational signs of calculations (+, −, etc.) for students to trace the steps in a calculation.

ILLUSTRATION 9-16 Annual depreciation expense for a plant asset using the production-unit method

Plant asset: Truck Original cost: $18,200.00 Estimated salvage value: $2,000.00 Estimated total depreciation: $16,200.00 Estimated useful life: 90,000 miles Depreciation rate: $0.18 per mile driven				
Year	**Beginning Book Value**	**Miles Driven**	**Annual Depreciation**	**Ending Book Value**
1	$18,200.00	9,000	$ 1,620.00	$16,580.00
2	16,580.00	23,000	4,140.00	12,440.00
3	12,440.00	25,000	4,500.00	7,940.00
4	7,940.00	22,000	3,960.00	3,980.00
5	3,980.00	8,000	1,440.00	2,540.00
Totals	—	87,000	$15,660.00	—

Depreciation expense for each year of the truck's estimated useful life is calculated at 18 cents per mile driven. As shown in Illustration 9-16, the truck's total depreciation at the end of five years is $15,660.00.

CALCULATING DEPRECIATION EXPENSE FOR INCOME TAX PURPOSES

FYI

The Accelerated Cost Recovery System (ACRS) depreciation method was put in place in 1981. The ACRS method of depreciation was changed in 1986. The new system was called the Modified Accelerated Cost Recovery System (MACRS) and was enacted by the Tax Reform Act of 1986.

Most businesses use one of the generally accepted accounting methods to calculate depreciation for financial reporting purposes. However, the Internal Revenue Service requires that for most plant assets placed in service after 1986, the IRS' Modified Accelerated Cost Recovery System depreciation method be used for income tax calculation purposes. A depreciation method required by the Internal Revenue Service to be used for income tax calculation purposes for most plant assets placed in service after 1986 is called the **Modified Accelerated Cost Recovery System.** This depreciation system is generally referred to as MACRS, the initials of its full name.

MACRS is a depreciation method with prescribed periods for eight classes of useful life for plant assets. Property is assigned to a specified class based on the property's characteristics and general life expectancy. The two most common classes, other than real estate, are the five-year and the seven-year property classes. The five-year property class includes cars, general purpose trucks, computers, manufacturing equipment, and office machinery. The seven-year property class includes office furniture and fixtures. The depreciation for these two property classes approximates the use of the declining-balance method using twice the straight-line rate.

To calculate depreciation using MACRS, the Internal Revenue Service has prescribed methods that use annual percentage rates to

CLOSURE

Use Audit Your Understanding questions.

ASSESS

- Administer Problem Test Chapter 9.
- Administer a MicroExam test for Chapter 9.

TEACHING STRATEGIES: TEACHING TIP

Gather financial statements from several businesses. Use these financial statements for demonstration purposes or on a bulletin board to demonstrate disclosure requirements for the method of calculating depreciation used by each business.

determine depreciation for each class of plant asset. These rates are applied to the total cost of the plant asset without considering a salvage value. All plant assets are assumed to be placed in service in the middle of the year and taken out of service in the middle of the year. For example, the five-year property class depreciation is spread over six years, as shown in the MACRS schedule of depreciation rates below.

Year	Five-Year Class Depreciation Rates
1	20.00%
2	32.00%
3	19.20%
4	11.52%
5	11.52%
6	5.76%
Total	100.00%

TEACHING STRATEGIES: DIFFERENT LEARNING STYLES

Visual Learner. Formulas, such as those used to calculate depreciation expense, should be illustrated on the chalkboard to assist visual learners. The instructor should also complete the calculations for a few depreciable assets to show the process to visual learners.

FYI

The differences between ACRS and MACRS are the class lives designed for particular assets and the depreciation methods allowed for recovering their cost.

Annual depreciation expense for Appliance Center's printer using MACRS is shown in Illustration 9-17. Annual depreciation is calculated by multiplying the plant asset's original cost times the depreciation rate for the specific class of plant asset. A printer is classed as five-year property. The first year's depreciation expense using MACRS for five-year property is calculated as shown below.

Year	Original Cost	×	Depreciation Rate	=	Annual Depreciation
1	$2,000.00	×	20.0%	=	$400.00

ILLUSTRATION 9-17

Depreciation for financial reporting purposes using MACRS for tax calculation purposes

Plant asset: Printer
Original cost: $2,000.00
Depreciation method: MACRS
Property class: 5-year

Year	Depreciation Rate	Annual Depreciation
1	20.00%	$ 400.00
2	32.00%	640.00
3	19.20%	384.00
4	11.52%	230.40
5	11.52%	230.40
6	5.76%	115.20
Totals	100.00%	$2,000.00

TEACHING STRATEGIES: COOPERATIVE LEARNING

Divide the class into groups of four or five students each. Using Cases for Critical Thinking, each group analyzes the cases and arrives at agreed-upon solutions. One member of each group is appointed the recorder and presents the group's analysis to the class. This cooperative learning activity should not take more than 20 to 25 minutes of class time.

DEPLETION

Some plant assets decrease in value because part of the plant asset is physically removed in the operation of a business. For example, a lumber business owns land on which there are many trees. The business removes the trees to use for lumber. The land with the trees still growing on it is more valuable than the land after the trees have been removed. The decrease in the value of a plant asset because of the removal of a natural resource is called **depletion.**

McGladden Company owns land on which a coal mine is located. The land with the coal has an original cost of $100,000.00. The company's experts estimate that the land contains 50,000 tons of recoverable coal. Also, after the coal is removed, the estimated value of the remaining land is $12,250.00. Therefore, each ton of coal taken from the land decreases the land's value by $1.755. The depletion rate is calculated as shown below.

FYI

Each quantity of natural resource removed from the land decreases (depletes) the value of the plant asset.

Original Cost	–	**Estimated Salvage Value**	=	**Estimated Total Value of Coal**
$100,000.00	–	$12,250.00	=	$87,750.00
Estimated Total Value of Coal	÷	**Estimated Tons of Recoverable Coal**	=	**Depletion Rate Per Ton of Coal**
$87,750.00	÷	50,000	=	$1.755

In the first year of operation, the business removed 8,000 tons of coal. The depletion expense for the first year is $14,040.00 (tons removed, 8,000, *times* depletion rate, $1.755, *equals* depletion expense, $14,040.00).

McGladden uses general ledger accounts titled Mine, Accumulated Depletion—Mine, and Depletion Expense—Mine. To record depletion, Depletion Expense—Mine is debited and Accumulated Depletion—Mine is credited. Entries are similar to those for depreciation of other plant assets.

APPLIED SKILLS: LANGUAGE ARTS

Paraphrasing, writing complete sentences, and identifying subjects. For additional practice in language arts skills, direct students to answer the Accounting Terms and Questions for Individual Study at the end of the chapter. Students should write the answers in their own words and in complete sentences. To further practice language arts skills, ask students to underline the subject(s) in each sentence of their answers.

CALCULATING AND PAYING PROPERTY TAX

For tax purposes, state and federal governments define two kinds of property: real and personal. Land and anything attached to the land is called **real property.** Real property is sometimes referred to as real estate. All property not classified as real property is called **personal property.** For tax purposes, these definitions apply whether the property is owned by a business or an individual.

Assessed Value of Property

The value of an asset determined by tax authorities for the purpose of calculating taxes is called the **assessed value.** Assessed value is usually based on the judgment of persons referred to as assessors.

AUDIT YOUR UNDERSTANDING

1. One that is twice the straight-line rate.
2. Production-unit method.
3. For income tax calculation.
4. Natural resources such as trees, coal, and oil.
5. Land and anything attached to the land.

Assessors are elected by citizens or are specially trained employees of a governmental unit.

The assessed value of an asset may not be the same as the book value on the business' or individual's records. The assessed value is assigned to an asset for tax purposes only. Often the assessed value is only a part of the true value of the asset. However, many persons and businesses use the assessed value to estimate the market value of an asset.

Audit Your Understanding

1. What declining-balance rate is used by many businesses?
2. Which depreciation method is a business using if annual depreciation is based on miles driven?
3. For what purpose is the MACRS depreciation method used?
4. What type of assets are subject to depletion?
5. What is real property?

Calculating Property Tax on Plant Assets

Most governmental units with taxing power have a tax based on the value of real property. The real property tax is used on buildings and land. Some governmental units also tax personal property such as cars, boats, trailers, and airplanes.

A governmental taxing unit determines a tax rate to use in calculating taxes. The tax rate is multiplied by an asset's *assessed* value, not the book value recorded on a business' records.

Appliance Center's buildings and land have been assessed for a total of $65,000.00. The city tax rate is 5%. Appliance Center's annual property tax is calculated as shown below.

Assessed Value	×	Tax Rate	=	Annual Property Tax
$65,000.00	×	5%	=	$3,250.00

FYI

Property tax is classified as an operating expense.

Appliance Center is required to pay property tax in two installments. On May 1 and November 1 of each year, Appliance Center must pay the city $1,625.00 (annual tax, $3,250.00, *divided by* 2 *equals* each installment, $1,625.00).

Paying Property Tax on Plant Assets

On May 1, Appliance Center paid the first installment of its property tax.

May 1, 19--. Paid cash for first installment of property tax, $1,625.00. Check No. 122.

Property Tax Expense	
1,625.00	

Cash	
	1,625.00

Property Tax Expense is increased by a $1,625.00 debit. Cash is decreased by a $1,625.00 credit.

The journal entry to record payment of property tax is shown in Illustration 9-18.

Payment of all assessed taxes is necessary if a firm is to continue in business. Therefore, Appliance Center classifies property tax as an operating expense.

ILLUSTRATION 9-18 Journal entry to record payment of property tax

CASH PAYMENTS JOURNAL — PAGE 9

	DATE		ACCOUNT TITLE	CK. NO.	POST. REF.	1 GENERAL DEBIT	2 GENERAL CREDIT	3 ACCOUNTS PAYABLE DEBIT	4 PURCHASES DISCOUNT CREDIT	5 CASH CREDIT	
1	19-- May	1	*Property Tax Expense*	122		1625 00				1625 00	1
2											2

ACCOUNTING TERMS EPT(a)

What is the meaning of each of the following?

1. **plant asset record**
2. **straight-line method of depreciation**
3. **book value of a plant asset**
4. **declining-balance method of depreciation**
5. **sum-of-the-years-digits method of depreciation**
6. **production-unit method of depreciation**
7. **Modified Accelerated Cost Recovery System**
8. **depletion**
9. **real property**
10. **personal property**
11. **assessed value**

QUESTIONS FOR INDIVIDUAL STUDY EPT(b)

1. What accounts are affected, and how, when cash is paid for office equipment?
2. In order to match revenue with the expenses incurred to earn the revenue, the cost of a plant asset should be allocated to an expense over what period of time?
3. Which accounting concept is being applied when depreciation expense is recorded for plant assets?
4. Why is annual depreciation not recorded for land?
5. What three factors are used to calculate a plant asset's annual depreciation expense?
6. When using the straight-line method of depreciation, what are the two formulas used to calculate a plant asset's annual depreciation?
7. What is the smallest unit of time used to calculate depreciation?
8. In what two places does Appliance Center record annual depreciation for each plant asset?
9. What accounts are affected, and how, when office equipment with no remaining book value is discarded?
10. What does Appliance Center record on plant asset records for plant assets that have been discarded?
11. When an asset is disposed of after the beginning of the fiscal year, what entry may need to be recorded before an entry is made for the discarding of a plant asset?
12. What accounts are affected, and how, when office equipment with some remaining book value is discarded?
13. What accounts are affected, and how, when office equipment is sold for cash less than its book value?
14. What accounts are affected, and how, when warehouse equipment is sold for cash greater than the remaining book value?
15. What accounts are affected, and how, when cash is paid and old store equipment is traded for new store equipment?
16. In Question 15, what is the formula for calculating the new equipment's original cost?
17. How do the straight-line, declining-balance, and sum-of-the-years-digits methods of calculating depreciation compare?
18. What is the basis for the production-unit method of calculating depreciation?
19. How does a mining company calculate the amount of depletion for a year?
20. What accounts are affected, and how, by an entry to pay property tax?

ACCOUNTING TERMS

1. **plant asset record:** An accounting form on which a business records information about each plant asset. (p. 247)
2. **straight-line method of depreciation:** Charging an *equal* amount of depreciation expense for a plant asset in each year of useful life. (p. 250)
3. **book value of a plant asset:** The original cost of a plant asset minus accumulated depreciation. (p. 252)
4. **declining-balance method of depreciation:** Multiplying the book value at the end of each fiscal period by a constant depreciation rate. (p. 262)
5. **sum-of-the-years-digits method of depreciation:** Using fractions based on years of a plant asset's useful life. (p. 264)
6. **production-unit method of depreciation:** Calculating estimated annual depreciation expense based on the amount of production expected from a plant asset. (p. 266)
7. **Modified Cost Recovery System:** A depreciation method required by the Internal Revenue Service to be used for income tax calculation purposes for most plant assets placed in service after 1986. (p. 267)
8. **depletion:** The decrease in the value of a plant asset because of the removal of a natural resource. (p. 269)
9. **real property:** Land and anything attached to the land. (p. 269)
10. **personal property:** All property not classified as real property. (p. 269)
11. **assessed value:** The value of an asset determined by tax authorities for the purpose of calculating taxes. (p. 269)

QUESTIONS FOR INDIVIDUAL STUDY

1. Office Equipment is debited; Cash is credited. (p. 248)
2. Over the useful life of the plant asset. (p. 249)
3. Matching Expenses with Revenue concept. (p. 249)

QUESTIONS *(cont'd)*

4. Because of the permanent nature of land. Increases or decreases in land value are usually recorded only when land is sold or otherwise disposed of. (p. 249)

5. (a) Original cost. (b) Estimated salvage value. (c) Estimated useful life. (p. 249)

6. (a) Original cost *minus* estimated salvage value *equals* estimated total depreciation expense. (b) Estimated total depreciation expense *divided by* years of estimated useful life *equals* annual depreciation expense. (p. 250)

7. A calendar month. (p. 250)

8. (a) On the plant asset record. (b) As part of the adjusting entries which are posted to general ledger accounts. (p. 251)

9. Accumulated Depreciation—Office Equipment is debited; Office Equipment is credited. (p. 254)

10. A notation is made in section 2 of the plant asset record showing the date on which the plant asset was discarded and the book value at the time it was discarded. (p. 254)

11. Depreciation expense from the beginning of the current fiscal year to date of disposal is recorded. (p. 255)

12. Accumulated Depreciation—Office Equipment and Loss on Plant Assets are debited; Office Equipment is credited. (p. 256)

13. Cash, Accumulated Depreciation—Office Equipment, and Loss on Plant Assets are debited; Office Equipment is credited. (p. 257)

14. Cash and Accumulated Depreciation—Warehouse Equipment are debited; Warehouse Equipment and Gain on Plant Assets are credited. (p. 259)

15. Store Equipment is debited for the original cost of the new piece of equipment; Accumulated Depreciation—Store Equipment is debited; Cash is credited; Store Equipment is also credited for the original cost of the traded equipment. (p. 260)

16. Book value of asset traded plus cash paid equal original cost of new asset. (p. 260)

CASES FOR CRITICAL THINKING EPT(b)

CASE 1 A corporation's plant assets include office equipment, a building, and the land on which the building is located. The corporation's general ledger includes a single account titled **Plant Assets** and a single account titled **Accumulated Depreciation—Plant Assets.** The corporation's accountant suggests that the plant asset account be divided into three accounts titled **Office Equipment, Building,** and **Land.** The corporation's president does not think this is a good idea. With whom do you agree and why?

CASE 2 A corporation owns land on which there is both an active coal mine and timber. The corporation also owns an office building and the land on which it is located. The corporation uses three plant asset accounts: 1. **Land and Buildings** (depreciation calculated using the straight-line method). 2. **Timber** (depreciation calculated using the declining-balance method). 3. **Coal Mine** (depreciation calculated using the declining-balance method). Do you agree with the accounting procedures being used? Explain your answers.

APPLICATION PROBLEMS EPT(c,d,e,f,g)

PROBLEM 9-1 Journalizing entries to record buying plant assets

AUTOMATED

Mannings, Inc. uses three plant asset accounts: **Office Equipment, Store Equipment,** and **Warehouse Equipment.**

INSTRUCTIONS:

1. Journalize the following transactions completed during the current year. Use page 1 of a general journal and page 1 of a cash payments journal. General ledger accounts are: Office Equipment, 1225; Store Equipment, 1235; and Warehouse Equipment, 1245. Source documents are abbreviated as follows: check, C; memorandum, M.

Jan. 2. Paid cash for office file cabinet (plant asset number 1), $500.00: estimated salvage value, $50.00; estimated useful life, 5 years; Serial No., FC2467. C130.

Jan. 3. Bought office typewriter (plant asset number 2) on account from Darst, Inc., $400.00: estimated salvage value, none; estimated useful life, 5 years; Serial No., X4672Y101. M11.

Apr. 4. Bought hand truck (plant asset number 3) for warehouse on account from Boeser, Inc., $100.00: estimated salvage value, $25.00; estimated useful life, 5 years; Serial No., 23D4689. M24.

May 1. Paid cash for used truck (plant asset number 4) to be used between warehouses, $8,500.00: estimated salvage value, $1,000.00; estimated useful life, 5 years; Serial No., 45J3257XF29. C210.

July 1. Paid cash for store shelving (plant asset number 5), $500.00: estimated salvage value, $25.00; estimated useful life, 10 years; Serial No., none. C250.

2. Complete section 1 of a plant asset record similar to the one in Illustration 9-1 for each plant asset. Leave the line for annual depreciation blank.

The plant asset records used in Problem 9-1 are needed to complete Problems 9-2, 9-3, and 9-4.

PROBLEM 9-2 Calculating depreciation using the straight-line method

The plant asset records used in Problem 9-1 are needed to complete Problem 9-2.

MATHEMATICS

INSTRUCTIONS:

Use the plant asset records completed in Problem 9-1. Complete a depreciation table for each of the plant assets bought by Mannings, Inc. Enter the annual depreciation in section 1 of the plant asset records.

The depreciation tables completed in Problem 9-2 are needed to complete Problem 9-3.

CHECK FIGURES

See Teacher's Edition of the Working Papers for complete solutions.

Problem 9-1 Accounts debited in general journal: Jan. 3, Office Equipment; Apr. 4, Warehouse Equipment. Accounts debited in cash payments journal: Jan. 2, Office Equipment; May 1, Warehouse Equipment; July 1, Store Equipment.

Problem 9-2 Annual depreciation: File Cabinet, $90.00; Typewriter, $80.00; Hand Truck, $15.00; Truck, $1,500.00; Shelving, $47.50

PROBLEM 9-3 Journalizing annual depreciation expense

The plant asset records used in Problem 9-1 and the depreciation tables completed in Problem 9-2 are needed to complete Problem 9-3.

INSTRUCTIONS:

1. Use the plant asset records prepared in Problem 9-1. For each plant asset, record depreciation for 19X1 in section 3 of the plant asset record.
2. Use page 12 of a general journal and the depreciation tables prepared in Problem 9-2. Journalize the three adjusting entries for office, store, and warehouse depreciation expense on December 31, 19X1.
3. For each plant asset, record depreciation for 19X2, 19X3, and 19X4 in section 3 of the plant asset record.
4. Journalize the three adjusting entries for December 31, 19X2.

The plant asset records used in Problem 9-3 are needed to complete Problem 9-4.

PROBLEM 9-4 Recording disposal of plant assets

The plant asset records used in Problem 9-3 are needed to complete Problem 9-4.

MATHEMATICS

Mannings, Inc. completed the following transactions. Use the appropriate plant asset records from Problem 9-3 for additional information needed. Use page 1 of a general journal, page 6 of a cash receipts journal, and page 12 of a cash payments journal. Source documents are abbreviated as follows: check, C; memorandum, M; receipt, R.

Jan. 21, 19X5. Discarded office typewriter. M522.
Jan. 28, 19X5. Discarded office file cabinet. M523.
Mar. 29, 19X6. Received cash for sale of hand truck, $10.00. M575 and R645.
Dec. 31, 19X6. Received cash for sale of store shelving, $250.00. M631 and R733.
Dec. 31, 19X6. Paid cash, $8,000.00, plus old truck for new truck. M632 and C815.

INSTRUCTIONS:

1. For each transaction in 19X5, do the following:
   a. Journalize an entry for additional depreciation if needed.
   b. Journalize the disposal of the plant asset.
   c. Make appropriate notations in the plant asset record.
2. Complete each plant asset record for the year.
3. Repeat instructions 1 and 2 for 19X6.

PROBLEM 9-5 Recording the sale of land and building

MATHEMATICS

On January 2, 19X6, Jamestown, Inc. sold land and a company operations building it is no longer using. The following data, relating to the land and building, are obtained from the accounting records of Jamestown.

Cash received ($30,000.00 for land; $43,000.00 for building)	$ 73,000.00
Original cost of land	$ 20,000.00
Original cost of building	$100,000.00
Accumulated depreciation on building to 12/31/X5	$ 61,200.00

INSTRUCTIONS:

1. Journalize the sale of the land and building. Use page 12 of a cash receipts journal. The source document is Receipt 125.
2. Make appropriate notations in the plant asset records.

QUESTIONS (cont'd)

17. Straight-line method records the same depreciation expense for each year. Declining-balance method records a greater depreciation expense in the early years than is true of the straight-line method. Sum-of-the-years-digits method records a greater depreciation expense in the early years than is true of the straight-line method. (p. 265)

18. The amount of production expected from a plant asset. (p. 266)

19. Tons removed *times* depletion rate *equals* depletion expense. (p. 269)

20. Property Tax Expense is debited; Cash is credited. (p. 270)

CASES FOR CRITICAL THINKING

Case 1 Agree with the accountant. Annual depreciation expense should be recorded on the office equipment and the building but not on the land. When the amounts are recorded together, there is difficulty in keeping the information separate for financial statement reporting. *(CONCEPT: Adequate Disclosure)*

Case 2 Do not agree. Annual depreciation expense is calculated for buildings but not land. Therefore, the two kinds of plant assets should not be recorded in the same account. Timber and minerals are plant assets for which *depletion* expense rather than depreciation expense is recorded. Therefore, depletion expense should be calculated and recorded rather than using the declining-balance method of depreciation.

CHECK FIGURES (cont'd)

Problem 9-3 Depreciation expense adjusting entry for Dec. 31, 19X1: Office Equipment, $170.00; Store Equipment, $23.75; Warehouse Equipment, $1,011.25

Problem 9-4 Gains and losses on disposal of plant assets: Jan. 21, 19X5, $73.33 loss; Jan. 28, 19X5, $132.50 loss; Mar. 29, 19X6, $15.00 loss, Dec. 31, 19X6, $11.25 gain

Problem 9-5 Journal entry for sale of land and buildings: Debit Cash, $73,000.00 and Accumulated Depreciation—Building, $61,200.00; credit Land, $20,000.00, Building, $100,000.00, and Gain on Plant Assets, $14,200.00

CHECK FIGURES *(cont'd)*

Problem 9-6 First year depreciation: Straight-line method, $550.00; Declining-balance method, $1,200.00; Sum-of-the-years-digits method, $880.00

Problem 9-7 Annual depreciation: Year 1, $2,062.50; Year 2, $1,950.00; Year 3, $1,875.00; Year 4, $1,575.00; Year 5, $1,425.00

Problem 9-8 Annual depreciation: Year 1, $660.00; Year 2, $1,056.00; Year 3, $633.60; Year 4, $379.50; Year 5, $379.50; Year 6, $191.40

PROBLEM 9-6 Calculating depreciation expense using the straight-line, declining-balance, and sum-of-the-years-digits methods

AUTOMATED · SPREADSHEET · MATHEMATICS

The following data, relating to an office desk, are obtained from the accounting records of Byrum, Inc.

Original cost.	$2,400.00
Estimated salvage value.	$200.00
Estimated useful life.	4 years

INSTRUCTIONS:

Prepare a depreciation table, similar to Illustration 9-15, showing depreciation expense calculated using the straight-line, declining-balance, and sum-of-the-years-digits methods.

PROBLEM 9-7 Calculating depreciation expense using the production-unit method

SPREADSHEET · MATHEMATICS

The following data, relating to a truck, are obtained from the accounting records of Marcotte, Inc.

Original cost	$10,000.00
Estimated salvage value	$1,000.00
Estimated total depreciation	$9,000.00
Estimated useful life	120,000 miles
Depreciation rate	$0.075 per mile driven

INSTRUCTIONS:

Prepare a depreciation table for this truck, similar to Illustration 9-16, showing depreciation expense calculated using the production unit method.

PROBLEM 9-8 Calculating depreciation expense using MACRS

AUTOMATED · SPREADSHEET · MATHEMATICS

The following data, relating to a computer, are obtained from the accounting records of Caesar Company.

Original cost.	$3,300.00
Property class	5-year property

INSTRUCTIONS:

Prepare a depreciation table, similar to Illustration 9-17, showing depreciation expense calculated using MACRS.

PROBLEM 9-9 Calculating depletion expense

The following data, relating to a coal mine, are obtained from the accounting records of Geist, Inc.

Original cost	$45,000.00
Estimated salvage value	$1,000.00
Estimated total value of coal	$44,000.00
Estimated tons of recoverable coal	50,000 tons
Depletion rate	$0.88 per ton mined

INSTRUCTIONS:

Prepare a depletion table for this mine, similar to Illustration 9-16, showing depletion expense calculated using the production unit method.

PROBLEM 9-10 Calculating and journalizing property tax

Dependable Deliveries, Inc. has real property with an assessed value of $350,000.00. The tax rate in the city where the property is located is 4.5% of assessed value. Property tax is paid in two installments.

INSTRUCTIONS:

1. Calculate Dependable Deliveries' total annual property tax for the current year.
2. Journalize the payment of the first installment of property tax on February 1. Use page 3 of a cash payments journal. Check No. 124.

CHECK FIGURES *(cont'd)*

Problem 9-9 Book value end of Year 5, $4,432.00

Problem 9-10 Feb. 1 property tax payment, $7,875.00

Mastery Problem 9-M Gains and losses on disposal of plant assets: Jan. 2, $120.00 loss; Mar. 29, $25.00 loss; Mar. 30, $50.00 loss; June 29, $65.00 gain

ENRICHMENT PROBLEMS EPT(c,d,e,f)

MASTERY PROBLEM 9-M Recording entries for plant assets

Western, Inc. uses the straight-line method of calculating depreciation expense. Western uses one plant asset account, **Office Equipment**, account number, 1230. The plant asset records for Western are given in the working papers accompanying this textbook.

INSTRUCTIONS:

1. Journalize the following transactions completed during 19X9. Journalize an entry for additional depreciation expense if needed. Use page 1 of a general journal, page 6 of a cash receipts journal, and page 1 of a cash payments journal. Source documents are abbreviated as follows: check, C; memorandum, M; receipt, R.

Jan. 2. Paid cash for new typewriter, $1,900.00: estimated salvage value, $400.00; estimated useful life, 5 years; Serial No. SD345J267. C122.
Jan. 2. Discarded desk, Serial No. D3481. M47.
Mar. 29. Discarded table, Serial No. T3029. M52.
Mar. 30. Received cash from sale of typewriter, $100.00: Serial No. TM48194H32. M54 and R191.
June 29. Received cash from sale of filing cabinet, $150.00: Serial No. FC125. M62 and R224.
July 2. Paid cash, $500.00, plus old copying machine, Serial No. C56M203, for new copying machine: estimated salvage value of new machine, $100.00; estimated useful life of new machine, 5 years; Serial No. of new machine, C35194. M70 and C239.

2. Make needed notations on plant asset records or prepare new records.

275

CHECK FIGURES *(cont'd)*

Challenge Problem 9-C

Amounts debited to Accumulated Depreciation accounts: General journal—July 1, 19X3, $46.00; Cash receipts journal—December 31, 19X3, $311.67; Cash payments journal—January 2, 19X3, $125.00 and September 1, 19X3, $3,900.00

CHALLENGE PROBLEM 9-C Recording entries for plant assets

AUTOMATED

McNeilley, Inc. uses the straight-line method of calculating depreciation expense. McNeilley uses two plant asset accounts: **Office Equipment** and **Delivery Equipment.**

INSTRUCTIONS:

Journalize the following transactions. Use page 7 of a general journal, page 12 of a cash receipts journal, and page 1 of a cash payments journal. Source documents are abbreviated as follows: check, C; memorandum, M; receipt, R.

Jan. 1, 19X1. Paid cash for new office typewriter (plant asset number 1), $600.00: estimated salvage value, $100.00; estimated useful life, 8 years; Serial No., T45M3409. C130.

Mar. 1, 19X1. Paid cash for office desk (plant asset number 2), $700.00: estimated salvage value, $150.00; estimated useful life, 5 years; Serial No., D345. C190.

June 30, 19X1. Paid cash for office chair (plant asset number 3), $125.00: estimated salvage value, $10.00; estimated useful life, 5 years; Serial No., none. C200.

July 1, 19X1. Paid cash for delivery truck (plant asset number 4), $10,000.00: estimated salvage value, $1,000.00; estimated useful life, 5 years; Serial No., 345X32LD54. C220.

Jan. 2, 19X3. Paid cash, $400.00, plus old typewriter, Serial No. T45M3409, for new typewriter: estimated salvage value of new typewriter, $100.00; estimated useful life of new typewriter (plant asset number 5), 5 years; Serial No. of new typewriter, T64M4391. M50 and C300.

July 1, 19X3. Discarded office chair bought on June 30, 19X1. M66.

Sept. 1, 19X3. Paid cash, $5,500.00, plus old delivery truck, Serial No. 345X32LD54, for new delivery truck: estimated salvage value of new truck, $2,000.00; estimated useful life of new truck (plant asset number 6), 5 years; Serial No. of new truck, 432XY30LE25. M70 and C310.

Dec. 31, 19X3. Received cash from sale of office desk, $400.00; Serial No. D345. M81 and R146.

Preparing Depreciation Schedules

Calculating depreciation for plant assets and preparing depreciation schedules may be accomplished using either manual or automated methods. Appliance Center, Inc., the business described in Part 4, uses manual methods to calculate depreciation and prepare depreciation schedules.

Integrating Automated Accounting Topic 5 applies procedures for using automated accounting software to calculate depreciation and prepare schedules for the straight-line (SL), double-declining-balance (DDB), sum-of-the-years-digits (SYD), and the modified accelerated cost recovery (MACR) methods. The Automated Accounting Problems contain instructions for using automated accounting software to solve Chapter 9 Application Problems 9-1, 9-6, and 9-8 and Challenge Problem 9-C.

SOFTWARE FOCUS

The Automated Accounting Problems in this Integrating Automated Accounting topic use Application Problems 9-1, 9-6, 9-8, and Challenge Problem 9-C, Chapter 9, which students have already completed manually. Refer students back to these problems to complete the input forms. The problem instructions in *Automated Accounting 6.0* will lead students through automating the problems.

TEACHING STRATEGIES: ACCOUNTING PEDAGOGY

This textbook introduces manual methods for calculating depreciation before using automated accounting to calculate depreciation. It is important that students master accounting theory before relying on the computer to perform the repetitive functions.

LESSON PLAN A5

Materials

- Student pages 277–279
- Input forms for Automating Application Problems 9-1, 9-6, 9-8, and Challenge Problem 9-C are provided in the working papers that accompany this textbook. If additional input forms are needed, blackline masters are provided in the Blackline Masters Section of the Teacher's Resource Guide.
- Complete solutions for automated problems are provided in the Teacher's Resource Guide.
- Software: *Automated Accounting 6.0* or higher; Accounting Textbook Template, Advanced Course

Objectives

- Calculate depreciation for plant assets using an automated accounting system.
- Prepare depreciation schedules for plant assets using an automated accounting system.

FOCUS

In Chapter 9, manual procedures for calculating depreciation and preparing depreciation schedules for plant assets were described. Emphasize that automated accounting software may be used to speed depreciation calculations and the preparation of depreciation schedules. Explain that using automated accounting software, however, does not change accounting concepts. Only the methods change.

TEACH

Integrating Automated Accounting: Topic 5 is designed to be completed by students as Independent Practice. You may choose to have students work in pairs to increase their cooperative learning experiences. Student understanding may be assessed by checking student solutions to the automated problems. Use Chapter 9 of this textbook to reteach any misunderstood accounting concepts related to plant assets.

CHECK FIGURES

- Automating Application Problem 9-1: Plant Assets Report total 10,000
- Automating Application Problem 9-6: Plant Assets Report total 2,400
- Automating Application Problem 9-8: Plant Assets Report total 3,300
- Automating Challenge Problem 9-C: Plant Assets Report total 22,116.67

AUTOMATED ACCOUNTING PROBLEMS

AUTOMATING APPLICATION PROBLEM 9-1 Preparing depreciation schedules

INSTRUCTIONS:

1. Record the transactions from Problem 9-1, Chapter 9, on a plant assets input form. Use July 31 of the current year as the run date. Use the straight-line method of depreciation.
2. Load the *Automated Accounting 6.0* or higher software. Select File from the menu bar, and then select the Payroll/Assets/Bank Rec. command. Select data base A9-1 from the *CENTURY 21 ACCOUNTING Advanced Course* template. Read the Problem Instructions screen.
3. Use the Save As command and rename your data base file.
4. Key the depreciation data from the plant assets input form.
5. Display/print a plant assets report.
6. Display/print depreciation schedules for the five plant assets.
7. Display/print a monthly depreciation report.
8. Display/print a yearly depreciation report.

AUTOMATING APPLICATION PROBLEM 9-6 Calculating depreciation expense

INSTRUCTIONS:

1. Load the *Automated Accounting 6.0* or higher software. Select File from the menu bar, and then select the Payroll/Assets/Bank Rec. command. Select data base A9-6 from the *CENTURY 21 ACCOUNTING Advanced Course* template. Read the Problem Instructions screen.
2. Use the Save As command and rename your data base file.
3. Key the depreciation data from Problem 9-6, Chapter 9. The asset was bought on April 1. Use April 30 of the current year as the run date and the declining-balance method of depreciation.
4. Display/print a plant assets report.
5. Display/print a depreciation schedule.
6. Display/print a monthly depreciation report.
7. Display/print a yearly depreciation report.

AUTOMATING APPLICATION PROBLEM 9-8 Calculating depreciation expense using MACRS

INSTRUCTIONS:

1. Load the *Automated Accounting 6.0* or higher software. Select File from the menu bar, and then select the Payroll/Assets/Bank Rec. command. Select data base A9-8 from the *CENTURY 21 ACCOUNTING Advanced Course* template. Read the Problem Instructions screen.
2. Use the Save As command and rename your data base file.
3. Key the depreciation data from Problem 9-8, Chapter 9. The asset was bought on March 1. Use March 31 of the current year as the run date.
4. Display/print a plant assets report.
5. Display/print a depreciation schedule.
6. Display/print a monthly depreciation report.
7. Display/print a yearly depreciation report.

TEACHING STRATEGIES: TEACHING TIP

It is important for students to save a template file under another name before they begin work. This will keep the template file intact for future use.

AUTOMATED

AUTOMATING CHALLENGE PROBLEM 9-C Recording entries for plant assets

INSTRUCTIONS:

1. Record the transactions from Challenge Problem 9-C, Chapter 9, on a plant assets input form. Use December 31 of year 3 as the run date. Use the sum-of-the-years-digits method of depreciation.
2. Load the *Automated Accounting 6.0* or higher software. Select File from the menu bar, and then select the Payroll/Assets/Bank Rec. command. Select data base A9-C from the *CENTURY 21 ACCOUNTING Advanced Course* template. Read the Problem Instructions screen.
3. Use the Save As command and rename your data base file.
4. Key the depreciation data from the plant assets input form.
5. Display/print a plant assets report.
6. Display/print depreciation schedules for the six plant assets.
7. Display/print a monthly depreciation report.
8. Display/print a yearly depreciation report.

279

CHAPTER 10 OVERVIEW

Chapter 10 explains how notes receivable (promissory notes) are issued including calculating interest and maturity dates and recording the appropriate transactions. Prepaid expenses and accrued expenses and the adjusting, closing, and reversing entries for each are also covered.

GUIDE TO ACHIEVING LEARNING OBJECTIVES

	TEACH	APPLY	EXTEND/ENRICH					
Enabling Performance Tasks	**Lesson Plans**	**Application Problems**	**Mastery Problems**	**Challenge Problems**	**Cases for Critical Thinking**	**Recycling Problems**	**Reinforcement Activity**	
a. Define accounting terms related to notes payable, prepaid expenses, and accrued expenses.	10-1, 10-2, 10-3							
b. Identify accounting concepts and practices related to notes payable, prepaid expenses, and accrued expenses.	10-1, 10-2, 10-3				Cases 1, 2			
c. Journalize transactions for notes payable.	10-1	10-1	10-M	10-C		10-R	RA2	
d. Journalize adjusting and reversing entries for prepaid expenses initially recorded as expenses.	10-2	10-2	10-M	10-C		10-R	RA2	
e. Journalize adjusting and reversing entries for accrued expenses.	10-3	10-3	10-M	10-C		10-R	RA2	

ENRICHMENT

SPECIAL FEATURES
Professional Business Ethics, page 286
Careers in Accounting, page 295

TECHNOLOGY CONNECTION
Spreadsheet Template Problem 10-1

NEW, REVIEW, AND EXTENSION

ACTIVITIES/CONCEPTS/TRANSACTIONS	NEW	REVIEW/ EXTENSION
Issuing a note payable		✓
Calculating maturity date and interest		✓
Paying a note payable		✓
Discounting a note		✓
Prepaid expenses		✓
Supplies initially recorded as an expense		✓
Prepaid insurance initially recorded as an expense		✓
Prepaid interest initially recorded as an expense		✓
Adjusting, closing, and reversing entries for prepaid expenses		✓
Adjusting, closing, and reversing entries for accrued expenses		✓
Accrued interest expense		✓
Accrued salary expense		✓
Accrued employer payroll taxes expense		✓

	INFORMAL ASSESSMENT		FORMAL ASSESSMENT			
	Study Guide	**Audit Your Understanding**	**Chapter MicroExam**	**Chapter Problem Test**	**Unit Objective Test**	**Portfolio**
	Unit B	✓	✓		✓	
	Units A, C	✓	✓		✓	
				✓		✓
				✓		✓
				✓		✓

TEACHING MATERIALS
Teacher's Wraparound Edition of the Text
Teacher's Resource Guide
Teacher's Edition of Working Papers
MicroExam

APPLIED MATHEMATICS

APPLIED MATH/ACCOUNTING SKILL	APPLICATION
Calculating interest	Prob. 10-1
Calculating maturity dates	Prob. 10-1
Calculating bank discount and proceeds	Prob. 10-1

10

Accounting for Notes Payable, Prepaid Expenses, and Accrued Expenses

TEACHING STRATEGIES: ACCOUNTING PEDAGOGY

This textbook introduces accounting for notes payable, prepaid expenses, and accrued expenses. Businesses incur transactions that involve prepaid and accrued accounts. Students must understand that accounting records must show all information needed to prepare accurate financial statements for a business.

ENABLING PERFORMANCE TASKS

After studying Chapter 10, you will be able to:

- **a** Define accounting terms related to notes payable, prepaid expenses, and accrued expenses.
- **b** Identify accounting concepts and practices related to notes payable, prepaid expenses, and accrued expenses.
- **c** Journalize transactions for notes payable.
- **d** Journalize adjusting and reversing entries for prepaid expenses initially recorded as expenses.
- **e** Journalize adjusting and reversing entries for accrued expenses.

TERMS PREVIEW

promissory note • notes payable • date of a note • principal of a note • maturity date of a note • interest • interest rate of a note • interest expense • maturity value • bank discount • discounted note • proceeds • prepaid expenses • reversing entry • accrued expenses

SOFTWARE FOCUS

Software may be used for independent practice or enrichment/extension as the instructor deems appropriate. For this chapter, the Spreadsheet Template may be used with Problem 10-1.

Business transactions occur throughout a fiscal period. Some transactions begin in one accounting period and are completed in a different accounting period. Accounting records must show all information needed to prepare the financial statements of a business. *(CONCEPT: Adequate Disclosure)* Therefore, some financial activities require special accounting procedures. A business may borrow money in one period and repay it in another period. Interest owed for the current period must be included in the financial statements of the current period. *(CONCEPT: Matching Expenses with Revenue)*

NOTES PAYABLE

A written and signed promise to pay a sum of money at a specified time is called a **promissory note.** Promissory notes that a business issues to creditors are called **notes payable.** The day a note is issued is called the **date of a note.** The original amount of a note is called the **principal of a note.** The date a note is due is called the **maturity date of a note.** An amount paid for the use of money for a period of time is called **interest.**

FYI

Notes are usually issued for two purposes: to borrow money and for an extension of time on an account.

Issuing a Note Payable

Appliance Center occasionally borrows money from a bank. A note payable is issued to the bank as evidence of the debt.

March 2, 19--. Issued a 6-month, 15% note, $1,500.00. Note Payable No. 6.

Cash	
1,500.00	

Notes Payable	
	1,500.00

The percentage of the principal that is paid for use of the money is called the **interest rate of a note.** The interest rate for Note Payable No. 6 is 15%.

Cash is increased by a $1,500.00 debit, the amount received from the bank for Note Payable No. 6. Notes Payable is increased by a $1,500.00 credit.

The journal entry to record this transaction is shown in Illustration 10-1.

ILLUSTRATION 10-1 Journal entry to record issuing a note payable

CASH RECEIPTS JOURNAL — PAGE 5

	DATE		ACCOUNT TITLE	DOC. NO.	POST. REF.	1 GENERAL DEBIT	2 GENERAL CREDIT	3 ACCOUNTS RECEIVABLE CREDIT	4 SALES CREDIT	5 SALES TAX PAYABLE DEBIT	6 SALES TAX PAYABLE CREDIT	7 SALES DISCOUNT DEBIT	8 CASH DEBIT	
1	19-- Mar.	2	Notes Payable	NP6			1 500 00						1 500 00	1
2														2
3														3

LESSON PLAN 10-1

Materials

- Student pages 281–284
- Software: Spreadsheet Template

Objectives (Enabling Performance Tasks)

a. Define accounting terms related to notes payable, prepaid expenses, and accrued expenses.
b. Identify accounting concepts and practices related to notes payable, prepaid expenses, and accrued expenses.
c. Journalize transactions for notes payable.

FOCUS

- Businesses occasionally need to borrow money from a bank. Explain that the bank will usually require the business to sign a promise to repay the money. The bank will also charge the business for the use of the money. In this lesson, the procedures for issuing a note payable, calculating interest, and paying a note payable will be presented.
- Introduce vocabulary: promissory note, notes payable, date of a note, principal of a note, maturity date of a note, interest, interest rate of a note, interest expense, maturity value, bank discount, discounted note, proceeds.

TEACHING STRATEGIES: TEACHING TIP

Emphasize that when a note is issued, only the principal is recorded. The interest is not recorded at this time.

TEACH

Cover student pages 281–284 "Notes Payable." Explain the procedure for journalizing a note payable. Emphasize that notes are usually issued for two purposes: to borrow money and for an extension of time on an account. Demonstrate the procedures for calculating maturity date and interest for a note payable. Emphasize that when a note is issued, only the principal is recorded. The interest is not recorded at this time. Review percentages—15% is .15 when multiplying. Discuss the journal entry to record the payment of a note payable with interest. Describe the procedure for discounting a note payable. Emphasize that the bank discount is calculated on the principal of the note, not maturity value. Explain that when a note payable is discounted, interest expense is recorded at the time the note is issued.

FYI

The maturity value of a discounted note is the principal of the note.

Calculating Maturity Date and Interest

The length of time between the issuance and maturity date of a note may be expressed in months or in days. The time for Appliance Center's Note Payable No. 6 is 6 months.

Calculating Maturity Date with the Time Stated in Months. When the time of a note is stated in months, the maturity date is calculated by counting the number of months from the date of issuance. Therefore, the maturity date for Note Payable No. 6, a 6-month note issued March 2, is September 2.

Calculating Interest with the Time Stated in Months. When the time of a note is stated in months, the time used in calculating interest is stated as a fraction of 12 months. The interest expense for Appliance Center's Note Payable No. 6 is calculated as shown below.

Principal	×	Interest Rate	×	Time as Fraction of Year	=	Interest for Fraction of Year
$1,500.00	×	15%	×	$\frac{6}{12}$	=	$\frac{\$1,350.00}{12}$ = $112.50

Calculating Maturity Date with the Time Stated in Days. On March 2, Ronken Company issued a note payable with the time stated in days.

March 2, 19--. Issued a 180-day, 15% note, $2,000.00. Note Payable No. 3.

FYI

When calculating maturity dates, remember that April, June, September, and November have 30 days. All other months, except February, have 31 days.

When the time of a note is stated in days, the exact number of days are counted. To calculate the maturity date, find the number of days remaining in the month the note was written. Continue adding the number of days in each of the following months until the total equals the number of days of the note. The maturity date for Ronken's Note Payable No. 3 is August 29 and is calculated as shown below.

Time	Number of Days	
March 2 through March 31	29	(31 − 2 = 29)
April 1 through April 30	30	
May 1 through May 31	31	
June 1 through June 30	30	
July 1 through July 31	31	
August 1 through August 29	29	(Maturity date: August 29)
	180	days

TEACHING STRATEGIES: TEACHING TIP

Explain that notes are usually issued for two purposes: to borrow money and for an extension of time on an account.

Calculating Interest with the Time Stated in Days. When the time of a note is stated in days, the interest is calculated using 360 days in a year. The interest expense for Ronken's Note Payable No. 3 is calculated as shown below.

Principal	×	Interest Rate	×	Time as Fraction of Year	=	Interest for Fraction of Year
\$2,000.00	×	15%	×	$\frac{180}{360}$	=	$\frac{\$54{,}000.00}{360}$ = \$150.00

FYI

A 360-day year is used for all interest calculations in this text.

Agencies of the federal government generally use a 365-day year when calculating interest. Consumer interest is also generally calculated on a 365-day year. However, many banks use a 360-day year when calculating interest. Therefore, the interest calculations in this textbook use a 360-day year.

Paying a Note Payable

The interest accrued on money borrowed is called **interest expense.** On the maturity date, both the principal of the note payable and the interest expense is paid. The amount that is due on the maturity date of a note is called the **maturity value.** Appliance Center pays the maturity value of Note Payable No. 6 on its maturity date.

Notes Payable	
1,500.00	Bal. 1,500.00

Interest Expense	
112.50	

Cash	
	1,612.50

September 2, 19--. Paid cash for the maturity value of Note Payable No. 6: principal, \$1,500.00, plus interest, \$112.50; total, \$1,612.50. Check No. 359.

Notes Payable is decreased by a \$1,500.00 debit, the principal amount of the note. The \$1,500.00 debit cancels the \$1,500.00 credit recorded at the time the note was issued. Interest Expense is increased by a \$112.50 debit, Appliance Center's interest expense for use of the bank's money for six months. Cash is decreased by a \$1,612.50 credit, the total cash paid.

The journal entry to record this transaction is shown in Illustration 10-2.

Interest Expense is listed as an Other Expense on Appliance Center's chart of accounts.

ILLUSTRATION 10-2 Journal entry to record payment of maturity value of a note payable

CASH PAYMENTS JOURNAL — PAGE 17

	DATE		ACCOUNT TITLE	CK. NO.	POST. REF.	1 GENERAL DEBIT	2 GENERAL CREDIT	3 ACCOUNTS PAYABLE DEBIT	4 PURCHASES DISCOUNT CREDIT	5 CASH CREDIT	
1	19-- Sept.	2	Notes Payable	359		1 500 00				1 612 50	1
2			Interest Expense			112 50					2

APPLY

Draw T accounts on the chalkboard to analyze each transaction as it is presented. Write the formulas for calculating interest, discounts, and proceeds on the board and demonstrate all calculations. Demonstrate how to calculate the maturity date with the time stated in days.

Guided Practice

Guide students through the calculation of the maturity dates and total amount of interest due on the notes in Problem 10-1, Instructions 1 and 2. Working as a group, write the formulas on the board and have students calculate the maturity date and interest due for Note Payable No. 1. All students should agree with the answers before proceeding to the next note. Repeat the process until maturity dates and interest have been calculated for all three notes. The balance of Problem 10-1 can be assigned as Independent Practice.

Independent Practice

Assign Terms 1–12, Questions 1–4, and Problem 10-1.

TEACHING STRATEGIES: TEACHING TIP

Explain that many banks use a 360-day year when calculating interest. Therefore, a 360-day year is used for all interest calculations in this textbook.

AUDIT YOUR UNDERSTANDING

The AUDIT YOUR UNDERSTANDING feature appears at the end of each section of the chapter. Explain to your students that the word *audit* means to check or verify. AUDIT YOUR UNDERSTANDING may be used to check student comprehension of the section just studied. The answers are provided in Appendix D in the back of the textbook.

1. By counting the number of months from the date of issuance.
2. As a fraction of 12 months.
3. May 19 (March 31 − 20 = 11 days; April, 30 days; May, 19 days).
4. Interest on the note is paid in advance.

ASSESS

Assess student understanding by checking the solutions to the Independent Practice activities.

Reteach

- Refer students to Recycling Problem 10-R, Instruction 1. Using the chalkboard or overhead projector, demonstrate how to calculate the maturity dates for Notes Payable Nos. 1, 2, 3, and 4 while students complete the calculations at their desks.
- Assign Recycling Problem 10-R, Instructions 1 and 2.

Extend

- Assign Cases for Critical Thinking 1.
- Assign the Spreadsheet Template for Problem 10-1.

CLOSURE

Use Audit Your Understanding questions.

Audit Your Understanding

1. How is the maturity date calculated when the time of a note is stated in months?
2. How is the time used in calculating interest stated when the time of a note is stated in months?
3. What is the due date for a 60-day note payable issued on March 20?
4. What is the unique characteristic of a discounted note payable?

Discounting a Note Payable

Some banks require that the interest be paid at the time a note is issued. Interest collected in advance on a note is called a **bank discount.** A note on which interest is paid in advance is called a **discounted note.** The amount received for a note after the bank discount has been deducted is called **proceeds.**

Appliance Center issued a note on which interest was paid in advance.

December 1, 19--. Discounted at 15% a 60-day non-interest-bearing note, $1,200.00; proceeds, $1,170.00, interest, $30.00. Note Payable No. 7.

The amount of the discount and the proceeds are calculated as shown below.

Maturity Value	×	Discount Rate	×	Time as Fraction of Year	=	Bank Discount
$1,200.00	×	15%	×	$\frac{60}{360}$	=	$\frac{\$10,800.00}{360}$ = $30.00

Maturity Value	−	Bank Discount	=	Proceeds
$1,200.00	−	$30.00	=	$1,170.00

Cash	
Proceeds 1,170.00	

Interest Expense	
Discount 30.00	

Notes Payable	
	Principal 1,200.00

When the note was discounted at the bank, Appliance Center received cash equal to the proceeds, $1,170.00.

Cash is increased by a $1,170.00 debit, the proceeds from the note. Interest Expense is increased by a $30.00 debit, the amount of the bank discount. Notes Payable is increased by a $1,200.00 credit, the principal of the note.

When Note Payable 7 is paid, a check is written for the principal. No payment of interest expense is necessary at this time because the bank collected the interest in advance when the note was discounted. Therefore, the maturity value of a discounted note is the principal of the note.

The journal entry to record this transaction is shown in Illustration 10-3.

ILLUSTRATION 10-3 Journal entry to record discounting a note payable

CASH RECEIPTS JOURNAL — PAGE 23

	Date		Account Title	Doc. No.	Post. Ref.	1 General Debit	2 General Credit	3 Accounts Receivable Credit	4 Sales Credit	5 Sales Tax Payable Debit	6 Sales Tax Payable Credit	7 Sales Discount Debit	8 Cash Debit	
1	19-- Dec.	1	Interest Expense	NP7		30 00							1 170 00	1
2			Notes Payable				1 200 00							2
3														3
4														4

PREPAID EXPENSES

Expenses paid in one fiscal period but not reported as expenses until a later fiscal period are called **prepaid expenses.** Prepaid expenses include such items as supplies, prepaid insurance, and interest on discounted notes payable. Only that portion of prepaid expenses that has been used in the current fiscal period should be reported as an expense in that fiscal period. *(CONCEPT: Matching Expenses with Revenue)* Prepaid expenses may be initially recorded as assets or as expenses. MasterSport, described in Part 2, initially records supplies and prepaid insurance as assets. Appliance Center initially records prepaid expenses as expenses.

Prepaid expense amounts are assets until actually used. For example, Appliance Center has a quantity of sales supplies on hand on any given day during the year. These sales supplies will be used by Appliance Center in the current and future fiscal periods. The amount recorded in Supplies Expense—Sales is a mixture of expense (already used) and asset (not yet used). An adjusting entry could be made each day to separate the expense from the asset portion of this account's balance. However, as a practical accounting procedure, an adjusting entry is made only when financial statements need to be prepared. *(CONCEPT: Adequate Disclosure)*

Supplies Initially Recorded as an Expense

FYI

To initially record prepaid supplies as an expense, the supplies expense account is debited. To initially record prepaid supplies as an asset, the supplies account is debited.

When MasterSport, described in Part 2, buys office supplies, the asset Supplies—Office is debited and Cash is credited. However, when Appliance Center buys sales supplies, Supplies Expense—Sales is debited and Cash is credited. Both MasterSport and Appliance Center record adjusting entries for supplies at the end of a fiscal period. The adjusting entries are made so that the prepaid expenses actually used during a fiscal period are reported as expenses and the supplies not used are reported as assets. *(CONCEPT: Matching Expenses with Revenue)*

MasterSport's and Appliance Center's two related supplies accounts before adjusting entries are made at the end of a fiscal period are shown in the T accounts.

MASTERSPORT

Supplies—Office	
12/31 Bal. 12,700.00	

Supplies Expense—Office	

APPLIANCE CENTER

Supplies—Sales	

Supplies Expense—Sales	
12/31 Bal. 2,000.00	

MasterSport initially recorded the prepaid supplies in the asset account Supplies—Office. The $12,700.00 debit balance is the begin-

LESSON 10-2

Materials

- Student pages 285–291
- 3-Step Checklist for Making Ethical Decisions (TRG)

Objectives (Enabling Performance Tasks)

a. Define accounting terms related to notes payable, prepaid expenses, and accrued expenses.

b. Identify accounting concepts and practices related to notes payable, prepaid expenses, and accrued expenses.

d. Journalize adjusting and reversing entries for prepaid expenses initially recorded as expenses.

TEACHING STRATEGIES: TEACHING TIP

Emphasize that when supplies are initially recorded as assets, the adjustment for supplies is the amount of supplies used. When supplies are initially recorded as an expense, the adjustment for supplies is the amount of supplies inventory.

Professional Business Ethics

The PROFESSIONAL BUSINESS ETHICS feature stimulates critical thinking and decision making. It may be used in many ways such as an individual assignment, a class discussion, or a small group cooperative learning project. When these ethics cases are discussed in class, students can also gain a sense of individual diversity as students demonstrate individual opinions. If you wish to integrate word processing in your accounting course, you may direct students to word process their answers. If you wish to include the creation of tables, you might direct students to format their responses to resemble the ethical decision-making grid in a 3-column table. A blackline master of the 3-Step Checklist for Making Ethical Decisions is furnished in the Teacher's Resource Guide. Suggested solutions for the Professional Business Ethics feature are provided in the front of this teacher's edition.

FOCUS

- Explain that expenses may be paid in one fiscal period but not reported as expenses until a later fiscal period. These expenses may be initially recorded as assets or as expenses. Remind students that MasterSport, described in Part 2, initially records supplies and prepaid insurance as assets. In this lesson, the procedures used to initially record supplies and prepaid insurance as expenses will be presented.
- Introduce vocabulary: prepaid expenses, reversing entry.

PROFESSIONAL BUSINESS ETHICS

Is Salary Expense a Picnic?

Edgewood Manufacturing is under contract with the federal government to produce radar systems. The contract entitles Edgewood to sell the systems at its cost plus 15 percent. A government document specifically outlines which expenditures qualify as "contract costs."

To boost employee morale, Edgewood recently held a picnic for its employees and their families. The expenditure does not qualify as a contract cost according to the government contract. At the direction of management, however, the accountant (who is a CPA) recorded the expenditure as salary expense. Salaries do qualify as contract costs. "The workers will be more productive—for every dollar we spent, we'll save two dollars on our payroll," stated Edgewood's president.

INSTRUCTIONS Use the three-step checklist to analyze whether the accountant's recording of the picnic as salary expense demonstrated ethical behavior.

ning inventory of supplies plus the total amount of all office supplies bought during the fiscal period. Nothing has been recorded in MasterSport's office supplies expense account during the fiscal period.

Appliance Center initially records prepaid supplies in Supplies Expense—Sales. The $2,000.00 debit balance is the beginning sales supplies inventory plus the total amount of all sales supplies bought during the fiscal period. Nothing has been recorded in Appliance Center's sales supplies account during the fiscal period.

Adjusting Entry for Supplies. As described in Chapter 5, MasterSport determined that the office supplies inventory was $2,750.00 and the office supplies expense for the fiscal period was $9,950.00. On December 31, Appliance Center determined that the sales supplies ending inventory is $800.00.

MASTERSPORT

Supplies—Office

12/31 Bal.	12,700.00	12/31 Adj.	9,950.00
(New Bal.	*2,750.00)*		

Supplies Expense—Office

12/31 Adj.	9,950.00		

APPLIANCE CENTER

Supplies—Sales

12/31 Adj.	800.00		

Supplies Expense—Sales

12/31 Bal.	2,000.00	12/31 Adj.	800.00
(New Bal.	*1,200.00)*		

For MasterSport's accounts, Supplies—Office is decreased by a $9,950.00 credit. The new balance of this account, *$2,750.00,* is the ending office supplies inventory on December 31. Supplies Expense—Office is increased by a $9,950.00 debit. The new balance of this account, *$9,950.00,* is the supplies expense for the current year.

FYI

When supplies are initially recorded as an expense, the adjustment for supplies is the amount of supplies inventory. When supplies are initially recorded as an asset, the adjustment for supplies is the amount of supplies used.

For Appliance Center's accounts, Supplies—Sales is increased by an $800.00 debit. The new balance of this account, *$800.00,* is the ending sales supplies inventory on December 31. Supplies Expense—Sales is decreased by an $800.00 credit. The new balance of this account, *$1,200.00,* is the sales supplies expense for the current year.

Although MasterSport and Appliance Center use different procedures, both correctly separate and record the asset and expense portions of supplies costs.

MasterSport's adjusting entry for office supplies is shown on lines 8 and 9, Illustration 5-11, Chapter 5. Appliance Center's adjusting entry to record sales supplies is shown on lines 10 and 11 of Illustration 10-4.

ILLUSTRATION 10-4

Journal entry to record adjustment for supplies initially recorded as an expense

GENERAL JOURNAL — PAGE *13*

	DATE		ACCOUNT TITLE	DOC. NO.	POST. REF.	DEBIT	CREDIT	
1			*Adjusting Entries*					1
8		*31*	*Supplies—Administrative*			*272 94*		8
9			*Supplies Expense—Administrative*				*272 94*	9
10		*31*	*Supplies—Sales*			*800 00*		10
11			*Supplies Expense—Sales*				*800 00*	11
12		*31*	*Supplies—Warehouse*			*397 50*		12
13			*Supplies Expense—Warehouse*				*397 50*	13

Appliance Center makes a similar adjusting entry for Supplies Expense—Administrative and Supplies Expense—Warehouse as shown on lines 8 and 9 and 12 and 13 of Illustration 10-4.

Closing Entry for Supplies Expense. To prepare a general ledger for the next fiscal period, closing entries are journalized and posted. The effect of closing entries on MasterSport's and Appliance Center's supplies expense accounts is shown in the T accounts.

MASTERSPORT

Income Summary

Debit		Credit	
12/31 Clos.	9,950.00		

Supplies Expense—Office

Debit		Credit	
12/31 Adj.	9,950.00	12/31 Clos.	9,950.00
(New Bal. zero)			

APPLIANCE CENTER

Income Summary

Debit		Credit	
12/31 Clos.	1,200.00		

Supplies Expense—Sales

Debit		Credit	
12/31 Bal.	2,000.00	12/31 Adj.	800.00
(New Bal. zero)		12/31 Clos.	1,200.00

TEACH

Cover student pages 285–291 "Prepaid Expenses." Explain the procedure to account for supplies initially recorded as an expense including the journal entries when buying the supplies, the end-of-period adjusting entry, the closing entry, and the reversing entry. Emphasize that when supplies are initially recorded as assets, the adjustment is the amount of supplies used. When supplies are initially recorded as an expense, the adjustment is the amount of supplies inventory. Explain that the purpose of reversing entries is to prepare the accounts for the next accounting period. Discuss the reason for reversing entries and illustrate the potential problem if reversing entries are not made. Point out that reversing entries are the opposite of adjusting entries. Discuss the procedure to account for prepaid insurance initially recorded as an expense. Emphasize that when prepaid interest is initially recorded as an expense, the adjustment is the amount of the interest still prepaid.

APPLIED SKILLS: BUILDING STUDY SKILLS

Direct students to create a Quick Reference Guide (QRG) for adjusting and reversing entries for prepaid and accrued expenses. (1) Label a QRG PREPAID EXPENSES. (2) List each prepaid expense situation out of the chapter narrative. For example, supplies initially recorded as an expense. (3) Indicate what accounts are debited and credited to record the adjusting and reversing entries for each situation. (4) Repeat the process for ACCRUED EXPENSES.

APPLY

To lessen the difficulty with reversing entries, use T accounts on the chalkboard or overhead projector to analyze entries presented in this lesson. Refer students to Illustrations 10-4 and 10-5, respectively, as adjusting and reversing entries for supplies initially recorded as an expense are discussed.

Guided Practice

Guide students through the T account analysis of the adjusting entries in Problem 10-2, Instructions 1 and 2. Have students draw T accounts on a sheet of paper and analyze the adjusting entry for supplies. All students should agree with the analysis before proceeding to the adjustment for insurance. Next, working as a group, calculate the amount of prepaid interest on Note Payable No. 4. All students should agree with the amount before proceeding to the analysis of the adjusting entry for prepaid interest. The balance of Problem 10-2 can be assigned as Independent Practice.

Independent Practice

Assign Terms 13–14, Questions 5–12, and Problem 10-2.

The other supplies expense accounts are also closed as part of the closing entries for both MasterSport and Appliance Center.

FYI

Reversing entries are the opposite of adjusting entries.

Need for Reversing Entries. After the closing entries have been posted, MasterSport's general ledger accounts are ready for the next fiscal period. However, Appliance Center's general ledger accounts are not ready for the next fiscal period.

Appliance Center initially records the amount of all supplies bought in an expense account. On December 31, the amount of Appliance Center's sales supplies inventory, *$800.00,* is the debit balance of Supplies—Sales. On January 1, the $800.00 should be a debit in Supplies Expense—Sales. The $800.00 debit can then be added to the amount of sales supplies bought during the next year.

Some businesses that initially record prepaid items as expenses reverse the adjusting entries for prepaid expenses at the beginning of each fiscal period. An entry made at the beginning of one fiscal period to reverse an adjusting entry made in the previous fiscal period is called a **reversing entry.**

MasterSport initially records supplies as assets and *does not* record reversing entries. On December 31, the office supplies inventory, *$2,750.00,* is in the account where it can be added to the amount of supplies bought in the next fiscal period.

Appliance Center initially records supplies as expenses and *does* need to record reversing entries. Accountants use the following rule of thumb to determine if a reversing entry is needed. If an adjusting entry *creates* a balance in an asset or a liability account, the adjusting entry is reversed.

FYI

If an adjusting entry creates a balance in an asset or a liability account, the adjusting entry is reversed.

Reversing Entry for Supplies Expense. Because Appliance Center's adjusting entry for sales supplies created a balance in Supplies—Sales, a reversing entry is needed.

Supplies Expense—Sales

12/31 Bal.	2,000.00	12/31 Adj.	800.00
1/1 Rev.	800.00	12/31 Clos.	1,200.00
(New Bal.	*800.00)*		

Supplies—Sales

12/31 Adj.	800.00	1/1 Rev.	800.00
(New Bal. zero)			

Supplies Expense—Sales is increased by an $800.00 debit. On December 31, the sales supplies inventory, *$800.00,* is in the account where it can be added to the amount of supplies bought in the next fiscal period. Supplies—Sales is decreased by an $800.00 credit. The balance of Supplies—Sales is zero as it was before the adjusting entry.

Appliance Center's journal entries to record reversing entries for the supplies expense accounts are shown in Illustration 10-5. These reversing entries are the opposite of the adjusting entries shown in Illustration 10-4.

Prepaid Insurance Initially Recorded as an Expense

MasterSport, described in Part 2, initially records insurance premiums as an asset. MasterSport's adjusting entry for insurance is shown on lines 12 and 13, Illustration 5-11, Chapter 5.

Appliance Center initially records insurance premiums as expenses. When Appliance Center pays insurance premiums, Insurance Expense is debited and Cash is credited.

ILLUSTRATION 10-5 Journal entries to record reversing entries for supplies initially recorded as an expense

GENERAL JOURNAL PAGE *1*

	DATE		ACCOUNT TITLE	DOC. NO.	POST. REF.	DEBIT	CREDIT	
1			*Reversing Entries*					1
4		1	*Supplies Expense—Administrative*			272 94		4
5			*Supplies—Administrative*				272 94	5
6		1	*Supplies Expense—Sales*			800 00		6
7			*Supplies—Sales*				800 00	7
8		1	*Supplies Expense—Warehouse*			397 50		8
9			*Supplies—Warehouse*				397 50	9

Adjusting Entry for Prepaid Insurance. The amount of Appliance Center's unexpired insurance premiums on December 31 is $300.00. Prepaid Insurance is increased by a $300.00 debit. The new balance of this account, *$300.00,* is the amount of unexpired insurance premiums at the end of the fiscal period. Insurance Expense is decreased by a $300.00 credit. The new balance of this account, *$600.00,* is the insurance expense for the fiscal period.

Appliance Center's journal entry to record the adjustment for prepaid insurance is shown in Illustration 10-6.

Prepaid Insurance

Debit		Credit	
12/31 Adj.	300.00		

Insurance Expense

Debit		Credit	
12/31 Bal.	900.00	12/31 Adj.	300.00
(New Bal.	*600.00)*		

ILLUSTRATION 10-6 Journal entry to record adjustment for prepaid insurance initially recorded as an expense

GENERAL JOURNAL PAGE *13*

	DATE		ACCOUNT TITLE	DOC. NO.	POST. REF.	DEBIT	CREDIT	
1			*Adjusting Entries*					1
14		31	*Prepaid Insurance*			300 00		14
15			*Insurance Expense*				300 00	15

Income Summary

Debit		Credit	
12/31 Clos.	600.00		

Insurance Expense

Debit		Credit	
12/31 Bal.	900.00	12/31 Adj.	300.00
(New Bal. zero)		12/31 Clos.	600.00

Closing Entry for Insurance Expense. Insurance Expense is closed as part of Appliance Center's closing entries.

Reversing Entry for Prepaid Insurance Expense. MasterSport, described in Part 2, *does not* need to record a reversing entry for insurance expense. However, Appliance Center's adjusting entry for insurance expense created a balance in the asset account, Prepaid Insurance. Therefore, on January 1, Appliance Center *does* need a reversing entry for insurance expense.

ASSESS

Assess student understanding by checking the solutions to the Independent Practice activities.

Reteach

Using information from Recycling Problem 10-R, Instruction 3, demonstrate the T account analysis of the adjusting and reversing entries for the prepaid expense items. Have students draw T accounts at their desks and complete the analysis with you.

Enrich

Discuss the PROFESSIONAL BUSINESS ETHICS feature on page 286. You may wish to distribute copies of the 3-Step Checklist for Making Ethical Decisions. A blackline master is furnished in the Blackline Masters Section of the Teacher's Resource Guide.

CLOSURE

Use Audit Your Understanding questions.

TEACHING STRATEGIES: COOPERATIVE LEARNING

Assign students to work in pairs to analyze transactions presented in the text. One student analyzes transactions by drawing T accounts. The other student journalizes the transaction. Then they switch activities. Allow 30 minutes for the exercise. Then ask students what they learned from this activity.

Insurance Expense			
12/31 Bal.	900.00	12/31 Adj.	300.00
(New Bal. zero)		12/31 Clos.	600.00
1/1 Rev.	300.00		
(New Bal.	*300.00)*		

Prepaid Insurance			
12/31 Adj.	300.00	1/1 Rev.	300.00
(New Bal. zero)			

Insurance Expense is increased by a $300.00 debit. The new balance of this account, *$300.00,* can now be added to the amount of insurance premiums paid during the next fiscal period. Prepaid Insurance is decreased by a $300.00 credit. The new balance of this account is zero as it was before the adjusting entry.

Appliance Center's journal entry to record the reversing entry for insurance expense is shown in Illustration 10-7.

TEACHING STRATEGIES: EXPANDING BEYOND THE CLASSROOM

Assign students to contact various professional organizations to obtain information about the association. You may want to give the students some guidance as to what kind of information to request, such as purpose of the organization, membership enrollment, examples of activities, scholarship information, etc.

ILLUSTRATION 10-7

Journal entry to record reversing entry for prepaid insurance initially recorded as an expense

GENERAL JOURNAL — PAGE 1

	DATE		ACCOUNT TITLE	DOC. NO.	POST. REF.	DEBIT	CREDIT	
1			*Reversing Entries*					1
10		1	*Insurance Expense*			300 00		10
11			*Prepaid Insurance*				300 00	11

Prepaid Interest Initially Recorded as an Expense

FYI

When prepaid interest is initially recorded as an expense, the adjustment for interest is the amount of interest still prepaid.

Appliance Center initially records prepaid interest as an expense. When Appliance Center discounted Note Payable No. 7, the discount, *$30.00,* was debited to Interest Expense.

Adjusting Entry for Prepaid Interest. Note Payable No. 7 has existed from December 1 to December 31. On December 31, only 30 days of Appliance Center's prepaid interest expense has been earned by the bank during the current fiscal period. The remaining 30 days' interest is still prepaid. The interest for 30 days is calculated as shown below.

Principal	×	Interest Rate	×	Time as Fraction of Year	=	Interest for 30 Days
$1,200.00	×	15%	×	$\frac{30}{360}$	=	$\frac{\$5,400.00}{360}$ = $15.00

Prepaid Interest			
12/31 Adj.	15.00		

Interest Expense			
12/31 Bal.	142.50	12/31 Adj.	15.00
(New Bal.	*127.50)*		

Prepaid Interest is increased by a $15.00 debit. The new balance of this account, *$15.00,* is the amount of the remaining prepaid interest on Note Payable No. 7. Interest Expense is decreased by a $15.00 credit. The new balance of this account, *$127.50,* includes the interest expense on Note Payable No. 7 for the current fiscal period. *(CONCEPT: Matching Expenses with Revenue)*

Appliance Center's journal entry to record the adjustment for prepaid interest is shown in Illustration 10-8.

ILLUSTRATION 10-8

Journal entry to record adjustment for prepaid interest initially recorded as an expense

GENERAL JOURNAL PAGE *13*

	DATE		ACCOUNT TITLE	DOC. NO.	POST. REF.	DEBIT	CREDIT	
1			*Adjusting Entries*					1
16		31	*Prepaid Interest*			15 00		16
17			*Interest Expense*				15 00	17
18								18
19								19
20								20

Closing Entry for Interest Expense. Interest Expense is closed as part of Appliance Center's closing entries. The effect of this closing entry on the interest expense account is described later in this chapter.

Reversing Entry for Prepaid Interest Expense. The adjusting entry for prepaid interest created a balance in Appliance Center's asset Prepaid Interest. Therefore, on January 1, Appliance Center *does* need a reversing entry for interest expense.

Interest Expense

Debit		Credit	
12/31 Bal.	142.50	12/31 Adj. NP7	15.00
12/31 Adj. NP8	3.13	12/31 Clos.	130.63
1/1 Rev.	15.00		
(New Bal.	*15.00)*		

Prepaid Interest

Debit		Credit	
12/31 Adj.	15.00	1/1 Rev.	15.00
(New Bal. zero)			

Interest Expense is increased by a $15.00 debit. The new balance of this account, *$15.00,* can now be added to payments for additional prepaid interest during the next fiscal period. Prepaid Interest is decreased by a $15.00 credit. The new balance of this account is zero as it was before the adjusting entry.

The $3.13 debit in Interest Expense is for an adjusting entry described later in this chapter.

Appliance Center's journal entry to record the reversing entry for interest expense is shown in Illustration 10-9.

ILLUSTRATION 10-9

Journal entry to record reversing entry for prepaid interest initially recorded as an expense

GENERAL JOURNAL PAGE *1*

	DATE		ACCOUNT TITLE	DOC. NO.	POST. REF.	DEBIT	CREDIT	
1			*Reversing Entries*					1
12		1	*Interest Expense*			15 00		12
13			*Prepaid Interest*				15 00	13
14								14
15								15
16								16
17								17

TEACHING STRATEGIES: TEACHING TIP

To lessen the difficulty with reversing entries, use T accounts on the chalkboard or overhead projector to analyze entries presented in this chapter. Discuss the reason for reversing entries and illustrate the potential problem if reversing entries are NOT made.

AUDIT YOUR UNDERSTANDING

1. Supplies is debited; Supplies Expense is credited.
2. Because the adjusting entry creates a balance in an asset account.
3. On January 1 of the new fiscal period.
4. Prepaid Insurance is debited; Insurance Expense is credited.

LESSON 10-3

Materials

- Student pages 292–301
- Assess: Problem Test Chapter 10, MicroExam Chapter 10

Objectives (Enabling Performance Tasks)

a. Define accounting terms related to notes payable, prepaid expenses, and accrued expenses.

b. Identify accounting concepts and practices related to notes payable, prepaid expenses, and accrued expenses.

e. Journalize adjusting and reversing entries for accrued expenses.

Audit Your Understanding

1. What accounts are affected, and how, to record an adjusting entry for supplies initially recorded as an expense?
2. Why is a reversing entry needed when supplies are initially recorded as an expense?
3. On what date are reversing entries recorded?
4. What accounts are affected, and how, to record an adjusting entry for prepaid insurance initially recorded as an expense?

ACCRUED EXPENSES

Expenses incurred in one fiscal period but not paid until a later fiscal period are called **accrued expenses.** In any fiscal period, Appliance Center may have four kinds of accrued expenses. (1) Accrued interest expense. (2) Accrued salary expense. (3) Accrued employer payroll taxes expense. (4) Accrued federal income tax expense.

Journalizing Accrued Interest Expense

On December 31, Appliance Center has Note Payable No. 8, a 60-day, 10% note for $750.00, dated December 16, on which interest has accrued.

Adjusting Entry for Accrued Interest Expense. On December 31, Appliance Center owed 15 days accrued interest on Note Payable No. 8. The accrued interest expense for this note should be reported in the current fiscal period. *(CONCEPT: Matching Expenses with Revenue)* The accrued interest is calculated as shown below.

Principal	×	Interest Rate	×	Time as Fraction of Year	=	Interest for 15 Days
$750.00	×	10%	×	$\frac{15}{360}$	=	$\frac{\$1{,}125.00}{360}$ = $3.13

Interest Expense

Debit		Credit	
12/31 Bal.	142.50	12/31 Adj. NP7	15.00
12/31 Adj. NP8	3.13		
(New Bal.	*130.63)*		

Interest Payable

Debit		Credit	
		12/31 Adj. NP8	3.13

Interest Expense is increased by a $3.13 debit, the interest expense for Note Payable No. 8 for the current fiscal period. Interest Payable is increased by a $3.13 credit, the interest owed on Note Payable No. 8 at the end of the fiscal period.

The $15.00 credit in Interest Expense is the adjusting entry for Note Payable No. 7 prepaid interest described earlier in this chapter.

Appliance Center's journal entry to record the adjustment for accrued interest expense is shown in Illustration 10-10.

ILLUSTRATION 10-10 Journal entry to record adjustment for accrued interest expense

	DATE		ACCOUNT TITLE	DOC. NO.	POST. REF.	DEBIT	CREDIT	
1			*Adjusting Entries*					1
26		31	*Interest Expense*			3 13		26
27			*Interest Payable*				3 13	27

FYI

Interest Expense is closed to Income Summary.

Closing Entry for Interest Expense. Interest Expense is closed as part of Appliance Center's closing entries.

Income Summary

Debit		Credit	
12/31 Clos.	130.63		

Interest Expense

Debit		Credit	
12/31 Bal.	130.63	12/31 Clos.	130.63
(New Bal. zero)			

Reversing Entry for Accrued Interest Expense. Appliance Center's adjusting entries for accrued expenses created a balance in an asset and a liability account. Therefore, on January 1, Appliance Center *does* need reversing entries for accrued interest expenses.

Prepaid Interest

Debit		Credit	
12/31 Adj. NP7	15.00	1/1 Rev. NP7	15.00
(New Bal. zero)			

Interest Expense

Debit		Credit	
12/31 Bal.	142.50	12/31 Adj. NP7	15.00
12/31 Adj. NP8	3.13	12/31 Clos.	130.63
(New Bal. zero)			
1/1 Rev. NP7	15.00	1/1 Rev. NP8	3.13

Interest Payable

Debit		Credit	
1/1 Rev. NP8	3.13	12/31 Adj. NP8	3.13
		(New Bal. zero)	

Two reversing entries affect Interest Expense. One is for prepaid interest, *$15.00,* for Note Payable No. 7 described earlier in this chapter. The other is for accrued interest, *$3.13,* for Note Payable No. 8.

Appliance Center's journal entry to record the reversing entry for accrued interest expense is shown in Illustration 10-11.

ILLUSTRATION 10-11 Journal entry to record reversing entry for accrued interest expense

GENERAL JOURNAL PAGE *1*

	DATE		ACCOUNT TITLE	DOC. NO.	POST. REF.	DEBIT	CREDIT	
1			*Reversing Entries*					1
14		*1*	*Interest Payable*			*3 13*		14
15			*Interest Expense*				*3 13*	15
16								16

When Note Payable No. 8 is paid on February 14 of the following year, the total interest expense is $12.50. The total interest, which should be divided between the two fiscal periods, is calculated as shown below.

Interest Expense Recorded in Previous Period	+	Interest Expense to Be Recorded in Current Period	=	Total Interest Expense for Note Payable No. 8
$3.13	+	$9.37	=	$12.50

FOCUS

- Adjusting, closing, and reversing entries for prepaid expenses were presented earlier in this chapter. In this lesson, adjusting, closing, and reversing entries for another type of expenses will be described. These expenses are incurred in one fiscal period but not paid until a later fiscal period.
- Introduce vocabulary: accrued expenses.

TEACH

Cover student pages 292–301 "Accrued Expenses." Explain the procedure to account for accrued interest expense including the end-of-period adjusting entry, the closing entry, and the reversing entry. Reinforce how to determine if a reversing entry is needed and what could occur if a reversing entry is not made. Describe the procedure to account for accrued employer payroll taxes expense. Emphasize that reversing entries eliminate the need to remember that some of the payroll taxes were an expense for the previous accounting period. Discuss the procedure to account for accrued federal income tax expense. Explain that the adjusting entry for federal income tax expense is not reversed. This follows the trend of most corporations, allowing the federal income tax expense account to accurately reflect the quarterly payments made in the next fiscal period.

Notes Payable			
2/14 Pay.	750.00	12/31 Bal.	750.00
(New Bal. zero)			

Interest Payable			
1/1 Rev.	3.13	12/31 Adj.	3.13
		(New Bal. zero)	

Interest Expense			
2/14 Pay.	12.50	1/1 Rev.	3.13

Cash			
		2/14 Pay.	762.50

With a reversing entry, the analysis of a transaction to pay Note Payable No. 8 is shown in the T accounts.

Notes Payable is decreased by a $750.00 debit. Interest Expense is increased by a $12.50 debit. The $12.50 debit in Interest Expense is offset by the $3.13 credit from the reversing entry. The difference, *$9.37,* is the current fiscal period's interest expense on Note Payable No. 8. Cash is decreased by a $762.50 credit.

Without a reversing entry, $3.13 of the interest would be reported twice. The $3.13 amount is recorded once as an adjusting entry in the last fiscal period. The amount is recorded a second time as part of the $12.50 debit in the current fiscal period when the note is paid. The analysis of an entry to pay Note Payable No. 8 without reversing entries is shown in the T accounts.

The entry to pay Note Payable No. 8 affects the accounts in the same way as previously described. However, the result in Interest Expense is different. Before the payment is recorded, Interest Expense has a zero balance because of the closing entries on December 31. Interest Expense is increased by a $12.50 debit. There is no offsetting credit from a reversing entry. Therefore, the amount charged in the current period is $12.50 instead of $9.37. Also, the $3.13 credit in Interest Payable still remains as a liability after the payment is recorded.

Notes Payable			
2/14 Pay.	750.00	12/31 Bal.	750.00
(New Bal. zero)			

Interest Expense			
2/14 Pay.	12.50		

Interest Payable			
		12/31 Adj.	3.13

Cash			
		2/14 Pay.	762.50

The double charge might be avoided if accounting personnel are careful to divide the interest amount when the note is paid. The part of the interest chargeable to the previous fiscal period, *$3.13,* is recorded as a debit in Interest Payable. The part chargeable to the current fiscal period, *$9.37,* is recorded as a debit in Interest Expense. The analysis of an entry to split the interest is shown in the T accounts.

Notes Payable			
2/14 Pay.	750.00	12/31 Bal.	750.00
(New Bal. zero)			

Interest Payable			
2/14 Pay.	3.13	12/31 Adj.	3.13
(New Bal. zero)			

Interest Expense			
12/14 Pay.	9.37		

Cash			
		2/14 Pay.	762.50

Notes Payable is decreased by a $750.00 debit. Interest Payable is decreased by a $3.13 debit. The new balance of this liability account is zero as it was before the adjusting entry. Interest Expense is increased with a $9.37 debit, the current period's interest on Note Payable No. 8. Cash is decreased by a $762.50 credit.

Although the entry described above could be used to divide the interest between fiscal periods, Appliance Center prefers to use reversing entries. Appliance Center's accounting personnel do not have to remember to check an entry each time a note is paid to determine if interest should be divided.

TEACHING STRATEGIES: TEACHING TIP

To the extent possible, have students work end-of-chapter problems in class so that you will be available when questions arise.

CAREERS IN ACCOUNTING

Financial Securities Clerk

- *Reviews statements of transactions such as purchases and sales of securities*
- *Enters transaction details in journals*
- *Calculates cash balances, dividends, or other investment data*

FYI

Reversing entries eliminate the need to remember that some of the payroll taxes were an expense for the previous accounting period.

Journalizing Accrued Salary Expense

Appliance Center pays its employees each Friday for the time worked during the previous week. For example, on Friday, December 29, all employees are paid for the time they worked during the week ended on Friday, December 22. The employees do not work on Saturday or Sunday. Therefore, at the end of the current fiscal period, Appliance Center has accrued salary expense for five days from December 25 to December 29.

Adjusting Entry for Accrued Salary Expense. On December 31, Appliance Center owes, but has not paid, the employees for Monday through Friday of the previous week. On Friday, January 5, the employees will receive a paycheck that includes five days' pay from the previous fiscal period. On December 31, even though the employees have not been paid, salaries for five days are reported as an expense of the current fiscal period. *(CONCEPT: Matching Expenses with Revenue)* The financial statements must show all the business expenses for a fiscal period. *(CONCEPT: Adequate Disclosure)*

The salaries that Appliance Center owes on December 31 are listed below.

Administrative salaries owed	$750.00
Sales salaries owed	850.00
Warehouse salaries owed	450.00

Salary Expense—Administrative is increased by a $750.00 debit, the portion of the accrued salaries applicable to administration. Salary Expense—Sales is increased by an $850.00 debit, the portion of the accrued salaries applicable to sales. Salary Expense—Warehouse is increased by a $450.00 debit, the portion of the accrued salaries applicable to the warehouse. Salaries Payable is increased by a $2,050.00 credit, the total accrued salaries owed to employees on December 31.

Salary Expense—Administrative

Debit		Credit
12/31 Bal.	37,062.50	
12/31 Adj.	750.00	
(New Bal.	*37,812.50)*	

Salary Expense—Warehouse

Debit		Credit
12/31 Bal.	22,037.50	
12/31 Adj.	450.00	
(New Bal.	*22,487.50)*	

Salary Expense—Sales

Debit		Credit
12/31 Bal.	45,075.00	
12/31 Adj.	850.00	
(New Bal.	*45,925.00)*	

Salaries Payable

Debit	Credit	
	12/31 Adj.	2,050.00

Appliance Center's journal entry to record the adjustment for accrued salary expense is shown in Illustration 10-12.

CAREERS IN ACCOUNTING

The CAREERS feature box, FINANCIAL SECURITIES CLERK, comes from the Dictionary of Occupational Titles (DOT). The entry number for this job title is D.O.T. 219.482-010. Bring this dictionary to class and explain its purpose and how to use it. The career feature is designed to expose students to the exploration of different careers in accounting. The feature gives a realistic description of actual job duties. This feature can be used to demonstrate that the skills learned in this course are relevant.

APPLY

Write the formulas on the board for calculating accrued interest expense and demonstrate the calculation. Draw T accounts on the chalkboard or overhead projector to analyze entries presented in this lesson. Refer students to Illustrations 10-10 and 10-11, respectively, as adjusting and reversing entries for accrued interest expense are discussed.

Guided Practice

Guide students through the T account analysis of the adjusting and reversing entries in Problem 10-3. Have students draw T accounts on a sheet of paper and analyze the adjusting entry for accrued interest. All students should agree with the analysis before proceeding to the next adjustment. Repeat the process for the reversing entries. The balance of Problem 10-3 can be assigned as Independent Practice.

Independent Practice

- Assign Term 15, Questions 13–20, and Problem 10-3.
- Assign Study Guide 10 and Mastery Problem 10-M.

ASSESS

Assess student understanding by checking the solutions to the Independent Practice activities.

Reteach

- Using information from Recycling Problem 10-R, Instruction 3, demonstrate the T account analysis of the adjusting and reversing entries for the accrued expense items. Have students draw T accounts at their desks and complete the analysis with you.
- Assign Recycling Problem 10-R, Instructions 3 and 4.

Extend

- Assign Cases for Critical Thinking 2.
- Assign Challenge Problem 10-C. (The challenge is to journalize adjusting entries for prepaid expenses initially recorded as assets.)

Enrich

Assign the CAREERS IN ACCOUNTING feature on page 295. Have students discuss what a career as a financial securities clerk might be like.

ILLUSTRATION 10-12 Journal entry to record adjustment for accrued salary expense

GENERAL JOURNAL PAGE *13*

	DATE		ACCOUNT TITLE	DOC. NO.	POST. REF.	DEBIT	CREDIT	
1			*Adjusting Entries*					1
28		*31*	*Salary Expense—Administrative*			*750 00*		28
29			*Salary Expense—Sales*			*850 00*		29
30			*Salary Expense—Warehouse*			*450 00*		30
31			*Salaries Payable*				*2050 00*	31
32								32
33								33
34								34
35								35

Closing Entry for Salary Expense. The effect of this closing entry on the salary expense accounts is shown in the T accounts.

Income Summary

Debit		Credit	
12/31 Clos.	106,225.00		

Salary Expense—Sales

Debit		Credit	
12/31 Bal.	45,925.00	12/31 Clos.	45,925.00
(New Bal. zero)			

Salary Expense—Administrative

Debit		Credit	
12/31 Bal.	37,812.50	12/31 Clos.	37,812.50
(New Bal. zero)			

Salary Expense—Warehouse

Debit		Credit	
12/31 Bal.	22,487.50	12/31 Clos.	22,487.50
(New Bal. zero)			

Reversing Entry for Accrued Salary Expense. Salaries Payable is decreased by a $2,050.00 debit. Salary Expense—Administrative is decreased by a $750.00 credit. Salary Expense—Sales is decreased by an $850.00 credit. Salary Expense—Warehouse is decreased by a $450.00 credit. The three expense accounts have contra balances after the reversing entry. When the payroll is paid in January, a portion of the amount debited in each account is offset by the credit contra balance.

Salaries Payable

Debit		Credit	
1/1 Rev.	2,050.00	12/31 Adj.	2,050.00
		(New Bal. zero)	

Salary Expense—Sales

Debit		Credit	
12/31 Bal.	45,075.00	12/31 Clos.	45,925.00
12/31 Adj.	850.00	1/1 Rev.	850.00
		(New Bal.	*850.00)*

Salary Expense—Administrative

Debit		Credit	
12/31 Bal.	37,062.50	12/31 Clos.	37,812.50
12/31 Adj.	750.00	1/1 Rev.	750.00
		(New Bal.	*750.00)*

Salary Expense—Warehouse

Debit		Credit	
12/31 Bal.	22,037.50	12/31 Clos.	22,487.50
12/31 Adj.	450.00	1/1 Rev.	450.00
		(New Bal.	*450.00)*

Appliance Center's journal entry to record the reversing entry for accrued salary expense is shown in Illustration 10-13.

TEACHING STRATEGIES: APPLYING VISUALS

Direct students to Illustrations 10-12 and 10-13 to review the adjusting and reversing entries for accrued salary expense.

ILLUSTRATION 10-13 Journal entry to record reversing entry for accrued salary expense

GENERAL JOURNAL PAGE 1

	DATE		ACCOUNT TITLE	DOC. NO.	POST. REF.	DEBIT	CREDIT	
1			*Reversing Entries*					1
16		1	*Salaries Payable*			2050 00		16
17			*Salary Expense—Administrative*				750 00	17
18			*Salary Expense—Sales*				850 00	18
19			*Salary Expense—Warehouse*				450 00	19
20								20

Journalizing Accrued Employer Payroll Taxes Expense

Employer payroll taxes for accrued salaries must be recorded at the end of a fiscal period. Appliance Center has three employer payroll taxes: (1) FICA tax, (2) federal unemployment tax, and (3) state unemployment tax.

Adjusting Entry for Accrued Employer Payroll Taxes Expense. Appliance Center's accrued employer payroll taxes are calculated as shown below.

Tax	Taxable Accrued Salary	×	Tax Rate	=	Accrued Employer Payroll Tax Expense
FICA	$2,050.00		8.0%		$164.00
Federal Unemployment	450.00		0.8%		3.60
State Unemployment	450.00		5.4%		24.30
Total	—		—		$191.90

The taxable salaries for FICA and unemployment taxes are different. Only $450.00 of the $2,050.00 accrued salary is subject to unemployment taxes.

Payroll Taxes Expense

Debit		Credit	
12/31 Bal.	9,050.00		
12/31 Adj.	191.90		
(New Bal.	*9,241.90)*		

Unemployment Tax Payable—Federal

Debit		Credit	
		12/31 Bal.	32.00
		12/31 Adj.	3.60
		(New Bal.	*35.60)*

FICA Tax Payable

Debit		Credit	
		12/31 Bal.	659.50
		12/31 Adj.	164.00
		(New Bal.	*823.50)*

Unemployment Tax Payable—State

Debit		Credit	
		12/31 Bal.	210.90
		12/31 Adj.	24.30
		(New Bal.	*235.20)*

CLOSURE

- Use Audit Your Understanding questions.
- Review Summary Illustration 10-17, "Summary of Adjusting and Reversing Entries for Prepaid and Accrued Expenses."

ASSESS

- Administer Problem Test Chapter 10.
- Administer a MicroExam test for Chapter 10.

APPLIED SKILLS: WORD PROCESSING

If you wish to integrate word processing in your accounting course, you may direct students to answer the end-of-chapter Accounting Terms, Questions for Individual Study, and Cases for Critical Thinking using their word processing software.

Payroll Taxes Expense is increased by a $191.90 debit. FICA Tax Payable is increased by a $164.00 credit. Unemployment Tax Payable—Federal is increased by a $3.60 credit. Unemployment Tax Payable—State is increased by a $24.30 credit.

Appliance Center's journal entry to record the adjustment for accrued employer payroll taxes expense is shown in Illustration 10-14.

ILLUSTRATION 10-14 Journal entry to record adjustment for accrued employer payroll taxes expense

GENERAL JOURNAL — PAGE 13

	DATE		ACCOUNT TITLE	DOC. NO.	POST. REF.	DEBIT	CREDIT	
1			*Adjusting Entries*					1
32		31	*Payroll Taxes Expense*			191 90		32
33			*FICA Tax Payable*				164 00	33
34			*Unemployment Tax Payable—Federal*				3 60	34
35			*Unemployment Tax Payable—State*				24 30	35
36								36
37								37
38								38

TEACHING STRATEGIES: DIFFERENT LEARNING ABILITIES

At-Risk Students. Utilize the lesson plans provided in the teacher's edition to divide each chapter into smaller parts to create short units that provide frequent opportunities for assessment and goal attainment.

Closing Entry for Employer Payroll Taxes Expense.

The effect of Appliance Center's closing entry on the payroll taxes expense account is shown in the T accounts.

Income Summary

Debit		Credit	
12/31 Clos.	9,241.90		

Payroll Taxes Expense

Debit		Credit	
12/31 Bal.	9,241.90	12/31 Clos.	9,241.90
(New Bal. zero)			

Reversing Entry for Accrued Employer Payroll Taxes Expense.

The analysis of Appliance Center's reversing entry for accrued employer payroll taxes expense is shown in the T accounts.

FICA Tax Payable

Debit		Credit	
1/1 Rev.	164.00	12/31 Bal.	659.50
		12/31 Adj.	164.00
		(New Bal.	*659.50)*

Unemployment Tax Payable—State

Debit		Credit	
1/1 Rev.	24.30	12/31 Bal.	210.90
		12/31 Adj.	24.30
		(New Bal.	*210.90)*

Unemployment Tax Payable—Federal

Debit		Credit	
1/1 Rev.	3.60	12/31 Bal.	32.00
		12/31 Adj.	3.60
		(New Bal.	*32.00)*

Payroll Taxes Expense

Debit		Credit	
12/31 Bal.	9,050.00	12/31 Clos.	9,241.90
12/31 Adj.	191.90	12/31 Rev.	191.90
		(New Bal.	*191.90)*

APPLIED SKILLS: WRITING ACROSS THE CURRICULUM

Writing paragraphs and short essays. The Cases for Critical Thinking are short, practical applications of the accounting principles developed in the chapter. Some cases are planned to present problems related to the chapter but not specifically discussed and answered in the chapter. These cases present an opportunity for critical thinking and decision making. These cases also require more than a short objective-type response. Therefore they provide ideal practice in writing paragraphs and short essays.

Appliance Center's journal entry to record the reversing entry for accrued employer payroll taxes expense is shown in Illustration 10-15.

ILLUSTRATION 10-15 Journal entry to record reversing entry for accrued employer payroll taxes expense

GENERAL JOURNAL PAGE 1

	DATE		ACCOUNT TITLE	DOC. NO.	POST. REF.	DEBIT	CREDIT	
1			*Reversing Entries*					1
20		1	*FICA Tax Payable*			164 00		20
21			*Unemployment Tax Payable—Federal*			3 60		21
22			*Unemployment Tax Payable—State*			24 30		22
23			*Payroll Taxes Expense*				191 90	23
24								24
25								25
26								26

APPLIED SKILLS: LANGUAGE ARTS

Paraphrasing, writing complete sentences, and identifying direct objects. For additional practice in language arts skills, direct students to answer the Accounting Terms and Questions for Individual Study at the end of the chapter. Students should write the answers in their own words and in complete sentences. To further practice language arts skills, ask students to underline the direct object(s) in each sentence of their answers.

Journalizing Accrued Federal Income Tax Expense

FYI

The adjusting entry for federal income tax expense is not reversed.

Corporations must pay federal income tax on net income. At the beginning of each year, Appliance Center makes an estimate of its federal income tax. The estimated amount is paid in four quarterly payments. At the end of a year, Appliance Center calculates its actual income tax for the year. Any unpaid federal income tax is an accrued expense for which an adjusting entry is made.

Adjusting Entry for Accrued Federal Income Tax Expense. On December 31, Appliance Center's records show that four quarterly income tax payments have been made for a total of $9,000.00. On December 31, Appliance Center calculates that its actual income tax is $10,000.00. Thus, the accrued federal income tax remaining to be paid is $1,000.00 (total tax, $10,000.00, *minus* amount paid, $9,000.00).

Calculating the amount of accrued federal income tax expense using a work sheet is described in Chapter 14.

Federal Income Tax Expense

Debit		Credit
12/31 Bal.	9,000.00	
12/31 Adj.	1,000.00	
(New Bal.	*10,000.00)*	

Federal Income Tax Payable

Debit	Credit	
	12/31 Adj.	1,000.00

Federal Income Tax Expense is increased by a $1,000.00 debit. Federal Income Tax Payable is increased by a $1,000.00 credit.

Federal Income Tax Payable is a current liability account. Federal Income Tax Expense is an expense account located in a general ledger division titled *Income Tax*. These accounts are shown on Appliance Center's chart of accounts.

Appliance Center's journal entry to record the adjustment for accrued federal income tax expense is shown in Illustration 10-16.

TEACHING STRATEGIES: TEACHING TIP

Explain that the adjusting entry for federal income tax expense is not reversed. This follows the trend of most corporations, allowing the federal income tax expense account to accurately reflect the quarterly payments made in the next fiscal period.

ILLUSTRATION 10-16 Journal entry to record adjustment for accrued federal income tax expense

GENERAL JOURNAL PAGE 13

	DATE		ACCOUNT TITLE	DOC. NO.	POST. REF.	DEBIT	CREDIT	
1			*Adjusting Entries*					1
38		31	*Federal Income Tax Expense*			1 0 0 0 00		38
39			*Federal Income Tax Payable*				1 0 0 0 00	39
40								40

Closing Entry for Federal Income Tax Expense. The effect of Appliance Center's closing entry on the federal income tax expense account is shown in the T accounts.

Income Summary

Debit		Credit
12/31 Clos.	10,000.00	

Federal Income Tax Expense

Debit		Credit	
12/31 Bal.	10,000.00	12/31 Clos.	10,000.00
(New Bal. zero)			

Audit Your Understanding

1. What is meant by accrued expenses?
2. What is the formula for calculating accrued interest?
3. What accounts are affected, and how, to record an adjusting entry for accrued interest expense?
4. Which adjusting entry for an accrued expense is not reversed?

Appliance Center's adjusting entry for income tax expense does create a balance in the federal income tax payable account. During the new year, cash will be paid for accrued income tax expense for the previous year plus periodic payments for the current year's income tax expense. To avoid confusing the amount of tax expense recorded for each of these years and to provide year-to-date income tax expense information for each year, Appliance Center does not reverse this adjusting entry. For similar reasons, many corporations do not reverse accrued income tax adjusting entries.

A summary of the adjusting and reversing entries described in this chapter is given in Illustration 10-17.

AUDIT YOUR UNDERSTANDING

1. Expenses incurred in one fiscal period but not paid until a later fiscal period.
2. Principal times interest rate times time as a fraction of a year equals interest.
3. Interest Expense is debited; Interest Payable is credited.
4. The adjusting entry for accrued federal income tax expense.

300

SUMMARY ILLUSTRATION 10-17

Summary of adjusting and reversing entries for prepaid and accrued expenses

Item	Adjusting Entry		Reversing Entry	
	Account Debited	Account Credited	Account Debited	Account Credited
MasterSport's prepaid items initially recorded as assets: Supplies Insurance	 Supplies Expense Insurance Expense	 Supplies Prepaid Insurance	 no reversing entry made no reversing entry made	
Appliance Center's prepaid items initially recorded as expenses: Supplies Insurance Interest	 Supplies Prepaid Insurance Prepaid Interest	 Supplies Expense Insurance Expense Interest Expense	 Supplies Expense Insurance Expense Interest Expense	 Supplies Prepaid Insurance Prepaid Interest
Appliance Center's accrued items: Interest Salaries Employer Payroll Taxes	 Interest Expense Salary Expense Payroll Taxes Expense	 Interest Payable Salaries Payable FICA Tax Payable Unemployment Tax Payable—Federal Unemployment Tax Payable—State	 Interest Payable Salaries Payable FICA Tax Payable Unemployment Tax Payable—Federal Unemployment Tax Payable—State	 Interest Expense Salary Expense Payroll Taxes Expense
Federal Income Tax	Federal Income Tax Expense	Federal Income Tax Payable	no reversing entry made	

ACCOUNTING TERMS EPT(a)

What is the meaning of each of the following?

1. promissory note
2. notes payable
3. date of a note
4. principal of a note
5. maturity date of a note
6. interest
7. interest rate of a note
8. interest expense
9. maturity value
10. bank discount
11. discounted note
12. proceeds
13. prepaid expenses
14. reversing entry
15. accrued expenses

ACCOUNTING TERMS

1. **promissory note:** A written and signed promise to pay a sum of money at a specified time. (p. 281)
2. **notes payable:** Promissory notes that a business issues to creditors. (p. 281)
3. **date of a note:** The day a note is issued. (p. 281)
4. **principal of a note:** The original amount of a note. (p. 281)
5. **maturity date of a note:** The date a note is due. (p. 281)
6. **interest:** An amount paid for the use of money for a period of time. (p. 281)
7. **interest rate of a note:** The percentage of the principal that is paid for use of the money. (p. 281)
8. **interest expense:** The interest accrued on money borrowed. (p. 283)
9. **maturity value:** The amount that is due on the maturity date of a note. (p. 283)
10. **bank discount:** Interest collected in advance on a note. (p. 284)
11. **discounted note:** A note on which interest is paid in advance. (p. 284)
12. **proceeds:** The amount received for a note after the bank discount has been deducted. (p. 284)
13. **prepaid expenses:** Expenses paid in one fiscal period but not reported as expenses until a later fiscal period. (p. 285)
14. **reversing entry:** An entry made at the beginning of one fiscal period to reverse an adjusting entry made in the previous fiscal period. (p. 288)
15. **accrued expenses:** Expenses incurred in one fiscal period but not paid until a later fiscal period. (p. 292)

QUESTIONS FOR INDIVIDUAL STUDY

1. Cash is debited; Notes Payable is credited. (p. 281)
2. Principal *times* interest rate *times* time as fraction of year *equals* interest for fraction of year. (p. 282)
3. Notes Payable and Interest Expense are debited; Cash is credited. (p. 283)
4. Cash and Interest Expense are debited; Notes Payable is credited. (p. 284)
5. Supplies Expense—Sales is debited; Cash is credited. (p. 285)
6. Matching Expenses with Revenue concept. (p. 285)
7. To separate the asset and expense portions of the supplies cost recorded in the supplies expense account. (p. 286)
8. If an adjusting entry *creates* a balance in an asset or a liability account, the adjusting entry is reversed. (p. 288)
9. Supplies Expense—Sales is debited; Supplies—Sales is credited. (p. 288)
10. Insurance Expense is debited; Prepaid Insurance is credited. (p. 290)
11. Prepaid Interest is debited; Interest Expense is credited. (p. 290)
12. Interest Expense is debited; Prepaid Interest is credited. (p. 291)
13. (a) Accrued interest expense. (b) Accrued salary expense. (c) Accrued employer payroll taxes expense. (d) Accrued federal income tax expense. (p. 292)
14. Interest Expense is debited; Interest Payable is credited. (p. 292)
15. Interest Payable is debited; Interest Expense is credited. (p. 293)
16. Salary Expense—Administrative, Salary Expense—Sales, and Salary Expense—Warehouse are debited; Salaries Payable is credited. (p. 295)
17. Salaries Payable is debited; Salary Expense—Administrative, Salary Expense—Sales, and Salary Expense—Warehouse are credited. (p. 296)
18. Payroll Taxes Expense is debited; FICA Tax Payable, Unemployment Tax Payable—Federal, and Unemployment Tax Payable—State are credited. (p. 297)

QUESTIONS FOR INDIVIDUAL STUDY

EPT(b)

1. What general ledger accounts are affected, and how, when a note payable is issued for cash?
2. What is the formula Appliance Center uses to calculate interest on notes?
3. What accounts are affected, and how, when cash is paid for the maturity value of a note payable?
4. What accounts are affected, and how, when a discounted note payable is recorded?
5. What accounts are affected, and how, when sales supplies bought for cash are initially recorded as an expense?
6. Which accounting concept is being applied when an adjusting entry is recorded for prepaid expenses?
7. Why is an adjusting entry made for supplies at the end of a fiscal period?
8. What rule of thumb can accountants follow to determine if a reversing entry is needed?
9. What accounts are affected, and how, by a reversing entry for sales supplies expense when supplies are initially recorded as an expense?
10. What accounts are affected, and how, by a reversing entry for insurance expense when insurance is initially recorded as an expense?
11. What accounts are affected, and how, to record an adjusting entry for interest expense when prepaid interest is initially recorded as an expense?
12. What accounts are affected, and how, by a reversing entry for interest expense when prepaid interest is initially recorded as an expense?
13. As described in this chapter, what four kinds of accrued expenses might Appliance Center have at the end of a fiscal period?
14. What accounts are affected, and how, by an adjusting entry for accrued interest expense?
15. What accounts are affected, and how, by a reversing entry for accrued interest expense?
16. What accounts are affected, and how, by an adjusting entry for accrued salary expense?
17. What accounts are affected, and how, by a reversing entry for accrued salary expense?
18. What accounts are affected, and how, by an adjusting entry for accrued employer payroll taxes expense?
19. What accounts are affected, and how, by a reversing entry for accrued employer payroll taxes expense?
20. What accounts are affected, and how, by an adjusting entry for accrued federal income tax expense?

CASES FOR CRITICAL THINKING

EPT(b)

CASE 1 Roberta Wagner owns Wagner Books. At the end of each month, Wagner Books borrows money from a bank and uses the proceeds to pay all outstanding accounts payable. The business discounts a 15-day, 14% note payable for each loan. Each month to date, Wagner Books has been able to pay the notes payable when due. Mrs. Wagner uses this procedure to maintain good credit ratings with vendors. Is Mrs. Wagner's reasoning sound? Explain your answer.

CASE 2 Jennifer Pier, owner and manager of Pier, Inc., does not record adjusting or reversing entries for accrued payroll. Ms. Pier says that the matter is taken care of when the first payroll is recorded in the next month. The CPA who advises Ms. Pier suggests that the adjusting and reversing entries should be made. He states that omission of these entries affects the information reported on the business' financial statements. With whom do you agree? Explain your answer.

APPLICATION PROBLEMS EPT(c,d,e)

PROBLEM 10-1 Journalizing notes payable transactions

SPREADSHEET

MATHEMATICS

Raecker, Inc. completed the following transactions during the current year.

INSTRUCTIONS:

1. Calculate the maturity dates for each of the three notes. Source documents are abbreviated as follows: check, C; note payable, NP.

Aug. 1. Issued a 3-month, 11% note, $1,100.00. NP1.

Sept. 2. Discounted at 12% a 60-day non-interest-bearing note, $1,200.00; proceeds, $1,176.00, interest, $24.00. NP2.

Oct. 1. Issued a 60-day, 10% note, $800.00. NP3.

2. Calculate the total amount of interest due at maturity for each of the three notes.
3. Journalize the transactions on page 15 of a cash receipts journal.
4. Journalize the following transactions on page 21 of a cash payments journal. Use the maturity dates calculated in Instruction 1 and the interest amounts calculated in Instruction 2.

Paid cash for the maturity value of NP1. C45.
Paid cash for the maturity value of NP2. C52.
Paid cash for the maturity value of NP3. C59.

PROBLEM 10-2 Journalizing adjusting and reversing entries for prepaid expenses initially recorded as expenses

Dupre, Inc. has the following general ledger balances on December 31 of the current year before adjusting entries are recorded.

Supplies Expense—Administrative	$1,500.00
Supplies Expense—Sales	2,500.00
Insurance Expense	3,000.00
Interest Expense	56.53
Notes Payable	1,000.00

(Discounted at 12% the 60-day Note Payable No. 4 issued December 1.)

INSTRUCTIONS:

1. Use the following adjustment information. Journalize the adjusting entries for supplies and insurance on December 31 of the current year. Use page 13 of a general journal.

Adjustment Information, December 31

Administrative supplies inventory	$450.00
Sales supplies inventory	800.00
Value of prepaid insurance	720.00

2. Continue using page 13 of the general journal. Calculate the amount of prepaid interest on Note Payable No. 4 as of December 31. Journalize the adjusting entry for prepaid interest on Note Payable No. 4.
3. Journalize the reversing entries on January 1 of the next year. Use page 1 of a general journal.

PROBLEM 10-3 Journalizing adjusting and reversing entries for accrued expenses

The following data are obtained from the records of Marquette, Inc. on December 31 of the current year before adjusting entries are recorded.

QUESTIONS (cont'd)

19. FICA Tax Payable, Unemployment Tax Payable—Federal, and Unemployment Tax Payable—State are debited; Payroll Taxes Expense is credited. (p. 298)

20. Federal Income Tax Expense is debited; Federal Income Tax Payable is credited. (p. 299)

CASES FOR CRITICAL THINKING

Case 1 No, Mrs. Wagner's reasoning is not sound. In most cases, vendors do not penalize customers if payment on account is received within 30 days. If Wagner Books is able to pay the notes in 15 days, it could do the same with the accounts payable. Fifteen days is well within the 30 days usually allowed. By paying the vendors directly, the business would save the interest on the monthly notes payable.

Case 2 Agree with the CPA. If adjusting entries are not made for accrued payroll in any specific fiscal period, then liabilities are understated on the balance sheet, and the expenses are understated on the income statement for that period. Also, this means the net income or net loss for that period is not accurate. If adjusting entries are made for accrued payroll and accrued employer payroll taxes, then reversing entries should be made to facilitate recording the payroll entries in the next fiscal period.

CHECK FIGURES

See Teacher's Edition of the Working Papers for complete solutions.

Problem 10-1 Maturity dates: Note 1, November 1; Note 2, November 1; Note 3, November 30. Interest at maturity: Note 1, $30.25; Note 2, none—paid in advance; Note 3, $13.33.

Problem 10-2 Prepaid interest on Note 4 as of December 31: $10.00

Problem 10-3 Adjusting entries reversed: Interest Expense, Salary Expense—Admin., Salary Expense—Sales, and Payroll Taxes Expense

Adjustment Information, December 31

Accrued interest on notes payable	$ 5.15
Accrued salaries—administrative	600.00
Accrued salaries—sales	500.00
Accrued payroll taxes—FICA tax	88.00
Accrued payroll taxes—federal unemployment tax	8.80
Accrued payroll taxes—state unemployment tax	59.40
Accrued federal income tax	1,300.00

INSTRUCTIONS:

1. Journalize the adjusting entries for accrued interest, accrued payroll, accrued employer payroll taxes, and accrued federal income tax on December 31 of the current year. Use page 13 of a general journal.
2. Journalize the reversing entries on January 1 of the next year. Use page 1 of a general journal.

CHECK FIGURES *(cont'd)*

Mastery Problem 10-M Maturity dates on notes payable: Note 2, January 31; Note 3, January 30; Note 4, January 30

Challenge Problem 10-C Maturity dates of notes payable: Note 4, March 30; Note 5, February 28

ENRICHMENT PROBLEMS EPT(c,d,e)

MASTERY PROBLEM 10-M Journalizing adjusting and reversing entries for prepaid expenses initially recorded as expenses and for accrued expenses

Sass, Inc. completed the following transactions during the current year. Sass initially records prepaid expenses as expenses. Source documents are abbreviated as follows: check, C; note payable, NP.

July	1.	Issued a 2-month, 16% note, $700.00. NP1.
Sept.	1.	Paid cash for the maturity value of NP1: principal, $700.00, plus interest, $18.67; total, $718.67. C105.
Oct.	31.	Issued a 3-month, 10% note, $1,500.00. NP2.
Nov.	1.	Issued a 90-day, 10% note, $1,000.00. NP3.
Dec.	1.	Discounted at 10% a 60-day non-interest-bearing note, $900.00; proceeds, $885.00, interest, $15.00. NP4.

INSTRUCTIONS:

1. Calculate the maturity dates for Notes Payable Nos. 2, 3, and 4.
2. Journalize the transactions. Use page 13 of a cash receipts journal and page 17 of a cash payments journal.
3. Sass, Inc. has the following general ledger account balances on December 31 of the current year before adjusting entries are recorded.

Supplies Expense—Administrative	$400.00
Supplies Expense—Sales	600.00
Insurance Expense	900.00

Use the following adjustment information. Journalize the adjusting entries for prepaid and accrued expenses on December 31. Use page 13 of a general journal.

Adjustment Information, December 31

Administrative supplies inventory	$200.00
Sales supplies inventory	300.00
Value of prepaid insurance	350.00
Remaining prepaid interest	7.50
Accrued interest on notes payable	41.00
Accrued salaries—administrative	350.00
Accrued salaries—sales	415.00
Accrued payroll taxes—FICA tax	61.20
Accrued payroll taxes—federal unemployment tax	6.12
Accrued payroll taxes—state unemployment tax	41.31
Accrued federal income tax	800.00

4. Journalize the reversing entries on January 1 of the next year. Use page 1 of a general journal.

CHALLENGE PROBLEM 10-C Journalizing adjusting entries for prepaid expenses initially recorded as assets and adjusting and reversing entries for accrued expenses

Hetland, Inc. completed the following transactions during the current year. Hetland initially records prepaid expenses as assets. Source documents are abbreviated as follows: check, C; note payable, NP.

Aug. 1. A 3-month, 10% note was issued, $2,000.00. NP3.
Sept. 30. Issued a 6-month, 12% note, $1,200.00. NP4.
Nov. 1. The maturity value of NP3 was paid: principal, $2,000.00, plus interest, $50.00; total, $2,050.00. C95.
Nov. 30. Discounted at 10% a 90-day non-interest-bearing note, $500.00; proceeds, $487.50, interest, $12.50. NP5.

INSTRUCTIONS:

1. Calculate the maturity dates for Notes Payable Nos. 4 and 5.
2. Journalize the transactions. Use page 15 of a cash receipts journal and page 21 of a cash payments journal.
3. Hetland, Inc. has the following general ledger balances on December 31 of the current year before adjusting entries are recorded.

Supplies—Administrative	$500.00
Supplies—Sales	700.00
Prepaid Insurance	800.00
Prepaid Interest	44.86

Use the following adjustment information. Journalize the adjusting entries for prepaid and accrued expenses on December 31. Use page 13 of a general journal.

Adjustment Information, December 31

Administrative supplies inventory	$ 200.00
Sales supplies inventory	300.00
Value of prepaid insurance	550.00
Remaining prepaid interest	8.19
Accrued interest on notes payable	36.00
Accrued salaries—administrative	305.00
Accrued salaries—sales	425.00
Accrued payroll taxes—FICA tax	58.40
Accrued payroll taxes—federal unemployment tax	5.84
Accrued payroll taxes—state unemployment tax	39.42
Accrued federal income tax	1,000.00

4. Journalize the reversing entries on January 1 of the next year. Use page 1 of a general journal.

CHAPTER 11 OVERVIEW

Chapter 11 discusses procedures involved when accepting a note receivable. The discussion includes the journal entries for these transactions as well as entries for dishonored notes. Unearned revenue and accrued revenue and the appropriate adjusting, closing, and reversing entries are also included.

GUIDE TO ACHIEVING LEARNING OBJECTIVES

	TEACH	APPLY	EXTEND/ENRICH					
Enabling Performance Tasks	**Lesson Plans**	**Application Problems**	**Mastery Problems**	**Challenge Problems**	**Cases for Critical Thinking**	**Recycling Problems**	**Reinforcement Activity**	
a. Define accounting terms related to notes receivable, unearned revenue, and accrued revenue.	11-1, 11-2, 11-3							
b. Identify accounting concepts and practices related to notes receivable, unearned revenue, and accrued revenue.	11-1, 11-2, 11-3				Cases 1, 2			
c. Journalize transactions for notes receivable.	11-1	11-1	11-M	11-C		11-R	RA2	
d. Journalize adjusting and reversing entries for unearned revenue initially recorded as revenue.	11-2	11-2	11-M	11-C		11-R	RA2	
e. Journalize adjusting and reversing entries for accrued revenue.	11-3	11-3	11-M	11-C		11-R	RA2	

ENRICHMENT

SPECIAL FEATURES
Personal Visions in Business, page 315
Applied Communications, page 319

NEW, REVIEW, AND EXTENSION

ACTIVITIES/CONCEPTS/TRANSACTIONS	NEW	REVIEW/ EXTENSION
Notes receivable		✓
Accepting a note receivable		✓
Calculating maturity date and interest		✓
Receiving cash for a note receivable		✓
Dishonored notes receivable		✓
Unearned revenue	✓	
Unearned revenue initially recorded as a revenue	✓	
Unearned revenue initially recorded as a liability	✓	
Unearned rent	✓	
Adjusting, closing, and reversing entries for unearned revenue		✓
Accrued revenue		✓
Adjusting, closing, and reversing entries for accrued revenue		✓
Accrued interest income		✓

	INFORMAL ASSESSMENT		FORMAL ASSESSMENT			
	Study Guide	Audit Your Understanding	Chapter MicroExam	Chapter Problem Test	Unit Objective Test	Portfolio
	Unit A	✓	✓		✓	
	Units B, C	✓	✓		✓	
				✓		✓
				✓		✓
				✓		✓

TEACHING MATERIALS

Teaching Materials
Teacher's Wraparound Edition of the Text
Teacher's Resource Guide
Teacher's Edition of Working Papers
MicroExam

APPLIED MATHEMATICS

APPLIED MATH/ACCOUNTING SKILL	APPLICATION
Calculating interest	Prob. 11-3
Calculating maturity dates	Prob. 11-C
Calculating unearned rent	Prob. 11-C

Accounting for Notes Receivable, Unearned Revenue, and Accrued Revenue

TEACHING STRATEGIES: ACCOUNTING PEDAGOGY

This textbook continues accounting procedures for special adjustments. Accurate and up-to-date information about notes receivable and accrued revenue must be reported on financial statements at the end of the fiscal period.

ENABLING PERFORMANCE TASKS

After studying Chapter 11, you will be able to:

a Define accounting terms related to notes receivable, unearned revenue, and accrued revenue.

b Identify accounting concepts and practices related to notes receivable, unearned revenue, and accrued revenue.

c Journalize transactions for notes receivable.

d Journalize adjusting and reversing entries for unearned revenue initially recorded as revenue.

e Journalize adjusting and reversing entries for accrued revenue.

TERMS PREVIEW

notes receivable • dishonored note • unearned revenue • accrued revenue

TEACHING STRATEGIES: TEACHING TIP

To the extent possible, have students work end-of-chapter problems in class so that you will be available when questions arise.

Accurate and up-to-date information about notes receivable and accrued revenue must be reported on financial statements at the end of a fiscal period. *(CONCEPT: Adequate Disclosure)* Because of the nature of notes receivable and some types of revenue, special accounting procedures may be required at the end of a fiscal period. For example, a note receivable accepted in one fiscal period with a maturity date in the following fiscal period requires special accounting procedures. Also, special accounting procedures are required for two types of revenue. (1) Revenue received in one fiscal period but not earned until the next fiscal period. (2) Revenue earned in one fiscal period but not received until the next fiscal period.

NOTES RECEIVABLE

FYI

Notes receivable are classified as current assets.

Promissory notes that a business accepts from customers are called **notes receivable.** Notes receivable are usually due within a year. Therefore, notes receivable are classified as current assets.

Accepting a Note Receivable

Most notes receivable are accepted from customers who need an extension of time in which to pay on account.

> *April 3, 19--. Received a 30-day, 12% note from Duane Jansen for an extension of time on his account, $300.00. Note Receivable No. 11.*

GENERAL LEDGER

Notes Receivable

Debit	Credit
300.00	

Accounts Receivable

Debit	Credit
	300.00

ACCOUNTS RECEIVABLE LEDGER

Duane Jansen

Debit	Credit
Bal. 300.00	300.00

Notes Receivable is increased by a $300.00 debit. Accounts Receivable is decreased by a $300.00 credit. The amount to be received has been changed from an account receivable to a note receivable. In the accounts receivable ledger, the customer account, Duane Jansen, is also decreased by a $300.00 credit. The balance of the accounts receivable account for Mr. Jansen will be zero.

The journal entry to record this transaction is shown in Illustration 11-1.

ILLUSTRATION 11-1 Journal entry to record a note receivable

GENERAL JOURNAL PAGE 4

	DATE		ACCOUNT TITLE	DOC. NO.	POST. REF.	DEBIT	CREDIT	
1	19-- Apr.	3	Notes Receivable	NR11		300 00		1
2			Accounts Rec./Duane Jansen		/		300 00	2
3								3
4								4
5								5
6								6
7								7
8								8

LESSON PLAN 11-1

Materials

- Student pages 307–310
- Blackline Master for General Journal (TRG)
- Blackline Master for Cash Receipts Journal (TRG)

Objectives (Enabling Performance Tasks)

a. Define accounting terms related to notes receivable, unearned revenue, and accrued revenue.
b. Identify accounting concepts and practices related to notes receivable, unearned revenue, and accrued revenue.
c. Journalize transactions for notes receivable.

FOCUS

- Promissory notes were introduced in Chapter 10 and accounting for notes payable, promissory notes issued to creditors, was described. In this lesson, the accounting procedures for notes receivable, promissory notes accepted from customers, will be presented.
- Introduce vocabulary: notes receivable, dishonored note.

TEACHING STRATEGIES: DIFFERENT LEARNING ABILITIES

Visually-Impaired Students. Many sources exist for providing alternative teaching materials. Most states have schools for the blind and rehabilitation service agencies that can enlarge the textbook and working papers. Consult these organizations to identify the latest technologies available for assisting the students.

TEACH

Cover student pages 307–310 "Notes Receivable." Explain the procedure for journalizing acceptance of a note receivable from a customer for an extension of time on account. Discuss the entry to record the receipt of cash for a note receivable with interest. Review the formula for calculating interest. Emphasize that a 360-day year is used for all interest calculations. Describe the procedures for journalizing transactions related to a dishonored note receivable. Demonstrate how additional interest income on a dishonored note receivable is calculated.

Receiving Cash for a Note Receivable

May 3, 19--. Received cash for the maturity value of Note Receivable No. 11: principal, $300.00, plus interest, $3.00; total, $303.00. Receipt No. 452.

Cash	
303.00	

Notes Receivable	
Bal. 300.00	300.00

Intererest Income	
	3.00

Cash is increased by a $303.00 debit ($300.00 principal *plus* $3.00 interest income). **Notes Receivable** is decreased by a $300.00 credit, the principal of the note. This credit cancels the $300.00 debit recorded when the note was received. **Interest Income** is increased by a $3.00 credit ($300.00 *times* 12% *times* 30/360).

Interest Income is classified as Other Revenue, as shown on Appliance Center's chart of accounts.

The journal entry to record this transaction is shown in Illustration 11-2.

ILLUSTRATION 11-2 Journal entry to record receipt of maturity value for a note receivable

CASH RECEIPTS JOURNAL PAGE 9

	DATE		ACCOUNT TITLE	DOC. NO.	POST. REF.	1 GENERAL DEBIT	2 GENERAL CREDIT	3 ACCOUNTS RECEIVABLE CREDIT	4 SALES CREDIT	5 SALES TAX PAYABLE DEBIT	6 SALES TAX PAYABLE CREDIT	7 SALES DISCOUNT DEBIT	8 CASH DEBIT	
9		3	Notes Receivable	R452			300 00						303 00	9
10			Interest Income				3 00							10
11														11
12														12
13														13
14														14

Recording a Dishonored Note Receivable

FYI

Maturity date is when a note is due.

A note that is not paid when due is called a **dishonored note**. The notes receivable account balance should include only the amount of notes receivable that a business expects to collect. Otherwise **Notes Receivable** will be reported incorrectly on a balance sheet. *(CONCEPT: Adequate Disclosure)*

June 1, 19--. Ruth Javinsky dishonored Note Receivable No. 8, a 1-month, 12% note, maturity value due today: principal, $250.00; interest, $2.50; total, $252.50. Memorandum No. 120.

On June 1, the maturity date of Note Receivable No. 8, Miss Javinsky owes the principal, *$250.00,* plus interest, *$2.50.* Miss Javinsky failed to pay the maturity value of $252.50. Although the note is dishonored, Miss Javinsky still owes the money to Appliance Center. Therefore, the total amount owed, *$252.50,* must appear in the business' records.

TEACHING STRATEGIES: TEACHING TIP

Review the formula for calculating interest. Emphasize that a 360-day year is used for all interest calculations.

GENERAL LEDGER

Accounts Receivable

252.50	

Notes Receivable

May 1	250.00	250.00

Interest Income

	2.50

ACCOUNTS RECEIVABLE LEDGER

Ruth Javinsky

252.50	

This entry for a dishonored note receivable does not cancel the debt. Appliance Center continues to try to collect the account. However, the debt is transferred to Accounts Receivable and carried on the records until Miss Javinsky pays the amount or her account is declared uncollectible.

Accounts Receivable is increased by a $252.50 debit, the total amount owed by Miss Javinsky. Notes Receivable is decreased by a $250.00 credit, the principal of the dishonored note. Interest Income is increased by a $2.50 credit, the amount of interest earned to maturity on Note Receivable No. 8. In the accounts receivable ledger, Ruth Javinsky is increased by a $252.50 debit.

The journal entry to record this transaction is shown in Illustration 11-3.

ILLUSTRATION 11-3 Journal entry to record cash for a dishonored note receivable

GENERAL JOURNAL PAGE 6

	DATE		ACCOUNT TITLE	DOC. NO.	POST. REF.	DEBIT	CREDIT	
1	19-- June	1	Accounts Rec./Ruth Javinsky	M120	/	252 50		1
2			Notes Receivable				250 00	2
3			Interest Income				2 50	3
4								4
5								5

Receiving Cash for a Dishonored Note Receivable

Sometimes payment may be received on a previously dishonored note. When this happens, additional interest is charged from maturity date to payment date.

FYI

When calculating maturity dates, remember that April, June, September, and November have 30 days. All other months, except February, have 31 days.

September 30, 19--. Received cash from Ruth Javinsky for dishonored Note Receivable No. 8: maturity value, $252.50, plus additional interest, $10.18; total, $262.68. Receipt No. 201.

The additional days for which interest is owed are calculated as shown below.

Time	Number of Days	
June 1 through June 30	29	(30 − 1 = 29)
July 1 through July 31	31	
August 1 through August 31	31	
September 1 through September 30	30	
Total number of days	121	

APPLY

Draw T accounts on the chalkboard to analyze each transaction as it is presented. Write the formula for calculating interest on the board and demonstrate all calculations. Demonstrate how to calculate the additional days for which interest is owed when cash is received for a dishonored note receivable.

Guided Practice

Guide students through the T account analysis of the entries in Problem 11-1. Have students draw T accounts on a sheet of paper and analyze the first transaction. All students should agree with the analysis before proceeding to the next transaction. Repeat the process until all transactions have been analyzed. The balance of Problem 11-1 can be assigned as Independent Practice.

Independent Practice

Assign Terms 1–2, Questions 1–7, and Problem 11-1.

APPLIED SKILLS: WRITING ACROSS THE CURRICULUM

Writing paragraphs and short essays. The Cases for Critical Thinking are short, practical applications of the accounting principles developed in the chapter. Some cases are planned to present problems related to the chapter but not specifically discussed and answered in the chapter. These cases present an opportunity for critical thinking and decision making. These cases also require more than a short objective-type response. Therefore they provide ideal practice in writing paragraphs and short essays.

ASSESS

Assess student understanding by checking the solutions to the Independent Practice activities.

Reteach

Make transparencies of the general journal and cash receipts journal from the accounting forms masters provided in the Blackline Masters Section of the Teacher's Resource Guide. Refer students to Recycling Problem 11-R, Instruction 1. Ask students to use T accounts to analyze all transactions related to notes receivable (all transactions except November 1). Use the transparencies to demonstrate how the transactions are journalized.

Extend

Assign Cases for Critical Thinking 1.

Enrich

Assign the PERSONAL VISIONS IN BUSINESS feature on page 315.

CLOSURE

Use Audit Your Understanding questions.

LESSON PLAN 11-2

Materials

- Student pages 310–314
- Blackline Master for General Journal (TRG)
- Blackline Master for Cash Receipts Journal (TRG)

Objectives (Enabling Performance Tasks)

a. Define accounting terms related to notes receivable, unearned revenue, and accrued revenue.

b. Identify accounting concepts and practices related to notes receivable, unearned revenue, and accrued revenue.

d. Journalize adjusting and reversing entries for unearned revenue initially recorded as revenue.

The interest due is calculated as shown below.

Maturity Value	×	Interest Rate	×	Time as Fraction of Year	=	Additional Interest		
$252.50	×	12%	×	$\frac{121}{360}$	=	$\frac{\$3,666.30}{360}$	=	$10.18

GENERAL LEDGER

Cash

262.68	

Accounts Receivable

Bal. 252.50	252.50

Interest Income

	10.18

ACCOUNTS RECEIVABLE LEDGER

Ruth Javinsky

Bal. 252.50	252.50

The additional interest is based on the maturity value of the note on the date the note is dishonored, *$252.50.* The time begins when the note is dishonored, June 1, and ends on the day cash is received from Miss Javinsky, September 30.

Cash is increased by a $262.68 debit. This amount is the original maturity value of the note plus additional interest. Accounts Receivable is decreased by a $252.50 credit. This amount is the original maturity value of the note. Interest Income is increased by a $10.18 credit, the additional interest owed from June 1 to September 30. In the accounts receivable ledger, the customer account, Ruth Javinsky, is decreased by a $252.50 credit.

The journal entry to record this transaction is shown in Illustration 11-4.

ILLUSTRATION 11-4 Journal entry to record receipt of a dishonored note receivable

CASH RECEIPTS JOURNAL — PAGE 18

	DATE		ACCOUNT TITLE	DOC. NO.	POST. REF.	1 GENERAL DEBIT	2 GENERAL CREDIT	3 ACCOUNTS RECEIVABLE CREDIT	4 SALES CREDIT	5 SALES TAX PAYABLE DEBIT	6 SALES TAX PAYABLE CREDIT	7 SALES DISCOUNT DEBIT	8 CASH DEBIT	
1	19-- Sept.	30	Ruth Javinsky	R201				252 50					262 68	1
2			Interest Income				10 18							2
3														3
4														4

UNEARNED REVENUE

Some revenue is received during a fiscal period but is not actually earned until the next fiscal period. Revenue received in one fiscal period but not earned until the next fiscal period is called **unearned revenue.** Unearned revenue is also known as deferred revenue.

Unearned revenue may be initially recorded as a liability or as revenue. Moore, Inc. rents part of a building to Millville, Inc. and initially records the unearned revenue as a liability. Moore prefers to delay recording unearned revenue as revenue until it is actually earned as the space is used. Appliance Center also rents out part

FYI

Unearned revenue has been received but has not been earned.

APPLIED SKILLS: BUILDING STUDY SKILLS

Direct students to create a Quick Reference Guide (QRG) for adjusting and reversing entries for unearned and accrued revenue. (1) Label a QRG UNEARNED REVENUE. (2) Indicate what accounts are debited and credited to record the adjusting and reversing entries for unearned revenue initially recorded as a revenue. (3) Repeat the process for ACCRUED REVENUE.

of its building. However, Appliance Center initially records its unearned revenue as revenue.

Initially recording unearned revenue either as a liability or as revenue is acceptable accounting practice. Appliance Center prefers recording unearned revenue as revenue because the unearned revenue eventually will become revenue as the building space is used.

Audit Your Understanding

1. Under what classification of an income statement should Interest Income be reported?
2. What will be the balance of a customer's accounts in the accounts receivable ledger after the entry to record acceptance of a note receivable is posted?
3. If a note receivable is dishonored, what general ledger accounts are debited and credited?
4. In the entry to record cash received for a dishonored note, what does the credit to Interest Income represent?

Adjusting Entry for Unearned Revenue Initially Recorded as a Revenue

Moore received rent, *$6,000.00,* for three months in advance.

December 1, 19--. Received cash for three months' rent in advance from Millville, Inc., $6,000.00. Receipt No. 220.

Appliance Center also received $6,000.00 for three months' rent in advance.

December 1, 19--. Received cash for three months' rent in advance from Pace Delivery Service, $6,000.00. Receipt No. 294.

Moore initially records prepaid revenue as a liability. Appliance Center initially records prepaid revenue as revenue. The analysis of these transactions for both Moore and Appliance Center is shown in the T accounts.

MOORE

Cash (Debit)	Cash (Credit)
6,000.00	

Unearned Rent (Debit)	Unearned Rent (Credit)
	Bal. 22,000.00
	6,000.00

APPLIANCE CENTER

Cash (Debit)	Cash (Credit)
6,000.00	

Rent Income (Debit)	Rent Income (Credit)
	Bal. 22,000.00
	6,000.00

Moore's balance in Unearned Rent, *$22,000.00,* is the rent received for eleven months, January 1 to November 30. On December 1, Cash is increased by a $6,000.00 debit, and Unearned Rent is increased by a $6,000.00 credit for three months' rent.

Appliance Center's balance in Rent Income, *$22,000.00,* is the rent received for eleven months, January 1 to November 30. On December 1, Cash is increased by a $6,000.00 debit, and Rent Income is increased by a $6,000.00 credit for three months' rent.

FYI

Only the rent actually earned should be recorded as revenue in a fiscal period.

Only that part of rent actually earned should be recorded as revenue in a fiscal period. An adjusting entry is needed to separate the earned and unearned portions of the rent received in advance.

For Moore on December 31, one of the three months' rent has been earned and two months' rent is unearned. Therefore, two-thirds of the rent received in advance is still unearned. The same

APPLIED SKILLS: LANGUAGE ARTS

Paraphrasing, writing complete sentences, and identifying verbs. For additional practice in language arts skills, direct students to answer the Accounting Terms and Questions for Individual Study at the end of the chapter. Students should write the answers in their own words and in complete sentences. To further practice language arts skills, ask students to underline all verbs in their answers.

AUDIT YOUR UNDERSTANDING

The AUDIT YOUR UNDERSTANDING feature appears at the end of each section of the chapter. Explain to your students that the word *audit* means to check or verify. AUDIT YOUR UNDERSTANDING may be used to check student comprehension of the section just studied. The answers are provided in Appendix D in the back of the textbook.

1. Other Revenue.
2. Zero.
3. Accounts Receivable is debited; Notes Receivable and Interest Income are credited.
4. The additional interest charged from maturity date to payment date.

FOCUS

- Journalizing adjusting and reversing entries for prepaid expenses initially recorded as expenses was covered in Chapter 10. Explain that some revenue is received during a fiscal period but is not actually earned until the next fiscal period. This revenue may be initially recorded as a liability or as revenue. In this lesson, the procedures to journalize adjusting and reversing entries for unearned revenue initially recorded as revenue will be presented.
- Introduce vocabulary: unearned revenue.

TEACH

Cover student pages 310–314 "Unearned Revenue." Emphasize that unearned revenue has been received but has not been earned. Explain that each business decides how unearned revenue will be recorded initially—either as a liability or as a revenue. Either method is acceptable. Describe the procedure to record an adjusting entry for unearned revenue initially recorded as a revenue. Review the calculation for rent revenue for the current period. Explain how to record the closing and reversing entries for unearned revenue initially recorded as a revenue. Review the definition of a reversing entry. Discuss the reason for reversing entries and illustrate the potential problem if reversing entries are not made.

APPLY

To lessen the difficulty with reversing entries, use T accounts on the chalkboard or overhead projector to analyze entries presented in this lesson. Refer students to Illustrations 11-5 and 11-6, respectively, as adjusting and reversing entries for unearned rent initially recorded as a revenue are discussed.

Guided Practice

Guide students through the T account analysis of the adjusting entry in Problem 11-2, Instruction 1. Have students draw T accounts on a sheet of paper and analyze the adjustment for unearned rent. All students should agree with the analysis before proceeding. Repeat the process for the reversing entry in Instruction 2. The balance of Problem 11-2 can be assigned as Independent Practice.

Independent Practice

Assign Term 3, Questions 8–10, and Problem 11-2.

is true for Appliance Center. The amount of unearned rent is calculated as shown below.

Rent Received in Advance	×	**Fraction Still Unearned**	=	**Unearned Rent**
$6,000.00	×	$\frac{2}{3}$	=	$4,000.00
Total Rent Received	–	**Unearned Rent**	=	**Rent Revenue for Current Period**
$28,000.00	–	$4,000.00	=	$24,000.00

The analysis of the adjusting entries for unearned rent revenue is shown in the T accounts.

MOORE

Unearned Rent

Adj.	24,000.00	Dec. 31 Bal.	28,000.00
		(New Bal.	*4,000.00)*

Rent Income

		Adj.	24,000.00

APPLIANCE CENTER

Unearned Rent

		Adj.	4,000.00

Rent Income

Adj.	4,000.00	Dec. 31 Bal.	28,000.00
		(New Bal.	*24,000.00)*

Moore's liability account, Unearned Rent, is decreased by a $24,000.00 debit. The new balance of this account, *$4,000.00,* is the remaining unearned rent at the end of the current fiscal year. The revenue account, Rent Income, is increased by a $24,000.00 credit. The new balance of this account, *$24,000.00,* is Moore's rent revenue for the current year.

Appliance Center's liability account, Unearned Rent, is increased by a $4,000.00 credit. The new balance of this account, *$4,000.00,* is the remaining unearned rent at the end of the current fiscal year. The revenue account, Rent Income, is decreased by a $4,000.00 debit. The new balance of this account, *$24,000.00,* is Appliance Center's rent revenue for the current year.

Unearned Rent is classified as a Current Liability and Rent Income is classified as Other Revenue, as shown on Appliance Center's chart of accounts.

Appliance Center's journal entry to record the adjustment for unearned rent is shown in Illustration 11-5.

TEACHING STRATEGIES: TEACHING TIP

Stress that after adjusting entries for unearned revenue are recorded, the liability accounts of both businesses represent the amount of rent still unearned. The revenue accounts of both businesses represent the amount of rent earned.

ILLUSTRATION 11-5

Journal entry to record adjustment for unearned rent initially recorded as a revenue

GENERAL JOURNAL — PAGE 13

	DATE		ACCOUNT TITLE	DOC. NO.	POST. REF.	DEBIT	CREDIT	
1			*Adjusting Entries*					1
36		31	*Rent Income*			4 000 00		36
37			*Unearned Rent*				4 000 00	37
38								38
39								39

Closing Entry for Unearned Revenue Initially Recorded as a Revenue

On December 31, Rent Income is closed as part of both Moore's and Appliance Center's closing entries.

MOORE

Rent Income

Debit		Credit	
Clos.	24,000.00	Adj.	24,000.00
		(New Bal. zero)	

Income Summary

Debit		Credit	
		Clos.	24,000.00

APPLIANCE CENTER

Rent Income

Debit		Credit	
Adj.	4,000.00	Dec. 31 Bal.	28,000.00
Clos.	24,000.00	*(New Bal. zero)*	

Income Summary

Debit		Credit	
		Clos.	24,000.00

In Moore's closing entry, Rent Income is decreased and closed by a $24,000.00 debit. Income Summary is affected by a $24,000.00 credit. In Appliance Center's closing entry, Rent Income is also decreased and closed by a $24,000.00 debit and Income Summary is affected by a $24,000.00 credit.

Reversing Entry for Unearned Revenue Initially Recorded as a Revenue

Reversing entries for prepaid and accrued expenses are described in Chapter 10. If an adjusting entry *creates* a balance in an asset or liability account, the adjusting entry is reversed. Reversing entries for unearned revenue are made for the same reason as for prepaid expenses. The amount of unearned revenue must be returned to the account in which it was initially recorded. Moore's adjusting entry for unearned rent *did not* create a balance in the liability account. Therefore, Moore *does not* need to make a reversing entry.

Appliance Center's adjusting entry *did* create a balance in the liability account, Unearned Rent. Therefore, Appliance Center *does* need to make a reversing entry for unearned rent on January 1. After the closing entries are journalized and posted on December 31, Rent Income has a zero balance. A reversing entry is journalized on January 1.

FYI

A reversing entry is needed if an adjusting entry creates a balance in a liability account.

ASSESS

Assess student understanding by checking the solutions to the Independent Practice activities.

Reteach

Make transparencies of the general journal and cash receipts journal from the accounting forms masters provided in the Blackline Masters Section of the Teacher's Resource Guide. Refer students to Recycling Problem 11-R, Instruction 1. Ask students to use T accounts to analyze the November 1 transaction. Next, using information in Instruction 2, have students use T accounts to analyze the adjusting entry for unearned rent. Lastly, ask students to use T accounts to analyze the reversing entry for unearned rent. Use the transparencies to demonstrate how the transactions are journalized.

Extend

Assign Cases for Critical Thinking 2.

CLOSURE

Use Audit Your Understanding questions.

TEACHING STRATEGIES: TEACHING TIP

Review the definition of a reversing entry: An entry made at the beginning of one fiscal period to reverse an adjusting entry made in the previous fiscal period.

Unearned Rent

Rev.	4,000.00	Adj.	4,000.00
		(New Bal. zero)	

Rent Income

Adj.	4,000.00	Dec. 31 Bal.	28,000.00
Clos.	24,000.00	Rev.	4,000.00
		(New Bal.	*4,000.00)*

Unearned Rent is decreased by a $4,000.00 debit. The new balance of Unearned Rent is zero as it was before the adjusting entry. Rent Income is increased by a $4,000.00 credit. On January 1, after the reversing entry is posted, Rent Income has a $4,000.00 credit balance. The remaining rent received in advance, *$4,000.00,* is part of the rent revenue for the new fiscal period.

Appliance Center's journal entry to record the reversing entry for unearned rent revenue is shown in Illustration 11-6.

ILLUSTRATION 11-6 Journal entry to record reversing entry for unearned rent initially recorded as a revenue

GENERAL JOURNAL PAGE *1*

	DATE		ACCOUNT TITLE	DOC. NO.	POST. REF.	DEBIT	CREDIT	
1			*Reversing Entries*					1
24		1	*Unearned Rent*			4 000 00		24
25			*Rent Income*				4 000 00	25

ACCRUED REVENUE

Revenue earned in one fiscal period but not received until a later fiscal period is called **accrued revenue.** For example, a business accepts a 30-day note on December 15. During December, the business earned interest for 16 days. However, the business will not receive any of the interest until the note's maturity in January. Interest for the first 16 days must be recorded in the current fiscal period. *(CONCEPT: Matching Expenses with Revenue)*

Calculating Accrued Interest Income

On December 31, Appliance Center's records show that the business has two notes receivable still on hand.

Note Receivable No. 12. Date, December 1; principal, $500.00; interest rate, 10%; time, 60 days.

Note Receivable No. 13. Date, December 16; principal, $700.00; interest rate, 10%; time, 30 days.

Accrued interest on the two notes is calculated as shown on the following page.

Audit Your Understanding

1. What are the two ways unearned revenue may be initially recorded?
2. What account is credited when rent received in advance is initially recorded as revenue?
3. When rent received in advance is initially recorded as revenue, what accounts are debited and credited to record the adjusting entry?
4. Why is a reversing entry needed when unearned revenue is initially recorded as a revenue?

FYI

Accrue means to accumulate

AUDIT YOUR UNDERSTANDING

1. As a liability or as revenue.
2. Rent Income.
3. Rent Income is debited; Unearned Rent is credited.
4. The adjusting entry creates a balance in a liability account.

LESSON PLAN 11-3

Materials

- Student pages 314–317
- Assess: Problem Test Chapter 11, MicroExam Chapter 11, Objective Test No. 4

Objectives (Enabling Performance Tasks)

a. Define accounting terms related to notes receivable, unearned revenue, and accrued revenue.
b. Identify accounting concepts and practices related to notes receivable, unearned revenue, and accrued revenue.
e. Journalize adjusting and reversing entries for accrued revenue.

TEACHING STRATEGIES: COOPERATIVE LEARNING

Divide the class into two groups. Each group stands and faces each other. Teacher chooses selected Accounting Terms from Chapters 8 through 11. Teacher gives the term. The first student who raises his or her hand has the opportunity to give the correct definition. The group with the most correctly defined terms is declared the winner. This cooperative learning activity should not take more than 20 to 25 minutes of class time.

Note	Principal	×	Interest Rate	×	Time as Fraction of Year	=	Accrued Interest Income		
12	$500.00	×	10%	×	$\frac{30}{360}$	=	$\frac{\$1,500.00}{360}$	=	$4.17
13	$700.00	×	10%	×	$\frac{15}{360}$	=	$\frac{\$1,050.00}{360}$	=	$2.92
	Total accrued interest income, December 31								$7.09

Adjusting Entry for Accrued Interest Income

Interest Receivable	
Adj. 7.09	

Interest Income	
	Dec. 31 Bal. 65.70
	Adj. 7.09
	(New Bal. 72.79)

The analysis of Appliance Center's adjusting entry for accrued interest income is shown in the T accounts. Interest Receivable is increased by a $7.09 debit, the interest owed at the end of the fiscal period. Interest Income is increased by a $7.09 credit, the interest earned for the current fiscal period.

Interest Receivable is classified as a Current Asset, as shown on Appliance Center's chart of accounts.

■ Cynthia Reed ■

BRANCHES MEDICAL, INC.

Cynthia Reed studied accounting in high school and majored in accounting at Loyola University. She then worked in tax accounting before starting the business she now owns with her family. Cynthia's family helped her start Branches Medical, Inc., a distributor of medical and surgical supplies, such as tongue depressors, wheelchairs and crutches, and pharmaceuticals. They started small using family savings. They even worked out of their home until they could afford to move to a business address. Today, Branches Medical has offices in Lauderhill, Florida, and Miami and Chicago.

Reed is the company's president and chief financial officer. Her brothers Hamish and Arjester are the chief executive officer and chief operating officer of the company they all started in 1989.

Reed said that she thought it would be hard starting a business because she was both female and a minority. She thought the opportunities would be limited but was surprised at the vast number of opportunities available to female minorities. Reed says, "Students should take every high school course seriously. Everything you learn in high school you will use in the world of work, especially business courses."

Reed's very positive attitude about business shows when she advises, "The sun will not shine on you every day, but the good days will outweigh the not so good ones." Reed is a good example of following that advice. In the first year of running the business, just shortly after moving out of the family home and into a business address, a fire destroyed the office and all the inventory. Rather than giving up, she moved the business back home, restocked the inventory, and continued on with the business. Reed looks back on this experience with a sense of accomplishment. She says that it would have been so easy to just give up after the fire, but she refused to do so. "It was worth it!" she concluded.

Personal Visions in Business

FOCUS

- Adjusting, closing, and reversing entries for unearned revenue were presented earlier in this chapter. In this lesson, adjusting, closing, and reversing entries for another type of revenue will be described. This revenue is earned in one fiscal period but not received until a later fiscal period.
- Introduce vocabulary: accrued revenue.

TEACH

Cover student pages 314–317 "Accrued Revenue." Demonstrate the procedure for calculating accrued interest income. Explain the adjusting, closing, and reversing entries for accrued interest income. Point out that Interest Receivable is classified as a Current Asset. Remind students that when an adjusting entry creates a balance in an asset account, a reversing entry is needed.

Personal Visions in Business

This special student feature introduces students to successful entrepreneurs or business professionals. Each profile gives a flavor of what the actual business world is like and some of the opportunities available to students who study accounting. These features can be used to motivate students to pursue professional business careers in a wide variety of fields. The subjects of these profiles have been carefully chosen to represent the full spectrum of diverse ethnic and racial backgrounds of professional business people. As an optional activity, students can be encouraged to seek out and interview successful business people in their own communities.

APPLY

Write the formula on the board and demonstrate how accrued interest is calculated. Refer students to Illustrations 11-7 and 11-8, respectively, as adjusting and reversing entries for accrued interest income are discussed.

Guided Practice

Guide students through the calculation of the accrued interest income on Note Receivable No. 1 in Problem 11-3, Instruction 1. Working as a group, write the formula on the board and have students calculate the accrued interest income. The balance of Problem 11-3 can be assigned as Independent Practice.

Independent Practice

- Assign Term 4, Questions 11–12, and Problem 11-3.
- Assign Study Guide 11 and Mastery Problem 11-M.

ASSESS

Assess student understanding by checking the solutions to the Independent Practice activities.

Reteach

- Using information from Recycling Problem 11-R, Instruction 2, demonstrate the T account analysis of the adjusting and reversing entries for accrued interest on notes receivable.
- Assign Recycling Problem 11-R.

Extend

Assign Challenge Problem 11-C. (The challenge is to calculate maturity value of a note, accrued interest, and unearned rent.)

Enrich

Assign the APPLIED COMMUNICATIONS special feature on page 319.

CLOSURE

- Use Audit Your Understanding questions.
- Review Summary Illustration 11-9, "Summary of Adjusting and Reversing Entries for Unearned and Accrued Revenue."

ASSESS

- Administer Problem Test Chapter 11.
- Administer a MicroExam test for Chapter 11.
- Administer Objective Test No. 4.

Appliance Center's journal entry to record the adjustment for accrued interest income is shown in Illustration 11-7.

ILLUSTRATION 11-7 Journal entry to record adjustment for accrued interest income

GENERAL JOURNAL — PAGE 13

	DATE		ACCOUNT TITLE	DOC. NO.	POST. REF.	DEBIT	CREDIT	
1			*Adjusting Entries*					1
2	19-- Dec.	31	*Interest Receivable*			7 09		2
3			*Interest Income*				7 09	3
4								4

Closing Entry for Interest Income

Interest Income is closed as part of Appliance Center's closing entries.

Interest Income

Debit		Credit	
Clos.	72.79	Dec. 31 Bal.	65.70
		Adj.	7.09
		(New Bal. zero)	

Income Summary

Debit		Credit	
		Clos.	72.79

FYI

Reversing entries are the opposite of adjusting entries.

Reversing Entry for Accrued Interest Income

Interest Income has a zero balance after closing entries are journalized and posted on December 31. However, the adjusting entry for accrued interest income created a balance in the asset account Interest Receivable. Therefore, on January 1, Appliance Center *does* need a reversing entry for accrued interest income.

Interest Income is decreased by a $7.09 debit. The new debit balance of Interest Income is $7.09. Interest Receivable is decreased by a $7.09 credit. The new balance of Interest Receivable is zero as it was before the adjusting entry.

Appliance Center's journal entry to record the reversing entry for accrued interest income is shown in Illustration 11-8.

Interest Income

Debit		Credit	
Clos.	72.79	Dec. 31 Bal.	65.70
Rev.	7.09	Adj.	7.09
(New Bal.	*7.09)*		

Interest Receivable

Debit		Credit	
Adj.	7.09	Rev.	7.09
(New Bal. zero)			

ILLUSTRATION 11-8 Journal entry to record reversing entry for accrued interest income

GENERAL JOURNAL — PAGE 1

	DATE		ACCOUNT TITLE	DOC. NO.	POST. REF.	DEBIT	CREDIT	
1			*Reversing Entries*					1
2	19-- Jan.	1	*Interest Income*			7 09		2
3			*Interest Receivable*				7 09	3
4								4
5								5
6								6
7								7

A summary of the adjusting and reversing entries described in this chapter is shown in Illustration 11-9.

Audit Your Understanding

1. What is the formula for calculating accrued interest income?
2. Why is a reversing entry needed for accrued interest income?
3. What accounts are debited and credited to record the reversing entry for accrued interest income?

AUDIT YOUR UNDERSTANDING

1. Principal times interest rate times time as fraction of year equals accrued interest income.
2. The adjusting entry for accrued interest income created a balance in the asset account Interest Receivable.
3. Interest Income is debited; Interest Receivable is credited.

SUMMARY ILLUSTRATION 11-9

Summary of adjusting and reversing entries for unearned and accrued revenue

Item	Adjusting Entry		Reversing Entry	
	Account Debited	Account Credited	Account Debited	Account Credited
Unearned revenue initially recorded as a liability: Rent Income	Unearned Rent	Rent Income	no reversing entry made	
Unearned revenue initially recorded as revenue: Rent Income:	Rent Income	Unearned Rent	Unearned Rent	Rent Income
Accrued revenue: Interest Income	Interest Receivable	Interest Income	Interest Income	Interest Receivable

TEACHING STRATEGIES: APPLYING VISUALS

Direct students to Summary Illustration 11-9 and review the adjusting and reversing entries for unearned and accrued revenue.

APPLIED SKILLS: WORD PROCESSING

If you wish to integrate word processing in your accounting course, you may direct students to answer the end-of-chapter Accounting Terms, Questions for Individual Study, and Cases for Critical Thinking using their word processing software.

ACCOUNTING TERMS

1. **notes receivable:** Promissory notes that a business accepts from customers. (p. 307)
2. **dishonored note:** A note that is not paid when due. (p. 308)
3. **unearned revenue:** Revenue received in one fiscal period but not earned until the next fiscal period. (p. 310)
4. **accrued revenue:** Revenue earned in one fiscal period but not received until a later fiscal period. (p. 314)

QUESTIONS FOR INDIVIDUAL STUDY

1. Adequate Disclosure concept. (p. 307)
2. The customer may need an extension of time in which to pay on account. (p. 307)
3. Notes Receivable is debited; Accounts Receivable and the subsidiary account are credited. (p. 307)
4. Cash is debited; Notes Receivable and Interest Income are credited. (p. 308)
5. The maturity value of the note is transferred from Notes Receivable to Accounts Receivable. (p. 309)
6. Accounts Receivable and the subsidiary account are debited; Notes Receivable and Interest Income are credited. (p. 309)
7. Cash is debited; Accounts Receivable, the subsidiary account, and Interest Income are credited. (p. 310)
8. Cash is debited; Rent Income is credited. (p. 311)
9. Rent Income is debited; Unearned Rent is credited. (p. 312)
10. Unearned Rent is debited; Rent Income is credited. (p. 314)
11. Interest Receivable is debited; Interest Income is credited. (p. 315)
12. Interest Income is debited; Interest Receivable is credited. (p. 316)

CASES FOR CRITICAL THINKING

Case 1 Yes, the entries are incorrect. When dishonored, more than the note's face value was transferred out of the notes receivable account. When cash was received, Accounts Receivable should have been credited instead of Notes Receivable. In both entries, interest should have been recorded in Interest Income. The correct entries are:

ACCOUNTING TERMS EPT(a)

What is the meaning of each of the following?

1. **notes receivable**
2. **dishonored note**
3. **unearned revenue**
4. **accrued revenue**

QUESTIONS FOR INDIVIDUAL STUDY EPT(b)

1. Which accounting concept is being applied by assuring that financial statements show all information about notes receivable and revenue?
2. Why might a business accept a note receivable from a customer?
3. What accounts are affected, and how, by an entry to accept a note receivable?
4. What accounts are affected, and how, when cash is received for the maturity value of a note receivable?
5. What happens to the maturity value of a note when a note receivable is dishonored?
6. What accounts are affected, and how, by an entry to record a dishonored note?
7. What accounts are affected, and how, when cash is received for a dishonored note receivable?
8. What accounts are affected, and how, when rent received in advance is initially recorded as a revenue?
9. What accounts are affected, and how, to record an adjusting entry for rent revenue when unearned revenue is initially recorded as a revenue?
10. What accounts are affected, and how, by a reversing entry for rent revenue when unearned revenue is initially recorded as a revenue?
11. What accounts are affected, and how, by an adjusting entry for accrued interest income?
12. What accounts are affected, and how, by a reversing entry for accrued interest income?

CASES FOR CRITICAL THINKING EPT(b)

CASE 1 Farmland, Inc. received a 60-day, 12%, $600.00 note receivable from a customer. The customer dishonored the note at maturity. The accounting clerk recorded the dishonored note receivable by debiting **Accounts Receivable** and crediting **Notes Receivable** for the maturity value, $612.00. Thirty days later, the customer paid $618.12 for the dishonored note. The accounting clerk recorded this amount by debiting **Cash** and crediting **Notes Receivable.** Farmland's bookkeeper checked the work and decided that the journal entries were both incorrect. Are the journal entries incorrect? Explain your answer.

CASE 2 At the beginning of December, Maxim Floral, Inc. received three months' rent in advance. Maxim initially records unearned revenue as a revenue. On December 31, Maxim does not make an adjusting entry for unearned rent. What effect will this have on the firm's financial statements?

APPLIED COMMUNICATIONS

You have just been hired as the first internal auditor for Harrell and Company, a retail clothing store. While performing an audit of the accounting system relating to sales returns, you discover that sales clerks have the authority to refund cash to customers for returned items. Although the clerks must record the name of the customer, they are not required to have the customer sign a return slip, receive manager approval for the return, or obtain the customer's original sales receipt.

INSTRUCTIONS:

Prepare a memorandum to your supervisor, Erin Smith, that discusses the potential problems with this system.

APPLICATION PROBLEMS EPT(c,d,e)

PROBLEM 11-1 Journalizing transactions for notes receivable

Bellingham, Inc. completed the following transactions during the current year.

INSTRUCTIONS:

Journalize the following transactions. Use page 8 of a general journal and page 15 of a cash receipts journal. Source documents are abbreviated as follows: memorandum, M; note receivable, NR; receipt, R.

Aug. 1. Received a 60-day, 10% note from James Huber for an extension of time on his account, $200.00. NR1.

Aug. 1. Received a 2-month, 12% note from Frank Otto for an extension of time on his account, $300.00. NR2.

Sept. 30. James Huber dishonored NR1, a 60-day, 10% note, maturity value due today: principal, $200.00; interest, $3.33; total, $203.33. M12.

Oct. 1. Received a 2-month, 10% note from Melissa Carr for an extension of time on her account, $500.00. NR3.

Oct. 1. Received cash for the maturity value of NR2: principal, $300.00, plus interest, $6.00; total, $306.00. R10.

Dec. 1. Received cash from James Huber for dishonored NR1: maturity value, $203.33, plus additional interest, $3.50; total, $206.83. R32.

Dec. 1. Received cash for the maturity value of NR3: principal, $500.00, plus interest, $8.33; total, $508.33. R33.

PROBLEM 11-2 Journalizing adjusting and reversing entries for unearned revenue initially recorded as revenue

The following data are obtained from the records of Billies, Inc. on December 31 of the current year before adjusting entries are recorded. Billies initially records unearned revenue as revenue.

General ledger account balances:

Unearned Rent	zero
Rent Income	$20,000.00

Adjustment Information, December 31

Rent received in advance and still unearned	$ 1,800.00

INSTRUCTIONS:

1. Journalize the adjusting entry for unearned rent on December 31 of the current year. Use page 13 of a general journal.

APPLIED SKILLS: COMMUNICATIONS

Surveys of business managers show that communication skills are one of the most desired traits in new employees. The APPLIED COMMUNICATIONS activity provides an opportunity for students to practice their communication and language arts skills on topics that directly relate to accounting. This activity requires the student to prepare a memorandum explaining the potential internal control problems of the accounting system relating to sales returns.

CASES FOR CRITICAL THINKING *(cont'd)*

(1) When dishonored, debit Accounts Receivable, $612.00; credit Notes Receivable, $600.00; credit Interest Income, $12.00. (2) When cash is received, debit Cash, $618.12; credit Accounts Receivable, $612.00; credit Interest Income, $6.12.

Case 2 On the income statement, rental income and net income will be overstated. *(CONCEPT: Matching Expenses with Revenue)* On the balance sheet, owner's equity will be overstated and unearned rent, a current liability, will be understated.

APPLIED COMMUNICATIONS

Students' solutions will vary. Students should raise concerns that the system in place does not provide for proof that the customer actually received a refund and that the merchandise was actually purchased from the store. Additionally, there are no procedures in place for manager review of sales returns transactions.

CHECK FIGURES

See Teacher's Edition of the Working Papers for complete solutions.

Problem 11-1 September 30: Debit Accounts Receivable/James Huber; credit Notes Receivable and Interest Income.

Problem 11-2 Adjusting entry: Debit Rent Income, $1,800.00; credit Unearned Rent, $1,800.00.

CHECK FIGURES *(cont'd)*

Problem 11-3 Accrued interest income: Note 1, $3.33; Note 2, $2.50. Adjusting entry: Debit Interest Receivable, $5.83; credit Interest Income, $5.83.

Mastery Problem 11-M Adjusting entries: Debit Interest Receivable, $11.35; credit Interest Income, $11.35. Debit Rent Income, $500.00; credit Unearned Rent, $500.00.

Challenge Problem 11-C Adjusting entries: Debit Interest Receivable, $2.50; credit Interest Income, $2.50. Debit Rent Income, $1,600.00; credit Unearned Rent, $1,600.00.

2. Journalize the reversing entry for unearned rent on January 1 of the next year. Use page 1 of a general journal.

PROBLEM 11-3 Journalizing adjusting and reversing entries for accrued revenue

MATHEMATICS

On December 31, McNeilson, Inc. has two notes receivable.

Note Receivable No. 1. Date, November 1; principal, $200.00; interest rate, 10%; time, 90 days.

Note Receivable No. 2. Date, December 1; principal, $300.00; interest rate, 10%; time, 60 days.

INSTRUCTIONS:

1. Calculate the accrued interest on Notes Receivable Nos. 1 and 2 as of December 31.

2. Journalize the adjusting entry for accrued interest income on December 31 of the current year. Use page 13 of a general journal.

3. Journalize the reversing entry for accrued interest income on January 1 of the next year. Use page 1 of a general journal.

ENRICHMENT PROBLEMS EPT(c,d,e)

MASTERY PROBLEM 11-M Journalizing notes receivable, unearned revenue, and accrued revenue initially recorded as revenue transactions

Marier, Inc. completed the following transactions during the current year. Marier initially records prepaid and unearned items as revenue.

INSTRUCTIONS:

1. Journalize the following transactions. Use page 7 of a general journal and page 19 of a cash receipts journal. Source documents are abbreviated as follows: memorandum, M; note receivable, NR; receipt, R.

July 1. Received a 90-day, 10% note from Timothy Johnson for an extension of time on his account, $500.00. NR12.

July 5. Received a 3-month, 12% note from Gerald Kammer for an extension of time on his account, $600.00. NR13.

Sept. 29. Timothy Johnson dishonored NR12, a 90-day, 10% note, maturity value due today: principal, $500.00; interest, $12.50; total, $512.50. M32.

Oct. 5. Received cash for the maturity value of NR13: principal, $600.00, plus interest, $18.00; total, $618.00. R65.

Nov. 1. Received cash for three months' rent in advance from Centuria, Inc., $1,500.00. R70.

Dec. 1. Received cash from Timothy Johnson for dishonored NR12: maturity value, $512.50, plus additional interest, $8.97; total, $521.47. R81.

2. Continue using page 7 of the general journal. Journalize the adjusting entries using the following information.

Adjustment Information, December 31

Accrued interest on notes receivable.	$ 11.35
Rent received in advance and still unearned	500.00

3. Journalize the reversing entries on January 1 of the next year. Use page 1 of a general journal.

CHALLENGE PROBLEM 11-C Journalizing notes receivable, unearned revenue, and accrued revenue initially recorded as revenue transactions

Hillsdale, Inc. completed the following transactions during the current year. Hillsdale initially records unearned items as revenue.

320

MATHEMATICS

INSTRUCTIONS:

1. Journalize the following transactions. Calculate amounts as needed for each transaction. Use page 7 of a general journal and page 18 of a cash receipts journal. Source documents are abbreviated as follows: memorandum, M; note receivable, NR; receipt, R.

July 1. Received a 90-day, 14% note from Steven Bozeman for an extension of time on his account, $500.00. NR26.

Aug. 1. Received a 60-day, 12% note from Duane Mortenson for an extension of time on his account, $600.00. NR27.

Sept. 29. Steven Bozeman dishonored NR26, a 90-day, 14% note, maturity value due today. M45.

Sept. 30. Received cash for the maturity value of NR27. R70.

Nov. 15. Received cash from Steven Bozeman for dishonored NR26. R85.

Dec. 1. Received a 90-day, 10% note from Jana Vasques for an extension of time on her account, $300.00. NR28.

Dec. 1. Received cash for three months' rent in advance from Lenter, Inc., $2,400.00. R97.

2. Continue using page 7 of the general journal. Journalize the adjusting entries using the following information on December 31 of the current year.
   - **a.** Accrued interest income. Calculate the accrued interest for Note Receivable No. 28.
   - **b.** Unearned rent revenue. Calculate the unearned portion of the rent received in advance from Lenter, Inc.
3. Journalize the reversing entries on January 1 of the next year. Use page 1 of a general journal.

PART 5 OVERVIEW

STUDENT EDITION

STUDENT FEATURES

Professional Business Ethics

Ups and Downs of CEO Compensation, page 352

Careers In Accounting

Audit Clerk, page 373

Spreadsheet Options

Printing Spreadsheets and Graphs, page 384

Multicultural Awareness

Diverse Work Force, page 326

Global Perspective

International Packages and Customs Inspections, page 330

Personal Visions in Business

Dr. Yoshi Tsuchiya, page 383

Audit Your Understanding

This student activity can be found on pages 330, 335, 338, 349, 354, 359, 369, 379, 386

APPLIED SKILLS

Applied Communications

Page 340

Applied Mathematics

Pages 336, 337, 345–347, 349, 352–354, 356, 357, 361, 363, 368–370, 372–376, 378, 388, 389

SOFTWARE APPLICATIONS

Automated Accounting 6.0 Problems 14-2, 14-M, Reinforcement Activity 2
Spreadsheet Template Problems 12-M, 14-1, 14-M

TEACHER'S EDITION

APPLIED SKILLS

Communications, page 340
Language Arts, pages 327, 358, 368
Writing Across the Curriculum, pages 328, 348, 375
Building Study Skills, page 350
Word Processing, pages 330, 344, 365

TEACHING STRATEGIES

Accounting Pedagogy, pages 324, 325, 344, 364, 393
Assessment by Portfolio, pages 384, 398
Different Learning Abilities, page 358
Different Learning Styles, pages 332–334, 336, 337, 370, 374, 375, 377, 378
Cooperative Learning, pages 329, 350, 376, 394, 397
Expanding Beyond the Classroom, page 380
Applying Visuals, pages 338, 359, 366
Teaching Tip, pages 324, 326, 331, 335, 338, 345, 347, 355, 367, 371, 377, 395
Software Focus, pages 325, 364, 393, 396
Simulation, page 385
Milestone, page 386
Reinforcement Activity, pages 385, 396

ASSESSMENT

Assessment by Portfolio
MicroExam software for each chapter
Problem Test for each chapter
Objective Test 5

SOFTWARE

Automated Accounting 6.0
MicroExam
Excel (spreadsheet software)
Lotus (spreadsheet software)
Works (integrated software)

BIBLIOGRAPHY

Ehrlich, Virginia Z. *Gifted Children: A Guide for Parents and Teachers.* Unionville, NY: Trillium Press, 1985.

Evans, Thomas G., Martin E. Taylor, and Oscar Holzmann. *International Accounting and Reporting.* Cincinnati: South-Western Publishing Co., 1985.

Langenderfer, Harold Q., Willis C. Stevenson, Herbert C. Sieg, and James B. Bower. *Federal Income Taxation.* (Revised annually). Cincinnati: South-Western Publishing Co.

Langenderfer, Harold Q., Willis C. Stevenson, Herbert C. Sieg, and James B. Bower. *Personal Income Taxation.* (Revised annually). Cincinnati: South-Western Publishing Co.

Nattive, A. "Cooperative Learning: An Overview." *Journal of Humanistic Education* (1988).

Mager, Robert F. *Preparing Instructional Objectives.* 2d. ed., rev. Belmont: Pitman Learning, Inc., 1984.

Periodicals

CPA Journal, New York State Society of CPAs, New York, NY.
Management Accounting, National Association of Accountants, 10 Paragon Drive, Montvale, NJ.
Working Woman, New York, NY. (Multicultural awareness)

Technology

AICPA. *The Bottom Line: Inside Accounting Today,* 1987. (Video)
Mead Data Central, Inc. LEXIS/NEXIS (On-line database)

PART 5 OPENER

PART 5

Corporation Accounting

GENERAL GOALS

1. Know accounting terminology related to a corporation.
2. Understand accounting concepts and practices related to a corporation.
3. Demonstrate accounting procedures unique to a corporation.

OVERVIEW

Part 5 gives an in-depth view of corporation accounting.

Chapter 12 begins with organizing a corporation and paying dividends. Transactions to get a corporation started are described and illustrated.

Chapter 13 moves on to cover the acquisition of additional capital for a corporation including a discussion of treasury stock and corporate bonds.

Chapter 14 wraps up the end-of-fiscal-period work for a corporation. The work sheet and financial statements, as well as calculating federal income tax, are given detailed coverage. This chapter is followed by Integrating Automated Accounting—Topic 6 which automates the entire cycle.

Chapters 12–14 cover the accounting cycle for a corporation. It is important that the student see the entire accounting cycle as it applies to a particular form of business. It is also important that the student apply these concepts through the completion of the simulation, Four Seasons, Inc. and/or the reinforcement activity.

CHAPTER 12 OVERVIEW

Chapter 12 begins to describe many of the transactions that are unique to corporations, including the initial stock issue for forming a corporation, stock subscriptions, and declaring and paying dividends. Two kinds of capital stock, common and preferred, are described and the characteristics of each are detailed. The calculations for the dividends for each class of stock are described and highlighted. Forming a corporation is not achieved without some accompanying costs, and journalizing the organization cost, an intangible asset, is described in this chapter.

GUIDE TO ACHIEVING LEARNING OBJECTIVES

	TEACH	APPLY	EXTEND/ENRICH				
Enabling Performance Tasks	**Lesson Plans**	**Application Problems**	**Mastery Problems**	**Challenge Problems**	**Cases for Critical Thinking**	**Recycling Problems**	**Reinforcement Activity**
a. Define accounting terms related to corporate accounting.	12-1, 12-2, 12-3						
b. Identify accounting concepts and practices related to corporate accounting.	12-1, 12-2, 12-3				Cases 1, 2		
c. Journalize transactions for starting a corporation.	12-2	12-1, 12-2	12-M			12-R	
d. Prepare a balance sheet for a newly formed corporation.	12-2	12-2	12-M			12-R	
e. Calculate dividends for a corporation.	12-3	12-3	12-M	12-C		12-R	2
f. Journalize transactions for declaring and paying dividends for a corporation.	12-3	12-4	12-M	12-C		12-R	2

ENRICHMENT

SPECIAL FEATURES
Multicultural Awareness, page 326
Global Perspective, page 330
Applied Communications, page 340
TECHNOLOGY CONNECTION
Spreadsheet Template Problem 12-M

NEW, REVIEW, AND EXTENSION

ACTIVITIES/CONCEPTS/TRANSACTIONS	NEW	REVIEW/ EXTENSION
Nature of a corporation		✓
Rights of stockholders	✓	
Common stock		✓
Preferred stock	✓	
Capital accounts for a corporation		✓
Transactions for forming a corporation	✓	
Subscriptions for capital stock	✓	
Organization costs of a corporation	✓	
Declaring and paying dividends		✓
Calculating dividends for common and preferred stock	✓	

	INFORMAL ASSESSMENT		FORMAL ASSESSMENT			
	Study Guide	Audit Your Understanding	Chapter MicroExam	Chapter Problem Test	Unit Objective Test	Portfolio
	Unit A	✓	✓		✓	
	Units B, C	✓	✓		✓	
				✓		
				✓		
				✓		✓
				✓		✓

TEACHING MATERIALS

Teacher's Wraparound Edition of the Text
Teacher's Resource Guide
Teacher's Edition of Working Papers
MicroExam

APPLIED MATHEMATICS

APPLIED MATH/ACCOUNTING SKILL	APPLICATION
Calculating the value of common and preferred stock	Prob. 12-3
Calculating dividends for common and preferred stock	Prob. 12-3

TEACHING STRATEGIES: ACCOUNTING PEDAGOGY

A chart of accounts for the business that is used to illustrate each part of this textbook is provided at the beginning of each part. Charts of accounts are extremely important to companies because they drive the accounting system. Employees usually cannot even receive reimbursement for expenses without knowing which account the expense should be charged to. Pedagogically, the chart of accounts provides the following information: (1) Classification for each account—needed to determine how a transaction is analyzed. (2) Permanent accounts (balance sheet accounts) and temporary accounts (income statement accounts)—assists in analyzing transactions and recording closing entries. (3) Account number for every general ledger account—critical information in automated accounting, since transactions are entered by account number rather than account title.

CHART OF ACCOUNTS

This chart of accounts is for a merchandising business organized as a corporation. LampLight's chart of accounts is similar to that of Appliance Center's described in Part 4. The Assets section is divided into current, long-term, plant, and intangible assets.

The Stockholders' Equity section reflects the additional accounts needed to account for the organizing of a corporation, paying of dividends, and acquiring of additional capital.

The Operating Expenses section is divided into selling and administrative expenses. LampLight does not account for warehousing expenses separately.

Like Appliance Center's, LampLight's chart of accounts distinguishes between revenues and expenses that occur that are not the result of everyday business transactions. The classifications Other Revenue and Other Expenses are used to account for those transactions that are not directly related to the selling of merchandise inventory.

LampLight, Inc.

CHART OF ACCOUNTS

Balance Sheet Accounts

(1000) ASSETS
1100 Current Assets
1105 Cash
1110 Petty Cash
1115 Notes Receivable
1120 Interest Receivable
1125 Accounts Receivable
1130 Allowance for Uncollectible Accounts
1135 Subscriptions Receivable
1140 Merchandise Inventory
1145 Supplies—Sales
1150 Supplies—Administrative
1155 Prepaid Insurance
1160 Prepaid Interest
1200 Long-Term Investment
1205 Bond Sinking Fund
1300 Plant Assets
1305 Store Equipment
1310 Accumulated Depreciation—Store Equipment
1315 Building
1320 Accumulated Depreciation—Building
1325 Office Equipment
1330 Accumulated Depreciation—Office Equipment
1335 Land
1400 Intangible Asset
1405 Organization Costs

(2000) LIABILITIES
2100 Current Liabilities
2105 Notes Payable
2110 Interest Payable
2115 Accounts Payable
2120 Employee Income Tax Payable
2125 Federal Income Tax Payable
2130 FICA Tax Payable
2135 Salaries Payable
2140 Sales Tax Payable
2145 Unemployment Tax Payable—Federal
2150 Unemployment Tax Payable—State
2155 Health Insurance Premiums Payable
2160 Dividends Payable
2200 Long-Term Liability
2205 Bonds Payable

(3000) STOCKHOLDERS' EQUITY
3105 Capital Stock—Common
3110 Stock Subscribed—Common
3115 Paid-in Capital in Excess of Stated Value—Common
3120 Capital Stock—Preferred
3125 Stock Subscribed—Preferred
3130 Paid-in Capital in Excess of Par Value—Preferred
3135 Discount on Sale of Preferred Stock
3140 Treasury Stock
3145 Paid-in Capital from Sale of Treasury Stock
3150 Retained Earnings
3155 Dividends—Common
3160 Dividends—Preferred
3165 Income Summary

Income Statement Accounts

(4000) OPERATING REVENUE
4105 Sales
4110 Sales Discount
4115 Sales Returns and Allowances

(5000) COST OF MERCHANDISE
5105 Purchases
5110 Purchases Discount
5115 Purchases Returns and Allowances

(6000) OPERATING EXPENSES
6100 Selling Expenses
6105 Advertising Expense
6110 Credit Card Fee Expense
6115 Depreciation Expense—Store Equipment
6120 Miscellaneous Expense—Sales
6125 Salary Expense—Sales
6130 Supplies Expense—Sales
6200 Administrative Expenses
6205 Depreciation Expense—Building
6210 Depreciation Expense—Office Equipment
6215 Insurance Expense
6220 Miscellaneous Expense—Administrative
6225 Payroll Taxes Expense
6230 Property Tax Expense
6235 Salary Expense—Administrative
6240 Supplies Expense—Administrative
6245 Uncollectible Accounts Expense
6250 Utilities Expense

(7000) OTHER REVENUE
7105 Gain on Plant Assets
7110 Interest Income

(8000) OTHER EXPENSES
8105 Interest Expense
8110 Loss on Plant Assets
8115 Organization Expense

(9000) INCOME TAX
9105 Federal Income Tax Expense

The chart of accounts for LampLight is illustrated above for ready reference as you study Part 5 of this textbook.

TEACHING STRATEGIES: TEACHING TIP

Emphasize that students should refer to this chart of accounts throughout their study of Part 5. It will help them determine classification of accounts, which accounts are temporary and permanent accounts, and what account numbers to use for automated accounting. It will also be a useful reference for performing file maintenance activities.

12

Organizing a Corporation and Paying Dividends

ENABLING PERFORMANCE TASKS

After studying Chapter 12, you will be able to:

a Define accounting terms related to corporate accounting.

b Identify accounting concepts and practices related to corporate accounting.

c Journalize transactions for starting a corporation.

d Prepare a balance sheet for a newly formed corporation.

e Calculate dividends for a corporation.

f Journalize transactions for declaring and paying dividends for a corporation.

TERMS PREVIEW

board of directors • articles of incorporation • charter • common stock • preferred stock • stock certificate • par value • par-value stock • no-par-value stock • stated-value stock • subscribing for capital stock • organization costs • intangible assets • declaring a dividend • date of declaration • date of record • date of payment

TEACHING STRATEGIES: ACCOUNTING PEDAGOGY

This textbook acquaints students with procedures for organizing a corporation. It is important that students understand procedures for the start up of all forms of business.

SOFTWARE FOCUS

Software may be used for independent practice or enrichment/extension as the instructor deems appropriate. For this chapter, the Spreadsheet Template may be used with Mastery Problem 12-M.

MULTICULTURAL AWARENESS

The MULTICULTURAL AWARENESS feature is intended to expose students to the concept that our society is composed of people from many different cultural backgrounds. These features show both past contributions of many cultures and benefits of a culturally diverse society. (1) Read the feature. (2) Discuss the specific information in the feature. (3) Clarify any terms or questions.

LESSON PLAN 12-1

Materials

Student pages 326–330

Objectives (Enabling Performance Tasks)

a. Define accounting terms related to corporate accounting.

b. Identify accounting concepts and practices related to corporate accounting.

FOCUS

- In Chapter 1, the advantages and disadvantages of the corporation form of business organization were presented. Also, the businesses used for illustration purposes in Chapters 2, 3, and 4 were corporations. In this lesson, the legal requirements for forming a corporation, the rights of stockholders, and the kinds of capital stock a corporation can issue will be presented.
- Introduce vocabulary: board of directors, articles of incorporation, charter, common stock, preferred stock, stock certificate, par value, par-value stock, no-par-value stock, stated-value stock.

MULTICULTURAL AWARENESS

Diverse Work Force

The United States is one of the most culturally diverse nations in the world. America began as a country of immigrants and continues to encourage immigration. In addition to a large population of Caucasians from various Western European backgrounds, there are also large groups of people with Hispanic, Asian, and African backgrounds. And the original residents of the continent, the Native Americans, comprise another cultural group.

It is no surprise, then, that the work force is also culturally diverse. This diversity is a great challenge and opportunity for American businesses. With so many diverse cultures represented in the work force, American business is poised to expand global trade, calling on the knowledge and talents of its diverse work force.

FYI

While the format for articles of incorporation varies from one corporation to another, they usually address similar items.

Selecting the form of business ownership is an important decision of new business owners. An organization with the legal rights of a person and which may be owned by many persons is known as a corporation. *(CONCEPT: Business Entity)* A corporation is organized by law to exist separately and apart from its owners. Corporations differ from other forms of businesses principally in the nature of ownership and management.

A corporation's ownership is divided into units. Each unit of ownership in a corporation is known as a share of stock. Total shares of ownership in a corporation is known as capital stock. An owner of one or more shares of a corporation is known as a stockholder.

A corporation's earnings are shared by stockholders. Earnings distributed to stockholders are known as dividends. A new corporation may retain a portion of the earnings to finance future business expansion and improvement. However, most corporations distribute a portion of the earnings to stockholders.

NATURE OF A CORPORATION

A corporation may have many owners. A large number of owners could have difficulty participating in the management of a business. Therefore, the owners elect a small group to represent their combined interests and to be responsible for management of the corporation. A group of persons elected by the stockholders to manage a corporation is called a **board of directors.** A board of directors determines corporate policies and selects corporate officers to supervise the day-to-day management of the corporation.

Legal Requirements for Forming a Corporation

Persons wishing to form a corporation must submit an application to the designated officials of the state in which the company is to be incorporated. A written application requesting permission to form a corporation is called the **articles of incorporation.** Some articles of incorporation are submitted to the federal government, but most are submitted to a state government.

When the articles of incorporation are approved, a corporation comes into existence. The approved articles of incorporation are called a **charter.** A charter is also referred to as a certificate of incorporation.

LampLight, Inc. is a corporation that sells lighting fixtures to individuals and building contractors. The articles of incorporation submitted for LampLight, Inc. are shown in Illustration 12-1 on pages 328–329.

LampLight is organized as a corporation to sell light fixtures and accessories. However, in the articles of incorporation, Article II, the nature of the business is described in broad, general terms. With this broad purpose, LampLight may expand into other kinds of business activities without applying for a new charter.

TEACHING STRATEGIES: TEACHING TIP

Review the definitions of the following terms presented earlier in the textbook.
Corporation: An organization with the legal rights of a person and which may be owned by many persons.
Share of stock: Each unit of ownership in a corporation.
Capital stock: Total shares of ownership in a corporation.
Stockholder: An owner of one or more shares of a corporation.
Dividends: Earnings distributed to stockholders.

Rights of Stockholders

Most stockholders have three basic rights.

1. The right to vote at stockholders' meetings unless an exception is made for a particular kind of stock.
2. The right to share in a corporation's earnings.
3. The right to share in the distribution of a corporation's assets if a corporation ceases operations and sells all its assets.

Some corporations also provide stockholders with the right to maintain the same percentage of ownership in a corporation. If additional stock is issued, existing stockholders have first choice to buy additional shares to maintain their same percentage of ownership.

CAPITAL STOCK OF A CORPORATION

FYI

Most stock sold today is common stock.

Corporations may issue two basic kinds of stock: common and preferred. Stock that does not give stockholders any special preferences is called **common stock.** Stock that gives stockholders preference in earnings and other rights is called **preferred stock.** LampLight is authorized to issue both common and preferred stock as described in Article III, Illustration 12-1.

Corporate Records of Stock Issued

Written evidence of the number of shares each stockholder owns in a corporation is called a **stock certificate.** A corporation issues a stock certificate when full payment is received for stock. A stock certificate usually contains the issue date, certificate number, number of shares, and name of the stockholder.

A record is also kept of stock issued to each stockholder. A stockholder may later decide to sell some or all shares of stock owned. Changing ownership of stock is referred to as stock transfers. Some corporations handle the issuing and transferring of stock certificates as well as the record of stock ownership. Many corporations, however, engage a transfer agent, such as a bank, to issue certificates and keep stock ownership records.

Value of Stock

Shares of stock are frequently assigned a value. A value assigned to a share of stock and printed on the stock certificate is called **par value.** A share of stock that has an authorized value printed on the stock certificate is called **par-value stock.**

A share of stock that has no authorized value printed on the stock certificate is called **no-par-value stock.** Some states require that no-par-value stock be assigned a stated or specific value. No-

TEACH

Cover student pages 326–330 "Nature of a Corporation" and "Capital Stock of a Corporation." Review the definitions of the following terms presented in Chapter 1: corporation, share of stock, capital stock, stockholder, and dividends. Explain the management of a corporation, the procedures for forming a corporation, and the basic rights of stockholders. Describe par-value, no-par-value, and stated-value stock. Discuss the differences between common and preferred stock.

APPLIED SKILLS: LANGUAGE ARTS

Practicing capitalization skills. Special handouts for practicing capitalization skills can be created easily using word processing software. Key in some text, either something that you have written yourself or that has appeared in a newspaper or magazine. After checking to be sure you have keyed it correctly, use the change case feature of your word processor to change all uppercase letters to lowercase letters. Students can be directed to underline or circle all letters that should be capitalized. Student solutions can then be compared with the original copy for correctness.

APPLY

Have students identify businesses which are organized as corporations. Remind students that corporations may range from a local business owned by a single individual to an international business with thousands of stockholders.

Guided Practice

Guide students through a review of how a corporation differs from other forms of business organizations. Write the headings Advantages and Disadvantages on the chalkboard. Invite students to the board to list either an advantage or a disadvantage of a corporation until all points have been reviewed. Leave the lists on the board. Repeat the exercise for a proprietorship and a partnership.

Independent Practice

Assign Terms 1–10 and Questions 1–5.

ILLUSTRATION 12-1 Articles of Incorporation (page 1)

ARTICLES OF INCORPORATION
OF
LAMPLIGHT, INC.

We, the undersigned, for the purpose of forming a corporation for profit under the laws of the State of Tennessee, hereby adopt the following Articles of Incorporation:

Article I - Name

The name of this corporation is LampLight, Inc.

Article II - Nature of Business

This corporation may engage in any activity or business permitted under the laws of the United States and of the State of Tennessee.

Article III - Capital Stock

The maximum authorized capital stock is:

Common stock:	100,000 shares; $10.00 stated value.
Preferred stock:	50,000 shares; 8%; $100.00 par value.

Article IV - Initial Capital

The amount of capital with which this corporation will begin business is not less than Three Hundred Thousand Dollars ($300,000.00).

Article V - Term of Existence

This corporation shall have perpetual existence.

Article VI - Address

The present address of the principal office of this corporation is 1450 Eaglewood Lane, Nashville, TN 37207-2361.

The Board of Directors may from time to time move the corporation's principal office to another place in the State of Tennessee.

Article VII - Directors

The number of directors of this corporation shall be determined in accordance with the by-laws, but the number shall never be less than three.

Article VIII - Initial Directors

The names and addresses of the members of the first Board of Directors of this corporation are:

Richard P. McLaurin	19034 Westerly Drive	Nashville, TN 37221-1786
Amy B. Thacker	9083 N. 23rd Street	Nashville, TN 37209-8196
Cynthia M. Fazio	1607 Charles Court	Nashville, TN 37218-4207
Andre W. Fazio	1607 Charles Court	Nashville, TN 37218-4207
Daniel E. Sikorowski	40623 Northview Avenue	Nashville, TN 37216-3271
Susan P. Boyd	890 Welch Road	Franklin, TN 37064-5678

par-value stock that is assigned a value by a corporation is called **stated-value stock.** Stated-value stock is similar to par-value stock except that the value is not printed on the stock certificates.

Common Stock

If a corporation issues only one kind of stock, that stock is common stock. If a corporation issues only common stock, the common stockholders are entitled to all of the dividends. In most corporations, only owners of common stock have a right to vote on matters brought before the stockholders. LampLight is authorized to issue no-par-value common stock with a stated value of $10.00.

FYI

Preferences for preferred stock are not predominant in most preferred stock issued today.

Preferred Stock

To attract more investors, a corporation may offer preferred stock with preferences in some of the basic stockholders' rights. Preferred stockholders usually do not have voting rights and cannot influence when and how much is paid in dividends. Therefore, a typical pref-

APPLIED SKILLS: WRITING ACROSS THE CURRICULUM

Writing paragraphs and short essays. The Cases for Critical Thinking are short, practical applications of the accounting principles developed in the chapter. Some cases are planned to present problems related to the chapter but not specifically discussed and answered in the chapter. These cases present an opportunity for critical thinking and decision making. These cases also require more than a short objective-type response. Therefore, they provide ideal practice in writing paragraphs and short essays.

ILLUSTRATION 12-1 Articles of Incorporation (page 2)

Article IX - Incorporators and Initial Subscribers

The names and addresses of the persons signing these articles of incorporation as incorporators and as initial subscribers for stock are:

Richard P. McLaurin	19034 Westerly Drive	Nashville, TN 37221-1786
Amy B. Thacker	9083 N. 23rd Street	Nashville, TN 37209-8196
Cynthia M. Fazio	1607 Charles Court	Nashville, TN 37218-4207
Andre W. Fazio	1607 Charles Court	Nashville, TN 37218-4207
Daniel E. Sikorowski	40623 Northview Avenue	Nashville, TN 37216-3271
Susan P. Boyd	890 Welch Road	Franklin, TN 37064-5678

Article X - Beginning of Corporate Existence

Corporate existence shall begin when these articles of incorporation have been filed with and approved by the State of Tennessee and all filing fees and taxes have been paid.

Article XI - Amendments

This corporation reserves the right to amend or repeal any provisions contained in these articles of incorporation, or any amendment thereto, and any right conferred upon the stockholders is subject to this reservation.

IN WITNESS WHEREOF, we have executed and acknowledged these articles of incorporation this 12th day of December, 19--.

Richard P. McLaurin	Andre W. Fazio
Amy B. Thacker	Daniel E. Sikorowski
Cynthia M. Fazio	Susan P. Boyd

STATE OF TENNESSEE)
COUNTY OF DAVIDSON) ss:

Before me, an officer duly authorized in the State and County aforesaid, to take acknowledgments, personally appeared Richard P. McLaurin, Amy B. Thacker, Cynthia M. Fazio, Andre W. Fazio, Daniel E. Sikorowski, and Susan P. Boyd, to me known to be the persons described in and who executed the foregoing instrument, and they acknowledged before me that they executed the same.

WITNESS my hand and official seal in the County and State aforesaid, this 27th day of December, 19--.

Robert P. Knight
Notary Public, State of Tennessee

(Seal)

My commission expires June 30, 19--

erence given to preferred stockholders is to receive dividends before common stockholders. Other preferences granted preferred stockholders may include the following.

1. Unpaid dividends may accumulate from one year to another.

   In years that dividends are not paid, the preferred dividends accumulate and are paid in a later year. Accumulated preferred dividends must be paid before any common stock dividends are paid.

2. Dividends may be shared with common stockholders above a stated percentage or amount.

   Once the dividend to common stockholders equals the stated percentage of the preferred stock, additional dividends may be shared between preferred and common stockholders.

Every preference granted to preferred stockholders comes at the expense of common stockholders. For example, if preferred stockholders share in dividends above a stated percentage, then common stockholders give up a right to some dividends. A few corporations

FYI

A limited liability company (LLC) is a relatively new form of business organization that is growing in popularity. An LLC combines the most favorable features of a corporation and a partnership.

ASSESS

Assess student understanding by checking the solutions to the Independent Practice activities.

Reteach

Divide the class into groups of six to eight students. Have each group plan the organization of a corporation. Each corporation is to be authorized 240,000 shares of $1.00 stated-value common stock and 50,000 shares of 10%, $100.00 par-value preferred stock. Have each group draft an articles of incorporation following Illustration 12-1. Each group should decide on its own corporation name and address.

Extend

Assign Cases for Critical Thinking 1 and 2.

Enrich

Assign the Applied Communications special feature on page 340.

CLOSURE

Use Audit Your Understanding questions.

TEACHING STRATEGIES: Cooperative Learning

Divide the class into groups of four or five students each. Using Cases for Critical Thinking, each group analyzes the cases and arrives at agreed-upon solutions. One member of each group is appointed the recorder and presents the group's analysis to the class. This cooperative learning activity should not take more than 20 to 25 minutes of class time.

Global Perspective

The GLOBAL PERSPECTIVE feature is intended to expose students to some of the ways in which accounting and business in general differ in other countries. This GLOBAL PERSPECTIVE feature allows students to explore international package delivery services and customs inspections. The GLOBAL PERSPECTIVE activity requires students to research international package delivery services available in the area.

Answers to Global Perspective Activity

Obtaining guidelines for sending a package internationally should be a relatively easy task. There should be at least one local delivery service that has developed guidelines for sending packages internationally. Student answers will vary depending on the carrier and country that is chosen.

AUDIT YOUR UNDERSTANDING

The AUDIT YOUR UNDERSTANDING feature appears at the end of each section of the chapter. Explain to your students that the word *audit* means to check or verify. AUDIT YOUR UNDERSTANDING may be used to check student comprehension of the section just studied. The answers are provided in Appendix D in the back of the textbook.

1. Determine corporate policies and select corporate officers to supervise the day-to-day management of the corporation.
2. (1) The right to vote at stockholders' meetings. (2) The right to share in the corporation's earnings. (3) The right to share in the distribution of a corporation's assets if a corporation ceases operations and sells its assets.

LESSON PLAN 12-2

Materials

- Student pages 330–335
- Blackline Master for Cash Payments Journal (TRG)
- Blackline Master for General Journal (TRG)
- Blackline Master for Cash Receipts Journal (TRG)

Global Perspective

INTERNATIONAL PACKAGES AND CUSTOMS INSPECTIONS

When sending a package overseas, appropriate documentation must accompany the package to verify its contents. Customs officials will read the documentation and may open the package to verify its contents. If the proper documentation does not accompany the package, the shipment will be held until proper documentation is presented to Customs.

To reduce inconsistencies in the application of Customs and freight tariffs, all major trading nations use the Harmonized Commodity Description and Coding System (HS). HS establishes a single ten-digit code for each type of commodity. This code may be obtained from the Census Bureau's Foreign Trade Division.

There are certain restrictions as to the types of commodities that can be shipped. The Food and Drug Administration (FDA) regulates the import of items such as foods, pharmaceuticals, medical devices, and cosmetics. These restrictions protect American citizens from improperly tested items that could cause physical harm.

The U.S. Department of Agriculture (USDA) regulates the import of items such as meat and meat products, insects, plants, fruits, and vegetables. Restrictions on shipments protect domestic horticulture from infection by disease or insects.

The Federal Communications Commission (FCC) regulates the import of such items as cordless telephones, video games, microwave ovens, and radio transmitters. By regulating such items, the quality of consumer products can be protected.

GLOBAL PERSPECTIVE ACTIVITY:

Obtain a guide from a carrier that provides the guidelines for sending a package internationally. Select a foreign country and assume that you are sending a package that contains a ten page legal document. The package weighs less than two pounds.

1. Which forms must be completed to send the document?
2. How should you package the document?
3. How much will it cost?
4. When will it be delivered?
5. Does the company offer pick up service or must you take it to their location?

may give voting rights to preferred stockholders. If this situation occurs, then the voting influence of the common stockholders is decreased because more shares have voting rights. However, regardless of the kind of stock issued, no stockholder is entitled to dividends until a corporation's board of directors votes to pay dividends.

Audit Your Understanding

1. What are the responsibilities of a corporation's board of directors?
2. What three basic rights do stockholders usually have?

The number of preferred stock preferences normally is determined by demand for the stock and the corporation's need for additional capital. When demand for a corporation's preferred stock is low, more preferences are often added to the preferred stock being issued.

Preferred stock dividends may be stated as a percentage of par value or as an amount per share. For example, LampLight has authorized the issuance of 8%, $100.00 par-value preferred stock.

TRANSACTIONS WHEN STARTING A CORPORATION

LampLight's articles of incorporation, Illustration 12-1, were approved by the state of Tennessee on December 27. The resulting charter was received by the corporation on December 31. The char-

APPLIED SKILLS: WORD PROCESSING

If you wish to integrate word processing into your accounting course, you may direct students to answer the end-of-chapter Accounting Terms, Questions for Individual Study, and Cases for Critical Thinking using their word processing software.

ter is LampLight's legal approval to begin transacting business in the name of the corporation. The corporation needs assets to operate. The initial capital is obtained by selling stock to the incorporators.

Capital Accounts of a Corporation

FYI

The Securities and Exchange Commission (SEC), established in 1934, helps regulate the offering, buying, and selling of securities, including capital stock.

Because of the potential number of owners, a corporation does not keep a separate general ledger capital account for each stockholder. Instead, a single summary general ledger capital account is used for each kind of stock issued. When a corporation issues only common stock, the value of all stock issued is recorded in a single capital stock account. When a corporation issues both common and preferred stock, separate capital stock accounts are used for common and preferred stock.

A corporation's net income is recorded in a capital account titled Retained Earnings. Using this account keeps the net income separate from the recorded values of issued capital stock. A net income is credited and a net loss is debited to Retained Earnings. A debit balance in Retained Earnings is often referred to as a deficit.

Issuing Capital Stock When Forming a Corporation

When the corporation is formed, each of LampLight's six incorporators agrees to buy 5,000 shares of common stock at the stated value. Thus, a total of 30,000 shares of common stock, stated value $10.00, is issued for a total of $300,000.00.

January 5, 19--. Received cash from six incorporators for 30,000 shares of $10.00 stated-value common stock, $300,000.00. Receipt Nos. 1–6.

Cash	
300,000.00	

Capital Stock—Common	
	300,000.00

Cash is debited for $300,000.00. Capital Stock—Common is credited for $300,000.00, the value of the issued common stock.

The journal entry to record this transaction is shown in Illustration 12-2.

ILLUSTRATION 12-2 Journal entry to record cash received for common stock

CASH RECEIPTS JOURNAL — PAGE 1

	DATE		ACCOUNT TITLE	DOC. NO.	POST. REF.	1 GENERAL DEBIT	2 GENERAL CREDIT	3 ACCOUNTS RECEIVABLE CREDIT	4 SALES CREDIT	5 SALES TAX PAYABLE DEBIT	6 SALES TAX PAYABLE CREDIT	7 SALES DISCOUNT DEBIT	8 CASH DEBIT	
1	19-- Jan.	5	Capital Stock—Common	R1-6			300 000 00						300 000 00	1
2														2

Subscribing for Capital Stock

Corporations frequently contract with investors for the sale of capital stock with payment to be received at a later date. Future pay-

Objectives (Enabling Performance Tasks)

a. Define accounting terms related to corporate accounting.

b. Identify accounting concepts and practices related to corporate accounting.

c. Journalize transactions for starting a corporation.

d. Prepare a balance sheet for a newly formed corporation.

FOCUS

- The legal requirements for forming a corporation were presented earlier in this chapter. Explain that the charter received by the corporation is the approval to begin operating the business by issuing capital stock to the incorporators. In this lesson, the transactions to start a new corporation will be journalized. Explain that after these initial transactions are recorded, a balance sheet will be prepared.
- Introduce vocabulary: subscribing for capital stock, organization costs, intangible assets.

TEACHING STRATEGIES: TEACHING TIP

Make liberal use of T accounts on the chalkboard or an overhead projector to demonstrate analyzing transactions. Reinforce the procedure by having students draw T accounts at their desks while you are drawing them on the board or transparency.

TEACH

Cover student pages 330–335 "Transactions When Starting a Corporation," "Organization Costs of a Corporation," and "Balance Sheet of a Newly Formed Corporation." Explain the capital accounts used by a corporation. Emphasize that the retained earnings account is used to record a corporation's earnings. Explain how the entry to issue capital stock is recorded. Describe the entries required to journalize a stock subscription, cash received for a stock subscription, and issuance of stock previously subscribed. Point out that subscribed stock does not allow the subscriber to vote or receive dividends. Emphasize that only the initial issuance of stock is recorded in the books of the corporation; a stock transfer is not journalized. Explain the kinds of fees and expenses that may be included in organization costs and how these costs are recorded. Present the balance sheet of the newly formed corporation and discuss the difference between intangible assets, current assets, and plant assets.

FYI

Subscribed stock has no voting rights.

ment for the stock may be made all at one time or on an installment plan. Entering into an agreement with a corporation to buy capital stock and pay at a later date is called **subscribing for capital stock.**

Journalizing a Stock Subscription. On January 5, Daniel Herring subscribed for 2,000 shares of LampLight's common stock at $10.00 a share. He agreed to pay $10,000.00 on March 1 and $10,000.00 not later than July 1.

January 5, 19--. Received a subscription from Daniel Herring for 2,000 shares of $10.00 stated-value common stock, $20,000.00. Memorandum No. 1.

Subscriptions Receivable	
20,000.00	

Stock Subscribed—Common	
	20,000.00

Subscriptions Receivable is debited for $20,000.00. The asset account, Subscriptions Receivable, shows the unpaid amount of all subscriptions. Stock Subscribed—Common is credited for $20,000.00. The capital account, Stock Subscribed—Common, shows the total amount of stock subscribed but not issued. This capital account is used because stock certificates are issued only when the stock is fully paid for. The amounts are recorded in Capital Stock—Common only when stock is fully paid for and stock certificates are issued.

The journal entry to record this transaction is shown in Illustration 12-3.

ILLUSTRATION 12-3 Journal entry to record a stock subscription

GENERAL JOURNAL PAGE 1

	DATE		ACCOUNT TITLE	DOC. NO.	POST. REF.	DEBIT	CREDIT	
1	19-- Jan.	5	Subscriptions Receivable	M1		20 000 00		1
2			Stock Subscribed—Common				20 000 00	2
3								3

Journalizing Cash Received for a Stock Subscription. On March 1, LampLight received cash from Daniel Herring for half of his stock subscription.

March 1, 19--. Received cash from Daniel Herring in partial payment of stock subscription, $10,000.00. Receipt No. 45.

Cash	
Mar. 1 10,000.00	

Subscriptions Receivable	
Jan. 5 20,000.00 *(New Bal. 10,000.00)*	Mar. 1 10,000.00

Cash is debited for $10,000.00. Subscriptions Receivable is credited for $10,000.00. The new balance of this account, $10,000.00, is the amount still owed by Mr. Herring for his stock subscription.

The journal entry to record this transaction is shown in Illustration 12-4.

TEACHING STRATEGIES: DIFFERENT LEARNING STYLES

Auditory Learner. To reinforce the learning of journal entries, the auditory learner should verbally repeat the analysis of the transaction. The student should also verbally list the steps involved in making the entry.

ILLUSTRATION 12-4 Journal entry to record cash received for a stock subscription

CASH RECEIPTS JOURNAL — PAGE 3

	DATE		ACCOUNT TITLE	DOC. NO.	POST. REF.	1 GENERAL DEBIT	2 GENERAL CREDIT	3 ACCOUNTS RECEIVABLE CREDIT	4 SALES CREDIT	5 SALES TAX PAYABLE DEBIT	6 SALES TAX PAYABLE CREDIT	7 SALES DISCOUNT DEBIT	8 CASH DEBIT	
1	19-- Mar.	1	*Subscriptions Receivable*	R45			10,000 00						10,000 00	1

A similar journal entry is made on July 1 when Mr. Herring pays the second installment of the stock subscription as shown in the T accounts.

Cash

Debit		Credit	
Mar. 1	10,000.00		
July 1	10,000.00		
(New Bal.	*20,000.00)*		

Subscriptions Receivable

Debit		Credit	
Jan. 5	20,000.00	Mar. 1	10,000.00
		July 1	10,000.00
		(New Bal. zero)	

Journalizing Issuance of Stock Previously Subscribed. When a stock subscription is fully paid for, a stock certificate is issued to the stockholder.

July 1, 19--. Issued Stock Certificate No. 7 to Daniel Herring for 2,000 shares of $10.00 stated-value common stock. Memorandum No. 67.

Stock Subscribed—Common

Debit		Credit	
July 1	20,000.00	Jan. 5	20,000.00
		(New Bal. zero)	

Capital Stock—Common

Debit		Credit	
		Jan. 5	300,000.00
		July 1	20,000.00
		(New Bal.	*320,000.00)*

Stock Subscribed—Common is debited for $20,000.00. Capital Stock—Common is credited for $20,000.00. The new balance of this account, $320,000.00, is the value of all common stock issued by LampLight.

The journal entry to record the issuance of stock to Mr. Herring is shown in Illustration 12-5.

LampLight only records the issuance of stock to the original stockholder. A stockholder may later decide to sell shares of stock to another person. Such stock transfers are not journalized by LampLight because these transactions do not generate additional capital for the corporation. However, the name of the new stockholder must be entered in LampLight's stock ownership records for future dividend payments.

ILLUSTRATION 12-5 Journal entry to record issuance of stock previously subscribed

GENERAL JOURNAL — PAGE 7

	DATE		ACCOUNT TITLE	DOC. NO.	POST. REF.	DEBIT	CREDIT	
1	19-- July	1	*Stock Subscribed—Common*	M67		20,000 00		1
2			*Capital Stock—Common*				20,000 00	2
3								3

APPLY

Draw T accounts to analyze each transaction as it is presented in this lesson. Identify the balance side of the capital stock accounts. Refer students to Illustration 12-2 when the issuance of capital stock is discussed. Refer students to Illustrations 12-3, 12-4, and 12-5, respectively, as the three transactions related to a stock subscription are presented. Have students compare the balance sheet in Illustration 12-7 with the balance sheet in Illustration 5-10, Chapter 5.

Guided Practice

Guide students through the T account analysis of the transactions for starting a corporation in Problem 12-1. Have students draw T accounts on a sheet of paper and analyze the first transaction. All students should agree with the analysis before proceeding to the next transaction. Repeat the process until all transactions have been analyzed. The balance of Problem 12-1 can be completed as Independent Practice.

Independent Practice

Assign Terms 11–13, Questions 6–12, Problems 12-1 and 12-2.

TEACHING STRATEGIES: DIFFERENT LEARNING STYLES

Kinesthetic Learner. When covering journal entries with a kinesthetic learner, the instructor should give the student journal paper and have the student complete the entries as the instructor demonstrates on a transparency or chalkboard.

ASSESS

Assess student understanding by checking the solutions to the Independent Practice activities.

Reteach

Make transparencies of the cash payments, general, and cash receipts journals from the accounting forms masters provided in the Blackline Masters Section of the Teacher's Resource Guide. Refer students to Recycling Problem 12-R. Ask students to use T accounts to analyze the July 5, 8, 25, and August 10 transactions. Use the transparencies to demonstrate how the transactions are journalized. The balance of Recycling Problem 12-R can be completed during the next lesson.

Enrich

Assign students to read the MULTICULTURAL AWARENESS feature on page 326. Discuss with them how an understanding and appreciation of history and other cultures contributes to understanding civilization today.

CLOSURE

Use Audit Your Understanding questions.

ORGANIZATION COSTS OF A CORPORATION

Fees and other expenses of organizing a corporation are called **organization costs.** Organization costs may include the following three items.

1. An incorporation fee paid to the state when the articles of incorporation are submitted.
2. Attorney fees for legal services during the process of incorporation.
3. Other incidental expenses incurred prior to receiving a charter.

A corporation cannot be formed without organization costs. Until a charter is received, a corporation does not exist to pay the organization costs. Therefore, one of the incorporators usually agrees to pay these costs until the charter is granted. After a charter is received, a corporation usually reimburses the incorporator for the organization costs.

If substantial organization costs were recorded as an expense in a corporation's first year, net income could be reduced unreasonably during that first year. Furthermore, benefits derived from these expenditures extend over many years. Therefore, these costs are recorded in an asset account, Organization Costs, until charged as an expense. Adjusting entries to record portions of the organization costs as an expense each year are described in Chapter 14. *(CONCEPT: Matching Expenses with Revenue)*

FYI

To publicly sell large issues of stock, a corporation must have the approval of the Securities and Exchange Commission (SEC) to certify that information about the business is not being concealed.

Amy Thacker agreed to pay the organization costs for LampLight until its charter was received. On January 5, Mrs. Thacker submitted a statement of organization costs, $2,400.00, that she incurred prior to the receipt of the charter.

Organization Costs	
2,400.00	

Cash	
	2,400.00

January 5, 19--. Paid cash to Amy Thacker as reimbursement for organization costs, $2,400.00. Check No. 1.

Organization Costs is debited for $2,400.00. Cash is credited for $2,400.00.

The journal entry to record this transaction is shown in Illustration 12-6.

ILLUSTRATION 12-6 Journal entry to record payment of organization costs

CASH PAYMENTS JOURNAL — PAGE *1*

	DATE		ACCOUNT TITLE	CK. NO.	POST. REF.	1 GENERAL DEBIT	2 GENERAL CREDIT	3 ACCOUNTS PAYABLE DEBIT	4 PURCHASES DISCOUNT CREDIT	5 CASH CREDIT	
1	19-- *Jan.*	*5*	*Organization Costs*	*1*		*2 400 00*				*2 400 00*	1
2											2
3											3
4											4
5											5

TEACHING STRATEGIES: DIFFERENT LEARNING STYLES

Print Learner. When covering journal entries with a print learner, the instructor should discuss the entries, using the textbook examples and referring to the textbook. The print learner can later go back and study the entries.

BALANCE SHEET OF A NEWLY FORMED CORPORATION

Audit Your Understanding

1. In place of a general ledger capital account for each owner, how does a corporation show stock ownership?
2. What accounts are affected, and how, when common stock is initially sold and issued to a corporation's incorporators?
3. What three items may be included in the organization costs of a corporation?
4. The account Organization Costs is presented in which section of the corporation's balance sheet?

LampLight's balance sheet at the end of business on January 5 is shown in Illustration 12-7.

Assets of a non-physical nature that have value for a business are called **intangible assets.** The heading, Intangible Asset, is listed on the balance sheet as the last subdivision in the assets section. The asset account Organization Costs is presented in the intangible assets section. If a corporation has long-term investments and plant assets, these would be shown on a balance sheet before intangible assets.

LampLight's cash on hand, January 5, is the original $300,000.00 paid by the incorporators *minus* the $2,400.00 paid for organization costs. The subscriptions receivable on January 5 is the amount due from Daniel Herring.

Paid-in capital is a subdivision of the stockholders' equity section of a balance sheet. LampLight's paid-in capital on January 5 consists of $300,000.00 in issued common stock plus $20,000.00 in common stock subscribed. On this date, LampLight has not issued any preferred stock. Therefore, no amount for preferred stock is shown on the balance sheet.

AUDIT YOUR UNDERSTANDING

1. A single summary general ledger capital account is used for each kind of stock issued.
2. Cash is debited; Capital Stock—Common is credited.
3. (1) An incorporation fee paid to the state when the articles of incorporation are submitted. (2) Attorney fees for legal services during the process of incorporation. (3) Other incidental expenses incurred prior to receiving a charter.
4. Intangible Asset section.

ILLUSTRATION 12-7 Balance sheet of a corporation

LampLight, Inc.
Balance Sheet
January 5, 19--

ASSETS			
Current Assets:			
Cash	$297,600.00		
Subscriptions Receivable	20,000.00		
Total Current Assets		$317,600.00	
Intangible Asset:			
Organization Costs		2,400.00	
Total Assets			$320,000.00
STOCKHOLDERS' EQUITY			
Paid-in Capital:			
Capital Stock—Common (30,000 shares, $10.00 stated value)		$300,000.00	
Stock Subscribed— Common (2,000 shares)		20,000.00	
Total Paid-in Capital			320,000.00
Total Stockholders' Equity			$320,000.00

TEACHING STRATEGIES: TEACHING TIP

Request annual reports from several publicly-traded corporations familiar to the students. Addresses and phone numbers can be obtained from many sources, such as product labels and phone directory assistance. For each corporation, have students locate the number of shares of common and preferred stock issued and the annual dividends for the reported years.

LESSON PLAN 12-3

Materials

- Student pages 336–338
- Blackline Master for Cash Payments Journal (TRG)
- Blackline Master for General Journal (TRG)
- Software: Spreadsheet Template
- Assess: Problem Test Chapter 12, MicroExam Chapter 12

Objectives (Enabling Performance Tasks)

a. Define accounting terms related to corporate accounting.

b. Identify accounting concepts and practices related to corporate accounting.

e. Calculate dividends for a corporation.

f. Journalize transactions for declaring and paying dividends for a corporation.

FOCUS

- Forming a corporation and issuing capital stock to investors were presented earlier in this chapter. In this lesson, the transactions to distribute earnings of a corporation to stockholders (dividends) will be journalized. Explain that dividends are one reason stockholders invest in a corporation.
- Introduce vocabulary: declaring a dividend, date of declaration, date of record, date of payment.

TEACH

Cover student pages 336–338 "Dividends." Explain the three important dates involved in distributing a dividend: date of declaration, date of record, and date of payment. Emphasize that a corporation does not have to pay dividends. However, once declared, dividends must be paid. Demonstrate how to calculate dividends for preferred and common stock. Present the entries to journalize the declaration and payment of a dividend. Remind students that no journal entry is required on the date of record.

DIVIDENDS

FYI

No stockholder is guaranteed a dividend.

Once operations begin, a new corporation may retain a portion of net income to finance future business expansion and improvement. However, most corporations distribute a portion of the earnings to stockholders.

Corporate earnings distributed to stockholders are known as dividends. Action by a board of directors to distribute corporate earnings to stockholders is called **declaring a dividend.** The board determines when and what amount of the retained earnings will be distributed. A corporation has no obligation to distribute money to stockholders until the board of directors has declared a dividend.

Three important dates are involved in distributing a dividend.

1. *Date of declaration.* The date on which a board of directors votes to distribute a dividend is called the **date of declaration.**
2. *Date of record.* The date that determines which stockholders are to receive dividends is called the **date of record.** Stockholders may buy and sell stock at any time. However, only persons listed as stockholders on the date of record will receive dividends.
3. *Date of payment.* The date on which dividends are actually to be paid to stockholders is called the **date of payment.** Ordinarily the date of payment is several weeks after the date of record. Thus, a corporation has time to determine who is entitled to receive dividends and to prepare dividend checks for mailing on the date of payment.

Transactions are recorded in a corporation's accounts on two of the three dates: (1) date of declaration and (2) date of payment.

Journalizing Declaration of a Dividend

When a board of directors declares a dividend, the corporation is obligated to pay the dividend. A liability is, therefore, incurred by the corporation and must be recorded.

The board of directors of CompuForm, Inc. has decided to declare an annual dividend of $24,000.00. On the date of record, the corporation has issued 1,000 shares of 8%, $100.00 par-value preferred stock and 16,000 shares of $20.00 stated-value common stock. The value of the preferred and common stock is calculated as shown below.

Number of Preferred Shares	×	Par Value	=	Value of Preferred Stock
1,000	×	$100.00	=	$100,000.00
Number of Common Shares	**×**	**Stated Value**	**=**	**Value of Common Stock**
16,000	×	$20.00	=	$320,000.00

TEACHING STRATEGIES: DIFFERENT LEARNING STYLES

Tactile Learner. Tactile learners may benefit from using the computer to key journal entries and then print reports. A ruler can be positioned on the input forms as a guide when keying the entries. The student should also be encouraged to place a finger on each account title in the journal entries report and trace it over to the amount in the amount column of the report to check it for accuracy. Tactile learners should also be given the opportunity to journalize transactions from at least one simulation that contains source documents which must be handled to analyze, journalize, and file.

The value of preferred stock is used to calculate the dividend on preferred stock. The distribution of the $24,000.00 dividend between preferred and common stock is calculated as shown below.

Value of Preferred Stock	×	Preferred Dividend Rate	=	Preferred Dividend Amount
$100,000.00	×	8%	=	$8,000.00
Total Amount Available for Dividends	–	**Preferred Dividend Amount**	=	**Amount Available for Common Dividends**
$24,000.00	–	$8,000.00	=	$16,000.00

The dividend rate for common stock is calculated as shown below.

Common Dividend Amount	÷	Value of Common Stock	=	Common Dividend Rate
$16,000.00	÷	$320,000.00	=	5%

A summary of CompuForm's dividends is shown below.

	Amount	Rate
Preferred stock dividends.	$ 8,000.00	8%
Common stock dividends.	$16,000.00	5%

FYI

Dividends may be paid in additional capital stock, known as a stock dividend, instead of cash. Dividends Payable is debited and Capital Stock is credited when the stock is issued on the date of payment.

In subsequent years, CompuForm may elect to increase its annual dividend. None of the increase in dividends would be distributed to preferred stock. Thus, CompuForm's preferred stock dividend rate will never exceed 8%. Additional dividends would be distributed to common stock, increasing the common stock dividend rate. The common stock dividend rate may be less than, equal to, or greater than the preferred stock dividend rate.

December 15, 19--. CompuForm's board of directors declared an annual dividend of $24,000.00. Preferred stock issued is $100,000.00 of 8%, $100.00 par-value preferred stock. Common stock issued is $320,000.00 of $20.00 stated-value common stock. Date of payment is January 15. Memorandum No. 132.

Dividends—Common	
16,000.00	

Dividends Payable	
	24,000.00

Dividends—Preferred	
8,000.00	

TEACHING STRATEGIES: DIFFERENT LEARNING STYLES

Visual Learner. When covering journal entries with a visual learner, the instructor should discuss the entries, using a transparency or the chalkboard to record the entry. In addition, the student should be asked to mentally picture each part of the entry before the instructor actually writes it on the transparency or chalkboard.

APPLY

Draw T accounts to analyze the dividend transactions presented in this lesson. Refer students to Illustrations 12-8 and 12-9 as the entries to journalize declaration and payment of dividends are discussed.

Guided Practice

Guide students through the procedures for calculating the amount of dividends to be paid to preferred and common stockholders of the Batchelder Corporation in Problem 12-3. Write the formulas on the board for reference. Working as a group, have the students calculate the value of the preferred stock for the Batchelder Corporation. When all students agree on the value, have them calculate the amount of dividends to be paid each year to preferred and common shareholders. When all students agree on the correct amounts, direct students to record the amounts on the form in the working papers. The balance of Problem 12-3 can be completed as Independent Practice.

Independent Practice

- Assign Terms 14–17, Questions 13–14, and Problems 12-3 and 12-4.
- Assign Study Guide 12 and Mastery Problem 12-M.

ASSESS

Assess student understanding by checking the solutions to the Independent Practice activities.

Reteach

- Make transparencies of the general and cash payments journals from the accounting forms masters provided in the Blackline Masters Section of the Teacher's Resource Guide. Refer students to Recycling Problem 12-R, Instruction 3. Guide students through the calculation of the amount of dividends to be paid to preferred and common stockholders. Ask students to use T accounts to analyze the transactions for declaring and paying the dividends. Use the transparencies to demonstrate how the transactions are journalized.
- Assign Recycling Problem 12-R.

ASSESS (cont'd)

Extend

- Assign Challenge Problem 12-C. (The challenge is to calculate distribution of the dividend between preferred and common stock.)
- Assign the Spreadsheet Template for Mastery Problem 12-M.

Enrich

Assign and discuss the GLOBAL PERSPECTIVE feature on page 330.

AUDIT YOUR UNDERSTANDING

1. The board of directors.
2. The corporation is obligated to pay the dividend.
3. (1) To avoid a large number of entries in the corporation's cash payments journal. (2) To reserve cash specifically for paying dividends.

TEACHING STRATEGIES: APPLYING VISUALS

Direct students to Illustrations 12-8 and 12-9 to review the entries to declare and pay dividends.

CLOSURE

Use Audit Your Understanding questions.

ASSESS

- Administer Problem Test Chapter 12.
- Administer a MicroExam test for Chapter 12.

Dividends—Common is debited for $16,000.00. Dividends—Preferred is debited for $8,000.00. Dividends Payable is credited for $24,000.00.

The journal entry to record this transaction is shown in Illustration 12-8.

ILLUSTRATION 12-8 Journal entry to record declaring a dividend

GENERAL JOURNAL — PAGE 12

	DATE		ACCOUNT TITLE	DOC. NO.	POST. REF.	DEBIT	CREDIT	
1	19-- Dec.	15	Dividends—Common	M132		16 000 00		1
2			Dividends—Preferred			8 000 00		2
3			Dividends Payable				24 000 00	3

Audit Your Understanding

1. Who determines when and what amount of retained earnings of a corporation will be distributed as dividends?
2. Why does a corporation record a liability when a dividend is declared?
3. What are two reasons for using a special dividend checking account?

Journalizing Payment of a Dividend

On January 15, CompuForm issued a single check for the total amount of the dividends to be paid. The single check is deposited in a special dividend checking account. A separate check for each eligible stockholder is written against the special checking account. This procedure avoids a large number of entries in CompuForm's cash payments journal. The special dividend checking account also reserves cash specifically for paying the dividends.

CompuForm's dividend check is given to an agent who handles the details of preparing and mailing stockholders' checks. CompuForm's agent is the bank where the corporation has its checking account.

January 15, 19--. Paid cash for annual dividend declared December 15, $24,000.00. Check No. 432.

Dividends Payable

Debit		Credit	
Jan. 15	24,000.00	Dec. 15	24,000.00

Cash

Debit		Credit	
		Jan. 15	24,000.00

Dividends Payable is debited and Cash is credited for $24,000.00.

The journal entry to record this transaction is shown in Illustration 12-9.

ILLUSTRATION 12-9 Journal entry to record paying a dividend

CASH PAYMENTS JOURNAL — PAGE 1

	DATE	ACCOUNT TITLE	CK. NO.	POST. REF.	1 GENERAL DEBIT	2 GENERAL CREDIT	3 ACCOUNTS PAYABLE DEBIT	4 PURCHASES DISCOUNT CREDIT	5 CASH CREDIT	
18	15	Dividends Payable	432		24 000 00				24 000 00	18

TEACHING STRATEGIES: TEACHING TIP

Use T accounts to show that Dividends Payable is closed after the dividends are paid, but that the amount of dividends distributed remains in the Dividends account until closing entries are made.

ACCOUNTING TERMS EPT(a)

What is the meaning of each of the following?

1. board of directors
2. articles of incorporation
3. charter
4. common stock
5. preferred stock
6. stock certificate
7. par value
8. par-value stock
9. no-par-value stock
10. stated-value stock
11. subscribing for capital stock
12. organization costs
13. intangible assets
14. declaring a dividend
15. date of declaration
16. date of record
17. date of payment

QUESTIONS FOR INDIVIDUAL STUDY EPT(b)

1. What steps must be taken by individuals who wish to form a corporation?
2. When does a corporation actually come into existence?
3. What three basic rights do stockholders usually have?
4. What are the two basic kinds of stock a corporation might issue?
5. What usually determines the number of stock preferences given to preferred stock?
6. How is the initial capital of a corporation obtained?
7. What is the title of a corporation's capital account in which net income is recorded?
8. What accounts are affected, and how, when common stock is initially sold and issued to a corporation's incorporators?
9. What accounts are affected, and how, when a corporation receives a subscription for common stock?
10. What accounts are affected, and how, when a corporation issues common stock previously subscribed?
11. What accounts are affected, and how, when a corporation reimburses an incorporator for the costs of organizing a corporation?
12. Where is the Intangible Asset subdivision placed on a corporation's balance sheet?
13. What accounts are affected, and how, by a journal entry to record the declaration of dividends for both common and preferred stock?
14. What accounts are affected, and how, by a journal entry to record payment of dividends for common and preferred stock?

CASES FOR CRITICAL THINKING EPT(b)

CASE 1 Jennifer Hester is considering whether she should buy stock as an investment. She asks you whether it would be better to buy common stock or preferred stock. How would you answer her? Explain your suggestions.

CASE 2 Steven and Barbara Lambert currently own all the issued common stock, $250,000.00, in a newly formed corporation, City Hardware, Inc. No preferred stock has been issued. They both decide that the corporation needs $100,000.00 additional capital. They decide to sell additional stock. Mr. Lambert suggests that the corporation sell more common stock. Mrs. Lambert suggests that the corporation sell preferred stock. With whom do you agree? Explain your answer.

ACCOUNTING TERMS

1. **board of directors:** A group of persons elected by the stockholders to manage a corporation. (p. 326)
2. **articles of incorporation:** A written application requesting permission to form a corporation. (p. 326)
3. **charter:** The approved articles of incorporation. (p. 326)
4. **common stock:** Stock that does not give stockholders any special preferences. (p. 327)
5. **preferred stock:** Stock that gives stockholders preference in earnings and other rights. (p. 327)
6. **stock certificate:** Written evidence of the number of shares each stockholder owns in a corporation. (p. 327)
7. **par value:** A value assigned to a share of stock and printed on the stock certificate. (p. 327)
8. **par-value stock:** A share of stock that has an authorized value printed on the stock certificate. (p. 327)
9. **no-par-value stock:** A share of stock that has no authorized value printed on the stock certificate. (p. 327)
10. **stated-value stock:** No-par-value stock that is assigned a value by a corporation. (p. 328)
11. **subscribing for capital stock:** Entering into an agreement with a corporation to buy capital stock and pay at a later date. (p. 332)
12. **organization costs:** Fees and other expenses of organizing a corporation. (p. 334)
13. **intangible assets:** Assets of a nonphysical nature that have value for a business. (p. 335)
14. **declaring a dividend:** Action by a board of directors to distribute corporate earnings to stockholders. (p. 336)
15. **date of declaration:** The date on which a board of directors votes to distribute a dividend. (p. 336)
16. **date of record:** The date that determines which stockholders are to receive dividends. (p. 336)
17. **date of payment:** The date on which dividends are actually to be paid to the stockholders. (p. 336)

QUESTIONS FOR INDIVIDUAL STUDY

1. Submit an application to the designated officials of the state in which the company is to be incorporated. (p. 326)
2. When the articles of incorporation are approved. (p. 326)

APPLIED SKILLS: COMMUNICATIONS

Surveys of business managers show that communication skills are one of the most desired traits in new employees. The APPLIED COMMUNICATIONS activity provides an opportunity for students to practice their communication and language arts skills on topics that directly relate to accounting. This activity requires students to prepare an introduction for an accounting professional. Students should be encouraged to prepare an outline rather than a word-for-word written speech. Outlines help prevent an oral message from sounding like a prepared statement. Throughout the semester, the instructor should elect a student to introduce business professionals who make presentations in the class.

QUESTIONS *(cont'd)*

3. (a) The right to vote at stockholders' meetings. (b) The right to share in a corporation's earnings. (c) The right to share in the distribution of a corporation's assets if a corporation ceases operations and sells its assets. (p. 327)

4. Common and preferred. (p. 327)

5. The demand for a corporation's stock and the corporation's need for additional capital. (p. 330)

6. By selling stock to the incorporators. (p. 331)

7. Retained Earnings. (p. 331)

8. Cash is debited; Capital Stock—Common is credited. (p. 331)

9. Subscriptions Receivable is debited; Stock Subscribed—Common is credited. (p. 332)

10. Stock Subscribed—Common is debited; Capital Stock—Common is credited. (p. 333)

11. Organization Costs is debited; Cash is credited. (p. 334)

12. As the last subdivision in the assets section. (p. 335)

13. Dividends—Common and Dividends—Preferred are debited; Dividends Payable is credited. (p. 338)

14. Dividends Payable is debited; Cash is credited. (p. 338)

APPLIED COMMUNICATIONS

Most accountants actively participate in professional organizations. These organizations enable accounting professionals to share their knowledge and experience with others. Many organizations have periodic dinner meetings where guest speakers make presentations regarding current accounting topics. As a member of a professional organization, you may be asked to introduce a guest speaker.

INSTRUCTIONS:

Prepare an introduction for a business professional. Identify an individual you know personally or a business professional scheduled to speak to your class. Identify the individual's most significant professional qualifications to establish that he or she is qualified to speak on the topic. Include information regarding the speaker's community service and personal information to highlight the personal qualities of the speaker.

APPLICATION PROBLEMS

EPT(c,d,e,f)

PROBLEM 12-1 Journalizing transactions for starting a corporation

Fleming Corporation received its charter on January 6 of the current year. The corporation is authorized to issue 100,000 shares of $25.00 stated-value common stock.

INSTRUCTIONS:

Journalize the following transactions. Use page 1 of a cash receipts journal and a general journal. Source documents are abbreviated as follows: memorandum, M; receipt, R.

Jan. 6. Received cash from four incorporators for 8,000 shares of $25.00 stated-value common stock, $200,000.00. R1-4.
Jan. 8. Received a subscription from Alice McIlwain for 2,000 shares of $25.00 stated-value common stock, $50,000.00. M1.
Jan. 31. Received cash from Alice McIlwain in payment of stock subscription, $50,000.00. R22.
Jan. 31. Issued Stock Certificate No. 5 to Alice McIlwain for 2,000 shares of $25.00 stated-value common stock, $50,000.00. M4.

PROBLEM 12-2 Journalizing transactions for starting a corporation and preparing a balance sheet

Chadwick Corporation received its charter on January 4 of the current year. The corporation is authorized to issue 200,000 shares of $10.00 stated-value common stock and 50,000 shares of 12%, $100.00 par-value preferred stock.

INSTRUCTIONS:

1. Journalize the following transactions. Use page 1 of a cash receipts journal, a cash payments journal, and a general journal. Source documents are abbreviated as follows: check, C; memorandum, M; receipt, R.

Jan. 4. Received cash from three incorporators for 48,000 shares of $10.00 stated-value common stock, $480,000.00. R1-3.
Jan. 4. Paid cash to Myles Camp as reimbursement for organization costs, $2,000.00. C1.
Jan. 5. Received a subscription from Mary Nettles for 2,000 shares of $10.00 stated-value common stock, $20,000.00. M1.
Jan. 16. Received a subscription from Kenneth Bryant for 10,000 shares of $10.00 stated-value common stock, $100,000.00. M2.
Feb. 1. Received cash from Mary Nettles in payment of stock subscription, $20,000.00. R4.
Feb. 1. Issued Stock Certificate No. 4 to Mary Nettles for 2,000 shares of $10.00 stated-value common stock, $20,000.00. M3.

Feb. 8. Received cash from Kenneth Bryant in partial payment of stock subscription, $50,000.00. R5.

Feb. 15. Received a subscription from Leigh Brooks for 300 shares of $10.00 stated-value common stock, $3,000.00. M4.

Mar. 1. Received cash from Kenneth Bryant in final payment of stock subscription, $50,000.00. R6.

Mar. 1. Issued Stock Certificate No. 5 to Kenneth Bryant for 10,000 shares of $10.00 stated-value common stock, $100,000. M5.

2. Prepare a balance sheet for Chadwick Corporation as of March 2 of the current year.

PROBLEM 12-3 Calculating dividends for a corporation

MATHEMATICS

The following information is available from the accounting records of two different corporations.

	Corporations Batchelder	Carnes
Preferred stock:		
Description	$100.00 par-value	$50.00 par-value
Dividend rate	10%	8%
Shares issued	2,000	10,000
Common stock:		
Description	$2.00 stated-value	$1.00 stated-value
Shares issued	300,000	200,000
Annual dividend:		
Year 1	$25,000.00	$50,000.00
Year 2	$30,000.00	$60,000.00
Year 3	$35,000.00	$75,000.00

INSTRUCTIONS:

1. Calculate the value of preferred stock.
2. Calculate the amount of dividends to be paid each year to preferred and common shareholders.

PROBLEM 12-4 Journalizing transactions for declaring and paying dividends

Lightsey, Inc. completed the following transactions.

INSTRUCTIONS:

Journalize the following transactions. Use page 8 of a general journal and page 21 of a cash payments journal. Source documents are abbreviated as follows: check, C; memorandum, M.

Aug. 12. Lightsey's board of directors declared an annual dividend of $180,000.00. Preferred stock issued is $500,000.00 of 10%, $100.00 par-value preferred stock. Common stock issued is $1,000,000.00 of $1,000.00 stated-value common stock. Date of payment is November 15. M65.

Nov. 15. Paid cash for annual dividend declared August 12, $180,000.00. C139.

ENRICHMENT PROBLEMS EPT(c,d,e,f)

MASTERY PROBLEM 12-M Journalizing transactions for starting a corporation, declaring and paying dividends, and preparing a balance sheet

Naper, Inc. received its charter on August 1 of the current year. The corporation is authorized to issue 150,000 shares of $5.00 stated-value common stock and 50,000 shares of 10%, $100.00 par-value preferred stock.

CASES FOR CRITICAL THINKING

Case 1 Each kind of stock has its advantages and disadvantages. If Miss Hester seeks a stock through which she will be able to participate in a corporation's stockholder meetings, she will buy common stock which has voting rights. If Miss Hester desires only an income, she may want to buy preferred stock which is assured of participating in dividends before common stock does. If Miss Hester is seeking a stock that will increase in value, she should check what has been happening to the value of various common and preferred stocks. Before deciding to invest in stock, Miss Hester would be wise to consult with a specialist in the stock market.

Case 2 If the corporation sells more common stock, then the Lamberts must share voting rights and dividends with other stockholders. If the corporation sells preferred stock, then earnings must be used to pay dividends to these stockholders before any can be paid to the Lamberts. However, with preferred stock, voting rights do not need to be shared. A decision about which kind of stock to issue is complicated and must be studied carefully. Stock market specialists may have to be consulted.

APPLIED COMMUNICATIONS

Individual student outlines will vary; however, they should include the following elements: (1) Name. (2) Title. (3) Individual's most significant professional qualifications that establish the speaker's ability to speak on the topic. (4) Community service. (5) Personal information to highlight the personal qualities of the speaker. The instructor should also consider writing style and mechanics (grammar, spelling, punctuation, sentence structure) when grading this activity.

CHECK FIGURES

See Teacher's Edition of Working Papers for complete solutions.

Problem 12-1 Jan. 6 Cash Debit $200,000

Problem 12-2 Balance Sheet: Cap. Stk. $600,000; Stk. Sub. 3,000

Problem 12-3 Batchelder Total Val. Pref. $200,000; Pref. Dividend 20,000; Com. Dividend Year 1 5,000; Year 2 10,000; Year 3 15,000. Carnes Total Val. Pref. $500,000; Pref. Dividend 40,000; Com. Dividend Year 1 10,000; Year 2 20,000; Year 3 35,000.

Problem 12-4 Pref. Dividend $50,000; Com. Dividend $130,000

Mastery Problem 12-M Pref. Dividend $10,000; Com. Dividend $30,000; Cap. Stk. $267,500; Stk. Sub. 30,000

SPREADSHEET

INSTRUCTIONS:

1. Journalize the following transactions. Use page 1 of a cash receipts journal, a cash payments journal, and a general journal. Source documents are abbreviated as follows: check, C; memorandum, M; receipt, R.

Aug. 4. Received cash from ten incorporators for 50,000 shares of $5.00 stated-value common stock, $250,000.00. R1-10.
Aug. 4. Paid cash to Paul Kerwin as reimbursement for organization costs, $6,500.00. C1.
Aug. 6. Received a subscription from Deborah Andrews for 500 shares of $5.00 stated-value common stock, $2,500.00. M1.
Aug. 21. Received a subscription from Kevin Clark for 3,000 shares of $5.00 stated-value common, $15,000.00. M2.
Sept. 16. Received cash from Deborah Andrews in payment of stock subscription, $2,500.00. R11.
Sept. 16. Issued Stock Certificate No. 11 to Deborah Andrews for 500 shares of $5.00 stated-value common stock, $2,500.00. M3.
Oct. 1. Received cash from Kevin Clark in partial payment of stock subscription, $7,500.00. R12.
Oct. 15. Received a subscription from George Bagwell for 6,000 shares of $5.00 stated-value common stock, $30,000.00. M4.
Nov. 1. Received cash from Kevin Clark in final payment of stock subscription, $7,500.00. R13.
Nov. 1. Issued Stock Certificate No. 12 to Kevin Clark for 3,000 shares of $5.00 stated-value common stock, $15,000.00. M5.

2. Prepare a balance sheet for Naper, Inc. as of November 2 of the current year.
3. Journalize the following transactions completed during the following two years to record the declaration and payment of the dividends. Continue using page 1 of the general journal and the cash payments journal.

Nov. 15. Naper's board of directors declared an annual dividend of $40,000.00. Preferred stock issued is $100,000.00 of 10%, $100.00 par-value preferred stock. Common stock issued is $400,000.00 of $5.00 stated-value common stock. Date of payment is January 15. M206.
Jan. 15. Paid cash for annual dividend declared November 15, $40,000.00. C339.

CHECK FIGURES *(cont'd)*

Challenge Problem 12-C 19X1 Pref. 20,000 × 12% × $100 = $240,000; Com. $400,000 – $240,000 = $160,000. 19X2 Com. $450,000 – $240,000 = $210,000. 19X3 Pref. 20,000 shares + 1,000 shares = 21,000; 21,000 × 12% × $100 = $252,000; Com. $450,000 – $252,000 = $198,000.

CHALLENGE PROBLEM 12-C Journalizing transactions for a corporation

On January 1, 19X1, Northwest Casting Corporation has issued the following stock.

250,000 shares of $10.00 stated-value common stock.
20,000 shares of 12%, $100.00 par-value preferred stock.

INSTRUCTIONS:

Journalize the following transactions. Use page 12 of a cash receipts journal, page 14 of a cash payments journal, and page 6 of a general journal. Source documents are abbreviated as follows: check, C; memorandum, M; receipt, R.

19X1
June 7. A subscription was received from Thomas Heath for 2,000 shares of $10.00 stated-value common stock, $20,000.00. M234.
Oct. 15. Thomas Heath paid cash in partial payment of stock subscription, $10,000.00. R245.
Nov. 1. Northwest's board of directors declared an annual dividend of $400,000.00. Date of payment is January 15, 19X2. M245.

19X2
Jan. 15. The annual dividend declared November 1, $400,000.00, was paid. C1489.
Feb. 21. Thomas Heath paid cash in final payment of stock subscription, $10,000.00. R296.
Feb. 21. Issued Stock Certificate No. 132 to Thomas Heath for 2,000 shares of $10.00 stated-value common stock, $20,000.00. M262.

Oct. 12. A subscription was received from Anne Fowler for 1,000 shares of $100.00 par-value preferred stock, $100,000.00. M289.

Nov. 1. Northwest's board of directors declared an annual dividend of $450,000.00. Date of payment is January 15, 19X3. M292.

19X3

Jan. 15. Paid annual dividend declared November 1, $450,000.00. C1654.

May 12. Cash was received from Anne Fowler in full payment for 1,000 shares of $100.00 par-value preferred stock, $100,000.00. R312.

May 12. Stock Certificate No. 87 was issued to Anne Fowler for 1,000 shares of $100.00 par-value preferred stock, $100,000.00 M324.

Nov. 1. Northwest's board of directors declared an annual dividend of $450,000.00. Date of payment is January 15, 19X4. M364.

343

CHAPTER 13 OVERVIEW

This chapter focuses on acquiring additional capital for a corporation using the sale of stocks and bonds. Transactions for issuing preferred stock at par value and above and below par value are illustrated. Common stock transactions at various values are also presented. Treasury stock transactions and their effect on outstanding stock are analyzed. Transactions for bond issues are covered in the second part of the

GUIDE TO ACHIEVING LEARNING OBJECTIVES

	TEACH	APPLY	EXTEND/ENRICH					
Enabling Performance Tasks	**Lesson Plans**	**Application Problems**	**Mastery Problems**	**Challenge Problems**	**Cases for Critical Thinking**	**Recycling Problems**	**Reinforcement Activity**	
a. Define accounting terms related to acquiring capital for a corporation.	13-1, 13-2, 13-3							
b. Identify accounting concepts and practices related to acquiring capital for a corporation.	13-1, 13-2, 13-3				Cases 1, 2			
c. Journalize entries for issuing additional capital stock.	13-1	13-1	13-M	13-C		13-R	RA2	
d. Journalize entries for buying and selling treasury stock.	13-2	13-2	13-M	13-C		13-R	RA2	
e. Journalize entries for bonds payable.	13-3	13-3	13-M	13-C		13-R	RA2	

ENRICHMENT

SPECIAL FEATURES
Professional Business Ethics, page 352

NEW, REVIEW, AND EXTENSION

ACTIVITIES/CONCEPTS/TRANSACTIONS	NEW	REVIEW/ EXTENSION
Issuing preferred stock at par value		✓
Issuing preferred stock for more or less than par value	✓	
Issuing preferred stock for assets other than cash	✓	
Issuing common stock with no par value	✓	
Issuing common stock at stated value	✓	
Issuing common stock for more than stated value	✓	
Buying treasury stock	✓	
Selling treasury stock for original cost	✓	
Selling treasury stock for more or less than original cost	✓	
Issuing bonds	✓	
Paying interest on bonds	✓	
Recording deposit and interest earned on bond sinking fund	✓	
Retiring a bond issue	✓	

chapter, including the use of regular deposits to a bond sinking fund for retiring the bond issue. The chapter concludes by comparing the advantages and disadvantages of using stocks versus bonds for acquiring additional capital.

	INFORMAL ASSESSMENT		FORMAL ASSESSMENT			
	Study Guide	**Audit Your Understanding**	**Chapter MicroExam**	**Chapter Problem Test**	**Unit Objective Test**	**Portfolio**
	Unit B	✓	✓		✓	
	Units A, C	✓	✓		✓	
				✓		✓
				✓		✓
				✓		✓

TEACHING MATERIALS

- Teacher's Wraparound Edition of the Text
- Teacher's Resource Guide
- Teacher's Edition of Working Papers
- MicroExam

APPLIED MATHEMATICS

APPLIED MATH/ACCOUNTING SKILL	APPLICATION
Calculating paid-in capital in excess of par/stated value	Prob. 13-1
Calculating discount on capital stock	Prob. 13-1
Calculating paid-in capital from sale of treasury stock	Prob. 13-2
Calculating interest on bonds	Prob. 13-C
Calculating bond sinking fund deposits	Prob. 13-C

TEACHING STRATEGIES: ACCOUNTING PEDAGOGY

This textbook continues discussion on corporations and maintaining their financial status. Corporations need to continue to acquire capital as the company grows. It is important to understand that corporations do not stay stagnant.

13

Acquiring Additional Capital for a Corporation

ENABLING PERFORMANCE TASKS

After studying Chapter 13, you will be able to:

- **a** Define accounting terms related to acquiring capital for a corporation.
- **b** Identify accounting concepts and practices related to acquiring capital for a corporation.
- **c** Journalize entries for issuing additional capital stock.
- **d** Journalize entries for buying and selling treasury stock.
- **e** Journalize entries for bonds payable.

TERMS PREVIEW

discount on capital stock • treasury stock • bond • bond issue • trustee • bond sinking fund • retiring a bond issue • term bonds • serial bonds

APPLIED SKILLS: WORD PROCESSING

If you wish to integrate word processing in your accounting course, you may direct students to answer the end-of-chapter Accounting Terms, Questions for Individual Study, and Cases for Critical Thinking using their word processing software.

As a corporation grows, additional capital may be required to finance its expansion. The portion of a corporation's net income not paid to stockholders as dividends is a primary source of additional capital. Retained earnings may not, however, provide an adequate source of capital for a corporation. Both new and existing corporations may require a large increase in capital to finance rapid expansion. Thus, a corporation can acquire additional capital by selling stock to investors or borrowing money.

CAPITAL STOCK

Articles of incorporation are usually written to permit a corporation to issue more shares of stock than it sold to initial investors. As the need arises for more capital, a corporation can issue some of the remaining authorized stock. LampLight is authorized by its charter to issue a total of 100,000 shares of common stock and 50,000 shares of preferred stock. *(CONCEPT: Business Entity)* However, LampLight initially issued only 32,000 shares of common stock during its first year as described in Chapter 12. Thus, LampLight may sell some of the remaining shares of common or some shares of preferred stock to raise additional capital.

Issuing Preferred Stock at Par Value

FYI

Par value is not directly related to market value.

LampLight decided to issue preferred stock to raise additional capital. Brenda Henson paid par value, $100.00, for 800 shares of preferred stock. The amounts to be recorded are calculated as shown below.

No. of Shares	×	Par Value per Share	=	Total Par Value
800	×	$100.00	=	$80,000.00

Cash	
80,000.00	

Capital Stock—Preferred	
	80,000.00

March 1, 19--. Received cash from Brenda Henson for 800 shares of $100.00 par-value preferred stock at $100.00 per share, $80,000.00. Receipt No. 117.

Cash is debited for $80,000.00. Capital Stock—Preferred is credited for $80,000.00, the total par value of the issued preferred stock.

The journal entry to record this transaction is shown in Illustration 13-1 on page 346.

A stock certificate is issued to Ms. Henson.

Issuing Preferred Stock for More Than Par Value

Sometimes preferred stock is issued for more than its par value. LampLight sold 300 shares of preferred stock at $120.00 per share

LESSON PLAN 13-1

Materials

- Student pages 345–350
- Blackline Master for General Journal (TRG)
- Blackline Master for Cash Receipts Journal (TRG)

Objectives (Enabling Performance Tasks)

a. Define accounting terms related to acquiring capital for a corporation.

b. Identify accounting concepts and practices related to acquiring capital for a corporation.

c. Journalize entries for issuing additional capital stock.

FOCUS

- Issuing capital stock to the initial investors in a newly formed corporation was presented in Chapter 12. Explain that after a corporation is in operation, investors most often purchase stock from a shareholder that currently owns stock in the corporation. Remind students that the corporation receives no money from this stock transfer; therefore, no journal entry is recorded by the corporation. Explain that only when the corporation decides to issue additional stock, can an investor purchase stock from the corporation. The entries to issue additional stock to acquire capital will be presented in this lesson.
- Introduce vocabulary: discount on capital stock.

TEACHING STRATEGIES: TEACHING TIP

Use the overhead projector or chalkboard to show the formulas and demonstrate how to calculate the amounts to be recorded for the capital stock, treasury stock, and bonds payable transactions.

TEACH

Cover student pages 345–350 "Capital Stock." Explain that a corporation may need to sell stock to raise additional capital for expansion. Emphasize that a corporation's articles of incorporation usually permit the corporation to issue more shares of stock than sold to initial investors. Present the transactions for issuing preferred stock at par value, for more than par value, and for less than par value. Stress that the credit to Capital Stock is always equal to the number of shares issued multiplied by the par value per share. Discuss the transaction for issuing preferred stock for assets other than cash. Point out that this entry is similar to the entry for issuing stock for cash, only the asset account changes. Describe the transactions for issuing common stock with no par value and for more than stated value. Review the transaction for issuing common stock at stated value that was presented in Chapter 12, Illustration 12-2.

ILLUSTRATION 13-1 Journal entry to record issuing preferred stock at par value

CASH RECEIPTS JOURNAL — PAGE 5

	DATE		ACCOUNT TITLE	DOC. NO.	POST. REF.	1 GENERAL DEBIT	2 GENERAL CREDIT	3 ACCOUNTS RECEIVABLE CREDIT	4 SALES CREDIT	5 SALES TAX PAYABLE DEBIT	6 SALES TAX PAYABLE CREDIT	7 SALES DISCOUNT DEBIT	8 CASH DEBIT	
1	19-- Mar.	1	Capital Stock—Preferred	R117			80 000 00						80 000 00	1
2														2
3														3
4														4

to Adam Kellogg. The amounts to be recorded for the 300 shares of preferred stock are calculated as shown below.

	No. of Shares	×	Value per Share	=	Value
Total received	300	×	$120.00	=	$36,000.00
Par value	300	×	100.00	=	30,000.00
Amount received in excess of par value					$ 6,000.00

April 6, 19--. Received cash from Adam Kellogg for 300 shares of $100.00 par-value preferred stock at $120.00 per share, $36,000.00. Receipt No. 127.

Cash			
Apr. 6	36,000.00		

Capital Stock—Preferred			
		Balance	80,000.00
		Apr. 6	30,000.00
		(New Bal.	*110,000.00)*

Paid-in Capital in Excess of Par Value—Preferred			
		Apr. 6	6,000.00

Cash is debited for $36,000.00, the total amount received. Capital Stock—Preferred is credited for $30,000.00, the total par value of the preferred stock issued. Paid-in Capital in Excess of Par Value—Preferred is credited for $6,000.00, the amount received in excess of the par value.

The journal entry to record this transaction is shown in Illustration 13-2.

ILLUSTRATION 13-2 Journal entry to record issuing preferred stock for more than par value

CASH RECEIPTS JOURNAL — PAGE 7

	DATE		ACCOUNT TITLE	DOC. NO.	POST. REF.	1 GENERAL DEBIT	2 GENERAL CREDIT	3 ACCOUNTS RECEIVABLE CREDIT	4 SALES CREDIT	5 SALES TAX PAYABLE DEBIT	6 SALES TAX PAYABLE CREDIT	7 SALES DISCOUNT DEBIT	8 CASH DEBIT	
1	19-- Apr.	6	Capital Stock—Preferred	R127			30 000 00						36 000 00	1
2			Paid-in Capital in Excess of											2
3			Par Value—Preferred				6 000 00							3
4														4
5														5
6														6
7														7

FYI

The credit to the preferred stock account always equals the par value of the stock issued.

Regardless of the amount received, the credit to the capital stock account always equals the par or stated value of the stock issued.

Issuing Preferred Stock for Less Than Par Value

An amount less than par or stated value at which capital stock is sold is called a **discount on capital stock.** The legal treatment of discounts on capital stock varies from state to state. In some states, a stockholder may be liable for the amount of discount on par-value stock if a corporation is unable to pay creditors. In other states, a stockholder is not liable for the amount of the discount.

LampLight sold 500 shares of $100.00 par-value preferred stock to Hazel Deloach at a price of $90.00 per share. The amounts to be recorded are calculated as shown below.

	No. of Shares	×	Value per Share	=	Value
Par value	500	×	$100.00	=	$50,000.00
Total received	500	×	90.00	=	45,000.00
Total discount					$ 5,000.00

Cash

Debit		Credit	
Aug. 9	45,000.00		

Discount on Sale of Preferred Stock

Debit		Credit	
Aug. 9	5,000.00		

Capital Stock—Preferred

Debit		Credit	
		Balance	110,000.00
		Aug. 9	50,000.00
		(New Bal.	*160,000.00)*

August 9, 19--. Received cash from Hazel Deloach for 500 shares of $100.00 par-value preferred stock at $90.00 per share, $45,000.00. Receipt No. 173.

Cash is debited for $45,000.00, the amount of cash received for the 500 shares of preferred stock. Discount on Sale of Preferred Stock is debited for $5,000.00, the discount amount. Capital Stock—Preferred is credited for $50,000.00, the par value of the 500 shares of preferred stock.

The journal entry to record this transaction is shown in Illustration 13-3.

ILLUSTRATION 13-3 Journal entry to record issuing preferred stock for less than par value

CASH RECEIPTS JOURNAL — PAGE 15

	DATE		ACCOUNT TITLE	DOC. NO.	POST. REF.	1 GENERAL DEBIT	2 GENERAL CREDIT	3 ACCOUNTS RECEIVABLE CREDIT	4 SALES CREDIT	5 SALES TAX PAYABLE DEBIT	6 SALES TAX PAYABLE CREDIT	7 SALES DISCOUNT DEBIT	8 CASH DEBIT	
8	19-- Aug.	9	Discount on Sale of											8
9			Preferred Stock	R173		5 000 00							45 000 00	9
10			Capital Stock—Preferred				50 000 00							10
11														11

APPLY

Draw T accounts on the chalkboard or overhead to analyze each transaction as it is presented in this lesson. Refer students to Illustrations 13-1, 13-2, 13-3, 13-4, 13-5, and 13-6, respectively, as each transaction related to issuing additional capital stock is discussed.

Guided Practice

Guide students through the T account analysis of the capital stock transactions in Problem 13-1. Have students draw T accounts on a sheet of paper and analyze the first transaction. All students should agree with the analysis before proceeding to the next transaction. Repeat the process until all transactions have been analyzed. The balance of Problem 13-1 can be completed as Independent Practice.

Independent Practice

Assign Term 1, Questions 1–6, and Problem 13-1.

TEACHING STRATEGIES: TEACHING TIP

Although students have not been studying accounts for proprietorships and partnerships, understanding can be helped by building on the knowledge they already have from previous accounting study. Use T accounts to show (a) investment of capital in each form of business (investment by owners in proprietorships and partnerships, selling stock for corporations) and (b) withdrawals by owners (drawing accounts for proprietorships and partnerships, dividends for corporations).

ASSESS

Assess student understanding by checking the solutions to the Independent Practice activities.

Reteach

Make transparencies of the cash receipts and general journals from the accounting forms masters provided in the Blackline Masters Section of the Teacher's Resource Guide. Refer students to Recycling Problem 13-R. Ask students to use T accounts to analyze the January 8, February 27, March 13, April 21, and July 12, 19X1, capital stock transactions. Use the transparencies to demonstrate how the transactions are journalized.

Extend

Assign Cases for Critical Thinking 1.

CLOSURE

Use Audit Your Understanding questions.

Issuing Preferred Stock for Assets Other Than Cash

Occasionally corporations issue capital stock in exchange for assets other than cash. When other assets are used to pay for capital stock, the investor and corporation must agree upon the value of the assets and the capital stock.

FYI

In 1990 the New York Stock Exchange processed the exchange of over 39 billion shares of stock.

LampLight issued 100 shares of preferred stock to Steven McBee in exchange for office equipment. The office equipment was accepted in full payment of the 100 shares of preferred stock. The agreed upon total value of the equipment is $12,000.00. Therefore, the equipment fully pays for the 100 shares of preferred stock.

Office Equipment

Debit		Credit	
Oct. 7	12,000.00		

Capital Stock—Preferred

Debit		Credit	
		Balance	160,000.00
		Oct. 7	10,000.00
		(New Bal.	*170,000.00)*

Paid-in Capital in Excess of Par Value—Preferred

Debit		Credit	
		Balance	6,000.00
		Oct. 7	2,000.00
		(New Bal.	*8,000.00)*

October 7, 19--. Received office equipment from Steven McBee at an agreed value of $12,000.00 for 100 shares of $100.00 par-value preferred stock. Memorandum No. 246.

Office Equipment is debited for $12,000.00. Capital Stock—Preferred is credited for $10,000.00, the total par value of the preferred stock issued. Paid-in Capital in Excess of Par Value—Preferred is credited for $2,000.00, the amount received in excess of the par value.

The journal entry to record this transaction is shown in Illustration 13-4.

ILLUSTRATION 13-4 Journal entry to record issuing preferred stock for assets other than cash

GENERAL JOURNAL PAGE *10*

	DATE		ACCOUNT TITLE	DOC. NO.	POST. REF.	DEBIT	CREDIT	
1	19-- Oct.	7	Office Equipment	M246		12 000 00		1
2			Capital Stock—Preferred				10 000 00	2
3			Paid-in Capital in Excess of					3
4			Par Value—Preferred				2 000 00	4
5								5

Issuing Common Stock with No Par Value

Common stock often has no par value assigned to it or printed on the stock certificates. With no-par-value stock, the entire amount paid by an investor is recorded in the capital stock account. Wheeler, Inc. sells no-par-value common stock.

July 8, 19--. Received cash from Elizabeth Griffin for 1,000 shares of no-par-value common stock at $14.00 per share, $14,000.00. Receipt No. 148.

APPLIED SKILLS: WRITING ACROSS THE CURRICULUM

Writing paragraphs and short essays. The Cases for Critical Thinking are short, practical applications of the accounting principles developed in the chapter. Some cases are planned to present problems related to the chapter but not specifically discussed and answered in the chapter. These cases present an opportunity for critical thinking and decision making. These cases also require more than a short objective-type response. Therefore, they provide ideal practice in writing paragraphs and short essays.

Cash	
14,000.00	

Capital Stock—Common	
	14,000.00

Cash is debited for $14,000.00, the total amount received. Capital Stock—Common is credited for $14,000.00, the total amount received for the 1,000 shares of stock.

The journal entry to record this transaction is shown in Illustration 13-5.

ILLUSTRATION 13-5 Journal entry to record issuing no-par-value common stock

CASH RECEIPTS JOURNAL — PAGE 13

	Date		Account Title	Doc. No.	Post. Ref.	1 General Debit	2 General Credit	3 Accounts Receivable Credit	4 Sales Credit	5 Sales Tax Payable Debit	6 Sales Tax Payable Credit	7 Sales Discount Debit	8 Cash Debit	
12	19-- July	8	Capital Stock—Common	R148			14 000 00						14 000 00	12
13														13
14														14
15														15
16														16
17														17
18														18
19														19

Audit Your Understanding

1. What accounts are affected, and how, when LampLight receives cash for preferred stock sold at par value?
2. What accounts are affected, and how, when LampLight receives cash for preferred stock sold for less than par value?

Issuing Common Stock at Stated Value

Some corporations assign a value to no-par-value common stock for purposes of recording its value. LampLight's common stock is no-par-value stock. However, LampLight has assigned a stated value of $10.00 to its common stock. No-par-value common stock with a stated value is recorded using the same procedures as par-value preferred stock. An entry for issuing common stock at stated value is shown in Illustration 12-2, Chapter 12.

Issuing Common Stock for More Than Stated Value

LampLight sold 100 shares of common stock to Alice Blake for $12.00 a share. The amounts to be recorded are calculated as shown below.

	No. of Shares	×	Value per Share	=	Value
Total received	100	×	$12.00	=	$1,200.00
Stated value	100	×	10.00	=	1,000.00
Amount received in excess of stated value					$ 200.00

AUDIT YOUR UNDERSTANDING

The AUDIT YOUR UNDERSTANDING feature appears at the end of each section of the chapter. Explain to your students that the word *audit* means to check or verify. AUDIT YOUR UNDERSTANDING may be used to check student comprehension of the section just studied. The answers are provided in Appendix D in the back of the textbook.

1. Cash is debited; Capital Stock—Preferred is credited.
2. Cash and Discount on Sale of Preferred Stock are debited; Capital Stock—Preferred is credited.

APPLIED SKILLS: BUILDING STUDY SKILLS

Instruct students to prepare Quick Reference Guides (QRG) for capital stock, treasury stock, and corporate bonds payable transactions. (1) Label a QRG CAPITAL STOCK. Copy the capital stock transactions out of the chapter narrative. Draw the T accounts that analyze the transactions. (2) Label a QRG TREASURY STOCK. Copy the treasury stock transactions out of the chapter. Draw the T accounts that analyze each transaction. (3) Label a QRG CORPORATE BONDS PAYABLE. Copy the bonds payable transactions out of the chapter. Draw the T accounts that analyze each transaction. These QRGs can be used when students are completing end-of-chapter activities.

Cash	
Oct. 10 1,200.00	

Capital Stock—Common	
	Balance 320,000.00
	Oct. 10 1,000.00
	(New Bal. 321,000.00)

Paid-in Capital in Excess of Stated Value—Common	
	Oct. 10 200.00

October 10, 19--. Received cash from Alice Blake for 100 shares of $10.00 stated-value common stock at $12.00 per share, $1,200.00. Receipt No. 181.

Cash is debited for $1,200.00, the total amount received. Capital Stock—Common is credited for $1,000.00, the total stated value of the 100 shares. Paid-in Capital in Excess of Stated Value—Common is credited for $200.00, the amount received in excess of the stated value.

The journal entry to record this transaction is shown in Illustration 13-6.

ILLUSTRATION 13-6 Journal entry to record issuing common stock for more than stated value

CASH RECEIPTS JOURNAL — PAGE 19

	DATE		ACCOUNT TITLE	DOC. NO.	POST. REF.	1 GENERAL DEBIT	2 GENERAL CREDIT	3 ACCOUNTS RECEIVABLE CREDIT	4 SALES CREDIT	5 SALES TAX PAYABLE DEBIT	6 SALES TAX PAYABLE CREDIT	7 SALES DISCOUNT DEBIT	8 CASH DEBIT	
1	19-- Oct.	10	Capital Stock—Common	R181			1 000 00						1 200 00	1
2			Paid-in Capital in Excess of											2
3			Stated Value—Common				200 00							3
4														4
5														5
6														6
7														7
8														8
9														9
10														10
11														11

LESSON PLAN 13-2

Materials

- Student pages 350–354
- Blackline Master for Cash Payments Journal (TRG)
- Blackline Master for Cash Receipts Journal (TRG)
- 3-Step Checklist for Making Ethical Decisions (TRG)

Objectives

a. Define accounting terms related to acquiring capital for a corporation.

b. Identify accounting concepts and practices related to acquiring capital for a corporation.

d. Journalize entries for buying and selling treasury stock.

TREASURY STOCK

A corporation's own stock that has been issued and reacquired is called **treasury stock.** When a corporation buys treasury stock, the number of shares outstanding is reduced. However, treasury stock is still considered to be issued stock. A corporation usually intends to use the treasury stock for a specific purpose. For example, a corporation may acquire treasury stock to be given to employees as bonus payments.

Treasury stock is not an asset of a corporation. Since treasury stock is not owned by a stockholder, the stock does not have voting rights. Dividends are not paid for the stock as long as the treasury stock is held by the issuing corporation. Once treasury stock is given or sold to a stockholder, it ceases to be treasury stock and is again capital stock outstanding.

FYI

The credit to the common stock account for stated-value stock always equals the stated value of the stock issued.

TEACHING STRATEGIES: COOPERATIVE LEARNING

Divide the class into groups of four or five students each. Have students brainstorm why a corporation would need (or want) to buy back shares of stock it had previously issued. One member of each group is appointed the recorder and writes the group's list on the board. This cooperative learning activity should not take more than 10 to 15 minutes of class time.

FYI

A corporation may acquire treasury stock to regain control of a corporation or to have additional stock to use for other purposes such as stock dividends.

Buying Treasury Stock

A corporation records treasury stock at the price paid regardless of the stock's par or stated value. *(CONCEPT: Historical Cost)*

October 24, 19--. Paid cash to Francis Burns for 500 shares of $10.00 stated-value common stock at $12.00 per share, $6,000.00. Check No. 502.

Treasury Stock	
6,000.00	

Cash	
	6,000.00

Treasury Stock is debited for $6,000.00, the amount paid for the 500 shares of treasury stock. Cash is credited for $6,000.00.

Capital stock accounts have normal credit balances. Treasury Stock is a contra capital stock account and, therefore, has a normal debit balance.

The journal entry to record this transaction is shown in Illustration 13-7.

ILLUSTRATION 13-7 Journal entry to record buying treasury stock

CASH PAYMENTS JOURNAL — PAGE 20

	DATE		ACCOUNT TITLE	CK. NO.	POST. REF.	1 GENERAL DEBIT	2 GENERAL CREDIT	3 ACCOUNTS PAYABLE DEBIT	4 PURCHASES DISCOUNT CREDIT	5 CASH CREDIT	
1	19-- Oct.	24	Treasury Stock	502		6 000 00				6 000 00	1
2											2
3											3
4											4
5											5
6											6
7											7
8											8
9											9
10											10

Selling Treasury Stock for Original Cost

LampLight sold some of its treasury stock at the $12.00 original cost.

Cash		
	1,200.00	

Treasury Stock		
Balance	6,000.00	1,200.00
(New Bal.	*4,800.00)*	

November 21, 19--. Received cash from Lisa Vance for 100 shares of treasury stock at $12.00 per share, $1,200.00. Treasury stock was bought on October 24 at $12.00 per share. Receipt No. 205.

Cash is debited for $1,200.00. Treasury Stock is credited for $1,200.00.

The journal entry to record this transaction is shown in Illustration 13-8.

FOCUS

- Issuing stock to acquire additional capital was presented earlier in this chapter. Explain that occasionally a corporation buys back some of its own stock. The entries to buy and sell this stock will be journalized in this lesson.
- Introduce vocabulary: treasury stock.

TEACH

Cover student pages 350–354 "Treasury Stock." Stress the difference between treasury stock and stock that has never been issued. Emphasize that treasury stock is not an asset of the corporation, does not have voting rights, and does not receive dividends as long as it is held by the corporation. Present the entries to buy and sell treasury stock. Emphasize that the Capital Stock account is NOT affected when treasury stock is bought or sold. The balance of the Capital Stock account is ALWAYS equal to the number of shares issued times the par value of the stock.

Professional Business Ethics

The PROFESSIONAL BUSINESS ETHICS feature stimulates critical thinking and decision making. It may be used in many ways such as an individual assignment, a class discussion, or a small group cooperative learning project. When these ethics cases are discussed in class, students can also gain a sense of individual diversity as students demonstrate individual opinions. If you wish to integrate word processing in your accounting course, you may direct students to word process their answers. If you wish to include the creation of tables, you might direct students to format their responses to resemble the ethical decision-making grid in a 3-column table. A blackline master of the 3-Step Checklist for Making Ethical Decisions is furnished in the Teacher's Resource Guide. Suggested solutions for the Professional Business Ethics feature are provided in the front of this teacher's edition.

APPLY

Draw T accounts on the chalkboard or overhead to analyze each transaction as it is presented in this lesson. Refer students to Illustrations 13-7, 13-8, 13-9, and 13-10, respectively, as the transactions related to buying and selling treasury stock are presented.

Guided Practice

Guide students through the T account analysis of the transactions for buying and selling treasury stock in Problem 13-2. Have students draw T accounts on a sheet of paper and analyze the first transaction. All students should agree with the analysis before proceeding to the next transaction. Repeat the process until all transactions have been analyzed. The balance of Problem 13-2 can be completed as Independent Practice.

Independent Practice

Assign Term 2, Questions 7–10, and Problem 13-2.

PROFESSIONAL BUSINESS ETHICS

Ups and Downs of CEO Compensation

A popular way to pay a chief executive officer (CEO) is for a corporation to give the CEO the right to purchase stock at a specified price. The right to purchase stock from a corporation at a specified price is called a **stock option.** The option price is typically set higher than the current market price. If the stock price increases above the option price, the option enables the individual to purchase the stock at less than the market price. If the stock's market price never exceeds the option price, the option is worthless.

Three years ago the board of directors of Teletron Industries gave its new CEO a $90,000 annual salary and 200,000 stock options at $25. The

ILLUSTRATION 13-8 Journal entry to record selling treasury stock for original cost

CASH RECEIPTS JOURNAL — PAGE 22

	DATE		ACCOUNT TITLE	DOC. NO.	POST. REF.	1 GENERAL DEBIT	2 GENERAL CREDIT	3 ACCOUNTS RECEIVABLE CREDIT	4 SALES CREDIT	5 SALES TAX PAYABLE DEBIT	6 SALES TAX PAYABLE CREDIT	7 SALES DISCOUNT DEBIT	8 CASH DEBIT	
1	19-- Nov.	21	Treasury Stock	R205			1 200 00						1 200 00	1
2														2
3														3

Selling Treasury Stock for More Than Original Cost

LampLight sold 200 shares of treasury stock to Mary Long for $15.00 per share. The amounts to be recorded are calculated as shown below.

	No. of Shares	×	Value per Share	=	Value
Total received	200	×	$15.00	=	$3,000.00
Original cost	200	×	12.00	=	2,400.00
Amount received in excess of original cost					$ 600.00

November 25, 19--. Received cash from Mary Long for 200 shares of treasury stock at $15.00 per share, $3,000.00. Treasury stock was bought on October 24 at $12.00 per share. Receipt No. 216.

Cash

Debit	Credit
3,000.00	

Treasury Stock

Debit	Credit
Balance 4,800.00	2,400.00
(New Bal. 2,400.00)	

Paid-in Capital from Sale of Treasury Stock

Debit	Credit
	600.00

Cash is debited for $3,000.00, the total amount received from the sale of the treasury stock. Treasury Stock is credited for $2,400.00, the original cost of the 200 shares of treasury stock. Paid-in Capital from Sale of Treasury Stock is credited for $600.00, the amount received in excess of the treasury stock's original cost.

stock was selling for $12 at the time. The stock options gave the CEO an incentive to increase the profitability of the corporation and, therefore, increase the stock's market price.

The new CEO successfully improved the corporation's profitability. As a result, the stock is currently selling for $40. When the CEO exercised stock options, 200,000 shares were purchased by the CEO from Teletron for $25 per share at a total of $5,000,000. The CEO immediately sold the stock on the stock exchange for $40 a share at a total of $8,000,000, earning a profit of $3,000,000.

INSTRUCTIONS Use the three-step checklist to analyze whether the use of stock options as executive salary demonstrates ethical behavior.

The journal entry to record this transaction is shown in Illustration 13-9.

ILLUSTRATION 13-9 Journal entry to record selling treasury stock for more than original cost

CASH RECEIPTS JOURNAL — PAGE 22

	DATE		ACCOUNT TITLE	DOC. NO.	POST. REF.	1 GENERAL DEBIT	2 GENERAL CREDIT	3 ACCOUNTS RECEIVABLE CREDIT	4 SALES CREDIT	5 SALES TAX PAYABLE DEBIT	6 SALES TAX PAYABLE CREDIT	7 SALES DISCOUNT DEBIT	8 CASH DEBIT	
8		25	*Treasury Stock*	*R216*			*2 400 00*						*3 000 00*	8
9			*Paid-in Capital from Sale of*											9
10			*Treasury Stock*				*600 00*							10
11														11
12														12
13														13
14														14

FYI

Treasury stock is considered to be issued stock but not outstanding stock. Therefore, dividends are not paid on treasury stock.

Selling Treasury Stock for Less Than Original Cost

LampLight sold 50 shares of treasury stock to Frank Demetz for $10.00 per share. The amounts to be recorded are calculated as shown below.

	No. of Shares	×	Value per Share	=	Value
Original cost	50	×	$12.00	=	$600.00
Total received	50	×	10.00	=	500.00
Amount received less than original cost					$100.00

ASSESS

Assess student understanding by checking the solutions to the Independent Practice activities.

Reteach

Make transparencies of the cash payments and cash receipts journals from the accounting forms masters provided in the Blackline Masters Section of the Teacher's Resource Guide. Refer students to Recycling Problem 13-R. Ask students to use T accounts to analyze the February 15, March 22, April 15, and July 30, 19X1, treasury stock transactions. Use the transparencies to demonstrate how the transactions are journalized.

Extend

In groups, have students brainstorm why a corporation would need (or want) to buy back shares of stock it had previously issued. Have each group write its list on the board.

Enrich

Discuss the PROFESSIONAL BUSINESS ETHICS feature on page 352. You may wish to distribute copies of the 3-Step Checklist for Making Ethical Decisions. A blackline master is furnished in the Blackline Masters Section of the Teacher's Resource Guide.

CLOSURE

Use Audit Your Understanding questions.

Cash	
500.00	

Paid-in Capital from Sale of Treasury Stock		
100.00	Balance	600.00
	(New Bal.	*500.00)*

Treasury Stock		
Balance	2,400.00	600.00
(New Bal.	*1,800.00)*	

December 22, 19--. Received cash from Frank Demetz for 50 shares of treasury stock at $10.00 per share, $500.00. Treasury stock was bought October 24 at $12.00 per share. Receipt No. 229.

Cash is debited for $500.00, the total amount of cash received. Paid-in Capital from Sale of Treasury Stock is debited for $100.00, the amount received less than the treasury stock's original cost. Treasury Stock is credited for $600.00, the original cost.

The journal entry to record this transaction is shown in Illustration 13-10.

ILLUSTRATION 13-10 Journal entry to record selling treasury stock for less than original cost

CASH RECEIPTS JOURNAL PAGE *24*

	DATE	ACCOUNT TITLE	DOC. NO.	POST. REF.	1 GENERAL DEBIT	2 GENERAL CREDIT	3 ACCOUNTS RECEIVABLE CREDIT	4 SALES CREDIT	5 SALES TAX PAYABLE DEBIT	6 SALES TAX PAYABLE CREDIT	7 SALES DISCOUNT DEBIT	8 CASH DEBIT	
10	22	*Paid-in Capital from*											10
11		*Sale of Treasury Stock*	*R229*		*100 00*							*500 00*	11
12		*Treasury Stock*				*600 00*							12
13													13
14													14

AUDIT YOUR UNDERSTANDING

1. Treasury Stock is debited; Cash is credited.
2. Cash is debited; Treasury Stock and Paid-in Capital from Sale of Treasury Stock are credited.

Audit Your Understanding

1. What accounts are affected, and how, when a corporation buys its own stock?
2. What accounts are affected, and how, when treasury stock is sold for more than its original cost?

When treasury stock transactions occur, no entry is made in Capital Stock—Common or Capital Stock—Preferred. Treasury stock is considered to be issued stock. The difference between the balances of the capital stock accounts and the treasury stock account is the value of outstanding stock. After the entry on December 22 to sell treasury stock, the number of LampLight's outstanding shares of capital stock is calculated as shown below.

	No. of Shares Issued	–	No. of Shares of Treasury Stock	=	No. of Shares Outstanding
Preferred	1,700	–	0	=	1,700
Common	32,100	–	150	=	31,950

CORPORATE BONDS PAYABLE

A business' management may find that needed capital for expansion could be obtained from retained net income during the next five to ten years. However, the business may need the additional

LESSON PLAN 13-3

Materials

- Student pages 354–359
- Blackline Master for Cash Receipts Journal (TRG)
- Blackline Master for Cash Payments Journal (TRG)
- Blackline Master for General Journal (TRG)
- Assess: Problem Test Chapter 13, MicroExam Chapter 13

Objectives (Enabling Performance Tasks)

a. Define accounting terms related to acquiring capital for a corporation.

b. Identify accounting concepts and practices related to acquiring capital for a corporation.

e. Journalize entries for bonds payable.

capital immediately. A corporation's board of directors must decide whether to raise the needed capital by selling additional stock or borrowing the money.

An advantage of selling stock is that the additional capital becomes part of a corporation's permanent capital. Permanent capital does not have to be returned to stockholders in the near future. Another advantage is that dividends do not have to be paid to stockholders unless the earnings are sufficient to warrant such payments. A disadvantage of selling more stock to raise additional capital is that the ownership is spread over more shares and more owners.

An advantage of borrowing the additional capital is that stockholders' equity is not spread over additional shares of stock. A disadvantage is that interest must be paid on the loan which decreases the net income. This decrease in net income may also decrease the amount available for dividends. Another disadvantage of borrowing additional capital is that the amount must be repaid in the future.

Large loans are sometimes difficult to obtain for short periods of time or from one bank or one individual. Therefore, corporations frequently borrow the needed capital with the provision that the loan is due several years in the future. The loan can be paid out of future earnings accumulated over several years.

A printed, long-term promise to pay a specified amount on a specified date, and to pay interest at stated intervals is called a **bond.** Bonds are similar to notes payable because both are written promises to pay. However, most notes payable are for one year or less while bonds generally run for a long period of time, such as 5, 10, or 20 years.

All the bonds representing the total amount of a loan are called a **bond issue.** A corporation usually sells an entire bond issue to a securities dealer who sells individual bonds to the public.

FYI

A limited liability company (LLC) provides the flexibility of a partnership by allowing earnings to flow through to its partners as personal income. This feature eliminates the double-taxation feature of a corporation.

Issuing Bonds

On July 1, LampLight borrowed $250,000.00 to expand its building. LampLight issued 250, 12%, $1,000.00 par-value bonds. The bonds are scheduled to mature in 5 years. Annual interest on the bonds is to be paid on July 1 of each year. The bond issue was sold at par value to a securities dealer.

July 1, 19--. Received cash for the face value of a 5-year, 12%, $1,000.00 par-value bond issue, $250,000.00. Receipt No. 246.

Cash	
250,000.00	

Bonds Payable	
	250,000.00

Cash is debited for $250,000.00. Bonds Payable is credited for $250,000.00.

The journal entry to record this transaction is shown in Illustration 13-11.

FOCUS

- Issuing stock to acquire additional capital was presented earlier in this chapter. Explain that another way for corporations to raise additional capital is by borrowing the money. In this lesson, transactions related to borrowing money to raise additional capital will be journalized.
- Introduce vocabulary: bond, bond issue, trustee, bond sinking fund, retiring a bond issue, term bonds, serial bonds.

TEACH

Cover student pages 354–359 "Corporate Bonds Payable" and "Comparison of Capital Stock and Bonds as a Source of Corporate Capital." Discuss the advantages and disadvantages of either selling stock or borrowing the additional capital. Explain how to journalize the transaction to issue bonds. Present the transactions for paying interest on bonds. Review how to calculate interest. Discuss the purpose of a bond sinking fund and the transactions to record the annual deposits to the fund. Explain the transactions related to retiring a bond issue.

TEACHING STRATEGIES: TEACHING TIP

Instruct students to check the financial pages of a daily newspaper to determine the kind of stock and bond information available, such as the kind of stock (common and preferred) and the terms of corporate bonds. Have volunteers report their findings.

APPLY

Use T accounts on the chalkboard or overhead to analyze each transaction as it is presented in this lesson. Refer students to Illustrations 13-11, 13-12, 13-13, 13-14, and 13-15, respectively, as the entries related to bonds payable are discussed.

Guided Practice

Guide students through the T account analysis of the transactions for bonds payable in Problem 13-3. Have students draw T accounts on a sheet of paper and analyze the first transaction. All students should agree with the analysis before proceeding to the next transaction. Repeat the process until all transactions have been analyzed. The balance of Problem 13-3 can be completed as Independent Practice.

Independent Practice

- Assign Terms 3–9, Questions 11–18, and Problem 13-3.
- Assign Study Guide 13 and Mastery Problem 13-M.

ILLUSTRATION 13-11 Journal entry to record issuing bonds

CASH RECEIPTS JOURNAL — PAGE 13

	DATE		ACCOUNT TITLE	DOC. NO.	POST. REF.	1 GENERAL DEBIT	2 GENERAL CREDIT	3 ACCOUNTS RECEIVABLE CREDIT	4 SALES CREDIT	5 SALES TAX PAYABLE DEBIT	6 SALES TAX PAYABLE CREDIT	7 SALES DISCOUNT DEBIT	8 CASH DEBIT	
1	19-- July	1	Bonds Payable	R246			250 000 00						250 000 00	1
2														2

Paying Interest on Bonds

FYI

The Securities and Exchange Commission (SEC) receives quarterly, annual, and special reports from over 11,000 United States companies.

A year's interest is paid to each bondholder on July 1 of each year until the bond's maturity date. A person or institution, usually a bank, who is given legal authorization to administer property for the benefit of property owners is called a **trustee.** LampLight pays the interest amount to a bond trustee who in turn handles the details of paying each individual bondholder.

The annual interest on the bond issue is calculated as shown below.

Balance Owed on Bond Issue	×	Bond Interest Rate	=	Annual Interest
$250,000.00	×	12%	=	$30,000.00

Interest Expense

Debit	Credit
30,000.00	

Cash

Debit	Credit
	30,000.00

July 1, 19--. Paid cash to bond trustee for annual interest on bond issue, $30,000.00. Check No. 562.

Interest Expense is debited for $30,000.00. Cash is credited for $30,000.00.

The journal entry to record this transaction is shown in Illustration 13-12.

ILLUSTRATION 13-12 Journal entry to record paying interest on bonds

CASH PAYMENTS JOURNAL — PAGE 13

	DATE		ACCOUNT TITLE	CK. NO.	POST. REF.	1 GENERAL DEBIT	2 GENERAL CREDIT	3 ACCOUNTS PAYABLE DEBIT	4 PURCHASES DISCOUNT CREDIT	5 CASH CREDIT	
1	19-- July	1	Interest Expense	562		30 000 00				30 000 00	1
2											2

Depositing Cash in a Bond Sinking Fund

Bondholders want assurance that a bond issue will be paid at maturity. Therefore, LampLight annually deposits a portion of the loan

FYI

If a bond is issued for *more* than its face value, it is said to be sold at a "premium." Cash is debited and Bonds Payable and Premium on Bonds Payable are credited.

value with the bond trustee. An amount set aside to pay a bond issue when due is called a **bond sinking fund.** Instead of paying $250,000.00 from a single year's earnings, LampLight spreads the amount over the five years that the bond issue is outstanding. The bond sinking fund is increased each year by $50,000.00, an amount equal to one-fifth of the total principal. On the bond issue's maturity date, a total of $250,000.00 will be available in the bond sinking fund to pay the bondholders.

Bond Sinking Fund	
50,000.00	

Cash	
	50,000.00

July 1, 19--. Paid cash to bond trustee for annual deposit to bond sinking fund, $50,000.00. Check No. 563.

Bond Sinking Fund is debited for $50,000.00. Cash is credited for $50,000.00.

The journal entry to record this transaction is shown in Illustration 13-13.

ILLUSTRATION 13-13 Journal entry to record depositing cash in a bond sinking fund

CASH PAYMENTS JOURNAL — PAGE 13

	DATE		ACCOUNT TITLE	CK. NO.	POST. REF.	1 GENERAL DEBIT	2 GENERAL CREDIT	3 ACCOUNTS PAYABLE DEBIT	4 PURCHASES DISCOUNT CREDIT	5 CASH CREDIT	
2		1	Bond Sinking Fund	563		50 000 00				50 000 00	2
3											3

FYI

If a bond is sold for *less* than its face value, it is said to be sold at a "discount." Cash and Discount on Bonds Payable are debited and Bonds Payable is credited.

A bond sinking fund is an asset to LampLight until the trustee makes payment to the bondholders. The bond trustee invests the sinking fund. The interest earned each year reduces the deposit that LampLight must make in that year. For example, the trustee reports to LampLight that the sinking fund investment earned $2,000.00. Therefore, on July 1, LampLight pays only $48,000.00 to the sinking fund trustee. This amount is calculated as shown below.

Amount of Increase in Sinking Fund	−	Interest Earned During Year	=	Amount to Be Deposited
$50,000.00	−	$2,000.00	=	$48,000.00

Bond Sinking Fund	
50,000.00	

Cash	
	48,000.00

Interest Income	
	2,000.00

July 1, 19--. Paid cash to bond trustee for annual deposit to bond sinking fund, $48,000.00, and recorded interest earned on bond sinking fund, $2,000.00. Check No. 610.

Bond Sinking Fund is debited for $50,000.00. Cash is credited for $48,000.00, the actual amount deposited. Interest Income is credited for $2,000.00, the amount of interest earned.

The journal entry to record this transaction is shown in Illustration 13-14.

ASSESS

Assess student understanding by checking the solutions to the Independent Practice activities.

Reteach

- Make transparencies of the cash receipts, cash payments, and general journals from the accounting forms masters provided in the Blackline Masters Section of the Teacher's Resource Guide. Refer students to Recycling Problem 13-R. Ask students to use T accounts to analyze the January 1 and July 1, 19X1, and the January 1 and 5, 19X2, bonds payable transactions. Use the transparencies to demonstrate how the transactions are journalized.
- Assign Recycling Problem 13-R.

Extend

- Assign Cases for Critical Thinking 2.
- Assign Challenge Problem 13-C. (The challenge is to calculate semiannual interest on bonds payable.)

CLOSURE

- Use Audit Your Understanding questions.
- Review "Comparison of Capital Stock and Bonds as a Source of Corporate Capital."

ASSESS

- Administer Problem Test Chapter 13.
- Administer a MicroExam test for Chapter 13.

TEACHING STRATEGIES: DIFFERENT LEARNING ABILITIES

Limited English Proficiency (LEP) Students. Although LEP students may feel at a disadvantage in the classroom, their knowledge of two languages provides them with excellent career opportunities in today's international business environment. LEP students should identify what unique career opportunities exist for them in various types of organizations, such as international businesses and government. Students could create a bulletin board to inform other students of these opportunities. Successful bulletin boards could also be used in the classrooms of younger students, or in elementary schools.

ILLUSTRATION 13-14 Journal entry to record annual interest earned on and deposit to a bond sinking fund

CASH PAYMENTS JOURNAL — PAGE 13

	DATE		ACCOUNT TITLE	CK. NO.	POST. REF.	1 GENERAL DEBIT	2 GENERAL CREDIT	3 ACCOUNTS PAYABLE DEBIT	4 PURCHASES DISCOUNT CREDIT	5 CASH CREDIT	
1	19-- July	1	Bond Sinking Fund	610		5000000				4800000	1
2			Interest Income				200000				2
3											3

As the bond sinking fund balance increases, the amount of interest earned in a year usually will increase. Thus, the amount LampLight must deposit each year will decrease.

Retiring a Bond Issue

FYI

One in five U.S. residents owns stocks or mutual funds that invest in stocks.

When LampLight's bonds are due, the bond trustee uses the bond sinking fund to pay the bondholders. Paying the amounts owed to bondholders for a bond issue is called **retiring a bond issue.**

July 1, 19--. Received notice from bond trustee that bond issue was retired using bond sinking fund, $250,000.00. Memorandum No. 600.

Bonds Payable

Debit		Credit	
Retired	250,000.00	Balance	250,000.00
		(New Bal. zero)	

Bond Sinking Fund

Debit		Credit	
Balance	250,000.00	Retired	250,000.00
(New Bal. zero)			

Bonds Payable is debited for $250,000.00, the total amount of the bond issue. Bond Sinking Fund is credited for $250,000.00, the amount in the fund used to retire the bond issue. After this entry is posted, both Bonds Payable and Bond Sinking Fund will have zero balances.

The journal entry to record this transaction is shown in Illustration 13-15.

ILLUSTRATION 13-15 Journal entry to record retiring a bond issue

GENERAL JOURNAL — PAGE 6

	DATE		ACCOUNT TITLE	DOC. NO.	POST. REF.	DEBIT	CREDIT	
1	19-- July	1	Bonds Payable	M600		25000000		1
2			Bond Sinking Fund				25000000	2
3								3

All of LampLight's bond issue matures on the same date. Bonds that all mature on the same date are called **term bonds.** Sometimes portions of a bond issue mature on different dates. Portions of a bond issue that mature on different dates are called **serial bonds.**

APPLIED SKILLS: LANGUAGE ARTS

Paraphrasing, writing complete sentences, and identifying objects of prepositional phrases. For additional practice in language arts skills, direct students to answer the Accounting Terms and Questions for Individual Study at the end of the chapter. Students should write the answers in their own words and in complete sentences. To further practice language arts skills, ask students to underline all the objects of prepositional phrases in their answers.

Audit Your Understanding

1. What are two advantages of raising needed capital by selling stock?
2. What is an advantage in raising additional capital by borrowing?
3. What is a disadvantage of borrowing additional capital?

For example, a 10-year bond issue with one-tenth of the bonds maturing every year is a serial bond issue. An advantage of serial bonds is that interest does not have to be paid on the total bond issue for the total 10 years.

COMPARISON OF CAPITAL STOCK AND BONDS AS A SOURCE OF CORPORATE CAPITAL

A comparison of capital stock and bonds as a source of corporate capital is shown in Illustration 13-16.

ILLUSTRATION 13-16 Comparison of capital stock and bonds as a source of corporate capital

Capital Stock	Bonds
1. Stockholders are corporate owners.	1. Bondholders are corporate creditors.
2. Capital Stock is a stockholders' equity account.	2. Bonds Payable is a liability account.
3. Stockholders have a secondary claim against corporate assets.	3. Bondholders have a primary, or first claim, against corporate assets.
4. Dividends are paid to stockholders out of corporate net income.	4. Interest paid to bondholders is a corporate expense.
5. Dividends are not fixed costs; dividends do not have to be paid if net income is insufficient.	5. Interest on bonds is a fixed expense; the expense must be paid when due; payment does not depend on amount of net income.
6. Amount received from sale of stock is relatively permanent capital; amount invested by stockholders does not have to be returned to them in foreseeable future.	6. Amount received from sale of bonds is not permanent; amount invested by bondholders must be returned to them on bonds' maturity date.

ACCOUNTING TERMS EPT(a)

What is the meaning of each of the following?

1. **discount on capital stock**
2. **treasury stock**
3. **bond**
4. **bond issue**
5. **trustee**
6. **bond sinking fund**
7. **retiring a bond issue**
8. **term bonds**
9. **serial bonds**

AUDIT YOUR UNDERSTANDING

1. (1) Additional capital becomes part of a corporation's permanent capital. (2) Dividends do not have to be paid unless earnings are sufficient.
2. Stockholders' equity is not spread over additional shares of stock.
3. Interest must be paid on the loan, which decreases net income.

TEACHING STRATEGIES: APPLYING VISUALS

Direct students to Illustration 13-16 to review the comparison of capital stock and bonds as a source of corporate capital.

ACCOUNTING TERMS

1. **discount on capital stock:** An amount less than par or stated value at which capital stock is sold. (p. 347)
2. **treasury stock:** A corporation's own stock that has been issued and reacquired. (p. 350)
3. **bond:** A printed, long-term promise to pay a specified amount on a specified date, and to pay interest at stated intervals. (p. 355)
4. **bond issue:** All the bonds representing the total amount of a loan. (p. 355)
5. **trustee:** A person or institution, usually a bank, who is given legal authorization to administer property for the benefit of property owners. (p. 356)
6. **bond sinking fund:** An amount set aside to pay a bond issue when due. (p. 357)
7. **retiring a bond issue:** Paying the amounts owed to bondholders for a bond issue. (p. 358)
8. **term bonds:** Bonds that all mature on the same date. (p. 358)
9. **serial bonds:** Portions of a bond issue that mature on different dates. (p. 358)

QUESTIONS FOR INDIVIDUAL STUDY

1. The portion of a corporation's net income not paid to stockholders as dividends. (p. 345)
2. So that additional shares of stock can be sold if additional capital is needed. (p. 345)
3. Cash is debited; Capital Stock—Preferred is credited. (p. 345)
4. Cash is debited; Capital Stock—Preferred and Paid-in Capital in Excess of Par Value—Preferred are credited. (p. 346)
5. Cash and Discount on Sale of Preferred Stock are debited; Capital Stock—Preferred is credited. (p. 347)
6. Cash is debited; Capital Stock—Common and Paid-in Capital in Excess of Stated Value—Common are credited. (p. 350)
7. Historical Cost concept. (p. 351)
8. Treasury Stock is debited; Cash is credited. (p. 351)
9. Cash is debited; Treasury Stock and Paid-in Capital from Sale of Treasury Stock are credited. (p. 352)
10. Cash and Paid-in Capital from Sale of Treasury Stock are debited; Treasury Stock is credited. (p. 354)
11. (a) Additional capital becomes part of a corporation's permanent capital. (b) Dividends do not have to be paid unless earnings are sufficient. (p. 355)
12. Stockholders' equity is not spread over additional shares of stock. (p. 355)
13. Interest must be paid on the loan, which decreases net income. (p. 355)
14. Cash is debited; Bonds Payable is credited. (p. 355)
15. Interest Expense is debited; Cash is credited. (p. 356)
16. Bond Sinking Fund is debited; Cash is credited. (p. 357)
17. Bond Sinking Fund is debited; Cash and Interest Income are credited. (p. 357)
18. Bonds Payable is debited; Bond Sinking Fund is credited. (p. 358)

QUESTIONS FOR INDIVIDUAL STUDY — EPT(b)

1. What is a primary source of additional capital for a corporation?
2. Why might a corporation obtain authorization for more shares of stock than will be issued when the corporation is first formed?
3. What accounts are affected, and how, when LampLight receives cash for preferred stock sold at par value?
4. What accounts are affected, and how, when LampLight receives cash for preferred stock sold for more than par value?
5. What accounts are affected, and how, when LampLight receives cash for preferred stock sold for less than par value?
6. What accounts are affected, and how, when LampLight receives cash for common stock sold for more than stated value?
7. Which accounting concept is being applied when a corporation records treasury stock at the price paid regardless of the stock's par or stated value?
8. What accounts are affected, and how, when a corporation buys its own stock?
9. What accounts are affected, and how, when treasury stock is sold for more than its original cost?
10. What accounts are affected, and how, when treasury stock is sold for less than its original cost?
11. What are two advantages of raising needed capital by selling stock?
12. What is an advantage in raising additional capital by borrowing?
13. What is a disadvantage of borrowing additional capital?
14. What accounts are affected, and how, when bonds are sold by a corporation?
15. What accounts are affected, and how, when a corporation pays interest to a bond trustee?
16. What accounts are affected, and how, when a corporation deposits cash with a trustee for the first payment of a bond issue's principal?
17. What accounts are affected, and how, when a corporation deposits cash with a trustee for partial payment of a bond issue's principal when interest has been earned on the bond sinking fund?
18. What accounts are affected, and how, when a corporation's bond issue is retired?

CASES FOR CRITICAL THINKING — EPT(b)

CASE 1 Cecil Thomas pays $12,000.00 for 2,000 shares of $5.00 stated-value common stock of Datkins, Inc. A year later, Mr. Thomas sells the 2,000 shares of stock to Sally Gilliam for a total of $14,000.00. Ms. Gilliam sends a notice to Datkins so that ownership can be changed on the corporation's stock records. An accounting clerk at Datkins is not sure what journal entry should be made so that the business' general ledger will reflect the correct information. What advice would you give the accounting clerk?

CASE 2 Spencer, Inc. estimates that with an additional $600,000.00 capital with which to expand the business, an additional $90,000.00 in net income can be earned. The board of directors is considering three alternatives for acquiring the additional capital. (1) Issue 600, 10-year, 10%, $1,000.00 face value bonds. (2) Sell 12,000 shares of 10%, $50.00 par-value preferred stock. (3) Sell 600,000 shares of $1.00 stated-value common stock. The corporation has been paying an annual $.08 per share dividend on common stock. The corporation's average tax rate on net income is 35%. What factors should you advise the corporation to consider before deciding on which alternative to use?

CASES FOR CRITICAL THINKING

Case 1 Change of stock ownership does not affect a corporation's general ledger accounts. Regardless of who owns the stock, the stock is still listed on the corporation's records as outstanding stock. No journal entry is made for stock transfer.

Case 2 1. Bonds: (a) The corporation must pay a total of $60,000 interest each year for ten years. This payment reduces the amount of net income available for stock dividends and for future use of the corporation. Also, the corporation must pay an additional $60,000.00 into a bond sinking fund each year for ten years. This means that the entire $600,000.00 is not available for use throughout the ten years. At the end of ten years, the money in the bond sinking fund must be returned to the investors. (b) The $600,000.00 is not a

APPLICATION PROBLEMS

EPT(c,d,e)

PROBLEM 13-1 Journalizing capital stock transactions

MATHEMATICS

Teel, Inc. is authorized to issue 200,000 shares of $5.00 stated-value common stock and 50,000 shares of 12%, $100.00 par-value preferred stock. Teel has 25,000 shares of common stock outstanding.

INSTRUCTIONS:

Journalize the following transactions completed during the current year. Use page 2 of a cash receipts journal and a general journal. Source documents are abbreviated as follows: memorandum, M; receipt, R.

Feb. 8. Received cash from Gladdis Jensen for 5,000 shares of $5.00 stated-value common stock at $5.00 per share, $25,000.00. R398.

Feb. 26. Received a parcel of land from Maria Vallejos at an agreed value of $30,000.00 for 300 shares of $100.00 par-value preferred stock. M67.

Apr. 15. Received cash from Michael Pettri for 400 shares of $100.00 par-value preferred stock at $100.00 per share, $40,000.00. R518.

Aug. 25. Received cash from Kimberly Sampson for 500 shares of $100.00 par-value preferred stock at $96.00 per share, $48,000.00. R601.

Dec. 11. Received cash from Harold Dankin for 200 shares of $100.00 par-value preferred stock at $102.00 per share, $20,400.00. R698.

PROBLEM 13-2 Journalizing treasury stock transactions

MATHEMATICS

Powers, Inc. is authorized to issue 150,000 shares of $10.00 stated-value common stock. Powers has 50,000 shares of stock outstanding.

INSTRUCTIONS:

Journalize the following transactions completed during the current year. Use page 2 of a cash receipts journal and page 3 of a cash payments journal. Source documents are abbreviated as follows: check, C; receipt, R.

Feb. 21. Paid cash to Chase Daniel for 400 shares of $10.00 stated-value common stock at $10.00 per share, $4,000.00. C87.

Feb. 27. Received cash from Sandra Teasley for 125 shares of treasury stock at $10.00 per share, $1,250.00. Treasury stock was bought on February 21 at $10.00 per share. R126.

Mar. 22. Paid cash to Lance Lupe for 750 shares of $10.00 stated-value common stock at $11.00 per share, $8,250.00. C138.

Apr. 15. Received cash from Mellisa Shannon for 275 shares of treasury stock at $12.00 per share, $3,300.00. Treasury stock was bought on February 21 at $10.00 per share. R151.

July 30. Received cash from John Glover for 300 shares of treasury stock at $10.00 per share, $3,000.00. Treasury stock was bought on March 22 at $11.00 per share. R203.

PROBLEM 13-3 Journalizing bonds payable transactions

On January 1, 19X1, Gifford, Inc. received cash, $200,000.00, for a bond issue. The bond agreement provides that a bond sinking fund is to be increased by $20,000.00 every six months for the next five years.

INSTRUCTIONS:

Journalize the following transactions. Use page 1 of a cash receipts journal, page 8 of a cash payments journal, and page 1 of a general journal. Source documents are abbreviated as follows: check, C; memorandum, M; receipt, R.

Jan. 1, 19X1. Received cash for the face value of a 5-year, 9%, $1,000.00 par-value bond issue, $200,000.00. R104.

CASES FOR CRITICAL THINKING *(cont'd)*

permanent investment in the business. If, at the end of ten years the additional earnings have not been as great as predicted, the corporation might still need the money but still must return the money to the bondholders. The investment is temporary. (c) Owners of bonds do not have a vote in stockholders' meetings. Control of the corporation is retained by the current owners of common stock. 2. Preferred Stock: (a) An annual dividend of $60,000.00 is required before any dividends can be paid on common stock. (b) Nothing has to be set aside each year to retire the stock. The investment in the corporation is permanent. (c) Owners of preferred stock do not have a vote in stockholders' meetings. Control of the corporation is retained by current owners of common stock. 3. Common Stock: (a) Although dividends may be paid each year on the common stock, if net income is insufficient, dividends need not be paid. If the corporation continues the previous dividend rate, a total of $48,000.00 would be paid each year on the additional common stock. (b) Nothing has to be set aside each year to retire the stock. The investment in the corporation is permanent. (c) Common stockholders have a vote in stockholders' meetings. The control of the business will be spread over more shares of stock. Recommendation: Issue bonds. Bonds and preferred stock will not change the control by current owners of common stock. Bonds and preferred stock will increase costs for interest and dividends. However, bonds will increase the cost for only ten years. Bonds will also decrease taxes for the ten years.

If the business does not anticipate paying dividends in the future, issuing common stock is the best source of additional capital. The investment would be permanent and incur no additional costs. However, few corporations anticipate that earnings will never be sufficient to pay dividends in the future. In addition, few persons are willing to pay for stock that has little chance of ever earning dividends.

CHECK FIGURES

See Teacher's Edition of Working Papers for complete solutions.

Problem 13-1 General Journal entry: Land dr. $30,000; Capital Stock—Preferred cr. $30,000

Problem 13-2 April 15 entry: Paid-in Capital from Sale of Treasury Stock is credited for $550.

Problem 13-3 Jan. 1, 19X1 entry: Cash is debited for $200,000.

July 1, 19X1. Paid cash to bond trustee for semiannual interest on bond issue, $9,000.00. C294.
July 1, 19X1. Paid cash to bond trustee for semiannual deposit to bond sinking fund, $20,000.00. C295.
Jan. 1, 19X2. Paid cash to bond trustee for semiannual interest on bond issue, $9,000.00. C504.
Jan. 1, 19X2. Paid cash to bond trustee for semiannual deposit to bond sinking fund, $19,200.00, and recorded interest earned on bond sinking fund, $800.00. C505.
Jan. 4, 19X6. Received notice from bond trustee that bond issue was retired using bond sinking fund, $200,000.00. M290.

ENRICHMENT PROBLEMS

EPT(c,d,e)

MASTERY PROBLEM 13-M Journalizing stocks and bonds transactions

Rohde, Inc. is authorized to issue 100,000 shares of $10.00 stated-value common stock, and 50,000 shares of 12%, $100.00 par-value preferred stock.

INSTRUCTIONS:

Journalize the following transactions. Use page 1 of a cash receipts journal, page 2 of a cash payments journal, and page 1 of a general journal. Source documents are abbreviated as follows: check, C; memorandum, M; receipt, R.

Jan. 1, 19X1. Received cash for the face value of a 5-year, 12%, $1,000.00 par-value bond issue, $50,000.00. R198.
Jan. 12, 19X1. Received cash from Jason Rooker for 1,000 shares of $10.00 stated-value common stock at $10.00 per share, $10,000.00. R210.
Feb. 21, 19X1. Paid cash to Charles Hepner for 900 shares of $10.00 stated-value common stock at $12.00 per share, $10,800.00. C97.
Feb. 28, 19X1. Received cash from Allen Edmonds for 500 shares of treasury stock at $12.00 per share, $6,000.00. Treasury stock was bought on February 21 at $12.00 per share. R215.
Mar. 13, 19X1. Received cash from Ora Damato for 200 shares of $10.00 stated-value common stock at $15.00 per share, $3,000.00. R220.
Mar. 22, 19X1. Paid cash to Emma Kellum for 2,000 shares of $10.00 stated-value common stock at $16.00 per share, $32,000.00. C138.
Apr. 8, 19X1. Received cash from Thomas Keller for 100 shares of $100.00 par-value preferred stock at $101.00 per share, $10,100.00. R226.
Apr. 15, 19X1. Received cash from Peter Kilborn for 300 shares of treasury stock at $18.00 per share, $5,400.00. Treasury stock was bought on February 21 at $12.00 per share. R231.
May 15, 19X1. Received cash from Patrick Emery for 800 shares of $100.00 par-value preferred stock at $97.50 per share, $78,000.00. R232.
July 1, 19X1. Paid cash to bond trustee for semiannual interest on bond issue, $3,000.00. C200.
July 1, 19X1. Paid cash to bond trustee for semiannual deposit to bond sinking fund, $5,000.00. C201.
July 14, 19X1. Received delivery equipment from Jane Bradley at an agreed value of $20,000.00 for 200 shares of $100.00 par-value preferred stock. M148.
July 23, 19X1. Received cash from Loretta Schnell for 300 shares of treasury stock at $14.00 per share, $4,200.00. One hundred shares of treasury stock were bought on February 21 at $12.00 per share. Two hundred shares were bought on March 22 at $16.00 per share. R353.
Jan. 1, 19X2. Paid cash to bond trustee for semiannual interest on bond issue, $3,000.00. C504.

CHECK FIGURES *(cont'd)*

Mastery Problem 13-M April 15, 19X1 entry: Paid-in Capital from Sale of Treasury Stock is credited for $1,800. Mar. 22, 19X2 entry: Cash is credited for $32,000.

Challenge Problem 13-C July 1 and Jan. 1 Int. Exp. $10,000

Jan. 1, 19X2. Paid cash to bond trustee for semiannual deposit to bond sinking fund, $4,600.00, and recorded interest earned on bond sinking fund, $400.00. C505.

Jan. 1, 19X6. Received notice from bond trustee that bond issue was retired using bond sinking fund, $50,000.00. M491.

CHALLENGE PROBLEM 13-C Journalizing stocks and bonds transactions

MATHEMATICS

Martin Industries, Inc. is authorized to issue 100,000 shares of $1.00 stated-value common stock and 25,000 shares of 10%, $100.00 par-value preferred stock. On January 1, 19X1, Martin has the following outstanding stock: common stock, 40,000 shares; preferred stock, 10,000 shares. Provisions of a bond issue, January 1, 19X1, include (a) interest on the bond issue is to be paid on July 1 and January 1 of each year, and (b) Martin must assure an increase of $20,000.00 in a bond sinking fund on July 1 and January 1 of each year.

INSTRUCTIONS:

Journalize the following transactions. Use page 1 of a cash receipts journal, page 2 of a cash payments journal, and page 1 of a general journal. Source documents are abbreviated as follows: check, C; memorandum, M; receipt, R.

Jan. 1, 19X1. Cash was received for the face value of a 10-year, 10%, $1,000.00 par-value bond issue, $200,000.00. R51.

Feb. 5, 19X1. Paid Janice Wiler for 5,000 shares of $1.00 stated-value common stock at $1.60 per share, $8,000.00. C120.

Feb. 12, 19X1. Cash was received from Robert Patterson for 15,000 shares of $1.00 stated-value common stock at $1.20 per share, $18,000.00. R64.

Feb. 20, 19X1. Darrel Stare paid cash for 500 shares of $100.00 par-value preferred stock at $100.00 per share, $50,000.00. R105.

Mar. 14, 19X1. Office equipment was received from Patricia Cannon at an agreed value of $7,000.00 for 5,000 shares of $1.00 stated-value common stock. M195.

Apr. 3, 19X1. Carolyn Petre paid cash for 1,000 shares of treasury stock at $1.50 per share, $1,500.00. Treasury stock was bought on February 5 at $1.60 per share. R210.

May 10, 19X1. Susan Rahis paid cash for 300 shares of $100.00 par-value preferred stock at $99.00 per share, $29,700.00. R387.

July 1, 19X1. Paid semiannual interest to bond trustee on bonds payable. C389.

July 1, 19X1. Paid to bond trustee for semiannual deposit to bond sinking fund, $20,000.00. C390.

Sept. 18, 19X1. Cash was received from Kenneth Miller for 2,500 shares of treasury stock at $2.00 per share, $5,000.00. Treasury stock was bought on February 5 at $1.60 per share. R561.

Oct. 14, 19X1. Gerald Mansk paid cash for 150 shares of $100.00 par-value preferred stock at $103.00 per share, $15,450.00. R600.

Jan. 1, 19X2. Paid cash to bond trustee for semiannual interest on bonds payable. C634.

Jan. 1, 19X2. Paid cash to bond trustee for semiannual deposit to bond sinking fund. Interest earned on money in sinking fund since last payment on July 1, $800.00. C635.

Jan. 2, 19X6. Received notice from bond trustee that bond issue was retired using bond sinking fund, $200,000.00. M428.

CHAPTER 14 OVERVIEW

Chapter 14 completes the accounting cycle for a corporation that began in Chapter 12. In addition to the usual end-of-fiscal-period work, including a work sheet, income statement, statement of stockholders' equity, balance sheet, adjusting entries, closing entries, reversing entries, and post-closing trial balance, several new kinds of financial statement analysis are introduced, such as price-earnings ratio, equity per

GUIDE TO ACHIEVING LEARNING OBJECTIVES

	TEACH	APPLY	EXTEND/ENRICH				
Enabling Performance Tasks	**Lesson Plans**	**Application Problems**	**Mastery Problems**	**Challenge Problems**	**Cases for Critical Thinking**	**Recycling Problems**	**Reinforcement Activity**
a. Define accounting terms related to financial analysis and reporting for a corporation.	14-1, 14-2,						
b. Identify accounting concepts and practices related to financial analysis and reporting for a corporation.	14-1, 14-2, 14-3				Cases 1, 2		
c. Journalize adjusting entries for amortizing an intangible asset.	14-3	14-6	14-M			14-R	2
d. Calculate federal income tax for a corporation.	14-1	14-1, 14-2	14-M	14-C		14-R	2
e. Prepare selected end-of-fiscal-period work for a corporation.	14-1, 14-2, 14-3	14-2, 14-3, 14-4, 14-5, 14-6	14-M			14-R	2
f. Analyze financial statements for a corporation.	14-2	14-3, 14-4, 14-5	14-M			14-R	2

ENRICHMENT

SPECIAL FEATURES
Spreadsheet Options, page 384
Personal Visions in Business, page 383
Careers in Accounting, page 373
TECHNOLOGY CONNECTION
Automated Accounting 6.0 Problems 14-2, 14-M
Spreadsheet Template Problems 14-1, 14-M

NEW, REVIEW, AND EXTENSION

ACTIVITIES/CONCEPTS/TRANSACTIONS	NEW	REVIEW/ EXTENSION
End-of-fiscal-period work for a corporation		✓
Adjustment to amortize corporation organization cost	✓	
Completing a work sheet for a corporation		✓
Calculating federal income tax	✓	
Completing and analyzing financial statements		✓
Calculating earnings per share		✓
Equity per share	✓	
Price-earnings ratio	✓	
Accounts receivable turnover ratio		✓
Rate earned on average stockholders' equity	✓	
Rate earned on average total assets	✓	
Adjusting, closing, and reversing entries		✓
Post-closing trial balance		✓
Dissolving a corporation		✓

share, and rate earned on average stockholders' equity. Percentages used for calculating federal income tax are provided and the method for amortizing a corporation's organization costs is described.

The work sheet completed in Problem 14-2 is needed to complete Problems 14-3, 14-4, 14-5, and 14-6.

INFORMAL ASSESSMENT		FORMAL ASSESSMENT			
Study Guide	**Audit Your Understanding**	**Chapter MicroExam**	**Chapter Problem Test**	**Unit Objective Test**	**Portfolio**
Unit A	✓	✓		✓	
Units B, C	✓	✓		✓	
			✓		✓
			✓		✓
			✓		✓
			✓		✓

TEACHING MATERIALS

Teacher's Wraparound Edition of the Text
Teacher's Resource Guide
Teacher's Edition of Working Papers
MicroExam
Key for Four Seasons, Inc. Simulation

APPLIED MATHEMATICS

APPLIED MATH/ACCOUNTING SKILL	APPLICATION
Calculating federal income tax	Prob. 14-1
Calculating component percentages	Prob. 14-3
Calculating earnings per share	Prob. 14-3
Calculating equity per share	Prob. 14-4
Calculating price-earnings ratio	Prob. 14-4
Calculating accounts receivable turnover ratio	Prob. 14-5
Calculating rate earned on average stockholders' equity	Prob. 14-5
Calculating rate earned on average total assets	Prob. 14-5

Financial Analysis and Reporting for a Corporation

TEACHING STRATEGIES: ACCOUNTING PEDAGOGY

This textbook covers financial reporting for a corporation. Critical thinking skills are applied to wrap up the entire accounting cycle for a corporation. Students not only complete the end-of-fiscal-period work, but they also improve their financial statement analysis skills.

ENABLING PERFORMANCE TASKS

After studying Chapter 14, you will be able to:

- **a** Define accounting terms related to financial analysis and reporting for a corporation.
- **b** Identify accounting concepts and practices related to financial analysis and reporting for a corporation.
- **c** Journalize adjusting entries for amortizing an intangible asset.
- **d** Calculate federal income tax for a corporation.
- **e** Prepare selected end-of-fiscal-period work for a corporation.
- **f** Analyze financial statements for a corporation.

TERMS PREVIEW

amortization • earnings per share • equity per share • market value • price-earnings ratio • rate earned on average stockholders' equity • rate earned on average total assets

SOFTWARE FOCUS

Software may be used for independent practice or enrichment/extension as the instructor deems appropriate. For this chapter, the following software may be used: *Automated Accounting 6.0* or higher with Problem 14-2, Mastery Problem 14-M, and Reinforcement Activity 2; Spreadsheet Template with Problem 14-1 and Mastery Problem 14-M.

Corporations prepare financial statements at the end of each fiscal period to report their financial progress and condition. Corporations normally provide an analysis of the financial statements to help interested persons understand and use the information. For example, a corporation's board of directors uses the information for making management decisions. The board of directors also uses the information to determine whether or not to distribute earnings to stockholders. Stockholders and other investors use the information to determine if they will begin or continue investing in the corporation. Creditors use the information to determine if the corporation will be able to meet its credit obligations. *(CONCEPT: Adequate Disclosure)*

WORK SHEET FOR A CORPORATION

FYI

Corporations whose stock is publicly traded are required to prepare financial statements on an annual basis.

LampLight's end-of-fiscal-period work includes preparation of a work sheet. The work sheet is used to prepare the financial statements. LampLight's work sheet for the fiscal year ended December 31 is shown in Illustration 14-1 on pages 366 and 367.

Planning Adjustments on a Work Sheet

Adjustments on LampLight's work sheet are similar to those described for MasterSport in Part 2. LampLight also records adjustments for organization expense and federal income tax expense.

Organization Expense Adjustment. Corporate organization costs are intangible assets. However, over a period of time, a business will have difficulty determining an intangible asset's continuing value. Therefore, most corporations do not carry organization costs indefinitely as an asset. Intangible assets are written off as an expense over a period of years. Recognizing a portion of an expense in each of several years is called **amortization.**

LampLight incurred total organization costs of $2,400.00. Instead of recording the entire $2,400.00 in an expense account in one year, the amount was spread over five years. Thus, one-fifth of this amount, $480.00, is amortized in each of the first five years. In the first year, $480.00 was amortized as an expense. An adjustment is planned on the work sheet for the second year's amortization.

Organization Expense

19X2 Adj. (k)	480.00		

Organization Costs

Bal.	2,400.00	19X1	480.00
(New Bal.	*1,440.00)*	19X2 Adj. (k)	480.00

Organization Expense is debited for $480.00. Organization Costs is credited for $480.00. The new balance of Organization Costs, *$1,440.00,* is the amount to be amortized in the next three years.

The adjustment for organization expense is shown as entry *(k)* on LampLight's work sheet, lines 21 and 74, Illustration 14-1.

Federal Income Tax Expense Adjustment. At the beginning of the year, LampLight estimated its annual net income and calculated its

LESSON PLAN 14-1

Materials

- Student pages 365–369
- Blackline Master of 8-Column Work Sheet (TRG)
- Software: Spreadsheet Template; *Automated Accounting 6.0* or higher; Accounting Textbook Template, Advanced Course

Objectives (Enabling Performance Tasks)

a. Define accounting terms related to financial analysis and reporting for a corporation.

b. Identify accounting concepts and practices related to financial analysis and reporting for a corporation.

d. Calculate federal income tax for a corporation.

e. Prepare selected end-of-fiscal-period work for a corporation.

APPLIED SKILLS: WORD PROCESSING

If you wish to integrate word processing into your accounting course, you may direct students to answer the end-of-chapter Accounting Terms, Questions for Individual Study, and Cases for Critical Thinking using their word processing software.

TEACHING STRATEGIES: APPLYING VISUALS

Direct students to Illustration 14-1 to review preparation of a corporate work sheet.

FOCUS

- Preparing a work sheet for a departmentalized corporation was presented in Chapter 5. In this lesson, steps for preparing a work sheet for a nondepartmentalized corporation will be reviewed. Explain that some of the organization costs, recorded in Chapter 12, will be written off as an expense. Therefore, a new adjustment for the organization expense will be planned on the work sheet. Also, the steps used to calculate federal income tax for a corporation will be introduced.
- Introduce vocabulary: amortization.

TEACH

Cover student pages 365–369 "Work Sheet for a Corporation." Review the adjustments planned on the work sheet. Remind students that the adjustments are similar to those presented in Chapter 5. Introduce the adjustment for organization expense. Discuss the steps used to calculate federal income tax for a corporation. Reinforce that the adjustment for federal income tax is the difference between what has been paid and total amount owed.

ILLUSTRATION 14-1 Corporate work sheet

LampLight, Inc.
Work Sheet
For Year Ended December 31, 19--

	ACCOUNT TITLE	1 TRIAL BALANCE DEBIT	2 TRIAL BALANCE CREDIT	3 ADJUSTMENTS DEBIT	4 ADJUSTMENTS CREDIT	5 INCOME STATEMENT DEBIT	6 INCOME STATEMENT CREDIT	7 BALANCE SHEET DEBIT	8 BALANCE SHEET CREDIT	
1	*Cash*	25,436.40						25,436.40		1
2	*Petty Cash*	250.00						250.00		2
3	*Notes Receivable*	10,000.00						10,000.00		3
4	*Interest Receivable*			(a) 1,000.00				1,000.00		4
5	*Accounts Receivable*	135,234.54						135,234.54		5
6	*Allow. for Uncoll. Accts.*		420.13		(b) 6,277.50				6,697.63	6
7	*Subscriptions Receivable*									7
8	*Merchandise Inventory*	267,453.09			(c) 8,697.90			258,755.19		8
9	*Supplies—Sales*	14,315.67			(d) 5,869.04			8,446.63		9
10	*Supplies—Administrative*	22,613.70			(e) 14,456.40			8,157.30		10
11	*Prepaid Insurance*	16,900.00			(f) 5,911.31			10,988.69		11
12	*Prepaid Interest*			(g) 10.47				10.47		12
13	*Bond Sinking Fund*	50,000.00						50,000.00		13
14	*Store Equipment*	142,983.34						142,983.34		14
15	*Accum. Depr.—Store Equip.*		15,123.00		(h) 16,753.00				31,876.00	15
16	*Building*	165,000.00						165,000.00		16
17	*Accum. Depr.—Building*		8,250.00		(i) 8,250.00				16,500.00	17
18	*Office Equipment*	73,928.23						73,928.23		18
19	*Accum. Depr.—Office Equip.*		7,652.00		(j) 9,734.13				17,386.13	19
20	*Land*	133,000.00						133,000.00		20
21	*Organization Costs*	1,920.00			(k) 480.00			1,440.00		21
22	*Notes Payable*		2,500.00						2,500.00	22
23	*Interest Payable*				(l) 15,000.00				15,000.00	23
24	*Accounts Payable*		28,085.40						28,085.40	24
25	*Employee Income Tax Pay.*		1,238.90						1,238.90	25
26	*Federal Income Tax Payable*				(o) 2,392.76				2,392.76	26
27	*FICA Tax Payable*		768.90		(n) 50.70				819.60	27
28	*Salaries Payable*				(m) 633.73				633.73	28
29	*Sales Tax Payable*		2,154.74						2,154.74	29
30	*Unemploy. Tax Pay.—Federal*		87.45		(n) 1.20				88.65	30
31	*Unemploy. Tax Pay.—State*		590.29		(n) 8.10				598.39	31
32	*Health Ins. Premiums Payable*		428.00						428.00	32
33	*Dividends Payable*		29,575.00						29,575.00	33
34	*Bonds Payable*		250,000.00						250,000.00	34
35	*Capital Stock—Common*		321,000.00						321,000.00	35
36	*Stock Subscribed—Common*									36

estimated federal income tax for the year to be $32,000.00. LampLight paid the estimated tax to the federal government in four equal quarterly installments of $8,000.00 each. As of December 31, Lamp-

	Account Title	Trial Balance Debit	Trial Balance Credit	Adjustments Debit	Adjustments Credit	Income Statement Debit	Income Statement Credit	Balance Sheet Debit	Balance Sheet Credit	
37	Pd.-in Cap. in Exc. of St. Val.—Com.		20000						20000	37
38	Capital Stock—Preferred		17000000						17000000	38
39	Stock Subscribed—Preferred									39
40	Pd.-in Cap. in Exc. of Par Val.—Pref.		800000						800000	40
41	Disc. on Sale of Preferred Stock	500000						500000		41
42	Treasury Stock	180000						180000		42
43	Pd.-in Cap. from Sale of Tr. Stock		50000						50000	43
44	Retained Earnings		5858835						5858835	44
45	Dividends—Common	1597500						1597500		45
46	Dividends—Preferred	1360000						1360000		46
47	Income Summary			(c) 869790		869790				47
48	Sales		87295240				87295240			48
49	Sales Discount	869512				869512				49
50	Sales Ret. and Allow.	290056				290056				50
51	Purchases	45539648				45539648				51
52	Purchases Discount		671035				671035			52
53	Purchases Ret. and Allow.		267000				267000			53
54	Advertising Expense	1778200				1778200				54
55	Credit Card Fee Expense	628500				628500				55
56	Depr. Exp.—Store Equip.			(h) 1675300		1675300				56
57	Miscellaneous Exp.—Sales	940612				940612				57
58	Salary Expense—Sales	6322600		(m) 45789		6368389				58
59	Supplies Expense—Sales			(d) 586904		586904				59
60	Depr. Expense—Building			(i) 825000		825000				60
61	Depr. Exp.—Office Equip.			(j) 973413		973413				61
62	Insurance Expense			(f) 591131		591131				62
63	Miscellaneous Exp.—Admin.	1257068				1257068				63
64	Payroll Taxes Expense	990240		(n) 6000		996240				64
65	Property Tax Expense	670000				670000				65
66	Salary Expense—Admin.	2364333		(m) 17584		2381917				66
67	Supplies Expense—Admin.			(e) 1445640		1445640				67
68	Uncollectible Accounts Exp.			(b) 627750		627750				68
69	Utilities Expense	2872725				2872725				69
70	Gain on Plant Assets									70
71	Interest Income		45000		(a) 100000		145000			71
72	Interest Expense	1530000		(l) 1500000	(g) 1047	3028953				72
73	Loss on Plant Assets									73
74	Organization Expense			(k) 48000		48000				74
75	Federal Inc. Tax Expense	3200000		(o) 239276		3439276				75
76		178794491	178794491	9552624	9552624	78704024	88378275	106100579	96426328	76
77	Net Inc. after Fed. Inc. Tax					9674251			9674251	77
78						88378275	88378275	106100579	106100579	78

Light calculated its *actual* federal income tax to determine if additional income tax is due. An adjustment is planned on the work sheet for the additional tax.

APPLY

Refer students to Illustration 14-1 as the preparation of the work sheet is discussed. Draw T accounts on the chalkboard or overhead and record the amounts for the adjustments as they are presented. Place several examples on the board or overhead to show how the tax rate table is used to calculate federal income tax.

Guided Practice

Guide students through the calculation of federal income tax for Corporation A in Problem 14-1. Refer students to Problem 14-1 and the tax rate table in their textbooks. As a group, calculate the amount of tax. When all students agree, have them record the correct amount on the form provided in their working papers. The balance of Problem 14-1 can be completed as Independent Practice.

Independent Practice

Assign Term 1, Questions 1–6, and Problems 14-1 and 14-2.

TEACHING STRATEGIES: TEACHING TIP

Before starting work on Problem 14-2, have students work together and use T accounts to review the analysis of adjustments into debit and credit parts. This exercise will help students reduce the time needed for actual completion of the work sheet.

ASSESS

Assess student understanding by checking the solutions to the Independent Practice activities.

Reteach

- Make a transparency of the 8-column work sheet from the accounting forms masters provided in the Blackline Masters Section of the Teacher's Resource Guide. Refer students to Recycling Problem 14-R. Using the transparency, demonstrate how the trial balance is recorded on the work sheet. Ask students to use T accounts to analyze the adjustments. Using the transparency, demonstrate how the adjustments are recorded on the work sheet. Demonstrate how the balances, except Federal Income Tax Expense, are extended to the Income Statement columns. Review the steps for calculating the amount of federal income tax and recording the adjustment on the work sheet.
- Assign Recycling Problem 14-R, Instruction 1.

Extend

- Assign the Spreadsheet Template for Problem 14-1.
- Use *Automated Accounting 6.0* or higher with Accounting Textbook Template, Advanced Course with Problem 14-2.

Enrich

Assign the SPREADSHEET OPTIONS feature on page 384.

CLOSURE

Use Audit Your Understanding questions.

FYI

Large securities exchanges are located in Amsterdam, Brussels, Chicago, Frankfurt, Hong Kong, Johannesburg, Los Angeles, Milan, Osaka, Paris, Seoul, Sidney, Singapore, Stockholm, and Toronto.

The following steps are used to calculate the total amount of federal income tax expense and the amount of the adjustment on the work sheet.

1. Complete the work sheet's Adjustments columns except for the federal income tax expense adjustment. Do not total the Adjustments columns at this time.
2. Extend all amounts, except the balance of Federal Income Tax Expense, to the work sheet's Income Statement columns.
3. Total the work sheet's Income Statement column totals using a calculator. Do not record the column totals on the work sheet. Calculate the difference between the two totals. The difference is the net income before federal income tax. LampLight's net income before federal income tax is calculated as shown below.

Income Statement Credit Column Total	–	Income Statement Debit Column Total before Federal Income Tax	=	Net Income before Federal Income Tax
$883,782.75	–	$752,647.48	=	$131,135.27

4. Calculate the amount of federal income tax using a tax rate table furnished by the Internal Revenue Service. LampLight's actual federal income tax is calculated using the tax rate table shown below.

15% of net income before taxes, zero to $50,000.00.
Plus 25% of net income before taxes, $50,000.00 to $75,000.00.
Plus 34% of net income before taxes, $75,000.00 to $100,000.00.
Plus 39% of net income before taxes, $100,000.00 to $335,000.00.
Plus 34% of net income before taxes over $335,000.00.

Tax rate tables showing income tax rates for corporations are distributed each year by the Internal Revenue Service. Each corporation should check a current table to find the applicable rates. Corporation rates that were current when this text was written were used to calculate federal income tax for LampLight as shown below.

Net Income before Taxes		Tax Rate		Federal Income Tax Amount
$ 50,000.00	×	15%	=	$ 7,500.00
Plus 25,000.00	×	25%	=	6,250.00
Plus 25,000.00	×	34%	=	8,500.00
Plus 31,135.27	×	39%	=	12,142.76
$131,135.27				$34,392.76

APPLIED SKILLS: LANGUAGE ARTS

Paraphrasing, writing complete sentences, and identifying adjectives and the words they modify. For additional practice in language arts skills, direct students to answer the Accounting Terms and Questions for Individual Study at the end of the chapter. Students should write the answers in their own words and in complete sentences. To further practice language arts skills, ask students to underline the adjectives and circle the words they modify in their answers.

5 Calculate the amount of accrued federal income tax expense.

Total Federal Income Tax Expense	–	Estimated Federal Income Tax Already Paid	=	Accrued Federal Income Tax Expense
$34,392.76	–	$32,000.00	=	$2,392.76

The tax already paid, *$32,000.00*, is the balance of Federal Income Tax Expense as shown in the work sheet's Trial Balance Debit column, line 75.

6 Record the federal income tax expense adjustment in the work sheet's Adjustments columns. This adjustment is shown as entry *(o)* on lines 26 and 75 of the work sheet.

7 Extend the new balance of Federal Income Tax Payable, *$2,392.76*, to the Balance Sheet Credit column. Extend the new balance of Federal Income Tax Expense, *$34,392.76*, to the Income Statement Debit column.

An adjustment on the work sheet is recorded for the year's federal income tax expense.

Federal Income Tax Expense

Dec. 31 Bal.	32,000.00		
Adj. (o)	2,392.76		
(New Bal.	*34,392.76)*		

Federal Income Tax Payable

		Adj. (o)	2,392.76

Federal Income Tax Expense is debited for $2,392.76. Federal Income Tax Payable is credited for $2,392.76. The new balance of Federal Income Tax Expense, *$34,392.76*, is the total amount of federal income tax due based on the net income before federal income tax.

Audit Your Understanding

1. How often does a corporation pay its estimated federal income tax to the federal government?
2. What three steps are used to calculate net income before federal income tax on a work sheet?

Completing a Work Sheet

The work sheet's Adjustments, Income Statement, and Balance Sheet columns are totaled and the work sheet is completed as shown on lines 76–78.

INCOME STATEMENT FOR A CORPORATION

LampLight prepares three important financial statements. (1) Income statement. (2) Statement of stockholders' equity. (3) Balance sheet. *(CONCEPT: Adequate Disclosure)*

AUDIT YOUR UNDERSTANDING

The AUDIT YOUR UNDERSTANDING feature appears at the end of each section of the chapter. Explain to your students that the word *audit* means to check or verify. AUDIT YOUR UNDERSTANDING may be used to check student comprehension of the section just studied. The answers are provided in Appendix D in the back of the textbook.

1. Quarterly.
2. (1) Complete the work sheet's Adjustments columns except for the federal income tax expense adjustment. (2) Extend all amounts, except the balance of Federal Income Tax Expense, to the work sheet's Income Statement columns. (3) Total the work sheet's Income Statement column totals using a calculator. Calculate the difference between the two totals. The difference is the net income before federal income tax.

LESSON PLAN 14-2

Materials

- Student pages 369–379
- Blackline Master of 3-Column Financial Statement (TRG)
- Blackline Master of 4-Column Financial Statement (TRG)

Objectives (Enabling Performance Tasks)

a. Define accounting terms related to financial analysis and reporting for a corporation.

b. Identify accounting concepts and practices related to financial analysis and reporting for a corporation.

e. Prepare selected end-of-fiscal-period work for a corporation.

f. Analyze financial statements for a corporation.

FOCUS

- In Chapter 5, four financial statements were prepared by the departmentalized corporation, and component percentages were calculated to analyze the reports. Explain that LampLight prepares three of the same statements—an income statement, a statement of stockholders' equity, and a balance sheet. In this lesson, the preparation of these three statements will be reviewed, and analysis of the statements will be expanded beyond the calculation of component percentages.
- Introduce vocabulary: earnings per share, equity per share, market value, price-earnings ratio, rate earned on average stockholders' equity, rate earned on average total assets.

FYI

Financial statements are only beneficial to the extent that they are analyzed and used by the corporation to measure progress.

Preparing an Income Statement

Unlike sole proprietorships and partnerships, a corporation must pay federal income tax. Both net income before and after federal income tax are shown on a corporate income statement. This method of reporting shows how much of a corporation's income is used to pay federal income tax.

LampLight's income statement is shown in Illustration 14-2, page 371.

Analyzing an Income Statement

Lamplight analyzes several items related to information on an income statement. (1) Component percentages. (2) Earnings per share.

Component Percentages. The percentage relationship between one financial statement item and the total that includes that item is known as a component percentage. LampLight calculates component percentages for each major item on its income statement. LampLight uses net sales as the basis for calculating component percentages. For example, LampLight's component percentage for selling expenses is calculated as shown below.

Total Selling Expenses	÷	Net Sales	=	Total Selling Expenses Component Percentage
$119,779.05	÷	$861,356.72	=	13.9%

The component percentage, *13.9%*, means that for each dollar of net sales, *$0.139*, is paid for selling expenses. Component percentages for each major item on LampLight's income statement are listed in a separate column as shown in Illustration 14-2.

LampLight compared their component percentages with previous years' income statements and with industry standards. LampLight determined acceptable component percentages for each major item of cost, expense, and income on its income statement. Similar to MasterSport in Chapter 5, LampLight does not analyze component percentages for federal income tax expense and net income after federal income tax. For comparative purposes, LampLight's acceptable and actual component percentages are shown in Illustration 14-3, page 372.

Achieving acceptable component percentages for the major income statement items indicates that the business is keeping costs and expenses at an acceptable level compared with revenue. If the component percentage of any item for a fiscal period varies from the acceptable percentage, that item is reviewed to

TEACHING STRATEGIES: DIFFERENT LEARNING STYLES

Auditory Learner. The auditory learner can reinforce the learning of formulas by verbally explaining the formula and/or calculations to other students in a small group. In a group of three, for example, each student should get the opportunity to "teach" the formula to the other two students. Through this process, each student in the group will "teach" the formula once and "learn" the formula two times.

ILLUSTRATION 14-2 Income statement for a corporation

LampLight, Inc.
Income Statement
For Year Ended December 31, 19--

					*% of Net Sales
Operating Revenue:					
Sales			$872,952.40		
Less: Sales Discount		$ 8,695.12			
Sales Returns and Allowances		2,900.56	11,595.68		
Net Sales				$861,356.72	100.0
Cost of Merchandise Sold:					
Merchandise Inventory, Jan. 1, 19--			$267,453.09		
Purchases		$455,396.48			
Less: Purchases Discount	$6,710.35				
Purchases Returns and Allowances	2,670.00	9,380.35			
Net Purchases			446,016.13		
Total Cost of Merchandise Available for Sale			$713,469.22		
Less Merchandise Inventory, Dec. 31, 19--			258,755.19		
Cost of Merchandise Sold				454,714.03	52.8
Gross Profit on Operations				$406,642.69	47.2
Operating Expenses:					
Selling Expenses:					
Advertising Expense		$ 17,782.00			
Credit Card Fee Expense		6,285.00			
Depreciation Expense—Store Equipment		16,753.00			
Miscellaneous Expense—Sales		9,406.12			
Salary Expense—Sales		63,683.89			
Supplies Expense—Sales		5,869.04			
Total Selling Expenses			$119,779.05		13.9
Administrative Expenses:					
Depreciation Expense—Building		$ 8,250.00			
Depreciation Expense—Office Equipment		9,734.13			
Insurance Expense		5,911.31			
Miscellaneous Expense—Administrative		12,570.68			
Payroll Taxes Expense		9,962.40			
Property Tax Expense		6,700.00			
Salary Expense—Administrative		23,819.17			
Supplies Expense—Administrative		14,456.40			
Uncollectible Accounts Expense		6,277.50			
Utilities Expense		28,727.25			
Total Administrative Expenses			126,408.84		14.7
Total Operating Expenses				246,187.89	28.6
Income from Operations				$160,454.80	18.6
Other Revenue:					
Interest Income			$ 1,450.00		
Other Expenses:					
Interest Expense		$ 30,289.53			
Organization Expense		480.00			
Total Other Expenses			$ 30,769.53		
Net Deduction				29,319.53	3.4
Net Income before Federal Income Tax				$131,135.27	15.2
Less Federal Income Tax Expense				34,392.76	4.0
Net Income after Federal Income Tax				$ 96,742.51	11.2

*Rounded to nearest 0.1%

TEACH

Cover student pages 369–379 "Income Statement for a Corporation," "Statement of Stockholders' Equity for a Corporation," and "Balance Sheet for a Corporation." Present the income statement and review its format. Review the definition of component percentages and how they are calculated. Discuss why some component percentages are acceptable and others are not. Demonstrate how earnings per share is calculated. Inform students that earnings per share is the most common measure of a corporation's earnings. Present the statement of stockholders' equity. Review the two major kinds of equity accounts used in a corporation—Paid-in Capital and Retained Earnings. Demonstrate how equity per share is calculated and used in analysis. Point out that the equity per share of preferred stock is always equal to the stock's par value. Discuss market value per share. Demonstrate how price-earnings ratio is calculated and used in analysis. Present the balance sheet and review its format. Demonstrate how to calculate the accounts receivable turnover ratio, the rate earned on average stockholders' equity, and the rate earned on average total assets. Explain how each is used to analyze the balance sheet. Point out that financial analysts consider a minimum acceptable rate earned on average stockholders equity to be 4% to 6% above the current prime lending rate.

TEACHING STRATEGIES: TEACHING TIP

Review the format of a corporation's financial statements by inviting students to the board to list the major headings of each statement.

APPLY

Refer students to Illustration 14-2, 14-4, and 14-5, respectively, as the income statement, statement of stockholders' equity, and balance sheet are discussed. Review the format of each financial statement by having students go to the board and write the major headings. As each formula used for financial statement analysis is discussed, write it on the board for reference.

Guided Practice

Guide students through the preparation of the income statement, statement of stockholders' equity, and balance sheet from Instruction 1 of Problems 14-3, 14-4, and 14-5. Students will need the work sheet prepared in Problem 14-2. As a group, prepare the three financial statements. All students must agree before they write any amounts on the forms provided in the working papers. The balance of Problems 14-3, 14-4, and 14-5 can be completed as Independent Practice.

Independent Practice

Assign Terms 2–7; Questions 7–14; and Problems 14-3, 14-4, and 14-5.

ILLUSTRATION 14-3 Acceptable and actual component percentages

Income Statement Items	Acceptable Component Percentages	Actual Component Percentages
Cost of merchandise sold	Not more than 55.0%	52.8%
Gross profit on operations	Not less than 45.0%	47.2%
Total selling expenses	Not more than 12.0%	13.9%
Total administrative expenses	Not more than 18.0%	14.7%
Total operating expenses	Not more than 30.0%	28.6%
Income from operations	Not less than 15.0%	18.6%
Net deduction from other expenses	Not more than 4.0%	3.4%
Net income before federal income tax	Not less than 11.0%	15.2%

FYI

Financial statements of publicly traded corporations must meet the standards set by the Securities and Exchange Commission (SEC).

determine the reason. Management can then seek ways to bring the item within acceptable limits.

For the current year ended December 31, LampLight has achieved acceptable percentages for most items. However, the component percentage for total selling expenses, 13.9%, is higher than the maximum acceptable percentage, 12.0%, a negative result. Thus, LampLight's managers further analyze the expense accounts which comprise selling expenses. This analysis enables the managers to correct negative situations or revise the acceptable percentage for the next fiscal period. For example, the managers' investigation revealed that the component percentage for advertising expense was significantly higher than the acceptable percentage, a negative result. Further investigation revealed a sharp increase in the price of television advertising. To correct this situation for the next fiscal period, LampLight's managers can select one of two alternatives. LampLight can reduce advertising costs by using alternate forms of advertising, such as radio, and continue using 12.0% as the maximum acceptable component percentage. However, television advertising may be LampLight's only effective means of advertising. Thus, LampLight could continue using television advertising and increase the maximum acceptable component percentage.

Earnings Per Share. The total earnings for outstanding preferred stock, equal to the 8% dividend specified on the stock certificates, is calculated as shown below.

Total Par Value	×	Dividend Rate	=	Preferred Stock's Share of Net Income
$170,000.00	×	8%	=	$13,600.00

The total share of net income for common stock is the remainder of the net income after the preferred stock's share is deducted.

Total Net Income	−	Preferred Stock's Share of Net Income	=	Common Stock's Share of Net Income
$96,742.51	−	$13,600.00	=	$83,142.51

FYI

Many investors use earnings per share as a measure to determine which stocks to purchase.

The amount of net income belonging to a single share of stock is called **earnings per share.** Earnings per share is typically only calculated on the number of common shares outstanding. For example, LampLight has 32,100 shares of common stock issued. However, 150 of these shares are treasury stock and, therefore, not outstanding stock. LampLight has 31,950 shares of outstanding common stock (32,100 shares *less* 150 shares *equals* 31,950).

For the year ended December 31, LampLight's earnings per share on common stock is calculated as shown below.

Share of Net Income	÷	Shares of Stock Outstanding	=	Earnings per Share
$83,142.51	÷	31,950	=	$2.60

STATEMENT OF STOCKHOLDERS' EQUITY FOR A CORPORATION

CAREERS IN ACCOUNTING

AUDIT CLERK

- *Verifies accuracy of figures, calculations, and postings pertaining to business transactions recorded by other workers*
- *Examines expense accounts, cash receipts, sales tickets, bank tickets, and similar items to verify accuracy of recorded data*
- *Corrects errors or lists discrepancies for adjustments*
- *Calculates totals and compares results with recorded entries*

A statement of stockholders' equity shows changes occurring in the stockholders' equity for a fiscal period.

Preparing a Statement of Stockholders' Equity

LampLight's statement of stockholders' equity has two major sections: (1) Paid-in Capital and (2) Retained Earnings. LampLight's statement of stockholders' equity prepared on December 31 is shown in Illustration 14-4 on page 374.

> Some businesses prepare a statement of retained earnings instead of a statement of stockholders' equity. A statement of retained earnings includes only information about the changes in retained earnings during a fiscal period. The remainder of the information about changes in paid-in capital is placed on the corporation's balance sheet. However, LampLight prepares a statement of stockholders' equity so that all the information does not need to be placed on the balance sheet.

As of December 31, LampLight has issued $321,000.00 in common stock and $170,000.00 in preferred stock for a total stock issue of $491,000.00. LampLight also has $1,800.00 in treasury stock. Therefore, the total stock outstanding is $489,200.00. The total stockholders' equity, *$618,655.86,* is shown on the last line of the statement of stockholders' equity.

ASSESS

Assess student understanding by checking the solutions to the Independent Practice activities.

Reteach

- Make transparencies of the appropriate 3- and 4-column financial statement paper from the accounting forms masters provided in the Blackline Masters Section of the Teacher's Resource Guide. Using the transparencies and the work sheet prepared in Recycling Problem 14-R, Instruction 1, demonstrate how to prepare an income statement, a statement of stockholders' equity, and a balance sheet.
- Assign Recycling Problem 14-R, Instructions 2–8.

Extend

Assign Cases for Critical Thinking 1 and 2.

Enrich

- Have students bring in the financial section of the newspaper. Ask them to locate the stock information that has been covered in class.
- Assign the CAREERS IN ACCOUNTING feature on page 373. Have students discuss what a career as an audit clerk might be like.

CAREERS IN ACCOUNTING

The CAREERS feature box, AUDIT CLERK, comes from the Dictionary of Occupational Titles (DOT). The entry number for this job title is D.O.T. 210.382.010. Bring this dictionary to class and explain its purpose and how to use it. The career feature is designed to expose students to the exploration of different careers in accounting. The feature gives a realistic description of actual job duties. This feature can be used to demonstrate that the skills learned in this course are relevant.

CLOSURE

Use Audit Your Understanding questions.

ILLUSTRATION 14-4 Statement of stockholders' equity for a corporation

LampLight, Inc.
Statement of Stockholders' Equity
For Year Ended December 31, 19--

Paid-in Capital:			
Common Stock, $10.00 Stated Value:			
January 1, 19--, 32,000 Shares Issued	$320,000.00		
Issued during Current Year, 100 Shares	1,000.00		
Balance, December 31, 19--, 32,100 Shares Issued		$321,000.00	
Preferred Stock, 8%, $100.00 Par Value:			
January 1, 19--, No Shares Issued	-0-		
Issued during Current Year, 1,700 Shares	170,000.00		
Balance, Dec. 31, 19--, 1,700 Shares Issued		170,000.00	
Total Value of Capital Stock Issued			$491,000.00
Additional Paid-in Capital:			
Paid-in Capital in Excess of Stated Value—Common	$ 200.00		
Paid-in Capital in Excess of Par Value—Preferred	8,000.00		
Paid-in Capital from Sale of Treasury Stock	500.00	$ 8,700.00	
Less Discount on Sale of Preferred Stock		5,000.00	
Total Additional Paid-in Capital			3,700.00
Total Paid-in Capital			$494,700.00
Retained Earnings:			
Balance, January 1, 19--		$ 58,588.35	
Net Income after Federal Income Tax for 19--	$ 96,742.51		
Less Dividends Declared during 19--	29,575.00		
Net Increase during 19--		67,167.51	
Balance, December 31, 19--			125,755.86
Total Paid-in Capital and Retained Earnings			$620,455.86
Less Treasury Stock, 150 Shares of Common Stock December 31, 19--			1,800.00
Total Stockholders' Equity, December 31, 19--			$618,655.86

Analyzing a Statement of Stockholders' Equity

LampLight analyzes three items related to information on its statement of stockholders' equity. (1) Equity per share. (2) Market value per share. (3) Price-earnings ratio.

Equity Per Share. The amount of total stockholders' equity belonging to a single share of stock is called **equity per share.** The equity per share for LampLight's preferred and common stock is calculated as shown below.

	Total Stockholders' Equity	÷	Shares of Capital Stock Outstanding	=	Equity per Share
Preferred	$170,000.00	÷	1,700	=	$100.00
Common	448,655.86	÷	31,950	=	14.04
Total	$618,655.86				

TEACHING STRATEGIES: DIFFERENT LEARNING STYLES

Kinesthetic Learner. The kinesthetic learner should have the opportunity to perform the calculations to solve the formula. One way to accomplish this is to develop several situations using different dividend rates for preferred stock and different amounts of net income. The student should calculate the earnings per share for each situation.

The equity of preferred stock is equal to its total par value, *$170,000.00*, or $100.00 per share. The remainder of the total stockholders' equity is the equity of the common stock, *$448,655.86*, or $14.04 per share. Most businesses consider common stock equity at least equal to its stated value to be acceptable. LampLight's common stock equity per share is greater than its stated value of $10.00 per share and is acceptable.

FYI

Many stock prices can be found in daily newspaper listings. NYSE stands for New York Stock Exchange in the stock listings in the newspaper.

Market Value Per Share. The price at which a share of stock may be sold on the stock market is called **market value.** The market value is determined by how much a buyer is willing to pay for the stock. Therefore, market price is established by investors' buying and selling the corporation's stock on the stock market. If a business is profitable and pays adequate dividends, investors often will offer to pay a market price higher than the stock's par or stated value. If a business is not profitable or does not pay regular dividends, investors often will offer to pay a market price lower than the stock's par or stated value.

Stock is recorded on a corporation's records at the par or stated value. The market value of stock is not recorded on corporate records.

TEACHING STRATEGIES: DIFFERENT LEARNING STYLES

Print Learner. When learning formulas, the print learner would prefer to be able to study the formula as given in the textbook or as printed on a separate handout. The print material should show the formula as well as an example of performing the calculations.

Price-Earnings Ratio. The relationship between the market value per share and earnings per share of a stock is called the **price-earnings ratio.** Investors usually want to buy stock in companies that are earning a reasonable amount of net income. One way to determine if a company is earning a reasonable amount of net income is to calculate the price-earnings ratio. The ratio is then compared to standards for similar companies.

LampLight's earnings per share on common stock is $2.60 as previously described. Using stock market reports on December 31, the price-earnings ratio for common stock is calculated as shown below.

Market Price per Share	÷	Earnings per Share	=	Price-Earnings Ratio
$19.50	÷	$2.60	=	7.5 times

The common stock price-earnings ratio, *7.5 times*, means that the stock is selling for 7.5 times its share of the earnings. For businesses similar to LampLight, a common stock price-earnings ratio between 6.0 and 10.0 times is considered acceptable. LampLight's price-earnings ratio for common stock is acceptable.

BALANCE SHEET FOR A CORPORATION

A corporate balance sheet reports assets, liabilities, and stockholders' equity on a specific date.

APPLIED SKILLS: WRITING ACROSS THE CURRICULUM

Writing paragraphs and short essays. The Cases for Critical Thinking are short, practical applications of the accounting principles developed in the chapter. Some cases are planned to present problems related to the chapter but not specifically discussed and answered in the chapter. These cases present an opportunity for critical thinking and decision making. These cases also require more than a short objective-type response. Therefore, they provide ideal practice in writing paragraphs and short essays.

TEACHING STRATEGIES: COOPERATIVE LEARNING

Research project: Assign students to groups of two. Each group researches the financial statements (through the annual report) of a company in which they are interested, perhaps because they are familiar with the product. Students look for a list of specific items such as: what kinds of stock is the corporation authorized to issue, what categories of assets are listed on the balance sheet, what is the total of current liabilities, did net income increase/decrease from the previous period, etc. After the research is done, the group must plan and deliver a presentation of the data to the entire class. Time frame: class time = 45 minutes to plan presentation; additional time outside of class is needed to complete research and prepare presentation.

FYI

The statement of cash flows, described in Appendix A, has largely replaced the outdated statement of changes in financial position.

Preparing a Balance Sheet

LampLight's December 31 balance sheet is shown in Illustration 14-5 on page 377. LampLight's balance sheet is similar to the one described for MasterSport in Chapter 5. However, LampLight includes two additional accounts: Bond Sinking Fund and Organization Costs. Bond Sinking Fund is listed in the balance sheet's Assets section under the heading *Long-Term Investment.* Organization Costs is listed in the Assets section under the heading *Intangible Assets.*

Only the total stockholders' equity obtained from the stockholders' equity statement is included under the heading *Stockholders' Equity.* If more detail is needed, LampLight's statement of stockholders' equity can be read.

Analyzing a Balance Sheet

LampLight calculates three ratios based on information from its balance sheet items. (1) Accounts receivable turnover ratio. (2) Rate earned on average stockholders' equity. (3) Rate earned on average total assets.

Accounts Receivable Turnover Ratio. The number of times the average amount of accounts receivable is collected annually is known as the accounts receivable turnover ratio. LampLight calculates this ratio as shown below.

1 Calculate the average book value of accounts receivable.

Accounts Receivable Beginning Balance	–	Allowance for Uncollectible Accounts Beginning Balance	=	Beginning Book Value
$124,983.89	–	$4,362.18	=	$120,621.71
Accounts Receivable Ending Balance	**–**	**Allowance for Uncollectible Accounts Ending Balance**	**=**	**Ending Book Value**
$135,234.54	–	$6,697.63	=	$128,536.91

(Beginning Book Value of Accounts Receivable	+	Ending Book Value of Accounts Receivable)	÷ 2	=	Average Book Value of Accounts Receivable
($120,621.71	+	$128,536.91)	÷ 2	=	$124,579.31

Beginning balances are obtained from the financial statements of the prior year. Ending balances are obtained from the work sheet for the current year.

2 Calculate the accounts receivable turnover ratio.

Net Sales on Account	÷	Average Book Value of Accounts Receivable	=	Accounts Receivable Turnover Ratio
$861,356.72	÷	$124,579.31	=	6.9 times

ILLUSTRATION 14-5 Balance sheet for a corporation

LampLight, Inc.
Balance Sheet
December 31, 19--

ASSETS			
Current Assets:			
Cash		$ 25,436.40	
Petty Cash		250.00	
Notes Receivable		10,000.00	
Interest Receivable		1,000.00	
Accounts Receivable	$135,234.54		
Less Allowance for Uncollectible Accounts	6,697.63	128,536.91	
Merchandise Inventory		258,755.19	
Supplies—Sales		8,446.63	
Supplies—Administrative		8,157.30	
Prepaid Insurance		10,988.69	
Prepaid Interest		10.47	
Total Current Assets			$451,581.59
Long-Term Investment:			
Bond Sinking Fund			50,000.00
Plant Assets:			
Store Equipment	$142,983.34		
Less Accumulated Depreciation—Store Equipment	31,876.00	$111,107.34	
Building	$165,000.00		
Less Accumulated Depreciation—Building	16,500.00	148,500.00	
Office Equipment	$ 73,928.23		
Less Accumulated Depreciation—Office Equipment	17,386.13	56,542.10	
Land		133,000.00	
Total Plant Assets			449,149.44
Intangible Assets:			
Organization Costs			1,440.00
Total Assets			$952,171.03
LIABILITIES			
Current Liabilities:			
Notes Payable	$ 2,500.00		
Interest Payable	15,000.00		
Accounts Payable	28,085.40		
Employee Income Tax Payable	1,238.90		
Federal Income Tax Payable	2,392.76		
FICA Tax Payable	819.60		
Salaries Payable	633.73		
Sales Tax Payable	2,154.74		
Unemployment Tax Payable—Federal	88.65		
Unemployment Tax Payable—State	598.39		
Health Insurance Premiums Payable	428.00		
Dividends Payable	29,575.00		
Total Current Liabilities		$ 83,515.17	
Long-Term Liability:			
Bonds Payable		250,000.00	
Total Liabilities			$333,515.17
STOCKHOLDERS' EQUITY			
Total Stockholders' Equity			618,655.86
Total Liabilities and Stockholders' Equity			$952,171.03

TEACHING STRATEGIES: TEACHING TIP

Ask for four or five volunteers to bring in the financial section of the newspaper. Pass the samples around so that all students have a chance to become familiar with the financial section. Ask students to locate stock information that has been covered in class. Have students list the stock exchanges available for trading stock.

TEACHING STRATEGIES: DIFFERENT LEARNING STYLES

Visually-Impaired Students. The use of software should not be overlooked for visually impaired students, particularly if oversized monitors with larger displays are available.

TEACHING STRATEGIES: DIFFERENT LEARNING STYLES

Tactile Learner. Suggest using a calculator with a printed tape to perform mathematical calculations. Better calculators also print the operational signs of calculations (+, −, etc.) for students to trace the steps in a calculation.

Some businesses record in separate accounts the amount of cash sales and net sales on account. Net sales as reported on the income statement should be used as net sales on account if the business does not record this information.

3 Calculate the average number of days for payment.

Days in Year	÷	Accounts Receivable Turnover Ratio	=	Average Number of Days for Payment
365	÷	6.9	=	53

LampLight's terms of sales are 2/10, n/30. Therefore, LampLight expects payment within 30 days. The expected accounts receivable turnover ratio is 12.2 times (365 days in a year ÷ 30 days). LampLight's average number of days for payment, *53,* is greater than the expected level of 30 days. Therefore, LampLight's accounts receivable turnover ratio, *6.9 times,* is unacceptable. LampLight needs to consider ways to encourage customers to pay their accounts within the credit period.

FYI

In 1989, 46% of Americans between 3 and 17 years old used a computer either at home or at school.

Rate Earned on Average Stockholders' Equity. The relationship between net income and average stockholders' equity is called the **rate earned on average stockholders' equity.** The rate earned on average stockholders' equity for LampLight is calculated as shown below.

(January 1 Stockholders' Equity	+	December 31 Stockholders' Equity)	÷	2	=	Average Stockholders' Equity
($378,588.35	+	$618,655.86)	÷	2	=	$498,622.11
Net Income after Federal Income Tax	÷	Average Stockholders' Equity			=	Rate Earned on Average Stockholders' Equity
$96,742.51	÷	$498,622.11			=	19.4%

For each dollar stockholders have invested, LampLight is earning $0.194 in net income. The best investment is in a corporation with the highest rate earned on average stockholders' equity. For example, Midtown, Inc. has a rate earned on average stockholders' equity of 14.2% compared to LampLight's rate of 19.4%. *Based on this one analysis,* an investor would choose to invest in LampLight's stock rather than Midtown's.

Rate Earned on Average Total Assets. The relationship between net income and average total assets is called **rate earned on average total assets.** This rate for LampLight is calculated as shown on the following page.

TEACHING STRATEGIES: DIFFERENT LEARNING STYLES

Visual Learner. Formulas, such as those used to calculate earnings per share, should be illustrated on the chalkboard to assist visual learners. The instructor should also complete the calculations for several different situations to show the process to visual learners.

(January 1 Total Assets	+	December 31 Total Assets)	÷ 2 =	Average Total Assets
($724,976.34	+	$952,171.03)	÷ 2 =	$838,573.69

Net Income after Federal Income Tax	÷	Average Total Assets	=	Rate Earned on Average Total Assets
$96,742.51	÷	$838,573.69	=	11.5%

For each dollar of assets owned by the corporation, the business has earnings of $0.115 after federal income tax is paid. Information published by trade organizations shows that businesses similar to LampLight tend to have a rate earned on average total assets between 10.0% and 14.0%. LampLight's rate, 11.5%, is acceptable.

Other methods of analyzing corporate financial statement items are described in Chapter 17.

Audit Your Understanding

1. What is the formula for calculating the component percentage for total selling expenses?
2. What should be done if the component percentage of any item for a fiscal period varies from the acceptable percentage?
3. What will cause investors to offer to pay a market price higher than the stock's par or stated value?
4. What is the formula for calculating the price-earnings ratio?
5. What is the formula for calculating the average book value of accounts receivable?
6. What is the formula for calculating the average number of days for payment?

OTHER END-OF-FISCAL-PERIOD WORK

In addition to a work sheet and financial statements, LampLight also prepares adjusting entries, closing entries, a post-closing trial balance, and reversing entries.

Adjusting Entries

LampLight's December 31 adjusting entries are shown in Illustration 14-6 on page 380.

Closing Entries

LampLight records four closing entries at the end of a fiscal period.

1. Closing entry for income statement accounts with credit balances (revenue and contra cost accounts).
2. Closing entry for income statement accounts with debit balances (cost, contra revenue, and expense accounts).
3. Closing entry to record net income or net loss in the retained earnings account and close the income summary account.
4. Closing entry for the dividends accounts.

LampLight's December 31 closing entries are shown in Illustration 14-7 on page 381.

LampLight's closing entries are similar to those described for MasterSport in Chapter 5.

FYI

Dividend accounts are closed into Retained Earnings.

AUDIT YOUR UNDERSTANDING

1. Total selling expenses divided by net sales.
2. Review the item to determine the reason.
3. If a business is profitable and pays adequate dividends.
4. Market price per share divided by earnings per share.
5. Beginning book value of accounts receivable plus ending book value of accounts receivable divided by two.
6. Days in year divided by accounts receivable turnover ratio.

LESSON PLAN 14-3

Materials

- Student pages 379–386
- Blackline Master of General Journal (TRG)
- Software: Spreadsheet Template; *Automated Accounting 6.0* or higher; Accounting Textbook Template, Advanced Course
- Assess: Problem Test Chapter 14, MicroExam Chapter 14, Objective Test No. 5

Objectives (Enabling Performance Tasks)

b. Identify accounting concepts and practices related to financial analysis and reporting for a corporation.

c. Journalize adjusting entries for amortizing an intangible asset.

e. Prepare selected end-of-fiscal-period work for a corporation.

FOCUS

Adjusting and closing entries for a departmentalized corporation were journalized in Chapter 5. Explain that similar entries are recorded for a nondepartmentalized business. In this lesson, information from the work sheet prepared earlier in this chapter will be used to journalize LampLight's adjusting and closing entries. Additional end-of-fiscal-period work, including a post-closing trial balance, reversing entries, and a corporate income tax return, will be presented.

ILLUSTRATION 14-6 Adjusting entries for a corporation

GENERAL JOURNAL — PAGE 13

	DATE		ACCOUNT TITLE	DOC. NO.	POST. REF.	DEBIT	CREDIT	
1			*Adjusting Entries*					1
2	19-- Dec.	31	*Interest Receivable*			1000 00		2
3			*Interest Income*				1000 00	3
4		31	*Uncollectible Accounts Expense*			6277 50		4
5			*Allowance for Uncoll. Accts.*				6277 50	5
6		31	*Income Summary*			8697 90		6
7			*Merchandise Inventory*				8697 90	7
8		31	*Supplies Expense—Sales*			5869 04		8
9			*Supplies—Sales*				5869 04	9
10		31	*Supplies Expense—Admin.*			14456 40		10
11			*Supplies—Admin.*				14456 40	11
12		31	*Insurance Expense*			5911 31		12
13			*Prepaid Insurance*				5911 31	13
14		31	*Prepaid Interest*			10 47		14
15			*Interest Expense*				10 47	15
16		31	*Depreciation Exp.—Store Equip.*			16753 00		16
17			*Accum. Depr.—Store Equip.*				16753 00	17
18		31	*Depreciation Exp.—Building*			8250 00		18
19			*Accum. Depr.—Building*				8250 00	19
20		31	*Depreciation Exp.—Office Equip.*			9734 13		20
21			*Accum. Depr.—Office Equip.*				9734 13	21
22		31	*Organization Expense*			480 00		22
23			*Organization Costs*				480 00	23
24		31	*Interest Expense*			15000 00		24
25			*Interest Payable*				15000 00	25
26		31	*Salary Expense—Sales*			457 89		26
27			*Salary Expense—Admin.*			175 84		27
28			*Salaries Payable*				633 73	28
29		31	*Payroll Taxes Expense*			60 00		29
30			*FICA Tax Payable*				50 70	30
31			*Unemploy. Tax Pay.—Federal*				1 20	31
32			*Unemploy. Tax Pay.—State*				8 10	32
33		31	*Federal Income Tax Expense*			2392 76		33
34			*Federal Income Tax Payable*				2392 76	34
35								35
36								36
37								37
38								38
39								39
40								40

Post-Closing Trial Balance

LampLight's December 31 post-closing trial balance is shown in Illustration 14-8 on page 382.

TEACHING STRATEGIES: EXPANDING BEYOND THE CLASSROOM

Invite an accountant from a merchandising business to the classroom to address the importance of the closing process, how long it takes, and what procedures are actually followed to close the books at the end of the period.

ILLUSTRATION 14-7 Closing entries for a corporation

GENERAL JOURNAL PAGE 14

	DATE		ACCOUNT TITLE	DOC. NO.	POST. REF.	DEBIT	CREDIT	
1			*Closing Entries*					1
2	*19-- Dec.*	*31*	*Sales*			*872 952 40*		2
3			*Purchases Discount*			*6 710 35*		3
4			*Purchases Returns and Allowances*			*2 670 00*		4
5			*Interest Income*			*1 450 00*		5
6			*Income Summary*				*883 782 75*	6
7		*31*	*Income Summary*			*778 342 34*		7
8			*Sales Discount*				*8 695 12*	8
9			*Sales Returns and Allowances*				*2 900 56*	9
10			*Purchases*				*455 396 48*	10
11			*Advertising Expense*				*17 782 00*	11
12			*Credit Card Fee Expense*				*6 285 00*	12
13			*Depreciation Exp.—Store Equip.*				*16 753 00*	13
14			*Miscellaneous Exp.—Sales*				*9 406 12*	14
15			*Salary Expense—Sales*				*63 683 89*	15
16			*Supplies Expense—Sales*				*5 869 04*	16
17			*Depreciation Exp.—Building*				*8 250 00*	17
18			*Depreciation Exp.—Office Equip.*				*9 734 13*	18
19			*Insurance Expense*				*5 911 31*	19
20			*Miscellaneous Exp.—Admin.*				*12 570 68*	20
21			*Payroll Taxes Expense*				*9 962 40*	21
22			*Property Tax Expense*				*6 700 00*	22
23			*Salary Expense—Admin.*				*23 819 17*	23
24			*Supplies Expense—Admin.*				*14 456 40*	24
25			*Uncollectible Accounts Expense*				*6 277 50*	25
26			*Utilities Expense*				*28 727 25*	26
27			*Interest Expense*				*30 289 53*	27
28			*Organization Expense*				*480 00*	28
29			*Federal Income Tax Expense*				*34 392 76*	29
30		*31*	*Income Summary*			*96 742 51*		30
31			*Retained Earnings*				*96 742 51*	31
32		*31*	*Retained Earnings*			*29 575 00*		32
33			*Dividends—Common*				*15 975 00*	33
34			*Dividends—Preferred*				*13 600 00*	34
35								35
36								36
37								37
38								38
39								39
40								40

FYI

Usually, a reversing entry is needed if an adjusting entry creates a balance in an asset or a liability account.

Reversing Entries

If an adjusting entry creates a balance in an asset or liability account, LampLight reverses the adjusting entry. Like most corpo-

TEACH

Cover student pages 379–386 "Other End-of-Fiscal-Period Work," "Federal Income Tax Return," and "Dissolving a Corporation." Discuss the importance of adjusting and closing entries. Review the steps for journalizing the four closing entries. Review the purpose of a post-closing trial balance. Discuss when reversing entries are needed. Emphasize that the adjustment for federal income tax is not reversed. Remind students that a corporation is considered to be an entity and, therefore, is subject to taxes. Discuss the income tax return, Form 1120, that a corporation must file. Review how a corporation is dissolved.

APPLY

Refer students to Illustrations 14-6, 14-7, 14-8, 14-9, respectively, as adjusting entries, closing entries, the post-closing trial balance, and reversing entries are discussed. Refer students to Illustration 14-10 as the preparation of Form 1120 is explained.

Guided Practice

Guide students through the use of T accounts to record the four closing entries in Problem 14-6, Instruction 2. Students will need the work sheet prepared in Problem 14-2. Have students draw T accounts on a sheet of paper for each account to be closed and record the December 31 balances in the accounts. Working as a group, record the first closing entry in the T accounts. Label each part of the entry (1). All students should agree before proceeding to the second closing entry. Repeat the process until all four closing entries have been recorded in the T accounts. The balance of Problem 14-6 can be completed as Independent Practice.

Independent Practice

- Assign Questions 15–16 and Problem 14-6.
- Assign Study Guide 14 and Mastery Problem 14-M.

ILLUSTRATION 14-8 Post-closing trial balance for a corporation

LampLight, Inc.
Post-Closing Trial Balance
December 31, 19--

Account Title	Debit	Credit
Cash	$ 25,436.40	
Petty Cash	250.00	
Notes Receivable	10,000.00	
Interest Receivable	1,000.00	
Accounts Receivable	135,234.54	
Allowance for Uncollectible Accounts		$ 6,697.63
Subscriptions Receivable		
Merchandise Inventory	258,755.19	
Supplies—Sales	8,446.63	
Supplies—Administrative	8,157.30	
Prepaid Insurance	10,988.69	
Prepaid Interest	10.47	
Bond Sinking Fund	50,000.00	
Store Equipment	142,983.34	
Accumulated Depreciation—Store Equipment		31,876.00
Building	165,000.00	
Accumulated Depreciation—Building		16,500.00
Office Equipment	73,928.23	
Accumulated Depreciation—Office Equipment		17,386.13
Land	133,000.00	
Organization Costs	1,440.00	
Notes Payable		2,500.00
Interest Payable		15,000.00
Accounts Payable		28,085.40
Employee Income Tax Payable		1,238.90
Federal Income Tax Payable		2,392.76
FICA Tax Payable		819.60
Salaries Payable		633.73
Sales Tax Payable		2,154.74
Unemployment Tax Payable—Federal		88.65
Unemployment Tax Payable—State		598.39
Health Insurance Premiums Payable		428.00
Dividends Payable		29,575.00
Bonds Payable		250,000.00
Capital Stock—Common		321,000.00
Stock Subscribed—Common		
Paid-in Capital in Excess of Stated Value—Common		200.00
Capital Stock—Preferred		170,000.00
Stock Subscribed—Preferred		
Paid-in Capital in Excess of Par Value—Preferred		8,000.00
Discount on Sale of Preferred Stock	5,000.00	
Treasury Stock	1,800.00	
Paid-in Capital from Sale of Treasury Stock		500.00
Retained Earnings		125,755.86
Totals	$1,031,430.79	$1,031,430.79

rations, however, LampLight does not reverse the adjusting entry that records federal income tax. LampLight's reversing entries recorded on January 1 are shown in Illustration 14-9.

ILLUSTRATION 14-9 Reversing entries for a corporation

GENERAL JOURNAL PAGE *15*

	DATE		ACCOUNT TITLE	DOC. NO.	POST. REF.	DEBIT	CREDIT	
1			*Reversing Entries*					1
2	*19-- Jan.*	*1*	*Interest Income*			*1 000 00*		2
3			*Interest Receivable*				*1 000 00*	3
4		*1*	*Interest Expense*			*10 47*		4
5			*Prepaid Interest*				*10 47*	5
6		*1*	*Interest Payable*			*15 000 00*		6
7			*Interest Expense*				*15 000 00*	7
8		*1*	*Salaries Payable*			*633 73*		8
9			*Salary Expense—Sales*				*457 89*	9
10			*Salary Expense—Administrative*				*175 84*	10
11		*1*	*FICA Tax Payable*			*50 70*		11
12			*Unemploy. Tax Pay.—Federal*			*1 20*		12
13			*Unemploy. Tax Pay.—State*			*8 10*		13
14			*Payroll Taxes Expense*				*60 00*	14

■ Dr. Yoshi Tsuchiya ■

HAMAGAMI LABORATORY

Dr. Yoshi Tsuchiya studied chemical engineering in Japan. After coming to America, he studied biochemistry and experimental medicine. When he arrived from Japan he had very little money but wanted to start his own laboratory. Therefore, he worked a second job at the end of business each day in order to keep his company alive.

Tsuchiya says that when he joined the medical laboratory in the 60s, there were few regulations on medical research, which surprised him. "Of course, today," he states, "that has all changed, and now there are many restrictions. The restrictions do make it more expensive to do business and that is why medical laboratory service often costs so much."

Tsuchiya did not have any formal education in business subjects. However, he spent a lot of time reading about business management and learning how to run a business. He learned a lot about accounting just from having to keep the records for his new business. However, he feels that a background in accounting would have been of great value in understanding the various federal, state, and local taxes that his business had to comply with.

Shortly after he came to America, Tsuchiya's mentor, Dr. Hamagami, became seriously ill, leaving all the responsibility for running the business to Tsuchiya. He said, "I not only had to learn the business, but I also had to learn the American culture. It took a lot of hard work and perseverance, but I was able to overcome this tragic event and grow the business."

"Believe in yourself" is Tsuchiya's advice to students. "If you desire to do something, you must make a commitment to do it and have a strong will to see it through. While money is important, it is not the key to success—the key is hard work. Hard work will make money."

Personal Visions in Business

ASSESS

Assess student understanding by checking the solutions to the Independent Practice activities.

Reteach

- Make transparencies of the general journal from the accounting forms masters provided in the Blackline Masters Section of the Teacher's Resource Guide. Use information from the work sheet prepared in Recycling Problem 14-R, Instruction 1, and the transparencies to demonstrate how adjusting, closing, and reversing entries are recorded.
- Assign Recycling Problem 14-R, Instructions 9–11.

Extend

- Assign Challenge Problem 14-C. (The challenge is to prepare a Form 1120.)
- Assign Reinforcement Activity 2.
- Assign the Spreadsheet Template for Mastery Problem 14-M.
- Use *Automated Accounting 6.0* or higher with Accounting Textbook Template, Advanced Course with Mastery Problem 14-M and Reinforcement Activity 2.

Enrich

- Assign FOUR SEASONS, INC.: A Business Simulation.
- Assign the PERSONAL VISIONS IN BUSINESS feature on page 383.

Personal Visions in Business

This special student feature introduces students to successful entrepreneurs or business professionals. Each profile gives a flavor of what the actual business world is like and some of the opportunities available to students who study accounting. These features can be used to motivate students to pursue professional business careers in a wide variety of fields. The subjects of these profiles have been carefully chosen to represent the full spectrum of diverse ethnic and racial backgrounds of professional business people. As an optional activity, students can be encouraged to seek out and interview successful business people in their own communities.

SPREADSHEET OPTIONS

The SPREADSHEET OPTIONS feature is intended to expose students to a variety of ways to use spreadsheets. As an optional activity, students may use their spreadsheet software to duplicate the example shown in the spreadsheet options feature. They may also create new sets of data to do what-if analyses.

CLOSURE

Use Audit Your Understanding questions.

SPREADSHEET OPTIONS

PRINTING SPREADSHEETS AND GRAPHS

Budgets are an excellent application for electronic spreadsheets. Once the mathematical relationships are created with formulas, a variety of information can be keyed to answer "what if" questions. As shown in the illustration, the spreadsheet can enhance the accountant's understanding of the calculated budget information by displaying selected information in a graph.

Once the final budget has been prepared, the accountant must print the budget to share the information with management. The budget may contain several components, such as a sales budget, purchases budget, and cash budget. Rather than printing the entire spreadsheet at one time, the accountant may elect to print only one portion of the spreadsheet. By identifying the upper left and lower right corner of a range of cells, the spreadsheet allows the user to print only a select portion of the spreadsheet. For example, the sales budget partially displayed in this screen would be printed by identifying the print range A1..H16. The cells in the rectangle formed by cells A1 and H16 would be included in the print range.

Graphs can also be printed to a printer or a file if the computer has a printer card and the printer is equipped for printing graphs. Printing a graph to a file on a disk allows other software, such as word processing software, to incorporate the graph into a written document.

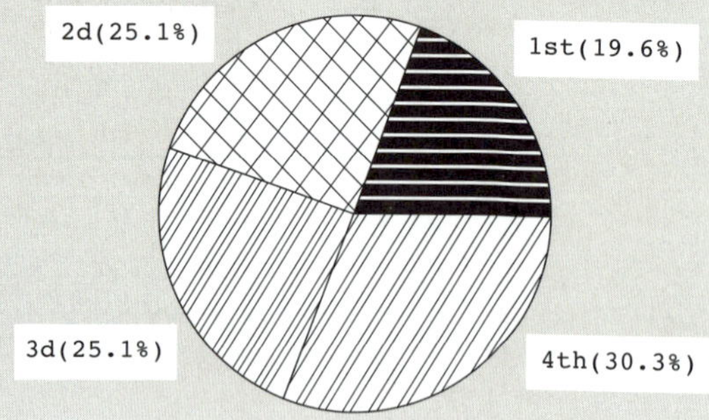

Sales Percentage by Quarter

```
    A B      C           D       E       F             G              H
 1
 2                                          Wilkes Corporation
 3                                         Sales Budget Schedule
 4                                  For Year Ended December 31, 19X3
 5  ================================================================
 6                                                                Quarter
 7                                        Annual     ---------------------
 8                                        Budget         1st          2d
 9  ----------------------------------------------------------------
10  Actual Unit Sales, 19X2......       216,364       42,342      54,332
11  Sales Percentage by Quarter..                      19.6%        25.1%
12  Projected Unit Sales, 19X3...       250,000       49,000      62,800
13  Times Unit Sales Price.......                     $35.00      $35.00
14                                 --------------------------------
15  Net Sales...................  $9,041,200 $1,715,000 $2,198,000
16                                 ================================
```

FEDERAL INCOME TAX RETURN

LampLight must file a federal income tax return and pay income taxes. Page 1 of LampLight's Form 1120, U.S. Corporation Income Tax Return, is shown in Illustration 14-10.

All corporations report their net income using the same tax form. The amounts reported on the tax form are often presented differently on corporations' income statements. For example, LampLight presents both payroll tax expense and property tax expense on its income statement. LampLight's managers require this information to make sound business decisions. However, the tax form requires LampLight to report only the total of all taxes. Thus, some amounts reported on a corporation's income statement must be modified to complete the tax return.

FYI

When earnings are retained rather than paid out as dividends, they are invested in assets, which helps a corporation grow.

TEACHING STRATEGIES: Assessment by Portfolio

An ideal specimen for inclusion in a portfolio to demonstrate mastery of the procedures and concepts involved in the complete accounting cycle is an extended activity that simulates the accounting cycle. For this part, you may wish to have students complete and include in their portfolios either Reinforcement Activity 2 or FOUR SEASONS, INC.: A Business Simulation. You may also wish to include both a manual version and an automated version for either or both of these activities.

ILLUSTRATION 14-10 Form 1120, U.S. Corporation Income Tax Return

Form **1120** Department of the Treasury Internal Revenue Service

U.S. Corporation Income Tax Return

For calendar year 19-- or tax year beginning ...., 19--, ending ...., 19 ...
▶ **Instructions are separate. See page 1 for Paperwork Reduction Act Notice.**

OMB No. 1545-0123 — **19--**

A Check if a: (1) Consolidated return (attach Form 851) ☐ (2) Personal holding co. (attach Sch. PH) ☐ (3) Personal service corp. (as defined in Temporary Regs. sec. 1.441-4T—see instructions) ☐

Use IRS label. Otherwise, please print or type.

Name: LampLight, Inc.
Number, street, and room or suite no. (If a P.O. box, see page 6 of instructions.): 1450 Eaglewood Lane
City or town, state, and ZIP code: Nashville, TN 37207-2361

B Employer identification number: 74-1334457
C Date incorporated: 12/26/--
D Total assets (see Specific Instructions): $ 952,171 03

E Check applicable boxes: (1) ☐ Initial return (2) ☐ Final return (3) ☐ Change in address

Income

Line	Description		Amount
1a	Gross receipts or sales 864,257 28; b Less returns and allowances 2,900 56; c Bal ▶	1c	861,356 72
2	Cost of goods sold (Schedule A, line 8)	2	454,714 03
3	Gross profit. Subtract line 2 from line 1c	3	406,642 69
4	Dividends (Schedule C, line 19)	4	-0-
5	Interest	5	1,450 00
6	Gross rents	6	-0-
7	Gross royalties	7	-0-
8	Capital gain net income (attach Schedule D (Form 1120))	8	-0-
9	Net gain or (loss) from Form 4797, Part II, line 20 (attach Form 4797)	9	-0-
10	Other income (see instructions—attach schedule)	10	-0-
11	**Total income.** Add lines 3 through 10 ▶	11	408,092 69

Deductions (See instructions for limitations on deductions.)

Line	Description		Amount
12	Compensation of officers (Schedule E, line 4)	12	28,432 50
13a	Salaries and wages 59,070 56; b Less jobs credit -0-; c Balance ▶	13c	59,070 56
14	Repairs	14	-0-
15	Bad debts	15	6,277 50
16	Rents	16	-0-
17	Taxes	17	16,662 40
18	Interest	18	30,289 53
19	Charitable contributions (**see instructions for 10% limitation**)	19	-0-
20	Depreciation (attach Form 4562) — 20: 34,737 13		
21	Less depreciation claimed on Schedule A and elsewhere on return — 21a: -0-	21b	34,737 13
22	Depletion	22	-0-
23	Advertising	23	17,782 00
24	Pension, profit-sharing, etc., plans	24	-0-
25	Employee benefit programs	25	-0-
26	Other deductions (attach schedule)	26	83,705 80
27	**Total deductions.** Add lines 12 through 26 ▶	27	276,957 42
28	Taxable income before net operating loss deduction and special deductions. Subtract line 27 from line 11	28	131,135 27
29	**Less:** a Net operating loss deduction (see instructions) — 29a: -0-; b Special deductions (Schedule C, line 20) — 29b: -0-	29c	-0-

Tax and Payments

Line	Description		Amount
30	**Taxable income.** Subtract line 29c from line 28	30	131,135 27
31	**Total tax** (Schedule J, line 10)	31	34,392 76
32	**Payments:** a 19-- overpayment credited to 19-- — 32a: -0-		
b	19-- estimated tax payments — 32b: 32,000 00		
c	Less 19-- refund applied for on Form 4466 — 32c: (-0-); d Bal ▶ 32d: 32,000 00		
e	Tax deposited with Form 7004 — 32e: -0-		
f	Credit from regulated investment companies (attach Form 2439) — 32f: -0-		
g	Credit for Federal tax on fuels (attach Form 4136). See instructions — 32g: -0-	32h	32,000 00
33	Estimated tax penalty (see instructions). Check if Form 2220 is attached ▶ ☐	33	-0-
34	**Tax due.** If line 32h is smaller than the total of lines 31 and 33, enter amount owed	34	2,392 76
35	**Overpayment.** If line 32h is larger than the total of lines 31 and 33, enter amount overpaid	35	
36	Enter amount of line 35 you want: **Credited to 19-- estimated tax** ▶ **Refunded** ▶	36	

Please Sign Here — Under penalties of perjury, I declare that I have examined this return, including accompanying schedules and statements, and to the best of my knowledge and belief, it is true, correct, and complete. Declaration of preparer (other than taxpayer) is based on all information of which preparer has any knowledge.

▶ Susan P. Boyd — Signature of officer | 3/15/-- — Date | ▶ Treasurer — Title

Paid Preparer's Use Only — Preparer's signature ▶ | Date | Check if self-employed ☐ | Preparer's social security number
Firm's name (or yours if self-employed) and address ▶ | E.I. No. ▶ | ZIP code ▶

ASSESS

- Administer Problem Test Chapter 14.
- Administer a MicroExam test for Chapter 14.
- Administer Objective Test No. 5.

REINFORCEMENT ACTIVITY

Reinforcement Activity 2 covers the complete accounting cycle for a departmentalized merchandising business organized as a corporation. Blackline masters for audit tests for Reinforcement Activity 2 are available in the Teacher's Resource Guide in three options: Part A only, Part B only, and Parts A and B combined. In addition, *Automated Accounting 6.0* or higher can be used to automate Reinforcement Activity 2.

SIMULATION

To give students an opportunity to apply accounting concepts for a merchandising business organized as a corporation, assign students to complete FOUR SEASONS, INC.: A Business Simulation. FOUR SEASONS, INC. may also be automated using *Automated Accounting 6.0* or higher.

DISSOLVING A CORPORATION

When a corporation is dissolved legal requirements must be met and correct accounting procedures must be followed. However, it is rare that a corporation is dissolved. When an owner (stockholder) decides not to participate in the corporation, the stockholder merely sells all shares of stock owned. The corporation is not dissolved.

The dissolution of a corporation involves many legal procedures and documents. Documents that must be filed include a notice to the state in which the business was incorporated and a notice to all creditors of the corporation. Since the dissolution of a corporation is complex, the board of directors should seek legal advice.

Once a corporation is dissolved, the liquidation process can begin. The procedure for selling noncash assets is similar to that for proprietorships and partnerships. However, since a corporation is a taxable entity, the gains and losses on the sale of noncash assets are subject to taxation. Therefore, additional tax reports for the corporation must be filed. The accounting aspects of actually liquidating a corporation are extremely complex. Therefore, obtaining professional accounting services to assist in the liquidation of a corporation is recommended.

Audit Your Understanding

1. What four closing entries does LampLight record at the end of a fiscal period?
2. What two items are listed differently on LampLight's income statements than on LampLight's income tax form?

AUDIT YOUR UNDERSTANDING

1. (1) Closing entry for income statement accounts with credit balances. (2) Closing entry for income statement accounts with debit balances. (3) Closing entry to record net income or net loss in the retained earnings account and close the income summary account. (4) Closing entry for the dividends accounts.
2. Both payroll tax expense and property tax expense are presented on LampLight's income statement. The tax form requires LampLight to report only the total of all taxes.

MILESTONE

The first five parts of this book concentrated on financial accounting procedures for corporations. It is assumed that these chapters have been mastered as the chapters to follow will expand upon this foundation with concepts of increasing complexity, such as management and cost accounting.

ACCOUNTING TERMS EPT(a)

What is the meaning of each of the following?

1. **amortization**
2. **earnings per share**
3. **equity per share**
4. **market value**
5. **price-earnings ratio**
6. **rate earned on average stockholders' equity**
7. **rate earned on average total assets**

QUESTIONS FOR INDIVIDUAL STUDY EPT(b)

1. Which accounting concept is being applied when financial information is reported to stockholders, investors, and creditors?
2. What accounts are affected, and how, by LampLight's adjustment for organization expense?
3. How often does a corporation pay its estimated federal income tax to the federal government?
4. What three steps are used to calculate net income before federal income tax on a work sheet?
5. Who distributes corporate tax rate tables?
6. What accounts are affected, and how, by LampLight's adjustment for federal income tax?
7. What is the formula for calculating the component percentage for total selling expenses?
8. What two actions can managers take when an analysis of component percentages reveals a negative result of an expense item?
9. What is the formula for calculating the earnings per share of a corporation?
10. What is the formula for calculating the equity per share for a corporation?
11. What determines the market value of the stock of a corporation?
12. What is the formula for calculating the price-earnings ratio?
13. What is the formula for calculating the accounts receivable turnover ratio?
14. What is the formula for calculating the rate earned on average stockholders' equity?
15. What guide does LampLight use in determining if a reversing entry should be recorded?
16. What form is used by LampLight to report annual income for federal income tax purposes?

CASES FOR CRITICAL THINKING EPT(b)

CASE 1 A corporation president suggests to the accounting department that the statement of stockholders' equity be dropped from the end-of-fiscal-period work. The president's reason is that the same information is reported on the corporation's balance sheet. The accounting department wants to continue using the statement. Which would you recommend? Why?

CASE 2 Kevin Edwards has $20,000.00 in a savings account which is earning 6% interest. He is thinking of investing the money in stock that has a stated value and a current market price of $100.00 per share. For the past three years the stock dividends have amounted to $9.00 per share per year. Mr. Edwards asks your advice. What would you recommend? Explain your answer.

ACCOUNTING TERMS

1. **amortization:** Recognizing a portion of an expense in each of several years. (p. 365)
2. **earnings per share:** The amount of net income belonging to a single share of stock. (p. 373)
3. **equity per share:** The amount of total stockholders' equity belonging to a single share of stock. (p. 374)
4. **market value:** The price at which a share of stock may be sold on the stock market. (p. 375)
5. **price-earnings ratio:** The relationship between the market value per share and earnings per share of a stock. (p. 375)
6. **rate earned on average stockholders' equity:** The relationship between net income and average stockholders' equity. (p. 378)
7. **rate earned on average total assets:** The relationship between net income and average total assets. (p. 378)

QUESTIONS FOR INDIVIDUAL STUDY

1. Adequate Disclosure concept. (p. 365)
2. Organization Expense is debited; Organization Costs is credited. (p. 365)
3. Quarterly. (p. 366)
4. (a) Complete the work sheet's Adjustments columns except for the federal income tax expense adjustment. (b) Extend all amounts, except the balance of Federal Income Tax Expense, to the work sheet's Income Statement columns. (c) Total the work sheet's Income Statement column totals using a calculator. Calculate the difference between the two totals. The difference is the net income before federal income tax. (p. 368)
5. The Internal Revenue Service. (p. 368)
6. Federal Income Tax Expense is debited; Federal Income Tax Payable is credited. (p. 369)
7. Total selling expenses divided by net sales. (p. 370)
8. Managers can correct negative situations or revise the acceptable percentage for the next fiscal period. (p. 372)
9. Share of net income divided by shares of stock outstanding. (p. 373)

QUESTIONS *(cont'd)*

10. Total stockholders' equity divided by shares of capital stock outstanding. (p. 374)

11. How much a buyer is willing to pay for the stock. (p. 375)

12. Market price per share divided by earnings per share. (p. 375)

13. Net sales on account divided by average book value of accounts receivable. (p. 376)

14. Net income after federal income tax divided by average stockholders' equity. (p. 378)

15. If an adjusting entry creates a balance in an asset or liability account, the adjusting entry is reversed. (p. 381)

16. Form 1120, U.S. Corporation Income Tax Return. (p. 384)

CASES FOR CRITICAL THINKING

Case 1 Recommend that the corporation prepare both a statement of stockholders' equity and a balance sheet. On the balance sheet show only summary information from the statement of stockholders' equity. This procedure will result in a shorter balance sheet which will be easier to read.

Case 2 If Mr. Edwards is saving his money for sometime in the future, investing in the stock will likely be better. The higher rate of return from dividends over several years will offset the broker's commissions when stock is bought and sold. However, the full 6% interest on a savings account will be paid in each of the future years. A stockholder has no assurance that a corporation will pay dividends in future years.

APPLICATION PROBLEMS EPT(c,d,e,f)

PROBLEM 14-1 Calculating federal income taxes

SPREADSHEET

During the past year, three corporations earned the following net income before federal income taxes: Corporation A, $73,932.56; Corporation B, $467,032.45; and Corporation C, $38,296.44.

INSTRUCTIONS:

Calculate the amount of federal income tax expense for each of the three corporations. Use the tax rate table on page 368 in this chapter.

MATHEMATICS

PROBLEM 14-2 Preparing a work sheet for a corporation

AUTOMATED

General ledger account titles and balances for Trexler, Inc. are recorded on a work sheet in the working papers accompanying this textbook.

INSTRUCTIONS:

Complete the work sheet for the current year ended December 31. Record the adjustments on the work sheet using the following information.

Adjustment Information, December 31

Accrued interest income	$ 160.17
Uncollectible accounts expense estimated as 1.0% of sales on account. Sales on account for year, $126,405.00.	
Merchandise inventory	51,450.23
Sales supplies inventory	1,202.70
Administrative supplies inventory	959.85
Value of prepaid insurance	1,436.58
Prepaid interest	1.85
Annual depreciation expense—store equipment	1,294.57
Annual depreciation expense—building	2,900.00
Annual depreciation expense—office equipment	3,018.64
Organization expense	50.00
Accrued interest expense	4,002.57
Accrued salaries—sales	153.97
Accrued salaries—administrative	593.49
Accrued payroll taxes—FICA tax	59.80
Accrued payroll taxes—federal unemployment tax	1.72
Accrued payroll taxes—state unemployment tax	11.61
Federal income taxes are based on the tax rate table in this chapter.	

The work sheet prepared in this problem is needed to complete Problems 14-3, 14-4, 14-5, and 14-6.

PROBLEM 14-3 Preparing an income statement for a corporation

The work sheet prepared in Problem 14-2 is needed to complete this problem.

MATHEMATICS

INSTRUCTIONS:

1. Prepare an income statement for the year ended December 31 of the current year.
2. Calculate and record the following component percentages. (a) Cost of merchandise sold. (b) Gross profit on operations. (c) Total selling expenses. (d) Total administrative expenses. (e) Total operating expenses. (f) Income from operations. (g) Net addition or deduction

resulting from other revenue and expenses. (h) Net income before federal income tax. (i) Federal income tax expense. (j) Net income after federal income tax. Round the percentage calculations to the nearest 0.1%.

3. Use the Income Statement Analysis table given in the working papers accompanying this textbook. Analyze Trexler's income statement by determining if component percentages are within acceptable levels. If any component percentage is not within an acceptable level, suggest steps that the company should take.
4. Calculate earnings per share. Round the calculation to the nearest cent. Trexler has 10,900 shares of $10.00 stated-value common stock issued and 420 shares of $100.00 par-value preferred stock issued. Treasury stock consists of 70 shares of common stock. The dividend rate on preferred stock is 10%.

PROBLEM 14-4 Preparing a statement of stockholders' equity for a corporation

The work sheet prepared in Problem 14-2 is needed to complete this problem.

INSTRUCTIONS:

1. Prepare a statement of stockholders' equity for the year ended December 31 of the current year. Use the following additional information.

	January 1 Balance	Issued During the Year	December 31 Balance
Common stock:			
No. of shares	8,000	2,900	10,900
Amount	$80,000.00	$29,000.00	$109,000.00
Preferred stock:			
No. of shares	150	270	420
Amount	$15,000.00	$27,000.00	$ 42,000.00

Treasury stock consists of 70 shares of common stock.
The January 1 balance of Retained Earnings was $13,411.26.

2. Calculate the following items. (a) Equity per share of stock. (b) Price-earnings ratio. The market price of common stock on December 31 is $24.00.

The statement of stockholders' equity prepared in this problem is needed to complete Problem 14-5.

PROBLEM 14-5 Preparing a balance sheet for a corporation

The work sheet prepared in Problem 14-2 and the statement of stockholders' equity prepared in Problem 14-4 are needed to complete this problem.

INSTRUCTIONS:

1. Prepare a balance sheet for December 31 of the current year.
2. Calculate the following items. (a) Accounts receivable turnover ratio. Net sales on account are $126,405.00. Accounts receivable and allowance for uncollectible accounts on January 1 were $26,495.72 and $1,142.37, respectively. (b) Rate earned on average stockholders' equity. Total stockholders' equity on January 1 was $106,951.26. (c) Rate earned on average total assets. Total assets on January 1 were $233,699.75.

CHECK FIGURES

See Teacher's Edition of Working Papers for complete solutions.

Problem 14-1 Inc. Tax $ 13,483.14; 158,791.03; 5,744.47

Problem 14-2 Suggestion: A 10-column work sheet may be used. Fed. Inc. Tax Exp. $6,001.50

Problem 14-3 (2) (a) 46.7; (b) 53.3; (c) 12.0; (d) 17.3; (e) 29.3; (f) 24.0; (g) 3.3; (h) 20.7; (i) 3.1; (j) 17.6.

Problem 14-4 (2) (a) $100.00, 15.69; (b) 8.7

Problem 14-5 (2) (a) $ 27,413.65, 4.6; (b) $159,418.77, 21.3; (c) $251,768.40, 13.5

CHECK FIGURES *(cont'd)*

Problem 14-6 Closing entry #3: Income Summary dr. 34,008.51; Retained Earnings cr. 34,008.51. Closing entry #4: Retained Earnings dr. 9,073.50; Dividends—Common cr. 4,873.50 and Dividends—Preferred 4,200.00.

Mastery Problem 14-M Fed. Inc. Tax Exp. $20,126.97. (2) (a) 40.6; (b) 59.4; (c) 17.8; (d) 13.6; (e) 31.5; (f) 27.9; (g) 2.9; (h) 25.0; (i) 5.4; (j) 19.6. (4) Earnings per share Pref. $10.00, Com. 3.63. (8) (a) $50,528.60, 4.2; (b) $327,838.61, 22.5; (c) $432,311.07, 17.0.

PROBLEM 14-6 Completing other end-of-fiscal-period work

The work sheet prepared in Problem 14-2 is needed to complete this problem.

INSTRUCTIONS:

1. Journalize the adjusting entries. Use page 13 of a general journal.
2. Journalize the closing entries. Use page 14 of a general journal.
3. Journalize the reversing entries. Use page 1 of a general journal. Use January 1 of the year following the current year as the date.

ENRICHMENT PROBLEMS EPT(c,d,e,f)

MASTERY PROBLEM 14-M Completing end-of-fiscal-period work for a corporation

AUTOMATED

SPREADSHEET

The general ledger account titles and balances for Lander, Inc. are recorded on a work sheet in the working papers accompanying this textbook.

INSTRUCTIONS:

1. Complete the work sheet for December 31 of the current year. Record the adjustments on the work sheet using the following information.

Adjustment Information, December 31

Accrued interest income	$ 277.18
Uncollectible accounts expense estimated as 1.0% of sales on account. Sales on account for year, $213,441.00.	
Merchandise inventory	86,876.38
Sales supplies inventory	9,808.79
Administrative supplies inventory	3,620.75
Value of prepaid insurance	2,363.94
Prepaid interest	3.12
Annual depreciation expense—store equipment	9,746.00
Annual depreciation expense—building	2,400.00
Annual depreciation expense—office equipment	2,185.95
Organization expense	75.00
Accrued interest expense	7,004.34
Accrued salaries—sales	375.65
Accrued salaries—administrative	1,002.13
Accrued payroll taxes—FICA tax	110.22
Accrued payroll taxes—federal unemployment tax	1.27
Accrued payroll taxes—state unemployment tax	8.59
Federal income taxes are based on the tax rate table in this chapter.	

2. Prepare an income statement. Calculate and record the following component percentages. (a) Cost of merchandise sold. (b) Gross profit on operations. (c) Total selling expenses. (d) Total administrative expenses. (e) Total operating expenses. (f) Income from operations. (g) Net addition or deduction resulting from other revenue and expenses. (h) Net income before federal income tax. (i) Federal income tax expense. (j) Net income after federal income tax. Round percentage calculations to the nearest 0.1%.
3. Use the Income Statement Analysis table given in the working papers accompanying this textbook. Analyze Lander's income statement by determining if component percentages are within acceptable levels. If any component percentage is not within an acceptable level, suggest steps that the company should take.

4. Calculate earnings per share. Round the calculation to the nearest cent. Lander has 18,400 shares of $10.00 stated-value common stock issued and 720 shares of $100.00 par-value preferred stock issued. Treasury stock consists of 90 shares of common stock. The dividend rate on preferred stock is 10%.

5. Prepare a statement of stockholders' equity for the year ended December 31 of the current year. Use the following additional information.

	January 1 Balance	Issued During the Year	December 31 Balance
Common stock:			
No. of shares	18,000	400	18,400
Amount	$180,000.00	$ 4,000.00	$184,000.00
Preferred stock:			
No. of shares	600	120	720
Amount	$ 60,000.00	$12,000.00	$ 72,000.00

The January 1 balance of Retained Earnings was $22,645.60.

6. Calculate the following items based on information on the statement of stockholders' equity. (a) Equity per share of stock. (b) Price-earnings ratio. The market price of common stock on December 31 is $30.00.

7. Prepare a balance sheet for December 31 of the current year.

8. Calculate the following items based on information from the balance sheet. (a) Net sales on account are $213,441.00. Accounts receivable turnover ratio. Accounts receivable and allowance for doubtful accounts on January 1 were $49,435.32 and $2,146.40, respectively. (b) Rate earned on average stockholders' equity. Total stockholders' equity on January 1 was $290,485.60. (c) Rate earned on average total assets. Total assets on January 1 were $392,691.70.

9. Journalize the adjusting entries. Use page 13 of a general journal.

10. Journalize the closing entries. Use page 14 of a general journal.

11. Journalize the reversing entries. Use page 1 of a general journal. Use January 1 of the year following the current year as the date.

CHALLENGE PROBLEM 14-C Preparing a Form 1120, U.S. Corporation Income Tax Return

Goldstein, Inc. has completed its work sheet and financial statements for the fiscal year ending on December 31 of the current year. The income statement for Goldstein is in the working papers accompanying this textbook.

Other information required to prepare the tax return is obtained from company records.

Employer identification number: 65-074738
Date incorporated: January 5, 19--
Address: 7834 Industrial Road, Oxford, MS 38655-1500
Total assets: $786,986.50
Compensation of officers: $7,217.60
Estimated tax payments: $42,000.00

INSTRUCTIONS:

1. Complete the company name and address in the spaces provided on the tax form.

2. Use the information provided above to complete lines D–F. Write the amount of compensation of officers on line 12. Write the estimated tax payments on line 32b.

3. Use the amounts on the income statement to complete the following lines of the tax form.

CHECK FIGURES *(cont'd)*

Challenge Problem 14-C Form 1120: Line 11 $443,611.80; Line 31 45,977.13; Line 34 3,977.13

Tax Form Line	Income Statement Account(s)
1a	Sales less Sales Discount
1b	Sales Returns and Allowances
2	Cost of Merchandise Sold
5	Interest Income
13a	Salary Expense—Sales plus Salary Expense—Administrative less Compensation of officers
15	Uncollectible Accounts Expense
17	Payroll Taxes Expense plus Property Taxes
18	Interest Expense
20	The sum of the three depreciation expense accounts
23	Advertising Expense
26	All other expenses not reported on other lines
31	Federal Income Tax Expense

4. Calculate the amounts on lines 1c, 3, 11, 13c, 21b, 27, 30, 32h, and 34 using the instructions provided on the tax form.

5. Check the accuracy of the completed tax form by comparing the amount on line 30 of the tax form to Net Income before Federal Income Tax on the income statement.

6. Write -0- on the remaining blank lines on the tax form.

392

End-of-Fiscal-Period Work

Chapter 14 describes LampLight's manual accounting procedures for completing end-of-fiscal-period work for a corporation. Integrating Automated Accounting Topic 6 applies procedures for using automated accounting software to complete end-of-fiscal-period work for a corporation. The Automated Accounting Problems contain instructions for using automated accounting software to solve Application Problem 14-2 and Mastery Problem 14-M from Chapter 14.

AUTOMATED

AUTOMATED ACCOUNTING PROBLEMS

AUTOMATING APPLICATION PROBLEM 14-2 Completing end-of-fiscal-period work for a corporation

INSTRUCTIONS:

1. Load the *Automated Accounting 6.0* or higher software. Select data base A14-2 from the *CENTURY 21 ACCOUNTING Advanced Course* template. Read the Problem Instructions screen.
2. Rename the file.
3. Display/print a trial balance.
4. Display/print a chart of accounts.
5. Journalize the adjusting entries on a general journal input form using the following information. Use December 31 of the current year as the run date.

TEACHING STRATEGIES: ACCOUNTING PEDAGOGY

This textbook introduces the manual procedures for preparing end-of-fiscal-period financial statements before using automated accounting to prepare end-of-fiscal-period financial statements. It is important that students master accounting theory before relying on the computer to do the repetitive functions.

LESSON PLAN A6

Materials

- Student pages 393–395
- Input forms for Automating Application Problem 14-2 and Mastery Problem 14-M are provided in the working papers that accompany this textbook. If additional input forms are needed, blackline masters are provided in the Blackline Masters Section of the Teacher's Resource Guide.
- Complete solutions for automated problems are provided in the Teacher's Resource Guide.
- Software: *Automated Accounting 6.0* or higher; Accounting Textbook Template, Advanced Course

Objective

Complete end-of-fiscal-period work for a corporation using an automated accounting system.

SOFTWARE FOCUS

The Automated Accounting Problems in this Integrating Automated Accounting topic use Application Problem 14-2 and Mastery Problem 14-M, Chapter 14, which students have already completed manually. Refer students back to these problems to complete the input forms. The problem instructions in *Automated Accounting 6.0* will lead students through automating the problems.

FOCUS

In Chapter 14, manual procedures for completing end-of-fiscal-period work for a corporation were described. Emphasize that using an automated accounting system speeds the processing of end-of-fiscal-period work by (1) eliminating the need to prepare a work sheet, (2) having all financial reports prepared by a computer, and (3) having the software generate closing entries.

TEACH

Integrating Automated Accounting: Topic 6 is designed to be completed by students as Independent Practice. You may choose to have students work in pairs to increase their cooperative learning experiences. Student understanding may be assessed by checking student solutions to the automated problems. Use Chapter 14 of this textbook to reteach any misunderstood accounting concepts related to completing end-of-fiscal-period work for a corporation. To enrich student learning assign Reinforcement Activity 2 and FOUR SEASONS, INC.: An Automated Business Simulation.

CHECK FIGURES

- Automating Application Problem 14-2: General Journal (Adj. Ent.) totals 22,567.86; Income Statement: Net Income after Income Tax: 34,008.51; Balance Sheet: Total Liabilities & Equity: 269,837.04; Post-closing Trial Balance totals: 288,713.62; General Journal (Rev.Ent.) totals: 4,985.18.
- Automating Mastery Problem 14-M: General Journal (Adj. Ent.) totals 44,373.40; Income Statement: Net Income after Income Tax: 73,628.81; Balance Sheet: Total Liabilities & Equity: 471,930.44; Post-closing Trial Balance totals 508,325.85; General Journal (Rev. Ent.) totals 8,782.50.

Adjustment Information, December 31

Accrued interest income	$ 160.17
Uncollectible accounts expense estimated as 1.0% of sales on account. Sales on account for year, $126,405.00.	
Merchandise inventory	51,450.23
Sales supplies inventory	1,202.70
Administrative supplies inventory	959.85
Value of prepaid insurance	1,436.58
Prepaid interest	1.85
Annual depreciation expense—store equipment	1,294.57
Annual depreciation expense—building	2,900.00
Annual depreciation expense—office equipment	3,018.64
Organization expense	50.00
Accrued interest expense	4,002.57
Accrued salaries—sales	153.97
Accrued salaries—administrative	593.49
Accrued payroll taxes—FICA tax	59.80
Accrued payroll taxes—federal unemployment tax	1.72
Accrued payroll taxes—state unemployment tax	11.61
Federal income tax expense for the year	6,001.50

6. Key the adjusting entries from the general journal input form.
7. Display/print the general journal report.
8. Display/print the income statement and the balance sheet.
9. Perform period-end closing.
10. Display/print a post-closing trial balance.
11. Journalize the reversing entries on a general journal input form. Use January 1 of the following year as the run date.
12. Key the reversing entries from the general journal input form.
13. Display/print the general journal report.

AUTOMATED

AUTOMATING MASTERY PROBLEM 14-M Completing end-of-fiscal-period work for a corporation

INSTRUCTIONS:

1. Load the *Automated Accounting 6.0* or higher software. Select data base A14-M from the *CENTURY 21 ACCOUNTING Advanced Course* template. Read the Problem Instructions screen.
2. Rename the file.
3. Display/print a trial balance.
4. Display/print a chart of accounts.
5. Journalize the adjusting entries on a general journal input form using the information given below. Use December 31 of the current year as the run date.

Adjustment Information, December 31

Accrued interest income	$ 277.18
Uncollectible accounts expense estimated as 1.0% of sales on account for year, $213,441.00.	
Merchandise inventory	86,876.38
Sales supplies inventory	9,808.79
Administrative supplies inventory	3,620.75
Value of prepaid insurance	2,363.94
Prepaid interest	3.12
Annual depreciation expense—store equipment	9,746.00
Annual depreciation expense—building	2,400.00
Annual depreciation expense—office equipment	2,185.95
Organization expense	75.00

TEACHING STRATEGIES: COOPERATIVE LEARNING

Using automated accounting software to complete accounting problems is an ideal cooperative learning experience. Students working in groups can collaborate on completing input forms and keying data.

Accrued interest expense	7,004.34
Accrued salaries—sales	375.65
Accrued salaries—administrative	1,002.13
Accrued payroll taxes—FICA tax	110.22
Accrued payroll taxes—federal unemployment tax	1.27
Accrued payroll taxes—state unemployment tax	8.59
Federal income tax expense for the year	20,126.97

6. Key the adjusting entries from the general journal input form.
7. Display/print the general journal report.
8. Display/print the income statement and the balance sheet.
9. Perform period-end closing.
10. Display/print a post-closing trial balance.
11. Journalize the reversing entries on a general journal input form. Use January 1 of the year following the current year as the run date.
12. Key the reversing entries from the general journal input form.
13. Display/print the general journal report.

TEACHING STRATEGIES: TEACHING TIP

It is important for students to save a template file under another name before they begin work. This will keep the template file intact for future use.

REINFORCEMENT ACTIVITY 2

Processing and Reporting Accounting Data for a Corporation

TEACHING STRATEGIES: REINFORCEMENT ACTIVITY

Reinforcement Activity 2 covers the complete accounting cycle for a departmentalized merchandising business organized as a corporation. Blackline masters for audit tests for Reinforcement Activity 2 are available in the Teacher's Resource Guide in three options: Part A only, Part B only, and Parts A and B combined. In addition, *Automated Accounting 6.0* or higher can be used to automate Reinforcement Activity 2.

AUTOMATED

This activity reinforces selected learnings from Parts 4 and 5, Chapters 8 through 14.

WHITEHURST, INC.

The accounting activities are for Whitehurst, Inc., a merchandising business organized as a corporation. Whitehurst sells plumbing and related products to building contractors, homeowners, and other consumers. Whitehurst's fiscal year is from January 1 through December 31.

PART A: JOURNALIZING TRANSACTIONS

In Part A of this reinforcement activity, selected transactions for Whitehurst, Inc., completed during December of the current year, are journalized.

Whitehurst uses the chart of accounts shown on page 397. The journals used by Whitehurst are similar to those illustrated in Parts 4 and 5.

RECORDING TRANSACTIONS

INSTRUCTIONS:

1. Journalize the following transactions completed during December of the current year. Use page 23 of a cash receipts journal, page 23 of a cash payments journal, and page 12 of a general journal. Whitehurst records prepaid interest expense initially as an expense and rent received in advance as revenue. Other prepaid and unearned items are recorded initially as assets and liabilities. Source documents are abbreviated as follows: check, C; memorandum, M; note payable, NP; note receivable, NR; receipt, R.

Dec. 1. Whitehurst's board of directors declared an annual dividend of $15,820.00. Preferred stock issued is $40,400.00 of 10%, $100.00 par-value preferred stock. Common stock issued is $11,780.00 of $10.00 stated-value common stock. Date of payment is December 30. M316.

1. Wrote off Susan Vine's past-due account as uncollectible, $427.50. M317.

1. Received cash for three months' rent in advance from Woodcrest, Inc., $2,400.00. R126.

1. Discarded a store fixture: original cost, $1,050.00; total accumulated depreciation through December 31 of last year, $840.00; additional depreciation to be recorded through December 1 of the current year, $210.00. M318.

1. Received a subscription from Delmar Adams for 30 shares of $100.00 par-value preferred stock, $3,000.00. M319.

2. Paid cash for office equipment, $2,650.00. C476.

4. Patrick Carson dishonored NR4, a 30-day, 10% note, maturity value due today: principal, $150.00; interest, $1.25; total, $151.25. M320.

SOFTWARE FOCUS

Automated Accounting 6.0 or higher can be used to complete Reinforcement Activity 2 using the computer.

WHITEHURST, INC.
CHART OF ACCOUNTS

Balance Sheet Accounts

(1000) ASSETS

1100 Current Assets

1105 Cash
1110 Petty Cash
1115 Notes Receivable
1120 Interest Receivable
1125 Accounts Receivable
1130 Allowance for Uncollectible Accounts
1135 Subscriptions Receivable
1140 Merchandise Inventory
1145 Supplies—Sales
1150 Supplies—Administrative
1155 Prepaid Insurance
1160 Prepaid Interest

1200 Long-Term Investment

1205 Bond Sinking Fund

1300 Plant Assets

1305 Store Equipment
1310 Accumulated Depreciation—Store Equipment
1315 Building
1320 Accumulated Depreciation—Building
1325 Office Equipment
1330 Accumulated Depreciation—Office Equipment
1335 Land

1400 Intangible Asset

1405 Organization Costs

(2000) LIABILITIES

2100 Current Liabilities

2105 Notes Payable
2110 Interest Payable
2115 Accounts Payable
2120 Employee Income Tax Payable
2125 Federal Income Tax Payable
2130 FICA Tax Payable
2135 Salaries Payable
2140 Sales Tax Payable
2145 Unearned Rent
2150 Unemployment Tax Payable—Federal
2155 Unemployment Tax Payable—State
2160 Health Insurance Premiums Payable
2165 Dividends Payable

2200 Long-Term Liability

2205 Bonds Payable

(3000) STOCKHOLDERS' EQUITY

3105 Capital Stock—Common
3110 Stock Subscribed—Common
3115 Paid-in Capital in Excess of Stated Value—Common
3120 Capital Stock—Preferred
3125 Stock Subscribed—Preferred
3130 Paid-in Capital in Excess of Par Value—Preferred
3135 Treasury Stock
3140 Paid-in Capital from Sale of Treasury Stock
3145 Retained Earnings
3150 Dividends—Common
3155 Dividends—Preferred
3160 Income Summary

Income Statement Accounts

(4000) OPERATING REVENUE

4105 Sales
4110 Sales Discount
4115 Sales Returns and Allowances

(5000) COST OF MERCHANDISE

5105 Purchases
5110 Purchases Discount
5115 Purchases Returns and Allowances

(6000) OPERATING EXPENSES

6100 Selling Expenses

6105 Advertising Expense
6110 Credit Card Fee Expense
6115 Depreciation Expense—Store Equipment
6120 Miscellaneous Expense—Sales
6125 Salary Expense—Sales
6130 Supplies Expense—Sales

6200 Administrative Expenses

6205 Depreciation Expense—Building
6210 Depreciation Expense—Office Equipment
6215 Insurance Expense
6220 Miscellaneous Expense—Administrative
6225 Payroll Taxes Expense
6230 Property Tax Expense
6235 Salary Expense—Administrative
6240 Supplies Expense—Administrative
6245 Uncollectible Accounts Expense
6250 Utilities Expense

(7000) OTHER REVENUE

7105 Gain on Plant Assets
7110 Interest Income
7115 Rent Income

(8000) OTHER EXPENSES

8105 Interest Expense
8110 Loss on Plant Assets
8115 Organization Expense

(9000) INCOME TAX

9105 Federal Income Tax Expense

TEACHING STRATEGIES: COOPERATIVE LEARNING

Divide the class into groups of two students each. After completing the recording of transactions as a homework assignment, students evaluate each other's work in class. Students are permitted to correct their work based on their partner's evaluation. This cooperative learning activity should not take more than 15 to 20 minutes of class time. The same kind of group activity can be used after students have completed the end-of-fiscal-period work.

TEACHING STRATEGIES: ASSESSMENT BY PORTFOLIO

If you intend to use Reinforcement Activity 2 as part of an assessment by portfolio evaluation, advise students that their work on this activity will be included in their portfolio.

Dec. 4. Discarded an office table: original cost, $250.00; total accumulated depreciation through December 31 of last year, $150.00; additional depreciation to be recorded through December 4 of the current year, $50.00. M321.

4. Received a 60-day, 10% note from Leigh Calhoun for an extension of time on her account, $500.00. NR5.

5. Issued a 6-month, 10% note, $10,000.00. NP6.

5. Paid cash to bond trustee for annual interest on bond issue, $24,000.00. C482.

5. Paid cash to bond trustee for annual deposit to bond sinking fund, $18,400.00, and recorded interest earned on bond sinking fund, $1,600.00. C487.

6. Received cash from Leslie Johns for 700 shares of $10.00 stated-value common stock at $11.00 per share, $7,700.00. R134.

7. Received cash for the maturity value of NR1, principal, $150.00, plus interest, $2.47; total, $152.47. R136.

11. Received cash from sale of office equipment, $70.00: original cost, $700.00; total accumulated depreciation through December 31 of last year, $500.00; additional depreciation to be recorded through December 11 of the current year, $100.00. M322 and R138.

11. Paid cash to Marlin Pratt for 60 shares of $10.00 stated-value common stock at $9.00 per share, $540.00. C502.

12. Paid cash for the maturity value of NP4: principal, $300.00, plus interest, $6.00; total, $306.00. C503.

13. Received cash from Robert Shull for 200 shares of $10.00 stated-value common stock at $10.00 per share, $2,000.00. R140.

14. Received cash for the maturity value of NR2: principal, $247.50, plus interest, $4.07; total, $251.57. R141.

16. Paid cash for the maturity value of NP3: principal, $1,000.00, plus interest, $16.44; total, $1,016.44. C509.

19. Received office equipment from Valerie DeLong at an agreed value of $1,000.00 for 10 shares of $100.00 par-value preferred stock. M323.

20. Received cash in full payment of Susan Vine's account, previously written off as uncollectible, $427.50. M324 and R143.

21. Paid cash, $2,000.00, plus an office microcomputer, for a new microcomputer: original cost of old microcomputer, $3,500.00; total accumulated depreciation through December 31 of last year, $2,100.00; additional depreciation to be recorded through December 21 of the current year, $700.00. M325 and C515.

27. Discounted at 12% a 60-day non-interest-bearing note, $5,000.00; proceeds, $4,900.00; interest, $100.00. NP7.

28. Received cash from James Dier for 10 shares of treasury stock at $13.00 per share, $130.00. Treasury stock was bought on December 11 at $9.00 per share. R146.

29. Received cash from sale of an old cash register used in sales, $800.00: original cost, $1,600.00; total accumulated depreciation through December 31 of last year, $896.00; additional depreciation to be recorded through December 29 of the current year, $144.00. M326 and R147.

29. Received cash from Patrick Carson for dishonored NR4: principal, $151.25, plus additional interest, $1.05; total, $152.30. R148.

29. Received cash from Delmar Adams in payment of stock subscription, $3,000.00. R149.

29. Issued Stock Certificate No. 14 to Delmar Adams for 30 shares of $100.00 par-value preferred stock, $3,000.00. M327.

30. Paid cash for annual dividend declared December 1, $15,820.00. C519.

2. Prove and rule the cash receipts and cash payments journals.

PART B: END-OF-FISCAL-PERIOD WORK

In Part B, Whitehurst's end-of-fiscal-period work is completed. This work is similar to activities described in Chapter 14. The December 31 trial balance is recorded on a work sheet in the working papers accompanying this textbook.

INSTRUCTIONS:

3. Complete the work sheet for the year ended December 31 of the current year. Record the adjustments on the work sheet using the following additional information.

Adjustment Information, December 31

Accrued interest income	$ 95.70
Uncollectible accounts expense estimated as 0.1% of net sales on account. Net sales on account for year, $343,472.60.	
Merchandise inventory	206,618.63
Sales supplies inventory	1,456.06
Administrative supplies inventory	730.00
Value of prepaid insurance	970.00
Prepaid interest	93.33
Annual depreciation expense—store equipment	8,300.00
Annual depreciation expense—building	1,500.00
Annual depreciation expense—office equipment	1,150.00
Organization expense	300.00
Accrued interest expense	2,025.00
Accrued salaries—sales	3,232.04
Accrued salaries—administrative	716.50
Accrued payroll taxes—FICA tax	315.88
Accrued payroll taxes—federal unemployment tax	15.79
Accrued payroll taxes—state unemployment tax	106.58
Rent received in advance and still unearned	1,200.00

Federal income tax expense for the year is calculated at the following rates:
15% of net income before taxes, zero to $50,000.00.
Plus 25% of net income before taxes, $50,000.00 to $75,000.00.
Plus 34% of net income before taxes, $75,000.00 to $100,000.00.
Plus 39% of net income before taxes, $100,000.00 to $335,000.00.
Plus 34% of the net income before taxes over $335,000.00.

4. Prepare an income statement. Calculate and record the following component percentages. (a) Cost of merchandise sold. (b) Gross profit on operations. (c) Total selling expenses. (d) Total administrative expenses. (e) Total operating expenses. (f) Income from operations. (g) Net addition or deduction resulting from other revenue and expenses. (h) Net income before federal income tax. (i) Federal income tax expense. (j) Net income after federal income tax. Round percentage calculations to the nearest 0.1%.

5. Analyze Whitehurst's income statement by determining if component percentages are within acceptable levels. If any component percentage is not within an acceptable level, suggest steps that the company should take. Acceptable component percentages are given in the working papers.

6. Calculate earnings per share. Round the calculation to the nearest cent. Whitehurst has 12,680 shares of $10.00 stated-value common stock issued and 444 shares of 10%, $100.00 par-value preferred stock issued. Treasury stock consists of 50 shares of common stock.

7. Prepare a statement of stockholders' equity. Use the following additional information.

	January 1 Balance	**Issued During the Year**	**December 31 Balance**
Common stock:			
No. of shares	11,780	900	12,680
Amount	$117,800.00	$ 9,000.00	$126,800.00
Preferred stock:			
No. of shares	404	40	444
Amount	$ 40,400.00	$ 4,000.00	$ 44,400.00

The January 1 balance of Retained Earnings was $26,759.39.

399

8. Calculate the following items based on information on the statement of stockholders' equity. (a) Equity per share of stock. (b) Price-earnings ratio. The market price of common stock on December 31 is $13.50.
9. Prepare a balance sheet for December 31 of the current year.
10. Calculate the following items based on information from the balance sheet. (a) Accounts receivable turnover ratio. Accounts receivable and allowance for uncollectible accounts on January 1 were $36,785.45 and $698.35, respectively. (b) Rate earned on average stockholders' equity. Total stockholders' equity on January 1 was $186,459.39. (c) Rate earned on average total assets. Total assets on January 1 were $458,204.24.
11. Use pages 13 and 14 of a general journal. Journalize the adjusting entries.
12. Use pages 14 and 15 of a general journal. Do not skip a line. Journalize the closing entries.
13. Use page 1 of a general journal. Journalize the reversing entries. Use January 1 of the year following the current year as the date.

Four Seasons, Inc. is a merchandising business organized as a corporation. This business simulation covers the realistic transactions completed by Four Seasons, Inc., which sells garden equipment. The activities included in the accounting cycle for Four Seasons, Inc. are listed below.

This simulation is available from the publisher in either manual or automated versions.

Activities in Four Seasons, Inc.

1. Recording transactions in special journals and a general journal.
2. Posting items to be posted individually to a general ledger and subsidiary ledgers.
3. Proving and ruling journals.
4. Posting column totals to a general ledger.
5. Preparing schedules of accounts receivable and accounts payable.
6. Preparing a trial balance on a work sheet.
7. Planning adjustments and completing a work sheet.
8. Preparing financial statements.
9. Journalizing and posting adjusting entries.
10. Journalizing and posting closing entries.
11. Preparing a post-closing trial balance.

401

STUDENT EDITION

STUDENT FEATURES

Professional Business Ethics
Smooth Sailing With Client Referrals, page 452

Careers In Accounting
Budget Accountant, page 439

Multicultural Awareness
Calculators, page 411

Global Perspective
International Organizations, page 474

Personal Visions In Business
Bonnie Combs, page 422

Audit Your Understanding
This student activity can be found on pages 409, 421, 429, 443, 455, 471, 479, 485

APPLIED SKILLS

Applied Communications
Page 431

Applied Mathematics
Pages 413–415, 423, 431, 432, 440, 443–445, 447, 453–455, 457–459, 464, 465, 471–473, 475–478, 480–485, 487, 488

SOFTWARE APPLICATIONS

Automated Accounting 6.0 Problem 15-C
Spreadsheet Template Problems 15-1, 15-2, 15-3, 16-1, 16-3, 16-4, 16-5, 16-6, 17-1, 17-2, 17-M

TEACHER'S EDITION

APPLIED SKILLS

Communications, page 431
Language Arts, pages 428, 454, 478
Writing Across the Curriculum, pages 416, 469
Building Study Skills, page 445
Word Processing, pages 427, 449, 484

TEACHING STRATEGIES

Accounting Pedagogy, pages 404, 405, 436, 438, 462
Different Learning Abilities, pages 418, 451, 470
Different Learning Styles, pages 440, 444, 446, 447, 453
Cooperative Learning, pages 419, 452, 480
Expanding Beyond the Classroom, pages 410, 450, 477
Applying Visuals, pages 427, 449, 468
Teaching Tip, pages 404, 412, 417, 420, 426, 437, 439, 441, 442, 448, 464, 465, 468, 472, 475
Software Focus, pages 405, 437, 451, 462

ASSESSMENT

MicroExam software for each chapter
Problem Test for each chapter
Objective Test 6

SOFTWARE

Automated Accounting 6.0
MicroExam
Excel (spreadsheet software)
Lotus (spreadsheet software)
Works (integrated software)

BIBLIOGRAPHY

Gordon, Gus. *Understanding Financial Statements.* Cincinnati: South-Western Publishing Co., 1992.
Hamilton, D. *Cooperative Learning in the Classroom.* Bloomington, IN: Phi Delta Kappa Educational Foundation, 1990.
Magill, Harry T., and Gary J. Previts. *CPA Professional Responsibilities: A Guide.* Cincinnati: South-Western Publishing Co., 1991.
Parker, Jeanette Plauché. *Instructional Strategies for Teaching the Gifted.* Allyn and Bacon, 1989.
Shim, Jay K., and Joel G. Siefel. *Encyclopedic Dictionary of Accounting & Finance.* Englewood Cliffs, NJ: Prentice Hall, 1989.
U.S. Department of Commerce. *Basic Guide to Exporting.* 1986.

Periodicals

Accounting Horizons, American Accounting Association, Sarasota, FL.
Accounting Today, Lebhar-Friedman, Inc., New York, NY.
Multicultural Review, Greenwood Press Inc., Westport, CT. (Multicultural awareness)

Technology

AICPA, *Take Action Now! The Treadway Report.* (video)
Research Institute of America. *OnPoint CD-ROM Tax Library* (Tax research CD-ROM database)

PART 6 OPENER

PART 6

Management Accounting

GENERAL GOALS

1. Know accounting terminology related to management accounting for a corporation.
2. Understand accounting concepts and practices related to management accounting for a corporation.
3. Demonstrate management accounting procedures for a corporation.

OVERVIEW

Part 6 takes a look at management accounting. One important aspect of management accounting, budgetary planning and control, is covered in Chapter 15. Topics such as budget functions, design procedures, and planning are discussed and illustrated. Following Chapter 15 is Integrating Automated Accounting—Topic 7 that integrates computer application of the manual procedures that have been introduced in this chapter.

Chapter 16 explores analyzing income statements so that managers can gain an understanding of the relationship among sales, costs, and expenses. Chapter 17 progresses to financial statement analysis and how this information can be used to make wise management decisions.

CHAPTER 15 OVERVIEW

This chapter guides students through the intricate process of preparing budgets for a business. After describing some of the details and procedures in general terms, specific procedures for calculating data for the various components of a budget are examined. A comparative income statement is examined to

GUIDE TO ACHIEVING LEARNING OBJECTIVES

	TEACH	APPLY	EXTEND/ENRICH				
Enabling Performance Tasks	**Lesson Plans**	**Application Problems**	**Mastery Problems**	**Challenge Problems**	**Cases for Critical Thinking**	**Recycling Problems**	**Reinforcement Activity**
a. Define accounting terms related to budgetary planning and control.	15-1, 15-3						
b. Identify accounting concepts and practices related to preparing and analyzing budgeted income statements and cash budgets.	15-1, 15-2, 15-3				Cases 1, 2		
c. Prepare a budgeted income statement.	15-2	15-1, 15-2	15-M			15-R	
d. Prepare a cash budget.	15-3	15-3	15-M			15-R	
e. Prepare a performance report.	15-3			15-C			

ENRICHMENT

SPECIAL FEATURES
Multicultural Awareness, page 411
Personal Visions in Business, page 422
Applied Communications, page 431
TECHNOLOGY CONNECTION
Automated Accounting 6.0 Problem 15-C
Spreadsheet Template Problems 15-1, 15-2, 15-3

NEW, REVIEW, AND EXTENSION

ACTIVITIES/CONCEPTS/TRANSACTIONS	NEW	REVIEW/ EXTENSION
Budget functions	✓	
Budget design	✓	
Budgeted income statement		✓
Sales budget schedule	✓	
Purchases budget schedule	✓	
Selling expenses budget schedule	✓	
Administrative expenses budget schedule	✓	
Other revenue and expenses budget schedule	✓	
Sales budget schedule	✓	
Cash receipts budget schedule	✓	
Cash payments budget schedule	✓	
Cash budget	✓	
Performance report	✓	

begin the process of preparing sales and purchases budget schedules. After expenses are projected, a budgeted income statement is prepared. Then cash payments and receipts are estimated and planned on schedules for preparing the year's cash budget.

	INFORMAL ASSESSMENT		FORMAL ASSESSMENT			
	Study Guide	**Audit Your Understanding**	**Chapter MicroExam**	**Chapter Problem Test**	**Unit Objective Test**	**Portfolio**
	Unit A	✓	✓		✓	
	Units B, C	✓	✓		✓	
				✓		
				✓		
				✓		

TEACHING MATERIALS

Teacher's Wraparound Edition of the Text
Teacher's Resource Guide
Teacher's Edition of Working Papers
MicroExam

APPLIED MATHEMATICS

APPLIED MATH/ACCOUNTING SKILL	APPLICATION
Calculating projected quarterly sales	Prob. 15-1
Calculating projected quarterly ending inventory	Prob. 15-1
Calculating projected quarterly purchases	Prob. 15-1
Calculating projected quarterly expenses	Prob. 15-2
Calculating projected federal income tax expense	Prob. 15-2
Calculating projected quarterly cash receipts	Prob. 15-3
Calculating projected quarterly cash payments	Prob. 15-3

TEACHING STRATEGIES: ACCOUNTING PEDAGOGY

A chart of accounts for the business that is used to illustrate each part of this textbook is provided at the beginning of each part. Charts of accounts are extremely important to companies because they drive the accounting system. Employees usually cannot even receive reimbursement for expenses without knowing which account the expense should be charged to. Pedagogically, the chart of accounts provides the following information: (1) Classification for each account—needed to determine how a transaction is analyzed. (2) Permanent accounts (balance sheet accounts) and temporary accounts (income statement accounts)—assist in analyzing transactions and recording closing entries. (3) Account number for every general ledger account—critical information in automated accounting, since transactions are entered by account number rather than account title.

CHART OF ACCOUNTS

This chart of accounts is for a merchandising business organized as a corporation. Reflection's chart of accounts is similar to that of Appliance Center's and LampLight's described in Part 4 and Part 5. One difference is that Reflection distinguishes between delivery equipment, office equipment, warehouse equipment, and buildings when accounting for plant assets and their related depreciation. Another difference is that when accounting for salary expenses, Reflection distinguishes between commissions, regular salaries, and salaries for administrative personnel.

Reflection, Inc.

CHART OF ACCOUNTS

Balance Sheet Accounts

(1000) ASSETS

1100 Current Assets
1105 Cash
1110 Petty Cash
1115 Notes Receivable
1120 Interest Receivable
1125 Accounts Receivable
1130 Allowance for Uncollectible Accounts
1135 Merchandise Inventory
1140 Supplies—Sales
1145 Supplies—Administrative
1150 Prepaid Insurance

1200 Plant Assets
1205 Equipment—Delivery
1210 Accumulated Depreciation—Delivery Equipment
1215 Equipment—Office
1220 Accumulated Depreciation—Office Equipment
1225 Equipment—Warehouse
1230 Accumulated Depreciation—Warehouse Equipment
1235 Building
1240 Accumulated Depreciation—Building
1245 Land

(2000) LIABILITIES

2100 Current Liabilities
2105 Notes Payable
2110 Interest Payable
2115 Accounts Payable
2120 Employee Income Tax Payable
2125 Federal Income Tax Payable
2130 FICA Tax Payable
2135 Sales Tax Payable
2140 Unemployment Tax Payable—Federal
2145 Unemployment Tax Payable—State
2150 Dividends Payable

2200 Long-Term Liability
2205 Mortgage Payable

(3000) CAPITAL
3105 Capital Stock
3110 Retained Earnings
3115 Dividends
3120 Income Summary

Income Statement Accounts

(4000) OPERATING REVENUE
4105 Sales
4110 Sales Discount
4115 Sales Returns and Allowances

(5000) COST OF MERCHANDISE
5105 Purchases
5110 Purchases Discount
5115 Purchases Returns and Allowances

(6000) OPERATING EXPENSES

6100 Selling Expenses
6105 Advertising Expense
6110 Delivery Expense
6115 Depreciation Expense—Delivery Equipment
6120 Depreciation Expense—Warehouse Equipment
6125 Miscellaneous Expense—Sales
6130 Salary Expense—Commissions
6135 Salary Expense—Regular
6140 Supplies Expense—Sales

6200 Administrative Expenses
6205 Depreciation Expense—Office Equipment
6210 Insurance Expense
6215 Miscellaneous Expense—Administrative
6220 Payroll Taxes Expense
6225 Rent Expense
6230 Salary Expense—Administrative
6235 Supplies Expense—Administrative
6240 Uncollectible Accounts Expense
6245 Utilities Expense

(7000) OTHER REVENUE
7105 Gain on Plant Assets
7110 Interest Income

(8000) OTHER EXPENSES
8105 Interest Expense
8110 Loss on Plant Assets

(9000) INCOME TAX
9105 Federal Income Tax Expense

The chart of accounts for Reflection, Inc. is illustrated above for ready reference as you study Part 6 of this textbook.

TEACHING STRATEGIES: TEACHING TIP

Emphasize that students should refer to this chart of accounts throughout their study of Part 6. It will help them determine classification of accounts, which accounts are temporary and permanent accounts, and what account numbers to use for automated accounting. It will also be a useful reference for performing file maintenance activities.

15

Budgetary Planning and Control

TEACHING STRATEGIES: ACCOUNTING PEDAGOGY

This textbook presents budgetary planning and control as a tool to improve profitability. Internal control is continually emphasized as a key to success.

ENABLING PERFORMANCE TASKS

After studying Chapter 15, you will be able to:

a Define accounting terms related to budgetary planning and control.

b Identify accounting concepts and practices related to preparing and analyzing budgeted income statements and cash budgets.

c Prepare a budgeted income statement.

d Prepare a cash budget.

e Prepare a performance report.

TERMS PREVIEW

budgeting • budget • budget period • comparative income statement • performance report

SOFTWARE FOCUS

Software may be used for independent practice or enrichment/extension as the instructor deems appropriate. For this chapter, the following software may be used: *Automated Accounting 6.0* or higher with Challenge Problem 15-C; Spreadsheet Template with Problems 15-1, 15-2, and 15-3.

Business managers must make a variety of business decisions each day. The quality of these decisions has a direct impact on the business' ability to improve profitability. Financial planning is one tool managers use to improve profitability. A business must earn a net income to continue in existence. *(CONCEPT: Going Concern)*

Planning the financial operations of a business is called **budgeting.** A written financial plan of a business for a specific period of time, expressed in dollars, is called a **budget.** *(CONCEPT: Unit of Measurement)* A business prepares a variety of budgets. Each budget provides managers with detailed information about a specific area of the business' operations.

BUDGET FUNCTIONS

FYI

Budgeting is one of the most important uses of historical financial statements.

Budgets are projections or estimates of what will happen in the future expressed in financial terms. A carefully prepared budget reflects the best projections possible by those persons who prepare the plan. A completed budget shows the projected course of action for a business. A budget serves three important business functions. (1) Planning. (2) Operational control. (3) Department coordination.

Planning

In preparing a budget, managers must project what will probably happen in the future. This view of the future helps a manager plan actions that will meet desired goals. The budgeting process forces a manager to decide which actions should be emphasized to achieve the desired goals.

Operational Control

A budget reports the projected accomplishments of a business—the kind as well as the amount of projected activities. By comparing actual performance with projected performance, a manager can judge how well a business is achieving its goals.

By comparing actual expenses with projected expenses, a business also can identify where action is needed to control expenses. Comparison of actual amounts with budgeted amounts identifies items for which amounts are higher than projected. After high expense items are identified, a business can concentrate on actions to reduce these amounts.

Department Coordination

Profitable business growth requires that all managers be aware of the company's future plans. A budget reflects these plans. Each phase of a business operation must be coordinated with all other related phases. For example, if projected sales are to be achieved, the purchasing department must know when and how much merchandise to purchase. Therefore, all management personnel must

LESSON PLAN 15-1

Materials

Student pages 406–410

Objectives (Enabling Performance Tasks)

a. Define accounting terms related to budgetary planning and control.

b. Identify accounting concepts and practices related to preparing and analyzing budgeted income statements and cash budgets.

FOCUS

- Chapter 14 presented the analysis of financial statements to measure past performance. In this lesson, the concept of financial planning for the future through the use of budgets will be introduced. This lesson also looks at the procedures typically followed to design budgets.
- Introduce vocabulary: budgeting, budget, budget period, comparative income statement.

help plan and use a budget as a guide to control and to coordinate sales, costs, and expenses.

BUDGET DESIGN PROCEDURES

A budget is a view into the future—a plan of projected financial activities. Therefore, budget preparation begins with company goals. Company goals might be to increase sales, reduce cost of merchandise sold, or increase net income. All of these goals affect budget preparation because the budget is a business' financial plan.

Budget Period

The length of time covered by a budget is called the **budget period.** Usually this period is one year. Some companies also prepare a long-range budget of five years or more for special projects and plant and equipment purchases. However, the annual budget is the one used to compare current financial performance with budget plans.

An annual budget is normally prepared for a company's fiscal year. The annual budget is commonly divided into quarterly and monthly budgets. Such budget subdivisions provide frequent opportunities to evaluate how actual operations compare with budgeted operations.

A budget must be prepared in sufficient time to be communicated to the appropriate managers prior to the beginning of a budget period. If a company is large and complex, gathering budget information will start long before the beginning of a new budget year. Gathering information, making analysis, making decisions, preparing the budget, and approving and communicating the budget take considerable time.

Budget Type

Businesses frequently prepare two types of annual budgets. (1) Budgeted income statement. (2) Cash budget.

Budgeted Income Statement. A budgeted income statement is a projection of a business' sales, costs, expenses, and net income for a fiscal period. The budgeted income statement is similar to a regular income statement and is sometimes known as an operating budget.

Cash Budget. A cash budget is a projection of a business' cash receipts and payments for a fiscal period. For example, if a cash budget shows a projected cash shortage as of April 30, the company can arrange to borrow cash prior to April 30. If a cash budget shows a projected surplus of cash on July 31, the company can plan how to invest the extra cash.

FYI

Beginning in 1994, answers to essay questions on the CPA exam are being graded for the candidates' writing skills.

TEACH

Cover student pages 406–410 "Budget Functions" and "Budget Design Procedures." Emphasize the three functions of budgeting: planning, operational control, department coordination. Discuss the two types of budgets frequently prepared by businesses and the sources of information for these budgets. Stress that unless budgets are based on realistic assumptions, their value in operational control is lessened. Discuss the comparative income statement. Explain that the percentage of increase or decrease is one of many pieces of information managers use to project future activity.

APPLY

- Ask for volunteers to list the three functions of budgeting on the board. Ask students to give examples of what could happen if the budgets weren't coordinated with all departments.
- Refer students to Illustration 15-1 as the comparative income statement is discussed. Demonstrate how the amount and percentage of increase (decrease) are calculated for each line of the Selling Expenses section.

Guided Practice

Guide students through a comparison of the budget design procedures for a business with the budget design procedures for a family. Write on the board the headings Business and Family. As a group, discuss each design procedure given in the textbook and decide if a family would use the same or a different procedure. As a decision is reached, have a volunteer come to the board and write the procedure for a business and a family under the appropriate heading.

Independent Practice

Assign Terms 1–4 and Questions 1–9.

ASSESS

Assess student understanding by checking the solutions to the Independent Practice activities.

Reteach

Put students in pairs. Student 1 reads the first paragraph in the lesson material and explains its content to Student 2. Student 2 asks questions until both students understand the material. Student 2 then reads the next paragraph and explains its content to Student 1, who asks questions until both students understand the material. Continue until all paragraphs are covered.

Enrich

Assign the MULTICULTURAL AWARENESS feature on page 411.

Information Sources

Budgets should be based on information from company records of past operations, current general economic information, consultation with company personnel, and good judgment. Budgets cannot be exact since only projected sales, costs, and expenses are shown. However, a company should make the best projection of what will occur in future operations.

Company Records. The accounting and sales records of a business contain much of the information needed to prepare budgets. Accounting information about previous years' operations is used to determine trends in sales, purchases, and operating expenses. Expected price changes, sales promotion plans, and market research studies also are important in projecting activity for a budget period.

FYI

National magazines and newspapers are a good source of information regarding general economic conditions.

General Economic Information. A general slowdown or speedup in the national economy may affect budget decisions. Unusually high inflation rates will affect amounts budgeted. A labor strike may affect some related industries and thus affect company operations. New product development, changes in consumer buying habits, availability of merchandise, international trade, and general business conditions all must be considered when preparing budgets.

Company Staff and Managers. Sales personnel estimate the amount of projected sales. Considering projected sales for the new budget period, other department managers project budget items for their area of responsibility of the business.

Good Judgment. Good judgment by the individuals preparing the budgets is essential to realistic budgets. Even after evaluating all available information, answers to many budget questions are seldom obvious. Since some information will be in conflict with other information, final budget decisions are based on good judgment.

Preparation for Budget Planning

All available financial information should be analyzed as a basis for preparing new budgets. An analysis of previous years' sales, cost, and expense amounts is an important part of budget preparation. A variety of other sources of information may also be used.

Reflection, Inc. is a corporation that sells custom-cut mirrors. Reflection makes the following decisions and analysis as a basis for preparing its annual budget.

1. Previous years' sales, costs, and expenses are analyzed.
2. General and industry economic conditions are analyzed to determine probable changes in sales volume for the coming year.
3. Company goals are set for costs and expenses as a percent of sales.

FYI

Comparative financial statements may be prepared for a fiscal year or a month.

An income statement containing sales, cost, and expense information for two or more years is called a **comparative income statement.** A comparative income statement provides the information for Reflection's analysis of previous years' sales, costs, and expenses. This statement shows trends that may be taking place in these items. The statement also highlights items that may be increasing or decreasing at a higher rate than other items on the statement. Reflection's comparative income statement is shown in Illustration 15-1, page 410.

The first column of Reflection's comparative income statement shows actual sales, costs, and expenses for 19X2, the current year. The second column shows actual amounts for 19X1, the prior year. The third column shows the amount of increase or decrease from the prior year, 19X1, to the current year, 19X2. (For example, 19X2 cost of merchandise sold, \$1,231,720, *less* 19X1 cost of merchandise sold, \$1,105,000, *equals* the increase, \$126,720.) The fourth column shows the percentage the current year amount increased or decreased from the prior year amount. (For example, the cost of merchandise sold increase, \$126,720, *divided by* the 19X1 amount, \$1,105,000, *equals* the percent of increase, 11.5%.) Reflection rounds percentages to the nearest 0.1%.

Managers carefully review each increase or decrease amount on the comparative income statement. The percent of increase or decrease provides an indication of whether the change is favorable, unfavorable, or normal compared with net sales. If a cost or expense item increase is a higher percentage than the net sales increase, net income is unfavorably affected by this change. However, if the net sales increase is a higher percentage than cost and expense items, net income is favorably affected. Decreases have the opposite effect. If a cost or expense item decrease is a higher percentage than the net sales decrease, net income is favorably affected. If the net sales decrease is a higher percentage than cost and expense items, net income is unfavorably affected.

Beginning with net sales, Reflection analyzed the items on its comparative income statement. If the trend of an item is unfavorable, further inquiry is made to determine the cause. Reflection's net sales increased 10.6% over 19X1. The goal for 19X2 was to increase sales volume by 10.0%. The actual 10.6% increase resulted from an increase in units sold from 340,000 to 376,000 square feet of mirrors. The unit sales price remained at \$5.00. Management attributed the increase to two factors. (1) A more intensive advertising campaign increased market share from 42.0% to 45.0%. (2) Favorable economic conditions spurred new home building and created a greater demand for mirrors.

Reflection analyzed each cost and expense item on its comparative income statement. For example, cost of merchandise sold increased 11.5% over 19X1. Most of the increase resulted from the 10.6% increase in the number of units sold. Also, the purchase price per square foot of mirrors increased during 19X2 from \$3.25 per square

Audit Your Understanding

1. What three important business functions does a budget serve?
2. How does the budgeting process help control expenses?
3. What is the length of time generally covered by a company's budget?
4. What is a budgeted income statement?

CLOSURE

Use Audit Your Understanding questions.

AUDIT YOUR UNDERSTANDING

The AUDIT YOUR UNDERSTANDING feature appears at the end of each section of the chapter. Explain to your students that the word *audit* means to check or verify. AUDIT YOUR UNDERSTANDING may be used to check student comprehension of the section just studied. The answers are provided in Appendix D in the back of the textbook.

1. (1) Planning. (2) Operational control. (3) Department coordination.
2. A business can control expenses by comparing actual expenses with projected expenses. The comparison identifies differences where costs are higher than projected. The business can then take action to correct the differences.
3. One year.
4. A projection of a business' sales, costs, expenses, and net income for a fiscal period.

ILLUSTRATION 15-1 Comparative income statement

Reflection, Inc.
Comparative Income Statement
For Years Ended December 31, 19X1 and 19X2

	19X2	19X1	Increase (Decrease)	
			Amount	Percentage*
Operating Revenue:				
Net Sales	$1,880,000	$1,700,000	$180,000	10.6
Cost of Merchandise Sold	1,231,720	1,105,000	126,720	11.5
Gross Profit on Operations	$ 648,280	$ 595,000	$ 53,280	9.0
Operating Expenses:				
Selling Expenses:				
Advertising Expense	$ 45,120	$ 37,800	$ 7,320	19.4
Delivery Expense	150,410	140,640	9,770	6.9
Depr. Expense—Delivery Equipment	7,200	7,000	200	2.9
Depr. Expense—Warehouse Equipment	10,800	10,800	0	0.0
Miscellaneous Expense—Sales	11,490	11,960	(470)	(3.9)
Salary Expense—Commissions	75,200	68,000	7,200	10.6
Salary Expense—Regular	34,160	28,320	5,840	20.6
Supplies Expense—Sales	11,280	10,850	430	4.0
Total Selling Expenses	$ 345,660	$ 315,370	$ 30,290	9.6
Administrative Expenses:				
Depr. Expense—Office Equipment	$ 14,400	$ 12,000	$ 2,400	20.0
Insurance Expense	4,800	4,500	300	6.7
Miscellaneous Expense—Administrative	38,770	33,640	5,130	15.2
Depr. Expense—Warehouse Equipment	19,200	19,200	0	0.0
Payroll Taxes Expense	22,540	20,590	1,950	9.5
Rent Expense	30,000	30,000	0	0.0
Salary Expense—Administrative	77,830	75,240	2,590	3.4
Supplies Expense—Administrative	13,620	14,600	(980)	(6.7)
Uncollectible Accounts Expense	11,280	10,230	1,050	10.3
Utilities Expense	10,080	7,320	2,760	37.7
Total Administrative Expenses	$ 242,520	$ 227,320	$ 15,200	6.7
Total Operating Expenses	$ 588,180	$ 542,690	$ 45,490	8.4
Income from Operations	$ 60,100	$ 52,310	$ 7,790	14.9
Other Expenses:				
Interest Expense	$ 3,000	$ 6,500	($ 3,500)	(53.8)
Net Income before Federal Income Tax	$ 57,100	$ 45,810	$ 11,290	24.6
Federal Income Tax Expense	9,280	6,870	2,410	35.1
Net Income after Federal Income Tax	$ 47,820	$ 38,940	$ 8,880	22.8
Units (sq. ft.) of Mirror Sold	376,000	340,000	36,000	10.6

*Percentages rounded to the nearest 0.1%.

TEACHING STRATEGIES: EXPANDING BEYOND THE CLASSROOM

Invite a local businessperson to speak to the class about the budgeting process used by the speaker's business. Ask the speaker to emphasize the procedures used to project amounts in the budget and what actions are taken when actual amounts differ from projected amounts.

foot to $3.30. Advertising expense increased 19.4% over 19X1. The increase is consistent with the successful effort to expand market share. Management believes that more expensive television advertising resulted in a significant increase in third and fourth quarter unit sales.

MULTICULTURAL AWARENESS

Calculators

Calculators are not a new invention but have been around for hundreds of years. The word calculator is a Latin term that means calculus or pebble. The first calculator used in Roman times was a system that used tiny stones that were inserted in grooves of a counting board. The counting board was divided into columns for ones, tens, hundreds, etc. This allowed the merchants to keep track of their business transactions.

Blaise Pascal, a French mathematician, developed the first adding calculating machine in 1642. This machine was called the Pascaline and was the forerunner of today's modern calculator.

BUDGETED INCOME STATEMENT PLANNING

After previous years' records have been analyzed, a business may set goals, develop operational plans, and prepare projection of sales, costs, and expenses for the coming year.

A business' executive officers and planners generally determine the goals and operational plan. The operational plan is converted to a more precise plan expressed in dollars by preparing a budgeted income statement. Reflection prepares separate schedules for the major parts of the budgeted income statement. Separate schedules are prepared for sales, purchases, selling expenses, administrative expenses, and other revenue and expenses. To permit more frequent comparisons with budgeted amounts, schedules for the budget are separated into quarterly projections.

At Reflection, the accounting department is responsible for coordinating budget preparation. The sales manager is responsible for preparing the sales, purchases, and selling expenses budget schedules. The administrative manager is responsible for preparing the administrative expenses budget and the other revenue and expenses budget schedules. The accounting department then prepares the budgeted income statement from these schedules. The completed budget, with attached schedules, is submitted to the budget committee for approval. The budget committee consists of the president and two members of Reflection's board of directors.

Annual Operational Plans and Goals

Annual company projections establish goals the company will work toward in the coming year. Goals help a company coordinate the efforts of all areas toward a common direction. An operational plan provides general guidelines for achieving the company's goals. Operational plans and goals generally are determined by a planning group consisting of the company's executive officers and department managers.

At Reflection, the planning group includes the president and all department managers. The planning group reviews the analysis of the previous years' comparative income statement and considers possible changes in economic conditions that may affect the company. From these discussions, the company's operational plan and goals are determined for the coming year.

After reviewing company records and considering general economic conditions, Reflection's planning group develops the following planning guidelines.

1. The economy is projected to remain strong throughout 19X3. Therefore, the sales goal is to increase unit sales to 400,000 units, about a 6.4% increase. The unit sales price will be increased in the second quarter from $5.00 to $5.25 per square foot to recover merchandise cost increases in 19X2 and projected increases in the budget year.
2. Sales distribution by quarters is projected to be consistent with prior quarters.

MULTICULTURAL AWARENESS

The MULTICULTURAL AWARENESS feature is intended to expose students to the concept that our society is composed of people from many different cultural backgrounds. These features show both past contributions of many cultures and benefits of a culturally diverse society. (1) Read the feature. (2) Discuss the specific information in the feature. (3) Clarify any terms or questions.

LESSON PLAN 15-2

Materials

- Student pages 411–421
- Blackline Master for Budget Schedule (TRG)
- Software: Spreadsheet Template

Objectives (Enabling Performance Tasks)

b. Identify accounting concepts and practices related to preparing and analyzing budgeted income statements and cash budgets.

c. Prepare a budgeted income statement.

FOCUS

The importance and design of budgets were presented earlier in this chapter. In this lesson, the actual budgeting process begins by preparing a budgeted income statement. Explain that the budgeted income statement is actually a combination of several more specific budget schedules. Preparation of these budget schedules will be covered in this lesson.

3. The unit cost of merchandise is projected to rise from $3.30 to $3.40 in the first quarter, a 3.0% increase.
4. An automated cutting machine has been ordered. The machine will cost $20,000 and is projected to save approximately $10,000 per year in salary expense.
5. All employees on salary will receive a 5.0% increase in wage rate.
6. Rigid controls on all expenditures will be exercised.

Sales Budget Schedule

FYI

Even though budgets are based on estimates, much care is taken to insure the estimates are as accurate as possible.

A sales budget schedule shows the projected net sales for a budget period. The sales budget schedule is usually the first schedule prepared, because the other schedules are affected by the projected net sales. Before a business can project the merchandise to purchase, an accurate estimate is needed for projected sales. Projected net sales also determines the amount that may be spent for salaries, advertising, and other selling and administrative expenses.

Reflection's sales manager, with knowledge of the budget guidelines and with the assistance of sales representatives, prepares a sales budget schedule. In preparing a sales budget schedule, previous net sales and the trend in net sales for a period of several years are considered. Also considered are general economic conditions, consumer buying trends, competition, new products on the market, and such activities as planned special sales.

Previous years' income statement trends, the current economic conditions, and the competitive situation support Reflection's planning group goal of a 6.4% increase in unit sales. Based on a projected 6.4% increase, the unit sales projection is set at 400,000 units.

After considering the budget guidelines, reviewing competitors' selling prices, and analyzing projected costs of merchandise, the sales manager increased the unit sales price in the second quarter from $5.00 to $5.25. When all factors that may affect sales have been considered, the sales budget schedule is prepared. The sales budget schedule for Reflection is shown in Illustration 15-2.

TEACHING STRATEGIES: TEACHING TIP

Collect copies of budgets from organizations familiar to students: school clubs and local businesses, if available. Review in class the sales, cost, and expense items on the budget schedules. Emphasize the importance for each of these groups to accurately project sales and expenditures that can be made from the projected sales.

ILLUSTRATION 15-2 Sales budget schedule

Reflection, Inc.
Sales Budget Schedule
For Year Ended December 31, 19X3 **Schedule 1**

	Annual Budget	Quarter			
		1st	2d	3d	4th
Actual Unit Sales, 19X2	376,000	91,600	99,000	103,800	81,600
Sales Percentage by Quarter		24.4%	26.3%	27.6%	21.7%
Projected Unit Sales, 19X3	400,000	97,600	105,200	110,400	86,800
Times Unit Sales Price		$5.00	$5.25	$5.25	$5.25
Net Sales	$2,075,600	$488,000	$552,300	$579,000	$455,700

FYI

Most budgets are based on forecasts of increases or decreases over previous years' performances. In zero-based budgeting, however, data are prepared as though operations were being started for the first time.

Accurate projections are important for effective budgeting. However, since budgets are based on estimates, most businesses round the projected amounts to simplify the budgeting process. Reflection rounds unit projections to the nearest hundred units and dollar projections to the nearest $10.

Reflection prepares its annual budget in quarterly segments to provide more frequent opportunities to compare actual with budgeted operations. Quarterly sales are based on a projected percentage of the annual budget similar to previous years' quarterly sales percentages and on projected activities for specific quarters. The first quarter's sales percentage is calculated as follows.

19X2 Actual Unit Sales First Quarter	÷	19X2 Actual Unit Sales	=	19X2 Sales Percentage First Quarter
91,600	÷	376,000	=	24.4%

Reflection's planning group believes quarterly sales percentages will remain the same. Thus, Reflection believes that 24.4% of its projected net sales will occur in the first quarter. Using the planned $5.00 unit sales price, a projection of net sales for the first quarter is calculated as shown below.

19X2 Sales Percentage First Quarter	×	19X3 Projected Unit Sales	=	19X3 Projected Unit Sales First Quarter
24.4%	×	400,000	=	97,600
19X3 Projected Unit Sales First Quarter	**×**	**Unit Sales Price**	**=**	**19X3 Projected Net Sales First Quarter**
97,600	×	$5.00	=	$488,000

The completed sales budget schedule is approved by the planning group before other budget schedules are prepared.

Purchases Budget Schedule

A purchases budget schedule is prepared to show the projected amount of purchases that will be required during a budget period. Since the amount of purchases depends on projected net sales, the purchases budget schedule is prepared after the sales budget schedule.

In planning a purchases budget schedule, the following factors are considered.

1. The projection of unit sales as shown in the sales budget schedule.

TEACH

Cover student pages 411–421 "Budgeted Income Statement Planning." Discuss how a business sets goals, develops operational plans, and projects sales, costs, and expenses. Stress that the sales budget schedule is the base for all other budget schedules. Refer back to the sales budget schedule as other budget schedules are introduced. Emphasize the purpose of each budget schedule and how each is connected to other budget schedules. When discussing the budgeted income statement, make sure students know where all the information is obtained. Review the procedure for calculating federal income tax for a corporation.

APPLY

Refer students to Illustrations 15-2, 15-3, 15-4, 15-5, and 15-6, respectively, as the sales, purchases, selling expenses, administrative expenses, and other revenue and expenses budget schedules are discussed. Demonstrate all calculations on the board or overhead projector. Refer students to Illustration 15-7 as the budgeted income statement is presented.

Guided Practice

- Guide students through the preparation of the 1st quarter of the sales budget schedule and the purchases budget schedule in Problem 15-1, Instructions 1 and 2. As a group, calculate the amounts and percentages. When all students agree on the correct amounts, direct students to record the answers in the forms provided in the working papers. The balance of Problem 15-1 can be completed as Independent Practice.
- Guide students through the preparation of the 1st quarter of the selling expenses budget schedule and the administrative expenses budget schedule in Problem 15-2, Instructions 1 and 2. As a group, calculate the amounts. When all students agree on the correct amounts, direct students to record the answers in the forms provided in the working papers. The balance of Problem 15-2 can be completed as Independent Practice.

Independent Practice

Assign Questions 10–16 and Problems 15-1 and 15-2.

2. The quantity of merchandise on hand at the beginning of the budget period.
3. The quantity of merchandise needed to fill projected net sales orders without having excessive inventory on hand at any one time.
4. The price trends of merchandise to be purchased.

The sales manager prepares the purchases budget schedule shown in Illustration 15-3.

ILLUSTRATION 15-3 Purchases budget schedule

Reflection, Inc.
Purchases Budget Schedule
For Year Ended December 31, 19X3 **Schedule 2**

	Quarter			
	1st	**2d**	**3d**	**4th**
Ending Inventory	42,100	44,200	34,700	40,000
Unit Sales for Quarter	97,600	105,200	110,400	86,800
Total Units Needed	139,700	149,400	145,100	126,800
Less Beginning Inventory	39,200	42,100	44,200	34,700
Purchases	100,500	107,300	100,900	92,100
Times Unit Cost	$3.40	$3.40	$3.40	$3.40
Cost of Purchases	$341,700	$364,820	$343,060	$313,140

Quarterly unit sales are obtained from the sales budget schedule. The sales manager determined that the number of units for ending inventory should be about 40.0% of the number of units projected to be sold in the subsequent quarter. The first quarter's projected ending inventory is calculated as shown below.

19X3 Unit Sales Second Quarter	×	Ending Inventory Unit Sales Percentage	=	19X3 Ending Inventory First Quarter
105,200	×	40.0%	=	42,080

Reflection rounds unit projections to the nearest hundred. Therefore, 42,100 units will be recorded in the purchases budget schedule for the first quarter's projected ending inventory.

Purchases are made in advance of sales to allow for delivery of the merchandise. Enough total units are needed to meet sales demand while new units are being purchased. The 42,100 units in the first quarter's ending inventory will assure that an adequate supply of mirrors is available for sale in April.

FYI

The budgets of most governmental units are public information.

The ending inventory plus the quarter's unit sales equals the number of units Reflection needs during the quarter. The number of units in beginning inventory is subtracted from the units needed to calculate unit purchases. Reflection had 39,200 units in its January 1 beginning inventory. Reflection's first quarter's projected purchases are calculated as shown below.

Ending Inventory	+	Unit Sales for Quarter	=	Total Units Needed	−	Beginning Inventory	=	Projected Purchases
42,100	+	97,600	=	139,700	−	39,200	=	100,500

Reflection's planning group has projected that material costs per unit will rise from $3.30 to $3.40 per unit in the first quarter of 19X3. The projected cost of purchases for the first quarter is calculated as shown below.

Purchases First Quarter	×	Unit Cost	=	Cost of Purchases First Quarter
100,500	×	$3.40	=	$341,700

Similar calculations are made for subsequent quarters. Beginning inventory for a quarter is equal to the ending inventory for the previous quarter. The ending inventory for the fourth quarter is calculated using a projection of unit sales for the first quarter following the budget year. Reflection's sales manager projected first quarter net sales in the year following the budget year as 100,000 units. Therefore, the fourth quarter's ending inventory is projected as 40,000 units (100,000 × 40.0% = 40,000).

Selling Expenses Budget Schedule

A selling expenses budget schedule is prepared to show projected expenditures related directly to the selling operations. The sales manager projects the information for the selling expenses budget schedule. However, other sales personnel may provide specific information. For example, the advertising manager supplies much of the advertising expense information. After selling expenses information has been projected, a selling expenses budget schedule is prepared.

Some selling expense items are relatively stable and require little budget planning. For example, delivery and warehouse equipment depreciation expenses are reasonably stable from year to year unless new equipment is bought. On the other hand, several selling expenses increase and decrease in relation to sales increases and decreases. Reflection has a seasonal business with higher sales during the second and third quarters. The company hires more personnel and spends more for advertising and sales supplies during the heavy sales season. All of these factors are considered in making a selling expenses budget schedule. Reflection's selling expenses budget schedule is shown in Illustration 15-4.

FYI

Accountants often use parentheses around a number that represents a deduction rather than a minus sign.

ASSESS

Assess student understanding by checking the solutions to the Independent Practice activities.

Reteach

- Make transparencies of the budget schedule from the accounting forms masters provided in the Blackline Masters Section of the Teacher's Resource Guide. Using information from Recycling Problem 15-R and the transparencies, demonstrate how the 1st quarter amounts and percentages are calculated and recorded on Schedules 1–5. Using these budget schedules, develop the 1st quarter of a budgeted income statement. As each supporting schedule is used, display it on the overhead and circle the amounts used on the budgeted income statement.
- Assign Recycling Problem 15-R, Instructions 1–6.

Extend

- Assign Cases for Critical Thinking 1.
- Assign Spreadsheet Template for Problems 15-1 and 15-2.

Enrich

Assign the APPLIED COMMUNICATIONS special feature on page 431.

CLOSURE

Use Audit Your Understanding questions.

ILLUSTRATION 15-4 Selling expenses budget schedule

Reflection, Inc.
Selling Expenses Budget Schedule
For Year Ended December 31, 19X3

Schedule 3

	Annual Budget	Quarter			
		1st	2d	3d	4th
Advertising Expense	$ 49,820	$11,710	$13,260	$ 13,910	$10,940
Delivery Expense	160,000	39,040	42,080	44,160	34,720
Depr. Expense—Delivery Equipment	7,200	1,800	1,800	1,800	1,800
Depr. Expense—Warehouse Equipment	13,800	2,700	3,700	3,700	3,700
Miscellaneous Expense—Sales	10,380	2,440	2,760	2,900	2,280
Salary Expense—Commissions	83,020	19,520	22,090	23,180	18,230
Salary Expense—Regular	25,370	6,190	6,670	7,000	5,510
Supplies Expense—Sales	12,450	2,930	3,310	3,480	2,730
Total Selling Expenses	$362,040	$86,330	$95,670	$100,130	$79,910

APPLIED SKILLS: WRITING ACROSS THE CURRICULUM

Writing paragraphs and short essays. The Cases for Critical Thinking are short, practical applications of the accounting principles developed in the chapter. Some cases are planned to present problems related to the chapter but not specifically discussed and answered in the chapter. These cases present an opportunity for critical thinking and decision making. These cases also require more than a short objective-type response. Therefore, they provide ideal practice in writing paragraphs and short essays.

Reflection's sales manager uses a number of approaches to project the various selling expenses. Most selling expenses are linked closely to the amount of quarterly net sales. Reflection's managers have the following projection guides to prepare its selling expenses budget schedule.

1. Advertising expense: Advertising expense is closely related to sales and sales promotions for the year. The comparative income statement shows that advertising expense for 19X2 was 2.4% ($45,120 ÷ $1,880,000) of net sales. Sales promotion emphasis will be maintained at about the same level this year. Thus, Reflection will use 2.4% of each quarter's projected net sales from the sales budget schedule to project advertising expense. First quarter's projected advertising expense is $11,710 (2.4% × $488,000 = $11,712, rounded to $11,710).

FYI

Many budgetary items are based on the budgeted estimate of sales. Therefore, the budget is only as accurate as the sales forecast.

2. Delivery expense: Delivery expense is closely related to the number of units sold and delivered. The previous year's delivery expense increased significantly because an external freight company was used for increased deliveries until Reflection could acquire an additional truck. Rigid cost control measures will be applied to reduce future unit delivery expenses. Delivery expense is projected to be $0.40 per unit (sq. ft.) sold times each quarter's projected unit sales from the sales budget schedule. First quarter's projected delivery expense is $39,040 ($0.40 × 97,600 units).
3. Depreciation expense—delivery equipment: No new delivery equipment will be added. Thus, depreciation expense will remain the same as the previous year ($1,800 per quarter). Since the depreciation of assets occurs over a period of time, an equal amount of depreciation expense is recorded in each quarter.
4. Depreciation expense—warehouse equipment: A new automated cutter will be acquired at the beginning of the second

quarter, increasing quarterly depreciation expense in the second quarter from $2,700 to $3,700.

5. Miscellaneous expense—sales: Closely related to net sales, miscellaneous expense was 0.6% ($11,490 ÷ $1,880,000) of net sales on the 19X2 comparative income statement. Management is committed to reducing miscellaneous expense to 0.5% of projected quarterly net sales from the 19X3 sales budget schedule. First quarter's miscellaneous expense is projected as $2,440 (0.5% × $488,000).
6. Salary expense—commissions: Salespersons will continue to earn a 4.0% commission on quarterly net sales from the 19X3 sales budget schedule. First quarter's commissions are projected as $19,520 (4.0% × $488,000).
7. Salary expense—regular: Regular salary expense is determined by salary increases and changes in activity which affects the number of people employed. The new automated cutter will reduce regular salary expense by $10,000. A 5.0% raise will be added to remaining salaries. Thus, the projected annual amount is calculated as shown below.

Salary expense, 19X2 comparative income statement	$34,160
Less reduction from automated cutter	−10,000
Total	$24,160
Plus 5.0% rate increase	+1,210
Projected salary expense—regular	$25,370

   The projected amount is allocated among the four quarters in relation to the sales percentage from the sales budget schedule. First quarter's regular salaries are projected as $6,190 (24.4% × $25,370).

8. Supplies expense—sales: Closely related to net sales, supplies expense was 0.6% ($11,280 ÷ $1,880,000) of net sales in 19X2. Supplies expense is projected to be 0.6% of net sales each quarter, the same percentage as last year. First quarter's supplies expense is projected as $2,930 (0.6% × $488,000 = $2,928, rounded to $2,930).

For amounts calculated by quarter, the annual budget amounts are the sum of quarterly amounts.

TEACHING STRATEGIES: TEACHING TIP

Explain how each expense is calculated on the selling expenses budget schedule and the administrative expenses budget schedule. Demonstrate the calculations on the chalkboard or overhead projector.

Administrative Expenses Budget Schedule

An administrative expenses budget schedule shows the projected expenses for all operating expenses not directly related to selling operations. The administrative manager is responsible for projecting most of the information in this budget. Information for this budget comes from a study of past records, an evaluation of company plans, the sales and selling expenses budget schedules, and discussions with other managers. After the administrative expenses have been projected, the administrative expenses budget schedule is prepared. Reflection's administrative expenses budget schedule is shown in Illustration 15-5.

FYI

Budgets are usually revised many times before they are finalized. Spreadsheet software is ideal for preparing repeated changes to projections.

ILLUSTRATION 15-5 Administrative expenses budget schedule

Reflection, Inc.
Administrative Expenses Budget Schedule
For Year Ended December 31, 19X3

Schedule 4

	Annual Budget	Quarter			
		1st	2d	3d	4th
Depr. Expense—Office Equipment	$ 14,400	$ 3,600	$ 3,600	$ 3,600	$ 3,600
Insurance Expense	5,600	1,400	1,400	1,400	1,400
Miscellaneous Expense—Administrative	36,760	9,190	9,190	9,190	9,190
Payroll Taxes Expense	22,810	5,540	5,900	6,070	5,300
Rent Expense	30,000	7,500	7,500	7,500	7,500
Salary Expense—Administrative	81,720	20,430	20,430	20,430	20,430
Supplies Expense—Administrative	14,540	3,420	3,870	4,060	3,190
Uncollectible Accounts Expense	12,450	2,930	3,310	3,480	2,730
Utilities Expense	10,980	4,870	1,470	1,610	3,030
Total Administrative Expenses	$229,260	$58,880	$56,670	$57,340	$56,370

Reflection's administrative manager uses a number of approaches to project expenses. Most administrative expenses are known and remain the same each period. Some administrative expenses need to be budgeted as a percent of another amount from another budget. The following information was used to prepare the administrative expenses budget schedule.

1. Depreciation expense—office equipment: Recently purchased office equipment increased annual depreciation to $14,400. Annual depreciation is divided equally over the four quarters.
2. Insurance expense: Annual insurance is projected to increase to $5,600 primarily because of added coverage for the new automated cutting machine. An equal amount is paid each quarter.
3. Miscellaneous expense—administrative: Closely related to administrative salaries, miscellaneous expense was 49.8% ($38,770 ÷ $77,830) of administrative salaries in 19X2. Management is committed to reducing miscellaneous expense to 45.0% of projected administrative salaries this year. First quarter's miscellaneous expense is projected as $9,190 (45.0% × $20,430 = $9,194, rounded to $9,190).
4. Payroll taxes expense: Based on current payroll tax rates, payroll taxes expense is 12.0% of all salaries each quarter. First quarter's salaries are projected as $46,140 ($19,520 + 6,190 + 20,430). Thus, payroll taxes expense is projected as $5,540 (12.0% × $46,140 = $5,537, rounded to $5,540).
5. Rent expense: Reflection leases the building for a known rental fee of $2,500 per month. Thus, rent expense can be projected accurately at $7,500 each quarter.
6. Salary expense—administrative: No new administrative personnel will be hired. Salary expense is projected as $81,720, equal to the 19X2 amount, $77,830, adjusted for a 5.0% salary rate increase. An equal amount is paid each quarter. Thus, each quarter's salary expense is projected as $20,430 ($81,720 ÷ 4).

TEACHING STRATEGIES: DIFFERENT LEARNING ABILITIES

Specific Learning Disability (SLD) Students. Exposing students to actual business situations can be an excellent motivational device. Arrange a field trip to a local business familiar to the students, such as a grocery store. Before the field trip, require the students to identify questions to ask the managers of the business. Allow students to ask these questions during the field trip. After the field trip, lead a class discussion which allows students the opportunity to share what they learned.

FYI

Individuals prepare budgets too. Many individuals prepare a weekly or monthly personal budget.

7. Supplies expense—administrative: Closely related to net sales, supplies expense was 0.7% ($13,620 ÷ $1,880,000) of net sales for 19X2. Supplies expense is projected to be 0.7% of net sales each quarter this year, the same percentage as last year. First quarter's supplies expense is projected as $3,420 (0.7% × $488,000 = $3,416, rounded to $3,420).
8. Uncollectible accounts expense: Closely related to net sales, uncollectible accounts expense was 0.6% ($11,280 ÷ $1,880,000) of net sales in 19X2. First quarter's uncollectible accounts expense is projected as $2,930 (0.6% × $488,000 = $2,928, rounded to $2,930).
9. Utilities expense: Utilities expense is based on the amount of power, heat, telephone, and other utilities used in 19X2. Costs are projected to increase by 9.0%, consisting of a 5.0% projected increase in activity and a 4.0% increase in rates. Utilities expense by quarter in 19X2 is multiplied by 109% (100.0% + 9.0%) to calculate 19X3's projected utilities expense as shown below.

	19X2 Actual Utilities Expense				19X3 Projected Utilities Expense
1st Quarter	$ 4,470	×	109%	=	$ 4,870
2d Quarter	1,350	×	109%	=	1,470
3d Quarter	1,480	×	109%	=	1,610
4th Quarter	2,780	×	109%	=	3,030
Total	$10,080				$10,980

TEACHING STRATEGIES: COOPERATIVE LEARNING

Divide the class into groups of three or four students each. Using the textbook as a guide, have each group compare the budget design procedures for a business with the budget design procedures for a family. Each group should appoint a leader who will present the list of similarities and differences to the class. This cooperative learning activity should not take more than 15 or 20 minutes of class time.

Other Revenue and Expenses Budget Schedule

Budgeted revenue and expenses from activities other than normal operations are shown in an other revenue and expenses budget schedule. Typical items in this budget are interest income, interest expense, and gains or losses on the sale of plant assets. Reflection's other revenue and expenses budget schedule is shown in Illustration 15-6. Reflection has only one other expense item and no other revenue items.

ILLUSTRATION 15-6 Other revenue and expenses budget schedule

Reflection, Inc.
Other Revenue and Expenses Budget Schedule
For Year Ended December 31, 19X3
Schedule 5

	Annual Budget	Quarter 1st	2d	3d	4th
Other Expenses:					
Interest Expense	$2,250	$750	$750	$750	

Reflection's administrative manager is responsible for projecting the information in the other revenue and expenses budget schedule. Projected interest expense, the only item in the budget, is based on the interest due on a $20,000 loan used to acquire the automated cutter. Reflection plans to repay the $20,000 loan at the beginning of the fourth quarter.

Budgeted Income Statement

A budgeted income statement shows projected sales, costs, expenses, and net income of a company. Reflection prepares the budgeted income statement from information in the sales, purchases, selling expenses, administrative expenses, and other revenue and expenses budget schedules. Since the budget schedules contain detailed items, Reflection prepares a shortened budgeted income statement and then attaches the budget schedules. Reflection's budgeted income statement is shown in Illustration 15-7.

TEACHING STRATEGIES: TEACHING TIP

Demonstrate how the tax rate table is used to calculate projected federal income tax for a corporation. Change the amount of projected net income and work several different calculations. You may wish to have students calculate the tax at their desks as you demonstrate the procedure on the chalkboard or overhead projector.

ILLUSTRATION 15-7 Budgeted income statement

Reflection, Inc.
Budgeted Income Statement
For Year Ended December 31, 19X3

	Annual Budget	Quarter			
		1st	2d	3d	4th
Operating Revenue:					
Net Sales (Schedule 1)	$2,075,600	$488,000	$552,300	$579,600	$455,700
Cost of Merchandise Sold:					
Beginning Inventory	$ 129,360	$129,360	$143,140	$150,280	$117,980
Purchases (Schedule 2)	1,362,720	341,700	364,820	343,060	313,140
Total Merchandise Available	$1,492,080	$471,060	$507,960	$493,340	$431,120
Less Ending Inventory	136,000	143,140	150,280	117,980	136,000
Cost of Merchandise Sold	$1,356,080	$327,920	$357,680	$375,360	$295,120
Gross Profit on Operations	$ 719,520	$160,080	$194,620	$204,240	$160,580
Operating Expenses:					
Selling Expenses (Schedule 3)	$ 362,040	$ 86,330	$ 95,670	$100,130	$ 79,910
Administrative Expenses (Schedule 4)	229,260	58,880	56,670	57,340	56,370
Total Operating Expenses	$ 591,300	$145,210	$152,340	$157,470	$136,280
Income from Operations	$ 128,220	$ 14,870	$ 42,280	$ 46,770	$ 24,300
Net Deduction (Schedule 5)	$ 2,250	$ 750	$ 750	$ 750	
Net Income before Federal Income Tax	$ 125,970	$ 14,120	$ 41,530	$ 46,020	$ 24,300
Federal Income Tax Expense	32,380	8,100	8,100	8,100	8,080
Net Income after Federal Income Tax	$ 93,590	$ 6,020	$ 33,430	$ 37,920	$ 16,220

The dollar amounts of beginning and ending inventories are calculated using the unit quantities from the purchases budget schedule. The first quarter's beginning inventory, *$129,360,* is calculated using the 19X2 unit cost, *$3.30,* multiplied by the 39,200 units in beginning inventory. Other inventory amounts are calculated using the unit cost for 19X3, *$3.40.* The first quarter's ending inventory is $143,140 (42,100 units × $3.40 = $143,140).

Amounts from the five budget schedules allow Reflection to project net income before federal income tax. To complete the budgeted income statement, federal income taxes are calculated using a tax rate table furnished by the Internal Revenue Service. Reflection's projected federal income tax is calculated using the tax rate table shown below.

15% of net income before taxes, zero to $50,000.00.
Plus 25% of net income before taxes, $50,000.00 to $75,000.00.
Plus 34% of net income before taxes, $75,000.00 to $100,000.00.
Plus 39% of net income before taxes, $100,000.00 to $335,000.00.
Plus 34% of net income before taxes over $335,000.00.

Corporation rates current when this text was written were used to calculate the federal income tax for Reflection as follows.

Net Income Before Federal Income Tax		Tax Rate		Federal Income Tax Expense
$ 50,000	×	15%	=	$ 7,500
25,000	×	25%	=	6,250
25,000	×	34%	=	8,500
25,970	×	39%	=	10,128
$125,970				$32,378, rounded to $32,380

Audit Your Understanding

1. How do annual goals help a company?
2. What factors are considered in preparing a sales budget schedule?

Quarterly federal income tax expense amounts are based on the projected annual federal income tax expense amount. Quarterly income tax payments are one fourth, *$8,095* ($32,380 ÷ 4 = $8,095, rounded to $8,100), of the annual federal income tax expense. Thus, Reflection's payments equal $24,300 ($8,100 × 3 quarters) through the third quarter. The fourth quarter's amount equals the unpaid amount of federal income taxes, *$8,080* ($32,380 − $24,300). Federal income tax payments equal the quarterly federal income tax expense amounts on the budgeted income statement.

CASH BUDGET PLANNING

Good cash management requires the planning and controlling of cash so that it will be available to meet obligations when due. Reliable cash management requires a knowledge of beginning cash balances, projected cash receipts, and projected cash payments during a budget period.

Reflection's cash budget is prepared by the treasurer in consultation with the budget committee. A corporation treasurer is an officer of the corporation who is usually responsible for planning the

AUDIT YOUR UNDERSTANDING

1. Establish targets to work toward in the coming year. Help coordinate the efforts of all areas toward a common direction.
2. Previous net sales and the trend in net sales for a period of several years, general economic conditions, consumer buying trends, competition, new products on the market, and such activities as planned special sales.

LESSON PLAN 15-3

Materials

- Student pages 421–429
- Blackline Master for Budget Schedule (TRG)
- Software: Spreadsheet Template; *Automated Accounting 6.0* or higher; Accounting Textbook Template, Advanced Course
- Assess: Problem Test Chapter 15, MicroExam Chapter 15

Objectives (Enabling Performance Tasks)

a. Define accounting terms related to budgetary planning and control.
b. Identify accounting concepts and practices related to preparing and analyzing budgeted income statements and cash budgets.
d. Prepare a cash budget.
e. Prepare a performance report.

FOCUS

- The procedures for planning and preparing a budgeted income statement were presented earlier in this chapter. Explain that a business also needs to plan and control the amount of cash on hand. In this lesson, a cash budget will be planned and prepared. Remind students that a function of budgeting is operational control. In this lesson, a report will be prepared that compares actual expenses with projected expenses. Managers use this report to judge how well a business is achieving its financial goals.
- Introduce vocabulary: performance report.

Personal Visions in Business

This special student feature introduces students to successful entrepreneurs or business professionals. Each profile gives a flavor of what the actual business world is like and some of the opportunities available to students who study accounting. These features can be used to motivate students to pursue professional business careers in a wide variety of fields. The subjects of these profiles have been carefully chosen to represent the full spectrum of diverse ethnic and racial backgrounds of professional business people. As an optional activity, students can be encouraged to seek out and interview successful business people in their own communities.

the corporation's requirement for and use of cash. A detailed analysis is made of projected receipts from cash sales, customers on account, and other sources. Also, an analysis is made of the projected cash payments for ordinary expenses such as rent, payroll, and payments to vendors on account. In addition, consideration is given to other cash payments such as buying plant assets or supplies. Since a cash budget reports projected cash receipts and payments, Reflection prepares two budget schedules, one for cash receipts and one for cash payments. Total amounts are then recorded on the cash budget.

Cash Receipts Budget Schedule

Projected cash receipts for a budget period are reported on a cash receipts budget schedule. The following projections are made in preparing a cash receipts budget schedule.

1. A projection of quarterly cash sales.
2. A projection of quarterly collections on account from customers. The amounts received from customers will not be the same as the amount of sales on account. Normally, cash is

■ Bonnie Combs ■

BONNIE'S HALLMARK

Bonnie Combs owns and operates a retail greeting card store called Bonnie's Hallmark. Bonnie and her husband bought the first store with some savings and other family funds. Before starting the retail enterprise, she worked as an administrative secretary for a university and as a teller in a bank. Because she had no formal training in accounting, she had to rely on someone else to help in financial matters. However, her husband's business degree and accounting background did help.

Combs learned some lessons about retail operations early in her career. She says that you have to use your own judgment with wholesalers from whom you purchase your merchandise. "They will emphatically state that every product they provide will be a hot seller in your store," Combs says. "It is simply not true, however. You are the best judge of what you can sell in your location, not the wholesaler."

Operating a retail store is hard work. If you are located in a mall, you probably will have to be open for business eleven or twelve hours a day, every day of the week. If you as owner wish to have any personal time at all, you need to hire employees to help operate the store when you cannot be there. Combs said that it's important to establish fair employment policies and stick to them.

Combs learned a lot about customers in operating her store. She was surprised that some customers try to take advantage of store owners. She said, "Customers try to bend store policies. If you run a promotion that includes one free item for the first item bought, some customers will try to get two, three, or even more free items. They don't seem to understand that you are trying to earn a living and that you have to sell merchandise at a reasonable profit to survive."

Combs suggests that continuing your education, especially with college courses in accounting and management, can be critical to success in the business world. "Business courses help you learn to operate in the financial world," Combs says. She also says that the owner of a retail store needs to be open-minded, yet aggressive, whether dealing with suppliers, customers, or employees.

Personal Visions in Business

received for sales on account made during the previous one or two months. Also, some sales returns and allowances and uncollectible accounts are likely.

3. A projection of cash to be received quarterly from other sources.

Reflection's cash receipts budget schedule is shown in Illustration 15-8.

ILLUSTRATION 15-8 Cash receipts budget schedule

Reflection, Inc.
Cash Receipts Budget Schedule
For Year Ended December 31, 19X3 **Schedule A**

	Quarter			
	1st	**2d**	**3d**	**4th**
From Sales:				
Prior Year's 4th Quarter ($408,000)	$ 79,150			
1st Quarter Sales ($488,000)	390,400	$ 94,670		
2d Quarter Sales ($552,300)		441,840	$107,150	
3d Quarter Sales ($579,600)			463,680	$112,440
4th Quarter Sales ($455,700)				364,560
Total Receipts from Sales	$469,550	$536,510	$570,830	$477,000
From Other Sources:				
Note Payable to Bank	20,000			
Total Cash Receipts	$489,550	$536,510	$570,830	$477,000

An analysis of Reflection's sales for previous years shows the following pattern of net sales. In any quarter, about 60.0% of all net sales are cash sales. About 20.0% are sales on account collected in the same quarter. Thus, 80.0% of a quarter's net sales are collected during the same quarter. About 19.4% are collected in the following quarter. About 0.6% of net sales prove to be uncollectible and, therefore, are never collected.

In the second quarter, Reflection collected $441,840 from second quarter net sales, calculated as shown below.

Collection Percentage	×	Second Quarter Net Sales	=	Second Quarter Cash Receipts
80.0%	×	$552,300	=	$441,840

Also in the second quarter, Reflection collected cash from sales on account made in the first quarter. Cash receipts from first quarter sales on account are calculated as shown below.

Collection Percentage	×	First Quarter Net Sales	=	Second Quarter Cash Receipts
19.4%	×	$488,000	=	$94,672, rounded to $94,670

TEACH

Cover student pages 421–429 "Cash Budget Planning" and "Performance Report Preparation and Analysis." Discuss the projections made when preparing a cash receipts budget schedule. Remind students that sales are of two types: cash and on account. Sales on account are collected over the next weeks or months. Discuss the projections made when preparing a cash payments budget schedule. Remind students that purchases can be for cash or on account. Purchases on account are paid over the next weeks or months. Explain how information from the cash receipts and cash payments budget schedules is used to prepare the cash budget. Emphasize that if a business knows in advance that it will need to borrow cash, it can make arrangements to borrow money at the lowest possible interest rate. Discuss the preparation of a performance report. Stress the importance of a performance report to managers who control operations.

APPLY

Refer students to Illustrations 15-8, 15-9, and 15-10, respectively, as the cash receipts and cash payments budget schedules and the cash budget are discussed. Write all formulas on the board and demonstrate the calculations. Refer students to Illustration 15-12 as preparation of a performance report is discussed. Demonstrate the calculations for several lines of the report.

Guided Practice

Guide students through the preparation of the 1st quarter of the cash receipts budget schedule and the cash payments budget schedule in Problem 15-3, Instructions 1 and 2. As a group, calculate the amounts and percentages. When all students agree on the correct amounts, direct students to record the answers in the forms provided in the working papers. The balance of Problem 15-3 can be completed as Independent Practice.

Independent Practice

- Assign Term 5, Questions 17–20, and Problem 15-3.
- Assign Study Guide 15 and Mastery Problem 15-M.

Cash receipts in the first quarter include $79,150 from 19X2's fourth quarter sales on account (19.4% × $408,000 = $79,152, rounded to $79,150).

Cash sales and collections on account generally provide most of the cash receipts. However, if additional cash is needed, other sources of cash should be planned. After preliminary planning of projected cash receipts and cash payments, the treasurer determines that cash on hand will be reduced in the first quarter to an unusually low level. This condition could prevent the company from making timely payments for its expenditures. Therefore, the treasurer makes arrangements to borrow $20,000 during the first quarter.

Cash Payments Budget Schedule

Projected cash payments for a budget period are reported on a cash payments budget schedule. To prepare a cash payments budget schedule, the accountant and treasurer project quarterly cash payments. The following projections are made in preparing a cash payments budget schedule.

1. A projection of quarterly cash payments for accounts payable or notes payable to vendors.
2. A projection of quarterly cash payments for each expense item. This projection requires an analysis of the selling expenses, administrative expenses, and other revenue and expenses budget schedules.
3. A projection of quarterly cash payments for buying equipment and other assets.
4. A projection of quarterly cash payments for dividends.
5. A projection of quarterly cash payments for investments.

Reflection's cash payments budget schedule is shown in Illustration 15-9.

Cash Payments for Merchandise. An analysis of past records for payments to vendors on account shows the following cash payment pattern. About 10.0% of all purchases are cash purchases. About 60.0% are purchases on account paid for in the quarter. Thus, 70.0% (10.0% + 60.0%) of a quarter's purchases are paid for during the same quarter. The remaining 30.0% are purchases on account paid for in the following quarter. Cash payments are calculated using the same procedure used for cash receipts. Purchase amounts are from the purchases budget schedule. First quarter cash payments for first quarter purchases are $239,190 (70.0% × $341,700).

FYI

Remember that cash is not paid for depreciation and uncollectible accounts expenses.

Cash Payments for Operating Expenses. Cash payments for most operating expenses are made in the quarter the expense is incurred. However, the selling expenses budget schedule, Illustration 15-4, and the administrative expenses budget schedule, Illustration 15-5, include some projected items for which cash will not be paid. For example, cash is not paid for depreciation and uncollectible

ILLUSTRATION 15-9 Cash payments budget schedule

Reflection, Inc.
Cash Payments Budget Schedule
For Year Ended December 31, 19X3
Schedule B

	Quarter			
	1st	2d	3d	4th
For Merchandise:				
Prior Year's 4th Quarter Purchases ($212,500)	$ 63,750			
1st Quarter Purchases ($341,700)	239,190	$102,510		
2d Quarter Purchases ($364,820)		255,370	$109,450	
3d Quarter Purchases ($343,060)			240,140	$102,920
4th Quarter Purchases ($313,140)				219,200
Total Cash Payments for Purchases	$302,940	$357,880	$349,590	$322,120
For Operating Expenses:				
Cash Selling Expenses	$ 81,830	$ 90,170	$ 94,630	$ 74,410
Cash Administrative Expenses	52,350	49,760	50,260	50,040
Total Cash Operating Expenses	$134,180	$139,930	$144,890	$124,450
For Other Cash Payments:				
Federal Income Tax Expense	$ 8,100	$ 8,100	$ 8,100	$ 8,080
Automated Cutting Machine	20,000			
Cash Dividend		50,000		50,000
Investment				25,000
Note Payable and Interest				22,250
Total Other Cash Payments	$ 28,100	$ 58,100	$ 8,100	$105,330
Total Cash Payments	$465,220	$555,910	$502,580	$551,900

accounts expenses. Therefore, these amounts are not included in the cash payments budget schedule. The first quarter's cash payment for selling expenses is calculated as shown below.

Selling Expenses		$86,330
Less: Depr. Expense—Delivery Equipment	$1,800	
Depr. Expense—Warehouse Equipment	2,700	4,500
Cash Payment for Selling Expenses		$81,830

Cash payments for administrative expenses are calculated by subtracting depreciation expense and uncollectible accounts expense amounts from the quarterly totals of administrative expenses.

Other Cash Payments. Reflection also plans for cash payments other than for merchandise, selling expenses, and administrative expenses. Federal income tax payments equal the quarterly federal income tax expense amounts on the budgeted income statement. Reflection also plans to buy a new automated cutting machine for

ASSESS

Assess student understanding by checking the solutions to the Independent Practice activities.

Reteach

- Make transparencies of the budget schedule from the accounting forms masters provided in the Blackline Masters Section of the Teacher's Resource Guide. Using information from Recycling Problem 15-R and the transparencies, demonstrate how the 1st quarter amounts and percentages are calculated and recorded on Schedules A and B. Using these budget schedules, develop the 1st quarter of a cash budget. As each supporting schedule is used, display it on the overhead and circle the amounts used on the cash budget.
- Assign Recycling Problem 15-R, Instructions 7–9.

Extend

- Assign Cases for Critical Thinking 2.
- Assign Challenge Problem 15-C. (The challenge is to prepare a performance report.)
- Assign the Spreadsheet Template for Problem 15-3.

Enrich

- Assign the PERSONAL VISIONS IN BUSINESS feature on page 422.
- Use *Automated Accounting 6.0* or higher with Accounting Textbook Template, Advanced Course with Problem 15-C.

CLOSURE

- Use Audit Your Understanding questions.
- Review Summary Illustration 15-11, "Summary of Budget Planning."

ASSESS

- Administer Problem Test Chapter 15.
- Administer a MicroExam test for Chapter 15.

TEACHING STRATEGIES: TEACHING TIP

Encourage students with allowances or part-time jobs to prepare a cash budget schedule for the next 12 months. Alternately, a cash budget schedule can be prepared for a parent, relative, or friend.

$20,000 at the end of the first quarter. The company expects to pay a $50,000 cash dividend to stockholders in each of the second and fourth quarters. Since a large cash balance is projected for the third quarter, Reflection plans a $25,000 interest-earning investment in the fourth quarter. Also, plans call for repaying the promissory note plus interest, *$22,250*, at the beginning of the fourth quarter.

The last line of the cash payments budget schedule shows the total cash payments projected each quarter. This total indicates the minimum amount of cash that must be available each quarter.

Cash Budget

A cash budget shows for each month or quarter a projection of a company's beginning cash balance, cash receipts, cash payments, and ending cash balance. Reflection's cash budget is prepared from the information in the cash receipts budget schedule and the cash payments budget schedule. The first quarter's beginning cash balance is from the balance sheet on December 31, 19X2. Reflection's cash budget is shown in Illustration 15-10.

ILLUSTRATION 15-10 Cash budget

Reflection, Inc.
Cash Budget
For Year Ended December 31, 19X3

	Quarter			
	1st	2d	3d	4th
Cash Balance—Beginning	$ 21,780	$ 46,110	$ 26,710	$ 94,960
Cash Receipts (Schedule A)	489,550	536,510	570,830	477,000
Cash Available	$511,330	$582,620	$597,540	$571,960
Less Cash Payments (Schedule B)	465,220	555,910	502,580	551,900
Cash Balance—Ending	$ 46,110	$ 26,710	$ 94,960	$ 20,060

At the end of each quarter of a budget period, Reflection compares the actual cash balance with the projected cash balance as shown in the cash budget. If the actual cash balance is less than the projected balance, the reasons for the decrease are determined and action is taken to correct the problem. One reason may be that some customers are not paying their accounts when they should. Another may be that expenses are exceeding budget projections. If the decrease continues, the company could have a quarter in which there is not enough cash to make all the required cash payments. If this shortage does occur, the business will have to borrow money until receipts and payments are brought into balance.

The process for preparing the budgeted income statement and cash budget is shown in Illustration 15-11.

SUMMARY ILLUSTRATION 15-11

Summary of budget planning

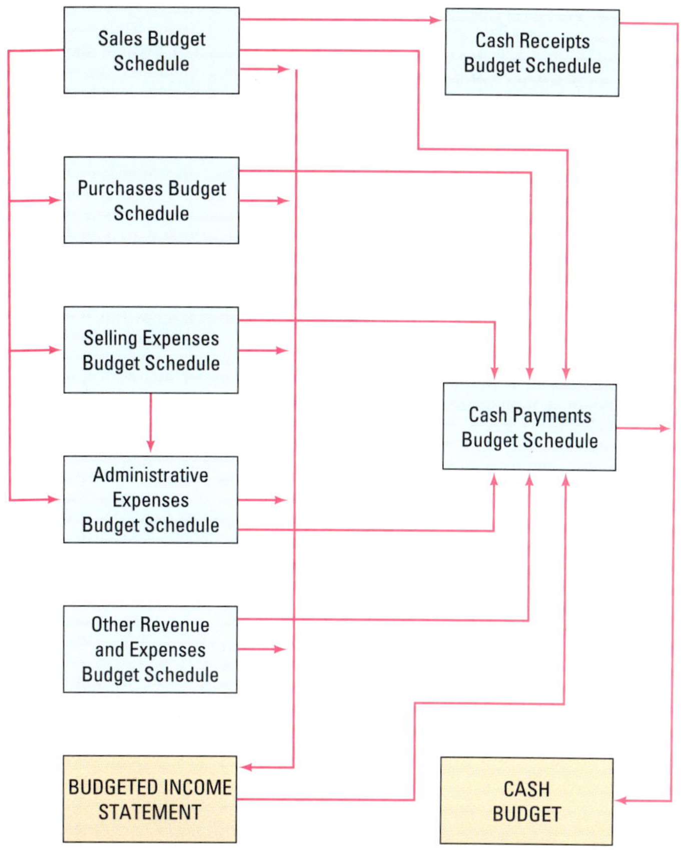

TEACHING STRATEGIES: APPLYING VISUALS

Direct students to Summary Illustration 15-11 to review the summary of budget planning.

APPLIED SKILLS: WORD PROCESSING

If you wish to integrate word processing into your accounting course, you may direct students to answer the end-of-chapter Accounting Terms, Questions for Individual Study, and Cases for Critical Thinking using their word processing software.

PERFORMANCE REPORT PREPARATION AND ANALYSIS

FYI

Actual performance must be compared with budgeted estimates in order for a business to evaluate its budgeting procedures.

At the end of each quarter, a business prepares an income statement that compares actual amounts with the budgeted income statement for that period. This comparison shows variations between actual and projected items. A report showing a comparison of projected and actual amounts for a specific period of time is called a **performance report.**

Reflection prepares a quarterly performance report. This report is sent to the sales manager and the administrative manager. Knowing about significant differences between projected and actual income statement amounts helps the managers identify areas that need to be reviewed. By identifying large variations early, managers may be able to make changes that will correct negative effects on net income for the year. If conditions change significantly, the budget for the remainder of the year can be revised. For the first quarter, Reflection prepares the performance report shown in Illustration 15-12.

Preparation of a performance report is similar to preparation of a comparative income statement. However, a performance report

APPLIED SKILLS: LANGUAGE ARTS

Exploring spelling checker software. Students may wish to rely too heavily on the spelling checker feature of their word processing software. A word may be spelled correctly, but it may not be the word that should be used. Spend some time giving examples of incorrect words that the spelling checker cannot identify as misspelled ("if" instead of "is"; "its" instead of "it's"; "the" instead of "them"). Ask students to supply other pairs of words.

ILLUSTRATION 15-12 Performance report

Reflection, Inc.
Performance Report
For Quarter Ended March 31, 19X3

	Budget	Actual	Increase (Decrease)	
			Amount	Percentage*
Unit Sales (sq. ft.)	97,600	98,500	900	0.9
Operating Revenue:				
Net Sales	$488,000	$492,500	$4,500	0.9
Cost of Merchandise Sold	327,920	330,680	2,760	0.8
Gross Profit on Operations	$160,080	$161,820	$1,740	1.1
Operating Expenses:				
Selling Expenses:				
Advertising Expense	$ 11,710	$ 12,050	$ 340	2.9
Delivery Expense	39,040	38,735	(305)	(0.8)
Depr. Expense—Delivery Equipment	1,800	1,800		
Depr. Expense—Warehouse Equipment	2,700	2,700		
Miscellaneous Expense—Sales	2,440	2,530	90	3.7
Salary Expense—Commissions	19,520	19,620	100	0.5
Salary Expense—Regular	6,190	6,190		
Supplies Expense—Sales	2,930	2,900	(30)	(1.0)
Total Selling Expenses	$ 86,330	$ 86,525	$ 195	0.2
Administrative Expenses:				
Depr. Expense—Office Equipment	$ 3,600	$ 3,600		
Insurance Expense	1,400	1,400		
Miscellaneous Expense—Administrative	9,190	9,350	$ 160	1.7
Payroll Taxes Expense	5,540	5,550	10	0.2
Rent Expense	7,500	7,500		
Salary Expense—Administrative	20,430	20,430		
Supplies Expense—Administrative	3,420	3,490	70	2.0
Uncollectible Accounts Expense	2,930	2,800	(130)	(4.4)
Utilities Expense	4,870	5,180	310	6.4
Total Administrative Expenses	$ 58,880	$ 59,300	$ 420	0.7
Total Operating Expenses	$145,210	$145,825	$ 615	0.4
Income from Operations	14,870	15,995	$1,125	7.6
Net Deduction	$ 750	$ 750	0	0.0
Net Income before Federal Income Tax	$ 14,120	$ 15,245	$1,125	8.0
Federal Income Tax Expense	8,100	8,100	0	0.0
Net Income after Federal Income Tax	$ 6,020	$ 7,145	$1,125	18.7

*Percentages rounded to the nearest 0.1%.

compares actual amounts with projected amounts for the same fiscal period. A comparative income statement compares actual amounts of one fiscal period with actual amounts of a prior fiscal period.

The first amount column of the performance report shows the amounts projected for the first quarter. The second amount column shows the actual sales, costs, and expenses for the quarter. The third amount column shows how much the actual amount varies from the projected amount. For example, actual net sales, $492,500, *less* projected net sales, $488,000, *equals* the increase, $4,500. The fourth column shows the percentage, the actual amount increased or decreased from the projected amount. For example, the net sales increase, $4,500, *divided by* projected net sales, $488,000, *equals* the percent of increase, 0.9%. Percentages are rounded to the nearest 0.1%.

An analysis is made of all significant differences to determine why the differences occurred. Normally, Reflection only considers changes of 5.0% or more to be significant. However, because the items influencing gross profit are large dollar amounts, small percentage changes affect net income significantly. Therefore, Reflection's sales manager reviews changes in net sales and cost of merchandise sold regardless of the amount of change.

This report alerts the managers to changes in sales, costs, and expenses as well as how those changes affect net income. The performance report indicates that three items should be reviewed: net sales, cost of merchandise sold, and utilities expense. Managers should determine what actions, if any, can correct the unfavorable situations such as the 6.4% increase in utilities expense. If the utility service cost has increased, the manager cannot change that. However, if power is being wasted, procedures may need to be changed to avoid the waste.

Managers should also determine what actions caused favorable results, such as the 0.9% increase in net sales and encourage a continuation of those favorable actions.

Audit Your Understanding

1. Why is a cash budget important?
2. What information is reported in a cash budget?
3. What information is reported in a performance report?
4. How is a performance report different than a comparative income statement?

AUDIT YOUR UNDERSTANDING

1. Good cash management requires the planning and controlling of cash so that cash will be available to meet obligations when due.
2. Projected beginning cash balance, cash receipts, cash payments, and ending cash balance.
3. A comparison of projected and actual amounts for a specific period of time.
4. A performance report compares actual amounts with projected amounts for the same fiscal period. A comparative income statement compares actual amounts of one fiscal period with actual amounts of a prior fiscal period.

ACCOUNTING TERMS

1. **budgeting:** Planning the financial operations of a business. (p. 406)
2. **budget:** A written financial plan of a business for a specific period of time, expressed in dollars. (p. 406)
3. **budget period:** The length of time covered by a budget. (p. 407)
4. **comparative income statement:** An income statement containing sales, cost, and expense information for two or more years. (p. 409)
5. **performance report:** A report showing a comparison of projected and actual amounts for a specific period of time. (p. 427)

QUESTIONS FOR INDIVIDUAL STUDY

1. Unit of Measurement concept. (p. 406)
2. (a) Planning. (b) Operational control. (c) Department coordination. (p. 406)
3. In preparing a budget, managers must project what will probably happen in the future. This view of the future helps a manager plan actions that will meet desired goals. The budgeting process forces a manager to decide which actions should be emphasized to achieve the desired goals. (p. 406)
4. A business can control expenses by comparing actual expenses with projected expenses. The comparison identifies differences where costs are higher than projected. The business can then take action to correct the differences. (p. 406)
5. One year. Some companies also prepare a long-range budget of five years or more for special projects and plant and equipment purchases. (p. 407)
6. Such budget subdivisions provide frequent opportunities to evaluate how actual operations compare with budgeted operations. (p. 407)
7. A projection of a business' sales, costs, expenses, and net income for a fiscal period. (p. 407)
8. A projection of a business' cash receipts and payments for a fiscal period. (p. 407)
9. Trends that may be taking place in certain sales, cost, or expense items. The statement also highlights items that may be increasing or decreasing at a higher rate than other items on the statement. (p. 409)

ACCOUNTING TERMS — EPT(a)

What is the meaning of each of the following?

1. **budgeting**
2. **budget**
3. **budget period**
4. **comparative income statement**
5. **performance report**

QUESTIONS FOR INDIVIDUAL STUDY — EPT(b)

1. Which accounting concept is being applied when financial information is expressed in dollars on a budget?
2. What three important business functions does a budget serve?
3. In preparing a budget, what must managers do?
4. How does the budgeting process help control expenses?
5. What is the length of time generally covered by a company's budget?
6. Why are annual budgets commonly divided into quarterly and monthly budgets?
7. What is a budgeted income statement?
8. What is a cash budget?
9. What kind of information does a comparative income statement show?
10. How do annual goals help a company?
11. Why is the sales budget schedule prepared first?
12. What factors are considered in preparing a sales budget schedule?
13. What factors are considered in preparing a purchases budget schedule?
14. Why do some items in a selling expenses budget schedule stay about the same from period to period, while other items vary a great deal?
15. Where is the information obtained to prepare an administrative expenses budget schedule?
16. What are three typical items in an other revenue and expenses budget schedule?
17. Why is a cash budget important?
18. What projections are made in preparing a cash receipts budget schedule?
19. What projections are made in preparing a cash payments budget schedule?
20. Why do many companies prepare a performance report at the end of each quarter?

CASES FOR CRITICAL THINKING — EPT(b)

CASE 1 Thomas Baker, president of Brundage Corporation, says he has observed that an increase in sales almost always results in an increase in net income. Therefore, he is considering recommending the company set a sales goal increase of 15.0% for next year and "spare no expense" to achieve this goal. Mr. Baker asks for your opinion regarding his recommendation. How would you respond?

CASE 2 Camille Stibbe is general manager of Alden Corporation. She suggests that the budgeted income statement and the cash budget seem to show the same information. Therefore, she recommends that one of the statements be eliminated to reduce accounting costs. What response would you make to Mrs. Stibbe?

10. Annual company goals establish targets the company will work toward in the coming year. Goals help a company coordinate the efforts of all areas toward a common direction. (p. 411)
11. Because the other schedules are affected by the projected net sales. (p. 412)
12. Previous net sales and the trend in net sales for a period of several years, general economic conditions, consumer buying trends, competition, new products on the market, and such activities as planned special sales. (p. 412)
13. (a) The projection of unit sales as shown in the sales budget schedule; (b) the quantity of merchandise on hand at the beginning of the budget period; (c) the quantity of merchandise needed to fill projected sales orders without having excessive inventory on hand at any one time; and (d) the price trends of merchandise to be purchased. (pp. 413–414)

APPLIED COMMUNICATIONS

People often think that only accountants need to know accounting. Many students may not consider taking accounting because they have no interest in being an accountant. Whether students aspire to be doctors, teachers, lawyers, scientists, florists, or artists, they will need to use accounting to control the financial resources of their business or organization.

INSTRUCTIONS:

Create a presentation that could be made to your high school counselor, student body, or incoming students to persuade the audience that everyone needs accounting. Use the following guidelines.

1. Prepare a list of skills learned in accounting that can be used in everyday life.
2. Elaborate by writing a paragraph to discuss each skill and how advantageous it is for a person to gain these skills.
3. Prepare graphic aids such as transparency masters that could be used to present the material.

APPLICATION PROBLEMS — EPT(c,d)

PROBLEM 15-1 Preparing a sales budget schedule and a purchases budget schedule

Paradise Corporation plans to prepare a sales budget schedule and a purchases budget schedule for 19X3. Management has set a sales goal of 250,000 units. After reviewing price trends, the sales manager projects that Paradise Corporation will need to increase its unit sales price from $12.50 to $14.00 in the first quarter.

The sales manager, after checking with the company's merchandise suppliers, projects that the cost of merchandise will increase from $7.00 to $7.50 per unit in the first quarter of 19X3.

Quarterly unit sales for 19X2 are as follows.

1st quarter	58,500 units	3d quarter.	68,900 units
2d quarter.	62,700 units	4th quarter	43,900 units

After considering the time required to reorder merchandise, the sales manager requests that 30.0% of the next quarter's unit sales be available in the prior quarter's ending inventory. Ending inventory for 19X2 is 27,700 units. Management projects that 65,000 units will be sold in the first quarter of 19X4.

INSTRUCTIONS:

Prepare the following budget schedules for the four quarters ended December 31, 19X3. Round unit amounts to the nearest hundred units, dollar amounts to the nearest $10, and percentage amounts to the nearest 0.1%.

1. Prepare a sales budget schedule (Schedule 1).
2. Prepare a purchases budget schedule (Schedule 2).

PROBLEM 15-2 Preparing a budgeted income statement

The sales manager and administrative manager of Manor Corporation have made the following projections to be used in preparing a budgeted income statement.

a. Total net sales for 19X3 are projected to be $1,400,000. In each quarter the following percentages of total net sales were made.

1st quarter	20.0%	3d quarter.	25.0%
2d quarter.	25.0%	4th quarter	30.0%

b. Purchases and merchandise ending inventories are projected as follows. Ending inventory for 19X2 was $88,250.

APPLIED SKILLS: Communications

Surveys of business managers show that communication skills are one of the most desired traits in new employees. The APPLIED COMMUNICATIONS activity provides an opportunity for students to practice their communication and language arts skills on topics that directly relate to accounting. This activity requires students to create a skills list, write a short paper, and prepare teaching masters for a presentation that could be made to a high school counselor, student body, or incoming students to persuade the audience that everyone needs accounting.

QUESTIONS (cont'd)

14. Some selling expense items are relatively stable like depreciation expenses. For example, delivery and warehouse equipment depreciation expenses are reasonably stable unless new equipment is bought. On the other hand, several selling expenses increase and decrease in relation to sales increases and decreases. For example, during the heavy sales season, Reflection hires more personnel and spends more for advertising and supplies. (p. 415)
15. A study of past records, an evaluation of company plans, the sales and selling expenses budget schedules, and discussions with other managers. (p. 417)
16. Interest income, interest expense, and gains or losses on the sale of plant assets. (p. 419)
17. Good cash management requires the planning and controlling of cash so that cash will be available to meet obligations when due. (p. 421)
18. A projection of (a) quarterly cash sales, (b) quarterly collections on account from customers, and (c) cash to be received quarterly from other sources. (pp. 422–423)
19. A projection of (a) quarterly cash payments for accounts payable or notes payable to vendors; (b) quarterly cash payments for each expense item; (c) quarterly cash payments for buying equipment and other assets; (d) quarterly cash payments for dividends; and (e) quarterly cash payments for investments. (p. 424)
20. A statement showing variations between projected and actual income statement amounts helps the managers identify areas that need to be reviewed. By identifying large variations early, managers may be able to make changes that will correct negative effects on net income for the year. (pp. 427–428)

APPLIED COMMUNICATIONS

This activity requires students to create a skills list, write a short paper, and prepare teaching masters. Students' solutions will vary. The instructor should consider the following items when grading the activity: (1) thorough list, (2) understandable explanation of each skill, (3) creativity, (3) writing style, and (4) mechanics (grammar, spelling, punctuation, and sentence structure).

CASES FOR CRITICAL THINKING

Case 1 Increasing sales does not guarantee an increase in net income. If costs and expenses increase at a higher rate than sales, net income may actually decrease. Many factors should be considered when setting a sales budget schedule—projected economic conditions, projections of the sales personnel, an evaluation of previous years' sales, and the ability of the company to make and/or deliver the increased volume of sales. If the sales budget schedule is unrealistically high, the company may overspend in an effort to meet its sales goal, possibly resulting in lower net income. Recommend Mr. Baker consider all the factors discussed above. Based on an evaluation of all these factors, set a realistic sales budget level.

Case 2 The statements are different and each reports valuable information that should help managers run the company more efficiently and profitably. A budgeted income statement reports the projected net income and all the major items affecting net income (revenue, cost of merchandise, expenses) of a company for a specified period. If the budgeted income statement has been carefully and accurately planned, it provides a reliable base for comparisons (monthly or quarterly) and provides managers with opportunities to identify and correct problems that are affecting net income. The principal purpose of this statement is to help mangers manage efficiently so the company can maximize net income. The principal purpose of a cash budget is to plan for a company's cash needs so that adequate cash will be available to meet the company's obligations when due. Both statements are important to the efficient operation of a business.

	Purchases	Ending Inventory
1st quarter.	$201,000	$111,500
2d quarter	242,500	110,500
3d quarter	283,000	132,500
4th quarter.	246,250	99,250

c. Expenses for 19X3 are projected as follows. Except where noted, percentages are based on projected net sales. For these items, calculate each quarter's amount by multiplying the percentage times that quarter's net sales. Calculate the annual total by adding the four quarterly amounts. When a dollar amount is given, the total amount should be divided equally among the four quarters.

Selling Expenses	
Advertising Expense	1.5%
Delivery Expense.	2.7%
Depreciation Expense—Delivery Equipment	$3,400
Depreciation Expense—Store Equipment	$4,200
Miscellaneous Expense—Sales	$15,800
Salary Expense—Sales.	6.0%
Supplies Expense—Sales. . .	2.0%

Administrative Expenses	
Depreciation Expense—Office Equipment	$4,800
Insurance Expense.	$6,000
Miscellaneous Expense—Administrative	$5,600
Payroll Taxes Expense	13.2% of salaries
Rent Expense	$12,800
Salary Expense—Administrative	$46,000
Supplies Expense—Administrative	$4,240
Uncollectible Accounts Expense.	0.8%
Utilities Expense.	$18,400

Federal income taxes are calculated using the tax rate table shown in this chapter. Equal quarterly income tax payments are based on the projected annual federal income tax expense.

INSTRUCTIONS:

Prepare the following budget schedules for the four quarters ended December 31, 19X3. Round all amounts to the nearest $10.

1. Prepare a selling expenses budget schedule (Schedule 3).
2. Prepare an administrative expenses budget schedule (Schedule 4).
3. Prepare a budgeted income statement.

PROBLEM 15-3 Preparing a cash budget with supporting schedules

The following table shows Windsor Company's projected net sales, purchases, and cash payments for expenses for 19X3.

			Cash Payments for Expenses	
Quarter	Net Sales	Purchases	Selling	Administrative
1st	$646,300	$558,300	$32,100	$38,600
2d	674,900	571,600	36,200	38,900
3d	661,800	561,200	42,400	39,700
4th	681,600	582,300	36,800	39,800

Additional information is listed as follows.

a. Actual amounts for the fourth quarter of 19X2: sales, $639,200; purchases, $548,240.

b. The balance of cash on hand on January 1, 19X3, is $35,720.

c. In each quarter, cash sales are 10.0% and collections of accounts receivable are 50.0% of the projected net sales for the current quarter. Collections from the preceding quarter's net sales are 39.5% of that quarter. Uncollectible accounts expense is 0.5% of net sales.

d. In each quarter, cash payments for cash purchases are 10.0% and for accounts payable 30.0% of the purchases for the current quarter. Cash payments for purchases of the preceding quarter are 60.0% of that quarter.

e. Projected cash payments for expenses are listed in the table shown previously. Record only total projected cash payments for expenses.

f. In the second quarter, $35,000 will be borrowed on a promissory note, and equipment costing $31,600 will be purchased for cash. In the third quarter dividends of $30,000 will be paid in cash. In the fourth quarter, the promissory note plus interest will be paid in cash, $37,500.

g. Equal quarterly income tax payments are based on projected annual federal income tax expense of $7,720.

INSTRUCTIONS:

Prepare the following budget schedules for the four quarters ended December 31, 19X3. Round all amounts to the nearest $10.

1. Prepare a cash receipts budget schedule (Schedule A).
2. Prepare a cash payments budget schedule (Schedule B).
3. Prepare a cash budget.

ENRICHMENT PROBLEMS EPT(c,d,e)

MASTERY PROBLEM 15-M Preparing a budgeted income statement and a cash budget with supporting budget schedules

On December 31, 19X2, the accounting records of Quintex, Inc. show the following unit sales for 19X2.

1st quarter	22,000 units	3d quarter.	34,800 units
2d quarter.	34,400 units	4th quarter	28,800 units

The following are additional actual amounts for the 4th quarter of 19X2.

Sales (28,800 units @ $5.60)	$161,280
Purchases (26,400 units @ $4.00) . . .	105,600
Ending inventory.	12,500 units

Management has established a unit sales goal of 130,000 units for 19X3 and 24,000 units for the first quarter of 19X4. The sales manager, after reviewing price trends and checking with the company's merchandise suppliers, projects the unit cost of merchandise will increase from $4.00 to $4.25 in the first quarter of 19X3. Because of the increase in costs, the company will need to increase its unit sales price from $5.60 to $6.00 in the first quarter of 19X3.

After considering the time required to reorder merchandise, the sales manager requests that 40.0% of each quarter's unit sales be available in the prior quarter's ending inventory.

CHECK FIGURES

See Teacher's Edition of Working Papers for complete solutions.

Problem 15-1 (1) Net Sales $3,500,000; 875,000; 938,000; 1,029,000; 658,000. (2) Cost of Purchases $411,750; 517,500; 491,250; 393,000.

Problem 15-2 (1) Total Selling Expenses $194,200; 40,010; 48,550; 48,550; 57,090. (2) Total Admin. Expenses $126,200; 30,440; 31,550; 31,550; 32,660. (3) Net Inc. after Fed. Inc. Tax $88,640; 24,500; 19,100; 1,600; 43,440.

Problem 15-3 (1) Total Cash Receipts $640,260; 695,230; 663,670; 670,370. (2) Total Cash Payments $624,890; 672,250; 681,470; 685,670. (3) Cash Balance-Ending $51,090; 74,070; 56,270; 40,970.

Mastery Problem 15-M (1) Net Sales $780,000; 142,800; 223,800; 226,200; 187,200. (2) Cost of Purchases $111,350; 159,380; 149,180; 120,280. (3) Total Selling Expenses $71,480; 13,690; 20,180; 20,360; 17,250. (4) Total Admin. Expenses $74,820; 17,140; 19,570; 19,640; 18,470. (5) Other Expenses $5,000; 1,250; 1,250; 1,250; 1,250. (6) Net Inc. after Fed. Inc. Tax $64,090; 8,890; 20,460; 20,910; 13,830. (7) Total Cash Receipts $191,070; 182,440; 223,660; 205,340. (8) Total Cash Payments $179,950; 191,620; 202,030; 220,610. (9) Cash Balance–Ending $52,720; 43,540; 65,170; 49,900.

Expenses are projected as follows. Except where noted, percentages are based on quarterly projected net sales. For these items, calculate each quarter's amount by multiplying the percentage times that quarter's net sales. Calculate the annual total by adding the four quarterly amounts. When a dollar amount is given, the total amount should be divided equally among the four quarters.

Selling Expenses	
Advertising Expense	1.2%
Delivery Expense	0.6%
Depreciation Expense—Delivery Equipment	$2,400
Depreciation Expense—Store Equipment	$6,680
Miscellaneous Expense—Sales	0.4%
Salary Expense—Sales	5.0%
Supplies Expense—Sales	0.8%

Administrative Expenses	
Depreciation Expense—Office Equipment	$3,600
Insurance Expense	$4,200
Miscellaneous Expense—Administrative	$3,000
Payroll Taxes Expense	12.0% of salaries
Rent Expense	$9,600
Salary Expense—Administrative	$25,200
Supplies Expense—Administrative	$2,800
Uncollectible Accounts Expense	0.6%
Utilities Expense	1.8%

Interest expense for each quarter is projected to be $1,250.

Federal income taxes are calculated using the tax rate table shown in this chapter. Equal quarterly income tax payments are based on the projected annual federal income tax expense.

Additional information is listed as follows.

a. The balance of cash on hand on January 1, 19X3, is $41,600.

b. In each quarter, cash sales are 10.0% and collections of accounts receivable are 40.0% of the projected net sales for the current quarter. Collections from the preceding quarter's net sales are 49.4% of that quarter. Uncollectible accounts expense is 0.6% of net sales.

c. In each quarter, cash payments for cash purchases are 10.0% and for accounts payable 55.0% of the purchases for the current quarter. Cash payments for purchases of the preceding quarter are 35.0% of that quarter.

d. In the first quarter, $40,000 will be borrowed on a promissory note, and equipment costing $30,000 will be purchased for cash. In each quarter, dividends of $10,000 will be paid in cash. In the fourth quarter, the promissory note plus interest will be paid in cash, $45,000.

INSTRUCTIONS:

Prepare the following budget schedules for the year ended December 31, 19X3. Round percentage amounts to the nearest 0.1%, unit amounts to the nearest 100 units, and dollar amounts to the nearest $10.

1. Prepare a sales budget schedule (Schedule 1).
2. Prepare a purchases budget schedule (Schedule 2).
3. Prepare a selling expenses budget schedule (Schedule 3).
4. Prepare an administrative expenses budget schedule (Schedule 4).
5. Prepare an other revenue and expenses budget schedule (Schedule 5).
6. Prepare a budgeted income statement.
7. Prepare a cash receipts budget schedule (Schedule A).
8. Prepare a cash payments budget schedule (Schedule B).
9. Prepare a cash budget.

434

CHALLENGE PROBLEM 15-C Preparing a performance report

AUTOMATED

A partially completed performance report for Beaumont Corporation is in the working papers accompanying this textbook.

Beaumont Corporation has just completed its first quarter of the fiscal year ended December 31, 19X3. Management is interested in identifying significant favorable and unfavorable differences between projected and actual amounts. Beaumont only considers changes of 5.0% or more to be significant. Management reviews changes in net sales and cost of merchandise regardless of the amount of change.

INSTRUCTIONS:

1. Complete the performance report by calculating the increase (decrease) from budget and percentage increase (decrease) from budget.
2. Place an asterisk (*) in the right margin by every item which is significant.

CHECK FIGURES (cont'd)

Challenge Problem 15-C Net Inc. after Fed. Inc. Tax $20,690; 21,418; 728; 3.5%.

Preparing a Performance Report

TEACHING STRATEGIES: ACCOUNTING PEDAGOGY

This textbook introduces the procedures for preparing a performance report manually before using the computer to prepare a performance report. It is important that students master accounting theory before using the computer to perform repetitive functions.

A performance report may be prepared using either manual or automated methods. Reflection, Inc., the business described in Chapter 15, uses manual methods to calculate the amount of increase (decrease) from budget, the percentage of increase (decrease) from budget, and to prepare a performance report.

Integrating Automated Accounting Topic 7 applies procedures for using automated accounting software to prepare a performance report. The Automated Accounting Problem contains instructions for using automated accounting software to solve Challenge Problem 15-C, Chapter 15.

AUTOMATED

AUTOMATED ACCOUNTING PROBLEM

AUTOMATING CHALLENGE PROBLEM 15-C Preparing a performance report

INSTRUCTIONS:

1. Load the *Automated Accounting 6.0* or higher software. Select data base A15-C from the *CENTURY 21 ACCOUNTING Advanced Course* template. Read the Problem Instructions screen.
2. Rename the file.

LESSON PLAN A7

Materials

- Student pages 436–437
- No student input forms are needed for Automating Challenge Problem 15-C.
- Complete solutions for automated problems are provided in the Teacher's Resource Guide.
- Software: *Automated Accounting 6.0* or higher; Accounting Textbook Template, Advanced Course

Objective

Prepare a performance report using an automated accounting system.

3. Select Options from the menu bar and choose the Enter Budgets command. Key Beaumont Corporation's budget data as follows for the quarter ended 03/31/--.

Operating Revenue	$336,000.00
Cost of Merchandise Sold	184,000.00
Advertising Expense	2,500.00
Delivery Expense	4,320.00
Depreciation Expense—Delivery Equipment	4,260.00
Depreciation Expense—Warehouse Equipment	3,450.00
Miscellaneous Expense—Sales	1,670.00
Salary Expense—Commissions	10,080.00
Salary Expense—Regular	25,680.00
Supplies Expense—Sales	2,450.00
Depreciation Expense—Office Equipment	4,200.00
Insurance Expense	900.00
Miscellaneous Expense—Administrative	6,500.00
Payroll Taxes Expense	8,470.00
Rent Expense	2,500.00
Salary Expense—Administrative	34,800.00
Supplies Expense—Administrative	4,400.00
Uncollectible Accounts Expense	3,360.00
Utilities Expense	5,400.00
Interest Expense	1,200.00
Federal Income Tax Expense	5,170.00

4. Display/print a performance report.

FOCUS

In Chapter 15, manual procedures for preparing a performance report were described. Emphasize that automated accounting software may be used to speed the preparation of performance reports. Explain that using automated accounting software, however, does not change accounting concepts. Only the methods change.

TEACH

Integrating Automated Accounting: Topic 7 is designed to be completed by students as Independent Practice. You may choose to have students work in pairs to increase their cooperative learning experiences. Student understanding may be assessed by checking student solutions to the automated problem. Use Chapter 15 of this textbook to reteach any misunderstood accounting concepts related to preparing a performance report.

CHECK FIGURES

- Automating Challenge Problem 15-C: Net Income after Income Tax: Budget 20,690; Actual 21,418; Diff. From Budget 728; % Diff. From Budget 3.52

TEACHING STRATEGIES: TEACHING TIP

It is important for students to save a template file under another name before they begin work. This will keep the template file intact for future use.

SOFTWARE FOCUS

The Automated Accounting Problem in this Integrating Automated Accounting topic uses Challenge Problem 15-C, Chapter 15, which students have already completed manually. The problem instructions in *Automated Accounting 6.0* will lead students through automating this problem.

CHAPTER 16 OVERVIEW

Chapter 16 continues the presentation of financial analysis for management decisions. Contribution margin and the relationship between fixed and variable costs is presented as the foundation for the analysis in this chapter. The breakeven point is demonstrated and used for finding the sales needed for a new

GUIDE TO ACHIEVING LEARNING OBJECTIVES

	TEACH	APPLY	EXTEND/ENRICH				
Enabling Performance Tasks	**Lesson Plans**	**Application Problems**	**Mastery Problems**	**Challenge Problems**	**Cases for Critical Thinking**	**Recycling Problems**	**Reinforcement Activity**
a. Define accounting terms related to accounting information for management decisions.	16-1, 16-2						
b. Identify accounting concepts and practices related to preparing accounting information for management decisions.	16-1, 16-2				Cases 1, 2		
c. Prepare an income statement reporting contribution margin.	16-1	16-1	16-M			16-R	
d. Calculate the contribution margin rate and breakeven point.	16-2	16-2, 16-3, 16-4	16-M			16-R	
e. Calculate the sales dollars and sales units required to earn a planned amount of net income.	16-2	16-4	16-M			16-R	
f. Determine the effect of changes in sales volume, unit costs, and unit sales prices on net income.	16-2	16-4, 16-5	16-M	16-C		16-R	
g. Calculate a sales mix.	16-2	16-6					

ENRICHMENT

SPECIAL FEATURES
Professional Business Ethics, page 452
Careers in Accounting, page 439

TECHNOLOGY CONNECTION
Spreadsheet Template Problems 16-1, 16-3, 16-4, 16-5, 16-6

NEW, REVIEW, AND EXTENSION

ACTIVITIES/CONCEPTS/TRANSACTIONS	NEW	REVIEW/ EXTENSION
Unit costs	✓	
Variable costs	✓	
Fixed costs	✓	
Calculating contribution margin	✓	
Calculating breakeven point	✓	
Calculating contribution margin per unit	✓	
Calculating sales needed to achieve planned net income	✓	
Determining effects of changes on net income	✓	
Calculating sales mix	✓	

product, the sales needed to achieve planned net income, the effect of changes in volume, cost, and unit sales price on net income, and the appropriate sales mix of different products.

	INFORMAL ASSESSMENT		FORMAL ASSESSMENT			
	Study Guide	**Audit Your Understanding**	**Chapter MicroExam**	**Chapter Problem Test**	**Unit Objective Test**	**Portfolio**
	Unit A	✓	✓		✓	
	Units B, C	✓	✓		✓	
				✓		
				✓		
				✓		
				✓		

TEACHING MATERIALS

Teacher's Wraparound Edition of the Text
Teacher's Resource Guide
Teacher's Edition of Working Papers
MicroExam

APPLIED MATHEMATICS

APPLIED MATH/ACCOUNTING SKILL	APPLICATION
Calculating contribution margin	Prob. 16-1
Calculating contribution margin rate	Prob. 16-2
Calculating breakeven point	Prob. 16-2
Calculating contribution margin per unit	Prob. 16-3
Calculating sales required to maintain planned net income	Prob. 16-4
Calculating sales mix	Prob. 16-6

TEACHING STRATEGIES: ACCOUNTING PEDAGOGY

This textbook continues to emphasize that proper planning is vital for financial success. This chapter introduces the importance of financial statement analysis and critical thinking skills that management needs to possess in order to run a successful company.

16

Accounting Information for Management Decisions

ENABLING PERFORMANCE TASKS

After studying Chapter 16, you will be able to:

- **a** Define accounting terms related to accounting information for management decisions.
- **b** Identify accounting concepts and practices related to preparing accounting information for management decisions.
- **c** Prepare an income statement reporting contribution margin.
- **d** Calculate the contribution margin rate and breakeven point.
- **e** Calculate the sales dollars and sales units required to earn a planned amount of net income.
- **f** Determine the effect of changes in sales volume, unit costs, and unit sales prices on net income.
- **g** Calculate a sales mix.

TERMS PREVIEW

total costs • unit cost • variable costs • fixed costs • contribution margin • breakeven point • sales mix

CAREERS IN ACCOUNTING

BUDGET ACCOUNTANT

- *Analyzes records of present and past operations to project future revenues and expenses*
- *Maintains budgeting systems that provide control of expenditures made*
- *Advises management on matters such as effective use of resources*
- *Interprets budgets for management*
- *May develop manual or computer based budgeting system*

Financial statements provide management with the sales, cost, and expense information necessary to make good business decisions. By analyzing the income statement, managers can gain an understanding of the relationship among sales, costs, and expenses. An analysis of this information enables management to determine the level of sales necessary to achieve planned net income. By understanding these relationships, management can also evaluate the impact of changes in sales volume, unit sales prices, and unit costs on net income.

COST CHARACTERISTICS THAT INFLUENCE DECISIONS

Net income can be increased by increasing sales and/or decreasing costs and expenses. Managers, with the advice and assistance of accountants, identify the strengths and weaknesses of a company by analyzing relationships among sales, cost, and expense information. An income statement is one source of information on which a manager can base decisions. An income statement includes information about operating revenue, cost of merchandise sold, gross profit on operations, operating expenses, and net income or net loss.

Total Costs Versus Unit Cost

All costs for a specific period of time are called **total costs.** The abbreviated income statement in Illustration 16-1 shows that the total cost of merchandise sold by Reflection, Inc. during July was $118,800.00. Total selling expenses were $31,930.00. These totals show how many total dollars were spent for these activities during a specific period of time. *(CONCEPT: Accounting Period Cycle)*

ILLUSTRATION 16-1 Abbreviated income statement

Reflection, Inc.
Income Statement
For Month Ended July 31, 19--

Operating Revenue:		
Net Sales		$180,000.00
Cost of Merchandise Sold		118,800.00
Gross Profit on Operations		$ 61,200.00
Operating Expenses:		
Selling Expenses	$31,930.00	
Administrative Expenses	20,820.00	
Total Operating Expenses		52,750.00
Income from Operations		$ 8,450.00
Other Expenses		2,450.00
Net Income		$ 6,000.00

CAREERS IN ACCOUNTING

The CAREERS feature box, BUDGET ACCOUNTANT, comes from the Dictionary of Occupational Titles (DOT). The entry number for this job title is D.O.T. 160.162-022. Bring this dictionary to class and explain its purpose and how to use it. The career feature is designed to expose students to the exploration of different careers in accounting. The feature gives a realistic description of actual job duties. This feature can be used to demonstrate that the skills learned in this course are relevant.

LESSON PLAN 16-1

Materials

- Student pages 439–443
- Blackline Master for 2-Column Financial Statement (TRG)
- 3-Step Checklist for Making Ethical Decisions (TRG)
- Software: Spreadsheet Template

Objectives (Enabling Performance Tasks)

a. Define accounting terms related to accounting information for management decisions.

b. Identify accounting concepts and practices related to preparing accounting information for management decisions.

c. Prepare an income statement reporting contribution margin.

TEACHING STRATEGIES: TEACHING TIP

Write the formulas on the chalkboard or overhead projector as they are presented. Review each formula and demonstrate how each is calculated. Show the relationships between the formulas. For example, contribution margin rate is calculated as the first step in determining the breakeven point. In the second step, the contribution margin rate is part of the formula used to calculate sales dollar breakeven point. In the third step, sales dollar breakeven point is part of the formula used to calculate unit sales breakeven point.

FOCUS

- Explain that management uses financial information for a variety of reasons. Chapter 15 discussed how financial information is used for planning and control. This lesson introduces the use of financial information in decision making. The characteristics of costs and how they influence decisions will be presented.
- Introduce vocabulary: total costs, unit cost, variable costs, fixed costs, contribution margin.

TEACH

Cover student pages 439–443 "Cost Characteristics that Influence Decisions." Discuss the difference between total costs and unit cost. Discuss the difference between variable and fixed costs. Students must understand the difference between the two costs. Emphasize that if the number of units increases, total variable cost increases but total fixed costs do not change. Also emphasize that the unit variable cost does not change as the number of units changes. Discuss the differences between a typical income statement and one showing contribution margin. Point out that the selling and administrative costs are the same amounts on both; the costs are just grouped differently.

An amount spent for one of a specific product or service is called a **unit cost.** Reflection sold 36,000 square feet of mirrors during July at a total cost of $118,800.00. The unit cost of each square foot of mirrors is calculated as shown below.

Cost of Merchandise Sold Total Cost	÷	Units Sold	=	Cost of Merchandise Sold Unit Cost
$118,800.00	÷	36,000	=	$3.30

Units may be expressed in many different terms. However, units should be expressed in terms that are meaningful to the people who are responsible for the costs. Some examples of other unit terms are gallons, liters, pounds, kilograms, inches, yards, meters, and hours. Knowing unit costs can be helpful to a manager in setting unit selling prices and in planning cost control.

Variable Costs Versus Fixed Costs

Costs may be separated into two parts: variable and fixed.

FYI

The unit cost of a variable cost does not change as volume changes.

Variable Costs. Total costs which change in direct proportion to a change in the number of units are called **variable costs.** The *total* costs of a variable cost *varies* with a change in the number of units. The *unit* cost of a variable cost *remains the same* regardless of the number of units.

For example, a business buys one hour of radio advertising for $150.00. Later the business buys ten more hours of advertising for $1,500.00 (10 × $150.00 = $1,500.00). Regardless of the number of hours purchased, the unit cost of an hour of advertising is $150.00 per hour. Thus, radio advertising is a variable cost.

Reflection's mirror purchases for the months January through July are shown in Illustration 16-2.

ILLUSTRATION 16-2

Reflection's mirror purchases

Reflection, Inc.
Mirror Purchases
For Period January 1–July 31, 19--

Month	Units Purchased	Unit Cost per sq. ft.	Total Cost
January	27,300	$3.30	$ 90,090.00
February	26,100	3.30	86,130.00
March	29,200	3.30	96,360.00
April	33,500	3.30	110,550.00
May	30,400	3.30	100,320.00
June	35,100	3.30	115,830.00
July	36,000	3.30	118,800.00

TEACHING STRATEGIES: DIFFERENT LEARNING STYLES

Auditory Learner. The auditory learner can reinforce the learning of formulas by verbally explaining the formula and/or calculations to other students in a small group. In a group of three, for example, each student should get the opportunity to "teach" the formula to the other two students. Through this process, each student in the group will "teach" the formula once and "learn" the formula two times.

The volume of mirrors purchased ranges from a low of 26,100 square feet in February to a high of 36,000 square feet in July. However, the price paid per square foot (unit cost) remained at $3.30 throughout the seven month period. Therefore, these costs have the characteristics of variable costs.

Reflection's monthly costs for purchases of mirrors are plotted on the graph in Illustration 16-3. The line drawn between the plotted points represents the relationship between the square feet of mirrors purchased and the total cost of mirrors. The straight, upward sloped line shows that as the quantity of mirrors increases, the total cost of mirrors also increases. The line is straight because Reflection's unit cost per square foot remained the same even though the number of units purchased per month varied.

ILLUSTRATION 16-3 Variable costs characteristics

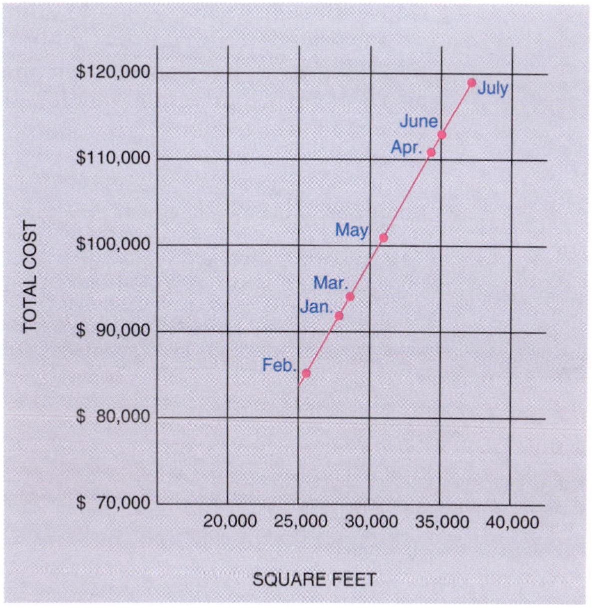

Fixed costs. Total costs that remain constant regardless of change in business activity are called **fixed costs**. For example, Reflection's rent is $2,500.00 per month. Rent is *fixed* because the amount has been set at $2,500.00 per month regardless of how many square feet of mirrors are purchased. If each monthly rental cost is plotted on a graph and connected, the chart will appear as shown in Illustration 16-4 on page 442. The fixed cost line is a straight line parallel to the base of the graph.

APPLY

Refer students to Illustrations 16-3 and 16-4 as variable and fixed costs are discussed. These graphs should help students visualize the difference between these two costs. Have students identify various costs of a business. As a group, decide which are variable, which are fixed, and which could be either fixed or variable depending on circumstances. Refer students to Illustrations 16-5 and 16-6 as the differences between a typical income statement and one showing contribution margin are discussed.

Guided Practice

Guide students through the partial preparation of the income statement with contribution margin in Problem 16-1. As a group, discuss what amounts are included in the Operating Revenue section. When all students agree on the amounts to be included in the Operating Revenue section, direct them to complete that section on the form provided in the working papers. Continue working as a group to decide which costs are included in the Variable Costs section. As agreement is reached on a cost, direct students to record that cost on their forms. Continue this procedure until the Variable Costs section is completed and contribution margin can be calculated. The balance of Problem 16-1 can be completed as Independent Practice.

Independent Practice

Assign Terms 1–5, Questions 1–7, and Problem 16-1.

TEACHING STRATEGIES: TEACHING TIP

Emphasize that total variable costs increase or decrease as the volume, such as sales, increases or decreases. Total fixed costs remain constant regardless of the volume. Students must understand the difference between variable and fixed costs.

ASSESS

Assess student understanding by checking the solutions to the Independent Practice activities.

Reteach

- Make a transparency of the 2-column financial statement from the accounting forms masters provided in the Blackline Masters Section of the Teacher's Resource Guide. Refer students to Recycling Problem 16-R. Ask students to determine which costs are variable and which are fixed. Use the transparency to demonstrate how the income statement with contribution margin is prepared.
- Assign Recycling Problem 16-R, Instruction 1.

Extend

- Assign Cases for Critical Thinking 1 and 2.
- Assign the Spreadsheet Template for Problem 16-1.

Enrich

Discuss the PROFESSIONAL BUSINESS ETHICS feature on page 452. You may wish to distribute copies of the 3-Step Checklist for Making Ethical Decisions. A blackline master is furnished in the Blackline Masters Section of the Teacher's Resource Guide.

CLOSURE

Use Audit Your Understanding questions.

ILLUSTRATION 16-4 Fixed costs characteristics

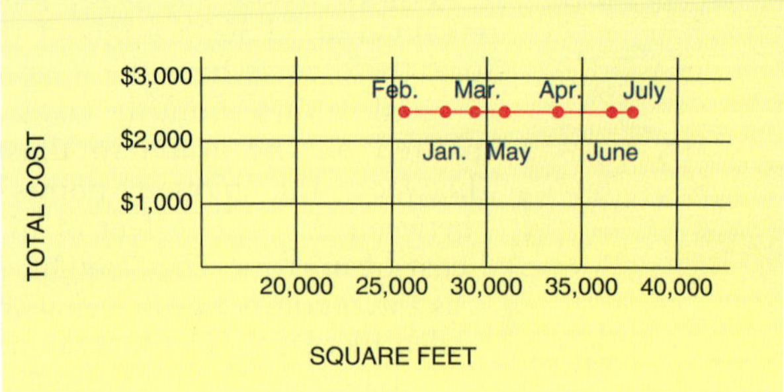

Contribution Margin Versus Gross Profit

FYI

Net sales minus cost of merchandise sold equals gross profit; net sales minus total variable costs equals contribution margin.

An income statement reports operating revenue, cost of merchandise sold, gross profit on operations, operating expenses, and net income or net loss. Gross profit is determined by subtracting cost of merchandise sold from net sales. On a typical income statement, as shown in Illustration 16-5, costs are shown as cost of merchandise sold, selling expenses, and administrative expenses.

Income determined by subtracting all variable costs from net sales is called **contribution margin.** Contribution margin is also known as marginal income. Reflection's income statement shown in Illustration 16-6 reports contribution margin and net

ILLUSTRATION 16-5 Abbreviated income statement

Reflection, Inc.
Income Statement
For Month Ended July 31, 19--

Operating Revenue:			
Net Sales (36,000 sq. ft. @ $5.00)			$180,000.00
Cost of Merchandise Sold (36,000 sq. ft. @ $3.30)			118,800.00
Gross Profit on Operations			$ 61,200.00
Operating Expenses:			
Selling Expenses:			
Sales Commission (36,000 sq. ft. @ $.20)	$ 7,200.00		
Delivery Costs (36,000 sq. ft. @ $.40)	14,400.00		
Other Variable Costs (36,000 sq. ft. @ $.15)	5,400.00		
Other Fixed Costs	4,930.00	$31,930.00	
Administrative Expenses:			
Rent	$ 2,500.00		
Insurance	400.00		
Other Variable Costs (36,000 sq. ft. @ $.20)	7,200.00		
Other Fixed Costs	10,720.00	20,820.00	
Total Operating Expenses			52,750.00
Income from Operations			$ 8,450.00
Other Expenses			2,450.00
Net Income			$ 6,000.00

TEACHING STRATEGIES: TEACHING TIP

Teach students how to interpret and use the graphs in Illustrations 16-3, 16-4, and 16-9.

ILLUSTRATION 16-6 Abbreviated income statement with contribution margin

Reflection, Inc.
Income Statement
For Month Ended July 31, 19--

Operating Revenue:		
Net Sales (36,000 sq. ft. @ $5.00)		$180,000.00
Variable Costs:		
Cost of Merchandise Sold (36,000 sq. ft. @ $3.30)	$118,800.00	
Sales Commission (36,000 sq. ft. @ $.20)	7,200.00	
Delivery Costs (36,000 sq. ft. @ $.40)	14,400.00	
Other Selling Costs (36,000 sq. ft. @ $.15)	5,400.00	
Other Administrative Costs (36,000 sq. ft. @ $.20)	7,200.00	
Total Variable Costs		153,000.00
Contribution Margin		$ 27,000.00
Fixed Costs:		
Rent	$ 2,500.00	
Insurance	400.00	
Other Selling Costs	4,930.00	
Other Administrative Costs	10,720.00	
Other Expenses	2,450.00	
Total Fixed Costs		21,000.00
Net Income		$ 6,000.00

income by grouping costs into two categories: variable costs and fixed costs.

Reflection's managers can determine from this income statement that the total contribution margin in July was $27,000.00. The contribution margin per unit is calculated as shown below.

Total Contribution Margin	÷	Units Sold	=	Contribution Margin per Unit
$27,000.00	÷	36,000	=	$0.75

Thus, Reflection determined that a $0.75 contribution margin will be earned for each square foot of mirrors sold. The manager also knows that the company will have $21,000.00 of fixed costs each month regardless of the number of square feet of mirrors sold.

Audit Your Understanding

1. If total monthly fixed costs for a company were plotted on a graph for seven months, would the line drawn between the plotted points be parallel to the base or sloped? Explain why.
2. How does contribution margin differ from gross profit?

DECISIONS THAT AFFECT INCOME

If a manager is to make decisions that yield a favorable net income for a company, two important kinds of information are needed. (1) The amount of merchandise or

AUDIT YOUR UNDERSTANDING

The AUDIT YOUR UNDERSTANDING feature appears at the end of each section of the chapter. Explain to your students that the word *audit* means to check or verify. AUDIT YOUR UNDERSTANDING may be used to check student comprehension of the section just studied. The answers are provided in Appendix D in the back of the textbook.

1. The line would be straight, parallel to the base. The line is straight because fixed costs are exactly the same for each month.
2. Gross profit is determined by subtracting only cost of merchandise sold from net sales. Contribution margin is determined by subtracting all variable costs from net sales.

LESSON PLAN 16-2

Materials

- Student pages 443–455
- Blackline Solution for Recycling Problem 16-R (TRG)
- Software: Spreadsheet Template
- Assess: Problem Test Chapter 16, MicroExam Chapter 16

Objectives (Enabling Performance Tasks)

a. Define accounting terms related to accounting information for management decisions.
b. Identify accounting concepts and practices related to preparing accounting information for management decisions.
d. Calculate the contribution margin rate and breakeven point.
e. Calculate the sales dollars and sales units required to earn a planned amount of net income.
f. Determine the effect of changes in sales volume, unit costs, and unit sales prices on net income.
g. Calculate a sales mix.

FOCUS

- The characteristics of variable and fixed costs and the procedures for calculating contribution margin on an income statement were presented earlier in this chapter. Variable costs, fixed costs, and contribution margin will be used in this lesson to determine the amount of sales to make a favorable net income and to determine the changes that affect net income. Explain that these are two important kinds of information managers need to make decisions.
- Introduce vocabulary: breakeven point, sales mix.

FYI

Remember that at the breakeven point, neither a net income nor a net loss occurs.

services the company must sell to make a favorable net income. (2) The factors that contribute most to net income.

Calculating the Breakeven Point

The amount of sales at which net sales is exactly the same as total costs is called the **breakeven point.** At the breakeven point, neither a net income nor a net loss will occur. Reflection calculates the breakeven point to determine how many dollars of merchandise must be sold before the company begins to earn a net income. The breakeven point can be stated in sales dollars or unit sales.

The amounts required to calculate a breakeven point are obtained from an income statement prepared to report contribution margin. A breakeven point is calculated using three steps.

1 Calculate the contribution margin rate. The contribution margin rate is calculated as shown below.

Contribution Margin	÷	Net Sales	=	Contribution Margin Rate
$27,000.00	÷	$180,000.00	=	.15 or 15%

Managers often use amounts from historical financial statements as projections of future sales and costs. Businesses usually round projected amounts to simplify the budgeting process. Reflection uses total amounts rounded to the nearest $10 in breakeven point calculations.

FYI

Contribution margin must cover fixed costs before any net income is earned.

The contribution margin rate means that for every $1.00 of revenue, $0.15 is contribution margin. The contribution rate is available to pay for fixed costs and provide net income. Variable costs change in direct proportion to changes in sales activity. Therefore, for every $1.00 of revenue, $0.85 is required for variable costs.

2 Calculate the sales dollar breakeven point. The sales dollar breakeven point is the amount of sales at which the entire contribution margin is used to pay for fixed costs. The sales dollar breakeven point is calculated as shown below.

Total Fixed Costs	÷	Contribution Margin Rate	=	Sales Dollar Breakeven Point
$21,000.00	÷	.15 or 15%	=	$140,000.00

Reflection must have total sales of $140,000.00 just to recover the fixed costs of doing business. Reflection's manager knows that more than $140,000.00 in sales must be made if the company is to earn a net income.

3 Calculate the unit sales breakeven point. Once the sales dollar breakeven point is calculated, Reflection can determine the

TEACHING STRATEGIES: DIFFERENT LEARNING STYLES

Print Learner. When learning formulas, the print learner would prefer to be able to study the formula as given in the textbook or as printed on a separate handout. The print material should show the formula as well as an example of performing the calculations.

quantity of mirrors which must be sold at $5.00 per square foot to achieve breakeven sales. The unit sales breakeven point is calculated as shown below.

Sales Dollar Breakeven Point	÷	Unit Sales Price	=	Unit Sales Breakeven Point
$140,000.00	÷	$5.00	=	28,000 units

FYI

Businesses with large fixed costs, such as airlines, public utilities, and railroads, are generally considered to be more risky.

Calculating Breakeven Point for New Products. When a business plans to introduce a new product, management is interested in knowing how many units must be sold to break even. Unfortunately, no financial statements exist from which sales and cost information can be obtained. Therefore, an alternative method of calculating the breakeven point is necessary that will use *the contribution margin per unit* rather than the *contribution margin rate.*

Reflection is considering selling desk lamps projected to sell at $18.00 per unit. Management also projects the variable costs at $12.00 per unit with fixed costs of $9,000.00 per month. Three steps are used to calculate the breakeven point.

1 Calculate the contribution margin per unit. The contribution margin per unit is calculated as shown below.

Unit Sales Price	−	Variable Cost per Unit	=	Contribution Margin per Unit
$18.00	−	$12.00	=	$6.00

2 Calculate the unit sales breakeven point. The unit sales breakeven point is calculated as shown below.

Total Fixed Costs	÷	Contribution Margin per Unit	=	Unit Sales Breakeven Point
$9,000.00	÷	$6.00	=	1,500 units

3 Calculate the sales dollar breakeven point. The sales dollar breakeven point is calculated as shown below.

Unit Sales Breakeven Point	×	Unit Sales Price	=	Sales Dollar Breakeven Point
1,500 units	×	$18.00	=	$27,000.00

Reflection must sell more than 1,500 desk lamps per month before the company begins to make a net income. Thus, management will begin selling desk lamps if it believes it can sell more than 1,500 desk lamps per month.

TEACH

Cover student pages 443–455 "Decisions that Affect Income." Explain that the amounts required to calculate a breakeven point are obtained from an income statement with contribution margin. Discuss the three steps for calculating the breakeven point and the procedure for verifying breakeven point calculations. Spend time explaining the importance of calculating the breakeven point for new products. Explain the effects of volume changes, cost changes, and sales price changes on net income. Explain the decisions that must be made when setting sales prices. Explain the importance of sales mix. Present the five steps used to calculate sales of more than one product to earn a planned net income.

APPLIED SKILLS: BUILDING STUDY SKILLS

Instruct students to prepare a Quick Reference Guide (QRG) for calculating breakeven point. (1) Label a QRG CALCULATING BREAKEVEN POINT. (2) Copy the three steps and formulas out of the chapter narrative. This QRG can be used when students are completing end-of-chapter activities. Additional QRGs could be prepared for other calculations and formulas presented in the chapter.

APPLY

Write the formulas on the board as the three steps for calculating breakeven point are described. Refer students to Illustration 16-7 as the procedure for verifying breakeven point calculations is presented. Refer students to Illustration 16-9 as the effect of volume changes are discussed. Write the formulas on the board as the five steps for calculating sales of more than one product are presented.

Guided Practice

Guide students through calculating contribution margin rate and breakeven point in Problem 16-2. Students will need the income statement prepared in Problem 16-1. Write the formula on the board for calculating the contribution margin rate. Working as a group, find the amounts on the income statement that are needed and do the calculation. When all students agree on the correct amounts, direct students to record the answers in the working papers. Repeat the process for the next two calculations.

Independent Practice

- Assign Terms 6–7; Questions 8–18; and Problems 16-3, 16-4, 16-5, and 16-6.
- Assign Study Guide 16 and Mastery Problem 16-M.

FYI

Fixed costs for your school might include the depreciation on the building and the principal's salary. These costs are the same no matter how many students there are enrolled.

This alternative method is also useful for calculating the breakeven point for existing products when complete financial statements are not available.

Verifying Breakeven Point Calculation. The simplest way to verify the accuracy of the breakeven calculation is to prepare an income statement using the breakeven point numbers. If the breakeven point is accurate, net income will be zero. The breakeven income statement in Illustration 16-7 shows the proof for Reflection's breakeven point for mirror sales.

ILLUSTRATION 16-7 Breakeven income statement

Reflection, Inc.
Breakeven Income Statement
For Month Ended July 31, 19--

Operating Revenue:		
Net Sales (28,000 sq. ft. @ $5.00)		$140,000.00
Variable Costs:		
Cost of Merchandise Sold (28,000 sq. ft. @ $3.30)	$92,400.00	
Sales Commission (28,000 sq. ft. @ $.20)	5,600.00	
Delivery Costs (28,000 sq. ft. @ $.40)	11,200.00	
Other Selling Costs (28,000 sq. ft. @ $.15)	4,200.00	
Other Administrative Costs (28,000 sq. ft. @ $.20)	5,600.00	
Total Variable Costs		119,000.00
Contribution Margin		$ 21,000.00
Fixed Costs:		
Rent	$ 2,500.00	
Insurance	400.00	
Other Selling Costs	4,930.00	
Other Administrative Costs	10,720.00	
Other Expenses	2,450.00	
Total Fixed Costs		21,000.00
Net Income		$ –0–

The breakeven income statement is a projection of sales and costs under specific assumptions. Reflection reports projected amounts to the nearest $10.

Total sales, *$140,000.00,* is equal to the sales dollar breakeven point. Each variable cost is calculated by multiplying the unit sales breakeven point, *28,000 units,* by the unit variable cost of each cost item. The amount of each fixed cost is taken from the July income statement. The contribution margin, *$21,000.00,* is 15% of net sales, *$140,000.00.* This verifies Reflection's contribution margin rate of 15%.

Calculating Sales to Earn Planned Net Income

Determining the breakeven point provides management with important information about the relationship of sales, variable costs, and fixed costs. Businesses do not, however, operate to merely

TEACHING STRATEGIES: DIFFERENT LEARNING STYLES

Tactile Learner. Suggest using a calculator with a printed tape to perform mathematical calculations. Better calculators also print the operational signs of calculations (+, −, etc.) for students to trace the steps in a calculation.

break even. Managers need information which will assist them in achieving planned net income.

Two steps are used to calculate the dollar sales and unit sales needed to earn any amount of planned net income.

1 Calculate the required contribution margin. The sum of total fixed costs and the planned net income is the contribution margin necessary to both cover fixed costs and earn the planned amount of net income. Reflection's managers want to know the amount of total sales required to earn $1,500.00 of net income. Reflection's contribution margin is calculated as shown below.

Total Fixed Costs	+	Planned Net Income	=	Required Contribution Margin
$21,000.00	+	$1,500.00	=	$22,500.00

2 Calculate the amount of sales dollars. The amount of sales dollars is calculated as shown below.

Required Contribution Margin	÷	Contribution Margin Rate	=	Sales Dollars
$22,500.00	÷	.15 or 15%	=	$150,000.00

Thus, Reflection must sell 30,000 square feet of mirrors ($150,000.00 total sales *divided by* the unit sales price of $5.00) to earn $1,500.00 of net income.

Also, the required contribution margin, *$22,500.00,* can be divided by the contribution margin per unit, *$0.75,* to calculate the number of units to be sold ($22,500.00 ÷ $0.75 = 30,000).

Determining the Effect of Changes on Net Income

Businesses must be able to determine the change in net income which would result from changes in the relationship of sales, variable costs, and fixed costs. Reflection's managers desire answers to questions such as what would be the net income if sales increase or decrease by 2,000 square feet from the breakeven point? Would it be profitable to change production methods to reduce variable costs by $0.25 but increase fixed costs by $7,500.00 per month? What will be the net income of a 10% decrease in unit sales price if sales volume increases by 20%?

FYI

Variable costs for your school might include the cost of computers, cafeteria lunches, and textbooks. These costs will increase or decrease depending on how many students there are enrolled.

Volume Changes. Reflection has calculated its unit sales breakeven point to be 28,000 square feet. Illustration 16-8 on page 448 shows how net income changes for a decrease and increase of 2,000 units.

For each square foot of mirrors Reflection sells, $0.75 of contribution margin is available for fixed costs and net income. At the

ASSESS

Assess student understanding by checking the solutions to the Independent Practice activities.

Reteach

- Make a transparency of the completed income statement reporting contribution margin prepared in Recycling Problem 16-R. The solution to Recycling Problem 16-R is provided in the Audit Tests and Solutions to Recycling Problems Section of the Teacher's Resource Guide. Using the information from this income statement, demonstrate how the contribution margin rate, sales dollar breakeven point, and unit sales breakeven point are calculated (Instructions 2–4 of Recycling Problem 16-R). Write the formulas on the board as each calculation is presented.
- Assign Recycling Problem 16-R, Instructions 5 and 6.

Extend

- Assign Challenge Problem 16-C.
- Assign the Spreadsheet Template for Problems 16-3, 16-4, 16-5, and 16-6.

Enrich

- Assign the CAREERS IN ACCOUNTING feature on page 439. Have students discuss what a career as a budget accountant might be like.
- Invite an accountant into the classroom to discuss how his/her business uses financial information to make decisions.

TEACHING STRATEGIES: DIFFERENT LEARNING STYLES

Kinesthetic Learner. The kinesthetic learner should have the opportunity to perform the calculations to solve the formula. One way to accomplish this is to develop several situations using different amounts for net sales. The student should calculate the contribution margin rate for each situation.

CLOSURE

Use Audit Your Understanding questions.

ASSESS

- Administer Problem Test Chapter 16.
- Administer a MicroExam test for Chapter 16.

ILLUSTRATION 16-8 Effect of volume changes on net income

1	2	3	4	5
	Per Unit	Number of Units		
		26,000	28,000	30,000
Net Sales	$5.00	$130,000.00	$140,000.00	$150,000.00
Variable Costs	4.25	110,500.00	119,000.00	127,500.00
Contribution Margin	$0.75	$ 19,500.00	$ 21,000.00	$ 22,500.00
Fixed Costs		21,000.00	21,000.00	21,000.00
Net Income (Loss)		$ (1,500.00)	$ -0-	$ 1,500.00

28,000 unit breakeven point, the $21,000.00 contribution margin pays for fixed costs leaving no remaining amount for net income. For each square foot of mirrors sold above 28,000 units, the $0.75 per square foot contribution margin will increase net income. Therefore, when 30,000 square feet of mirrors are sold, as shown in column 5, the contribution margin from the first 28,000 units pays the fixed costs. The contribution margin from the remaining 2,000 square feet results in a net income of $1,500.00 (2,000 square feet *times* $0.75 contribution margin per unit).

If only 26,000 square feet of mirrors are sold during the month, the contribution margin of $19,500.00 will not cover the fixed costs of $21,000.00. At this sales volume, a net loss of $1,500.00 will result as shown in column 3.

FYI

The intersection of the sales line and the cost line is the breakeven point.

The graph, Illustration 16-9, page 449, shows the relationship of sales, costs, and net income as the volume of units changes.

The sales line, beginning at zero, represents unit sales price times number of units sold. The total cost line starting at $21,000.00 (total fixed costs) represents the total fixed and variable costs for the number of units sold. The fixed costs are $21,000.00. No matter what the sales volume is, the fixed costs remain constant as shown by the horizontal line at the bottom of the graph. The variable cost area represents 85% of sales regardless of volume.

At the breakeven point, the 28,000 square feet of mirrors are sold for $140,000.00, the variable costs are $119,000.00, and fixed costs are $21,000.00. At this sales volume, the sales and total costs lines intersect, indicating that neither a net income nor a net loss will occur.

If 30,000 square feet of mirrors are sold, the sales line is above the total cost line. At this sales volume, sales of $150,000.00 are greater than the sum of fixed costs ($21,000.00) and variable costs ($127,500.00) resulting in net income of $1,500.00. If sales volume is below 28,000 square feet, the total cost line is above the sales line indicating that a net loss will occur.

Cost Changes. Two types of costs influence the decisions a company may make: variable costs and fixed costs. Total variable costs

TEACHING STRATEGIES: TEACHING TIP

Have students identify various costs of a business. As a group, decide which are variable, which are fixed, and which could be either fixed or variable depending on circumstances.

ILLUSTRATION 16-9 Effect of sales volume on net income

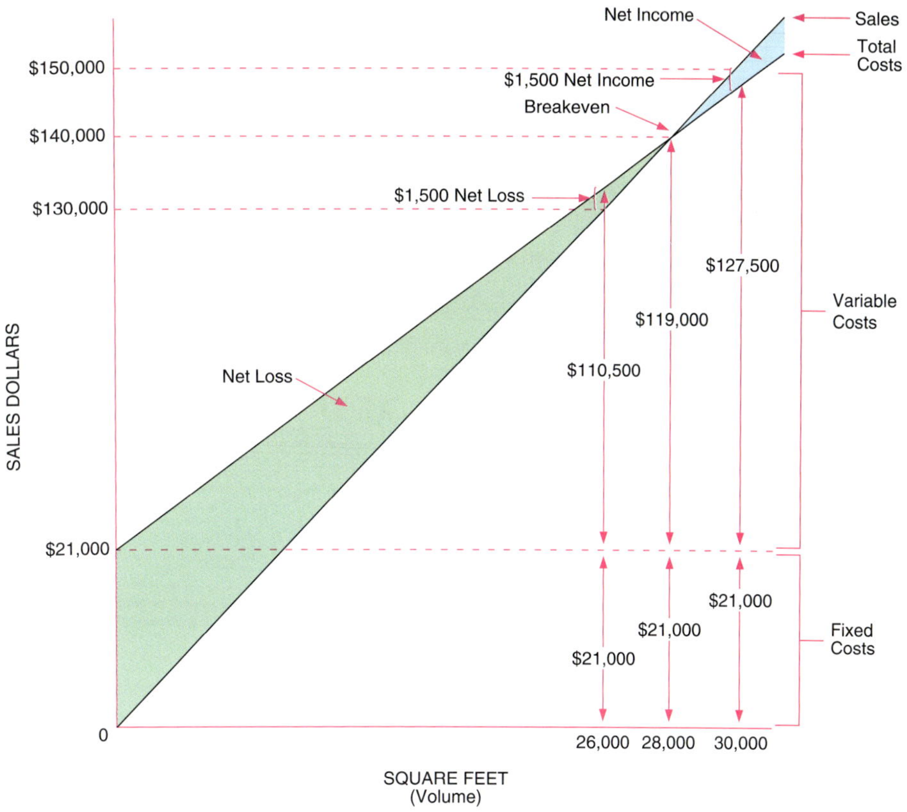

increase or decrease as sales increase or decrease. Total fixed costs remain constant regardless of sales amount.

Reflection is considering changing its production method. The relatively low contribution margin rate is making it difficult for the company to increase net income. Reflection is searching for ways to improve its percentage of net income per sales dollar.

Reflection has been paying a crew to manually cut mirrors to dimensions ordered by its customers. The variable cost of this crew is projected to be approximately $0.25 per square foot. The company is considering buying an automated cutter. If the automated cutter is bought, the crew that manually cuts the mirrors would be available to process orders of new product lines. Therefore, variable costs of mirrors will decrease by $0.25 per square foot to $4.00 per square foot. However, the new method will require buying the automated cutter and employing an experienced cutter at a fixed salary. Thus, fixed costs will increase by $7,500.00 per month to $28,500.00. The following is a cost analysis for the two alternatives.

FYI

Computers and spreadsheet or graphics software can be used to generate professional-looking graphs.

TEACHING STRATEGIES: APPLYING VISUALS

Direct students to Illustration 16-9 to review the effect of sales volume on net income.

APPLIED SKILLS: WORD PROCESSING

If you wish to integrate word processing in your accounting course, you may direct students to answer the end-of-chapter Accounting Terms, Questions for Individual Study, and Cases for Critical Thinking using their word processing software.

Alternative 1: *Manual cutting.* Variable costs per square foot of mirrors are $4.25. Fixed costs are $21,000.00 per month.

Alternative 2: *Automated cutting.* Variable costs per square foot of mirrors are projected to be $4.00 ($4.25 *minus* $0.25 savings). Fixed costs are projected to be $28,500.00 per month ($21,000.00 *plus* $7,500.00 additional fixed costs).

Sales have been averaging about 30,000 square feet of mirrors per month. A cost comparison is shown in Illustration 16-10 for the two alternative plans assuming sales volume continues at 30,000 square feet per month.

ILLUSTRATION 16-10 Effect of variable and fixed costs—average volume

	Alternative 1 Manual Cutting			Alternative 2 Automated Cutting		
	Per Unit	Units Sold	Total	Per Unit	Units Sold	Total
Net Sales	$5.00	30,000	$150,000.00	$5.00	30,000	$150,000.00
Variable Costs	4.25	30,000	127,500.00	4.00	30,000	120,000.00
Contribution Margin	$0.75	30,000	$ 22,500.00	$1.00	30,000	$ 30,000.00
Fixed Costs			21,000.00			28,500.00
Net Income (Loss)			$ 1,500.00			$ 1,500.00

At a 30,000 unit sales level, net income is the same for both alternatives. With Alternative 2, the contribution margin is higher but fixed costs also are higher. Thus, the higher fixed costs cancel out the higher contribution margin.

If Reflection expects increased sales, a cost comparison may be made for a higher sales rate. Cost comparisons with a sales volume of 32,000 units are shown in Illustration 16-11.

ILLUSTRATION 16-11 Effect of variable and fixed costs—above average volume

	Alternative 1 Manual Cutting			Alternative 2 Automated Cutting		
	Per Unit	Units Sold	Total	Per Unit	Units Sold	Total
Net Sales	$5.00	32,000	$160,000.00	$5.00	32,000	$160,000.00
Variable Costs	4.25	32,000	136,000.00	4.00	32,000	128,000.00
Contribution Margin	$0.75	32,000	$ 24,000.00	$1.00	32,000	$ 32,000.00
Fixed Costs			21,000.00			28,500.00
Net Income (Loss)			$ 3,000.00			$ 3,500.00

TEACHING STRATEGIES: EXPANDING BEYOND THE CLASSROOM

Invite a manager from a local business to talk to the class about important cost considerations that influence a manager's business decisions.

With the increased sales volume, Alternative 2 earns a higher net income. If Reflection expects a permanent sales increase, Alternative 2 would be more profitable than Alternative 1. However, if there is doubt whether sales will increase, the results could be much different. If the number of units actually sold falls below 30,000 units, the results will favor Alternative 1.

FYI

Many personal telephone bills have both fixed costs (the monthly charge) and variable costs (the cost per minute of each long-distance call).

What is the reason for the change in favorable alternatives? The contribution margin rate favors Alternative 2. Illustration 16-12 shows that the contribution margin rate for Alternative 1 is 15% ($22,500.00 contribution margin *divided by* $150,000.00 net sales) versus 20% ($30,000.00 contribution margin *divided by* $150,000.00 net sales) for Alternative 2. This means that for every $1.00 of sales from Alternative 1, $0.15 is available for fixed costs and net income. But for every $1.00 of sales from Alternative 2, $0.20 is available for fixed costs and net income.

SOFTWARE FOCUS

Software may be used for independent practice or enrichment/extension as the instructor deems appropriate. For this chapter, the Spreadsheet Template may be used with Problems 16-1, 16-3, 16-4, 16-5, and 16-6.

ILLUSTRATION 16-12 Effects of different variable costs on contribution margin rate

	Alternative 1 Manual Cutting		Alternative 2 Automated Cutting	
	Dollars	**Percent**	**Dollars**	**Percent**
Net Sales	$150,000.00	100%	$150,000.00	100%
Variable Costs	127,500.00	85%	120,000.00	80%
Contribution Margin	$ 22,500.00	15%	$ 30,000.00	20%

A high contribution margin rate is usually desirable. However, fixed costs must also be reasonable since the contribution margin must cover the fixed costs before any net income is earned. The contribution margin rate, *20%,* for the automated cutting method is more favorable. But, as shown in the cost comparison charts, fixed costs are $28,500.00—$7,500.00 more than fixed costs for the manual cutting method. Thus, if sales volume is reduced, the increased contribution margin is not enough to recover the increased fixed costs and a reduction in net income occurs.

A logical conclusion is that "Everything else being equal, the activity with the higher contribution margin rate is more profitable." If "everything else" is equal, selecting the more profitable choice is very simple. However, alternatives normally are not that simple because fixed costs probably will differ for each alternative. Therefore, an effective business looks for the best combination of fixed and variable costs.

Unit Sales Price Changes. Setting the selling price of a product is extremely important for a business that expects to make a reasonable net income. If the price is set too high, potential customers will buy from another business. If the price is set too low, the company may not earn enough money to cover costs and may suffer a

TEACHING STRATEGIES: DIFFERENT LEARNING ABILITIES

Limited English Proficiency (LEP) Students. LEP students, like visual learners, require a variety of visual clues to support the lesson and help them understand abstract ideas. Use transparencies, textbook illustrations, and software demonstrations to provide these clues.

Professional Business Ethics

The PROFESSIONAL BUSINESS ETHICS feature stimulates critical thinking and decision making. It may be used in many ways such as an individual assignment, a class discussion, or a small group cooperative learning project. When these ethics cases are discussed in class, students can also gain a sense of individual diversity as students demonstrate individual opinions. If you wish to integrate word processing in your accounting course, you may direct students to word process their answers. If you wish to include the creation of tables, you might direct students to format their responses to resemble the ethical decision-making grid in a 3-column table. A blackline master of the 3-Step Checklist for Making Ethical Decisions is furnished in the Teacher's Resource Guide. Suggested solutions for the Professional Business Ethics feature are provided in the front of this teacher's edition.

PROFESSIONAL BUSINESS ETHICS

Smooth Sailing with Client Referrals

Miller Steel Company has asked its public accounting firm, Williams & Associates, to develop a comprehensive health and retirement program. Knowing that it lacks the expertise to perform the work, Darryl Williams, a partner and CPA with Williams & Associates, refers Miller Steel to Tellish, Barde, & Scott, CPAs. Unknown to Miller Steel, partner Sandra Tellish shows her appreciation for the referral by giving Darryl Williams four tickets for a two-week Caribbean cruise.

INSTRUCTIONS Use the three-step checklist to analyze whether Darryl's accepting the tickets for a cruise demonstrates ethical behavior.

loss. The objective is to set selling prices which provide a reasonable amount of net income while keeping prices competitive.

Reflection earned record net income in July selling 36,000 units. Unfortunately, Reflection's managers believe a price reduction is necessary to sustain this level of sales volume. Management projected that a 5% reduction in the unit sales price would result in a 20% increase in the average number of units sold (from 30,000 to 36,000 units). Should Reflection implement this price reduction? Before making these changes, the schedule shown in Illustration 16-13 is prepared to project the effect of this price change on sales volume and net income. As the schedule shows, a 5% reduction in unit sales price and a 20% increase in sales volume results in a significant reduction in net income.

ILLUSTRATION 16-13 Effect of 5% reduction in sales price and 20% increase in units sold

	Current Price			Price Reduction and Sales Volume Increase		
	Per Unit	Units Sold	Total	Per Unit	Units Sold	Total
Net Sales	$5.00	30,000	$150,000.00	$4.75	36,000	$171,000.00
Variable Costs	4.25	30,000	127,500.00	4.25	36,000	153,000.00
Contribution Margin	$0.75	30,000	$ 22,500.00	$0.50	36,000	$ 18,000.00
Fixed Costs			21,000.00			21,000.00
Net Income (Loss)			$ 1,500.00			$ (3,000.00)

Price cutting can be dangerous. In July, Reflection had a $0.75 contribution margin per square foot of mirrors sold. Average sales of 30,000 units resulted in $22,500.00 total contribution margin. A unit sales price reduction of 5% ($0.25 per unit) to $4.75 per unit

TEACHING STRATEGIES: Cooperative Learning

Divide the class into groups of four or five students each. Using Cases for Critical Thinking, each group analyzes the cases and arrives at agreed-upon solutions. One member of each group is appointed the recorder and presents the group's analysis to the class. This cooperative learning activity should not take more than 20 to 25 minutes of class time.

reduces the contribution margin to $0.50. Thus, the contribution margin per unit would be reduced 33⅓% (from $0.75 to $0.50) even though the total selling price would be reduced only 5% (from $5.00 to $4.75).

The potential results of a price cut can be calculated. The unit sales required to maintain the net income using the new contribution margin is calculated as shown below.

Contribution Margin	÷	New Contribution Margin per Unit	=	Unit Sales Required to Maintain Planned Net Income
$22,500.00	÷	$0.50	=	45,000 units

A decrease in unit sales price from $5.00 to $4.75 is projected to increase average sales from 30,000 to 36,000 units. However, at $4.75, a total of 45,000 units would have to be sold to maintain the same net income as current sales at the $5.00 price. Reducing the unit sales price by $0.25 would not be a profitable decision if only 36,000 units can be sold.

TEACHING STRATEGIES: DIFFERENT LEARNING STYLES

Visual Learner. Formulas, such as those used to calculate contribution rate, should be illustrated on the chalkboard to assist visual learners. The instructor should also complete the calculations for several different situations to show the process to visual learners.

Sales Mix

FYI

Spreadsheet software is ideal for doing "what if" analysis on the effect of changes in sales mix. The results of many different mixes can be determined rapidly.

Businesses that sell two or more products can also use breakeven point calculations to assist managers in planning. Relative distribution of sales among various products is called **sales mix.** The sales mix must be calculated to determine the breakeven point for a company that sells more than one product. VideoPort, Inc. sells televisions and video cassette recorders (VCRs). The income statement in Illustration 16-14 reports VideoPort's sales and cost information for the month ended November 30.

ILLUSTRATION 16-14 Abbreviated income statement

VideoPort, Inc.
Income Statement
For Month Ended November 30, 19--

Operating Revenue:		
Net Sales		
Televisions (150 units @ $350)	$52,500.00	
VCRs (90 units @ $250)	22,500.00	$75,000.00
Variable Costs:		
Televisions (150 units @ $210)	$31,500.00	
VCRs (90 units @ $150)	13,500.00	45,000.00
Contribution Margin		$30,000.00
Fixed Costs		24,000.00
Net Income		$ 6,000.00

FYI

The sales mix may include many hundreds of different products.

VideoPort expects the relationship of television to VCR sales to remain relatively stable in future months. However, management has indicated its objective to improve monthly net income to $10,000.00. How many televisions and VCRs should VideoPort plan to purchase and sell?

The procedures used to calculate sales to earn a planned net income are similar to those previously described in this chapter. Five steps are used to calculate sales of more than one product to earn a planned net income.

APPLIED SKILLS: LANGUAGE ARTS

Paraphrasing, writing complete sentences, and identifying singular and plural nouns. For additional practice in language arts skills, direct students to answer the Accounting Terms and Questions for Individual Study at the end of the chapter. Students should write the answers in their own words and in complete sentences. To further practice language arts skills, ask students to underline the singular nouns and circle the plural nouns in each sentence of their answers.

1 Calculate the sales mix. Using sales information from the income statement, the sales mix is calculated as shown below.

	Product Sales	÷	Net Sales	=	Sales Mix
Television	$52,500.00	÷	$75,000.00	=	70%
VCR	$22,500.00	÷	$75,000.00	=	30%

2 Calculate the contribution margin rate. The contribution margin rate is calculated as follows.

Contribution Margin	÷	Net Sales	=	Contribution Margin Rate
$30,000.00	÷	$75,000.00	=	.40 or 40%

3 Calculate total sales dollars. Total sales dollars to earn $10,000.00 net income are calculated as shown below.

Total Fixed Costs	+	Planned Net Income	=	Required Contribution Margin
$24,000.00	+	$10,000.00	=	$34,000.00

Required Contribution Margin	÷	Contribution Margin Rate	=	Total Sales Dollars
$34,000.00	÷	.40 or 40%	=	$85,000.00

4 Calculate product sales dollars. Product sales dollars are calculated as shown below.

	Sales Mix	×	Total Sales Dollars	=	Product Sales Dollars
Television	70%	×	$85,000.00	=	$59,500.00
VCR	30%	×	$85,000.00	=	$25,500.00

454

5 Calculate product unit sales. Product unit sales are calculated as shown below.

	Product Sales Dollars	÷	Unit Sales Price	=	Product Unit Sales
Television	$59,500.00	÷	$350.00	=	170 units
VCR	$25,500.00	÷	$250.00	=	102 units

Managers of the television and VCR departments can now plan to accomplish these sales objectives. For example, the television department manager knows that 20 more televisions (170 − 150 = 20) must be sold each month. Thus, the manager can plan to increase purchases and devise new sales promotions and advertising campaigns to sell the increased number of televisions.

Audit Your Understanding

1. What is the simplest way to verify the accuracy of a breakeven calculation?
2. What is the formula for calculating the contribution margin rate?
3. To earn a planned net income, the required contribution margin must equal what two amounts?

AUDIT YOUR UNDERSTANDING

1. Prepare an income statement using the breakeven point numbers. If the breakeven point is accurate, net income will be zero.
2. Contribution margin divided by net sales equals contribution margin rate.
3. Total fixed costs plus planned net income equals required contribution margin.

ACCOUNTING TERMS

1. **total costs:** All costs for a specific period of time. (p. 439)
2. **unit cost:** An amount spent for one of a specific product or service. (p. 440)
3. **variable costs:** Total costs which change in direct proportion to a change in the number of units. (p. 440)
4. **fixed costs:** Total costs that remain constant regardless of change in business activity. (p. 441)
5. **contribution margin:** Income determined by subtracting all variable costs from net sales. (p. 442)
6. **breakeven point:** The amount of sales at which net sales is exactly the same as total costs. (p. 444)
7. **sales mix:** Relative distribution of sales among various products. (p. 453)

QUESTIONS FOR INDIVIDUAL STUDY

1. To gain an understanding of the relationship among sales, costs, and expenses. (p. 439)
2. By analyzing relationships among sales, cost, and expense information. (p. 439)
3. The unit cost of a variable cost remains the same regardless of the number of units. (p. 440)
4. The line would be a straight, upward sloped line from the base. The upward sloped line shows that as the quantity of units increases, the total cost of the units also increases. The line is straight because the unit cost remains the same even though the number of units per month varies. (p. 441)
5. The line would be a straight line, parallel to the base. The line is straight because fixed costs are exactly the same for each month. (p. 441)
6. Gross profit is determined by subtracting only cost of merchandise sold from net sales. Contribution margin is determined by subtracting all variable costs from net sales. (p. 442)
7. Total contribution margin ÷ units sold = contribution margin per unit. (p. 443)
8. Sales dollars or unit sales. (p. 444)
9. An income statement prepared to report contribution margin. (p. 444)
10. Contribution margin ÷ net sales = contribution margin rate. (p. 444)

ACCOUNTING TERMS EPT(a)

What is the meaning of each of the following?

1. **total costs**
2. **unit cost**
3. **variable costs**
4. **fixed costs**
5. **contribution margin**
6. **breakeven point**
7. **sales mix**

QUESTIONS FOR INDIVIDUAL STUDY EPT(b)

1. Why do managers analyze the income statement?
2. How can a manager identify a company's strengths and weaknesses?
3. How does a change in the number of units affect the unit variable costs?
4. If total monthly variable costs for a company were plotted on a graph for seven months, would the line drawn between the plotted points be parallel to the base or sloped? Explain why.
5. If total monthly fixed costs for a company were plotted on a graph for seven months, would the line drawn between the plotted points be parallel to the base or sloped? Explain why.
6. How does contribution margin differ from gross profit?
7. How is contribution margin per unit calculated?
8. What are the two ways to state the breakeven point?
9. What is the source of the financial information required to calculate a company's breakeven point?
10. How is the contribution margin rate calculated?
11. What is the meaning of a 35% contribution margin rate?
12. How is the sales dollar breakeven point calculated?
13. How is the contribution margin per unit calculated?
14. How is the unit sales breakeven point calculated?
15. What is the simplest way to verify the accuracy of a breakeven calculation?
16. To earn a planned net income, the required contribution margin must equal what two amounts?
17. On a graph showing the relationship between sales volume and total costs, what is the significance of the point where the sales and total cost lines intersect?
18. What is the formula for calculating sales mix?

CASES FOR CRITICAL THINKING EPT(b)

CASE 1 George Edmonds, the new accountant for Zigler Company, has recommended that income statements reporting contribution margin be prepared rather than statements reporting gross profit. He states that the income statement with contribution margin provides better information. Kimberly Johnson, the manager, disagrees that one statement is better than the other. She says gross profit is the same as contribution margin so it does not make any difference which statement is prepared. Which person is correct? Explain.

CASE 2 Denise Young, an accountant for Chiles Corporation, has been asked to prepare an income statement which reports contribution margin. Miss Young has asked you to prepare an analysis of three month's costs as shown below.

Provide Miss Young with an analysis of this data which includes the unit cost of variable costs and monthly costs of fixed costs. Explain to Miss Young how you prepared your analysis.

	May	June	July
Unit Sales	400	500	600
Cost of Merchandise Sold	$8,000.00	$10,000.00	$12,000.00
Advertising Expense	2,300.00	2,300.00	2,300.00
Depreciation Expense	1,000.00	1,000.00	1,000.00
Payroll Taxes Expense	640.00	800.00	960.00
Rent Expense	2,000.00	2,000.00	2,000.00
Salary Expense	3,200.00	4,000.00	4,800.00
Supplies Expense	1,200.00	1,200.00	1,200.00
Utilities Expense	600.00	750.00	900.00

APPLICATION PROBLEMS EPT(c,d,e,f,g)

PROBLEM 16-1 Preparing an income statement reporting contribution margin

SPREADSHEET

MATHEMATICS

Blue Mountain Chair Company's income statement has been prepared for May of the current year.

Blue Mountain Chair Company
Income Statement
For Month Ended May 31, 19--

Operating Revenue:			
Net Sales (7,200 units @ $75.00)			$540,000.00
Cost of Merchandise Sold (7,200 units @ $42.00)			302,400.00
Gross Profit on Operations			$237,600.00
Operating Expenses:			
Selling Expenses:			
Sales Commission (7,200 units @ $5.25)	$37,800.00		
Delivery Costs (7,200 units @ $4.80)	34,560.00		
Other Variable Costs (7,200 units @ $2.25)	16,200.00		
Other Fixed Costs	19,850.00	$108,410.00	
Administrative Expenses:			
Rent	$ 5,000.00		
Insurance	2,400.00		
Other Variable Costs (7,200 units @ $4.20)	30,240.00		
Other Fixed Costs	31,575.00	69,215.00	
Total Operating Expenses			177,625.00
Income from Operations			$ 59,975.00
Other Expenses			4,700.00
Net Income			$ 55,275.00

QUESTIONS *(cont'd)*

11. For every $1.00 of revenue, $0.35 is contribution margin. Also, for every $1.00 of revenue, $0.65 is required for variable costs. (p. 444)

12. Total fixed costs ÷ contribution margin rate = sales dollar breakeven point. (p. 444)

13. Unit sales price − variable cost per unit = contribution margin per unit. (p. 445)

14. Total fixed costs ÷ contribution margin per unit = unit sales breakeven point. Or sales dollar breakeven point ÷ unit sales price = unit sales breakeven point. (p. 445)

15. Prepare an income statement using the breakeven point numbers. If the breakeven point is accurate, net income will be zero. (p. 446)

16. Total fixed costs + planned net income = required contribution margin. (p. 447)

17. The point indicates that neither a net income nor a net loss will occur. (p. 448)

18. Product sales ÷ net sales = sales mix. (p. 454)

CASES FOR CRITICAL THINKING

Case 1 Neither is completely accurate or necessarily better. Each reports different information. Gross profit is sales less cost of merchandise sold. Because cost of merchandise is such a significant amount of total costs, many businesses want to know how much is left after merchandise costs are deducted, i.e., gross profit.

Contribution margin is sales less variable costs. Cost of merchandise is one of the variable costs and may be listed separately. However, gross profit is not reported. Income statements with contribution margin provide information for profit planning, such as calculating breakeven amounts and amounts needed to earn a planned amount of net income. For profit planning purposes, the statement with contribution margin is more useful.

CHECK FIGURES

See Teacher's Edition of Working Papers for complete solutions.

Problem 16-1 Contribution Margin = $118,800

CASES FOR CRITICAL THINKING *(cont'd)*

Case 2 A fixed cost remains constant regardless of a change in the number of units sold. For example, advertising expense was $2,300.00 in each month even though the number of units increased. Thus, advertising is a fixed expense which is $2,300.00 each month.

A variable cost varies with a change in the number of units. For example, the cost of merchandise sold varied with the increase between May and July units sold. Thus, cost of merchandise sold is a variable cost. To calculate the unit cost, divide the total cost of any month by the number of units for that month. The cost of merchandise sold calculation, using July amounts, is: Total Cost $12,000.00 ÷ Number of Units 600 = Unit Variable Cost $20.00

CHECK FIGURES *(cont'd)*

Problem 16-2
(1) $118,800/540,000 = 22%; (2) $63,525/22% = $288,750; (3) $288,750/$75 = 3,850 units

Problem 16-3 (1) $60−$25 = $35; (2) $42,000/$35 = 1,200 units; (3) 1,200 × $60 = $72,000; (4) No

Problem 16-4 (1) (a) 27,000 units; (b) $405,000. (2) (a) 37,000 units; (b) $555,000. (3) (a) 34,000 units; (b) $510,000

Problem 16-5 (1) (a) $ 80,000; (b) 110,000; (c) 140,000. (2) $265,000 with employees. (3) $90,000 at $16.00

Problem 16-6
(a) $40,000/$100,000 = 40%; $60,000/$100,000 = 60%; (b) $40,000/$100,000 = 40%; (c) $38,000 + $10,000 = 48,000; $48,000/40% = $120,000; (d) 40% × $120,000 = 48,000; 60% × $120,000 = 72,000; (e) $48,000/$40 = 1,200 units; $72,000/$250 = 288 units

INSTRUCTIONS:

Prepare Blue Mountain Chair Company's May income statement reporting contribution margin. Use Illustration 16-6 on page 443 as a guide.

The income statement prepared in Problem 16-1 is needed to complete Problem 16-2.

PROBLEM 16-2 Calculating contribution margin rate and breakeven point

The income statement prepared in Problem 16-1 is needed to complete this problem.

The managers of Blue Mountain Chair Company are interested in knowing the number of chairs which must be sold to break even.

MATHEMATICS

INSTRUCTIONS:

1. Calculate the contribution margin rate.
2. Calculate the sales dollar breakeven point.
3. Calculate the unit sales breakeven point.

PROBLEM 16-3 Calculating contribution margin and breakeven point

SPREADSHEET

Farris Electronics is considering expanding its product line to include portable radios. Management projects that radios would sell for $60.00 each. Variable costs are projected to be $25.00 with total fixed costs of $42,000.00 per month.

INSTRUCTIONS:

1. Calculate the contribution margin per unit.
2. Calculate the unit sales breakeven point.
3. Calculate the sales dollar breakeven point.
4. Farris has projected that it could sell 1,000 units per month. Should the company expand its product line to sell the portable radios? Support your answer.

MATHEMATICS

PROBLEM 16-4 Calculating plans for net income

SPREADSHEET

Dennis Williams is projecting the coming year's net income potential for Williams Paint. The paint is sold for $15.00 a gallon. Variable costs per gallon are $10.00 and annual fixed costs are $135,000.00.

Complete each of the following instructions independently of the others.

INSTRUCTIONS:

1. Calculate the (a) unit sales and (b) sales dollar breakeven points.
2. If a $50,000.00 annual net income is planned, calculate the required (a) number of gallons of paint to be sold and (b) sales dollars.
3. Mr. Williams plans to purchase a new paint mixing machine which would reduce the cost of paint by $0.50 per gallon, but increase annual fixed costs by $52,000.00. Calculate the (a) sales dollar and (b) unit sales breakeven points. Should Mr. Williams purchase the mixing machine? Explain your answer.

MATHEMATICS

PROBLEM 16-5 Calculating the effects on net income of changes in unit sales price, variable costs, fixed costs, and volume

Edward Balinski, manager of Nerren Carpet Shop, is anticipating several price and cost changes next year. The Company sold 120,000 square yards of carpet last year with the following results

SPREADSHEET

MATHEMATICS

Nerren Carpet Shop Income Statement For Year Ended December 31, 19--	
Net Sales (120,000 sq. yd. @ $15.00)	$1,800,000.00
Less Variable Costs (120,000 sq. yd. @ $12.00)	1,440,000.00
Contribution Margin	$ 360,000.00
Less Fixed Costs	310,000.00
Net Income	$ 50,000.00

Complete each of the following instructions independently of the others.

INSTRUCTIONS:

1. Calculate the projected net income for sales volumes of (a) 130,000, (b) 140,000, and (c) 150,000 square yards of carpet.
2. Nerren currently hires independent contractors to install carpet at a cost of $2.00 per square yard. Mr. Balinski can hire and equip employees to install carpet for $125,000.00 per year, thus eliminating the need to hire independent contractors. Calculate the projected net income assuming a sales volume of 140,000 square yards of carpet. Should Nerren hire the employees? Explain your answer.
3. Mr. Balinski believes he can increase this year's net income by raising the unit sales price from $15.00 to $16.00 per square yard. The price increase is expected to reduce sales volume from 140,000 to 100,000 square yards. Calculate the planned net income. Should Mr. Nerren raise the unit sales price to $16.00? Explain your answer.

PROBLEM 16-6 Calculating sales mix

SPREADSHEET

MATHEMATICS

Schenk, Inc. sells desk lamps and desks. The following information is from the June income statement. Schenk's management is interested in knowing the number of lamps and desks it must sell to earn $10,000.00 of net income.

Schenk, Inc. Income Statement For Month Ended June 30, 19--		
Net Sales:		
Lamps (1,000 @ $40.00)	$40,000.00	
Desks (240 @ $250.00)	60,000.00	
Total Net Sales		$100,000.00
Variable Costs:		
Lamps (1,000 @ $30.00)	$30,000.00	
Desks (240 @ $125.00)	30,000.00	
Total Variable Costs		60,000.00
Contribution Margin		$ 40,000.00
Fixed Costs		38,000.00
Net Income		$ 2,000.00

INSTRUCTIONS:

Schenk's managers need sales information assuming the company earns $10,000.00 of monthly net income. Calculate the following amounts to achieve the $10,000.00 planned net income.

459

a. Sales mix.
b. Required contribution margin.
c. Total sales dollars.
d. Product sales dollars.
e. Product unit sales.

CHECK FIGURES *(cont'd)*

Mastery Problem 16-M
(1) Contribution Margin = $18,750;
(2) $18,750/$75,000 = 25%;
(3) $11,600/25% = $46,400;
(4) $46,400/$25 = 1,856 units;
(5) (a) $26,000/25% = $106,400;
(b) $106,400/$25 = 4,256 units;
(6) Current machines, $7,150; Computer based machines, $9,750

Challenge Problem 16-C (1) current, $770,000; decreased, $20,000. (2) purchase, $770,000; produce, $905,000

ENRICHMENT PROBLEMS

EPT(c,d,e,f)

MASTERY PROBLEM 16-M Calculating contribution margin and breakeven point; calculating sales dollars and unit sales for planned net income

Ratliff Corporation produces lawn fertilizer spreaders. Ratliff's income statement has been prepared for August of the current year.

Ratliff Corporation
Income Statement
For Month Ended August 31, 19--

Operating Revenue:			
Net Sales (3,000 units @ $25.00)			$75,000.00
Cost of Merchandise Sold (3,000 units @ $16.00)			48,000.00
Gross Profit on Operations			$27,000.00
Operating Expenses:			
Selling Expenses:			
Sales Commission (3,000 units @ $0.60)	$1,800.00		
Delivery Costs (3,000 units @ $0.75)	2,250.00		
Other Variable Costs (3,000 units @ $1.15)	3,450.00		
Other Fixed Costs	3,590.00	$11,090.00	
Administrative Expenses:			
Rent	$1,000.00		
Insurance	600.00		
Other Variable Costs (3,000 units @ $0.25)	750.00		
Other Fixed Costs	5,610.00	7,960.00	
Total Operating Expenses			19,050.00
Income from Operations			$ 7,950.00
Other Expenses			800.00
Net Income			$ 7,150.00

INSTRUCTIONS:

1. Prepare Ratliff's August income statement reporting contribution margin.
2. Calculate the contribution margin rate.
3. Calculate the sales dollar breakeven point.
4. Calculate the unit sales breakeven point.
5. If a $15,000.00 monthly net income is planned, calculate the required (a) sales dollars and (b) unit sales.
6. Ratliff is considering using computer-based machines to increase the productivity of the manufacturing process. The new machines would reduce variable costs by $4.20 per unit but increase monthly fixed costs by $10,000.00. Calculate the projected net income assuming 3,000 units are sold. Should Ratliff purchase the machines? Explain your answer.

460

CHALLENGE PROBLEM 16-C Calculating the effects on net income of changes in unit sales price, variable costs, and fixed costs

Millard, Inc. sold 68,000 computer printers last year with the following results.

Millard, Inc. Income Statement For Year Ended December 31, 19--	
Net Sales (68,000 units @ $250.00)	$17,000,000.00
Less Variable Costs (68,000 units @ $200.00)	13,600,000.00
Contribution Margin	$ 3,400,000.00
Less Fixed Costs	2,980,000.00
Net Income	$ 420,000.00

Complete each of the following instructions independently of the others.

INSTRUCTIONS:

1. Millard projects that 75,000 printers can be sold next year at the current $250.00 unit sales price. However, management believes it can increase net income by selling its printer below the unit sales price of its competitors. Millard's marketing department projects that 100,000 printers could be sold at a unit sales price of $230.00. Calculate the projected net income. Should Millard reduce the unit sales price to $230.00? Explain your answer.
2. Millard currently purchases the power cable from another manufacturer at a cost of $7.00 per unit. The company is considering producing the cable. Millard projects the cable can be produced for $2.00 each plus annual fixed costs of $240,000.00. Calculate the projected net income assuming a sales volume of 75,000 printers. Should Millard produce the power cables? Explain your answer.

CHAPTER 17 OVERVIEW

This chapter brings together all of the tools of financial analysis presented in previous chapters and explains and demonstrates new measures such as trend analysis, debit and equity ratios, working capital, current ratio, and acid-test ratio. Students see that analysis can be approached using trends and com-

GUIDE TO ACHIEVING LEARNING OBJECTIVES

	TEACH	APPLY	EXTEND/ENRICH					
Enabling Performance Tasks	**Lesson Plans**	**Application Problems**	**Mastery Problems**	**Challenge Problems**	**Cases for Critical Thinking**	**Recycling Problems**	**Reinforcement Activity**	
a. Define accounting terms related to financial statement analysis.	17-1, 17-3							
b. Identify accounting concepts and practices related to financial statement analysis.	17-1, 17-2, 17-3				Cases 1, 2			
c. Analyze financial statements.	17-1	17-1, 17-2	17-M	17-C		17-R		
d. Calculate earnings performance analysis.	17-2	17-3	17-M	17-C		17-R		
e. Calculate efficiency analysis.	17-2	17-4	17-M	17-C		17-R		
f. Calculate financial strength analysis.	17-3	17-5, 17-6	17-M	17-C		17-R		

ENRICHMENT

SPECIAL FEATURES
Global Perspective, page 474
TECHNOLOGY CONNECTION
Spreadsheet Template Problems 17-1, 17-2, 17-M

NEW, REVIEW, AND EXTENSION

ACTIVITIES/CONCEPTS/TRANSACTIONS	NEW	REVIEW/ EXTENSION
Trend analysis	✓	
Component percentage analysis		✓
Earnings performance analysis		
Earnings per share		✓
Price-earnings ratio		✓
Efficiency analysis		✓
Accounts receivable turnover ratio		✓
Average number of days for payment		✓
Merchandise inventory turnover ratio		✓
Average number of days' sales		✓
Financial strength analysis		✓
Working capital	✓	
Current and acid-test ratios	✓	
Debt and equity ratios	✓	
Equity per share		✓

ponent percentages of actual performance, as well as earnings performance, efficiency, and financial strength analysis.

The solution to Problem 17-1 is needed to complete Problems 17-3, 17-4, 17-5, and 17-6.

INFORMAL ASSESSMENT		FORMAL ASSESSMENT			
Study Guide	**Audit Your Understanding**	**Chapter MicroExam**	**Chapter Problem Test**	**Unit Objective Test**	**Portfolio**
Unit A	✓	✓		✓	
Units B, C	✓	✓		✓	
			✓		
			✓		
			✓		
			✓		

TEACHING MATERIALS

- Teacher's Wraparound Edition of the Text
- Teacher's Resource Guide
- Teacher's Edition of Working Papers
- MicroExam

APPLIED MATHEMATICS

APPLIED MATH/ACCOUNTING SKILL	APPLICATION
Calculating trend analysis	Prob. 17-1
Calculating component percentages	Prob. 17-2
Calculating rate earned on average total assets	Prob. 17-3
Calculating rate earned on average stockholders' equity	Prob. 17-3
Calculating rate earned on net sales	Prob. 17-3
Calculating earnings per share	Prob. 17-3
Calculating price-earnings ratio	Prob. 17-3
Calculating accounts receivable turnover ratio	Prob. 17-4
Calculating average number of days for payment	Prob. 17-4
Calculating merchandise inventory turnover ratio	Prob. 17-4
Calculating average number of days' sales in merchandise inventory	Prob. 17-4
Calculating working capital	Prob. 17-5
Calculating current ratio	Prob. 17-5
Calculating acid-test ratio	Prob. 17-5
Calculating debt ratio	Prob. 17-6
Calculating equity ratio	Prob. 17-6
Calculating equity per share	Prob. 17-6

17

Financial Statement Analysis

TEACHING STRATEGIES: ACCOUNTING PEDAGOGY

This textbook covers complete financial statement preparation and analysis including efficiency analysis. Financial statement analysis is reviewed and expanded upon in this chapter to help students improve their critical thinking skills.

ENABLING PERFORMANCE TASKS

After studying Chapter 17, you will be able to:

a Define accounting terms related to financial statement analysis.

b Identify accounting concepts and practices related to financial statement analysis.

c Analyze financial statements.

d Calculate earnings performance analysis.

e Calculate efficiency analysis.

f Calculate financial strength analysis.

TERMS PREVIEW

ratio • working capital • current ratio • quick assets • acid-test ratio • debt ratio • equity ratio

SOFTWARE FOCUS

Software may be used for independent practice or enrichment/extension as the instructor deems appropriate. For this chapter, the Spreadsheet Template may be used with Problems 17-1 and 17-2 and Mastery Problem 17-M.

Financial statements report the financial progress and condition of a business for a fiscal period. *(CONCEPT: Adequate Disclosure)* Financial information is used by many individuals to make business decisions. Managers use financial information to identify areas for improving profitability. Banks and lending agencies use the information to decide whether to loan money to a business. Owners and potential owners use the information to decide whether to buy, sell, or keep their investment. Each group uses the financial information in a different way to provide the best help in making decisions.

Although financial statements provide useful information, they can be difficult to understand. For example, is a significant increase in the cost of merchandise sold an unfavorable trend? This question cannot be answered without considering changes in other financial statement items, such as net sales. Financial statement analysis allows financial statement users to calculate relationships among financial statement items which provide more meaningful information.

FINANCIAL ANALYSIS

Before financial information can be analyzed effectively, several questions must be answered. (1) What are the objectives for making the analysis? (2) What sources of information are needed to make the analysis? (3) What kind of analysis is to be made? (4) What level of performance is acceptable?

Financial Analysis Objectives

Financial analysis objectives are determined by a business' characteristics and achievements that are important to the person making the analysis. Information is analyzed to obtain more knowledge about the business' strengths and weaknesses. Common objectives for analyzing financial information are to determine (1) profitability, (2) efficiency, (3) short-term financial strength, and (4) long-term financial strength.

Financial Information Sources

Financial statements, with supporting schedules, are the primary information sources to be analyzed. A statement showing two or more years' information permits a reader to compare year to year differences. Financial statements providing information for each of two or more fiscal periods are known as comparative financial statements. Thus, consistent preparation and reporting of financial information are essential. *(CONCEPT: Consistent Reporting)*

LESSON PLAN 17-1

Materials

- Student pages 463–471
- Blackline Master for Comparative Statement for Trend Analysis (TRG)
- Blackline Master for Comparative Statement for Component Percentage Analysis (TRG)
- Software: Spreadsheet Template

Objectives (Enabling Performance Tasks)

a. Define accounting terms related to financial statement analysis.

b. Identify accounting concepts and practices related to financial statement analysis.

c. Analyze financial statements.

FOCUS

- The analysis of financial statements has been discussed in previous chapters. Explain that this lesson introduces a more in-depth discussion of methods available to analyze financial statements.
- Introduce vocabulary: ratio.

FYI

Publications such as *Dun and Bradstreet* list various ratios for a variety of businesses.

Financial Analysis Procedures

Comparative financial statements report a business' current and past activity. However, most financial statement readers are also interested in how well a business will do in the future. Therefore, financial statements are analyzed to help predict how well a business will perform in the future. *(CONCEPT: Adequate Disclosure)*

Several different comparisons may be made to analyze financial statements. Three common comparisons are (1) ratio analysis, (2) trend analysis, and (3) component percentage analysis.

Ratio Analysis. A comparison between two numbers showing how many times one number exceeds the other is called a **ratio.** A ratio may be expressed as a stated ratio, percentage, or fraction. For a business with net sales of $2,000,000.00 and net income of $200,000.00, the relationship may be stated as any of the ratios calculated as follows.

a.	**Net Sales**	÷	**Net Income**	=	**Stated Ratio**
	$2,000,000.00	÷	$200,000.00	=	10 times (often stated as 10 to 1 or 10:1)

The stated ratio of net sales to net income is 10 times; that is, net sales is 10 times net income. Another way of stating this ratio is 10:1, or for each $1.00 of net income, the business has $10.00 of net sales.

b.	**Net Income**	÷	**Net Sales**	=	**Percentage Ratio**
	$200,000.00	÷	$2,000,000.00	=	.10 or 10%

Net income is 10% of net sales.

c.	**Net Income**	÷	**Net Sales**	=	**Fractional Ratio**
	$200,000.00	÷	$2,000,000.00	=	1/10

Net income is one tenth of net sales.

TEACHING STRATEGIES: TEACHING TIP

Write the formulas on the chalkboard or overhead projector as they are presented. Review each formula and demonstrate how each is calculated. Have volunteers explain what each calculation measures and how it is used.

All three methods of calculating and expressing ratios are correct and essentially the same. The method selected is usually determined by the statement user's preference.

Trend Analysis. Trends in a business' financial condition and operating results may not be apparent from a single year's financial information. Comparison of information for two or more fiscal periods may be needed to determine whether a business is making satisfactory progress. A comparison of the relationship between one item on a financial statement and the same item on a previous fiscal period's financial statement is known as trend analysis. Trend analysis is sometimes referred to as horizontal analysis. A trend analysis can be calculated for any financial statement item. A trend analysis for Hamilton Corporation's net sales is calculated as shown on the next page.

FYI

Horizontal analysis refers to the relationship between different amounts on more than one statement for several fiscal periods.

Current year net sales . . . $4,767,200.00				
Less prior year net sales . . . 3,633,000.00		Prior Year Net Sales		% Increase or Decrease in Net Sales
Increase or decrease in net sales . . . $1,134,200.00	÷	$3,633,000.00	=	31.2%

Hamilton's net sales increased 31.2% from last year's net sales, a favorable trend. The trend for each item on Hamilton's income statement is shown in Illustration 17-1. Some items are reported in

ILLUSTRATION 17-1 Comparative income statement with trend analysis

Hamilton Corporation
Comparative Income Statement
For Years Ended December 31, 19-- and 19--

	Current Year	Prior Year	Increase (Decrease) Amount	Increase (Decrease) Percentage*
Operating Revenue:				
Net Sales	$4,767,200	$3,633,000	$1,134,200	31.2
Cost of Merchandise Sold:				
Merchandise Inv., Jan. 1	$ 423,800	$ 232,300	$ 191,500	82.4
Net Purchases	2,726,900	2,226,900	500,000	22.5
Total Cost of Mdse. Avail. for Sale	$3,150,700	$2,459,200	$ 691,500	28.1
Less Mdse. Inventory, Dec. 31	547,900	423,800	124,100	29.3
Cost of Merchandise Sold	$2,602,800	$2,035,400	$ 567,400	27.9
Gross Profit on Operations	$2,164,400	$1,597,600	$ 566,800	35.5
Operating Expenses:				
Selling Expenses:				
Advertising Expense	$ 46,700	$ 30,100	$ 16,600	55.1
Delivery Expense	74,600	55,200	19,400	35.1
Salary Expense—Sales	912,400	696,800	215,600	30.9
Supplies Expense	81,600	63,800	17,800	27.9
Other Selling Expenses	102,900	78,700	24,200	30.7
Total Selling Expenses	$1,218,200	$ 924,600	$ 293,600	31.8
Administrative Expenses:				
Salary Expense—Administrative	$ 290,200	$ 229,600	$ 60,600	26.4
Uncollectible Accounts Expense	27,700	19,100	8,600	45.0
Other Administrative Expenses	229,500	189,200	40,300	21.3
Total Administrative Expenses	$ 547,400	$ 437,900	$ 109,500	25.0
Total Operating Expenses	$1,765,600	$1,362,500	$ 403,100	29.6
Income from Operations	$ 398,800	$ 235,100	$ 163,700	69.6
Other Expenses:				
Interest Expense	$ 62,000	$ 52,000	$ 10,000	19.2
Net Income before Fed. Inc. Tax	$ 336,800	$ 183,100	$ 153,700	83.9
Less Federal Income Tax Exp.	114,500	54,700	59,800	109.3
Net Income after Fed. Inc. Tax	$ 222,300	$ 128,400	$ 93,900	73.1

*Rounded to nearest 0.1%

TEACH

Cover student pages 463–471 "Financial Analysis." Remind students that objectives should be set BEFORE financial statements are analyzed. Discuss the three common comparisons made to analyze financial statements: ratio analysis, trend analysis, and component percentage analysis. Review the three ways of expressing a ratio. Review the definition of component percentage. Emphasize which amount is used for calculating component percentages for items on each financial statement. Discuss the acceptable levels of performance.

TEACHING STRATEGIES: TEACHING TIP

Review the definition of component percentage. The percentage relationship between one financial statement item and the total that includes that item.

APPLY

Write the formulas on the board as the calculations for ratio analysis and trend analysis are presented. Refer students to Illustrations 17-1, 17-2, and 17-3 as trend analysis is discussed. Refer students to Illustrations 17-4, 17-5, and 17-6 as component percentage analysis is reviewed. Demonstrate how several of the percentages are calculated on each of the statements illustrated. Bring in performance guide sources such as Dun & Bradstreet. Let students peruse the publications.

Guided Practice

Guide students through the first few calculations in Problems 17-1 and 17-2, Instruction 1 (a). Refer students to the comparative income statement provided in the working papers for Problem 17-1. Working as a group, calculate the trend analysis for Net Sales. When all students agree with the calculations, direct them to write the correct answer on the form provided in the working papers. Continue working as a group to calculate the trend analysis for Merchandise Inventory and Net Purchases. When students understand the calculations, refer them to Problem 17-2 and repeat the process for component percentage analysis. The balance of Problems 17-1 and 17-2 can be completed as Independent Practice.

Independent Practice

Assign Term 1, Questions 1–8, and Problems 17-1 and 17-2.

FYI

An unfavorable ratio in one year may be balanced by previous actual positive results and future expected positive results. The trend in a ratio may be more important than a particular year's ratio.

condensed form. For example, a number of selling expenses are combined under the income statement heading Other Selling Expenses. Also, a number of administrative expenses are combined under the heading Other Administrative Expenses.

The trend in stockholders' equity can be determined from information on Hamilton's comparative statement of stockholders' equity, Illustration 17-2. Total stockholders' equity increased 23.8% from the prior year. Further review shows the increase in stockholders' equity was caused by an increase in both capital stock and net income. Hamilton's management believes the prior year's stockholders' equity was unsatisfactorily low; thus, the trend is favorable.

ILLUSTRATION 17-2 Comparative statement of stockholders' equity with trend analysis

Hamilton Corporation
Comparative Statement of Stockholders' Equity
For Years Ended December 31, 19-- and 19--

	Current Year	Prior Year	Increase (Decrease) Amount	Increase (Decrease) Percentage*
Capital Stock:				
$10.00 Per Share				
Balance, January 1	$ 500,000	$500,000	$ -0-	0.0
Additional Capital Stock Issued	100,000	-0-	100,000	—
Balance, December 31	$ 600,000	$500,000	$100,000	20.0
Retained Earnings:				
Balance, January 1	$ 349,300	$320,900	$ 28,400	8.9
Net Income after Federal Income Tax	222,300	128,400	93,900	73.1
Total	$ 571,600	$449,300	$122,300	27.2
Less Dividends Declared	120,000	100,000	20,000	20.0
Balance, December 31	$ 451,600	$349,300	$102,300	29.3
Total Stockholders' Equity, December 31	$1,051,600	$849,300	$202,300	23.8
Capital Stock Shares Outstanding	60,000	50,000	10,000	20.0

*Rounded to nearest 0.1%

A percentage increase (decrease) cannot be calculated if the amount divided by is zero. Therefore, a dash (—) is recorded in the percentage column.

Changes in Hamilton's balance sheet accounts are shown in Illustration 17-3, page 467. Accounts Receivable and Plant Assets are reported at book value. Information on this statement shows that total assets increased 17.5% during the current year. This increase was caused by an 11.6% increase in total liabilities and a 23.8% increase in total stockholders' equity. This trend is considered favorable because assets are increasing and the increase came more from the significant increase in stockholders' equity than the increase in liabilities.

Component Percentage Analysis. The percentage relationship between one financial statement item and the total that includes

ILLUSTRATION 17-3 Comparative balance sheet with trend analysis

Hamilton Corporation
Comparative Balance Sheet
December 31, 19-- and 19--

	Current Year	Prior Year	Increase (Decrease) Amount	Increase (Decrease) Percentage*
ASSETS				
Current Assets:				
Cash	$ 206,100	$ 104,300	$101,800	97.6
Accounts Receivable (book value)	474,000	569,200	(95,200)	(16.7)
Merchandise Inventory	547,900	423,800	124,100	29.3
Other Current Assets	26,100	21,300	4,800	22.5
Total Current Assets	$1,254,100	$1,118,600	$135,500	12.1
Total Plant Assets (book value)	813,600	641,100	172,500	26.9
Total Assets	$2,067,700	$1,759,700	$308,000	17.5
LIABILITIES				
Current Liabilities:				
Notes Payable	$ 222,200	$ 241,600	$ (19,400)	(8.0)
Interest Payable	12,900	20,700	(7,800)	(37.7)
Accounts Payable	344,300	413,300	(69,000)	(16.7)
Federal Income Tax Payable	11,300	3,300	8,000	242.4
Other Current Liabilities	5,400	6,500	(1,100)	(16.9)
Total Current Liabilities	$ 596,100	$ 685,400	$ (89,300)	(13.0)
Long-Term Liability:				
Mortgage Payable	$ 420,000	$ 225,000	$195,000	86.7
Total Liabilities	$1,016,100	$ 910,400	$105,700	11.6
STOCKHOLDERS' EQUITY				
Capital Stock	$ 600,000	$ 500,000	$100,000	20.0
Retained Earnings	451,600	349,300	102,300	29.3
Total Stockholders' Equity	$1,051,600	$ 849,300	$202,300	23.8
Total Liabilities and Stockholders' Equity	$2,067,700	$1,759,700	$308,000	17.5

*Rounded to nearest 0.1%

that item is known as a component percentage. Component percentage analysis is also referred to as vertical analysis.

Component percentages for items on an income statement are normally calculated as a percentage of net sales. Hamilton calculates component percentages as described for MasterSport in Chapter 5 and LampLight in Chapter 14. The component percentage is shown in a separate percentage column. Hamilton's income statement with component percentages is shown in Illustration 17-4, page 468. For example, the component percentage column for the current year shows that cost of merchandise sold was 54.6%.

In addition, component percentages on comparative statements show changes in a specific item from year to year. For example, Hamilton's cost of merchandise sold decreased from 56.0% to 54.6% of net sales as shown in Illustration 17-4. These percentages show a favorable trend. The current year's percentage, *54.6%*, is lower than the prior year's percentage, *56.0%*.

ASSESS

Assess student understanding by checking the solutions to the Independent Practice activities.

Reteach

- Make transparencies of the comparative statements for trend analysis and component percentage analysis from the accounting forms masters provided in the Blackline Masters Section of the Teacher's Resource Guide. Using the information from Recycling Problem 17-R and the transparency for trend analysis, demonstrate how to prepare several lines of the comparative income statement. Have students calculate the percentages at their desks. Discuss whether the trend is favorable or unfavorable. Repeat the process for component percentage analysis.
- Assign Recycling Problem 17-R, Instructions 1–4.

Extend

- Assign Cases for Critical Thinking 1.
- Assign the Spreadsheet Template for Problems 17-1 and 17-2.

CLOSURE

Use Audit Your Understanding questions.

TEACHING STRATEGIES: APPLYING VISUALS

Direct students to Illustrations 17-4, 17-5, and 17-6 to review component percentage analysis.

TEACHING STRATEGIES: TEACHING TIP

Obtain copies of printed annual reports from several major corporations as well as local corporations. Display these reports on the bulletin board. Discuss and highlight the way in which the corporations present their financial statements. Note the comparative statements when included. Illustrate points in the written parts of the reports that show an analysis of items on the financial statements.

ILLUSTRATION 17-4 Comparative income statement with component percentage analysis

Hamilton Corporation
Comparative Income Statement
For Years Ended December 31, 19-- and 19--

	Current Year		Prior Year	
	Amount	**Percentage***	**Amount**	**Percentage***
Operating Revenue:				
Net Sales	$4,767,200	100.0	$3,633,000	100.0
Cost of Merchandise Sold:				
Merchandise Inv., Jan. 1	$ 423,800	8.9	$ 232,300	6.4
Net Purchases	2,726,900	57.2	2,226,900	61.3
Total Cost of Mdse. Avail. for Sale	$3,150,700	66.1	$2,459,200	67.7
Less Mdse. Inventory, Dec. 31	547,900	11.5	423,800	11.7
Cost of Merchandise Sold	$2,602,800	54.6	$2,035,400	56.0
Gross Profit on Operations	$2,164,400	45.4	$1,597,600	44.0
Operating Expenses:				
Selling Expenses:				
Advertising Expense	$ 46,700	1.0	$ 30,100	0.8
Delivery Expense	74,600	1.6	55,200	1.5
Salary Expense—Sales	912,400	19.1	696,800	19.2
Supplies Expense	81,600	1.7	63,800	1.8
Other Selling Expenses	102,900	2.2	78,700	2.2
Total Selling Expenses	$1,218,200	25.6	$ 924,600	25.5
Administrative Expenses:				
Salary Expense—Administrative	$ 290,200	6.1	$ 229,600	6.3
Uncollectible Accounts Expense	27,700	0.6	19,100	0.5
Other Administrative Expenses	229,500	4.8	189,200	5.2
Total Administrative Expenses	$ 547,400	11.5	$ 437,900	12.1
Total Operating Expenses	$1,765,600	37.0	$1,362,500	37.5
Income from Operations	$ 398,800	8.4	$ 235,100	6.5
Other Expenses:				
Interest Expense	$ 62,000	1.3	$ 52,000	1.4
Net Income before Fed. Inc. Tax	$ 336,800	7.1	$ 183,100	5.0
Less Federal Income Tax Exp.	114,500	2.4	54,700	1.5
Net Income after Fed. Inc. Tax	$ 222,300	4.7	$ 128,400	3.5

*Rounded to nearest 0.1%.
Percentage totals may not equal sum of parts because of rounding.

FYI

Vertical analysis refers to the relationship between different amounts on the same financial statement for a fiscal period.

This change indicates that the cost of merchandise sold took a smaller part of each sales dollar in the current year. Similar comparisons can be made for each item on the comparative income statement. The cause of significant unfavorable changes should be investigated so that corrective action can be taken.

Component percentages for items on a comparative statement of stockholders' equity are normally calculated as a percentage of total stockholders' equity. As shown in Illustration 17-5, 57.1% of Hamilton's current year's stockholders' equity consists of capital

ILLUSTRATION 17-5 Comparative statement of stockholders' equity with component percentage analysis

Hamilton Corporation
Comparative Statement of Stockholders' Equity
For Years Ended December 31, 19-- and 19--

	Current Year		Prior Year	
	Amount	**Percentage***	**Amount**	**Percentage***
Capital Stock:				
$10.00 Per Share				
Balance, January 1	$ 500,000	47.5	$500,000	58.9
Additional Capital Stock Issued	100,000	9.5	0	0.0
Balance, December 31	$ 600,000	57.1	$500,000	58.9
Retained Earnings:				
Balance, January 1	$ 349,300	33.2	$320,900	37.8
Net Income after Federal Income Tax	222,300	21.1	128,400	15.1
Total	$ 571,600	54.4	$449,300	52.9
Less Dividends Declared	120,000	11.4	100,000	11.8
Balance, December 31	$ 451,600	42.9	$349,300	41.1
Total Stockholders' Equity, December 31	$1,051,600	100.0	$849,300	100.0
Capital Stock Shares Outstanding	60,000		50,000	

*Rounded to nearest 0.1%.
Percentage totals may not equal sum of parts because of rounding.

stock and 42.9% consists of retained earnings. Respective percentages for the prior year are 58.9% and 41.1%. Thus, little change has occurred in the component makeup of total equity. However, the percentage of dividends declared decreased slightly from 11.8% to 11.4%, an unfavorable trend for stockholders.

Component percentages for asset amounts on a comparative balance sheet are normally calculated as a percentage of total assets. Liabilities and stockholders' equity amounts are calculated as a percentage of total liabilities and stockholders' equity. Information on Hamilton's comparative balance sheet, Illustration 17-6, page 470, shows that in the current year current liabilities were 28.8% of total liabilities and stockholders' equity, down from 38.9% in the prior year.

Since current liabilities were at a high percentage in the prior year, Hamilton considers the reduction from 38.9% to 28.8% as a very favorable change. Similar comparisons can be made for each item on the comparative balance sheet.

APPLIED SKILLS: WRITING ACROSS THE CURRICULUM

Writing paragraphs and short essays. The Cases for Critical Thinking are short, practical applications of the accounting principles developed in the chapter. Some cases are planned to present problems related to the chapter but not specifically discussed and answered in the chapter. These cases present an opportunity for critical thinking and decision making. These cases also require more than a short objective-type response. Therefore, they provide ideal practice in writing paragraphs and short essays.

Acceptable Levels of Financial Performance

Analyzing financial information shows relationships among parts of the information analyzed. However, for an analysis to be useful, a company needs to know what level of performance is acceptable for each analysis made. For example, Wiseman Grocery considers a

ILLUSTRATION 17-6 Comparative balance sheet with component percentage analysis

Hamilton Corporation
Comparative Balance Sheet
December 31, 19-- and 19--

	Current Year		Prior Year	
	Amount	Percentage*	Amount	Percentage*
ASSETS				
Current Assets:				
Cash	$ 206,100	10.0	$ 104,300	5.9
Accounts Receivable (book value)	474,000	22.9	569,200	32.3
Merchandise Inventory	547,900	26.5	423,800	24.1
Other Current Assets	26,100	1.3	21,300	1.2
Total Current Assets	$1,254,100	60.7	$1,118,600	63.6
Total Plant Assets (book value)	813,600	39.3	641,100	36.4
Total Assets	$2,067,700	100.0	$1,759,700	100.0
LIABILITIES				
Current Liabilities:				
Notes Payable	$ 222,200	10.7	$ 241,600	13.7
Interest Payable	12,900	0.6	20,700	1.2
Accounts Payable	344,300	16.7	413,300	23.5
Federal Income Tax Payable	11,300	0.5	3,300	0.2
Other Current Liabilities	5,400	0.3	6,500	0.4
Total Current Liabilities	$ 596,100	28.8	$ 685,400	38.9
Long-Term Liability:				
Mortgage Payable	$ 420,000	20.3	$ 225,000	12.8
Total Liabilities	$1,016,100	49.1	$ 910,400	51.7
STOCKHOLDERS' EQUITY				
Capital Stock	$ 600,000	29.0	$ 500,000	28.4
Retained Earnings	451,600	21.8	349,300	19.8
Total Stockholders' Equity	$1,051,600	50.9	$ 849,300	48.3
Total Liabilities and Stockholders' Equity	$2,067,700	100.0	$1,759,700	100.0

*Rounded to nearest 0.1%.
Percentage totals may not equal sum of parts because of rounding.

TEACHING STRATEGIES: DIFFERENT LEARNING ABILITIES

At-Risk Students. Assist students to understand how accounting is a useful skill in careers which interest them. This could be accomplished in many ways. For example, a student who shows interest in auto mechanics could be introduced to the owner of a local auto repair business. The student could then report his or her observations to the instructor in oral or written form. If no mentor is available, trade magazines often present articles to assist their readers in managing their businesses.

component percentage for net income before federal income tax of 3.0% to be very good. However, Mitchell Manufacturing Company considers a 3.0% component percentage for net income before federal income tax to be very poor. A 12.0% component percentage for Mitchell would be more desirable because the two companies have different financial characteristics. The grocery company has a low investment in plant assets and sells its inventory quickly. The manufacturing company has a high investment in plant assets and holds its inventory much longer because of the time required to manufacture and sell a finished product. Because of the manufacturing company's larger investment per sales dollar, the company must earn a higher rate on sales. Each company's management must determine the acceptable levels of performance for each financial analysis made.

Audit Your Understanding

1. What are four common objectives for analyzing a business' financial information?
2. What three types of comparisons are commonly used to analyze financial statements?

Many businesses use two major guides to determine acceptable levels of performance. (1) Trends are compared with prior company performances. (2) Company results are compared with industry performance standards that are published by industry organizations.

Other sources of performance guides are frequently used. (1) Financial and credit reporting companies such as Dun and Bradstreet. (2) The company's planned financial objectives (budget schedules). (3) Current interest rates that could be earned by investing capital elsewhere.

Each company's management should determine the acceptable performance level for each financial analysis made by the company.

AUDIT YOUR UNDERSTANDING

The AUDIT YOUR UNDERSTANDING feature appears at the end of each section of the chapter. Explain to your students that the word *audit* means to check or verify. AUDIT YOUR UNDERSTANDING may be used to check student comprehension of the section just studied. The answers are provided in Appendix D in the back of the textbook.

1. Determine (1) profitability, (2) efficiency, (3) short-term financial strength, and (4) long-term financial strength.
2. (1) Ratio analysis, (2) trend analysis, and (3) component percentage analysis.

EARNINGS PERFORMANCE ANALYSIS

Amount and consistency of earnings are important measures of a business' success. The earnings of a business must be satisfactory to continue operations. *(CONCEPT: Going Concern)* Consequently, managers, owners, and creditors are interested in an analysis of earnings performance. Hamilton calculates five earnings performance ratios for the two most recent years. (1) Rate earned on average total assets. (2) Rate earned on average stockholders' equity. (3) Rate earned on net sales. (4) Earnings per share. (5) Price-earnings ratio.

Rate Earned on Average Total Assets

A business uses its assets to earn net income. If all assets are used as efficiently as possible, a business should earn the best possible net income. The rate found by dividing net income after federal income tax by average total assets is known as the rate earned on average total assets. The rate earned on average total assets shows how well a business is using its assets to earn net income. Average total assets is the average amount of assets held during a year.

Hamilton's rate of return on average total assets is calculated from income statement and balance sheet information, Illustrations 17-4 and 17-6. This ratio for the current year is calculated as shown below.

STEP 1:

(January 1 Total Assets	+	December 31 Total Assets)	÷	2	=	Average Total Assets
($1,759,700.00	+	$2,067,700.00)	÷	2	=	$1,913,700.00

STEP 2:

Net Income after Federal Income Tax	÷	Average Total Assets	=	Rate Earned on Average Total Assets
$222,300.00	÷	$1,913,700.00	=	11.6%

LESSON PLAN 17-2

Materials

- Student pages 471–479
- Blackline Solution for Recycling Problem 17-R (TRG)

Objectives (Enabling Performance Tasks)

b. Identify accounting concepts and practices related to financial statement analysis.
d. Calculate earnings performance analysis.
e. Calculate efficiency analysis.

FOCUS

General financial statement analysis was presented earlier in this chapter. In this lesson, analysis will focus on the amount and consistency of the earnings of a business and the measures available to determine how efficiently a business is using its assets to make a profit.

January 1 total assets are the same as the total assets on the prior year's December 31 balance sheet.

An 11.6% rate earned on average total assets means that for each $1.00 of assets the business earned 11.6 cents. The following rates earned on average total assets are calculated for the current and prior years. (Some information for the prior year is taken from financial statements that are not illustrated.)

	Current Year	Prior Year
Net Income after Federal Income Tax . .	$ 222,300.00	$ 128,400.00
January 1 Total Assets	1,759,700.00	1,437,600.00
December 31 Total Assets	2,067,700.00	1,759,700.00
Average Total Assets	1,913,700.00	1,598,650.00
Rate Earned on Average Total Assets . . .	11.6%	8.0%

Hamilton determines an acceptable rate of return on total assets by reviewing the company's prior year's results and comparing rates of return on alternative investments. Hamilton's goal is to earn a rate of return on average total assets at least as high as investments available elsewhere. For example, if Hamilton can earn more by placing extra cash in savings deposits or government bonds, the company is not meeting its earnings goal.

Investment sources available to Hamilton are earning 10.0%. Also, the trend in rate earned is up significantly from 8.0% to 11.6%. Therefore, Hamilton believes a rate earned on total assets of 11.6% is satisfactory.

Rate Earned on Average Stockholders' Equity

FYI

Ratios are common in everyday life. Your car's gasoline mileage is a ratio of the number of miles driven to the number of gallons of gasoline used.

Stockholders are particularly interested in knowing how much net income their investment is earning. Also, potential investors may compare the rate earned on stockholders' equity for several businesses to determine in which business to invest. The rate found by dividing net income after federal income tax by average stockholders' equity is known as the rate earned on average stockholders' equity.

Hamilton's rate earned on average stockholders' equity is calculated from income statement and stockholders' equity statement information, Illustrations 17-4 and 17-5. This ratio for the current year is calculated as shown below.

STEP 1:

(January 1 Stockholders' Equity	+	December 31 Stockholders' Equity)	÷	2	=	Average Stockholders' Equity
($849,300.00	+	$1,051,600.00)	÷	2	=	$950,450.00

STEP 2:

Net Income after Federal Income Tax	÷	Average Stockholders' Equity	=	Rate Earned on Average Stockholders' Equity
$222,300.00	÷	$950,450.00	=	23.4%

TEACHING STRATEGIES: TEACHING TIP

Bring in sources of performance guides such as Dun & Bradstreet. Let students peruse the publications.

January 1 stockholders' equity is the same as the stockholders' equity on the prior year's December 31 statement of stockholders' equity.

The following rates earned on average stockholders' equity are calculated for the current and prior years. (Some information for the prior year is taken from financial statements that are not illustrated.)

	Current Year	Prior Year
Net Income after Federal Income Tax	$ 222,300.00	$128,400.00
January 1 Stockholders' Equity	849,300.00	820,900.00
December 31 Stockholders' Equity	1,051,600.00	849,300.00
Average Stockholders' Equity	950,450.00	835,100.00
Rate Earned on Average Stockholders' Equity	23.4%	15.4%

Hamilton determines an acceptable rate earned on average stockholders' equity by reviewing the company's prior year's results. The company also compares its rate earned on average stockholders' equity with rates earned by other companies in the same industry. Minimum industry standards for the last two years have been 20.0%.

A review of the analysis shows that Hamilton did not meet the minimum acceptable rate of earnings on average stockholders' equity in the prior year. However, the rate of earnings increased significantly from 15.4% to 23.4%. Based upon the trend and comparison with industry standards, Hamilton achieved a satisfactory rate earned on average stockholders' equity.

FYI

"Garbage-in, garbage-out" is a term that applies to using software to process financial data. If incorrect amounts are entered (garbage-in), the resulting analysis will also be incorrect (garbage-out).

Rate Earned on Net Sales

A business that carefully controls costs should earn about the same or higher percentage of net income compared to sales dollar from year to year. However, if costs suddenly change, the rate earned on net sales will also change.

From income statement information, Illustration 17-4, Hamilton's rate earned on net sales for the current year is calculated as shown below.

Net Income after Federal Income Tax	÷	Net Sales	=	Rate Earned on Net Sales
$222,300.00	÷	$4,767,200.00	=	4.7%

The following rates earned on net sales are calculated for the current and prior years.

	Current Year	Prior Year
Net Income after Federal Income Tax	$ 222,300.00	$ 128,400.00
Net Sales	4,767,200.00	3,633,000.00
Rate Earned on Net Sales	4.7%	3.5%

TEACH

Cover student pages 471–479 "Earnings Performance Analysis" and "Efficiency Analysis." Present the five earnings performance ratios. Stress what each ratio measures and how it is used. Point out the similarities in the procedures for all calculations. Discuss what is an acceptable rate for each. Explain that earnings per share is one of the most widely recognized financial ratios. However, earnings per share are not comparable to other businesses since each business issues a different number of shares at various par or stated values. Present the two ratios to measure efficiency. Emphasize that a high accounts receivable turnover ratio is generally considered to be favorable. Also, the fewer average number of days for payment, the more favorable the results. Explain the importance of sufficient inventory to a merchandising business.

Global Perspective

The GLOBAL PERSPECTIVE feature is intended to expose students to some of the ways in which accounting and business in general differ in other countries. This GLOBAL PERSPECTIVE feature allows students to explore international organizations that establish trade regulations and standards. The Global Perspective Activity requires students to research the creation, policies, and accomplishments of an international organization.

Answers to Global Perspective Activity

Students' solutions will vary depending on the organization chosen. The instructor should consider the following items when grading the activity: (1) thoroughness of research, (2) identification of facts, (3) writing style, and (4) mechanics (grammar, spelling, punctuation, sentence structure).

Global Perspective

INTERNATIONAL ORGANIZATIONS

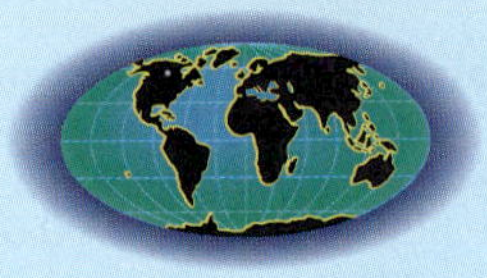

There are many international organizations that establish trade regulations and standards. These regulations and standards facilitate conducting business among the various countries in the world. The United States is a member of several trade related organizations.

- The United Nations plays an important role in foreign trade and has many organizations that make contributions. For example, The International Court of Justice (ICJ) decides disputes between nations, The International Monetary Fund (IMF) promotes international monetary cooperation and currency stabilization among member nations, The Universal Postal Union (UPU) promotes international cooperation in postal service, and the United Nations Children's Fund (UNICEF) provides aid to children and mothers in developing countries.
- The International Chamber of Commerce (ICC) serves traders in over 100 countries. Its most important function is to issue rules on international trade practices. It is not a government agency and confines its activities to business issues rather than national policy issues.
- The General Agreement on Tariffs and Trade (GATT) promotes economic growth by liberalizing world trade through requiring its member governments to reduce artificial trade restraints. There are 90 members of GATT, and the U.S. is a charter member.
- The European Community (EC) is a group of 12 European democracies—Belgium, Denmark, France, Germany, Greece, the Republic of Ireland, Italy, Luxembourg, the Netherlands, Portugal, Spain, and the United Kingdom. The EC has a short-term goal to integrate member nation's economies so members will act as a single nation for trade purposes. The EC's long-term goal is to unite member nations into a political union.
- The Latin American Integration Association (LAIA) was formerly called the Latin American Free Trade Association. It is a regional common market and charges member countries low duty or no duty on member-country imports. LAIA membership includes Argentina, Bolivia, Brazil, Chile, Columbia, Ecuador, Mexico, Paraguay, Uruguay, and Venezuela.
- The Carribean Community (CARICOM) is a common market of 13 English-speaking countries in the Carribean, including Barbados, Jamaica, Trinidad, and Tobago. CARICOM charges member countries low duty or no duty on member-country imports.
- The Central American Common Market (CACM) is a common market and encourages trade by charging member countries low duty or no duty on member-country imports. CACM members are Costa Rica, El Salvador, Guatemala, Honduras, and Nicaragua.

GLOBAL PERSPECTIVE ACTIVITY:

Select one of the above organizations (or another one not described), and research the organization's creation, policies, and accomplishments.

The component percentage for net income after federal income tax, Illustration 17-4, is the same percentage as the rate earned on net sales as calculated on the previous page. In both calculations, net income is calculated as a percentage of net sales.

When evaluating an acceptable rate earned on net sales, Hamilton considers what is normal for other similar businesses and the company's own past experience. Businesses similar to Hamilton have been earning about a 4.0% rate on net sales for the last two or three years. Based on a comparison of similar businesses, Hamilton's rate earned on net sales of 3.5% in the prior year was unsatisfactory. The trend in rate earned increased to 4.7% in the current year, a satisfactory rate. This trend should be watched closely for any future declines. When the rate earned on net sales declines, the company must increase sales or reduce costs to overcome the lower rate.

Earnings Per Share

FYI

Earnings per share is one of the most widely recognized financial ratios.

The amount of net income earned on one share of common stock during a fiscal period is known as earnings per share. Stockholders and management frequently use earnings per share as a measure of success. As earnings per share increase, more people become interested in buying stock. This demand for stock causes stock prices to go up. The company then finds it easier to issue stock or borrow money.

From income statement and statement of stockholders' equity information, Illustrations 17-4 and 17-5, Hamilton's earnings per share for the current year are calculated as shown below.

Net Income after Federal Income Tax	÷	Shares of Capital Stock Outstanding	=	Earnings Per Share
$222,300.00	÷	60,000	=	$3.71

The following earnings per share are calculated for the current and prior years.

	Current Year	Prior Year
Net Income after Federal Income Tax . .	$222,300.00	$128,400.00
Shares of Capital Stock Outstanding. . . .	60,000	50,000
Earnings Per Share.	$3.71	$2.57

A trend of increasing earnings per share is important to stockholders. This trend is one signal to stockholders that the company is continuing to increase the net income earned for each share. Therefore, Hamilton considers a trend of increasing earnings per share important to the company. Earnings per share increased significantly from $2.57 to $3.71, a very favorable trend.

Price-Earnings Ratio

Investors want to buy stock in companies that will earn a reasonable return on their investment. The relationship between the earnings per share and the market value per share of stock is known as the price-earnings ratio. As described in Chapter 14, the price-earnings ratio of a company's stock relates profitability to the amount the investors currently pay for the stock. The price-earnings ratio is usually expressed as a stated ratio.

Hamilton's capital stock sold for $43.50 per share on December 31 of the current year. Hamilton's price-earnings ratio for the current year is calculated as shown on the next page.

APPLY

Write the formulas on the board for reference as each earning performance ratio and efficiency ratio is discussed. Demonstrate all calculations. Refer students to Illustrations 17-4, 17-5, and 17-6, when appropriate, for information for the calculations.

Guided Practice

- Guide students through the calculation of the rate earned on average total assets in Problem 17-3, Instruction 1 (a). The comparative statements prepared in Problem 17-1 are needed. Working as a group, calculate the ratio for the current year. When all students agree with the calculations, direct them to write the correct answer on the form provided in the working papers. Repeat the process for the prior year. Discuss whether the trend is favorable or unfavorable. The balance of Problem 17-3 can be completed as Independent Practice.
- Guide students through the calculation of the accounts receivable turnover ratio and average number of days for payment in Problem 17-4, Instructions 1 (a) and (b). The comparative statements prepared in Problem 17-1 are needed. Working as a group, calculate the accounts receivable turnover ratio and the average number of days for payment for the current year. When all students agree with the calculations, direct them to write the correct answers on the form provided in the working papers. Repeat the process for the prior year. Discuss whether the trend is favorable or unfavorable. The balance of Problem 17-4 can be completed as Independent Practice.

Independent Practice

Assign Questions 9–16 and Problems 17-3 and 17-4.

TEACHING STRATEGIES: TEACHING TIP

Emphasize that earnings per share is one of the most widely recognized financial ratios.

ASSESS

Assess student understanding by checking the solutions to the Independent Practice activities.

Reteach

- Make transparencies of the financial statements prepared in Recycling Problem 17-R. The solution to Recycling Problem 17-R is provided in the Audit Tests and Solutions to Recycling Problems Section of the Teacher's Resource Guide. Using the information from these financial statements, demonstrate how to calculate the rate earned on average stockholders' equity, rate earned on net sales, and merchandise inventory turnover ratio.
- Assign Recycling Problem 17-R, Instructions 5 (a) and (b) and 6.

Extend

Assign Cases for Critical Thinking 2.

Enrich

Assign and discuss the GLOBAL PERSPECTIVE feature on page 474.

CLOSURE

Use Audit Your Understanding questions.

Market Price Per Share	÷	Earnings Per Share	=	Price-Earnings Ratio
$43.50	÷	$3.71	=	11.7 times

The following price-earnings ratios are calculated for the current and prior years.

	Current Year	Prior Year
Market Price Per Share	$43.50	$24.50
Earnings Per Share..................	3.71	2.57
Price-Earnings Ratio..................	11.7 times	9.5 times

FYI

The *Wall Street Journal* and many local newspapers report price-earnings ratios for many companies in their stock quotations.

The market price of a share of stock is determined by the amount investors are willing to pay for the stock. If investors think a company's profitability is increasing, they will usually pay more for the stock. Thus, the market price of a company's stock is influenced strongly by what potential investors think the company's earnings will be in the future. Hamilton's price-earnings ratio increased from 9.5 to 11.7. This change indicates investors considered the stock more valuable and were willing to pay more for the stock per dollar earned by the corporation in the current year. This increased demand is a favorable trend for Hamilton.

EFFICIENCY ANALYSIS

The profitability and continued growth of a business are influenced by how efficiently the business utilizes its assets. The operating cycle of a merchandising business consists of three phases. (1) Purchase merchandise. (2) Sell merchandise, frequently on account. (3) Collect the accounts receivable. Much of a business' assets are in accounts receivable and merchandise inventory. The quicker a business can convert these assets to cash and begin another operating cycle, the more efficient and profitable the business will be.

Hamilton uses two ratios to measure its efficiency. (1) Accounts receivable turnover ratio. (2) Merchandise inventory turnover ratio.

Accounts Receivable Turnover Ratio

A business accepts accounts receivable to encourage sales. However, the earnings process is not complete until the business receives cash for the sales on account. Thus, an efficient company will closely monitor the length of time required to collect its receivables. The number of times the average amount of accounts receivable is collected annually is known as the accounts receivable turnover ratio. The accounts receivable turnover ratio can be used to monitor a business' accounts receivable collection efficiency.

From income statement and balance sheet information, Illustrations 17-4 and 17-6, Hamilton's accounts receivable turnover ratio for the current year is calculated as shown below.

STEP 1:

(Beginning Book Value of Accounts Receivable	+	Ending Book Value of Accounts Receivable)	÷	2	=	Average Book Value of Accounts Receivable
($569,200.00	+	$474,000.00)	÷	2	=	$521,600.00

STEP 2:

Net Sales on Account	÷	Average Book Value of Accounts Receivable	=	Accounts Receivable Turnover Ratio
$4,767,200.00	÷	$521,600.00	=	9.1 times

TEACHING STRATEGIES: EXPANDING BEYOND THE CLASSROOM

Invite an accountant into the classroom to discuss how his or her business uses financial measures to analyze financial statements.

FYI

Individual investors can subscribe to many different services that report the financial statement ratios for many companies.

The beginning book value of accounts receivable is the same as the ending book value of accounts receivable for the prior year. All of Hamilton's sales are on account.

Hamilton's turnover ratio of 9.1 indicates accounts are being collected 9.1 times a year. The average number of days for customers to pay their accounts based on a 9.1 turnover ratio is calculated as shown below.

Days in Year	÷	Accounts Receivable Turnover Ratio	=	Average Number of Days for Payment
365	÷	9.1	=	40 days

Hamilton had an average of 40 days from date of sale to date of collection for the average account receivable. The following accounts receivable turnover ratios are calculated for the current and prior years. (Some information for the prior year is taken from financial statements that are not illustrated.)

	Current Year	Prior Year
Beginning Book Value of Accounts Receivable	$ 569,200.00	$ 463,400.00
Ending Book Value of Accounts Receivable	474,000.00	569,200.00
Average Book Value of Accounts Receivable	521,600.00	516,300.00
Net Sales on Account	4,767,200.00	3,633,000.00
Accounts Receivable Turnover Ratio	9.1 times	7.0 times
Average Number of Days for Payment	40 days	52 days

The larger the accounts receivable turnover ratio, the more favorable the results. That is, accounts have been collected more times in a year. The fewer the average number of days for payment, the more favorable the results. The accounts are being collected quicker.

Hamilton's credit terms are n/30. Thus, the company's goal is to collect accounts receivable in 30 days or less. Neither years' results meet that goal, an unfavorable result. However, Hamilton increased its accounts receivable turnover ratio from 7.0 to 9.1. This favorable trend means the company is improving its collection efficiency by reducing collection of its accounts receivable from 52 to 40 days.

APPLIED SKILLS: LANGUAGE ARTS

Paraphrasing, writing complete sentences, and identifying adjectives and the words they modify. For additional practice in language arts skills, direct students to answer the Accounting Terms and Questions for Individual Study at the end of the chapter. Students should write the answers in their own words and in complete sentences. To further practice language arts skills, ask students to underline the adjectives and circle the words they modify in their answers.

Merchandise Inventory Turnover Ratio

FYI

Proper inventory management is essential to prevent over- or under-stocking.

A company earns income when merchandise is sold. Therefore, the quicker a business can sell its merchandise inventory, the more efficient and generally more profitable the business will be. The number of times the average amount of merchandise inventory is sold annually is known as the merchandise inventory turnover ratio. The merchandise inventory turnover ratio can be used to monitor a business' merchandise inventory efficiency.

The merchandise inventory turnover ratio is described in Chapter 7. Hamilton's merchandise inventory turnover ratio is calculated from income statement information, Illustration 17-4. This ratio for the current year is calculated as shown below.

STEP 1:

(January 1 Merchandise Inventory	+	December 31 Merchandise Inventory)	÷	2	=	Average Merchandise Inventory
($423,800.00	+	$547,900.00)	÷	2	=	$485,850.00

STEP 2:

Cost of Merchandise Sold	÷	Average Merchandise Inventory	=	Merchandise Inventory Turnover Ratio
$2,602,800.00	÷	$485,850.00	=	5.4 times

January 1 merchandise inventory is the same as the December 31 merchandise inventory on the prior year's income statement.

Hamilton's merchandise inventory turnover ratio of 5.4 indicates that the average amount of inventory is being sold 5.4 times in a year. The average number of days' sales in merchandise inventory based on a 5.4 turnover ratio is calculated as shown below.

Days in Year	÷	Merchandise Inventory Turnover Ratio	=	Average Number of Days' Sales in Merchandise Inventory
365	÷	5.4	=	68 days

Hamilton had an average of 68 days' sales in merchandise inventory. The following merchandise inventory ratios and average number of days' sales in merchandise inventory are calculated for the current and prior years.

	Current Year	Prior Year
January 1 Merchandise Inventory....	$ 423,800.00	$ 232,300.00
December 31 Merchandise Inventory.	547,900.00	423,800.00
Average Merchandise Inventory......	485,850.00	328,050.00
Cost of Merchandise Sold...........	2,602,800.00	2,035,400.00
Merchandise Inventory Turnover Ratio...................	5.4 times	6.2 times
Average Number of Days' Sales in Merchandise Inventory............	68 days	59 days

An optimum merchandise inventory turnover ratio is determined by two factors. (1) Amount of sales. (2) Number of days needed to replenish inventory. A business needs, as a minimum, enough merchandise on hand to fill all sales orders during the time required to order and receive new merchandise. If the inventory level gets too low, a business risks running out of merchandise to sell before new merchandise is received. However, if the inventory level is much higher than needed, a business has more money invested in inventory than is necessary which adds additional costs. An efficient business tries to maintain an optimum level of merchandise inventory—enough to meet sales demand but no more than is needed.

Audit Your Understanding

1. What does a rate earned on average total assets show?
2. What does a rate earned on average stockholders' equity show?
3. What are two ratios that can be used to analyze the efficiency of a business?
4. What does an accounts receivable turnover ratio of 9.1 indicate?

Previous experience has shown that Hamilton needs to maintain an inventory turnover ratio of about 6.0. This 6.0 ratio equates to an average number of days' sales in merchandise inventory of 61 days. Hamilton's days' sales in inventory was 59 days in the prior year. This lower than desired level of inventory resulted in lost sales because some items were out of stock before new inventory arrived. However, the current year inventory level, *68 days,* is back to a satisfactory amount.

SHORT-TERM FINANCIAL STRENGTH ANALYSIS

A successful business needs adequate capital. A business gets capital from two sources. (1) Owners' investments and retained earnings. (2) Loans. Some capital, either owned or borrowed, is to be used for long periods of time. Also, some capital is borrowed for short periods of time. A business can invest long-term capital in some assets (such as equipment and buildings) for long periods of time. A business also invests in assets (such as merchandise) that

AUDIT YOUR UNDERSTANDING

1. How well a business is using its assets to earn net income.
2. How much net income stockholders' investment is earning.
3. (1) Accounts receivable turnover ratio and (2) merchandise inventory turnover ratio.
4. Accounts are being collected 9.1 times a year.

LESSON PLAN 17-3

Materials

- Student pages 479–485
- Software: Spreadsheet Template
- Assess: Problem Test Chapter 17, MicroExam Chapter 17, Objective Test No. 6

Objectives (Enabling Performance Tasks)

a. Define accounting terms related to financial statement analysis.

b. Identify accounting concepts and practices related to financial statement analysis.

f. Calculate financial strength analysis.

FOCUS

- General financial statement analysis, earnings performance analysis, and efficiency analysis were presented earlier in this chapter. This lesson will cover the measures used to analyze both short-term and long-term financial strength.
- Introduce vocabulary: working capital, current ratio, quick assets, acid-test ratio, debt ratio, equity ratio.

TEACHING STRATEGIES: COOPERATIVE LEARNING

Divide the class into groups of three students each. Have each student select and explain to the other members of the group one of the three measures used to analyze short-term financial strength. This cooperative learning activity should not take more than 15 to 20 minutes of class time.

FYI

The position CIO has become common in large corporations. CIO stands for Chief Information Officer.

will be converted back to cash in a short period of time. Short-term assets are referred to as current assets because they are consumed in a business' daily activities or exchanged for cash. Long-term assets are referred to as plant assets and are used over a long period of time.

Hamilton uses three measures to analyze short-term financial strength. (1) Working capital. (2) Current ratio. (3) Acid-test ratio.

Working Capital

The amount of total current assets less total current liabilities is called **working capital.** Working capital, stated in dollars, is the amount of current assets available to the business after current liabilities are paid. From balance sheet information, Illustration 17-6, Hamilton's working capital for December 31 of the current year is calculated as shown below.

Total Current Assets	–	Total Current Liabilities	=	Working Capital
$1,254,100.00	–	$596,100.00	=	$658,000.00

Hamilton has $658,000.00 of current assets available after current liabilities are paid. However, this does not mean that Hamilton has $658,000.00 of cash available. Working capital is a useful measure. The amount of working capital can be compared from year to year to look for a trend. However, working capital cannot be easily used to compare Hamilton with other companies in the industry.

The following working capital amounts are calculated for the current and prior years.

	Current Year	Prior Year
Total Current Assets	$1,254,100.00	$1,118,600.00
Total Current Liabilities	−596,100.00	−685,400.00
Working Capital	$ 658,000.00	$ 433,200.00

Hamilton's working capital has increased from $433,200.00 to $658,000.00, a favorable trend. A review of other financial information suggests that part of the reason for the prior year's lower working capital was the company's fast expansion. Frequently, when a business expands too rapidly, money is borrowed to buy more inventory and to pay more employees. The rate of increased costs for merchandise and payroll may be initially greater than the rate of increase in sales and net income. Hamilton took action in the current year to lower its current liabilities by issuing more capital stock and long-term liabilities.

Current Ratio

A ratio that shows the numeric relationship of current assets to current liabilities is called the **current ratio.** Normally, current liabilities are expected to be paid from cash on hand plus cash soon to be received from other current assets.

The current ratio is calculated by dividing total current assets by total current liabilities. From balance sheet information, Illustration 17-6, Hamilton's current ratio for the current year is calculated as shown below.

Total Current Assets	÷	Total Current Liabilities	=	Current Ratio
$1,254,100.00	÷	$596,100.00	=	2.1 times

The current ratio of 2.1 means that Hamilton owns $2.10 in current assets for each $1.00 needed to pay current liabilities.

Businesses similar to Hamilton try to maintain a current ratio of 2.0 times. Industry experience has shown that a business with a current ratio less than 2.0 times will have difficulty raising ready cash to pay current liabilities on time. At the same time, industry experience shows that a current ratio can be too high. If the current ratio is 3.0 times or higher, the business has more capital invested in current assets than is needed to run the business.

A current ratio becomes more meaningful when compared to current ratios for other years. The following current ratios are calculated for the current and prior years.

	Current Year	Prior Year
Total Current Assets	$1,254,100.00	$1,118,600.00
Total Current Liabilities	596,100.00	685,400.00
Current Ratio	2.1 times	1.6 times

In the prior year, Hamilton's current ratio, *1.6,* was significantly below the desired ratio. However, the current year ratio, *2.1,* is back to a satisfactory level. A review of other financial information suggests that part of the reason for the prior year's lower current ratio was the company's fast expansion. Hamilton took action in the current year to lower its current liabilities by issuing more capital stock and long-term liabilities.

Acid-Test Ratio

FYI

Merchandise inventory is a current asset but not a quick asset.

Those current assets that are cash or that can be quickly turned into cash are called **quick assets.** Quick assets include cash, accounts receivable, and marketable securities, but not merchandise inventory or prepaid expenses. Merchandise inventory is a current asset that is expected to be turned into cash. However, the

TEACH

Cover student pages 479–485 "Short-Term Financial Strength Analysis" and "Long-Term Financial Strength Analysis." Present the three measures used to analyze short-term financial strength. Stress what each measures and how it is used. Discuss what is acceptable or favorable for each. Present the three measures used to analyze long-term financial strength. Discuss how Hamilton's debt and equity ratios compare with the industry averages.

APPLY

Write the formulas on the board for reference as each ratio is discussed. Demonstrate all calculations. Refer students to Illustration 17-6 for information for the calculations.

Guided Practice

- Guide students through the calculation of working capital in Problem 17-5, Instruction 1 (a). The comparative balance sheet prepared in Problem 17-1 is needed. Working as a group, calculate working capital for the current year. When all students agree with the calculations, direct them to write the correct answer on the form provided in the working papers. Repeat the process for the prior year. Discuss whether the trend is favorable or unfavorable. The balance of Problem 17-5 can be completed as Independent Practice.
- Guide students through the calculation of debt ratio in Problem 17-6, Instruction 1 (a). The comparative balance sheet prepared in Problem 17-1 is needed. Working as a group, calculate debt ratio for the current year. When all students agree with the calculations, direct them to write the correct answer on the form provided in the working papers. Repeat the process for the prior year. Discuss whether the trend is favorable or unfavorable. The balance of Problem 17-6 can be completed as Independent Practice.

Independent Practice

- Assign Terms 2–7, Questions 17–20, and Problems 17-5 and 17-6.
- Assign Study Guide 17 and Mastery Problem 17-M.

merchandise inventory first has to be sold and then accounts receivable have to be collected before cash is available. Therefore, merchandise inventory is not considered to be a quick asset. Also, prepaid expenses will seldom be converted to cash.

A ratio that shows the numeric relationship of quick assets to current liabilities is called the **acid-test ratio.** This ratio shows the ability of a business to pay all current liabilities almost immediately if necessary.

From balance sheet information, Illustration 17-6, Hamilton's acid-test ratio for the current year is calculated as shown below.

Total Quick Assets (Cash + Accounts Receivable)	÷	Total Current Liabilities	=	Acid-Test Ratio
($206,100.00 + $474,000.00)	÷	$596,100.00	=	1.1 times

The ratio indicates that for each $1.00 needed to pay current liabilities, Hamilton has $1.10 available in quick assets. For companies similar to Hamilton, the desired industry standard for an acid-test ratio is between 0.9 and 1.3.

The following acid-test ratios are calculated for the current and prior years.

	Current Year	Prior Year
Total Quick Assets	$680,100.00	$673,500.00
Total Current Liabilities	596,100.00	685,400.00
Acid-Test Ratio	1.1 times	1.0 times

Hamilton's acid-test ratio has increased from 1.0 to 1.1, a favorable trend. A review of financial statements shows that Hamilton issued additional capital stock and long-term liabilities in the current year. Part of the cash received from these activities was used to reduce the level of current liabilities and improve the acid-test ratio.

LONG-TERM FINANCIAL STRENGTH ANALYSIS

Businesses that are successful and are able to continue in business through both strong and weak economic periods usually have long-term financial strength. Long-term financial strength requires a balance between stockholders' capital and borrowed capital. A profitable business can be even more profitable by using borrowed capital wisely. However, borrowed capital must be repaid with interest. Continuing operation of a business with a large percentage of borrowed capital may be jeopardized if net income declines and loan payments cannot be made. Also, creditors are reluctant to loan additional money to companies with a high level of liabilities. A well-managed company monitors its long-term financial strength to insure that a reasonable balance between stockholders' capital and borrowed capital is maintained.

FYI

Many businesses are forced out of business because they do not have the cash to pay liabilities when due.

FYI

Investors are interested in both short-term and long-term financial strength.

Hamilton uses three measures to analyze long-term financial strength. (1) Debt ratio. (2) Equity ratio. (3) Equity per share.

Debt Ratio

The ratio found by dividing total liabilities by total assets is called the **debt ratio.** This ratio shows the percentage of assets that are financed with borrowed capital (liabilities).

From information on the comparative balance sheet, Illustration 17-6, Hamilton's debt ratio for the current year is calculated as shown below.

Total Liabilities	÷	Total Assets	=	Debt Ratio
$1,016,100.00	÷	$2,067,700.00	=	49.1%

This ratio, *49.1%,* indicates that for each $1.00 of assets owned by Hamilton, the company has borrowed 49.1 cents.

The following debt ratios are calculated for the current and prior years.

	Current Year	Prior Year
Total Liabilities	$1,016,100.00	$ 910,400.00
Total Assets	2,067,700.00	1,759,700.00
Debt Ratio	49.1%	51.7%

The average debt ratio for companies similar to Hamilton is 43.0%. Hamilton's ratios are above the industry average, an unfavorable condition. Rapid growth over the past two or three years, financed primarily through borrowed capital, has caused the unfavorable liabilities level. However, Hamilton issued additional capital stock in the current year which helped lower the debt ratio from 51.7% to 49.1%. The company should consider issuing more capital stock to reduce the total liabilities to an industry average of 43.0%.

Equity Ratio

The ratio found by dividing stockholders' equity by total assets is called the **equity ratio.** This ratio shows the percentage of assets that are provided by stockholders' equity.

From information on the comparative balance sheet, Illustration 17-6, Hamilton's equity ratio for the current year is calculated as shown below.

Total Stockholders' Equity	÷	Total Assets	=	Equity Ratio
$1,051,600.00	÷	$2,067,700.00	=	50.9%

ASSESS

Assess student understanding by checking the solutions to the Independent Practice activities.

Reteach

- Refer students to MasterSport's balance sheet shown in Illustration 5-10, Chapter 5. Using information from this balance sheet, demonstrate how to calculate the three measures used to analyze short-term financial strength and the three measures used to analyze long-term financial strength. Call on students for the formulas and amounts needed for the calculations.
- Assign Recycling Problem 17-R, Instructions 5 (c) and (d) and 6.

Extend

- Assign Challenge Problem 17-C.
- Assign the Spreadsheet Template for Mastery Problem 17-M.

CLOSURE

Use Audit Your Understanding questions.

ASSESS

- Administer Problem Test Chapter 17.
- Administer a MicroExam test for Chapter 17.
- Administer Objective Test No. 6.

APPLIED SKILLS: WORD PROCESSING

If you wish to integrate word processing into your accounting course, you may direct students to answer the end-of-chapter Accounting Terms, Questions for Individual Study, and Cases for Critical Thinking using their word processing software.

FYI

The Dow Jones Industrial Average is often used to determine the health of the stock market. This average measures the stock prices of 30 large corporations.

Hamilton's ratio, *50.9%*, indicates that for each $1.00 of assets owned by the company, 50.9 cents worth was acquired with stockholders' capital.

The following equity ratios are calculated for the current and prior years.

	Current Year	Prior Year
Total Stockholders' Equity	$1,051,600.00	$ 849,300.00
Total Assets	2,067,700.00	1,759,700.00
Equity Ratio	50.9%	48.3%

The average equity ratio for companies similar to Hamilton is 57.0%. Hamilton's ratios are below the industry average, an unfavorable condition. A review of two ratios, debt ratio and equity ratio, shows the mix of capital provided by borrowing and capital provided by stockholders. These ratios for Hamilton are shown below.

	Current Year	Prior Year
Debt Ratio	49.1%	51.7%
Equity Ratio	50.9%	48.3%
Totals	100.0%	100.0%

The sum of the two ratios equals 100%. This fact is always true because the total liabilities and stockholders' equity represent the source of all asset ownership. However, the relationship between the two ratios at Hamilton is changing. In the current year, a higher percentage of ownership comes from stockholders' equity. Hamilton's prior year stockholders' equity had declined to a level the company considered unfavorable. The company took action to increase the percentage of ownership provided by stockholders' equity by issuing more capital stock. Hamilton could also increase the equity ratio by paying some of its liabilities. However, Hamilton is expanding and needs the additional capital. Additional capital stock has been issued to help regain a favorable balance of stockholders' equity and liabilities.

Equity Per Share

The amount of total stockholders' equity belonging to a single share of stock is known as equity per share. Equity per share is also referred to as book value per share.

From information on the comparative stockholders' equity statement, Illustration 17-5, Hamilton's equity per share for the current year is calculated as shown below.

Total Stockholders' Equity	÷	Shares of Capital Stock Outstanding	=	Equity Per Share
$1,051,600.00	÷	60,000	=	$17.53

FYI

Typical ratios for various industries can be quickly obtained by using industry data bases.

Hamilton's equity per share, *$17.53*, indicates that on December 31 of the current year, each share of capital stock represents ownership in $17.53 of the assets.

The following equity per share amounts are calculated for the current and prior years.

	Current Year	Prior Year
Total Stockholders' Equity	$1,051,600.00	$849,300.00
Shares of Capital Stock Outstanding	60,000	50,000
Equity Per Share	$17.53	$16.99

Equity per share provides more meaningful information for individual stockholders. With this additional information, a stockholder knows how much ownership of a company each share represents. For example, a stockholder of Hamilton knows that each share of stock represents $17.53 ownership of the total company assets. Also, this ownership has increased from $16.99 per share in the prior year, a favorable trend.

Audit Your Understanding

1. What are two sources from which a business gets capital?
2. What is the formula for working capital?
3. What is the formula for acid-test ratio?
4. Why does a well-managed company monitor its long-term financial strength?
5. What is the formula for calculating debt ratio?
6. What is the formula for calculating equity per share?

AUDIT YOUR UNDERSTANDING

1. (1) Owners' investments and retained earnings. (2) Loans.
2. Total current assets minus total current liabilities equals working capital.
3. Total quick assets divided by total current liabilities equals acid-test ratio.
4. To insure that a reasonable balance between stockholders' capital and borrowed capital is maintained.
5. Total liabilities divided by total assets equals debt ratio.
6. Total stockholders' equity divided by shares of capital stock outstanding equals equity per share.

ACCOUNTING TERMS

EPT(a)

What is the meaning of each of the following?

1. ratio
2. working capital
3. current ratio
4. quick assets
5. acid-test ratio
6. debt ratio
7. equity ratio

QUESTIONS FOR INDIVIDUAL STUDY

EPT(b)

1. Why do managers, banks, lending agencies, and owners and potential owners need financial information of a business?
2. What questions should be answered to effectively analyze financial information?
3. What are four common objectives for analyzing a business' financial information?
4. Which accounting concept is being applied when comparative financial statements are prepared to provide useful information for statement users?
5. What three types of comparisons are commonly used to analyze financial statements?
6. How can trends in financial condition and operating results of a business be determined?
7. How is the percentage increase or decrease in net sales calculated?
8. Which comparative analysis should be used to determine whether cost of merchandise sold is too high a percentage of net sales compared with other years?
9. What are five ratios that can be used to analyze earnings performance of a business?
10. What does a rate earned on average total assets show?
11. How should a company determine an acceptable rate earned on total assets?
12. What does a rate earned on average stockholders' equity show?
13. What determines the market price of a share of stock?
14. How does efficient management of accounts receivable and merchandise inventory contribute to a business' profitability?
15. What are two ratios that can be used to analyze the efficiency of a business?
16. What factors determine the optimum merchandise inventory turnover ratio for a business?
17. What three measures can be used to analyze short-term financial strength?
18. What is the major difference between current assets and quick assets?
19. What three measures can be used to analyze long-term financial strength?
20. What is the relationship between the two ratios: debt ratio and equity ratio?

CASES FOR CRITICAL THINKING

EPT(b)

CASE 1 Sheppard Corporation has had declining net income the past four years. The company president employs you as a consultant to review the company's operations in an effort to identify the reason for the decline. As part of your analysis, you make a component percentage analysis of the company's four most recent income statements. A part of that analysis is shown below. What are the implications from the information? What are the problems or potential problems evident from this analysis? What are your suggestions to the company?

	19X4	19X3	19X2	19X1
Cost of Merchandise Sold	62.1%	58.4%	55.2%	52.5%
Total Selling Expenses	12.1%	14.6%	15.7%	18.9%

CASE 2 Joyce Devine has received year-end information from her accountant, including financial statements. Among the information is a report that the accounts receivable turnover ratio in the prior year was 8.7 and for the current year is 6.2. Ms. Devine is overjoyed at the trend of the accounts receivable turnover ratio. Do you agree with Devine's interpretation? Explain your answer.

ACCOUNTING TERMS

1. **ratio:** A comparison between two numbers showing how many times one number exceeds the other. (p. 464)
2. **working capital:** The amount of total current assets less total current liabilities. (p. 480)
3. **current ratio:** A ratio that shows the numeric relationship of current assets to current liabilities. (p. 481)
4. **quick assets:** Those current assets that are cash or that can be quickly turned into cash. (p. 481)
5. **acid-test ratio:** A ratio that shows the numeric relationship of quick assets to current liabilities. (p. 482)
6. **debt ratio:** The ratio found by dividing total liabilities by total assets. (p. 483)
7. **equity ratio:** The ratio found by dividing stockholders' equity by total assets. (p. 483)

QUESTIONS FOR INDIVIDUAL STUDY

1. Managers use financial information to identify areas for improving profitability. Banks and lending agencies use the information to decide whether to loan money to a business. Owners and potential owners use the information to decide whether to buy, sell, or keep their investment. (p. 463)
2. (a) What are the objectives for making the analysis? (b) What sources of information are needed to make the analysis? (c) What kind of analysis is to be made? (d) What level of performance is acceptable? (p. 463)
3. Determine (a) profitability, (b) efficiency, (c) short-term financial strength, and (d) long-term financial strength. (p. 463)
4. Consistent Reporting concept. (p. 463)
5. (a) Ratio analysis, (b) trend analysis, and (c) component percentage analysis. (p. 464)
6. Information for several fiscal periods must be compared to determine whether a business is making satisfactory progress. (p. 464)
7. Current year net sales less prior year net sales divided by prior year net sales. (p. 465)
8. Component percentage analysis. (p. 467)
9. (a) Rate earned on average total assets, (b) rate earned on average stockholders' equity, (c) rate earned on net sales, (d) earnings per share, and (e) price-earnings ratio. (p. 471)
10. How well a business is using its assets to earn net income. (p. 471)
11. By reviewing the company's prior year's results and comparing rates of return on alternative investments. (p. 472)
12. How much net income stockholders' investment is earning. (p. 472)
13. The amount investors are willing to pay for the stock. (p. 476)
14. The quicker a business can convert accounts receivable and merchandise inventory to cash and begin another operating cycle, the more efficient and profitable the business is. (p. 476)
15. (a) Accounts receivable turnover ratio and (b) merchandise inventory turnover ratio. (p. 476)
16. (a) Amount of sales and (b) number of days needed to replenish inventory. (p. 479)
17. (a) Working capital, (b) current ratio, and (c) acid-test ratio. (p. 480)

APPLICATION PROBLEMS EPT(c,d,e,f)

PROBLEM 17-1 Analyzing comparative financial statements using trend analysis

SPREADSHEET

MATHEMATICS

The comparative financial statements for Mallette Corporation are in the working papers which accompany this textbook. The financial statements have been completed up to the trend analysis section.

The following information is taken from the financial records of Mallette for the two fiscal years ended December 31.

	Current Year	Prior Year
Accounts receivable (book value), January 1	$ 76,820.00	$ 69,450.00
Total assets, January 1	670,670.00	544,200.00
Market price per share of stock, December 31	23.50	16.50

INSTRUCTIONS:

1. Complete the following comparative financial statements using trend analysis. Round percentage calculations to the nearest 0.1%.
   a. Comparative income statement
   b. Comparative stockholders' equity statement
   c. Comparative balance sheet
2. Use the financial statements' trend analysis to determine if the trend from the prior to current year for each of the following items appears to be favorable or unfavorable. Give reasons for these trends.
   a. Net sales
   b. Net income
   c. Total stockholders' equity
   d. Total assets

The comparative financial statements prepared in Problem 17-1 are needed to complete Problems 17-3, 17-4, 17-5, and 17-6.

PROBLEM 17-2 Analyzing comparative financial statements using component percentage analysis

SPREADSHEET

MATHEMATICS

The comparative financial statements for Mallette Corporation are in the working papers which accompany this textbook. The financial statements have been completed up to the comparative analysis section.

INSTRUCTIONS:

1. Complete the following comparative financial statements using component percentage analysis. Round percentage calculations to the nearest 0.1%.
   a. Comparative income statement
   b. Comparative stockholders' equity statement
   c. Comparative balance sheet
2. Use the financial statements' component percentage analysis to determine if the current year's results for the following items, compared with the prior year, appear to be favorable or unfavorable. Give reasons for your responses.
   a. As a percentage of net sales:
      (1) Cost of merchandise sold
      (2) Gross profit on operations
      (3) Total operating expenses
      (4) Net income after federal income tax
   b. As a percentage of total stockholders' equity:
      (1) Retained earnings
      (2) Capital stock

QUESTIONS (cont'd)

18. Quick assets do not include merchandise inventory or prepaid expenses. Merchandise inventory first has to be sold and then accounts receivable have to be collected before cash is available. Prepaid expenses will seldom be converted into cash. (pp. 481–482)

19. (a) Debt ratio, (b) equity ratio, and (c) equity per share. (p. 483)

20. The sum of the two ratios always equals 100% because the two provide the source of all asset ownership. If one ratio decreases, the other ratio will increase by the same percentage. (p. 484)

CASES FOR CRITICAL THINKING

Case 1 Two trends are evident that can hurt the company's profits. First, cost of merchandise sold has been steadily rising. This means the cost of merchandise has been going up but the company has not been increasing its selling prices to match the increased costs. Second, selling expenses have been steadily declining which is desirable. The cost of merchandise has been increasing more rapidly than the total expenses have been decreasing. Well-managed companies always try to reduce expenses to a minimum level that will accomplish the necessary activities. However, if selling expenses are cut too much, the company may actually be reducing essential selling activities that will eventually cause sales to decline. Recommend the company review its pricing policy as well as essential costs and expenses. If costs are reasonable, selling prices must be increased if the company is to continue making a profit.

CHECK FIGURES

See Teacher's Edition of the Working Papers for complete solutions.

Problem 17-1 (2) (a) 13.9% Fav. (b) 56.0% Fav. (c) 30.7% Fav. (d) 19.1% Fav.

Problem 17-2 (2a) (1) 70.0%, 75.9% Fav. (2) 30.0%, 24.1% Fav. (3) 12.4%, 11.9% Unfav. (4) 11.3%, 8.2% Fav. (2b) (1) 45.3%, 42.9% Fav. (2) 54.7%, 57.1% Fav. (2c) (1) 68.3%, 66.5% Fav. (2) 32.7%, 32.9% Fav.

CASES (cont'd)

Case 2 Devine's interpretation of the accounts receivable turnover ratio trend is incorrect. The trend is unfavorable, not favorable. The ratio indicates the number of times the average accounts receivable balance has been collected during the year. If the accounts receivable are collected 8.7 times per year, they are collected more often than if collected only 6.2 times in a year.

The turnover ratio can be converted to number of days' sales in accounts receivable by dividing 365 (days in a year) by the accounts receivable turnover ratio. This calculation provides the following information.

	Current Year	Prior Year
Days in Year	365	365
Accounts Receivable Turnover Ratio	6.2 times	8.7 times
Number of Days for Payment	59 days	42 days

These results show that Devine's company had an average of 42 days from date of sale to date of collection for the average account receivable during the prior year. The amount increased to 59 days in the current year. An efficient business wants to collect accounts receivable as quickly as possible. Thus the trend is unfavorable.

c. As a percentage of total assets or total liabilities and stockholders' equity:
(1) Current assets
(2) Current liabilities

PROBLEM 17-3 Analyzing earnings performance from comparative financial statements

The comparative statements prepared in Problem 17-1 are needed to complete this problem.

MATHEMATICS

INSTRUCTIONS:

1. Based on Mallette's comparative financial statements prepared in Problem 17-1 and the information given in the text for Problem 17-1, calculate the following for each year.
   a. Rate earned on average total assets
   b. Rate earned on average stockholders' equity
   c. Rate earned on net sales
   d. Earnings per share
   e. Price-earnings ratio
2. For each analysis, indicate if there appears to be a favorable or an unfavorable trend from the prior to current year. Give reasons for these trends.

PROBLEM 17-4 Analyzing efficiency from comparative financial statements

The comparative statements prepared in Problem 17-1 are needed to complete this problem.

MATHEMATICS

INSTRUCTIONS:

1. Based on Mallette's comparative financial statements prepared in Problem 17-1 and the information given in the text for Problem 17-1, calculate the following for each year. All of Mallette's sales are on account.
   a. Accounts receivable turnover ratio
   b. Average number of days for payment
   c. Merchandise inventory turnover ratio
   d. Average number of days' sales in merchandise inventory
2. For each analysis, indicate if there appears to be a favorable or an unfavorable trend from prior to current year. Give reasons for these trends.

PROBLEM 17-5 Analyzing short-term financial strength from a comparative balance sheet

The comparative balance sheet prepared in Problem 17-1 is needed to complete this problem.

MATHEMATICS

INSTRUCTIONS:

1. Based on Mallette's comparative balance sheet prepared in Problem 17-1, calculate the following for each year.
   a. Working capital
   b. Current ratio
   c. Acid-test ratio
2. For each analysis, indicate if there appears to be a favorable or an unfavorable trend from the prior to current year. Give reasons for these trends.

PROBLEM 17-6 Analyzing long-term financial strength from a comparative balance sheet

The comparative balance sheet prepared in Problem 17-1 is needed to complete this problem.

MATHEMATICS

INSTRUCTIONS:

1. Based on Mallette's comparative balance sheet prepared in Problem 17-1, calculate the following for each year.
   a. Debt ratio

488

   b. Equity ratio
   c. Equity per share
2. For each analysis, indicate if there appears to be a favorable or an unfavorable trend from the prior to current year. Give reasons for these trends.

ENRICHMENT PROBLEMS — EPT(c,d,e,f)

MASTERY PROBLEM 17-M Analyzing comparative financial statements

The comparative financial statements for Lancaster, Inc. are in the working papers which accompany this textbook. The financial statements have been completed up to the financial analysis section.

SPREADSHEET

The following information is taken from the financial records of Lancaster for two fiscal years ended December 31.

	Current Year	Prior Year
Accounts receivable (book value), January 1	$242,890.00	$236,580.00
Merchandise inventory, January 1	172,890.00	53,760.00
Total assets, January 1	762,860.00	693,200.00
Stockholders' equity, January 1	413,160.00	306,780.00
Shares of capital stock outstanding	48,000	40,000
Market price per share of stock, December 31	42.50	30.00

INSTRUCTIONS:

1. Complete the following comparative financial statements using trend analysis. Round percentage calculations to the nearest 0.1%.
   a. Comparative income statement
   b. Comparative stockholders' equity statement
   c. Comparative balance sheet
2. Use the financial statements' trend analysis to determine if the trend from the prior to current year for each of the following items appears to be favorable or unfavorable. Give reasons for these trends.
   a. Net sales
   b. Net income
   c. Total stockholders' equity
   d. Total assets
3. Complete the comparative income statement using component percentage analysis. Round percentage calculations to the nearest 0.1%.
4. Record from the statement prepared in Instruction 3 or calculate the component percentages for each of the following. Determine if the current year's results, compared with the prior year, appear to be favorable or unfavorable. Give reasons for your responses.
   a. As a percentage of net sales:
      (1) Cost of merchandise sold
      (2) Gross profit on operations
      (3) Total operating expenses
      (4) Net income after federal income tax
   b. As a percentage of total stockholders' equity:
      (1) Retained earnings
      (2) Capital stock
   c. As a percentage of total assets or total liabilities and stockholders' equity:
      (1) Current assets
      (2) Current liabilities

CHECK FIGURES *(cont'd)*

Problem 17-3 (1) (a) 16.0%, 12.4% Fav. (b) 29.1%, 22.6% Fav. (c) 11.3%, 8.2% Fav. (d) $2.35, $1.88 Fav. (e) 10.0, 8.8 Fav.

Problem 17-4 (1) (a) 13.4, 12.5 Fav. (b) 27, 29 Fav. (c) 2.7, 4.0 Unfav. (d) 135, 91 Unfav.

Problem 17-5 (1) (a) $284,380, $225,670 Fav. (b) 2.1, 2.0 Fav. (c) 0.8, 1.0 Unfav.

Problem 17-6 (1) (a) 42.8%, 47.8% Fav. (b) 57.2%, 52.2% Fav. (c) $9.15, $8.75 Fav.

Mastery Problem 17-M (2) (a) 32.0% Fav. (b) 76.2% Fav. (c) 44.2% Fav. (d) 18.5% Fav. (4a) (1) 59.8%, 63.3% Fav. (2) 40.2%, 36.7% Fav. (3) 25.4%, 25.8% Fav. (4) 9.1%, 6.8% Fav. (4b) (1) 55.4%, 46.4% Fav. (2) 44.6%, 53.6% Fav. (4c) (1) 53.3%, 59.9% Unfav. (2) 21.1%, 32.7% Fav. (5a) (1) 22.5%, 14.6% Fav. (2) 41.1%, 31.3% Fav. (3) 9.1%, 6.8% Fav. (4) $3.90, $2.66 Fav. (5) 10.9, 11.3 Unfav. (5b) (1) 9.3, 6.5 Fav. (2) 6.7, 8.7 Unfav. (5c) (1) $291,060, $207,160 Fav. (2) 2.5, 1.8 Fav. (3) 1.4, 1.1 Fav. (5d) (1) 40.5%, 51.1% Fav. (2) 59.5%, 48.9% Fav. (3) $11.21, $9.33 Fav.

5. Based on Lancaster's comparative financial statements, calculate the following ratios for each year.
   a. Profitability ratios:
      (1) Rate earned on average total assets
      (2) Rate earned on average stockholders' equity
      (3) Rate earned on net sales
      (4) Earnings per share
      (5) Price-earnings ratio
   b. Efficiency ratios:
      (1) Accounts receivable turnover ratio
      (2) Merchandise inventory turnover ratio
   c. Short-term financial strength ratios:
      (1) Working capital
      (2) Current ratio
      (3) Acid-test ratio
   d. Long-term financial strength ratios:
      (1) Debt ratio
      (2) Equity ratio
      (3) Equity per share
6. For each of the items in Instruction 5, indicate if there appears to be a favorable or an unfavorable trend from the prior to current year. Give reasons for these trends.

CHALLENGE PROBLEM 17-C Analyzing comparative financial statements

CHECK FIGURES *(cont'd)*

Challenge Problem 17-C

(2) (a) −16.0% Unfav. (b) −61.4% Unfav. (c) −4.6% Unfav. (d) −6.5% Unfav. (4a) (1) 70.9%, 66.5% Unfav. (2) 29.1%, 33.5% Unfav. (3) 24.1%, 25.7% Fav. (4) 2.2%, 4.8% Unfav. (4b) (1) 10.2%, 14.4% Unfav. (2) 89.8%, 85.6% Unfav. (4c) (1) 65.9%, 66.8% Unfav. (2) 26.8%, 28.6% Fav. (5a) (1) 3.0%, 7.3% Unfav. (2) 6.2%, 16.2% Unfav. (3) 2.2%, 4.8% Unfav. (4) $1.42, $3.69 Unfav. (5) 5.3, 8.0 Unfav. (5b) (1) 13.3, 13.2 Fav. (2) 2.8, 3.3 Unfav. (5c) (1) $357,780, $373,360 Unfav. (2) 2.5, 2.3 Fav. (3) 0.5, 0.7 Unfav. (5d) (1) 51.4%, 52.3% Fav. (2) 48.6%, 47.7% Fav. (3) $22.27, 23.35 Unfav.

The comparative financial statements for Fondren Corporation are in the working papers which accompany this textbook. The financial statements have been completed up to the financial analysis section.

The following information is taken from the financial records of Fondren for two fiscal years ended December 31.

	Current Year	Prior Year
Accounts receivable (book value), January 1	$105,500.00	$ 126,400.00
Total assets, January 1	979,660.00	1,052,400.00
Market price per share of stock, December 31	7.50	29.50

INSTRUCTIONS:

1. Prepare the following comparative financial statements using trend analysis. Round percentage calculations to the nearest 0.1%.
   a. Comparative income statement
   b. Comparative stockholders' equity statement
   c. Comparative balance sheet
2. Use the financial statements' trend analysis to determine if the trend from the prior to current year for each of the following items appears to be favorable or unfavorable. Give reasons for these trends.
   a. Net sales
   b. Net income
   c. Total stockholders' equity
   d. Total assets
3. Complete the comparative income statement using component percentage analysis. Round percentage calculations to the nearest 0.1%.
4. Record from the statement prepared in Instruction 3 or calculate the component percentages for each of the following. Determine if the current year's results, compared with the prior year, appear to be favorable or unfavorable. Give reasons for your responses.

a. As a percentage of net sales:
   (1) Cost of merchandise sold
   (2) Gross profit on operations
   (3) Total operating expenses
   (4) Net income after federal income tax
b. As a percentage of total stockholders' equity:
   (1) Retained earnings
   (2) Capital stock
c. As a percentage of total assets or total liabilities and stockholders' equity:
   (1) Current assets
   (2) Current liabilities

5. Based on Fondren's comparative financial statements, calculate the following ratios for each year.
   a. Profitability ratios:
      (1) Rate earned on average total assets
      (2) Rate earned on average stockholders' equity
      (3) Rate earned on net sales
      (4) Earnings per share
      (5) Price-earnings ratio
   b. Efficiency ratios:
      (1) Accounts receivable turnover ratio
      (2) Merchandise inventory turnover ratio
   c. Short-term financial strength ratios:
      (1) Working capital
      (2) Current ratio
      (3) Acid-test ratio
   d. Long-term financial strength ratios:
      (1) Debt ratio
      (2) Equity ratio
      (3) Equity per share
6. For each of the items in Instruction 5, indicate if there appears to be a favorable or an unfavorable trend from the prior to current year. Give reasons for these trends.

491

PART 7 OVERVIEW

STUDENT EDITION

STUDENT FEATURES

Professional Business Ethics

Legislate Competition Away, page 506

Careers in Accounting

Cost Accountant, page 516

Spreadsheet Options

Using the Numerical Format Option, page 544

Multicultural Awareness

Women Business Owners, page 497

Global Perspective

International Travel, page 523

Personal Visions in Business

Glenn D. Southard, page 542

Audit Your Understanding

This student activity can be found on pages 498, 504, 509, 519, 528, 545, 552

APPLIED SKILLS

Applied Communications

Page 554

Applied Mathematics

Pages 504, 506, 512, 525–527, 530–532

SOFTWARE APPLICATIONS

Automated Accounting 6.0 Problem 18-2, 18-M
Spreadsheet Template Problems 18-M, 19-1, 20-3

TEACHER'S EDITION

APPLIED SKILLS

Communications, page 554
Language Arts, pages 508, 527, 544
Writing Across the Curriculum, pages 502, 520, 539
Building Study Skills, page 526
Word Processing, pages 506, 522, 542

TEACHING STRATEGIES

Accounting Pedagogy, pages 494, 495, 514, 515, 534
Assessment by Portfolio, pages 551, 558
Different Learning Abilities, pages 507, 521, 538
Different Learning Styles, pages 535, 537, 540, 541, 543
Cooperative Learning, pages 497, 527, 546, 559
Expanding Beyond the Classroom, pages 503, 517, 547
Applying Visuals, pages 500, 519, 536
Teaching Tip, pages 494, 496, 498, 499, 501, 505, 514, 518, 519, 525, 528, 536, 540, 541, 550
Software Focus, pages 495, 515, 534
Simulation, page 551
Milestone, page 550
Reinforcement Activity, pages 551, 558

ASSESSMENT

Assessment by Portfolio
MicroExam software for each chapter
Problem Test for each chapter
Objective Test 7

SOFTWARE

Automated Accounting 6.0
MicroExam
Lotus (spreadsheet)
Ventura Publisher (desktop publishing software)
WordPerfect (word processing)
Windows (operating system)

BIBLIOGRAPHY

Johnson, D., and R. Johnson. *Cooperation and Competition.* Hillsdale, NJ: Lawrence Eribaum, 1987.

National Society of Public Accountants. *Portfolio of Accounting Systems for Small and Medium-Sized Businesses.* Revised. Englewood Cliffs, NJ: Prentice Hall, 1977.

Sarkees, Michelle Donnelly, and John L. Scott. *Vocation Special Needs,* Second Edition. American Technical Publishers, 1986.

U.S. Department of Labor. *Occupational Outlook Handbook.*

Weirich, Thomas R., and Alan Reinstein. *Accounting and Auditing Research: A Practical Guide.* Third Edition. Cincinnati: South-Western Publishing Co., 1992.

Periodicals

Accounting News, Warren, Gorham & Lamont, New York, NY.

Journal of Business Ethics, Kluwer Academic Publishers, Norwell, CA.

Technology

AICPA. *Serving America: A Tradition of Excellence,* 1986. (Video)

Dun & Bradstreet Information Services. *Dun's Direct Access* (On-line database of U.S. companies)

PART 7 OPENER

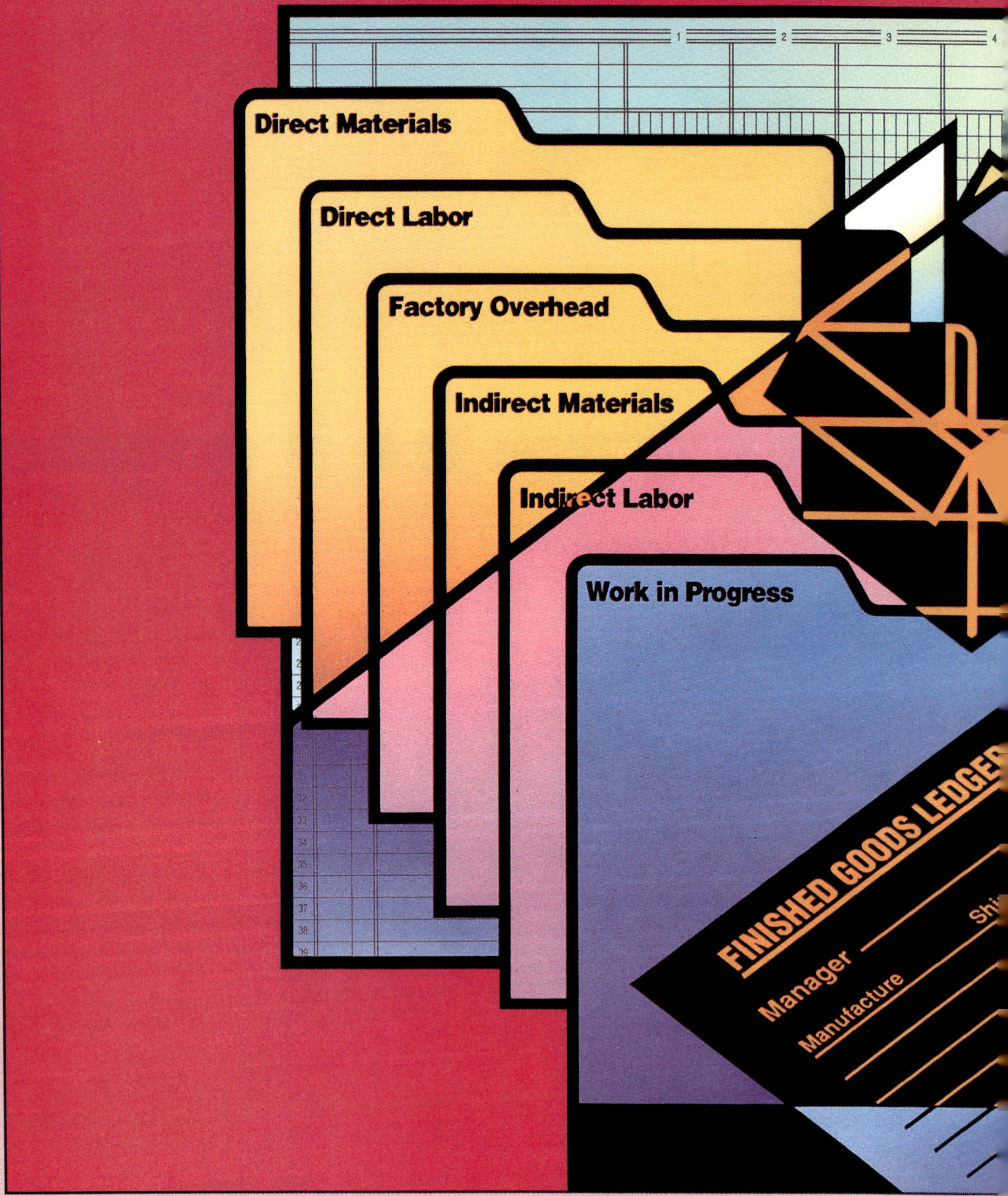

PART 7

Cost Accounting

GENERAL GOALS

1. Know accounting terminology related to cost accounting.
2. Understand accounting concepts and practices related to cost accounting.
3. Demonstrate cost accounting procedures.

OVERVIEW

Part 7 introduces cost accounting for both merchandising and manufacturing businesses.

Chapter 18 discusses the accurate, timely statements of revenue, costs, and expenses necessary for a merchandising business to be profitable. Responsibility accounting is discussed as well as the end-of-fiscal-period work that is necessary.

Chapter 19 then shows how a manufacturing business buys materials and, by using labor and machines, changes the form of the materials into a finished product. The elements of manufacturing costs are covered, as well as the other important topics that relate to manufacturing and controlling inventory.

Chapter 20 concludes with the accounting transactions and financial reporting for a manufacturing business.

Part 7 wraps up with an opportunity for students to apply what they have learned about cost accounting for a manufacturing business through completion of the simulation, Bombay Leather, Inc., and/or Reinforcement Activity 3.

CHAPTER 18 OVERVIEW

Chapter 18 describes how costs and cost controls are analyzed for a merchandising business with two selling departments. The chapter distinguishes between direct and indirect costs and describes the preparation of departmental margin statements which show the direct costs controlled by a department. The margin statements are analyzed to determine effective cost controls. The completion of a 12-column work sheet is illustrated and the usual end-of-fiscal-period preparation of financial statements and analysis are described.

The work sheet completed in Problem 18-2 is needed to complete Problems 18-3 and 18-4.

GUIDE TO ACHIEVING LEARNING OBJECTIVES

	TEACH	APPLY	EXTEND/ENRICH					
Enabling Performance Tasks	**Lesson Plans**	**Application Problems**	**Mastery Problems**	**Challenge Problems**	**Cases for Critical Thinking**	**Recycling Problems**	**Reinforcement Activity**	
a. Define accounting terms related to cost accounting for a departmentalized merchandising business.	18-1, 18-3							
b. Identify accounting concepts and practices related to cost accounting for a departmentalized merchandising business.	18-1, 18-2, 18-3				Cases 1, 2			
c. Journalize entries for direct and indirect expenses.	18-1	18-1						
d. Prepare selected end-of-fiscal-period work for a departmentalized merchandising business using departmental margins.	18-2, 18-3	18-2, 18-3, 18-4	18-M	18-C		18-R		

ENRICHMENT

SPECIAL FEATURES
Professional Business Ethics, page 506
Multicultural Awareness, page 497
TECHNOLOGY CONNECTION
Automated Accounting 6.0 Problems 18-2, 18-M
Spreadsheet Template Problem 18-M

NEW, REVIEW, AND EXTENSION

ACTIVITIES/CONCEPTS/TRANSACTIONS	NEW	REVIEW/ EXTENSION
Responsibility accounting	✓	
Recording direct and indirect costs		✓
Completing a 12-column work sheet with departmental margin columns		✓
Work sheet adjustments		✓
Departmental margin columns on a work sheet		✓
Preparing departmental margin statements		✓
Calculating component percentage for departmental margin		✓
Preparing an income statement with departmental margin amounts		✓

INFORMAL ASSESSMENT		FORMAL ASSESSMENT			
Study Guide	**Audit Your Understanding**	**Chapter MicroExam**	**Chapter Problem Test**	**Unit Objective Test**	**Portfolio**
Unit B	✓	✓		✓	
Units A, C	✓	✓		✓	
			✓		
			✓		

TEACHING MATERIALS

Teacher's Wraparound Edition of the Text
Teacher's Resource Guide
Teacher's Edition of Working Papers
MicroExam

APPLIED MATHEMATICS

APPLIED MATH/ACCOUNTING SKILL	APPLICATION
Calculating component percentages	Prob. 18-3

TEACHING STRATEGIES: ACCOUNTING PEDAGOGY

A chart of accounts for the business that is used to illustrate each part of this textbook is provided at the beginning of each part. Charts of accounts are extremely important to companies because they drive the accounting system. Employees usually cannot even receive reimbursement for expenses without knowing which account the expense should be charged to. Pedagogically, the chart of accounts provides the following information: (1) Classification for each account—needed to determine how a transaction is analyzed. (2) Permanent accounts (balance sheet accounts) and temporary accounts (income statement accounts)—assist in analyzing transactions and recording closing entries. (3) Account number for every general ledger account—critical information in automated accounting, since transactions are entered by account number rather than account title.

CHART OF ACCOUNTS

This chart of accounts is for a merchandising business organized as a corporation that uses cost accounting principles to determine and control costs. Because the business is also departmentalized, many accounts are divided into departments. In the Assets section, there is a merchandise inventory account for each department. In the stockholders' equity section, there is an income summary account for each department and also a general income summary account. The Operating Revenue and Cost of Merchandise accounts are all departmentalized.

The Direct Expenses section is divided to indicate the operating expenses that are identifiable with and chargeable to the operation of one of the two different departments. The Indirect Expenses section is used to account for expenses of the business that are chargeable to overall business operations but are not identifiable with a specific department.

AQUACRUISER, INC.

CHART OF ACCOUNTS

Balance Sheet Accounts

(1000) ASSETS

1100 Current Assets

1105 Cash
1110 Accounts Receivable
1115 Allowance for Uncollectible Accounts
1120 Merchandise Inventory—Accessories
1125 Merchandise Inventory—Boats
1130 Supplies
1135 Prepaid Insurance

1200 Plant Assets

1205 Delivery Equipment—Boats
1210 Accumulated Depreciation—Delivery Equipment, Boats
1215 Office Equipment
1220 Accumulated Depreciation—Office Equipment
1225 Store Equipment—Accessories
1230 Accumulated Depreciation—Store Equipment, Accessories
1235 Store Equipment—Boats
1240 Accumulated Depreciation—Store Equipment, Boats

(2000) LIABILITIES

2100 Current Liabilities

2105 Accounts Payable
2110 Employee Income Tax Payable
2115 Federal Income Tax Payable
2120 FICA Tax Payable
2125 Salaries Payable
2130 Sales Tax Payable
2135 Unemployment Tax Payable—Federal
2140 Unemployment Tax Payable—State
2145 Dividends Payable

(3000) STOCKHOLDERS' EQUITY

3105 Capital Stock
3110 Retained Earnings
3115 Dividends
3120 Income Summary—Accessories
3125 Income Summary—Boats
3130 Income Summary—General

Income Statement Accounts

(4000) OPERATING REVENUE

4105 Sales—Accessories
4110 Sales Discount—Accessories
4115 Sales Returns and Allowances—Accessories
4120 Sales—Boats
4125 Sales Discount—Boats
4130 Sales Returns and Allowances—Boats

(5000) COST OF MERCHANDISE

5105 Purchases—Accessories
5110 Purchases Discount—Accessories
5115 Purchases Returns and Allowances—Accessories
5120 Purchases—Boats
5125 Purchases Discount—Boats
5130 Purchases Returns and Allowances—Boats

(6000) DIRECT EXPENSES

6100 Direct Expenses—Accessories

6105 Advertising Expense—Accessories
6110 Depreciation Expense—Store Equipment, Accessories
6115 Insurance Expense—Accessories
6120 Payroll Taxes Expense—Accessories
6125 Salary Expense—Accessories
6130 Supplies Expense—Accessories

6200 Direct Expenses—Boats

6205 Advertising Expense—Boats
6210 Delivery Expense—Boats
6215 Depreciation Expense—Delivery Equipment, Boats
6220 Depreciation Expense—Store Equipment, Boats
6225 Insurance Expense—Boats
6230 Payroll Taxes Expense—Boats
6235 Salary Expense—Boats
6240 Supplies Expense—Boats
6245 Uncollectible Accounts Expense—Boats

(7000) INDIRECT EXPENSES

7105 Credit Card Fee Expense
7110 Depreciation Expense—Office Equipment
7115 Insurance Expense—Administrative
7120 Miscellaneous Expense
7125 Payroll Taxes Expense—Administrative
7130 Rent Expense
7135 Salary Expense—Administrative
7140 Supplies Expense—Administrative
7145 Utilities Expense

(8000) INCOME TAX

8105 Federal Income Tax Expense

The chart of accounts for AquaCruiser, Inc. is illustrated above for ready reference as you study Chapter 18 of this textbook.

TEACHING STRATEGIES: TEACHING TIP

Emphasize that students should refer to this chart of accounts throughout their study of Chapter 18 of Part 7. It will help them determine classification of accounts, which accounts are temporary and permanent accounts, and what account numbers to use for automated accounting. It will also be a useful reference for performing file maintenance activities.

18

Cost Accounting for a Merchandising Business

TEACHING STRATEGIES: ACCOUNTING PEDAGOGY

This textbook presents cost accounting for a merchandising business so that students understand the importance of a business needing accurate, timely statements of revenue, costs, and expenses to operate a profitable business.

ENABLING PERFORMANCE TASKS

After studying Chapter 18, you will be able to:

a Define accounting terms related to cost accounting for a departmentalized merchandising business.

b Identify accounting concepts and practices related to cost accounting for a departmentalized merchandising business.

c Journalize entries for direct and indirect expenses.

d Prepare selected end-of-fiscal-period work for a departmentalized merchandising business using departmental margins.

TERMS PREVIEW

responsibility accounting • direct expense • indirect expense • departmental margin • departmental margin statement • responsibility statements

SOFTWARE FOCUS

Software may be used for independent practice or enrichment/extension as the instructor deems appropriate. For this chapter, the following software may be used: *Automated Accounting 6.0* or higher with Problem 18-2 and Mastery Problem 18-M; Spreadsheet Template with Mastery Problem 18-M.

Businesses make many different products available to meet the many needs of consumers. To meet these needs efficiently, businesses normally specialize in a part of the total process necessary to make and deliver these products to consumers. Manufacturing businesses make the products. Each manufacturing business normally concentrates on making only a few similar types of products. Merchandising businesses purchase and display products from many different manufacturers to provide consumers a selection of products in one location. Regardless of the type of business, a company needs accurate, timely statements of revenue, costs, and expenses to operate a profitable business. *(CONCEPT: Adequate Disclosure)*

RESPONSIBILITY ACCOUNTING FOR A MERCHANDISING BUSINESS

Controlling costs is essential to a business' success. However, who should control a business' costs? Good management practices require that each manager is responsible for controlling all costs incurred by the manager's business unit. Assigning control of business revenues, costs, and expenses as a responsibility of a specific manager is called **responsibility accounting.**

Merchandising businesses with effective cost controls generally use some kind of responsibility accounting. A successful responsibility accounting system has two important features.

1. Each manager is assigned responsibility for only those revenues, costs, and expenses for which the manager can make decisions and affect the outcome.
2. The revenues, costs, and expenses for which a manager is responsible must be readily identifiable with the manager's unit. For example, if a manager is responsible for supplies expense, that manager should make decisions about the use of supplies. Also, a separate record should be kept for the manager's supplies expense. Thus, responsibility accounting traces revenues, costs, and expenses to the individual managers who are responsible for making decisions about those revenues, costs, and expenses. *(CONCEPT: Adequate Disclosure)*

FYI

The typical income statement is not as useful to a department manager as statements that show departmental costs broken down by department.

A typical merchandising business income statement reports net income earned during a fiscal period. *(CONCEPT: Accounting Period Cycle)* However, an income statement usually does not report specific information which a department manager can use to control departmental costs. Therefore, merchandising businesses often prepare departmental statements to show each department's contribution to the net income earned by the business.

In responsibility accounting, operating expenses are classified as either direct or indirect expenses. An operating expense identifiable with and chargeable to the operation of a specific department is

LESSON PLAN 18-1

Materials

- Student pages 496–498
- 3-Step Checklist for Making Ethical Decisions (TRG)

Objectives (Enabling Performance Tasks)

a. Define accounting terms related to cost accounting for a departmentalized merchandising business.

b. Identify accounting concepts and practices related to cost accounting for a departmentalized merchandising business.

c. Journalize entries for direct and indirect expenses.

FOCUS

- Chapters 2–5 presented the accounting cycle for a departmentalized merchandising business. Explain that Chapter 18 covers the accounting procedures used to determine and control costs for a departmentalized merchandising business. In this lesson, the use of responsibility accounting to help control costs and expenses will be presented. The recording of revenue, cost, and expense transactions will be reviewed.
- Introduce vocabulary: responsibility accounting, direct expense, indirect expense, departmental margin, departmental margin statement.

TEACHING STRATEGIES: TEACHING TIP

Review the definition of cost accounting: The determination and control of costs of a business enterprise.

called a **direct expense.** The cost of supplies used by a specific department is an example of a direct expense. An operating expense chargeable to overall business operations and not identifiable with a specific department is called an **indirect expense.** The cost of electricity used by a business' overall operation is an example of an indirect expense.

The revenue earned by a department less its cost of merchandise sold and less its direct expenses is called **departmental margin.** A statement that reports departmental margin for a specific department is called a **departmental margin statement.**

AquaCruiser, Inc. uses responsibility accounting to help control costs and expenses. AquaCruiser has two merchandising departments: accessories and boats. Each department's revenue, cost of merchandise sold, and direct expenses are recorded in separate departmental general ledger accounts as shown in AquaCruiser's chart of accounts.

> Each business develops a chart of accounts that best accommodates its accounting transactions and financial statements. MasterSport, in Part 2, and AquaCruiser, in this chapter, are both departmentalized businesses. MasterSport, adds a *-1* and *-2* to the separate departmental accounts to permit sorting by departments. AquaCruiser prefers to group accounts by types of accounts, such as revenue, cost of merchandise, direct expenses, and indirect expenses. For example, Direct Expenses—Accessories are 6100 numbers. Direct Expenses—Boats are 6200 numbers. Each business develops a chart of accounts that best meets its needs.

REVENUE, COST, AND EXPENSE TRANSACTIONS FOR A DEPARTMENTALIZED MERCHANDISING BUSINESS

Procedures for recording revenue, cost, and expense transactions are similar for most merchandising businesses. Journalizing procedures used by MasterSport in Chapters 2 and 3 are similar to procedures used by AquaCruiser. AquaCruiser has separate accounts as does MasterSport for each department's merchandise inventory, sales, and purchases. MasterSport uses these departmental accounts to calculate and report gross profit for each department. In addition to these accounts, AquaCruiser has separate accounts in the general ledger for each department's direct expenses, such as advertising, salaries, and supplies. Separate departmental accounts for sales, merchandise inventory, purchases, and direct expenses provide information needed to prepare departmental margin statements.

A journal entry prepared by AquaCruiser to record a direct expense is shown in Illustration 18-1.

AquaCruiser's accessories department manager decided to buy the advertising services recorded in Illustration 18-1. The advertising promotes the department's sale of boat accessories. Since the

FYI

Indirect expenses are not reported in departmental margin statements.

MULTICULTURAL AWARENESS

Women Business Owners

Some organizations were formed to support the interest of professional women. Examples of these organizations are American Society of Women Accountants, National Association for Female Executives, and National Association of Women Business Owners.

Women are an important component of business ownership. By the end of 1992, women owned more than 6.5 million businesses in the United States, an increase of over 2.4 million businesses since 1987. Sales of the 50 largest businesses owned by women in the United States range from $60 million to $2.4 billion.

TEACH

Cover student pages 496–498 "Responsibility Accounting for a Merchandising Business" and "Revenue, Cost, and Expense Transactions for a Departmentalized Merchandising Business." Discuss the features of a responsibility accounting system. Emphasize the importance of managerial responsibilities. Explain direct and indirect expenses and list examples on the board. Explain how AquaCruiser's procedures for recording revenue, cost, and expense transactions are similar to those of MasterSport presented in Chapters 2 and 3. Point out the differences since AquaCruiser uses separate accounts for each department's direct expenses.

APPLY

Direct students to turn to the chart of accounts for MasterSport, in Part 2, and AquaCruiser, in Part 7. Compare the types of accounts and their numbers. Refer students to Illustrations 18-1 and 18-2 as journalizing direct and indirect expenses is discussed.

Guided Practice

Guide students through the T account analysis of the transactions in Problem 18-1. Have students draw T accounts on a sheet of paper and analyze the first transaction. All students should agree with the analysis before proceeding to the next transaction. Repeat the process until all transactions have been analyzed. The balance of Problem 18-1 can be completed as Independent Practice.

Independent Practice

Assign Terms 1–5, Questions 1–11, and Problem 18-1.

MULTICULTURAL AWARENESS

The MULTICULTURAL AWARENESS feature is intended to expose students to the concept that our society is composed of people from many different cultural backgrounds. These features show both past contributions of many cultures and benefits of a culturally diverse society. (1) Read the feature. (2) Discuss the specific information in the feature. (3) Clarify any terms or questions.

TEACHING STRATEGIES: COOPERATIVE LEARNING

Divide the class into groups of two or three students each. Have each group discuss and prepare a list of the direct and indirect expenses incurred in operating a household. Each group should appoint a leader who will present the list to the class. This cooperative learning activity should not take more than 15 to 20 minutes of class time.

ILLUSTRATION 18-1 Journal entry to record a direct expense

CASH PAYMENTS JOURNAL — PAGE 16

	DATE		ACCOUNT TITLE	CK. NO.	POST. REF.	1 GENERAL DEBIT	2 GENERAL CREDIT	3 ACCOUNTS PAYABLE DEBIT	4 PURCH. DISCOUNT CR. ACCESS.	5 PURCH. DISCOUNT CR. BOATS	6 CASH CREDIT	
1	19-- Apr.	1	Advertising Exp.—Access.	610		400 00					400 00	1

Audit Your Understanding

1. What two features are required for responsibility accounting to be successful?
2. What information is not reported by an income statement of a merchandising business?
3. What is a direct expense?
4. What is meant by the term "departmental margin"?
5. For what type of expenses does AquaCruiser have separate departmental accounts in the general ledger?

department manager controls the advertising expense and the department receives the benefits, the expense is classified as a direct expense. To insure that such expenses are recorded as direct expenses, the account title also includes the department's name, Advertising Expense—Accessories.

A journal entry prepared by AquaCruiser to record an indirect expense is shown in Illustration 18-2.

The accessories department uses a portion of the space rented by AquaCruiser. However, the decision to rent the specific facility was made by the company president, not the accessories department manager. Also, the rent expense is not separated by departments but is one payment for the entire facility used by all departments. Since this expense is not separated by departments, the expense is recorded as an indirect expense. Indirect expenses are reported in the company's income statement but not in departmental margin statements. Direct and indirect expenses are reported in the same way each fiscal period. *(CONCEPT: Consistent Reporting)*

ILLUSTRATION 18-2 Journal entry to record an indirect expense

CASH PAYMENTS JOURNAL — PAGE 16

	DATE		ACCOUNT TITLE	CK. NO.	POST. REF.	1 GENERAL DEBIT	2 GENERAL CREDIT	3 ACCOUNTS PAYABLE DEBIT	4 PURCH. DISCOUNT CR. ACCESS.	5 PURCH. DISCOUNT CR. BOATS	6 CASH CREDIT	
2		1	Rent Expense	611		6 000 00					6 000 00	2

END-OF-FISCAL-PERIOD WORK FOR A MERCHANDISING BUSINESS USING RESPONSIBILITY ACCOUNTING

AquaCruiser uses an expanded work sheet to help sort information needed for departmental margin statements. The 12-column work sheet prepared by AquaCruiser on April 30 is shown in Illustration 18-3, pages 500–501.

ASSESS

Assess student understanding by checking the solutions to the Independent Practice activities.

Reteach

Have students identify the direct and indirect expenses likely to be incurred by a local merchandising business. As students classify the expenses by logical departments, create the Direct Expenses and Indirect Expenses sections of a chart of accounts on the chalkboard or overhead projector.

Enrich

Discuss the PROFESSIONAL BUSINESS ETHICS feature on page 506. You may wish to distribute copies of the 3-Step Checklist for Making Ethical Decisions. A Blackline Master is furnished in the Blackline Masters Section of the Teacher's Resource Guide.

CLOSURE

Use Audit Your Understanding questions.

AUDIT YOUR UNDERSTANDING

The AUDIT YOUR UNDERSTANDING feature appears at the end of each section of the chapter. Explain to your students that the word *audit* means to check or verify. AUDIT YOUR UNDERSTANDING may be used to check student comprehension of the section just studied. The answers are provided in Appendix D in the back of the textbook.

1. (1) Each manager is assigned responsibility for those revenues, costs, and expenses for which the manager can make decisions and affect the outcome. (2) The revenues, costs, and expenses must be readily identifiable with the manager's unit.
2. The specific information a department manager can use to control departmental costs.
3. An operating expense identifiable with and chargeable to the operation of a specific department.
4. The revenue earned by a department less its cost of merchandise sold and less its direct expenses.
5. Direct expenses.

TEACHING STRATEGIES: TEACHING TIP

List examples of direct and indirect expenses on the chalkboard or overhead projector.

Eight amount columns on the work sheet are the same as described previously. Four additional columns are used by AquaCruiser: Departmental Margin Statement—Accessories Debit and Credit and Departmental Margin Statement—Boats Debit and Credit. Information in these four additional columns is used to prepare departmental margin statements.

Trial Balance on a Work Sheet

FYI

The trial balance will include an income summary account for each department.

A trial balance is prepared by AquaCruiser in the same way as previously described for other kinds of businesses. The trial balance prepared by AquaCruiser on April 30 is on the work sheet, Illustration 18-3. All general ledger accounts are listed whether they have balances or not. Three income summary accounts are used. Two are used for adjusting inventory accounts related to separate departments, Income Summary—Accessories and Income Summary—Boats. They are also used to close revenue, cost, and direct expense accounts of both departments. Income Summary—General is used for other closing entries.

AquaCruiser writes the account Federal Income Tax Expense on the work sheet two lines below Departmental Margin—Boats. This location simplifies subtotaling the income statement columns and calculating additional income tax expense. Procedures for calculating corporate income tax are described in Chapter 14.

Adjustments on a Work Sheet with Departmental Margins

The following information is needed for adjusting AquaCruiser's general ledger accounts for the month ended April 30 of the current year.

Adjustment Information, April 30

Uncollectible accounts expense—boats estimated as 1.0% of sales on account. Sales on account for year, $75,000.00.	
Merchandise inventory—accessories	$168,306.00
Merchandise inventory—boats	219,634.00
Supplies used—accessories	1,279.00
Supplies used—boats	1,121.00
Supplies used—administrative	922.00
Insurance expired—accessories	114.00
Insurance expired—boats	152.00
Insurance expired—administrative	28.00
Depreciation expense—delivery equipment, boats	570.00
Depreciation expense—office equipment	200.00
Depreciation expense—store equipment, accessories	506.00
Depreciation expense—store equipment, boats	125.00
Federal income tax expense for April	11,460.00

AquaCruiser's adjustments are in the work sheet's Adjustments columns, Illustration 18-3. The departmental merchandise inven-

LESSON PLAN 18-2

Materials

- Student pages 498–504
- Blackline Master for 12-Column Work Sheet (TRG)
- Software: *Automated Accounting 6.0* or higher; Accounting Textbook Template, Advanced Course

Objectives (Enabling Performance Tasks)

b. Identify accounting concepts and practices related to cost accounting for a departmentalized merchandising business.

d. Prepare selected end-of-fiscal-period work for a departmentalized merchandising business using departmental margins.

TEACHING STRATEGIES: TEACHING TIP

Have students compare the 12-column work sheet in Illustration 18-3 with the 8-column work sheet shown in Illustration 5-5, Chapter 5. Emphasize that the only major difference is the addition of separate columns to sort balances of departmental accounts.

TEACHING STRATEGIES: APPLYING VISUALS

Direct students to Illustration 18-3 to review preparation of the 12-column work sheet.

FOCUS

Preparation of an 8-column work sheet for a departmentalized merchandising business was presented in Chapter 5. Responsibility accounting was introduced earlier in this chapter. In this lesson, an expanded 12-column work sheet will be prepared to sort the information needed for the departmental margin statements used in responsibility accounting.

ILLUSTRATION 18-3 Work sheet with departmental margin statement columns

AquaCruiser, Inc.
Work Sheet
For Month Ended April 30, 19--

		1	2	3	4	5	6	7	8	9	10	11	12	
	ACCOUNT TITLE	TRIAL BALANCE		ADJUSTMENTS		DEPARTMENTAL MARGIN STATEMENTS				INCOME STATEMENT		BALANCE SHEET		
						ACCESSORIES		BOATS						
		DEBIT	CREDIT	DEBIT	CREDIT	DEBIT	CREDIT	DEBIT	CREDIT	DEBIT	CREDIT	DEBIT	CREDIT	
1	Cash	104315 00										104315 00		1
2	Accounts Receivable	68204 00										68204 00		2
3	Allow. for Uncoll. Accts.		134 00		(a) 750 00								884 00	3
4	Mdse. Inv.—Accessories	155838 00		(b) 12468 00								168306 00		4
5	Mdse. Inv.—Boats	203364 00		(c) 16270 00								219634 00		5
6	Supplies	6276 00			(d) 3322 00							2954 00		6
7	Prepaid Insurance	2350 00			(e) 294 00							2056 00		7
8	Delivery Equip.—Boats	33960 00										33960 00		8
9	Accum. Depr.—Del. Equip., Boats		10200 00		(f) 570 00								10770 00	9
10	Office Equipment	11990 00										11990 00		10
11	Accum. Depr.—Office Equipment		1800 00		(g) 200 00								2000 00	11
12	Store Equipment—Access.	30270 00										30270 00		12
13	Accum. Depr.—Store Equip., Access.		9080 00		(h) 506 00								9586 00	13
14	Store Equipment—Boats	7600 00										7600 00		14
15	Accum. Depr.—Store Equip., Boats		2280 00		(i) 125 00								2405 00	15
16	Accounts Payable		98510 00										98510 00	16
17	Employee Income Tax Payable		5390 00										5390 00	17
18	Federal Income Tax Payable				(j) 11460 00								11460 00	18
19	FICA Tax Payable		9600 00										9600 00	19
20	Salaries Payable													20
21	Sales Tax Payable		16880 00										16880 00	21
22	Unemploy. Tax Pay.—Federal		384 00										384 00	22
23	Unemploy. Tax Pay.—State		2592 00										2592 00	23
24	Dividends Payable													24
25	Capital Stock		300000 00										300000 00	25
26	Retained Earnings		186582 00										186582 00	26
27	Dividends	30000 00										30000 00		27
28	Income Summary—Access.				(b) 12468 00		12468 00							28
29	Income Summary—Boats				(c) 16270 00				16270 00					29
30	Income Summary—General													30
31	Sales—Accessories		131800 00				131800 00							31
32	Sales Discount—Accessories	440 00				440 00								32

33	Sales Ret. and Allow.—Access.	11000				11000								33
34	Sales—Boats		15151000						15151000					34
35	Sales Discount—Boats	75700						75700						35
36	Sales Ret. and Allow.—Boats	72500						72500						36
37	Purchases—Accessories	8831300				8831300								37
38	Purch. Discount—Accessories		44100				44100							38
39	Purch. Ret. and Allow.—Access.		39000				39000							39
40	Purchases—Boats	8976500						8976500						40
41	Purch. Discount—Boats		54000						54000					41
42	Purch. Ret. and Allow.—Boats		36300						36300					42
43	Advertising Exp.—Access.	165000				165000								43
44	Depr. Exp.—Store Equip., Access.			(h) 50600		50600								44
45	Insurance Exp.—Access.			(e) 11400		11400								45
46	Payroll Taxes Exp.—Access.	252100				252100								46
47	Salary Expense—Access.	1950000				1950000								47
48	Supplies Expense—Access.			(d) 127900		127900								48
49	Advertising Expense—Boats	233500						233500						49
50	Delivery Expense—Boats	475000						475000						50
51	Depr. Exp.—Del. Equip., Boats			(f) 57000				57000						51
52	Depr. Exp.—Store Equip., Boats			(i) 12500				12500						52
53	Insurance Expense—Boats			(e) 15200				15200						53
54	Payroll Taxes Exp.—Boats	233900						233900						54
55	Salary Expense—Boats	1800000						1800000						55
56	Supplies Expense—Boats			(d) 112100				112100						56
57	Uncollect. Accts. Expense—Boats			(a) 75000				75000						57
58	Credit Card Fee Expense	368500								368500				58
59	Depr. Exp.—Office Equip.			(g) 20000						20000				59
60	Insurance Expense—Admin.			(e) 2800						2800				60
61	Miscellaneous Expense	504700								504700				61
62	Payroll Taxes Exp.—Admin.	291600								291600				62
63	Rent Expense	600000								600000				63
64	Salary Expense—Admin.	2250000								2250000				64
65	Supplies Expense—Admin.			(d) 92200						92200				65
66	Utilities Expense	295600								295600				66
67						11443300	14509900	12138900	16868300					67
68	Dept. Margin—Access.					3066600					3066600			68
69	Dept. Margin—Boats							4729400			4729400			69
70						14509900	14509900	16868300	16868300					70
71	Federal Income Tax Expense			(i) 1146000						1146000				71
72		92847600	92847600	4596500	4596500					5571400	7796000	65704300		72
73	Net Income after Fed. Inc. Tax									2224600			2224600	73
74										7796000	7796000	67928900	67928900	74

TEACH

Cover student pages 498–504 "End-of-Fiscal-Period Work for a Merchandising Business Using Responsibility Accounting." Explain the four additional columns on the work sheet used in responsibility accounting. Review the preparation of the Trial Balance columns. Review how adjustments are planned on a work sheet. Emphasize that the adjustments for supplies and prepaid insurance are made in the same manner as for businesses that do not use responsibility accounting. However, the amounts are charged against the appropriate department. Explain the steps for completing a work sheet with departmental margin statement columns. Review the procedure for calculating federal income tax.

TEACHING STRATEGIES: TEACHING TIP

Have students compare the expense accounts used by AquaCruiser with the expense accounts used by MasterSport in Part 2.

APPLY

Refer students to Illustration 18-3 as preparation of the 12-column work sheet is discussed. Use T accounts on the overhead projector or chalkboard to analyze each adjustment in this lesson.

Guided Practice

Guide students through the T account analysis of the adjustments in Problem 18-2, Instruction 1. Refer students to the work sheet provided in the working papers for general ledger account balances. Have students draw T accounts on a sheet of paper and analyze the first adjustment. All students should agree with the analysis before proceeding to the next adjustment. Repeat the process until all adjustments have been analyzed. The balance of Problem 18-2 can be completed as Independent Practice.

Independent Practice

Assign Questions 12–15 and Problem 18-2.

FYI

Segregation of duties for internal control can reduce the risk of embezzlement (the taking of an asset by the person who has responsibility for the asset). More than one person will then have responsibility for an asset.

tory adjustments are recorded in each department's appropriate income summary account.

Adjustments are made for uncollectible accounts expense, changes in departmental merchandise inventory, supplies used, insurance expired, depreciation, and estimated federal income tax expense.

AquaCruiser keeps a record of supplies used by each department so supplies expense can be charged to the appropriate department. The effect of the supplies adjustment for April is shown in the T accounts.

Supplies Expense—Accessories	
Adj. (d) 1,279.00	

Supplies Expense—Administrative	
Adj. (d) 922.00	

Supplies Expense—Boats	
Adj. (d) 1,121.00	

Supplies	
Apr. 1 Bal. 6,276.00	Adj. (d) 3,322.00

AquaCruiser also analyzes insurance records each month to determine how much insurance expense each department has incurred. The effect of the adjustment to record insurance expired for each department is shown in the T accounts.

Insurance Expense—Accessories	
Adj. (e) 114.00	

Insurance Expense—Administrative	
Adj. (e) 28.00	

Insurance Expense—Boats	
Adj. (e) 152.00	

Prepaid Insurance	
Apr. 1 Bal. 2,350.00	Adj. (e) 294.00

These adjustments record expenses associated with producing revenue for a fiscal period. *(CONCEPT: Matching Expenses with Revenue)*

Uncollectible Accounts Expense is included in the direct expenses section of AquaCruiser's departmental margin statement—boats because only boats are sold on credit. Therefore, uncollectible accounts expense is charged only to this department. In some companies uncollectible accounts expense is divided among various departments. In other companies uncollectible accounts expense is considered an administrative expense and is listed in the indirect expenses section of the income statement.

Completing a Work Sheet with Departmental Margin Columns

FYI

The Institute of Certified Management Accountants offers a Certificate in Management Accounting (CMA) program that requires a two-day examination.

Seven basic steps are followed in completing a work sheet with departmental margin columns. AquaCruiser's work sheet is shown in Illustration 18-3.

1 Extend balance sheet items to the Balance Sheet Debit and Credit columns. (Lines 1-27.)

- The procedure for extending the balance sheet amounts is the same as previously described in this textbook. When an

APPLIED SKILLS: WRITING ACROSS THE CURRICULUM

Writing paragraphs and short essays. The Cases for Critical Thinking are short, practical applications of the accounting principles developed in the chapter. Some cases are planned to present problems related to the chapter but not specifically discussed and answered in the chapter. These cases present an opportunity for critical thinking and decision making. These cases also require more than a short objective-type response. Therefore, they provide ideal practice in writing paragraphs and short essays.

account is not affected by an adjustment, the amount in the Trial Balance Debit or Credit column is extended to either the Balance Sheet Debit or Credit column. When an account is affected by an adjustment, the new balance is calculated and extended to either the Balance Sheet Debit or Credit column.

FYI

Revenue, cost, and direct expense items are extended to the Departmental Margin Statements columns of the work sheet.

2 Extend revenue, cost, and direct expense items for the accessories department to the Departmental Margin—Accessories Debit and Credit columns. (Lines 28, 31–33, 37–39, and 43–48.)

- The procedure for extending these income statement amounts is the same as previously described. The difference is that the amounts are extended to the Departmental Margin Statements—Accessories Debit and Credit columns.

3 Extend the revenue, cost, and direct expense items for the boats department to the Departmental Margin Statements—Boats Debit and Credit columns. (Lines 29, 34–36, 40–42, and 49–57.)

- The procedure for extending these income statement amounts is the same as that for the accessories department amounts described in Step 2.

4 Extend the indirect expense items to the Income Statement Debit column. (Lines 58–66.)

5 Calculate the departmental margin for each department. (Lines 68 and 69.)

- Rule a single line across the Departmental Margin Statements—Accessories Debit and Credit columns on the line with the last expense account, line 66. Add each column and write the totals under the ruled line. Subtract the smaller total from the larger total ($145,099.00 – $114,433.00 = $30,666.00). Write the difference, $30,666.00, in the Departmental Margin Statements—Accessories Debit column on the next line, line 68. Also, write the same amount in the Income Statement Credit column on the same line. Write the words *Dept. Margin—Access.* on the same line in the Account Title column. The amount written on this line, $30,666.00, is the departmental margin for the accessories department for the month ended April 30 of the current year.
- The same procedure is followed to calculate departmental margin for the boats department. The totals for the Boats Debit and Credit columns are written on the same line as the totals of the Accessories columns. This departmental margin is recorded in the work sheet's Departmental Margin Statements—Boats Debit column and in the Income Statement Credit column. The amounts are written on the line below the departmental margin for the accessories department, line 69.
- The Departmental Margin Statements columns for the two departments are totaled and ruled as shown on line 70.

FYI

Departmental margins are extended to the Income Statement columns of the work sheet.

ASSESS

Assess student understanding by checking the solutions to the Independent Practice activities.

Reteach

- Make a transparency of the 12-column work sheet from the accounting forms masters provided in the Blackline Masters Section of the Teacher's Resource Guide. Use data from Recycling Problem 18-R, Instructions 1–3, and the transparency to demonstrate how to prepare a work sheet for a merchandising business using responsibility accounting.
- Assign Recycling Problem 18-R, Instructions 1–3.

Extend

- Have students calculate the federal income tax for AquaCruiser. Use the corporate tax rate table given in Chapter 14. The amount of estimated annual net income before federal income tax is $404,472.00.
- Use *Automated Accounting 6.0* or higher with Accounting Textbook Template, Advanced Course with Problem 18-2.

Enrich

Assign students to read the MULTICULTURAL AWARENESS feature on page 497. Discuss with them how an understanding and appreciation of history and other cultures contributes to understanding civilization today.

TEACHING STRATEGIES: EXPANDING BEYOND THE CLASSROOM

Invite an accountant from a merchandising business to the classroom to address the importance of responsibility accounting.

CLOSURE

Use Audit Your Understanding questions.

AUDIT YOUR UNDERSTANDING

1. Departmental margin statements.
2. Departmental Margin Statements—Boats Debit.
3. Multiply the month's net income before federal income tax by 12 to determine estimated annual net income. Calculate the estimated federal income tax on annual net income. Divide the estimated federal income tax by 12.

LESSON PLAN 18-3

Materials

- Student pages 504–509
- Blackline Master for 4-Column Financial Statement With % of Net Sales (TRG)
- Blackline Master for 4-Column Financial Statement With % of Net Sales (Dept./Co.) (TRG)
- Software: Spreadsheet Template; *Automated Accounting 6.0* or higher; Accounting Textbook Template, Advanced Course
- Assess: Problem Test Chapter 18, MicroExam Chapter 18

6 Calculate the federal income tax expense and record it on the work sheet.

- The procedure for calculating estimated federal income tax expense is the same as described in Chapter 14 except AquaCruiser estimates the amount for one month. The monthly net income before Federal Income Tax is multiplied by 12 to determine estimated annual net income before federal income tax. Estimated tax is calculated on annual net income using the procedure described in Chapter 14. The federal income tax amount is divided by 12 to obtain the estimated federal income tax expense for the month. AquaCruiser calculated the estimated federal income tax expense for April as follows.

April net income before federal income tax	$ 33,706.00
Multiplied by 12	× 12
Estimated annual net income before federal income tax	$404,472.00
Federal income tax	$137,520.48
Divided by 12	÷ 12
Estimated federal income tax expense for April	$ 11,460.04*

*Since amount is an estimate, AquaCruiser rounds the amount to the nearest dollar.

Audit Your Understanding

1. Which financial statements are prepared from information in the four additional columns of AquaCruiser's work sheet?
2. To which column are direct expense items of the boat department extended on the work sheet?
3. How is federal income tax expense estimated for one month?

7 Total the Adjustments, Income Statement, and Balance Sheet columns. Calculate and record net income after federal income tax. Rule the work sheet as shown on lines 72–74.

Generally, procedures for completing a 12-column work sheet are the same as for work sheets previously described. However, the procedures differ for (1) extending amounts to Departmental Margin Statements columns, (2) calculating departmental margin, and (3) extending departmental margins to Income Statement columns.

RESPONSIBILITY STATEMENTS FOR A MERCHANDISING BUSINESS

Financial statements reporting revenue, costs, and direct expenses under a specific department's control are called **responsibility statements.** AquaCruiser prepares the usual end-of-fiscal-period financial statements: income statement, statement of stockholders' equity, and balance sheet. In addition, AquaCruiser prepares two responsibility statements: (1) departmental margin statement accessories and (2) departmental margin statement—boats. *(CONCEPT: Adequate Disclosure)*

Departmental Margin Statements

FYI

Departmental margin statements are used only by internal users, such as department managers and company officers.

Major responsibility for improving AquaCruiser's financial condition rests with the management, including the department managers. To help these managers make management decisions, two responsibility statements are prepared to provide information about the two departments' progress.

AquaCruiser's departmental margin statement—accessories for the month ended April 30 is shown in Illustration 18-4. Information for this statement is obtained from the Departmental Margin Statements—Accessories columns of the work sheet, Illustration 18-3.

ILLUSTRATION 18-4 Departmental margin statement for a merchandising business

AquaCruiser, Inc.
Departmental Margin Statement—Accessories
For Month Ended April 30, 19--

					*% of Net Sales
Operating Revenue:					
Sales			$131,800.00		100.4
Less: Sales Discount		$ 440.00			0.3
Sales Returns and Allowances		110.00	550.00		0.1
Net Sales				$131,250.00	100.0
Cost of Merchandise Sold:					
Merchandise Inv., April 1, 19–			155,838.00		118.7
Purchases		$88,313.00			67.3
Less: Purchases Discount	$441.00				0.3
Purchases Returns and Allowances	390.00	831.00			0.3
Net Purchases			87,482.00		66.7
Total Cost of Mdse. Avail. for Sale			$243,320.00		185.4
Less Mdse. Inv., April 30, 19–			168,306.00		128.2
Cost of Merchandise Sold				75,014.00	57.2
Gross Profit on Operations				$ 56,236.00	42.8
Direct Expenses:					
Advertising Expense			$ 1,650.00		1.3
Depreciation Expense—Store Equipment			506.00		0.4
Insurance Expense			114.00		0.1
Payroll Taxes Expense			2,521.00		1.9
Salary Expense			19,500.00		14.9
Supplies Expense			1,279.00		1.0
Total Direct Expenses				25,570.00	19.5
Departmental Margin				$ 30,666.00	23.4

*Rounded to nearest 0.1%

The departmental margin statement, Illustration 18-4, includes information about operating revenue, cost of merchandise sold, and the direct expenses which can be identified with AquaCruiser's accessories department. The departmental margin statement is similar to an income statement for the accessories department. The

Objectives (Enabling Performance Tasks)

a. Define accounting terms related to cost accounting for a departmentalized merchandising business.

b. Identify accounting concepts and practices related to cost accounting for a departmentalized merchandising business.

d. Prepare selected end-of-fiscal-period work for a departmentalized merchandising business using departmental margins.

FOCUS

- Preparation of a 12-column work sheet for a merchandising business using responsibility accounting was presented earlier in this chapter. In this lesson, the work sheet will be used to prepare the usual end-of-fiscal-period financial statements plus the departmental margin statements.
- Introduce vocabulary: responsibility statements.

TEACHING STRATEGIES: TEACHING TIP

Have students compare the departmental margin statement in Illustration 18-4 with the departmental statement of gross profit shown in Illustration 5-6, Chapter 5. Ask students to identify the differences and similarities.

Professional Business Ethics

The PROFESSIONAL BUSINESS ETHICS feature stimulates critical thinking and decision making. It may be used in many ways, such as an individual assignment, a class discussion, or a small group cooperative learning project. When these ethics cases are discussed in class, students can also gain a sense of individual diversity as students demonstrate individual opinions. If you wish to integrate word processing in your accounting course, you may direct students to word process their answers. If you wish to include the creation of tables, you might direct students to format their responses to resemble the ethical decision-making grid in a 3-column table. A Blackline Master of the 3-Step Checklist for Making Ethical Decisions is furnished in the Teacher's Resource Guide. Suggested solutions for the Professional Business Ethics feature are provided in the front of this teacher's edition.

TEACH

Cover student pages 504–509 "Responsibility Statements for a Merchandising Business." Present the departmental margin statement. Have students compare the departmental margin statement with the departmental statement of gross profit shown in Illustration 5-6, Chapter 5. Discuss the differences and the reasons for using a departmental margin statement. Review the calculation of a component percentage. Explain the steps for preparing the income statement with departmental margin. Discuss how the amounts in the departmental margin statements are reported on the income statement. Have students compare the income statement with departmental margin with the income statement shown in Illustration 5-8, Chapter 5.

PROFESSIONAL BUSINESS ETHICS

Legislate Competition Away

Foreign manufacturers have severely hurt the dominance of American companies in selling a certain piece of electronic equipment. A lobbyist for an industrial association successfully convinces Congress to enact a bill that requires all manufacturers of all electronic equipment sold in the United States to follow certain affirmative action employment rules. This means that no manufacturer can sell equipment unless its staff meets certain requirements for minorities. Foreign companies are generally not able to follow these rules and, therefore, are unable to market their product in the United States.

INSTRUCTIONS Use the three-step checklist to analyze whether the industrial association's action demonstrates ethical behavior.

statement is prepared in much the same format as an income statement. However, only direct expenses for the accessories department are included on the departmental margin statement.

FYI

On departmental margin statements, component percentages are based on departmental net sales.

AquaCruiser calculates component percentages on departmental margin statements to help interpret the information. The component percentages are calculated by dividing the amount on each line by the amount of departmental net sales. For the departmental margin statement—accessories, the departmental margin component percentage is calculated as follows.

Departmental Margin	÷	Net Sales	=	Component Percentage for Departmental Margin
$30,666.00	÷	$131,250.00	=	23.4%

A company may set departmental margin goals for each of its departments to encourage and determine acceptable performance by each department. AquaCruiser has set a minimum departmental margin goal of 22.0% for the accessories department. Departmental goals are determined by reviewing the department's previous achievements and evaluating changes in selling prices and department costs.

Component percentages for the current fiscal period also are compared to component percentages for previous fiscal periods. The accessories department's departmental margin component percentages for the current and two preceding months are shown below.

	Component Percentages		
	April	March	February
Departmental Margin	23.4%	22.5%	22.2%

Since a department has control of and can affect its departmental margin by specific departmental action, this component per-

APPLIED SKILLS: Word Processing

If you wish to integrate word processing into your accounting course, you may direct students to answer the end-of-chapter Accounting Terms, Questions for Individual Study, and Cases for Critical Thinking using their word processing software.

FYI

Managerial accounting data is usually limited to internal use. If such data were obtained, competitors might gain an unfair advantage.

centage is an excellent measure of a department's performance. AquaCruiser's accessories department manager can determine if the department is performing satisfactorily by making two comparisons. (1) Current period's departmental margin component percentage compared with the company assigned goal of at least 22.0% departmental margin. The department exceeded the company assigned goal during February through April, a desirable result. (2) Current period's departmental margin component percentage compared with previous periods' departmental margin component percentages. The accessories department increased its departmental margin component percentage from 22.2% to 23.4% in two months, a favorable trend.

When changes in component percentages occur for an item on the departmental margin statement, the department manager seeks the reasons for the changes. If changes are good, the policies resulting in favorable changes are continued. If changes are not good, the manager seeks to change policies to prevent unfavorable changes.

Sometimes departmental revenue increases because of special sales and advertising programs. Sometimes the cost of merchandise changes because lower prices are obtained when merchandise is purchased. At other times the component percentages change because of an increase or decrease in direct expenses. Without the information on the departmental margin statement, a department manager will not know which policies to continue and which to change. *(CONCEPT: Adequate Disclosure)*

Thus, departmental margin statements provide information to help managers identify unusual changes in revenue and cost amounts. The statements also provide information to assist company officers as well as department managers in evaluating departmental performance.

AquaCruiser prepares a departmental margin statement for the boats department as well as for the accessories department. The departmental margin statement—boats for the month ended April 30 is shown in Illustration 18-5, page 508.

Income Statement

AquaCruiser's income statement reports operating revenue, cost of merchandise sold, gross profit, direct expenses, departmental margin, indirect expenses, federal income tax expense, and net income. AquaCruiser's income statement for the month ended April 30 is shown in Illustration 18-6, page 509.

The information for AquaCruiser's income statement is obtained from the two departmental margin statements, Illustrations 18-4 and 18-5, and from the Income Statement columns of the work sheet, Illustration 18-3.

The income statement is prepared with five columns: two for departmental amounts and three for company amounts and component percentages. The income statement is prepared as follows.

1 Write the heading. Use the same format as for income statements previously described.

FYI

Service businesses also need management accounting information, such as the cost of providing a service, in order to be able to charge a profitable price.

APPLY

Refer students to Illustrations 18-4 and 18-5 as the departmental margin statements are discussed. Refer students to Illustration 18-6 as the preparation of the income statement is discussed.

Guided Practice

Guide students through the preparation of the departmental margin statement for the clothing department in Problem 18-3. Students will need the work sheet prepared in Problem 18-2. Working as a group, have students determine the amounts to be recorded in the Operating Revenue section. When students agree, direct them to record the amounts on the form provided in the working papers. Continue this procedure with each section until the statement has been completed. Working as a group, calculate the component percentages. Students should agree on each percentage before they record it on the statement. The balance of Problem 18-3 can be completed as Independent Practice.

Independent Practice

- Assign Term 6, Questions 16–20, and Problems 18-3 and 18-4.
- Assign Study Guide 18 and Mastery Problem 18-M.

TEACHING STRATEGIES: DIFFERENT LEARNING ABILITIES

Limited English Proficiency (LEP) Students. Rather than asking students whether they understand what you have said, ask them to restate what you have said in their own words.

ASSESS

Assess student understanding by checking the solutions to the Independent Practice activities.

Reteach

- Make transparencies of the 4-column financial statement with percentage of net sales column and the departmental 4-column financial statement with percentage of net sales column from the accounting forms masters provided in the Blackline Masters Section of the Teacher's Resource Guide. Using the transparencies and the amounts from the work sheet prepared in Recycling Problem 18-R, demonstrate how to prepare the departmental margin statements and the income statement with departmental margin. The solution to Recycling Problem 18-R is provided in the Audit Tests and Solutions to Recycling Problems Section of the Teacher's Resource Guide.
- Assign Recycling Problem 18-R, Instructions 4 and 5.

Extend

- Assign Cases for Critical Thinking 1 and 2.
- Assign Challenge Problem 18-C. (The challenge is to calculate changes in percentage of net sales from 19X6 to 19X7 and analyze the trends.)

Enrich

- Assign the Spreadsheet Template for Mastery Problem 18-M.
- Use *Automated Accounting 6.0* or higher with Accounting Textbook Template, Advanced Course with Mastery Problem 18-M.

ILLUSTRATION 18-5 Departmental margin statement for a merchandising business

AquaCruiser, Inc.
Departmental Margin Statement—Boats
For Month Ended April 30, 19--

					*% of Net Sales
Operating Revenue:					
Sales			$151,510.00		101.0
Less: Sales Discount		$ 757.00			0.5
Sales Returns and Allowances		725.00	1,482.00		0.5
Net Sales				$150,028.00	100.0
Cost of Merchandise Sold:					
Merchandise Inv., April 1, 19–			$203,364.00		135.6
Purchases		$89,765.00			59.8
Less: Purchases Discount	$540.00				0.4
Purchases Returns and Allowances	363.00	903.00			0.2
Net Purchases			88,862.00		59.2
Total Cost of Mdse. Avail. for Sale			$292,226.00		194.8
Less Mdse. Inv., April 30, 19–			219,634.00		146.4
Cost of Merchandise Sold				72,592.00	48.4
Gross Profit on Operations				$ 77,436.00	51.6
Direct Expenses:					
Advertising Expense			$ 2,335.00		1.6
Delivery Expense			4,750.00		3.2
Depreciation Expense—Delivery Equipment			570.00		0.4
Depreciation Expense—Store Equipment			125.00		0.1
Insurance Expense			152.00		0.1
Payroll Taxes Expense			2,339.00		1.6
Salary Expense			18,000.00		12.0
Supplies Expense			1,121.00		0.7
Uncollectible Accounts Expense			750.00		0.5
Total Direct Expenses				30,142.00	20.1
Departmental Margin				$ 47,294.00	31.5

*Rounded to nearest 0.1%

2 Prepare the net sales section. Information is obtained from the departmental margin statements.

3 Prepare the cost of merchandise sold section. Information is obtained from the departmental margin statements.

4 Prepare the gross profit section. Information is obtained from the departmental margin statements.

5 Prepare the direct expenses section. Information is obtained from the departmental margin statements.

Details about direct expenses are not listed. If managers need these calculations, they refer to departmental margin statements.

APPLIED SKILLS: LANGUAGE ARTS

Using pronouns and identifying their antecedents. For additional practice in language arts skills, direct students to answer the Cases for Critical Thinking. Students should write in complete sentences and consciously use personal pronouns. Ask students to underline each personal pronoun they use and its antecedent. Suggest that if they have not used personal pronouns, they are probably overusing the business owner's name.

ILLUSTRATION 18-6 Income statement with departmental margin

AquaCruiser, Inc.
Income Statement
For Month Ended April 30, 19--

	Departmental: Accessories	Departmental: Boats		Company: Amounts	Company: *% of Net Sales
Net Sales	$131,250.00	$150,028.00		$281,278.00	100.0
Cost of Merchandise Sold	75,014.00	72,592.00		147,606.00	52.5
Gross Profit on Operations	$ 56,236.00	$ 77,436.00		$133,672.00	47.5
Direct Expenses	25,570.00	30,142.00		55,712.00	19.8
Departmental Margin	$ 30,666.00	$ 47,294.00		$ 77,960.00	27.7
Indirect Expenses:					
Credit Card Fee Expense			$ 3,685.00		1.3
Depreciation Exp.—Office Equipment			200.00		0.1
Insurance Expense—Administrative			28.00		0.0
Miscellaneous Expense			5,047.00		1.8
Payroll Taxes Exp.—Administrative			2,916.00		1.0
Rent Expense			6,000.00		2.1
Salary Expense—Administrative			22,500.00		8.0
Supplies Expense—Administrative			922.00		0.3
Utilities Expense			2,956.00		1.1
Total Indirect Expenses				44,254.00	15.7
Net Income before Federal Income Tax				$ 33,706.00	12.0
Less Federal Income Tax Exp.				11,460.00	4.1
Net Income after Fed. Inc. Tax				$ 22,246.00	7.9

*Rounded to nearest 0.1%
Percentage totals may not equal sum of parts due to rounding.

Audit Your Understanding

1. What ratio is useful to interpret the information presented in a departmental margin statement?
2. How is the component percentage for departmental margin calculated?
3. Where does AquaCruiser obtain information to prepare the direct expenses section of the income statement?
4. Where does AquaCruiser obtain information to prepare the indirect expenses section of the income statement?

6 Prepare the departmental margin section. Information is obtained from the departmental margin statements.

Company amounts in steps 2 through 6 are totals of departmental amounts.

7 Prepare the indirect expenses section. Account titles and balances are obtained from the Income Statement columns of the work sheet, Illustration 18-3.

8 Complete the income statement. The procedure is the same as for income statements previously described. AquaCruiser has no Other Revenue or Other Expenses. However, if these items are included, the same procedure as previously described is followed.

9 Calculate the component percentages. The procedure is the same as calculating the percentages of net sales on departmental margin statements. However, the percentages are based on company net sales.

CLOSURE

Use Audit Your Understanding questions.

ASSESS

- Administer Problem Test Chapter 18.
- Administer a MicroExam test for Chapter 18.

AUDIT YOUR UNDERSTANDING

1. The component percentage for departmental margin.
2. Departmental margin divided by departmental net sales equals component percentage for departmental margin.
3. The departmental margin statements.
4. The Income Statement columns of the work sheet.

ACCOUNTING TERMS

1. **responsibility accounting:** Assigning control of business revenues, costs, and expenses as a responsibility of a specific manager. (p. 496)
2. **direct expense:** An operating expense identifiable with and chargeable to the operation of a specific department. (p. 497)
3. **indirect expense:** An operating expense chargeable to overall business operations and not identifiable with a specific department. (p. 497)
4. **departmental margin:** The revenue earned by a department less its cost of merchandise sold and less its direct expenses. (p. 497)
5. **departmental margin statement:** A statement that reports departmental margin for a specific department. (p. 497)
6. **responsibility statements:** Financial statements reporting revenue, costs, and direct expenses under a specific department's control. (p. 504)

QUESTIONS FOR INDIVIDUAL STUDY

1. Manufacturing businesses and merchandising businesses. Manufacturing businesses make the products. Merchandising businesses purchase and display products from many different manufacturers to provide consumers a selection of products in one location. (p. 496)
2. Accurate, timely statements of revenue, costs, and expenses. (p. 496)
3. Good management practices require that each manager is responsible for controlling all costs incurred by the manager's business unit. (p. 496)
4. (a) Each manager is assigned responsibility for only those revenues, costs, and expenses for which the manager can make decisions and affect the outcome. (b) The revenues, costs, and expenses for which a manager is responsible must be readily identifiable with the manager's unit. (p. 496)
5. Accounting Period Cycle concept. (p. 496)
6. A direct expense is identifiable with and chargeable to the operation of a specific department. An indirect expense is chargeable to over all business operations and not identifiable with a specific department. (pp. 496–497)
7. Direct expenses are recorded in separate departmental general ledger accounts. (p. 497)

ACCOUNTING TERMS — EPT(a)

What is the meaning of each of the following?

1. **responsibility accounting**
2. **direct expense**
3. **indirect expense**
4. **departmental margin**
5. **departmental margin statement**
6. **responsibility statements**

QUESTIONS FOR INDIVIDUAL STUDY — EPT(b)

1. What types of businesses are needed to meet the needs of consumers and what part does each type play?
2. What kind of statements does a company need to operate a profitable business?
3. According to good management practices, who should control a business' costs?
4. What two important features does a successful responsibility accounting system have?
5. Which accounting concept is being applied when a business reports net income earned for each fiscal period?
6. What is the major difference between a direct expense and an indirect expense?
7. How are supplies that are a specific department's direct expenses accounted for differently from supplies for the entire business?
8. What separate departmental accounts are needed to prepare departmental margin statements?
9. What two factors should exist for an expense to be classified as a direct expense of a department?
10. How should an expense that is not separated by departments be reported on a company's income statement?
11. Which accounting concept is being applied when a business reports direct and indirect expenses in the same way each fiscal period?
12. Why does AquaCruiser use an expanded work sheet?
13. Why does AquaCruiser have three income summary accounts?
14. To which column on a work sheet is the balance of Insurance Expense—Accessories extended?
15. How do the procedures differ for completing the 12-column work sheet described in this chapter from work sheets previously described?
16. What is the difference between a departmental margin statement and a company income statement?
17. Why should a company set departmental margin goals for each of its departments?
18. What two comparisons can be made to determine if a department is performing satisfactorily?
19. Departmental margin statements provide information to help managers in what two ways?
20. Where does AquaCruiser obtain information to prepare an income statement?

CASES FOR CRITICAL THINKING — EPT(b)

CASE 1 Superior Corporation prepares departmental margin statements for each of its four departments. A new company accountant listed the sum of the departmental margins as the company's net income on the tax return. Is the accountant's procedure correct? Explain.

CASE 2 Kelley's Hardware has three departments: plumbing, electrical, and household. The departmental margins reported for the three departments for the year ended December 31 are: plumbing, $51,400.00; electrical, $54,300.00; household, $1,780.00. These amounts are similar to the departmental margins reported for the past four years. The owner is considering closing the household department because of the consistently low departmental margin. Before taking action, he asks for your recommendation. What is your reply? What factors should be considered before a decision is made to close the department?

APPLICATION PROBLEMS

EPT(c,d)

PROBLEM 18-1 Journalizing direct and indirect expenses

Wall Designs, a paint and wallpaper merchandising business, uses an accounting system that provides information needed to prepare departmental margin statements as well as an income statement. The company has two departments: paint and wallpaper.

INSTRUCTIONS:

Journalize the following transactions completed during March of the current year. Use page 5 of a cash payments journal. Expenses not identified with a specific department are recorded as indirect expenses.

Mar. 1. Paid cash for March rent, $5,000.00. C234. (Used by all departments.)

4. Paid cash for paint department advertising, $50.00. C262.

11. Paid cash for wallpaper department delivery expense, $84.00. C316.

16. Paid cash for telephone bill, $124.00. C331. (A miscellaneous expense used by all departments.)

23. Paid cash for wallpaper department advertising, $73.00. C394.

30. Paid cash for electric bill, $2,840.00. C437. (Amount used cannot be identified with each department.)

31. Paid cash for wallpaper department's monthly payroll, $3,888.00 (total payroll, $4,800.00, less deductions: employee income tax, $528.00; FICA tax, $384.00). C486.

PROBLEM 18-2 Preparing a work sheet with departmental margins

AUTOMATED

AllSports Center is a merchandising business that sells sports clothing and equipment. The company uses a monthly fiscal period. AllSports Center's July 31 trial balance is recorded on a 12-column work sheet in the working papers accompanying this textbook.

INSTRUCTIONS:

1. Complete a work sheet for the month ended July 31 of the current year. Record the adjustments on the work sheet using the following information.

Adjustment Information, July 31

Uncollectible accounts expense—equipment estimated as 1.0% of sales on account. Sales on account for the month are $20,520.00.

Merchandise inventory—clothing	$37,821.30
Merchandise inventory—equipment	55,978.80
Supplies used—clothing	298.40
Supplies used—equipment	370.80
Supplies used—administrative	164.80
Insurance expired—clothing	60.30
Insurance expired—equipment	115.60
Insurance expired—administrative	20.10
Depreciation expense—delivery equipment, equipment	198.00
Depreciation expense—office equipment	28.00
Depreciation expense—store equipment, clothing	185.50
Depreciation expense—store equipment, equipment	32.00
Federal income tax expense for the month	2,156.00

2. Extend amounts to the proper debit and credit columns for Departmental Margin Statement—Clothing, Departmental Margin Statement —Equipment, Income Statement, and Balance Sheet. Accounts on trial balance lines 58–66 are classified as indirect expenses.

The work sheet prepared in this problem is needed to complete Problems 18-3 and 18-4.

QUESTIONS (cont'd)

8. Sales, merchandise inventory, purchases, and direct expenses. (p. 497)

9. The departmental manager should control the expense and the department should receive the benefits. (pp. 497–498)

10. As an indirect expense. (p. 498)

11. Consistent Reporting Concept. (p. 498)

12. To help sort information needed for departmental margin statements. (p. 498)

13. Two accounts are used for adjusting inventory accounts related to separate departments—Accessories and Boats, and to close revenue, cost, and direct expense accounts of both departments. Income Summary—General is used for other closing entries. (p. 499)

14. To the Departmental Margin Statement—Accessories Debit column. (p. 503)

15. (a) Extending amounts to Departmental Margin Statements columns, (b) calculating departmental margin, and (c) extending departmental margins to Income Statement columns. (p. 504)

16. A departmental margin statement reports operating revenue, cost of merchandise sold, and direct expenses for a department. The statement is prepared in much the same format as an income statement. However, only direct expenses for a department are included on the departmental margin statement. (pp. 505–506)

17. To encourage and determine acceptable performance by each department. (p. 506)

18. (a) Compare current period's departmental margin component percentage with the company assigned departmental margin goal. (b) Compare current period's departmental margin component percentage with previous periods' departmental margin component percentages. (p. 507)

19. (a) To help managers identify unusual changes in revenue and cost amounts. (b) To assist company officers and managers in evaluating departmental performance. (p. 507)

20. From the two departmental margin statements and the Income Statement columns of the work sheet. (p. 507)

CHECK FIGURES

See Teacher's Edition of Working Papers for complete solutions.

Problem 18-1 General debit entries are recorded for the wallpaper department on March 11, 23, and 31; general debit entries for the paint department on March 4.

Problem 18-2 Work sheet column totals: adjustments, $16,352.80; clothing, $32,786.80; equipment, $38,102.40; income statement, $22,926.80; balance sheet, $177,333.20. Departmental margins: clothing, $11,612.10; equipment, $11,314.70. Net Income after Federal Income Tax: $6,950.40.

CASES FOR CRITICAL THINKING

Case 1 The procedure is incorrect. Departmental margin is calculated by subtracting from revenue the cost of merchandise sold and direct departmental expenses. Net income is calculated by subtracting from the sum of all departmental margins the indirect expenses. The accountant is overstating the company's net income by not deducting the indirect expenses.

Case 2 The household department is contributing very little of the business' net income. However, other factors should be considered before a decision is made. Do the products in this department attract customers who may then buy merchandise from the other departments? By having a complete line of hardware items, more customers may be persuaded to come into the store. Are selling prices of household items set at a reasonable yet competitive level? Selling prices may be set so low that there is no possibility of making a departmental margin. Have costs of merchandise and direct expenses been reviewed? Maybe some direct expenses could be reduced or eliminated without affecting sales in the household department. Maybe Kelley's can purchase merchandise for less from other suppliers. Maybe merchandise can be purchased in larger quantities at a lower cost. Conclusion: A low departmental margin from one department is not justification for eliminating the department. However, this information is a signal to investigate the reasons for the low margin. After a thorough review, corrective action can be taken to improve the departmental margin or make the decision to eliminate the department.

PROBLEM 18-3 Preparing departmental margin statements

The work sheet prepared in Problem 18-2 is needed to complete this problem.

MATHEMATICS

INSTRUCTIONS:

Prepare departmental margin statements for AllSports Center's clothing department and equipment department. Prepare statements similar to the ones described in this chapter. Calculate and record the component percentages for each item on the statements. Round percentage calculations to the nearest 0.1%.

The statements prepared in this problem are needed to complete Problem 18-4.

PROBLEM 18-4 Preparing an income statement with departmental margins

The work sheet prepared in Problem 18-2 and statements prepared in Problem 18-3 are needed to complete this problem.

INSTRUCTIONS:

Prepare an income statement for AllSports Center. Prepare a statement similar to the one described in this chapter. Calculate and record the component percentages for each item on the statements. Round the percentage calculations to the nearest 0.1%.

ENRICHMENT PROBLEMS

EPT(d)

MASTERY PROBLEM 18-M Completing end-of-fiscal-period work for a merchandising business using departmental margins

AUTOMATED

SPREADSHEET

Furniture DeCor, Inc. is a merchandising business that specializes in custom furniture and accessories. The company uses a yearly fiscal period. Furniture DeCor's December 31 trial balance is recorded on a 12-column work sheet in the working papers accompanying this textbook.

INSTRUCTIONS:

1. Complete a work sheet for the year ended December 31 of the current year. Record the adjustments using the following information.

Adjustment Information, December 31

Uncollectible accounts expense—furniture estimated as 1.0% of sales on account. Sales on account for year, $10,160.00.

Merchandise inventory—furniture	$112,460.00
Merchandise inventory—accessories	46,543.80
Supplies used—furniture	1,409.00
Supplies used—accessories	896.30
Supplies used—administrative	422.70
Insurance expired—furniture	1,395.00
Insurance expired—accessories	1,395.00
Insurance expired—administrative	325.00
Depreciation expense—office equipment	529.50
Depreciation expense—store equipment, furniture	2,131.30
Depreciation expense—store equipment, accessories	981.70
Federal income tax expense for the year	2,958.60

2. Extend amounts to the proper debit and credit columns for Departmental Margin Statement—Furniture, Departmental Margin Statement —Accessories, Income Statement, and Balance Sheet. Accounts on trial balance lines 54–62 are classified as indirect expenses.

3. Prepare departmental margin statements for each department. Calculate and record the percentages for each item on the statements. Round percentage calculations to the nearest 0.1%.
4. Prepare an income statement for Furniture DeCor, Inc. Calculate and record the component percentages for each item on the statement. Round percentage calculations to the nearest 0.1%.

CHALLENGE PROBLEM 18-C Analyzing a Departmental Margin Statement

The departmental margin statement for the camcorder department of Ultra Video, Inc. for the years 19X6 and 19X7 is given in the working papers accompanying this textbook. The company has set a goal for the camcorder department to contribute a minimum of 25.0% departmental margin. For the years 19X1 through 19X6, the departmental margin for the camcorder department has varied from 25.5% to 29.0% of net sales.

INSTRUCTIONS:

1. Calculate and record the component percentages for each item on the 19X7 departmental margin statement. Round percentage calculations to the nearest 0.1%.
2. Calculate the changes in *% of Net Sales* from 19X6 to 19X7 for the following items: (a) cost of merchandise sold, (b) gross profit, (c) total direct departmental expenses, and (d) departmental margin.
3. From an analysis of the departmental margin statement and the amounts obtained from Instructions 1 and 2, answer the following questions.
   a. Is the departmental margin for the camcorder department at a satisfactory percentage of sales? Explain why it is or is not satisfactory.
   b. Is the trend of the cost of merchandise sold percentage favorable or unfavorable? Explain why it is or is not favorable. Suggest some possible reasons for the change in cost of merchandise sold from 19X6 to 19X7.
   c. Is the trend of the total direct departmental expenses percentage favorable or unfavorable? Explain why the trend is or is not favorable.

CHECK FIGURES *(cont'd)*

Problem 18-3 Departmental Margins and component percentage: clothing, $11,612.10, 42.8%; equipment, $11,314.70, 36.8%.

Problem 18-4 Company Departmental Margin and component percentage: $22,926.80, 39.6%; Net Income after Federal Income Tax: $6,950.40, 12.0%.

Mastery Problem 18-M
(1) Adjustment column total, $29,518.50. (2) Column Totals: Furniture, $368,794.50; Accessories, $123,742.70; Income Statement, $75,142.50; Balance Sheet, $256,556.20. (3) Departmental Margins and component percentage: Furniture, $63,855.10, 17.9%; Accessories, $11,287.40, 10.1%. (4) Company Departmental Margin and component percentage: $75,142.50, 16.1%; Net Income after Federal Income Tax: $16,765.40, 3.6%.

Challenge Problem 18-C
(1) Departmental Margin, 22.6%. (2) (a) Cost of Merchandise Sold, +4.0%. (b) Gross Profit, −4.0%. (c) Total Direct Departmental Expenses, +1.3%. (d) Departmental Margin, −5.3%. (3) (a) Not satisfactory. (b) Unfavorable. (c) Unfavorable.

CHAPTER 19 OVERVIEW

This chapter introduces the records kept for information about manufacturing costs. The three manufacturing ledgers—materials, cost, and finished goods—are described as are the three manufacturing inventories—materials, work in process, and finished goods. Manufacturing costs flow through these inventories and different records are kept at each stage of the manufacturing process. The different bases for estimating factory overhead are described so that applied factory overhead can be recorded on the cost sheets.

GUIDE TO ACHIEVING LEARNING OBJECTIVES

	TEACH	APPLY	EXTEND/ENRICH						
Enabling Performance Tasks	**Lesson Plans**	**Application Problems**	**Mastery Problems**	**Challenge Problems**	**Cases for Critical Thinking**	**Recycling Problems**	**Reinforcement Activity**	
a. Define accounting terms related to cost accounting for a manufacturing business.	19-1, 19-2							
b. Identify accounting concepts and practices related to cost accounting for a manufacturing business.	19-1, 19-2				Cases 1, 2			
c. Identify the elements of manufacturing costs: (1) direct materials, (2) direct labor, and (3) factory overhead.	19-1	19-2	19-M	19-C	Cases 1, 2	19-R	3A	
d. Identify the flow of costs through the manufacturing process.	19-1							
e. Record entries related to cost records for a manufacturing business.	19-2	19-1, 19-3, 19-4	19-M	19-C		19-R	3A	
f. Prepare selected ledgers and cost sheets for a manufacturing business.	19-2	19-1, 19-3, 19-4	19-M	19-C		19-R	3B	

ENRICHMENT

SPECIAL FEATURES

Global Perspective, page 523

Careers in Accounting, page 516

TECHNOLOGY CONNECTION

Spreadsheet Template Problem 19-1

NEW, REVIEW, AND EXTENSION

ACTIVITIES/CONCEPTS/TRANSACTIONS	NEW	REVIEW/ EXTENSION
Cost accounting	✓	
Direct materials	✓	
Direct labor	✓	
Materials inventory	✓	
Work in process inventory	✓	
Finished goods inventory	✓	
Completing a direct materials requisition	✓	
Completing a cost sheet	✓	
Completing a finished goods ledger card	✓	
Calculating and recording factory overhead	✓	

	INFORMAL ASSESSMENT		FORMAL ASSESSMENT			
	Study Guide	Audit Your Understanding	Chapter MicroExam	Chapter Problem Test	Unit Objective Test	Portfolio
	Unit A	✓	✓		✓	
	Units B, C	✓	✓		✓	
		✓	✓	✓	✓	✓
		✓	✓		✓	
				✓		✓
				✓		✓

TEACHING MATERIALS

- Teacher's Wraparound Edition of the Text
- Teacher's Resource Guide
- Teacher's Edition of Working Papers
- MicroExam

APPLIED MATHEMATICS

APPLIED MATH/ACCOUNTING SKILL	APPLICATION
Estimating direct labor cost	Prob. 19-C
Calculating the factory overhead applied rate	Prob. 19-2
Calculating applied factory overhead	Prob. 19-3
Calculating manufacturing cost per unit	Prob. 19-3

TEACHING STRATEGIES: Accounting Pedagogy

A chart of accounts for the business that is used to illustrate each part of this textbook is provided at the beginning of each part. Charts of accounts are extremely important to companies because they drive the accounting system. Employees usually cannot even receive reimbursement for expenses without knowing which account the expense should be charged to. Pedagogically, the chart of accounts provides the following information: (1) Classification for each account—needed to determine how a transaction is analyzed. (2) Permanent accounts (balance sheet accounts) and temporary accounts (income statement accounts)—assist in analyzing transactions and recording closing entries. (3) Account number for every general ledger account—critical information in automated accounting, since transactions are entered by account number rather than account title.

CHART OF ACCOUNTS

This chart of accounts is for a manufacturing business organized as a corporation that uses cost accounting principles to determine and control costs. Because the business is not departmentalized, accounts are not divided into departments as they were for AquaCruiser in Chapter 18. The major difference between a chart of accounts for a merchandising business and a manufacturing business can be found in the Costs sections. FaxaVision uses a Cost of Sales and a Manufacturing Costs section to account for the costs associated with the three inventory accounts related to the products manufactured. (1) Materials. (2) Work in Process. (3) Finished Goods.

The Operating Expenses section is divided into selling and administrative expenses. Administrative expenses are expenses of the business that do not clearly relate to the sales effort, such as salaries and supplies of the office staff.

FAXAVISION, INC.

CHART OF ACCOUNTS

Balance Sheet Accounts

(1000) ASSETS

1100 Current Assets

1105 Cash
1110 Petty Cash
1115 Accounts Receivable
1120 Allowance for Uncollectible Accounts
1125 Materials
1130 Work in Process
1135 Finished Goods
1140 Supplies—Factory
1145 Supplies—Sales
1150 Supplies—Administrative
1155 Prepaid Insurance

1200 Plant Assets

1205 Factory Equipment
1210 Accumulated Depreciation—Factory Equipment
1215 Office Equipment
1220 Accumulated Depreciation—Office Equipment
1225 Store Equipment
1230 Accumulated Depreciation—Store Equipment
1235 Building
1240 Accumulated Depreciation—Building
1245 Land

(2000) LIABILITIES

2100 Current Liabilities

2105 Accounts Payable
2110 Employee Income Tax Payable
2115 Federal Income Tax Payable
2120 FICA Tax Payable
2125 Salaries Payable
2130 Unemployment Tax Payable—Federal
2135 Unemployment Tax Payable—State
2140 Dividends Payable

2200 Long-Term Liability

2205 Mortgage Payable

(3000) STOCKHOLDERS' EQUITY

3105 Capital Stock
3110 Retained Earnings
3115 Dividends
3120 Income Summary

Income Statement Accounts

(4000) OPERATING REVENUE

4105 Sales

(5000) COST OF SALES

5105 Cost of Goods Sold

(5500) MANUFACTURING COSTS

5505 Factory Overhead
5510 Depreciation Expense—Factory Equipment
5515 Depreciation Expense—Building
5520 Heat, Light, and Power Expense
5525 Insurance Expense—Factory
5530 Miscellaneous Expense—Factory
5535 Payroll Taxes Expense—Factory
5540 Property Tax Expense—Factory
5545 Supplies Expense—Factory

(6000) OPERATING EXPENSES

6100 Selling Expenses

6105 Advertising Expense
6110 Delivery Expense
6115 Depreciation Expense—Store Equipment
6120 Miscellaneous Expense—Sales
6125 Salary Expense—Sales
6130 Supplies Expense—Sales

6200 Administrative Expenses

6205 Depreciation Expense—Office Equipment
6210 Insurance Expense—Administrative
6215 Miscellaneous Expense—Administrative
6220 Payroll Taxes Expense—Administrative
6225 Property Tax Expense—Administrative
6230 Salary Expense—Administrative
6235 Supplies Expense—Administrative
6240 Uncollectible Accounts Expense
6245 Utilities Expense—Administrative

(7000) OTHER REVENUE

7105 Gain on Plant Assets
7110 Miscellaneous Revenue

(8000) OTHER EXPENSES

8105 Interest Expense
8110 Loss on Plant Assets

(9000) INCOME TAX

9105 Federal Income Tax Expense

The chart of accounts for FaxaVision, Inc. is illustrated above for ready reference as you study Chapters 19 and 20 of this textbook.

TEACHING STRATEGIES: Teaching Tip

Emphasize that students should refer to this chart of accounts throughout their study of Chapters 19 and 20 of Part 7. It will help them determine classification of accounts, which accounts are temporary and permanent accounts, and what account numbers to use for automated accounting. It will also be a useful reference for performing file maintenance activities.

19

Cost Accounting for a Manufacturing Business

TEACHING STRATEGIES: ACCOUNTING PEDAGOGY

This textbook presents cost accounting for a manufacturing business so that students understand the difference in procedures between merchandising and manufacturing businesses.

ENABLING PERFORMANCE TASKS

After studying Chapter 19, you will be able to:

a Define accounting terms related to cost accounting for a manufacturing business.

b Identify accounting concepts and practices related to cost accounting for a manufacturing business.

c Identify the elements of manufacturing costs: (1) direct materials, (2) direct labor, and (3) factory overhead.

d Identify the flow of costs through the manufacturing process.

e Record entries related to cost records for a manufacturing business.

f Prepare selected ledgers and cost sheets for a manufacturing business.

TERMS PREVIEW

direct materials • direct labor • factory overhead • indirect materials • indirect labor • work in process • finished goods • materials ledger • cost ledger • finished goods ledger • applied overhead

SOFTWARE FOCUS

Software may be used for independent practice or enrichment/extension as the instructor deems appropriate. For this chapter, the Spreadsheet Template may be used with Problem 19-1.

CAREERS IN ACCOUNTING

The CAREERS feature box, ACCOUNTANT, COST, comes from the Dictionary of Occupational Titles (DOT). The entry number for this job title is D.O.T. 160.167-030. Bring this dictionary to class and explain its purpose and how to use it. The career feature is designed to expose students to the exploration of different careers in accounting. The feature gives a realistic description of actual job duties. This feature can be used to demonstrate that the skills learned in this course are relevant.

CAREERS IN ACCOUNTING

ACCOUNTANT, COST

- *Collects data to determine costs such as raw materials, purchases, inventory, and labor*
- *Analyzes data obtained and records results*
- *Analyzes actual manufacturing costs and prepares periodic reports comparing standard costs to actual production costs*
- *Provides management with reports comparing factors affecting profitability*
- *Analyzes changes in product design, manufacturing methods, etc., to determine effects on costs*

Many different kinds of products and services are required to meet the needs of customers. One business cannot assemble the expertise and resources necessary to provide all the services and products needed by customers. Therefore, businesses specialize as to type as well as kinds of services or products they provide. However, all businesses earn revenue, incur expenses, and intend to earn net income. *(CONCEPT: Going Concern)* The three general types of businesses are service, merchandising, and manufacturing.

Service businesses provide a needed service for their customers. Examples of service businesses are accounting firms, law firms, and medical practices. These businesses provide accounting, legal, and medical service and advice for their customers.

Merchandising businesses sell products to their customers. A merchandising business purchases products and, without changing the products' form, sells those products to customers. Department stores and grocery stores are examples of merchandising businesses.

A manufacturing business buys materials and, by using labor and machines, changes the form of the materials into a finished product. A manufacturing business generally sells the finished product to a merchandising business which then sells the product to customers.

FaxaVision, Inc. a facsimile manufacturing business, buys modems, print motors, cutter assemblies, document sensors, and other materials. By using labor and machines, FaxaVision combines the materials to make facsimile machines, commonly referred to as fax machines. Merchandising businesses buy the fax machines from FaxaVision for resale to customers.

A service business needs to know the cost of providing services in order to calculate net income. A merchandising business also needs to know the cost of merchandise sold to calculate net income. For the same reason, a manufacturing company needs to know the cost of finished products sold. To know how much finished products cost, FaxaVision keeps records of all costs involved in making the products.

Selling and administrative activities of a manufacturing business normally are similar to those of service and merchandising businesses. Procedures for recording the selling and administrative expenses are also similar in all three types of businesses.

FYI

Public accountants can play an important role in protecting the environment by assisting clients in accounting for projects for environmental protection.

ELEMENTS OF MANUFACTURING COST

The manufacturing cost of any finished product includes three cost elements: (1) direct materials, (2) direct labor, and (3) factory overhead.

Direct Materials

Materials that are of significant value in the cost of and that become an identifiable part of a finished product are called **direct materials**.

LESSON PLAN 19-1

Materials

Student pages 516–519

Objectives (Enabling Performance Tasks)

a. Define accounting terms related to cost accounting for a manufacturing business.

b. Identify accounting concepts and practices related to cost accounting for a manufacturing business.

c. Identify the elements of manufacturing costs: (1) direct materials, (2) direct labor, and (3) factory overhead.

d. Identify the flow of costs through the manufacturing process.

Direct materials include all items used in the manufacturing process that have sufficient value to justify charging the cost directly to the product. *(CONCEPT: Materiality)* Examples of direct materials are the modems and print motors used in the manufacture of fax machines.

Direct Labor

FYI

With the increased use of robotics in the manufacturing process, direct labor is becoming a smaller component of manufacturing cost.

Salaries of factory workers who make a product are called **direct labor.** Direct labor includes only salaries of persons working directly on a product. Salaries of supervisors, maintenance workers, and others whose efforts do not apply directly to the manufacture of a product are not direct labor.

Factory Overhead

All expenses other than direct materials and direct labor that apply to the making of products are called **factory overhead.**

Some materials used in manufacturing a product cost a very small amount for each unit produced. Materials used in the completion of a product but that are of insignificant value to justify accounting for separately are called **indirect materials.** Indirect materials may include items such as glue, solder, bolts, and rivets. Materials and supplies used by the factory such as cleaning supplies and lubricants for the machinery are also classified as indirect materials.

FYI

Indirect materials and indirect labor are components of factory overhead.

Some factory workers devote their time to supervisory, clerical, and maintenance tasks necessary to operate the factory. Such workers include time clerks, supervisors, maintenance people, receiving clerks, and inspectors. Salaries paid to factory workers who are not actually making products are called **indirect labor.**

Other costs are also incurred in the manufacturing process. (1) Depreciation of factory buildings and equipment. (2) Repairs to factory buildings and equipment. (3) Insurance on building, equipment, and stock. (4) Taxes on property owned. (5) Heat, light, and power. All of these expenses, including indirect materials and indirect labor, make up factory overhead.

INVENTORIES FOR A MANUFACTURING BUSINESS

A merchandising business normally has one general ledger account for merchandise inventory. However, a manufacturing business has three inventory accounts related to the products manufactured. (1) Materials. (2) Work in Process. (3) Finished Goods.

A materials inventory account shows the costs of materials on hand that have not yet been used in making a product. Products that are being manufactured but are not yet complete are called **work in process.** A work in process inventory account, therefore, shows all costs that have been spent on products that are not yet

FOCUS

- Chapter 18 presented cost accounting for a merchandising business. Chapter 19 extends cost accounting concepts and practices to a manufacturing business. In this lesson, the elements of manufacturing costs and the inventories and cost records used by manufacturing businesses will be introduced.
- Introduce vocabulary: direct materials, direct labor, factory overhead, indirect materials, indirect labor, work in process, finished goods, materials ledger, cost ledger, finished goods ledger.

TEACH

Cover student pages 516–519 "Elements of Manufacturing Cost," "Inventories for a Manufacturing Business," and "Cost Records." Review the three types of businesses: service, merchandising, and manufacturing. Discuss the three elements of cost in a manufacturing business. Explain the three inventory accounts used by a manufacturing business. Discuss the kinds of cost records kept by a manufacturing business. Review the definition of a perpetual inventory. Discuss the flow of costs from raw materials through work in process to finished goods.

TEACHING STRATEGIES: EXPANDING BEYOND THE CLASSROOM

Arrange a field trip to a manufacturing business. Inform the business contact that the major purpose of the trip is to learn what direct and indirect materials are used in production. After the trip, have students compile a list of the direct and indirect materials they identified.

APPLY

Refer students to Illustration 19-1 to review the cost flow and forms used to record manufacturing costs.

Guided Practice

Guide students through an analysis of direct and indirect materials used to manufacture an item in the classroom, such as a desk. Working as a group, compile a list of all the materials used to manufacture the item. Next, have students decide the most likely classification of each material on the list. As a decision is reached, write the item under the appropriate heading on the chalkboard or overhead projector. Continue the process until all items have been classified.

Independent Practice

Assign Terms 1–10 and Questions 1–9.

ASSESS

Assess student understanding by checking the solutions to the Independent Practice activities.

Reteach

Illustrate the flow of costs from raw materials through work in process to finished goods, by sketching the flow on the chalkboard or overhead projector.

Extend

Assign Cases for Critical Thinking 1.

Enrich

Assign the CAREERS IN ACCOUNTING feature on page 516. Have students discuss what a career as a cost accountant might be like.

CLOSURE

Use Audit Your Understanding questions.

complete. Manufactured products that are fully completed are called **finished goods.** A finished goods inventory account, therefore, shows the cost of completed products still on hand and unsold.

COST RECORDS

Manufacturing businesses keep detailed cost records for three purposes. (1) To determine accurate costs for each product made. (2) To provide specific cost information to managers who must identify high cost areas so that corrective action can be taken. (3) To provide cost summary information for journal entries.

Subsidiary Cost Ledgers

Three subsidiary ledgers are kept to provide detailed cost information for the three manufacturing inventory accounts.

FYI

Manufacturing companies are usually at greater risk than merchandising companies for liabilities involving damaging the environment.

Materials Ledger. Merchandise inventory determined by keeping a continuous record of increases, decreases, and balance on hand is known as perpetual inventory. FaxaVision uses a perpetual inventory system for direct and indirect materials. A perpetual inventory record is kept to provide detailed cost information about each kind of material. A ledger containing all records of materials is called a **materials ledger.**

Cost Ledger. A record is kept of all charges for direct materials, direct labor, and factory overhead for each specific job. The record is known as a cost sheet. A cost sheet is maintained for each manufacturing job. A ledger containing all cost sheets for products in the process of being manufactured is called a **cost ledger.**

Finished Goods Ledger. A record is kept of each kind of finished good to provide a perpetual inventory of each product produced and its cost. A ledger containing records of all finished goods on hand is called a **finished goods ledger.** This ledger is similar to a materials ledger.

Manufacturing Cost Flows

Manufacturing costs are recorded on cost forms as costs occur. The forms used and sequence of steps followed for recording FaxaVision's manufacturing costs are shown in Illustration 19-1.

FYI

Cost accountants monitor factory overhead during the year. If actual costs vary significantly from projected costs, the factory overhead applied rate should be changed.

1 When both direct and indirect materials are purchased, the number and cost of each kind of material are recorded on materials ledger cards.

2 When direct materials are issued for use in the factory, a materials requisition is prepared. The amount of direct materials issued is recorded as a reduction on the materials ledger

TEACHING STRATEGIES: TEACHING TIP

Review the definition of a perpetual inventory: A merchandise inventory determined by keeping a continuous record of increases, decreases, and balance on hand.

ILLUSTRATION 19-1 Cost flow and forms used to record manufacturing costs

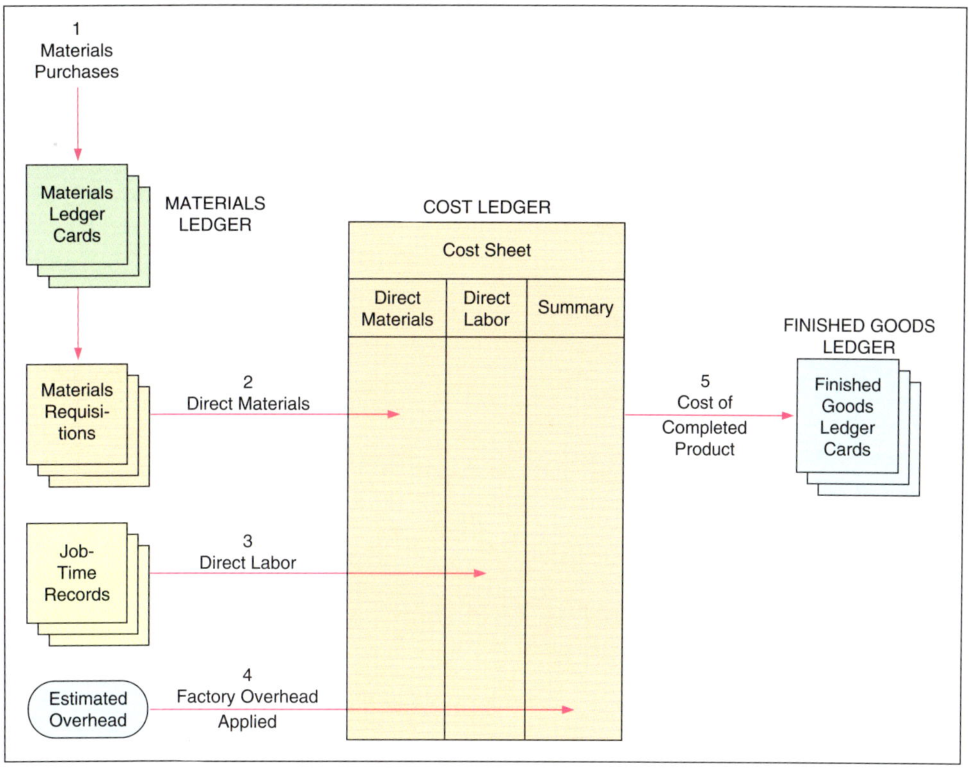

TEACHING STRATEGIES: APPLYING VISUALS

Direct students to Illustration 19-1 to review the cost flow and forms used to record manufacturing costs.

card and an increase in the Direct Materials column of the cost sheet.

3 When direct labor is used, job-time records are prepared. Time record amounts are recorded in the Direct Labor column of the cost sheet.

4 When a product is completed, the amount of factory overhead is estimated and recorded in the Summary column of the cost sheet. Estimating factory overhead is described later in this chapter.

5 When a product is completed, amounts on the cost sheet are totaled and recorded on a finished goods ledger card.

Journal entries for job costs are described in Chapter 20.

Audit Your Understanding

1. What are the three elements of the manufacturing cost of a finished product?
2. How would the salary of a production line supervisor be classified in the accounting records?
3. What is the term used to describe products that are being manufactured but are not yet complete?
4. What is the purpose of a cost sheet?

AUDIT YOUR UNDERSTANDING

The AUDIT YOUR UNDERSTANDING feature appears at the end of each section of the chapter. Explain to your students that the word *audit* means to check or verify. AUDIT YOUR UNDERSTANDING may be used to check student comprehension of the section just studied. The answers are provided in Appendix D in the back of the textbook

1. (1) Direct materials, (2) direct labor, (3) factory overhead.
2. As indirect labor, a part of factory overhead.
3. Work in process.
4. To keep a record of all charges for direct materials, direct labor, and factory overhead for each specific job.

TEACHING STRATEGIES: TEACHING TIP

Create a bulletin board to illustrate the forms used and the sequence of steps followed for recording manufacturing costs. You may be able to get some actual forms from a local manufacturing business or use forms from a business simulation.

LESSON PLAN 19-2

Materials

- Student pages 520–528
- Blackline Master for Materials Ledger Card (TRG)
- Blackline Master for Cost Sheet (TRG)
- Software: Spreadsheet Template
- Assess: Problem Test Chapter 19, MicroExam Chapter 19

Objectives (Enabling Performance Tasks)

a. Define accounting terms related to cost accounting for a manufacturing business.

b. Identify accounting concepts and practices related to cost accounting for a manufacturing business.

e. Record entries related to cost records for a manufacturing business.

f. Prepare selected ledgers and cost sheets for a manufacturing business.

RECORDS FOR MATERIALS

Manufacturers usually maintain detailed materials records for several purposes. A manufacturing business keeps a record of materials used in the manufacturing process. In addition, sufficient materials should be on hand so that the manufacturing process will not be interrupted. However, too great a stock of materials requires needless investment in inventory. To provide a perpetual inventory and detailed cost information about materials, FaxaVision keeps a materials ledger card for each kind of material.

Preparing a Materials Ledger

A materials ledger contains a materials ledger card for each kind of material kept in the storeroom. FaxaVision's materials ledger card is shown in Illustration 19-2.

ILLUSTRATION 19-2 Materials ledger card

MATERIALS LEDGER CARD

Article *28S Print Motor* Acct. No. *145*

Reorder *300* Minimum *220* Location *B-16*

ORDERED			RECEIVED					ISSUED					BALANCE			
DATE	PURCHASE ORDER NO.	QUANTITY	DATE	PURCHASE ORDER NO.	QUANTITY	UNIT PRICE	VALUE	DATE	REQUISITION NO.	QUANTITY	UNIT PRICE	VALUE	DATE	QUANTITY	UNIT PRICE	VALUE
													19-- Jan. 2	*220*	*78.00*	*17,160.00*
19-- Jan. 3	*461*	*300*						*19-- Jan. 3*	*730*	*100*	*78.00*	*7,800.00*	*3*	*120*	*78.00*	*9,360.00*
								10	*752*	*100*	*78.00*	*7,800.00*	*10*	*20*	*78.00*	*1,560.00*
			19-- Jan. 13	*461*	*300*	*78.00*	*23,400.00*						*13*	*320*	*78.00*	*24,960.00*

The name and account number of the item are entered at the top of each materials ledger card. The reorder quantity and minimum quantities to be kept in stock are shown on the second line. When the number on hand equals the minimum, the materials clerk notifies the purchasing agent and a new order is placed.

Recording Purchases of Materials

FYI

Reordering materials when the number on hand equals the minimum quantity is critical to a continuous manufacturing process.

On January 3, FaxaVision ordered 300 print motors from Electro Company on Purchase Order No. 461. A completed form authorizing a seller to deliver goods with payment to be made later is known as a purchase order. The date of the order, the purchase order number, and the quantity ordered are recorded on the materials ledger card in the Ordered columns, as shown in Illustration 19-2. Information about quantities ordered is recorded on the card to avoid placing duplicate orders.

APPLIED SKILLS: WRITING ACROSS THE CURRICULUM

Writing paragraphs and short essays. The Cases for Critical Thinking are short, practical applications of the accounting principles developed in the chapter. Some cases are planned to present problems related to the chapter but not specifically discussed and answered in the chapter. These cases present an opportunity for critical thinking and decision making. These cases also require more than a short objective-type response. Therefore, they provide ideal practice in writing paragraphs and short essays.

When the items ordered are received, an entry is made in the Received columns on the card as shown in Illustration 19-2. The quantity and value are added to the previous balance and extended into the Balance columns. The total value for all the materials ledger cards equals the balance of the materials general ledger account.

The relationship of the general ledger accounts to the forms and ledgers described in this chapter is explained in Chapter 20.

RECORDS FOR WORK IN PROCESS

During the manufacturing process, all costs of making a product must be recorded. All charges for direct materials, direct labor, and factory overhead for a particular job are recorded on a cost sheet. A job number is recorded on each cost sheet to identify the specific job.

Preparing Cost Sheets

When a factory department is ready to start a new job, the factory department supervisor requests a job number from the cost accounting department. The cost accounting department assigns a job number and prepares a cost sheet for the job. All costs then can be charged to a specific job number.

On January 17, FaxaVision started Job No. 791 for 50 FM25 Fax Machines. The heading of the cost sheet for Job No. 791 is shown in Illustration 19-3.

ILLUSTRATION 19-3 Cost sheet

COST SHEET

Job No. *791* — Date *January 17, 19--*
Item *FM25 Fax Machine* — Date wanted *January 24, 19--*
No. of items *50* — Date completed
Ordered for *Stock*

DIRECT MATERIALS		DIRECT LABOR				SUMMARY	
REQ. NO.	AMOUNT	DATE	AMOUNT	DATE	AMOUNT	ITEM	AMOUNT

Recording Direct Materials Requisitions

Direct materials, when needed, are requested from the storeroom. A materials requisition form is used to authorize transfer of items from the storeroom to the factory. The materials requisition is prepared in triplicate and signed by a person in authority, usually the factory superintendent or factory department supervisor.

FOCUS

- The elements of manufacturing costs and the cost flow and forms used to record manufacturing costs were introduced earlier in this chapter. In this lesson, the procedures for preparing the cost forms and recording manufacturing costs on the forms will be presented.
- Introduce vocabulary: applied overhead.

TEACHING STRATEGIES: DIFFERENT LEARNING ABILITIES

Visually-Impaired Students. Many visually-impaired individuals are successful business professionals. It is important for visually-impaired students to have confidence in their ability to participate fully within the business world. Assign students to prepare an oral or written report which profiles a successful visually-impaired business professional.

TEACH

Cover student pages 520–528 "Records for Materials," "Records for Work in Process," and "Records for Finished Goods." Explain how a materials ledger card is used. Discuss the preparation of a cost sheet. Explain that the sources of the entries in the Direct Materials column of the cost sheet are materials requisitions. Explain the sources of the entries in the Direct Labor column of the cost sheet—job time records. Discuss the steps to determine factory overhead applied rate. Emphasize that applied overhead is estimated. Explain how to complete a cost sheet. Discuss the preparation of the finished goods ledger card. Review the first-in, first-out (FIFO) inventory costing method.

One copy of a materials requisition is kept in the factory. Two copies are sent to the materials storeroom. The unit price, total cost, and materials issued date are recorded on both storeroom requisition copies. The materials clerk initials the requisition to show that the materials have been issued. One copy of the completed materials requisition is kept in the storeroom. The original requisition is sent to the cost accounting department. The completed Materials Requisition No. 774 is shown in Illustration 19-4.

ILLUSTRATION 19-4 Completed materials requisition

MATERIALS REQUISITION

☑ Direct
☐ Indirect

REQUISITION NO. *774* DATE *January 17* 19 *--*

REQUISITIONED BY *Mark Jansen* POSITION *Supervisor*

JOB NO.	QUANTITY	DESCRIPTION	UNIT PRICE	TOTAL COST
791	*50*	*28S Print Motor*	*78.00*	*3,900 00*

MATERIALS ISSUED *January 17* 19 *--*
BY *DGD*
MATERIALS CLERK

RECORDED:

From the materials requisition copy, an entry is made in the materials ledger. The entry for Materials Requisition No. 774 on the materials ledger card is shown in Illustration 19-5. The requisition is first summarized in the Issued columns. Then the quantity and value entered in the Issued columns are subtracted from the amounts in the Balance columns to show the new balance.

ILLUSTRATION 19-5 Materials ledger card after entering a materials requisition

MATERIALS LEDGER CARD

Article *28S Print Motor* Acct. No. *145*
Reorder *300* Minimum *220* Location *B-16*

ORDERED			RECEIVED					ISSUED					BALANCE			
DATE	PURCHASE ORDER NO.	QUANTITY	DATE	PURCHASE ORDER NO.	QUANTITY	UNIT PRICE	VALUE	DATE	REQUISITION NO.	QUANTITY	UNIT PRICE	VALUE	DATE	QUANTITY	UNIT PRICE	VALUE
			19-- Jan. 13	*461*	*300*	*78.00*	*23,400.00*						*19-- Jan. 13*	*320*	*78.00*	*24,960.00*
								19-- Jan. 17	*774*	*50*	*78.00*	*3,900.00*	*17*	*270*	*78.00*	*21,060.00*

APPLIED SKILLS: Word Processing

If you wish to integrate word processing in your accounting course, you may direct students to answer the end-of-chapter Accounting Terms, Questions for Individual Study, and Cases for Critical Thinking using their word processing software.

Global Perspective

INTERNATIONAL TRAVEL

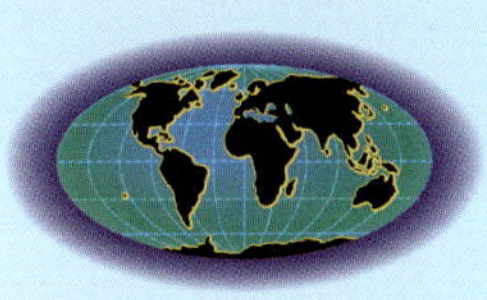

International travel usually requires a passport. A passport is a formal document that allows exit from and reentry into a country. It proves citizenship and provides identity for the traveler.

For the first-time passport applicant to receive a passport, a passport application must be completed. The application may be obtained from a United States Postal Service office and must be submitted with the following:

1. Proof of U.S. citizenship. Proof of U.S. citizenship is usually a certified birth certificate.
2. Proof of identity. Proof of identity is a document such as a driver's license.
3. Two photographs. Two photographs must be submitted that are identical and 2″ × 2″ in size. These photos cannot be snapshots as they must meet certain criteria. There are many local photo studios that advertise passport photo service.
4. Fee. The applicable fee when this textbook was written was $65. The passport is valid for ten years.

This information must be sent to a designated postal service employee at a selected postal service office; a clerk of a federal or state court of record or a judge or clerk of a probate court who accepts applications; a U.S. consular official; or an agent at a passport agency in Boston, Chicago, Honolulu, Houston, Los Angeles, Miami, New Orleans, New York, Philadelphia, San Francisco, Seattle, Stamford, or Washington, D.C.

Some countries require an additional endorsement or stamp by foreign country officials to be placed on the U.S. passport that allows entrance into that country. This stamp is known as a visa. Visas may be obtained from the appropriate embassy of the country being visited.

Immunizations are sometimes required by countries under the International Health Regulations adopted by the World Health Organization. Be sure to check with the Centers for Disease Control to see if vaccinations, such as those to prevent yellow fever or cholera, are necessary before entering a particular country.

GLOBAL PERSPECTIVE ACTIVITY:
Complete the following information that will be transferable to a passport application.

NAME: first name, middle name, last name
ADDRESS: street, city, state, zip, country
PLACE OF BIRTH: city, state (or province), country
DATE OF BIRTH: month, day, year
PERSONAL: SOCIAL SECURITY NUMBER, HEIGHT, COLOR OF HAIR, COLOR OF EYES
PHONE NUMBER: area code and home phone
FAMILY: FATHER'S NAME, BIRTHPLACE, BIRTH DATE, U.S. CITIZEN (yes or no)
MOTHER'S NAME, BIRTHPLACE, BIRTH DATE, U.S. CITIZEN (yes or no)

Global Perspective

The GLOBAL PERSPECTIVE feature is intended to expose students to some of the ways in which accounting and business in general differ in other countries. This GLOBAL PERSPECTIVE feature allows students to explore international travel requirements. The GLOBAL PERSPECTIVE activity requires students to provide the information that would be transferable to a passport application.

Answers to Global Perspective Activity

Students' solutions will vary. The instructor should consider the following items when grading the activity:
(1) accuracy of information and
(2) mechanics (grammar, spelling, punctuation).

FYI

In a job order cost system, a cost sheet is maintained for each manufacturing job. In a process cost system, the costs are accumulated by department rather than by job.

Recording Direct Materials on a Cost Sheet

The original copy of each materials requisition is sent to the cost accounting department. As requisitions are received, they are recorded on the cost sheets for the jobs to be charged. For example, Materials Requisition No. 774 is for direct materials, $3,900.00, Job No. 791. The entries for direct materials are in the Direct Materials columns of the cost sheet shown in Illustration 19-6, page 524.

Recording Direct Labor on a Cost Sheet

Factory employees may work on a number of different jobs each day. Therefore, a job-time record is kept showing the amount of time spent on each job. At the end of each day, all job-time records are summarized. The total direct labor cost for each job is recorded on each job's cost sheet. A job-time record for one FaxaVision

APPLY

- Refer students to Illustrations 19-2, 19-8, and 19-9. Review the procedures for preparing the records for materials, work in process, and finished goods.
- Demonstrate the three steps followed to determine a factory overhead applied rate. Write the formulas on the chalkboard or overhead projector for reference during the discussion.

Guided Practice

Guide students through partial preparation of the materials ledger card in Problem 19-1. Make a transparency of the materials ledger card from the accounting forms masters provided in the Blackline Masters Section of the Teacher's Resource Guide. Refer students to Problem 19-1. Working as a group, have students use the information from Instruction 1 to complete the top of the materials ledger card provided in the working papers as you demonstrate using the transparency. Use the same procedure to record the beginning balance, Instruction 2, and the July 1, 2, and 5 transactions in Instruction 3. Be sure students have recorded each transaction correctly before proceeding. The balance of Problem 19-1 can be completed as Independent Practice.

Independent Practice

- Assign Term 11, Questions 10–20, and Problems 19-1, 19-2, 19-3, and 19-4.
- Assign Study Guide 19 and Mastery Problem 19-M.

ILLUSTRATION 19-6 Cost sheet with direct materials and direct labor entries

COST SHEET

Job No. *791* — Date *January 17, 19--*
Item *FM25 Fax Machine* — Date wanted *January 24, 19--*
No. of items *50* — Date completed
Ordered for *Stock*

DIRECT MATERIALS		DIRECT LABOR				SUMMARY	
REQ. NO.	AMOUNT	DATE	AMOUNT	DATE	AMOUNT	ITEM	AMOUNT
773	*$ 197.00*	*Jan. 17*	*$ 556.00*				
774	*3,900.00*	*18*	*966.00*				
778	*620.60*	*19*	*949.00*				
779	*639.80*	*20*	*992.00*				
783	*811.00*	*23*	*1,010.00*				
786	*356.50*	*24*	*551.00*				
787	*1,244.40*		*$5,024.00*				
	$7,769.30						

employee working 4 hours on Job No. 791 is shown in Illustration 19-7.

ILLUSTRATION 19-7 Job-time record

JOB – TIME RECORD

Employee Number *20* Job Number *791*
Date *1/17/--*
Time started *1 p.m.*
Time finished *5 p.m.*
Total time spent on job . . . . *4.0 hrs.*

All the direct labor costs for Job No. 791 are recorded in the Direct Labor columns of the cost sheet shown in Illustration 19-6.

FYI

The use of robots in manufacturing may increase factory overhead because of increases in depreciation, maintenance, and repairs.

Calculating and Recording Factory Overhead on a Cost Sheet

Some factory overhead expenses occur regularly throughout a fiscal period while others occur irregularly. Also, many factory overhead expenses are not known until the end of a fiscal period. Therefore, factory overhead expenses normally are charged to jobs by using an application rate based on a known cost such as direct

FYI

Applied overhead is an estimate; actual overhead can only be determined at the end of the fiscal period.

labor. This method applies factory overhead expenses to all jobs and permits a company to record overhead on a cost sheet when a job is completed. The estimated amount of factory overhead recorded on cost sheets is called **applied overhead.**

Applied overhead is recorded on cost sheets during the fiscal period and before all factory overhead for the current period is known. *(CONCEPT: Matching Expenses with Revenue)* Therefore, the factory overhead applied rate used to determine applied overhead is calculated before the fiscal period begins.

Three steps are followed to determine a factory overhead applied rate.

1 Estimate the amount of factory overhead costs for the next fiscal period. Generally, three factors are considered in estimating factory overhead. (a) Amount of factory overhead for the past several fiscal periods. (b) Number of products the factory expects to produce in the next fiscal period. (c) Expected increase in unit costs of factory overhead items. FaxaVision expects to produce 10,000 fax machines during the coming year. Considering this volume, previous years' overhead, and anticipated cost increases, FaxaVision estimates next year's factory overhead as $800,000.00.

2 Estimate the number of base units that will be used in the next fiscal period. Base units are usually cost items that can be identified easily. Direct labor cost, direct labor hours, and direct material cost are common bases. A base unit should be selected that most closely relates to actual overhead costs. FaxaVision uses direct labor cost as a base unit because there is a close relationship between the amount of direct labor cost and factory overhead costs. FaxaVision estimates next year's direct labor cost as $1,000,000.00. This amount is calculated as shown below.

Estimated No. of Units (Fax Machines) Produced	×	Estimated Direct Labor Hours per Unit	×	Estimated Salary Rate per Hour	=	Estimated Total Direct Labor Cost
10,000	×	8	×	$12.50	=	$1,000,000.00

3 Calculate the factory overhead applied rate. Divide estimated factory overhead costs by the estimated base unit. FaxaVision's factory overhead applied rate is 80% of direct labor cost. The rate is calculated as shown below.

Estimated Factory Overhead	÷	Estimated Direct Labor Cost	=	Factory Overhead Applied Rate
$800,000.00	÷	$1,000,000.00	=	.80 or 80%

ASSESS

Assess student understanding by checking the solutions to the Independent Practice activities.

Reteach

- Make a transparency of the cost sheet from the accounting forms masters provided in the Blackline Masters Section of the Teacher's Resource Guide. Use data from Recycling Problem 19-R, Instructions 1–3, and the transparency to demonstrate how to calculate the factory overhead applied rate and complete a cost sheet.
- Assign Recycling Problem 19-R.

Extend

- Assign Cases for Critical Thinking 2.
- Assign Challenge Problem 19-C. (The challenges are to calculate factory overhead applied rate for three bases and to use the last-in, first-out method to record inventory costs.)
- Assign the Spreadsheet Template for Problem 19-1.

Enrich

Assign and discuss the GLOBAL PERSPECTIVE feature on page 523.

TEACHING STRATEGIES: TEACHING TIP

Demonstrate the steps to determine a factory overhead applied rate. Emphasize that applied overhead is estimated.

CLOSURE

Use Audit Your Understanding questions.

ASSESS

- Administer Problem Test Chapter 19.
- Administer a MicroExam test for Chapter 19.

During the coming year, FaxaVision will record factory overhead costs of 80% of direct labor costs on each cost sheet. This overhead amount is the applied overhead. The total direct labor for Job No. 791 is $5,024.00 as shown in Illustration 19-6. The amount of applied overhead, $4,019.20, recorded on the cost sheet for Job No. 791 is calculated as shown below.

Total Direct Labor Costs (Job No. 791)	×	Factory Overhead Applied Rate	=	Applied Overhead (Job No. 791)
$5,024.00	×	80%	=	$4,019.20

Completing a Cost Sheet

The completed cost sheet for Job No. 791 is shown in Illustration 19-8.

ILLUSTRATION 19-8 Completed cost sheet

COST SHEET

Job No. *791* Date *January 17, 19--*

Item *FM25 Fax Machine* Date wanted *January 24, 19--*

No. of items *50* Date completed *January 24, 19--*

Ordered for *Stock*

DIRECT MATERIALS		DIRECT LABOR				SUMMARY	
REQ. NO.	AMOUNT	DATE	AMOUNT	DATE	AMOUNT	ITEM	AMOUNT
773	*$ 197.00*	*Jan. 17*	*$ 556.00*			*Direct Materials*	*$ 7,769.30*
774	*3,900.00*	*18*	*966.00*			*Direct Labor*	*5,024.00*
778	*620.60*	*19*	*949.00*			*Factory Overhead*	
779	*639.80*	*20*	*992.00*			*(80% of direct*	
783	*811.00*	*23*	*1,010.00*			*labor costs)*	*4,019.20*
786	*356.50*	*24*	*551.00*			*Total Cost*	*$16,812.50*
787	*1,244.40*		*$5,024.00*				
	$7,769.30					*No. of units finished*	*50*
						Cost per unit	*$ 336.25*

FYI

Robots are used to manufacture products in many factories. The use of automated equipment to perform routine, repetitive manufacturing tasks is often referred to as "computer-integrated manufacturing" (CIM).

When a job is completed, total costs are calculated and recorded in the Summary columns of the cost sheet. Direct Materials and Direct Labor columns on the cost sheet are totaled and the totals are recorded in the Summary columns. For Job No. 791, FaxaVision recorded Direct Materials, $7,769.30, and Direct Labor, $5,024.00, in the Summary columns. Applied overhead is calculated and recorded in the cost sheet's Summary columns. FaxaVision records factory overhead for Job No. 791, *$4,019.20,* which is 80% of direct labor cost ($5,024.00 × 80% = $4,019.20).

Next, the three cost element amounts recorded in the cost sheet's Summary columns, direct materials, direct labor, and fac-

APPLIED SKILLS: BUILDING STUDY SKILLS

Direct students to prepare a Quick Reference Guide (QRG) for calculating the applied overhead. (1) Label the QRG CALCULATING FACTORY OVERHEAD. (2) List the three steps for determining a factory overhead applied rate. Copy the formulas out of the chapter. (3) Copy the formula for calculating the amount of applied overhead. This QRG can be used when students are completing end-of-chapter problems.

tory overhead, are totaled. This total amount is the total cost of the job. Total cost for FaxaVision's Job No. 791 is $16,812.50 as shown in Illustration 19-8.

The cost of each fax machine manufactured in Job No. 791, *$336.25,* is calculated as shown below.

Total Costs (Job No. 791)	÷	No. of Units	=	Cost per Unit
$16,812.50	÷	50	=	$336.25

FYI

The total value of all cost sheets for work in process equals the balance of the general ledger account Work in Process.

This information is recorded on the cost sheet for Job No. 791 so that the cost per unit is available when needed.

The total value for all cost sheets for work still in process equals the balance of the work in process account in the general ledger. Thus, at the end of a fiscal period, cost sheets for work in process are totaled to determine ending inventory for the general ledger account Work in Process.

APPLIED SKILLS: LANGUAGE ARTS

Paraphrasing, writing complete sentences, and identifying verbs. For additional practice in language arts skills, direct students to answer the Accounting Terms and Questions for Individual Study at the end of the chapter. Students should write the answers in their own words and in complete sentences. To further practice language arts skills, ask students to underline all verbs in their answers.

RECORDS FOR FINISHED GOODS

FYI

The total value of all finished goods ledger cards equals the balance of the general ledger account Finished Goods.

When a job is completed, the finished goods are placed in the finished goods stock area until shipped to customers. When finished goods are moved to the stock area, summary information from the cost sheet is recorded on the completed product's finished goods ledger card.

The entry for the completed Job No. 791 is recorded on the finished goods ledger card shown in Illustration 19-9.

ILLUSTRATION 19-9 Finished goods ledger card

FINISHED GOODS LEDGER CARD

Description *Fax Machine* Stock No. *FM25*
Minimum *75* Location *S-5*

MANUFACTURED/RECEIVED					SHIPPED/ISSUED					BALANCE			
DATE	JOB NO.	QUANTITY	UNIT COST	TOTAL COST	DATE	SALES INVOICE NO.	QUANTITY	UNIT COST	TOTAL COST	DATE	QUANTITY	UNIT COST	TOTAL COST
										19-- Jan. 1	*120*	*335.00*	*40,200.00*
					19-- Jan. 6	*515*	*40*	*335.00*	*13,400.00*	*6*	*80*	*335.00*	*26,800.00*
19-- Jan. 10	*766*	*140*	*339.30*	*47,502.00*						*10*	*80*	*335.00*	
											140	*339.30*	*74,302.00*
					11	*521*	*60*	*335.00*	*20,100.00*	*11*	*20*	*335.00*	
											140	*339.30*	*54,202.00*
					17	*528*	*20*	*335.00*					
							30	*339.30*	*16,879.00*	*17*	*110*	*339.30*	*37,323.00*
24	*791*	*50*	*336.25*	*16,812.50*						*24*	*110*	*339.30*	
											50	*336.25*	*54,135.50*

TEACHING STRATEGIES: COOPERATIVE LEARNING

Divide the class into groups of three or four students each. Have each group discuss and prepare a list of manufacturing businesses in the local community. Each group appoints a leader who will present the list and products being manufactured to the class. This cooperative learning activity should not take more than 15 or 20 minutes of class time.

AUDIT YOUR UNDERSTANDING

1. Ordered, received, issued, and balance.
2. Purchase order.
3. To authorize transfer of items from the storeroom to the factory.
4. Estimated factory overhead divided by estimated direct labor cost equals factory overhead applied rate.
5. Because the unit costs of each job frequently are different.

Audit Your Understanding

1. What are the four sets of columns on a materials ledger card?
2. What is the name of the form used to authorize a seller to deliver goods with payment to be made later?
3. What is the purpose of the materials requisition?
4. What is the formula for calculating the factory overhead applied rate?
5. Why are unit costs kept separate on the finished goods ledger card?

When FaxaVision's Job No. 791 is complete, five cost sheet items are recorded in the Manufactured/Received columns of the FM25 Fax Machine finished goods ledger card. (1) Date job is completed, 24. (2) Job No., 791. (3) Quantity of products, 50. (4) Unit cost of product, $336.25. (5) Total cost of the job, $16,812.50.

The Balance columns are calculated by adding the costs of Job No. 791 to the previous balance. Since unit costs for each job frequently are different amounts, unit costs are kept separate. However, the total cost balance is combined for all units in the finished goods inventory. FaxaVision uses the first-in, first-out inventory method. Thus, the cost recorded first is the cost removed from inventory first when units are sold.

The total value for all finished goods ledger cards equals the finished goods inventory account balance in the general ledger. After FaxaVision's Job No. 791 is completed and recorded, the company has 160 FM25 Fax Machines on hand at a total cost of $54,135.50 (110 units @ $339.30 *plus* 50 units @ $336.25).

Different amounts of direct materials and direct labor cause the difference in unit costs of different jobs.

TEACHING STRATEGIES: TEACHING TIP

Review the definition of the first-in, first-out inventory costing method: Using the price of merchandise purchased (costs recorded) first to calculate the cost of merchandise (units) sold first.

ACCOUNTING TERMS EPT(a)

What is the meaning of each of the following?

1. **direct materials**
2. **direct labor**
3. **factory overhead**
4. **indirect materials**
5. **indirect labor**
6. **work in process**
7. **finished goods**
8. **materials ledger**
9. **cost ledger**
10. **finished goods ledger**
11. **applied overhead**

QUESTIONS FOR INDIVIDUAL STUDY EPT(b,c,d)

1. How are a service business, merchandising business, and manufacturing business similar?
2. How do service and merchandising businesses differ from manufacturing businesses?
3. What are the three elements of manufacturing cost for any finished product?
4. Which accounting concept is being applied when a business records only the identifiable part of a finished product as direct materials that have sufficient value to justify charging directly to the product?
5. Why are the salaries of a manufacturing plant's maintenance workers not recorded as direct labor?
6. What are some of the overhead expenses incurred in manufacturing?
7. What three inventory accounts does a manufacturing company generally keep?
8. Why do manufacturing businesses keep detailed cost records?
9. What are the three subsidiary cost ledgers that are kept to provide detailed cost information of the manufacturing inventory accounts?
10. Why do manufacturers usually maintain detailed materials records?
11. What is the relationship between the total value balances for all the materials ledger cards and the general ledger?
12. What is the process generally used to authorize transfer of direct materials from the storeroom to the factory?
13. Where is the information obtained for the Direct Materials section of each cost sheet?
14. What information is recorded daily on each cost sheet?
15. Where is the information obtained for the Direct Labor section of each cost sheet?
16. How are factory overhead expenses normally distributed to a specific job?
17. What three factors generally are considered in estimating factory overhead?
18. What are some common base units used in calculating the applied overhead?
19. How is a factory overhead applied rate calculated?
20. What is the source of information for making entries in the finished goods ledger for newly completed products?

ACCOUNTING TERMS

1. **direct materials:** Materials that are of significant value in the cost of and that become an identifiable part of a finished product. (p. 516)
2. **direct labor:** Salaries of factory workers who make a product. (p. 517)
3. **factory overhead:** All expenses other than direct materials and direct labor that apply to the making of products. (p. 517)
4. **indirect materials:** Materials used in the completion of a product but that are of insignificant value to justify accounting for separately. (p. 517)
5. **indirect labor:** Salaries paid to factory workers who are not actually making products. (p. 517)
6. **work in process:** Products that are being manufactured but are not yet complete. (p. 517)
7. **finished goods:** Manufactured products that are fully completed. (p. 518)
8. **materials ledger:** A ledger containing all records of materials. (p. 518)
9. **cost ledger:** A ledger containing all cost sheets for products in the process of being manufactured. (p. 518)
10. **finished goods ledger:** A ledger containing records of all finished goods on hand. (p. 518)
11. **applied overhead:** The estimated amount of factory overhead recorded on cost sheets. (p. 525)

QUESTIONS FOR INDIVIDUAL STUDY

1. Each type of business provides services or products, earns revenue, incurs expenses, and intends to earn net income. (p. 516)
2. A service business sells services to customers. A merchandising business purchases products and, without changing the products' form, sells those products to customers. A manufacturing business buys materials and, by using labor and machines, changes the form of the materials into a finished product. A manufacturing business then generally sells the finished product to a merchandising business which then sells the product to customers. (p. 516)
3. (a) Direct materials, (b) direct labor, (c) factory overhead. (p. 516)
4. Materiality concept. (p. 517)
5. Their efforts do not apply directly to the manufacturing of a product (p. 517)

QUESTIONS *(cont'd)*

6. Depreciation of factory buildings and equipment; repairs to factory buildings and equipment; insurance on building, equipment, and inventory; taxes on property owned; heat, light, and power; and indirect materials and indirect labor. (p. 517)

7. (a) Materials, (b) Work in Process, and (c) Finished Goods. (p. 517)

8. (a) To determine accurate costs for each product made. (b) To provide specific cost information to managers who must identify high cost areas so that corrective action can be taken. (c) To provide cost summary information for journal entries. (p. 518)

9. (a) Materials ledger, (b) cost ledger, and (c) finished goods ledger. (p. 518)

10. (a) To have a record of materials used in the manufacturing process. (b) To make sure sufficient materials are on hand so that the manufacturing process will not be interrupted. (c) To avoid too great a stock of materials which requires needless investment in inventory. (p. 520)

11. The total value for all the materials ledger cards equals the balance of the materials general ledger account. (p. 521)

12. A materials requisition for the needed direct materials is prepared in triplicate and signed by a person in authority, usually the factory superintendent or factory department supervisor. (p. 521)

13. From the materials requisitions. (p. 523)

14. Direct labor cost. (p. 523)

15. From a summary of the job-time records. (p. 523)

16. Factory overhead expenses normally are charged to jobs by using an application rate based on a known cost such as direct labor. (p. 524)

17. (a) Amount of factory overhead for the past several fiscal periods. (b) Number of products the factory expects to produce in the next fiscal period. (c) Expected increase in unit costs of factory overhead items. (p. 525)

18. Direct labor cost, direct labor hours, and direct materials cost. (p. 525)

19. Estimated factory overhead costs divided by the estimated base unit. (p. 525)

CASES FOR CRITICAL THINKING — EPT(b,c)

CASE 1 Century Fan Company manufactures ceiling fans. During the current year, payments were made for the following items. A new clerk classified the cost items. Are the cost items classified correctly? If not, give the correct classification and explain the reason for your corrected classification. (1) Wood to be used for fan blades. (Factory Overhead) (2) Insurance premium on the factory building. (Direct Materials) (3) Salary of factory workers assembling fans. (Factory Overhead) (4) Bolts used in assembling the fans. (Direct Materials) (5) Salary of factory supervisor. (Direct Labor) (6) Brooms used to sweep the factory floors. (Direct Materials) (7) Salary of packer who packs fan crates for shipping. (Direct Labor) (8) Paint and stain to be used on the fans. (Direct Materials)

CASE 2 Astro Company has found that total factory overhead is usually about 60% of direct labor cost. The business manufactures one product that is processed in three different manufacturing departments: A, B, and C. In Department A, much expensive machinery is used. In Department B, some machinery is used. In Department C, virtually no machinery is used, all the work being manual work. There is a great difference in the amount of time required to process various jobs in the different departments. Under these circumstances do you believe that the company should charge factory overhead to each job at the rate of 60% of direct labor? If not, what would you recommend?

APPLICATION PROBLEMS — EPT(c,e,f)

PROBLEM 19-1 Recording direct materials in a materials ledger

SPREADSHEET

Secure, Inc. manufactures home security systems. The company maintains a materials ledger for all direct materials.

INSTRUCTIONS:

1. Prepare a materials ledger card for H-8 sensors. The sensor is Account No. 91. Reorder quantity is set at 1,000 sensors; minimum at 200 sensors. Inventory location is Area A16.
2. Record the beginning balance on July 1 of the current year of 200 H-8 sensors at a unit price of $12.75.
3. Record the following transactions.

July 1. Ordered 1,000 H-8 sensors. Purchase Order No. 285.
2. Issued 50 H-8 sensors. Materials Requisition No. 260.
5. Received 1,000 H-8 sensors; unit price, $12.75. Purchase Order No. 285.
8. Issued 150 H-8 sensors. Materials Requisition No. 268.
16. Issued 125 H-8 sensors. Materials Requisition No. 274.
22. Issued 50 H-8 sensors. Materials Requisition No. 289.
30. Issued 160 H-8 sensors. Materials Requisition No. 303.

PROBLEM 19-2 Calculating factory overhead applied rate

MATHEMATICS

AutoAnswer, Inc., a manufacturer of telephone answering machines, uses a factory overhead applied rate to charge overhead costs to its manufactured products.

The company manager estimates AutoAnswer will manufacture 30,000 units next year. For this amount of production, the cost accountant estimates total factory overhead costs to be $336,000.00. Estimated direct labor cost for next year is $420,000.00.

INSTRUCTIONS:

Calculate AutoAnswer's factory overhead applied rate for next year as a percentage of direct labor cost.

20. Summary information from the cost sheet. (p. 527)

CHECK FIGURES

See Teacher's Edition of Working Papers for complete solutions.

Problem 19-1 July 30 balance, 665 units, $12.75 unit price, $8,478.75 value.

Problem 19-2 Factory overhead applied rate, 80%.

PROBLEM 19-3 Preparing a cost sheet

MATHEMATICS

On July 1, Esquire Tables, Inc. began work on Job No. 309. The order is for 45 No. ET42 game tables for stock, date wanted July 10.

INSTRUCTIONS:

1. Open a cost sheet and record the following items.

July	1.	Direct materials, $641.25. Materials Requisition No. 432.
	1.	Direct labor, $465.00. Daily summary of job-time records.
	2.	Direct materials, $345.00. Materials Requisition No. 438.
	2.	Direct labor, $364.50. Daily summary of job-time records.
	3.	Direct labor, $301.50. Daily summary of job-time records.
	5.	Direct materials, $261.00. Materials Requisition No. 447.
	5.	Direct labor, $285.00. Daily summary of job-time records.
	8.	Direct labor, $201.00. Daily summary of job-time records.

2. Complete the cost sheet, recording factory overhead at the applied rate of 75% of direct labor costs.

PROBLEM 19-4 Recording entries in a finished goods ledger

Eye Design, Inc. maintains a finished goods ledger for all of its manufactured products.

INSTRUCTIONS:

1. Prepare a finished goods ledger card for Stock No. ED78 sunglasses. Minimum quantity is set at 160. Inventory location is Area D-45.
2. Record the beginning balance on July 1 of the current year for 340 ED78 sunglasses at a unit cost of $12.10. Eye Design uses the first-in, first-out method to record inventory costs.
3. Record the following transactions.

July	1.	Sold 120 ED78 sunglasses. Sales Invoice No. 534.
	3.	Sold 60 ED78 sunglasses. Sales Invoice No. 547.
	5.	Received 180 ED78 sunglasses; unit cost, $12.10. Job No. 409.
	9.	Sold 80 ED78 sunglasses. Sales Invoice No. 562.
	12.	Received 200 ED78 sunglasses; unit cost, $12.60. Job No. 418.
	19.	Sold 100 ED78 sunglasses. Sales Invoice No. 590.
	23.	Received 180 ED78 sunglasses; unit cost, $12.60. Job No. 432.
	26.	Sold 270 ED78 sunglasses. Sales Invoice No. 593.
	30.	Received 100 ED78 sunglasses; unit cost, $12.80. Job No. 446.

ENRICHMENT PROBLEMS

EPT(c,e,f)

MASTERY PROBLEM 19-M Preparing cost records

Gemini manufactures athletic shoes. The company records manufacturing costs by job number and uses a factory overhead applied rate to charge overhead costs to its products.

The company estimates Gemini will manufacture 50,000 shoes next year. For this amount of production, total factory overhead is estimated to be $398,800.00. Estimated direct labor costs for next year are $498,500.00.

INSTRUCTIONS:

1. Calculate Gemini's factory overhead applied rate for next year as a percentage of direct labor cost.

On May 3, Gemini began work on Job No. 283. The order is for 150 pairs of No. 52L athletic shoes for stock, date wanted May 13.

CASES FOR CRITICAL THINKING

Case 1 Several cost items are incorrectly classified. Correct classifications with reasons follow. (1) Direct Materials. The wood is a part of the finished product. (2) Factory Overhead. Insurance premiums are not part of the finished product. (3) Direct Labor. Time of the fan assembler is devoted to actual work on the finished product. (4) Direct Materials. The bolts are part of the finished product. However, because of their relatively small part of materials cost, they also may be classified as factory overhead. (5) Factory Overhead. The factory supervisor does not work directly on the finished product. (6) Factory Overhead. The brooms are not part of the finished product. (7) Factory Overhead. The packer does not work directly on the finished product. (8) Direct Materials. The paint and stain are part of the finished product. If the paint and stain are a relatively small part of the product's cost, they may be classified as factory overhead.

Case 2 Since Astro Company has found that total factory overhead is usually about 60% of total direct labor cost, applying factory overhead to each job at 60% of total direct labor cost on that job provides an easy and relatively accurate way of applying factory overhead. However, if the records are to be departmentalized, then a different method of applying factory overhead should be used since there are such wide variations in factory overhead expenses applicable to each department. Each factory overhead expense should be distributed to the three departments on an equitable basis, such as depreciation expense based on the value of the machinery in the department or rent expense based on the space occupied by the department.

CHECK FIGURES *(cont'd)*

Problem 19-3 Direct materials, $1,247.25; direct labor, $1,617.00; factory overhead, $1,212.75. Units finished, 45, $90.60 each.

Problem 19-4 July 30 balance, 270 units at $12.60 each and 100 units at $12.80 each; finished goods final total, $4,682.00.

CHECK FIGURES *(cont'd)*

Mastery Problem 19-M (1) Factory overhead applied rate, 80%. (3) Direct Materials, $1,695.00; direct labor, $1,480.00; factory overhead, $1,184.00. Units finished, 150, $29.06 each. (6) May 18 balance, 50 units at $30.45 each and 150 units at $29.06 each; finished goods final total, $5,881.50.

2. Open a cost sheet for Job No. 283 and record the following items.

May 3. Direct materials, $862.50. Materials Requisition No. 392.
3. Direct labor, $129.00. Daily summary of job-time records.
4. Direct labor, $248.00. Daily summary of job-time records.
5. Direct materials, $472.50. Materials Requisition No. 399.
5. Direct labor, $175.00. Daily summary of job-time records.
6. Direct labor, $192.00. Daily summary of job-time records.
7. Direct labor, $295.00. Daily summary of job-time records.
10. Direct materials, $360.00. Materials Requisition No. 428.
10. Direct labor, $165.00. Daily summary of job-time records.
11. Direct labor, $152.00. Daily summary of job-time records.
12. Direct labor, $124.00. Daily summary of job-time records.

3. Complete the cost sheet, recording factory overhead at the rate calculated in Instruction 1.

4. Prepare a finished goods ledger card for Stock No. 52L athletic shoes. Minimum quantity is set at 100. Inventory location is Area C-50.

5. Record on the finished goods ledger card the beginning balance on May 1. The May 1 balance of 52L athletic shoes is 140 units at a unit cost of $30.45. Gemini uses the first-in, first-out method to record inventory costs.

6. Record the following transactions on the finished goods ledger card for 52L athletic shoes.

May 5. Sold 60 pairs of 52L athletic shoes. Sales Invoice No. 633.
12. Received 150 pairs of 52L athletic shoes. Record cost from cost sheet for Job No. 283.
18. Sold 30 pairs of 52L athletic shoes. Sales Invoice No. 652.

CHECK FIGURES *(cont'd)*

Challenge Problem 19-C (1) (a) 75% of direct materials cost, (b) 120% of direct labor cost, (c) $15.00 per direct labor hour. (3) Direct Materials, $4,499.00; direct labor, $2,873.75; factory overhead, $3,374.25. Units finished, 55, $195.40 each. (6) May 25 balance, 30 units at $191.50 each; finished goods final total, $5,745.00.

CHALLENGE PROBLEM 19-C Preparing cost records

MATHEMATICS

Sea Explor manufactures deep-sea diving suits. The company records manufacturing costs by job number and uses a factory overhead applied rate to charge overhead costs to its products.

Sea Explor estimates they will manufacture 10,000 diving suits next year. For this amount of production, total factory overhead is estimated to be $600,000.00. Estimated direct materials costs for next year are $80.00 for each suit manufactured. Estimated direct labor for next year is 4 labor hours for each suit at $12.50 per hour.

INSTRUCTIONS:

1. Calculate Sea Explor's factory overhead applied rate for next year for each of the following three bases. (a) Direct materials cost. (b) Direct labor cost. (c) Direct labor hours.

On May 9, Sea Explor began work on Job No. 365. The order is for 55 SE80 diving suits for stock, dated wanted May 19.

2. Open a cost sheet for Job No. 365 and record the following items.

May 9. Direct materials, $1,160.50. Materials Requisition No. 421.
9. Direct labor, $274.75. Daily summary of job-time records.
10. Direct labor, $441.00. Daily summary of job-time records.
11. Direct materials, $2,321.00. Materials Requisition No. 430.
11. Direct labor, $392.00. Daily summary of job-time records.
12. Direct labor, $423.00. Daily summary of job-time records.
13. Direct labor, $440.00. Daily summary of job-time records.
16. Direct materials, $1,017.50. Materials Requisition No. 438.
16. Direct labor, $370.00. Daily summary of job-time records.
17. Direct labor, $352.00. Daily summary of job-time records.
18. Direct labor, $181.00. Daily summary of job-time records.

3. Complete the cost sheet, recording factory overhead at the direct materials cost rate calculated in Instruction 1.

4. Prepare a finished goods ledger card for Stock No. SE80 diving suit. Minimum quantity is set at 30. Inventory location is Area J16.
5. Record on the finished goods ledger card the beginning balance on May 1. The May 1 balance of SE80 diving suits is 40 units at a unit cost of $191.50. Sea Explor uses the last-in, first-out method to record inventory costs.
6. Record the following transactions on the finished goods ledger card for SE80 diving suits.

May 11. Sold 10 SE80 diving suits. Sales Invoice No. 450.
18. Received 55 SE80 diving suits. Record cost from cost sheet for Job No. 365.
23. Sold 30 SE80 diving suits. Sales Invoice No. 494.
25. Sold 25 SE80 diving suits. Sales Invoice No. 523.

533

CHAPTER 20 OVERVIEW

Chapter 20 concludes the accounting cycle for a manufacturing business. The first part of the chapter covers journalizing and posting payroll, materials purchase, sales, and factory overhead transactions that are necessary to distribute the appropriate costs to the inventory accounts. The chapter then presents the usual end-of-fiscal-period work, including an 8-column work sheet and adjustments, and the finan-

GUIDE TO ACHIEVING LEARNING OBJECTIVES

	TEACH	APPLY	EXTEND/ENRICH					
Enabling Performance Tasks	**Lesson Plans**	**Application Problems**	**Mastery Problems**	**Challenge Problems**	**Cases for Critical Thinking**	**Recycling Problems**	**Reinforcement Activity**	
a. Define accounting terms related to accounting transactions and financial reporting for a manufacturing business.	20-1, 20-2							
b. Identify accounting concepts and practices related to accounting transactions and financial reporting for a manufacturing business.	20-1, 20-2				Case 1			
c. Journalize transactions for a manufacturing business.	20-1	20-1, 20-2	20-M	20-C		20-R	3A	
d. Prepare selected financial statements for a manufacturing business.	20-2	20-3	20-M	20-C		20-R	3B	

ENRICHMENT

SPECIAL FEATURES	TECHNOLOGY CONNECTION
Spreadsheet Options, page 544	Spreadsheet Template Problem 20-3
Personal Visions in Business, page 542	
Applied Communications, page 554	

cial statements. The statement of costs of goods manufactured is unique to manufacturing businesses. The income statement and balance sheet also have some features unique to a manufacturing business.

The ledger and journals prepared in Problem 20-2 are needed to complete Problem 20-3.

	INFORMAL ASSESSMENT		FORMAL ASSESSMENT			
	Study Guide	Audit Your Understanding	Chapter MicroExam	Chapter Problem Test	Unit Objective Test	Portfolio
		✓	✓		✓	
	Units A, B, C	✓	✓		✓	
				✓		✓
				✓		✓

NEW, REVIEW, AND EXTENSION

ACTIVITIES/CONCEPTS/TRANSACTIONS	NEW	REVIEW/ EXTENSION
Journalizing manufacturing accounting transactions		✓
Recording payroll transactions		✓
Recording materials transactions	✓	
Recording factory overhead transactions	✓	
Overapplied and underapplied factory overhead	✓	
Recording finished goods transactions	✓	
Recording sales and cost of goods sold transactions		✓
Work sheet for a manufacturing business		✓
Statement of cost of goods manufactured	✓	
Income statement for a manufacturing business		✓
Balance sheet for a manufacturing business		✓

TEACHING MATERIALS

Teacher's Wraparound Edition of the Text
Teacher's Resource Guide
Teacher's Edition of Working Papers
MicroExam
Key for Bombay Leather, Inc. Simulation

20

Accounting Transactions and Financial Reporting for a Manufacturing Business

TEACHING STRATEGIES: ACCOUNTING PEDAGOGY

This textbook covers financial reporting for a manufacturing business. Critical thinking skills are applied to complete the financial reporting requirements for a manufacturing business organized as a corporation. Students record manufacturing accounting transactions, complete the end-of-fiscal-period work, and improve their financial statement analysis skills.

ENABLING PERFORMANCE TASKS

After studying Chapter 20, you will be able to:

a Define accounting terms related to accounting transactions and financial reporting for a manufacturing business.

b Identify accounting concepts and practices related to accounting transactions and financial reporting for a manufacturing business.

c Journalize transactions for a manufacturing business.

d Prepare selected financial statements for a manufacturing business.

TERMS PREVIEW

underapplied overhead • overapplied overhead • statement of cost of goods manufactured

534

SOFTWARE FOCUS

Software may be used for independent practice or enrichment/extension as the instructor deems appropriate. For this chapter, the Spreadsheet Template may be used with Problem 20-3.

Managing a manufacturing business requires more elaborate planning and control than a merchandising business. In addition to sales and administrative activities required of both types of businesses, a manufacturing business must also provide the knowledge and resources needed to make the product.

Accounting for a manufacturing business is more complex than accounting for a merchandising business. To provide usable financial information for a manufacturing business, detailed cost records must be maintained throughout the manufacturing process. These detailed manufacturing cost records provide a business with information needed to price its product, analyze manufacturing costs, and make other important management decisions. Procedures for maintaining detailed manufacturing cost records are described in Chapter 19.

In addition to detailed cost records, a manufacturing business also needs accurate financial statements. To provide financial statements, journal entries must be made to reflect cost transactions in general ledger accounts.

Manufacturing cost data are generally recorded daily to provide up-to-date cost information. However, most manufacturing costs are recorded only when up-to-date account balances are needed to prepare financial statements. These end-of-fiscal-period journal entries update the general ledger manufacturing accounts before financial statements are prepared.

JOURNALIZING MANUFACTURING ACCOUNTING TRANSACTIONS

All manufacturing costs flow through the manufacturing accounts. Therefore, these costs are recorded through each phase of the manufacturing process. The flow of manufacturing costs through the general ledger accounts is shown in Illustration 20-1. Seven journal entries involving manufacturing accounts are normally recorded.

1 Record materials purchased by debiting Materials and crediting Accounts Payable.

2 Record direct materials transferred to the factory by crediting Materials and debiting Work in Process. Record indirect materials transferred to the factory by crediting Materials and debiting Factory Overhead.

3 Record factory payroll by debiting direct labor to Work in Process, debiting indirect labor to Factory Overhead, crediting payroll liability accounts, and crediting Cash.

4 Close individual manufacturing expense accounts by debiting Factory Overhead and crediting each manufacturing expense account for its balance.

5 Record applied overhead by debiting Work in Process and crediting Factory Overhead for the total overhead amount applied during the fiscal period.

FYI

Cost accountants work closely with engineers and purchasing agents to identify strategies for reducing the cost of manufacturing.

LESSON PLAN 20-1

Materials

Student pages 535–545

Objectives (Enabling Performance Tasks)

a. Define accounting terms related to accounting transactions and financial reporting for a manufacturing business.

b. Identify accounting concepts and practices related to accounting transactions and financial reporting for a manufacturing business.

c. Journalize transactions for a manufacturing business.

TEACHING STRATEGIES: DIFFERENT LEARNING STYLES

Auditory Learner. To reinforce the learning of journal entries, the auditory learner should verbally repeat the analysis of the transaction. The student should also verbally list the steps involved in making the entry.

TEACHING STRATEGIES: APPLYING VISUALS

Direct students to Illustration 20-1 to review the flow of manufacturing costs through general ledger accounts.

FOCUS

- In Chapter 19, the procedures for recording manufacturing costs in the materials ledger, cost ledger, and finished goods ledger were presented. In this lesson, the seven journal entries normally used to record these costs in the general ledger manufacturing accounts will be introduced.
- Introduce vocabulary: underapplied overhead, overapplied overhead.

ILLUSTRATION 20-1 Flow of manufacturing costs through general ledger accounts

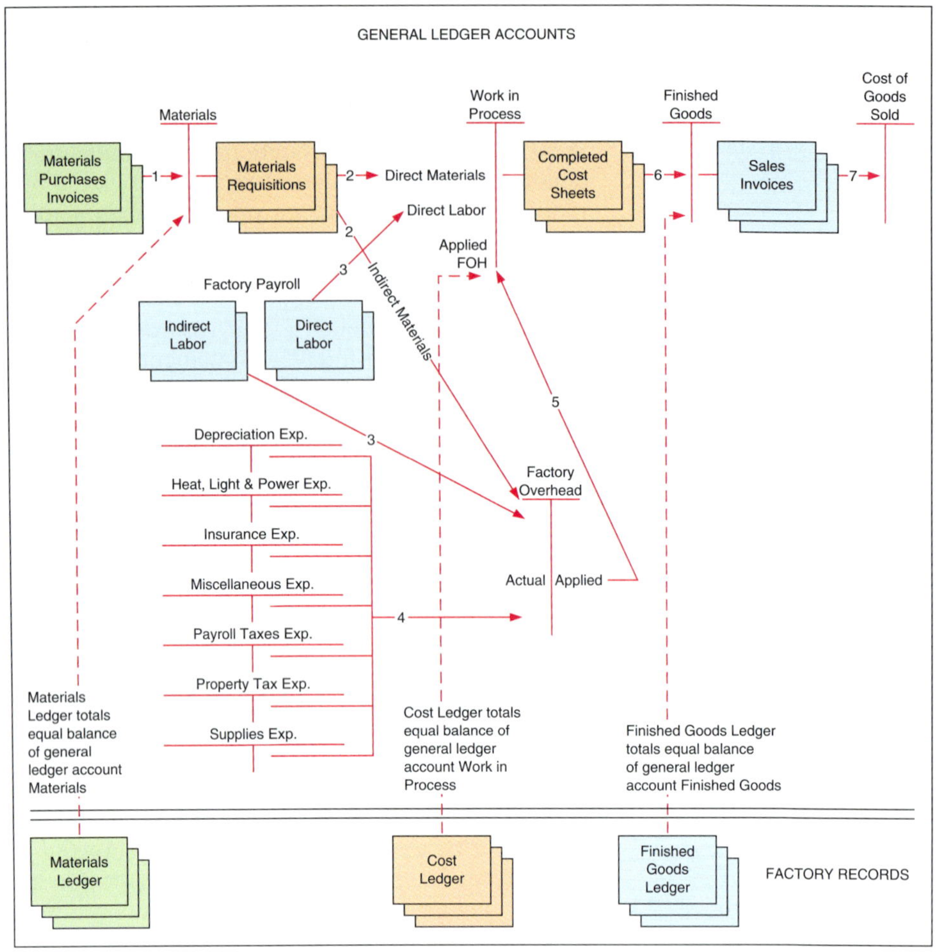

6 Record cost of products completed by crediting Work in Process and debiting Finished Goods.

7 Record cost of products sold by crediting Finished Goods and debiting Cost of Goods Sold.

FYI

American companies that manufacture products to be sold outside the U.S. largely use the metric system of measurement because most countries other than the U.S. use the metric system.

FaxaVision uses cost sheets to record direct materials, direct labor, and overhead costs of each job. This method permits the company to determine the unit costs of completed jobs. The unit costs are recorded in the company's perpetual inventory of finished goods. Summary journal entries update general ledger accounts for costs incurred in completing jobs. Thus, end-of-fiscal-period inventory adjustments are not required.

TEACHING STRATEGIES: TEACHING TIP

On a chalkboard or overhead projector, sketch the flowchart shown in Illustration 20-1. Describe the flow of manufacturing costs through the general ledger accounts as the chart is drawn. Emphasize the relationship between the subsidiary cost ledgers and the general ledger accounts.

Payroll Transactions

FaxaVision pays all factory employees semi-monthly. A separate payroll register is prepared for factory employees. A cash payments journal entry is prepared for each factory payroll. Two factory accounts are debited: Work in Process for direct labor, and Factory Overhead for indirect labor. Two tax withholding accounts are credited: Employee Income Tax Payable and FICA Tax Payable. Cash is credited for the net amount.

Work in Process

Debit		Credit	
Bal.	82,579.00		
Jan. 15	39,245.00		
Jan. 31	44,255.00		

FICA Tax Payable

Debit		Credit	
		Jan. 15	4,081.52
		Jan. 31	4,602.48

Factory Overhead

Debit		Credit	
Jan. 15	11,774.00		
Jan. 31	13,276.00		

Cash

Debit		Credit	
		Jan. 15	41,325.38
		Jan. 31	46,600.12

Employee Income Tax Payable

Debit		Credit	
		Jan. 15	5,612.10
		Jan. 31	6,328.40

FaxaVision prepared the factory payrolls on January 15 and January 31. The journal entries to record the two payrolls are shown in Illustration 20-2.

ILLUSTRATION 20-2 Journal entries to record factory payroll for a month

CASH PAYMENTS JOURNAL PAGE 2

	DATE		ACCOUNT TITLE	CK. NO.	POST. REF.	1 GENERAL DEBIT	2 GENERAL CREDIT	3 ACCOUNTS PAYABLE DEBIT	4 PURCHASES DISCOUNT CREDIT	5 CASH CREDIT	
1	19-- Jan.	15	Work in Process	1194		39 245 00				41 325 38	1
2			Factory Overhead			11 774 00					2
3			Employee Income Tax Payable				5 612 10				3
4			FICA Tax Payable				4 081 52				4
21		31	Work in Process	1211		44 255 00				46 600 12	21
22			Factory Overhead			13 276 00					22
23			Employee Income Tax Payable				6 328 40				23
24			FICA Tax Payable				4 602 48				24

Materials Transactions

FaxaVision records the amount of direct and indirect materials purchased and issued in the general ledger account Materials. FaxaVision uses a perpetual inventory in the factory which permits the company to charge cost of materials to a job as materials are issued. *(CONCEPT: Matching Expenses with Revenue)*

TEACH

Cover student pages 535–545 "Journalizing Manufacturing Accounting Transactions." Describe how the manufacturing costs flow through the general ledger accounts. Discuss the relationships between the three subsidiary cost ledgers and the general ledger accounts. Review which items are considered as direct materials, direct labor, and overhead costs. Discuss the payroll transactions. Present the materials transactions. Explain that the materials account is a controlling account for the materials ledger. Discuss the factory overhead transactions. Review what items are included in factory overhead. Remind students that applied overhead is an estimated amount. Therefore, applied factory overhead may not equal actual factory overhead. Discuss the finished goods transactions.

TEACHING STRATEGIES: DIFFERENT LEARNING STYLES

Kinesthetic Learner. When covering journal entries with a kinesthetic learner, the instructor should give the student journal paper and have the student complete the entries as the instructor demonstrates on a transparency or chalkboard.

APPLY

Refer students to Illustration 20-1 as the flow of manufacturing costs through the general ledger accounts is described. Use T accounts on the overhead projector or chalkboard to show how each transaction in this lesson is analyzed. Refer students to Illustration 20-10 to show the effect of posting the cost entries to the manufacturing accounts.

Guided Practice

Guide students through the T account analysis of the transactions in Problem 20-1. Have students draw T accounts on a sheet of paper and analyze the first transaction. All students should agree with the analysis before proceeding to the next transaction. Repeat the process until all transactions have been analyzed. The balance of Problem 20-1 can be assigned as Independent Practice.

Independent Practice

Assign Terms 1–2, Questions 1–17, and Problems 20-1 and 20-2.

Materials Purchases. Purchases of materials are frequent. Thus, FaxaVision uses a special materials purchases journal to record direct and indirect materials purchases. The journal has a single amount column headed Materials Dr./Accts. Pay. Cr. All purchases on account of materials are debited to Materials and credited to Accounts Payable in the general ledger. The journal entry to record a purchase of materials in the materials purchases journal is shown in Illustration 20-3.

ILLUSTRATION 20-3 Journal entry to record purchase of materials

MATERIALS PURCHASES JOURNAL — PAGE 1

	DATE		ACCOUNT CREDITED	PURCH. NO.	POST. REF.	MATERIALS DR. ACCTS. PAY. CR.	
1	19-- Jan.	4	Oakley Electronics	621		7 097 80	1
24		31	Total			168 642 60	24

At the end of a month, the total of the materials purchases journal is posted to two general ledger accounts, Materials and Accounts Payable.

Materials

Debit		Credit
Jan. 1 Bal.	121,231.20	
Jan. 31	168,642.60	

Accounts Payable

Debit	Credit	
	Jan. 31	168,642.60

In the materials account, the January 1 debit balance, *$121,231.20,* is the materials inventory at the beginning of the month. The January 31 debit, *$168,642.60,* is the total posted from the materials purchases journal. This last entry is the total cost of direct and indirect materials purchased during the month.

FYI

Materials are sometimes referred to as raw materials.

Materials Requisitions. A materials requisition is prepared for direct materials issued for a specific job. After materials are issued, the requisition amount is recorded on a cost sheet and the requisition placed in a materials requisitions file for direct materials. At the end of a month, the total value of all direct materials issued to specific jobs must be transferred from Materials to Work in Process.

A materials requisition is also prepared for indirect materials used in the factory. These materials are used in making the product, such as solder, bolts, and rivets. However, the cost of these items for each job is so small that FaxaVision records these costs in Factory Overhead. After the indirect materials are issued to the factory, the requisition is placed in a materials requisition file for indirect materials. At the end of the month, the total value of all indirect materials issued is transferred from Materials to Factory Overhead.

FaxaVision prepares a memorandum with monthly summary information of the direct materials requisitions total, *$156,477.00,* and the indirect materials total, *$11,447.50.* The general journal entry to transfer these amounts is shown in Illustration 20-4.

The first debit amount in the work in process account, *$82,579.00,* is the beginning inventory of Work in Process. The second

TEACHING STRATEGIES: DIFFERENT LEARNING ABILITIES

Specific Learning Disability (SLD) Students. When feasible, SLD students should become involved in work-study programs that are consistent with course content. When work-study opportunities are unavailable, simulations can be used to provide a simulated work environment. Field trips are an excellent method to expose students to the business world.

ILLUSTRATION 20-4 Journal entry to record materials requisitions for a month

GENERAL JOURNAL PAGE 1

	DATE		ACCOUNT TITLE	DOC. NO.	POST. REF.	DEBIT	CREDIT	
1	19-- Jan.	31	Work in Process	M240		156 477 00		1
2			Factory Overhead			11 447 50		2
3			Materials				167 924 50	3

and third debit amounts, *$39,245.00* and *$44,255.00,* are the total amounts of direct labor used for all jobs during the month. The last debit amount, *$156,477.00,* is the total amount of direct materials placed in process on all jobs during the month.

Work in Process

Debit		Credit
Bal.	82,579.00	
Jan. 15 Dir. Lab.	39,245.00	
Jan. 31 Dir. Lab.	44,255.00	
Jan. 31 Dir. Mat.	156,477.00	

Materials

Debit		Credit	
Bal.	121,231.20	Jan. 31 Dir. Issued	156,477.00
Jan. 31 Purch.	168,642.60	Jan. 31 Ind. Issued	11,447.50

Factory Overhead

Debit		Credit
Jan. 15 Ind. Lab.	11,774.00	
Jan. 31 Ind. Lab.	13,276.00	
Jan. 31 Ind. Mat.	11,447.50	

The first and second debit amounts in the factory overhead account, *$11,774.00* and *$13,276.00,* are the total amounts of indirect labor used during the month. The last debit amount, *$11,447.50,* is the total amount of indirect materials issued during the month.

The first debit amount in the materials account, *$121,231.20,* is the materials inventory at the beginning of the month. The second debit amount, *$168,642.60,* is the total amount of materials purchased during the month. The first credit amount, *$156,477.00,* is the total amount of all direct materials issued during the month. The second credit amount, *$11,447.50,* is the total of all indirect materials issued during the month.

FYI

Public accountants may become involved in litigation support. In this growing field, accountants may be hired to serve as expert witnesses in trials involving financial matters.

Materials Account. The materials account is a controlling account for the materials ledger described in Chapter 19. The materials purchases total as shown in the materials purchases journal is debited to the general ledger account Materials. Each materials purchase is also recorded in the Received columns of a materials ledger card after the invoice has been received.

The total of all direct and indirect materials requisitions is recorded in the general journal as a credit to the general ledger account Materials. Each materials requisition is recorded in the Issued columns of a materials ledger card. Therefore, the balance of the general ledger account Materials must equal the sum of the balances of all records in the materials ledger.

ASSESS

Assess student understanding by checking the solutions to the Independent Practice activities.

Reteach

- On the overhead projector or chalkboard, draw T accounts and record the balances for information items in (a), (b), and (c) of Recycling Problem 20-R. Use the T accounts to analyze each of the transactions given in Instructions 2–6. Label each transaction on the T accounts.
- Assign Recycling Problem 20-R, Instructions 1–6.

Extend

Assign Cases for Critical Thinking 1.

Enrich

- Assign the APPLIED COMMUNICATIONS special feature on page 554.
- Assign the PERSONAL VISIONS IN BUSINESS feature on page 542.

CLOSURE

Use Audit Your Understanding questions.

APPLIED SKILLS: WRITING ACROSS THE CURRICULUM

Writing paragraphs and short essays. The Cases for Critical Thinking are short, practical applications of the accounting principles developed in the chapter. Some cases are planned to present problems related to the chapter but not specifically discussed and answered in the chapter. These cases present an opportunity for critical thinking and decision making. These cases also require more than a short objective-type response. Therefore they provide ideal practice in writing paragraphs and short essays.

Factory Overhead Transactions

FYI

All expenses other than direct materials and direct labor that apply to manufacturing a product are included in factory overhead.

Factory overhead includes various indirect factory expenses such as indirect labor, indirect materials, taxes, depreciation, and insurance. Actual factory overhead expenses are summarized in an account titled Factory Overhead.

TEACHING STRATEGIES: TEACHING TIP

Review which items are included in factory overhead. Remind students that since applied overhead is an estimated amount, the amount may not equal actual factory overhead.

Journalizing Actual Factory Overhead. Indirect labor is posted directly to the factory overhead account from the factory payroll entry shown in Illustration 20-2. Indirect materials are posted directly to the factory overhead account from the general journal entry that records all materials issued to the factory shown in Illustration 20-4. Other indirect expenses are recorded throughout the month in other manufacturing expense accounts. At the end of each month, these indirect expense account balances are all transferred to the factory overhead account. The actual factory overhead can then be compared with the estimated amount of factory overhead recorded on the job cost sheets. The general journal entry to transfer actual overhead expenses to the factory overhead account is shown in Illustration 20-5.

ILLUSTRATION 20-5

Journal entry to close actual monthly factory overhead expenses to the factory overhead account

GENERAL JOURNAL — PAGE 1

	DATE	ACCOUNT TITLE	DOC. NO.	POST. REF.	DEBIT	CREDIT	
4	31	Factory Overhead	M241		30 456 00		4
5		Depr. Exp.—Factory Equip.				2 500 00	5
6		Depr. Exp.—Building				1 300 00	6
7		Heat, Light, and Power Exp.				6 158 50	7
8		Insurance Exp.—Factory				620 00	8
9		Miscellaneous Exp.—Factory				784 40	9
10		Payroll Taxes Exp.—Factory				15 414 10	10
11		Property Tax Exp.—Factory				1 463 60	11
12		Supplies Exp.—Factory				2 215 40	12
13							13

Adjusting entries are made at the end of a fiscal period prior to the entry to transfer actual factory overhead expenses to the factory overhead account. These adjusting entries resulted in amounts being debited to the depreciation expense, insurance expense, and supplies expense accounts.

Factory Overhead		
Jan. 15 Ind. Lab.	11,774.00	
Jan. 31 Ind. Lab.	13,276.00	
Jan. 31 Ind. Mat.	11,447.50	
Jan. 31 Act. OH	30,456.00	
(New Bal.	*66,953.50)*	

After posting the cash payments journal shown in Illustration 20-2, the general journal shown in Illustration 20-4, and the general journal shown in Illustration 20-5, all factory overhead expense accounts are summarized in the factory overhead account. The factory overhead account is debited for the actual fac-

TEACHING STRATEGIES: DIFFERENT LEARNING STYLES

Print Learner. When covering journal entries with a print learner, the instructor should discuss the entries, using the textbook examples and referring to the textbook. The print learner can later go back and study the entries.

tory overhead expenses for the month. These expenses are indirect labor, *$11,774.00* and *$13,276.00,* indirect materials, *$11,447.50,* plus the other actual factory overhead expenses, *$30,456.00.*

Journalizing Applied Factory Overhead to Work in Process. FaxaVision distributes estimated factory overhead as described in Chapter 19. Factory overhead is applied to each job at the rate of 80% of direct labor charges on each cost sheet.

At the end of each month, the applied factory overhead recorded on all job cost sheets during the month is totaled. FaxaVision's applied factory overhead for January is $66,800.00. The journal entry to record applied factory overhead is shown in Illustration 20-6.

> **TEACHING STRATEGIES: DIFFERENT LEARNING STYLES**
>
> ***Tactile Learner.*** Tactile learners should be given the opportunity to journalize transactions from at least one simulation that contains source documents which must be handled to analyze, journalize, and file.

ILLUSTRATION 20-6 Journal entry to record applied overhead

GENERAL JOURNAL PAGE *1*

	DATE	ACCOUNT TITLE	DOC. NO.	POST. REF.	DEBIT	CREDIT	
13	*31*	*Work in Process*	*M242*		*66 800 00*		13
14		*Factory Overhead*				*66 800 00*	14
15							15

Work in Process

Bal.	82,579.00
Jan. 15 Dir. Lab.	39,245.00
Jan. 31 Dir. Lab.	44,255.00
Jan. 31 Dir. Mat.	156,477.00
Jan. 31 Applied OH	66,800.00

Factory Overhead

Debit		Credit	
Jan. 31 Act. OH	66,953.50	Jan. 31 Applied OH	66,800.00
(New Bal.	*153.50)*		

The work in process account now shows beginning inventory, direct labor cost, direct materials cost, and applied factory overhead.

The factory overhead account debit, *$66,953.50,* is the actual factory overhead expense for the month. The credit, *$66,800.00,* is the applied factory overhead recorded on cost sheets during the month. The factory overhead account ending balance is a $153.50 debit. This debit balance results from recording less applied factory overhead than the amount of actual factory overhead expenses.

> **FYI**
>
> **If the ending balance of Factory Overhead is a debit, actual overhead is greater than applied overhead and there is underapplied overhead.**

Disposing of Overapplied and Underapplied Factory Overhead Balances. In theory, applied factory overhead should be equal to the actual factory overhead expenses. However, the rate used to calculate applied factory overhead is estimated and may not be absolutely accurate. Therefore, the factory overhead account may have an ending balance. The amount by which applied factory overhead is less than actual factory overhead is called **underapplied overhead.** The debit balance, *$153.50,* in FaxaVision's account

> **TEACHING STRATEGIES: TEACHING TIP**
>
> Have students compare the differences between the chart of accounts for Chapters 19 and 20 and the chart of accounts used in Chapter 18. Students should determine which accounts are different and why these accounts are needed in a manufacturing business but not in a merchandising business.

indicates underapplied overhead for January. This balance is closed to the income summary account. The journal entry to close the factory overhead account at the end of January is shown in Illustration 20-7.

ILLUSTRATION 20-7

Journal entry to close the factory overhead account with underapplied overhead

GENERAL JOURNAL — PAGE *1*

	DATE	ACCOUNT TITLE	DOC. NO.	POST. REF.	DEBIT	CREDIT	
15	*31*	*Income Summary*	*M243*		*1 5 3 50*		15
16		*Factory Overhead*				*1 5 3 50*	16

FYI

If the ending balance of Factory Overhead is a credit, applied overhead is greater than actual overhead and there is overapplied overhead.

A credit balance in the factory overhead account indicates that applied factory overhead is more than actual factory overhead. The amount by which applied factory overhead is more than actual factory overhead is called **overapplied overhead.** A credit ending balance in the factory overhead account indicates overapplied overhead. If the factory overhead account has a credit balance, Factory Overhead is debited and Income Summary is credited for the overapplied overhead amount.

Personal Visions in Business

This special student feature introduces students to successful entrepreneurs or business professionals. Each profile gives a flavor of what the actual business world is like and some of the opportunities available to students who study accounting. These features can be used to motivate students to pursue professional business careers in a wide variety of fields. The subjects of these profiles have been carefully chosen to represent the full spectrum of diverse ethnic and racial backgrounds of professional business people. As an optional activity, students can be encouraged to seek out and interview successful business people in their own communities.

Glenn D. Southard

SOUTHARD INSURANCE AGENCY

Glenn Southard knows what it's like to go from earning a regular paycheck working for someone else to hoping you can support your family working for yourself. Southard studied engineering in college and worked for General Motors. When he left General Motors, he used his severance pay to start his own insurance agency.

Southard had no other capital. He could only hope that hard work would keep his head above water. "Imagine how I felt," Southard says, "when I sold my first insurance policy. I was a success—this was something I was going to be able to do. I earned a commission of $6.00! Let me tell you, I had to sell a lot of policies to support a family of five."

Southard had no background in accounting or business courses in either high school or college. He admits that this lack of knowledge made it very hard for him to balance the books. "Fortunately," he says, "my wife had studied accounting so that helped us understand what we needed to do." Eventually Southard learned what he needed to know; however, it took more time than he thought it would.

Southard was surprised by the attitudes of some of the people he knew when he started his business. He said, "Some of my friends told me I would not last six months—this surprised me. Yet, some people stopped by and wished me good luck, even some people I barely knew. I was really encouraged by the number of people that did support me; I didn't realize that many people were pulling for me to succeed."

Personal Visions in Business

APPLIED SKILLS: WORD PROCESSING

If you wish to integrate word processing into your accounting course, you may direct students to answer the end-of-chapter Accounting Terms, Questions for Individual Study, and Cases for Critical Thinking using their word processing software.

If an overapplied or underapplied overhead amount is large, factory expense accounts should be reviewed to determine the reason for the significant difference. FaxaVision considers the amount to be significant if overapplied or underapplied overhead is 2% or more of actual factory overhead. Two situations may cause overapplied or underapplied overhead. (1) Actual expenses may be higher or lower than normal. This event requires closer control of expenditures. (2) The factory overhead applied rate may be inaccurate. This event requires more accurate estimating and calculating of the applied rate.

Finished Goods Transactions

After a job is completed, the cost sheet is filed. At the end of the month, total amounts on all cost sheets completed during the current month are totaled. The total of FaxaVision's completed cost sheets for January, *$280,352.50,* is the cost of work finished during the month. This total amount is transferred from Work in Process to Finished Goods to update these two inventory accounts. The journal entry to record this transaction is shown in Illustration 20-8.

TEACHING STRATEGIES: DIFFERENT LEARNING STYLES

Visual Learner. When covering journal entries with a visual learner, the instructor should discuss the entries, using a transparency or the chalkboard to record the entry. In addition, the student should be asked to mentally picture each part of the entry before the instructor actually writes it on the transparency or chalkboard.

ILLUSTRATION 20-8 Journal entry to record finished goods completed during a month

GENERAL JOURNAL — PAGE *1*

	DATE	ACCOUNT TITLE	DOC. NO.	POST. REF.	DEBIT	CREDIT	
17	*31*	*Finished Goods*	*M244*		*280 352 50*		17
18		*Work in Process*				*280 352 50*	18
19							19
20							20
21							21

Finished Goods

Debit		Credit
Bal.	115,140.00	
Jan. 31 Completed Cost Sheets	280,352.50	

Work in Process

Debit		Credit	
Bal.	82,579.00	Jan. 31 Completed Cost Sheets to Finished Goods	280,352.50
Jan. 15 Dir. Lab.	39,245.00		
Jan. 31 Dir. Lab.	44,255.00		
Jan. 31 Dir. Mat.	156,477.00		
Jan. 31 Applied OH	66,800.00		
(New Bal. Jan. 31	*109,003.50)*		

The first debit in the finished goods account, *$115,140.00,* is the beginning inventory of finished goods. The second debit, *$280,352.50,* is the cost of goods finished during the month. The credit to Work in Process, *$280,352.50,* is the cost of finished goods transferred from the factory to the stockroom. The work in process account balance, *$109,003.50,* is the total amount of direct materials, direct labor, and applied factory overhead charged to the jobs in the ending inventory of work in process.

Spreadsheet Options

The SPREADSHEET OPTIONS feature is intended to expose students to a variety of ways to use spreadsheets. As an optional activity, students may use their spreadsheet software to duplicate the example shown in the spreadsheet options feature. They may also create new sets of data to do what-if analyses.

Spreadsheet Options

USING THE NUMERICAL FORMAT OPTION

A financial ratio presents the relationship among two or more numbers. To improve users' understanding of these relationships, financial ratios should be displayed in generally accepted formats. The numerical format option allows a variety of formats to be used, as shown in the illustration. For example, the rate earned on net sales in cells F147 and G147 in the illustration is displayed as a percentage with one decimal place accuracy. The earnings per share in F152 and G152 is displayed in dollars and cents. The price-earnings ratio in cells F157 and G157 is displayed without a dollar sign to one decimal place accuracy.

The (C2) notation on the prompt line indicates that cell F152 is formatted with the currency format with two decimal place accuracy. Although the currency format is most frequently used on business spreadsheet templates, several other formats are available, including percentage, comma, and fixed with decimal place accuracy of 0 to 15 digits.

```
F152: (C2) [W15] +F150/F151                                          READY

     A B      C          D           E              F               G
139                      Financial Statement Analysis
140
141                                               Current          Prior
142                                                 Year            Year
143                                           ------------------------------
144    Rate Earned on Net Sales:
145      Net Income after Federal Income Tax...    $42,322         $38,976
146      Net Sales.............................    514,560         465,430
147      Rate Earned on Net Sales..............       8.2%            8.4%
148
149    Earnings per Share:
150      Net Income after Federal Income Tax...    $42,322         $38,976
151      Shares of Stock Outstanding...........     10,000          10,000
152      Earnings per Share....................      $4.23           $3.90
153
154    Price-earnings ratio:
155      Market Price per Share................     $25.00          $22.00
156      Earnings per Share....................      $4.23           $3.90
157      Price-earnings ratio..................        5.9             5.6
158
```

Sales and Cost of Goods Sold Transactions

FYI

Japanese factory assembly lines use about seven times more industrial robots than American assembly lines.

FaxaVision's procedures for recording sales are similar to those described in Chapter 3. However, since FaxaVision uses a perpetual inventory, a different procedure is used to determine and record cost of goods sold.

For each sale, a sales invoice is sent to the finished goods stockroom. A sales invoice provides authorization and information for shipping products. The number of products shipped is posted to the finished goods ledger from the sales invoice. The unit cost and total amount of products sold is recorded on the sales invoice. The sales invoice is then filed until the end of the month.

At the end of the month, cost information on all sales invoices is totaled. The total costs recorded on all of FaxaVision's sales for January, *$264,020.00,* is the cost of goods sold during the month. This total cost is transferred from the inventory account Finished Goods to the cost account Cost of Goods Sold. The journal entry to record this transaction is shown in Illustration 20-9.

APPLIED SKILLS: LANGUAGE ARTS

Paraphrasing, writing complete sentences, and identifying subjects. For additional practice in language arts skills, direct students to answer the Accounting Terms and Questions for Individual Study at the end of the chapter. Students should write the answers in their own words and in complete sentences. To further practice language arts skills, ask students to underline the subject(s) in each sentence of their answers.

ILLUSTRATION 20-9 Journal entry to record cost of goods sold for a month

GENERAL JOURNAL PAGE 1

	DATE		ACCOUNT TITLE	DOC. NO.	POST. REF.	DEBIT	CREDIT	
19		31	Cost of Goods Sold	M245		264 020 00		19
20			Finished Goods				264 020 00	20
21								21

Cost of Goods Sold

Debit		Credit	
Jan. 31 from Finished Goods	264,020.00		

Finished Goods

Debit		Credit	
Bal.	115,140.00	Jan. 31 Cost of Goods Sold	264,020.00
Jan. 31 Completed Cost Sheets	280,352.50		
(New Bal. Jan. 31	*131,472.50)*		

Audit Your Understanding

1. What accounts are debited for a payroll consisting of direct and indirect labor?
2. What accounts are debited and credited when the purchase of materials is recorded in the materials purchases journal?
3. What account is debited to record applied factory overhead at the end of the month?
4. What does a credit ending balance in Factory Overhead indicate?
5. What does a credit to Work in Process indicate?
6. What account is credited to record the cost of goods sold during the month?

The debit to Cost of Goods Sold, *$264,020.00,* is the cost of goods sold during the month. The credit to Finished Goods, *$264,020.00,* is the cost of finished goods sold during the month and removed from inventory. The finished goods account balance, *$131,472.50,* is the ending inventory of finished goods.

Manufacturing Accounts in the General Ledger

The effect of posting the entries described in this chapter is shown in Illustration 20-10, page 546.

PREPARING END-OF-FISCAL-PERIOD STATEMENTS

Several of the procedures used to prepare a manufacturing business' work sheet and financial statements are similar to the procedures used for a merchandising business.

Work Sheet

A work sheet is used to plan a manufacturing business' financial information for fiscal period statements just as it is for merchandising businesses. However, a manufacturing business' work sheet includes three factory inventory accounts and a cost of goods sold account. FaxaVision's work sheet for January is shown in Illustration 20-11, pages 548 and 549.

AUDIT YOUR UNDERSTANDING

The AUDIT YOUR UNDERSTANDING feature appears at the end of each section of the chapter. Explain to your students that the word *audit* means to check or verify. AUDIT YOUR UNDERSTANDING may be used to check student comprehension of the section just studied. The answers are provided in Appendix D in the back of the textbook.

1. Work in Process and Factory Overhead.
2. Materials is debited; Accounts Payable is credited.
3. Work in Process.
4. Overapplied overhead.
5. The cost of finished goods transferred from the factory to the stockroom.
6. Finished Goods.

LESSON PLAN 20-2

Materials

- Student pages 545–552
- Blackline Master for 1-Column Statement (TRG)
- Software: Spreadsheet Template
- Assess: Problem Test Chapter 20, MicroExam Chapter 20, Objective Test No. 7

Objectives (Enabling Performance Tasks)

a. Define accounting terms related to accounting transactions and financial reporting for a manufacturing business.

b. Identify accounting concepts and practices related to accounting transactions and financial reporting for a manufacturing business.

d. Prepare selected financial statements for a manufacturing business.

FOCUS

- Manufacturing cost transactions were journalized and posted to manufacturing accounts in the general ledger earlier in this chapter. In this lesson, the work sheet and end-of-fiscal-period statements will be presented. Explain that the information collected in the manufacturing accounts is used to prepare a new financial statement that supplements the income statement.
- Introduce vocabulary: statement of cost of goods manufactured.

ILLUSTRATION 20-10 Manufacturing accounts

ACCOUNT *Materials* ACCOUNT NO. *1125*

DATE		ITEM	POST. REF.	DEBIT	CREDIT	BALANCE DEBIT	BALANCE CREDIT
19-- Jan.	1	Balance	✓			121 231 20	
	31		MP1	168 642 60		289 873 80	
	31		G1		167 924 50	121 949 30	

ACCOUNT *Work in Process* ACCOUNT NO. *1130*

DATE		ITEM	POST. REF.	DEBIT	CREDIT	BALANCE DEBIT	BALANCE CREDIT
19-- Jan.	1	Balance	✓			82 579 00	
	15		CP2	39 245 00		121 824 00	
	31		CP2	44 255 00		166 079 00	
	31		G1	156 477 00		322 556 00	
	31		G1	66 800 00		389 356 00	
	31		G1		280 352 50	109 003 50	

ACCOUNT *Finished Goods* ACCOUNT NO. *1135*

DATE		ITEM	POST. REF.	DEBIT	CREDIT	BALANCE DEBIT	BALANCE CREDIT
19-- Jan.	1	Balance	✓			115 140 00	
	31		G1	280 352 50		395 492 50	
	31		G1		264 020 00	131 472 50	

ACCOUNT *Cost of Goods Sold* ACCOUNT NO. *5105*

DATE		ITEM	POST. REF.	DEBIT	CREDIT	BALANCE DEBIT	BALANCE CREDIT
19-- Jan.	31		G1	264 020 00		264 020 00	

ACCOUNT *Factory Overhead* ACCOUNT NO. *5505*

DATE		ITEM	POST. REF.	DEBIT	CREDIT	BALANCE DEBIT	BALANCE CREDIT
19-- Jan.	15		CP2	11 774 00		11 774 00	
	31		CP2	13 276 00		25 050 00	
	31		G1	11 447 50		36 497 50	
	31		G1	30 456 00		66 953 50	
	31		G1		66 800 00	153 50	
	31		G1		153 50	—	—

TEACHING STRATEGIES: COOPERATIVE LEARNING

Divide the class into two groups. Each group stands and faces each other. Teacher chooses selected Accounting Terms from Chapters 18 through 20. Teacher gives the term. The first student who raises his or her hand has the opportunity to give the correct definition. The group with the most correctly defined terms is declared the winner. This cooperative learning activity should not take more than 20 to 25 minutes of class time.

FaxaVision's work sheet, similar to the work sheets of other manufacturing businesses using the perpetual inventory method, has several unique characteristics.

1. The entries to record direct materials, work in process, and finished goods bring manufacturing inventory accounts up to date on January 31. Thus, the balances of Materials, Work in Process, and Finished Goods are brought up to date before a work sheet is prepared. Adjustments for these inventory accounts do not need to be planned on a work sheet.
2. Perpetual inventory subsidiary ledgers and detailed cost records are kept in the factory. Based on these subsidiary records, summary journal entries are made that record the flow of costs through the manufacturing process to the cost of goods sold account. Since all manufacturing costs flow toward the account Cost of Goods Sold, no manufacturing cost accounts on the work sheet have balances. Amounts in these accounts have been transferred to either one of the inventory accounts or the cost of goods sold account. The cost of goods sold amount, *$264,020.00,* is extended to the Income Statement Debit column.
3. Income Summary has a debit balance of $153.50. This balance resulted from closing the underapplied overhead to Income Summary. The amount represents additional manufacturing costs that are not already in the inventory or cost of goods sold account. The amount is extended to the Income Statement Debit column.

Extending other accounts to the Income Statement and Balance Sheet columns and calculating net income are similar to the procedures described for corporations in Chapter 14.

Financial Statements

A manufacturing business prepares an income statement, a statement of stockholders' equity, and a balance sheet. These statements are similar to those previously described for other kinds of businesses. Many manufacturing businesses also prepare a statement of cost of goods manufactured.

A statement of stockholders' equity for a manufacturing business is similar to that of a merchandising business described in Chapter 14. This statement is not illustrated in Chapter 20.

FYI

A statement of cost of goods manufactured supplements the income statement.

Statement of Cost of Goods Manufactured. An additional statement is prepared by many manufacturing businesses to report greater detail about costs of finished goods. A statement showing details about the cost of finished goods is called a **statement of cost of goods manufactured.** This statement shows the details of the cost elements—materials, direct labor, and factory overhead—spent on the goods completed in a fiscal period. A statement of cost of goods manufactured supplements the income statement. FaxaVision's

TEACH

Cover student pages 545–552 "Preparing End-of-Fiscal-Period Statements." Review the steps for preparing a work sheet. Explain why adjustments for the three manufacturing inventory accounts do not need to be planned on the work sheet. Discuss the procedures to complete a statement of cost of goods manufactured, an income statement, and a balance sheet. Have students compare the income statement of a manufacturing business with the income statement of a merchandising business shown in Illustration 18-6, Chapter 18.

TEACHING STRATEGIES: EXPANDING BEYOND THE CLASSROOM

Invite an accountant from a manufacturing business to the classroom to address the importance of cost accounting to a manufacturing business.

APPLY

Refer students to Illustration 20-12, 20-13, and 20-14, respectively, as the financial statements are discussed.

Guided Practice

Guide students through the preparation of the statement of cost of goods manufactured in Problem 20-3. Make a transparency of the 1-column statement paper from the accounting forms provided in the Blackline Masters Section of the Teacher's Resource Guide. Students will need the ledger and journals prepared in Problem 20-2. Working as a group, decide what amount should be recorded for direct materials. When all students agree on the amount, direct them to record the amount on the form provided in the working papers as you demonstrate on the overhead projector. Repeat the process for each line until the statement has been completed.

Independent Practice

- Assign Term 3 and Questions 18–20.
- Assign Study Guide 20 and Mastery Problem 20-M.

ILLUSTRATION 20-11 Work sheet for a manufacturing business

FaxaVision, Inc.
Work Sheet
For Month Ended January 31, 19--

	ACCOUNT TITLE	1 TRIAL BALANCE DEBIT	2 TRIAL BALANCE CREDIT	3 ADJUSTMENTS DEBIT	4 ADJUSTMENTS CREDIT	5 INCOME STATEMENT DEBIT	6 INCOME STATEMENT CREDIT	7 BALANCE SHEET DEBIT	8 BALANCE SHEET CREDIT	
1	Cash	182633 60						182633 60		1
2	Petty Cash	300 00						300 00		2
3	Accounts Receivable	224207 50						224207 50		3
4	Allow. for Uncoll. Accts.		4541 60		(a) 2056 60				6598 20	4
5	Materials	121949 30						121949 30		5
6	Work in Process	109003 50						109003 50		6
7	Finished Goods	131472 50						131472 50		7
8	Supplies—Factory	7258 70						7258 70		8
9	Supplies—Sales	9531 20			(b) 1850 20			7681 00		9
10	Supplies—Administrative	2425 80			(c) 468 40			1957 40		10
11	Prepaid Insurance	4198 60			(d) 130 60			4068 00		11
12	Factory Equipment	182000 00						182000 00		12
13	Accum. Depr.—Factory Equipment		54610 00						54610 00	13
14	Office Equipment	25260 00						25260 00		14
15	Accum. Depr.—Office Equipment		6200 00		(e) 530 00				6730 00	15
16	Store Equipment	22900 00						22900 00		16
17	Accum. Depr.—Store Equipment		6770 00		(f) 490 00				7260 00	17
18	Building	397000 00						397000 00		18
19	Accum. Depr.—Building		59500 00						59500 00	19
20	Land	177000 00						177000 00		20
21	Accounts Payable		189698 50						189698 50	21
22	Employee Income Tax Payable		11871 40						11871 40	22
23	Federal Income Tax Payable				(g) 20995 00				20995 00	23
24	FICA Tax Payable		17205 00						17205 00	24
25	Salaries Payable									25
26	Unemploy. Tax Payable—Federal		1268 40						1268 40	26
27	Unemploy. Tax Payable—State		8561 70						8561 70	27
28	Dividends Payable									28
29	Mortgage Payable		100000 00						100000 00	29
30	Capital Stock		600000 00						600000 00	30

31	Retained Earnings		469 638 80						469 638 80	31
32	Dividends									32
33	Income Summary	153 50				153 50				33
34	Sales		411 480 00				411 480 00			34
35	Cost of Goods Sold	264 020 00				264 020 00				35
36	Factory Overhead									36
37	Depr. Expense—Factory Equipment									37
38	Depr. Expense—Building									38
39	Heat, Light, and Power Expense									39
40	Insurance Expense—Factory									40
41	Miscellaneous Exp.—Factory									41
42	Payroll Taxes Exp.—Factory									42
43	Property Tax Exp.—Factory									43
44	Supplies Expense—Factory									44
45	Advertising Expense	4 784 40				4 784 40				45
46	Delivery Expense	11 058 60				11 058 60				46
47	Depr. Expense—Store Equipment			(f) 490 00		490 00				47
48	Miscellaneous Expenses—Sales	1 554 50				1 554 50				48
49	Salary Expense—Sales	28 078 00				28 078 00				49
50	Supplies Expense—Sales			(b) 1 850 20		1 850 20				50
51	Depr. Expense—Office Equipment			(e) 530 00		530 00				51
52	Insurance Expense—Admin.			(d) 130 60		130 60				52
53	Miscellaneous Exp.—Admin.	2 184 20				2 184 20				53
54	Payroll Taxes Exp.—Admin.	7 100 00				7 100 00				54
55	Property Tax Exp.—Admin.	159 80				159 80				55
56	Salary Expense—Admin.	21 922 00				21 922 00				56
57	Supplies Expense—Admin.			(c) 468 40		468 40				57
58	Uncollectible Accounts Expense			(a) 2 056 60		2 056 60				58
59	Utilities Expense—Admin.	1 543 80				1 543 80				59
60	Gain on Plant Assets									60
61	Miscellaneous Revenue									61
62	Interest Expense	1 500 00				1 500 00				62
63	Loss on Plant Assets	145 90				145 90				63
64	Federal Income Tax Expense			(g) 20 995 00		20 995 00				64
65		1941 345 40	1941 345 40	26 520 80	26 520 80	370 725 50	411 480 00	1594 691 50	1553 937 00	65
66	Net Income after Fed. Inc. Tax					40 754 50			40 754 50	66
67						411 480 00	411 480 00	1594 691 50	1594 691 50	67

ASSESS

Assess student understanding by checking the solutions to the Independent Practice activities.

Reteach

- Make a transparency of the 1-column statement paper from the accounting forms provided in the Blackline Masters Section of the Teacher's Resource Guide. Using the ledger and journals prepared in Recycling Problem 20-R and the transparency, demonstrate how the statement of cost of goods manufactured is prepared. The solution to Recycling Problem 20-R is provided in the Audit Tests and Solutions to Recycling Problems section of the Teacher's Resource Guide.
- Assign Recycling Problem 20-R, Instruction 7.

Extend

- Assign Cases for Critical Thinking 2.
- Assign Challenge Problem 20-C. (The challenge is to prepare a work sheet, income statement, and balance sheet.)
- Assign Reinforcement Activity 3.
- Assign the Spreadsheet Template for Problem 20-3.

Enrich

- Assign the SPREADSHEET OPTIONS feature on page 544.
- Assign BOMBAY LEATHER, INC.: A Business Simulation.

CLOSURE

Use Audit Your Understanding questions.

ASSESS

- Administer Problem Test Chapter 20.
- Administer a MicroExam test for Chapter 20.
- Administer Objective Test No. 7.

statement of cost of goods manufactured is shown in Illustration 20-12.

ILLUSTRATION 20-12 Statement of cost of goods manufactured

FaxaVision, Inc. Statement of Cost of Goods Manufactured For Month Ended January 31, 19--	
Direct Materials	$156,477.00
Direct Labor	83,500.00
Factory Overhead Applied	66,800.00
Total Cost of Work Placed in Process	$306,777.00
Work in Process Inventory, Jan. 1, 19--	82,579.00
Total Cost of Work in Process During January	$389,356.00
Less Work in Process Inventory, Jan. 31, 19--	109,003.50
Cost of Goods Manufactured	$280,352.50

Information for the statement of cost of goods manufactured comes from four sources. (1) Direct materials, *$156,477.00,* is the amount debited to Work in Process in the general journal, Illustration 20-4. Direct materials is the total amount of direct materials requisitions. (2) Direct labor, *$83,500.00,* comes from the cash payments journal, Illustration 20-2. (3) Factory overhead applied, *$66,800.00,* comes from the general journal entry applying factory overhead to the work in process account, Illustration 20-6. The amount of factory overhead is the total of the applied factory overhead recorded on cost sheets. (4) Beginning and ending work in process inventories, *$82,579.00* and *$109,003.50,* come from the general ledger accounts, Illustration 20-10.

MILESTONE

The accounting principles for departmentalized accounting, corporation accounting, management accounting, and cost accounting have now been covered. It is assumed that the concepts presented in the first 20 chapters dealing with the most common accounting systems have been mastered as the chapters to follow will expand upon this knowledge by introducing two other accounting systems.

Income Statement. FaxaVision's income statement for the month of January is shown in Illustration 20-13.

Information for FaxaVision's income statement comes from three sources. (1) Beginning and ending finished goods inventories, *$115,140.00* and *$131,472.50,* come from the general ledger account, Illustration 20-10. (2) Cost of goods manufactured, *$280,352.50,* comes from the statement of cost of goods manufactured, Illustration 20-12. (3) All other amounts come from the Income Statement columns of the work sheet, Illustration 20-11.

FYI

In 1991, state income taxes raised more revenue for 33 states than any other source; sales taxes were the largest revenue source for 15 states.

This income statement differs in two ways from the income statements of merchandising businesses shown in previous chapters.

1. Cost of goods manufactured is used instead of purchases. Details of the cost of goods manufactured are given on the statement of cost of goods manufactured.

TEACHING STRATEGIES: Teaching Tip

Have the class review the income statement and balance sheet shown in Illustrations 20-13 and 20-14. Have the class make an oral analysis of the sections of each of these statements.

ILLUSTRATION 20-13 Income statement for a manufacturing business

FaxaVision, Inc.
Income Statement
For Month Ended January 31, 19--

				***% of Net Sales**
Operating Revenue:				
Sales			$411,480.00	100.0
Cost of Goods Sold:				
Finished Goods Inventory, Jan. 1, 19--		$115,140.00		
Cost of Goods Manufactured		280,352.50		
Total Cost of Finished Goods Available for Sale		$395,492.50		
Less Finished Goods Inventory, Jan. 31, 19--		131,472.50		
Cost of Goods Sold		$264,020.00		
Underapplied Overhead		153.50		
Net Cost of Goods Sold			264,173.50	64.2
Gross Profit on Operations			$147,306.50	35.8
Operating Expenses:				
Selling Expenses:				
Advertising Expense	$ 4,784.40			
Delivery Expense	11,058.60			
Depreciation Expense—Store Equipment	490.00			
Miscellaneous Expense—Sales	1,554.50			
Salary Expense—Sales	28,078.00			
Supplies Expense—Sales	1,850.20			
Total Selling Expenses		$ 47,815.70		
Administrative Expenses:				
Depreciation Expense—Office Equipment	$ 530.00			
Insurance Expense—Administrative	130.60			
Miscellaneous Expense—Administrative	2,184.20			
Payroll Taxes Expense—Administrative	7,100.00			
Property Tax Expense—Administrative	159.80			
Salary Expense—Administrative	21,922.00			
Supplies Expense—Administrative	468.40			
Uncollectible Accounts Expense	2,056.60			
Utilities Expense—Administrative	1,543.80			
Total Administrative Expenses		$ 36,095.40		
Total Operating Expenses			83,911.10	20.4
Net Income from Operations			$ 63,395.40	15.4
Other Expenses:				
Interest Expense		$ 1,500.00		
Loss on Plant Assets		145.90		
Net Deduction			1,645.90	0.4
Net Income before Federal Income Tax			$ 61,749.50	15.0
Less Federal Income Tax Expense			20,995.00	5.1
Net Income after Federal Income Tax			$ 40,754.50	9.9

*Rounded to nearest 0.1%

REINFORCEMENT ACTIVITY

Reinforcement Activity 3 is the complete accounting cycle for a manufacturing business organized as a corporation. Job cost accounting processing and reporting is emphasized. Blackline masters for audit tests for Reinforcement Activity 3 are available in the Teacher's Resource Guide in three options: Part A only, Part B only, and Parts A and B combined.

2. The amount of underapplied overhead, *$153.50,* is added to the cost of goods sold. The amount is added because applied overhead, *$66,800.00,* is less than the actual overhead, *$66,953.50.*

SIMULATION

To give students an opportunity to apply accounting concepts for a manufacturing business, assign students to complete BOMBAY LEATHER, INC.: A Business Simulation.

TEACHING STRATEGIES: ASSESSMENT BY PORTFOLIO

An ideal specimen for inclusion in a portfolio to demonstrate mastery of the accounting principles that apply to a manufacturing business is an extended activity that simulates the accounting cycle for a manufacturing business. For this part, you may wish to have students complete and include in their portfolios either Reinforcement Activity 3 or BOMBAY LEATHER, INC.: A Business Simulation.

AUDIT YOUR UNDERSTANDING

1. Income Statement Debit column.
2. Underapplied overhead has been closed to Income Summary.
3. Direct materials, direct labor, and factory overhead.
4. Underapplied overhead is added to the cost of goods sold.
5. Current Assets.

Audit Your Understanding

1. To which work sheet column is the debit balance of Cost of Goods Sold extended?
2. What has occurred if Income Summary has a debit balance on the Trial Balance of a work sheet for a manufacturing business?
3. What are the three cost elements reported on a statement of cost of goods manufactured?
4. How is underapplied overhead accounted for on an income statement?
5. In which section of the balance sheet are the three inventory accounts of a manufacturing business listed?

If there had been overapplied overhead, the overhead included in the cost of goods manufactured would have been more than the actual overhead expenses. In that case, the amount of the overapplied overhead would have been subtracted from the cost of goods sold on the income statement.

Balance Sheet. The balance sheet prepared by FaxaVision on January 31, of the current year is shown in Illustration 20-14.

Except for the listing of inventories, the balance sheet of a manufacturing business is similar to the balance sheet of a merchandising business. In a manufacturing business, the current assets section of the balance sheet lists three types of inventories. (1) Materials. (2) Work in Process. (3) Finished Goods.

ACCOUNTING TERMS

1. **underapplied overhead:** The amount by which applied factory overhead is less than actual factory overhead. (p. 541)
2. **overapplied overhead:** The amount by which applied factory overhead is more than actual factory overhead. (p. 542)
3. **statement of cost of goods manufactured:** A statement showing details about the cost of finished goods. (p. 547)

ACCOUNTING TERMS EPT(a)

What is the meaning of each of the following?

1. **underapplied overhead**
2. **overapplied overhead**
3. **statement of cost of goods manufactured**

QUESTIONS FOR INDIVIDUAL STUDY

1. Detailed cost records must be maintained throughout the manufacturing process. (p. 535)
2. At the end of a fiscal period. (p. 535)
3. Inventories are up to date after journal entries are posted. Thus, end-of-fiscal-period inventory adjustments are not required. (p. 536)
4. Work in Process and Factory Overhead. (p. 537)
5. Matching Expenses with Revenue. (p. 537)
6. Materials is debited; Accounts Payable is credited. (p. 538)

QUESTIONS FOR INDIVIDUAL STUDY EPT(b)

1. What is needed to provide usable financial information for a manufacturing business?
2. When are most general ledger entries made for manufacturing costs?
3. What is the reason for a manufacturing company to use the perpetual inventory method to record materials, work in process, and finished goods?
4. What two accounts are debited when a factory payroll is recorded in a cash payments journal?
5. Which accounting concept is being applied when cost of materials is charged to a job as materials are used?
6. What accounts are affected, and how, when materials are purchased on account?
7. What accounts are affected, and how, when the total value of all direct and indirect materials requisitions is recorded in the general journal at the end of a month?
8. What amount does the balance of the general ledger account Materials equal?
9. What are some examples of factory overhead expenses?
10. What accounts are affected, and how, when overhead is applied for the month?
11. After the journal entry for applied overhead has

ILLUSTRATION 20-14 Balance sheet for a manufacturing business

FaxaVision, Inc.
Balance Sheet
January 31, 19--

ASSETS			
Current Assets:			
Cash		$182,633.60	
Petty Cash		300.00	
Accounts Receivable	$224,207.50		
Less Allowance for Uncollectible Accounts	6,598.20	217,609.30	
Materials		121,949.30	
Work in Process		109,003.50	
Finished Goods		131,472.50	
Supplies—Factory		7,258.70	
Supplies—Sales		7,681.00	
Supplies—Administrative		1,957.40	
Prepaid Insurance		4,068.00	
Total Current Assets			$ 783,933.30
Plant Assets:			
Factory Equipment	$182,000.00		
Less Accumulated Depreciation—Factory Equipment	54,610.00	$127,390.00	
Office Equipment	$ 25,260.00		
Less Accumulated Depreciation—Office Equipment	6,730.00	18,530.00	
Store Equipment	$ 22,900.00		
Less Accumulated Depreciation—Store Equipment	7,260.00	15,640.00	
Building	$397,000.00		
Less Accumulated Depreciation—Building	59,500.00	337,500.00	
Land		177,000.00	
Total Plant Assets			676,060.00
Total Assets			$1,459,993.30
LIABILITIES			
Current Liabilities:			
Accounts Payable		$189,698.50	
Employee Income Tax Payable		11,871.40	
Federal Income Tax Payable		20,995.00	
FICA Tax Payable		17,205.00	
Unemployment Tax Payable—Federal		1,268.40	
Unemployment Tax Payable—State		8,561.70	
Total Current Liabilities			$ 249,600.00
Long-Term Liability:			
Mortgage Payable			100,000.00
Total Liabilities			$ 349,600.00
STOCKHOLDERS' EQUITY			
Capital Stock		$600,000.00	
Retained Earnings		510,393.30	
Total Stockholders' Equity			1,110,393.30
Total Liabilities and Stockholders' Equity			$1,459,993.30

QUESTIONS *(cont'd)*

7. Work in Process is debited for the amount of direct materials issued and Factory Overhead is debited for the amount of indirect materials issued. Materials is credited for the total amount issued. (pp. 538–539)

8. The account balance must equal the sum of the balances of all records in the materials ledger. (p. 539)

9. Indirect labor, indirect materials, taxes, depreciation, and insurance. (p. 540)

10. Work in Process is debited; Factory Overhead is credited. (p. 541)

11. The factory overhead account debit is the actual factory overhead expense for the month. The credit is the total of applied factory overhead recorded on cost sheets during the month. (p. 541)

12. A debit balance. (pp. 541–542)

13. Factory Overhead is debited; Income Summary is credited. (p. 542)

14. (a) Actual expenses may be higher or lower than normal. This event requires closer control of expenditures. (b) The factory overhead applied rate may be inaccurate. This event requires more accurate estimating and calculating of the applied rate. (p. 543)

15. At the end of the month, total amounts on all cost sheets completed during the current month are totaled. (p. 543)

16. Finished Goods is debited; Work in Process is credited. (p. 543)

17. Cost of Goods Sold is debited; Finished Goods is credited. (p. 545)

18. The details of the cost elements—materials, direct labor, and factory overhead—spent on the goods completed in a fiscal period. (p. 547)

19. (a) Cost of goods manufactured is used instead of purchases. Details of the cost of goods manufactured are given on the statement of cost of goods manufactured. (b) The amount of underapplied overhead is added to the cost of goods sold if applied overhead is less than the actual overhead. The amount of overapplied overhead is subtracted from the cost of goods sold if applied overhead is more than actual overhead. (pp. 550–552)

20. FaxaVision's current assets section lists three types of inventories—Materials, Work in Process, and Finished Goods. (p. 552)

been posted, what do the debit and credit amounts in the factory overhead account represent?

12. When there is underapplied overhead at the end of a month, does the factory overhead account have a debit balance or a credit balance?
13. What accounts are affected, and how, when the factory overhead account is closed and there is overapplied overhead?
14. What two reasons may cause a difference between actual and applied overhead? What should be done to correct the difference?
15. How does FaxaVision determine the amount of work finished during a month?
16. What accounts are affected, and how, to record the finished goods manufactured during the month?
17. What accounts are affected, and how, to record costs of sales for a business using a perpetual inventory?
18. What is reported on a statement of cost of goods manufactured?
19. FaxaVision's income statement differs in what two ways from income statements of merchandising businesses shown in previous chapters?
20. How does FaxaVision's balance sheet differ from a merchandising business' balance sheet?

CASES FOR CRITICAL THINKING

EPT(b)

CASE 1 Kingston Corporation, a manufacturing company, uses the perpetual inventory method for all inventory accounts. Direct materials, direct labor, and applied overhead are recorded on cost sheets similar to FaxaVision's. At the end of each month, general journal entries are made to update the general ledger manufacturing accounts. Overapplied or Underapplied Overhead is closed to **Income Summary** and reported separately on the income statement as an adjustment to the cost of goods sold.

A new accountant suggests that the company could save considerable time if a number of accounting changes are made: (a) Use the periodic inventory method, (b) drop the use of applied overhead, and (c) close all manufacturing accounts into **Income Summary** similar to the procedure used by merchandising businesses. The accountant indicates that these new procedures would provide adequate information to prepare the income statement with a substantial time and cost saving.

Should the changes in accounting procedures be made? Will the changes provide adequate information? How will the changes affect the information now provided?

CASE 2 Southwest Corporation is a small manufacturing company. At the end of each fiscal period, the company prepares an income statement and a balance sheet. However, the company does not prepare a statement of goods manufactured. A consultant told the company president that a statement of cost of goods manufactured is absolutely essential. Do you agree with the consultant or not? Why?

APPLIED COMMUNICATIONS

Competition is the key to free enterprise in our economy. There are many companies that produce nearly the same products or provide nearly the same services. Competition makes these businesses provide better products and services for the consumer. However, businesses compete not only by providing better products and services, but also through avenues such as advertising, hours of operation, providing a difference in products that are similar, and business location.

INSTRUCTIONS:

Select two local competitors in either the food, clothing, or hair salons industries. Create a graph that lists competitive factors such as hours, advertising, location, prices, etc. Analyze your two choices and select which business you think is the competitive leader. Then write a paragraph on your findings.

CASES FOR CRITICAL THINKING

Case 1 The accounting changes should not be made. The suggested procedure would require less time. However, without the information provided by the existing procedures, cost control would be more limited and management information less available.

Periodic inventory would not provide cost information for each job or unit manufactured. If an applied overhead rate is not used, overhead could not be charged to manufacturing costs until the end of the accounting period and then would be only a total amount. Overhead cost information would not be available for each job. If cost sheets were not used for each job, unit manufacturing costs could not be calculated. If all costs are closed into Income Summary, cost of goods sold could not be determined without separate computations.

APPLIED SKILLS: COMMUNICATIONS

Surveys of business managers show that communication skills are one of the most desired traits in new employees. The APPLIED COMMUNICATIONS activity provides an opportunity for students to practice their communication and language arts skills on topics that directly relate to accounting. This activity requires students to create a graph for two competitive businesses. Students should summarize the competitive features about both businesses and draw a conclusion. If available, students should use software that permits the display of graphics within the text.

APPLICATION PROBLEMS

EPT(c,d)

PROBLEM 20-1 Journalizing cost accounting transactions for a manufacturing company

Dillard, Inc., a manufacturing business, completed the following factory cost transactions during March of the current year.

INSTRUCTIONS:

1. Journalize the following transactions. Use page 3 of a materials purchases journal and page 6 of a cash payments journal. Source documents are abbreviated as follows: check, C; purchase invoice, P.

Mar. 7. Purchased materials on account from Scotsman Company, $3,840.00. P162.
10. Paid cash for machinery repairs, $186.90. C333. (Miscellaneous Expense—Factory)
15. Paid cash for factory supplies, $412.90. C341.
22. Purchased materials on account from North Company, $1,394.70. P163.
23. Paid cash for a new stitching machine, $1,265.30. C352. (Factory Equipment)
25. Paid cash for monthly factory payroll, $5,709.80 (direct labor, $5,100.00, and indirect labor, $1,950.00; less deductions: employee income tax, $776.20; FICA tax, $564.00). C367.

2. Total and rule the materials purchases journal.
3. Prove and rule the cash payments journal.

PROBLEM 20-2 Journalizing and posting entries that summarize cost records at the end of a fiscal period

The following information is taken from the records of Cramer Corporation on March 31 of the current year. The accounts and balances needed to complete this problem are given in the working papers accompanying this textbook.

a. The total factory payroll for the month according to the payroll register is $122,530.00, distributed as follows.

Work in Process	$102,570.00
Factory Overhead	19,960.00
Cash	99,249.10
Employee Income Tax Payable	13,478.50
FICA Tax Payable	9,802.40

b. The total of all requisitions of direct materials issued during the month is $139,419.80. The total of all requisitions of indirect materials issued during the month is $4,505.00.
c. The factory overhead to be charged to **Work in Process** is 68% of the direct labor cost.
d. The total of all cost sheets completed during the month is $294,313.50.
e. The total of costs recorded on all sales invoices for March is $395,800.00.

INSTRUCTIONS:

1. Journalize the factory payroll entry on page 6 of a cash payments journal. C371. Post the general debit and general credit amounts.
2. Journalize the following entries on page 3 of a general journal. Post the entries.
   a. An entry to transfer the total of all direct materials requisitions to **Work in Process** and indirect materials to **Factory Overhead**. M34.
   b. An entry to close all individual manufacturing expense accounts to **Factory Overhead**. M35.
   c. An entry to record applied factory overhead to **Work in Process**. M36.
3. Continue using page 3 of the general journal. Journalize and post the entry to close the balance of the factory overhead account to **Income Summary**. M37.
4. Journalize and post the entry to transfer the total of all cost sheets completed from **Work in Process** to **Finished Goods**. M38.
5. Journalize and post the entry to transfer the cost of products sold from **Finished Goods** to **Cost of Goods Sold**. M39.

The ledger and journals prepared in this problem are needed to complete Problem 20-3.

CASES FOR CRITICAL THINKING *(cont'd)*

Case 2 Do not agree with consultant. Accurate records should be kept so that the cost of goods manufactured can be accurately calculated. However, a statement of cost of goods manufactured is not "absolutely essential." The statement does show detail about the cost of goods manufactured. The detail is used by many managers in making decisions related to the manufacturing process. However, not all managers require this much detailed cost information. Two alternatives could be used to report cost of goods manufactured information. (1) Report only the cost of goods manufactured amount on the cost of goods sold section of the income statement. (2) Expand the cost of goods sold section of the income statement to include the detail normally reported on a statement of cost of goods manufactured. This approach would make the income statement longer but a separate statement would not be required. Most manufacturing businesses do, however, prepare a separate statement of cost of goods manufactured.

APPLIED COMMUNICATIONS

This activity requires students to create a graph for two competitive businesses. Students should summarize the competitive features about both businesses and draw a conclusion. Students' solutions will vary. The instructor should consider the following items when grading the activity: (1) is the graph thorough, (2) did they identify the leader, (3) writing style, and (4) mechanics (grammar, spelling, punctuation, and sentence structure).

CHECK FIGURES

See Teacher's Edition of Working Papers for complete solutions.

Problem 20-1 Materials Purchases Journal total, $5,234.70; Cash Payments Journal totals, $8,915.10, $1,340.20, $7,574.90.

Problem 20-2 (2c) Applied factory overhead, $69,747.60. (3) Underapplied overhead, $767.80.

CHECK FIGURES *(cont'd)*

Problem 20-3 Cost of Goods Manufactured, $294,313.50.

Mastery Problem 20-M (2c) Applied factory overhead, $46,528.00. (3) Underapplied overhead, $444.80. (6) Cost of Goods Manufactured, $166,425.00.

Challenge Problem 20-C (2c) Applied factory overhead, $44,270.00. (3) Overapplied overhead, $191.83. (6) Cost of Goods Manufactured, $140,984.00. (7) Work sheet adjustments column total, $10,357.06. (8b) Gross Profit on Operations, $71,595.00. (8h) Net Income after Federal Income Tax, $20,068.28. (9) Total Assets, $729,259.42.

PROBLEM 20-3 Preparing a statement of cost of goods manufactured

The ledger and journals prepared in Problem 20-2 are needed to complete this problem.

SPREADSHEET

INSTRUCTIONS:

Prepare a statement of cost of goods manufactured for Cramer Corporation. The statement is for the month ended March 31 of the current year. Use the information from Problem 20-2 to prepare the statement.

ENRICHMENT PROBLEMS

EPT(c,d)

MASTERY PROBLEM 20-M Journalizing entries that summarize cost records at the end of a fiscal period

The following information is taken from the records of Simmons Corporation on May 31 of the current year. The accounts and balances needed to complete this problem are given in the working papers accompanying this textbook.

a. The total factory payroll for the month according to the payroll register is $77,430.00, distributed as follows.

Work in Process	$58,160.00
Factory Overhead	19,270.00
Cash	62,608.10
Employee Income Tax Payable	8,627.50
FICA Tax Payable	6,194.40

b. The total of all requisitions of direct materials issued during the month is $64,344.00. The total of all requisitions of indirect materials issued during the month is $5,835.00.

c. The factory overhead to be charged to Work in Process is 80% of the direct labor cost.

d. The total of all cost sheets completed during the month is $166,425.00.

e. The total of costs recorded on all sales invoices for May is $258,705.00.

INSTRUCTIONS:

1. Journalize the factory payroll entry on page 10 of a cash payments journal. C711. Post the general debit and general credit amounts.
2. Journalize the following entries on page 5 of a general journal. Post the debit and credit amounts.
   - **a.** An entry to transfer the total of all direct materials requisitions to Work in Process and indirect materials to Factory Overhead. M211.
   - **b.** An entry to close all individual manufacturing expense accounts to Factory Overhead. M212.
   - **c.** An entry to record applied factory overhead to Work in Process. M213.
3. Continue using page 5 of the general journal. Journalize and post the entry to close the balance of the factory overhead account to Income Summary. M214.
4. Journalize and post the entry to transfer the total of all cost sheets completed from Work in Process to Finished Goods. M215.
5. Journalize and post the entry to transfer the cost of products sold from Finished Goods to Cost of Goods Sold. M216.
6. Prepare a statement of cost of goods manufactured for the month ended May 31 of the current year.

CHALLENGE PROBLEM 20-C Journalizing entries that summarize cost records at the end of a fiscal period; preparing financial statements

The following information is taken from the records of Cozart Company on July 31 of the current year. The accounts and balances needed to complete this problem are given in the working papers accompanying this textbook.

556

a. The total factory payroll for the month according to the payroll register is $63,000.00, distributed as follows.

Work in Process	$46,600.00
Factory Overhead	16,400.00
Cash	51,030.00
Employee Income Tax Payable	6,930.00
FICA Tax Payable	5,040.00

b. The total of all requisitions of direct materials issued during the month is $67,760.00. The total of all requisitions of indirect materials issued during the month is $6,990.00.

c. The factory overhead to be charged to **Work in Process** is 95% of the direct labor cost.

d. The total of all cost sheets completed during the month is $140,984.00.

e. The total of costs recorded on all sales invoices for July is $112,176.83.

INSTRUCTIONS:

1. Journalize the factory payroll entry on page 14 of a cash payments journal. C341. Post the general debit and general credit amounts.
2. Journalize the following entries on page 7 of a general journal. Post the entries.
   a. An entry to transfer the total of all direct materials requisitions to **Work in Process** and indirect materials to **Factory Overhead.** M698.
   b. An entry to close all individual manufacturing expense accounts to **Factory Overhead.** M699.
   c. An entry to record applied factory overhead to **Work in Process.** M700.
3. Continue using page 7 of the general journal. Journalize and post the entry to close the balance of the factory overhead account to **Income Summary.** M701.
4. Journalize and post the entry to transfer the total of all cost sheets completed from **Work in Process** to **Finished Goods.** M702.
5. Journalize and post the entry to transfer the cost of products sold from **Finished Goods** to **Cost of Goods Sold.** M703.
6. Prepare a statement of cost of goods manufactured for the month ended July 31 of the current year.

Cozart's general ledger accounts and their balances on July 31 of the current year are given on the work sheet in the working papers accompanying this textbook. (The Employee Income Tax Payable and FICA Tax Payable balances differ from your ledger account balances due to additional postings completed for payroll taxes and sales and administrative salaries.)

7. Prepare an 8-column work sheet for the month ended July 31 of the current year. Record the adjustments on the work sheet using the following information.

Adjustment Information, July 31

Uncollectible accounts expense estimated as 1.0% of total sales on account. Sales on account for year, $76,275.00.

Sales supplies inventory	$1,762.50
Administrative supplies inventory	520.74
Value of prepaid administrative insurance	1,383.30
Monthly depreciation expense—office equipment	68.51
Monthly depreciation expense—store equipment	61.88
Federal income tax expense estimated for the month	7,807.00

8. Prepare an income statement for the month ended July 31 of the current year. Calculate and record the following component percentages. (a) Net cost of goods sold. (b) Gross profit on operations. (c) Total operating expenses. (d) Income from operations. (e) Net addition or deduction resulting from other revenue and expenses. (f) Net income before federal income tax. (g) Federal income tax expense. (h) Net income after federal income tax. Round percentage calculations to the nearest 0.1%.
9. Prepare a balance sheet for July 31 of the current year. A statement of stockholders' equity is not prepared. Therefore, add the amount of net income after federal income tax to the beginning balance of **Retained Earnings** to obtain the ending balance.

Processing and Reporting Cost Accounting Data for a Manufacturing Business

TEACHING STRATEGIES: REINFORCEMENT ACTIVITY

Reinforcement Activity 3 is the complete accounting cycle for a manufacturing business organized as a corporation. Job cost accounting processing and reporting is emphasized. Blackline masters for audit tests for Reinforcement Activity 3 are available in the Teacher's Resource Guide in three options: Part A only, Part B only, and Parts A and B combined.

This activity reinforces selected learnings from Chapters 19 and 20. Job cost accounting processing and reporting is emphasized for a manufacturing company organized as a corporation.

FURNITURE DECOR, INC.

Furniture Decor, Inc. is a corporation that manufactures office furniture. Furniture Decor uses a job cost accounting system to record manufacturing costs. The fiscal year is from January 1 through December 31. Monthly financial statements are prepared.

PART A: RECORDING COST ACCOUNTING ACTIVITIES

In Part A of this reinforcement activity, Furniture Decor's daily cost accounting activities for one month will be recorded.

Furniture Decor uses the chart of accounts shown on the following page. The journals and ledgers used by Furniture Decor are similar to those illustrated in Chapters 19 and 20. The job cost sheets, selected general ledger accounts, and other accounting records or forms needed to do the cost accounting activities are provided in the working papers accompanying this textbook. Beginning balances have been recorded.

The January 31 general ledger balances are the result of posting completed during the month of January. Note that **Accounts Payable** has a debit balance for this reason. Also, the balances of the payroll liability accounts are the amounts posted for sales and administrative salaries for January.

CALCULATING FACTORY OVERHEAD APPLIED RATE

INSTRUCTIONS:

1. Calculate the factory overhead applied rate based on direct labor costs. Estimated annual factory overhead costs for the current year are $306,000.00. Estimated direct labor hours to be used during the current year are 17,000 hours at an estimated rate of $15.00 per hour. Retain the calculations for use later in this reinforcement activity.

RECORDING TRANSACTIONS

INSTRUCTIONS:

2. Record the following transactions completed during January of the current year in the appropriate cost records and journals. Use page 1 of a materials purchases journal,

TEACHING STRATEGIES: ASSESSMENT BY PORTFOLIO

If you intend to use Reinforcement Activity 3 as part of an assessment by portfolio evaluation, advise students that their work on this activity will be included in their portfolio.

FURNITURE DECOR, INC.
CHART OF ACCOUNTS

Balance Sheet Accounts

(1000) ASSETS

1100 Current Assets

1105 Cash
1110 Petty Cash
1115 Accounts Receivable
1120 Allowance for Uncollectible Accounts
1125 Materials
1130 Work in Process
1135 Finished Goods
1140 Supplies—Factory
1145 Supplies—Sales
1150 Supplies—Administrative
1155 Prepaid Insurance

1200 Plant Assets

1205 Factory Equipment
1210 Accumulated Depreciation—Factory Equipment
1215 Office Equipment
1220 Accumulated Depreciation—Office Equipment
1225 Store Equipment
1230 Accumulated Depreciation—Store Equipment
1235 Building
1240 Accumulated Depreciation—Building
1245 Land

(2000) LIABILITIES

2100 Current Liabilities

2105 Accounts Payable
2110 Employee Income Tax Payable
2115 Federal Income Tax Payable
2120 FICA Tax Payable
2125 Salaries Payable
2130 Unemployment Tax Payable—Federal
2135 Unemployment Tax Payable—State
2140 Dividends Payable

2200 Long-Term Liability

2205 Mortgage Payable

(3000) STOCKHOLDERS' EQUITY

3105 Capital Stock
3110 Retained Earnings
3115 Dividends
3120 Income Summary

Income Statement Accounts

(4000) OPERATING REVENUE

4105 Sales

(5000) COST OF SALES

5105 Cost of Goods Sold

(5500) MANUFACTURING COSTS

5505 Factory Overhead
5510 Depreciation Expense—Factory Equipment
5515 Depreciation Expense—Building
5520 Heat, Light, and Power Expense
5525 Insurance Expense—Factory
5530 Miscellaneous Expense—Factory
5535 Payroll Taxes Expense—Factory
5540 Property Tax Expense—Factory
5545 Supplies Expense—Factory

(6000) OPERATING EXPENSES

6100 Selling Expenses

6105 Advertising Expense
6110 Delivery Expense
6115 Depreciation Expense—Store Equipment
6120 Miscellaneous Expense—Sales
6125 Salary Expense—Sales
6130 Supplies Expense—Sales

6200 Administrative Expenses

6205 Depreciation Expense—Office Equipment
6210 Insurance Expense—Administrative
6215 Miscellaneous Expense—Administrative
6220 Payroll Taxes Expense—Administrative
6225 Property Tax Expense—Administrative
6230 Salary Expense—Administrative
6235 Supplies Expense—Administrative
6240 Uncollectible Accounts Expense
6245 Utilities Expense—Administrative

(7000) OTHER REVENUE

7105 Gain on Plant Assets
7110 Miscellaneous Revenue

(8000) OTHER EXPENSES

8105 Interest Expense
8110 Loss on Plant Assets

(9000) INCOME TAX

9105 Federal Income Tax Expense

TEACHING STRATEGIES: COOPERATIVE LEARNING

Divide the class into groups of two students each. After completing the recording of transactions as a homework assignment, students evaluate each other's work in class. Students are permitted to correct their work based on their partner's evaluation. This cooperative learning activity should not take more than 15 to 20 minutes of class time. The same kind of group activity can be used after students have completed the end-of-fiscal-period work.

general journal, and cash payments journal. Recording instructions are provided only for the first occurrence of each kind of transaction. Source documents are abbreviated as follows: check, C; memorandum, M; materials requisition, MR; purchase order, PO; sales invoice, S.

Jan. 3. Opened a cost sheet for Job No. 232, 250 C200 computer desks ordered for stock. Date wanted, January 12.

3. Issued direct materials to factory for Job No. 232, $5,100.00. MR750.
   Materials list: 6,000 square feet base wood @ $0.20 per square foot
   6,000 square feet laminate @ $0.60 per square foot
   187.5 pounds adhesive @ $1.60 per pound
   Record the direct materials in the materials ledger and the cost ledger.

5. Opened a cost sheet for Job No. 233, 200 P150 printer tables ordered for stock. Date wanted, January 17.

5. Issued direct materials to factory for Job No. 233, $3,400.00. MR751.
   Materials list: 4,000 square feet base wood @ $0.20 per square foot
   4,000 square feet laminate @ $0.60 per square foot
   125 pounds adhesive @ $1.60 per pound

5. Ordered 30,000 square feet base wood. P0520.
   Record the purchase order in the materials ledger.

5. Ordered 20,000 square feet laminate. P0521.

7. Ordered 1,600 casters. P0522.

7. Issued direct materials to factory for Job No. 232, $1,250.00. MR752.
   Materials list: 1,000 casters @ $1.25 each

7. Ordered 1,000 sets hinges. P0523.

7. Recorded weekly summary of job-time records to cost ledger.
   Job No. 232 $3,300.00
   Job No. 233 1,125.00

7. Ordered 1,000 pounds adhesive. P0524.

10. Issued direct materials to factory for Job No. 233, $1,200.00. MR753.
    Materials list: 800 casters @ $1.25 each
    200 sets metal glides @ $1.00 per set

10. Ordered 300 sets of metal glides. P0525.

10. Sold 100 C200 computer desks to Office Mart. S323.
    Record only the cost in the finished goods ledger. Furniture Decor uses the first-in, first-out inventory method. Thus, the cost recorded first is the cost removed from inventory first when units are sold.

10. Ordered 1,000 fasteners. P0526.

10. Received at materials stockroom 20,000 square feet of laminate @ $0.60 per square foot. Materials were purchased on account from Plastics Unlimited, $12,000.00. P0521.
    Record all receipts of materials in the materials ledger and purchases journal.

11. Completed Job No. 232. Apply factory overhead to job. Use the rate calculated in Instruction 1. Complete the cost sheet. Interim summary of job-time records for Job No. 232, $1,387.50.
    When jobs are completed in the middle of a week, Furniture Decor makes a special interim summary of job-time records for these jobs. Therefore, direct labor costs will be complete. Record the finished goods in the finished goods ledger.

12. Opened a cost sheet for Job No. 234, 120 E400 entertainment centers ordered for stock. Date wanted, January 18.

12. Issued direct materials to factory for Job No. 234, $5,100.00. MR754.
    Materials list: 6,000 square feet base wood @ $0.20 per square foot
    6,000 square feet laminate @ $0.60 per square foot
    187.5 pounds adhesive @ $1.60 per pound

Jan. 12. Received at materials stockroom 30,000 square feet of base wood @ $0.20 per square foot. Materials were purchased on account from Wood Craft, Inc., $6,000.00. P0520.

12. Received at materials stockroom 1,600 casters @ $1.25 each. Materials were purchased on account from Wheels Galore, $2,000.00. P0522.

12. Received at materials stockroom 300 sets of metal glides @ $1.00 per set. Materials were purchased on account from Simpson Company, $300.00. P0525.

14. Opened a cost sheet for Job No. 235, 150 V110 video tape cabinets for stock. Date wanted, January 27.

14. Issued direct materials to factory for Job No. 235, $2,040.00. MR755.
    Materials list: 2,400 square feet base wood @ $0.20 per square foot
    2,400 square feet laminate @ $0.60 per square foot
    75 pounds adhesive @ $1.60 per pound

14. Recorded weekly summary of job-time records to cost ledger.
    Job No. 233 $1,875.00
    Job No. 234 1,800.00
    Job No. 235 225.00

14. Completed Job No. 233.

17. Paid cash for semimonthly factory payroll, $11,080.80 (direct labor, $9,712.50, and indirect labor, $3,967.50, less deductions: employee income tax, $1,504.80; FICA tax, $1,094.40). C782.
    Record the payroll entry in the cash payments journal. Post the general debit and general credit amounts.

17. Recorded employer factory payroll taxes, $1,942.56, for the semimonthly pay period ended January 15. Taxes owed are FICA tax, $1,094.40; federal unemployment tax, $109.44; state unemployment tax, $738.72. M308.
    Record the entry in the general journal. Post the amounts.

17. Sold 150 P150 printer tables to CompuFurnishings. S324.

18. Issued direct materials to factory for Job No. 234, $420.00. MR756.
    Materials list: 240 sets of hinges @ $1.00 per set
    240 fasteners @ $0.75 each

18. Opened a cost sheet for Job No. 236, 200 B160 bookcases ordered for stock. Date wanted, January 28.

18. Issued direct materials to factory for Job No. 236, $6,800.00. MR757.
    Materials list: 8,000 square feet base wood @ $0.20 per square foot
    8,000 square feet laminate @ $0.60 per square foot
    250 pounds adhesive @ $1.60 per pound

19. Completed Job No. 234. Interim summary of job-time record for Job No. 234, $1,800.00.

20. Sold 60 T120 TV carts to Office Mart. S325.

21. Issued direct materials to factory for Job No. 235, $825.00. MR758.
    Materials list: 300 sets metal glides @ $1.00 per set
    300 sets hinges @ $1.00 per set
    300 fasteners @ $0.75 each

21. Received at materials stockroom 1,000 pounds adhesive @ $1.60 per pound. Materials were purchased on account from Cal Adhesives, $1,600.00. P0524.

21. Received at materials stockroom 1,000 fasteners @ $0.75 each. Materials were purchased on account from Simpson Company, $750.00. P0526.

21. Ordered 300 sets metal glides. P0527.

21. Posted weekly summary of job-time records to cost ledger.
    Job No. 235 $1,125.00
    Job No. 236 2,250.00

24. Ordered 20,000 square feet laminate. P0528.

24. Received at materials stockroom 1,000 sets of hinges @ $1.00 per set. Materials were purchased on account from Simpson Company, $1,000.00. P0523.

561

Jan. 25. Issued direct materials to factory for Job No. 236, $700.00. MR759.
Materials list: 400 sets of hinges @ $1.00 per set
400 fasteners @ $0.75 each

25. Opened a cost sheet for Job No. 237, 160 T120 TV carts ordered for stock. Date wanted, January 31.

25. Issued direct materials to factory for Job No. 237, $1,904.00. MR760.
Materials list: 2,240 square feet base wood @ $0.20 per square foot
2,240 square feet laminate @ $0.60 per square foot
70 pounds adhesive @ $1.60 per pound

26. Sold 90 E400 entertainment centers to BizFurn. S326.

27. Completed Job No. 235. Interim summary of job-time records for Job No. 235, $900.00.

27. Sold 200 V110 video tape cabinets to CompuFurnishings. S327.

28. Issued direct materials to factory for Job No. 237, $800.00. MR761.
Materials list: 640 casters @ $1.25 each

28. Opened a cost sheet for Job No. 238, 200 C200 computer desks ordered for stock. Date wanted, February 8.

28. Issued direct materials to factory for Job No. 238, $4,080.00. MR762.
Materials list: 4,800 square feet base wood @ $0.20 per square foot
4,800 square feet laminate @ $0.60 per square foot
150 pounds adhesive @ $1.60 per pound

28. Posted weekly summary of job-time records to cost ledger.
Job No. 236 $2,250.00
Job No. 237 1,440.00
Job No. 238 630.00

28. Completed Job No. 236.

28. Sold 120 B160 bookcases to Office Mart. S328.

31. Received at materials stockroom 300 metal glides @ $1.00 per set. Materials were purchased on account from Simpson Company, $300.00. P0527.

31. Received at materials stockroom indirect materials (bolts, screws, and nails). Materials were purchased on account from Grant Hardware Supplies, $1,200.00. PO519.
Record indirect materials purchases only in the materials purchases journal.

31. Posted summary of job-time records for January 31 to cost ledger.
Job No. 237 $360.00
Job No. 238 630.00

31. Sold 200 C200 computer desks to Straight Arrow, Inc. S329.

31. Completed Job No. 237.

31. Paid cash for semimonthly factory payroll, $12,988.20 (direct labor, $11,385.00, and indirect labor, $4,650.00, less deductions: employee income tax, $1,764.00; FICA tax, $1,282.80). C856.

31. Recorded employer factory payroll taxes, $2,276.97, for the semimonthly pay period ended January 31. Taxes owed are FICA tax, $1,282.80; federal unemployment tax, $128.28; state unemployment tax, $865.89. M345.

COMPLETING COST RECORDS

INSTRUCTIONS:

3. Jobs not completed on January 31 are work in process. The factory overhead for the month of January on work in process must be recorded. Apply the factory overhead rate to the direct labor costs recorded on the cost sheet for work in process. Record this amount in the Summary column with the item description *Factory Overhead for January* and the explanation of how this was calculated.

4. Total and rule the materials purchases journal. Post the total. Do not post the individual amounts. The abbreviation for the materials purchases journal is MP.

5. Prove and rule the cash payments journal. Do not post the total of the Cash Cr. column.

562

6. Record the following entries. Continue using page 1 of the general journal. Use January 31 as the date. Post after journalizing each entry.
   a. An entry to transfer the total of all direct materials requisitions to **Work in Process** and indirect materials to **Factory Overhead.** The total of all requisitions of direct materials issued during January is $33,619.00. The total of all requisitions of indirect materials issued is $1,181.00. M346.
   b. An entry to close all individual manufacturing expense accounts to **Factory Overhead.** M347.
   c. An entry to record applied factory overhead to **Work in Process.** (Sum of factory overhead applied to cost sheets for the month.) M348.
7. Continue using page 1 of the general journal. Journalize and post the entry to close the balance of the factory overhead account to **Income Summary.** M349.
8. Journalize and post the entry to transfer the total of all cost sheets completed from **Work in Process** to **Finished Goods.** M350.
9. Journalize and post the entry to transfer the cost of products sold from **Finished Goods** to **Cost of Goods Sold.** The total cost recorded on all sales invoices for January is $61,137.50. M351.
10. Prove the subsidiary ledgers as follows.
    a. Add the ending balances in the materials ledger. The ending balance of the indirect materials is $1,369.00. The total of the materials ledger must equal the ending balance of **Materials** in the general ledger.
    b. Add the costs recorded on all cost sheets in the cost ledger that have not been completed. This total must equal the ending balance of **Work in Process** in the general ledger.
    c. Add the ending balances in the finished goods ledger. This total must equal the ending balance of **Finished Goods** in the general ledger.
11. Prepare a statement of cost of goods manufactured for Furniture Decor, Inc. for the month ended January 31 of the current year.

PART B: COMPLETING END-OF-FISCAL-PERIOD ACTIVITIES

In Part B of this reinforcement activity, all accounting activities have been completed up to, but not including, a trial balance for the month of January.

The January 31 balances of the general ledger accounts not provided in Part A are recorded on an 8-column work sheet in the working papers accompanying this textbook.

INSTRUCTIONS:

12. Record the January 31 balances from the general ledger accounts used in Part A on the work sheet for Furniture Decor, Inc. Complete the Trial Balance columns of the work sheet.
13. Complete the work sheet for the month ended January 31 of the current year. Record the adjustments on the work sheet using the following information.

Adjustment Information, January 31

Uncollectible accounts expense estimated as 1.0% of sales on account. Sales on account for month, $27,000.00.	
Sales supplies inventory	$1,111.35
Administrative supplies inventory	302.47
Value of prepaid administrative insurance	257.40
Monthly depreciation expense—office equipment	34.25
Monthly depreciation expense—store equipment	31.00
Federal income tax expense estimated for the month	3,682.38

14. Prepare an income statement for the month ended January 31 of the current year. Calculate and record the following component percentages. (a) Cost of goods sold. (b) Gross profit on operations. (c) Total operating expenses. (d) Income from operations. (e) Net

addition or deduction resulting from other revenue and expenses. (f) Net income before federal income tax. (g) Federal income tax. (h) Net income after federal income tax. Round percentage calculations to the nearest 0.1%.

15. Prepare a balance sheet for January 31 of the current year. A statement of stockholders' equity is not prepared. Therefore, add the amount of net income after federal income taxes to the beginning balance of **Retained Earnings** to obtain the ending balance.

564

Bombay Leather, Inc. is a manufacturing business organized as a corporation. This business simulation covers the realistic transactions completed by Bombay Leather, Inc., which manufactures suitcases, garment bags, and briefcases. The activities included in the accounting cycle for Bombay Leather, Inc. are listed below.

Activities in Bombay Leather, Inc.

1. Recording transactions in special journals and a general journal.
2. Recording items in materials ledgers, cost sheets, and finished goods ledgers.
3. Posting items to be posted individually to a general ledger and subsidiary ledgers.
4. Proving and ruling journals.
5. Recording and posting general journal entries that summarize cost records.
6. Proving the subsidiary ledgers.
7. Preparing a trial balance on a work sheet.
8. Planning adjustments and completing a work sheet.
9. Preparing financial statements.
10. Journalizing and posting adjusting entries.
11. Journalizing and posting closing entries.
12. Preparing a post-closing trial balance.

565

PART 8 OVERVIEW

STUDENT EDITION

STUDENT FEATURES

Professional Business Ethics

Keeping A Trade Secret, page 620

Careers In Accounting

Revenue Officer, page 595
Auditor, County or City, page 640

Multicultural Awareness

Minority Recruiting, page 572

Global Perspective

International Mail, page 592

Personal Visions In Business

Ruth Smith, page 645

Audit Your Understanding

This student activity can be found on pages 574, 579, 593, 598, 604, 618, 628, 639, 643, 646

APPLIED SKILLS

Communications

Page 581

Mathematics

Pages 575, 576, 578, 582, 583, 587, 588, 589, 590, 591, 601, 603, 605, 606, 607, 639, 648

SOFTWARE APPLICATIONS

Automated Accounting 6.0 Problem 24-1
Spreadsheet Template Problems 21-4, 21-5, 22-1, 22-M, 24-M

TEACHER'S EDITION

APPLIED SKILLS

Communications, page 581
Language Arts, pages 579, 599, 615, 637
Writing Across the Curriculum, pages 572, 601, 602, 624, 646
Building Study Skills, pages 574, 619, 645
Word Processing, pages 575, 589, 616, 642

TEACHING STRATEGIES

Accounting Pedagogy, pages 568, 569, 586, 608, 609, 634
Different Learning Abilities, pages 578, 598, 625, 641
Cooperative Learning, pages 571, 590, 627, 644
Expanding Beyond the Classroom, pages 573, 626
Applying Visuals, pages 571, 590, 616, 644
Teaching Tip, pages 568, 570, 573, 576, 577, 588, 592, 597, 600, 608, 610, 611, 613, 614, 617, 635, 636, 638, 640
Software Focus, pages 569, 586, 634

ASSESSMENT

MicroExam software for each chapter
Problem Test for each chapter
Objective Test 8

SOFTWARE

Automated Accounting 6.0
MicroExam
Excel (spreadsheet software)
Lotus (spreadsheet software)
Windows (operating system software)
WordPerfect (word processing software)
Works (integrated software)

BIBLIOGRAPHY

Henke, Emerson O. *Introduction to Nonprofit Organization Accounting.* Fourth Edition. Cincinnati: South-Western Publishing Co., 1992.

Johnson, D., and R. Johnson. *Social Skills for Successful Group Work.* Educational Leadership, 1990.

Slavin, R. *Using Student Team Learning.* Baltimore: John Hopkins University Press, 1986.

Periodicals

Accounting, Organizations and Society, Pergamon Press, Inc., Tarrytown, NY.

Multinational Business, Economist Newspaper, New York, NY. (Global business)

Technology

AICPA. *The Bottom Line: Inside Accounting Today,* 1987. (Video)

AICPA. *TOTAL (Total On-line Tax and Accounting Library)* (Tax and accounting on-line database)

PART 8 OPENER

PART 8

Other Accounting Systems

OVERVIEW

Part 8 concludes the text with coverage of other important accounting systems.

Chapter 21 thoroughly discusses forming a partnership and the other aspects of the structure of this form of ownership. Chapter 22 takes this a step further and covers the financial reporting for a partnership.

Chapter 23 investigates budgeting and accounting for a not-for-profit organization. Chapter 24 then covers the financial reporting for a not-for-profit organization.

GENERAL GOALS

1. Know accounting terminology related to partnership accounting and accounting for not-for-profit organizations.
2. Understand accounting concepts and practices related to partnership accounting and accounting for not-for-profit organizations.
3. Demonstrate accounting procedures unique to partnerships and not-for-profit organizations.

CHAPTER 21 OVERVIEW

Chapter 21 begins by describing how businesses organized as partnerships are formed and emphasizes the importance and characteristics of a partnership agreement. The journal entry for the initial formation of a partnership is illustrated and discussed. The rest of the chapter describes different scenarios for admitting new partners to an existing partnership, including cases in which there is no increase in equity, investment equal to equity, and the recognition of goodwill.

GUIDE TO ACHIEVING LEARNING OBJECTIVES

	TEACH	APPLY	EXTEND/ENRICH				
Enabling Performance Tasks	**Lesson Plans**	**Application Problems**	**Mastery Problems**	**Challenge Problems**	**Cases for Critical Thinking**	**Recycling Problems**	**Reinforcement Activity**
a. Define accounting terms related to forming and expanding a partnership.	21-1, 21-2						
b. Identify accounting concepts and practices related to forming and expanding a partnership.	21-1, 21-2				Cases 1, 2		
c. Journalize transactions related to forming and expanding a partnership.	21-1, 21-2	21-1, 21-2, 21-3, 21-4, 21-5	21-M	21-C		21-R	

ENRICHMENT

SPECIAL FEATURES
Multicultural Awareness, page 572
Applied Communications, page 581
TECHNOLOGY CONNECTION
Spreadsheet Template Problems 21-4, 21-5

NEW, REVIEW, AND EXTENSION

ACTIVITIES/CONCEPTS/TRANSACTIONS	NEW	REVIEW/ EXTENSION
Characteristics of a partnership		✓
Formation of a partnership		✓
Partnership agreement		✓
Recording partners' initial investments		✓
Admitting new partner with no change in total equity	✓	
Admitting new partner with equity equal to investment	✓	
Admitting new partner with equity greater than investment	✓	
Admitting new partner with goodwill	✓	

	INFORMAL ASSESSMENT		FORMAL ASSESSMENT			
	Study Guide	**Audit Your Understanding**	**Chapter MicroExam**	**Chapter Problem Test**	**Unit Objective Test**	**Portfolio**
		✓	✓		✓	
	Units A, B, C	✓	✓		✓	
				✓		

TEACHING MATERIALS

Teacher's Wraparound Edition of the Text
Teacher's Resource Guide
Teacher's Edition of Working Papers
MicroExam

APPLIED MATHEMATICS

APPLIED MATH/ACCOUNTING SKILL	APPLICATION
Calculating share of partnership equity	Prob. 21-2
Calculating equity greater than partner's investment	Prob. 21-4
Calculating goodwill	Prob. 21-5

TEACHING STRATEGIES: ACCOUNTING PEDAGOGY

A chart of accounts for the business that is used to illustrate each part of this textbook is provided at the beginning of each part. Charts of accounts are extremely important to companies because they drive the accounting system. Employees usually cannot even receive reimbursement for expenses without knowing which account the expense should be charged to. Pedagogically, the chart of accounts provides the following information: (1) Classification for each account—needed to determine how a transaction is analyzed. (2) Permanent accounts (balance sheet accounts) and temporary accounts (income statement accounts)—assist in analyzing transactions and recording closing entries. (3) Account number for every general ledger account—critical information in automated accounting, since transactions are entered by account number rather than account title.

CHART OF ACCOUNTS

This chart of accounts is for a service business organized as a partnership. The business does not sell merchandise. For this reason, the business does not need general ledger accounts for merchandise inventory, purchases, purchases discount, and purchases returns and allowances. The partners, who provide all the services to customers, are not employees of the partnership; therefore, a general ledger account for salary expenses is not needed. In the owners' equity section, there is a capital and drawing account for each of the two partners.

MaLin Carpet Design

CHART OF ACCOUNTS

Balance Sheet Accounts

(1000) ASSETS

1100 Current Assets

1105 Cash
1110 Petty Cash
1115 Accounts Receivable
1120 Allowance for Uncollectible Accounts
1125 Supplies—Carpet
1130 Supplies—Office
1135 Prepaid Insurance

1200 Plant Assets

1205 Equipment
1210 Accumulated Depreciation—Equipment
1215 Truck
1220 Accumulated Depreciation—Truck

(2000) LIABILITIES
2105 Accounts Payable

(3000) OWNERS' EQUITY
3105 May Baker, Capital
3110 May Baker, Drawing
3115 Lindel Mattingly, Capital
3120 Lindel Mattingly, Drawing
3125 Income Summary

Income Statement Accounts

(4000) OPERATING REVENUE
4105 Sales

(5000) OPERATING EXPENSES
5105 Advertising Expense
5110 Depreciation Expense—Equipment
5115 Depreciation Expense—Truck
5120 Insurance Expense
5125 Miscellaneous Expense
5130 Rent Expense
5135 Supplies Expense—Carpet
5140 Supplies Expense—Office
5145 Truck Expense
5150 Uncollectible Accounts Expense
5155 Utilities Expense

The chart of accounts for MaLin Carpet Design is illustrated above for ready reference as you study Chapters 21 and 22 of this textbook.

TEACHING STRATEGIES: TEACHING TIP

Emphasize that students should refer to this chart of accounts throughout their study of Chapters 21 and 22 of Part 8. It will help them determine classification of accounts, which accounts are temporary and permanent accounts, and what account numbers to use for automated accounting. It will also be a useful reference for performing file maintenance activities.

21

Organizational Structure of a Partnership

ENABLING PERFORMANCE TASKS

After studying Chapter 21, you will be able to:

a Define accounting terms related to forming and expanding a partnership.

b Identify accounting concepts and practices related to forming and expanding a partnership.

c Journalize transactions related to forming and expanding a partnership.

TERMS PREVIEW

partnership agreement • mutual agency • goodwill

TEACHING STRATEGIES: ACCOUNTING PEDAGOGY

This textbook discusses the organizational structure of a partnership. It is important for students to understand the technical aspects of the partnership form of business and be able to distinguish the differences between the structure of a corporation and a partnership.

SOFTWARE FOCUS

Software may be used for independent practice or enrichment/extension as the instructor deems appropriate. For this chapter, the Spreadsheet Template may be used with Problems 21-4 and 21-5.

A corporation is one form of business that may be owned by many persons. Another form of business may also have more than one owner. A business in which two or more persons combine their assets and skills is known as a partnership. Each member of a partnership is known as a partner. Except for recording owners' equity and income taxes, accounting procedures for a partnership are similar to those for a corporation.

LESSON PLAN 21-1

Materials

- Student pages 570–574
- Blackline Master for Cash Receipts Journal (TRG)

Objectives (Enabling Performance Tasks)

a. Define accounting terms related to forming and expanding a partnership.

b. Identify accounting concepts and practices related to forming and expanding a partnership.

c. Journalize transactions related to forming and expanding a partnership.

FOCUS

- The advantages and disadvantages of the partnership form of organization were covered in Chapter 1. In this lesson, the procedures for forming a partnership and journalizing the partners' initial investments will be presented.
- Introduce vocabulary: partnership agreement, mutual agency.

FORMING A PARTNERSHIP

FYI

A partnership can have an unlimited number of partners.

A partnership is created when two or more persons agree orally or in writing to form a business using the partnership form of organization. As in other forms of business, a partnership's financial records are kept separate from those of the partners. *(CONCEPT: Business Entity)*

May Baker and Lindel Mattingly agree to form a partnership called MaLin Carpet Design. Prior to forming the partnership, Ms. Baker owned a similar business and Mr. Mattingly was employed as a carpet layer.

MaLin Carpet Design provides carpet installation services to homeowners, housing developers, and businesses. The business does not sell merchandise. For this reason, the business does not need general ledger accounts for merchandise inventory, purchases, purchases discount, and purchases returns and allowances. The partners, who provide all the services to customers, are not employees of the partnership. The Internal Revenue Service does not consider the money partners receive from a partnership to be salaries. Therefore, the business does not need accounts for recording salaries and payroll taxes.

Partnership Agreement

A written agreement setting forth the conditions under which a partnership is to operate is called a **partnership agreement.** A partnership's life is limited to the length of time agreed on by the partners. A partnership is terminated by the partners' mutual agreement, death of a partner, withdrawal of one partner, or admission of a new partner. In comparison, a corporation has unlimited life.

Each partner can bind a partnership to any contract. The right of all partners to contract for a partnership is called **mutual agency.** Each partner is an agent of the partnership unless restricted by agreement.

Legally, a partnership agreement may be either written or oral. Some but not all states require that a partnership agreement be in writing. However, to avoid misunderstandings, a partnership agreement should be in writing.

FYI

Public accounting firms are often organized as partnerships.

TEACHING STRATEGIES: TEACHING TIP

Review the definition of a partnership: A business in which two or more persons combine their assets and skills.

With an attorney's assistance, Ms. Baker and Mr. Mattingly prepare the partnership agreement shown in Illustration 21-1.

ILLUSTRATION 21-1 Partnership agreement

PARTNERSHIP AGREEMENT

THIS CONTRACT is made and entered into this thirty-first day of December, 19--, by and between May Baker and Lindel Mattingly, of Petersburg, VA.

WITNESSETH: That the said parties have this date formed a partnership to engage in and conduct a business under the following stipulations which are a part of this contract. The partnership will begin operation January 1, 19--.

FIRST: The business shall be conducted under the name of MaLin Carpet Design, located initially at 1910 South Crater Road, Petersburg, VA 23801-2343.

SECOND: The investment of each partner is: May Baker: Equity in a business located at 1910 South Crater Road, Petersburg, VA 23801-2343, and as shown in a balance sheet to be provided by Ms. Baker on December 31, 19--. Total investment, $22,880.00. Lindel Mattingly: Cash equal to one-half of the initial investment of Ms. Baker. Total investment, $11,440.00.

THIRD: Both partners are to (a) participate in all general policy-making decisions, (b) devote full time and attention to the partnership business, and (c) engage in no other business enterprise without the written consent of the other partner. Ms. Baker is to be general manager of the business' operations.

FOURTH: Neither partner is to become a surety or bonding agent for anyone without the written consent of the other partner.

FIFTH: The partners' shares in earnings and losses of the partnership are: Ms. Baker: 5% interest on equity as of January 1 of each year; salary, $5,000.00 per year; remaining income or loss, 50%. Mr. Mattingly: 5% interest on equity as of January 1 of each year; salary, $3,000.00 per year; remaining income or loss, 50%.

SIXTH: No partner is to withdraw assets in excess of the agreed upon interest and salary without the other partner's written consent.

SEVENTH: All partnership transactions are to be recorded in accordance with standard and generally accepted accounting procedures and concepts. The partnership records are to be open at all times for inspection by either partner.

EIGHTH: In case of either partner's death or legal disability, the equity of the partners is to be determined as of the time of the death or disability of the one partner. The continuing partner is to have first option to buy the deceased/disabled partner's equity at recorded book value.

NINTH: This partnership agreement is to continue indefinitely unless (a) terminated by death of one partner, (b) terminated by either partner by giving the other partner written notice at least ninety (90) days prior to the termination date, or (c) terminated by written mutual agreement signed by both partners.

TENTH: At the termination of this partnership agreement, the partnership's assets, after all liabilities are paid, will be distributed according to the balance in partners' capital accounts.

IN WITNESS WHEREOF, the parties to this contract have set their hands and seals on the date and year written.

Signed *May Baker* (Seal) Date *December 31, 19--*

Signed *Lindel Mattingly* (Seal) Date *December 31, 19--*

Both partners sign three copies of the partnership agreement. Each partner receives a copy for personal records, and the third copy becomes part of the partnership's records.

Partnership Capital Accounts

The owners' equity division of a partnership's general ledger has two capital accounts for each partner.

TEACHING STRATEGIES: APPLYING VISUALS

Direct students to Illustration 21-1 to review the terms included in a partnership agreement.

TEACH

Cover student pages 570–574 "Forming a Partnership." Review the advantages and disadvantages of the partnership form of organization. Emphasize that each partner is individually responsible for the total liabilities of the partnership. Discuss the two capital accounts used for each partner—Capital and Drawing. Review the definition of withdrawals. Emphasize that the value of non-cash assets invested in a partnership are recorded at a value agreed upon by the partners—not the book value of the assets recorded in the previous business.

TEACHING STRATEGIES: COOPERATIVE LEARNING

Divide the class into groups of two or three students each. Each group decides on a service business to form as a partnership. Each group must write a partnership agreement and record the partners' initial investments. Encourage students to use their word processing software to prepare the partnership agreement. The teacher provides journal forms necessary to record the transactions. Time frame: class time = 30 minutes to plan the partnership; additional time outside of class is needed to complete the partnership agreement and record the transactions.

MULTICULTURAL AWARENESS

The MULTICULTURAL AWARENESS feature is intended to expose students to the concept that our society is composed of people from many different cultural backgrounds. These features show both past contributions of many cultures and benefits of a culturally diverse society. (1) Read the feature. (2) Discuss the specific information in the feature; (3) clarify any terms or questions.

APPLY

Draw T accounts on the overhead projector or chalkboard to analyze the transactions to record partners' initial investments. Refer students to Illustration 21-3 as journalizing the entries is discussed.

Guided Practice

Guide students through the T account analysis of the transactions in Problem 21-1. Have students draw T accounts on a sheet of paper and analyze the first transaction. All students should agree with the analysis before proceeding to the second transaction. The balance of Problem 21-1 can be completed as Independent Practice.

Independent Practice

Assign Terms 1–2, Questions 1–8, and Problem 21-1.

MULTICULTURAL AWARENESS

Minority Recruiting

Companies today are very interested in achieving a balance in the work force. They recognize that there are advantages in a work force that has the same ethnic and cultural composition as their customers. This attitude creates opportunity for minorities, including Native Americans, African-Americans, Hispanic-Americans, and Asian-Americans. Many cities have annual "multicultural" or "work force diversity" job fairs in which those looking for jobs meet employers looking for employees. At these minority job fairs, a wide range of jobs may be available. Companies are especially interested in minority hiring in sales, marketing, and customer service. However, companies are also interested in diversity in their technical and administrative positions.

Business interest in recruiting minorities grew in the 1990s. While some companies are motivated by fair employment practice regulations, most companies are interested in hiring a diverse work force because they can benefit from the diverse contributions of such a work force.

1. An account in which to record a partner's equity includes the word *capital* in the title. The two equity accounts in MaLin's general ledger are titled May Baker, Capital and Lindel Mattingly, Capital.
2. An account in which the earnings taken out of the partnership during the fiscal period are recorded includes the word *drawing* in the title. Assets taken out of a business for the owner's personal use are known as withdrawals. The two accounts in MaLin's general ledger used to record withdrawals are titled May Baker, Drawing and Lindel Mattingly, Drawing.

Partners' withdrawals can be a cause of misunderstandings. For this reason, most partnership agreements include a statement controlling withdrawals. MaLin's partnership agreement has a controlling statement in item six as shown in Illustration 21-1.

Partners' Initial Investments

Ms. Baker invests the assets of her existing business in the new partnership. According to item two of the partnership agreement, Ms. Baker will provide a December 31 balance sheet for her existing business. Ms. Baker's balance sheet is shown in Illustration 21-2 on page 573.

A value for all invested assets is agreed on by the two partners on the date the partnership begins, January 1. Ms. Baker's initial investment is $22,880.00, the agreed upon value of her equity in her previous business. Mr. Mattingly's initial investment is cash of $11,440.00.

Journal Entries to Record Partners' Initial Investments

A separate journal entry is made for each partner's initial investment.

Journalizing Initial Investment of Cash Only. A journal entry is made for Mr. Mattingly's initial cash investment.

January 1, 19--. Received cash from partner, Lindel Mattingly, as an initial investment, $11,440.00. Receipt No. 1.

The journal entry to record this transaction is shown on line 1 of Illustration 21-3 on page 573.

Cash	
11,440.00	

Lindel Mattingly, Capital	
	11,440.00

Journalizing Initial Investment of Cash, Other Assets, and Liabilities. Ms. Baker's investment includes cash, other assets, and liabilities from her prior existing business. A copy of the balance sheet from Ms. Baker's previous business, Illustration 21-2, is

APPLIED SKILLS: WRITING ACROSS THE CURRICULUM

Writing paragraphs and short essays. The Cases for Critical Thinking are short, practical applications of the accounting principles developed in the chapter. Some cases are planned to present problems related to the chapter but not specifically discussed and answered in the chapter. These cases present an opportunity for critical thinking and decision making. These cases also require more than a short objective-type response. Therefore, they provide ideal practice in writing paragraphs and short essays.

ILLUSTRATION 21-2 Balance sheet of an existing business invested in a partnership

Baker's Carpet Design
Balance Sheet
December 31, 19--

ASSETS			
Current Assets:			
Cash		$ 9,097.48	
Accounts Receivable	$1,947.94		
Less Allowance for Uncollectible Accounts	58.76	1,889.18	
Supplies—Carpet		2,194.39	
Supplies—Office		900.00	
Prepaid Insurance		116.86	
Total Current Assets			$14,197.91
Plant Assets:			
Equipment		$10,881.73	
Truck		4,900.00	
Total Plant Assets			15,781.73
Total Assets			$29,979.64
LIABILITIES			
Accounts Payable			$ 7,099.64
OWNER'S EQUITY			
May Baker, Capital			22,880.00
Total Liabilities and Owner's Equity			$29,979.64

ILLUSTRATION 21-3 Journal entries for partners' initial investments

CASH RECEIPTS JOURNAL — PAGE 1

	DATE		ACCOUNT TITLE	DOC. NO.	POST. REF.	1 GENERAL DEBIT	2 GENERAL CREDIT	3 ACCOUNTS RECEIVABLE CREDIT	4 SALES CREDIT	5 SALES TAX PAYABLE CREDIT	6 CASH DEBIT	
1	19-- Jan.	1	Lindel Mattingly, Capital	R1			11440 00				11440 00	1
2		1	Accounts Receivable	R2		1947 94					9097 48	2
3			Supplies—Carpet			2194 39						3
4			Supplies—Office			900 00						4
5			Prepaid Insurance			116 86						5
6			Equipment			10881 73						6
7			Truck			4900 00						7
8			Allow. for Uncoll. Accts.				58 76					8
9			Accounts Payable				7099 64					9
10			May Baker, Capital				22880 00					10

FYI

The use of several individuals' names in the name of a business is often an indication of a partnership.

attached to a receipt to provide needed details. *(CONCEPT: Objective Evidence)*

January 1, 19--. Accepted assets and liabilities of May Baker's existing business as an initial investment, $22,880.00. Receipt No. 2.

ASSESS

Assess student understanding by checking the solutions to the Independent Practice activities.

Reteach

Make a transparency of the cash receipts journal from the accounting forms masters provided in the Blackline Masters Section of the Teacher's Resource Guide. Refer students to Recycling Problem 21-R. Ask students to use T accounts to analyze the January 1 transactions for the partners' initial investment. Use the transparency to demonstrate how to journalize the transactions.

Extend

Assign Cases for Critical Thinking 1 and 2.

Enrich

Assign the MULTICULTURAL AWARENESS feature on page 572.

CLOSURE

Use Audit Your Understanding questions.

TEACHING STRATEGIES: TEACHING TIP

Review the definition of withdrawals: Assets taken out of a business for the owner's personal use.

TEACHING STRATEGIES: EXPANDING BEYOND THE CLASSROOM

Invite a lawyer, certified public accountant, or partner from a local partnership to speak to the class. Have the individual explain why the partnership form of organization is the best for that business.

AUDIT YOUR UNDERSTANDING

The AUDIT YOUR UNDERSTANDING feature appears at the end of each section of the chapter. Explain to your students that the word *audit* means to check or verify. AUDIT YOUR UNDERSTANDING may be used to check student comprehension of the section just studied. The answers are provided in Appendix D in the back of the textbook.

1. To avoid misunderstandings. Some states require that partnership agreements be in writing.
2. The existing partnership is terminated.
3. The right of all partners to contract for a partnership.
4. Drawing.

LESSON PLAN 21-2

Materials

- Student pages 574–579
- Blackline Master for Cash Receipts Journal (TRG)
- Blackline Master for General Journal (TRG)
- Software: Spreadsheet Template
- Assess: Problem Test Chapter 21, MicroExam Chapter 21

Objectives (Enabling Performance Tasks)

a. Define accounting terms related to forming and expanding a partnership.
b. Identify accounting concepts and practices related to forming and expanding a partnership.
c. Journalize transactions related to forming and expanding a partnership.

Cash	
9,097.48	

Accounts Receivable	
1,947.94	

Supplies—Carpet	
2,194.39	

Supplies—Office	
900.00	

Prepaid Insurance	
116.86	

Equipment	
10,881.73	

Truck	
4,900.00	

Allowance for Uncollectible Accounts	
	58.76

Accounts Payable	
	7,099.64

May Baker, Capital	
	22,880.00

The journal entry to record this transaction is shown on lines 2 through 10 of Illustration 21-3 on page 573.

Audit Your Understanding

1. Why should a partnership agreement be in writing?
2. What happens to an existing partnership if a partner dies?
3. What is meant by mutual agency?
4. What is the title of the account used to record earnings taken out of a partnership during the fiscal year?

ADMITTING PARTNERS TO EXISTING PARTNERSHIPS

Any change in the number of partners terminates an existing partnership agreement. When a new partner is admitted, a new partnership agreement is signed by the new partners.

When a new partner is admitted, the old partnership's accounting records are often continued for the new partnership. As a result, initial investment journal entries for all partners are not always needed. Journal entries are needed, however, to show clearly how the partners' equity has changed. One or both of the following journal entries may be needed.

1. A journal entry to show how much the new partner invests.
2. A journal entry to show how the new partner's admission affects existing partners' capital accounts.

FYI

One reason for admitting a new partner with greater equity than investment is when a celebrity joins the partnership, bringing name recognition and increased sales.

Admitting a Partner with No Change in Total Equity

Elaine Jenkins and Anna Panopoulos are partners in an existing business. Fred Kirchhoff has considerable experience in the same kind of business and desires to join the partnership. The two existing partners agree that Mr. Kirchhoff's skills are needed by the partnership. However, the business does not need additional capital at the present time. Therefore, Ms. Jenkins and Mrs. Panopoulos agree to sell part of their existing equity to Mr. Kirchhoff.

APPLIED SKILLS: BUILDING STUDY SKILLS

Direct students to prepare a Quick Reference Guide (QRG) for transactions to admit partners to existing partnerships. (1) Label the QRG ADMITTING PARTNERS. (2) Copy the transactions out of the chapter narrative. (3) Show the calculations to determine the new partner's equity. (4) Draw T accounts to analyze how the transactions affect capital accounts. This QRG can be used when students are completing end-of-chapter activities.

FYI

If partners agree to sell part of their existing equity to a new partner, the receipt of cash is a personal transaction and is not recorded on the partnership's records.

The existing partners each have $30,000.00 equity in the existing partnership. The three partners of the new partnership agree that Mr. Kirchhoff is to pay $20,000.00 for a one-third equity in the new partnership. The two partners personally receive cash from Mr. Kirchhoff for equity in the partnership. The partnership does not receive the cash from the sale of equity. The equity for Mr. Kirchhoff is calculated as shown below.

Total Equity		×	Share of Equity	=	Kirchhoff's Equity
Jenkins	$30,000.00				
Panopoulos	+ 30,000.00				
Total Equity	$60,000.00	×	1/3	=	$20,000.00

The two existing partners are each entitled to one-half of the price Mr. Kirchhoff pays to buy a one-third share of the partnership. Therefore, Mr. Kirchhoff pays $10,000.00 to each of the existing partners. Also, $20,000.00 of the existing equity is transferred to Mr. Kirchhoff on the partnership's records.

June 1, 19--. Journalized personal sale of equity to new partner, Fred Kirchhoff, $20,000.00, distributed as follows: from Elaine Jenkins, $10,000.00; from Anna Panopoulos, $10,000.00. Memorandum No. 23.

Elaine Jenkins, Capital	
10,000.00	Bal. 30,000.00

Anna Panopoulos, Capital	
10,000.00	Bal. 30,000.00

Fred Kirchhoff, Capital	
	20,000.00

The receipt of cash, a personal transaction among Ms. Jenkins, Mrs. Panopoulos, and Mr. Kirchhoff, is not recorded on the partnership's records. However, the redistribution of capital is a partnership entry and is journalized as shown in Illustration 21-4.

ILLUSTRATION 21-4 Journal entry to admit new partner with no change in total equity

GENERAL JOURNAL PAGE 6

	DATE		ACCOUNT TITLE	DOC. NO.	POST. REF.	DEBIT	CREDIT	
1	19-- June	1	*Elaine Jenkins, Capital*	M23		10 000 00		1
2			*Anna Panopoulos, Capital*			10 000 00		2
3			*Fred Kirchhoff, Capital*				20 000 00	3
4								4

Admitting a Partner with Equity Equal to New Partner's Investment

John Costello and Juliet Ramirez are partners in an existing partnership. Each partner's equity is $30,000.00 for a total equity of

FOCUS

- Forming a partnership and journalizing the partners' initial investments were presented earlier in this chapter. Explain that a new partner may be admitted to an existing partnership. When this occurs, a new partnership agreement must be written and signed. However, the new partnership can continue to use the old partnership's accounting records. In this lesson, the journal entries used to record the admission of a new partner will be presented.
- Introduce vocabulary: goodwill.

TEACH

Cover student pages 574–579 "Admitting Partners to Existing Partnerships." Discuss why a new partner might be admitted. Explain how the equity of the existing partners changes when a new partner is admitted. Show how the equity of the new partner is calculated. Emphasize that the amount of the new partner's investment is not necessarily the same amount as the new partner's equity. Discuss goodwill and show how the value of goodwill is calculated. Emphasize that a new partner's offer to pay more for a given share than the equity of that share can be a basis for revaluing the equity of the existing partners.

APPLIED SKILLS: WORD PROCESSING

If you wish to integrate word processing into your accounting course, you may direct students to answer the end-of-chapter Accounting Terms, Questions for Individual Study, and Cases for Critical Thinking using their word processing software.

APPLY

Demonstrate how the equity of each new partner is calculated. Draw T accounts on the chalkboard or overhead projector to analyze each of the transactions to admit a new partner and show the affect of the transaction on the partners' capital accounts.

Guided Practice

Guide students through the T account analysis of the transactions in Problems 21-4 and 21-5. Have students draw T accounts on a sheet of paper and analyze the transaction in Problem 21-4. All students should agree with the analysis before proceeding to the transaction in Problem 21-5. The balance of Problems 21-4 and 21-5 can be completed as Independent Practice.

Independent Practice

- Assign Term 3, Questions 9–15, and Problems 21-2, 21-3, 21-4, and 21-5.
- Assign Study Guide 21 and Mastery Problem 21-M.

$60,000.00. The existing partners agree to admit Alan Spears as a partner with a one-fourth interest for a $20,000.00 cash investment.

Alan Spears' equity is calculated as shown below.

Total Equity		×	Share of Equity	=	Spears' Equity
Costello	$30,000.00				
Ramirez	30,000.00				
Spears	+ 20,000.00				
Total Equity	$80,000.00	×	1/4	=	$20,000.00

July 1, 19--. Received cash from new partner, Alan Spears, for a one-fourth equity in the business, $20,000.00. Receipt No. 150.

Cash	
20,000.00	

Juliet Ramirez, Capital	
	Bal. 30,000.00

John Costello, Capital	
	Bal. 30,000.00

Alan Spears, Capital	
	20,000.00

The transaction does not change the equity of Mr. Costello or Ms. Ramirez. The journal entry to record this transaction is shown in Illustration 21-5.

ILLUSTRATION 21-5 Journal entry to record cash investment of a new partner

CASH RECEIPTS JOURNAL — PAGE 13

	DATE		ACCOUNT TITLE	DOC. NO.	POST. REF.	1 GENERAL DEBIT	2 GENERAL CREDIT	3 ACCOUNTS RECEIVABLE CREDIT	4 SALES CREDIT	5 SALES TAX PAYABLE CREDIT	6 CASH DEBIT	
1	19-- July	1	Alan Spears, Capital	R150			20 000 00				20 000 00	1

Admitting a Partner with Equity Greater than New Partner's Investment

FYI

The amount of a new partner's investment is not necessarily the same amount as the new partner's equity.

James Weisman and Lisa Redman have equity of $33,000.00 each in an existing partnership. The existing partners agree to admit Lois Wood as a partner with a one-third interest for a $24,000.00 cash investment. Miss Wood's equity is calculated as shown below.

Total Equity		×	Share of Equity	=	Wood's Equity
Weisman	$33,000.00				
Redman	33,000.00				
Wood	+ 24,000.00				
Total Equity	$90,000.00	×	1/3	=	$30,000.00

TEACHING STRATEGIES: TEACHING TIP

Emphasize that the amount of a new partner's investment is not necessarily the same as the new partner's equity.

September 1, 19--. Received cash from new partner, Lois Wood, for a one-third equity in the business, $24,000.00. Existing equity is redistributed as follows: from James Weisman, $3,000.00; from Lisa Redman, $3,000.00. Receipt No. 125 and Memorandum No. 45.

Cash	
24,000.00	

Lois Wood, Capital	
	24,000.00

Two journal entries are required to record this transaction. (1) Receipt of cash is recorded. (2) Redistribution of existing equity is recorded. The analysis of the receipt of cash is shown in the T accounts.

The journal entry to record the receipt of cash is shown in Illustration 21-6.

ILLUSTRATION 21-6 Journal entry to record a cash investment by a new partner

CASH RECEIPTS JOURNAL — PAGE 17

	DATE		ACCOUNT TITLE	DOC. NO.	POST. REF.	1 GENERAL DEBIT	2 GENERAL CREDIT	3 ACCOUNTS RECEIVABLE CREDIT	4 SALES CREDIT	5 SALES TAX PAYABLE CREDIT	6 CASH DEBIT	
1	19-- Sept.	1	Lois Wood, Capital	R125			24 000 00				24 000 00	1

James Weisman, Capital	
3,000.00	Bal. 33,000.00

Lisa Redman, Capital	
3,000.00	Bal. 33,000.00

Lois Wood, Capital	
	Bal. 24,000.00
	6,000.00

The analysis of the redistribution of existing equity is shown in the T accounts.

Miss Wood paid $24,000.00 for a one-third equity share which is worth $30,000.00 in the business' equity. The additional $6,000.00 above Miss Wood's cash investment comes from the equity of the two existing partners. The existing partnership agreement between Mr. Weisman and Mrs. Redman provides that they share equally in equity increases and decreases. Therefore, half of the $6,000.00, or $3,000.00, is transferred from the capital account of each partner to Miss Wood's capital account.

The journal entry to record the redistribution of equity is shown in Illustration 21-7.

ILLUSTRATION 21-7 Journal entry to record transfer of equity to a new partner admitted with equity greater than investment

GENERAL JOURNAL — PAGE 9

	DATE		ACCOUNT TITLE	DOC. NO.	POST. REF.	DEBIT	CREDIT	
1	19-- Sept.	1	James Weisman, Capital	M45		3 000 00		1
2			Lisa Redman, Capital			3 000 00		2
3			Lois Wood, Capital				6 000 00	3

Admitting a Partner when Goodwill Is Recognized

Keith Hess and Ralph Grimes are partners in an existing business. Each partner's equity is $30,000.00, for a total equity of $60,000.00. The existing partners agree to admit Julie Spencer as a partner with

ASSESS

Assess student understanding by checking the solutions to the Independent Practice activities.

Reteach

- Make transparencies of the cash receipts journal and general journal from the accounting forms masters provided in the Blackline Masters Section of the Teacher's Resource Guide. Refer students to Recycling Problem 21-R. Ask students to use T accounts to analyze the March 1, August 1, September 2, and November 1 transactions to admit new partners. Use the transparencies to demonstrate how to journalize the transactions.
- Assign Recycling Problem 21-R.

Extend

- Assign Challenge Problem 21-C. (The challenge is to calculate redistribution of equity.)
- Assign the Spreadsheet Template for Problem 21-4 and 21-5.

Enrich

Assign the APPLIED COMMUNICATIONS special feature on page 581.

TEACHING STRATEGIES: TEACHING TIP

Have students compare the chart of accounts for Chapters 21 and 22 with the chart of accounts for Part 5. The purpose is to discover which accounts used by a corporation and by a partnership are the same and which are different.

CLOSURE

Use Audit Your Understanding questions.

ASSESS

- Administer Problem Test Chapter 21.
- Administer a MicroExam test for Chapter 21.

a one-third interest for a $40,000.00 cash investment. Ms. Spencer is willing to pay $40,000.00 for a one-third equity. She believes the total equity value is worth $120,000.00 after her investment. This value is calculated as shown below.

Spencer's Total Equity	×	3	=	Total Agreed Value of Equity of Partnership
$40,000.00	×	3	=	$120,000.00

FYI

The division of goodwill should be stated in the partnership agreement.

The value of a business in excess of the total investment of owners is called **goodwill**. The partners agree that Ms. Spencer's willingness to pay $40,000.00 for a one-third interest is evidence that goodwill exists. After Ms. Spencer invests her $40,000.00, the total capital on record is $100,000.00 ($30,000.00 + $30,000.00 + $40,000.00). The value of goodwill is calculated as shown below.

Total Agreed Value of Equity	–	Total Recorded Equity	=	Increase in Equity from Goodwill
$120,000.00	–	$100,000.00	=	$20,000.00

FYI

The account Goodwill is located in the Intangible Assets section of a general ledger.

The $20,000.00 amount of equity in excess of the total recorded investment of the three partners is the value of goodwill.

September 1, 19--. Received cash from new partner, Julie Spencer, for a one-third equity in the business, $40,000.00. Goodwill, $20,000.00, is distributed as follows: Keith Hess, $10,000.00; Ralph Grimes, $10,000.00. Receipt No. 120 and Memorandum No. 60.

Cash	
40,000.00	

Julie Spencer, Capital	
	40,000.00

Two journal entries are required for this transaction. (1) Receipt of cash is recorded. (2) Distribution of goodwill is recorded.

The analysis of the receipt of cash is shown in the T accounts.

The journal entry to record this cash investment is similar to the one shown in Illustration 21-6.

Based on prior partnership agreement, the goodwill is divided equally between Mr. Hess and Mr. Grimes with each partner receiving $10,000.00. The total equity after admission of Ms. Spencer as a partner is distributed as shown below.

	Previous Equity	+	Share of Goodwill	=	New Equity
Hess	$ 30,000.00	+	$10,000.00	=	$ 40,000.00
Grimes	30,000.00	+	10,000.00	=	40,000.00
Spencer	+ 40,000.00	+	—	=	40,000.00
Total	$100,000.00	+	$20,000.00	=	$120,000.00

TEACHING STRATEGIES: DIFFERENT LEARNING ABILITIES

Gifted Students. Partnerships are an effective form of business organization only when there is effective communication and cooperation among partners. Gifted students can best learn about the opportunities, problems, and challenges of a partnership by forming a real partnership. Encourage gifted students to form a partnership to sell a service or product of their selection. The students should prepare the partnership agreement, operate the business, and report the results of operations. Suggest that the students consult businesspersons, such as lawyers and accountants, for assistance.

Goodwill	
20,000.00	

Keith Hess, Capital	
	Bal. 30,000.00
	10,000.00

Ralph Grimes, Capital	
	Bal. 30,000.00
	10,000.00

The analysis of the distribution of goodwill is shown in the T accounts.

None of the goodwill is recorded in Julie Spencer's capital account. She invested $40,000.00 for a one-third share of the business. One-third of the total equity, *$120,000.00,* equals the current balance of Ms. Spencer's capital account, *$40,000.00.*

When used, the account Goodwill is located in a general ledger's *Intangible Assets* section. If MaLin Carpet Design has goodwill to record, this account will be added to its general ledger.

The journal entry to record the goodwill is shown in Illustration 21-8.

ILLUSTRATION 21-8 Journal entry to record goodwill

GENERAL JOURNAL PAGE 9

	DATE		ACCOUNT TITLE	DOC. NO.	POST. REF.	DEBIT	CREDIT	
1	19-- Sept.	1	Goodwill	M60		20 000 00		1
2			Keith Hess, Capital				10 000 00	2
3			Ralph Grimes, Capital				10 000 00	3

Audit Your Understanding

1. What happens to an existing partnership if a new partner is admitted?
2. When admitting a new partner, how is the new partner's equity calculated?
3. What two journal entries are required to record admitting a partner with equity greater than the new partner's investment?
4. What accounts are debited and credited to record the distribution of goodwill when a new partner is admitted?

AUDIT YOUR UNDERSTANDING

1. The existing partnership is terminated.
2. Total equity (including investment by new partner) multiplied by new partner's share of equity equals the new partner's equity.
3. (1) Receipt of cash is recorded. (2) Redistribution of existing equity is recorded.
4. Goodwill is debited; existing partners' capital accounts are credited.

APPLIED SKILLS: LANGUAGE ARTS

Paraphrasing, writing complete sentences, and identifying direct objects. For additional practice in language arts skills, direct students to answer the Accounting Terms and Questions For Individual Study at the end of the chapter. Students should write the answers in their own words and in complete sentences. To further practice language arts skills, ask students to underline the direct object(s) in each sentence of their answers.

ACCOUNTING TERMS

1. **partnership agreement:** A written agreement setting forth the conditions under which a partnership is to operate. (p. 570)
2. **mutual agency:** The right of all partners to contract for a partnership. (p. 570)
3. **goodwill:** The value of a business in excess of the total investment of owners. (p. 578)

QUESTIONS FOR INDIVIDUAL STUDY

1. Recording owners' equity and income taxes. (p. 570)
2. When two or more persons agree to form a business using the partnership form of organization. (p. 570)
3. Business Entity concept. (p. 570)
4. The existing partnership is terminated. (p. 570)
5. To avoid misunderstandings. (p. 570)
6. A capital account and a drawing account. (p. 572)
7. Cash is debited; Partner A, Capital is credited. (p. 572)
8. Cash and Equipment are debited; Accounts Payable and Partner B, Capital are credited. (p. 574)
9. The existing partnership is terminated and a new partnership is formed. (p. 574)
10. (a) An entry to show the new partner's investment. (b) An entry to show how the new partner's admission affects existing partners' capital accounts. (p. 574)
11. Partner A, Capital and Partner B, Capital are debited; Partner C, Capital is credited. (p. 575)
12. Cash is debited; Partner C, Capital is credited. (p. 576)
13. (a) Cash is debited; Partner C, Capital is credited. (b) Partner A, Capital and Partner B, Capital are debited; Partner C, Capital is credited. (p. 577)
14. (a) Cash is debited; Partner C, Capital is credited. (b) Goodwill is debited; Partner A, Capital and Partner B, Capital are credited. (pp. 578–579)
15. Intangible Asset. (p. 579)

ACCOUNTING TERMS EPT(a)

What is the meaning of each of the following?

1. **partnership agreement**
2. **mutual agency**
3. **goodwill**

QUESTIONS FOR INDIVIDUAL STUDY EPT(b)

1. In what way do accounting procedures for a partnership differ from accounting procedures for a corporation?
2. When does a partnership come into existence?
3. Which accounting concept is being applied when partnership records are kept separate from those of the partners?
4. What happens to an existing partnership if a partner dies?
5. Why should a partnership agreement be in writing?
6. Which two capital accounts for each partner are kept in a partnership's general ledger?
7. What accounts are affected, and how, when Partner A invests only cash to form a partnership?
8. What accounts are affected, and how, when Partner B invests cash, equipment, and accounts payable to form a partnership?
9. What happens to the existence of a partnership when a new partner is admitted?
10. When a new partnership is created and the records of a previous partnership are continued, what two kinds of entries may be needed?
11. What accounts are affected, and how, when cash is paid to Partners A and B for admission of Partner C with no change in total equity?
12. What accounts are affected, and how, when Partners A and B admit Partner C with an equity equal to Partner C's cash investment?
13. What accounts are affected, and how, when Partners A and B admit Partner C for an equity share greater than Partner C's cash investment?
14. What accounts are affected, and how, to record goodwill when Partner C's investment creates goodwill?
15. What is the general ledger classification of the goodwill account?

CASES FOR CRITICAL THINKING EPT(b)

CASE 1 Partner A contracted with a vendor to buy a computer for the partnership. Partner A did not discuss the transaction with Partner B or get Partner B's approval. Partner B refused to approve payment for the computer when it was delivered, claiming the vendor cannot force payment because all partners did not agree to buy the computer. The vendor claims that the transaction is valid, and the partnership must pay for the computer. Is Partner B or the vendor correct? Explain.

CASE 2 Helen Cole, her husband, and her son were partners in a business. Mrs. Cole's husband died, leaving his equity in the partnership to Mrs. Cole. Mrs. Cole and her son plan to form a new partnership and continue the business. Mrs. Cole's brother owns a similar business. The brother suggests that they combine the two businesses into a corporation. What questions do you suggest Mrs. Cole answer before she decides whether to form a partnership with her son or a corporation with her son and brother?

APPLIED COMMUNICATIONS

Partnerships, like other forms of business, have operating expenses each month. Advertising, depreciation, and rent expense are examples of those operating expenses. Controlling these expenses affects the net income of the business.

INSTRUCTIONS:

Identify the operating expenses for MaLin Carpet Design in this chapter. Prepare a brief report, including a pie graph, that depicts the operating expenses for the year ended December 31. Do you think MaLin is controlling its operating expenses?

APPLICATION PROBLEMS EPT(c)

PROBLEM 21-1 Forming a partnership

Denise Wood and Anne Cortez agree to form a partnership on June 1 of the current year. The partnership assumes the assets and liabilities of Mrs. Wood's existing business. Miss Cortez invests cash equal to the investment of Mrs. Wood. Partners share equally in all changes in equity. The May 31 balance sheet for Mrs. Wood's existing business is as follows.

Wood Crafts
Balance Sheet
May 31, 19--

ASSETS			
Current Assets:			
Cash		$10,764.44	
Accounts Receivable	$2,775.16		
Less Allowance for Uncollectible Accounts	55.49	2,719.67	
Merchandise Inventory		19,480.25	
Supplies		496.73	
Total Current Assets			$33,461.09
Plant Assets:			
Equipment			7,023.04
Total Assets			$40,484.13
LIABILITIES			
Accounts Payable			$ 9,484.13
OWNER'S EQUITY			
Denise Wood, Capital			31,000.00
Total Liabilities and Owner's Equity			$40,484.13

INSTRUCTIONS:

Journalize the following transactions. Use page 1 of a cash receipts journal. Use June 1 of the current year as the date.

June 1. Received cash from partner, Anne Cortez, as an initial investment, $31,000.00. R1.

1. Accepted assets and liabilities of Denise Wood's existing business as an initial investment, $31,000.00. R2.

APPLIED SKILLS: COMMUNICATIONS

Surveys of business managers show that communication skills are one of the most desired traits in new employees. The APPLIED COMMUNICATIONS activity provides an opportunity for students to practice their communication and language arts skills on topics that directly relate to accounting. This activity requires students to identify and analyze the expenditures of their local community. Students should be encouraged to share their perceptions regarding the efficient expenditures of the funds. If available, students should use software that permits the display of graphics within the text.

CASES FOR CRITICAL THINKING

Case 1 The vendor is correct. Each partner is an agent of the partnership and may bind the partnership to contracts with outside vendors.

Case 2 (1) Can the business succeed as a two-owner partnership or are the skills and assets of the brother-in-law needed? (2) In a partnership, can Mrs. Cole and her son work together successfully as partners? (3) What will forming a corporation do to the income tax liabilities of the new business as compared to a partnership? (4) In a corporation, can the three persons work together successfully as stockholders/officers?

APPLIED COMMUNICATIONS

Students' solutions will vary. The instructor should consider the following items when grading the activity: (1) identification of facts, (2) analysis of expenditure efficiency, (3) writing style, and (4) mechanics (grammar, spelling, punctuation, and sentence structure).

CHECK FIGURES

See Teacher's Edition of Working Papers for complete solutions.

Problem 21-1 Each partner's capital is credited for $31,000. Total Cash invested, $41,764.44.

CHECK FIGURES *(cont'd)*

Problem 21-2 Debit original partners' capital, $10,000 each. Credit new partner's capital, $20,000.

Problem 21-3 Credit new partner's capital, debit Cash, $60,000.

Problem 21-4 Credit new partner's capital account, debit Cash, $22,000. Debit existing partners' capital, $6,000 each; credit new partner's capital, $12,000.

Problem 21-5 Credit new partner's capital, debit Cash, $36,000. Debit Goodwill $18,000; credit original partners' capital, $9,000 each.

Mastery Problem 21-M General journal transactions: Aug. 1, debit existing partners' capital, $4,000 each; credit new partner's capital, $8,000. Oct. 20, debit original partners' capital, $200 each; credit new partner's capital, $800. Dec. 5, debit Goodwill, $2,000, credit original partners' capital, $400 each.

Challenge Problem 21-C General journal transactions: July 1, debit Merchandise Inventory and credit new partner's capital, $12,000. July 20, debit new partner's capital, $2,250, credit existing partners' capital, $750 each. Nov. 5, debit Goodwill, $1,000.00, credit existing partners' capital, $250 each.

PROBLEM 21-2 Admitting a partner with no change in total equity

MATHEMATICS

Steven Myer and William Riggs are partners in an existing business. Each partner has equity of $30,000.00. On October 1 of the current year, the two partners agree to admit Sandra DeVito as a third partner. The partners agree to personally sell Mrs. DeVito $10,000.00 each of their equity and to give her a one-third share of ownership. Mrs. DeVito is to pay the money directly to the two original partners.

INSTRUCTIONS:

Journalize the following transaction. Use page 12 of a general journal.

Oct. 1. Journalized personal sale of equity to new partner, Sandra DeVito, $20,000.00, distributed as follows: from Steven Myer, $10,000.00; from William Riggs, $10,000.00. M24.

PROBLEM 21-3 Admitting a partner with equity equal to new partner's investment

Susan Wang and Lelah Burch are partners in an existing business. Each partner has $60,000.00 equity in the partnership. Partners share equally in all changes in equity. On April 1 of the current year, the two partners agree to admit Daryl Wetzel as a partner with a one-third share of the total equity.

INSTRUCTIONS:

Journalize the following transaction. Use page 13 of a cash receipts journal.

Apr. 1. Received cash from new partner, Daryl Wetzel, for a one-third equity in the business, $60,000.00. R95.

PROBLEM 21-4 Admitting a partner with equity greater than new partner's investment

SPREADSHEET

MATHEMATICS

Stanley Neal and Helen Jobe each have equity of $40,000.00 in an existing partnership. The partners share equally in all changes in equity. On August 1 of the current year, the existing partners agree to admit Greg Talbot with a one-third share of the total equity.

INSTRUCTIONS:

Journalize the following transaction. Use page 14 of a cash receipts journal and page 7 of a general journal.

Aug. 1. Received cash from new partner, Greg Talbot, for a one-third equity in the business, $22,000.00. Existing equity is redistributed as follows: from Stanley Neal, $6,000.00; from Helen Jobe, $6,000.00. R116 and M25.

PROBLEM 21-5 Admitting a partner when goodwill is recognized

SPREADSHEET

MATHEMATICS

Arthur Jansky and Edward Thayer are partners, each with $27,000.00 equity in an existing business. The partners share equally in all changes in equity. On March 1 of the current year, Dean McGee is admitted as a new partner with a one-third share of the total equity.

INSTRUCTIONS:

Journalize the following transaction. Use page 5 of a cash receipts journal and page 3 of a general journal.

Mar. 1. Received cash from new partner, Dean McGee, for a one-third equity in the business, $36,000.00. Goodwill, $18,000.00, is distributed as follows: Arthur Jansky, $9,000.00; Edward Thayer, $9,000.00. R67 and M10.

ENRICHMENT PROBLEMS

EPT(c)

MASTERY PROBLEM 21-M Forming and expanding a partnership

On July 1 of the current year, Roy Hatfield and Michelle Allen form a partnership. The partners share equally in all changes in equity. The partnership assumes the assets and liabilities of Mr. Hatfield's existing business. Miss Allen invests cash equal to Mr. Hatfield's investment. The June 30 balance sheet for Mr. Hatfield's existing business is as follows.

Hatfield Financial Services
Balance Sheet
June 30, 19--

ASSETS			
Current Assets:			
Cash		$4,291.23	
Accounts Receivable	$3,303.60		
Less Allowance for Uncollectible Accounts	35.79	3,267.81	
Supplies		290.19	
Total Current Assets			$ 7,849.23
Plant Assets:			
Equipment			4,378.14
Total Assets			$12,227.37
LIABILITIES			
Accounts Payable			$ 227.37
OWNER'S EQUITY			
Roy Hatfield, Capital			12,000.00
Total Liabilities and Owner's Equity			$12,227.37

INSTRUCTIONS:

Journalize the following transactions. Use page 1 of a cash receipts journal and page 1 of a general journal.

July 1. Received cash from partner, Michelle Allen, as an initial investment, $12,000.00. R1.
1. Accepted assets and liabilities of Roy Hatfield's existing business as an initial investment, $12,000.00. R2.

Aug. 1. Journalized personal sale of equity to new partner, Frank Boyd, $8,000.00, distributed as follows: from Michelle Allen, $4,000.00; from Roy Hatfield, $4,000.00. M8.

Oct. 1. Received cash from new partner, Danita McGrew, for a one-fourth equity in the business, $8,000.00. R80.

Oct. 20. Received cash from new partner, Donna Wells, for a one-fifth equity in the business, $7,000.00. Existing equity is redistributed as follows: Michelle Allen, $200.00; from Roy Hatfield, $200.00; from Frank Boyd, $200.00; from Danita McGrew, $200.00. R92 and M18.

Dec. 5. Received cash from new partner, Pearl Morgan, for a one-sixth equity in the business, $8,200.00. Goodwill, $2,000.00, is distributed as follows: Roy Hatfield, $400.00; Michelle Allen, $400.00; Frank Boyd, $400.00; Danita McGrew, $400.00; Donna Wells, $400.00. R118 and M24.

CHALLENGE PROBLEM 21-C Forming and expanding a partnership

MATHEMATICS

On May 1 of the current year, Marsha Huerta and John Ward form a partnership. The partnership assumes the assets and liabilities of the two partners' existing businesses. Partners share equally in all changes in equity. The May 1 balance sheets for the existing businesses are as follows.

Marsha's Party Planner
Balance Sheet
May 1, 19--

ASSETS			
Current Assets:			
Cash		$4,258.32	
Accounts Receivable	$2,280.56		
Less Allowance for Uncollectible Accounts	35.43	2,245.13	
Merchandise Inventory		6,237.29	
Total Current Assets			$12,740.74
Plant Assets:			
Office Equipment			2,943.49
Total Assets			$15,684.23
LIABILITIES			
Accounts Payable			$ 3,684.23
OWNER'S EQUITY			
Marsha Huerta, Capital			12,000.00
Total Liabilities and Owner's Equity			$15,684.23

Ward's Wedding Chapel
Balance Sheet
May 1, 19--

ASSETS		
Current Assets:		
Cash	$4,323.49	
Supplies	2,075.21	
Merchandise Inventory	6,342.04	
Total Current Assets		$12,740.74
Plant Assets:		
Office Equipment		2,959.88
Total Assets		$15,700.62
LIABILITIES		
Accounts Payable		$ 3,700.62
OWNER'S EQUITY		
John Ward, Capital		12,000.00
Total Liabilities and Owner's Equity		$15,700.62

INSTRUCTIONS:

Journalize the following transactions. Use page 8 of a cash receipts journal and page 4 of a general journal.

May 1. Accepted assets and liabilities of Marsha Huerta's existing business as an initial investment. R1.

1. Accepted assets and liabilities of John Ward's existing business as an initial investment. R2.

July 1. Accepted assets of Dan Ogden's existing business as an investment of new partner for a one-third equity in the business. M80. Mr. Ogden's July 1 balance sheet is as follows.

Dan Ogden
Balance Sheet
July 1, 19--

ASSETS	
Merchandise Inventory	$12,000.00
OWNER'S EQUITY	
Dan Ogden, Capital	$12,000.00

July 20. Received cash from new partner, Pam Wise, for a one-fourth equity in the business, $15,000.00. R24 and M85.

Nov. 5. Accepted assets of Rodney Stein's existing business as an investment of new partner for a one-fifth equity in the business. Goodwill, $1,000.00, is distributed as follows: Marsha Huerta, $250.00; John Ward, $250.00; Dan Ogden, $250.00; Pam Wise, $250.00. R92 and M105. Mr. Stein's November 5 balance sheet is as follows.

Stein Supplies
Balance Sheet
November 5, 19--

ASSETS	
Cash	$ 5,000.00
Merchandise Inventory	8,000.00
Total Assets	$13,000.00
OWNER'S EQUITY	
Rodney Stein, Capital	$13,000.00

585

CHAPTER 22 OVERVIEW

Chapter 22 concludes the coverage for a partnership by focusing on end-of-fiscal-period work. Four separate methods of distributing partnership net income and a combination of methods are described. The chapter also shows how to distribute a partnership deficit to partners. A work sheet is prepared and an income statement, distribution of net income statement, owners' equity statement, and balance sheet

GUIDE TO ACHIEVING LEARNING OBJECTIVES

	TEACH	APPLY	EXTEND/ENRICH					
Enabling Performance Tasks	**Lesson Plans**	**Application Problems**	**Mastery Problems**	**Challenge Problems**	**Cases for Critical Thinking**	**Recycling Problems**	**Reinforcement Activity**	
a. Define accounting terms related to distributing earnings and completing end-of-fiscal-period work for a partnership.	22-1, 22-2, 22-3							
b. Identify accounting concepts and practices related to distributing earnings and completing end-of-fiscal-period work for a partnership.	22-1, 22-2, 22-3				Cases 1, 2			
c. Prepare a distribution of net income statement for a partnership.	22-1	22-1	22-M	22-C		22-R		
d. Journalize entries for withdrawal of partnership earnings.	22-1	22-2						
e. Complete end-of-fiscal-period work for a partnership.	22-2	22-3	22-M	22-C		22-R		
f. Journalize entries for liquidating a partnership.	22-3	22-4						

ENRICHMENT

SPECIAL FEATURES
Global Perspective, page 592
Careers in Accounting, page 595
TECHNOLOGY CONNECTION
Spreadsheet Template Problems 22-1, 22-M

NEW, REVIEW, AND EXTENSION

ACTIVITIES/CONCEPTS/TRANSACTIONS	NEW	REVIEW/ EXTENSION
Distributing partnership earnings using fixed percentages		✓
Distributing partnership earnings using percentage of total equity and using interest on equity	✓	
Distributing partnership earnings using salaries	✓	
Distributing partnership earnings using a combination of methods	✓	
Distribution of net income statement		✓
Recording partners' cash withdrawals and noncash assets		✓
Work sheet for a partnership		✓
Financial statements for a partnership		✓
Adjusting and closing entries for a partnership		✓
Liquidation of a partnership		✓
Gains and losses on realization		✓

are prepared. Then adjusting and closing entries for a partnership are discussed, followed by a description of how federal income tax applies for a partnership. The rest of the chapter demonstrates how a partnership is liquidated, with assets sold at gains and losses, liabilities paid, and remaining cash distributed to the partners.

INFORMAL ASSESSMENT		FORMAL ASSESSMENT			
Study Guide	**Audit Your Understanding**	**Chapter MicroExam**	**Chapter Problem Test**	**Unit Objective Test**	**Portfolio**
Unit A	✓	✓		✓	
Units B, C, D	✓	✓		✓	
			✓		
			✓		
			✓		
			✓		

TEACHING MATERIALS

- Teacher's Wraparound Edition of the Text
- Teacher's Resource Guide
- Teacher's Edition of Working Papers
- MicroExam

APPLIED MATHEMATICS

APPLIED MATH/ACCOUNTING SKILL	APPLICATION
Calculating distribution of partnership net income using:	
Fixed percentage	Prob. 22-1
Percentage of total equity	Prob. 22-1
Interest on equity	Prob. 22-1
Salaries	Prob. 22-1
Combination of methods	Prob. 22-1
Calculating distribution of partnership deficit	Prob. 22-1
Calculating distribution of loss and gain on realization	Prob. 22-4

22

TEACHING STRATEGIES: ACCOUNTING PEDAGOGY

This textbook covers financial reporting for a partnership. It is important for students to understand how the financial reporting for a partnership differs from a corporation.

Financial Reporting for a Partnership

ENABLING PERFORMANCE TASKS

After studying Chapter 22, you will be able to:

a Define accounting terms related to distributing earnings and completing end-of-fiscal-period work for a partnership.

b Identify accounting concepts and practices related to distributing earnings and completing end-of-fiscal-period work for a partnership.

c Prepare a distribution of net income statement for a partnership.

d Journalize entries for withdrawal of partnership earnings.

e Complete end-of-fiscal-period work for a partnership.

f Journalize entries for liquidating a partnership.

TERMS PREVIEW

distribution of net income statement • deficit • owners' equity statement • liquidation of a partnership • realization

586

SOFTWARE FOCUS

Software may be used for independent practice or enrichment/extension as the instructor deems appropriate. For this chapter, the Spreadsheet Template may be used with Problem 22-1 and Mastery Problem 22-M.

Most end-of-fiscal-period work is similar for corporations, proprietorships, and partnerships. Two major procedures are different. (1) A corporation calculates and pays income tax on its net income; partnerships and proprietorships do not. (2) A corporation maintains separate accounts for contributed capital (Capital Stock) and earned capital (Retained Earnings). Partnerships and proprietorships combine contributed and earned capital in one account for each owner.

A corporation may distribute some, but usually not all, of its earnings to stockholders as dividends. However, partnerships, like proprietorships, distribute all earnings of the business to the owners' capital accounts. The owners may then withdraw the earnings or leave them in the business.

DISTRIBUTION OF PARTNERSHIP EARNINGS

All earnings of a partnership are distributed to the partners. Five methods are commonly used for calculating the distribution of partnership earnings.

1. Fixed percentage.
2. Percentage of total equity.
3. Interest on equity.
4. Salaries.
5. Combination of methods.

Fixed Percentage

FYI

Many sports teams are owned by partnerships.

The basis on which a partnership's earnings are distributed is usually stated in the partnership agreement. If a partnership agreement does not indicate how to divide the earnings, most state laws stipulate that partners share the earnings equally. For example, if there are two partners, earnings are shared on a fixed percentage of 50% and 50%. The law applies regardless of differences in the partners' investments, abilities, or time devoted to partnership business.

Scott Costa and Gary McKee are partners. On January 1, the partners' equities are: Mr. Costa, $50,000.00; Mr. McKee, $30,000.00. The net income for the year ended December 31 is $20,000.00. The partnership agreement states that Mr. Costa is to receive 60% and Mr. McKee is to receive 40% of the net income or net loss. The distribution of net income is calculated as shown below.

	Total Net Income	×	Fixed Percentage	=	Share of Net Income
Costa	$20,000.00	×	60%	=	$12,000.00
McKee	$20,000.00	×	40%	=	8,000.00
Total					$20,000.00

LESSON PLAN 22-1

Materials

- Student pages 587–593
- Blackline Master for 2-Column Statement (TRG)
- Software: Spreadsheet Template

Objectives (Enabling Performance Tasks)

a. Define accounting terms related to distributing earnings and completing end-of-fiscal-period work for a partnership.

b. Identify accounting concepts and practices related to distributing earnings and completing end-of-fiscal-period work for a partnership.

c. Prepare a distribution of net income statement for a partnership.

d. Journalize entries for withdrawal of partnership earnings.

FOCUS

- Chapter 21 presented the journal entries to form a partnership and to admit a new partner to an existing partnership. In this lesson, the methods used to distribute a partnership's earnings to the partners will be introduced. Also, the entries used to record partners' withdrawals of earnings will be presented.
- Introduce vocabulary: distribution of net income statement, deficit.

Percentage of Total Equity

Partners often agree to use capital account balances on the first day of a fiscal year as the basis for calculating the distribution of partnership earnings. If Mr. Costa and Mr. McKee had agreed to use this method, referred to as the percentage of total equity method, the percentages would be calculated as shown below.

	Partner's Equity	÷	Total Equity	=	Percentage of Total Equity
Costa	$50,000.00	÷	$80,000.00	=	62.5%
McKee	30,000.00	÷	$80,000.00	=	37.5%
Total	$80,000.00				

	Total Net Income	×	Percentage of Total Equity	=	Share of Net Income
Costa	$20,000.00	×	62.5%	=	$12,500.00
McKee	$20,000.00	×	37.5%	=	7,500.00
Total					$20,000.00

Interest on Equity

FYI

The rate of interest on equity is often related to the current bank prime lending rate.

Interest on equity is often used as a method to distribute earnings when partners invest different amounts in a partnership. Partners often agree to use capital account balances on the first day of a fiscal year as the basis for this income distribution method. The partnership agreement states the interest rate.

MaLin Carpet Design's partnership agreement, Item Five, Illustration 21-1, Chapter 21, stipulates that each partner is to receive 5% interest on equity. On January 1, Ms. Baker's equity is $22,880.00 and Mr. Mattingly's equity is $11,440.00. The interest on equity is calculated as shown below.

	Partner's Equity	×	Interest Rate	=	Interest on Equity
Baker	$22,880.00	×	5%	=	$1,144.00
Mattingly	$11,440.00	×	5%	=	$ 572.00

When the interest on equity method is used, the remaining net income or net loss is distributed using another income distribution method as described later in this chapter.

Salaries

FYI

A partner's salary is not an expense to the business.

Salaries are often used as a method to distribute earnings when partners contribute different amounts of personal service or bring different prior experience to a partnership. The amount of salary for each partner is stated in the partnership agreement.

MaLin's partnership agreement states that salaries are to be paid as follows: Ms. Baker, $5,000.00; Mr. Mattingly, $3,000.00.

TEACHING STRATEGIES: TEACHING TIP

Emphasize that the IRS classifies the partners as self-employed persons whose salaries are not an expense of the partnership. Therefore, partners' salaries are considered to be withdrawals of partnership earnings.

When salaries are used, the remaining net income or net loss is distributed using another income distribution method as described later in this chapter.

Combination of Methods

A combination of income distribution methods may be used for distributing partnership earnings. MaLin's partnership agreement states the earnings distribution as shown below.

	Interest on Equity	Salary	Distribution of Remaining Net Income or Net Loss
Baker	5%	$5,000.00	50%
Mattingly	5%	$3,000.00	50%

The distribution of MaLin's net income, *$37,400.00*, is calculated as follows.

	Baker	Mattingly	Distribution
Total Net Income			$37,400.00
Interest on Equity	$ 1,144.00	$ 572.00	
Salary	5,000.00	3,000.00	
Total	$ 6,144.00	$ 3,572.00	9,716.00
Remaining Net Income			$27,684.00
Distribution of Remaining Net Income	13,842.00	13,842.00	
Total Distribution	$19,986.00	$17,414.00	$37,400.00

DISTRIBUTION OF NET INCOME STATEMENT FOR A PARTNERSHIP

A partnership financial statement showing distribution of net income or net loss to partners is called a **distribution of net income statement.**

Distribution of Net Income Statement Showing a Net Income

MaLin's distribution of net income statement is shown in Illustration 22-1 on page 590.

FYI

There is not always enough net income to cover each partner's allowance. Partners must share the deficit according to the partnership agreement.

Distribution of Net Income Statement Showing a Deficit

When salaries or interest on equity are stipulated, the amounts are allowed whether or not there is sufficient net income available. The amount by which allowances to partners exceed net income is

TEACH

Cover student pages 587–593 "Distribution of Partnership Earnings," "Distribution of Net Income Statement for a Partnership," and "Withdrawal of Partnership Earnings." Discuss and demonstrate the five methods for calculating the distribution of partnership earnings. Emphasize the two steps for calculating the percentage of total equity. (1) Divide each partner's equity by total equity. (2) Multiply the total net income by the percentage of total equity. Stress that partner's salaries are not an expense to the business. Present the distribution of net income statement. Emphasize that there is not always a large enough net income to cover each partner's allowance. When this situation occurs, partners must share the deficit according to the partnership agreement. Review the entries to record withdrawals of cash or other assets from the partnership.

APPLIED SKILLS: WORD PROCESSING

If you wish to integrate word processing into your accounting course, you may direct students to answer the end-of-chapter Accounting Terms, Questions for Individual Study, and Cases for Critical Thinking using their word processing software.

TEACHING STRATEGIES: APPLYING VISUALS

Direct students to Illustration 22-1 to review the distribution of net income statement.

APPLY

Write the formulas on the chalkboard and demonstrate how to calculate the distribution of partnership earnings. Refer students to Illustrations 22-1 and 22-2 as the distribution of net income statement is discussed. Demonstrate how each partner's share of a deficit is calculated.

Guided Practice

Guide students through the calculations to distribute the net income in Problem 22-1, Instructions 1 (a), (b), (c), and (d). Working as a group, calculate the distribution of net income for case (a). When all students agree with the answer, repeat the process for cases (b), (c), and (d). The balance of Problem 22-1 can be assigned as Independent Practice.

Independent Practice

Assign Terms 1–2, Questions 1–6, and Problems 22-1 and 22-2.

ILLUSTRATION 22-1 Distribution of net income statement showing a net income

MaLin Carpet Design
Distribution of Net Income Statement
For Year Ended December 31, 19--

May Baker:		
5% Interest on Equity	$ 1,144.00	
Salary	5,000.00	
Share of Remaining Net Income	13,842.00	
Total Share on Net Income		$19,986.00
Lindel Mattingly:		
5% Interest on Equity	$ 572.00	
Salary	3,000.00	
Share of Remaining Net Income	13,842.00	
Total Share of Net Income		17,414.00
Total Net Income		$37,400.00

FYI

Fields of accounting become extremely specialized as technical requirements increase. For example, some accountants specialize in accounting only for the gas and oil industry.

called a **deficit.** If the net income is less than the total allowed, partners share in the resulting deficit according to the partnership agreement.

On January 1, the equity of two partners is as follows: Jason Ford, $60,000.00; Celia Pope, $54,000.00. The partners each receive a 10% annual interest on equity and share any remaining income or deficit on a fixed percentage of 60% and 40%, respectively. For the month of January, the partnership earned a net income of $750.00. The monthly amounts due each partner are calculated as shown below.

	Partner's Equity	×	Interest Rate	×	Time as Fraction of Year	=	Monthly Interest
Ford	($60,000.00	×	10%)	×	1/12	=	$500.00
Pope	($54,000.00	×	10%)	×	1/12	=	450.00
Total							$950.00

The 10% interest rate on equity is for a year. To find the monthly interest, the annual amount is multiplied by the time expressed as a fraction of a year. One month is one-twelfth of a year.

Total Net Income	−	Total Allowance	=	Deficit
$750.00	−	$950.00	=	$200.00

The total interest is more than the net income available. The difference between the net income available and the allowances is a deficit. The distribution of the deficit is calculated as follows.

TEACHING STRATEGIES: COOPERATIVE LEARNING

Divide the class into groups of three or four students each. Have each group create a problem similar to Problem 22-1. The problem should use numerous methods for calculating the distribution of partnership earnings. Next, have the groups exchange problems, work the problem, and prepare a solution. This cooperative learning activity should not take more than 15 to 20 minutes.

	Deficit	×	Fixed Percentage	=	Partner's Share of Deficit
Ford	$200.00	×	60%	=	$120.00
Pope	$200.00	×	40%	=	80.00
Total					$200.00

The partnership's distribution of net income statement is shown in Illustration 22-2.

ILLUSTRATION 22-2 Distribution of net income statement showing a deficit

Ford and Pope
Distribution of Net Income Statement
For Month Ended January 31, 19--

Jason Ford:		
10% Interest on Equity	$500.00	
Less Share of Deficit	120.00	
Total Share of Net Income		$380.00
Celia Pope:		
10% Interest on Equity	$450.00	
Less Share of Deficit	80.00	
Total Share of Net Income		370.00
Total Net Income		$750.00

WITHDRAWAL OF PARTNERSHIP EARNINGS

FYI

A partner may have a large capital balance, yet be unable to withdraw any assets from the partnership. Cash or other assets must be available for a partner to make a withdrawal.

A partner often needs a portion of the annual net income before the end of a fiscal year when the actual net income is known. Thus, during a fiscal year, partners take assets out of the partnership in anticipation of the net income for the year. Assets taken out of a business for the owner's personal use are known as withdrawals. Usually the partnership agreement indicates limits on the amount of assets that may be withdrawn.

Withdrawal of Cash

May 30, 19--. May Baker, partner, withdrew cash for personal use, $600.00. Check No. 95.

May Baker, Drawing	
600.00	

Cash	
	600.00

May Baker, Drawing is debited for $600.00. Cash is credited for $600.00. The account balance of May Baker, Drawing a contra capital account, is a deduction from the account balance of May Baker, Capital.

The journal entry to record this transaction is shown in Illustration 22-3, page 592.

ASSESS

Assess student understanding by checking the solutions to the Independent Practice activities.

Reteach

Make a transparency of the 2-column financial statement paper from the accounting forms masters provided in the Blackline Masters Section of the Teacher's Resource Guide. Use the cases given in Problem 22-1, Instruction 1 (e) and (f), but change some key amounts such as net income, partners' salary, percentage of interest, etc. Demonstrate how the distribution of net income is calculated in each case. Use the information and the transparency to show how a distribution of net income statement is prepared for each case.

Extend

- Assign Cases for Critical Thinking 1.
- Assign the Spreadsheet Template for Problem 22-1.

Enrich

Accountants often write procedure manuals to provide accounting clerks with instructions for recording routine transactions. Have students write instructions for recording a partner's withdrawal of cash or other assets.

Global Perspective

The GLOBAL PERSPECTIVE feature is intended to expose students to some of the ways in which accounting and business in general differ in other countries. This GLOBAL PERSPECTIVE feature allows students to explore international mail services and rates. The GLOBAL PERSPECTIVE activity requires students to research the mailing options available and their costs.

Answers to Global Perspective Activity

Obtaining a schedule of costs and restrictions for international mail from the United States Postal Service or another mail service should be a relatively easy task. Student answers will vary depending on the mail service and country that is chosen.

Global Perspective

INTERNATIONAL MAIL

When doing business internationally, correspondence that includes written communication or published materials must be sent to foreign countries. Sometimes transmitting documents, such as legal agreements, by fax may not be acceptable and documents must be mailed.

When sending documents internationally, there are three categories of mail:

1. LC mail (initials for the French *lettres* and *cartes postale*—meaning "letters" and "postcards"). LC mail consists mainly of letters and postcards. Items that are generally considered communications, such as letters or letter packages, are mailed at the letter rate of postage. This service is airmail delivery.
2. AO mail (initials for the French *Autres Objets*—meaning "other things"). AO mail usually consists of items considered printed materials, such as books, periodicals, and braille publications. This service is usually by ship and is slower than airmail.
3. CP mail (initials for the French *par Colis Postal*—meaning "by parcel post"). CP mail is the equivalent of American parcel post. Parcel post resembles fourth class domestic mail but is mail other than personal correspondence. It is the only class of mail that can be insured. This service is also usually by ship and, again, is slower than airmail.

If special delivery services are required, there are also special services that are offered:

1. Express mail, which will offer a faster delivery than regular airmail for a higher price.
2. International Priority Airmail, which is intended for bulk items except parcel post.
3. Registered mail, which is for items that require a proof of delivery.

GLOBAL PERSPECTIVE ACTIVITY:

Contact the local United States Postal Service or another mail service to obtain a schedule of costs and restrictions for international mail. Select a foreign country and obtain information to mail a ten-ounce document.

1. What are the costs per ounce for each type of mail?
2. What is the usual delivery time for each type of mail?
3. How much do special delivery services cost? What is included in the service?

ILLUSTRATION 22-3 Journal entry to record withdrawal of cash by a partner

CASH PAYMENTS JOURNAL — PAGE *10*

	DATE		ACCOUNT TITLE	CK. NO.	POST. REF.	1 GENERAL DEBIT	2 GENERAL CREDIT	3 ACCOUNTS PAYABLE DEBIT	4 CASH CREDIT	
21		*30*	*May Baker, Drawing*	*95*		*600 00*			*600 00*	21

Withdrawal of Assets Other than Cash

July 10, 19--. Lindel Mattingly, partner, withdrew office supplies for personal use, $50.00. Memorandum No. 14.

Lindel Mattingly, Drawing	
50.00	

Supplies—Office	
	50.00

Because office supplies withdrawn from a partnership are not a business expense, the amount cannot be debited to the office supplies expense account. This transaction reduces the partnership's office supplies inventory and, therefore, Supplies—Office is credited.

TEACHING STRATEGIES: TEACHING TIP

Emphasize that although partners typically withdraw cash, partners can also withdraw inventory, supplies, and other useful assets.

Lindel Mattingly, Drawing is debited for $50.00. Supplies—Office is credited for $50.00.

The journal entry to record this transaction is shown in Illustration 22-4.

ILLUSTRATION 22-4 Journal entry to record withdrawal of assets other than cash by a partner

GENERAL JOURNAL PAGE 7

	DATE		ACCOUNT TITLE	DOC. NO.	POST. REF.	DEBIT	CREDIT	
1	July[19--]	10	*Lindel Mattingly, Drawing*	*M14*		50 00		1
2			*Supplies—Office*				50 00	2

Audit Your Understanding

1. Where should the method of distributing partnership earnings be stated?
2. What are five common methods for distributing partnership earnings?
3. When does a deficit occur?
4. What account is debited when a partner withdraws cash for personal use?
5. What account is debited when a partner withdraws supplies for personal use?

END-OF-FISCAL-PERIOD WORK FOR A PARTNERSHIP

End-of-fiscal-period work for a partnership is similar to that for a corporation. In preparing partnership financial statements, accounting principles are applied in the same way during each fiscal period. *(CONCEPT: Consistent Reporting)*

Work Sheet

MaLin's work sheet is shown in Illustration 22-5 on page 594. All accounts in MaLin's general ledger are listed in the Account Title column. This procedure is the same as that used by corporations.

Needed adjustments are planned on a partnership work sheet in the same manner as on a corporate work sheet, with one exception. No adjustment for accrued federal income tax is *ever* planned on a partnership work sheet because partnerships do not pay federal income tax.

As described later in this chapter, partnership net income is reported to the Internal Revenue Service on the partners' personal tax returns.

Because MaLin Carpet Design does not sell merchandise, an adjustment for merchandise inventory is not needed.

Income Statement

MaLin's income statement is shown in Illustration 22-6, page 595.

Because MaLin does not sell merchandise, the income statement does not include a cost of merchandise sold section. MaLin needs

FYI

Limited partnerships include owners who have limited liability and limited operating responsibilities. Limited partnerships are sometimes formed for special projects such as Broadway plays.

CLOSURE

Use Audit Your Understanding questions.

AUDIT YOUR UNDERSTANDING

The AUDIT YOUR UNDERSTANDING feature appears at the end of each section of the chapter. Explain to your students that the word *audit* means to check or verify. AUDIT YOUR UNDERSTANDING may be used to check student comprehension of the section just studied. The answers are provided in Appendix D in the back of the textbook.

1. In the partnership agreement.
2. (1) Fixed percentage. (2) Percentage of total equity. (3) Interest on equity. (4) Salaries. (5) Combination of methods.
3. When the amount of allowances to partners exceed net income.
4. The partner's Drawing account.
5. The partner's Drawing account.

LESSON PLAN 22-2

Materials

- Student pages 593–599
- Blackline Master for 2-Column Statement (TRG)
- Blackline Master for 3-Column Statement (TRG)

Objectives (Enabling Performance Tasks)

a. Define accounting terms related to distributing earnings and completing end-of-fiscal-period work for a partnership.
b. Identify accounting concepts and practices related to distributing earnings and completing end-of-fiscal-period work for a partnership.
e. Complete end-of-fiscal-period work for a partnership.

FOCUS

- End-of-fiscal-period work for a merchandising business organized as corporation was introduced in Chapter 5 and expanded in Chapters 14 and 17. In this lesson, the end-of-fiscal-period work for a service business organized as a partnership will be presented. Explain that the end-of-fiscal-period work for a partnership is similar to that for a corporation.
- Introduce vocabulary: owners' equity statement.

ILLUSTRATION 22-5 Work sheet

MaLin Carpet Design
Work Sheet
For Year Ended December 31, 19--

		1	2	3	4	5	6	7	8	
	ACCOUNT TITLE	TRIAL BALANCE		ADJUSTMENTS		INCOME STATEMENT		BALANCE SHEET		
		DEBIT	CREDIT	DEBIT	CREDIT	DEBIT	CREDIT	DEBIT	CREDIT	
1	Cash	42,802.47						42,802.47		1
2	Petty Cash	200.00						200.00		2
3	Accounts Receivable	11,992.51						11,992.51		3
4	Allow. for Uncollectible Accts.		19.92		(a) 119.55				139.47	4
5	Supplies—Carpet	9,305.00			(b) 7,676.50			1,628.50		5
6	Supplies—Office	1,845.00			(c) 1,420.00			425.00		6
7	Prepaid Insurance	1,349.70			(d) 503.20			846.50		7
8	Equipment	12,504.97						12,504.97		8
9	Accum. Depr.—Equipment				(e) 1,250.50				1,250.50	9
10	Truck	4,900.00						4,900.00		10
11	Accum. Depr.—Truck				(f) 918.75				918.75	11
12	Accounts Payable		8,521.23						8,521.23	12
13	May Baker, Capital		22,880.00						22,880.00	13
14	May Baker, Drawing	4,500.00						4,500.00		14
15	Lindel Mattingly, Capital		11,440.00						11,440.00	15
16	Lindel Mattingly, Drawing	2,750.00						2,750.00		16
17	Income Summary									17
18	Sales		72,020.27				72,020.27			18
19	Advertising Expense	985.00				985.00				19
20	Depr. Expense—Equipment			(e) 1,250.50		1,250.50				20
21	Depr. Expense—Truck			(f) 918.75		918.75				21
22	Insurance Expense			(d) 503.20		503.20				22
23	Miscellaneous Expense	2,869.21				2,869.21				23
24	Rent Expense	8,400.00				8,400.00				24
25	Supplies Expense—Carpet			(b) 7,676.50		7,676.50				25
26	Supplies Expense—Office			(c) 1,420.00		1,420.00				26
27	Truck Expense	8,477.56				8,477.56				27
28	Uncollectible Accounts Expense			(a) 119.55		119.55				28
29	Utilities Expense	2,000.00				2,000.00				29
30		114,881.42	114,881.42	11,888.50	11,888.50	34,620.27	72,020.27	82,549.95	45,149.95	30
31	Net Income					37,400.00			37,400.00	31
32						72,020.27	72,020.27	82,549.95	82,549.95	32

ILLUSTRATION 22-6 Income statement

MaLin Carpet Design Income Statement For Year Ended December 31, 19--			*% of Sales
Operating Revenue:			
Sales		$72,020.27	100.0
Operating Expenses:			
Advertising Expense	$ 985.00		
Depreciation Expense—Equipment	1,250.50		
Depreciation Expense—Truck	918.75		
Insurance Expense	503.20		
Miscellaneous Expense	2,869.21		
Rent Expense	8,400.00		
Supplies Expense—Carpet	7,676.50		
Supplies Expense—Office	1,420.00		
Truck Expense	8,477.56		
Uncollectible Accounts Expense	119.55		
Utilities Expense	2,000.00		
Total Operating Expenses		34,620.27	48.1
Net Income		$37,400.00	51.9

*Rounded to the nearest 0.1%.

relatively few expense accounts. Therefore, the partnership does not subdivide the operating expenses.

MaLin calculates two component percentages on its income statement.

1. Operating expenses component percentage. MaLin expects a component percentage not more than 55.0%. Therefore, MaLin's operating expenses component percentage of 48.1% is acceptable.
2. Net income component percentage. MaLin expects a component percentage not less than 45.0%. Therefore, MaLin's net income component percentage of 51.9% is acceptable.

The net income component percentage is often high for partnerships that sell only services because there is no cost of merchandise sold. Also, the partners' salaries are not expenses of the partnership.

Distribution of Net Income Statement

MaLin's distribution of net income statement is shown in Illustration 22-1.

Owners' Equity Statement

A corporation's equity is reported on a statement of stockholders' equity. The statement summarizes changes in equity during a fiscal period. A similar statement is prepared for a partnership. A finan-

CAREERS IN ACCOUNTING

REVENUE OFFICER

- *Investigates overdue tax cases*
- *Confers with business representatives to determine amount of overdue tax and enforce collection*
- *Selects appropriate remedy for overdue taxes*
- *Directs service of legal documents*
- *Recommends criminal prosecutions and civil penalties when necessary*
- *Writes reports of actions taken for departmental files*

TEACH

Cover student pages 593–599 "End-of-Fiscal-Period Work for a Partnership." Discuss the work sheet. Reinforce that partnerships do not pay federal income tax. Explain that this partnership is a service business and does not plan an adjustment for merchandise inventory. Discuss the income statement. Point out that a service business does not include a cost of merchandise sold section on its income statement. Review component percentages. Remind students that the distribution of net income statement must be prepared before the owners' equity statement. Describe the owners' equity statement. Discuss the balance sheet. Emphasize that owner's equity is reported in a different manner than for a corporation. Review the adjusting and closing entries. Emphasize the entries that are different than those for a corporation.

CAREERS IN ACCOUNTING

The CAREERS feature box, REVENUE OFFICER, comes from the Dictionary of Occupational Titles (DOT). The entry number for this job title is D.O.T. 188.167-074. Bring this dictionary to class and explain its purpose and how to use it. The career feature is designed to expose students to the exploration of different careers in accounting. The feature gives a realistic description of actual job duties. This feature can be used to demonstrate that the skills learned in this course are relevant.

APPLY

Refer students to Illustrations 22-5, 22-6, 22-7, and 22-8, respectively, as the work sheet and financial statements are discussed. Refer students to Illustration 22-10 as the five closing entries are presented.

Guided Practice

Guide students through the T account analysis of the closing entries in Problem 22-3, Instruction 6. Have students draw T accounts on a sheet of paper and analyze the first entry. All students should agree with the analysis before proceeding to the second entry. Repeat the process until all five closing entries have been analyzed. The balance of Problem 22-3 can be completed as Independent Practice.

Independent Practice

Assign Term 3, Questions 7–11, and Problem 22-3.

cial statement that summarizes the changes in owners' equity during a fiscal period is called an **owners' equity statement.** The partners review the owners' equity statement to determine the changes occurring in equity.

MaLin's owners' equity statement is shown in Illustration 22-7.

ILLUSTRATION 22-7 Owners' equity statement

MaLin Carpet Design
Owners' Equity Statement
For Year Ended December 31, 19--

May Baker:			
Capital, January 1, 19–		$22,880.00	
Share of Net Income	$19,986.00		
Less Withdrawals	4,500.00		
Net Increase in Capital		15,486.00	
Capital, December 31, 19–			$38,366.00
Lindel Mattingly:			
Capital, January 1, 19–		$11,440.00	
Share of Net Income	$17,414.00		
Less Withdrawals	2,750.00		
Net Increase in Capital		14,664.00	
Capital, December 31, 19–			26,104.00
Total Owners' Equity, December 31, 19–			$64,470.00

The following information is reported on a partnership's owners' equity statement.

1. Each partner's capital at the beginning of the fiscal period. This balance is found in each partner's capital account in the general ledger.
2. Each partner's total share of net income. These amounts are obtained from the distribution of net income statement.
3. Each partner's withdrawals during the fiscal period. This amount is found on the work sheet.
4. Each partner's net increase in capital during the fiscal period.
5. Each partner's capital on the last day of the fiscal period.
6. The partnership's total owners' equity on the last day of the fiscal period.

FYI

Some areas of specialization for accountants include the banking industry, insurance, and nonprofit organizations.

Balance Sheet

A balance sheet for a partnership is similar to a balance sheet for a corporation. The major difference is how the owners' equity is reported. On a corporate balance sheet, summarized information about capital stock is reported under the heading *Stockholders' Equity.* No information is reported about the equity of individual stockholders. On a partnership balance sheet, each partner's ending capital is reported under the heading *Owners' Equity.* The amount of ending owners' equity is obtained from the owners' equity statement.

MaLin's balance sheet is shown in Illustration 22-8.

ILLUSTRATION 22-8 Balance sheet

MaLin Carpet Design
Balance Sheet
December 31, 19--

ASSETS			
Current Assets:			
Cash		$42,802.47	
Petty Cash		200.00	
Accounts Receivable	$11,992.51		
Less Allowance for Uncollectible Accounts	139.47	11,853.04	
Supplies—Carpet		1,628.50	
Supplies—Office		425.00	
Prepaid Insurance		846.50	
Total Current Assets			$57,755.51
Plant Assets:			
Equipment	$12,504.97		
Less Accumulated Depreciation—Equipment	1,250.50	$11,254.47	
Truck	4,900.00		
Less Accumulated Depreciation—Truck	$ 918.75	3,981.25	
Total Plant Assets			15,235.72
Total Assets			$72,991.23
LIABILITIES			
Accounts Payable			$ 8,521.23
OWNERS' EQUITY			
May Baker, Capital		$38,366.00	
Lindel Mattingly, Capital		26,104.00	
Total Owners' Equity			64,470.00
Total Liabilities and Owners' Equity			$72,991.23

Adjusting Entries

MaLin's adjusting entries are made to record expenses in the fiscal period to which they apply. *(CONCEPT: Matching Expenses with Revenue)*

Partnerships often need to make the same adjusting entries made by corporations. However, MaLin does not sell merchandise, does not accept notes receivable, has not issued any notes payable, and does not pay federal income tax. Also, because the business has no employees, no accrued salaries need to be recorded. Therefore, MaLin does not need adjusting entries for merchandise inventory, prepaid interest expense, accrued interest expense, interest income, accrued federal income tax, or accrued payroll.

MaLin's adjusting entries are shown in Illustration 22-9.

FYI

Professional businesses, such as accounting firms, law firms, and medical practices, frequently organize as partnerships.

ASSESS

Assess student understanding by checking the solutions to the Independent Practice activities.

Reteach

- Make transparencies of the appropriate financial statement paper from the accounting forms masters provided in the Blackline Masters Section of the Teacher's Resource Guide. Use data from Recycling Problem 22-R and the transparencies to demonstrate how to prepare an income statement, a distribution of net income statement, an owners' equity statement, and a balance sheet.
- Assign Recycling Problem 22-R.

Extend

Assign Cases for Critical Thinking 2.

Enrich

Assign the CAREERS IN ACCOUNTING feature on page 595. Have students discuss what a career as a revenue officer might be like.

CLOSURE

Use Audit Your Understanding questions.

TEACHING STRATEGIES: TEACHING TIP

Reinforce that partnerships do not pay federal income tax on their earnings.

TEACHING STRATEGIES: DIFFERENT LEARNING ABILITIES

Limited English Proficiency (LEP) Students. Be cautious if there are no interruptions or questions. It may mean that very little has been understood.

AUDIT YOUR UNDERSTANDING

1. To summarize the changes in owners' equity during the fiscal period.
2. Because a partnership does not pay federal income tax.
3. Share of Net Income less Withdrawals equals Net Increase in Capital.
4. The partner's capital account.

ILLUSTRATION 22-9 Adjusting entries

GENERAL JOURNAL PAGE *12*

	DATE		ACCOUNT TITLE	DOC. NO.	POST. REF.	DEBIT	CREDIT	
1			*Adjusting Entries*					1
2	*19-- Dec.*	*31*	*Uncollectible Accounts Expense*			*119 55*		2
3			*Allowance for Uncoll. Accts.*				*119 55*	3
4		*31*	*Supplies Expense—Carpet*			*7 676 50*		4
5			*Supplies—Carpet*				*7 676 50*	5
6		*31*	*Supplies Expense—Office*			*1 420 00*		6
7			*Supplies—Office*				*1 420 00*	7
8		*31*	*Insurance Expense*			*503 20*		8
9			*Prepaid Insurance*				*503 20*	9
10		*31*	*Depreciation Expense—Equipment*			*1 250 50*		10
11			*Accum. Depreciation—Equipment*				*1 250 50*	11
12		*31*	*Depreciation Expense—Truck*			*918 75*		12
13			*Accum. Depreciation—Truck*				*918 75*	13

Closing Entries

Closing entries for a partnership are similar to those of a corporation. The major difference is in recording distribution of earnings to the partners.

MaLin's closing entries, recorded on December 31, are shown in Illustration 22-10 on page 599.

MaLin records five closing entries.

1. The first entry closes income statement accounts with credit balances as shown on lines 15–16.
2. The second entry closes income statement accounts with debit balances as shown on lines 17–28.
3. The third entry closes the income summary account and distributes earnings to the partners' capital accounts as shown on lines 29–31. The amount credited to each partner's capital account is obtained from the distribution of net income statement, Illustration 22-1. When this closing entry is posted, the income summary account is closed. Each partner's capital account is increased by the partner's share of the net income for the year.
4. The fourth and fifth entries close each partner's drawing account and transfer the balances to each partner's capital account as shown on lines 32–35.

Audit Your Understanding

1. What is the purpose of the owners' equity statement?
2. Why is an adjustment for accrued federal income tax never planned on a partnership work sheet?
3. How is a partner's net increase in capital calculated on the owners' equity statement?
4. Into which account is a partner's drawing account closed?

Post-Closing Trial Balance

After adjusting and closing entries have been posted, MaLin prepares a post-closing trial balance listing all general ledger accounts with balances. MaLin's post-closing trial balance, similar to that of a corporation, is shown in Illustration 22-11.

ILLUSTRATION 22-10 Closing entries

GENERAL JOURNAL PAGE 12

	DATE		ACCOUNT TITLE	DOC. NO.	POST. REF.	DEBIT	CREDIT	
14			*Closing Entries*					14
15		31	*Sales*			72020 27		15
16			*Income Summary*				72020 27	16
17		31	*Income Summary*			34620 27		17
18			*Advertising Expense*				985 00	18
19			*Depreciation Exp.—Equipment*				1250 50	19
20			*Depreciation Exp.—Truck*				918 75	20
21			*Insurance Expense*				503 20	21
22			*Miscellaneous Expense*				2869 21	22
23			*Rent Expense*				8400 00	23
24			*Supplies Expense—Carpet*				7676 50	24
25			*Supplies Expense—Office*				1420 00	25
26			*Truck Expense*				8477 56	26
27			*Uncollectible Accts. Expense*				119 55	27
28			*Utilities Expense*				2000 00	28
29		31	*Income Summary*			37400 00		29
30			*May Baker, Capital*				19986 00	30
31			*Lindel Mattingly, Capital*				17414 00	31
32		31	*May Baker, Capital*			4500 00		32
33			*May Baker, Drawing*				4500 00	33
34		31	*Lindel Mattingly, Capital*			2750 00		34
35			*Lindel Mattingly, Drawing*				2750 00	35

APPLIED SKILLS: LANGUAGE ARTS

Paraphrasing, writing complete sentences, and identifying objects of prepositional phrases. For additional practice in language arts skills, direct students to answer the Accounting Terms and Questions for Individual Study at the end of the chapter. Students should write the answers in their own words and in complete sentences. To further practice language arts skills, ask students to underline all the objects of prepositional phrases in their answers.

ILLUSTRATION 22-11 Post-closing trial balance

MaLin Carpet Design
Post-Closing Trial Balance
December 31, 19--

Account Title	Debit	Credit
Cash	$42,802.47	
Petty Cash	200.00	
Accounts Receivable	11,992.51	
Allowance for Uncollectible Accounts		$ 139.47
Supplies—Carpet	1,628.50	
Supplies—Office	425.00	
Prepaid Insurance	846.50	
Equipment	12,504.97	
Accumulated Depreciation—Equipment		1,250.50
Truck	4,900.00	
Accumulated Depreciation—Truck		918.75
Accounts Payable		8,521.23
May Baker, Capital		38,366.00
Lindel Mattingly, Capital		26,104.00
	$75,299.95	$75,299.95

LESSON PLAN 22-3

Materials

- Student pages 600–604
- Software: Spreadsheet Template
- Assess: Problem Test Chapter 22, MicroExam Chapter 22

Objectives (Enabling Performance Tasks)

a. Define accounting terms related to distributing earnings and completing end-of-fiscal-period work for a partnership.

b. Identify accounting concepts and practices related to distributing earnings and completing end-of-fiscal-period work for a partnership.

f. Journalize entries for liquidating a partnership.

FOCUS

- Chapter 21 covered the formation of a partnership. In this lesson, the procedures followed if a partnership goes out of business will be presented.
- Introduce vocabulary: liquidation of a partnership, realization.

FYI

Partners may have to pay self-employment tax on their share of net income.

FEDERAL INCOME TAXES OF A PARTNERSHIP

MaLin's distribution of net income statement, Illustration 22-1, shows salaries for each of the partners. However, the Internal Revenue Service does not consider partners to be employees of the partnership they own. The IRS classifies the partners as self-employed persons whose salaries are not an expense of the partnership. Therefore, partners' salaries are considered to be withdrawals of partnership earnings and not expenses.

A partnership does not pay income tax on its earnings. However, a partnership does submit to the IRS a partnership tax return that reports the earnings distributed to each partner. In addition, partners include their respective share of the partnership net income or net loss on their personal income tax returns.

As self-employed persons, partners are entitled to old-age, survivors, disability, and hospitalization insurance benefits known collectively as social security. Each partner personally pays a self-employment tax in order to qualify for social security coverage. Therefore, the self-employment tax rate is double that of an employed individual's FICA tax rate. Thus, the same total amount of FICA tax is paid for both self-employed persons and employees. The self-employment taxes are personal expenses of the partners, not of the partnership. Therefore, partners' self-employment FICA taxes are not recorded on partnership records. *(CONCEPT: Business Entity)*

FYI

A partnership usually tries to sell the business before it begins the process of liquidation.

LIQUIDATION OF A PARTNERSHIP

If a partnership goes out of business, the assets are distributed to the creditors and partners. The process of paying a partnership's liabilities and distributing remaining assets to the partners is called **liquidation of a partnership.**

Recording Realization

Cash received from the sale of assets during liquidation of a partnership is called **realization.** Typically, when a partnership is liquidated, the noncash assets are sold, and the available cash is used to pay the creditors. Any remaining cash is distributed to the partners according to each partner's total equity.

On July 31, Adam Walker and Shirley Jeter liquidated their partnership. At that time, financial statements were prepared and adjusting and closing entries were journalized and posted. After the end-of-fiscal-period work was completed, the partnership had account balances as shown in the T accounts.

Account	Debit	Credit
Cash	11,000.00	
Supplies	1,000.00	
Truck	15,000.00	
Accumulated Depreciation—Truck		5,000.00
Accounts Payable		2,500.00
Adam Walker, Capital		10,000.00
Shirley Jeter, Capital		9,500.00

Gain on Realization. Noncash assets might be sold for more than the recorded book value. When this happens, the amount received in excess of the book value is recorded as a gain on real-

TEACHING STRATEGIES: TEACHING TIP

Explain that when a business is liquidated the following steps are completed: (1) Sell noncash assets. (2) Pay all liabilities. (3) Distribute remaining cash to partners according to partnership agreement.

ization. The gain is recorded as a credit in an account titled Loss and Gain on Realization.

August 1, 19--. Received cash from sale of truck, $12,000.00: original cost, $15,000.00; total accumulated depreciation recorded to date, $5,000.00. Receipt No. 316.

The partnership's gain on the sale of the truck is calculated as shown below.

Value of Asset Received	–	Book Value of Asset Sold		=	Gain on Realization
		Cost	$15,000.00		
		Accum. Depr.	5,000.00		
Cash $12,000.00	–	Book Value	$10,000.00	=	$2,000.00

Cash

	Debit	Credit
Bal.	11,000.00	
	12,000.00	
(New Bal.	*23,000.00)*	

Accumulated Depreciation—Truck

Debit	Credit	
5,000.00	Bal.	5,000.00

Truck

	Debit	Credit
Bal.	15,000.00	15,000.00

Loss and Gain on Realization

Debit	Credit
	2,000.00

The analysis of this transaction is shown in the T accounts.

Cash is debited for the total amount received, *$12,000.00*. Accumulated Depreciation—Truck is debited for the total depreciation recorded to date, *$5,000.00*. Truck is credited for the cost of the truck, *$15,000.00*. Loss and Gain on Realization is credited for the amount received in excess of the truck's book value, *$2,000.00*.

The journal entry to record this transaction is shown in Illustration 22-12, lines 1–3.

Loss on Realization. Sometimes during liquidation, the sale of an asset brings in less cash than the recorded book value.

August 1, 19--. Received cash from sale of supplies, $800.00; balance of supplies account, $1,000.00. Receipt No. 317.

ILLUSTRATION 22-12 Journal entries to record loss and gain on realization

CASH RECEIPTS JOURNAL — PAGE *15*

	DATE		ACCOUNT TITLE	DOC. NO.	POST. REF.	1 GENERAL DEBIT	2 GENERAL CREDIT	3 ACCOUNTS RECEIVABLE CREDIT	4 SALES CREDIT	5 SALES TAX PAYABLE CREDIT	6 CASH DEBIT	
1	19-- Aug.	1	Accum. Depr.—Truck	R316		5 000 00					12 000 00	1
2			Truck				15 000 00					2
3			Loss and Gain on Realization				2 000 00					3
4		1	Loss and Gain on Realization	R317		200 00					800 00	4
5			Supplies				1 000 00					5
6												6

TEACH

Cover student pages 600–604 "Federal Income Taxes of a Partnership" and "Liquidation of a Partnership." Remind students that the Internal Revenue Service does not consider partners to be employees of the partnership they own. Explain self-employment tax. Bring in the IRS form for calculating self-employment tax, Schedule SE, and explain how it is completed. Discuss liquidation of a partnership. Explain that when a business is liquidated the following steps are completed: (1) Sell noncash assets. (2) Pay all liabilities. (3) Distribute remaining cash to partners according to partnership agreement. Describe the entries to record a gain or loss on realization, to liquidate liabilities, to distribute loss or gain on realization to partners, and to distribute remaining cash to partners.

APPLIED SKILLS: WRITING ACROSS THE CURRICULUM

Writing paragraphs and short essays. The Cases for Critical Thinking are short, practical applications of the accounting principles developed in the chapter. Some cases are planned to present problems related to the chapter but not specifically discussed and answered in the chapter. These cases present an opportunity for critical thinking and decision making. These cases also require more than a short objective-type response. Therefore, they provide ideal practice in writing paragraphs and short essays.

APPLY

Draw T accounts on the chalkboard to analyze the transactions to liquidate a partnership. Write the formulas on the board and demonstrate how to calculate gain on realization and each partner's share of the balance of Loss or Gain on Realization.

Guided Practice

Guide students through the T account analysis of the transactions in Problem 22-4. Have students draw T accounts on a sheet of paper and analyze the first transaction. All students should agree with the analysis before proceeding to the second transaction. Repeat the process until all transactions have been analyzed. The balance of Problem 22-4 can be completed as Independent Practice.

Independent Practice

- Assign Terms 4–5, Questions 12–17, and Problem 22-4.
- Assign Study Guide 22 and Mastery Problem 22-M.

Cash

Debit		Credit	
Bal.	23,000.00		
	800.00		
(New Bal.	*23,800.00)*		

Loss and Gain on Realization

Debit		Credit	
	200.00	Bal.	2,000.00
		(New Bal.	*1,800.00)*

Supplies

Debit		Credit	
Bal.	1,000.00		1,000.00

Cash is debited for the amount received, *$800.00.* Loss and Gain on Realization is debited for the difference between the amount received and the recorded value of the supplies, *$200.00.* Supplies is credited for the recorded value of the supplies sold, *$1,000.00.*

The journal entry to record this transaction is shown in Illustration 22-12, lines 4 through 5. After these journal entries are recorded, the balance of Loss and Gain on Realization, *$1,800.00,* is the amount received in excess of the value of the truck and supplies combined.

Liquidating Liabilities

Noncash assets are sold; the available cash is used to pay creditors.

August 4, 19--. Paid cash to all creditors for the amounts owed, $2,500.00. Check No. 422.

Accounts Payable

Debit		Credit	
	2,500.00	Bal.	2,500.00

Cash

Debit		Credit	
Bal.	23,800.00		2,500.00
(New Bal.	*21,300.00)*		

Accounts Payable is debited for $2,500.00. Cash is credited for the same amount.

The journal entry to record this transaction is shown in Illustration 22-13.

ILLUSTRATION 22-13 Journal entry to record liquidation of liabilities

CASH PAYMENTS JOURNAL — PAGE 15

	DATE		ACCOUNT TITLE	CK. NO.	POST. REF.	1 GENERAL DEBIT	2 GENERAL CREDIT	3 ACCOUNTS PAYABLE DEBIT	4 CASH CREDIT	
1	19-- Aug.	4	Accounts Payable	422		2,500 00			2,500 00	1

When this transaction has been journalized and posted, the partnership has only four general ledger accounts with balances as shown in the T accounts.

Cash

Debit		Credit	
Bal.	21,300.00		

Shirley Jeter, Capital

Debit		Credit	
		Bal.	9,500.00

Adam Walker, Capital

Debit		Credit	
		Bal.	10,000.00

Loss and Gain on Realization

Debit		Credit	
		Bal.	1,800.00

Distributing Loss or Gain on Realization to Partners

When all creditors have been paid, the balance of Loss and Gain on Realization is distributed to the partners. A credit balance indicates a gain on realization. A debit balance indicates a loss. The distribution is based on the method of distributing net income or net loss as stated in the partnership agreement. The percentages for the Walker and Jeter partnership are: Mr. Walker, 60%; Ms. Jeter, 40%. The distribution of the balance of Loss and Gain on Realization is calculated as shown on the following page.

TEACHING STRATEGIES: TEACHING TIP

Before students begin working the end-of-chapter problems, demonstrate on the chalkboard and explain the formulas for distributing partnership net income.

	Balance of Loss and Gain on Realization	×	Fixed Percentage	=	Share of the Balance of Loss and Gain on Realization
Walker	$1,800.00	×	60%	=	$1,080.00
Jeter	1,800.00	×	40%	=	720.00
Total					$1,800.00

August 6, 19--. Recorded distribution of gain on realization: to Adam Walker, $1,080.00; to Shirley Jeter, $720.00. Memorandum No. 412.

Loss and Gain on Realization

Debit		Credit
1,800.00	Bal.	1,800.00

Adam Walker, Capital

Debit		Credit
	Bal.	10,000.00
		1,080.00
	(New Bal.	*11,080.00)*

Shirley Jeter, Capital

Debit		Credit
	Bal.	9,500.00
		720.00
	(New Bal.	*10,220.00)*

Loss and Gain on Realization is debited for $1,800.00 to close this account. Adam Walker, Capital is credited for $1,080.00, his share of the gain on realization. Shirley Jeter, Capital is credited for $720.00, her share of the gain on realization.

The journal entry to record this transaction is shown in Illustration 22-14.

If a loss on realization is distributed to the partners, Loss and Gain on Realization is credited to close the account. Each partner's capital account is debited for the partner's share of the loss on realization.

ILLUSTRATION 22-14 Journal entry to record distribution of gain on realization

GENERAL JOURNAL PAGE 8

	DATE		ACCOUNT TITLE	DOC. NO.	POST. REF.	DEBIT	CREDIT	
1	19-- Aug.	6	*Loss and Gain on Realization*	M412		1800 00		1
2			*Adam Walker, Capital*				1080 00	2
3			*Shirley Jeter, Capital*				720 00	3

Distributing Remaining Cash to Partners

The final step in liquidating a partnership is to distribute any remaining cash to the partners. The cash is distributed according to each partner's capital account balance regardless of the method used to distribute net income or net loss.

Adam Walker, Capital

Debit		Credit
11,080.00	Bal.	11,080.00

Shirley Jeter, Capital

Debit		Credit
10,220.00	Bal.	10,220.00

Cash

	Debit	Credit
Bal.	21,300.00	21,300.00

August 6, 19--. Recorded final distribution of remaining cash to partners: to Adam Walker, $11,080.00; to Shirley Jeter, $10,220.00. Check Nos. 423 and 424.

Adam Walker, Capital is debited for $11,080.00. Shirley Jeter, Capital is debited for $10,220.00. Cash is credited for $21,300.00.

The journal entry to record this transaction is shown in Illustration 22-15.

ASSESS

Assess student understanding by checking the solutions to the Independent Practice activities.

Reteach

Bring several inexpensive items to class to be the fixed assets of a hypothetical partnership. Prepare a balance sheet for the partnership, assigning values to each item, recording an accounts payable for the real cost of the items, and making the class equal partners. Auction the items to the students, recording the gain or loss on realization for each transaction. Liquidate the partnership by distributing the available cash. Record each transaction on the board using T accounts.

Extend

- Assign Challenge Problem 22-C. (The challenge is to distribute a net loss.)
- Assign the Spreadsheet Template for Mastery Problem 22-M.

Enrich

Assign and discuss the GLOBAL PERSPECTIVE feature on page 592.

CLOSURE

Use Audit Your Understanding questions.

ASSESS

- Administer Problem Test Chapter 22.
- Administer a MicroExam test for Chapter 22.

ILLUSTRATION 22-15 Journal entry to record distribution of remaining cash to partners

CASH PAYMENTS JOURNAL PAGE 15

	DATE		ACCOUNT TITLE	CK. NO.	POST. REF.	1 GENERAL DEBIT	2 GENERAL CREDIT	3 ACCOUNTS PAYABLE DEBIT	4 CASH CREDIT	
2		6	Adam Walker, Capital	423		11 080 00			21 300 00	2
3			Shirley Jeter, Capital	424		10 220 00				3

Audit Your Understanding

1. Why does the IRS classify partners as self-employed persons?
2. Why does a partnership file a tax return?
3. What is meant by the term "realization"?
4. Is the account Loss and Gain on Realization debited or credited to record a loss on realization?
5. What accounts are debited when distributing remaining cash to partners during liquidation?

After this journal entry is journalized and posted, all of the partnership's general ledger accounts will have zero balances. The partnership is liquidated.

ACCOUNTING TERMS EPT(a)

What is the meaning of each of the following?

1. **distribution of net income statement**
2. **deficit**
3. **owners' equity statement**
4. **liquidation of a partnership**
5. **realization**

QUESTIONS FOR INDIVIDUAL STUDY EPT(b)

1. What are two major differences between corporations and partnerships for end-of-fiscal-period procedures?
2. What are five common methods of dividing partnership earnings?
3. If a partnership agreement does not state how earnings are to be distributed, how are the earnings distributed?
4. What is the formula for calculating each partner's percentage of total equity?

AUDIT YOUR UNDERSTANDING

1. Because the IRS does not consider partners to be employees of the partnership they own.
2. To report to the IRS the earnings distributed to each partner.
3. Cash received from the sale of assets during liquidation of a partnership.
4. Debited.
5. The partners' capital accounts.

ACCOUNTING TERMS

1. **distribution of net income statement:** A partnership financial statement showing distribution of net income or net loss to partners. (p. 589)
2. **deficit:** The amount by which allowances to partners exceed net income. (p. 590)
3. **owners' equity statement:** A financial statement that summarizes the changes in owners' equity during a fiscal period. (p. 596)
4. **liquidation of a partnership:** The process of paying a partnership's liabilities and distributing remaining assets to the partners. (p. 600)
5. **realization:** Cash received from the sale of assets during liquidation of a partnership. (p. 600)

QUESTIONS FOR INDIVIDUAL STUDY

1. (a) A corporation calculates and pays income tax on its net income; partnerships do not. (b) A corporation maintains separate accounts for contributed capital and earned capital. Partnerships combine contributed and earned capital in one account for each owner. (p. 587)

5. What is done when there are insufficient earnings to cover the salaries or interest allowed to partners?
6. What accounts are affected, and how, when Partner A withdraws office supplies for personal use?
7. Which accounting concept is being applied when partnership financial statements are prepared using the same procedures in each fiscal period?
8. What adjustment planned on a corporate work sheet is never found on a partnership work sheet? Why not?
9. Which accounting concept is being applied when adjusting entries are journalized and posted?
10. What are the five closing entries recorded by MaLin Carpet Design?
11. What accounts are affected, and how, by MaLin's closing entry to record distribution of the partnership's net income?
12. Why are partners' salaries not recorded as a partnership expense?
13. What information does a partnership report to the IRS?
14. What accounts are affected, and how, when a truck is sold for more than its book value during liquidation?
15. What accounts are affected, and how, when supplies are sold for less than their book value during liquidation?
16. What accounts are affected, and how, when distributing a gain on realization to partners?
17. What accounts are affected, and how, when distributing remaining cash to partners during liquidation?

CASES FOR CRITICAL THINKING

EPT(b)

CASE 1 Lola Stroud invests $30,000.00 in a partnership. Her partner, Juan Santo, invests $50,000.00. Miss Stroud has 10 years' experience in a similar business, and Mr. Santo has no experience. Miss Stroud is to spend about 20 hours a week working for the partnership. Mr. Santo is to work full time. Which method of distributing partnership earnings would you suggest for this partnership? Explain your answer.

CASE 2 The P & A partnership does not prepare a distribution of net income statement or an owners' equity statement at the end of a fiscal period. Instead, the information is all reported in detail on the partnership's balance sheet. Is this an acceptable practice? Explain your answer.

APPLICATION PROBLEMS

EPT(c,d,e,f)

PROBLEM 22-1 Calculating partnership earnings and preparing a distribution of net income statement

SPREADSHEET

MATHEMATICS

Margorie Sims and Donna Kelly are partners in a business called Sims and Kelly. On December 31 of the current year, the partners' equities are: Miss Sims, $40,000.00; Ms. Kelly, $60,000.00. The net income for the year is $40,000.00.

INSTRUCTIONS:

1. For each of the following cases, calculate how the $40,000.00 net income will be distributed to the two partners.
   a. Each partner receives a fixed percentage of 50% of net income.
   b. Each partner receives a percentage of net income based on the percentage of total equity.
   c. Each partner receives 10% interest on equity. The partners share remaining net income, net loss, or deficit equally.
   d. Miss Sims receives a salary of $12,000.00; Ms. Kelly receives a salary of $15,000.00. The partners share remaining net income, net loss, or deficit on a fixed percentage of: Miss Sims, 40%; and Ms. Kelly, 60%.

CHECK FIGURES

See Teacher's Edition of Working Papers for complete solutions.

Problem 22-1 (a) $20,000 each. (b) Sims $16,000; Kelly 24,000. (c) Sims $19,000; Kelly 21,000. (d) Sims $17,200; Kelly 22,000. (e) Sims $17,700; Kelly 22,300. (f) Sims $17,300; Kelly 22,700.

QUESTIONS *(cont'd)*

2. (a) Fixed percentage. (b) Percentage of total equity. (c) Interest on equity. (d) Salaries. (e) Combination of methods. (p. 587)
3. Partners share equally. (p. 587)
4. Partner's equity ÷ total equity = percentage of total equity. (p. 588)
5. The salaries and interest are allowed whether or not there is sufficient net income. The resulting deficit is shared by the partners according to the partnership agreement. (pp. 589–590)
6. Partner A, Drawing is debited; Supplies—Office is credited. (p. 592)
7. Consistent Reporting concept. (p. 593)
8. Adjustment for accrued federal income tax. Partnerships do not pay federal income tax. The net income is personally reported by the partners on their personal income tax forms. (p. 593)
9. Matching Expenses with Revenue concept. (p. 597)
10. (1) Close income statement accounts with credit balances. (2) Close income statement accounts with debit balances. (3) Close the income summary account and distribute earnings to the partners' capital accounts. (4) and (5) Close each partner's drawing account and transfer the balances to each partner's capital account. (p. 598)
11. Income Summary is debited; May Baker, Capital and Lindel Mattingly, Capital are credited. (p. 599)
12. Partners are not considered employees of the partnership. They are classified as self-employed. Therefore, partners' salaries are withdrawals of partnership earnings and not expenses. (p. 600)
13. A partnership tax return that reports the earnings distributed to each partner. (p. 600)
14. Cash and Accumulated Depreciation—Truck are debited; Truck and Loss and Gain on Realization are credited. (p. 601)
15. Cash and Loss and Gain on Realization are debited; Supplies is credited. (p. 602)
16. Loss and Gain on Realization is debited; partners' capital accounts are credited. (p. 603)
17. Partners' capital accounts are debited; Cash is credited. (p. 603)

e. Miss Sims is to receive 8% interest on equity and a salary of $12,000.00. Ms. Kelly is to receive 8% interest on equity and a salary of $15,000.00. The partners share remaining net income, net loss, or deficit equally.

f. Miss Sims is to receive 12% interest on equity and a salary of $15,000.00. Ms. Kelly is to receive 12% interest on equity and a salary of $18,000.00. The partners share remaining net income, net loss, or deficit equally.

2. From the information calculated in Instruction 1, letter *e*, prepare a distribution of net income statement.
3. From the information calculated in Instruction 1, letter *f*, prepare a distribution of net income statement.

PROBLEM 22-2 Journalizing partners' withdrawals

Karen Mayes and Roger Getz are partners in a business. Each partner withdraws assets during May of the current year.

INSTRUCTIONS:

Journalize the following transactions. Use page 10 of a cash payments journal and page 5 of a general journal.

May 5. Karen Mayes, partner, withdrew office supplies for personal use, $300.00. M32.
26. Roger Getz, partner, withdrew cash for personal use, $350.00. C240.

PROBLEM 22-3 Completing end-of-fiscal-period work for a partnership

Susan Poole and Ann Dodd are partners in a business called Plantasia. The partnership's work sheet for the year ended December 31 of the current year is given in the working papers accompanying this textbook.

INSTRUCTIONS:

1. Prepare an income statement. Calculate and record the component percentages for total operating expenses and net income. Round percentage calculations to the nearest 0.1%.
2. Prepare a distribution of net income statement. The partners share in net income, net loss, or deficit according to each partner's percentage of total equity. The January 1 equity is: Ms. Poole, $23,400.00; Mrs. Dodd, $12,600.00. Round percentage calculations to the nearest 0.1%.
3. Prepare an owners' equity statement.
4. Prepare a balance sheet.
5. Journalize the adjusting entries. Use page 12 of a general journal.
6. Continue using page 12 of the general journal. Journalize the closing entries.

PROBLEM 22-4 Liquidating a partnership

MATHEMATICS

Donald Winn and Judy Reed agreed to liquidate their partnership on June 30 of the current year. On that date, after financial statements were prepared and closing entries were posted, the general ledger accounts had the following balances.

Cash	$ 5,000.00
Supplies	500.00
Office Equipment	10,000.00
Accumulated Depreciation—Office Equipment	5,500.00
Truck	17,000.00
Accumulated Depreciation—Truck	12,200.00
Accounts Payable	500.00
Donald Winn, Capital	7,300.00
Judy Reed, Capital	7,000.00

INSTRUCTIONS:

Journalize the following transactions. Use page 13 of a cash receipts journal, page 13 of a cash payments journal, and page 7 of a general journal.

CASES FOR CRITICAL THINKING

Case 1 Use a combination of methods. (a) Interest on equity. Mr. Santo should receive recognition for investing more equity. (b) Salary. Mr. Santo should receive recognition for working more hours, and Miss Stroud should receive recognition for her prior experience. (c) Divide remaining net income, net loss, or deficit according to a fixed percentage.

Case 2 The procedure is acceptable. However, the partnership's balance sheet is longer than it needs to be. The balance sheet is not as easy to read as it would be if some of the equity details were removed. Preparing the distribution of net income statement and the owners' equity statement reduces the size of the balance sheet. If interested persons still need the details, they can read the two statements in addition to the balance sheet.

CHECK FIGURES *(cont'd)*

Problem 22-2 May 5, debit Karen Mayes, Drawing and credit Supplies—Office, $300.00. May 26, debit Roger Getz, Drawing and credit Cash, $350.00.

Problem 22-3 (1) Net Income, $24,600.00, 46.1%. (2) Poole $15,990; Dodd 8,610. (3) Poole $34,990; Dodd 18,610. (4) Total Assets $59,548.52; Total Owners' Equity $53,600.00.

Problem 22-4 July 6, debit Winn, Capital $390; debit Reed, Capital, $210; credit Loss and Gain on Realization, $600. July 6, debit Winn, Capital, $6,910; debit Reed, Capital, $6,790; credit Cash, $13,700.

Mastery Problem 22-M (1) Net Income, $38,000, 45.9%. (2) Saxon $16,650; Rolf 21,350. (3) Saxon $23,650; Rolf 23,350. (4) Total Assets $52,490.32; Total Owners' Equity $47,000.00.

Challenge Problem 22-C (1) Net Loss, $4,600, 10.4%. (2) Doran $2,721.25; Eden 1,878.75. (3) Doran $15,528.75; Eden 14,621.25. (4) Total Assets $34,989.02; Total Owners' Equity $30,150.00.

July 1. Received cash from sale of office equipment, $4,000.00. R114.
1. Received cash from sale of supplies, $200.00. R115.
3. Received cash from sale of truck, $5,000.00. R116.
5. Paid cash to all creditors for amounts owed. C156.
6. Distributed balance of **Loss and Gain on Realization** to Donald Winn, 65%; to Judy Reed, 35%. M34.
6. Distributed remaining cash to partners. C157 and C158.

ENRICHMENT PROBLEMS EPT(c,e)

MASTERY PROBLEM 22-M Completing end-of-fiscal-period work for a partnership

SPREADSHEET

MATHEMATICS

Sarah Saxon and Jane Rolf are partners in a business called J & L Service. The partnership's work sheet for the year ended December 31 of the current year is given in the working papers accompanying this textbook.

INSTRUCTIONS:

1. Prepare an income statement. Calculate and record the component percentage for total operating expenses and net income. Round percentage computations to the nearest 0.1%.
2. Prepare a distribution of net income statement. Each partner is to receive 10% interest on January 1 equity. The January 1 equity is: Mrs. Saxon, $15,000.00; Miss Rolf, $12,000.00. Also, partners' salaries are: Mrs. Saxon, $10,000.00; Miss Rolf, $15,000.00. The partners share remaining net income, net loss, or deficit equally.
3. Prepare an owners' equity statement.
4. Prepare a balance sheet.
5. Journalize the adjusting entries. Use page 12 of a general journal.
6. Continue using page 12 of the general journal. Journalize the closing entries.

CHALLENGE PROBLEM 22-C Completing end-of-fiscal-period work for a partnership

Theresa Doran and Roy Eden are partners in a business called D & E Sales. The partnership's work sheet for the year ended December 31 of the current year is given in the working papers accompanying this textbook.

INSTRUCTIONS:

1. Prepare an income statement. Calculate and record the component percentages for cost of merchandise sold, gross profit on operations, total operating expenses, and net income or net loss. Round percentage calculations to the nearest 0.1%. If there is a net loss, use a minus sign with the component percentage.
2. Prepare a distribution of net income statement. Each partner is to receive 10% interest on January 1 equity. The January 1 equity is: Mrs. Doran, $24,250.00; Mr. Eden, $21,500.00. Also, partners' salaries are: Mrs. Doran, $12,000.00; Mr. Eden, $10,000.00. The remaining net income, net loss, or deficit is shared as follows: Mrs. Doran, 55%; Mr. Eden, 45%.
3. Prepare an owners' equity statement.
4. Prepare a balance sheet.

607

CHAPTER 23 OVERVIEW

Chapter 23 begins a two-chapter section on not-for-profit organizations, using a town government to illustrate the procedures. This first chapter describes the characteristics of a governmental unit that require different accounting procedures than those of for-profit businesses. The chapter describes the

GUIDE TO ACHIEVING LEARNING OBJECTIVES

	TEACH	APPLY	EXTEND/ENRICH					
Enabling Performance Tasks	**Lesson Plans**	**Application Problems**	**Mastery Problems**	**Challenge Problems**	**Cases for Critical Thinking**	**Recycling Problems**	**Reinforcement Activity**	
a. Define accounting terms related to budgeting and accounting for a not-for-profit governmental organization.	23-1, 23-2							
b. Identify accounting concepts and practices related to budgeting and accounting for a not-for-profit governmental organization.	23-1, 23-2				Cases 1, 2			
c. Journalize budget, revenues, expenditures, encumbrances, and other transactions for a not-for-profit governmental organization.	23-1, 23-2	23-1, 23-2, 23-3	23-M	23-C		23-R		

ENRICHMENT

SPECIAL FEATURES
Professional Business Ethics, page 620

procedures for developing an annual budget and then explains and illustrates the kinds of transactions that are journalized in the operations of the town.

	INFORMAL ASSESSMENT		FORMAL ASSESSMENT			
	Study Guide	**Audit Your Understanding**	**Chapter MicroExam**	**Chapter Problem Test**	**Unit Objective Test**	**Portfolio**
	Unit A	✓	✓		✓	
	Units B, C	✓	✓		✓	
				✓		

NEW, REVIEW, AND EXTENSION

ACTIVITIES/CONCEPTS/TRANSACTIONS	NEW	REVIEW/ EXTENSION
Nature of not-for-profit organizations	✓	
Characteristics of governmental accounting systems	✓	✓
Developing an operating budget	✓	✓
Journalizing an approved operating budget	✓	✓
Journalizing property tax revenue		✓
Journalizing collection of current property taxes		✓
Journalizing other revenue		✓
Journalizing collection of delinquent property taxes		✓
Journalizing expenditures		✓
Journalizing encumbrances		✓
Journalizing expenditures for amounts encumbered		✓
Journalizing expenditures benefiting future periods		✓
Journalizing issuance and payment of liabilities		✓
Journalizing short-term investments		✓

TEACHING MATERIALS

Teacher's Wraparound Edition of the Text
Teacher's Resource Guide
Teacher's Edition of Working Papers
MicroExam

TOWN OF SPARTA GENERAL FUND

CHART OF ACCOUNTS

Balance Sheet Accounts

(1000) ASSETS

1010 Cash
1020 Taxes Receivable—Current
1030 Allowance for Uncollectible Taxes—Current
1040 Taxes Receivable—Delinquent
1050 Allowance for Uncollectible Taxes—Delinquent
1060 Interest Receivable
1070 Allowance for Uncollectible Interest
1080 Inventory of Supplies
1090 Investments—Short Term

(2000) LIABILITIES

2010 Accounts Payable
2020 Notes Payable

(3000) FUND EQUITY

3010 Unreserved Fund Balance
3020 Reserve for Encumbrances—Current Year
3030 Reserve for Encumbrances—Prior Year
3040 Reserve for Inventory of Supplies

Revenue and Expenditure Accounts

(4000) REVENUES

4010 Property Tax Revenue
4020 Interest Revenue
4030 Other Revenue

(5000) EXPENDITURES

5100 General Government

5110 Expenditure—Personnel, General Government
5120 Expenditure—Supplies, General Government
5130 Expenditure—Other Charges, General Government
5140 Expenditure—Capital Outlays, General Government

5200 Public Safety

5210 Expenditure—Personnel, Public Safety
5220 Expenditure—Supplies, Public Safety
5230 Expenditure—Other Charges, Public Safety
5240 Expenditure—Capital Outlays, Public Safety

5300 Public Works

5310 Expenditure—Personnel, Public Works
5320 Expenditure—Supplies, Public Works
5330 Expenditure—Other Charges, Public Works
5340 Expenditure—Capital Outlays, Public Works

Revenue and Expenditure Accounts (cont.)

(5000) EXPENDITURES (cont.)

5400 Recreation

5410 Expenditure—Personnel, Recreation
5420 Expenditure—Supplies, Recreation
5430 Expenditure—Other Charges, Recreation
5440 Expenditure—Capital Outlays, Recreation

Budgetary Accounts

(6000) BUDGETARY

6010 Estimated Revenues
6020 Appropriations
6030 Budgetary Fund Balance

6100 General Government

6110 Encumbrance—Personnel, General Government
6120 Encumbrance—Supplies, General Government
6130 Encumbrance—Other Charges, General Government
6140 Encumbrance—Capital Outlays, General Government

6200 Public Safety

6210 Encumbrance—Personnel, Public Safety
6220 Encumbrance—Supplies, Public Safety
6230 Encumbrance—Other Charges, Public Safety
6240 Encumbrance—Capital Outlays, Public Safety

6300 Public Works

6310 Encumbrance—Personnel, Public Works
6320 Encumbrance—Supplies, Public Works
6330 Encumbrance—Other Charges, Public Works
6340 Encumbrance—Capital Outlays, Public Works

6400 Recreation

6410 Encumbrance—Personnel, Recreation
6420 Encumbrance—Supplies, Recreation
6430 Encumbrance—Other Charges, Recreation
6440 Encumbrance—Capital Outlays, Recreation

The chart of accounts for Sparta is illustrated above for ready reference as you study Chapters 23 and 24 of this textbook.

TEACHING STRATEGIES: ACCOUNTING PEDAGOGY

A chart of accounts for the business that is used to illustrate each part of this textbook is provided at the beginning of each part. Charts of accounts are extremely important to companies because they drive the accounting system. Employees usually cannot even receive reimbursement for expenses without knowing which account the expense should be charged to. Pedagogically, the chart of accounts provides the following information: (1) Classification for each account—needed to determine how a transaction is analyzed. (2) Permanent accounts (balance sheet accounts) and temporary accounts (income statement accounts)—assists in analyzing transactions and recording closing entries. (3) Account number for every general ledger account—critical information in automated accounting, since transactions are entered by account number rather than account title.

CHART OF ACCOUNTS

This chart of accounts is for a general fund of a not-for-profit organization. Because the differences between a business corporation and a governmental organization are significant, the differences in their respective chart of accounts will be significant. The chart of accounts reflects Sparta's use of a fund accounting system which emphasizes strong controls on the use of funds. Unlike a business corporation, a not-for-profit organization uses modified accrual accounting. This fact is reflected in the Expenditures section of the chart of accounts.

TEACHING STRATEGIES: TEACHING TIP

Emphasize that students should refer to this chart of accounts throughout their study of Chapters 23 and 24 of Part 8. It will help them determine classification of accounts, which accounts are temporary and permanent accounts, and what account numbers to use for automated accounting. It will also be a useful reference for performing file maintenance activities.

23

Budgeting and Accounting for a Not-for-Profit Organization

TEACHING STRATEGIES: ACCOUNTING PEDAGOGY

This textbook presents information for a not-for-profit organization. This is a timely subject as not-for-profit accounting is becoming an increasingly important sector of the accounting profession.

ENABLING PERFORMANCE TASKS

After studying Chapter 23, you will be able to:

a Define accounting terms related to budgeting and accounting for a not-for-profit governmental organization.

b Identify accounting concepts and practices related to budgeting and accounting for a not-for-profit governmental organization.

c Journalize budget, revenues, expenditures, encumbrances, and other transactions for a not-for-profit governmental organization.

TERMS PREVIEW

not-for-profit organization • fund • expenditures • operating budget • appropriations • tax levy • encumbrance • general fixed assets • certificate of deposit

LESSON PLAN 23-1

Materials

- Student pages 610–618
- Blackline Master for Multi-Column Journal (TRG)
- 3-Step Checklist for Making Ethical Decisions (TRG)

Objectives (Enabling Performance Tasks)

a. Define accounting terms related to budgeting and accounting for a not-for-profit governmental organization.

b. Identify accounting concepts and practices related to budgeting and accounting for a not-for-profit governmental organization.

c. Journalize budget, revenues, expenditures, encumbrances, and other transactions for a not-for-profit governmental organization.

All businesses, whether organized as proprietorships, partnerships, or corporations, have a common objective—to earn a profit. Other kinds of organizations are formed for purposes other than earning a profit. An organization providing goods or services with neither a conscious motive nor expectation of earning a profit is called a **not-for-profit organization.** Not-for-profit organizations are also referred to as nonprofit organizations.

FYI

Most college accounting programs have a course on governmental accounting.

Both businesses and not-for-profit organizations provide goods and/or services. Business owners generally invest in a business for the purpose of earning a profit. Not-for-profit organizations, however, are formed to provide needed goods or services to a group of individuals without regard to earning a profit. The primary purpose of the organization is to make available the needed goods or services that may not be available otherwise.

THE NATURE OF NOT-FOR-PROFIT ORGANIZATIONS

Not-for-profit organizations may differ in types of goods or services provided, sources of revenues, or procedures for selecting their leaders or managers. Major types of not-for-profit organizations are as follows.

1. Governmental, such as federal, state, county, city, town, and village.
2. Educational, such as elementary, secondary, and post-secondary schools.
3. Health, such as hospitals and nursing homes.
4. Charitable, such as United Way, United Fund, and American Red Cross.
5. Foundational, including trusts and corporations organized for charitable and educational purposes, such as the Carnegie Foundation and the Ford Foundation.
6. Religious, such as churches and other religious organizations.

Since not-for-profit organizations have a common objective, they all have many of the same needs for financial information. Thus, the accounting system and many of the financial reports are similar for all not-for-profit organizations. However, because of differences in goods or services provided, sources of revenues, or methods of leadership selection, accounting procedures and reports are modified for the specific type of organization.

All individuals are affected by or are members of one or more governmental organizations. Also, more individuals are employed by governmental organizations than any other type of not-for-profit organization. Therefore, Chapters 23 and 24 emphasize accounting for local governmental organizations.

TEACHING STRATEGIES: TEACHING TIP

Have students compare the differences between the chart of accounts for Chapters 23 and 24 and the corporation chart of accounts used in Part 5. As students identify those differences, list them on a chalkboard. Solicit responses until the major differences, such as the following, are identified: (a) Corporations use expense accounts. (b) Not-for-profit organizations use expenditure and encumbrance accounts. (c) Not-for-profit organizations do not have fund accounts for long-term assets or liabilities, nor do they have plant and equipment accounts.

Characteristics of Governmental Organizations that Affect the Accounting System

A governmental organization's purpose is normally to provide needed goods or services that would be impossible for individuals to provide for themselves. For example, the federal government provides national defense for all citizens of the nation. Individual states and cities would find it difficult and very inefficient to provide for their own defense from foreign pressures. Similarly, cities provide police and fire protection that would be very expensive and inefficient for individuals to provide for themselves.

A governmental organization has four major characteristics that affect the accounting system.

FYI

Accountants are often asked to assist not-for-profit organizations in organizing and managing their accounting systems.

1. No profit motive exists. A business' success can be measured by whether or not a profit is earned. If a business is inefficient or not competitive, a profit will not be earned. Without profits, a business will soon be unable to continue operations. However, since a governmental organization does not intend to earn a profit, success is much more difficult to measure. As long as money is available, a governmental organization can continue to operate regardless of its efficiency or inefficiency.
2. Leadership is subject to frequent change. Policy-making bodies of governmental organizations are generally elected by popular vote of the group's members. Thus, the leadership is dependent upon the political process and may change frequently. Therefore, policies and long-range goals may change when the leadership changes. These frequent changes make effective long-range planning difficult.
3. Users of services do not necessarily pay for the services. Revenues for governmental organizations are provided primarily by taxation on property, retail sales, or income. Organization members who have the greatest amount of property or income provide the greatest amount of revenues. However, the goods or services are normally provided to all members of the organization based on need. The amount individuals pay is not directly related to the benefits they receive. Therefore, individuals have decreased incentive for insuring that services are administered efficiently.
4. Conflicting pressures for differing objectives exist. No direct relationship exists between who pays for and who receives the services provided by a governmental organization. Therefore, individuals generally support the organizational objective most advantageous to themselves. For example, some citizens of a city may place the construction of a city library high on their list of priorities. Others, who seldom use a library, may place this project low on their list of priorities. Consequently, services provided by a governmental organization are usually determined through negotiation and compromise among the different interest groups. This procedure does not necessarily provide for the best services or the most efficiency.

FOCUS

- A complete accounting cycle for a governmental organization is described in Chapters 23 and 24. In this lesson, the unique characteristics of not-for-profit accounting, the development of an annual budget, and the journal entry to record an approved operating budget will be presented.
- Introduce vocabulary: not-for-profit organization, fund, expenditures, operating budget, appropriations.

TEACHING STRATEGIES: TEACHING TIP

Have students compare the differences and similarities in accounting practices and procedures for corporations and governmental organizations. As students identify these differences and similarities, list them on the board.

TEACH

Cover student pages 610–618 "The Nature of Not-for-Profit Organizations," "Developing an Annual Governmental Operating Budget," and "Journalizing an Approved Annual Governmental Operating Budget." Involve students in a discussion of the differences between a business corporation and a governmental organization (city or county). Explain the profit motive and discuss why the profit motive is not appropriate for a not-for-profit organization. Emphasize and discuss the differences between accrual and modified accrual accounting. Review the differences and similarities of a corporation's and a governmental organization's financial statements. Explain the similarities and differences in the purpose and preparation procedures of budgets for corporations and governmental organizations. Discuss the reason for journalizing a governmental organization's budget. Introduce the multi-column journal used by Sparta.

The characteristics of governmental organizations have affected the development of governmental accounting systems. As a result, numerous financial and legal regulations for determining the source and amount of revenues and for planning and executing expenditures of funds are required.

Characteristics of Governmental Accounting Systems

Six accounting practices are similar for business and governmental organizations.

1. The accounting equation, assets equal liabilities plus equities, is applied.
2. An appropriate chart of accounts is prepared.
3. Transactions are analyzed into debit and credit parts.
4. Transactions are journalized and posted to ledgers.
5. Financial statements are prepared for each fiscal period.
6. Most of the same accounting concepts are applied.

FYI

Many governmental organizations have a fiscal period that ends on June 30.

The characteristics of governmental organizations and the conditions in which they operate create information and control requirements different from those of businesses. Because of these differences, governmental accounting and financial reporting differ in several ways from business accounting and financial reporting.

Fund Accounting. The accounting system for a business includes a single accounting entity. That is, all accounts used to record accounting transactions for the entire business are part of a single set of accounts. Within this set of accounts, net assets must equal liabilities plus equities. A governmental accounting entity with a set of accounts in which assets always equal liabilities plus equities is called a **fund.** A governmental unit, such as a city, may have several different funds.

A fund accounting system emphasizes strong controls on the use of funds. The amount in a fund can be spent only for the specified purpose of the fund. Different funds may be created for different purposes. For example, the town of Eastfield has two funds: (1) a general fund and (2) a library fund. Balance sheets for the two funds are shown in Illustration 23-1.

The town of Eastfield has total assets of $470,000.00 (general fund, $400,00.00, *plus* library fund, $70,000.00). However, the assets are accounted for separately. Assets in the library fund may be used for library purposes only. General fund assets may be used for other authorized town expenditures. Each fund is kept as a separate set of accounts.

FYI

Governmental accounting equation: Assets equal liabilities plus fund equity.

The fund equity, similar to owners' equity for a business, is the net amount of assets available for use. For example, Eastfield's library fund equity is $65,000.00 (assets, $70,000.00, *less* liabilities, $5,000.00). If $6,000.00 cash is spent for library salaries, total assets available for spending would be reduced to $64,000.00 ($70,000.00 *less* $6,000.00). The fund equity account, Fund Balance, would be reduced to $59,000.00 (assets, $64,000.00, *less* liabilities, $5,000.00).

ILLUSTRATION 23-1 Balance sheets for two funds

Eastfield General Fund

ASSETS	
Cash	$350,000.00
Taxes Receivable	50,000.00
Total Assets	$400,000.00
LIABILITIES AND FUND EQUITY	
Liabilities:	
Accounts Payable	$ 60,000.00
Fund Equity:	
Fund Balance	340,000.00
Total Liabilities and Fund Equity	$400,000.00

Eastfield Library Fund

ASSETS	
Cash	$70,000.00
LIABILITIES AND FUND EQUITY	
Liabilities:	
Accounts Payable	$ 5,000.00
Fund Equity:	
Fund Balance	65,000.00
Total Liabilities and Fund Equity	$70,000.00

After this transaction, the fund remains in balance. The governmental accounting equation, assets equal liabilities plus fund equity, is in balance.

Types of funds vary with the type of not-for-profit organization and the types of goods or services provided. A unique set of funds normally is used for each type of organization—federal government, state and local governments, hospitals, schools, etc.

Modified Accrual Accounting. Most businesses use accrual accounting so that revenue and expenses incurred during a fiscal period determine the resulting net income for the period. *(CONCEPT: Matching Expenses with Revenue)* In governmental accounting, modified accrual accounting is used. In modified accrual accounting, revenues are recorded in the accounting period in which they become measurable and available. For example, property taxes become measurable and available as soon as the amount is determined and tax statements are sent to property owners. However, sales taxes cannot be determined until sales are made. Thus, sales tax revenue is recognized when the taxes are received from merchants.

FYI

Governmental organizations record expenditures rather than expenses.

Cash disbursements and liabilities incurred for the cost of goods delivered or services rendered are called **expenditures.** In modified accrual accounting, expenditures are generally recognized when a liability is incurred. Therefore, governmental organizations record expenditures rather than expenses. An important distinction is made between expenditures and expenses. Businesses emphasize matching expenses with revenue in each fiscal period. However, governmental accounting emphasizes determining and controlling revenues and expenditures during a fiscal period. For example, if a business buys a truck, Plant Asset or Truck is debited and Cash or Notes Payable is credited. No expense is incurred until the truck is used. If a governmental organization buys a truck, Expenditure is debited and Cash or Notes Payable is credited. The amount of money spent or

APPLY

Refer students to Illustration 23-2 as the operating budget is discussed and Illustration 23-3 as the multi-column journal is introduced.

Guided Practice

Guide students through the T account analysis of the entries to record operating budgets in Problem 23-1. Have students draw T accounts on a sheet of paper and analyze the entry for the first town. All students should agree with the analysis before proceeding to the entry for the second town. Repeat the process until all three entries have been analyzed. The balance of Problem 23-1 can be completed as Independent Practice.

Independent Practice

Assign Terms 1–5, Questions 1–10, and Problem 23-1.

TEACHING STRATEGIES: TEACHING TIP

Discuss the differences and similarities of a corporation's and a governmental organization's balance sheets.

ASSESS

Assess student understanding by checking the solutions to the Independent Practice activities.

Reteach

Make a transparency of the multi-column journal from the accounting forms masters provided in the Blackline Masters Section of the Teacher's Resource Guide. Refer students to Recycling Problem 23-R. Ask students to use T accounts to analyze the January 2 transaction to record the approved operating budget. Use the transparency to demonstrate how to journalize the transaction.

Extend

Assign Cases for Critical Thinking 1.

Enrich

Discuss the PROFESSIONAL BUSINESS ETHICS feature on page 620. You may wish to distribute copies of the 3-Step Checklist for Making Ethical Decisions. A blackline master is furnished in the Blackline Masters Section of the Teacher's Resource Guide.

liability incurred is recorded, not the expense. Thus, expenditures are decreases in net financial resources. Emphasis is placed on control of the net financial resources, not on matching expenses with revenue. Thus, modified accrual accounting is used for measuring financial position and operating results of governmental organizations.

Financial Reporting Emphasis. Both business and governmental organizations prepare financial statements at the end of a fiscal period. *(CONCEPT: Accounting Period Cycle)* However, because the organizations have different objectives, the statements also differ. The two most common financial statements prepared by businesses are an income statement and a balance sheet. The two most common financial statements prepared by governmental organizations are a statement of revenues, expenditures, and changes in fund balance and a balance sheet (described in Chapter 24).

FYI

Governmental organizations do not prepare income statements.

Businesses prepare income statements to report the amount of net income earned during a fiscal period. Earning a net income is not an objective of governmental organizations. However, identifying and controlling the sources of revenues and the expenditure of funds is emphasized as part of the control process. Therefore, a statement of revenues, expenditures, and changes in fund balance is prepared.

A business' balance sheet reports the assets, liabilities, and owners' equity of the business at the end of a fiscal period. A governmental organization's balance sheet also reports the current assets and liabilities of the organization at the end of a fiscal period. However, no specific ownership of a governmental organization exists. Therefore, assets less liabilities is reported as fund equity.

Budgeting. Budgets are prepared by both businesses and governmental organizations. The primary purpose of all budgets is planning and control. For businesses, planning is required to prepare the budget. During the fiscal period, budgeted amounts are compared with actual amounts to provide information to management about the effectiveness of cost control. Planning is also required to prepare a budget for a governmental organization. However, an approved governmental budget becomes (1) a legal authorization to spend and (2) a legal limit on the amount that can be spent.

DEVELOPING AN ANNUAL GOVERNMENTAL OPERATING BUDGET

A plan of current expenditures and the proposed means of financing those expenditures is called an **operating budget.** A governmental fund's annual operating budget authorizes and provides the basis for control of financial operations during a fiscal year. Since each governmental fund is a separate accounting entity, an operating budget is normally prepared for each fund. Some basic proce-

TEACHING STRATEGIES: TEACHING TIP

Discuss the similarities and differences in the purpose and preparation procedures of budgets for corporations and governmental organizations.

CLOSURE

Use Audit Your Understanding questions.

dures are followed to prepare an annual governmental operating budget.

1 Departments of the governmental organization submit budget requests to the chief executive of the organization. Requests are based on an analysis of expenditures for the previous year and expected changes in expenditures for the coming year.

2 The chief executive reviews budget requests with department heads. When budget requests are acceptable to the chief executive, departmental requests are consolidated into a single budget request for the organization. The chief executive then submits the operating budget to the legislative body. The legislative body is a group of persons normally elected by the citizens of the organization and granted authority to make laws for the organization.

3 The legislative body approves the operating budget. The approved operating budget becomes an authorization to spend the amounts listed in the budget. Before the operating budget can be approved, revenues plus the available amount of fund equity must be at least as great as the expenditures. If the expenditures are more than the total of expected revenues and available fund equity, the expected sources of revenue must be increased or expenditures decreased.

In some states, the operating budget is not officially approved until reviewed by tax committees at the county and state level.

FYI

Not-for-profit organizations can include governments, hospitals, colleges and universities, voluntary health and welfare organizations, museums, churches, associations, political parties, and cemeteries.

Sparta is a small town with a town manager and five town council members. The council members are elected to their positions. One member of the council serves as mayor. The council serves as the legislative body for Sparta. The council appoints the town manager who works full time as chief executive of the town. Sparta has three department heads: public safety director, public works director, and recreation director. Because Sparta is small and most of its revenues come from property taxes, the accounting system contains only one fund—a general fund.

At the request of the town manager, Sparta's three department heads analyze the current year's expenditures and expected changes, then prepare budget requests for the next year. The town manager reviews the budget requests with each department head. The requests are then combined into a single operating budget for Sparta's general fund for next year and submitted to the town council. The town council represents the interests of all the town's citizens. Thus, the council should evaluate the operating budget from at least four viewpoints. (1) Are adequate services being provided? (2) Are the services desired by a majority of citizens? (3) Are the amounts requested essential to provide the desired level of services? (4) Does the city have the financial capacity to support the budget?

The approved operating budget determines the amount of revenues needed for the year. The town tax rate needed to provide the

APPLIED SKILLS: LANGUAGE ARTS

Paraphrasing, writing complete sentences, and identifying adjectives and the words they modify. For additional practice in language arts skills, direct students to answer the Accounting Terms and Questions for Individual Study at the end of the chapter. Students should write the answers in their own words and in complete sentences. To further practice language arts skills, ask students to underline the adjectives and circle the words they modify in their answers.

FYI

Local and state laws may prohibit governmental organizations from expending more funds than they receive.

necessary funds for the approved operating budget is then determined.

After completing their review, the Sparta council formally approves next year's governmental operating budget. The approved governmental operating budget becomes authorization for the town manager and department heads to make expenditures as specified in the budget. The approved annual governmental operating budget for Sparta's general fund is shown in Illustration 23-2.

Sparta organizes revenue accounts by source of revenue. Expenditure accounts are organized by department and type of expenditure. Some organizations maintain subsidiary accounts for each of the general ledger accounts to provide greater detail about the

TEACHING STRATEGIES: APPLYING VISUALS

Direct students to Illustration 23-2 and review the annual governmental operating budget.

ILLUSTRATION 23-2 Annual governmental operating budget for general fund

Town of Sparta Annual Operating Budget—General Fund For Year Ended December 31, 19--		
ESTIMATED REVENUES		
Property Tax	$1,594,000.00	
Interest	10,000.00	
Other	2,500.00	
Total Estimated Revenues		$1,606,500.00
ESTIMATED EXPENDITURES AND BUDGETARY FUND BALANCE		
General Government:		
Personnel	$ 263,280.00	
Supplies	12,150.00	
Other Charges	113,400.00	
Capital Outlays	16,220.00	
Total General Government		$ 405,050.00
Public Safety:		
Personnel	$ 589,200.00	
Supplies	20,000.00	
Other Charges	153,150.00	
Capital Outlays	90,300.00	
Total Public Safety		852,650.00
Public Works:		
Personnel	$ 113,400.00	
Supplies	5,600.00	
Other Charges	47,500.00	
Capital Outlays	51,500.00	
Total Public Works		218,000.00
Recreation:		
Personnel	$ 58,260.00	
Supplies	1,970.00	
Other Charges	25,250.00	
Capital Outlays	11,620.00	
Total Recreation		97,100.00
Total Estimated Expenditures		$1,572,800.00
Budgetary Fund Balance		33,700.00
Total Estimated Expenditures and Budgetary Fund Balance		$1,606,500.00

APPLIED SKILLS: WORD PROCESSING

If you wish to integrate word processing into your accounting course, you may direct students to answer the end-of-chapter Accounting Terms, Questions for Individual Study, and Cases for Critical Thinking using their word processing software.

sources of revenues and types of expenditures. Because of its small size, Sparta maintains only the general ledger accounts listed in its chart of accounts.

JOURNALIZING AN APPROVED ANNUAL GOVERNMENTAL OPERATING BUDGET

Approval of an annual governmental operating budget by the proper authorities provides legal authorization for expenditures to be made in accordance with the approved budget. Authorizations to make expenditures for specified purposes are called **appropriations.** Sparta's approved operating budget has appropriations that authorize expenditures up to the amounts stated in the budget. The tax rate is then set at a rate that will raise at least enough revenue to cover the appropriations.

FYI

At one time the state of New York had approximately 5,000 different funds; however, the general trend today is to reduce the number of funds.

TEACHING STRATEGIES: TEACHING TIP

Explain that governmental organizations use a variety of journals depending upon the size and complexity of the organization and the number of transactions. Medium and large cities generally use computers to record transactions. Small towns and villages may use a multi-column journal, a general journal, or special journals adapted to the organization's needs. Regardless of the method used, the accounting procedures for journalizing are similar. To keep the journalizing process as simple as possible for a small town, the chapter illustrations and end-of-chapter problems use a multi-column journal.

Many governmental organizations have restrictions on the amount of tax increase permitted. Public hearings may be required to increase taxes. A formal vote in an election may also be required. If a proposed operating budget exceeds the amount of taxes and other estimated revenue, the budget may need to be reduced to the level of available revenues.

As an additional control measure, Sparta journalizes its approved operating budget in the budgetary accounts, Estimated Revenues and Appropriations. Budgetary accounts are for control purposes and are closed at the end of a fiscal period.

Total estimated revenues, as shown on Sparta's operating budget, Illustration 23-2, are $1,606,500.00. Sparta's appropriations (total estimated expenditures) are $1,572,800.00.

Governmental organizations, just as businesses, record accounting transactions initially in a journal. Also, source documents are the basis for recording the journal entries. Governmental organizations may use a multi-column journal, a general journal, or special journals adapted to the organization's needs. Sparta uses a multi-column journal to record all its journal entries.

January 2, 19--. Recorded Sparta's approved operating budget: estimated revenues, $1,606,500.00; appropriations, $1,572,800.00; budgetary fund balance, $33,700.00. Memorandum No. 35.

Estimated Revenues	
1,606,500.00	

Appropriations	
	1,572,800.00

Budgetary Fund Balance	
	33,700.00

Estimated Revenues is increased by a debit for the amount of budgeted revenues, *$1,606,500.00.* Estimated Revenues has a normal debit balance. This debit balance is opposite the normal credit balance of an actual revenue account. Appropriations is increased by a credit for the amount of Sparta's budgeted expenditures, *$1,572,800.00.* Appropriations has a normal credit balance. This credit balance is opposite the normal debit balance of the actual expenditure accounts. Budgetary Fund Balance is increased by a credit, *$33,700.00* (estimated revenues, $1,606,500.00, *less* appropriations, $1,572,800.00).

The journal entry to record Sparta's approved operating budget is shown in Illustration 23-3 on page 618.

AUDIT YOUR UNDERSTANDING

The AUDIT YOUR UNDERSTANDING feature appears at the end of each section of the chapter. Explain to your students that the word *audit* means to check or verify. AUDIT YOUR UNDERSTANDING may be used to check student comprehension of the section just studied. The answers are provided in Appendix D in the back of the textbook.

1. (1) No profit motive exists. (2) Leadership is subject to frequent change. (3) Users of services do not necessarily pay for the services. (4) Conflicting pressures for differing objectives exist.
2. A governmental accounting entity with a set of accounts in which assets always equal liabilities plus equities.
3. To authorize and provide the basis for control of financial operations during a fiscal year.
4. Estimated Revenues is debited; Appropriations and Budgetary Fund Balance are credited.

LESSON PLAN 23-2

Materials

- Student pages 618–629
- Blackline Master for Multi-Column Journal (TRG)
- Assess: Problem Test Chapter 23, MicroExam Chapter 23

Objectives (Enabling Performance Tasks)

a. Define accounting terms related to budgeting and accounting for a not-for-profit governmental organization.

b. Identify accounting concepts and practices related to budgeting and accounting for a not-for-profit governmental organization.

c. Journalize budget, revenues, expenditures, encumbrances, and other transactions for a not-for-profit governmental organization.

ILLUSTRATION 23-3 Journal entry to record an approved annual governmental operating budget

JOURNAL PAGE 1

	DATE		ACCOUNT TITLE	DOC. NO.	POST. REF.	GENERAL DEBIT (1)	GENERAL CREDIT (2)	CASH DEBIT (3)	CASH CREDIT (4)	
1	19-- Jan.	2	Estimated Revenues	M35		1606 500 00				1
2			Appropriations				1572 800 00			2
3			Budgetary Fund Balance				33 700 00			3

A separate revenue account will be credited as revenues are earned. Balances of the two accounts, Estimated Revenues and Revenues, can be reviewed to determine the amount of actual revenues earned compared with the amount of revenues estimated to be earned. If actual revenues are not as great as expected, expenditures may need to be reduced to avoid exceeding available funds. Recording the estimated revenues in the budgetary account Estimated Revenues provides this additional planning and control information.

Separate expenditure accounts will be debited as actual expenditures are made. Insuring that expenditures do not exceed the appropriations (budgeted expenditures) is essential for governmental organizations. Periodically, the appropriations account balance can be compared with the total of expenditure account balances to avoid overspending appropriations. Appropriations less total expenditures is the amount still available for spending. Recording appropriations in the budgetary account Appropriations provides this additional control information. Each department also keeps records of its appropriated and expended amounts to insure each department's appropriation amounts are not exceeded.

If appropriations exceed estimated revenues, Budgetary Fund Balance is debited to make the total debits equal the total credits. However, most governmental organizations normally set their revenue sources slightly above appropriations to avoid exceeding appropriations.

Audit Your Understanding

1. What are the four characteristics that affect the accounting system for a governmental organization?
2. What is a fund?
3. What is the purpose of a governmental operating budget?
4. What accounts are debited and credited to journalize a governmental organization's approved operating budget?

JOURNALIZING REVENUES

Governmental fund revenues are recorded in the accounting period in which the revenues become measurable and available.

FYI

Property taxes can be levied on both personal and real property. Personal property includes furniture, boats, and cars. Real property includes land and buildings.

Current Property Tax Revenue

When property tax rates have been set and tax amounts calculated, taxes are levied on all taxable property. Authorized action taken by a governmental organization to collect taxes by legal authority is

FYI

The Government Accounting Standards Board (GASB) provides standards for accounting for governmental units.

called a **tax levy.** When property taxes are levied, the taxes are considered measurable and available because they are now a legal obligation of property owners. Therefore, when the levy is made, a journal entry is made to record property tax revenue. Although tax levies are legal obligations of property owners, some property owners do not pay their taxes. Legal action may eventually be taken against these property owners in an effort to collect the taxes. Even with these actions, a government generally does not collect all the taxes levied. On January 2, Sparta authorized its tax levy and sent out property tax statements to property owners. Sparta estimated that $16,000.00 of property taxes will not be collected.

January 2, 19--. Recorded property tax levy: taxes receivable—current, $1,610,000.00; allowance for uncollectible taxes—current, $16,000.00; property tax revenue, $1,594,000.00. Memorandum No. 36.

Taxes Receivable—Current	
1,610,000.00	

Allowance for Uncollectible Taxes—Current	
	16,000.00

Property Tax Revenue	
	1,594,000.00

Taxes Receivable—Current is increased by a debit for the total amount of tax levied, *$1,610,000.00.* This amount is the total of the tax statements sent to taxpayers. The contra asset account, Allowance for Uncollectible Taxes—Current, is increased by a credit for the amount of estimated loss, *$16,000.00.* The revenue account, Property Tax Revenue, is increased by a credit for the amount of revenue recognized, *$1,594,000.00.* This amount is the total tax levy, $1,610,000.00, *less* the allowance for current uncollectible taxes, $16,000.00.

The journal entry to record this transaction is shown in Illustration 23-4.

ILLUSTRATION 23-4 Journal entry to record current property tax revenue

JOURNAL PAGE 1

	DATE		ACCOUNT TITLE	DOC. NO.	POST. REF.	1 GENERAL DEBIT	2 GENERAL CREDIT	3 CASH DEBIT	4 CASH CREDIT	
4		2	Taxes Receivable—Current	M36		1610 000 00				4
5			Allowance for Uncollectible Taxes—Current				16 000 00			5
6			Property Tax Revenue				1594 000 00			6
7										7

Collection of Current Property Taxes

Cash received for property taxes reduces the taxes receivable account. A journal entry was recorded for revenue when property taxes were levied.

January 10, 19--. Received cash for current taxes receivable, $194,000.00. Receipt No. 371.

FOCUS

- The nature of not-for-profit organizations and developing and journalizing an annual budget were presented earlier in the chapter. In this lesson, journalizing transactions for a governmental organization will be described.
- Introduce vocabulary: tax levy, encumbrance, general fixed assets, certificate of deposit.

APPLIED SKILLS: BUILDING STUDY SKILLS

Numerous new accounts unique to governmental organizations are introduced in this chapter. Direct students to create a Quick Reference Guide (QRG) on a sheet of paper to use as an aid in analyzing transactions. Instruct students to draw a T account for each new account as it is introduced and label the debit, credit, increase, and decrease sides.

Professional Business Ethics

The PROFESSIONAL BUSINESS ETHICS feature stimulates critical thinking and decision making. It may be used in many ways such as an individual assignment, a class discussion, or a small group cooperative learning project. When these ethics cases are discussed in class, students can also gain a sense of individual diversity as students demonstrate individual opinions. If you wish to integrate word processing in your accounting course, you may direct students to word process their answers. If you wish to include the creation of tables, you might direct students to format their responses to resemble the ethical decision-making grid in a 3-column table. A blackline master of the 3-Step Checklist for Making Ethical Decisions is furnished in the Teacher's Resource Guide. Suggested solutions for the Professional Business Ethics feature are provided in the front of this teacher's edition.

TEACH

Cover student pages 618–629 "Journalizing Revenues," "Journalizing Expenditures and Encumbrances," and "Journalizing Other Transactions." Present the procedures for journalizing revenues. Ask students if they are familiar with the term tax levy. Discuss the reason for journalizing property tax revenue before cash is received. Ask students if they know when property taxes are collected in your area. Present the procedures for journalizing expenditures and encumbrances. Discuss the difference between expenses and expenditures. Then discuss the difference between expenditures and encumbrances. Describe how the accounting procedure for the purchase of a computer by a corporation differs from the procedure of a governmental organization. Present the procedures for journalizing other transactions.

PROFESSIONAL BUSINESS ETHICS

Keeping a Trade Secret

Frank Polk, CPA, has just completed the audit of a hospital that is a not-for-profit business. During the audit, Mr. Polk learned of the hospital's plan to build a new wing.

The person who is in charge of receiving bids told Mr. Polk that several bids were expected. Two bids had already been received. While Mr. Polk was completing the audit, he accidentally picked up the folder with the two bids. Out of curiosity, he read the bids.

The next day Mr. Polk was talking to a client who happens to be a builder. Mr. Polk casually mentioned the amount of the two bids for the wing. He then suggested to the builder that the builder should submit a bid for the project.

INSTRUCTIONS Use the three-step checklist to analyze whether Frank Polk's recommendation to the contractor to submit a bid demonstrates ethical behavior.

Cash	
194,000.00	

Taxes Receivable—Current	
Bal. 1,610,000.00	194,000.00

Cash is increased by a debit for the amount of cash received, *$194,000.00*. Taxes Receivable—Current is decreased by a credit for the same amount, *$194,000.00*.

The journal entry to record this transaction is shown in Illustration 23-5.

ILLUSTRATION 23-5 Journal entry to record collection of current property taxes

JOURNAL PAGE *3*

	DATE		ACCOUNT TITLE	DOC. NO.	POST. REF.	GENERAL DEBIT (1)	GENERAL CREDIT (2)	CASH DEBIT (3)	CASH CREDIT (4)	
12		*10*	*Taxes Receivable—Current*	*R371*			*194 000 00*	*194 000 00*		12

Other Revenue

Some revenues, such as fines, inspection charges, parking meter receipts, and penalties, are normally not known, and, thus, are not measurable until cash is received. A journal entry to record such revenues, therefore, is generally made only when cash is received.

January 15, 19--. Received cash from traffic fines, $85.00. Receipt No. 386.

Cash	
85.00	

Other Revenue	
	85.00

Cash is increased by a debit for the amount of cash received, *$85.00*. Other Revenue is increased by a credit for the same amount, *$85.00*.

The journal entry to record this transaction is shown in Illustration 23-6.

ILLUSTRATION 23-6 Journal entry to record other revenue

JOURNAL — PAGE 3

	DATE		ACCOUNT TITLE	DOC. NO.	POST. REF.	GENERAL DEBIT (1)	GENERAL CREDIT (2)	CASH DEBIT (3)	CASH CREDIT (4)	
17		15	Other Revenue	R386			85 00	85 00		17
18										18

Delinquent Property Taxes

FYI

Taxes not paid by a specified date are reclassified as delinquent.

Property taxes normally are due and payable by a date specified on the tax statements. Taxes not paid by the specified date are reclassified as delinquent to distinguish them from current taxes. Sparta's property taxes are due on February 28. On March 1, taxes not paid are considered delinquent. On that date, a journal entry is made to transfer uncollected taxes from current to delinquent status.

Taxes that Sparta expects to collect are accounted for by using two accounts, Taxes Receivable—Current and Allowance for Uncollectible Taxes—Current. On March 1 of each year, the remaining balance of Taxes Receivable—Current is considered to be a delinquent amount. Delinquent taxes are accounted for by using two accounts, Taxes Receivable—Delinquent and Allowance for Uncollectible Taxes—Delinquent. Thus, on March 1 of each year, the balances of the two current accounts are transferred to the two delinquent accounts.

March 1, 19--. Recorded reclassification of current taxes receivable to delinquent status, $64,200.00, and the accompanying allowance for uncollectible accounts, $16,000.00. Memorandum No. 65.

Taxes Receivable—Delinquent	
64,200.00	

Allowance for Uncollectible Taxes—Current	
16,000.00	Bal. 16,000.00

Taxes Receivable—Current	
Bal. 64,200.00	64,200.00

Allowance for Uncollectible Taxes—Delinquent	
	16,000.00

Taxes Receivable—Delinquent is increased by a debit for the amount of current taxes becoming delinquent, *$64,200.00*. The contra asset account Allowance for Uncollectible Taxes—Current is decreased by a debit for the balance in that account, *$16,000.00*. Taxes Receivable—Current is decreased by a credit for the amount of current taxes becoming delinquent, *$64,200.00*. Allowance for Uncollectible Taxes—Delinquent is increased by a credit for the amount of allowance on the delinquent taxes, *$16,000.00*. When this entry is posted, the delinquent taxes and the accompanying uncollectible allowance amount will be transferred from current to delinquent status.

The journal entry to record this transaction is shown in Illustration 23-7 on page 622.

Collection of Delinquent Property Taxes

Even though some taxes become delinquent, Sparta continues efforts to collect these taxes. Cash received for delinquent taxes reduces Taxes Receivable—Delinquent.

APPLY

Use T accounts on an overhead projector or chalkboard to emphasize the debit and credit parts of transactions illustrated in this lesson. Explain each transaction as it is recorded in the T accounts.

Guided Practice

Guide students through the T account analysis of the transactions in Problems 23-2 and 23-3. Have students draw T accounts on a sheet of paper and analyze the first transaction of Problem 23-2. All students should agree with the analysis before proceeding to the next transaction. Repeat the process until all transactions in Problems 23-2 and 23-3 have been analyzed. The balance of Problems 23-2 and 23-3 can be completed as Independent Practice.

Independent Practice

- Assign Terms 6–9, Questions 11–20, and Problems 23-2 and 23-3.
- Assign Study Guide 23 and Mastery Problem 23-M.

ASSESS

Assess student understanding by checking the solutions to the Independent Practice activities.

Reteach

- Make a transparency of the multi-column journal from the accounting forms masters provided in the Blackline Masters Section of the Teacher's Resource Guide. Refer students to Recycling Problem 23-R. Ask students to use T accounts to analyze the transactions. Use the transparency to demonstrate how to journalize the January transactions.
- Assign Recycling Problem 23-R.

Extend

- Assign Cases for Critical Thinking 2.
- Assign Challenge Problem 23-C. (The challenge is to record a budget in which appropriations exceed revenues.)

ILLUSTRATION 23-7 Journal entry to record delinquent property taxes

JOURNAL PAGE *21*

	DATE		ACCOUNT TITLE	DOC. NO.	POST. REF.	GENERAL DEBIT (1)	GENERAL CREDIT (2)	CASH DEBIT (3)	CASH CREDIT (4)	
1	*Mar.*	*1*	*Taxes Receivable—Delinquent*	*M65*		*64 200 00*				1
2			*Allowance for Uncollectible Taxes—Current*			*16 000 00*				2
3			*Taxes Receivable—Current*				*64 200 00*			3
4			*Allowance for Uncollectible Taxes—Delinquent*				*16 000 00*			4
5										5
6										6
7										7

Cash	
12,000.00	

Taxes Receivable—Delinquent	
Bal. 64,200.00	12,000.00

March 20, 19--. Received cash for delinquent taxes receivable, $12,000.00. Receipt No. 420.

Cash is increased by a debit for the amount of cash received, *$12,000.00.* Taxes Receivable—Delinquent is decreased by a credit for the same amount, *$12,000.00.*

The journal entry to record this transaction is shown in Illustration 23-8.

ILLUSTRATION 23-8 Journal entry to record collection of delinquent property taxes

JOURNAL PAGE *22*

	DATE		ACCOUNT TITLE	DOC. NO.	POST. REF.	GENERAL DEBIT (1)	GENERAL CREDIT (2)	CASH DEBIT (3)	CASH CREDIT (4)	
20		*20*	*Taxes Receivable—Delinquent*	*R420*			*12 000 00*	*12 000 00*		20
21										21

JOURNALIZING EXPENDITURES AND ENCUMBRANCES

A primary objective of governmental accounting is to control the financial resources. Governmental accounting focuses on measuring changes in financial resources rather than determining net income. Therefore, in governmental accounting, expenditures rather than expenses are recorded.

Control of expenditures is enhanced by the use of two special accounting procedures.

1. Expenditures are classified into several categories to assign specific responsibility for the expenditure and to analyze the purpose of the expenditure. For example, Expenditure—Personnel,

FYI

One responsibility of the General Accounting Office of the federal government is to improve the federal government's financial management and efficiency.

FYI

Some hospitals are not for-profit businesses. Many not-for-profit hospitals are operated by federal, state, or local governments, but many more are voluntary not-for-profit organizations.

Public Safety is one of Sparta's expenditure accounts. Personnel indicates the type of expenditure (salaries for personnel). Public Safety indicates the department for which the personnel expenditures were made.

2. Budgetary accounts are used to record estimated amounts of expenditures to protect against overspending the budgeted amounts. To accomplish this control procedure, encumbrance accounts are used. A commitment to pay for goods or services which have been ordered but not yet provided is called an **encumbrance.** When an order is placed that will require a future expenditure, a budgetary encumbrance account is debited for the estimated amount. This entry reduces the fund balance and insures that commitments and expenditures will not be greater than funds available.

CLOSURE

Use Audit Your Understanding questions.

ASSESS

- Administer Problem Test Chapter 23.
- Administer a MicroExam test for Chapter 23.

Expenditures

Exact amounts of some expenditures are known as soon as the obligation is determined. For example, the amount and due date of payment for utility costs is known when the utility statement is received.

Expenditure—Other Charges, Public Safety	
290.00	

Cash	
	290.00

January 10, 19--. Paid cash for electrical service in public safety department, $290.00. Check No. 355.

Expenditure—Other Charges, Public Safety is increased by a debit for the cost of the electrical service, *$290.00.* Cash is decreased by a credit for the same amount, *$290.00.*

The journal entry to record this transaction is shown in Illustration 23-9.

ILLUSTRATION 23-9 Journal entry to record an expenditure for electrical service

JOURNAL PAGE 3

	DATE		ACCOUNT TITLE	DOC. NO.	POST. REF.	GENERAL DEBIT (1)	GENERAL CREDIT (2)	CASH DEBIT (3)	CASH CREDIT (4)	
1	19-- Jan.	10	Expenditure—Other Charges, Public Safety	C355		290 00			290 00	1

The major control of expenditures is achieved by holding department heads accountable for expenditures in their unit. Classification of expenditures is used to analyze major types of expenditures within each department. For Sparta, each department's expenditures are recorded in one of four classifications: personnel, supplies, other charges, or capital outlays. The other charges classification is used for all expenditures except: salaries and related personnel expenditures, supplies expenditures, and capital outlays. Capital outlays is used for expenditures that will benefit future years.

Encumbrances

FYI

Local governmental accounting systems must effectively monitor how public funds are spent. Many federal grants require local governments to report that funds were expended only on "allowable expenses."

To avoid spending more resources than are available, encumbrance accounts are used. When goods or services are ordered that will be provided at a later date, an obligation for a future expenditure is made. Resources have not yet been used, but there is a promise to give up those resources when ordered goods or services are delivered. Encumbering resources is a way of setting aside the amount estimated to be needed to pay for the ordered goods or services. When the goods or services are delivered, the estimated amount is removed from the encumbrance account and the exact amount of the expenditure is journalized in an expenditure account.

January 12, 19--. Encumbered estimated amount for supplies in public works department, $380.00. Memorandum No. 40.

APPLIED SKILLS: WRITING ACROSS THE CURRICULUM

Writing paragraphs and short essays. The Cases for Critical Thinking are short, practical applications of the accounting principles developed in the chapter. Some cases are planned to present problems related to the chapter but not specifically discussed and answered in the chapter. These cases present an opportunity for critical thinking and decision making. These cases also require more than a short objective-type response. Therefore, they provide ideal practice in writing paragraphs and short essays.

Encumbrance—Supplies, Public Works	
380.00	

Reserve for Encumbrances—Current Year	
	380.00

The budgetary account Encumbrance—Supplies, Public Works is increased by a debit for the amount of the order, *$380.00.* The fund equity account Reserve for Encumbrances—Current Year is increased by a credit for the amount of the supplies order, *$380.00.* This account serves as an offsetting account for the encumbrance account and shows that this amount of the fund equity is reserved for an encumbrance.

The journal entry to record this transaction is shown in Illustration 23-10.

ILLUSTRATION 23-10 Journal entry to record an encumbrance for supplies ordered

JOURNAL PAGE 3

	DATE		ACCOUNT TITLE	DOC. NO.	POST. REF.	1 GENERAL DEBIT	2 GENERAL CREDIT	3 CASH DEBIT	4 CASH CREDIT	
12		*12*	*Encumbrance—Supplies, Public Works*	*M40*		*380 00*				12
13			*Reserve for Encumbrances—Current Year*				*380 00*			13

Expenditures plus encumbrances for a specific account equal the total commitment that has been made against the appropriated amount for that account. The appropriated amount less the encumbrances and expenditures equals the amount that can still be spent. For example, Sparta appropriated $5,600.00 for supplies for the public works department. If expenditures are $900.00 and encumbrances are $380.00, then $4,320.00 is still available for public works supplies expenditures ($5,600.00 *less* $900.00 *less* $380.00).

Expenditures for Amounts Encumbered

When goods or services that have been encumbered are received, two entries must be made. (1) The encumbrance entry is reversed

624

to remove the estimated amount from the encumbrance and reserve for encumbrance accounts. (2) The expenditure is recorded.

January 25, 19--. Paid cash for public works department supplies, $375.00, encumbered January 12 per Memorandum No. 40. Memorandum No. 46 and Check No. 362.

The analysis of the first entry to reverse the encumbrance entry for the supplies ordered is shown in the T accounts.

Reserve for Encumbrances—Current Year

Debit		Credit	
Jan. 25	380.00	Jan. 12	380.00
		(New Bal. zero)	

Encumbrance—Supplies, Public Works

Debit		Credit	
Jan. 12	380.00	Jan. 25	380.00
(New Bal. zero)			

The encumbrance was for an estimated amount, *$380.00*. When the supplies were delivered, the actual cost was $375.00. The actual amount of an expenditure sometimes differs from the amount estimated when an order is placed. Reserve for Encumbrances—Current Year is decreased by a debit for the amount of the entry made to this fund equity account when the encumbrance was initially recorded, *$380.00*. Encumbrance—Supplies, Public Works is credited for the amount of the encumbrance in this budgetary account, *$380.00*. This entry cancels the encumbrance, which is no longer needed. The order has been received and the expenditure will be journalized. Thus, an encumbrance is no longer outstanding.

The analysis of the entry to record the expenditure is shown in the T accounts.

Expenditure—Supplies, Public Works

Debit	Credit
375.00	

Cash

Debit	Credit
	375.00

Expenditure—Supplies, Public Works is increased by a debit for the actual cost of supplies, *$375.00*. Cash is decreased by a credit for the same amount, *$375.00*.

The journal entries to record reversing the encumbrance and to record the actual expenditure for supplies are shown in Illustration 23-11.

ILLUSTRATION 23-11 Journal entries to record reversing an encumbrance and to record an actual expenditure

JOURNAL PAGE 6

	DATE	ACCOUNT TITLE	DOC. NO.	POST. REF.	1 GENERAL DEBIT	2 GENERAL CREDIT	3 CASH DEBIT	4 CASH CREDIT	
10	25	Reserve for Encumbrances—Current Year	M46		380 00				10
11		Encumbrance—Supplies, Public Works				380 00			11
12	25	Expenditure—Supplies, Public Works	C362		375 00			375 00	12
13									13

Expenditures Benefiting Future Periods

FYI

Expenditures classified as capital outlays will benefit future years.

Governmental organizations are formed to provide needed services for their members, not to earn a profit. A business records the cost of property, such as a computer, as an asset. The business then depreciates the asset over its useful life. Recording depreciation spreads the cost of the asset over the asset's life. The depreciation

TEACHING STRATEGIES: DIFFERENT LEARNING ABILITIES

At-Risk Students. Many at-risk students can become motivated to begin self improvement only when they recognize that they have a need to improve. One method of promoting self evaluation is to have students identify the qualities they would require of another individual. Have students imagine that they are considering hiring employees for an office position. Require the student to prepare a job description that includes both skill and personal characteristics that applicants should possess. This activity should enable students to compare their qualifications with the job descriptions they have developed.

expense is matched with revenue earned in each fiscal period. Since governmental organizations do not earn net income, they have no need for expense information. However, controlling the expenditure of funds is important. When money is spent for capital outlays, the amount is recorded as an expenditure in the period spent even though the item may benefit several accounting periods.

On March 10, Sparta's general government department bought a new computer.

March 10, 19--. Paid cash for a computer for general government department, $900.00. Check No. 400.

Expenditure—Capital Outlays, General Government	
900.00	

Cash	
	900.00

Expenditure—Capital Outlays, General Government is increased by a debit for the cost of the computer, *$900.00*. Cash is decreased by a credit for the same amount, *$900.00*.

The journal entry to record the expenditure for property that will benefit future periods is shown in Illustration 23-12.

TEACHING STRATEGIES: EXPANDING BEYOND THE CLASSROOM

Invite a guest speaker who is knowledgeable in not-for-profit accounting to speak to your class. Potential speakers are: city finance directors (or possibly the city clerk for smaller towns), county auditors, and CPAs who audit not-for-profit organizations. Request the speaker to describe the unique characteristics of not-for-profit organizations.

ILLUSTRATION 23-12 Journal entry to record an expenditure benefiting future periods

JOURNAL PAGE 21

	DATE		ACCOUNT TITLE	DOC. NO.	POST. REF.	1 GENERAL DEBIT	2 GENERAL CREDIT	3 CASH DEBIT	4 CASH CREDIT	
17		10	*Expenditure—Capital Outlays, Gen. Gov't.*	C400		900 00			900 00	17
18										18
19										19

Governmental properties that benefit future periods are called **general fixed assets.** Most governmental organizations keep some kind of record of general fixed assets. The purpose of the record is to help safeguard the government's ownership of the property. Sparta keeps a card file with needed information about each general fixed asset.

JOURNALIZING OTHER TRANSACTIONS

Sometimes governmental organizations need to borrow cash for short periods until tax money is received. At other times, these organizations have cash to invest for short periods until the cash is needed to pay expenditures.

FYI

Businesses may also use similar types of funds, such as bond sinking funds or pension funds.

Issuance and Payment of Liabilities

Sparta sends tax statements to property owners on January 1 each year. Taxes can be paid anytime from January 1 through February 28. Consequently, the town may need to borrow cash until taxes are received.

Cash	
100,000.00	

Notes Payable	
	100,000.00

January 4, 19--. Issued a 1-month, 9% note, $100,000.00. Note Payable No. 26.

Cash is increased by a debit for the amount of cash received, *$100,000.00*. Notes Payable is increased by a credit for the same amount, *$100,000.00*.

The journal entry to record this transaction is shown in Illustration 23-13.

ILLUSTRATION 23-13 Journal entry to record issuance of a note payable

JOURNAL PAGE 1

	DATE		ACCOUNT TITLE	DOC. NO.	POST. REF.	1 GENERAL DEBIT	2 GENERAL CREDIT	3 CASH DEBIT	4 CASH CREDIT	
15		4	Notes Payable	NP26			100 000 00	100 000 00		15
16										16

When Sparta's note payable is due on February 4, the amount of the note plus interest expense is paid to the bank.

Notes Payable	
Feb. 4 100,000.00	Jan. 4 100,000.00

Expenditure—Other Charges, General Government	
Feb. 4 750.00	

Cash	
	Feb. 4 100,750.00

February 4, 19--. Paid cash for the maturity value of NP26: principal, $100,000.00, plus interest, $750.00; total, $100,750.00. Check No. 370.

Notes Payable is decreased by a debit, *$100,000.00*. Expenditure—Other Charges, General Government is increased by a debit for the amount of interest expense, *$750.00*. Cash is decreased by a credit for the total amount paid, *$100,750.00*.

The journal entry to record payment of the note payable is shown in Illustration 23-14.

ILLUSTRATION 23-14 Journal entry to record payment of a note payable with interest

JOURNAL PAGE 8

	DATE		ACCOUNT TITLE	DOC. NO.	POST. REF.	1 GENERAL DEBIT	2 GENERAL CREDIT	3 CASH DEBIT	4 CASH CREDIT	
22		4	Notes Payable	C370		100 000 00			100 750 00	22
23			Expenditure—Other Charges, Gen. Gov't.			750 00				23
24										24

FYI

The interest rate of a certificate of deposit usually increases as the time period increases.

Short-Term Investments

Most of Sparta's property taxes, the major portion of the town's revenue, are collected by March 1 each year. Cash that will not be needed for several months is placed in short-term investments. Interest on these investments provides additional revenue.

TEACHING STRATEGIES: COOPERATIVE LEARNING

Select two auditing groups made up of three or four students per group. One group serves as auditors for Chapter 23 and the other serves as auditors for Chapter 24. Each auditing group is responsible for assisting other class members as well as correcting homework assignments. A lead auditor is appointed by the group and is responsible for turning in completed homework assignments to the teacher.

March 1, 19--. Paid cash for a 4-month, 8% certificate of deposit, $300,000.00. Check No. 385.

Investments—Short Term	
300,000.00	

Cash	
	300,000.00

A document issued by a bank as evidence of money invested with the bank is called a **certificate of deposit.** The time and interest rate to be paid are included on the certificate.

Investments—Short Term is increased by a debit for the amount of the certificate, *$300,000.00*. Cash is decreased by a credit for the same amount, *$300,000.00*.

The journal entry to record this transaction is shown in Illustration 23-15.

ILLUSTRATION 23-15 Journal entry to record a short-term investment

JOURNAL PAGE 21

	DATE		ACCOUNT TITLE	DOC. NO.	POST. REF.	1 GENERAL DEBIT	2 GENERAL CREDIT	3 CASH DEBIT	4 CASH CREDIT	
19		1	*Investments—Short Term*	*C385*		*300 000 00*			*300 000 00*	19
20										20

Cash	
308,000.00	

Investments—Short Term	
	300,000.00

Interest Revenue	
	8,000.00

When the certificate of deposit is due on July 1, cash is received for the original cost of the investment plus interest revenue earned.

July 1, 19--. Received cash for the maturity value of certificate of deposit due today: principal, $300,000.00, plus interest, $8,000.00; total, $308,000.00. Receipt No. 572.

Cash is increased by a debit for the amount of cash received, *$308,000.00*. Investments—Short Term is decreased by a credit for the certificate of deposit's original cost, *$300,000.00*. Interest Revenue is increased by a credit for the amount of interest earned, *$8,000.00*.

The journal entry to record this transaction is shown in Illustration 23-16.

Audit Your Understanding

1. When is a journal entry made to record property tax revenue?
2. What accounts are affected, and how, when a taxpayer pays property taxes two months after the due date?
3. What is an encumbrance?
4. Why does a governmental organization not record depreciation expense?
5. What is a certificate of deposit?

AUDIT YOUR UNDERSTANDING

1. When property taxes are levied.
2. Cash is debited; Taxes Receivable—Delinquent is credited.
3. A commitment to pay for goods or services which have been ordered but not yet provided.
4. Because the organization does not earn a net income and, therefore, has no need for expense information.
5. A document issued by a bank as evidence of money invested with the bank.

ILLUSTRATION 23-16 Journal entry to record cash received for a short-term investment plus interest

JOURNAL PAGE 51

	DATE	ACCOUNT TITLE	DOC. NO.	POST. REF.	GENERAL DEBIT (1)	GENERAL CREDIT (2)	CASH DEBIT (3)	CASH CREDIT (4)	
22	1	*Investments—Short Term*	*R572*			300 000 00	308 000 00		22
23		*Interest Revenue*				8 000 00			23
24									24
25									25

ACCOUNTING TERMS EPT(a)

What is the meaning of each of the following?

1. **not-for-profit organization**
2. **fund**
3. **expenditures**
4. **operating budget**
5. **appropriations**
6. **tax levy**
7. **encumbrance**
8. **general fixed assets**
9. **certificate of deposit**

QUESTIONS FOR INDIVIDUAL STUDY EPT(b)

1. What is the major purpose of a not-for-profit organization?
2. What are six types of not-for-profit organizations?
3. What are the four characteristics of a governmental organization that affect the accounting system?
4. How have the characteristics of governmental organizations affected the development of governmental accounting systems?
5. Which accounting practices are applied by both businesses and governmental organizations?
6. What is the accounting equation for governmental organizations?
7. Which accounting concept is being applied when financial statements are prepared at the end of a fiscal period?
8. What are the two most common financial statements prepared by governmental organizations?
9. What two control functions does an approved governmental budget serve?
10. What general procedures are followed to prepare a governmental operating budget?
11. When is a journal entry made to record property tax revenue?
12. What accounts are affected, and how, when a governmental organization levies property taxes?
13. When is a journal entry made to record traffic fines as revenue?
14. What accounts are affected, and how, when Sparta collects traffic fines?
15. What is the purpose of using encumbrance accounts?

ACCOUNTING TERMS

1. **not-for-profit organization:** An organization providing goods or services with neither a conscious motive nor expectation of earning a profit. (p. 610)
2. **fund:** A governmental accounting entity with a set of accounts in which assets always equal liabilities plus equities. (p. 612)
3. **expenditures:** Cash disbursements and liabilities incurred for the cost of goods delivered or services rendered. (p. 613)
4. **operating budget:** A plan of current expenditures and the proposed means of financing those expenditures. (p. 614)
5. **appropriations:** Authorizations to make expenditures for specified purposes. (p. 617)
6. **tax levy:** Authorized action taken by a governmental organization to collect taxes by legal authority. (p. 619)
7. **encumbrance:** A commitment to pay for goods or services which have been ordered but not yet provided. (p. 623)
8. **general fixed assets:** Governmental properties that benefit future periods. (p. 626)
9. **certificate of deposit:** A document issued by a bank as evidence of money invested with the bank. (p. 628)

QUESTIONS FOR INDIVIDUAL STUDY

1. To provide needed goods or services to a group of individuals without regard to earning a profit. (p. 610)
2. (a) Governmental, (b) Educational, (c) Health, (d) Charitable, (e) Foundational, and (f) Religious. (p. 610)
3. (a) No profit motive exists, (b) leadership is subject to frequent change, (c) users of services do not necessarily pay for the services, (d) conflicting pressures for differing objectives exist. (p. 611)

QUESTIONS (cont'd)

4. Numerous financial and legal regulations for determining the source and amount of revenues and for planning and executing expenditures of funds are required. (p. 612)
5. (a) The accounting equation, assets equal liabilities plus equities, is applied, (b) an appropriate chart of accounts is prepared, (c) transactions are analyzed into debit and credit parts, (d) transactions are journalized and posted to ledgers, (e) financial statements are prepared for each fiscal period, (f) most of the same accounting concepts are applied. (p. 612)
6. Assets = Liabilities + Fund Equity. (p. 612)
7. Accounting Period Cycle concept. (p. 614)
8. A statement of revenues, expenditures, and changes in fund balance and a balance sheet. (p. 614)
9. (a) A legal authorization to spend. (b) A legal limit on the amount that can be spent. (p. 614)
10. (a) Departments of the governmental organization submit budget requests to the chief executive of the organization. (b) The chief executive reviews budget requests with department heads. (c) The legislative body approves the operating budget. (pp. 614–615)
11. Property tax revenue is recorded when levied. (p. 619)
12. Taxes Receivable—Current is debited; Allowance for Uncollectible Taxes—Current and Property Tax Revenue are credited. (p. 619)
13. Traffic fines are recorded as revenue when cash is received. (p. 620)
14. Cash is debited; Other Revenue is credited. (p. 620)
15. To record estimated amounts of expenditures to avoid spending more resources than are available. (p. 623)
16. (a) The encumbrance entry is reversed to remove the estimated amount from the encumbrance and reserve for encumbrance accounts. (b) The expenditure is recorded. (pp. 624–625)
17. The actual amount of an expenditure sometimes differs from the amount estimated when an order is placed. (p. 625)

16. What two journal entries must be made when goods or services are received that have been encumbered?
17. Why may the amount for an encumbrance entry be different than the amount for the related expenditure entry?
18. What accounts are affected, and how, when a governmental organization buys a computer?
19. What accounts are affected, and how, when a governmental organization issues a note payable?
20. What accounts are affected, and how, when a governmental organization pays a note payable plus interest expense?

CASES FOR CRITICAL THINKING EPT(b)

CASE 1 The town of Oneida has three funds in its accounting system—general, library, and recreation. Oneida's new town manager, Donna Ward, has questioned the necessity of having three separate governmental funds. Ms. Ward suggests combining all the funds into a single general fund. What do you recommend? Explain your answer.

CASE 2 Edwin Mansky, a new accounting clerk with the town of Thornton, has been struggling with accounting entries involving encumbrances. He suggests that no entries be made until goods or services are received. When goods are received, an expenditure would be recorded. Encumbrances would not be necessary and the final results would be the same. What is your response to Mr. Mansky's suggestion? Explain your answer.

APPLICATION PROBLEMS EPT(c)

PROBLEM 23-1 Journalizing governmental operating budgets

Three towns, Burns, Milner, and Pinewood, approved their annual general fund operating budgets effective January 1 of the current year.

INSTRUCTIONS:

Journalize the entry to record the following operating budgets for each of the three towns. Use page 1 of a journal.

	Estimated Revenues	Appropriations	Budgetary Fund Balance
Burns......	$1,056,000.00	$1,009,000.00	$47,000.00
Milner	794,500.00	789,200.00	5,300.00
Pinewood ..	1,754,000.00	1,722,500.00	31,500.00

PROBLEM 23-2 Journalizing governmental revenue transactions

Deerwood's town council recently approved the town's general fund operating budget for the current year.

INSTRUCTIONS:

Journalize the following transactions. Use page 1 of a journal.

Jan. 1. Recorded property tax levy: taxes receivable—current, $1,300,000.00; allowance for uncollectible taxes—current, $13,000.00; property tax revenue, $1,287,000.00. M88.
8. Received cash for current taxes receivable, $97,600.00. R134.
14. Received cash from traffic fines, $56.00. R147. (Other Revenue)
Feb. 11. Received cash for current taxes receivable, $172,350.00. R194.
16. Received cash from parking meter receipts, $274.50. R212. (Other Revenue)

Mar. 1. Recorded reclassification of current taxes receivable to delinquent status, $56,800.00, and the accompanying allowance for uncollectible accounts, $13,000.00. M107.
12. Received cash for delinquent taxes receivable, $10,700.00. R259.

PROBLEM 23-3 Journalizing governmental encumbrances, expenditures, and other transactions

The town of Tioga uses a general fund for all financial transactions. Expenditures are recorded by type of expenditure and by department. The four categories of expenditures are: personnel, supplies, other charges, and capital outlays. Departments are: General Government, Public Safety, Public Works, and Recreation.

INSTRUCTIONS:

Journalize the following transactions completed during the current year. Use page 1 of a journal.

Jan. 11. Paid cash for electrical service in public works department, $195.00. C244.
15. Encumbered estimated amount for supplies in public safety department, $135.00. M33.
16. Issued a one-month, 10% note, $150,000.00. NP6.
28. Paid cash for public safety department supplies, $132.00, encumbered January 15 per M33. M40 and C258.

Feb. 5. Paid cash for calculator for general government department, $255.00. C267. (Capital Outlays)
16. Paid cash for the maturity value of NP6: principal, $150,000.00, plus interest, $1,250.00; total, $151,250.00. C279.
28. Encumbered estimated amount for supplies in public works department, $276.00. M49.

Mar. 15. Paid cash for a 3-month, 8% certificate of deposit, $200,000.00. C296.
18. Paid cash for public works department supplies, $278.00, encumbered February 28 per M49. M58 and C315.
21. Paid cash for consultant's services in recreation department, $360.00. C322. (Personnel)

June 15. Received cash for the maturity value of certificate of deposit due today: principal, $200,000.00, plus interest, $4,000.00; total, $204,000.00. R184.

ENRICHMENT PROBLEMS

EPT(c)

MASTERY PROBLEM 23-M Journalizing governmental transactions

The town of Ingalls uses a general fund for all financial transactions. Expenditures are recorded by type of expenditure and by department. The four categories of expenditures are: personnel, supplies, other charges, and capital outlays. Departments are: General Government, Public Safety, Public Works, and Recreation.

INSTRUCTIONS:

Journalize the following transactions completed during the current year. Use page 1 of a journal.

Jan. 2. Recorded current year's approved operating budget: estimated revenues, $1,270,000.00; appropriations, $1,224,000.00; budgetary fund balance, $46,000.00. M42.
2. Recorded current year's property tax levy: taxes receivable—current, $1,220,000.00; allowance for uncollectible taxes—current, $12,200.00; property tax revenue, $1,207,800.00. M43.

QUESTIONS *(cont'd)*

18. Expenditure—Capital Outlays, General Government is debited; Cash is credited. (p. 626)

19. Cash is debited; Notes Payable is credited. (p. 627)

20. Notes Payable is debited for the amount of the note; Expenditure—Other Charges, General Government is debited for the amount of interest expense; Cash is credited for the total amount paid. (p. 627)

CASES FOR CRITICAL THINKING

Case 1 Before any change in funds is considered, the original purpose for establishing the three funds should be determined. The funds may have been established by action of the town council. The funds may be required by county or state regulations. Normally, separate funds are created to place greater restrictions and control on the use of funds. Special taxing authority may have been approved by the town citizens to support specific services such as libraries or recreation. If a portion of the taxes is designated for the special purposes (libraries and recreation), then the separate funds should be retained. If there is no specific requirement or need for maintaining the special funds, such as town council authority or county or state regulations, then the three funds could be combined into a single general fund.

Case 2 When goods are ordered that will be delivered at some future date, a commitment is made to use resources when the goods arrive. However, to insure that commitments are not made for more than is authorized, entries for encumbrances are made. An encumbrance reserves the resources necessary to pay for the goods when they arrive. This process protects the organization from obligating itself for more than is authorized. Governmental organizations do not have a profit objective and thus cannot measure efficiency by the amount of profit earned. Consequently, greater control is placed on the use of financial resources by a governmental organization. An important part of the control is implemented through the development of budgets which, when approved, become authorizations to spend specific amounts for specific purposes.

CHECK FIGURES

See Teacher's Edition of Working Papers for complete solutions.

Problem 23-1 General debit and general credit totals, $3,604,500.00.

Problem 23-2 Column totals: general debit, $1,369,800.00, general credit, $1,650,780.50; Cash debit, $280,980.50.

Problem 23-3 Column totals: general debit, $353,292.00; general credit, $354,822.00; Cash debit, $354,000.00; Cash credit, $352,470.00.

Mastery Problem 23-M Column totals: general debit, $3,158,681.00; general credit, $3,240,721.00; Cash debit, $686,525.00; Cash credit, $604,485.00.

Jan. 9. Received cash for current taxes receivable, $57,300.00. R105.
11. Paid cash for gas utility service in general government department, $234.00. C168.
12. Issued a 2-month, 9% note, $200,000.00. NP7.
16. Encumbered estimated amount for supplies in public works department, $165.00. M54.
20. Received cash from traffic fines, $225.00. R111. (Other Revenue)
30. Paid cash for lawn mower for public works department, $450.00. (Capital Outlays) C182.

Feb. 6. Paid cash for public works department supplies, $170.00, encumbered January 16 per M54. M58 and C190.
24. Encumbered estimated amount for supplies in recreation department, $133.00. M69.

Mar. 1. Recorded reclassification of current taxes receivable to delinquent status, $51,400.00, and the accompanying allowance for uncollectible accounts, $12,200.00. M76.
12. Paid cash for the maturity value of NP7: principal, $200,000.00, plus interest, $3,000.00; total, $203,000.00. C222.
20. Paid cash for a 3-month, 8% certificate of deposit, $400,000.00. C234.
22. Paid cash for recreation department supplies, $131.00, encumbered February 24 per M69. M88 and C241.

Apr. 10. Received cash for delinquent taxes receivable, $21,000.00. R355.
25. Paid cash for consultant's services in recreation department, $500.00. C266. (Personnel)

June 20. Received cash for the maturity value of certificate of deposit due today: principal, $400,000.00, plus interest, $8,000.00; total, $408,000.00. R497.

CHECK FIGURES *(cont'd)*

Challenge Problem 23-C
Column totals: general debit, $3,849,241.00; general credit, $3,947,178.00; Cash debit, $778,358.00; Cash credit, $680,421.00.

CHALLENGE PROBLEM 23-C Journalizing governmental transactions

The town of Mabank uses a general fund for all financial transactions. Expenditures are recorded by type of expenditure and by department. The four categories of expenditures are: personnel, supplies, other charges, and capital outlays. Departments are: General Government, Public Safety, Public Works, and Recreation.

INSTRUCTIONS:

Journalize the following transactions completed during the current year. Use page 1 of a journal.

Jan. 2. Recorded current year's approved operating budget: estimated revenues, $1,528,000.00; appropriations, $1,542,100.00; budgetary fund balance, $14,100.00. M88.

(Note: Most towns prohibit deficit spending. In this case, a town would be prohibited from having a debit balance in the budgetary fund balance account. However, if sufficient fund equity is available at the beginning of a year, a town council may choose to appropriate more than the estimated revenues. The available fund equity would then be used for the amount that expenditures exceed revenues for the current period.)

2. Recorded current year's property tax levy: total amount of tax statements sent, $1,452,000.00; uncollectible taxes estimated at 1% of total tax levy. M89.
9. Received cash for current taxes receivable, $64,700.00. R111.
17. Paid cash for electric utility service in public works department, $286.00. C131.
20. Issued a 2-month, 12% note, $175,000.00. NP14.
25. Encumbered estimated amount for supplies in public safety department, $170.00. M102.

Feb. 3. Received cash from parking meter receipts, $1,158.00. R152.
10. Paid cash for public safety department supplies, $162.00, encumbered January 25 per M102. M130 and C188.
21. Paid cash for swing set for recreation department, $575.00. C199. (Capital Outlays)

Mar. 1. Recorded reclassification of current taxes receivable to delinquent status, $158,100.00, and the accompanying allowance for uncollectible accounts. M154.

Mar. 15. Paid cash for a 4-month, 9% certificate of deposit, $500,000.00. C220.

20. Paid cash for the maturity value of NP14: principal, $175,000.00, plus interest. C230.

21. Received cash for delinquent taxes receivable, $22,500.00. R206.

Apr. 4. Encumbered estimated amount for printer in general government department, $880.00. M178. (Capital Outlays)

16. Paid cash for general government department printer, $898.00, encumbered April 4 per M178. M190 and C267.

July 15. Received cash for the maturity value of certificate of deposit due today, $500,000.00, plus interest. R289.

633

CHAPTER 24 OVERVIEW

This final chapter presents the end-of-fiscal-period work for a not-for-profit governmental organization. The usual work sheet and adjustments are prepared and the excess of revenues over expenditures is calculated. Instead of an income statement, a statement of revenues, expenditures, and changes in fund balance—budget and actual—is prepared. Then a balance sheet reporting changes in fund equity is described and illustrated. Finally, adjusting and closing entries are recorded and a post-closing trial balance is prepared. This concludes the accounting cycle for a not-for-profit organization.

The work sheet prepared in Problem 24-1 is needed to complete Problems 24-2, 24-3, and 24-4.

GUIDE TO ACHIEVING LEARNING OBJECTIVES

	TEACH	APPLY	EXTEND/ENRICH						
Enabling Performance Tasks	**Lesson Plans**	**Application Problems**	**Mastery Problems**	**Challenge Problems**	**Cases for Critical Thinking**	**Recycling Problems**	**Reinforcement Activity**	
a. Identify accounting concepts and practices related to financial reporting for a not-for-profit governmental organization.	24-1, 24-2, 24-3				Cases 1, 2			
b. Complete end-of-fiscal-period work for a not-for-profit governmental organization.	24-1, 24-2, 24-3	24-1, 24-2, 24-3, 24-4	24-M	24-C		24-R		

ENRICHMENT

SPECIAL FEATURES
Careers in Accounting, page 640
Personal Visions in Business, page 645
TECHNOLOGY CONNECTION
Automated Accounting 6.0 Problem 24-1
Spreadsheet Template Problem 24-M

NEW, REVIEW, AND EXTENSION

ACTIVITIES/CONCEPTS/TRANSACTIONS	NEW	REVIEW/ EXTENSION
Work sheet for a governmental organization		✓
Adjustments for a governmental organization		✓
Excess of revenues over expenditures		✓
Financial statements for a governmental organization		✓
Statement of revenues, expenditures, and changes in fund balance—budget and actual		✓
Balance sheet for a governmental organization		✓
Adjusting and closing entries for a governmental organization		✓
Post-closing trial balance for a governmental organization		✓

	INFORMAL ASSESSMENT		FORMAL ASSESSMENT			
	Study Guide	**Audit Your Understanding**	**Chapter MicroExam**	**Chapter Problem Test**	**Unit Objective Test**	**Portfolio**
	Units A, B, C	✓	✓		✓	
				✓		

TEACHING MATERIALS

Teacher's Wraparound Edition of the Text
Teacher's Resource Guide
Teacher's Edition of Working Papers
MicroExam

APPLIED MATHEMATICS

APPLIED MATH/ACCOUNTING SKILL	APPLICATION
Calculating excess of revenues over expenditures	Prob. 24-1

24

Financial Reporting for a Not-for-Profit Organization

TEACHING STRATEGIES: ACCOUNTING PEDAGOGY

This textbook covers financial reporting for a not-for-profit organization. It is important not only to learn about the not-for-profit organization, but also to apply critical thinking skills and complete the financial reporting responsibilities.

ENABLING PERFORMANCE TASKS

After studying Chapter 24, you will be able to:

a Identify accounting concepts and practices related to financial reporting for a not-for-profit governmental organization.

b Complete end-of-fiscal-period work for a not-for-profit governmental organization.

Both businesses and not-for-profit organizations prepare financial statements periodically to report the results of financial activities. *(CONCEPT: Accounting Period Cycle)* However, financial information needed for not-for-profit organizations differs from that needed for businesses. A business' performance is measured primarily through determining the amount of net income. Thus, the accounting records are designed to emphasize the measurement of net income. However, a not-for-profit organization's performance is

SOFTWARE FOCUS

Software may be used for independent practice or enrichment/extension as the instructor deems appropriate. For this chapter, the following software may be used: *Automated Accounting 6.0* or higher with Problem 24-1; Spreadsheet Template with Mastery Problem 24-M.

measured primarily by the services provided and the efficiency with which resources are used. Therefore, a not-for-profit organization's financial statements are designed to provide information for the following purposes.

1. To make decisions about the use of resources.
2. To assess services provided and the ability to provide those services.
3. To assess management's financial accountability and performance.
4. To determine the assets, liabilities, and fund equity of the organization.

PREPARING A WORK SHEET FOR A GOVERNMENTAL ORGANIZATION

FYI

Governments often issue bonds to pay for large projects, such as building schools and highways. Investors are not required to pay federal income tax on the interest income.

The town of Sparta uses an eight-column work sheet similar to the one used by Lamplight, Inc. in Part 5. However, the work sheets differ in one set of columns. Sparta's work sheet has Revenues/Expenditures Debit and Credit columns. Lamplight's work sheet has Income Statement Debit and Credit columns.

Recording a Trial Balance on a Work Sheet

A trial balance is entered in the Trial Balance columns as the first step in preparing a work sheet. All general ledger accounts except encumbrances are listed in the Account Title column in the same order as they appear in the general ledger. Only encumbrance accounts with balances are listed. The Trial Balance columns are totaled to prove the equality of debits and credits.

Sparta's trial balance on December 31 is shown on the work sheet in Illustration 24-1 (on page 636).

Planning Adjustments on a Work Sheet

Some general ledger accounts for governmental funds need to be brought up to date before financial statements are prepared. However, since governmental funds report expenditures and not expenses, no adjustments are needed for expense accounts. The actual amounts that have been spent and recorded as expenditures are the amounts reported.

Since governmental funds recognize revenues when the revenues become measurable and available, an adjustment may be needed to record some revenues.

Adjustments are planned on a work sheet. Sparta makes adjustments to three accounts. (1) Inventory of Supplies. (2) Interest Revenue. (3) Reserve for Encumbrances—Current Year.

FYI

Inventory of Supplies is an asset account; Reserve for Inventory of Supplies is a restricted fund equity account.

Inventory of Supplies Adjustment. When supplies are bought, an expenditure account is debited. Some supplies may be unused at the end of a fiscal period. These unused supplies should be reported

LESSON PLAN 24-1

Materials

- Student pages 635–639
- Blackline Master for 8-Column Work Sheet (TRG)
- Software: *Automated Accounting 6.0* or higher; Accounting Textbook Template, Advanced Course

Objectives (Enabling Performance Tasks)

a. Identify accounting concepts and practices related to financial reporting for a not-for-profit governmental organization.

b. Complete end-of-fiscal-period work for a not-for-profit governmental organization.

FOCUS

The unique characteristics of not-for-profit accounting, the development of an annual budget, and transactions for a governmental organization were presented in Chapter 23. In this lesson, preparing a work sheet for a not-for-profit governmental organization will be described.

TEACHING STRATEGIES: TEACHING TIP

Review the definition of encumbrances: A commitment to pay for goods or services which have been ordered but not yet provided.

TEACH

Cover student pages 635–639 "Preparing a Work Sheet for a Governmental Organization." Present the work sheet. Point out that Sparta's work sheet uses the heading Revenues/Expenditures rather than Income Statement. Emphasize that only encumbrances accounts with balances are listed in the Account Title column and included in the trial balance. Explain the adjustments that a governmental organization must plan on the work sheet. Review the definition of encumbrances. Describe how amounts are extended to the Revenues/Expenditures and Balance Sheet columns of the work sheet. Emphasize that the balance of Reserve for Encumbrances—Prior Year is extended to the Revenues/Expenditures columns. Explain how a work sheet is completed. Emphasize that a not-for-profit governmental organization does not calculate net income; excess of revenues over expenditures is calculated. Point out how expenditures for each department are totaled and recorded on the work sheet after the work sheet is completed.

ILLUSTRATION 24-1 Work sheet for a governmental organization

Town of Sparta General Fund
Work Sheet
For Year Ended December 31, 19--

	ACCOUNT TITLE	1 TRIAL BALANCE DEBIT	2 TRIAL BALANCE CREDIT	3 ADJUSTMENTS DEBIT	4 ADJUSTMENTS CREDIT	5 REVENUES/EXPENDITURES DEBIT	6 REVENUES/EXPENDITURES CREDIT	7 BALANCE SHEET DEBIT	8 BALANCE SHEET CREDIT	
1	Cash	78360 00						78360 00		1
2	Taxes Receivable—Current									2
3	Allow. for Uncoll. Taxes—Cur.									3
4	Taxes Receivable—Delinquent	15640 00						15640 00		4
5	Allow. for Uncoll. Taxes—Delin.		8750 00						8750 00	5
6	Interest Receivable			(b) 2565 00				2565 00		6
7	Allow. for Uncoll. Interest				(b) 513 00				513 00	7
8	Inventory of Supplies			(a) 2820 00				2820 00		8
9	Investments—Short Term									9
10	Accounts Payable		36125 00						36125 00	10
11	Notes Payable									11
12	Unreserved Fund Balance		11705 00						11705 00	12
13	Res. for Encum.—Current Year		1640 00	(c) 1640 00						13
14	Res. for Encum.—Prior Year				(c) 1640 00		1640 00			14
15	Reserve for Inv. of Supplies				(a) 2820 00				2820 00	15
16	Property Tax Revenue		1594000 00				1594000 00			16
17	Interest Revenue		8785 00		(b) 2052 00		10837 00			17
18	Other Revenue		2625 00				2625 00			18
19	Expend.—Personnel, Gen. Gov't.	263175 00				263175 00				19
20	Expend.—Supplies, Gen. Gov't.	11940 00				11940 00				20
21	Expend.—Other Chgs., Gen. Gov't.	112380 00				112380 00				21
22	Expend.—Cap. Outlays, Gen. Gov't.	16000 00				16000 00				22
23	Expend.—Personnel, Public Safety	588650 00				403495 00 588650 00				23
24	Expend.—Supplies, Public Safety	19790 00				19790 00				24
25	Expend.—Other Chgs., Pub. Safety	152635 00				152635 00				25
26	Expend.—Cap. Outlays, Pub. Safety	89350 00				89350 00				26
27	Expend.—Personnel, Public Works	113300 00				850425 00 113300 00				27
28	Expend.—Supplies, Public Works	5540 00				5540 00				28
29	Expend.—Other Chgs., Pub. Works	47340 00				47340 00				29
30	Expend.—Cap. Outlays, Pub. Works	51175 00				51175 00				30
31	Expend.—Personnel, Recreation	58110 00				217355 00 58110 00				31
32	Expend.—Supplies, Recreation	1960 00				1960 00				32
33	Expend.—Other Chgs., Recreation	25105 00				25105 00				33
34	Expend.—Cap. Outlays, Recreation	11540 00				11540 00				34
35	Estimated Revenues	1606500 00				96715 00 1606500 00				35
36	Appropriations		1572800 00				1572800 00			36
37	Budgetary Fund Balance		33700 00				33700 00			37
38	Encum.—Supplies, Public Safety	1640 00				1640 00				38
39		3270130 00	3270130 00	7025 00	7025 00	3176130 00	3215602 00	99385 00	59913 00	39
40	Excess of Revenues Over Expend.					39472 00			39472 00	40
41						3215602 00	3215602 00	99385 00	99385 00	41

as an asset. *(CONCEPT: Adequate Disclosure)* Thus, an adjustment is made at the end of a fiscal period to record the remaining amount of supplies inventory as an asset. Expenditure accounts debited when supplies were bought are not adjusted. When an expenditure

TEACHING STRATEGIES: TEACHING TIP

Use T accounts on an overhead projector or chalkboard to emphasize the debit and credit parts of the adjusting and closing entries illustrated in this chapter. Discuss each entry as it is recorded in the T accounts.

is made during a fiscal period, the expenditure is reported regardless of the purpose.

The total account balances of a governmental fund represent the equity of that fund. Thus, assets *less* liabilities *equals* total fund equity, which, unless reserved for a specified purpose, should represent resources that are available for appropriations and spending. The inventory of supplies, however, will be used by the organization. Therefore, this asset is not available for spending. To show that this asset, Inventory of Supplies, is not available for other uses, an equal amount of fund equity is reserved. Thus, the amount is credited to a restricted fund equity account titled Reserve for Inventory of Supplies.

Inventory of Supplies	
Adj. (a) 2,820.00	

Reserve for Inventory of Supplies	
	Adj. (a) 2,820.00

The analysis of the adjustment for supplies on hand is shown in the T accounts. Inventory of Supplies, an asset account, is increased by a debit for the amount of supplies on hand, *$2,820.00*. Reserve for Inventory of Supplies is increased by a credit for the same amount, *$2,820.00*.

The adjustment for inventory of supplies is shown as adjustment (a) on the work sheet, lines 8 and 15, Illustration 24-1.

FYI

Allowance for Uncollectible Interest is a contra asset account that reduces the balance of Interest Receivable on the balance sheet.

Interest Revenue Adjustment. Interest is assessed on all delinquent taxes. Interest on delinquent taxes becomes measurable and available when the interest is assessed. Thus, to bring the accounts up to date and record revenue earned but not collected at the end of the year, an adjustment is made.

Sparta's interest due but not yet collected on December 31 is $2,565.00. Past experience has shown that approximately 20% of this amount, *$513.00* ($2,565.00 × 20%), will not be collected. Thus, the amount expected to be collected, *$2,052.00* ($2,565.00 − $513.00), is recorded as revenue.

Interest Receivable	
Adj. (b) 2,565.00	

Allowance for Uncollectible Interest	
	Adj. (b) 513.00

Interest Revenue	
	Adj. (b) 2,052.00

The analysis of the adjustment for interest revenue and allowance for uncollectible interest is shown in the T accounts. Interest Receivable, an asset account, is increased by a debit for the amount earned but not collected, *$2,565.00*. Allowance for Uncollectible Interest, a contra asset account, is increased by a credit for the amount of interest that is not expected to be collected, *$513.00*. Interest Revenue is increased by a credit for the amount of interest that is expected to be collected, *$2,052.00*.

The adjustment for interest revenue is shown as adjustment (b) on the work sheet, lines 6, 7, and 17, Illustration 24-1.

FYI

The reserve for encumbrances—current year adjustment prevents charging expenditures of one year to another year's appropriations.

Reserve for Encumbrances—Current Year Adjustment. At the end of a fiscal year, a governmental organization may have outstanding encumbrances—orders that have not yet been delivered. When goods are delivered that were encumbered against the preceding year's appropriations, the amount should not be recorded as an expenditure of the current period. Therefore, at the end of a fiscal period, the balance of Reserve for Encumbrances—Current Year, the amount of encumbrances outstanding, should be reclassified to prior year status. Then, when prior year's orders arrive, they can be debited to Reserve for Encumbrances—Prior Year, rather than current

APPLY

Refer students to Illustration 24-1 as preparation of a governmental organization's work sheet is discussed. Draw T accounts on the chalkboard to analyze the adjustments presented in this lesson.

Guided Practice

Guide students through the T account analysis of the adjusting entries in Problem 24-1, Instruction 1. Have students draw T accounts on a sheet of paper and analyze the first adjustment. All students should agree with the analysis before proceeding to the second adjustment. Repeat the process until all adjustments have been analyzed. The balance of Problem 24-1 can be completed as Independent Practice.

Independent Practice

Assign Questions 1–8 and Problem 24-1.

APPLIED SKILLS: LANGUAGE ARTS

Paraphrasing, writing complete sentences, and identifying subjects. For additional practice in language arts skills, direct students to answer the Questions for Individual Study at the end of the chapter. Students should write the answers in their own words and in complete sentences. To further practice language arts skills, ask students to underline the subject(s) in each sentence of their answers.

ASSESS

Assess student understanding by checking the solutions to the Independent Practice activities.

Reteach

- Make a transparency of the 8-column work sheet from the accounting forms masters provided in the Blackline Masters Section of the Teacher's Resource Guide. Refer students to Recycling Problem 24-R. Ask students to use T accounts to analyze the adjustments in Instruction 2. Use the transparency to demonstrate how to prepare a work sheet for a governmental organization.
- Assign Recycling Problem 24-R, Instructions 1–3.

Extend

Use *Automated Accounting 6.0* or higher with Accounting Textbook Template, Advanced Course with Problem 24-1.

Enrich

Assign the CAREERS IN ACCOUNTING feature on page 640. Have students discuss what a career as a county auditor might be like.

year's expenditures. This procedure prevents charging expenditures of one year to another year's appropriations.

On December 31, the balance of Sparta's Reserve for Encumbrances—Current Year is $1,640.00. The analysis of the adjustment to reclassify this fund equity account is shown in the T accounts.

Reserve for Encumbrances—Current Year

Adj. (c)	1,640.00	Bal. *(New Bal. zero)*	1,640.00

Reserve for Encumbrances—Prior Year

		Adj. (c)	1,640.00

Reserve for Encumbrances—Current Year is decreased by a debit, *$1,640.00*. Reserve for Encumbrances—Prior Year is increased by a credit, *$1,640.00*. Reserve for Encumbrances—Current Year has a zero balance after this adjustment. Reserve for Encumbrances—Prior Year has a $1,640.00 balance after this adjustment.

The adjustment for reserve for encumbrances—current year is shown as adjustment (c) on the work sheet, lines 13 and 14, Illustration 24-1.

Extending Amounts to Revenues/Expenditures and Balance Sheet Columns

FYI

Governmental budgetary accounts are temporary accounts that are extended to the work sheet Revenues/Expenditures columns and closed at the end of the fiscal year.

All asset, liability, and fund equity account balances except Reserve for Encumbrances—Prior Year are extended to the Balance Sheet columns as shown on the work sheet, lines 1 through 12 and line 15, Illustration 24-1.

The reserve for encumbrances accounts are listed as balance sheet accounts in the chart of accounts. During a fiscal period, the current year reserve for encumbrances account is used as a balancing account for the encumbrance accounts. Fund equity is not actually reduced when encumbrances are recorded. Therefore, the current year's reserve for encumbrances account is considered to be a budgetary account until accounts are closed at the end of a fiscal period. Therefore, the balance of Reserve for Encumbrances—Prior Year is extended to the Revenues/Expenditures columns as shown on the work sheet, line 14.

The balances of all temporary accounts are also extended to the work sheet's Revenues/Expenditures columns. Temporary accounts are those accounts that are closed at the end of each fiscal period. Temporary accounts include all revenue, expenditure, and budgetary accounts. Revenue accounts are extended to the Revenues/Expenditures columns as shown on the work sheet, lines 16 through 18. Expenditure accounts are shown on lines 19 through 34. Budgetary accounts are shown on line 14 and lines 35 through 38.

Completing a Work Sheet

FYI

Most not-for-profit organizations, excluding governmental agencies, are required to file information tax returns with the IRS.

The Revenues/Expenditures and Balance Sheet columns are totaled. Totals are written as shown on the work sheet, line 39, Illustration 24-1. The difference between the Revenues/Expenditures Credit column total and the Debit column total is the excess of revenues over expenditures. If the Debit column total is larger, the difference is the excess of expenditures over revenues.

Sparta has an excess of revenues over expenditures calculated as shown on the next page.

TEACHING STRATEGIES: TEACHING TIP

Emphasize that a not-for-profit governmental organization does not calculate net income on a work sheet. The governmental organization calculates excess of revenues over expenditures and writes the amount under the Revenues/Expenditures Debit column total.

Revenues/Expenditures Credit column total (line 39)	$3,215,602.00
Less Revenues/Expenditures Debit column total (line 39) .	3,176,130.00
Equals excess of revenues over expenditures	$ 39,472.00

The excess of revenues over expenditures, *$39,472.00,* is written under the work sheet's Revenues/Expenditures Debit column total on line 40 to make the two Revenues/Expenditures columns balance. The words *Excess of Revenues Over Expend.* are written in the Account Title column on the same line.

Sparta's excess of revenues over expenditures, *$39,472.00,* is also written under the Balance Sheet Credit column total on line 40 to make the two Balance Sheet columns balance.

When there is an excess of expenditures over revenues, the excess amount is written on a work sheet in the Revenues/Expenditures Credit and Balance Sheet Debit columns.

After the excess of revenues over expenditures is recorded on the work sheet, the last four columns are totaled again. Each pair of these new totals, as shown on line 41, must be the same. Sparta's Revenues/Expenditures column totals are the same, *$3,215,602.00.* The Balance Sheet column totals are the same, *$99,385.00.* When the totals of each pair of columns are the same, the work sheet is assumed to be correct. The work sheet is then ruled as shown on line 41.

After the work sheet is completed, expenditures in the Revenues/Expenditures Debit column are totaled for each department. These totals are used in the preparation of financial statements. Departmental totals are written in small numbers below the amount of the last listed expenditure for the department. For General Government, lines 19 through 22, the total, *$403,495.00,* is written below line 22. For Public Safety, lines 23 through 26, the total, *$850,425.00,* is written below line 26. For Public Works, lines 27 through 30, the total, *$217,355.00,* is written below line 30. For Recreation, lines 31 through 34, the total, *$96,715.00,* is written below line 34.

Audit Your Understanding

1. What columns on a governmental organization's work sheet replace the Income Statement columns on a business' work sheet?
2. What accounts are affected, and how, when an interest revenue adjustment is recorded for a governmental organization?
3. To which column of a work sheet is the balance of Reserve for Encumbrances—Prior Year extended?
4. How is the excess of revenues over expenditures calculated on the work sheet?

PREPARING FINANCIAL STATEMENTS FOR A GOVERNMENTAL ORGANIZATION

FYI

Governmental financial statements are often published in local newspapers.

Financial statements are prepared to report a governmental organization's financial activity for a fiscal period and financial condition on a specific date. Financial statements are prepared for each governmental fund. *(CONCEPT: Adequate Disclosure)* Sparta prepares two financial statements for its general fund. (1) Statement

CLOSURE

Use Audit Your Understanding questions.

AUDIT YOUR UNDERSTANDING

The AUDIT YOUR UNDERSTANDING feature appears at the end of each section of the chapter. Explain to your students that the word *audit* means to check or verify. AUDIT YOUR UNDERSTANDING may be used to check student comprehension of the section just studied. The answers are provided in Appendix D in the back of the textbook.

1. Revenues/Expenditures.
2. Interest Receivable is debited; Allowance for Uncollectible Interest and Interest Revenue are credited.
3. Revenues/Expenditures Credit column.
4. Revenues/Expenditures Credit column total less Revenues/Expenditures Debit column total equals excess of revenues over expenditures.

LESSON PLAN 24-2

Materials

- Student pages 639–643
- Blackline Master for Statement of Revenues, Expenditures, and Changes in Fund Balance (TRG)
- Blackline Master for Balance Sheet (TRG)

Objectives (Enabling Performance Tasks)

a. Identify accounting concepts and practices related to financial reporting for a not-for-profit governmental organization.

b. Complete end-of-fiscal-period work for a not-for-profit governmental organization.

CAREERS IN ACCOUNTING

The CAREERS feature box, AUDITOR, COUNTY OR CITY, comes from the Dictionary of Occupational Titles (DOT). The entry number for this job title is D.O.T. 160.167-030. Bring this dictionary to class and explain its purpose and how to use it. The career feature is designed to expose students to the exploration of different careers in accounting. The feature gives a realistic description of actual job duties. This feature can be used to demonstrate that the skills learned in this course are relevant.

FOCUS

Preparing a work sheet for a governmental organization was presented earlier in this chapter. In this lesson, using information from the work sheet to prepare financial statements for a governmental organization will be described.

TEACH

Cover student pages 639–643 "Preparing Financial Statements for a Governmental Organization." Explain that financial statements are prepared for each governmental fund. Present the statement of revenues, expenditures, and changes in fund balance—budget and actual—and discuss how it is different from the income statement of a corporation. Describe the three sections and the three amount columns of the statement. Emphasize that information for the statement is obtained from the annual operating budget, the work sheet, and the prior year's balance sheet. Review the steps to complete the statement of revenues, expenditures, and changes in fund balance—budget and actual. Discuss how variances are calculated and which are favorable and unfavorable. Present the governmental fund balance sheet and discuss how it is different from the balance sheet of a corporation. Emphasize that total assets must equal total liabilities and fund equity.

CAREERS IN ACCOUNTING

AUDITOR, COUNTY OR CITY

- *Directs activities of workers recording deeds*
- *Directs activities of workers keeping records of accounts*
- *Directs activities of workers compiling and transmitting fiscal records to state officials*
- *Directs activities of workers preparing financial statements for publication in local newspapers*
- *Directs activities of workers auditing books of city or county offices and departments*

of revenues, expenditures, and changes in fund balance—budget and actual. (2) Balance sheet. In the preparation of financial statements, accounting concepts are applied the same way from one fiscal period to the next. *(CONCEPT: Consistent Reporting)*

Statement of Revenues, Expenditures, and Changes in Fund Balance—Budget and Actual

A statement of revenues, expenditures, and changes in fund balance—budget and actual reports the amount of revenues earned and expenditures made for a fiscal period. The changes in the unreserved fund balance from the beginning to the end of the fiscal period are also reported. *(CONCEPT: Accounting Period Cycle)* In addition, actual revenues, expenditures, and unreserved fund balance are compared with budgeted amounts for a fiscal period. *(CONCEPT: Accounting Period Cycle)*

Sparta's general fund statement of revenues, expenditures, and changes in fund balance—budget and actual for the fiscal year ended December 31 is shown in Illustration 24-2.

This statement has three sections: (1) revenues, (2) expenditures, and (3) changes in unreserved fund balance. This statement has three amount columns: (1) Budget, (2) Actual, and (3) Variance—Favorable (Unfavorable).

Information used to prepare the Budget column is obtained from the annual operating budget shown in Chapter 23, Illustration 23-3. Information needed to prepare the Actual column is obtained

ILLUSTRATION 24-2 Statement of revenues, expenditures, and changes in fund balance—budget and actual

Town of Sparta General Fund
Statement of Revenues, Expenditures, and Changes in Fund Balance—Budget and Actual
For Year Ended December 31, 19--

	Budget	Actual	Variance—Favorable (Unfavorable)
Revenues:			
Property Tax Revenue	$1,594,000.00	$1,594,000.00	—
Interest Revenue	10,000.00	10,837.00	$ 837.00
Other Revenue	2,500.00	2,625.00	125.00
Total Revenues	$1,606,500.00	$1,607,462.00	$ 962.00
Expenditures:			
General Government	$ 405,050.00	$ 403,495.00	$ 1,555.00
Public Safety	852,650.00	850,425.00	2,225.00
Public Works	218,000.00	217,355.00	645.00
Recreation	97,100.00	96,715.00	385.00
Total Expenditures	$1,572,800.00	$1,567,990.00	$ 4,810.00
Excess of Revenues Over Expenditures	$ 33,700.00	$ 39,472.00	$ 5,772.00
Less Outstanding Encumbrances, Dec. 31, 19--	—	1,640.00	(1,640.00)
Increase in Unreserved Fund Balance for Year	$ 33,700.00	$ 37,832.00	$ 4,132.00
Unreserved Fund Balance, Jan. 1, 19--	11,705.00	11,705.00	—
Unreserved Fund Balance, Dec. 31, 19--	$ 45,405.00	$ 49,537.00	$ 4,132.00

TEACHING STRATEGIES: TEACHING TIP

Instruct students to compare the differences and similarities between the statement of revenues, expenditures, and changes in fund balance—budget and actual in this chapter, Illustration 24-2, and the income statement for a corporation in Chapter 14, Illustration 14-2. List the differences and similarities on the chalkboard as students identify them. Instruct students to make a similar comparison of the balance sheet in this chapter, Illustration 24-3, and the balance sheet for a corporation in Chapter 14, Illustration 14-5. List the differences and similarities on the chalkboard as students identify them.

FYI

Not-for-profit organizations receive annual revenues of over $750 billion.

from the work sheet's Revenues/Expenditures columns shown in Illustration 24-1. The beginning fund balance that is used in both the Budget and Actual columns is obtained from the prior year's balance sheet.

The following steps are used to prepare a statement of revenues, expenditures, and changes in fund balance—budget and actual.

1. List revenues by source. Sparta has three sources of revenues: property taxes, interest, and other. The total of all three sources of revenues is also shown.
2. List expenditures as totals for each department. Departments are responsible for controlling expenditures through budgeting and appropriations of specific amounts for each department. Thus, to aid the control process, amounts actually spent are reported for each responsible department. The total expenditures for the whole fund are also shown on the statement.
3. Calculate the excess of revenues over expenditures.

   If expenditures exceed revenues, the difference is labeled "excess of expenditures over revenues."
4. Calculate the changes in the unreserved fund balance.
   - Record any outstanding encumbrances for the current year. Outstanding encumbrances are not deducted in figuring excess of revenues over expenditures. However, funds will be required in the future when the goods for which the encumbrances were made are delivered. Therefore, current year's encumbrances should be reported as a reduction in the current year's excess of revenues rather than in the next year when goods are paid for. Because no amount is budgeted for the encumbrances, the amount shown in the budget column is zero.
   - Deduct outstanding encumbrances from excess of revenues over expenditures to determine the change in the unreserved fund balance for the year. The remaining excess of revenues over expenditures is an increase in the unreserved fund balance for the current year.
   - Record the beginning unreserved fund balance. This January 1 balance is obtained from the prior year's balance sheet.
   - Calculate the ending unreserved fund balance. The increase in the unreserved fund balance for the year plus the beginning unreserved fund balance equals the ending unreserved fund balance.

FYI

Parentheses are placed around unfavorable variances to show negative results.

Each amount recorded in the Variance column is the difference between the budget and actual amounts for the item. For example, the variance for other revenue is $125.00 (actual, $2,625.00, *less* budget, $2,500.00). Variances are considered favorable if actual results are better than the amount budgeted for that item. When

APPLY

Refer students to Illustration 24-2 as the statement of revenues, expenditures, and changes in fund balance—budget and actual is discussed. Refer students to Illustration 24-3 as the balance sheet for a governmental organization is explained.

Guided Practice

Guide students through the preparation of the Revenues section of the statement of revenues, expenditures, and changes in fund balance—budget and actual in Problem 24-2. Students will need the work sheet completed in Problem 24-1. Working as a group, determine the budget and actual amounts to be recorded for Property Tax Revenue. When all students agree on the amounts, direct them to record the amounts on the form provided in the working papers. Continue to work as a group to determine the variance. When all students agree, direct them to record the amount on the form in the working papers. Repeat the process until the Revenues section has been completed. The balance of Problem 24-2 can be completed as Independent Practice.

Independent Practice

Assign Questions 9–20 and Problems 24-2 and 24-3.

TEACHING STRATEGIES: DIFFERENT LEARNING ABILITIES

Visually-Impaired Students. New technologies are continually being developed that assist visually-impaired students to participate fully in both school and business. Students must be aware of these technologies and know how to continually learn of new technologies. Using government agencies as a resource, assist the students in preparing a report concerning anticipated technologies.

ASSESS

Assess student understanding by checking the solutions to the Independent Practice activities.

Reteach

- Make transparencies of the statement paper for a statement of revenues, expenditures, and changes in fund balance and a balance sheet from the accounting forms masters provided in the Blackline Masters Section of the Teacher's Resource Guide. Use information from Recycling Problem 24-R and the transparencies to demonstrate how to prepare a statement of revenues, expenditures, and changes in fund balance and a balance sheet for a governmental organization. The solution to Recycling Problem 24-R is provided in the Audit Tests and Solutions to Recycling Problems Section of the Teacher's Resource Guide.
- Assign Recycling Problem 24-R, Instructions 4 and 5.

Extend

Assign Cases for Critical Thinking 1.

actual revenues are more than budgeted revenues, variances are favorable. When actual revenues are less than budgeted revenues, variances are unfavorable. When actual expenditures are less than budgeted expenditures, variances are favorable. When actual expenditures are more than budgeted expenditures, variances are unfavorable. A reserve for encumbrances variance has the same effect as an expenditure variance. Because encumbrances are not budgeted, any variance will be unfavorable since an actual encumbrance will cause an increase. Unfavorable variances are indicated by placing the amounts in parentheses.

Balance Sheet

A governmental fund balance sheet reports information about assets, liabilities, and fund equity for a specific date, usually the last day of a fiscal period. *(CONCEPT: Adequate Disclosure)*

FYI

The difference between assets and liabilities is reported as fund equity on a balance sheet.

Assets and liabilities reported on a governmental fund balance sheet have similar characteristics to those reported on a corporation's balance sheet. However, a governmental fund does not have specific owners. Therefore, a governmental fund has no owners' equity section. Instead, the difference between assets and liabilities is reported as fund equity. Thus, unless restricted, fund equity represents the amount that is available for expenditures or encumbrances.

Sparta's general fund balance sheet for December 31 is shown in Illustration 24-3.

On December 31, Sparta's fund equity, consisting of three fund equity account balances, is $53,997.00. The unreserved fund bal-

ILLUSTRATION 24-3 Balance sheet for a governmental organization

Town of Sparta General Fund
Balance Sheet
December 31, 19--

ASSETS		
Cash		$78,360.00
Taxes Receivable—Delinquent	$15,640.00	
Less Allowance for Uncollectible Taxes—Delinquent	8,750.00	6,890.00
Interest Receivable	$ 2,565.00	
Less Allowance for Uncollectible Interest	513.00	2,052.00
Inventory of Supplies		2,820.00
Total Assets		$90,122.00
LIABILITIES AND FUND EQUITY		
Liabilities:		
Accounts Payable		$36,125.00
Fund Equity:		
Unreserved Fund Balance	$49,537.00	
Reserve for Encumbrances—Prior Year	1,640.00	
Reserve for Inventory of Supplies	2,820.00	
Total Fund Equity		53,997.00
Total Liabilities and Fund Equity		$90,122.00

APPLIED SKILLS: WORD PROCESSING

If you wish to integrate word processing into your accounting course, you may direct students to answer the end-of-chapter Questions for Individual Study and Cases for Critical Thinking using their word processing software.

Reserve for Encumbrances—Prior Year			
Current Year	1,640.00	Bal. (New Bal. zero)	1,640.00

Cash			
		Current Year	1,640.00

ance, *$49,537.00,* represents equity in the fund that has no restrictions (Total fund equity, $53,997.00, *less* Reserve for Encumbrances—Prior Year, $1,640.00, and *less* Reserve for Inventory of Supplies, $2,820.00). With proper authorization, Sparta may appropriate this amount for expenditures.

Two of the fund equity account balances are reserved for specific purposes. The Reserve for Encumbrances—Prior Year, *$1,640.00,* is an amount of equity set aside for an encumbrance outstanding on December 31 of the prior year. This encumbrance will be paid for when the order arrives in the current year. When goods arrive and are paid for in the current year for an order that was encumbered in a prior year, Reserve for Encumbrances—Prior Year is debited rather than Expenditures.

Payment of the prior year's order closes the reserve for encumbrances account. The entry also avoids recording an expenditure in the current year for goods ordered in a prior year.

The reserve for inventory of supplies, *$2,820.00,* represents the equity in inventory of supplies. Although supplies are assets, they are available for use, not spending. Therefore, part of the fund equity is reserved for the amount of supplies on hand. This reserve avoids appropriating the amount of equity that is represented by the asset supplies.

On a governmental fund balance sheet, total assets must equal total liabilities and fund equity. Sparta's balance sheet has total assets of $90,122.00. The total liabilities and fund equity is the same amount. The balance sheet is in balance and assumed to be correct.

Audit Your Understanding

1. What are the three sections of a statement of revenues, expenditures, and changes in fund balance—budget and actual?
2. From where is the information obtained to prepare the Actual column of the statement of revenues, expenditures, and changes in fund balance—budget and actual?
3. When actual expenditures are less than budgeted expenditures, is the variance favorable or unfavorable?
4. What must total assets equal on a governmental fund balance sheet?

RECORDING ADJUSTING AND CLOSING ENTRIES FOR A GOVERNMENTAL ORGANIZATION

Adjusting and closing entries are journalized and posted to the general ledger accounts for governmental funds as they are for businesses.

Adjusting Entries

Sparta's adjusting entries recorded on December 31 are shown in Illustration 24-4 on page 644.

Information needed for Sparta's adjusting entries is obtained from the work sheet's Adjustments columns, Illustration 24-1.

Closing Entries

Sparta's closing entries, recorded on December 31, are shown in Illustration 24-5 on page 644.

FYI

All revenue, expenditure, and budgetary accounts are closed at the end of a fiscal period.

CLOSURE

Use Audit Your Understanding questions.

AUDIT YOUR UNDERSTANDING

1. (1) Revenues. (2) Expenditures. (3) Changes in unreserved fund balance.
2. The work sheet.
3. Favorable.
4. Total assets must equal total liabilities and fund equity.

LESSON PLAN 24-3

Materials

- Student pages 643–646
- Blackline Master for Multi-Column Journal (TRG)
- Software: Spreadsheet Template
- Assess: Problem Test Chapter 24, MicroExam Chapter 24, Objective Test No. 8

Objectives (Enabling Performance Tasks)

a. Identify accounting concepts and practices related to financial reporting for a not-for-profit governmental organization.

b. Complete end-of-fiscal-period work for a not-for-profit governmental organization.

FOCUS

The preparation of financial statements for a governmental organization was presented earlier in this chapter. In this lesson, journalizing adjusting and closing entries and preparing a post-closing trial balance for a governmental organization will be described.

TEACH

Cover student pages 643–646 "Recording Adjusting and Closing Entries for a Governmental Organization" and "Preparing a Post-Closing Trial Balance for a Governmental Organization." Review the adjusting entries recorded by a governmental organization. Explain the four entries used to close the temporary and budgetary accounts of a governmental organization. Emphasize that the entry to close the budgetary accounts is the opposite of the original entry to record the operating budget. Discuss the post-closing trial balance prepared by a governmental organization.

TEACHING STRATEGIES: APPLYING VISUALS

Direct students to Illustration 24-5 to review closing entries for a governmental organization.

APPLY

Refer students to Illustration 24-5 as the closing entries for a governmental organization are discussed.

Guided Practice

Guide students through the T account analysis of the closing entries in Problem 24-4. Students will need the work sheet prepared in Problem 24-1. Have students draw T accounts on a sheet of paper and analyze the first closing entry. All students should agree with the analysis before proceeding to the second closing entry. Repeat the process until all four closing entries have been analyzed. The balance of Problem 24-4 can be completed as Independent Practice.

Independent Practice

- Assign Problem 24-4.
- Assign Study Guide 24 and Mastery Problem 24-M.

ILLUSTRATION 24-4 Adjusting entries for a governmental organization

JOURNAL — PAGE 48

	DATE		ACCOUNT TITLE	DOC. NO.	POST. REF.	GENERAL 1 DEBIT	GENERAL 2 CREDIT	CASH 3 DEBIT	CASH 4 CREDIT	
1			*Adjusting Entries*							1
2	19-- Dec.	31	*Inventory of Supplies*			2,820.00				2
3			*Reserve for Inventory of Supplies*				2,820.00			3
4		31	*Interest Receivable*			2,565.00				4
5			*Allowance for Uncollectible Interest*				513.00			5
6			*Interest Revenue*				2,052.00			6
7		31	*Reserve for Encumbrances—Current Year*			1,640.00				7
8			*Reserve for Encumbrances—Prior Year*				1,640.00			8

ILLUSTRATION 24-5 Closing entries for a governmental organization

JOURNAL — PAGE 48

	DATE		ACCOUNT TITLE	DOC. NO.	POST. REF.	GENERAL 1 DEBIT	GENERAL 2 CREDIT	CASH 3 DEBIT	CASH 4 CREDIT	
9			*Closing Entries*							9
10		31	*Property Tax Revenue*			1,594,000.00				10
11			*Interest Revenue*			10,837.00				11
12			*Other Revenue*			2,625.00				12
13			*Unreserved Fund Balance*				1,607,462.00			13
14		31	*Unreserved Fund Balance*			1,567,990.00				14
15			*Expenditure—Personnel, General Government*				263,175.00			15
16			*Expenditure—Supplies, General Government*				11,940.00			16
17			*Expenditure—Other Charges, General Government*				112,380.00			17
18			*Expenditure—Capital Outlays, General Government*				16,000.00			18
19			*Expenditure—Personnel, Public Safety*				588,650.00			19
20			*Expenditure—Supplies, Public Safety*				19,790.00			20
21			*Expenditure—Other Charges, Public Safety*				152,635.00			21
22			*Expenditure—Capital Outlays, Public Safety*				89,350.00			22
23			*Expenditure—Personnel, Public Works*				113,300.00			23
24			*Expenditure—Supplies, Public Works*				5,540.00			24
25			*Expenditure—Other Charges, Public Works*				47,340.00			25
26			*Expenditure—Capital Outlays, Public Works*				51,175.00			26
27			*Expenditure—Personnel, Recreation*				58,110.00			27
28			*Expenditure—Supplies, Recreation*				1,960.00			28
29			*Expenditure—Other Charges, Recreation*				25,105.00			29
30			*Expenditure—Capital Outlays, Recreation*				11,540.00			30
31		31	*Appropriations*			1,572,800.00				31
32			*Budgetary Fund Balance*			33,700.00				32
33			*Estimated Revenues*				1,606,500.00			33
34		31	*Unreserved Fund Balance*			1,640.00				34
35			*Encumbrance—Supplies, Public Safety*				1,640.00			35
36										36

TEACHING STRATEGIES: COOPERATIVE LEARNING

Divide the class into groups of four or five students each. Using Cases for Critical Thinking, each group analyzes the cases and arrives at agreed-upon solutions. One member of each group is appointed the recorder and presents the group's analysis to the class. This cooperative learning activity should not take more than 20 to 25 minutes of class time.

Information needed for Sparta's closing entries is obtained from the work sheet's Revenues/Expenditures columns. Sparta records four entries to close the temporary and budgetary accounts.

1. Close all revenue accounts to the unreserved fund balance account as shown on lines 10 through 13 of the journal, Illustration 24-5.
2. Close all expenditure accounts to the unreserved fund balance account as shown on lines 14 through 30 of the journal.
3. Close the budgetary accounts. At the beginning of the fiscal year, estimated revenues and appropriations were recorded based on the approved operating budget. This entry provides control by permitting comparisons of estimated versus actual revenue and appropriations versus expenditures. At the end of the fiscal year, these budgetary accounts are no longer needed. Thus they are closed as shown on lines 31 through 33 of the journal. This entry is the opposite of the original entry to record the operating budget.
4. Close the outstanding encumbrance accounts to the unreserved fund balance account as shown on lines 34 and 35 of the

FYI

A major difference between for-profit and not-for-profit organizations is that only the for-profit organizations pay taxes on income.

■ Ruth Smith ■

AMERICAN INDIAN HERITAGE CENTER OF TEXAS

Ruth Smith, an American Indian of Cherokee heritage, started the nonprofit American Indian Heritage Center of Texas. The center is dedicated to the preservation of American Indian heritage in Texas.

Smith started the center with a small amount of her own personal savings. She continues to finance the center through memberships, her own earnings, and Sequoyah House, a retail store associated with the center. Smith assumed that a worthy cause like the preservation of Native American heritage would receive instant community support. However, contributions and grants are hard to get because most people assume that the not-for-profit agency is funded by the federal government. However, that is not the case. The center has never received any federal funds.

When she started the Heritage Center, Smith used all of her start-up money to rent an office and obtain phone service. The first week the center was open she had only a phone in her office. Smith said, "I had to sit on the floor, and I had no desk. It wasn't until a while later that someone donated a desk and chair for me to use. Until then, I conducted all business sitting on the floor with my back up against the wall for support."

Although Smith majored in English in college, she saw the value of accounting as a background for one day owning her own business so she took a course in it. She believes that accounting and other business courses can help prepare you for handling business matters as well as your personal affairs. Her own accounting background helps her prepare budgets and proposals for donations from corporations. It also helps her run the retail store and account for its finances within the Heritage Center. She was able to save some money because she could keep all the records herself without hiring additional services.

Smith states that you have to be "tenacious and persistent" to succeed in business. "Believe in yourself and what you are doing and take as many business courses as you can," Smith advises. She also thinks it is important to get to know someone who is successful and learn from them.

Personal Visions in Business

APPLIED SKILLS: BUILDING STUDY SKILLS

Direct students to prepare a Quick Reference Guide (QRG) for recording the four closing entries recorded by a governmental organization. Students should use this QRG as a reference as they complete the end-of-chapter problems.

ASSESS

Assess student understanding by checking the solutions to the Independent Practice activities.

Reteach

- Make a transparency of the multi-column journal from the accounting forms masters provided in the Blackline Masters Section of the Teacher's Resource Guide. Students will need the work sheet completed in Recycling Problem 24-R, Instruction 3. Ask students to use T accounts to analyze the adjusting and closing entries. Use the transparency to demonstrate how to journalize the adjusting and closing entries for a governmental organization. The solution to Recycling Problem 24-R is provided in the Audit Tests and Solutions to Recycling Problems Section of the Teacher's Resource Guide.
- Assign Recycling Problem 24-R, Instruction 6.

Extend

- Assign Cases for Critical Thinking 2.
- Assign Challenge Problem 24-C. (The challenge is to work with actual amounts that exceed budgeted amounts.)
- Assign the Spreadsheet Template for Mastery Problem 24-M.

Extend

Assign the PERSONAL VISIONS IN BUSINESS feature on page 645.

Personal Visions in Business

This special student feature introduces students to successful entrepreneurs or business professionals. Each profile gives a flavor of what the actual business world is like and some of the opportunities available to students who study accounting. These features can be used to motivate students to pursue professional business careers in a wide variety of fields. The subjects of these profiles have been carefully chosen to represent the full spectrum of diverse ethnic and racial backgrounds of professional business people. As an optional activity, students can be encouraged to seek out and interview successful business people in their own communities.

AUDIT YOUR UNDERSTANDING

1. Unreserved Fund Balance.
2. Appropriations and Budgetary Fund Balance are debited; Estimated Revenues is credited.
3. Reserve for Encumbrances—Prior Year; Taxes Receivable—Delinquent; Unreserved Fund Balance.

CLOSURE

Use Audit Your Understanding questions.

ASSESS

- Administer Problem Test Chapter 24.
- Administer a MicroExam test for Chapter 24.
- Administer Objective Test No. 8.

Audit Your Understanding

1. Into what account are revenue and expenditure accounts closed?
2. What accounts are debited and credited to close the budgetary accounts?
3. Which of the following accounts will appear on a post-closing trial balance: Appropriations, Reserve for Encumbrances—Prior Year, Property Tax Revenue, Taxes Receivable—Delinquent, Budgetary Fund Balance, Unreserved Fund Balance?

journal. This entry reduces the unreserved fund balance account by the amount of the outstanding encumbrance for supplies, public safety, *$1,640.00.*

The balance of Reserve for Encumbrances—Prior Year, *$1,640.00,* has been a budgetary account balance. Thus, the account balance is listed in the work sheet's Revenues/Expenditures Credit column. However, after the outstanding encumbrance account is closed to Unreserved Fund Balance, Reserve for Encumbrances—Prior Year is considered a fund equity account. The account, therefore, is not closed even though it has an amount in the work sheet's Revenues/Expenditures Credit column. This account balance now is the amount of total fund equity that is reserved for outstanding encumbrances.

After closing journal entries are posted, all temporary accounts have zero balances and are prepared for a new fiscal period. The difference between revenues and expenditures has been transferred to the unreserved fund balance account. Fund equity amounts that are not available for appropriations are recorded in reserve accounts.

PREPARING A POST-CLOSING TRIAL BALANCE FOR A GOVERNMENTAL ORGANIZATION

After all end-of-fiscal-period activities are complete, a post-closing trial balance is prepared to prove the equality of debits and credits in the account balances. Sparta's post-closing trial balance is shown in Illustration 24-6.

Debits and credits on Sparta's post-closing trial balance both equal $99,385.00. Because the debit and credit balance totals equal, the general ledger accounts are ready for the new fiscal period. *(CONCEPT: Accounting Period Cycle)*

ILLUSTRATION 24-6 Post-closing trial balance for a governmental organization

Town of Sparta General Fund
Post-Closing Trial Balance
December 31, 19--

Account	Debit	Credit
Cash	$78,360.00	
Taxes Receivable—Delinquent	15,640.00	
Allowance for Uncollectible Taxes—Delinquent		$ 8,750.00
Interest Receivable	2,565.00	
Allowance for Uncollectible Interest		513.00
Inventory of Supplies	2,820.00	
Accounts Payable		36,125.00
Reserve for Encumbrances—Prior Year		1,640.00
Reserve for Inventory of Supplies		2,820.00
Unreserved Fund Balance		49,537.00
Totals	$99,385.00	$99,385.00

APPLIED SKILLS: WRITING ACROSS THE CURRICULUM

Writing paragraphs and short essays. The Cases for Critical Thinking are short, practical applications of the accounting principles developed in the chapter. Some cases are planned to present problems related to the chapter but not specifically discussed and answered in the chapter. These cases present an opportunity for critical thinking and decision making. These cases also require more than a short objective-type response. Therefore, they provide ideal practice in writing paragraphs and short essays.

QUESTIONS FOR INDIVIDUAL STUDY EPT(a)

1. How is a not-for-profit organization's performance measured?
2. For what purposes are financial statements prepared for a not-for-profit organization?
3. For what three accounts does Sparta make adjustments on its work sheet before financial statements are prepared?
4. What is the purpose of an adjustment for Inventory of Supplies?
5. What two accounts are affected, and how, when an inventory of supplies adjustment is recorded for a governmental organization?
6. What is the purpose of an adjustment for Reserve for Encumbrances—Current Year?
7. What accounts are affected, and how, when an adjustment for Reserve for Encumbrances—Current Year is recorded?
8. What are the temporary accounts of a governmental organization?
9. Which accounting concept is being applied when financial statements are prepared for each governmental fund?
10. What two financial statements does Sparta prepare for its general fund?
11. Which accounting concept is being applied when financial statements are prepared the same way from one fiscal period to the next?
12. What does a statement of revenues, expenditures, and changes in fund balance—budget and actual report?
13. What are the three sections of a statement of revenues, expenditures, and changes in fund balance—budget and actual?
14. From where is the information obtained to prepare a statement of revenues, expenditures, and changes in fund balance—budget and actual?
15. What steps are followed in preparing a statement of revenues, expenditures, and changes in fund balance—budget and actual?
16. What does the amount in the Variance column of the statement of revenues, expenditures, and changes in fund balance—budget and actual represent?
17. What are favorable variances on a statement of revenues, expenditures and changes in fund balance—budget and actual?
18. What does a governmental fund balance sheet report?
19. How is the difference between assets and liabilities reported on a governmental fund balance sheet?
20. What does fund equity on a governmental fund balance sheet represent?

CASES FOR CRITICAL THINKING EPT(a)

CASE 1 The town of Spearman's statement of revenue, expenditures, and changes in fund balance—budget and actual lists expenditures by type. Expenditures listed are personnel, supplies, other charges, and capital outlays. Charles Lambert, a new accountant, suggested that expenditures be reported on this statement by departmental organization. Do you agree with Mr. Lambert? Explain your response.

CASE 2 Vicki Bonilla, a new accounting clerk for the town of Evergreen, recorded the closing entries for the current year. Miss Bonilla questions the necessity of making a closing entry for encumbrance accounts with balances. She suggests not closing the encumbrances. Then when items are received for which the encumbrances were recorded, make the regular journal entries. That is, (1) reverse the encumbrance entry and (2) debit **Expenditures** and credit **Cash.** Do you agree with Miss Bonilla? Explain your response.

APPLICATION PROBLEMS EPT(b)

PROBLEM 24-1 Preparing a work sheet for a governmental organization

The town of Windsor uses a general fund. The trial balance for December 31 of the current year is recorded on a work sheet in the working papers accompanying this textbook.

ACCOUNTING TERMS

No new terms are defined in Chapter 24.

QUESTIONS FOR INDIVIDUAL STUDY

1. Primarily by the services provided and the efficiency with which resources are used. (pp. 634–635)
2. (a) To make decisions about the use of resources. (b) To assess services provided and the ability to provide those services. (c) To assess management's financial accountability and performance. (d) To determine the assets, liabilities, and fund equity of the organization. (p. 635)
3. (a) Inventory of Supplies, (b) Interest Revenue, and (c) Reserve for Encumbrances—Current Year. (p. 635)
4. When supplies are bought, an expenditure account is debited. Some supplies may be unused at the end of a fiscal period. These unused supplies should be reported as an asset. (pp. 635–636)
5. Inventory of Supplies is debited; Reserve for Inventory of Supplies is credited. (p. 637)
6. At the end of a fiscal year, a governmental organization may have outstanding encumbrances—orders that have not been delivered. When goods are delivered that were encumbered against the preceding year's appropriations, the amount should not be recorded as an expenditure of the current period. Therefore, at the end of a fiscal period, the balance of Reserve for Encumbrances—Current Year, the amount of encumbrances outstanding, should be reclassified to prior year status. Then, when prior year's orders arrive, they can be debited to Reserve for Encumbrances—Prior Year, rather than current year's expenditures. This procedure prevents charging expenditures of one year to another year's appropriations. (pp. 637–638)
7. Reserve for Encumbrances—Current Year is debited; Reserve for Encumbrances—Prior Year is credited. (p. 638)
8. Temporary accounts include all revenue, expenditure, and budgetary accounts. (p. 638)
9. Adequate Disclosure concept. (p. 639)

CHECK FIGURES

See Teacher's Edition of Working Papers for complete solutions.

Problem 24-1 Column totals: Trial Balance, $3,035,490.00; Adjustments, $8,674.00; Revenues/Expenditures, $2,954,286.00; Balance Sheet, $98,264.00. Excess of Revenue Over Expenditures, $10,626.00.

INSTRUCTIONS:

1. Analyze the following adjustment information and record the adjustments on the work sheet.

Adjustment Information, December 31

Supplies inventory	$3,534.00
Interest revenue due but not collected	2,900.00

An estimated 20% of the interest revenue due will not be collected.
The reserve for encumbrances for the current year is reclassified to prior year status.

2. Complete the work sheet.

The work sheet prepared in this problem is needed to complete Problems 24-2, 24-3, and 24-4.

PROBLEM 24-2 Preparing a statement of revenues, expenditures, and changes in fund balance—budget and actual for a governmental organization

The work sheet prepared in Problem 24-1 is needed to complete this problem.

The town of Windsor's general fund operating budget for the current fiscal year is as follows.

Town of Windsor
Annual Operating Budget—General Fund
For Year Ended December 31, 19--

ESTIMATED REVENUES		
Property Tax	$1,459,000.00	
Interest	8,950.00	
Other	9,000.00	
Total Estimated Revenues		$1,476,950.00
ESTIMATED EXPENDITURES AND BUDGETARY FUND BALANCE		
General Government:		
Personnel	$ 250,250.00	
Supplies	13,230.00	
Other Charges	124,740.00	
Capital Outlays	14,600.00	
Total General Government		$ 402,820.00
Public Safety:		
Personnel	$ 414,740.00	
Supplies	22,000.00	
Other Charges	168,460.00	
Capital Outlays	81,270.00	
Total Public Safety		686,470.00
Public Works:		
Personnel	$ 157,730.00	
Supplies	6,160.00	
Other Charges	52,250.00	
Capital Outlays	46,350.00	
Total Public Works		262,490.00
Recreation:		
Personnel	$ 55,350.00	
Supplies	22,170.00	
Other Charges	27,780.00	
Capital Outlays	10,460.00	
Total Recreation		115,760.00
Total Estimated Expenditures		$1,467,540.00
Budgetary Fund Balance		9,410.00
Total Estimated Expenditures and Budgetary Fund Balance		$1,476,950.00

QUESTIONS *(cont'd)*

10. (a) Statement of revenues, expenditures, and changes in fund balance—budget and actual. (b) Balance sheet. (pp. 639–640)

11. Consistent Reporting concept. (p. 640)

12. The amount of revenues earned and expenditures made for a fiscal period are reported. The changes in the unreserved fund balance from the beginning to the end of the fiscal period are also reported. In addition, actual revenues, expenditures, and unreserved fund balance are compared with budgeted amounts for a fiscal period. (p. 640)

13. (a) Revenues, (b) expenditures, and (c) changes in unreserved fund balance. (p. 640)

14. Information used to prepare the Budget column is obtained from the annual operating budget. Information needed to prepare the Actual column is obtained from the work sheet's Revenues/Expenditures columns. The beginning fund balance that is used in both the Budget and Actual columns is obtained from the prior year's balance sheet. (pp. 640–641)

15. (a) List revenues by source. (b) List expenditures as totals for each department. (c) Calculate the excess of revenues over expenditures. (d) Calculate the changes in the unreserved fund balance. (p. 641)

16. The difference between the budget and actual amounts for the item. (p. 641)

17. When actual revenues are more than budgeted revenues, variances are favorable. When actual expenditures are less than budgeted expenditures, variances are favorable. (pp. 641–642)

18. Information about assets, liabilities, and fund equity for a specific date, usually the last day of a fiscal period. (p. 642)

19. As fund equity. (p. 642)

20. Unless restricted, fund equity represents the amount that is available for expenditures or encumbrances. (p. 642)

CHECK FIGURES *(cont'd)*

Problem 24-2 Increase in Unreserved Fund Balance for the Year: Budget, $9,410.00; Actual, $8,386.00; Variance, $1,024.00, Unfavorable.

INSTRUCTIONS:

Prepare a statement of revenues, expenditures, and changes in fund balance—budget and actual for the year ended December 31 of the current year. The unreserved fund balance on January 1 was $41,244.00.

The statement of revenues, expenditures, and changes in fund balance—budget and actual prepared in this problem is needed to complete Problem 24-3.

PROBLEM 24-3 Preparing a balance sheet for a governmental organization

The work sheet and statement of revenues, expenditures, and changes in fund balance—budget and actual prepared in Problems 24-1 and 24-2 are needed to complete this problem.

INSTRUCTIONS:

Prepare a balance sheet for December 31 of the current year.

PROBLEM 24-4 Journalizing adjusting and closing entries for a governmental organization

The work sheet prepared in Problem 24-1 is needed to complete this problem.

INSTRUCTIONS:

1. Use page 48 of a journal. Journalize the adjusting entries.
2. Continue using page 48 of the journal. Journalize the closing entries.

ENRICHMENT PROBLEMS

EPT(b)

MASTERY PROBLEM 24-M Completing end-of-fiscal-period work for a governmental organization

SPREADSHEET

The town of Durham uses a general fund. The trial balance for December 31 of the current year is recorded on a work sheet in the working papers accompanying this textbook.

INSTRUCTIONS:

1. Analyze the following adjustment information and record the adjustments on the work sheet.

Adjustment Information, December 31

Supplies inventory	$2,900.00
Interest revenue due but not collected	2,350.00

An estimated 20% of the interest revenue due will not be collected.
The reserve for encumbrances for the current year is reclassified to prior year status.

2. Complete the work sheet.

   Durham's general fund operating budget for the current fiscal year is shown on page 650.

3. Prepare a statement of revenues, expenditures, and changes in fund balance—budget and actual for the year ended December 31 of the current year. The unreserved fund balance on January 1 was $35,550.00.
4. Prepare a balance sheet for December 31 of the current year.
5. Use page 42 of a journal. Journalize the adjusting entries. Continue using page 42 of the journal. Journalize the closing entries.

CHECK FIGURES *(cont'd)*

Problem 24-3 Total Assets, $89,724.00; Unreserved Fund Balance, $49,630.00; Total Fund Equity, $55,404.00.

Problem 24-4 10 Debit entries; 23 Credit entries.

Mastery Problem 24-M (2) Work Sheet column totals: Trial Balance, $2,633,500.00; Adjustments, $7,120.00; Revenues/Expenditures, $2,563,550.00; Balance Sheet, $119,070.00. Excess of Revenue Over Expenditures, $43,870.00. (3) Increase in Unreserved Fund Balance for the Year: Budget, $40,000.00; Actual, $42,000.00; Variance, $2,000.00, Favorable (4) Total Assets, $111,660.00; Unreserved Fund Balance, $77,550.00; Total Fund Equity, $82,320.00. (5) 10 Debit entries; 23 Credit entries.

CASES FOR CRITICAL THINKING

Case 1 Yes, agree with Mr. Lambert. Financial control is a major purpose for governmental accounting since there is no profit motive to encourage good financial management. Control is generally implemented by assigning to each departmental manager of an organization accountability for financial control of the department. This is achieved by appropriating or budgeting a specified amount for each department's operations. By reporting the budgeted and actual amounts expended by each department for an accounting period, statement readers can determine how well each department controlled its expenditures. Also, the managers know that they are accountable for operating within their budgeted amount. Thus, emphasis is placed on relating expenditures to the units accountable for those expenditures—a major part of the control process.

However, expenditures should be recorded by type of expenditure, also, to help each manager analyze the way in which funds are expended.

Case 2 No, disagree with Ms. Bonilla's suggestion. Encumbrances are recorded when a commitment is made to spend money. However, the expenditure transaction has not yet occurred. Thus the encumbrance account is a budgetary account and the reserve for encumbrances is a balancing account for encumbrances. If Encumbrances is not closed, this budgetary account balance would have to be reported on the only statement with account balances at year end—the balance sheet. A balance sheet reports only assets, liabilities, and fund equity. Commitments to spend money in the future, encumbrances should not be reported on a balance sheet.

The correct procedure was used when encumbrances were closed by debiting Unreserved Fund Balance and crediting Encumbrances. This procedure reduces the balance of Unreserved Fund Balance and causes Reserve for Encumbrances—Prior Year to become an equity account. Thus, the reserve for encumbrances account now reserves equity for the outstanding commitments made in the current period for the use of assets in a future period. Also the unreserved fund balance is now the amount available for future commitments.

Ms. Bonilla's suggested procedure would also record the expenditure for

CASES *(cont'd)*

this outstanding encumbrance in the next year. Governmental accounting requires that expenditures be recorded in the period for which they are budgeted.

Town of Durham
Annual Operating Budget—General Fund
For Year Ended December 31, 19--

ESTIMATED REVENUES		
Property Tax	$1,265,000.00	
Interest	7,250.00	
Other	7,750.00	
Total Estimated Revenues		$1,280,000.00
ESTIMATED EXPENDITURES AND BUDGETARY FUND BALANCE		
General Government:		
Personnel	$ 211,750.00	
Supplies	11,360.00	
Other Charges	106,700.00	
Capital Outlays	12,390.00	
Total General Government		$ 342,200.00
Public Safety:		
Personnel	$ 397,590.00	
Supplies	18,900.00	
Other Charges	144,290.00	
Capital Outlays	72,320.00	
Total Public Safety		633,100.00
Public Works:		
Personnel	$ 92,270.00	
Supplies	5,280.00	
Other Charges	44,770.00	
Capital Outlays	39,680.00	
Total Public Works		182,000.00
Recreation:		
Personnel	$ 48,220.00	
Supplies	1,880.00	
Other Charges	23,690.00	
Capital Outlays	8,910.00	
Total Recreation		82,700.00
Total Estimated Expenditures		$1,240,000.00
Budgetary Fund Balance		40,000.00
Total Estimated Expenditures and Budgetary Fund Balance		$1,280,000.00

CHECK FIGURES *(cont'd)*

Challenge Problem 24-C (2) Work Sheet column totals: Trial Balance, $3,104,485.00; Adjustments, $10,538.00; Revenues/Expenditures, $3,020,263.00; Balance Sheet, $115,089.00. Excess of Expenditures Over Revenues, $21,405.00. (3) Decrease in Unreserved Fund Balance for the Year: Budget, $25,320.00; Actual, $22,481.00; Variance, $2,839.00, Favorable. (4) Total Assets, $81,243.00; Unreserved Fund Balance, $40,969.00; Total Fund Equity, $45,427.00. (5) 9 Debit entries; 24 Credit entries.

CHALLENGE PROBLEM 24-C Completing end-of-fiscal-period work for a governmental organization

The town of Fairmont uses a general fund. The trial balance for December 31 of the current year is recorded on a work sheet in the working papers accompanying this textbook.

INSTRUCTIONS:

1. Analyze the following adjustment information and record the adjustments on the work sheet.

Adjustment Information, December 31

Supplies inventory	$3,382.00
Interest revenue due but not collected	6,080.00

An estimated 20% of the interest revenue due will not be collected.
The reserve for encumbrances for the current year is reclassified to prior year status.

2. Complete the work sheet.

Fairmont's general fund operating budget for the current fiscal year follows. Fairmont's town council permits departmental managers to exceed budgeted amounts for supplies, other charges, and capital outlays. However, total amounts expended for these three types of expenditure must be within the total budget amounts for these three items within each department.

Fairmont is prohibited from deficit spending. However, if sufficient funds are on hand at the beginning of a year, the town council may choose to appropriate more than the estimated revenues. Sufficient funds are on hand when the beginning fund balance plus estimated revenues equals or exceeds appropriations.

Town of Fairmont
Annual Operating Budget—General Fund
For Year Ended December 31, 19--

ESTIMATED REVENUES AND BUDGETARY FUND BALANCE		
Property Tax	$1,455,900.00	
Interest	13,360.00	
Other	16,580.00	
Total Estimated Revenues		$1,485,840.00
Budgetary Fund Balance		25,320.00
Estimated Revenues and Budgetary Fund Balance		$1,511,160.00
ESTIMATED EXPENDITURES		
General Government:		
Personnel	$ 260,480.00	
Supplies	14,280.00	
Other Charges	130,240.00	
Capital Outlays	15,130.00	
Total General Government		$ 420,130.00
Public Safety:		
Personnel	$ 484,610.00	
Supplies	23,080.00	
Other Charges	176,920.00	
Capital Outlays	84,920.00	
Total Public Safety		769,530.00
Public Works:		
Personnel	$ 113,300.00	
Supplies	6,660.00	
Other Charges	53,120.00	
Capital Outlays	48,875.00	
Total Public Works		221,955.00
Recreation:		
Personnel	$ 56,855.00	
Supplies	2,790.00	
Other Charges	28,925.00	
Capital Outlays	10,975.00	
Total Recreation		99,545.00
Total Estimated Expenditures		$1,511,160.00

3. Prepare a statement of revenues, expenditures, and changes in fund balance—budget and actual for the year ended December 31 of the current year. The unreserved fund balance on January 1 was $63,450.00.
4. Prepare a balance sheet for December 31 of the current year.
5. Use page 40 of a journal. Journalize the adjusting entries. Continue using page 40 of the journal. Journalize the closing entries.

APPENDIX A

Statement of Cash Flows

Financial statements provide managers, investors, and other individuals with financial information about the operating efficiency and financial condition of a business. The income statement, balance sheet, and statement of stockholders' equity are prepared using accounting records of a business. These financial statements report the financial activity and condition of a business using the accrual basis of accounting.

Accrual-based financial statements report useful information. Some individuals, however, may need more information about the cash flows of a business. An ample supply of cash is necessary to allow a business to purchase merchandise, pay its expenses and debts, and provide its owners with a return on their investment.

REPORTING CASH FLOWS

A financial statement which reports the cash flows of a business for a fiscal period is called a **statement of cash flows.** The statement reports the source of cash receipts and cash payments during a fiscal period. The statement of cash flows for Hamilton Corporation for the fiscal year ended December 31 is shown in Illustration A-1 on page A-2.

The statement of cash flows is divided into three sections: cash flows from operating activities, cash flows from investing activities, and cash flows from financing activities.

ILLUSTRATION A-1 Statement of cash flows

Hamilton Corporation
Statement of Cash Flows
For Year Ended December 31, 19--

Cash flows from operating activities:			
Net income after federal income tax			$222,300
Adjustments to reconcile net income to net cash provided by operating activities:			
Add:			
Depreciation	$125,000		
Decrease in accounts receivable	95,200		
Increase in federal income tax payable	8,000	$228,200	
Deduct:			
Decrease in interest payable	$ 7,800		
Decrease in accounts payable	69,000		
Increase in merchandise inventory	124,100		
Increase in other current assets	4,800		
Decrease in other current liabilities	1,100	206,800	
Total adjustments			21,400
Net cash flow provided by operating activities			$243,700
Cash flows from investing activities:			
Cash paid for purchase of equipment and buildings		297,500	
Net cash flow used in investing activities			(297,500)
Cash flows from financing activities:			
Cash received from issuance of mortgage payable	$195,000		
Cash received from sale of common stock	100,000	$295,000	
Less:			
Cash paid to retire short-term notes payable	$ 19,400		
Cash paid for dividends	120,000	139,400	
Net cash flow provided by financing activities			155,600
Increase in cash			$101,800
Cash on January 1, 19--			104,300
Cash on December 31, 19--			$206,100

Cash Flows from Operating Activities

Cash receipts and payments for revenue and expense transactions from the normal operations of a business are called **cash flows from operating activities.** The amount of cash provided by operating activities reports important information about the efficient and effective operations of a business. A sufficient amount of cash must be provided from operating activities for a business to continue in existence. Thus, the amount of cash flows from operating activities is reported first on the statement of cash flows.

Cash receipts and payments from operating activities are calculated using income statement amounts, adjusted for changes in related current asset and current liability accounts. Hamilton's comparative income statement and balance sheet are shown in Chapter 17, Illustrations 17-1 and 17-3.

Hamilton Corporation's net income after federal income tax, *$222,300,* provides the starting point for calculating the cash flows from operating activities. However, the income statement reports revenue and expense transactions using the accrual basis of accounting. Thus, certain adjustments are necessary to calculate the cash flow resulting from these transactions.

Adjustments are reported for revenue and expense transactions that do not affect cash. For example, the journal entries to record Hamilton's depreciation expense of $125,000 did not affect the cash account. Since depreciation expense does not use cash, the amount is added to net income after federal income tax to calculate the cash provided by operating activities.

Hamilton's depreciation expense is reported as part of **Other Selling Expenses** and **Other Administrative Expenses** on its comparative income statement, Illustration 17-1.

Adjustments are reported for changes in certain current asset and liability accounts. For example, the $124,100 increase in Hamilton's merchandise inventory account indicates that Hamilton's purchases exceeded cost of goods sold. Thus, the amount is subtracted from net income after federal income tax to calculate the cash provided by operating activities.

After reporting the adjustments to net income after federal income tax, Hamilton Corporation generated $243,700 of cash from operating activities.

Cash Flows from Investing Activities

Cash receipts and payments relating to the sale and purchase of assets used to earn revenue over a period of time are called **cash flows from investing activities.** The second section of the statement of cash flows reports the cash affect of these activities. Investing activities provide creditors and owners with important information about the future financial strength and profitability of a business.

Cash receipts and payments from investing activities are determined from the changes in investment and plant asset accounts reported on a comparative balance sheet. Hamilton's comparative balance sheet is shown in Illustration 17-3.

An efficient business should invest its excess cash in interest-bearing investments until the money is required for business operations. The purchase of plant assets, such as equipment and buildings, allows a business to expand and increase its profits. These activities are necessary if the business is to remain profitable.

Hamilton Corporation purchased $297,500 of equipment and buildings during the year. Hamilton plans to use these assets to increase sales and net income.

The cost of plant assets purchased, *$297,500,* is obtained from the general ledger.

Cash Flows from Financing Activities

Cash receipts and cash payments involving transactions with creditors and investors are called **cash flows from financing activities.**

Financing activities are reported in the last section of the statement of cash flows. Creditors and owners are especially interested in this section since it reports the transactions between them and the business.

Cash receipts and payments from financing activities are determined from the changes in long-term debt and stockholder equity accounts. Changes in these accounts are reported on Hamilton's comparative statement of stockholders' equity and balance sheet, Illustrations 17-2 and 17-3.

The investing activities of a business may use more cash than is provided by its operating activities. Further, owners typically expect to receive a return on their investment. To retain a positive cash balance, a business must borrow money from creditors or issue capital stock.

Hamilton Corporation used more cash in its investing activities than was provided by operating activities. Further, Hamilton retired a $19,400 short-term note payable and paid $120,000 in dividends to stockholders. Additional cash was required to retain a positive cash balance. Therefore, Hamilton issued a $195,000 mortgage payable and sold $100,000 of common stock. The net cash provided from these financing activities was $155,600.

Reconciling the Cash Balance

The sum of the operating, investing, and financing activities sections of the statement of cash flows are added to calculate the increase or decrease in cash. If all cash transactions have been accounted for, the change in cash plus the beginning cash balance should equal the ending cash balance reported on the comparative balance sheet.

Hamilton's increase in cash, *$101,800,* is added to the beginning cash balance, *$104,300,* to calculate the ending cash balance, *$206,100.* The ending cash balance equals the cash balance reported on the comparative balance sheet, Illustration 17-3. Thus, the statement of cash flows has been prepared accurately.

APPENDIX B

Using a Calculator and Computer Keypad

KINDS OF CALCULATORS

Many different models of calculators, both desktop and hand held, are available. All calculators have their own features and particular placement of operating keys. Therefore, it is necessary to refer to the operator's manual for specific instructions and locations of the operating keys for the calculator being used. A typical keyboard of a desktop calculator is shown in Illustration B-1.

ILLUSTRATION B-1 Typical desktop calculator keyboard

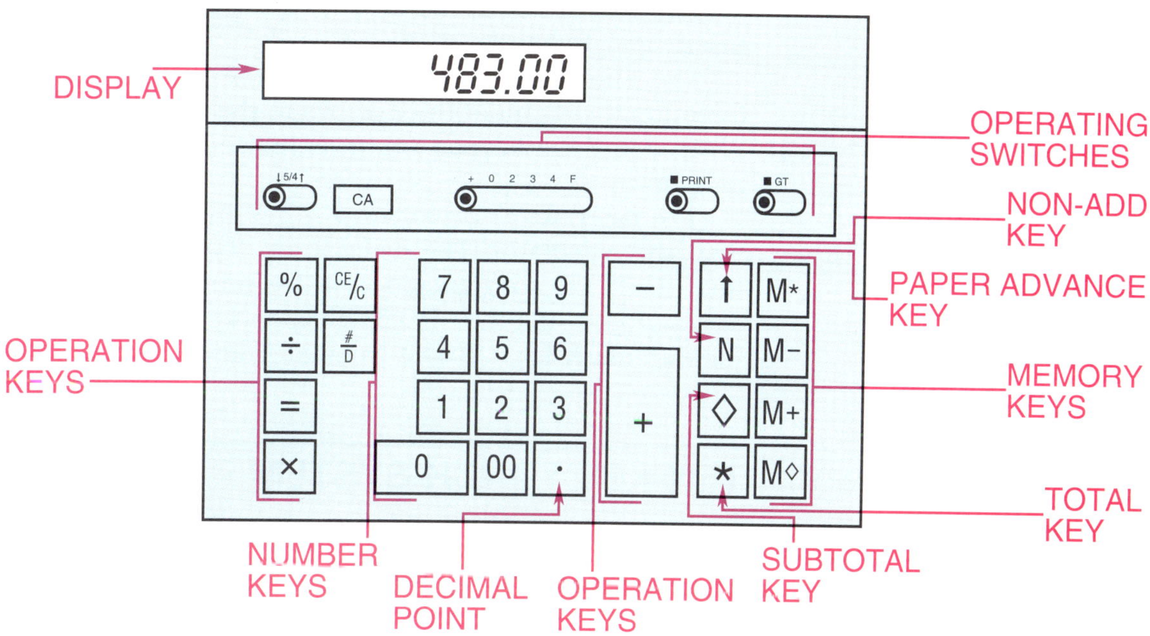

DESKTOP CALCULATOR SETTINGS

Several operating switches on a desktop calculator must be engaged before the calculator will produce the desired results.

The *decimal selector* sets the appropriate decimal places necessary for the numbers that will be entered. For example, if the decimal selector is set at 2, both the numbers entered and the answer will have two decimal places. If the decimal selector is set at F, the calculator automatically sets the decimal places. The F setting allows the answer to be unrounded and carried out to the maximum number of decimal places possible.

The *decimal rounding selector* rounds the answers. The down arrow position will drop any digits beyond the last digit desired. The up arrow position will drop any digits beyond the last digit desired and round the last digit up. In the 5/4 position, the calculator rounds the last desired digit up only when the following digit is 5 or greater. If the following digit is less than 5, the last desired digit remains unchanged.

The *GT* or *grand total switch* in the on position accumulates totals.

KINDS OF COMPUTER KEYBOARDS

The computer has a keypad on the right side of the keyboard called the **numeric keypad.** Even though several styles of keyboards for the IBM® and compatible computers are found, there are two basic layouts for the numeric keypad. The standard layout and enhanced layout are shown in Illustration B-2 on page B-3. On the standard keyboard the directional arrow keys are found on the number keys. To use the numbers, press the key called **Num Lock.** (This key is found above the "7" key.) When the Num Lock is turned on, numbers are entered when the keys on the keypad are pressed. When the Num Lock is off, the arrow, Home, Page Up, Page Down, End, Insert, and Delete keys can be used.

The enhanced keyboards have the arrow keys and the other directional keys mentioned above to the left of the numeric keypad. When using the keypad on an enhanced keyboard, Num Lock can remain on.

The asterisk (*) performs a different function on the computer than the calculator. The asterisk on the calculator is used for the total while the computer uses it for multiplication.

Another difference is the division key. The computer key is the forward slash key (/). The calculator key uses the division key (÷).

TEN-KEY TOUCH SYSTEM

Striking the numbers 0 to 9 on a calculator or numeric keypad without looking at the keyboard is called the **touch system.** Using the touch system develops both speed and accuracy.

ILLUSTRATION B-2 Standard and enhanced keypads

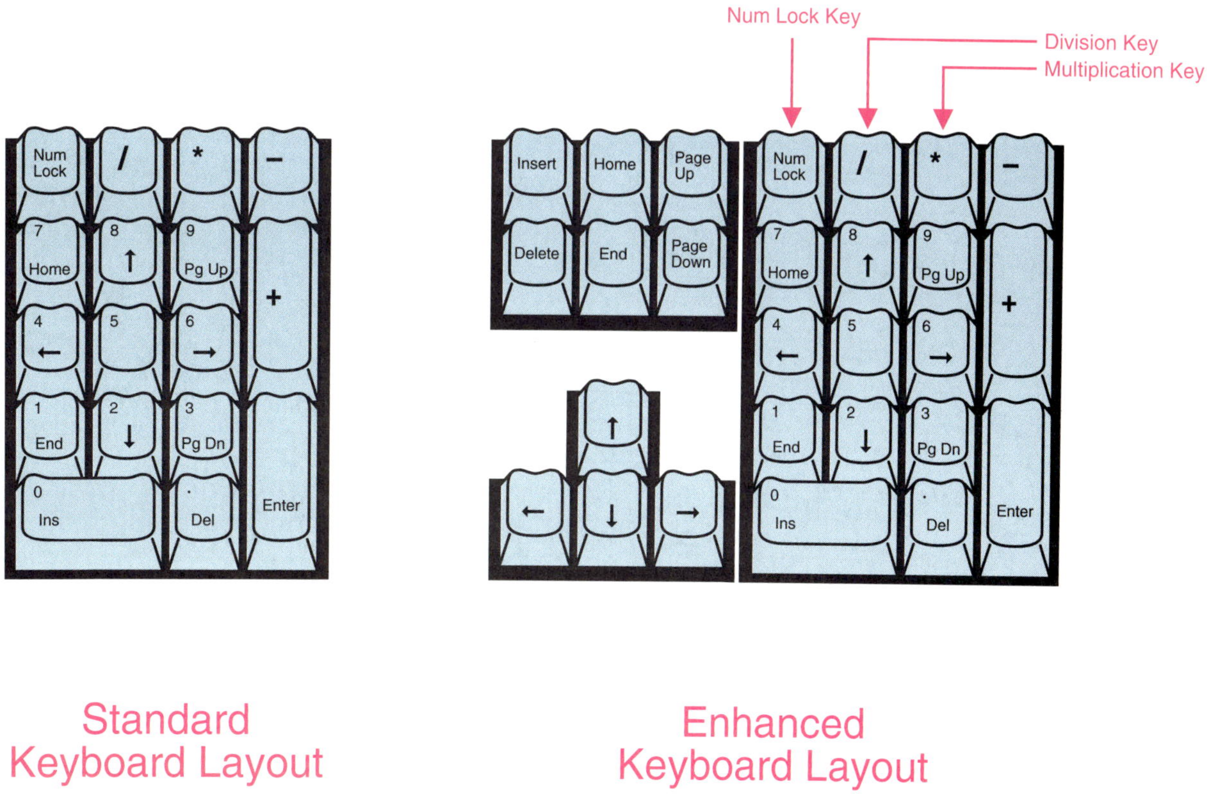

The 4, 5, and 6 keys are called the **home row.** If the right hand is used for the keyboard, the index finger is placed on the 4 key, the middle finger on the 5 key, and the ring finger on the 6 key. If the left hand is used, the ring finger is placed on the 4 key, the middle finger on the 5 key, and the index finger on the 6 key.

Place the fingers on the home row keys. Curve the fingers and keep the wrist straight. These keys may feel slightly concaved or the 5 key may have a raised dot. The differences in the home row allow the operator to recognize the home row by touch rather than by sight.

Maintain the position of the fingers on the home row. The finger used to strike the 4 key will also strike the 7 key and the 1 key. Stretch the finger up to reach the 7; then stretch the finger down to reach the 1 key. Visualize the position of these keys.

Again, place the fingers on the home row. Stretch the finger that strikes the 5 key up to reach the 8 key, then down to reach the 2 key. Likewise, stretch the finger that strikes the 6 key up to strike the 9 and down to strike the 3 key. This same finger will stretch down again to hit the decimal point.

If the right hand is used, the thumb will be used to strike the 0 and 00 keys and the little finger to strike the addition key. If the left hand is used, the little finger will be used to strike the 0 and 00 keys and the thumb to strike the addition key.

HAND-HELD CALCULATORS

Hand-held calculators are slightly different from desktop calculators, not only in their size and features but also in their operation. Refer to the operator's manual for specific instructions for the calculator being used.

On a hand-held calculator, the numeric keys are usually very close together. In addition, the keys do not respond to touch as easily as on a desktop calculator. Therefore, the touch system is usually not used on a hand-held calculator.

PERFORMING MATHEMATICAL OPERATIONS ON DESKTOP CALCULATORS

Mathematical operations can be performed on a calculator both quickly and efficiently. The basic operations of addition, subtraction, multiplication, and division are used frequently on a calculator.

Addition

Each number to be added is called an **addend.** The answer to an addition problem is called the **sum.**

Addition is performed by entering an addend and striking the addition key (+). All numbers are entered on a calculator in the exact order they are given. To enter the number 4,455.65, strike the 4, 4, 5, 5, decimal, 6, and 5 keys in that order, and then strike the addition key. Commas are not entered. Continue in this manner until all addends have been entered. To obtain the sum, strike the total key on the calculator.

Subtraction

The top number or first number of a subtraction problem is called the **minuend.** The number to be subtracted from the minuend is called the **subtrahend.** The answer to a subtraction problem is called the **difference.**

Subtraction is performed by first entering the minuend and striking the addition key (+). The subtrahend is then entered, followed by the minus key (−), followed by the total key.

Multiplication

The number to be multiplied is called the **multiplicand.** The number of times the multiplicand will be multiplied is called the **multiplier.** The answer to a multiplication problem is called the **product.**

Multiplication is performed by entering the multiplicand and striking the multiplication key (×). The multiplier is then entered, followed by the equals key (=). The calculator will automatically multiply and give the product.

Division

The number to be divided is called the **dividend.** The number the dividend will be divided by is called the **divisor.** The answer to a division problem is called the **quotient.**

Division is performed by entering the dividend and striking the division key (÷). The divisor is then entered, followed by the equals key (=). The calculator will automatically divide and give the quotient.

Correcting Errors

If an error is made while using a calculator, several methods of correction may be used. If an incorrect number has been entered and the addition key or equals key has not yet been struck, strike the clear entry (CE) key one time. This key will clear only the last number that was entered. However, if the clear entry key is depressed more than one time, the entire problem will be cleared on some calculators. If an incorrect number has been entered and the addition key has been struck, strike the minus key one time only. This will automatically subtract the last number added, thus removing it from the total.

PERFORMING MATHEMATICAL OPERATIONS ON COMPUTERS AND HAND-HELD CALCULATORS

On a computer keypad or a hand-held calculator, addition is performed in much the same way as on a desktop calculator. However, after the + key is depressed, the display usually shows the accumulated total. Therefore, the total key is not found. Some computer programs will not calculate the total until Enter is pressed.

Subtraction is performed differently on many computer keypads and hand-held calculators. The minuend is usually entered, followed by the minus (−) key. Then the subtrahend is entered. Pressing either the + key or the = key will display the difference. Some computer programs will not calculate the difference until Enter is pressed.

Multiplication and division are performed the same way on a computer keypad and hand-held calculator as on a desktop calculator. Keep in mind that computers use the * for multiplication and / for division.

SAFETY CONCERNS

Whenever electrical equipment such as a calculator or computer is being operated in a classroom or office, several safety rules apply. These rules protect the operator of the equipment, other persons in the environment, and the equipment itself.

1. Do not unplug equipment by pulling on the electrical cord. Instead, grasp the plug at the outlet and remove it.

2. Do not stretch electrical cords across an aisle where someone might trip over them.

3. Avoid food and beverages near the equipment where a spill might result in an electrical short.

4. Do not attempt to remove the cover of a calculator, computer, or keyboard for any reason while the power is turned on.

5. Do not attempt to repair equipment while it is plugged in.

6. Always turn the power off or unplug equipment when finished using it.

CALCULATION DRILLS

INSTRUCTIONS FOR DESKTOP CALCULATORS

Complete each drill using the touch method. Set the decimal selector at the setting indicated in each drill. Compare the answer on the calculator to the answer in the book. If the two are the same, progress to the next problem. It is not necessary to enter 00 in the cents column if the decimal selector is set at 0-F. However, digits other than zeros in the cents column must be entered preceded by a decimal point.

INSTRUCTIONS FOR COMPUTER KEYPADS

Complete each drill using the touch method. There is no decimal selector on computer keypads. Set the number of decimal places as directed in the instructions for the computer program. In spreadsheets, for example, use the formatting options to set the number of decimal places. When the drill indicates "F" for floating, leave the computer application in its default format. Compare the answer on the computer monitor to the answer in the book. If the two are the same, progress to the next problem. It is not necessary to enter 00 in the cents column. However, digits other than zeros in the cents column must be entered preceded by a decimal point.

DRILL D-1 **Performing addition using the home row keys**
Decimal Selector—2

4.00	44.00	444.00	4,444.00	44,444.00
5.00	55.00	555.00	5,555.00	55,555.00
6.00	66.00	666.00	6,666.00	66,666.00
5.00	45.00	455.00	4,455.00	44,556.00
4.00	46.00	466.00	4,466.00	44,565.00
5.00	54.00	544.00	5,544.00	55,446.00
6.00	56.00	566.00	5,566.00	55,664.00
5.00	65.00	655.00	6,655.00	66,554.00
4.00	64.00	644.00	6,644.00	66,555.00
5.00	66.00	654.00	6,545.00	65,465.00
49.00	561.00	5,649.00	56,540.00	565,470.00

DRILL D-2 **Performing addition using the 0, 1, 4, and 7 keys**
Decimal Selector—2

4.00	11.00	444.00	4,440.00	44,000.00
7.00	44.00	777.00	7,770.00	77,000.00
4.00	74.00	111.00	1,110.00	11,000.00
1.00	71.00	741.00	4,400.00	41,000.00
4.00	70.00	740.00	1,100.00	71,000.00
7.00	10.00	101.00	4,007.00	10,000.00
4.00	14.00	140.00	7,001.00	10,100.00
1.00	17.00	701.00	1,007.00	40,100.00
4.00	40.00	700.00	1,004.00	70,100.00
7.00	77.00	407.00	7,700.00	74,100.00
43.00	428.00	4,862.00	39,539.00	448,400.00

DRILL D-3 **Performing addition using the 2, 5, and 8 keys**
Decimal Selector—2

5.00	58.00	588.00	8,888.00	88,855.00
8.00	52.00	522.00	5,555.00	88,822.00
5.00	85.00	888.00	2,222.00	88,852.00
2.00	52.00	222.00	8,525.00	88,222.00
5.00	25.00	258.00	2,585.00	85,258.00
8.00	58.00	852.00	8,258.00	22,255.00
5.00	82.00	225.00	8,585.00	22,288.00
2.00	28.00	885.00	5,258.00	22,258.00
5.00	88.00	882.00	2,852.00	22,888.00
8.00	22.00	228.00	2,288.00	25,852.00
53.00	550.00	5,550.00	55,016.00	555,550.00

DRILL D-4 **Performing addition using the 3, 6, 9, and decimal point keys**
Decimal Selector—2

6.00	66.66	666.66	6,666.99	66,699.33
9.00	99.99	999.99	9,999.66	99,966.66
6.00	33.33	333.33	3,333.99	33,366.33
3.00	33.66	666.99	3,366.99	36,963.36
6.36	33.99	999.66	6,699.33	69,636.36
3.36	99.66	333.66	9,966.33	33,333.66
9.36	99.33	696.36	9,636.69	66,666.99
9.63	33.36	369.63	3,696.36	99,999.33
6.33	33.69	336.69	6,963.99	96,369.63
9.93	69.63	963.36	6,699.33	36,963.36
68.97	603.30	6,366.33	67,029.66	639,965.01

DRILL D-5 **Performing subtraction using all number keys**
Decimal Selector—F

456.73	789.01	741.00	852.55	987.98
123.21	−456.00	−258.10	−369.88	−102.55
333.52	333.01	482.90	482.67	885.43

DRILL D-6 **Performing multiplication using all number keys**
Decimal Selector—F

654.05	975.01	487.10	123.56	803.75
× 12.66	× 27.19	× 30.21	× 50.09	× 1.45
8,280.273	26,510.5219	14,715.291	6,189.1204	1,165.4375

DRILL D-7 **Performing division using all number keys**
Decimal Selector—F

900.56	÷	450.28	=	2.
500.25	÷	100.05	=	5.
135.66	÷	6.65	=	20.4
269.155	÷	105.55	=	2.550023685*
985.66	÷	22.66	=	43.49779346*

**Number of decimal places may vary due to machine capacity.*

Recycling Problems

NOTE: No recycling problems are provided for Chapter 1.

RECYCLING PROBLEM 2-R1 Performing file maintenance activities; journalizing departmental purchases and cash payments

The Floor Store has two departments: Carpeting and Linoleum.

The following is Floor Store's partial general ledger chart of accounts.

6105	Advertising Expense
6110	Depreciation Expense—Store Equipment
6115-1	Salary Expense—Carpet
6115-2	Salary Expense—Linoleum

INSTRUCTIONS:

1. Add Credit Card Fee Expense and Supplies Expense—Store to the general ledger chart of accounts using the unused middle number method described in this chapter.
2. Journalize the following transactions completed during November of the current year. Use page 11 of a purchases journal and a purchases returns and allowances journal and page 21 of a cash payments journal. All vendors from whom merchandise is purchased on account offer terms of 2/10, n/30. Source documents are abbreviated as follows: check, C; debit memorandum, DM; purchase invoice, P.

Check figures: Pur. journal totals—$16,715.00 8,335.00 8,380.00

Nov. 1. Paid cash for office supplies, $62.50. C301.
2. Paid cash for rent, $1,000.00. C302.
4. Paid cash on account to Lyndale Linoleum, $2,763.60, covering P176 for linoleum for $2,820.00, less discount, $56.40. C303.
5. Purchased carpeting on account from King Carpets, $3,740.00. P178.
7. Paid cash on account to Floors and More, $1,651.30, covering P177 for linoleum for $1,685.00, less discount, $33.70. C304.
8. Returned carpeting to King Carpets, $186.00, from P178. DM19.
10. Purchased linoleum on account from Mercury Floors, $2,680.00. P179.
12. Paid cash on account to King Carpets, $3,482.92, covering P178 for carpeting for $3,740.00, less DM19 for $186.00, and less discount, $71.08. C305.

PR&A journal totals—$848.40 636.00 212.40

14. Purchased carpeting on account from Carpet Distributors, $2,670.00. P180.
14. Paid cash for advertising, $82.50. C306.
15. Returned linoleum to Floors and More, $212.40, from P177. DM20.
15. Returned carpeting to Carpet Distributors, $450.00, from P180. DM21.
17. Paid cash on account to Mercury Floors, $2,626.40, covering P179 for linoleum for $2,680.00, less discount, $53.60. C307.

Cash Pay. journal totals— $ 2,010.45 14,319.00 115.48 170.90 16,043.07

Nov. 18. Purchased linoleum on account from Mercury Floors, $1,360.00. P181.
19. Paid cash for store supplies, $62.75. C308.
21. Paid cash on account to Carpet Distributors, $2,175.60, covering P180 for carpeting for $2,670.00, less DM21 for $450.00, and less discount, $44.40. C309.
24. Purchased carpeting on account from King Carpets, $1,925.00. P182.
25. Paid cash on account to Mercury Floors, $1,332.80, covering P181 for linoleum for $1,360.00, less discount, $27.20. C310.
28. Purchased linoleum on account from Lyndale Linoleum, $4,340.00. P183.
30. Paid cash to replenish the petty cash fund, $214.00: office supplies, $65.50; advertising, $87.30; miscellaneous, $61.20. C311.
30. Received bank statement showing November bank service charge, $21.20. M22.
30. Recorded credit card fee expense for November, $567.50. M23.

3. Prove and rule the journals.

Check figure: Adjusted checkbook and bank balance $28,235.80

RECYCLING PROBLEM 2-R2 Reconciling a bank statement

On September 30 of the current year, Boone, Inc. received a bank statement dated September 28. The following information is obtained from the bank statement and from the records of the business.

Bank statement balance	$27,160.00
Bank service charge	10.40
Bank credit card charge	393.80
Outstanding deposit: September 29	3,157.20
Outstanding checks:	
No. 231	1,221.00
No. 232	860.40
Checkbook balance on Check Stub No. 233	28,640.00

INSTRUCTIONS:

Prepare a bank statement reconciliation. Use September 30 of the current year as the date.

RECYCLING PROBLEM 3-R Journalizing departmental sales, sales returns and allowances, and cash receipts

Highcrest Computers, Inc. has two departments: Hardware and Software.

INSTRUCTIONS:

1. Journalize the following transactions completed during April of the current year. Calculate and record sales tax on all sales and sales returns and allowances as described in this chapter. Use page 4 of a sales journal and a sales returns and allowances journal and page 7 of a cash receipts journal. Highcrest offers its customers terms of 2/10, n/30. The sales tax rate is 5%. Source documents are abbreviated as follows: credit memorandum, CM; receipt, R; sales invoice, S; cash register tape, T.

Apr. 1. Sold hardware on account to Allen Davis, $1,640.00, plus sales tax. S119.
2. Recorded cash and credit card sales: hardware, $3,170.00; software, $2,690.00; plus sales tax. T2.
5. Received cash on account from Westen Co., covering S116 for software ($168.00 plus sales tax), less discount and less sales tax. R72.
5. Granted credit to Gloria Odum for software returned, $30.00, plus sales tax, from S118. CM21.
8. Sold software on account to Geig Enterprises, $680.00, plus sales tax. S120.
8. Received cash on account from Travis O'Leary, covering S117 for hardware ($850.00 plus sales tax), less discount and less sales tax. R73.
9. Received cash on account from Gloria Odum, covering S118 for software ($168.00 plus sales tax), less CM21 ($30.00 plus sales tax), less discount and less sales tax. R74.
9. Recorded cash and credit card sales: hardware, $5,780.00; software, $4,620.00; plus sales tax. T9.

Check figures: Sales Journal totals— $4,763.75 148.75 3,760.00 855.00 SR&A Journal totals— $50.40 2.40 48.00 Cash Receipts Journal totals— $ 4,213.65 4.02 2,333.50 25,680.00 20,990.00 59.40 20.86 53,132.87

Apr. 11. Received cash on account from Allen Davis, covering S119 for hardware ($1,640.00 plus sales tax), less discount and less sales tax. R75.
13. Sold software on account to Susan Neuman, $75.00, plus sales tax. S121.
15. Sold hardware on account to Travis O'Leary, $480.00, plus sales tax. S122.
16. Recorded cash and credit card sales: hardware, $6,210.00; software, $5,030.00; plus sales tax. T16.
18. Received cash on account from Geig Enterprises, covering S120 for software ($680.00 plus sales tax), less discount and less sales tax. R76.
19. Granted credit to Susan Neuman for software returned, $18.00, plus sales tax, from S121. CM22.
22. Sold hardware on account to Melrose Schools, $1,640.00; no sales tax. S123.
23. Received cash on account from Susan Neuman, covering S121 for software ($75.00 plus sales tax), less CM22 ($18.00 plus sales tax), less discount and less sales tax. R77.
23. Recorded cash and credit card sales: hardware, $6,630.00; software, $4,720.00; plus sales tax. T23.
25. Received cash on account from Travis O'Leary, covering S122 for hardware ($480.00 plus sales tax), less discount and less sales tax. R78.
27. Sold software on account to Gloria Odum, $100.00; plus sales tax. S124.
30. Recorded cash and credit card sales: hardware, $3,890.00; software, $3,930.00; plus sales tax. T30.

2. Prove and rule the sales journal and the sales returns and allowances journal.
3. Prove the cash receipts journal.
4. Prove cash. The cash balance on hand on April 1 was $36,930.00. The total of the cash credit column of the cash payments journal is $42,870.95. The balance on the next unused check stub is $47,191.92.
5. Rule the cash receipts journal.

RECYCLING PROBLEM 4-R Completing payroll records, journalizing payment of a payroll, and journalizing payroll taxes

Sheridan Shoes has two departments: Men's Shoes and Women's Shoes. A biweekly payroll system of 26 pay periods per year is used. Salesclerks and employees in the accounting department are paid on an hourly basis and receive 1½ times the regular hourly rate for all hours worked over 80 each pay period. A time card is used for hourly employees to record hours worked. Departmental supervisors are paid a biweekly salary and receive monthly commissions of 1% of net sales. Commissions are paid in the first pay period of the following month.

Sheridan Shoes provides the same employee benefits as MasterSport in Chapter 4. The employee benefits provided are in the employee benefits schedule shown in Illustration 4-1.

INSTRUCTIONS:

1. Prepare Joan Aldrich's benefits record for the first four biweekly pay periods of the current year. Use the following information.

Employee No.: 1 Employee Name: Joan J. Aldrich
Department: Women's Shoes Date of Initial Employment: February 15, 1984

Pay Period	Regular Hours	Employee Benefits Available			Employee Benefits Used		
1/2	80	V66	S41	P19	V8	S0	P2
1/16	80	______	______	______	V0	S3	P4
1/30	80	______	______	______	V24	S4	P0
2/13	80	______	______	______	V4	S0	P3

V = Vacation time; S = Sick leave time; P = Personal leave time

2. Prepare the commissions record for each departmental supervisor for the month ended January 31 of the current year. Use the basic payroll information given in the table below. The following additional information is needed to complete the commissions records.
   a. Men's Shoes department: sales on account, $5,143.77; cash and credit card sales, $9,656.04; sales discount, $115.17; sales returns and allowances, $389.94.
   b. Women's Shoes department: sales on account, $6,712.50; cash and credit card sales, $ 9,320.40; sales discount, $124.30; sales returns and allowances, $517.60.

Employee No.	Employee Name	Position	Dept.	Marital Status	Allow.	Total Hours	Regular Pay	Overtime Pay
1	Aldrich, Joan J.	Salesclerk	W	M	2	83	$520.00	$29.25
2	Bryant, Mark K.	Supervisor	M	S	1	—	525.00	—
3	Colfax, Mary D.	Clerk	A	S	2	82	520.00	19.50
4	Emerson, Theodore A.	Salesclerk	M	M	3	80	464.00	—
5	James, Kelly A.	Salesclerk	W	M	2	84	432.00	32.40
6	Newton, Loretta M.	Supervisor	W	M	4	—	550.00	—
7	Penn, Joseph P.	Clerk	A	M	3	82	448.00	16.80
8	Russell, Eileen R.	Salesclerk	M	S	1	84	440.00	33.00
9	Thomas, Emily R.	Salesclerk	M	S	1	83	456.00	25.65
10	Washburn, Mark S.	Salesclerk	W	M	2	83	448.00	25.20

Departments: Men's Shoes, M; Women's Shoes, W; Administrative, A

Check figures: Tot. Payroll $5,281.66 Tot. Ded. 1,311.22 Net Pay 3,970.44

3. Prepare Sheridan Shoes' payroll register for the biweekly pay period ended February 13 and paid February 20 of the current year. The following additional data is needed to complete the payroll register.
   a. A deduction for federal tax is to be made from each employee's total earnings. Use the appropriate income tax withholding tables shown in Chapter 4, Illustration 4-7.
   b. A deduction of 4.5% for state income tax is to be made from each employee's total earnings.
   c. A deduction of 8% for FICA tax is to be made from each employee's total earnings.
   d. All employees have dental insurance, $9.10, and health insurance, $13.40, deducted from their pay each biweekly pay period. The letter *D* is to be written in front of the dental insurance deduction. The letter *H* is to be written in front of the health insurance deduction.
4. Complete Joan Aldrich's employee earnings record for the fourth pay period ended February 13 of the current year. The following data about Joan Aldrich is needed to complete the record.
   a. Hourly rate, $6.50.
   b. Social security number, 514-30-2258.
   c. Accumulated earnings for the first three payroll periods, $1,503.00.
5. Journalize the February 20 payroll payment on page 4 of a cash payments journal. The source document is Check No. 125.
6. Journalize the employer payroll taxes on page 4 of a general journal. Use February 20 of the current year as the date. The source document is Memorandum No. 10. Employer tax rates are: FICA, 8%; federal unemployment, 0.8%; and state unemployment, 5.4%.

RECYCLING PROBLEM 5-R1 Estimating ending merchandise inventory; preparing an interim departmental statement of gross profit; calculating and recording component percentages

Shoreline Shoes has two departments: Men's Shoes and Women's Shoes. The following data were obtained from the accounting records on March 31 of the current year.

Check figures: Estimated Ending Inventory— Men's $66,926.59 Women's 57,515.32

	Men's Shoes	Women's Shoes
Beginning inventory, January 1	$65,340.30	$58,120.50
Estimated beginning inventory, March 1	65,144.59	60,154.72
Net purchases, January 1 to February 28	22,178.40	25,420.60
Net sales, January 1 to February 28	40,680.20	42,520.70
Net purchases for March	9,746.00	6,270.60
Net sales for March	14,480.00	16,200.00
Gross profit on operations as a percent of sales	45.0%	45.0%

INSTRUCTIONS:

1. Prepare an estimated merchandise inventory sheet, similar to the one in Chapter 5, for each department for the month ended March 31 of the current year.
2. Prepare an interim departmental statement of gross profit. Calculate and enter departmental and total component percentages for cost of merchandise sold and gross profit on operations. Round percentage calculations to the nearest 0.1%.

RECYCLING PROBLEM 5-R2 Preparing end-of-fiscal-period work for a departmentalized business

Deluxe Decorating, Inc. has two departments: Paint and Wallpaper. On December 31 of the current year, Deluxe Decorating has the following general ledger accounts and balances.

Account Title	Account Balance
Cash	$ 46,086.18
Petty Cash	500.00
Accounts Receivable	22,470.20
Allow. for Uncoll. Acc.	296.60
Mdse. Inventory—Paint	190,382.60
Mdse. Inventory—Wallpaper	163,740.30
Supplies—Office	12,930.00
Supplies—Store	10,640.30
Prepaid Insurance	7,560.00
Office Equipment	16,820.00
Accum. Depr.—Off. Equip.	8,760.00
Store Equipment	19,380.00
Accum. Depr.—Store Equip.	11,270.00
Accounts Payable	26,138.00
Employ. Inc. Tax Pay.—Fed.	1,630.60
Employ. Inc. Tax Pay.—State	960.50
Fed. Inc. Tax Pay.	—
FICA Tax Payable	1,102.00
Sales Tax Payable	7,108.10
Unemploy. Tax Pay.—Fed.	21.30
Unemploy. Tax Pay.—State	143.78
Health Ins. Premiums Pay.	2,810.60
Dividends Payable	—
Capital Stock	200,000.00
Dividends	40,000.00
Retained Earnings	182,181.92
Income Summary—Paint	—
Income Summary—Wallpaper	—
Income Summary—General	—
Sales—Paint	369,891.10
Sales—Wallpaper	352,840.30
Sales Discount—Paint	3,120.50
Sales Discount—Wallpaper	2,910.30

Account Title	Account Balance
Sales Ret. and Allow.—Paint	2,830.60
Sales Ret. and Allow.—Wallpaper	3,060.00
Purchases—Paint	194,938.72
Purchases—Wallpaper	193,696.10
Purch. Disc.—Paint	2,940.20
Purch. Disc.—Wallpaper	3,180.90
Purch. Ret. and Allow.—Paint	3,480.60
Purch. Ret. and Allow.—Wallpaper	4,260.00
Advertising Expense	6,340.00
Credit Card Fee Expense	5,210.30
Depr. Exp.—Store Equip.	—
Salary Expense—Paint	76,920.00
Salary Expense—Wallpaper	73,680.00
Supplies Expense—Store	—
Depr. Exp.—Office Equip.	—
Insurance Expense	—
Miscellaneous Expense	3,960.40
Payroll Taxes Expense	17,420.00
Rent Expense	15,600.00
Salary Exp.—Admin.	38,320.00
Supplies Expense—Office	—
Uncoll. Accounts Exp.	—
Federal Income Tax Expense	10,800.00

INSTRUCTIONS:

Check figures: Adjustments
a) $ 2,140.60
b) 3,642.40
c) 1,720.40
d) 11,319.70
e) 7,380.10
f) 5,040.00
g) 1,320.00
h) 1,480.00
i) 1,195.95
Net Inc. after Fed. Inc. Tax $55,987.83
Tot. Stock-holder's Eq. $398,169.75
Tot. Assets $439,580.58

1. Complete the departmental work sheet for the year ended December 31 of the current year. Record the adjustments on the work sheet using the following information.

Adjustment Information, December 31

Uncollectible accounts expense estimated as 1.0% of sales on account. Sales on account for year, $214,060.00.

Merchandise inventory—paint	$186,740.20
Merchandise inventory—wallpaper	165,460.70
Office supplies inventory	1,610.30
Store supplies inventory	3,260.20
Value of prepaid insurance	2,520.00
Annual depreciation expense—office equipment	1,320.00
Annual depreciation expense—store equipment	1,480.00
Federal income tax expense for the year	11,995.95

2. Prepare a departmental statement of gross profit. Calculate and record component percentages for cost of merchandise sold and gross profit on operations. Round percentage calculations to the nearest 0.1%.

3. Prepare an income statement. Record the component percentages for cost of merchandise sold and gross profit on operations from the departmental statement of gross profit. Calculate and record the component percentages for total operating expenses and net income before and after federal income tax. Round percentage calculations to the nearest 0.1%.

4. Prepare a statement of stockholders' equity. Use the following additional information.

January 1 balance of capital stock account (2,000 shares issued for $100.00 per share)	$200,000.00
No additional capital stock issued.	
January 1 balance of retained earnings account	182,181.92
Dividends declared during the current year	40,000.00

5. Prepare a balance sheet.

6. Journalize the adjusting entries. Use page 14 of a general journal.

7. Journalize the closing entries. Continue using page 14 of a general journal. Do not skip a line between the adjusting and closing entries.

RECYCLING PROBLEM 6-R Journalizing transactions in a voucher system

Walston Company uses a voucher system, including a voucher register and a check register, similar to those described in Chapter 6.

Check figures: Voucher Reg. Vouchers Pay. $10,067.46 Check Reg. Vouchers Pay. $3,483.75 Nov. 30 Bank Balance $7,388.88

INSTRUCTIONS:

1. Use page 7 of a check register. Record the bank balance brought forward on May 1 of the current year, $6,597.66.
2. Journalize the following transactions completed during May of the current year. Use page 8 of a voucher register and page 7 of a check register. When a voucher is paid or canceled, make appropriate notations in the voucher register. Source documents are abbreviated as follows: check, C; debit memorandum, DM; voucher, V.

May 1. Purchased merchandise on account from Moraska Company, $790.00. V30.
2. Bought sales supplies on account from Waldoch Supplies, $159.78. V31.
4. Bought store equipment on account from Murphy Equipment, $1,449.77. V32.
8. Purchased merchandise on account from Westhaven Company, $1,278.00. V33.
8. Paid cash to Moraska Company, $774.20, covering V30 for $790.00, less 2% discount, $15.80. C19.
10. Made a deposit in the checking account, $2,957.50.
14. Received invoice for delivery service from Davis Delivery, $29.50. V34.
14. Paid cash to Davis Delivery, $29.50, covering V34. C20.
14. Issued DM5 to Westhaven Company for return of merchandise purchased, $170.00. Cancel V33. V35.
15. Paid cash to Westhaven Company, $1,085.84, covering V35 for $1,108.00, less 2% discount, $22.16. C21.
16. Recorded voucher for semimonthly payroll for period ended May 15, $1,396.47 (total payroll: sales, $1,116.00; administrative, $744.00; less deductions: employee income tax payable—federal, $280.50; employee income tax payable—state, $34.23; FICA tax payable, $148.80). V36.
16. Paid cash for semimonthly payroll, $1,396.47, covering V36. C22.
22. Paid cash to Waldoch Supplies, $159.78, covering V31. C23.
25. Bought office equipment on account from Yurik Company, $1,979.99. V37.
29. Made a deposit in the checking account, $1,279.51.
30. Purchased merchandise on account from Moraska Company, $1,875.95. V38.

3. Prove and rule both the voucher register and the check register.

RECYCLING PROBLEM 7-R Determining cost of merchandise inventory; estimating cost of merchandise using estimating methods; calculating merchandise inventory turnover ratio and average number of days' sales in merchandise inventory

On December 31 of the current year, Rackley, Inc. took a periodic inventory. The following selected information is obtained from Rackley's records.

Stock No.	January 1 Inventory		First Purchase		Second Purchase		December 31 Inventory	Market Price
	No.	Unit Price	No.	Unit Price	No.	Unit Price		
A12	12	$10.00	12	$ 9.00	15	$8.00	18	$9.50
B70	15	10.00	15	10.00	15	9.00	9	9.00
D62	35	3.00	25	4.00	20	5.00	30	6.00
G29	20	10.00	10	9.00	10	8.00	15	6.00
J72	24	5.00	10	5.00	10	6.00	20	9.00

Check figures:
2. Total Cost $603.00
604.00
605.24

INSTRUCTIONS:

1. Calculate the inventory costs using the fifo, lifo, and weighted-average inventory costing methods. Use a form similar to the following.

Check figure:
3. Total $550.46

Stock No.	Dec. 31 Inventory	Inventory Costing Method					
		Fifo		Lifo		Weighted-Average	
		Unit Price	Total Cost	Unit Price	Total Cost	Unit Price	Total Cost
Total Costs							

2. Total the three Total Cost columns.
3. Rackley uses the weighted-average costing method to determine the cost of inventory. Use the market price given in the form at the beginning of the problem to determine the cost of inventory using the lower of cost or market method. Total the Lower of Cost or Market column. Use a form similar to the following.

Check figure:
4. $640.00

Stock No.	Weighted-Average Cost	Market Price			Lower of Cost or Market
		Inventory	Unit Price	Total Cost	
Total					

Check figure:
5. $679.65

4. Calculate the corporation's estimated ending inventory using the gross profit method of estimating inventory. The following information is obtained from the corporation's records on December 31 of the current year.

Item	Cost	Retail
Beginning merchandise inventory	$ 400.00	$ 670.00
Net purchases to date	3,000.00	5,080.00
Net sales to date	—	4,600.00
Gross profit percentage	40%	

Check figure:
6. 5.3

5. Calculate the corporation's estimated ending inventory using the retail method of estimating inventory. Round the percentage to the nearest 0.1%.
6. Use the information and the estimated inventory calculated in Instruction 4. Calculate the corporation's merchandise inventory turnover ratio. Round the ratio to the nearest 0.1%.
7. Calculate the corporation's average number of days' sales in merchandise inventory. Round the amount to the nearest day.

Check figure:
7. 69

RECYCLING PROBLEM 8-R Estimating and journalizing uncollectible accounts using a percentage of net sales—allowance method; calculating and journalizing the adjusting entry for uncollectible accounts expense

Motion, Inc. uses the allowance method of recording uncollectible accounts expense.

INSTRUCTIONS:

1. Journalize the following transactions completed during the current year. Use page 1 of a general journal and page 1 of a cash receipts journal.

Jan. 18. Wrote off Judith Tessman's past-due account as uncollectible, $43.96. M25.
Mar. 4. Wrote off James York's past-due account as uncollectible, $80.85. M34.
Mar. 28. Received cash in full payment of Judith Tessman's account, previously written off as uncollectible, $43.96. M45 and R83.
June 20. Wrote off Beverly Axel's past-due account as uncollectible, $17.16. M63.
Oct. 7. Wrote off Tanya Wadsworth's past-due account as uncollectible, $108.15. M79.
Dec. 11. Received cash in full payment of James York's account, previously written off as uncollectible, $80.85. M87 and R97.

Check figure: $509.94

2. Journalize the adjusting entry for uncollectible accounts expense on December 31 of the current year. Motion, Inc. has the following account balances on December 31 before adjusting entries are recorded.

Accounts Receivable	$ 19,768.25
Sales	104,463.79
Sales Discount	1,573.58
Sales Returns and Allowances	901.42

Motion, Inc. estimates that the amount of uncollectible accounts expense is equal to 0.5% of net sales.

Check figure: $1,819.24

3. If all the entries recorded in the general journal and cash receipts journal were posted, including the adjusting entry, what would be the new balance of Allowance for Uncollectible Accounts? The January 1 balance of Allowance for Uncollectible Accounts, before the transactions for the year were recorded, was $1,434.61.

RECYCLING PROBLEM 9-R1 Journalizing transactions for plant assets

Ludden, Inc. uses the straight-line method of calculating depreciation expense. Ludden uses one plant asset account, Office Equipment.

Check figure: No check figure available

INSTRUCTIONS:

Journalize the following transactions. Journalize an entry for additional depreciation expense if needed. Use page 1 of a general journal, page 5 of a cash receipts journal, and page 5 of a cash payments journal.

Jan. 5, 19X1. Paid cash for chair, $200.00: estimated salvage value, none; estimated useful life, 2 years; Serial No., none. C30.
Mar. 3, 19X1. Paid cash for desk, $650.00: estimated salvage value, $150.00; estimated useful life, 4 years; Serial No., D125. C45.
Jan. 5, 19X2. Paid cash for file cabinet, $300.00: estimated salvage value, $75.00; estimated useful life, 5 years; Serial No., F325. C115.
July 3, 19X2. Paid cash for table, $270.00: estimated salvage value, $20.00; estimated useful life, 10 years; Serial No., none. C170.
Jan. 3, 19X3. Discarded chair bought in 19X1. M50
Mar. 5, 19X3. Received cash for sale of desk, Serial No., D125, $300.00. M55 and R50.
June 29, 19X3. Paid cash, $200.00, plus old file cabinet, Serial No. F325, for new file cabinet: estimated salvage value of new cabinet, $80.00; estimated useful life of new cabinet, 5 years; Serial No. of new cabinet, F915. M70 and C200.
July 1, 19X3. Paid cash for typewriter, $1,000.00: estimated salvage value, $200.00; estimated useful life, 5 years; Serial No., A6501M341. C230.

RECYCLING PROBLEM 9-R2 Calculating depreciation expense

On January 5 of the current year, Burdick, Inc. paid cash for a new company car, $15,000.00: estimated salvage value, $1,500.00; estimated useful life, 5 years.

INSTRUCTIONS:

Check figures: Book Value $1,500.00 for each

1. Prepare a depreciation table, similar to Illustration 9-14, showing depreciation expense calculated using the straight-line, declining-balance, and sum-of-the-years-digits methods.
2. Assume that Burdick's car has an estimated useful life of 100,000 miles. Also assume that the car is driven the following number of miles: 1st year, 27,000; 2d year, 23,000; 3d year, 15,000; 4th year, 20,000; 5th year, 15,000. Prepare a depreciation table, similar to Illustration 9-15, using the production-unit method of calculating depreciation expense.

RECYCLING PROBLEM 9-R3 Calculating and journalizing property tax

Amluxson, Inc. has real property with an assessed value of $400,000.00. The tax rate in the city where the property is located is 5% of assessed value. Property tax is paid in two installments.

INSTRUCTIONS:

Check figure: $20,000.00 for year

1. Calculate Amluxson's total annual property tax for the current year.
2. Journalize the payment of the first installment of property tax on May 1. Use page 9 of a cash payments journal. Check No. 142.

RECYCLING PROBLEM 10-R Journalizing adjusting and reversing entries for prepaid expenses initially recorded as expenses and for accrued expenses

Sutton, Inc. completed the following transactions during the current year. Sutton initially records prepaid expenses as expenses. Source documents are abbreviated as follows: check, C; note payable, NP.

Check figures: Maturity dates: Jan. 29, Jan. 29, Jan. 30

Aug. 1. Issued a 1-month, 10% note, $700.00. NP1.
Sept. 1. Paid cash for the maturity value of NP1: principal, $700.00, plus interest, $5.83; total, $705.83. C95.
Sept. 1. Issued a 150-day, 10% note, $1,300.00. NP2.
Oct. 1. Issued a 120-day, 12% note, $1,500.00. NP3.
Dec. 1. Discounted at 12% a 60-day non-interest-bearing note, $800.00; proceeds, $784.00, interest, $16.00. NP4.

INSTRUCTIONS:

1. Calculate the maturity dates for Notes Payable Nos. 2, 3, and 4.
2. Journalize the transactions. Use page 15 of a cash receipts journal and page 17 of a cash payments journal.
3. Sutton, Inc. has the following general ledger balances on December 31 of the current year before adjusting entries are recorded.

Supplies Expense—Administrative	$600.00
Supplies Expense—Sales	900.00
Insurance Expense	800.00

Use the following adjustment information. Journalize the adjusting entries for prepaid and accrued expenses on December 31. Use page 13 of a general journal.

Adjustment Information, December 31

Administrative supplies inventory	$300.00
Sales supplies inventory	350.00
Value of prepaid insurance	400.00
Remaining prepaid interest	8.00
Accrued interest on notes payable	89.19
Accrued salaries—administrative	250.00
Accrued salaries—sales	215.00
Accrued payroll taxes—FICA tax	37.20

Adjustment Information, December 31

Accrued payroll taxes—federal unemployment tax	3.72
Accrued payroll taxes—state unemployment tax	25.11
Accrued federal income tax	400.00

4. Journalize the reversing entries on January 1 of the next year. Use page 1 of a general journal.

RECYCLING PROBLEM 11-R Journalizing notes receivable, unearned revenue, and accrued revenue initially recorded as revenue transactions

Check figure: No check figure available

Marastreet, Inc. completed the following transactions during the current year. Marastreet initially records unearned items as revenue.

INSTRUCTIONS:

1. Journalize the following transactions. Use page 7 of a general journal and page 17 of a cash receipts journal. Source documents are abbreviated as follows: memorandum, M; note receivable, NR; receipt, R.

July 1. Received a 60-day, 10% note from Juan Beldoza for an extension of time on his account, $200.00. NR20.
July 5. Received a 2-month, 12% note from David Symanski for an extension of time on his account, $400.00. NR21.
Aug. 30. Juan Beldoza dishonored NR20, a 60-day, 10% note, maturity value due today: principal, $200.00; interest $3.33; total, $203.33. M39.
Sept. 5. Received cash for the maturity value of NR21: principal, $400.00, plus interest, $8.00; total, $408.00. R70.
Nov. 1. Received cash for three months' rent in advance from Clarkson, Inc., $1,800.00. R75.
Nov. 29. Received cash from Juan Beldoza for dishonored NR20: maturity value, $203.33, plus additional interest, $5.14; total, $208.47. R90.

2. Continue using page 7 of the general journal. Journalize the adjusting entries using the following information.

Adjustment Information, December 31

Accrued interest on notes receivable	$ 17.57
Rent received in advance and still unearned	600.00

3. Journalize the reversing entries on January 1 of the next year. Use page 1 of a general journal.

RECYCLING PROBLEM 12-R Journalizing transactions for starting a corporation, paying dividends, and preparing a balance sheet

Hillcrest, Inc. received its charter on July 1 of the current year. The corporation is authorized to issue 500,000 shares of $1.00 stated-value common stock and 1,000 shares of 8%, $50.00 par-value preferred stock.

INSTRUCTIONS:

1. Journalize the following transactions. Use page 1 of a cash receipts journal, a cash payments journal, and a general journal.

Check figures: Cap. Stk. $355,000 Stk. Sub. 30,000

July 5. Received cash from five incorporators for 300,000 shares of $1.00 stated-value common stock, $300,000.00. R1-5.
July 8. Paid cash to George Quitman as reimbursement for organization costs, $4,000.00. C1.
July 12. Received a subscription from Angela Smith for 50,000 shares of $1.00 stated-value common stock, $50,000.00. M1.
July 25. Received a subscription from Dayne Wilson for 5,000 shares of $1.00 stated-value common stock, $5,000.00. M2.
Aug. 10. Received cash from Dayne Wilson in payment of stock subscription, $5,000.00. R6.
Aug. 10. Issued Stock Certificate No. 6 to Dayne Wilson for 5,000 shares of $1.00 stated-value common stock, $5,000.00. M3.

Oct. 1. Received cash from Angela Smith in partial payment of stock subscription, $25,000.00. R7.

Oct. 15. Received a subscription from Lance Mosier for 30,000 shares of $1.00 stated-value common stock, $30,000.00. M4.

Nov. 1. Received cash from Angela Smith in final payment of stock subscription, $25,000.00. R8.

Nov. 1. Issued Stock Certificate No. 7 to Angela Smith for 50,000 shares of $1.00 stated-value common stock, $50,000.00. M5.

Check figures: Pref. $250,000 × 8% = $20,000 Com. $50,000 − 20,000 = $30,000

2. Prepare a balance sheet for Hillcrest, Inc. as of November 2 of the current year.

3. Journalize the following transactions completed during the following two years to record the declaration and payment of the dividends. Continue using page 1 of the general journal and the cash payments journal.

Nov. 24. Hillcrest's board of directors declared an annual dividend of $50,000.00. Preferred stock issued is $250,000.00 of 8%, $50.00 par-value preferred stock. Common stock issued is $400,000.00 of $1.00 stated-value common stock. Date of payment is January 15. M106.

Jan. 15. Paid cash for annual dividend declared November 24, $50,000.00. C257.

Check figure: No check figure available

RECYCLING PROBLEM 13-R Journalizing stocks and bonds transactions

Fleming, Inc. is authorized to issue 200,000 shares of $20.00 stated-value common stock and 50,000 shares of 12%, $200.00 par-value preferred stock.

INSTRUCTIONS:

Journalize the following transactions. Use page 1 of a cash receipts journal, page 2 of a cash payments journal, and page 7 of a general journal.

Jan. 1, 19X1. Received cash for the face value of a 5-year, 10%, $1,000.00 par-value bond issue, $100,000.00. R104.

Jan. 8, 19X1. Received cash from Mary Brooker for 800 shares of $20.00 stated-value common stock at $20.00 per share, $16,000.00. R110.

Feb. 15, 19X1. Paid cash to Alfred Clark for 800 shares of $20.00 stated-value common stock at $21.00 per share, $16,800.00. C124.

Feb. 27, 19X1. Received cash from Connie Boyle for 300 shares of $200.00 par-value preferred stock at $198.00 per share, $59,400.00. R127.

Mar. 13, 19X1. Received cash from Edward Timmell for 100 shares of $20.00 stated-value common stock at $21.00 per share, $2,100.00. R143.

Mar. 22, 19X1. Received cash from Carol Petre for 200 shares of treasury stock at $21.00 per share, $4,200.00. Treasury stock was bought on February 15 at $21.00 per share. R149.

Apr. 15, 19X1. Received cash from Dennis Cochran for 100 shares of treasury stock at $22.00 per share, $2,200.00. Treasury stock was bought on February 15 at $21.00 per share. R155.

Apr. 21, 19X1. Received cash from David Vassel for 300 shares of $200.00 par-value preferred stock at $202.00 per share, $60,600.00. R156.

July 1, 19X1. Paid cash to bond trustee for semiannual interest on bond issue, $5,000.00. C308.

July 1, 19X1. Paid cash to bond trustee for semiannual deposit to bond sinking fund, $10,000.00. C309.

July 12, 19X1. Received store equipment from Jake Smith at an agreed value of $50,000.00 for 250 shares of $200.00 par-value preferred stock. M361.

July 30, 19X1. Received cash from Lester Branch for 100 shares of treasury stock at $20.50 per share, $2,050.00. Treasury stock was bought on February 15 at $21.00 per share. R215.

Jan. 1, 19X2. Paid cash to bond trustee for semiannual interest on bond issue, $5,000.00. C519.

Jan. 1, 19X2. Paid cash to bond trustee for semiannual deposit to bond sinking fund, $9,700.00, and recorded interest earned on bond sinking fund, $300.00. C520.

Jan. 5, 19X6. Received notice from bond trustee that bond issue was retired using bond sinking fund, $100,000.00. M491.

RECYCLING PROBLEM 14-R End-of-fiscal-period work for a corporation

On December 31 of the current year, Nichol, Inc. has the following general ledger account balances.

Cash	$ 16,923.38
Petty Cash	600.00
Notes Receivable	12,030.37
Interest Receivable	—
Accounts Receivable	67,676.52
Allow. for Uncoll. Accts.	203.03
Subscriptions Receivable	—
Merchandise Inventory	113,290.49
Supplies—Sales	14,415.10
Supplies—Administrative	11,031.27
Prepaid Insurance	8,933.30
Prepaid Interest	—
Bond Sinking Fund	9,000.00
Store Equipment	66,932.08
Accum. Depr.—Store Equip.	6,760.14
Building	63,000.00
Accum. Depr.—Building	6,993.00
Office Equipment	90,348.15
Accum. Depr.—Office Equip.	6,558.19
Land	47,170.53
Organization Costs	400.00
Notes Payable	2,676.77
Interest Payable	—
Accounts Payable	609.09
Employ. Inc. Tax Pay.	541.41
Federal Income Tax Payable	—
FICA Tax Payable	326.64
Salaries Payable	—
Sales Tax Payable	947.47
Unemploy. Tax Pay.—Fed.	108.01
Unemploy. Tax Pay.—State	730.50
Health Ins. Premiums Pay.	203.03
Dividends Payable	21,320.00
Bonds Payable	90,000.00
Capital Stock—Common	120,000.00
Stock Subscribed—Common	—
Paid-in Cap. in Excess of Stated Value—Common	15,000.00
Capital Stock—Preferred	94,000.00
Stock Subscribed—Preferred	—
Paid-in Cap. in Excess of Par Value—Preferred	2,400.00
Discount on Sale of Preferred Stock	4,000.00
Treasury Stock	1,600.00
Paid-in Cap. from Sale of Treasury Stock (credit bal.)	320.00
Retained Earnings	29,439.29
Dividends—Common	11,920.00
Dividends—Preferred	9,400.00
Income Summary	—
Sales	492,897.38
Sales Discount	879.79
Sales Returns and Allow.	1,319.69
Purchases	204,352.79
Purch. Discount	3,440.00
Purch. Return and Allow.	1,214.12
Advertising Expense	5,143.42
Credit Card Fee Expense	5,820.18
Depr. Expense—Store Equip.	—
Misc. Expense—Sales	9,068.65
Salary Expense—Sales	30,725.14
Supplies Expense—Sale	—
Depr. Expense—Building	—
Depr. Exp.—Office Equip.	—
Insurance Expense	—
Misc. Expense—Admin.	7,173.71
Payroll Taxes Expense	6,423.57
Property Tax Expense	4,000.00
Salary Expense—Admin.	25,514.05
Supplies Expense—Admin.	—
Uncoll. Accts. Expense	—
Utilities Expense	12,114.10
Gain on Plant Assets	—
Interest Income	270.71
Interest Expense	5,752.50
Loss on Plant Assets	—
Organization Expense	—
Federal Inc. Tax Expense	30,000.00

INSTRUCTIONS:

1. Complete the work sheet. The following additional information is needed.

Adjustment Information, December 31

Accrued interest income	$ 122.33
Uncollectible accounts expense estimated as 1.0% of sales on account. Sales on account for year, $277,474.00.	
Merchandise inventory	110,939.29
Sales supplies inventory	4,951.42
Administrative supplies inventory	6,106.97

Check figures: Federal Income Tax $31,833.28

Adjustment Information, December 31

Value of prepaid insurance	3,153.46
Prepaid interest	4.06
Annual depreciation expense—store equipment	6,626.28
Annual depreciation expense—building	3,150.00
Annual depreciation expense—office equipment	8,965.31
Organization expense	100.00
Accrued interest expense	9,005.64
Accrued salaries—sales	488.36
Accrued salaries—administrative	1,302.77
Accrued payroll taxes—FICA tax	143.29
Accrued payroll taxes—federal unemployment tax	1.69
Accrued payroll taxes—state unemployment tax	11.39

Use the tax rate table on page 368 in Chapter 14 to calculate the federal income tax for the year.

Check figures: 41.2 58.8 13.7 16.8 30.5 28.3 2.9 25.4 6.5 18.9

2. Prepare an income statement. Calculate and record the following component percentages. (a) Cost of merchandise sold. (b) Gross profit on operations. (c) Total selling expenses. (d) Total administrative expenses. (e) Total operating expenses. (f) Income from operations. (g) Net addition or deduction resulting from other revenue and expenses. (h) Net income before federal income tax. (i) Federal income tax expense. (j) Net income after federal income tax. Round percentage calculations to the nearest 0.1%.
3. Analyze Nichol's income statement by determining if component percentages are within acceptable levels. If any component percentage is not within an acceptable level, suggest steps that the company should take. Nichol considers the following component percentages acceptable.

Cost of merchandise sold	Not more than 43.0%
Gross profit on operations	Not less than 57.0%
Total selling expenses	Not more than 13.0%
Total administrative expenses	Not more than 18.0%
Total operating expenses	Not more than 31.0%
Income from operations	Not less than 26.0%
Net deduction from other revenue and expenses	Not more than 8.0%
Net income before federal income tax	Not less than 18.0%

Check figures: 4. Pref. $10.00 Com. 3.50

4. Calculate earnings per share. Nichol's has 24,000 shares of $5.00 stated-value common stock issued and 940 shares of $100.00 par-value preferred stock issued. Treasury stock consists of 160 shares of common stock. The dividend rate on preferred stock is 10.0%.
5. Prepare a statement of stockholders' equity for the year ended December 31 of the current year. Use the following additional information.

	January 1 Balance	**Issued During the Year**	**December 31 Balance**
Common stock:			
No. of shares	20,000	4,000	24,000
Amount	$100,000.00	$20,000.00	$120,000.00
Preferred stock:			
No. of shares	900	40	940
Amount	$ 90,000.00	$ 4,000.00	$ 94,000.00

The January 1 balance of Retained Earnings was $29,439.29.

Check figures: 6a. Pref. $100.00 Com. 9.77 b. 6.9

6. Calculate the following items based on information from the statement of stockholders' equity. (a) Equity per share of stock. (b) Price-earnings ratio. The market price of common stock on December 31 is $24.25.
7. Prepare a balance sheet for December 31 of the current year.
8. Calculate the following items based on information from the balance sheet. (a) Net sales on account are $277,474.00. Accounts receivable turnover ratio. Accounts receivable and allowance for uncollectible accounts on January 1 were $64,984.46 and $2,482.57,

Check figures:
8a. $ 63,600.32
4.4
b. $271,768.91
34.1
c. $439,458.72
21.1

respectively. (b) Rate earned on average stockholders' equity. Total stockholders' equity on January 1 was $216,559.29. (c) Rate earned on average total assets. Total assets on January 1 were $421,689.57.

9. Journalize the adjusting entries. Use page 13 of a general journal.
10. Journalize the closing entries. Use page 14 of a general journal.
11. Journalize the reversing entries. Use page 1 of a general journal. Use January 1 of the following year as the date.

RECYCLING PROBLEM 15-R Preparing a budgeted income statement and a cash budget with supporting budget schedules

On December 31, 19X2, the accounting records of Reilly Corporation show the following unit sales for 19X2.

1st quarter	20,600 units	3d quarter	22,800 units
2d quarter	21,500 units	4th quarter	35,100 units

The following are additional actual amounts for the 4th quarter of 19X2.

Sales (35,100 units @ $5.00)	$175,500
Purchases (29,400 units @ $2.60)	76,440
Ending inventory	11,500 units

Management has established a unit sales goal of 120,000 units for 19X3 and 25,000 units for the first quarter of 19X4. The sales manager, after reviewing price trends and checking with the company's merchandise suppliers, projects the unit cost of merchandise will increase from $2.60 to $2.80 in the first quarter of 19X3. Because of the increase in costs, the company will need to increase its unit sales price from $5.00 to $5.20 in the first quarter of 19X3.

After considering the time required to reorder merchandise, the sales manager requests that 50.0% of each quarter's unit sales be available in the prior quarter's ending inventory.

Expenses are projected as follows. Except where noted, percentages are based on quarterly projected net sales. For these items, calculate each quarter's amount by multiplying the percentage times that quarter's net sales. Calculate the annual total by adding the four quarterly amounts. When a dollar amount is given, the total amount should be divided equally among the four quarters.

Check figures
1. $624,000
128,440
134,160
142,480
218,920
2. $ 73,080
74,480
97,440
93,800
3. $ 57,790
12,170
12,630
13,320
19,670
4. $ 61,550
14,660
14,810
15,030
17,050
7. $165,450
130,370
137,240
176,160
8. $143,570
126,140
141,340
170,120
9. $ 44,420
48,650
44,550
50,590

Selling Expenses	
Advertising Expense	1.2%
Delivery Expense	0.7%
Depreciation Expense—Delivery Equipment	$4,200
Depreciation Expense—Store Equipment	$1,800
Miscellaneous Expense—Sales	0.2%
Salary Expense—Sales	5.4%
Supplies Expense—Sales	0.8%

Administrative Expenses	
Depreciation Expense—Office Equipment	$1,440
Insurance Expense	$3,640
Miscellaneous Expense—Administrative	$2,400
Payroll Taxes Expense	12.0% of salaries
Rent Expense	$6,640
Salary Expense—Administrative	$26,000
Supplies Expense—Administrative	$1,800
Uncollectible Accounts Expense	0.5%
Utilities Expense	1.5%

Interest expense for each quarter is projected to be $450.

Federal income taxes are calculated using the tax rate table shown in Chapter 17. Equal quarterly income tax payments are based on the projected annual federal income tax expense.

Additional information is listed as follows.

a. The balance of cash on hand on January 1, 19X3, is $22,540.
b. In each quarter, cash sales are 20.0% and collections of accounts receivable are 25.0% of

the projected net sales for the current quarter. Collections from the preceding quarter's net sales are 54.5% of that quarter. Uncollectible accounts expense is 0.5% of net sales.

c. In each quarter, cash payments for cash purchases are 10.0% and for accounts payable 50.0% of the purchases for the current quarter. Cash payments for purchases of the preceding quarter are 40.0% of that quarter.

d. In the first quarter, $12,000 will be borrowed on a promissory note, and equipment costing $17,500 will be purchased for cash. In each quarter, dividends of $15,000 will be paid in cash. In the fourth quarter, the promissory note plus interest will be paid in cash, $13,800.

INSTRUCTIONS:

Prepare the following budget schedules for the year ended December 31, 19X3. Round percentage amounts to the nearest 0.1%, unit amounts to the nearest 100 units, and dollar amounts to the nearest $10.

1. Prepare a sales budget schedule (Schedule 1).
2. Prepare a purchases budget schedule (Schedule 2).
3. Prepare a selling expenses budget schedule (Schedule 3).
4. Prepare an administrative expenses budget schedule (Schedule 4).
5. Prepare an other revenue and expenses budget schedule (Schedule 5).
6. Prepare a budgeted income statement.
7. Prepare a cash receipts budget schedule (Schedule A).
8. Prepare a cash payments budget schedule (Schedule B).
9. Prepare a cash budget.

RECYCLING PROBLEM 16-R Calculating contribution margin and breakeven point; calculating sales dollars and unit sales for planned net income

NewWave Cycle, Inc. manufactures and sells racing bicycles. The company's income statement has been prepared for January of the current year.

Check figures:
2. $40,500/ $135,000 = 30%
3. $27,000/ 30% = $90,000
4. $90,000/ $750 = 120 units
5. (a) $45,000/ 30% = $150,000
(b) $150,000/ $750 = 200 units

NewWave Cycle, Inc.
Income Statement
For Month Ended January 31, 19--

Operating Revenue:			
Net Sales (180 units @ $750.00)			$135,000.00
Cost of Merchandise Sold (180 units @ $460.00)			82,800.00
Gross Profit on Operations			$ 52,200.00
Operating Expenses:			
Selling Expenses:			
Sales Commission (180 units @ $25.00)	$ 4,500.00		
Delivery Costs (180 units @ $15.00)	2,700.00		
Other Variable Costs (180 units @ $18.20)	3,276.00		
Other Fixed Costs	6,450.00	$16,926.00	
Administrative Expenses:			
Rent	$ 1,200.00		
Insurance	450.00		
Other Variable Costs (180 units @ $6.80)	1,224.00		
Other Fixed Costs	15,900.00	18,774.00	
Total Operating Expenses			35,700.00
Income from Operations			$ 16,500.00
Other Expenses			3,000.00
Net Income			$ 13,500.00

INSTRUCTIONS:

1. Prepare NewWave Cycle's January income statement reporting contribution margin.
2. Calculate the contribution margin rate.

3. Calculate the sales dollar breakeven point.
4. Calculate the unit sales breakeven point.
5. If an $18,000.00 monthly net income is planned, calculate the required (a) sales dollars and (b) number of cycles to be sold.
6. NewWave Cycle currently produces one of the components of its cycles. However, the company can also purchase the component from another company, reducing fixed costs by $5,000.00 per month, but increasing variable costs by $25.00 per cycle. Calculate the projected net income assuming NewWave Cycle sells 180 cycles per month. Should NewWave Cycle purchase the component from another company? Explain your answer.

RECYCLING PROBLEM 17-R Preparing and analyzing comparative financial statements

The following information is taken from the financial records of Reardon Corporation for two fiscal years ended December 31.

	Current Year	Prior Year
Cash	$ 66,560.00	$ 45,230.00
Accounts Receivable (book value)	84,340.00	62,430.00
Merchandise Inventory	347,960.00	229,690.00
Other Current Assets	8,320.00	8,470.00
Plant Assets (book value)	136,800.00	147,360.00
Notes Payable	66,530.00	10,830.00
Interest Payable	2,500.00	1,800.00
Accounts Payable	125,100.00	45,020.00
Federal Income Tax Payable	500.00	500.00
Other Current Liabilities	19,210.00	2,040.00
Mortgage Payable (long-term liability)	73,920.00	83,130.00
Capital Stock	300,000.00	300,000.00
Retained Earnings (after closing entries)	56,220.00	49,860.00
Net Sales	859,600.00	780,800.00
Net Purchases	783,440.00	704,840.00
Advertising Expense	14,190.00	13,880.00
Delivery Expense	15,610.00	14,500.00
Salary Expense—Regular	50,380.00	47,310.00
Supplies Expense—Sales	2,130.00	2,520.00
Other Selling Expenses	4,260.00	4,420.00
Salary Expense—Administrative	29,090.00	32,170.00
Uncollectible Accounts Expense	8,520.00	3,780.00
Other Administrative Expenses	16,320.00	17,030.00
Interest Expense	17,030.00	11,990.00
Federal Income Tax Expense	5,540.00	5,580.00
Additional information:		
Dividends Declared	$ 25,000.00	$ 25,000.00
Shares of capital stock outstanding	3,000	3,000
Accounts Receivable (book value), January 1	$ 62,430.00	$ 59,480.00
Merchandise Inventory, January 1	229,690.00	120,830.00
Total Assets, January 1	493,180.00	421,200.00
Capital Stock, January 1	300,000.00	300,000.00
Retained Earnings, January 1	49,860.00	43,220.00
Market price per share of stock, December 31	112.50	123.00

INSTRUCTIONS:

1. Prepare the following comparative financial statements using trend analysis. Round percentage calculations to the nearest 0.1%.
   a. Comparative income statement
   b. Comparative stockholders' equity statement

Check figures:
2. (a) 10.1% (b) -0.9% (c) 1.8% (d) 30.6%
4a. (1) 77.4%, 76.3% (2) 22.6%, 23.7% (3) 16.3%, 17.4% (4) 3.6%, 4.1%
4b. (1) 15.8%, 14.3% (2) 84.2%, 85.7%
4c. (1) 78.8%, 70.1% (2) 33.2%, 12.2%
5a. (1) 5.5%, 6.9% (2) 8.9%, 9.1% (3) 3.6%, 4.1% (4) $10.45, $10.55 (5) 10.8, 11.7
5b. (1) 11.7, 12.8 (2) 2.3, 3.4
5c. (1) 2.4, 5.7 (2) 0.7, 1.8
5d. (1) 44.7%, 29.1% (2) 55.3%, 70.9% (3) $118.74, $116.62

c. Comparative balance sheet

2. Use the financial statements' trend analysis to determine if the trend from the prior to current year for each of the following items appears to be favorable or unfavorable. Give reasons for these trends.
  a. Net sales
  b. Net income
  c. Total stockholders' equity
  d. Total assets

3. Prepare a comparative income statement using component percentage analysis. Round percentage calculations to the nearest 0.1%.

4. Record from the statement prepared in Instruction 3 or calculate the component percentages for each of the following. Determine if the current year's results, compared with the prior year, appear to be favorable or unfavorable. Give reasons for your responses.
  a. As a percentage of net sales:
    (1) Cost of merchandise sold
    (2) Gross profit on operations
    (3) Total operating expenses
    (4) Net income after federal income tax
  b. As a percentage of total stockholders' equity:
    (1) Retained earnings
    (2) Capital stock
  c. As a percentage of total assets or total liabilities and stockholders' equity:
    (1) Current assets
    (2) Current liabilities

5. Based on Reardon's comparative financial statements, calculate the following ratios for each year.
  a. Profitability ratios:
    (1) Rate earned on average total assets
    (2) Rate earned on average stockholders' equity
    (3) Rate earned on net sales
    (4) Earnings per share
    (5) Price-earnings ratio
  b. Efficiency ratios:
    (1) Accounts receivable turnover ratio
    (2) Merchandise inventory turnover ratio
  c. Short-term financial strength ratios:
    (1) Working capital
    (2) Current ratio
    (3) Acid-test ratio
  d. Long-term financial strength ratios:
    (1) Debt ratio
    (2) Equity ratio
    (3) Equity per share

6. For each of the items in Instruction 5, indicate if there appears to be a favorable or an unfavorable trend from the prior to current year. Give reasons for these trends.

RECYCLING PROBLEM 18-R Completing end-of-fiscal-period work for a merchandising business using departmental margins

Lawn Care is a merchandising business that specializes in lawn mowers and mower parts. Lawn Care has the following general ledger account balances on December 31 of the current year.

Cash	$ 67,576.80	Supplies	9,776.00
Accounts Receivable	53,312.60	Prepaid Insurance	9,300.00
Allowance for Uncoll. Accts.	86.50	Office Equipment	3,694.20
Mdse. Inv.—Mowers	65,251.50	Accum. Depr.— Office Equip.	396.30
Mdse. Inv.—Parts	51,732.70	Store Equipment—Mowers	10,584.60

Accum. Depr.—	
Store Equip., Mowers	2,449.40
Store Equip.—Parts	7,595.90
Accum. Depr.—	
Store Equip., Parts	1,542.00
Accounts Payable	16,287.40
Employee Income Tax Pay.	1,064.30
Federal Income Tax Pay.	—
FICA Tax Payable	1,474.40
Salaries Payable	—
Sales Tax Payable	2,728.90
Unemploy. Tax Pay.—Fed.	14.40
Unemploy. Tax Pay.—State	97.20
Dividends Pay.	—
Capital Stock	150,000.00
Retained Earnings	69,493.40
Dividends	10,000.00
Income Sum.—Mowers	—
Income Sum.—Parts	—
Income Sum.—General	—
Sales—Mowers	242,546.90
Sales Discount—Mowers	601.20
Sales Returns and Allow.—	
Mowers	400.90
Sales—Parts	281,081.30
Sales Discount—Parts	772.00
Sales Ret. and Allow.—Parts	631.70
Purchases—Mowers	139,180.60
Purch. Discount—Mowers	267.80
Purchases Ret. and Allow.—	
Mowers	401.70
Purchases—Parts	143,913.20
Purch. Discount—Parts	331.20
Purch. Ret. and Allow.—Parts	271.10
Advertising Exp.—Mowers	2,957.60
Delivery Exp.—Mowers	6,114.40
Depr. Exp.—Store Equip.,	
Mowers	—
Insurance Exp.—Mowers	—
Payroll Taxes Exp.—Mowers	3,593.00
Salary Expense—Mowers	34,219.00
Supplies Expense—Mowers	—
Uncoll. Accounts Expense—	
Mowers	—
Advertising Exp.—Parts	4,239.60
Depr. Exp.—Store Equip.,	
Parts	—
Insurance Expense—Parts	—
Payroll Taxes Exp.—Parts	3,320.60
Salary Expense—Parts	31,628.00
Supplies Expense—Parts	—
Credit Card Fee Expense	5,263.70
Depr. Exp.—Office Equip.	—
Insurance Exp.—Admin.	—
Misc. Expense	18,318.20
Payroll Taxes Exp.—Admin.	4,562.00
Rent Expense	23,440.00
Salary Expense—Admin.	44,733.00
Supplies Expense—Admin.	—
Utilities Expense	8,621.20
Federal Income Tax Expense	5,200.00

Check figure: Trial Bal. $770,534.20

INSTRUCTIONS:

1. Prepare a trial balance on a 12-column work sheet. List all accounts with or without a balance. Skip four lines after Utilities Expenses before entering Federal Income Tax Expense.
2. Complete a work sheet for the year ended December 31 of the current year. Record the adjustments on the work sheet using the following information.

Adjustment Information, December 31

Uncollectible accounts expense—mowers estimated as 1.0% of sales on account. Sales on account for year, $78,000.00.

Merchandise inventory—mowers	$67,623.30
Merchandise inventory—parts	52,611.10
Supplies used—mowers	2,413.80
Supplies used—parts	4,023.00
Supplies used—administrative	1,609.20
Insurance expired—mowers	2,220.00
Insurance expired—parts	2,775.00
Insurance expired—administrative	555.00
Depreciation expense—office equipment	123.90
Depreciation expense—store equipment, mowers	896.10
Depreciation expense—store equipment, parts	232.30
Federal income tax expense for the year	5,401.80

3. Extend amounts to the proper debit and credit columns for Departmental Margin Statement—Mowers, Departmental Margin Statement—Parts, Income Statement, and Balance Sheet. Accounts on trial balance lines 55–63 are classified as indirect expenses.

Check figure: Net Inc. After Tax, $30,610.20

4. Prepare a departmental margin statement for each department. Calculate and record the component percentages for each item on the statements. Round percentage calculations to the nearest 0.1%.
5. Prepare an income statement similar to the one described in Chapter 18. Calculate and record the component percentages for each item on the statements. Round percentage calculations to the nearest 0.1%.

RECYCLING PROBLEM 19-R Preparing cost records

Air Wave, Inc. manufactures CB (citizen band) radios. The company records manufacturing costs by job number and uses a factory overhead applied rate to charge overhead costs to its products.

The company estimates it will manufacture 5,000 radios next year. For this amount of production, total factory overhead is estimated to be $198,000.00. Estimated direct labor costs for next year are $220,000.00.

INSTRUCTIONS:

1. Calculate Air Wave's factory overhead applied rate for next year as a percentage of direct labor cost.

On November 6, Air Wave began work on Job No. 753. The order is for 30 No. LR75 CB radios for stock, date wanted November 21.

Check figures: 30 units finished $136.60 ea.

2. Open a cost sheet for Job No. 753 and record the following items.

Nov. 6. Direct materials, $762.00. Materials Requisition No. 524.
6. Direct labor, $120.00. Daily summary of job-time records.
7. Direct labor, $180.00. Daily summary of job-time records.
8. Direct materials, $230.00. Materials Requisition No. 535.
8. Direct labor, $136.00. Daily summary of job-time records.
9. Direct labor, $126.00. Daily summary of job-time records.
10. Direct materials, $185.00. Materials Requisition No. 542.
10. Direct labor, $210.00. Daily summary of job-time records.
13. Direct materials, $156.00. Materials Requisition No. 548.
13. Direct labor, $198.00. Daily summary of job-time records.
14. Direct materials, $112.00. Materials Requisition No. 556.
14. Direct labor, $186.00. Daily summary of job-time records.
15. Direct materials, $145.00. Materials Requisition No. 563.
15. Direct labor, $112.00. Daily summary of job-time records.
16. Direct labor, $52.00. Daily summary of job-time records.

3. Complete the cost sheet, recording factory overhead at the rate calculated in Instruction 1.
4. Prepare a finished goods ledger card for Stock No. LR75 CB radio. Minimum quantity is set at 10. Inventory location is Area B-11.
5. Record on the finished goods ledger card the beginning balance on November 1. The November 1 balance of LR75 CB radios is 20 units at a unit cost of $133.50. Air Wave uses the first-in, first-out method to record inventory costs.
6. Record the following transactions on the finished goods ledger card for LR75 CB radios.

Check figures: Finished goods final total $3,005.20

Nov. 10. Sold 8 LR75 CB radios. Sales Invoice No. 743.
16. Received 30 LR75 CB radios. Record cost from cost sheet for Job No. 753.
21. Sold 20 LR75 CB radios. Sales Invoice No. 757.

RECYCLING PROBLEM 20-R Journalizing entries that summarize cost records at the end of a fiscal period; preparing statement of cost of goods manufactured

The following information is taken from the records of Bartley Company on January 31 of the current year.

a. The various general ledger accounts used in recording actual factory overhead expenses during the month have the following balances on January 31.

5510	Depreciation Expense—Factory Equipment	$ 2,885.12
5515	Depreciation Expense—Building	1,411.20
5520	Heat, Light, and Power Expense	4,527.60
5525	Insurance Expense—Factory	752.64
5530	Miscellaneous Expense—Factory	6,890.24
5535	Payroll Taxes Expense—Factory	21,868.00
5540	Property Tax Expense—Factory	3,044.16
5545	Supplies Expense—Factory	9,031.68

b. Inventory accounts have the following balances on January 1.

Account No. 1125	Materials	$272,244.00
Account No. 1130	Work in Process	95,961.60
Account No. 1135	Finished Goods	71,442.00

c. The following accounts are needed for completing the posting. No beginning balances are needed.

2110	Employee Income Tax Payable
2120	FICA Tax Payable
3120	Income Summary
5105	Cost of Goods Sold
5505	Factory Overhead

d. The total factory payroll for the month according to the payroll register is $154,000.00, distributed as follows.

Work in Process	$114,520.00
Factory Overhead	39,480.00
Cash	124,740.00
Employee Income Tax Payable	16,940.00
FICA Tax Payable	12,320.00

e. The total of all requisitions of direct materials issued during the month is $126,115.00. The total of all requisitions of indirect materials issued during the month is $10,085.00.

f. The factory overhead to be charged to **Work in Process** is 87% of the direct labor cost.

g. The total of all cost sheets completed during the month is $314,440.00.

h. The total of costs recorded on all sales invoices for January is $327,026.00.

INSTRUCTIONS:

Check figure: Cost of Goods Manu. $314,440.00

1. Open ledger accounts and record balances for information items in (a), (b), and (c).
2. Journalize the factory payroll entry on page 2 of a cash payments journal. C1012. Post the general debit and general credit amounts.
3. Journalize the following entries on page 1 of a general journal. Post the entries.
   - **a.** An entry to transfer the total of all direct materials requisitions to **Work in Process** and indirect materials to **Factory Overhead.** M844.
   - **b.** An entry to close all individual manufacturing expense accounts to **Factory Overhead.** M845.
   - **c.** An entry to record applied factory overhead to **Work in Process.** M846.
4. Continue using page 1 of the general journal. Journalize and post the entry to close the balance of the factory overhead account to **Income Summary.** M847.
5. Journalize and post the entry to transfer the total of all cost sheets completed from **Work in Process** to **Finished Goods.** M848.
6. Journalize and post the entry to transfer the cost of products sold from **Finished Goods** to **Cost of Goods Sold.** M849.
7. Prepare for Bartley Company a statement of cost of goods manufactured for the month ended January 31 of the current year.

RECYCLING PROBLEM 21-R Forming and expanding a partnership

On January 1 of the current year, Richard Meyer and Susan Rusk form a partnership. The partnership accepts the assets and liabilities of Mr. Meyer's existing business. Miss Rusk invests cash equal to Mr. Meyer's investment. The partners share equally in all changes in equity. The January 1 balance sheet for Mr. Meyer's existing business is as follows.

Meyer Computer Doctor
Balance Sheet
January 1, 19--

ASSETS			
Current Assets:			
Cash		$3,291.23	
Accounts Receivable	$1,800.00		
Less Allowance for Uncollectible Accounts	15.39	1,784.61	
Supplies		300.00	
Total Current Assets			$5,375.84
Plant Assets:			
Equipment			2,200.00
Total Assets			$7,575.84
LIABILITIES			
Accounts Payable			$1,575.84
OWNER'S EQUITY			
Richard Meyer, Capital			6,000.00
Total Liabilities and Owner's Equity			$7,575.84

Check figure: No check figure available

INSTRUCTIONS:

Journalize the following transactions. Use page 1 of a cash receipts journal and page 1 of a general journal. Source documents are abbreviated as follows: memorandum, M; receipt, R.

Jan. 1. Received cash from partner, Susan Rusk, as an initial investment, $6,000.00. R1.
1. Accepted assets and liabilities of Richard Meyer's existing business as an initial investment, $6,000.00. R2.

Mar. 1. Journalized personal sale of equity to new partner, Luke Chin, $4,000.00, distributed as follows: from Richard Meyer, $2,000.00; from Susan Rusk, $2,000.00. M18.

Aug. 1. Received cash from new partner, Penney Cory, for a one-fourth equity in the business, $4,000.00. R92.

Sept. 2. Received cash from new partner, Chad Breslau, for a one-fifth equity in the business, $3,600.00. Existing equity is redistributed as follows: from Richard Meyer, $80.00; from Susan Rusk, $80.00; from Luke Chin, $80.00; from Penney Cory, $80.00. R121 and M32.

Nov. 1. Received cash from new partner, Sharon Logan, for a one-sixth equity in the business, $4,200.00. Goodwill, $1,400.00, is distributed as follows: Richard Meyer, $280.00; Susan Rusk, $280.00; Luke Chin, $280.00; Penney Cory, $280.00; Chad Breslau, $280.00. R181 and M42.

RECYCLING PROBLEM 22-R Completing end-of-fiscal-period work for a partnership

James Dyson and Gerald Nickle are partners in a partnership called Fast Service Plumbing. The partnership's work sheet for the year ended December 31 of the current year is shown on page C-23.

INSTRUCTIONS:

1. Prepare an income statement. Calculate and record the component percentages for total operating expenses and for net income. Round percentage calculations to the nearest 0.1%.

Fast Service Plumbing
Work Sheet
For Year Ended December 31, 19--

	Account Title	1 Trial Balance Debit	2 Trial Balance Credit	3 Adjustments Debit	4 Adjustments Credit	5 Income Statement Debit	6 Income Statement Credit	7 Balance Sheet Debit	8 Balance Sheet Credit	
1	Cash	26762 02						26762 02		1
2	Petty Cash	300 00						300 00		2
3	Accounts Receivable	1529 47						1529 47		3
4	Allow. for Uncoll. Accts.		32 15		(a) 90 00				122 15	4
5	Supplies—Plumbing	7142 61			(b) 5892 56			1250 05		5
6	Supplies—Office	1360 00			(c) 1088 76			271 24		6
7	Prepaid Insurance	1236 00			(d) 383 82			852 18		7
8	Equipment	21527 00						21527 00		8
9	Accum. Depr.—Equip.		4305 00		(e) 2152 70				6457 70	9
10	Truck	17000 00						17000 00		10
11	Accum. Depr.—Truck		3400 00		(f) 1700 00				5100 00	11
12	Accounts Payable		4677 65						4677 65	12
13	James Dyson, Capital		22000 00						22000 00	13
14	James Dyson, Drawing	7000 00						7000 00		14
15	Gerald Nickle, Capital		20000 00						20000 00	15
16	Gerald Nickle, Drawing	7000 00						7000 00		16
17	Income Summary									17
18	Sales		52793 30				52793 30			18
19	Advertising Expense	600 00				600 00				19
20	Depr. Exp.—Equipment			(e) 2152 70		2152 70				20
21	Depr. Exp.—Truck			(f) 1700 00		1700 00				21
22	Insurance Expense			(d) 383 82		383 82				22
23	Miscellaneous Expense	900 00				900 00				23
24	Rent Expense	8400 00				8400 00				24
25	Supplies Exp.—Plumbing			(b) 5892 56		5892 56				25
26	Supplies Exp.—Office			(c) 1088 76		1088 76				26
27	Truck Expense	5126 00				5126 00				27
28	Uncollectible Accts. Exp.			(a) 90 00		90 00				28
29	Utilities Expense	1325 00				1325 00				29
30		107208 10	107208 10	11307 84	11307 84	27658 84	52793 30	83491 96	58357 50	30
31	Net Income					25134 46			25134 46	31
32						52793 30	52793 30	83491 96	83491 96	32

Check figures:
3. Dyson $28,647.23
Nickle 24,487.23

2. Prepare a distribution of net income statement. Each partner is to receive 8% interest on January 1 equity. The January 1 equity is: Mr. Dyson, $22,000.00; Mr. Nickle, $20,000.00. Also, the partners' salaries are: Mr. Dyson, $10,000.00; Mr. Nickle, $8,000.00. The partners share remaining net income, net loss, or deficit equally.
3. Prepare an owners' equity statement.
4. Prepare a balance sheet.
5. Journalize the adjusting entries. Use page 12 of a general journal.
6. Continue using page 12 of the general journal. Journalize the closing entries.

RECYCLING PROBLEM 23-R Journalizing governmental transactions

The town of Osage uses a general fund for all financial transactions. Expenditures are recorded by type of expenditure and by department. The four categories of expenditures are: personnel, supplies, other charges, and capital outlays. Departments are: General Government, Public Safety, Public Works, and Recreation.

Check figure: No check figure available

INSTRUCTIONS:

Journalize the following transactions completed during the current year. Use page 1 of a journal.

Jan. 2. Recorded current year's approved operating budget: estimated revenues, $1,148,500.00; appropriations, $1,113,000.00; budgetary fund balance, $35,500.00. M35.

2. Recorded current year's property tax levy: taxes receivable—current, $1,033,000.00; allowance for uncollectible taxes—current, $15,500.00; property tax revenue, $1,017,500.00. M36.

9. Paid cash for gas utility service in recreation department, $182.00. C134.

15. Issued a 1-month, 9% note, $100,000.00. NP7.

16. Received cash for current taxes receivable, $61,200.00. R85.

19. Encumbered estimated amount for supplies in general government department, $120.00. M52.

31. Received cash from traffic fines, $490.00. R100. (Other Revenue)

Feb. 3. Paid cash for general government department supplies, $117.00, encumbered January 19 per M52. M61 and C155.

15. Paid cash for the maturity value of NP7: principal, $100,000.00, plus interest, $750.00; total, $100,750.00. C189.

22. Paid cash for library books for recreation department, $450.00. C192. (Capital Outlays)

Mar. 1. Recorded reclassification of current taxes receivable to delinquent status, $72,000.00, and the accompanying allowance for uncollectible accounts, $15,500.00. M73.

15. Paid cash for a 4-month, 8% certificate of deposit, $300,000.00. C209.

Apr. 5. Encumbered estimated amount for supplies in public safety department, $250.00. M94.

18. Received cash for delinquent taxes receivable, $34,500.00. R255.

26. Paid cash for public safety department supplies, $254.00, encumbered April 5 per M94. M102 and C244.

May 8. Paid cash for consultant's services in general government department, $500.00. C265. (Personnel)

July 15. Received cash for the maturity value of certificate of deposit due today: principal, $300,000.00, plus interest, $8,000.00; total $308,000.00. R314.

RECYCLING PROBLEM 24-R Completing end-of-fiscal-period work for a governmental organization

The town of Weston uses a general fund. The general ledger account balances for December 31 of the current year are as follows.

Account Title	Debit	Credit
Cash	$ 87,390.00	
Taxes Receivable—Current	—	—
Allowance for Uncollectible Taxes—Current	—	—
Taxes Receivable—Delinquent	20,760.00	
Allow. for Uncoll. Taxes—Delinquent		$ 7,950.00
Interest Receivable	—	—
Allow. for Uncoll. Interest	—	—
Inventory of Supplies	—	—
Investments—Short Term	—	—
Accounts Payable		25,640.00
Notes Payable	—	—
Unreserved Fund Balance		47,610.00
Reserve for Encumbrances—Current Year		1,780.00
Reserve for Encumbrances—Prior Year	—	—
Reserve for Inventory of Supplies	—	—
Property Tax Revenue		1,139,200.00
Interest Revenue		6,610.00
Other Revenue		14,840.00
Expenditure—Personnel, Gen. Gov't.	196,460.00	
Expenditure—Supplies, Gen. Gov't.	11,580.00	
Expenditure—Other Charges, Gen. Gov't.	96,700.00	
Expenditure—Capital Outlays, Gen. Gov't.	13,200.00	
Expenditure—Personnel, Public Safety	352,150.00	
Expenditure—Supplies, Public Safety	16,690.00	
Expenditure—Other Charges, Public Safety	128,900.00	
Expenditure—Capital Outlays, Public Safety	64,300.00	
Expenditure—Personnel, Public Works	88,100.00	
Expenditure—Supplies, Public Works	5,890.00	
Expenditure—Other Charges, Public Works	40,120.00	
Expenditure—Capital Outlays, Public Works	37,750.00	
Expenditure—Personnel, Recreation	46,490.00	
Expenditure—Supplies, Recreation	3,290.00	
Expenditure—Other Charges, Recreation	23,500.00	
Expenditure—Capital Outlays, Recreation	8,580.00	
Estimated Revenues	1,163,300.00	
Appropriations		1,135,200.00
Budgetary Fund Balance		28,100.00
Encumbrance—Supplies, Public Works	1,780.00	

Check figure: Excess of Rev. over Expend. $29,870

INSTRUCTIONS:

1. Record the trial balance on a work sheet.
2. Analyze the following adjustment information and record the adjustments on the work sheet.

Adjustment Information, December 31

Supplies inventory	$3,380.00
Interest revenue due but not collected	3,650.00

An estimated 20% of the interest revenue due will not be collected.
The reserve for encumbrances for the current year is reclassified to prior year status.

3. Complete the work sheet.

Weston's general fund operating budget for the current fiscal year is shown on page C-26.

4. Prepare a statement of revenues, expenditures, and changes in fund balance—budget and actual for the year ended December 31 of the current year. The unreserved fund balance on January 1 was $47,610.00.

Town of Weston
Annual Operating Budget—General Fund
For Year Ended December 31, 19--

ESTIMATED REVENUES		
Property Tax	$1,139,200.00	
Interest	9,500.00	
Other	14,600.00	
Total Estimated Revenues		$1,163,300.00
ESTIMATED EXPENDITURES AND BUDGETARY FUND BALANCE		
General Government:		
Personnel	$ 196,560.00	
Supplies	11,610.00	
Other Charges	96,780.00	
Capital Outlays	13,250.00	
Total General Government		$ 318,200.00
Public Safety:		
Personnel	$ 352,420.00	
Supplies	16,730.00	
Other Charges	129,220.00	
Capital Outlays	64,330.00	
Total Public Safety		562,700.00
Public Works:		
Personnel	$ 88,300.00	
Supplies	6,020.00	
Other Charges	40,140.00	
Capital Outlays	37,790.00	
Total Public Works		172,250.00
Recreation:		
Personnel	$ 46,490.00	
Supplies	3,340.00	
Other Charges	23,630.00	
Capital Outlays	8,590.00	
Total Recreation		82,050.00
Total Estimated Expenditures		$1,135,200.00
Budgetary Fund Balance		28,100.00
Total Estimated Expenditures and Budgetary Fund Balance		$1,163,300.00

5. Prepare a balance sheet for December 31 of the current year.
6. Use page 48 of a journal. Journalize the adjusting entries. Continue using page 48 of the journal. Journalize the closing entries.

APPENDIX D

Answers to Audit Your Understanding

CHAPTER 1, PAGE 8

1. The economy, economic events, government units, competitors, and customers.
2. Managers, owners, creditors, bankers, inventors, and government units.
3. Financial accounting, managerial accounting, cost accounting, tax accounting, accounting systems, auditing, and personal financial planning.
4. To assist individuals to interpret financial information and determine which investments will maximize their investment income.

CHAPTER 1, PAGE 11

1. Similar: both typically specialize in one field of accounting. Different: private accountants work for only one business; public accountants sell professional services to many businesses.
2. Certified Public Accountant (CPA), Certified Management Accountant (CMA), and Certified Internal Auditor (CIA).
3. When an individual disregards his or her principles of right and wrong by choosing the wrong action.
4. Employees, owners, customers, the local community, and society.

CHAPTER 1, PAGE 21

1. Proprietorship and partnership.
2. Corporation.
3. Development of standards for financial accounting and reporting.
4. American Institute of Certified Public Accountants (AICPA); Institute of Management Accountants (IMA); American Accounting Association (AAA).
5. Materiality concept.

CHAPTER 2, PAGE 32

1. Assets = Liabilities + Owner's Equity
2. **(a)** A separate numeric listing is provided for each ledger division.
   (b) A predesigned arrangement of numbers is provided within each ledger division.
   (c) Enough account number digits are provided to allow the addition of new accounts.

CHAPTER 2, PAGE 38

1. Purchases—Tennis is debited; Accounts Payable is credited.
2. Accounts Payable is debited; Purchases Returns and Allowances—Tennis is credited.

CHAPTER 2, PAGE 45

1. Accounts Payable is debited; Cash and Purchases Discount—Tennis are credited.
2. To assure that all expenses are recorded during the fiscal period in which they occurred.
3. Memorandum.

CHAPTER 3, PAGE 70

1. Accounts Receivable is debited; Sales Tax Payable and Sales—Golf are credited.
2. Sales Tax Payable and Sales Returns and Allowances—Tennis are debited; Accounts Receivable is credited.

CHAPTER 3, PAGE 76

1. Cash, Sales Tax Payable, and Sales Discount—Golf are debited; Accounts Receivable is credited.
2. Cash is debited; Sales Tax Payable, Sales—Golf, and Sales—Tennis are credited.
3. Cash on hand at the beginning of the month *plus* total cash received during the month *less* total cash paid during the month *equals* cash on hand at the end of the month.

CHAPTER 4, PAGE 97

1. Because the taxes represent a business transaction with dollar amounts large enough to affect business decisions.

2. As a reward for continuous service.
3. $60.00 (5 hours *times* $8.00 *times* 1.5).
4. Federal income tax and FICA tax.

CHAPTER 4, PAGE 104

1. The Other Deductions column.
2. Total Earnings *minus* Total Deductions *equals* Net Pay.
3. Total earnings for the pay period.

CHAPTER 4, PAGE 109

1. Cash.
2. **(a)** Employer FICA tax.
   (b) Federal unemployment tax.
   (c) State unemployment tax.
3. The amount owed.

CHAPTER 5, PAGE 121

1. Reports about how well each department is doing.
2. Periodic inventory and perpetual inventory.
3. Operating Revenue, Cost of Merchandise Sold, Gross Profit on Operations.

CHAPTER 5, PAGE 130

1. Schedule of accounts receivable and schedule of accounts payable.
2. Uncollectible Accounts Expense is debited; Allowance for Uncollectible Accounts is credited.
3. Asset, liability, and stockholders' equity.

CHAPTER 5, PAGE 141

1. Departmental statement of gross profit, income statement, statement of stockholders' equity, balance sheet.
2. Total Operating Expenses *divided by* Net Sales *equals* Total Operating Expenses Component Percentage.
3. Capital Stock and Retained Earnings.

CHAPTER 6, PAGE 174

1. Vouchers Payable.
2. To serve as an additional control; all vouchers can be accounted for.
3. Purchases journal.
4. When the vouchers are approved.

CHAPTER 6, PAGE 179

1. Cash payments journal.
2. According to the name of the vendor.
3. In a check register.
4. Vouchers Payable.

CHAPTER 6, PAGE 184

1. Vouchers Payable is debited; Purchases Returns and Allowances is credited.
2. Remove the voucher from the unpaid voucher file and write *Canceled* across Section 5.
3. A payroll register.
4. The procedure helps assure payment of invoices within the discount periods.

CHAPTER 7, PAGE 198

1. **(1)** Cost of beginning merchandise inventory. **(2)** Cost of the net purchases added to the inventory during the fiscal period.
2. Understated.
3. **(1)** By physically counting the items. **(2)** By keeping a continuous record showing the number purchased and sold for each item.
4. Once each fiscal period.

CHAPTER 7, PAGE 203

1. A method that best matches the revenue and costs for that business during the fiscal period.
2. The last-in, first-out (lifo) method.
3. The first-in, first-out (fifo) method.
4. **(1)** The cost of the inventory using the fifo, lifo, or weighted-average method. **(2)** The current market price of the inventory.

CHAPTER 7, PAGE 208

1. That a continuing relationship exists between gross profit and net sales.
2. Separate records of both cost and retail prices for net purchases, net sales, and beginning merchandise inventory.
3. That the business sold the average merchandise inventory five times during the current year.
4. Days in year (365) divided by merchandise inventory turnover ratio equals average number of days' sales in merchandise inventory.

CHAPTER 8, PAGE 228

1. Canceling the balance of a customer account because the customer does not pay.
2. Uncollectible Accounts Expense.
3. **(1)** A general journal entry to reopen the customer account. **(2)** A cash receipts journal entry to record the cash received on account.
4. Collection of Uncollectible Accounts.

CHAPTER 8, PAGE 236

1. Matching Expenses with Revenue concept.
2. Total sales *minus* sales discount *minus* sales returns and allowances *equals* net sales.
3. **(1)** Estimating the amount of uncollectible accounts by aging accounts receivable. **(2)** Estimating the amount of uncollectible accounts by using a percentage of the accounts receivable account balance.
4. Allowance for Uncollectible Accounts.

CHAPTER 8, PAGE 240

1. A business needs cash to purchase additional merchandise to sell and to pay for operating expenses.

2. Total accounts receivable *minus* allowance for uncollectible accounts *equals* book value of accounts receivable.
3. Net sales on account *divided by* average book value of accounts receivable *equals* accounts receivable turnover ratio.
4. Days in year (365) *divided by* accounts receivable turnover ratio *equals* actual average number of days for payment.

CHAPTER 9, PAGE 252

1. General journal.
2. Over the useful life of the plant asset.
3. **(1)** Original cost *minus* estimated salvage value *equals* estimated total depreciation expense. **(2)** Estimated total depreciation expense *divided by* years of estimated useful life *equals* annual depreciation expense.
4. Original cost of a plant asset *minus* accumulated depreciation *equals* book value of a plant asset.
5. Depreciation Expense—Store Equipment is debited; Accumulated Depreciation—Office Equipment is credited.

CHAPTER 9, PAGE 261

1. **(1)** Discarded because no useful life remains. **(2)** Sold because the plant asset is no longer needed even though it might still be usable. **(3)** Traded for another plant asset of the same kind.
2. **(1)** Removes the original cost of the plant asset and its related accumulated depreciation. **(2)** Recognizes the cash received. **(3)** Recognizes the loss on disposal of the asset.
3. Book value of asset sold *minus* value of asset received *equals* loss on disposal.
4. The original cost of the land.

CHAPTER 9, PAGE 270

1. One that is twice the straight-line rate.
2. Production-unit method.
3. For income tax calculation.
4. Natural resources such as trees, coal, and oil.
5. Land and anything attached to the land.

CHAPTER 10, PAGE 284

1. By counting the number of months from the date of issuance.
2. As a fraction of 12 months.
3. May 19 (March 31 − 20 = 11 days; April, 30 days; May, 19 days).
4. Interest on the note is paid in advance.

CHAPTER 10, PAGE 292

1. Supplies is debited; Supplies Expense is credited.
2. Because the adjusting entry creates a balance in an asset account.
3. On January 1 of the new fiscal period.
4. Prepaid Insurance is debited; Insurance Expense is credited.

CHAPTER 10, PAGE 300

1. Expenses incurred in one fiscal period but not paid until a later fiscal period.
2. Principal *times* interest rate *times* time as a fraction *equals* interest.
3. Interest Expense is debited; Interest Payable is credited.
4. The adjusting entry for accrued federal income tax expense.

CHAPTER 11, PAGE 311

1. Other Revenue.
2. Zero.
3. Accounts Receivable is debited; Notes Receivable and Interest Income are credited.
4. The additional interest charged from maturity date to payment date.

CHAPTER 11, PAGE 314

1. As a liability or as revenue.
2. Rent Income.
3. Rent Income is debited; Unearned Rent is credited.
4. The adjusting entry creates a balance in a liability account.

CHAPTER 11, PAGE 317

1. Principal *times* interest rate *times* time as fraction of year *equals* accrued interest income.
2. The adjusting entry for accrued interest income created a balance in the asset account Interest Receivable.
3. Interest Income is debited; Interest Receivable is credited.

CHAPTER 12, PAGE 330

1. Determine corporate policies and select corporate officers to supervise the day-to-day management of the corporation.
2. **(1)** The right to vote at stockholders' meetings.
   (2) The right to share in the corporation's earnings.
   (3) The right to share in the distribution of a corporation's assets if a corporation ceases operations and sells its assets.

CHAPTER 12, PAGE 335

1. A single summary general ledger capital account is used for each kind of stock issued.
2. Cash is debited; Capital Stock—Common is credited.
3. **(1)** An incorporation fee paid to the state when the articles of incorporation are submitted.
   (2) Attorney fees for legal services during the process of incorporation.

(3) Other incidental expenses incurred prior to receiving a charter.

4. Intangible Asset section.

CHAPTER 12, PAGE 338

1. The board of directors.
2. The corporation is obligated to pay the dividend.
3. **(1)** To avoid a large number of entries in the corporation's cash payments journal.
   (2) To reserve cash specifically for paying dividends.

CHAPTER 13, PAGE 349

1. Cash is debited; Capital Stock—Preferred is credited.
2. Cash and Discount on Sale of Preferred Stock are debited; Capital Stock—Preferred is credited.

CHAPTER 13, PAGE 354

1. Treasury Stock is debited; Cash is credited.
2. Cash is debited; Treasury Stock and Paid-in Capital from Sale of Treasury Stock are credited.

CHAPTER 13, PAGE 359

1. **(1)** Additional capital becomes part of a corporation's permanent capital.
   (2) Dividends do not have to be paid unless earnings are sufficient.
2. Stockholders' equity is not spread over additional shares of stock.
3. Interest must be paid on the loan, which decreases net income.

CHAPTER 14, PAGE 369

1. Quarterly.
2. **(1)** Complete the work sheet's Adjustments columns except for the federal income tax expense adjustment.
   (2) Extend all amounts, except the balance of Federal Income Tax Expense, to the work sheet's Revenues/Expenditures columns.
   (3) Total the work sheet's Revenues/Expenditures column totals using a calculator. Calculate the difference between the two totals. The difference is the net income before federal income tax.

CHAPTER 14, PAGE 379

1. Total selling expenses *divided by* net sales.
2. Review the item to determine the reason.
3. If a business is profitable and pays adequate dividends.
4. Market price per share *divided by* earnings per share.
5. Beginning book value of accounts receivable *plus* ending book value of accounts receivable *divided by* two.
6. Days in year *divided by* accounts receivable turnover ratio.

CHAPTER 14, PAGE 386

1. **(1)** Closing entry for income statement accounts with credit balances.
   (2) Closing entry for income statement accounts with debit balances.
   (3) Closing entry to record net income or net loss in the retained earnings account and close the income summary account.
   (4) Closing entry for the dividends accounts.
2. Both payroll tax expense and property tax expense are presented on LampLight's income statement. The tax form requires LampLight to report only the total of all taxes.

CHAPTER 15, PAGE 409

1. **(1)** Planning. **(2)** Operational control. **(3)** Department coordination.
2. A business can control expenses by comparing actual expenses with projected expenses. The comparison identifies differences where costs are higher than projected. The business can then take action to correct the differences.
3. One year.
4. A projection of a business' sales, costs, expenses, and net income for a fiscal period.

CHAPTER 15, PAGE 421

1. Establish targets to work toward in the coming year. Help coordinate the efforts of all areas toward a common direction.
2. Previous net sales and the trend in net sales for a period of several years, general economic conditions, consumer buying trends, competition, new products on the market, and such activities as planned special sales.

CHAPTER 15, PAGE 429

1. Good cash management requires the planning and controlling of cash so that cash will be available to meet obligations when due.
2. Projected beginning cash balance, cash receipts, cash payments, and ending cash balance.
3. A comparison of projected and actual amounts for a specific period of time.
4. A performance report compares actual amounts with projected amounts for the same fiscal period. A comparative income statement compares actual amounts of one fiscal period with actual amounts of a prior fiscal period.

CHAPTER 16, PAGE 443

1. The line would be straight, parallel to the base. The line is straight because fixed costs are exactly the same for each month.
2. Gross profit is determined by subtracting only

cost of merchandise sold from net sales. Contribution margin is determined by subtracting all variable costs from net sales.

CHAPTER 16, PAGE 455

1. Prepare an income statement using the breakeven point numbers. If the breakeven point is accurate, net income will be zero.
2. Contribution margin *divided by* net sales *equals* contribution margin rate.
3. Total fixed costs *plus* planned net income *equals* required contribution margin.

CHAPTER 17, PAGE 471

1. Determine **(1)** profitability, **(2)** efficiency, **(3)** short-term financial strength, and **(4)** long-term financial strength.
2. **(1)** Ratio analysis, **(2)** trend analysis, and **(3)** component percentage analysis.

CHAPTER 17, PAGE 479

1. How well a business is using its assets to earn net income.
2. How much net income stockholders' investment is earning.
3. **(1)** Accounts receivable turnover ratio and **(2)** merchandise inventory turnover ratio.
4. Accounts are being collected 9.1 times a year.

CHAPTER 17, PAGE 485

1. **(1)** Owners' investments and retained earnings. **(2)** Loans.
2. Total current assets *minus* total current liabilities *equals* working capital.
3. Total quick assets *divided by* total current liabilities *equals* acid-test ratio.
4. To insure that a reasonable balance between stockholders' capital and borrowed capital is maintained.
5. Total liabilities *divided by* total assets *equals* debt ratio.
6. Total stockholders' equity *divided by* shares of capital stock outstanding *equals* equity per share.

CHAPTER 18, PAGE 498

1. **(1)** Each manager is assigned responsibility for those revenues, costs, and expenses for which the manager can make decisions and affect the outcome. **(2)** The revenues, costs, and expenses must be readily identifiable with the manager's unit.
2. The specific information a department manager can use to control departmental costs.
3. An operating expense identifiable with and chargeable to the operation of a specific department.
4. The revenue earned by a department less its cost of merchandise sold and less its direct expenses.
5. Direct expenses.

CHAPTER 18, PAGE 504

1. Departmental margin statements.
2. Departmental Margin Statements—Boats Debit.
3. Multiply the month's net income before federal income tax by 12 to determine estimated annual net income. Calculate the estimated federal income tax on annual net income. Divide the estimated federal income tax by 12.

CHAPTER 18, PAGE 509

1. The component percentage for departmental margin.
2. Departmental margin *divided by* departmental net sales *equals* component percentage for departmental margin.
3. The departmental margin statements.
4. The Income Statement columns of the work sheet.

CHAPTER 19, PAGE 519

1. **(1)** Direct materials, **(2)** direct labor, **(3)** factory overhead.
2. As indirect labor, a part of factory overhead.
3. Work in process.
4. To keep a record of all charges for direct materials, direct labor, and factory overhead for each specific job.

CHAPTER 19, PAGE 528

1. Ordered, received, issued, and balance.
2. Purchase order.
3. To authorize transfer of items from the storeroom to the factory.
4. Estimated factory overhead *divided by* estimated direct labor cost *equals* factory overhead applied rate.
5. Because the unit costs of each job frequently are different.

CHAPTER 20, PAGE 545

1. Work in Process and Factory Overhead.
2. Materials is debited; Accounts Payable is credited.
3. Work in Process.
4. Overapplied overhead.
5. The cost of finished goods transferred from the factory to the stockroom.
6. Finished Goods.

CHAPTER 20, PAGE 552

1. Income Statement Debit column.
2. Underapplied overhead has been closed to Income Summary.
3. Direct materials, direct labor, and factory overhead.

4. Underapplied overhead is added to the cost of goods sold.
5. Current Assets.

CHAPTER 21, PAGE 574

1. To avoid misunderstandings. Some states require that partnership agreements be in writing.
2. The existing partnership is terminated.
3. The right of all partners to contract for a partnership.
4. Drawing.

CHAPTER 21, PAGE 579

1. The existing partnership is terminated.
2. Total equity (including investment by new partner) *multiplied by* new partner's share of equity *equals* the new partner's equity.
3. **(1)** Receipt of cash is recorded. **(2)** Redistribution of existing equity is recorded.
4. Goodwill is debited; existing partners' capital accounts are credited.

CHAPTER 22, PAGE 593

1. In the partnership agreement.
2. **(1)** Fixed percentage. **(2)** Percentage of total equity. **(3)** Interest on equity. **(4)** Salaries. **(5)** Combination of methods.
3. When the amount of allowances to partners exceed net income.
4. The partner's drawing account.
5. The partner's drawing account.

CHAPTER 22, PAGE 598

1. To summarize the changes in owners' equity during the fiscal period.
2. Because a partnership does not pay federal income tax.
3. Share of Net Income *less* Withdrawals *equals* Net Increase in Capital.
4. The partner's capital account.

CHAPTER 22, PAGE 604

1. Because the IRS does not consider partners to be employees of the partnership they own.
2. To report to the IRS the earnings distributed to each partner.
3. Cash received from the sale of assets during liquidation of a partnership.
4. Debited.
5. The partners' capital accounts.

CHAPTER 23, PAGE 618

1. **(1)** No profit motive exists. **(2)** Leadership is subject to frequent change. **(3)** Users of services do not necessarily pay for the services. **(4)** Conflicting pressures for differing objectives exist.
2. A governmental accounting entity with a set of accounts in which assets always equal liabilities plus equities.
3. To authorize and provide the basis for control of financial operations during a fiscal year.
4. Estimated Revenues is debited; Appropriations and Budgetary Fund Balance are credited.

CHAPTER 23, PAGE 628

1. When property taxes are levied.
2. Cash is debited; Taxes Receivable—Delinquent is credited.
3. A commitment to pay for goods or services which have been ordered but not yet provided.
4. Because the organization does not earn a net income and, therefore, has no need for expense information.
5. A document issued by a bank as evidence of money invested with the bank.

CHAPTER 24, PAGE 639

1. Revenues/Expenditures.
2. Interest Receivable is debited; Allowance for Uncollectible Interest and Interest Revenue are credited.
3. Revenues/Expenditures Credit column.
4. Revenue/Expenditures Credit column total *less* Revenues/Expenditures Debit column total *equals* excess of revenues over expenditures.

CHAPTER 24, PAGE 643

1. **(1)** Revenues. **(2)** Expenditures. **(3)** Changes in unreserved fund balance.
2. The work sheet.
3. Favorable.
4. Total assets must equal total liabilities and fund equity.

CHAPTER 24, PAGE 646

1. Unreserved Fund Balance.
2. Appropriations and Budgetary Fund Balance are debited; Estimated Revenues is credited.
3. Reserve for Encumbrances—Prior Year, Taxes Receivable—Delinquent, Unreserved Fund Balance.

Glossary

Account: a record summarizing all the information pertaining to a single item in the accounting equation. (p. 30)

Account balance: the amount in an account. (p. 30)

Accounting: planning, recording, analyzing, and interpreting financial information. (p. 5)

Accounting cycle: the series of accounting activities included in recording financial information for a fiscal period. (p. 141)

Accounting equation: an equation showing the relationship among assets, liabilities, and owner's equity. (p. 28)

Accounting records: organized summaries of a business' financial activities. (p. 6)

Accounting system: a planned process for providing financial information that will be useful to management. (p. 6)

Accounts receivable turnover ratio: the number of times the average amount of accounts receivable is collected during a specified period. (p. 237)

Accrued expenses: expenses incurred in one fiscal period but not paid until a later fiscal period. (p. 292)

Accrued revenue: revenue earned in one fiscal period but not received until a later fiscal period. (p. 314)

Acid-test ratio: a ratio that shows the numeric relationship of quick assets to current liabilities. (p. 481)

Adjusting entries: journal entries recorded to update general ledger accounts at the end of a fiscal period. (p. 138)

Aging accounts receivable: analyzing accounts receivable according to when they are due. (p. 232)

Allowance method of recording losses from uncollectible accounts: crediting the estimated value of uncollectible accounts to a contra account. (p. 229)

Amortization: recognizing a portion of an expense in each of several years. (p. 365)

Applied overhead: the estimated amount of factory overhead recorded on cost sheets. (p. 525)

Appropriations: authorizations to make expenditures for specified purposes. (p. 617)

Articles of incorporation: a written application requesting permission to form a corporation. (p. 326)

Assessed value: the value of an asset determined by tax authorities for the purpose of calculating taxes. (p. 269)

Asset: anything of value that is owned. (p. 28)

Auditing: the independent reviewing and issuing of an opinion on the reliability of accounting records. (p. 7)

Auditor: a person who examines the records that support the financial records of a business to assure that generally accepted accounting principles (GAAP) are being followed. (p. 7)

Automated accounting: an accounting system in which data are recorded and reported mostly by using automated machines. (p. 53)

Automatic check deposit: depositing payroll checks directly to an employee's checking or savings account in a specific bank. (p. 104)

Average number of days' sales in merchandise inventory: the period of time needed to sell an average amount of merchandise inventory. (p. 208)

Bad debts: see *uncollectible accounts*.

Balance sheet: a financial statement that reports assets, liabilities, and owner's equity on a specific date. (p. 136)

Bank discount: interest collected in advance on a note. (p. 284)

Bank statement: a report of deposits, withdrawals, and bank balance sent to a depositor by a bank. (p. 43)

Batch: a group of journal entries. (p. 57)

Board of directors: a group of persons elected by the stockholders to manage a corporation. (p. 326)

Bond: a printed, long-term promise to pay a specified amount on a specified date and to pay interest at stated intervals. (p. 355)

Bond issue: all the bonds representing the total amount of a loan. (p. 355)

Bond sinking fund: an amount set aside to pay a bond issue when due. (p. 357)

Book inventory: see *perpetual inventory.*

Book value of accounts receivable: the difference between the balance of Accounts Receivable and its contra account, Allowance for Uncollectible Accounts. (p. 237)

Book value of a plant asset: the original cost of a plant asset minus accumulated depreciation. (p. 252)

Book value per share: see *equity per share.*

Breakeven point: the amount of sales at which net sales is exactly the same as total costs. (p. 444)

Budget: a written financial plan of a business for a specific period of time, expressed in dollars. (p. 406)

Budgeting: planning the financial operations of a business. (p. 406)

Budget period: the length of time covered by a budget. (p. 407)

Capital stock: total shares of ownership in a corporation. (p. 14)

Cash discount: a deduction that a vendor allows on the invoice amount to encourage prompt payment. (p. 38)

Certificate of deposit: a document issued by a bank as evidence of money invested with the bank. (p. 628)

Charter: the approved articles of incorporation. (p. 326)

Check register: a journal used in a voucher system to record cash payments. (p. 177)

Closing entries: journal entries used to prepare temporary accounts for a new fiscal period. (p. 138)

Common stock: stock that does not give stockholders any special preferences. (p. 327)

Comparative financial statements: financial statements providing information for each of two or more fiscal periods. (p. 465)

Comparative income statement: an income statement containing sales, cost, and expense information for two or more years. (p. 409)

Component percentage: the percentage relationship between one financial statement item and the total that includes that item. (p. 120)

Consignee: the person or business who receives goods on consignment. (p. 195)

Consignment: goods that are given to a business to sell, but for which title to the goods remains with the vendor. (p. 195)

Consignor: the person or business who gives goods on consignment. (p. 195)

Contra account: an account that reduces a related account on a financial statement. (p. 37)

Contra balance: an account balance that is opposite the normal balance. (p. 38)

Contribution margin: income determined by subtracting all variable costs from net sales. (p. 442)

Controlling account: an account in a general ledger that summarizes all accounts in a subsidiary ledger. (p. 31)

Corporation: an organization with the legal rights of a person and which may be owned by many persons. (p. 13)

Cost accounting: the determination and control of costs of a business enterprise. (p. 7)

Cost ledger: a ledger containing all cost sheets for products in the process of being manufactured. (p. 518)

Credit memorandum: a form prepared by the vendor showing the amount deducted for returns and allowances. (p. 68)

Current ratio: a ratio that shows the numeric relationship of current assets to current liabilities. (p. 481)

Data base: a pre-arranged file in which data can be entered and retrieved. (p. 54)

Date of a note: the day a note is issued. (p. 281)

Date of declaration: the date on which a board of directors votes to distribute a dividend. (p. 336)

Date of payment: the date on which dividends are actually to be paid to stockholders. (p. 336)

Date of record: the date that determines which stockholders are to receive dividends. (p. 336)

Debit memorandum: a form prepared by the customer showing the price deduction taken by the customer for returns and allowances. (p. 36)

Debt ratio: the ratio found by dividing total liabilities by total assets. (p. 483)

Declaring a dividend: action by a board of directors to distribute corporate earnings to stockholders. (p. 336)

Declining-balance method of depreciation: multiplying the book value at the end of each fiscal period by a constant depreciation rate. (p. 262)

Deferred revenue: see *unearned revenue*.

Deficit: the amount by which allowances to partners exceed net income. (p. 590)

Departmental accounting system: an accounting system showing accounting information for two or more departments. (p. 33)

Departmental margin: the revenue earned by a department less its cost of merchandise sold and less its direct expenses. (p. 497)

Departmental margin statement: a statement that reports departmental margin for a specific department. (p. 497)

Departmental statement of gross profit: a statement prepared at the end of a fiscal period showing the gross profit for each department. (p. 117)

Depletion: the decrease in the value of a plant asset because of the removal of a natural resource. (p. 269)

Depreciation expense: the portion of a plant asset's cost that is transferred to an expense account in each fiscal period during a plant asset's useful life. (p. 128)

Direct expense: an operating expense identifiable with and chargeable to the operation of a specific department. (p. 497)

Direct labor: salaries of factory workers who make a product. (p. 517)

Direct materials: materials that are of significant value in the cost of and that become an identifiable part of a finished product. (p. 516)

Direct write-off method of recording losses from uncollectible accounts: recording uncollectible accounts expense only when an amount is actually known to be uncollectible. (p. 226)

Discounted note: a note on which interest is paid in advance. (p. 284)

Discount on capital stock: an amount less than par or stated value at which capital stock is sold. (p. 347)

Dishonored note: a note that is not paid when due. (p. 308)

Distribution of net income statement: a partnership financial statement showing distribution of net income or net loss to partners. (p. 589)

Dividends: earnings distributed to stockholders. (p. 136)

Double-entry accounting: the recording of debit and credit parts of a transaction. (p. 29)

Earnings per share: the amount of net income belonging to a single share of stock. (p. 373)

Employee benefits: payments to employees for nonworking hours and to insurance and retirement programs. (p. 89)

Employee earnings record: a business form used to record details affecting payments made to an employee. (p. 103)

Encumbrance: a commitment to pay for goods or services that have been ordered but not yet provided. (p. 623)

Equities: financial rights to the assets of a business. (p. 28)

Equity per share: the amount of total stockholders' equity belonging to a single share of stock. (p. 374)

Equity ratio: the ratio found by dividing stockholders' equity by total assets. (p. 483)

Estimated salvage value: the amount an owner expects to receive when a plant asset is removed from use. (p. 249)

Ethics: the principles of right and wrong that guide an individual in making decisions. (p. 10)

Expenditures: cash disbursements and liabilities incurred for the cost of goods delivered or services rendered. (p. 613)

Factory overhead: all expenses other than direct materials and direct labor that apply to the making of products. (p. 517)

FICA tax: a federal tax paid by employees and employers for old-age, survivors, disability, and hospitalization insurance. (p. 97)

Fifo: see *first-in, first out inventory costing method*.

File maintenance: the procedure for arranging accounts in a general ledger, assigning account numbers, and keeping records current. (pp. 31, 54)

Financial accounting: the recording of a business' financial activities and the periodic preparation of financial reports. (p. 6)

Finished goods: manufactured products that are fully completed. (p. 518)

Finished goods ledger: a ledger containing records of all finished goods on hand. (p. 518)

First-in, first-out inventory costing method: using the price of merchandise purchased first to calculate the cost of merchandise sold first. (p. 198)

Fiscal period: the length of time for which a business summarizes and reports financial information. (p. 117)

Fixed assets: see *plant assets*.

Fixed costs: total costs that remain constant regardless of change in business activity. (p. 441)

FOB shipping point: the buyer agrees to pay transportation charges. (p. 194)

Fund: a governmental accounting entity with a set of accounts in which assets always equal liabilities plus equities. (p. 612)

General fixed assets: governmental properties that benefit future periods. (p. 626)

General ledger: a ledger that contains all accounts needed to prepare financial statements. (p. 31)

Goodwill: the value of a business in excess of the total investment of owners. (p. 578)

Gross profit method of estimating an inventory: estimating inventory by using the previous year's percentage of gross profit on operations. (p. 118)

Horizontal analysis: see *trend analysis.*

Income statement: a financial statement showing the revenue and expenses for a fiscal period. (p. 132)

Indirect expense: an operating expense chargeable to overall business operations and not identifiable with a specific department. (p. 497)

Indirect labor: salaries paid to factory workers who are not actually making products. (p. 517)

Indirect materials: materials used in the completion of a product but that are of insignificant value to justify accounting for separately. (p. 517)

Intangible assets: assets of a non-physical nature that have value for a business. (p. 335)

Interest: an amount paid for the use of money for a period of time. (p. 281)

Interest expense: the interest accrued on money borrowed. (p. 283)

Interest rate of a note: the percentage of the principal that is paid for use of the money. (p. 281)

Interim departmental statement of gross profit: a statement showing gross profit for each department for a portion of a fiscal period. (p. 117)

Internal auditor: see *auditor.*

Inventory record: a form used during a periodic inventory to record information about each item of merchandise on hand. (p. 197)

Journal: a form for recording transactions in chronological order. (p. 29)

Last-in, first-out inventory costing method: using the price of merchandise purchased last to calculate the cost of merchandise sold first. (p. 199)

Ledger: a group of accounts. (p. 31)

Liability: an amount owed by a business. (p. 28)

Lifo: see *last-in, first-out inventory costing method.*

Liquidation of a partnership: the process of paying a partnership's liabilities and distributing remaining assets to the partners. (p. 600)

Long-term assets: see *plant assets.*

Lower of cost or market inventory costing method: using the lower of cost or market price to calculate the cost of ending merchandise inventory. (p. 202)

MACRS: see *Modified Accelerated Cost Recovery System.*

Management advisory services: management advice provided to an organization by a private accountant. (p. 8)

Managerial accounting: the analysis, measurement, and interpretation of financial accounting information. (p. 6)

Manual accounting: an accounting system in which data are recorded and reported mostly by hand. (p. 53)

Marginal income: see *contribution margin.*

Market value: the price at which a share of stock may be sold on the stock market. (p. 375)

Materials ledger: a ledger containing all records of materials. (p. 518)

Maturity date of a note: the date a note is due. (p. 281)

Maturity value: the amount that is due on the maturity date of a note. (p. 283)

Menu: a list of commands from which an activity may be selected. (p. 55)

Merchandise inventory turnover ratio: the number of times the average amount of merchandise inventory is sold during a specific period of time. (p. 206)

Merchandising business: a business that purchases and sells goods. (p. 33)

Modified Accelerated Cost Recovery System: a depreciation method required by the Internal Revenue Service to be used for income tax calculation purposes for most plant assets placed in service after 1986. (p. 267)

Mutual agency: the right of all partners to contract for a partnership. (p. 570)

Nonprofit organization: see *not-for-profit organization.*

No-par-value stock: a share of stock that has no authorized value printed on the stock certificate. (p. 327)

Note: see *promissory note*.

Notes payable: promissory notes that a business issues to creditors. (p. 281)

Notes receivable: promissory notes that a business accepts from customers. (p. 307)

Not-for-profit organization: an organization providing goods or services with neither a conscious motive nor expectation of earning a profit. (p. 610)

Operating budget: a plan of current expenditures and the proposed means of financing those expenditures. (p. 614)

Organization costs: fees and other expenses of organizing a corporation. (p. 334)

Overapplied overhead: the amount by which applied factory overhead is more than actual factory overhead. (p. 542)

Overhead: see *factory overhead*.

Owner's equity: the amount remaining after the value of all liabilities is subtracted from the value of all assets. (p. 28)

Owners' equity statement: a financial statement that summarizes the changes in owners' equity during a fiscal period. (p. 596)

Partnership: a business in which two or more persons combine their assets and skills. (p. 13)

Partnership agreement: a written agreement setting forth the conditions under which a partnership is to operate. (p. 570)

Par value: a value assigned to a share of stock and printed on the stock certificate. (p. 327)

Par-value stock: a share of stock that has an authorized value printed on the stock certificate. (p. 327)

Passport: a formal document that allows exit from and reentry into a country. (p. 523)

Pay period: the period covered by a salary payment. (p. 89)

Payroll: the total amount earned by all employees for a pay period. (p. 89)

Payroll register: a business form used to record payroll information. (p. 97)

Payroll taxes: taxes based on the payroll of a business. (p. 89)

Performance report: a report showing a comparison of projected and actual amounts for a specific period of time. (p. 427)

Periodic inventory: a merchandise inventory determined by counting, weighing, or measuring items of merchandise on hand. (p. 117)

Perpetual inventory: a merchandise inventory determined by keeping a continuous record of increases, decreases, and balance on hand. (p. 118)

Personal financial planning: assisting individuals in managing their personal investments. (p. 7)

Personal property: all property not classified as real property. (p. 269)

Petty cash: an amount of cash kept on hand and used for making small payments. (p. 42)

Physical inventory: see *periodic inventory*.

Plant asset record: an accounting form on which a business records information about each plant asset. (p. 247)

Plant assets: assets that will be used for a number of years in the operation of a business. (p. 128)

Post-closing trial balance: a trial balance prepared after the closing entries are posted. (p. 141)

Posting: transferring information from a journal entry to a ledger account. (p. 34)

Preferred stock: stock that gives stockholders preference in earnings and other rights. (p. 327)

Prepaid expenses: expenses paid in one fiscal period but not reported as expenses until a later fiscal period. (p. 285)

Price-earnings ratio: the relationship between the market value per share and earnings per share of a stock. (p. 375)

Principal of a note: the original amount of a note. (p. 281)

Proceeds: the amount received for a note after the bank discount has been deducted. (p. 284)

Production-unit method of depreciation: calculating estimated annual depreciation expense based on the amount of production expected from a plant asset. (p. 266)

Promissory note: a written and signed promise to pay a sum of money at a specified time. (p. 281)

Proprietorship: a business owned by one person. (p. 13)

Proving cash: determining that the amount of cash agrees with the accounting records. (p. 75)

Purchase order: a completed form authorizing a seller to deliver goods with payment to be made later. (p. 196)

Purchases discount: a cash discount on purchases taken by a customer. (p. 38)

Quick assets: those current assets that are cash or that can be quickly turned into cash. (p. 481)

Rate earned on average stockholders' equity: the relationship between net income and average stockholders' equity. (p. 378)

Rate earned on average total assets: the relationship between net income and average total assets. (p. 378)

Ratio: a comparison between two numbers showing how many times one number exceeds the other. (p. 464)

Real estate: see *real property*.

Realization: cash received from the sale of assets during liquidation of a partnership. (p. 600)

Real property: land and anything attached to the land. (p. 269)

Relative cell reference: the spreadsheet formula that is copied automatically changes to reflect where it was moved. (p. 239)

Residual value: see *estimated salvage value*.

Responsibility accounting: assigning control of business revenues, costs, and expenses as a responsibility of a specific manager. (p. 496)

Responsibility statements: financial statements reporting revenue, costs, and direct expenses under a specific department's control. (p. 504)

Retail method of estimating inventory: estimating inventory by using a percentage based on both cost and retail prices. (p. 205)

Retained earnings: an amount earned by a corporation and not yet distributed to stockholders. (p. 136)

Retiring a bond issue: paying the amounts owed to bondholders for a bond issue. (p. 358)

Reversing entry: an entry made at the beginning of one fiscal period to reverse an adjusting entry made in the previous fiscal period. (p. 288)

Salary: the money paid for employee services. (p. 89)

Sales discount: a cash discount on sales. (p. 70)

Sales mix: relative distribution of sales among various products. (p. 453)

Salvage value: see *estimated salvage value*.

Schedule of accounts payable: a listing of vendor accounts, account balances, and total amount due all vendors. (p. 122)

Schedule of accounts receivable: a listing of customer accounts, account balances, and total amount due from all customers. (p. 122)

Scrap value: see *estimated salvage value*.

Serial bonds: portions of a bond issue that mature on different dates. (p. 358)

Share of stock: each unit of ownership in a corporation. (p. 13)

Social security tax: see *FICA tax*.

Sole proprietorship: see *proprietorship*.

Source document: a business paper from which information is obtained for a journal entry. (p. 28)

Special journal: a journal used to record only one kind of transaction. (p. 29)

Spreadsheet titles command: allows part of the spreadsheet to be locked or frozen on the screen. (p. 94)

Stated-value stock: no-par-value stock that is assigned a value by a corporation. (p. 328)

Statement of cost of goods manufactured: a statement showing details about the cost of finished goods. (p. 547)

Statement of stockholders' equity: a financial statement that shows changes in a corporation's ownership for a fiscal period. (p. 135)

Stock certificate: written evidence of the number of shares each stockholder owns in a corporation. (p. 327)

Stockholder: an owner of one or more shares of a corporation. (p. 14)

Stockholder's equity: value of the owner's equity in a corporation. (p. 135)

Stock ledger: a file of stock records for all merchandise on hand. (p. 196)

Stock record: a form used to show the kind of merchandise, quantity received, quantity sold, and balance on hand. (p. 196)

Straight-line method of depreciation: charging an equal amount of depreciation expense for a plant asset in each year of useful life. (p. 250)

Subscribing for capital stock: entering into an agreement with a corporation to buy capital stock and pay at a later date. (p. 332)

Subsidiary ledger: a ledger that is summarized in a single general ledger account. (p. 31)

Sum-of-the-years-digits method of depreciation: using fractions based on years of a plant asset's useful life. (p. 264)

Taking an inventory: see *periodic inventory*.

Tax accounting: the preparation of tax returns as well as tax planning. (p. 7)

Tax base: the maximum amount of earnings on which a tax is calculated. (p. 101)

Tax levy: authorized action taken by a governmental organization to collect taxes by legal authority. (p. 619)

Template: a model of a computer application stored on a computer disk for repeated use. (p. 54)

Term bonds: bonds that all mature on the same date. (p. 358)

Total costs: all costs for a specific period of time. (p. 439)

Trade-in value: see *estimated salvage value.*

Treasury stock: a corporation's own stock that has been issued and reacquired. (p. 350)

Trend analysis: a comparison of the relationship between one item on a financial statement and the same item on a previous fiscal period's financial statement. (p. 464)

Trial balance: a proof of the equality of debits and credits in a general ledger. (p. 123)

Trustee: a person or institution, usually a bank, who is given legal authorization to administer property for the benefit of property owners. (p. 356)

Uncollectible accounts: accounts receivable that cannot be collected. (p. 226)

Underapplied overhead: the amount by which applied factory overhead is less than actual factory overhead. (p. 541)

Unearned revenue: revenue received in one fiscal period but not earned until the next fiscal period. (p. 318)

Unit cost: an amount spent for one of a specific product or service. (p. 440)

Variable costs: total costs that change in direct proportion to a change in the number of units. (p. 440)

Vertical analysis: see *component percentage.*

Voucher: a business form used to show an authorized person's approval for a cash payment. (p. 168)

Voucher check: a check with space for writing details about a cash payment. (p. 175)

Voucher jacket: see *voucher.*

Voucher register: a journal used to record vouchers. (p. 171)

Voucher system: a set of procedures for controlling cash payments by preparing and approving vouchers before payments are made. (p. 168)

Weighted-average inventory costing method: using the average cost of beginning inventory plus merchandise purchased during a fiscal period to calculate the cost of merchandise sold. (p. 200)

Withholding allowance: a deduction from total earnings for each person legally supported by a taxpayer. (p. 98)

Working capital: the amount of total current assets less total current liabilities. (p. 480)

Work in process: products that are being manufactured but are not yet complete. (p. 517)

Work sheet: a columnar accounting form used to summarize the general ledger information needed to prepare financial statements. (p. 123)

Writing off an account: canceling the balance of a customer account because the customer does not pay. (p. 226)

Index

Bold page numbers indicate illustrations.

E